DICTIONARY OF
THE HISTORY OF IDEAS

DICTIONARY
OF THE HISTORY
OF IDEAS

Studies of Selected Pivotal Ideas

PHILIP P. WIENER

EDITOR IN CHIEF

VOLUME III

Law, Concept of

TO

Protest Movements

CHARLES SCRIBNER'S SONS · NEW YORK

Copyright © 1973 Charles Scribner's Sons

The Publishers are grateful for permission to quote from
previously published works in the following articles:

"Newton and the Method of Analysis"
from Galileo Galilei, *Dialogue Concerning the Two Chief World
Systems-Ptolemaic and Copernican*, trans. Stillman Drake, foreword
by Albert Einstein, 2nd rev. ed. © 1967, originally published
by the University of California Press, reprinted by permission
of The Regents of the University of California

"Prophecy in Hebrew Scripture"
from *Basic Writings of Saint Augustine*, ed. W. J. Oates, copyright
1948, by permission of Random House, Inc.

from *The Old Testament: An American Translation*, ed. J. M.
Powis Smith, 1927, rev. ed. copyright 1941 by The University
of Chicago, all rights reserved

from *The Torah: A New Translation*, © 1962, by permission of
The Jewish Publication Society of America

DICTIONARY OF
THE HISTORY OF IDEAS

CONCEPT OF LAW

A LEGAL system is the most explicit, institutionalized, and complex mode of regulating human conduct. At the same time it plays only one part in the congeries of rules which influence behavior, for social and moral rules of a less institutionalized kind are also of great importance. The complexity of the organization and operations of a legal system has led to disagreements about the best terms in which to describe the nature of law, while the coexistence of law with social and moral rules affecting conduct has generated discussion about the exact nature of the relationships between the different sets of rules. A further source of difficulty is caused by the opposition or tension that sometimes exists between legal and moral rules, as when a legal prescription appears to violate the dictates of conscience. This has led to discussion of the relationship between the concept of law and ethical criteria.

I

In primitive societies legal rules are often not sharply distinguished from religious prescriptions and the dictates of social morality or convention. It is only with the emergence of law as a distinct and organized form of social control in a relatively advanced civilization that the problems mentioned above become apparent. The Greek Sophists raised such questions in the fourth and fifth centuries B.C. They distinguished between nature (*physis*) and convention or law (*nomos*) and regarded law as an artificial, man-made scheme of regulation which encroached upon natural freedoms. In their view there could be no explanation of lawmaking and no reason for obedience to law other than self-interest. This is a position which recurs throughout later thought about law; it is echoed in the writings of Thomas Hobbes. But it should be noticed that while this position seems to deny the possibility of incorporating natural reason in positive law, it does at the same time leave room for an argument that there are good reasons for complying with the law. This argument would be that the security and relative satisfaction of desires guaranteed by a legal system are to be preferred to the constant conflict of an anarchic society, where even the strongest cannot expect peace. This argument from enlightened self-interest, so strongly urged by Hobbes, also characterizes nineteenth-century utilitarianism. Discussion in the 1960's of the obligation to obey the law tended to rely less on utilitarian considerations and more on arguments of fairness derived from notions of reciprocity (Wasserstrom [1963], passim).

The Sophists' view of law as an arbitrary expression of self-interest was opposed, even in the ancient world, by the more hopeful tendencies of Platonic and Aristotelian thought. Plato denied that law could be constituted by the mere application of coercive power; he defined it rather as public regulations which express the results of a process of reasoning (*Laws* 644D). Aristotle, though he was concerned more with an analysis of justice than with the concept of law or a legal system, spoke always of law as "order" or "reason." This opposition in Greek thought, between those who viewed positive law as simply the working out of coercive power and those who saw in law some necessary expression of reason, continues to be a matter of debate in modern legal theory.

II

The pattern of discourse about the concept of law in modern legal philosophy emerges in the nineteenth century with the work of the English jurist, John Austin. Austin described law as a set of general commands issuing from a sovereign. The sovereign he defined as a determinate human superior who receives habitual obedience from the bulk of a given society and is not himself in the habit of obedience to any superior. The command of the sovereign is characterized by the sanction which is held out as a threat in the event of noncompliance and such a command backed by a sanction imposes a duty on the citizen. Command, sanction, and duty are thus key terms in the Austinian scheme.

Austin was bent on freeing the concept of positive law from entanglements and confusion with notions of justice and natural law. Not only did he select hard and concrete key terms for his description of law but he also insisted explicitly on the separation of law and morals. "The existence of law is one thing; its merit or demerit is another. Whether it be or be not is one enquiry; whether it be or be not conformable to an assumed standard, is a different enquiry" (1954, p. 184). This severance of the realms of law and morality has characterized a continuing school of legal philosophy which is sometimes known as analytical positivism, signifying its preoccupation with the analysis of the content and structure of law as found (*positum*) in a given legal system. Austin's position on this issue is reiterated in the work of the most distinguished contemporary analytical positivist, H. L. A. Hart. But while the positivist thesis on the separation of law and morals has held firm, there has been radical revision since Austin's time of the terms used in elucidating the nature of positive law.

Here the foremost architect of the modern positivist position has been the Austrian legal philosopher, Hans Kelsen, who has lived for many years in the United States. Kelsen, in two celebrated works, *Allgemeine*

1

Staatslehre (*General Theory of Law and State*, 1925) and *Reine Rechtslehre* (*The Pure Theory of Law*, 1934), departed from Austin's attempt to describe law in terms of a human commander laying down rules for subjects and substituted as his key concept the notion of laws as consisting of normative ought-propositions which, in a legal system, are all linked together and acquire unity through their common derivation from a basic ought-proposition or set of propositions which he called the *Grundnorm*. The most concrete and particular propositions of law in a legal system ultimately derive their validity through a process of tracing back to the basic norms of the system. So the proposition that X ought to pay Y $100 may be valid because it is contained in a contract duly made in conformity with general rules of the legal system which prescribe how binding agreements may be made. These general rules in turn are valid because they are contained in a statute or in decisions of the courts. The statute or decisions of the courts are valid because they have been enacted or decided in conformity with constitutional provisions which prescribe the proper procedures for enacting statutes and for appointing judges with definitions of their jurisdiction and powers. If we ask why the provisions of the constitution are valid we must, according to Kelsen, simply accept as necessary for comprehending the existence of a legal system the proposition that the provisions of the constitution ought to be complied with.

It is apparent that when Kelsen uses the term "valid" with reference to a particular rule of the system it has no connotation of approbation or moral approval but signifies only that the rule has been identified as belonging to the system by the criteria of recognition. To speak of the basic norm as "valid," however, introduces an element of confusion, since this cannot be a question of identification by further formal criteria of recognition, but must refer either to an empirical observation about actual acceptance in society or to a moral precept that functioning coercive orders ought to be obeyed. The failure to clarify the precise import of his assertion that the basic norm has validity has been a source of difficulty with Kelsen's theory of the nature of law.

With respect to the relation between law and morals Kelsen is squarely within the positivist tradition. In *What is Justice?* . . . (1956, p. 4) he tells us that questions of justice "cannot be answered by means of rational cognition," and takes up a thoroughly noncognitivist position in ethics, asserting that choices about values and ends ultimately rest on intuitions. His basic concept of the *Grundnorm* can encompass the totalitarian society as easily as the democratic, vicious and depraved laws as well as just and beneficent ones. Kelsen's system is a powerful demonstration of the unity and scheme of action of a legal system. His pyramidal image of a set of norms linked ascendingly to a basic norm reveals the essentially common features of the legislative and judicial roles, for both judge and legislator are creating new legal norms while at the same time drawing upon and applying superior norms which confer validity upon their actions. Just as Austin insisted on the central place of sanctions in a legal system, so does Kelsen find the distinctive element of law in the element of coercion institutionally applied through the normative structure. For Kelsen all legal norms are directives to officials to apply force in certain prescribed circumstances though this may not be superficially obvious. For example, a rule that directs that a will should have two witnesses appears to say nothing directly about the imposition of coercion. For Kelsen, however, the aspect of the rule which gives it a legal character is to be found in the proposition that coercion will be applied to those who seek to act in defiance of the terms of a valid will. This, in Kelsen's scheme, is the primary rule, and the direction to private citizens about how they should make a will is a secondary or derivative rule. The terms "secondary" or "derivative" here do not imply any sense of precedence or superiority but are only a figurative way of expressing the notion that the distinctive characteristic of a legal rule is in its reference to the prescribed circumstances for the application of institutional force.

The most powerful and subtle contemporary exponent of analytical positivism is the English jurist, H. L. A. Hart. In his book, *The Concept of Law* (1961), Hart offers a devastating critique of Austin's attempt to elucidate the nature of law in terms of a human superior issuing commands, backed up by sanctions which create duties. This elucidation, Hart argues, will not serve to explain the nature of laws which confer powers (such as the power to make a will) and which cannot be seen as imposing duties, while the notion of law being founded in the habit of obedience to a sovereign commander does not explain the continuity of a legal system which, by the operation of basic constitutional procedures of succession, proceeds uninterruptedly after the death of the head of state. Who, after all, are those determinate human beings whose commands the law could be said to be? The members of the legislature know only a little of the law and are themselves bound by the law. (Similar criticisms of the Austinian position have been made by Scandinavian jurists, notably Karl Olivecrona.)

Hart suggests that the key to understanding the nature of a legal system is to distinguish between what he calls primary and secondary rules. Primary rules are those which impose duties and secondary rules are those which confer powers. It is the union of primary and secondary rules which gives a legal system its dynamic, highly structured, and rapidly creative character as compared with a body of customary rules. Secondary rules are rules about rules. They provide procedures for the creation, modification, and abrogation of primary rules. At the base of a legal system we find secondary rules which are fundamental rules of recognition and which embody the constitutional procedures for valid lawmaking in the system.

It is apparent that Hart's analysis owes a great deal to the earlier work of Kelsen but it differs in some significant aspects. For Hart the basic rules of recognition are not described in terms of validity which Kelsen used in constructing his concept of the *Grundnorm*. The existence of a basic rule of recognition is presented rather as an empirical phenomenon evidenced by the actual acceptance of the rules in a given society. The notions of obligation and duty are also analyzed by Hart in more subtle and complex terms than Kelsen's reduction of all legal rules to a uniform pattern of directives to officials about the application of coercion. Hart elucidates the meaning of statements about duty and obligation in the context of a legal system as involving social practices of reference to certain standards. In the light of these standards we justify criticism and condemnation of the behavior of others and the application of sanctions to them, and we offer reasons to explain and justify our own behavior. The maintenance of a general system of coercion in society no doubt psychologically sustains feelings of obligation, but statements of obligation are not simply statements of the probability that coercion will be applied. Our ordinary speechways evidence this, for we do not cease to speak of a person as being in breach of an obligatory rule simply because he has effectively removed himself from the jurisdiction and so from any threat of sanction. Statements of obligation do entail a general acceptance in society of the basic rule which is taken to validate the primary rules which formulate particular duties, but this is to be distinguished from an individual's acceptance of any particular rule. So if I say that X has broken his legal obligations by smoking opium, this does imply my recognition that the rule against smoking opium (primary rule) is properly derived from the constitutional procedures for lawmaking in the jurisdiction (basic rule). But it does not logically entail the prediction that X will probably be prosecuted and punished, and it says nothing at all about what I or X may feel about the sense and wisdom of the particular law in question.

III

Hart's introduction of the concept of acceptance of a basic rule as the foundation of the legal order immediately raises questions about the connection between analytical and philosophical enquiries into the nature of law and, on the other hand, enquiries which employ the concepts and methodology of the social sciences. Law is, after all, eminently a social phenomenon. A legal system is more than a structure of rules on paper. It is a system of rules in action, for without some minimal effectiveness in the life of a community a set of rules would not be said to constitute a legal system at all. This was recognized by Kelsen in his statement that a *Grundnorm* must be minimally effective, and by Hart in his reference to the acceptance of basic rules of recognition.

Long before the rise of the modern social science disciplines European jurists had concerned themselves with the social aspects of law through the medium of studies in legal history. In the eleventh century the study of Roman law was revived in the universities of Italy and France, and this study deepened as Roman law was received as the foundation of the legal systems of Western European societies. The basis for modern scholarship was laid by social interpretation of law in the work of the French jurist, Jacques Cujas, in the sixteenth century, and there is a continuing link between this early movement and the great German school of historical jurisprudence in the nineteenth century whose finest exponent was F. K. von Savigny. These historical jurists were not very consciously or explicitly sociological in their emphasis, but the necessity for them to elucidate doctrines of Roman law in terms of historical change inevitably led them to advert to the relationship between legal concepts and social phenomena. In this way they lead into the Germanic school of sociological jurisprudence which counts as its leading figure the Austrian jurist, Eugen Ehrlich.

Ehrlich insisted that if our interest and enquiry are into the forms of social control we must acknowledge that formal law plays only a part, and sometimes no part at all, even in areas where it purports to regulate. A full statement of the "living law" which applies in any sector of human conduct could be made only after careful observation of actual behavior in that context. After such observation we would often find that morality, custom, and commercial practice play a large part as sources of the norms to which people actually adhere, and that in some instances the norms of positive law are in practice largely ignored. As an analysis of the reality of social regulation this is patently true, but it is not particularly helpful as an elucidation of the concept of law where the enquiry is rather into what distinguishes the norms of positive law from those of morality, custom, and commercial practice. If a rule of positive law is in practice ignored both by citizens and by law enforcement officials, this may be a good reason for deciding that it is not a part of the "living law" but it is not so clear whether we can for this

3

reason decide that it has also lost its character as positive law.

Ehrlich's insistence on a constant comparison of the formal content of the norms of positive law with the reality of social practice set a theme for legal philosophy which has continued to be strongly influential in the twentieth century. In Scandinavia a school of jurists has developed who, in a strongly empiricist vein which owes something to the logical positivist movement in philosophy, have analyzed the concept of obligation as it appears in a legal order in psychological terms. The most interesting of these writers is the Danish jurist, Alf Ross, who in his book *On Law and Justice* (1958) invites us to begin an analysis of the nature of a legal system by considering the analogy of the rules of a game. He suggests that if we were watching two people playing a game, say chess, and we wished to know what were the rules of the game, we could not necessarily rely on the statement of the rules as issued by some governing body such as the International Chess Federation, for it may well be that the two players are not following all of these rules but are playing some modified version of the game. But then again we could not deduce the rules of the game simply by watching and observing the moves that the players made, for on that evidence alone we could never distinguish between what was done or not done because of the demands made by the rules and what was done or not done out of tactical considerations. To comprehend the rules of the game, suggests Ross, we have to introduce the notion of an ideology common to the players, so that the rules of the game they are playing can be defined as those directives with which they comply because they respond to them as binding. When we transpose this analysis to the elucidation of a legal system, the transition is not free from difficulty for it is not immediately apparent whom we are to characterize as the players of the law game. It seems that for Ross the players are the officials of the system so that a valid law for Ross would be a directive to which officials adhere because they have a reaction of feelings of obligation. He would thus accept a position much the same as that of Ehrlich, to the effect that a purported statement of law on the statute book which is in fact ignored by officials is not to be regarded as the statement of a valid law.

In the last few years of the nineteenth century a distinctively American voice began to be heard in legal philosophy, that of Justice Oliver Wendell Holmes. Holmes turned the attention of jurists to the role of the judge and the process of decision making as vital elements to be incorporated in any elucidation of the nature of law. Holmes's new emphasis was underscored by the voluminous writings of the Harvard jurist,

Roscoe Pound, who also introduced the American legal public to the thinking of European sociological jurists. The seeds planted by Holmes and Pound germinated in the third and fourth decades of this century in a movement which is usually referred to as "legal realism" and which continues to be influential in a modified form.

The Realists reacted sharply against traditional presentations of law as a system of rules which by reasoned application to the facts of a dispute could yield a predictable decision. They stressed the discretionary role of judge and jury in finding the "facts" of a case, and the further creative role in choosing between competing rules and principles for application. They deprecated the emphasis traditionally given in legal education to the study of the decisions of appellate courts, and stressed the importance of close observation of the practice of decision makers at all levels of the legal system. In their more extreme statements they came close to denying that rules had any significant role in a legal system and suggested that they were mere tokens that were manipulated by decision makers to give a facade of certainty and predictability to their decisions. So Jerome Frank stressed the importance of the psychology of the judge in his book, *Law and the Modern Mind* (1930), and Karl Llewellyn in a famous statement defined law as "what officials do about disputes" (*The Bramble Bush* [1930], p. 3).

The Realist movement had a great impact on the nature of legal education in the United States and so indirectly on the whole English-speaking world. But its philosophical position has come under telling attack, particularly in the writings of H. L. A. Hart. He has argued that the authoritative position of decision makers is not a good reason for defining law in terms of what these decision makers do. So the concept of the "score" in a game would not be adequately elucidated in terms only of what the scorer says. It is true that the score is what the scorer says it is but this is only to say something about it and something which, taken alone, is positively misleading. For it suggests that the score might be anything that the scorer at his whim might choose to say and nobody who has played or watched a game would accept that proposition. When we play baseball or football we do not think we are playing a game of "scorer's discretion." We know that the scorer has discretion but one that is limited by rules and exercised within the framework of rules. Rules, Hart argues, have a core of settled meaning and a penumbral area where their application to a set of facts is debatable, and where no judgment in either direction could in any absolute way be demonstrated to be right or wrong. The American Realists, he contends, were preoccupied with the problems of this penumbra to an extent that led them to distort the importance of rules in legal decision making.

IV

Contemporary discussion of the concept of law reveals several diverse trends in legal philosophy. One of the most influential is the application of the English school of analytical or ordinary language philosophy to the analysis of the concept of law and legal concepts. This is best exemplified in the work of H. L. A. Hart referred to above. This movement is strongest in England but it now has numerous practitioners in the other English-speaking countries. While writers in this vein are for the most part professional philosophers whose work appears in the philosophical journals, this movement in recent years has had some influence in law schools and its impact can be detected in the writings of some law professors and in the pages of the professional legal journals. While acknowledging the importance of properly conducted sociological studies, analytical jurists tend to concern themselves for the most part with such questions as the elucidation of the concept of a legal system; the relationship between legal and moral obligation or between law and coercion; concepts of responsibility; and, finally, analyses of legal concepts such as rights, duties, powers, and privileges.

In the United States the interest in analytical studies has been accompanied by a continuing influence from the Realist movement which in its central thesis and concern was dubious about the utility of the analytical approach. One of the leading exponents of a neo-realist position is Myres McDougal, who insists on the importance of law in a modern community as a creative instrument of social change. He exhorts decision makers in a legal system to make the fullest and most sensitive enquiries into the social implications of their potential decisions, and to manipulate legal rules and principles (which he refers to as *miranda*) in the interests of maximizing values which serve human dignity on the national and international scene.

America, like Western Europe, has also witnessed something of a revival in natural law thinking. The barbarities of European dictatorships in this century, and in particular the hideous brutalities of the Nazi regime in Germany, left many jurists unhappy with the traditional positivist insistence that an elucidation of the concept of law could not properly include a reference to any element of morality. The positivist view that the criteria for identifying valid law were purely formal was thought in some quarters to be one reason why the German judiciary for the most part so meekly accepted the Nazi edicts. One aspect of this antipositivist reaction has been the strengthening of the traditional Catholic school of neo-Thomist jurists who have been very influential in French legal philosophy in the twentieth century (e.g., Jean Dabin), and also occupy a position of importance in the United States.

In the secular world Lon Fuller in the United States has consistently mounted attacks on the positivist position which are expounded in his book *The Morality of Law* (1964). Fuller stresses the purposive element in the institution of law. He argues that often human conduct and institutions can be best understood and can only be adequately described in terms of their purpose. A description of the arrangement of parts in an automobile would give us very little insight into its social significance, if we did not include in our description a reference to its purpose in providing transportation. The very notion of an automobile thus incorporates the idea that it is at least minimally fit to fulfill a certain social function. If we transpose this argument into the discussion of a legal system then we can also argue that not everything which has a certain formal stamp is to be counted as law, but only those collections of rules which at least minimally serve human purposes of mutual regulation in the interests of furthering certain basic values.

The overlap between the concept of law and morality is, in Fuller's view, further demonstrated by a consideration of certain conditions which a legal system must fulfill if it is to be minimally efficient in achieving orderly regulation of social life. So we cannot contemplate an orderly society in which all rules would be retrospective or where all rules were secret or where tribunals in adjudicating disputes never made reference to the rules that they were charged with applying. But these conditions which are necessary for law to exist at all are at the same time attributes of the concept of justice, and in this way what Fuller calls the "internal morality of law" exhibits a necessary connection with minimal notions of justice.

Of late there has been a concentration of interest by legal philosophers on the nature of legal reasoning, and this promises a revision in the analytical approach to the concept of law. It is now acknowledged that legal reasoning cannot be properly described according to a deductive or an inductive model but consists rather of a marshalling of more or less persuasive arguments—which is peculiar only in the way in which a structure of authoritative precedent is intertwined with the kinds of criteria which go into everyday moral and prudential decision making. In this way a study of legal reasoning involves a revival of the classical notions of rhetoric. Important pioneering work in this field has been done by the Belgian legal philosophers, Chaim Perelman and L. Olbrechts-Tyteca in their book *Traité de l'argumentation* (1958). These studies cast some doubt on the traditional positivist insistence on elucidating the concept of law primarily in terms of a structure of valid rules. If more diffuse principles and maxims play a vital role at all levels of decision making in a legal system, one can perceive how considerations of ethics and policy are built into the fabric of the legal system more easily than under the traditional positivist position. The sharp separation between law and morals which has characterized the positivist position becomes difficult to defend when the close similarities between legal and moral reasoning are pointed out. In this way contemporary studies of legal reasoning hold out some promise of bridging the ancient division between positivist and natural law traditions.

BIBLIOGRAPHY

John Austin, *The Province of Jurisprudence Determined*, ed. H. L. A. Hart (1832; London, 1954; reprint New York). H. Cairns, *Legal Philosophy from Plato to Hegel* (Baltimore, 1949). E. Ehrlich, *Grundlegung der Soziologie des Rechts* (1913), trans. W. L. Moll as *Fundamental Principles of the Sociology of Law* (Cambridge, Mass., 1936). W. Friedmann, *Legal Theory*, 5th ed. (London, 1967). L. Fuller, *The Morality of Law* (New Haven, 1964). H. L. A. Hart, *The Concept of Law* (Oxford and New York, 1961). G. Hughes, ed., *Law, Reason and Justice* (New York, 1969). H. Kelsen, *Allgemeine Staatslehre* (1925), trans. Anders Wedberg as *General Theory of Law and State* (Cambridge, Mass., 1945; rev. ed., New York, 1961); idem, *Reine Rechtslehre* (1934; 2nd rev. ed., Vienna, 1960), trans. Max Knight as *The Pure Theory of Law* (Berkeley, 1967). K. Llewellyn, *The Common Law Tradition: Deciding Appeals* (Boston, 1960). M. S. McDougal and H. D. Lasswell, "Legal Education and Public Policy: Professional Training in the Public Interest," *Yale Law Journal*, **52** (1943), 203. C. Perelman and L. Olbrechts-Tyteca, *Traité de l'argumentation*, 2 vols. (Paris, 1958). A. Ross, *On Law and Justice* (London, 1958; Berkeley, 1959). J. Stone, *Legal Systems and Lawyers' Reasonings* (Stanford, 1964). R. Summers, ed., *Essays in Legal Philosophy* (Oxford and Berkeley, 1968). R. Wasserstrom, "The Obligation to Obey the Law," *University of California at Los Angeles Law Review*, **10** (1963), 780–807.

GRAHAM HUGHES

[See also **Equity; Justice; Law, Common, Natural and Natural Rights; Legal Precedent; Legal Responsibility;** Positivism; Utilitarianism.]

DUE PROCESS IN LAW

A GENERALIZED and regular procedure becomes established in man's historical and cultural life when hunters who cooperate, or the governing institutions, demand minimum standards of such procedural conduct for all. Whenever, at some point in his history, man claimed as his "due" that substance or property to which he was rightly entitled, he resorted to a procedure to obtain it which was customary, or accepted, in whatever activity he engaged. This economic, political, or cultural process, respectively, became due to persons as a right and was not necessarily the same in different nations, or even in regions or localities within a nation; regardless of what the formal or informal standards of procedure were, they were justified in some manner and continued to be claimed and variously applied as different needs arose over the years.

There is a second and more particularized aspect of such process that is one's due, which comes with a broadening of the meaning of "due." The term continues to mean an entitlement or right, but now has added a regularity or institutionalized formality of a legalistic nature. One reason for this addition is that a continuing basis for the civilization which characterizes all developed nations is a need for, and reliance upon, some regular form of procedure to apply the law as a means of social control. In every such country the law is usually divided and applied in both a procedural and substantive manner. The latter ordinarily deals with the content of the rules and principles which apply to those governed, while the former deals with the methods whereby the content of the law is applied in particular cases. For example, the Ten Commandments are concerned almost exclusively with substance and give the moral laws which are to be followed and obeyed, as does the Golden Rule. It appears that where a formalized belief impinges upon and determines the conduct and control of a relatively small group, detailed legalistic procedures are not urgently needed, as such religious forms dominate. But where a nation is large or controls an empire it must codify its laws and evolve uniform procedures to expedite the handling of cases, e.g., the Babylonian Code of King Hammurabi (ca. 2100? B.C.), the Roman Law of the Twelve Tables, and the English common law.

Historically the idea and content of due process of law arose in very ancient times. The earliest records disclose the difficulty of the Egyptian King Harmhab in finding "two judges . . . acquainted with [the] procedure of the palace and the laws of the court." And his instructions to the judges included an admonition not to decide a case "without hearing the other" party. The oldest court record (ca. 2500 B.C.) shows that the Egyptian legal procedure included allegations of a claim, denials by the other, and the requirement that the first party produce "credible witnesses who will make oath" supporting him; otherwise the case is to be decided negatively (Wigmore, I, 15, 33f.). The earliest Mesopotamian legal records (ca. 2000 B.C.) disclose similar procedures, and the Hebraic Ninth Commandment is "Neither shalt thou bear false witness against thy neighbor." Hindu and Chinese records of the same era are hardly available, but China's reliance upon its past enables its earliest known codes to indicate procedures analogous to the preceding, and even the heterogeneous and religion-oriented peoples of India were given a monarchical personal form of justice which included such minimal procedures.

These minimal procedures seem to include some form of what is today called "notice" that charges are being preferred against a person, then a trial or hearing on them before a (disinterested) court which determines the matter; all these and other details are condensed into the phrase "notice and hearing." This phrase seems to entail universal standards of elementary procedural regularity and fairness. There apparently was no requirement of any degree of formality in these details, although eventually they evolved into generally adopted conventional forms. And there does not initially appear to be any general rationale to support the original necessity for these particular requirements, religious, legal, or political.

Homer's description of the shield made by Hephaestus (Vulcan) for Achilles in the Trojan War depicts, in one part, the marketplace where the people "swarm" for a lawsuit; the parties each pleaded, their witnesses appeared, "The rev'rend Elders nodded o'er the Case" before they each proposed judgments, and the jury, i.e., "the partial People," then chose one proposal by acclamation and so decided the case (*The Iliad*, Book XVIII). In addition to this concept of a jury the Athenians added professional advocacy, with skill in argumentation and oratory, such as that of Demosthenes, to sway the crowds. The Roman Twelve Tables also required analogous notice and hearing, although soon a court of justice or Basilica was used for trials; eventually the Roman Emperors substituted praetors, i.e., professional judges, for the lay juries. These judicial methods were generally assimilated by the *jus gentium* which Roman tribunals applied universally, although other nations, e.g., the Celts, Gauls, and Germanic tribes, had long histories of analogous procedures. Even into the eleventh century such procedural requirements may be found, as in the decree of Conrad II in 1037 that "no man shall be deprived of a fief . . . but by the laws of the empire and the judgment of his peers . . ." (Stubbs, p. 147). The most famous trial in history occurred in the Praetorium at Jerusalem with notice via His arrest, the preferment of charges, a tribunal to hear, the giving of evidence, the opportunity to reply, and the judgment and sentencing. This idea of due process of law seems to appear early in history whenever a person was charged or accused in what is today called an "accusatorial" (criminal) or "adversary" (civil) proceeding. By contrast, the inquisitorial proceeding is applied to a person who may never even be accused but is still subjected to an inquiry and determination without knowing the charges, and who may also be compelled to give evidence which convicts him. This inquisitorial proceeding is to be differentiated from the preliminary investigatory one which may precede a criminal accusatory proceeding.

At the beginning of the modern period we find that in France the Declaration of the Rights of Man and of the Citizen (*Droits de l'homme et du citoyen*), promulgated in 1789 and made a part of the Constitution of 1793, required in Article 7 that "No man should be accused, arrested, or held in confinement, except in cases determined by the law, and according to the forms which it has prescribed." In other countries other forms and hybrids developed. The Universal Declaration of Human Rights, approved by the General Assembly of the United Nations in 1948, attempted to formulate such general principles applicable everywhere (Art. 10).

For the English-speaking peoples it may be that Article 39 of Magna Carta (June 15, 1215) and its subsequent interpretation settled any doubts as to preferment of the accusatorial-adversary procedures. Its language eventually safeguarded the "free man" from being "in any way ruined . . . except by the lawful judgement of his peers or by the law of the land." In addition to this general clause the Great Charter contained other specific procedural ones although, as James Madison remarked in 1789 when proposing the future Bill of Rights, "Magna Charta does not contain any one provision for the security of those rights, respecting which the people of America are most alarmed" (1 Annals 453). Magna Carta nevertheless became a sacred text in England and famous as the precursor of the phrase, "due process of law," first used by Edward III in a statute of 1354 (28 Edw. III, c. 3). It was, however, Sir Edward Coke's Second Institute which emphasized the concept and insisted that "law of the land" meant "due process of law"; it thus became a part of the common law and was given a natural-law interpretation and flavor.

The American colonial reception and modification of the idea of due process of law is disclosed in the early charters granted by the Crown, the laws of the colonists, the documents preceding and following the American Revolution, and the various state and federal constitutions. Colonial statutes and documents continued the Crown charters' general references but also became more specific. For example, acting under the grant by Charles I in 1629, the Massachusetts colonists agreed "to frame a body or grounds of laws in resemblance to a *magna charta*," and their 1641 Body of Liberties provided somewhat detailed procedures (J. Winthrop, *The History of New England from 1630–1649*, Boston [1826], II, 57). The New England Confederation of 1643, the Dutch provisions for New Amsterdam in 1663, and the New York "Charter of Libertyes and Priviledges" of 1683, all provided for a form of due process, and due process was claimed as a right by the Congress of the Colonies held in New York in 1765. Similarly, the First Continental Congress of 1774 resolved that the colonists "are entitled to life, liberty and property . . . [and] to the common law of England," and following its suggestion the colonies promulgated their own Constitutions. The famous Declaration of Rights adopted by Virginia in 1776 included the guarantee "that no man be deprived of his liberty, except by the law of the land, or the judgment of his peers," and with minor changes in language this was the general type of clause used. It was also found in the famous Northwest Ordinance of 1787.

The Constitutional Convention of 1787 discussed briefly and adopted a few procedural rights. In some of the state ratifying conventions bare majorities were obtained only because of promised amendments. Seven ratifying States appended lengthy proposals; New York's included "That no Person ought to be . . . deprived of his Privileges, Franchises, Life, Liberty or Property but by due process of Law" (*Documentary History of the Constitution*, Washington, D.C. [1894] II, 192), and this may be the first use of this clause in the United States. In 1789 James Madison called the attention of the House of Representatives to these obligations and his proposals included the clause which eventually became part of the Fifth Amendment, that "No person shall . . . be deprived of life, liberty, or property, without due process of law" (1 *Annals* 451–52). Curiously, not a single word appears in the *Annals* discussing or concerning the meaning of due process of law, but it undoubtedly was not meant to include the other substantive and procedural specifics which were discussed in some detail. Of the ten amendments to the American Constitution ratified in 1791, the first eight are generally termed the Bill of Rights. The question whether these limited the federal government only, or also the states, arose in 1833. Chief Justice Marshall held in effect that they were a limitation solely on the federal government (*Barron v. City of Baltimore*, 7 Pet. 243).

In the first important case involving the Due Process Clause it was determined that the language was "undoubtedly intended to convey the same meaning as the words 'by the law of the land,' in Magna Charta" (*Murray's Lessees v. The Hoboken Land & Improvement Co.*, 18 How. 272, 276 [1856]). This dictum limited the Clause to procedural notice and hearing, with the notice required to be adequate and the hearing fair, and subsequent opinions also followed this view (of course, "adequate" and "fair" themselves had to be interpreted, defined, and applied). Until 1868 this limitation and interpretation was not disturbed; in that year the Fourteenth Amendment was ratified, and its first section, second sentence, opens with "No State shall . . . deprive any person of," and then repeats verbatim the Fifth Amendment's language quoted above. There are thus two Due Process Clauses, the earlier one limiting the federal and the later one the state governments. Although the language is practically identical in both, their interpretation is not necessarily so (*French v. Barber Asphalt Paving Co.*, 181 U.S. 324, 328 [1901]); for practical purposes, however, they may be and here are treated as somewhat alike.

The colonial and American idea of due process which now emerges, especially in the light of its English background, indicates only a procedural content. This idea is not limited to judicial or quasi-judicial proceedings. As disclosed at the outset, due process is found in many nonlegal areas such as unions, educational institutions, the church, fraternal organizations, political conventions, and various disciplinary or other proceedings (Forkosch, "American Democracy . . . ," p. 173). However, while due process in the nonjudicial fields in the United States has generally been restricted to procedure, in the judicial area it has been interpreted so as to include substantive rights. The basis for this is found in the separation of the Clause's language into first "life, liberty, or property," and then into "due process of law," terming them respectively substantive and procedural due process. The judiciary in effect has said that the substantive portion may stand alone as a limitation upon the governments, preventing them from depriving a person of these rights when it felt this should not occur; when permitting the deprivation, however, the Justices then insist that the procedural requirements be observed, that is, the term "without" is now activated.

The earliest questioning of a solely procedural content in the Clause is found in a little-publicized opinion of 1819 (*The Bank of Columbia v. Okely*, 4 Wheat. 235, 244), and in the same year that Murray (noted above) was decided, New York's highest court rejected that state's exercise of power "even by the forms of due process of law" (*Wynehamer v. People*, 13 N.Y. 378 [1856]). The following year Chief Justice Taney, despite his earlier acquiescence in the Murray opinion, wrote that "it is beyond the powers conferred on the

Federal Government" to deprive a citizen of his property (*Dred Scott v. Sandford,* 19 How. 393, 451 [1857]). After the ratification of the Fourteenth Amendment the first major case to mention the new Clause was the *Slaughter-House Cases* of 1873 (16 Wall. 36). In his dissenting opinion Justice Bradley pointed up its usefulness, and then rejected the "great fears" that this would lead to Congressional interference "with the internal affairs of the states . . . and thus abolishing the state governments in everything but name . . ." (at 122f.).

This judicial self-abnegation, however, did not last long. Aroused by the 1876 *Granger Cases* (94 U.S. 113) which upheld a state's police power to prescribe rates charged by businesses affected with a public interest, the American bar influenced the Supreme Court to strike down "State laws, regulatory of business and industrial conditions, because they [were] unwise, improvident, or out of harmony with a particular school of thought" (Justice Douglas in *Williamson v. Lee Optical Co.,* 348 U.S. 483, 488 [1955]). By 1890, with three dissenters, the Supreme Court took a decisive plunge into the substantive due process waters by requiring judicial review of a railroad commission's rate-making determination, as well as its procedure (*Chicago, Milwaukee, & St. Paul Ry. Co. v. Minnesota,* 134 U.S. 418 [1890]). Thus in 1927 Justice Brandeis could write: "Despite arguments to the contrary which had seemed to me persuasive, it is well settled that the due process clause . . . applies to matters of substantive law as well as to matters of procedure" (dissenting in *Whitney v. California,* 271 U.S. 357, 373). The substantive limitation may therefore be enforced against a government independently of the second requirement, that is, a government may not have any power whatever to act regardless of the excellence of its procedural methods; or, even if it has such a substantive power, it may be acting poorly in its procedural method. The consequences in each situation are different, for if a government cannot exercise a particular substantive power then it cannot act at all under it unless a judicial reversal occurs, a constitutional amendment is ratified, or another and separate power can be exercised; if, however, it is only the procedure which is bad, this may be properly corrected and the otherwise same law now upheld.

The subsequent exercise of this power by the Supreme Court, even though in exceptional cases the federal and state governments were permitted a degree of control, produced outcries of indignation from laymen and jurists. For example, in the debate on the nomination of Chief Justice Hughes in 1930, Senator William E. Borah denounced the Court as "the economic dictator" of the country; Brandeis felt the majority was exercising "the powers of a super-legislature" (dissenting in *Jay Burns Baking Co. v. Bryan,* 264 U.S. 504, 534 [1924]), while Holmes castigated their use of "no guide but" their "own discretion" so that he could "see hardly any limit but the sky to the invalidating of those [constitutional rights of the States] if they happen to strike a majority of this Court as for any reason undesirable" (dissenting in *Baldwin v. Missouri,* 281 U.S. 586, 595 [1930]).

The turn came with the New Deal era of 1932. The judicial retreat began with its upholding of federal and state legislation by reversing many of the earlier cases, expanding the use of the Constitution's Commerce Clause (in Art. I, §8, cl. 3) to support new laws directed against economic and social evils, and withdrawing from its due process supervisory role. However, although in 1965 it reiterated that "We do not sit as a superlegislature to determine the wisdom, need, and propriety of laws that touch economic problems, business affairs, or social conditions" (*Griswold v. Connecticut,* 381 U.S. 479, 482), the Court still retains and exercises such powers albeit their scope and depth have been voluntarily reduced and narrowed (e.g., *Nebbia v. New York,* 291 U.S. 502 [1934], and especially *Ferguson v. Skrupa,* 372 U.S. 726 [1963]). The Justices have now transferred their major directing role from the economic to other areas, in effect becoming modern Platonic philosopher-kings in determining the minimal procedural and substantive due process of law which must be accorded all persons; nowhere else in the free nations is there such a concentration of this definitional power delegated to nine appointed individuals. These conclusions are supported by what follows.

In 1954 the Court's new form of activism began with the *Desegregation Case* (*Brown v. Board of Education,* 347 U.S. 483), which used the Fourteenth Amendment's Equal Protection Clause to strike down a state's educational segregation; simultaneously, however, the Fifth Amendment's Due Process Clause was used to denounce similar federal conduct in the District of Columbia, the Court saying "It would be unthinkable that the same Constitution would impose a lesser duty on the Federal Government" (*Bolling v. Sharpe,* 347 U.S. 497, 500). This new approach presaged an extended further broadening of the content of the Due Process Clause, and in this regard another question arose, namely, did the Barron case, mentioned above, still limit the use of the Bill of Rights only against the federal government or could it now also so limit the states? As part of their rejection of a generalized natural law content in the Due Process Clause, Justices Black and Douglas urged that the specifics of the entire Bill of Rights be embraced in that Clause (*Adamson*

9

v. California, 322 U.S. 46 [1947], in effect following the like view of the first Justice Harlan in *Hurtado v. California,* 110 U.S. 516, 550 [1884]). The Supreme Court has never accepted this "total incorporation" view but utilizes a selective case-by-case approach, handling each Clause in the first eight Amendments separately. The result has nevertheless been an almost total incorporation, with only a few Amendments and Clauses not so embraced.

The Due Process Clauses thus impose limitations upon both federal and state governments in civil, criminal, and administrative proceedings, as well as upon their acting through legislative, executive, and (state) judicial branches when they "exceed" their substantive or procedural (constitutional) powers. For example, in civil matters notice continues to be vital, even though a sufficiency of (minimum) contacts enables personal jurisdiction to be obtained upon a nonresident person, and a fair hearing remains an important requirement in every type of adversary proceeding. In criminal matters a virtual revolution occurred during the 1960's. The rights of persons include not only such procedural ones but also, e.g., all of the First Amendment's substantive clauses involving free speech, religion, press, and assembly. For example, the rights to associate and also peacefully to picket and handbill within broad limits whether for labor, consumer, political, or other reasons, are protected, as are teachers and public servants protected against loyalty oaths, vague requirements, and "fishing investigations"; and education and religion are generally not intermixed.

Summary. Due process, whether in the general area of human conduct or the particular one of law, thus connotes a procedure or method which includes regularity, fairness, equality, and a degree of justice. The idea is found in the internal disciplinary and other procedures used by labor unions, athletic organizations, social clubs, educational boards, business firms, and even religious groups, to mention but a few. The use of the term by the judiciary in the United States at first tended to follow the early procedural formulation; since the 1890's, however, a substantive content gradually broadened the meaning of due process.

BIBLIOGRAPHY

C. Fairman, "Does the Fourteenth Amendment Incorporate the Bill of Rights?," *Stanford Law Review,* **2** (Dec. 1949), 5–139. M. D. Forkosch, "American Democracy and Procedural Due Process," *Brooklyn Law Review,* **24** (April 1958), 173–253; idem, *Constitutional Law,* 2d ed. (New York, 1969). O. W. Holmes, *The Common Law* (Boston, 1881). J. C. Holt, *Magna Carta* (Cambridge, 1965). H. S. Maine, *Early Law and Custom* (New York, 1886). L. P. McGehee, *Due Process of Law Under the Federal Constitution* (New York, 1906). C. H. McIlwain, "Due Process of Law in Magna Carta," *Columbia Law Review,* **14** (Jan. 1914), 27–51. R. L. Mott, *Due Process of Law* (Indianapolis, Ind., 1926). F. C. Newman, "Natural Justice, Due Process and the New International Covenants on Human Rights: Prospectus," *Public Law* (Winter 1967), 274–313. F. M. Powicke, *Magna Carta Commemoration Essays,* ed. H. G. Malden (London, 1917). W. Stubbs, *Germany in the Middle Ages, 476–1250,* ed. A. Hassall (London, 1908). H. Taylor, *Due Process of Law* (Chicago, 1917). J. W. Thompson, *Economic and Social History of the Middle Ages* (New York, 1928). B. R. Twiss, *Lawyers and the Constitution* (Princeton, 1942). U.N. Commission on Human Rights, *Study of the Right of Everyone to be Free, etc.* (New York, 1964, Doc. E/CN. 4/826/rev. l). J. H. Wigmore, *A Panorama of the World's Legal Systems,* 3 vols. (St. Paul, Minn., 1928). E. M. Wise, "International Standards of Criminal Law and Administration," *International Criminal Law,* ed. G. O. W. Mueller and E. M. Wise (London, 1965), Ch. 2.

MORRIS D. FORKOSCH

[See also Civil Disobedience; Constitutionalism; **Equality; Justice;** Law, Ancient Greek, Ancient Roman, Common, **Equal Protection, Natural; Legal Responsibility;** Property; Social Contract; State.]

EQUAL PROTECTION IN LAW

Ancient Roots. The idea of equal protection seems originally to be rooted in the individual's relations to nature and to God. In relation to nature, men have always primordially and collectively feared other creatures and the elements, and thereby found a common ground for mutual protection, sharing an empathic sense of a levelling equality. For example, the seasonal overflowing of the Nile made all helpless equally, regardless of station. In his relation to God, man believed that a higher will rewarded all the faithful equally in a later, if not the present, world. In both the natural and supernatural domains, however, differences were undeniably recognized: a stronger physique was better for hunting, whereas an older head might be preferred for advice. These dissimilarities undoubtedly led to a social stratification of chieftains and priests in an hierarchical, if not a caste, system, with varied supporting justifications such as hereditary innate differences or divine dispensation. Economic and social distinctions eventually followed, and wars and conquests also resulted in the capture and enslavement of man by his fellows.

The originally felt need for equality of protection is found even among early civilized peoples, who at the same time also practiced inequality. However, the idea of justice functioned to compel equal protection in various ways. Thus Egypt's kings were divine, and they sanctioned oppressive regimes, but Thutmose III (ca. 1500 B.C.) nevertheless charged his new chief justice that "thou shalt act alike to all"; in the Coffin Text a god announced he had "made every man like his fellow" and "made the floodwaters of the Nile for the benefit of the poor man and the great man alike, and given all men equal access to the kingdom of the dead" (Muller, p. 58). So the Hebraic theocracy set up the Ten Commandments to be administered evenly among the chosen tribes, while the Mesopotamian King Hammurabi (ca. 2100? B.C.) legalized inequality by adjusting penalties and damages to rank.

The Greeks felt united against all others, whom they called *barbaroi*, and practiced a form of political equality in that a marketplace assemblage of all the citizens (*demokratia*) made the laws and administered justice, as did the Germanic tribes a thousand years later. Greek society was democratic and unequal, and Janus-like, presented two faces, best exemplified in the ideas of Plato and Aristotle. "Equality consists in the same treatment of similar persons," wrote Aristotle; "equality [is] not, however, for all, but only for equals. And inequality is . . . only for unequals" (*Politics* 1280a). What the Greeks so taught and practiced was continued in subsequent years and centuries; for example, Rome applied to all equally the same general principles of the *jus gentium*.

The sense and practice of inequality in society and religion continued into the Middle Ages, with Saint Augustine defending government, private property, and slavery, and Aquinas also expounding different "just" prices for each separate class in society. The Renaissance revolt against authoritarianism in all fields of knowledge and belief, for example, Luther, Rabelais, and Ramus (1515–72), may have inspired subsequent centuries, but without exception every nation then upheld the inequality of classes and the unequal treatment or protection in the distribution of land and wealth. The Reformation was not much better; Luther exalted the God-derived power of the prince and glorified the state and its class system, while Hobbes's sophisticated liberalism gave it support in a rationalist political philosophy.

Nevertheless, the idea of man's supremacy over nature led to a great levelling movement in Western political, religious, and social history, with a consequent desire for equality and like treatment. This was translated in many countries and in various ways, e.g., the English Revolution of 1688, which projected Locke's idea of a social contract among men who were all equal, an idea which the German Enlightenment

reciprocated, for example, in Wolff's (1679–1754) view that all men are equal before nature. And this view is, of course, the essence of the American Declaration of Independence of 1776, which exalted the doctrine that "all men are created equal," and of the French Declaration of the Rights of Man and of the Citizen (1789) which stated "Men are born, and always continue, free and equal in respect of their rights." Through both these documents the middle class achieved political power; Adam Smith's (1723–90) idea of free competition put all persons on a plane of original economic equality; in the nineteenth century Darwin gave a scientific *imprimatur* to man's basic equality, at least in forebears; and the nineteenth- and twentieth-century nationalization and internationalization of democratic ideas adopted the Enlightenment's idea of man's political right to equality everywhere.

This levelling movement was, however, not uniform in time or degree; even the Constitution of the United States partly repudiated the Declaration's egalitarian statement by supporting a system which safeguarded property and class distinctions to a degree; and, despite the idea's growth, questions were asked concerning what sort of equality it was which taxed all equally regardless of differences in wealth. As Anatole France formulated it: "The law in its majestic equality, forbids the rich as well as the poor to sleep under the bridges, to beg in the streets, and steal bread." And when the consequences of such individual equality resulted in an economic laissez-faire exploitation with inequality and hardships occurring, many people and nations rejected the practice if not the theory of such a definition and application of the idea.

Legal Aspect. The translation of this historical amalgam of religion, politics, and economics into the current legalistic concept of equal protection followed a similar kind of circularity. First, the law had to recognize the fact that differences existed among men, corporations, and institutions. And even if there were no identifiable differences some would have to be provided, e.g., geographical ones, because millions of persons were involved. Second, on the basis of such natural or man-made differences, whom and how could the governments then affect? It is at this point that equal protection, based on an acceptable or valid group classification, emerges; once properly classified, groups may be treated differently but, within themselves, all persons must be treated equally or alike. In every new or old nation, whether representative or monarchical, socialist or otherwise, such identifiable differences, and others which conform to their own mores and laws, are used, but without universal uniformity being required (although note the efforts of the U.N., below). 11

This classification and then equal protection or treatment may each or both be required in a country as the result of custom and history, a law, or a constitution; for example, English custom before and after the Norman Conquest of 1066, and the French Declaration of 1789 (par. XIII). There can, of course, be a negation of such classifications, as is found in the Universal Declaration of Human Rights adopted by the General Assembly of the United Nations in 1948, that all human beings are entitled to all their rights and freedoms "without distinction of any kind . . ." (Art. 2, par. 1).

In every country, whether by custom, law, or constitution, such classification and equal treatment are initiated and regulated by its parliament, legislature, or congress, with the judiciary entering in a minor and interpretive role, as in England (e.g., the House of Lords), France (*Cour de Cassation*), Germany (Constitutional Court or *Bundesverfassungsgericht*), and India (Supreme Court). In the United States, however, the legislative and executive branches seem to be only the proposers, with the Supreme Court acting as the determiner in each such aspect of classification and treatment. This is brought about by the language and interpretation of a portion of the Fourteenth Amendment to the Constitution which is binding upon the states directly, and to some extent upon the federal government by judicial interpretation: "No State shall . . . deny to any person within its jurisdiction the equal protection of the laws" (§1, sentence 2).

While this Equal Protection Clause does not specifically mention classification, the judiciary necessarily permits this; as Justice Frankfurter said in 1943, "The right to legislate implies the right to classify." Classification is the jugular vein of equal protection. For example, if the government desires to separate XY, the line drawn between them, or the classification X/Y, must be a valid one, that is, constitutionally permitted. If this classification is upheld then all in X may ordinarily receive more or less than all in Y, and so long as all X's and all Y's receive more or less equally, i.e., if they are all treated alike within their own classifications, then they have all received equal protection. This permits one to view equal protection as equal discrimination; that is, the class receiving less is discriminated against with respect to the other class, but so long as this discrimination is spread equally among all within the lesser class, there is no violation of the Clause. If, however, X/Y is held to be an invalid classification, then one XY group results; and so all X's and all Y's must now be treated as one XY group, that is, alike and not differently, as when they were classified separately.

The initial question may therefore be whether the government has the power to classify in this manner. In the United States this ordinarily becomes a question of Due Process of Law in its substantive aspects, that is, whether or not the legislature has power to classify in this fashion for this purpose is ordinarily to be determined by this Clause. In 1966, in an exceptional situation, a "requirement of some [degree of] rationality in the nature of the class singled out" seems to have been suggested (*Rinaldi v. Yaeger*, 384 U.S. 305, 308). However, assuming that such a classification—and also any subclassification—is upheld then one may next question whether all in each class are receiving equal or like treatment. In other words, equal protection now enters. (Of course a government may not have any power at all to act for or against the persons regardless of a valid classification, which is a completely separate question brought under any constitutional clause, or there may be a lack of procedural due process, but these are technical legal problems not pertinent here.)

In this analysis the classification question is generally decisive (assuming government power to act as it desires). Whether or not a particular classification is good or bad, i.e., constitutional or not, is, however, not only a reflection of a nation's historic background and culture but of all of its current and changing attitudes, as well as of how all this is interpreted and applied by those having this power. In the United States the judicial view is to uphold legislative or executive classifications when these are not arbitrary or capricious but are rational and reasonable. In 1928 Justice Brandeis wrote that "the classification must rest upon a difference which is real, as distinguished from one which is speculative, remote or negligible."

The American judiciary has upheld classifications involving or based upon sex, age, income, wages, hours, etc., although repudiating illegitimacy as "an invidious discrimination against a particular class" where only legitimates were permitted to sue for the wrongful death of a next of kin. In several instances the High Court has first upheld, and later denounced, classifications. For example, in 1894, in *Plessy v. Ferguson*, a state's classification of persons on the basis of color was upheld for the purpose of requiring all black people to ride in railroad coaches reserved for them, so long as these coaches were physically equal to those reserved for the non-black. In 1954 the *Desegregation Case* reversed this holding because, in the light of new social discoveries and knowledge, such a classification in education on the basis of color was wrong. Subsequent rulings extended this rejection of a color classification. And, in a remarkably viable decision in 1968, the Court upheld §1 of the Civil Rights Act of 1866 as authorized by the Thirteenth Amendment so that federal courts could restrain racial discrimination by private individuals in the sale of realty (*Jones v. Mayer Co.*, 392 U.S. 409).

This humanistic attitude toward people, as distinguished from associations, corporations, and all impersonal groups subsumed under the constitutional term "persons" in the Equal Protection Clause, makes for a greater equality in protection and in treatment. In this respect the United States has permitted its judges to lead in determining whether or not such Clause is to be extended beyond its former boundaries. But equal protection is not limited to this Clause; it is accorded in many and different ways, in addition to the voluntary methods adopted by religious and other groups, and individuals. For example, there are other Clauses available, as well as various legislatures and chief executives who may also so act, either independently or in conjunction.

There is thus a broadening of equality and equal protection, a greater inclusion of people within its concepts, with more extensive and deeper protection accorded, even while the built-in historical method of classification remains. For example, equal protection in its general and not necessarily legalistic sense, is also found through the negative use of the Due Process Clause, which generally limits governments in the United States when these seek to prevent permanent resident aliens from working, operating businesses, or otherwise earning a living. The Constitution's Commerce Clause (Art. I, §8, cl. 3) is also used to enable the federal government to prevent inequities and provide for a degree of equality, for example, through desegregation of motels and restaurants which may not be otherwise reachable. The Bill of Rights, among other things, enables all persons to demonstrate peacefully and to speak and protest so as to obtain equality in all facets of life, and gives any accused the right to counsel regardless of financial inability to pay. The legislatures, either federal or state, may strike at discrimination and the unequal treatment of black people, aliens, or others in job opportunities. The chief executives, whether federal, state, or local, may exert similar negative and positive powers with respect to their armed and police forces, and otherwise.

Other Countries. What the United States is doing through its various powers and organs, and what its people do voluntarily, meet with varying degrees of opposition; such opposition is also found elsewhere in the world, sometimes in a repressive fashion. Rhodesia is only one example. Nevertheless, the idea of equal protection and treatment has spread during the last two centuries to the point where the United Nations' purposes include the development of "friendly relations among nations based on respect for the principle of equal rights," etc. (Charter, Art. 1, par. 2). So, too,

does India's Constitution provide for equality (Arts. 14–18) and other rights, as does that of the Philippines, which contains a Bill of Rights. In 1968 the new Canadian Prime Minister reportedly promised "to strive for a just society with all possible freedom for individuals and equal sharing of the country's wealth."

The desire for equal protection and treatment politically, economically, educationally, and in all other aspects of human behavior and conduct has spread with the "revolt of the masses" envisaged since Christ. This current desire and need for such negative and positive equal protection is aggressive, that is, the people press for it, but is also defensive, that is, persons and nations which can aid do so not only for humanitarian reasons but also for self-interest. Some feel that this glacial movement toward equality will result in a complete levelling of differences and the elimination of all classifications, but this is impossible. What appears more likely to happen is a general raising of the economic standards of living, equal participation in government and culture, and otherwise the enjoying of more of the good life by those once classed as inferiors.

BIBLIOGRAPHY

Additional bibliographies are contained in several of the following, and cases and citations are found throughout. L. Abbott, *The Rights of Man* (Boston, 1901). Aristotle, *Politics*, trans. B. Jowett (Oxford, 1885), pp. 79–80, 232. M. Berger, *Equality by Statute*, rev. ed. (New York, 1967), biblio., pp. 230–36. C. F. Emerick, *The Struggle for Equality in the United States* (New York, 1914). M. D. Forkosch, *Constitutional Law*, 2d ed. (New York, 1969), and idem, "The Desegregation Opinion Revisited: Legal or Sociological," *Vanderbilt Law Review*, 21 (Dec. 1967), 47–76. R. J. Harris, *The Quest for Equality* (Baton Rouge, La., 1960). H. J. Muller, *Freedom in the Ancient World* (New York, 1961), p. 58. H. A. Myers, *Are Men Equal?* (Ithaca, N.Y., 1945). J. H. Wigmore, *A Panorama of the World's Legal Systems*, 3 vols. (St. Paul, Minn., 1928), I, 16.

MORRIS D. FORKOSCH

[See also Class; **Democracy;** Enlightenment; **Equality;** Hierarchy; **Justice;** Law, Due Process, Natural; Property.]

NATURAL LAW AND NATURAL RIGHTS

I. *DEFINITIONS*

THE EXPRESSION "natural law" includes the ideas of *nature* and *law*, two nouns which do not lend themselves to univocal objective definition or even at least to general or commonly accepted usage. One recent author Erik Wolf (*Das Problem* . . . , Ch. I, Part III) enumerates twelve meanings of "nature" and ten meanings of "law," which yield 120 possible combinations and almost as many definitions of the expression "natural law." We may add that if it is theoretically possible to think of supporting a specific agreement as to the present meaning of "nature"—again in this case not overlooking all the other historically accepted meanings—on the other hand, it is certain that there is no hope of finding a similar agreement about the idea of "law": the definition of law entails reference to philosophical presuppositions and consequently is not susceptible to supporting an indispensable general consensus. The definition of law is indeed the rock of Sisyphus.

To define natural law in an objective manner by disengaging it from its environment, from the schools which employ the expression, or from the political and legal organs which make use of it, is therefore an undertaking doomed to failure from the start. Hence it is necessary, if we wish to avoid confusion, always to qualify the expression: for example, classical natural law (to make the Aristotelian or Thomist conception precise); Stoic natural law; Protestant natural law; positive natural law characteristic of one of the forms of contemporary natural law (the legal sense of natural law); and so forth.

Furthermore, certain essential features of natural law can be formulated by specifying it in contrast with conventional law: nature opposed to convention, justice to legal right, even unwritten law opposed to written law, the permanence of certain human values confronting the transitory character of other values derived especially from the state. Seen in this light natural law appears as a group of principles that transcend the law of different epochs and regrouping a set of norms endowed with a certain continuity by opposition to the law of a given epoch, which is transitory and changing; for the law of any epoch is the interpreter of the preceding one, whereas natural law is the law which outlives the times.

Though the expression "natural law" is equivocal, the idea of "natural rights" presents much less ambiguity. By "natural rights" we understand the subjective rights that man possesses as a human being, which are granted to his person for the protection of certain essential interests. These rights are considered the irreducible legal patrimony of every human being as part of his very nature. They are based on the idea that only a human being is a person, and that every human being is a person. As a consequence, these rights are inalienable and imprescriptible. Inalienable, because if these rights would be given up, man would cease to be a person and become a case of alienation;

imprescriptible, because if these rights ceased to exist (extinctive prescription), man would likewise cease to be a person in his prescribed condition.

Natural rights thus appear as a manifestation of individualism, man being considered in his own nature independently of his political allegiance. They consecrate the idea of the dignity of the human person considered as such.

II. HISTORICAL ORIGINS

Greece and Rome. The idea of natural law is tied to the conception of an organized universe; the idea can be disengaged only after a society has become aware of the regularity, the succession, the repetition of natural phenomena, the existence of cycles and the ability to make predictions, predictability based on the existence of interrelations with the physical world. Natural law assumes a spatiotemporal representation of the universe. Hence it is at a loss when confronted with the many discrepancies in the magical condition of societies lacking any ordered structuring. But as soon as the idea becomes clear that there exist laws governing natural phenomena, there develops immediately the conception of a general principle and ubiquitous organizer of the initial chaos.

In Greece the idea came to a head quickly. Incoherence gave way to order. Since certain phenomena in nature answer to laws, it was logical to believe that all phenomena answer to laws and that notably societies, peoples, and relations among individuals would also answer to a preestablished integral order which needed only to be sought and discovered. It was namely the idea of *Kosmos*, the order of things in contrast to disorder, confusion, and chaos. The single directing principle was supposed to govern everything including men placed at the center of the universe and societies having the same characteristics as the other elements in the external world. Whence the idea that there exists a set of general and universal norms inherent in nature itself, especially in human nature, and which would be imposed upon man's will insofar as his will manifests itself in the form of custom or law. Heraclitus, for example, defined wisdom as consisting of "a single thing, to know the thought which governs all things everywhere" (Heraclitus, frag. 41; Jean Voilquin, p. 76). This thought is the "Logos" whose meaning is surely difficult to comprehend exactly, but which—as Voilquin proposes (p. 76, note 48)—appears really to be reason insofar as it is common to all creatures, because reason contains the laws that govern the world: "It would be in some manner the communality of universal thought, the wisdom which is one, excluding the neo-Platonic and Stoic meaning" (ibid.).

In such a conception the world does not develop

in an order according to time, but in an order according to thought, which moreover sees the world as one. The laws, besides, are not due to man's will alone or maintained solely by human support, but "are nourished by a single divine law which rules over all, as it pleases, sufficing and surpassing in all things" (Voilquin, frag. 114). Thought is considered the highest virtue, and wisdom consists in saying what is true and in acting according to nature by listening to its voice.

We find again a moving and coordinating principle of a similar or at least analogous nature, in Anaxagoras of Clazomena, in the form of *voῦs* ("mind") infinite and autonomous, mingling with nothing, "alone with itself and by itself." It is at once the directing principle and the moving principle; it is the ordering principle of the universe: *μάνια διέκοτμησε voῦs*. The idea of a law higher than human law can be perceived to emerge here with the opposition between nature and convention. The idea of nature is extended farther. Besides purely physical nature, education is capable of producing kinds of conduct which are so well integrated with our personality that they are indistinguishably fused with natural sorts of behavior. "Nature and education are close to each other, for education transforms man, but through this transformation creates in him a second nature" (Voilquin, frag. 33).

The opposition between a higher law inherent in the logos, which organizes the world, and man-made law finds its dramatic illustration in the fifth century B.C. in Sophocles' *Antigone* (ca. 454–450), putting into relief the contrast between Creon's edict and the Gods' unwritten and infallible laws. Let us not be mistaken about it, however; it is less a matter in this case of appealing to a natural rather than to a supernatural law against the state, but it was more specifically a case of a moral against a legal duty. In fact, Antigone appealed to piety.

Recourse to an organizing principle of the cosmos as evidence of intelligence is found again in Socrates in the form of the tendencies according to which it is normal to live, whereas Plato does not refer to empirical phenomena but to ideas realized in the "eternity of nature." Moreover, Plato defines justice in the *Republic* as conforming to nature (*Republic*, IV, 444d). Justice and nature are thereafter indissolubly linked. Furthermore, he distinguishes the written law from the unwritten law; the former governs cities, the latter issues from custom and manners, that is to say, from natural conduct.

Aristotle brings to natural law theory an essentially new contribution by deriving the concept of right from the idea of justice, the latter being the appropriate mean that the judge maintains between the parties in court (*Nicom. Ethics*, Book V, Ch. IV, 8). The right is

called δίκαιον "because the division is made in two equal parts" (δίχα); it is as though one were to say "divided in two" (δίχαιον) and the word for judge (δικαστής) is synonymous with "he who divides in two" (διχαστής). In other terms, the judge apportions to each his due, that is, fixes in fair proportion the goods and benefits which men share within the city. It is a specific instance of justice within the idea of general justice. The magistrate is just in the largest sense for in exercising his power he is the guardian of this general justice. And where there is justice, there is also equality (*Ethics*, Book V, Ch. VI, 5). The aim of judicial activity is therefore the right, the right of the city, a political right insofar as it aims to establish this equality. Now this political right exists either by natural origin or by its basis in law (*Ethics*, Book V, Ch. VII, 1).

Aristotle envisages nature as the source of justice even if beside nature there exists legal justice. Justice is thus sought in nature itself, that is, outside of man in a world external to man. Justice is no longer taken from the principle organizing chaos, nor from internal reason, but from the observation of the world. The criterion of original nature is found, Aristotle says, in what "everywhere has the same effect and does not depend on diverse opinions" (*Ethics*, ibid.) in contrast with what is based on law. Furthermore, he argues against those who would question whether right can be in part natural on the ground that what is natural should be immutable and have the same effect everywhere, whereas right is always changing. For Aristotle, nature in fact is susceptible to modification and is not immutable; skill can be acquired and modify nature (the handicrafts are an example). It is up to man consequently to discern by observation and by interrogating nature what is natural and what conforms to its order, natural right consisting precisely in finding that justice is in consistent harmony with the natural order and thereby objective. There is accordingly a common external reference to individuals to which one may have recourse in order to determine what is each one's just due. The totality of these conclusions forms natural right whose content tends to evolve to the extent that nature itself evolves, and to change in proportion to which man tends to change. A theory of this sort leads necessarily to casuistry.

The Stoic doctrine by comparison with Aristotle's theory marks a return to a less legalistic conception, being almost entirely part of a moral theory. Nonetheless, nature occupies a fundamental place in it. Nature is an "hexis," an essence which is self-moving through seminal reasons, producing and containing what she provides in limited periods of time, and giving birth to things similar to those from which she has been detached. Her aim is both utilitarian and agreeable.

15

As for the world in general, it is governed by a destiny which is the linkage of the causes of things, or again, reason.

We see something of the sort reappear in a logos, a part of which is attributed to man in the form of rational faculties; but it is clearly no longer the logos of Heraclitus. On the contrary, the world "is a living reasonable being, animated and intelligible," according to Chrysippus. Man can, therefore, perceive the structures of this rationally intelligible world through reason as interpreter. Reason, having been given to reasonable animals in a more perfect fashion, to live according to their nature, becomes for them the same as to live according to reason which is the regulator of instinct. To live in conformity with nature is conducive also to living in accord with virtue, for nature leads to virtue.

Furthermore nature's gifts consist of good instincts only. Hence justice can result only from nature and not by human decree, as is also the case with law and right opinion. Hence the subordination of decree and convention to a higher norm which integrates the just. This higher norm is surely not juridicial, and Michel Villey (I, 135) was correct in challenging the view that it is, but it is a means of knowing the right rule and consequently, of singling out the norms that can qualify as natural, for these norms are in conformity with nature or with the intelligible structure of reality. Undoubtedly the norms thus singled out are not what observation of nature shows, but they are what a rational process yields. As a consequence, we have another meaning here for the expression "natural law" but this meaning is destined to have profound repercussions. In any case it is a declaration that the just is not a matter of convention. Moreover, by virtue of the fact that this theory is inscribed in an ethics in which corruption is absent, reference is made to man. Applied to jurisprudence such a theory by its very nature leads one to scrutinize the nature of man and to place man at the center of the legal construction of right. Whence, the idea of "natural rights" comes to the fore.

On these foundations the idea of natural law penetrated Roman law. But before approaching this problem it is important to show briefly that the natural law doctrine was far from encountering unanimity in Greek philosophy.

In opposition to the current of natural law, there was in fact a steady stream of what, for lack of any more adequate expression, may be described as positivist thought. Archelaus, the teacher of Socrates, thought that "the just and unjust are not such by nature, but by custom." Similarly the Pyrrhonians and Epicureans, on the grounds of their philosophy, subscribed to the same point of view since the essence of things could not be perceived. There is an echo of this doctrine in Lucretius' *De rerum natura*. The coexistence, consequently, within philosophy itself of two irreconcilable, irreducibly opposed tendencies is found, moreover, again in nearly every period.

Roman Law. It was through the path laid down by middle Stoicism that the doctrine of natural law reached Roman jurisprudence. The very ancient Roman law knew nothing in fact of natural law. Every law was tied to political allegiance. Once this allegiance was over, the law also terminated and the legal bonds which united the individual to the city were severed, so that the city was then deprived of any legal prerogative.

The penetration of Greek ideas was, however, to modify this point of view, especially after 146 B.C. when Greece was annexed. The praetor's edict and the jurisconsults' works were the vehicle for this penetration, so long as the jurisconsults belonged to the intellectual aristocracy and kept a share of the power, their influence was consequently decisive on the evolution of Roman law.

Middle Stoicism, notably that of Panaetius and Posidonius, made the matter easy moreover, for it revised the very narrow positions held by the original Stoics, yielding on certain points, and proposing especially an active morality. "The wise man does not live in the desert, for he is sociable by nature and made for action. He exercises to strengthen his body, and he will pray to the Gods and make vows to obtain their blessings."

However, the thought of Plato and Aristotle was for all that not neglected. They are the source of those famous definitions: of Law (*Jus*) as "the art of the good and the equitable" (*Jus est ars boni et aequi*) by Celsus, and of Justice as "the constant and perpetual will to attribute to each his due" (*Iusticia est constans et perpetua voluntas ius suum cuique tribuendi*) by Ulpian. These definitions were undoubtedly of Greek origin.

The famous definition, not of natural right but of natural law, is formulated by Cicero in his *De republica* (3.22.33): "True law is right reason which conforms to nature" (*Est quaedam vera lex recta ratio, naturae congruens*); it is nonetheless Stoic and constitutive of an ethics whose content is made clear in *De inventione* (2.53.161), namely, the law engraved in our hearts, as are religion, piety, gratitude, vengeance, respect, and truth.

But if the distinction between law and justice is not too clear-cut, the distinction between natural law and the law of the city was soon adopted by the jurisconsults who with much less oratory took up again the

Stoics' notion of natural reason enabling one to distinguish among the norms those that would qualify as natural. Gaius, in Book I of his *Institutes* (*Digest*, I.t.1;9) taught that "all the civilized peoples govern themselves partly through the law common to all peoples, and partly through the law peculiar to themselves, for when a nation creates a law, it becomes its own 'civil law,' while the law established by natural reason among all men is observed equally everywhere and is called the law of all people (*lex gentium*), obligatory on all nations."

The separation is clearly made, for lack of being well made: this law of peoples, product of natural reason, is necessarily the most ancient "for it was born with the human species" and the compelling character of natural reason with respect to positive law is undeniable. Hence civil law cannot be arbitrary for it is limited by *natural reason* (*naturalis ratio*).

Probably even more stoical is the tripartite division of Ulpian: natural law, human law, and civil law. This division reveals the wish to allow nature to play as extensive a role as possible.

Is the influence of natural law, conceived as stemming from natural reason, only an ornament of Roman law, a kind of addition to its basis which was probably quite different, a general introduction to a law which would have had no use for it?

The answer appears to us subtle. It is certain that the analysis of the *Digest* proves that the part played by natural law in the regulation of an institution like marriage is important (*Digest*, Book XXIII, title II, law 14, sec. 2). As a single example: the *cognatio servilis* ("slave status") prevents the marriage of a liberated slave with his mother, his sister, or his sister's daughter, and reciprocally a liberated father could not marry a liberated daughter. The reason: "in marriage the natural law and the feeling of decency are to be observed" (*in contratendis matrimonis naturale jus et pudor inspiciendus est*). Likewise, the evolution of the status of the slave seems to be well based on the Stoic idea that all men are equal—a line of reasoning contrary to that of Aristotle. At first, the slave's acquisition of a name, then of limited property (*peculum*), and finally, of the right to manifest and declare his freedom as a person—all that indicates an evolution based on a principle borrowed from the Porch of Stoicism.

As for the law of contractual obligations, there seems to be no exception to its having been conceived with the theory of natural obligations. On the other hand, it is true that most of the jurists' works remain works of casuistry, and to this extent they may be claimed to be more Aristotelian than Stoical since natural law never appears in their works dressed in the form of a deductive system.

The Christian Contribution. The influence of Stoic thought came to fruition with the advent of Christianity. Humanitarian Stoicism, at the time of the Antonines, led Roman society to Christianity, while the jurists were welcoming the idea of a justice superior to human laws. We have already indicated the definitions of Celsus and Ulpian. Saint Augustine, in his *City of God*, was to be the first to formulate clearly the doctrine by which participation in God's thought and creative work is imposed as a moral and obligatory end. Natural law is nothing but the formulation of this moral order. Now, there is an undeniable hierarchy: the superiority of life over organic matter, and among living creatures, the primacy of the life of the mind over that of the senses.

The subordination of matter to the mind and the subjection of the senses to reason were to become the fundamental principles of natural law. At all times in every period and in every place, actions are considered just and others unjust, licit or illicit, authorized or forbidden; forbidden: to betray one's country, to steal, to kill, not to do unto others what one would not have others do unto one. This emphasizes at the same time the recognition in man of preexisting rights in the form of individual rights, natural rights which were to be recognized in every individual as his irreducible patrimony.

The reconciliation of Stoic with Christian thought is appropriately referred to Saint Paul. The principal text is that of the Epistle to the Romans 2:14–15 which declares that nature has given the pagans something, a law engraved in their heart, to which their conscience bears witness as well as their thoughts. Here was an undeniable coming together of reason, natural law, and consciousness of this law. This uniting was already present in Judaism.

Teaching about the natural consciousness of good and evil was taken up again by Justinian. God is believed to have confirmed natural law or to have given it to mankind.

However, this reconciliation which led to a form of rational law was not to be without frequent vehement opposition: Lactantius strongly opposed Zeno's maxim "to live according to nature" and "to live according to reason." In any case, the appeal to reason as the regulating element of individual life and the recognition of natural law in men's hearts were triumphantly expressed by Saint Ambrose in an explicitly Paulist perspective. Saint Augustine's position is a more complex one; the text of the Epistle to the Romans should be interpreted in the sense that all the natural virtues can be considered as virtue only through grace. There is no nature which can lead to virtue apart from grace, so that natural law is natural by reference to God. The **17** idea of reason is surely not eliminated, it is referred to divine reason and reinforced by divine will. Furthermore, it may be inferred that God imposes only commandments conforming to an order called natural.

The Stoic influence is nevertheless assured even though there is little unanimity about purely rational natural law. The whole problem of ontology is posed here. However, the existence of a natural law categorically opposed to positive law is not questioned and the definition of these respective laws remains a classical question just as it was in Roman law.

Isidore of Seville, in his *Etymologies* (ca. 633), announced the dichotomy: "All laws are either divine or human" (*Omnes leges aut divinae sunt, aut humanae*). The former flow from the "constant Divine nature," and the others from human customs and manners (*humanae moribus constant*). Divinity and nature in that way form again an indissolubly linked pair. However, the Roman tripartite division of Ulpian was not formally abandoned, but was to undergo a profound modification. Natural law is common to all peoples, the civil law appropriate to each people, the *jus gentium* is used among the majority of peoples. Natural law is the same everywhere, for it is not the work of an initial institution but the result of a genuine instinct, based on nature independently of the vacillations of opinion with divergent views of civil law.

Isidore's classification, though it preserves the formal framework of Ulpian, still profoundly modifies the content of the ideas. Natural law (*jus naturale*) included the law common to man and animals and the law common to all men. The category of *jus gentium* thus became dispensable and was to be used in order to rearrange the rules of public international law utilized by most nations, such as rules about the occupation of vacated lands, their organization and defense; rules about war and the aftermath of war, rules about treaties, captivity, postwar boundaries, immunity of elected officials, as well as interdictions of marriage between foreigners which would be one of the matters subject to the law of peoples until the end of the eighteenth century.

These ideas were taken up again and even highlighted by Gratianus (fl. 1140). The beginning of the Decretal of 1140 is in fact a gloss on the first of Isidore's classifications: "the human race is governed by two things, natural law and custom."

The confusion between divine law and natural law was complete. Besides, Gratianus was as clumsy as Isidore in reconciling this bipartite division with the tripartite division of natural law, law of peoples, and civil law.

Natural law is the oldest, going back, as it does, to the origins of mankind. Civil laws afterward codified the habits and customs of men. Natural law is the most stable, without variation in each era. Finally, natural law transcends positive law in such wise that if certain things are accepted by custom or by written law but are contrary to natural law, they are null and void (*vana et irrita sunt habenda*).

The Decretal played an important role in the evolution of Christian thought; actually influenced by the reflections of jurists and theologians, the Decretal was enriched by a whole battery of commentaries and ideas, at times profound and always ingenious.

The idea of natural law was to be put to the test. The decretalists were divided on the question whether there exists a law common to men and animals. Rufinus eliminated this idea which Etienne de Tournai, on the other side, defended, admitting at the same time the *jus gentium* which identifies the law arising from the community of civilized peoples with natural law, reserved for men. On the whole, thought on the subject was wavering; the meanings given to the expression "natural law" multiplied; they were not only numerous but also irreconcilable (see, for example, the *Summa Lipsiensis* of 1186 which set up six successive definitions going from miraculous revelation to the teaching of reason and to simple morality). However, a deepening of thought should be noted, one resulting from the analysis of the rules of natural law. Not all of them are equally constraining.

Thanks to these analyses, natural law takes on an eminent value, differing from positive law with respect to four distinctive characteristics:

(1) its origin (natural law goes back to the beginning of mankind);
(2) its domain (it is common to all);
(3) its worth (it is a measure or standard);
(4) its rigor (it is immutable in two of its three parts).

The theologians' task is more explicative than analytical; they explain the Bible by relating it to natural law (Exodus 3, 22; the polygamy of patriarchs, fornication, etc.). However, certain theologians contribute important matters with respect to the idea itself; such was the case with William of Auxerre (fl. 1231) who insisted on the innateness of natural law and its close association with synteresis, or innate moral sense, which as an activity starts with the contemplation of God or with the knowledge of observable things. Then there was Albert the Great (1206–80) who defended vigorously the idea that natural law is the rational feature of human law, certain precepts being at the same time natural and rational (conservation of the species, for example), other precepts being simply rational (those of religion). The rational is not opposed to nature, for human nature is rational.

End of the Middle Ages and William of Ockham.
The intransigeant Augustinian conception of Christianity was thus subdued and a return to the ancient sources was bound to occur. Saint Thomas Aquinas was going to refer back to these sources, more particularly to Aristotle's natural law. From Aristotle he borrowed the evolutionary feature of a changing natural law, for human nature is variable. Hence, laws are themselves susceptible to variations. The precepts of natural law are the first principles of human action. Man's initiative returned to the forefront in the quest and discovery of law.

In short, Aquinas viewed the universe as governed by eternal law; man is subject to natural law, which is only the reflection of divine reason, and finally human law simply applies the precepts and principles of natural law by adapting them to the particular needs and circumstances of social life. The eternal or divine law integrates natural law, but natural law is distinct from divine law in that the latter includes the many truths of a supernatural order foreign to natural law. Natural law appears here not as natural in the first sense of the term, but as rational human law for man is a reasonable creature.

Natural law consists henceforth in fundamental primordial judgments of a moral order; synteresis is its habitus or way of functioning. Natural law is therefore not the synteresis but its object. The system thus is clear: natural law constitutes the principle of universal order and archetype of all law; natural law permits man to participate through his reason in divine or eternal law; finally, human law is integrated in natural law by being a projection of it as the function of fulfilling social needs. Hence it is possible to resist unjust laws. Since natural law is the intended product of natural reason, it participates in nature.

What then happens to the universality and immutability of natural law? Universality holds only through certain universal principles (act according to sound reason), immutability is relative by virtue of the very nature of man. Man is impelled by sound reason towards the quest of the common good, for an individual's ideal is realizable only to the extent that the community's ideal is realized.

The voluntarist current was not however obliterated, and the return to this position was very plainly discernible in William of Ockham, in the fourteenth century. He opposed both Aristotle's realism and Aquinas' moderate form of realism. For Ockham, only individuals exist; man as an abstract category is a creation of the mind—such is his essentially nominalist thesis. Hence, there arises the tendency to think of law chiefly as starting from the individual and not by virtue of relationships among individuals, which tendency will lead ultimately to formulating individual prerogatives and to setting down exactly the rights of individuals. The very idea of natural order appeared to Ockham contrary to divine omnipotence. Participation in any reason (*logos*) whatever, which would impose on God rules external to Him, would be unacceptable.

Henceforth legal precepts are not and cannot be based on reason, nor possess any intrinsically good value. God, all powerful, can order what He pleases. The law thus finds the justification of its validity simply in the fact that it is a command. Consequently, Ockham cannot recognize as sources of civil law any other laws than the expression of the will, and no longer of nature. Natural law, in such a conception, becomes again justice "contained . . . in writing" (*in scripturis . . . continetur*), and no longer the group of rationally necessary precepts.

The Renaissance. The Renaissance was, in the person of the French thinker, Jean Bodin, to announce the return to a Stoic natural law. In his picture of universal law, Jean Bodin resumed the bipartite division of common law: natural law, human law. Natural law is called so because it is innate, ever since the origin of mankind, and that is why it is always equitable and just. Bodin extrapolates from the *De inventione* (2, 53, 161), but refuses to accept Ulpian's idea of a law common to man and animals. Opposing human law to natural law, he depicts natural law as instituted by men in conformity with nature and in view of their needs. He includes in natural law the law of peoples (in Gaius' sense) and the civil law belonging properly to each nation, but dispenses with natural law for this purpose when it is a question of defining the art of law. In Bodin's *Republic*, the natural faculties of individuals are recognized as equivalent to laws (natural laws). Positive law has no other aim than to assure the individual the legitimate prerogatives which he holds by virtue of his nature, by the needs and aspirations of his being. All this does not, however, prevent the State from being the true sovereign, and the will of the Prince from being its voice. Absolutism is not in any case complete for this sovereignty is exercised only with regard to the positive law. Above the State and binding it is natural law; the danger is thus conjured away.

The School of Natural Law. The so-called school of Protestant natural law arose in the seventeenth century with Grotius, incorrectly described as the father of natural law. His originality is undeniable, but a great part of his natural law work is only the consolidation of tradition. The Aristotelian and Thomistic foundation is unmistakable. Man is characterized by a nature at once sociable and reasonable. Whence it follows that all the norms, which in the light of man's reason favor his life in society, are in harmony with his nature. Man has a genuine instinct for sociability; as soon as he perceives the necessity of human interdependence, he proposes a rule to obey laws that he is reasonably expected to observe as actually necessary to his life. It is of the nature of an intelligent and free man to accept this rule; but differing from physical laws, man's laws may not be obeyed, and therefore it is necessary to supply them with sanctions; these sanctions should have to be rarely applied for otherwise there would be anarchy leading to the disappearance of social life.

Natural law is thus a presentation of right reason according to which we necessarily judge an action to be just or immoral depending on its conformity with reasonable and social nature. God, the author of nature, may thus defend some laws and condemn others (Grotius, *De jure belli ac pacis,* Vol. I, Ch. IX, 1). On the other hand, the originality of Grotius is to have pushed the thought of Saint Thomas to its extreme limits. In fact, reason is no longer the reflection of the divine nature, but is inherent in the very nature of man; everything "would take place somehow even if it were admitted that there is no God (an impiety which cannot be anything but a possible crime), or if there is a God, that he is not concerned with human matters" (Grotius, ibid., Prolegomena, para. 2). The idea is not a formally new one, since Hugh of Saint Victor had already expressed it, and Suarez after him, but it was no longer a scholastic hypothesis. Natural law was secularized in germ by Saint Thomas who offered an entire intellectual attempt aimed at giving natural law an objective basis. Moreover, Grotius' method opened the door to the construction of a rational law no longer verified by experience but deduced abstractly, without considering "any particular fact," taking as initially given only the nature of man. It was a very sharp break with Aristotelian and Thomistic empiricism which was to lead to "rational natural law" and to enjoy an enormous success until the beginning of the nineteenth century; it has been severely criticized since then.

Grotius' teaching was confirmed and amply developed. Spinoza's *Ethics* brought philosophical support by affirming that each being tries necessarily to persevere in its nature. Man consequently is opposed to everything which can destroy his existence, and natural law will help him realize this aim.

It was in 1672 that Samuel Pufendorf, in his *De jure naturae et gentium* (8 vols.), and in 1673 in *De officio hominis et civis juxta legem naturalem* (2 vols.), extended considerably the ideas of Grotius. Natural reason is concerned with terrestrial duties and allows us to establish the scale of our duties imposed on us for the protection of human society. Theology is domiciled in an otherworldly domain.

Rational natural law was to acquire in that way an eminent place and was imposed as much on matters relating to personal individual law as to those of citizens and affairs of state and relations among states; we need recall only Cumberland, Barbeyrac, Wolff, and Burlamaqui in the eighteenth century. A common trait running through all these authors' writings, the permanent nature of man illuminated by right reason, has as its corollary universal rules of behavior logically deduced and indispensable for the survival of any society. Although the impulse seemed irresistible, and man in such a system enlightened by his reason can deduce all of law and then discover the universal rules governing human actions, nevertheless there were still solid points of resistance. Adopting the viewpoint of Montaigne, Pascal in his *Pensées* (Sec. V) was to make a harsh criticism of this universal justice and rational law. Pascal's aim was obviously apologetic: the unity of religion opposing the heterogeneity of law or positivist position.

Hobbes occupies a special place by himself with his critical stand on sociability. His *De cive* contains a sharp criticism of Aristotle's idea of man as a social creature. Far from being impelled by a natural desire to be united, men being equal by definition, distrust one another and fight and injure each other often in seeking the same thing. The natural state of men is a perpetual war of all against all. Men, no doubt, are not intrinsically bad, but they have a complex nature. In any case, however, in the state of nature they are selfish and hence enemies. As the supreme evil is suffering and death, they consequently go ahead and unite in a society under the influence of fear and insecurity and delegate their powers to an authority which would be all the more absolute insofar as Hobbes made the social contract the basis of a civil state. All powers were in that way to be concentrated in the hands of the sovereign.

The law of nature rationally demands respect for this pact and regard for the justice emanating from the sovereign. The *Leviathan's* universal society thus appears as an anthropomorphic creation intended to guarantee the security and protection of men. As for natural law, it holds only in the state of nature, but in a politically organized society the positive law emanating from the sovereign is obligatory, a consequent return to positivism.

The Eighteenth and Nineteenth Centuries. The preceding historical exposition has enabled us to discern at least four forms of natural law: classical, Stoic, voluntarist, and rational natural law, justifying what we said about the necessity to qualify the expression. The school of natural law met with such great success that it affected the whole political philosophy of the eighteenth century. Without minimizing the influence of Grotius and Pufendorf, it was John Locke who marked most profoundly the later development of this philosophy in the domain of natural rights and thereby of individualism, as the result of the publication in 1689/1690 of his *Two Treatises of Government*. The individual is at the center of this work which counterbalanced Hobbes's work. Men are by nature in a state of perfect freedom and complete equality. However, freedom is not license. The state of nature possesses a law which is reason, and reason teaches that no one should injure another's life, health, freedom, or property. Every human being, furthermore, should have the right to protect his prerogatives drawn from natural law, chiefly to remain in the free state of nature and not to be subjected to the political power of anyone else.

If men do unite in a society, it is by their consent, and they then form a community. But this community can live effectively only when a method of arriving at decisions is adopted, namely, the law of majority vote. He who enters a society remits power consequently and necessarily to the majority of the members. The theory of the social contract is in that way clearly expressed. Now, through this contract the individual does not give up all his natural rights, but only the part necessary for the good of the whole society. He preserves his individual rights, and political authority is limited in its action by the unconditional respect for these rights. There is thus a sharing of things. Power which does not aim at the common good or invokes the domain reserved for individual rights is tyrannical and may be resisted by force. Locke's work had an immediate and enormous success, not only in England, but also in France and in Germany.

The ideas of Montesquieu, brought up in the school of natural law, are no less important for the evolution of political society. His *The Spirit of the Laws* is built on natural law in a unified framework: "the laws are the necessary relations derived from the nature of things." Justice is prior to every contingent aspect: "To say that there is nothing just or unjust except what the laws order or forbid, is to say that before a circle is drawn the radii are not equal." Natural law then forms the framework and boundary of the powers of the civil laws, as shown by the title of his famous chapter "On Civil Laws which are contrary to Natural Law."

Montesquieu's essential contribution is not, however, in the sphere of natural law, which he does not question or improve upon, but rather in the matter of natural rights: defense of freedom, essential prerogatives which flow from freedom, guarantees against arbitrariness on the part of governing rulers.

In the sphere of ideas, the role of Jean Jacques Rousseau and of his version of the social contract is just as important as that of Locke and Montesquieu although Rousseau's predilection for natural law is more questionable. He surely admits the postulates of natural law: men's native freedom and equality. But the state of nature cannot be maintained among them. Hence, the necessity of shaping a form of association which defends and protects with all the common force the person and property of each; in this association each one, by uniting with all, obeys only himself, however, and remains as free as before. This form was elaborated by starting with a genuine fiction "the general will."

Through the "social contract," which entails "the complete alienation or surrender of each member *with all his rights* to the community," the moral collectivity called the State is established. The aim of the State is to carry out the general will which cannot err since no one is unjust to himself. The social contract gives the State an absolute power; the general will expressed by the majority necessarily implies the assent of the less enlightened minority. Of course, citizens will preserve a "natural right" as individual persons, but the sovereign alone will judge the importance of this right. This absolutism of the law contained in germ the absolutism of the State.

All these theories were soon to find a field of application. The accession to independence by the United States had brought with it published declarations which were marked by national and individualistic natural law ideas guaranteeing citizens against abuses by the sovereign power. The Constitution of the State of Virginia (1776) is prefaced by such a declaration, and the same is true of the constitutions of the states of Pennsylvania, Maryland, South Carolina, Vermont, Massachusetts, and New Hampshire which were adopted between September 1776 and October 1783.

The French Declaration of the Rights of Man was inspired by these examples. Recall that this Declaration proclaimed that the aim of every political association is "the preservation of the natural and imprescriptible rights of man," liberty, property, security, and the right of resistance to oppression.

Natural law and natural rights triumphed, but the very extension of the victory of rational natural law was going to bring about its defeat. The French codes presented as works of reason—which, moreover, they were not—appeared as models of legislation which were supposed to be applicable to other States; this extrapolation brought in its wake some severe reactions, despite the philosophical support given to Rousseau's idea by Kant, for example. Kant, in fact, defended the classical distinction between natural law and positive law by basing natural law on the rules that reason recognizes *a priori*. He thereby made a rational place for freedom in his otherwise mechanistically oriented and formal system. Post-Kantians, like Fichte, put a heavy emphasis on this *a priori* idea which gave the idea of law a supremely abstract character (Stammler).

The reaction came to be organized in Germany as well as in England and France. The German historical school was under the leadership of von Savigny, who published his famous work *On the Call of our Time for Legislation and Science of Law* (1814). It contested the idea that law could be rational, law being on the contrary the expression of the soul of a people whose law is latent in its manners and expressed in its customs. This is, of course, an historical conception, but it is also a romantic one, and Hegel, who presented himself as an adversary of Savigny, shared with him an opposition to natural law. Hegel, on the other hand, identified the rational with the real. Therefore, the real allows one to know the rational; the development of history progressively reveals the mind. Besides, man matures not through living as an individual, but does so collectively. The State is presented as the synthetic center of the general interest and good, being the reality of the moral Idea.

Hegelianism, revived by Kohler at the end of the nineteenth century, was to find some disciples also in the Third Reich's official builders of its ideology.

In England, the reaction against natural law began with Bentham's *Principles of Morals and Legislation* (1789). Bentham denounced the theory of natural law as arbitrary and based his doctrine on social utility. John Stuart Mill and Herbert Spencer enlarged this idea, which had an equivalent expression in Germany in the teleological view of law held by Jhering.

The French reactionary movement was directed not so much against natural law as against natural rights. It was led by Joseph de Maistre and Louis de Bonald who took sharp exception to the abstract nature of man in their attack on natural law.

The utopian socialism of Saint-Simon and Fourier, on the other hand, placed the whole emphasis on society rather than on the individual and gave no value to law itself. Proudhon is more subtle. Auguste Comte, finally, set natural law aside for the sake of social physics.

Marx and Engels cannot be confined to any national setting because of the widespread import of their message. The *Communist Manifesto*, issued in 1847, took a firm stand against the idea of objective immutable or eternal truths. Law results from the economy which is the substructure (*Unterbau*) whereas law is the superstructure (*Ueberbau*). Law is the will of the ruling class erected in statutes whose aim is determined by the material conditions of existence of this class. If one questions this by asking, "Are there no eternal truths

like liberty, justice, etc. which are true of the whole society?" the sharp answer is, "Communism abolishes eternal truths; instead of transforming religion and morals, it abolishes them." Positivism appeared, then, to triumph and natural law seemed destined for an irrecoverable decline.

But again, a reaction took place. A number of philosophers and jurists were indeed frightened by the possible consequences of strictly positivistic theories of law which ran the risk of validating the worst iniquities. Thus a new effort soon emerged in jurisprudence on the side of natural law.

The Contemporary Period. The tendency to return to the principles of natural law appeared at the end of the nineteenth century and soon grew rapidly.

Beudant published *Individual Law and the State* (1891); Saleilles, in 1902, spoke of "the renaissance of natural law," an expression which Charmont picked up for the title of a volume in which he put together a series of lectures he had given during the academic year 1908–09 at Montpellier, translated soon after into English and published by A. W. Spencer (Boston, 1916).

The second volume of Geny's four-volume work on *Science and Technique in Positive Law* (1921–30) bears the epigraph "irreducible natural law." It was a new declaration of a law above the legislator, and opposed the voluntarism of legal positivism. For some it was a matter of moral truth that would be imposed on the legislator, but for others it was really a matter of a distinctive legal order with the capacity to limit and even to replace the standards of positive law contrary to its imperatives.

Man would remain at the center of this renewed conception of natural law, the idea revolving entirely around the eminent dignity of the human personality basic to a series of obligations: respect for life, liberty, honor, etc. The needs of social life also entail some obligations: respect for contractual agreements, for example. The relations of the State and citizen are subject to these essential rules. Rational ethical duties are combined with social needs. These theories of natural law are not, however, reducible to a unified system.

The Neo-Thomist school challenges the absolute separation that Kant and more recently Kelsen have established between the "is" and the "ought." Man has an ultimate end directed towards the good by virtue of man's divine essence, whence the principles of justice are to be found at the center of natural law. The rational development of these principles should lead to a check on positive law, and to adapt the latter to social requirements by respecting the moral requirements. On this theme there exist many variations (Leclercq, Coste-Floret, Massis, Maritain, and others).

Michel Villey occupies a marginal place in this movement because he is a resolute Thomist and Aristotelian. Thanks to his profound analysis, however, he renewed the usual meaning given to the message of Thomas Aquinas and Aristotle.

Law is confounded with the quest of justice. Natural law implies a specific method: that of controversy; it links up with the studies, in the domain of casuistry, of the Belgian National Center of Logical Research.

The Protestant school, or better the Protestant vision of natural law, tries, following Brunner, to construct a reformed theory of society. Natural law is based neither on a cosmic nature nor on the abstract individual, but on man as the concrete bearer of the moral values of freedom which are prior to positive law, and on man as a social creature whose vocation is fulfilled within the social matrix. This idea is not far from Thomism. The reaction here is accountable as one due to the amoral character of strictly positive law. The restricted cognizance, in rules of law, of norms satisfying only formal requirements clashes too violently with that dynamic store of moral values carried by social man within himself, and leads to too many inadmissible ethical consequences. This reaction can be seen historically in the fields of both the philosophy of law and of political philosophy (cf. the Declaration of the Rights of Man, 1789). It has a non-negligible place in what Wiederkehr calls the "philosophy of the manuals," that is, the philosophy which is not expounded by those specializing in philosophy of law, but by writers expounding a branch of positive law. It is found in various countries in diverse forms (Georges Scelle, Hauriou, Roubier, Battifol, Del Vecchio, d'Entrèves, de Jouvenel, and others) and even in Germany, where Helmut Coïng in 1947 wrote on "The Supreme Principle of Law, an Inquiry into a new foundation for Natural Law" (*Die obersten Grundsätze des Rechts, Ein Versuch zur Neubegrundung des Naturrechts*). To Coïng, what is permanent in law are the basic situations assumed by him to be repeated constantly in history because of the constant condition of man and his nature. Among the spiritual needs of man is the sense of right which renders to each his due (*suum cuique*) and to the moral values required by human coexistence, values which have their source in human nature. Finally, natural law has preserved and does preserve a non-negligible place in judicial decisions, a fact which leads us to formulate a theory of positive natural law, that is to say, a law which emerges from the living judicial scene.

Seen from this angle, a certain number of general principles of law, after being approximated and brought together, benefit from a common consensus. On the other hand, natural law continues, as in every epoch, to experience serious resistance on the part of positivists whether they are state socialists or sociologists (Ripert, De Page, Kelsen, Bobbio, Eisemann, and others).

The validity of legal norms cannot be based on two eventually irreconcilable foundations; to recognize the primacy of natural law would mean destroying that of positive law. Without positive law, however, natural law would be inexact. Finally, the adversaries of natural law, analyzing the idea of natural law, challenge especially its conformity with human nature.

These objections do not appear to be decisive; the first sin by excess of logic, since the hierarchy established between natural law and positive law suffices to eliminate this objection; since the second objection is justified only to a lesser degree, it would be more exact to say that natural law allows the extraction of general rather than inexact rules; the third objection is acceptable only to the degree that this law would necessarily be innate, which is only one way to look at it. Moreover, historical study asserts that the debate is far from ended.

III. ANALYSIS OF THE ACTUAL CONCEPT OF NATURAL LAW AND ITS FUNCTIONS

Natural law appears as a model of positive law (when the meaning given to this expression is law imposed by authority, whether it be legislative or judicial), but it is nothing but a model. Natural law appears equally as a limitation of positive law, in the sense that it seeks to guarantee a certain irreducible content of the law, thereby limiting the liberty of the one who imposes the law whether he be a legislator or a judge. But it is no more than a limitation.

Natural law is really nothing but a model or a limit because it is realized in positive law, as actual judicial experience proves. Therefore, there is no necessary conflict between ideal law which ought to be and positive law which is. The opposition or antinomy, on the other hand, generally tends to diminish as positive law takes in a sufficient share of natural law even as it always takes in a minimum amount of moral value. But the amount of natural law taken in by positive law does not affect its quality. Natural law and positive law are neither opposed to each other nor are they placed side by side as the elements of a mosaic; they are complementary to each other and they are intertwined. Hence we have to separate out the functions of natural law in order to analyze it with circumspection.

To our understanding, natural law has three juridical functions: a supplementary function; a function of control or regulation; a motivating or creative function. The supplementary function comes into play when it is proper to close up the gaps in positive law. The legislator cannot foresee every case of conflict and consequently cannot formulate rules for all conflicts. In the same way the judge is limited in his mission by the cases submitted to him. Judicial rule is thus necessarily limited even when it has the unconditional value of obligatory precedent. Certainly many cases are solved, either by reference to the law, or by reference to precedent, but there are many hypotheses where there is an absence both of legislative norms and of precedents. The juridical order of law (judge-made law) then has a lacuna or deficiency.

Now, it is a principle that the judge must judge (see, for example, article 4 of the French civil code) and cannot abscond from his duty under the pretext of the law's silence; the *non liquet* ("the case is not clear") is in fact exceptional.

In such a case the judge must himself formulate a rule or a norm which would undoubtedly be decisive but which under these circumstances would perforce not be arbitrary. Accordingly, the judge's tendency is to refer to principles, and among these, when the personality of a man is involved in the conflict, the reference in particular is to the principles of natural law on account of the human values it comprehends. Natural law is thus called upon to meet the deficiencies of judicial ordinances and to supplement positive law; thereby the rule of natural law becomes the rule of positive law.

Under these circumstances natural law's function of control or regulation is nonetheless assured. Indeed, experience proves that the jurist brings judgments to bear on the rule of law, conspicuously in countries of written law. Undoubtedly, positivists challenge this prerogative: "the judge judges according to the law, he does not judge the law," they write freely. But the contrary is verifiable: the fact is that the jurist compares the positive rule with the model of natural law, and limits or departs from the rule of positive law when it seems too obviously to contradict this model. Judges do so today, and they always have done so.

This regulative function of natural law is obviously much more disputed than its supplementary role. The dogma of the separation of powers is really put to the test since the judicial power eventually understands it is censuring the work of the legislative power, and is doing so not by virtue of a fundamental law of the State charter (the Constitution) but by virtue of unwritten principles, essential principles of justice which would be imposed over any legislation for the sake of justice. Such a function is obviously inconceivable in Kelsen's system or in any system of so-called pure law. Yet experimental verification leads to the sure conclusion that at least some judges do not hesitate to test the internal content or intrinsic basis of the rule of law, and to limit or put aside the rule if its content is too obviously contrary to the so-called principles of natural law.

A variant of this attitude is seen in an intermediate position which consists in putting aside the rule set by authority insofar as the legislative power has not clearly expressed its will to infringe, in a limited domain, upon a principle generally known to be one of natural law. In short, the motivating or creative role of natural law no longer seems disputable. The rule of natural law serves the legislator as a support for creating a legal norm and to give the law in this case more of a declarative value than a created one. The rule is then supposed to have existed always, if not in its form at least in its basis, which falls back on the idea of legal retroactivity, the declarative norm being only the recognition of a preexisting legal principle. We need only think of the judgments relating to war crimes brought under the positive law of different countries in the aftermath of the second world war.

But beside its juridical functions, natural law also has a metajuridical or political function which is at least as important; again, as De Page has so subtly remarked, it is less in this case the notion of natural law than the idea of natural right which is involved.

A society's law is not a static but a dynamic affair. Called upon to govern social relations, it is not indifferent to the transformation of these relations, and must therefore follow this evolution more often than it leads it. This observation has been made for thousands of years and the principle of law arising from the fact was already recognized in the "rule of the old law" (*regulae juris antique*) in the *Digest* of Justinian. This necessary adjustment can be realized thanks to the adaptation of the existing system of law through the methods of judicial interpretation, which is in fact both explicative and creative. However, the possibilities of active interpretation are limited by technical reasons. First of all, interpretation has to operate under certain conditions. Although it is possible, by questioning the clarity of a juridical rule, to attribute a new meaning to it, still the jurist being essentially conservative, will not admit departing too far from the old rule. Abrupt mutations do occur, but they are exceptional and pointed out as such by the doctrine. Furthermore, the process of interpretation is relatively slow in its action and in its effects. A sudden change in jurisprudence has to be prepared. Coming out of the lower courts it has to be progressively confirmed by the higher courts. Moreover, a sufficient number of cases must be presented for the new theory to be elaborated, made exactly clear, and confirmed. Now it is a matter of chance as to which kinds of cases that will allow this new construction. These kinds of cases for this very reason extend over a relatively long period of time.

Finally, interpretation only solves a fraction of the problems that it sets out to resolve, bearing only on those limited aspects of a case that are necessary for its litigation. The result is that though the juridical interpretation plays a central role in the evolution of the law by acting within the system, it will not always answer adequately to the requirements of a society in rapid evolution. In this case the whole system is contested and its replacement by a new system (judged to be more just, more adequate, and better adapted to the new needs) is urged by a minority that does not have the power to change the system. They must then, for lack of power, convince the others rather than impose on them; whence, a dialectical phenomenon, the obligation to justify and to find a basis for the new system. The passage from the old to the new system is effective on the rhetorical, that is, argumentative level. Now what better argument is there than to maintain that the new system is more in conformity with the nature of things than the old one, that is to say, with the model that is provided by natural law? But it appears immediately that on this hypothesis it is not natural law so much as the *idea* of natural law which is called upon to validate and establish the new system.

This reversal, demanded in the name of an order judged to be higher, plays its part no longer on the level of jurisprudence but on the political plane. It is the accomplishment of a group of protesters who, starting with a small number, will try to add to its ranks an increasingly important mass of citizens and urge them to demand no longer the evolution of the existing system but its disqualification and its replacement eventually by force. The idea of natural law is then called upon to play a metajuridical or political role by validating a new system intended to be a substitute for the old one.

We have, in summary, remarked that the notion of natural right and the idea of natural law play a complex role, that the functions of natural law or of the idea of natural right are many whether we remain inside the legal system or go outside of it, that the concept of natural right is dynamic and not static, and that its very imprecise nature permits one to have recourse to it in many hypotheses. Must we add that because of this very imprecision, the multiplicity of its possible meanings, and the diversity of its functions, agreement about natural law and rights is very hard to obtain in any controversy? That is why there is such an extraordinary proliferation of irreconcilable opinions on the subject.

IV. ANALYSIS OF THE CURRENT IDEA OF NATURAL RIGHTS

According to the theory of natural rights, the dignity of the human person is supposed to take precedence over any social order. With Alfred Verdross we may formulate five propositions which follow from this axiom:

(1) each social order must recognize in the person a sphere within which the person may act as a free and responsible agent;
(2) the law must protect and guarantee the free exercise of a person's action;
(3) the authority of the governing body must be limited;
(4) respect for this limitation must be guaranteed;
(5) respect for authority is not absolute, but subordinate to the dignity of the human person.

Natural rights, being tied by hypothesis to the very nature of man and prior to any social order, cannot be conferred by political authority, but should be recognized and declared by the latter. Despite the lack of such declarations, these rights exist nonetheless. Declarations are therefore only a solemn affirmation of these rights and only a catalogue of the latter, as well as an expression of the wish to protect these rights.

Natural rights presuppose a fundamental postulate of equality. They are indeed tied to the idea of justice, that is, to equal treatment for all those who belong essentially to the same category. Natural rights, in short, imply the notion of a human family, in which no discrimination is permitted whether based on sex, race, religion, or any other criterion.

The first of these natural rights is obviously freedom. From it follow the other basic rights, notably property, the patrimonially protected prolongation of freedom, the security of guarantees of the free enjoyment and right of resistance to oppression, which is the supreme remedy against a political power's failure to respect natural rights or to be constrained by legal means to respect those rights. These are, moreover, the other basic rights recognized by the French Declaration of the Rights of Man of 1789 (article 2) and restated in the Constitution of 1791: "the aim of every political association is the consecration of the natural and inalienable rights of man. These rights are freedom, property, security, and the right of resistance to oppression."

The expression "natural rights" is consequently often a synonym for the "rights of man." In a more technical sense the expression is reserved for the right of existence, bodily safety, health, sexual life, personality, respect for mortal remains, etc.

Bound up with a historico-critical development, the **25**

idea of natural rights is subject to evolution and thereby to a growing enrichment; a comparison of recent declarations with those of the eighteenth century is very enlightening in this respect. The extension of natural rights to new domains is a constant one, for example, in the social or cultural domain (see the Universal Declaration of the Rights of Man of December 10, 1948 which was accepted by the General Assembly of the United Nations).

CONCLUSION

Nobody today believes in an objective natural law inscribed in the nature of things which, if it were transcribed, would suffice to yield a positive law. But there are very few people today who admit the conception of positive law as a law arbitrarily imposed by a legally recognized legislative power.

Though it is true, in any case, that law is a human product, it is not true that it can be arbitrarily imposed without consideration for the social function which it must fill. Beyond what Professor Lon Fuller calls the "inner morality of law," which consists of a set of rules that are related to what the Americans call "due process," there is room to consider, in the elaboration and application of the law, the so-called "nature of things," although this "nature of things," cannot by itself prescribe precise rules of law.

Let us take the example of a piece of legislation which for the first time authorizes the legislator to arrange with the greatest liberty a traffic code; no general principle of law, no rule of justice in this domain limits his legislative power. Let us suppose he announces the rule that every vehicle must be driven on the right side of the road, in the direction it is moving. In principle, there is no opposition to this regulation. However, the nature of things intervenes in the form of a mountainous road where two vehicles cannot cross at any point, and when a permanent one-way road cannot be established, it goes without saying that the local administration, or the judge in its absence, will have to define the conditions for utilization of this road, taking account of the location of the places and the needs of the community. Here, priority would be given, either to a certain type of vehicle; whether it were ascending or descending; or temporary or alternative one-way roads or a completely different solution, compatible with the technical condition and with the most rational possible utilization of the existing road, would be organized. But it would not occur to anybody to claim that the adopted regulation could be considered completely arbitrary.

A similar problem appears where "the nature of things" is not of a purely technical matter, but institutional or moral. Given what is considered marriage in our society, with the relationships between husband and wife, between parents and their children, what should the judge do in the present state of legislation, if in a family that has an infant child, one of the parents, for example, the father, changes his sex? The "nature of things" will oblige the judge not to refer to a predetermined solution, but to find a solution compatible with the family relationships and with the interests of all those who are involved in this unusual situation.

That which has traditionally been qualified as "natural law" presents a collection of limitations of every sort left to the discretion of the legislator, of the administrator or of the judge, by drawing their attention to a collection of exigencies which they must respect in order that the law may fulfill its avowed function. If the legislator, who acts in a general manner, does not fulfill this task, the administration or the judicial power will take charge. If that is not possible for them, for any reason, the social discontent which would result, depending on its intensity and extent, may lead to an opposition to power, to a reversal of the majority, or even to a reversal of the system.

Indeed, it is only to the degree to which those who have the authority to legislate, to govern, or to judge, fulfill their mission in a manner that does not displease the governed too much, that their authority will suffice to maintain, without too much effort, obedience to the law. But, if we admit that this obedience is the function, not only of brute force, but also of the respect which the system and its directors inspire, we come to the conclusion that any realistic study of law cannot neglect this aspect of the adaptation of juridical solutions to social exigencies, permanent or lasting, which is historically summed up in the idea of natural law or natural rights.

BIBLIOGRAPHY

Joseph Charmont, *La Renaissance du droit naturel*, 2nd ed. (Paris, 1927). Helmut Coïng, *Grundzüge des Rechtsphilosophie* (Berlin, 1950). Jean Dabin, *Théorie générale du droit* (Brussels, 1953). Georges del Vecchio, *Philosophie du droit*, French trans. (Paris, 1953). Passerin d'Entrèves, *Natural Law* (London, 1951). Henri de Page, *L'idée de droit naturel* (Brussels, 1938); idem, *Droit naturel et positivisme juridique* (Brussels, 1939). Paul Foriers, "Le juriste et le droit naturel, essai de définition d'un droit naturel positif," *Revue de Philosophie Internationale*, **65** (1965); issue devoted to Natural Law. Carl Joachim Friedrich, *The Philosophy of Law in Historical Perspective* (Chicago, 1958; revised ed., 1963). François Geny, *Science et technique en droit positif*, 4 vols. (Paris, 1921–30). Hugo Grotius, *De jure belli ac Pacis Libri tres*, trans. F. W. Kelsey, 2 vols. (Oxford, 1925). Thomas Hobbes, *De Cive or, The Citizen* (New York, 1949). Jacques

Leclercq, *Cours de droit naturel; Du droit naturel à la sociologie,* 2 vols. (Paris, 1960). John Locke, *Two Treatises of Government* (London, 1698); ed. P. Laslett (Cambridge, 1960). Dom Odon Lottin, *Le droit naturel chez Saint Thomas d'Aquin et ses prédécesseurs,* 2nd ed. (Bruges, 1931). Jacques Maritain, *The Rights of Man and Natural Law* (London, 1958); idem, *Man and the State* (Chicago, 1951). Karl Marx and Friedrich Engels, *Manifesto of the Communist Party* (1847, and many reprints). Chaim Perelman, *Justice* (New York, 1967). Samuel Pufendorf, *Droit de la nature et des gens,* trans. from Latin to French by Jean de Barbeyrac (Basel, 1732). Leo Strauss, *Natural Right and History* (Chicago, 1955). Emmerich de Vattel, *Le droit des gens ou Principes de la loi naturelle appliqués à la conduite et aux affaires des nations et des souverains* (Amsterdam, 1775). Alfred Verdross, *Abendländische Rechtsphilosophie* (Vienna, 1958). Michel Villey, *Cours d'histoire de la philosophie du droit,* Vols. 2, 3, 4 (Paris, 1963, 1964, 1965). Jean Voilquin, *Les penseurs grecs avant Socrate: de Thales à Prodicos* (Paris, 1964). Erik Wolf, *Das Problem der Naturrechtslehre, Versuch einer Orientierung* (Karlsruhe, 1955), Ch. I. *Le droit naturel:* ("Natural Law"), H. Kelsen, Chaim Perelman, A. P. d'Entrèves, B. de Jouvenal, N. Bobbio, M. Prelot, Ch. Eisenmann (Paris, 1959).

PAUL FORIERS and CHAIM PERELMAN

[See also Constitutionalism; Equality; Freedom; General Will; Hegelian . . . ; **Justice; Law, Common, Concept of,** Due Process; **Nature;** Positivism; **Right and Good;** Romanticism in Post-Kantian Philosophy; **Social Contract; State;** Stoicism.]

LEGAL PRECEDENT

I. GENERAL

As A GENERAL idea "precedent" is not restricted to juristic situations or the determination of legal controversies. Human conduct in general is largely based upon past experience. Thus precedent serves not only as an aid to resolve instant problems by reference to past practice but also is used consciously or unconsciously to direct the course of legal or other social developments. Psychologist, sociologist, philosopher, and lawyer, whose paths may diverge on many issues, are here on common ground. Resort to precedent anticipates the evolution of ideas and theories regarding it. Hoebel, a social anthropologist writes:

Regularity is what law in the legal sense has in common with law in a scientific sense. Regularity, it must be warned, does not mean absolute certainty. There can be no true certainty where human beings enter. . . . In law, the doctrine of precedent is not the unique possession of the Anglo-American common law jurist. . . . [P]rimitive law also builds

on precedents, for there too, new decisions rest on old rules of law or norms of custom, and new decisions which are sound tend to supply the foundations of future action (Hoebel, p. 28).

The psychological motivation to accept—at first unquestioningly—the validity of the conduct patterns of the past has been noted by many. Thus F. Pollock, of an older generation, thought it ". . . not unlikely that this is the manner in which the ideas of precedent and custom are formed. What has been done before is done again, not because it seems the best thing to do, but because there is an unreasoning tendency to do it" (Pollock, p. 165). K. Llewellyn, who concludes that "case law in some form" is found wherever there is law and that precedent is operative even before the idea is consciously recognized, asserts: "Towards its operation drive all those phases of human makeup which build habit in the individual and institutions in the group" (Llewellyn, "Case Law").

If there is a general natural inclination to regard past experience and decisions as guides to future action, lawyers more than other groups perhaps have used and elaborated the concept of precedent in many ways, in many legal systems, and in many epochs. Juristic theory and judicial practice may often seem to conflict—sometimes for quite creditable reasons. Though precedent may first have been recognized and accepted through irrational or unreflecting attitudes, the idea or concept of legal precedent has been supported by a variety of cogent arguments. In particular it has been said from Aristotle or Chaim Perelman to be a basic principle of the administration of justice that like cases should be decided alike. Such at least is the equality of "formal" justice. "The rules of justice," says Perelman, "arise from a tendency natural to the human mind to consider as normal and rational . . . behaviour in conformity with precedents" (Perelman, p. 86). Without the guidance of precedent based on the accumulated wisdom of the past and declared as the basis of decision by the authorized oracle, whether judge or jurist, men, it is said, would have no certainty of the law or confidence in equality before an evenhanded justice. Precedent assists the litigant or his adviser to assess the extent of his rights and duties and restricts the scope of litigation. Nor is it the party litigant or accused alone who rejects the idea of arbitrary justice. The judge or other lawgiver, unless he claims to speak as the medium of the gods with access to supernatural revelation or as an autocrat, prefers as a rule to show preexisting legal justification for the decision or sentence which he pronounces. Judges of lesser ability and experience may be fortified by the opinions of the most eminent. Moreover, in the busiest courts where most justice is administered, the machinery would break down if all judges took it on themselves to reexamine, in disregard of precedent, each aspect of every case before them. It is not indolence alone that suggests conformity to established practice. If justice requires that like cases be decided alike, this implies equality before the law. Yet, no more than two men's fingerprints are identical, are all the facts of two legal proceedings. The law itself selects—either by general rules or by the individuation of equity—what facts are relevant to exclude precedent. J. Stone comments: "Unfortunately, as lawyers have come to see, the question whether an earlier case *is* a 'precedent' for the present situation depends on an assessment of 'essential similarities' and 'differences' between the two" (Stone, p. 328).

Thus the law itself does not treat all persons as "equal"—for benefit or detriment. The young, the mentally ill, the female, the foreigner, the professional man, and the law officer are not necessarily weighed on the same scales. Changes of social mores or economic circumstance and the passage of time itself may supply good reasons for rejecting or distinguishing earlier precedents and developing the law by interstitial judicial lawmaking. Some systems are more rigid than other in veneration of past decisions. To some the idea of legal precedent is almost abhorrent.

A propensity to decide according to precedent has been criticized on the grounds that true justice is precluded when before argument or evidence one scale of the balance is already weighted by a previous decision on similar facts. Hence, as J. P. Dawson, a leading apostle of case law, has shrewdly discerned, "[T]he German for 'precedent' is *Präjudiz*. Its primary meaning is 'prejudgment' but it also verges on 'prejudice.'" A similar word (*praeiudicia*) was occasionally used by Roman jurists as a description of prior court decisions; as *préjugés* with the same meaning it appeared in pre-revolutionary France. Whether taken as 'prejudgment' or 'prejudice' it carries an implication that is distinctly unpleasant; it suggests that minds have been at least partly closed" (Dawson, p. xv). Philippe de Beaumanoir indeed argued that a judge who had participated in the decision of a case should be disqualified on grounds of bias from ruling in the future on another similar matter. Perhaps, however, the main argument which has been mounted against legal precedent based on case law is that decisions should always be based upon laws already declared by legislative power and should not be restricted by reference to decisions of judges on particular cases. It is, of course, fallacious to assume that any legal system has been or could be so formulated as to cover completely all legal relationships and situations. Moreover, the meaning of legal rules, whether contained in codes, juristic writings, or case law can only be manifested through a continuous process of interpretation, which itself tends to become guided by precedent.

Whatever the strength of arguments for and against doctrines of legal precedent in the abstract, in fact the doctrine is found to apply generally, though with differences in rigidity of application and of theoretical rationalization. A broad distinction may be made between systems where precedent has persuasive force and systems in which adherence—related to an hierarchic system of courts—is regarded as obligatory. Precedent is a useful legal tool; but misuse can result and has resulted in rigidity and injustice. Anthropologists have demonstrated that laws of precedent operate in simple societies, and legal historians have traced the application of case law in *inter alia* Semitic and Jewish law, under the code of Hammurabi, in Islamic law, in the systems of China and Japan before the impact of Western influence. For the Western world the legal traditions which have particularly molded attitudes to legal precedent are derived from Roman and English law.

II. ROMAN LAW—THE CIVIL LAW SYSTEMS

Woldemar Engelmann as late as 1938 wrote: "Precedent-justice is not only illogical but pernicious, because it interferes with the wiser conclusion of a later judge through the 'prejudice' of the earlier judge and serves the comfort of the indolent judge. . . . A mark of Rome's high legal culture is its systematic prohibition" (Engelmann, p. 29). This exaggerated statement, which is in fact mistaken, focusses sharply what has often been claimed as the main distinction between the Roman and English legal traditions, but stresses usefully a difference in attitude towards precedent which for centuries characterized these two traditions. If development of English law, built up from precedent to precedent, depended upon the preeminence of a small centralized professional judiciary assisted by a technically expert bar, legal development in Roman law was mainly the contribution of legislator and jurist using a different technique of precedent. Roman law owed its excellence to the work of its jurists.

Until the middle of the third century A.D. under Roman procedure an action usually took place at two stages, neither of which was before a professional judge, but before respected and responsible laymen who sought expert advice. At the first stage the parties settled with the *praetor* the issue to be tried and at the second the *iudex* ("judge") actually tried the case and pronounced judgment.

In early Roman law an aristocratic priesthood had exercised a monopoly of legal knowledge, and gave opinions (*responsa*) on matters of procedure and interpretation. Their opinions, of which copies were kept in the archives of the pontifical college, were binding on the magistrates. These opinions no doubt provided precedents for the pontiffs themselves. About the third century B.C., however, the pontifical monopoly was breached when a number of lay jurists appeared, sharing with the priests access to legal lore. Secularization of the role of jurist was, however, a gradual process and for a period many experts on legal matters continued to be members of the aristocratic priesthood, who in any event claimed no supernatural or spiritual gifts. The lay jurists possessed no formal authority and received no remuneration for their services, but by virtue of their high social status and personal prestige as experts, eventually superseded the pontiffs as interpreters of secular law. Under the formulary system (introduced about 150 B.C.) a party seeking redress was allowed to submit a draft *formula* embodying his claim for the *praetor's* approval, and would seek a jurist's advice in the drafting. In deciding whether to allow a novel type of *formula*, the *praetor* was accustomed to take the advice of the jurists on his council. The latter were thus enabled indirectly through the *praetor* to extend the scope of legal remedies, and thus make new law. They also exercised their influence through the medium of the *praetor's* Edict. On entering on his year of office a *praetor* issued an edict in which he proclaimed the policy in granting actions which he intended to follow. He was morally, and later legally, obliged to implement its terms, though he was not debarred from granting an action not contained in the edict. In drawing up his edict the *praetor* was again advised by his council of jurists, and, as he was not bound to follow the policies of his predecessors (until the Edict was given permanent form about A.D. 130) the jurists had scope for cautious and experimental development of the law, giving weight to the claims of continuity and innovation.

At the trial stage the judge (who like the *praetor* was an eminent layman) could also seek the advice of a council of jurists or seek an opinion from a jurist of reputation. The class of lay jurists, however, held themselves available to give gratuitous advice to all who sought it. Their opinions (*responsa*) in due course were published and they engaged in legal writing based on the style of *responsa*. Augustus granted to certain patented jurists the right to give opinions by the Emperor's authority and these carried special weight. In due course the opinions and writings of the jurists (*responsa prudentium*) were recognized among the sources of written law, and were cited as authority. The jurists were, on the whole, content to give solutions based on particular problems without elaborate theoretical analysis and reference to first principles. Though the work of the jurists was often in effect comparable to that of English "case lawyers," they did not cite judicial decisions but juristic opinions, and were not dependent on the actual adjudication of disputes to develop the law. The learned men, rather than the judges, were the elite or *honoratiores* of the Roman system, a factor which has influenced attitudes in the successors to Rome's legal heritage.

When, in the Roman system, a professional judiciary was established it was too much overshadowed by imperial authority to introduce an effective system of precedent by judicial decisions, and in A.D. 534 Justinian's *Corpus Juris Civilis* was promulgated. Justinian conceived of this as a "complete code of laws without contradiction or imperfection," and arrogated to himself the authority of interpretation. He laid down (C 7.45.13) that "decisions should be rendered in accordance, not with examples, but with laws." This pronouncement, misconstrued in its emphasis and implication, was often seized on after the "reception" in Europe of the Roman Law (from the twelfth century) to disavow judicial precedent as a source of law, though in reconciling Roman law with custom, judicial acceptance of custom was recognized. In Italy by 1500 the judges, to protect themselves against accusation of deciding wrongly, relied on the advice of legal scholars, the successors to the jurists of classical Roman law. In Germany, despite a considerable contribution of the judges before and after the reception, and many collections of judicial decisions, primacy again was for centuries secured by the learned men who professed the systematized Romanistic law and were not generally disposed to recognize judicial decisions as a source of law unless they had the effect of declaring "custom." The German Civil Code (*Bürgerliches Gesetzbuch* or B. G. B.), which came into force in 1900, was highly conceptual in structure and was expected to restrict the judicial role to that of interpretation rather than that of creating and developing law by decision. However, the duty to interpret "the general clauses" in the code and the pressure of unforeseen circumstances following two wars compelled the judges to take a leading part in developing German law by judicial decision. Extensive use has been made of interpretation of the code by analogy to develop the law. It seems now to be widely accepted that German judges can and do make law, though, as in the United States, there are differing views as to how far the judiciary should take the initiative in introducing new trends of moral attitude or social policy. Though there are differences in attitudes and techniques, J. P. Dawson concludes that there is a close resemblance between the administration of case law in Germany and the United States, and that "all the devices for close and critical reading of judicial opinions are known and used in Germany" (Dawson, p. 505). Thus, for example, cases may be narrowly distinguished on their facts if a court does not wish to follow a policy suggested in an earlier decision. However, subject to possible qualifications with regard to precedents of the *Bundesverfassungsgericht* ("Constitutional Court"), in Germany no higher court's decision in theory binds a lower court in a subsequent case, and no court is precluded from overruling its own decisions. In practice, however, decisions of the *Bundesgerichtshof* or of an appeal court will be followed by lower courts, while the form of judicial opinions and an elaborate reporting system facilitate the use of judicial precedents. Though hitherto decisions have been collegiate, a bill was prepared in 1968 with the object of recognizing opinions of individual judges and allowing dissents in the Constitutional Court. It follows that German ideas on precedent have undergone considerable transmutation over the centuries.

In France before the Revolution, though the law was largely Romanized, its administration differed substantially from the patterns of Italy and Germany. The highest courts (*Parlements*) played a considerable part in developing private law, but, though the judges themselves sought to achieve consistency through precedent in their own decisions, their motives were not readily accessible for practitioners. The *Parlements* were empowered by *arrêts de règlement* to make judicial pronouncements which were essentially legislative in character, and, because the *Parlements* tended to pursue reactionary policies, powers of judicial lawmaking were regarded with hostility after the Revolution. Article 5 of the *Code Napoléon* forbids judges to pronounce decisions so as to make general rules or precedents for the future. It was intended to abolish decisions made by judges as a source of law, not as an echo of Justinian but because of distrust of judges based on French experience. However, while academic writers emphasized the supremacy of the written law of the codes, law reports multiplied. Moreover, "While ostensibly disclaiming lawmaking power, the judges assumed it, while adopting a cryptic style of opinion writing whose main purpose was to prove their dutiful submission, but which in fact left them more free" (Dawson, p. 431). Still, though counsel in France rely greatly on precedents (which are extensively reported) the court in theory always applies the legal rule derived from the appropriate code, and the highest court (*Cour de Cassation*) refrains from citing previous cases to avoid the appearance of violating Article 5. Theoretically a French judge is entitled to ignore the previous decisions of other courts and of his own, but in fact judges tend to adopt the interpretation of courts higher in the hierarchy unless for special reason, and will also tend to follow a course of decisions in courts of coordinate jurisdiction. Judges will also be influenced by the attitude of legal scholars to particular decisions. Courts normally follow their own previous decisions, but all, including the *Cour de Cassation*, may reject a prior ruling on grounds, for example, of social or economic change. Thus the words of the code may be reinterpreted from time to time.

The French pattern is, on the whole, typical of Western Europe, because of the wide dissemination of the *Code Napoléon*, but Spanish law (which has influenced South America) provides that a lower court is obliged to follow a principle expressed in two judgments of the highest court. European civil law jurists regard this rule as unsound and calculated to result in casuistic distinctions in cases where the lower courts should anticipate that the highest court would not itself any longer follow the principle formerly enunciated. In civilian systems, generally, decisions are pronounced by a collegiate court and dissenting opinions are excluded. Moreover, the precedent is a proposition stating a legal principle, while Anglo-American techniques often leave this to inference closely linked to findings in fact. The primary technique of judicial decision in civilian systems is deductive and in Anglo-American systems inductive.

III. ANGLO-AMERICAN COMMON LAW SYSTEMS

English law is rightly regarded as the system which has given greatest veneration to legal precedent. Founded neither on the received Roman law nor on a code, the system itself was built up precedent by precedent from the Middle Ages by a remarkably small centralized judiciary working intuitively with a restricted number of practitioners at the bar. Previous decisions provided the means for building up the common law of England from other customs of the realm and was closely linked to procedural forms and techniques. Though the doctrine of precedent in a general sense is of ancient origin in English law, the doctrine of strict precedent (*stare decisis*) whereby a single decision may have binding force is more modern.

The common law was evolved by the fiction that the whole law was to be found in the bosoms of the judges (*in gremio iudicum*) and was conjured up from that repository as occasion required. Naturally therefore from the twelfth century onwards the courts were referred to earlier decisions. Bracton, who had access to the original plea rolls (the court records), cited in his writings many cases on a selective basis and accustomed lawyers of the thirteenth and fourteenth centuries to discuss them. The Year Books (ca. 1260–1535) were the earliest available law reports and, concentrating on procedural matters rather than on decided cases, supplied an account of accepted professional practice. The lawyers of this period did not evolve theories of precedent, though they attached importance to decisions recalled by judges and pleaders. They did not feel themselves compelled to perpetuate the error of a precedent which seemed clearly wrong. Until an orderly hierarchy of courts was ordained and until reliable law reports became available covering the facts in issue, counsels' arguments and judgments thereon, a strict doctrine of precedent could not develop, and from the early seventeenth until the mid-eighteenth century English law was poorly served by private reporters. Moreover, until the late eighteenth century the highest court of appeal, the House of Lords, forbade reporting of its decisions. In C. K. Allen's words: "To sum up the position at the end of the eighteenth century: the application of precedent was powerful and constant, but no Judge would have been found to admit that he was 'absolutely bound' by any decision of any tribunal" (Allen, p. 150). In 1833 Chief Justice Park stated clearly the view that rules derived from precedents must be followed unless "plainly unreasonable" for the sake of conformity, consistency, and certainty. Jeremy Bentham and John Austin had already exposed the "declaratory" theory of judicial precedent in England, i.e., that the law reposed *in gremio iudicum*, but while Bentham denounced the "retrospective legislation" of judges, Austin criticized them for being too obsequious to past authority.

Private law reporting improved in the later eighteenth century and eventually the current semi-official series of Law Reports was instituted in 1865. The Judicature Acts 1873–75 ordained a hierarchy of courts ascending from the High Court, to the Court of Appeal, to the House of Lords. Thus the whole apparatus for a strict doctrine of precedent was assembled, the decisions of courts higher in the hierarchy binding those inferior, and in the alleged cause of certainty the House of Lords in 1898 held itself bound by its own previous decisions. Probably because of the resulting rigidity, English jurists have since engaged in extensive and conflicting casuistic writing seeking to determine the binding element or proposition of law (*ratio decidendi*) in a precedent, as contrasted with an incidental judicial statement (*obiter dictum*). In fact the "general rule" of a precedent may be construed subsequently either broadly or narrowly according to whether the court considering it wishes and feels free to restrict or develop the underlying judicial policy. Though theoretically many a precedent could be "dis-

tinguished" because its "material" facts differed from those of the instant case, the handling of case law is an art partly learned in the course of practice and partly dependent on judicial temperament and placing in the judicial hierarchy. "Notwithstanding all the apparatus of authority, the judge has nearly always some degree of choice"—at least in the higher echelons. On the whole, nevertheless, English judges have been more anxious to preserve "certainty" through precedent than have judges of most other systems in the Anglo-American tradition. R. Cross, the leading modern English writer on precedent, declines to regard the distinction between *ratio decidendi* and *obiter dictum* as "entirely chimerical" in English law and concludes that to accept the views of Judge Jerome Frank and the American realists would be to impute hypocrisy to English judges who follow, while disliking "the rule" laid down by earlier cases. The "realists" by way of contrast with the stress placed by orthodox English judicial theory on the binding force of *ratio decidendi* emphasize the liberty of judges to disregard the views of their predecessors, though they may pay lip service to precedent. In 1966 the Lord Chancellor announced that the Lords of Appeal in Ordinary recognized that too rigid an adherence to precedent could result in injustice and restrict unduly development of the law. Accordingly they declared that in the future they would not be strictly bound by their own earlier decisions. This relaxation resulted from the initiative of Scots lawyers whose system, though not derived from English law, is subject to the appellate jurisdiction of the House of Lords. Subsequently, in 1968, the English Court of Appeal held that it would be bound by its own previous decisions. The Court of Session in Scotland is not so fettered. Scots law, like other systems derived from Roman law but influenced by Anglo-American law—such as those of Ceylon, Quebec, Louisiana, and South Africa—reflects that influence by accepting a doctrine of *stare decisis* (the authority of a single, binding precedent) similar to, if more liberal than, that of English law.

Courts of the United States, while accepting the principle that precedents should normally be followed, and in general using the same techniques and pronouncing opinions of the same general pattern as those of English judges, have introduced greater flexibility. American law, like English law and unlike civilian systems in general, distinguishes between the proposition of law (*ratio decidendi*) for which a precedent is authority and *obiter dicta*, and, moreover, recognizes the doctrine of *stare decisis*. Eugene Wambaugh, the American jurist, writing at the end of the nineteenth century, propounded one of the most important theories for isolating the true *ratio decidendi* of a case. 31

Judge Benjamin N. Cardozo has observed that though in exceptional cases precedents may be disregarded,

Stare decisis is at least the everyday working rule of our law. [T]he work of deciding cases in accordance with precedents that plainly fit them is similar to deciding cases in accordance with a statute. It is a process of search, comparison and little more. . . . The sample nearest in shade supplies the applicable rule. But, of course, . . . no judge of a high court, worthy of his office, views the function of his place so narrowly. . . . It is when . . . there is no decisive precedent, that the serious business of the judge begins. He must then fashion law for the litigants before him. In fashioning it for them, he will be fashioning it for others (Cardozo, pp. 20–21).

The Supreme Court of the United States and the appellate courts of the different states do not regard themselves as absolutely bound by their own previous decisions, and in certain exceptional cases lower courts may not follow a precedent of a higher court. The multiplicity of jurisdictions, and consequently of law reports, has resulted in a system of law school training based on the detailed study of cases from different American jurisdictions with a view to determining the best solutions to problems. Close attention is paid to the facts of cases in their sociological and economic context, and the creative role of the judge is stressed. Judges and legal scholars alike have appreciated realistically the judicial function, and have shed many inhibitions of English lawyers. Thus the "problem oriented" American judge will take into account trends of decision in other United States jurisdictions and apply principles of legal philosophy much more readily than his English counterpart. In certain sectors of the law, such as commercial law and property law, courts may be more reluctant than in other sectors to innovate by departing from precedent.

Where constitutional matters are in issue the Supreme Court has, most noticeably in recent years, declined to be strictly bound by its own previous decisions. Amendment of a constitution is not readily secured, and if the constitution has been previously interpreted in different social and economic conditions, public policy may make expedient judicial reinterpretation. The constitution itself remains fundamental. To a limited extent American courts have used the technique of "prospective overruling" by declaring that a precedent shall be reversed for the future but not as affects the legal relations of the litigants before the court. Strictly it would seem such a pronouncement should not be a binding precedent in a similar future case, but the technique has secured the approval of the Supreme Court.

IV. CONCLUSION

The idea of precedent is not restricted to the citation of authority within a single jurisdiction or nation-state. Systems sharing the same jurisprudential origins—e.g., the Napoleonic Code or the English Common law—may invoke each other's precedents; and there is authority in the United States and the Netherlands for the courts' adopting a "harmonizing construction" of domestic law by using comparative techniques to ascertain the solutions to a particular social problem of foreign legal systems of various types. Moreover, decisions of international courts and tribunals have persuasive authority in public international law and the Statute of the International Court of Justice (article 38) accepts national judicial decisions as a subsidiary source of law.

In sum, legal precedent in its conservative and creative aspects is encountered in all legal systems, though in different forms. It has been said: "Tradition and Conscience are the two wings given to the human soul to reach the truth" (T. M. Taylor, *Speaking to Graduates*, Edinburgh, 1965). Both are implicit in legal precedent. The judicial function is not or should not be that of an animated index to the law reports, nor is justice by computer a tolerable thought, however helpful computers may prove to be in tracking available authority. Julius Stone, who has written extensively on all aspects of precedent, echoes in that content the injunction of the father of cybernetics, Norbert Wiener, "Render unto man what is man's, and unto the machine only that which is the machine's."

BIBLIOGRAPHY

C. K. Allen, *Law in the Making*, 2nd ed. (Oxford, 1930). B. N. Cardozo, *The Nature of the Judicial Process* (New Haven, 1932). R. Cross, *Precedent in English Law* (Oxford, 1961). J. P. Dawson, *The Oracles of the Law* (Ann Arbor, 1968). R. W. M. Dias, *A Bibliography of Jurisprudence* (London, 1964). Woldemar Engelmann, *Die Wiedergeburt der Rechtskultur in Italien* (Leipzig, 1938). J. N. Frank, *Law and the Modern Mind* (New York, 1930; London, 1949). W. Friedmann, *Legal Theory*, 4th ed. (London, 1960). A. L. Goodhart, *Essays in Jurisprudence and the Common Law* (Cambridge, 1937); idem, "Precedent in English and Continental Law," *Law Quarterly Review*, **50** (1934), 40. J. C. Gray, *The Nature and Sources of the Law* (New York, 1921). H. R. Hahlo and E. Kahn, *The South African Legal System and Its Background* (Cape Town, 1968). E. A. Hoebel, *The Law of Primitive Man* (Cambridge, Mass., 1964). H. F. Jolowicz, *Historical Introduction to the Study of Roman Law*, 2nd ed. (Cambridge, 1952). K. Lipstein, "The Doctrines of Precedent in Continental Law with Special Reference to French and German Law," *Journal of Criminal Law*, **28** (1946), 34. K. Llewellyn, *The Bramble Bush* (New York, 1930); idem, "Case Law," *Encyclopedia of the Social Sci-*

ences (New York, 1930), III, 249. Y. Loussouarn, "The Relative Importance of Legislation, Custom, Doctrine and Precedent in French Law," *Louisiana Law Review*, **18** (1957), 235. D. N. MacCormick, "Can Stare Decisis be Abolished?" *Juridical Review* (1966), 197. Chaim Perelman, *The Idea of Justice and the Problem of Argument* (London and New York, 1963). T. Plucknett, *A Concise History of the Common Law*, 5th ed. (London, 1956). F. Pollock, *Jurisprudence and Legal Essays*, ed. A. L. Goodhart (London, 1961). R. Pound, "The Theory of Judicial Decision," *Harvard Law Review*, **36** (1922–23), 641, 802. R. B. Schlesinger, *Comparative Law*, 2nd ed. (London, 1960). T. B. Smith, *The Doctrines of Judicial Precedent in Scots Law* (Edinburgh, 1952). J. Stone, *Legal System and Lawyers' Reasoning* (London and Stanford, 1964); idem, *Human Law and Human Justice* (London and Stanford, 1965); idem, *Social Dimensions of Law and Justice* (London and Stanford, 1966). A. Taylor, "Functional Aspects of the Lawyer's Concept of Justice," *Juridical Review* (1966), 13. J. Vanderlinden, "Some Reflections on the Law Making Powers of the French Judiciary," *Juridical Review* (1968), 1. A. T. Von Mehren, *The Civil Law System* (Englewood Cliffs, N.J., 1957).

T. B. SMITH

[See also Casuistry; Certainty; Equality; Equity; **Justice; Law, Ancient Roman, Common.**]

LEGAL RESPONSIBILITY

WE SEEK with law to achieve order through the governance of men by rules. This reliance upon rules presupposes that men are responsible in two senses. First, law governs the conduct of those capable of understanding the meaning of rules and capable of making choices guided by this understanding. Law is not a technique designed to govern the conduct of those who are not responsible, creatures human and nonhuman, who lack either the capacity to understand or the capacity, given understanding, to conform their conduct to rules. There are rules with respect to those who are not responsible; there are none designed to govern them.

Second, law also requires for its existence at least some individuals disposed to exercise self-restraint, individuals who are responsible in the sense of caring for their fellow human beings, caring for the objects sought to be achieved by law, and thus caring to comply with the rules which exist to realize those objects. Those who are unwilling, in the absence of threats of harm, to exercise restraint are the irresponsible, at the extreme, the psychopaths, and if their number becomes too great, there is no longer law. In its place are threats supported by force and relations between individuals

are, perhaps, best describable as those of war. Law exists, then, only when not all persons are irresponsible, at least some are responsible; and a substantial number of those for whom the rules are intended are disposed to follow the rules for reasons other than fear of harm if they do not.

At the core of law are rules which, if generally obeyed, provide benefits for all persons who value such matters as continuance of life, bodily security, security of possessions, and predictability. These rules define spheres within which each person is immune from interference by others. Connected with these core rules are others prescribing responses if there is a failure to comply with rules of the first kind. A failure to comply typically initiates a process that may be divided for purposes of analysis into three stages. First, a charge or complaint is brought. If it is a criminal action, normally initiated by an authority representing the state, a charge is levelled that the party before the court has violated a law. If it is a civil suit, normally initiated by a private person, there is a complaint of breach of some duty owed to the injured person. There is then an inquiry into, among other things, who or what *was responsible for* the violation or the breach with an opportunity provided to answer the charge or complaint. Second, there is a decision, intimately connected with the earlier inquiry, that the party before the tribunal is or is not *to be held responsible* or, what is the equivalent in the law, *held liable*. Third, the system provides for execution of a judgment of liability, that is, in a criminal case the exacting of punishment and in a civil case the order to pay damages or to do or forbear from doing certain acts.

The concept of legal responsibility is not univocal in meaning. There are, first, within the law criteria to differentiate those who are from those who are not legally responsible persons. Infants, imbeciles, and psychotics fall into the latter class. Second, responsible persons are sometimes said to have specific legal responsibilities such as those imposed upon parents with respect to providing for their children and guardians with respect to their wards. These responsibilities are with respect to the future. Third, the law is concerned with whether or not a person is responsible for something that has happened, for example, a burned building or the death of a human being. And finally, there is a decision to "hold responsible" or "hold liable" that is generally, but not always, closely connected with a finding of individual responsibility for something that has happened. "Being responsible for" some happening and "being held liable" particularly require further consideration.

What, then, is involved in holding a person legally liable? First, a decision of legal liability implies the 33 existence of applicable legal standards or legal rules. The retaliation by one country, for example, against another, where there is no recognized international law, is not a case of legal liability. Second, holding a party liable implies that the party is appropriately subject to what is commonly regarded as some deprivation or disadvantage. A decision that a party is liable is, then, incompatible with disregarding the offense or wrong for which one is held liable, excusing it, or, *a fortiori*, rewarding the party. Third, holding a party liable is a response justified by some offense or wrong. Neither preventive measures nor compelled therapy, divorced as these modes of response are from the idea of a deprivation justified by some violation or wrong done, is connected with the idea of liability. Fourth, holding one liable and the deprivation, essentially linked to it, are deliberate acts. They are not spontaneous responses to some injury suffered. They are to be contrasted with striking out in anger when we are struck. Fifth, a decision to hold a particular party legally liable is a decision made by authorized persons who hold defined adjudicative roles within the society. A private person who judges that some wrong has been done to him and who seeks and achieves revenge against the alleged wrongdoer is not holding the wrongdoer legally liable nor punishing because of liability. The deprivation he visits upon the wrongdoer is neither grounded on a decision made by authorities of the system nor within the control of such authorities.

A person's being responsible for some occurrence is a pervasive requirement in legal systems for holding the person liable for the occurrence. It is also commonly supplemented by a requirement of fault. Each of these grounds of liability deserves attention.

A person may challenge his being responsible for some happening in a variety of ways, all of which may fairly be described as relating, in one way or another, to the absence of a causal connection between the individual as a person and the occurrence. A person may claim that he was not involved at all, and that it was another who was responsible for the occurrence. "I was nowhere near the scene of the crime. You have the wrong man." This claim may be of no avail if the law specifically imposes on a class of persons liability for the conduct of another class, and it was this conduct that was responsible for the occurrence. The law sometimes proceeds in this manner with parents and their children, employers and their employees, owners and their animals. Second, a person may admit that his body was involved causally in some injury and deny that he, as a person was, for he may argue that the movements of his body were not under his control, or that he was totally unconscious when the movements took place. In these cases, in which voluntariness is

absent there is no responsibility. Third, a party may claim absence of responsibility for some occurrence, not by denying his part as a person in what came about but, by denying the claimed causal connection between his voluntary conduct and the occurrence. Thus, if a person shoots at what he takes to be a live human being and the bullet is in fact entering what is a corpse, the person is not responsible for killing a human being. Finally, in a situation where the result which has come about may not have come about except for the individual's conduct and still, the result was only remotely connected with the conduct or it came about too accidentally or because of the intervening act of another human being, then there is no responsibility for the occurrence.

Liability is normally grounded on some finding of fault in addition to a finding of responsibility for some occurrence. When is there legal fault? First, there is legal fault provided there is conduct determined to be a violation of some rule. There is no legal fault if there is no rule in existence the person is alleged to have violated. And there is no fault if the conduct falls within legal definitions of justifiable conduct. Thus, one may be without fault if acting in self-defense. Second, there is some culpable state of the person with respect to the conduct. The culpable states typically made relevant by law are intentionally doing, knowingly doing, doing in conscious disregard of risk, and doing without taking care. There is no fault if none of these conditions are satisfied. Neither ignorance of the legal proscription, however, nor the commendability of one's motives is generally made relevant to legal fault. Third, fault is absent or, at least, diminished if a person lacks ability to appreciate the significance of what he is doing or the ability to conform his conduct to the rules. Thus, some impairment in one's control over conduct, due to provocation or to mental illness or drugs or alcohol, may lead either to a conclusion there was no fault or that its degree is less than it would be had the condition not been present.

All legal systems include principles of liability that are exceptions to the generalization that legal liability is grounded on a finding of responsibility and fault. First, questions of causation may sometimes be irrelevant to the issue of liability because a wrong is not defined in terms of causing or bringing about a result. This is so, for example, in the criminal law governing attempts, conspiracy, and possession of narcotics. Second, conduct prohibited by law may involve injury to others but a person may be held liable who is not responsible in a causal sense for the harm. This is so with vicarious liability where the basis for liability is one's relation to another who was causally responsible for some harm. Third, within both the civil and criminal law there are rules permitting liability without fault. This is so, for example, when there is objective liability, that is, where a standard is employed to determine the existence of fault which makes irrelevant the actual fault of the person charged with an offense. His testimony, for example, on his actual state of mind will be treated as irrelevant. There may also be an absence of fault in cases of vicarious liability. And finally, there are those cases of strict or absolute liability in which the definition of the offense or wrong obviates inquiry into fault, even fault tested by objective standards.

We have before us now a sketch of a familiar and complicated system of liability. But, of course, such a system is the product of a long evolution. In the earliest period injury of one person by another meets with an attempt at retaliation. Primitive conduct that first suggests the concept of liability arises when a member of one kin group injures a member of another kin group, and there is an accepted alternative to retaliation. The vengeance desired by the injured party and his kin may be bought off. With time and the growing desire for peace vengeance ceases to be a recognized option; there must be acceptance of the offer to buy off the vengeance. The idea of composition is introduced. It is an agreed upon amount, usually definitely fixed, depending upon the injury done, which quiets the feelings and dissolves the need for returning injury with injury. Soon composition is determined not by what it takes to buy off the vengeance but by the injury done; and the idea of compensation comes into existence.

For primitive societies, punishment, with its condemnatory connotation, is a response reserved for injury done to a member of the same group; for cases where there is no discernible injury, but some wrong done, such as incest; and for cases where there is a developed sense of the impropriety of accepting some material benefit for offense done.

Primitive modes of response to wrongdoing which differ from those of more developed societies may be accounted for by three pervasive characteristics of primitive culture: belief in unity of nature, belief in unity of the individual and the group, and focus on the physically observable. First, then, divisions between men and the rest of nature, pronounced in our own way of looking at the world, assume little significance in primitive societies. If there is some disaster, caused not by man but by some natural force, this may be looked upon as a punishment for transgression. But nature does not only mete out punishment; it is thought to justifiably receive it. So, a tree which has fallen on a man may be destroyed in a ritual of punishment. Second, the dominant primitive conceptions are not of individual but of collective responsibility and liability. When an individual acts, it is the group acting, the group that is responsible, and it is the group that is held liable for the damage that has been done. Third, the familiar distinction between what a man does and the mental state with which he does it, gives way to a focus on the harm done despite the state of mind of the actor. The primary impulse is to repair injury and not the assessment of fault.

Ezekiel's words: ". . . the righteousness of the righteous shall be upon him, and the wickedness of the wicked shall be upon him" (18:20) signals a revolution in ways of conceiving responsibility. There have been few such periods in human history. There is evidence that the twentieth century is one such period. Serious doubt exists whether or not the law is responding to men as it ought. The future promises a confrontation between opposing ideologies on the subject of legal responsibility. The doctrine of legal liability, particularly in the criminal law, is more than ever before, under attack. There is, first, a serious doubt, one long with us, about the morality of punishment. Developments in the behavioral sciences lead some to believe that no one is guilty, that fault is an outmoded concept that does not apply to men as they are, that holding persons liable and punishing them are outmoded responses appropriate for an earlier era when we knew less than we now do, and that rationality suggests prevention and cure and not punishment. Second, conclusions similar to these may be reached through skepticism. A system of liability connected with findings of fault presupposes that we can make justifiable claims about the state of mind of another, and this some deny on philosophical grounds or simply on grounds of the difficulty in coming by reliable evidence, particularly when the inquiry relates to a state of mind accompanying past conduct. There are, third, doubts about the efficacy of punishment. Some believe that punishment hardly serves to reduce wrongdoing but only increases it.

There are, then, powerful assaults on the concept of individual responsibility. They leave us with difficult questions. Is it possible for men to give up the idea of individual fault or responsibility? If the criminal law as we now understand it should disappear and in its place there were to be a system of social control scrupulously avoiding judgments of fault and responsibility, would we be better or worse off? There are those who argue forcefully that were this to come about we would lose much that we value in human freedom and much that we value in being viewed by others as responsible creatures, capable of wrongdoing and worthy of being responded to as wrongdoers, and not animals or sick persons.

BIBLIOGRAPHY

A. S. Diamond, *Primitive Law* (London, 1935). P. Fauconnet, *La Responsabilité* (Paris, 1920). C. J. Friedrich, ed., *Responsibility* (New York, 1960). H. L. A. Hart and A. Honoré, *Causation in the Law* (Oxford, 1959). H. L. A. Hart, *Punishment and Responsibility* (Oxford, 1968). E. A. Hoebel, *The Law of Primitive Man* (Cambridge, Mass., 1954). O. W. Holmes, *The Common Law* (Boston, 1881). W. Moberly, *Responsibility* (Oxford, 1951). H. Morris, ed., *Freedom and Responsibility* (Stanford, 1961). R. Pound, *An Introduction to the Philosophy of Law* (New Haven, 1922), pp. 144–90. G. de Tarde, *Penal Philosophy* (Boston, 1912). B. Wootton, *Crime and the Criminal Law* (London, 1963).

HERBERT MORRIS

[See also **Civil Disobedience; Freedom, Legal Concept of;** Law, Common; **Legal Precedent.**]

LIBERALISM

INTRODUCTION

THE LIBERAL is concerned with aspects of freedom that have come to be important only in the modern age that begins with the Renaissance and the Reformation. Not that his idea of freedom is unrelated to older ones, for its emergence in the West was no sharp break with the past. The causes of the emergence are as much cultural and intellectual as they are social and economic. An idea—or, as in this case, a family of ideas—has its ideological ancestry as well as social circumstances propitious to its birth.

The liberal idea (or ideas) of freedom emerged in a part of the world deeply affected by Greek philosophy, by Roman conceptions of law, and by a religion affirming the closeness of man's relations with God. How far there were, outside the West, philosophies of the Greek type (concerned to dissect and define man's ideas about himself, his mental processes, his moral ideals and social practices), or conceptions of law like the Roman ones, or religions as intimately personal as Christianity, we do not know; but that these things—to speak for the moment only of things ideological—have had a deep influence on how we think about freedom in the West cannot be denied. These ways of thinking are common to us all, and they are—as we shall try to show later—essentially liberal, even though there are now many people who think in these ways and refuse to call themselves liberals. Liberal ideas of freedom are far more widespread than the readiness to admit that one's ideas of freedom are liberal; which does not mean, of course, that the re-

pudiator of liberalism does not also hold ideas inconsistent with his ideas of freedom.

The liberal idea of freedom, though it emerged in a society deeply influenced by Greek philosophy, Roman law, and Christianity, is not to be found in ancient Greece or Rome, or in Christian countries before the Reformation. No doubt, the consistent liberal (the man who understands the implications of his liberal faith) sets great store by much that the Greeks or Romans or early and medieval Christians valued highly, as, for example, by self-knowledge and self-discipline, or the impartial administration of law and the integrity of officials, or sincerity of belief. He sets store by them because they are closely connected with the freedom precious to him. But, though indispensable to that freedom, they are distinct from it.

The modern or liberal idea of freedom emerges with the attribution of rights of the mere individual against those in authority over him. By the mere individual we mean the individual considered apart from any specific social role. The rights of the priest against the civil magistrate, rights often asserted in the Middle Ages, are his by virtue of his office. So, too, are the rights of inferiors against their superiors in a hierarchy, unless the rights are claimed for them merely on the ground that they are men, without reference to any service or duty expected of them. But the rights whose exercise constitutes freedom, as the liberal conceives of it, are held to be universal and important. To have them, it is enough to be a man—or to have specifically human capacities. This is the essence of the liberal claim for man; though the claim, as soon as it is made, is qualified in a variety of ways. It is admitted that these rights are not to be exercised to the injury of others, or that in practice not everyone can exercise them, or that their universal exercise is a gradual achievement. These and other qualifications we shall consider later, both in the context of the times they were made and more generally.

Political philosophers have differed considerably in their explanations of these rights, and also about the limits to be placed on them. Yet they all have, in some measure, the liberal idea of freedom if they claim for man, by reason of his humanity, the right, within limits strictly or loosely defined, to order his life as seems good to him. This is not to say that whoever makes this claim must be called a liberal or aspires to the name. For he may make the claim and then qualify it in such a way that, in practice, it comes to very little. There are differences of opinion as to whether, say, Hegel was a liberal. But, even if we refuse to call him one, we cannot deny that he made for the human being, on the mere ground of his capacity to reason and to form purposes, claims of a kind that Aristotle,

Aquinas, and Machiavelli never made. The modern or liberal idea of freedom is prominent in his political philosophy, no matter how well founded the complaint that that philosophy is dangerous to freedom. Indeed, he makes much more of the idea than, for example, does Montesquieu, though Montesquieu has the better claim to be reckoned a liberal.

It is not always the more liberal thinker who contributes most to explain or justify or refine upon the liberal conception of freedom. Locke, Kant, and Mill had much to say about freedom, and their right to be called liberal thinkers is seldom contested; and yet, in what they say about freedom and its conditions, psychological and social, they are no more perceptive and original than is Rousseau, whom it would be odd and misleading to call a liberal. A writer with moving, and even profound, things to say about freedom may speak with two voices, one liberal and the other not.

Individualism, in the sense of concern for the quality of the individual's life, is much older than liberalism. Plato had an elaborate conception of a good life to be lived by those capable of it, and he valued that life for itself and not only as a means to political stability and social harmony. So too did Aristotle. Though it is quite often said of a political thinker that he "sacrifices" the individual to the state or to society, not even Plato or Rousseau cared primarily for the character of the social or political order and only secondarily for the quality of the individual's life.

The Christian political thinker is often more of an individualist in this sense than either Plato or Aristotle, without being noticeably liberal. He cares little or nothing for the social or political order except as it affects the individual, and is concerned above all for his relations with God. If to be an individualist is to attach supreme importance to how the individual lives, to his feelings, intentions, and capacities, and to his welfare, and almost no importance to the social and political order, except as it affects him, then some of the most passionate individualists are not liberals. A liberal, no doubt, is always, in this sense, an individualist, but not necessarily more so than the man who rejects his idea of freedom or has not heard of it.

In the Renaissance many writers, among them Machiavelli, admired the self-assertive man who knows what he wants and acts resolutely and intelligently in the endeavor to get it. They admired him even when he did not allow conventional morality and fear of public opinion to deter him from the pursuit of his aims. They admired self-reliance and independence of mind as much as John Stuart Mill did, though they expressed their admiration differently and with a greater desire to shock. The man who, in the pursuit of what he wants, especially when what he wants is

to prove his "worth" to himself and to others, is not deterred by ordinary scruples, and who dares do what most men dare not, has been admired in societies far more remote culturally from ours than was Renaissance Italy. He has been admired when successful, or when close to success in some spectacular or moving way, as a hero. The hero is free, or freer at least than the ordinary run of men; and the cult of the hero is common to many societies in which freedom, as the liberal thinks of it, means nothing.

I. HISTORICAL CAUSES

The liberal idea of freedom arose slowly with the rise of the modern state and the gradual acceptance of religious diversity in a part of the world where the church was a unique institution and personal faith of peculiar importance.

1. The Modern State. The modern state, as no political community before it, is both highly centralized and highly populated; its authority is extensive and pervasive. The modern state includes millions of persons. So, too, did many of the old empires; but these empires were bureaucracies superimposed on a vast number of small communities having a large measure of autonomy, while the modern state controls closely the lives of all its citizens. The old empires were chiefly tax-gathering and military organizations, though they also maintained some important public works, such as roads and water supplies, and administered justice between persons from different communities or enjoying a special status. These local communities were self-governing even where the authority of the supreme ruler was held to be absolute—as, for example, in the Ottoman Empire. Thus, in these empires, supreme authority, though extensive, was not pervasive, for most people most of the time were not directly affected by it, whereas in the modern state it is extensive and pervasive.

In the city-states, in Greece, Italy, and elsewhere, supreme authority, though pervasive, was not extensive; and quite often a considerable minority of the persons subject to it took part in deciding how it should be exercised or who should exercise it. Supreme authority was "close" to the persons over whom it was exercised.

Of the modern state it is often said that its authority is "remote." This is true or false, depending on how we take it. The holders of supreme authority are not personally known to the vast majority of the citizens, or are known to them only as much advertised public figures, and to that extent are remote from them. But there are state officials everywhere, and the citizen has more to do with them than ever before. Though he rarely meets any of the men who take the important decisions, he sees pictures of them and reads or hears their words repeatedly. The "state" in one way or another is very present to him.

This state, even where it is federal, is a tightly knit organization in which everyone's rights and duties are clearly defined. It is also quickly changing. To do what is expected of it, it must be highly adaptable and must have elaborate and precise rules for the guidance of its officers. It could not be adaptable unless procedures, powers, and obligations inside it were carefully defined.

In the modern state the rights and obligations of the mere citizen, of the man without public authority, are also well defined. He has a variety of social roles; and his rights and duties in them, as a husband or father, as an employer or hired worker, as a man with a particular trade or profession, are defined not only—nor even principally—by custom but also by statute and by contract. He sees himself, and is seen by others, as a bearer of rights and obligations that are or ought to be definite and yet liable to change since he belongs to a changing society and his roles in it also change. Apart from the rights and duties attaching to some particular occupation or role, he has others that he shares with all citizens, or with all of his sex or age; or he has rights and obligations merely because he resides within the jurisdiction of the state.

He is ordinarily more mobile socially and geographically than his ancestors were: he is more likely to enter a profession or trade different from his father's, more likely also to change it, and more likely to move from one place to another. Some of his rights and obligations change with his occupation or place of residence, while others remain the same. His right to choose his occupation and to change it, and his right to move from place to place, are not tied to any particular status or role; they are rights he shares with everyone, or at least with many, in his state.

Thus, even in the most authoritarian or "illiberal" of modern states, men and women have a variety of rights and duties that they share with everyone, or with most people. These rights and duties are not justified, as are other narrower ones, by appeals to custom or to needs peculiar to an occupation, social role, or locality.

Increased mobility, social and geographical, is associated historically with two developments: with the rise of the modern state, a highly centralized structure of authority which is both "remote" from and "close" to the persons subject to it, and with the emergence of an elaborate legal system in which the rights and obligations of the mere citizen, or of the mere human being, are distinguished as never before from rights and obligations attaching to particular occupations and roles.

The authority of the modern state is "impersonal" in the sense that the persons who exercise it are not concerned with the persons subject to it as unique individuals but rather as belonging to some category or other. This authority differs, therefore, not only from that of parents over their children, but also from that of elders or chiefs in small custom-bound communities. Moreover, where it exists, it affects the exercise of authority in the smaller communities within the larger one, even though in them personal ties are still close. It does so partly, but only partly, because the individual is freer to move out of whatever small communities he belongs to. For example, he is freer to leave the parental home.

Though the authority of the state can be the more oppressive for being "impersonal," this "impersonality" is also, as we shall see, a condition of freedom as the liberal understands it, a necessary but by no means sufficient condition. The individual is treated as someone to whom a certain description applies; he is "categorized." Therefore, all he need do to make good his claims is to show that a certain description does indeed apply to him. The quality of intercourse between the possessor of authority and whoever is subject to it is not what it is in intimate and custom-bound communities; it allows both of new kinds of freedom and new kinds of oppression.

It used to be claimed for the modern state—whether it was liberal (as in Britain in Gladstone's time) or authoritarian (as in Bismarck's Germany)—that it is essentially a *Rechtstaat;* a political community in which the powers of everyone having public authority are carefully defined and the citizen has a legal remedy against abuses of power. This claim is no longer made since the emergence of communist and fascist states, whose "modernity" can hardly be denied. Nazi Germany was not, Communist Russia is not, a *Rechtstaat.*

And yet in the modern state, if we compare it with older systems, there are always elaborate rules defining the rights and obligations, not merely of private persons, but of holders of public authority. Though the private citizen often lacks a remedy against official abuses of power, lesser officials are more strictly responsible to greater ones. There is also a sharper distinction made between rights and duties attached to particular occupations or social roles and more general ones. The citizen is at least encouraged to look upon himself as a citizen. Even though he has little remedy against abuses of public authority, this is not officially admitted. The official claim is that his rights are well defined and adequately protected. The modern state claims to be constitutional; to be so organized that public authority is exercised according to definite rules, and the citizen has effective remedies against abuses of authority. It is part of the myth of the modern state that it is "constitutional," just as it is part of its myth that it is "democratic."

No doubt, respect for constitutional rules and for "the rule of law" is dismissed in some modern states as a "bourgeois" prejudice. But this dismissal is always equivocal; for these states also claim to be constitutional. Their rulers are revolutionaries who got power illegally and who keep it by methods different from those of the their predecessors, methods that involve denying to their subjects rights previously enjoyed or widely aspired to, or even proclaimed by their own revolutionary creed. To give the appearance of legitimacy to their power and to achieve their other aims, they always set up a constitution and proclaim rights that they often cannot afford to respect. Within their own circles they take this constitution and these rights for what they are—for pretences serving to cover up the realities of power. Outside these circles, they speak of them differently and more respectfully, denying that they are mere pretences. The respect is usually to some extent genuine; for they would like things to be as they say they are, and even deceive themselves into believing that the reality is nearer the appearance than in fact it is.

Yet behind the appearance, there emerges a structure of power which—precisely because it is centralized, extensive, and pervasive, and has to be adapted to changing needs and purposes—cannot rest on custom but must operate in accordance with definite and deliberately-made rules. Unless it were so, it would not be effective; it would not serve to control millions of people in the many different ways that their rulers want them controlled in order to achieve their diverse and changing purposes. Nor could these people be effectively controlled for these purposes unless many of their rights and obligations were fairly well defined. If the activities of millions of persons are to be directed to the achievement of large and new aims, if society is to be transformed, there must be an elaborate system of rules for the guidance of both those who govern and those who are governed, and there must be procedures established for changing the rules. There must be some kind of effective political and legal order, even though there is alongside it an order that is not effective and exists largely for show—whether it expresses genuine aspirations or serves to keep up appearances which those who profit by them do not take seriously.

No doubt, revolutionaries who get control of a state sometimes fail of their purposes; they do not transform society the way they want to, and the reality behind the façade is not an effective political and legal order. Nevertheless, if they are really concerned to transform society, they cannot achieve their aims unless they establish such an order.

The idea of the modern state is the idea of an extensive and elaborate structure of authority carefully defined and organized, and deliberately changed to meet changing needs; and there arises along with it the need to define more precisely the rights and obligations of the individual, distinguishing those that are his in some particular capacity from those that are not. These ways of thinking about public authority and private rights are common to all societies in which the modern state arises whether they are liberal or authoritarian. In all of them the individual acquires precious rights he did not have before, or had to a smaller extent, rights not attached to any particular occupation, status, or role: as, for example, the right to choose his occupation, or to choose whom he shall marry, or to decide where he shall live. Women acquire rights hitherto confined to men; and the adult of either sex enjoys a greater independence, taking for himself or herself decisions that used to be taken by parents or by seniors in the family or clan or local community. This severing of old ties, this acquisition of new rights, is inevitable in an economy calling for greater social mobility. Wherever these rights are acquired, whether in a liberal or an authoritarian society, the acquisition is apt to be seen as a liberation.

The modern state also claims to be democratic. It did not do so in the beginning, if we take that beginning as far back as the sixteenth and seventeenth centuries. The modern state was, in its early days, a monarchy or oligarchy. But in those days it was much less centralized than it became later, and its authority much less pervasive. As that authority increased, as local autonomies lessened or survived only within limits defined by the central power, as the individual found himself more and more controlled by that power, his desire to control it grew stronger. This desire arose first among the wealthy but spread in time to other classes. In Britain the powers of the king and of parliament increased together, long before parliament became democratic. In France, when the French equivalent of the British parliament was revived and reformed at the revolution, the popularly elected legislature was reduced to impotence by a group of extreme radicals. And for generations afterwards, the only legislatures that were not quickly rendered powerless were elected on a narrow franchise. France had no democracy that lasted more than two or three years before the Third Republic. Yet democracy seemed inevitable long before it came; and even to those who despaired of its coming, or who argued that it could not be genuine, the desire for it and belief in it seemed rooted in social conditions that arise with the modern state. Modern society is by nature democratic; it needs the illusion of democracy even where it cannot have the reality.

Political theory in the West has had a "bias" towards democracy from the time that the modern state arose and long before it became democratic. It has held that the legitimacy of government derives from the consent of the governed, and has spoken of this consent as if it consisted, not in mere acquiescence or acceptance of custom, but in a specific act, a social contract. No doubt, it began by relegating this contract to a mythical past; and yet contract implies deliberate agreement. This is already clear in Locke's political philosophy, when he says that every man must consent for himself, since the consent of his ancestors cannot bind him. Locke, of course, was no democrat, and qualified his initial assertions so as to draw no democratic conclusions from them. But he spoke of rights that all men have, merely because they are men, and he argued that governments are obliged to protect these rights, and that subjects have the right to resist or remove governments when they fail in this duty. His argument has democratic implications, though neither he nor his contemporaries drew them.

Marxists and others, to explain how such a thinker as Locke came to speak as he did, have said that a rising class, though themselves a minority, when they challenge the supremacy of another class, try to gain popularity by using arguments that appeal to the people generally. They try to make the interest of their class look as if it were the interest of all. This is what happened in the seventeenth century, when the rising bourgeoisie challenged the supremacy of the old nobility, especially in England. Rights that could in fact, given social conditions at that time, be exercised effectively only by the wealthy and the educated were claimed for the whole people, or for some part of them supposed to be acting as their representatives.

This Marxist argument is akin to another, which has perhaps more to be said for it. According to this second argument, a new kind of economy and social order required the assertion of rights to be shared by all, or by all adult males, regardless of status, occupation, or wealth. Though this economy and social order allow of great inequalities of status, wealth, and education, there are rights that all men must have if the economy and social order are to function properly. These rights are asserted in all societies where commerce and industry are growing fast, and there is increasing social mobility; where the least educated are required to be literate, and where the maintenance of social discipline takes the form of the modern state.

2. Liberty of Conscience. In Europe in the Middle Ages two ideas were widely accepted: that salvation, or union with God in an afterlife, depends not just on leading a good life, but on holding certain beliefs about God and his relations to man; and that there is a church, a community of the faithful, having sole authority from God to teach the beliefs (and administer the sacraments) necessary to salvation. To most people in medieval Europe, these two ideas may have meant very little, for most people were illiterate and incapable of understanding them. No doubt, to most people everywhere, religion has been more a matter of ritual than of doctrine. But these ideas were important to persons in authority, both clerical and lay.

At the Reformation the first of these ideas—that salvation depends on holding certain beliefs— was not challenged, and the second was challenged only up to a point. Luther rejected the authority of the pope and of other ecclesiastical superiors who disagreed with him; and he taught that every Christian must interpret for himself the Holy Scriptures containing the truths necessary to salvation. Yet he proved in the end unwilling to admit that avowed Christians whose interpretations of the Scriptures differed widely from his own should be allowed to propagate their beliefs. It is arguable that he wanted them silenced only because he thought their doctrines dangerous to the social order and not because they had misinterpreted Holy Scripture. But the Lutherans after him certainly wanted some of their opponents silenced on the ground that their doctrines were false and not merely dangerous. So too did the Calvinists. What is more, the idea of a true church with sole authority to teach a faith necessary to salvation long remained widely attractive to Protestants, even though their beliefs about how the faithful should be organized were sometimes incompatible with this idea. So there were soon, over large parts of Western Europe, several organized bodies of Christians, each claiming, if not a monopoly of the truth, a privileged status in declaring it and in deciding what false beliefs were intolerable. Most of them were intolerant, though some less so than others; and the more tolerant were so often from motives of prudence, being more liable to persecution by others than able to persecute them.

Nevertheless, with time, belief in toleration grew stronger. In the wake of a growing belief that toleration is expedient, there grew another—that it is just. Yet toleration was mostly from motives of expediency until quite recent times. Governments learned by experience that they were more likely to provoke disorder by trying to establish uniformity of religious belief by force than by allowing diversity. Religious leaders learned that the number of the faithful was as likely to grow if they gave up being persecutors where they were strong in return for not being persecuted where they were weak.

The long period of religious conflict that started with Luther's defiance of the papacy had two lasting effects. It strengthened and spread more widely the belief that "faith" is important, and it made people keener to associate for the defense and propagation of beliefs that they cared deeply about. These beliefs were at first mostly religious, but they came in time to be much more than merely religious, or ceased altogether to be so. Beliefs about how men should live and society be organized had long been associated with beliefs about God and his purposes for man. As the association between these two kinds of belief weakened and for many people (agnostics and atheists) was quite severed, beliefs about man, morals, and society still kept something of the "sacred" character of religious beliefs. The idea survived that nothing matters more about a man than his faith, than the beliefs he cares deeply about because they form or justify his aspirations or his way of life.

The idea that faith is important can be used to justify either persecution and indoctrination or toleration and freedom of speech. It was used at first much more for the first purpose than the second, and in our day is still used widely for both purposes. In the West it is now more often used for the second purpose. And yet, though it was used for this second, this "liberal," purpose later than for the first, there has been no steady movement away from the first use to the second.

Tolerance and freedom of speech are not, of course, peculiarly modern any more than are persecution and indoctrination. There was a great deal of tolerance and of this freedom, in some places at some times, in the ancient world. But it is in the modern age and in the West, in a part of the world where persecution and indoctrination were for a long time peculiarly fierce and thorough, with bitter conflicts between rival faiths, that tolerance and freedom of speech are most highly prized. This is not to suggest that periods of persecution and indoctrination are always followed by periods of toleration and freedom of speech; but to suggest only that, in a part of the world where peculiar importance was attached to faith, after a long period of conflict between persecuting and proselytizing churches and sects, none of which gained complete ascendency, tolerance and freedom of speech came to be more highly valued than they had ever been anywhere before. They were not merely practiced, as they had been in other places and other times; they were put forward as principles that ought to be practiced as far as possible.

In the West until the eighteenth century, persecutors and advocates of toleration were concerned mostly with religious beliefs, and have since that time turned their attention more to social and moral doctrines. Or, rather, the beliefs that now concern them are less often religious, as well as social and moral, than they used to be; for religious beliefs that have attracted persecution have nearly always been closely connected with social and moral doctrines.

So, too, since the eighteenth century, the impulse to form associations to maintain and propagate religious beliefs and practices has broadened into a readiness to form them to promote and protect any beliefs and practices important to those who share them. The right to associate for such purposes has been widely asserted and recognized as one of the most precious of all.

In the West in the Middle Ages it was the church rather than the state that was responsible for defending as well as teaching the true faith, the temporal magistrate acting rather as an auxiliary to punish persons condemned by priests. Hence an idea more widely accepted in the West than in other parts of Christendom, that matters of faith are beyond the jurisdiction of the state, that its business is to prevent people from acting harmfully rather than to ensure that they hold true beliefs. Defense of the church against the state, even when it has not been defense of religious freedom, has nevertheless been, or appeared to be, a defense of faith against the state or the Temporal Power, against organized force. For the organ of coercion has been the state or the Temporal Power and not the church, even when that Power has acted in defense of the church or to promote its aims. Hence in the West two important social functions, organized coercion and organized indoctrination, have long been separate or more nearly separate than elsewhere.

II. IDEAS AND ARGUMENTS ABOUT FREEDOM SINCE THE REFORMATION.

1. The Argument for Religious Freedom. It is often said that the modern idea of freedom first appeared, or at least first became formidable, in the Reformation. The first of its champions to make a mark in the world was Luther, who asserted the "priesthood of all believers," and who said that "God desires to be alone in our consciences, and desires that His word alone should prevail."

Certainly, implicit in some of Luther's utterances is the principle that the believer is responsible to God alone for his religious beliefs. Long before Luther, Socrates had felt an inner compulsion to teach what he believed was the truth, and had held fast to his truth when accused of corrupting the youth of Athens. But he had not proclaimed the right of anyone who felt as he did to act as he had done. His accusers, in any case, were not concerned to forbid the teaching of error, nor yet to uphold true beliefs "necessary to salvation," but to maintain outward respect for con- **41** ventional beliefs and manners. They no more saw themselves as champions of a true faith than Socrates saw himself as a martyr for liberty of conscience. And long before the Reformation, there were Christians who said that the believer must be allowed to follow God's Word without hindrance from the temporal magistrates, and there were accusations of heresy made against some priests by others (even subordinates in the hierarchy) and by laymen. Defiance of the church's authority in matters of faith did not begin with the Reformation. Yet Luther's doctrine of the priesthood of all believers was new and formidable. Though there were traces of it before his time, it was his version of it that excited and disturbed Christendom in the West.

It is arguable that Luther's hold on his own doctrine was not altogether firm, and that he failed to see its full implications. In practice, he sometimes denied to others the right to publish religious beliefs widely different from his own, and it is far from certain that he did so only because he thought the beliefs dangerous to the social order and not because he thought them false and abhorrent to God. In any case, the doctrine of the priesthood of believers is ambiguous. It invites the question: Who is to be reckoned a believer? Is anyone a believer who says that Holy Scripture is the Word of God, no matter how he interprets it? In that case, a man might be a Christian though his beliefs differed more from those of other Christians than from the beliefs of Mohammed. And if outrageous or absurd interpretations are condemned as insincere, and the believer's claim to be recognized and tolerated as such is rejected on that account, are not those who reject it saying that, after all, he is answerable to his fellow men for his beliefs, and not to God alone? Luther never put to himself such a question as this; he merely took it for granted that there are limits to what professed "believers" can be allowed to read into the Scriptures. In practice he was no more tolerant than Erasmus or than several other great writers of the age who never broke away from the old church.

Perhaps the finest plea for toleration made in the sixteenth century is Castellion's *De haereticis, an sint persequendi*, published in 1554. Belief, to be acceptable to God, must be sincere, which it cannot be, if it is forced. God is just, and therefore does not make it a condition of salvation that men should hold uncertain beliefs long disputed among Christians. Only beliefs that Christians have always accepted can be necessary to salvation; and to hold otherwise is to doubt the goodness of God. To punish men for beliefs they dare to avow is to risk punishing the sincere and to allow hypocrites to go unpunished. Castellion's arguments were directed at Calvin, who only a few months earlier

had had Servetus burned to death as a heretic. Castellion's plea was not only for a wide toleration; he condemned extreme measures against any heretic. He was concerned for the quality of faith, for the spiritual condition of the believer. Yet he did not advocate full liberty of conscience; he did not put it forward as a principle that anyone may hold and publish any religious beliefs, and may worship God as he pleases, provided he does not propagate beliefs and indulge in practices that endanger the peace and the secure enjoyment of rights.

This principle was not clearly and vigorously asserted until the end of the seventeenth century. Years of controversy and long and painful experience were needed to bring home to men two lessons: that domestic peace and security do not depend on people having the same, or even broadly similar, religious beliefs; and that persecution is unlikely to bring about uniformity of belief, even though it may silence the heterodox.

The first lesson disposes those who learn it to accept liberty of conscience on political grounds: let people hold and publish what religious opinions they choose, since the attempt to impose religious uniformity endangers the peace more than does religious diversity. The second lesson disposes them to accept it on religious and moral grounds: let individuals hold and publish what religious opinions they choose, since forbidding them to do so will not ensure that they accept with sincerity the opinions of those who impose the sanctions.

The case for liberty of conscience was refined and reduced to essentials by Spinoza, Locke, and Bayle. Spinoza, in the twentieth chapter of his *Tractatus theologico-politicus* (1670), asserted man's right to reason freely about everything and said that the sovereign invades this right if he prescribes to his subjects what they must accept as true or reject as false. Bayle, in his *Commentaire philosophique sur ces paroles de Jésus-Christ, "Contrains-les d'entrer"* (1686), argued that coercion in matters of belief encourages hypocrisy and corrupts society by destroying the good faith on which it depends. And it is absurd, as some people do, to condemn persecution when it is harsh and approve it when it is mild. Since faith is important, heresy, if it is a crime, must be a serious one and ought to be severely punished; and if it is not a crime, it ought not to be punished at all. The conscience that errs has rights as much entitled to respect as the conscience that possesses the truth. Even atheists should be tolerated; and if Catholics should not be, it is not on account of their faith, but because they are intolerant. For the doctrine that heretics should be persecuted is not religious but political; and it is pernicious because it makes for disorder and is destructive of good morals.

Locke's *Letter Concerning Toleration* (1689), shorter than Bayle's *Commentary* and more popular and less abstract than Spinoza's argument in the *Tractatus,* is the classical apology for liberty of conscience. Though it does not, any more than does Bayle's *Commentary,* put forward new ideas, it is clear and vigorous. Coming towards the end of a long period of religious wars and persecutions, it brings together into a coherent and compelling whole the most solid arguments for religious liberty. It is an act of completion, the last best word of its age for a kind of freedom that men had learned, slowly and painfully, to recognize and to value.

The proper business of civil government, according to Locke, is to protect and promote men's interests. Though everyone has the right to try to persuade others to hold beliefs which he thinks are true and important, nobody has the right to use force to that end. The civil magistrate has no authority from either God or man to require anyone to profess or refrain from professing a belief on the ground that it is true or false, necessary to salvation or incompatible with it. It is not for him to dispute with his subjects or to persuade them to a particular religion. Even if he could force them to adhere to it, he would not thereby save their souls, for salvation depends on a free adherence to what is true. A church is no more than an association of men who come together to worship God in the manner they think acceptable to him, and no church can claim authority from God to be the only teacher of the true faith. Like any other voluntary association it may make rules for its members, may admonish and exhort them, and may expel them for disobeying the rules. But it may not deprive them of their civil rights, or of any rights other than those they acquire by joining it, nor may it call upon the civil power to do so. No belief is to be suppressed merely because it is heretical, nor any practice merely because it is offensive to God. No doubt, what is offensive to God is sinful, but what is sinful is not punishable by man. No man deserves punishment at the hands of other men, unless he has offended some man, unless he has invaded his rights. Locke, in this *Letter,* seems at times to come close to saying what J. S. Mill was to say long afterwards: that men are answerable to civil authority only for their harmful and not their immoral actions. Yet he does not say it outright, nor even clearly imply it.

What he does say is that all beliefs are to be tolerated "unless they are contrary to human society" or to moral rules "necessary to the preservation of civil society." This is not a clear saying. What is to be reckoned *contrary to human society* or *necessary to the preservation of civil society?* Since Locke wrote his *Letter,* there have been many attempts to answer this question

or others like it. Locke held that there are rights that all men have, and we can perhaps ascribe to him the belief that anything is to be reckoned contrary to human society if it prevents the exercise of these rights, either directly or by subverting institutions on which their exercise depends. It is actions, therefore, rather than beliefs, that are directly contrary to human society. But actions are inspired by beliefs. Are people to be punished for expressing and publishing beliefs that inspire harmful actions? Or is it enough that such beliefs should be combated by argument, and their attractive power diminished by education?

Locke speaks of moral rules necessary to the preservation of society. Presumably, that promises be kept is such a rule. Yet all societies distinguish between enforceable promises (contracts) and promises that are not enforceable. Nor is the keeping of promises that are not enforceable any less necessary to the preservation of civil society than the keeping of the others. In all societies there are rules, supported only by "moral sanctions," no less necessary to preserving the social order than rules the breach of which is a punishable offence. If the breaker of these rules is not liable to punishment, should the man be so who teaches that they need not be kept—or not in all circumstances?

Locke's *Letter* closes one stage in the long debate on freedom of speech and association, and opens another. It puts forward, simply and persuasively, a number of important principles but goes only a little way in considering how they should be applied.

2. *The Rights of Man and Government by Consent.* The doctrine of the social contract, fashionable among political theorists in the late sixteenth and the seventeenth centuries and surviving into the eighteenth, was first used to support the claims of religious minorities, or of churches and sects anxious to assert their independence of the civil power. Huguenots and Jesuits both used it for this purpose. But the doctrine has egalitarian and libertarian implications that came eventually to seem more important than the first uses to which it was put. For it postulates an individual with rights and wants prior to the setting up of government whose proper business is to protect the rights and supply the wants. The state of nature, as the contract theorist imagines it, though it is not really presocial—for natural man lives in families, is capable of speech, uses tools, and cultivates the soil—is a condition of rough equality. Great inequalities arise only with the rise of government; and yet the social rules that government is established to enforce are in everyone's interest.

These implications of the idea of a social contract were first clearly drawn by Hobbes. For he, though he was no liberal, was an "individualist" in the sense that he built up his political philosophy on claims and needs that he ascribed to everyone and to which he appealed to demonstrate both the utility and the legitimacy of government. In this sense, at least, he was more markedly an individualist than were the Jesuit and Huguenot contract theorists, though he argued, as they did not, that only a ruler with unlimited authority can provide his subjects with the security they want.

Hobbes and Locke were both individualists in their assumptions and in the manner of their argument; they both argued to political conclusions from assumptions about needs and rights that everyone has. But Locke's conclusions, unlike Hobbes's and more clearly than any earlier thinker's, were liberal. Just as his *Letter Concerning Toleration* simplifies and draws together several arguments for religious freedom, and so adds to their persuasive power, so his *Second Treatise of Civil Government* (1690) brings together, and in so doing strengthens and clarifies, several arguments for limited government. Government exists to protect the life, liberty, and property of its subjects, whose obligation to obey it lasts only as long as it protects them adequately and does not abuse its powers; and subjects may take action to ensure that they get this protection and to put an end to abuses of power.

This principle is important but needs to be qualified. Before we can act upon it, we must raise and answer several questions. Men may differ as to whether or not basic rights are adequately protected. If they do, who is to judge between them? Again, rights may be invaded either by private persons or by the government and its agents. In the first case, a subject who appeals to the government for protection or redress, may find that it fails him for one or both of two reasons: because it lacks the power to do what he asks, or because it decides that no right of his has been invaded. This last decision, the subject may question either because he has in general no faith in the impartiality of the body or person that took it, or because he believes that this particular decision was wrong. He is ordinarily more willing to "accept" what he thinks is a wrong decision when the persons who take it seem to him impartial and their procedure fair than when they seem partial and unfair. Political power, according to Locke, is not legitimate unless those who exercise it do so with the consent of their subjects, who may take action to prevent abuses of power. Unfortunately, he failed to explain how we can know whether or not rulers have the consent of their subjects, or how we can decide whether or not there has been an abuse of power. If it is for subjects to decide, how can we know whether or not they have done so?

Locke did not see in the right of resistance the only safeguard against a government's being oppressive or its failing to protect basic rights. He wanted a separation of the executive and legislative powers, and a partly elected legislature. Yet he had little to say either about the distribution of authority within the government or about methods of ensuring that governments are responsible to their subjects. But he did raise tentatively (though without going far towards answering them) three questions of capital importance to the liberal: How should authority be distributed and its exercise regulated for the better protection of essential rights? How can it be contrived that authority is exercised in ways acceptable to those subject to it? When are subjects justified in resorting to illegal means to resist or get rid of their rulers?

Montesquieu went further than Locke towards answering the first of these questions. He not only explained, as Locke had not done, why it is expedient to separate the judicial from the executive and legislative powers; he also, in the twelfth book of *The Spirit of the Laws* (*De l'esprit des lois*, 1748; English trans., 1750), discussed in some detail what he called "the laws forming political liberty in relation to the subject." These are the laws and practices ensuring that no one is punished except for breaking the law, that accused persons get a fair trial, that the citizen can assert his rights effectively both against other citizens and against public officials.

With the second question Montesquieu dealt more perfunctorily. He took it for granted that authority exercised in customary ways is acceptable to those subject to it because they believe it is exercised to protect their rights and to meet their needs. On this point Burke and Hume agreed with him. Neither he nor they took much account of the fact that people's ideas about their needs and their rights change. They did not enquire how it could be contrived that forms of government can be changed legally and peacefully to ensure that rulers are more willing and better able to meet the changing requirements of their subjects.

Yet Montesquieu, in dealing with this second question, was more specific than Locke on three points. Though he too thought it desirable that part of the legislature should be elected, he excluded from the vote persons "in so mean a situation as to be deemed to have no will of their own." He denied that constituents ought to give specific instructions to their representatives. And, lastly, he held that the kind of limited and partly representative government which alone can be trusted to respect rights scrupulously is not suited to most peoples. It may well be that Locke, if he had been asked his opinion, would have agreed with Montesquieu on all three points. Yet Montesquieu is explicit where Locke is silent. Though Locke was no more a democrat than he was, the doctrine that democracy is dangerous to liberty is his rather than Locke's, as is also the doctrine that liberty is confined to some peoples. Montesquieu had more to say than Locke had about the conditions, social and otherwise, of political competence, and was therefore more obviously undemocratic. Democracy had long been attacked on the ground that it was likely to be unjust to the rich and the privileged. Montesquieu objected to it on this ground also, but it is in his writings that we find the confused beginnings of a new objection to it—that it destroys liberty.

To the third question: When are subjects justified in acting illegally to resist or get rid of their rulers?, Montesquieu had nothing to say. He was silent where Locke was bold.

It was not till the latter part of the eighteenth century that political writers had much to say about three rights which since that time have been subjects of continual controversy: the right to vote at free elections, the right to form associations to promote shared purposes and beliefs of all kinds, and freedom of the press. In the seventeenth century the supremely important beliefs were religious, and so argument turned on the right to hold and publish religious beliefs and on the right to associate for religious purposes. In the next century other beliefs and association for other purposes came to seem no less important.

In the eighteenth century, before the French revolution and the first shots in the long campaign for parliamentary reform in England, there was more concern for freedom of the press than for freedom of association and the right to vote. This was the freedom that Voltaire and other philosophers of his time cared most about. The educated classes to whom they addressed their books could meet easily enough for most purposes important to them, and had not yet learned to form associations to put pressure on governments. Freedom of association for other than religious purposes mattered more in Britain, where there was already a partly elected national legislature, than in countries like France, though even in Britain it was not widely and strongly upheld until the demand arose for extending the franchise. Where concern for freedom is confined to aristocratic and intellectual circles, the freedom most prized, after freedom of person and property, is apt to be freedom of discussion and of the press. Freedom of association and the right to vote come to seem important when leaders arise who have or aspire to have a large following. Such leaders want to "politicize" the people, or some broad section of them, to draw them into political activities, into organized bodies making demands on government. Even a "recluse" like Jeremy Bentham came to care greatly for freedom of association and extending the franchise, as experience taught him that no government would take the advice he gave unless popular pressure was brought to bear on it.

Freedom of association can be greatly prized where there is neither democracy nor a widespread demand for it. It was prized, for example, by French liberals during the Restoration and the July Monarchy, even though most of them wanted only a narrow electorate, just as it was in Britain in the first part of the nineteenth century by Utilitarians and other reformers who wanted only a modest extension of the franchise. Freedom of association is prized above all where there is an electorate to be mobilized for political purposes, and the right to vote where there is hope of creating or extending such an electorate.

The Jacobin Terror and the popular tyranny of Bonaparte between them produced a kind of liberalism hostile to democracy. Locke and Montesquieu are to be reckoned liberals "before the letter," for it was only later that champions of doctrines similar to theirs were called liberals, but they were neither democrats nor declared enemies of democracy. They never argued that its coming would destroy the liberties they valued most, nor did they, as Benjamin Constant did, fear democracy (see his two important works: *De l'esprit de conquête . . .* [1814], and *Principes de politique applicables à tous les gouvernements* [1815]).

Edmund Burke, of course, was an unrelenting enemy of democracy, who denounced it bitterly several years before the Jacobin Terror. He was, in his peculiar way, a champion of freedom. His concern for it was genuine enough, though different from that of Constant. For Constant, as he set about explaining what he thought were the essential liberties, pointed to the institutions and procedures needed to make them actual. Remembering vividly both Robespierre and Bonaparte, he abhorred radical demagogues and popular dictators as exploiters and perverters of the principles they professed. Rulers, he thought, will not respect liberty unless they are responsible only to those among their subjects who care about it and understand how it is secured, the educated and the propertied classes. The attempt to make them responsible to the whole people brings influence and power to irresponsible leaders, who destroy the liberties they pretend to secure to all, and brings with it a new kind of absolute rule more intrusive and oppressive than that of the dispossessed kings.

Anti-democratic liberalism, especially on the European Continent, took the form of attacks on the doctrines of Rousseau, attacks that misinterpret what they condemn. Rousseau proclaimed the sovereignty of the people, having in mind not representative assemblies elected by universal suffrage, but political communities 45 small enough for all adult men (but not women) to come together to make laws and major decisions of policy. To secure the popular assembly against pressures from groups pushing their interests to the detriment of others, he said that these groups ought not to be organized for political purposes. But these two doctrines of his—that the people are sovereign and that there must be no organized bodies to influence their decisions—when they were applied later to a country the size of France, where the people could not make law directly but only through their representatives, came to have implications undreamt of by him. To say with Rousseau that what the people in sovereign assembly decide must not be predetermined or challenged by lesser bodies, though it may be challenged and reversed in the assembly itself, is one thing; to make, as some of his disciples did, the same claim on behalf of a popularly elected representative assembly is quite another.

Rousseau, misrepresented by both admirers and critics, has served above all as a source of quotations for radicals to use in their attacks on liberal opponents. Respect for the constitutional forms and rights of the individual dear to the liberals has seemed to them an obstacle in the way of reforms urgently needed for the benefit of the poor. The poor, the socially weak, if they are to gain strength, need solidarity; they must organize themselves and be loyal to the organizations they form. This solidarity, or the appearance of it, is sometimes hard to achieve or preserve where the rights of minorities and of lone rebels are respected.

Democracy has been attacked on the ground that it threatens the rights of property of the well-to-do, and also on the ground that it threatens liberties that all men should have. Often, the attacker has attacked it on both these grounds without noticing that they differ, though one is as old as Aristotle and the other is modern. As soon as the difference is brought home to us, we are compelled to put questions that Locke and Montesquieu never put: How far must rights of property (from which in practice the rich benefit more than the poor do) be curtailed so that everyone may have certain rights and opportunities, the ones dignified by the name of freedom? How far does the attempt to ensure that everyone has them change their nature? And, lastly, how far is the attempt to make everyone free self-defeating, taking away with one hand what it gives with the other? These three questions, seldom if ever put in the eighteenth century, have been more widely raised in the nineteenth and twentieth. We can see how they arise as soon as we consider critically the dislike of democracy of such an impeccably liberal thinker as Constant.

These questions have seldom been discussed rigor-

ously and realistically. Hence the looseness and the ambiguity of much of the debate between liberals, who fear the growing power of the state and other large organizations, and Marxists and other socialists who attack "bourgeois liberalism" and yet claim to be "emancipators" of the exploited and oppressed classes. As we shall see later, liberals and Marxists have ideas about freedom that are much more alike than they appear to be on the surface, in spite of the bitterness of the quarrel between them.

Already in the eighteenth century, the notion of a social contract was rejected as unhistorical and unnecessary. First Hume and then Bentham argued that there is no need, if we want to show that men have interests, and therefore also claims or rights, that governments ought to promote or secure, to postulate a deliberate setting up of government to achieve these purposes. Even the ideas of natural law and natural right, as they had long been used, were rejected by Hume and Bentham. If there are rules, rights, and obligations common to all men everywhere, this is only because their wants and conditions are everywhere in important respects the same, so that everywhere experience teaches them that there are rules which it is everyone's interest should be generally observed, claims that everyone makes, and duties from which no one is exempt.

Yet the earlier critics of natural law and the social contract were closer to the writers they criticized than they thought they were. They too took it for granted that there are interests and claims common to all men everywhere, which they have even in the absence of government, and whose protection is the proper business of government. For them, too, political authority arises to enforce claims and obligations that are prior to it in the sense that they can be defined without reference to social conditions created by it or arising along with it.

Actually, the contract theorists did not, any more than their early critics, conceive of the condition of man before the emergence of civil government as an unsocial condition—though it has often been said that they did. They differed from these critics, not in thinking of the state of nature as an unsocial state (for they recognized that men in that state lived in families), but in making a sharper distinction between the human condition before the setting up of government and after it. Nor did they, as Hume did, point to the social origins of the rules and the rights that they thought common to mankind. Yet Hume and Bentham were like them in treating not only political but all social institutions as arising to serve conscious needs that could be defined without reference to them. For Hume, though he said that the rules common to men everywhere arise out of a social experience that is everywhere in some respects the same, took little interest in the effects of social institutions on men's needs and ideas. If it had been put to him that distinctively human needs, those not shared by man with the other animals, are essentially social, having no meaning outside a social context, he might well have agreed. But this idea, though consistent with his account of the origins of justice, is nowhere made explicitly in his social and political theory, and affects it hardly at all.

3. Man as Essentially a Social Being. The idea that man is *essentially* a social being, not only because his distinctively human capacities and needs are developed in social intercourse, but also because their exercise and satisfaction consists in social intercourse, was not invented by philosophers and political theorists of the late eighteenth and early nineteenth centuries. It is much older than that, for there is more than a trace of it in Aristotle and in later thinkers influenced by him. But it was in this period that it came to have a profound effect on the idea of freedom inherited from the Reformation and the contract theorists, the modern idea of freedom.

In his *Discourse on the Origins of Inequality among Men* (1754), Rousseau describes a state of nature which, unlike that of earlier thinkers, is emphatically not a social state. In it man, except that he has potentialities peculiar to his species, is like the other animals. He acquires distinctively human skills and needs only when he leaves the state of nature and comes to live permanently with other men. It is then that his animal needs are transformed into properly social needs, and it is his social needs that social institutions and civil government help to satisfy more or less adequately. In another of his works, *Émile* (1762), Rousseau describes a process of education which makes a rational and a moral being of a child that is neither to begin with, creating needs in him that are social. Only as a creature having such needs, making claims on others, and recognizing their claims on him, does Émile come to understand what it is to be free. Man, whose ability to reason and to will is developed in him as he learns to live with other men, cannot be *free* outside society nor *independent* inside it. To be free, he must be rational and able to make deliberate choices, he must have capacities that he acquires only in society; and to be independent, to be able to do without others, he must be without the needs that he acquires in acquiring these capacities; he must be unsocial.

Rousseau also introduced into social theory the idea of man "corrupted" by society. Now, society consists only of men and their modes of behavior; it is both a system of human behavior and an effect of what men have done. The social environment that "corrupts"

men would not be what it is unless they had sufficient motives for behaving as they do. This Rousseau admitted, at least by implication, and yet he claimed that they can be frustrated by their environment, can be moved to act in ways harmful to themselves and others. The wants and ambitions they acquire in society may be insatiable, or inconsistent with one another, or such that the means to satisfy them are lacking. But the more a man finds obstacles that are not natural but social or man-made in the way of his getting what he wants or becoming what he aspires to be, the less he is free.

Rousseau's ideal is therefore a condition in which the wants that society produces in men are fully satisfied. This condition we can aim at in two quite different ways: by indoctrination and discipline calculated to ensure that the individual has wants that are easily satisfied, or by so educating him that he forms his own ideas about how he should live and respects the right of others to do the same. Rousseau seems to prefer now one way and now another. The kind of private education described in *Émile* aims at producing a man of independent judgment, aware of his obligations to others, whereas the plan of public education which Rousseau proposed to the Poles in the *Considerations on the Government of Poland* aims rather at producing devoted citizens who think and feel alike. Thus, though there is an idea of freedom important to liberals to which Rousseau was the first to give powerful expression, it can hardly be said that he was himself a liberal thinker.

This is the freedom that in *The Social Contract* (*Contrat social*, 1762), he calls "moral freedom," saying that it makes man truly his own master, for it is obedience to a law which he has prescribed to himself (Book I, Ch. 8). This moral freedom is, in *The Social Contract*, connected with popular government. The citizens make their own laws, and because each of them is able to vote as he thinks right without being tricked or "pressured" to vote otherwise, he takes an equal part with the others in making the rules that all must obey, and so commits himself deliberately to this obedience. In *Émile*, what is essentially the same idea of freedom has a broader and less political significance. Émile does not take his principles on trust; he learns from experience that they are to his own and other people's advantage, and so adopts them as rules of conduct. Unless he did so, he could neither live comfortably with others nor form enduring purposes of his own to be pursued intelligently and with hope of success. Moral freedom is Rousseau's answer to the question: How can a man be free and yet subject to social rules?

Kant has a similar idea of freedom, as for example when he says in *The Fundamental Principles of the*

Metaphysic of Morals that "a free will and a will subject to moral laws are one and the same" (Kant, p. 66). But he makes a sharper distinction than Rousseau made between morality and legality. The business of the state is to make and enforce laws in the common interest; its concern is that men should keep the law and not that they should keep it from the right motive. If they keep it from fear of punishment, they do not keep it freely, as they do when they keep it from a sense that it is their duty to do so. Thus, for Kant, the freedom that consists in obedience to self-imposed laws belongs to a sphere with which the state is not directly concerned. Kant would not, of course, deny that the legal order maintained by the state is a condition of man's acquiring a moral will; nor would he say that any political and legal order is as propitious to moral freedom as any other. Yet he does not, as Rousseau does in *The Social Contract*, see a close connection between moral freedom and popular government.

It is implicit in this idea of moral freedom that being free consists in more than just having desires and not being prevented from satisfying them, that it involves having a will, being able to make decisions. Only a rational being, assessing the situations in which it acts, has this ability; and only a rational being can be moral, can recognize rules of conduct as obligatory upon itself and all other rational beings. Being free and being moral both involve being rational. But neither Rousseau nor Kant makes it clear why being free and being subject to moral law should be *identical*. Why should not a man be free if he can make decisions (or form purposes) and carry them out? Why must he be moral, if he is to be free?

To this question Kant seems to provide no answer. Indeed, he goes less far than Rousseau does towards answering it; for, though his explanations of what is involved in making decisions and in acting morally are fuller and better than Rousseau's, he rather asserts a connection between freedom and morality than explains what it is.

In this last respect, the improver on Rousseau is not Kant but Hegel. His explanation is not wholly convincing, and not only because it is mixed up with a metaphysic that few can understand, let alone accept; but it is ingenious and perceptive.

Hegel improves on Rousseau because he explains more elaborately and forcefully, both in *The Phenomenology of Mind* (1807) and in *The Philosophy of Right* (1821), what is involved in man's being essentially social. Man's ideas about himself, his purposes as distinct from his mere appetites, are related to the social order he belongs to. His ability to reason, to form purposes, and therefore to make decisions, is developed in the process of acquiring a cultural inheritance, a process that involves coming to have standards and to accept rules. Thus becoming rational, becoming purposeful, and becoming moral (not good or virtuous but able to make claims and recognize obligations) are all parts of the same course of development. It is as a social being with a place in a community, as a partaker in what Hegel calls ethical life, that the individual forms purposes and takes decisions that have a meaning only in a context of social relations defined by the rights and obligations that help to make them what they are. Only as a being whose needs and purposes are essentially social does man conceive of freedom and put a value on it. No doubt, we can ask of a creature that is not rational and social, that has only appetites and no purposes, whether there are obstacles to its getting what it wants, whether it is free. But this is not the freedom that men are willing to die for, or to exert themselves greatly to preserve or extend. What they deeply care about is the exercise of certain capacities and the having of certain rights and opportunities, and the obstacles they resent as curtailments of freedom frustrate these capacities, detract from these rights, deny these opportunities. To exercise these capacities and rights, and to take these opportunities, a man needs a self-discipline which is the fruit of an education that includes necessarily a social or external discipline. It is only as a creature under social discipline and capable of self-discipline, as a moral being, that man aspires to freedom.

The social rules that he learns to accept do not stand to his purposes as means to ends, for his purposes have no meaning apart from the social order he belongs to, the social relations in which he stands to others; and these relations are also moral relations, for to belong to a community with others is to make claims upon them and recognize obligations to them.

Men, as Hegel sees them, are progressive as well as moral beings; they develop their capacities as they create their institutions; the "subjective" and the "objective," their beliefs, wants, and dispositions, on the one hand, and their customs and conventions, on the other, are but aspects of one whole, and change together. And yet tensions or "contradictions" arise inevitably between these two aspects of human life, and progress consists in their emergence and in the overcoming of them. This progress is a growth in reason, a deeper understanding by men of themselves and their world, and especially that part of the world which is the system of their own activities, the social world, the world of culture; a deeper understanding and a fuller control over what they understand. This growth in reason is also a growth in freedom: in the ability to form consistent and realistic purposes and to remove obstacles to them.

The state, as Hegel conceives of it, is both an effect

and a condition of this greater understanding and control. The more social rules are made or declared by a legislature and by professional courts of justice, the more secure men's rights and the more definite their obligations, and the greater also their power to adapt their institutions to their needs and ideals. The state is the social order in its most rational aspect; for it is through its laws and policies that men express the most clearly and effectively their aspirations both for the individual and the community.

Hegel has been called an idolator of the state. The accusation is not wholly unjust and yet is misleading. He never preached unquestioning obedience to the laws or the government. Nor does it follow from his account of the state that all resistance to established authority, still less criticism of it, is wrong. But the bias of his argument is strongly against the challenger of authority, for he nowhere defines conditions in which, in his opinion, resistance is justified. His failure to do so, together with the extravagant and almost adulatory language in which he speaks of the state, explain and in part justify his reputation as an illiberal thinker.

Yet he puts forward, more forcefully and ingeniously than any thinker before him, four theses of which liberals since his day have taken large account: (1) only as a creature educated by social intercourse and having purposes and ideals that are meaningless outside a social context, does man come to conceive and to cherish the rights and opportunities that he dignifies by the name of freedom; (2) a long course of social and cultural evolution has gone to formulating these rights and opportunities and to inquiry into their social and political conditions; (3) this formulation and this inquiry are closely related to the emergence of the modern state; (4) the effective maintenance of these rights and opportunities requires a legal order of the sort we have in mind when we speak of the state.

The liberal who accepts these theses need not agree that there is a necessary progress towards a legal order that maintains freedom. For example, he can accept the fourth thesis and still argue that the state has often in the past, and will yet more often in the future, develop in ways that curtail freedom or prevent its enlargement. The state may be both a condition of freedom and a considerable and growing impediment to it.

The liberal often takes pride in being suspicious of the state. "The price of freedom is eternal vigilance"; and the liberal is, or claims to be, vigilant for freedom, presumably against those well placed to threaten it, who for the most part either hold public office or belong to organized bodies controlling or aspiring to control those who hold it. What he is suspicious of is not so much the idea of the state as the state as

it actually is, or some party or group that controls the state or aspires to do so. The laws and institutions of government may not be as he would have them, and he therefore wants them changed; and yet it is to them as they ought to be as much as to the energy and independence of mind of private citizens that he looks for the preservation of freedom. An Hegelian might say that the concern of a Wilhelm von Humboldt or a John Stuart Mill for the individual is conceivable only in a society in which the modern state has emerged. The state, say Humboldt and Mill, must not encroach on the sphere of the individual. But the statement is empty unless that sphere is defined, which it cannot be without using concepts, legal and moral, that have emerged or acquired precision in the modern state, either in courts of law and administrative departments or in controversies about their proper business. Nor can "the private sphere" be adequately protected except by the state; for the individual must have legal recourse, which is to say, recourse to the state, against whoever encroaches on that sphere. No doubt, the individual appeals also to public opinion, but the effectiveness of such appeals depends largely on the legal protection of carefully defined rights.

Humboldt and Mill, and Tocqueville also, feared paternal government no less than oppression by the state. If the state looks after the citizen too well, though with the best intentions, it weakens his self-reliance and independence of judgment, his ability to define his own problems and to set about solving them. Freedom is the school of freedom; the individual learns to value his essential rights, and to act responsibly, by being left, as far as possible, to act for himself, either alone or in free association with others.

This fear of paternalism as distinct from oppression is scarcely to be found in the eighteenth century. It comes, as might be expected, with the era of social reform; and if in the twentieth century there is less of it than there was in the nineteenth century, this is because liberals have come to believe that much more must be done for the individual to enable him to use the rights and opportunities they think he ought to have than Humboldt or Tocqueville or Mill imagined. The liberal is as vigilant as ever, and as suspicious of the state, but is less concerned to prevent the state trying to do too much than to ensure that it does what it must do if its subjects are to be effectively free.

In the nineteenth century fear of state paternalism often went with belief in "self-improvement." In the Middle Ages, and indeed much later, there had been in plenty a different kind of paternalism. The individual belonged to a community ruled by custom, and his "elders" interpreted this custom to him. The course of his life, in many respects, was traced out for him; he had not much scope for independence of judgment.

He had no career to make, for he belonged to a social order in which he had a well-defined place, and was brought up to fill it adequately. He was educated, not to improve himself or make the best of his talents, but to take the place he was born to take.

As we have seen already, the breakup of the custom-bound community and the increased social mobility that came with it were liberating influences. They encouraged the individual to be more self-reliant, to see himself as making a place for himself in society, to think of himself as the possessor of rights not tied to any particular occupation or social role. But they also, insofar as he felt himself to be weaker than others, encouraged him to look for protection and assistance to the state. He was made free of old ties and yet made to feel insecure and weak, and so disposed to look for protection from the strongest power of all, the state.

Tocqueville dwells upon this disposition and some of its consequences that he thinks are bad. He speaks of a democratic egalitarianism dangerous to liberty. More perhaps than any other writer of his age, he makes a contrast between equality and freedom, which is illuminating in some respects but misleading in others. He argues that, as the state grows stronger, so too does the passion for equality at the expense of freedom. He admits that in the old order before the French Revolution, there was more inequality, but the state, he says, was weaker and there was more freedom. We can agree with him that the state was weaker and the classes more unequal, and yet deny that there was greater freedom. The nobleman had larger privileges and in some respects was more free, but he was also kept out of many occupations and activities that might otherwise have attracted him by the prejudices of his class. The bourgeois and the peasant were less free. The movement, even in France, was not really from aristocratic freedom to democratic equality; it was from a social order in which the privileged had not much freedom, as the liberal understands it, to an order in which inequalities of birth counted for less and inequalities of wealth for more, and the formerly un-privileged had rights that were more secure and larger opportunities.

In the nineteenth century much more than in the century before it, social and political thinkers, liberals and others, spoke of the "development of human po-tentialities," "self-improvement," "moral autonomy," and "self-realization." They still do so in the twentieth century, though with a greater awareness that these are terms of uncertain meaning. If we are to judge by how they are used, they are not equivalent but are closely related.

What, then, is it to develop human potentialities? Is it to acquire dispositions or skills peculiar to human beings, no matter what they are? Presumably not, for this development is held to be desirable, whereas much that is peculiarly human is harmful or useless. Who then is to decide what dispositions and skills are worth having? The person who acquires them or the person who educates or trains him?

What kind of learning is "self-improvement," and what kind of teaching does it exclude? The trainer of animals teaches them and in so doing "develops their potentialities"; he does more than evoke responses in them; he so acts upon them that, when they have left his hands, they have dispositions and skills they did not have before. The trainer may not threaten or hurt his animals but may only coax and reward them, so that his training is not coercive. What they do as they learn may be as freely done as what they do when they act instinctively or on their own initiative to satisfy their appetites, without prompting from him. The training of little children is in some ways like the training of animals, when they acquire dispositions and skills useful to others or to themselves. Yet, presumably, this kind of training is not what is meant by "self-improvement," even though there is nothing coercive about it.

Can it be called "self-realization"? Only, if at all, when it is the training of little children, and then only to the extent that they acquire capacities that are peculiarly human. They learn to use words, to make choices, to pass judgments on themselves and others, to control themselves. They acquire the capacities we refer to when we speak of reason and will. Their early training, though it is not self-improvement, puts them in the way of acquiring self-knowledge and self-control; and this, perhaps, is the reason why it is sometimes spoken of as a stage in self-realization.

"Self-realization" is an ambiguous term. If we con-sider how it is used, it does not always imply that the individual sets up some ideal for himself, some concep-tion of the sort of person he would like to be or the kind of life he would like to live, and then tries to achieve it. For those who use the term often speak as if the individual came to understand himself, and to set up such ideals, in the process of realizing himself. As he grows in self-knowledge, he sets up and abandons several such ideals; his purposes and aspirations change. When he is young they are ill-defined or unrealistic or fickle; as he grows older they often, though by no means always, become more realistic and firmer. But this, so it would appear, is not a sufficient sign that he has "realized himself," or has come closer to doing so. For he may be no more than set in his ways or lacking in ambition. This notion of self-realization is elusive and obscure.

Does self-realization, at least at that stage of it that

involves setting up of ideals for the self and striving to attain them, entail self-improvement? If a man has base ambitions, mean or wicked self-ideals, and strives to achieve them, is he realizing himself? It would appear that he is not. Self-realization, where it involves pursuit of an ideal, would seem to imply—for most writers who use the term, if not for all—self-improvement. But how are we to decide whether or not someone is improving himself? If Napoleon had aimed at becoming the beneficent mayor of some small Corsican town, would he have improved or realized himself more or less than he did by becoming Emperor of the French? If a man, to be self-realizing or self-improving, must have admirable or worthwhile (even though not virtuous) ambitions, who is to decide whether he has them? And if he is to be taught or persuaded to have them, what forms may the teaching or persuasion take for the acquiring and pursuit of the ambitions to be reckoned self-improvement and not improvement by his betters? J. S. Mill, and perhaps T. H. Green also, went some little way towards answering these questions but not very far.

And what is moral autonomy? Psychologists and writers on education tell us that we acquire most of the ideals to which we are deeply attached while we are as yet incapable of assessing them critically. Our more enduring and realistic ambitions, we may acquire later, but they are shaped to a large extent by ideals that were ours before we had even learned to define them. So, too, the disposition, weak or strong, to tell the truth, or to be loyal to friends and colleagues, or to help the unfortunate, or to forgive injuries, or to be careful of the feelings of others, is formed in us before we are old enough to consider the reasons for and against acting on any of these principles. If to be morally autonomous is to accept on rational grounds the principles that govern one's conduct, then there are few or none who have moral autonomy. But if this autonomy involves no more than being able to apply such principles firmly and intelligently, then there may be many persons who are morally autonomous, though some of them more so than others. Indeed, if this is what moral autonomy is, then everyone who is moral is necessarily, to some extent, morally autonomous, for being moral involves being able to apply some such principles with some degree of firmness and intelligence.

To the extent that self-realization involves the pursuit of ambitions calling for the exercise of rare and much admired abilities, it may be incompatible with moral autonomy, or with more than a little of it. Napoleon might have had much smaller scope to exercise his rare abilities, had he had greater moral autonomy. It is said of him that he had a strong will; but,

though whoever has a high degree of moral autonomy has a strong will, the reverse is not true.

We have not pointed to the obscurities and ambiguities of such expressions as "self-realization," "self-improvement," and "moral autonomy" to suggest that there is little to them. They are used to refer to aspects of human experience and endeavor that are important, and if we dismiss them as insignificant, we may fail to notice these aspects. And, in any case, they are relevant to our theme, which is liberalism; they are an important part of its stock of ideas. They are much in favor, not only among self-styled liberals, but also among socialists and anarchists who attack "liberalism" as inadequate or old-fashioned, or even as a "bourgeois ideology."

The liberal, the socialist, and the anarchist seem all to accept three principles: that the individual should be so educated and so placed in society that he can form for himself ambitions and ideals whose pursuit is satisfying to him; that the worth of his ambitions and ideals depends partly on their pursuit being useful to society, partly on the satisfaction he gets from pursuing them, and partly on their pursuit bringing into play abilities that are admirable; and that the individual should accept willingly rules of conduct that he can defend on rational grounds and can act upon firmly and intelligently. These three principles, though socialists and anarchists (not to speak of many conservatives) accept them, are nevertheless properly called liberal. They are more closely and obviously connected with freedom than with the social control of production or the abolition of government or the preservation of established institutions; and the writers who have done most to explain and recommend them—as, for example, Humboldt, Mill, and T. H. Green—are widely acknowledged to be liberals.

These three principles may not cover all that is meant by "self-realization," "self-improvement," and "moral autonomy," but they are shared by most people who speak favorably of these things, and they are relatively clear. No doubt, with these as with all broad principles, questions arise that are difficult to answer as soon as we look closely at them. For example, if we take only the first principle, we are faced, as soon as we examine it critically, with two questions, neither of them easy to answer: What criteria must we use in deciding whether someone has formed his ambitions and ideals for himself? How do we decide whether his pursuit of them is satisfying to him? The putting forward of principles as broad as these is only a beginning, though it is important to begin aright, so that the principles, when closely examined, raise questions that can be answered and are relevant to problems that people who care for freedom feel strongly about. Or, 51 rather, the putting of them is neither a beginning nor an end, for we continually reformulate our principles in the light of our answers to the questions they suggest to us.

Most of the rights to which liberals in the West attach great importance can be, and often are, justified by reference to these principles. For example, the right to an education that enables you to assess the opportunities (the occupations and ways of life) that society offers to its members; the right to choose your occupation provided you have the requisite skills; the right to get the special training needed to acquire these skills, provided you are capable of profiting by it; the right to choose your partner in marriage; the right to be gainfully employed; the right to a minimal standard of living, whether or not you are so employed; the right to privacy, especially in your own home; the right to express and publish your opinions; the right to form or join associations for any purpose that appeals to you and does not invade the rights of others; the right to be tried for alleged offenses and to have your disputes settled by courts not subject to political pressures; the right to take part in choosing at free elections the persons who make policy, at least at the highest level, in the communities or associations you belong to. These rights are by no means the only ones to which liberals attach importance, but it is doubtful whether there are any that they hold more important. These formulations of them are brief and need to be qualified, but they are sufficient for the present purpose, which is only to indicate roughly the kind of rights of special concern to the liberal.

The last four of these rights are primarily political, though they are not confined to the political sphere. Many opinions important to their holders, many associations important to their members, are not political. Yet these rights may be called *political* because they are important above all in the political sphere. The other seven rights, in contrast with these four, may be called *social*, though they too impinge on the political sphere, since whether or not they are exercised partly determines the aims and methods of governments, what sort of persons get public office, and the ways in which political influence is acquired and used.

Countries in which the social rights are coming to be more widely enjoyed are not called liberal, if the political rights are denied to the people, even though denied much more in the political sphere than outside it. Nor do these countries claim to be liberal; for the word "liberal," unlike the word "democratic," is in them often a term of abuse. It is so at least in government circles and among supporters of the government. On the other hand, the liberal denies that these countries are democratic precisely on the ground that their peoples do not enjoy the political rights. He may allow that, if in fact the social rights are more widely enjoyed, people are becoming in important respects more free, but he denies that this is enough to make these countries either liberal or democratic. He denies it, not because he cares only for the political rights and not the social ones, but because he believes that the social rights are less secure and more restricted where the political rights are lacking.

Most countries now claim to be democratic, and a smaller number claim to be liberal as well. In the countries that make the first claim but not the second, people do not in fact enjoy the political rights, or do so only to a slight extent and precariously. How, then, do these countries (or their rulers) come to make this claim? When they make it, are they denying that our four political rights are essential to democracy? Or are they saying that their peoples in fact enjoy them? As we shall see in a moment, they turn and turn about, like weathercocks in shifting winds, swivelling and yet bold.

4. The Radical Attack on Liberalism. As we have seen, there were liberals after the French Revolution who thought democracy dangerous to freedom. Their fear of democracy made them suspect to the radicals, who therefore attacked them. The radicals attacked not freedom but liberalism, which they interpreted as concern for the privileges of the well-to-do masquerading as concern for freedom.

The quarrel between radicals and liberals has been genuine enough, though it has led to equivocation and self-deception. It was in France that it first came to the forefront of politics, especially during the July Monarchy and the Second Republic. The liberals wanted the political rights, and above all the right to vote at free elections, confined to persons capable of exercising them responsibly, who (in their opinion) were the educated and the well-to-do. If, in practice, they cared more for political than for social rights, this was not because they thought them more important in themselves but because they held that, at least in Western countries, they were less secure; as indeed they were, for the educated and the well-to-do, who in fact enjoyed their social more securely than their political rights. The liberal argument of that time might be put briefly into these words: the people as a whole will enjoy their rights more securely, if the most important of the political rights, the right to vote, is confined to those capable of exercising it responsibly; and therefore the right to vote is, of all rights, the one that must be extended the most cautiously, as education and political competence spread.

The radicals answered that the poor and the uneducated enjoyed their social rights precariously, and

LIBERALISM

lacked some altogether, precisely because they were
without political rights. They too, like the liberals,
treated the right to vote as the most immediately
important; the other political rights were of limited
use without it. To begin with, many radicals thought
it enough that the poor should have the vote, and that
their children should be educated at public expense.
This, they hoped, would enable them to exercise all
their rights effectively. Later they changed their minds,
and made progressively larger demands on behalf of
the poor, requiring that more and more services be
provided for those unable to pay for them; and to cover
the cost of these services, they advocated steeper taxation of the well-to-do. Also, to protect the economically
weak from the effects of crises and depressions, they
pressed for a wider control of the economy, whether
by the state or by lesser political communities or by
producers' associations.

The liberals too, self-styled or so-called by socialists
and others to the "left" of them, have changed with
the times. They have accepted first manhood and then
universal suffrage, a large provision of "social services"
at public expense, and a greater control of the economy. If a distinction is worth making between the
liberal and the radical, it is a distinction between
attitudes rather than doctrines. Both the liberal and
the radical accept the rights, social and political, that
were mentioned earlier, at least in the sense that they
admit that all men should have them, when conditions
allow. And they both accept the three liberal principles
used to justify these rights. They are both, therefore,
in the broad sense liberals. Yet there is a difference
between them worth noticing: the liberal is more concerned than is the radical that attempts to extend the
rights quickly should not emasculate or even destroy
them, while the radical is more concerned that they
should be extended quickly.

We distinguish here between two attitudes taken in
the abstract. Of course, there are people calling themselves liberals (and even called so by others) who care
above all for the privileges of a minority, just as there
are people calling themselves radicals (or socialists or
communists) who care above all for getting power and
exercising it over docile subjects. Such persons are
sometimes cynical, sometimes self-deceivers, and
sometimes both.

Thus, though there is nothing illiberal about radicalism—about the desire to extend, as far and as
quickly as possible, the rights, social and political,
whose exercise constitutes the freedom we have been
discussing—it is easy enough to see how radicals, as
assiduous and vocal champions of the poor, come to
appear illiberal to liberals. Nor is it always a matter
of appearances, for radicals may indeed be illiberal.

That is to say, they may do more than advocate policies
that postpone the coming of freedom without intending
to do so; they may want to deprive people of liberties
they already have.

For example, they may want to deprive some people
of political rights they already have while pretending
to give them to everyone; they may extend the franchise and abolish free elections, or they may form
associations and encourage people to join them, but
otherwise suppress freedom of association. They may
have illusions about their intentions or they may not.
They may even admit that they are suppressing some
liberties, taking them away from a minority who use
them to prevent urgently needed reforms. This minority are to be deprived for a time of some of their
freedom so that everyone may have freedom more
abundantly in the future. Or, as happens more often,
perhaps, they may deny that they want to deprive
anyone, even for a time, of any of the rights that
constitute freedom, and yet advocate courses that result
in this deprivation. Though they refuse to admit this
result, their policies are in fact illiberal if putting them
into effect curtails the liberties of some people without
extending those of others.

There is, as recent history proves, an "equivocation
of the Left" difficult to avoid. The champions of the
poor and the ignorant need their support if they are
to get for them what they hope to get. Their aim, they
say, is to "liberate the people," to ensure that they
acquire essential liberties (the rights, social and political, that we have been discussing, and others like
them); and they can hardly win the popular support
they need unless they assume, at least in public, that
the people understand and want the benefits intended
for them. They can hardly say to the poor and the
ignorant: "Support us in our endeavors to get for you
advantages that you do not understand, or understand
so little, that we shall not be able to let you have them
for some considerable time after we have got power
with your support." So they equivocate, both to keep
their followers loyal to them and to reassure themselves
as to their own intentions.

The more backward a country, the less social and
cultural conditions inside it allow the effective exercise
of these rights, the greater the temptation to equivocate, to declare publicly that the people do exercise
them while adopting policies that make sense only on
the assumption that they do not yet understand them
and so cannot exercise them. This equivocation is made
easier by attacks, often enough justified, on the hypocrisy of the well-to-do liberals, who pretend to care for
freedom in general when in fact they care only for
their own privileges. The rights precious to these liberals, say the attackers, have been too often used, in

53

their present forms, as excuses to prevent drastic but urgent reforms for the benefit of the poor at the expense of the rich. So these rights, in these forms, are denounced as "illusory" or "bourgeois." They are rights proper to a society in which there are great inequalities of wealth, and the rich can exercise them much more effectively than the poor can, even though, on paper, all classes have them. The radicals who attack bourgeois liberalism do not reject in principle even the political rights asserted by the liberals: they do not deny that governments should be responsible to the people, or that the people should be free to form associations to promote aims of their own choosing, or should be allowed to express their opinions freely. They say rather that these rights, in their so-called "bourgeois" or "liberal" forms, are not useful to the people generally but only to the rich. Unfortunately, they seldom make it clear how these bourgeois forms differ from other, and (in their opinion) more genuinely popular, forms.

That the poor, though they have these rights "on paper," cannot exercise them effectively while the rich retain their wealth and the advantages it brings, may or may not be true; or it may be true to an extent that varies with the circumstances. But, true or not, it is not obvious why, when great inequalities of wealth are removed, these rights must take forms very different from those they now have if all sections of the community are to exercise them effectively. In particular, the argument that political rights, if the people generally are really to have them, cannot take the forms they do while they are of little use except to the wealthy, is quite unconvincing. If the argument were merely that different political and legal institutions are required to ensure that a vast number of persons exercise their rights effectively from those that suffice to ensure that a small number do so, it would be more plausible at the first blush, though still not convincing, unless it were made clear what the differences would be and the reasons for them. But this is not the argument.

Not all radicals (as defined above) are given to this kind of equivocation. But the Marxists have been and are, and so, too, have socialists of other schools. Nor is this equivocation of the Left confined to socialists, for there are traces of it as far back at least as the Jacobinism of the seventeen-nineties.

There is also an equivocation of the Right. In its earlier forms, it was cruder and perhaps more widespread than it is now, but it still survives. This kind of equivocator, while he says that all men are equal in certain fundamental respects, though some are superior to the rest in other respects, fails to notice (or to admit) that the other respects are at bottom only

some of the fundamental ones described in different words. This sort of equivocation goes back at least as far as Montesquieu and Locke, and perhaps further.

Montesquieu, in *The Spirit of the Laws* (Book XI, Ch. 6), with the English form of government in mind, speaks of persons who ought not to have the vote because they are "in so mean a situation as to be deemed to have no will of their own." Yet in other parts of this same work, he takes it for granted that all men (except, presumably, infants and the mentally defective) are legally responsible for their actions. If someone of "mean situation" breaks the law or makes a contract, Montesquieu does not claim for him diminished responsibility on the ground that he has no "will of his own"; that his understanding of the circumstances in which he acts is such that he ought not to be held responsible for what he does, or ought to be so held less than if he were not in a "mean situation." He understands the law and the circumstances to which it applies quite well enough to be deemed to have a will of his own when he commits an offense or makes a contract, but when it comes to choosing lawmakers, he must have no say, because he then lacks a will of his own—that is to say, does not understand what law is about well enough to be of good judgment in deciding who shall take part in making or declaring the law.

Now, it may well be that the criteria of legal and political competence are not the same, so that we cannot say that someone who has understanding enough to be answerable to the courts for breaches of law or contract must have understanding enough to make a rational use of the vote. But Montesquieu never troubled to distinguish legal from political competence, and never explained why the "mean in situation" (presumably, the poor and the uneducated) should be deemed legally competent and politically incompetent. Even if it should happen that political is more rare than legal competence, it is not obvious that there is proportionately less of it to be found among the poor and the uneducated than among the others. And if there is less, may this not be due above all to their not exercising the rights denied to them on the ground that they are politically incompetent? Is not political competence acquired by exercising these rights rather than by going to school or having private tutors? And was this not so particularly in Montesquieu's day, when formal teaching was so largely classical and literary?

The truth is that while the criteria of legal competence (or legal responsibility) have been often discussed, the criteria of political competence have been so scarcely at all. Political competence consists, presumably, of a variety of capacities or skills, though for our purposes it is enough to distinguish, broadly, between four: *political judgment*, or being a good judge of what policies are likely to achieve some desired end or ends; *political sense*, or being good at discerning who has political judgment and can be trusted to exercise it responsibly; *political skill*, or knowing how to use established procedures to get the decisions you want; and *political power*, or being able to induce those who have political judgment or skill to exercise it as you want them to do.

Political judgment and political skill are kinds of competence acquired above all by being politically active, by taking part in government or by observing it closely. Being well-to-do and well-educated do not give this judgment or skill to a man except to the extent that they make it easier for him to take part in government or to observe it. Political sense and political power come mostly of the exercise of political rights, and are confined to the well-to-do and well-educated only while they alone have these rights. With the coming of democracy, the acquiring of political competence, in all four kinds, is not a product of forms of education or styles of life peculiar to any class; it is acquired either by professionals, whose business is government and politics, or the discussion and study of them, or else it comes of the exercise of political rights. The more widely these rights are shared, the more evenly distributed among all classes the kinds of competence that come of exercising them, and the more the kinds that are acquired professionally are at the service of all classes. For it is less the social origins, or the present status, of the politically active that matters than the extent to which their services are at the disposal of different sections of the community. It is the same with whole-time politicians as with other "professionals." Not long ago, doctors were not only drawn mostly from well-to-do families; they also mostly served them. Today they are drawn from them rather less often than they used to be; but what matters more is that their services are now much more widely available to the poor.

This is not to suggest that the idea of political competence is empty, and that adults ought never to be refused political rights on the ground that they are politically incompetent. It is to suggest only that people who use the idea, either by that name or another, often do not know what they are about. They say, on the one hand, that all classes or all races or the two sexes are equal in certain respects (often called "fundamental respects," to lend dignity to them), while on the other, overtly or by implication, they claim superiority for some classes or races, or for one of the sexes, without noticing that the respects in which they claim

it are identical, wholly or in part, with some of the respects they call fundamental.

There are, of course, people who do not admit that everyone ought, as far as possible, to enjoy the rights we have been discussing. In their case, there is none of the equivocation mentioned earlier, though their arguments may be defective for other reasons. The "equivocators" are all, in the broad sense, liberal; they agree that in principle everyone ought to have these rights. Their equivocation consists in their taking up, without noticing or at least admitting it, positions inconsistent with the principle. On the Left, they reject as bourgeois shams institutions needed to secure these rights, or some of them; on the Right, they make political competence a condition of people's having some of these rights, when in fact their having them is a condition of their acquiring political competence or of their being able to call on the services of the politically competent.

III. FREEDOM, EQUALITY, AND THE STATE

The desire to secure to the unprivileged rights held to be essential or to constitute freedom has been a strong motive behind reforms that have greatly increased the power of the state. This power has increased at the expense of the privileged, in the obvious sense that it has deprived them of powers they used to have. But it is not obvious that this decrease in their power has also diminished their freedom, not at least if freedom is understood as the liberal understands it. When the right to vote at free elections is confined to the well-to-do, each vote carries greater weight than when the right is extended to all. The rich man's political influence is then diminished, but his right to vote is as secure as ever. So, too, when only the well-to-do can publish their opinions or form associations to put pressure on governments, their political influence is greater than it is when the poor can do so as well; but their rights to publish and to associate for political purposes are not curtailed when democracy comes.

There are even some respects in which greater equality enlarges the rights of the well-to-do by destroying prejudices that prevent them doing what they are legally entitled to do, as, for example, by giving them a wider choice of marriage partners or of occupations. It can be said, therefore, that the reforms, which have been one important cause among others of the great increase in the power of the state, have enlarged in some respects the freedom of all classes, though they have done more for the poor than for the rich.

Yet the rich have been deprived of powers important to them, and the deprivation has seemed to them a loss of freedom. Whether the loss, in their eyes, is made up for by the benefits it brings to themselves (and others) depends on their tastes and principles. And these tastes and principles are affected by the reforms. It may be that their opportunities in a reformed society seem to them better worth having than the powers that the wealthy had before the reforms were made. Whether or not they seem so must depend largely on how the reforms are made. The more peacefully they are made, the more quickly the "dispossessed" are reconciled to them.

To the liberal, of course, it goes without saying that reforms aimed at ensuring that all men, regardless of wealth and social status, can exercise effectively the rights that constitute freedom, do more for the unprivileged than the privileged; for, in his eyes, the advantages of the privileged consist above all in their being better able to exercise these rights. They, too, before the reforms are made, may be less free (and even much less free) than they might be, but they are considerably more free than the unprivileged.

But the privileged, and even the unprivileged, do not always look at society and social change through liberal eyes. The privileged are often more attached to rights threatened by the reformers, especially rights of property, than to the liberties that the reforms are meant to enlarge. They may be willing to abandon some of these liberties—as, for example, the right to vote at free elections, or freedom of speech or association—rather than accept reforms that curtail their rights of property and their incomes. The unprivileged, too, are often willing to forego political rights for the sake of others, making do with considerably less freedom than the liberal claims for all men.

No doubt, the rights precious to the liberal would matter much less than they do, if nobody but the intellectual cared about them. Their attractive power depends on their usefulness to large or powerful social groups. If we consider them in the wide perspective attempted here, we can see how they arise in a certain kind of society, and we can say that they are typical of it. Yet they are not equally attractive to all groups in that society; and each group is willing to sacrifice some to preserve or acquire others, or to get other advantages. Every large group in a society of that kind is apt to be both liberal and dangerous to liberty.

The more these groups, to whom some of the essential rights or liberties are peculiarly attractive, organize effectively to define and push their claims, the more each of them has to take notice of the claims of the others. The groups learn to understand and respect each other's aspirations. Indeed, this is how, in some Western countries, there has come to be wide agreement about what rights are "essential liberties," though in practice every one of them means more to some groups than to others. Most political leaders, most acknowledged spokesmen for important groups, recognize these rights; and the recognition makes each group readier to make concessions to the others, whenever the concessions are justified on the ground that they extend these rights. But this respect for the claims of others, this readiness to make concessions, is always limited, so that there is always a good deal of resistance to reforms that enlarge freedom. Even the society that takes pride in being liberal is to some extent illiberal. Most groups inside it are sometimes willing to sacrifice their own freedom to other advantages or to resist reforms enlarging the freedom of others. They are willing to do so though they pretend not to be; they deny, not freedom, but that the advantages they seek are gained at the cost of it or that the reforms they resist enlarge it for others. In liberal societies, when freedom is sacrificed, it is so often in the name of freedom.

Reforms aimed at extending freedom have had two effects often regarded as dangerous to freedom: the increased power of the state and more intense competition. These reforms have not been the sole causes of these effects but they have been among the most important. Some writers concerned for liberty, for example, R. H. Tawney in both *The Acquisitive Society* and *Equality*, have criticized this competitiveness as a source of anxiety and self-centeredness, and also as deflecting people from occupations that might suit them better to others carrying greater rewards in terms of wealth, power, or status.

Anxiety, self-centeredness, and doing less suitable work are not in themselves diminutions of freedom; not at least if freedom consists in having the rights, social and political, that we have been discussing. For the competitiveness that produces these things itself arises because these rights are widely exercised. But, as we saw earlier, these rights are often justified by appeals to such notions as "self-realization," "self-improvement," and "moral autonomy"—and are so not only by self-styled liberals but by socialists and anarchists as well. The gist of these notions, or the parts of them more easily understood, we tried to formulate in three liberal principles, of which the first asserts that the individual should be so educated and placed socially that he can form for himself ambitions and ideals whose pursuit is satisfying to him. Now, these effects of "excessive" competition, though they may not prevent people from exercising "essential" rights or liberties, may yet impede the realization of a principle used to justify the rights. Thus the liberal, even though his concern is for freedom, must take account of this attack on the undesirable consequences of excessive competition; he cannot ignore it as, from his point of view, irrelevant on the ground that it has nothing to do with freedom. He must consider it, and if he finds it justified, must allow that his essential rights, though necessary, are not sufficient for the achievement of freedom.

The rise of the state has brought with it inequalities of power greater than any known before, and this rise has been to a considerable extent an effect of reforms aimed at extending freedom. So we have here what looks like a paradox: the more we ensure that all men are equal (that they all enjoy the "essential" rights), the greater the inequalities among them. We may resolve the paradox by pointing out that the respects in which they are equal are different from the respects in which they are not. They are equal in the sense that they all have certain rights, and they are unequal because some of them have much more power than others; and the inequalities of power are needed to ensure that everyone does in fact enjoy the rights. But this resolution of the paradox, though neat in the abstract, does not carry conviction. Great inequalities of power may be needed to ensure that everyone enjoys essential rights; but we cannot assume that wherever these rights are prized and sought, the inequalities that arise with the seeking do in fact secure the rights to everyone; that where social conditions produce the demand, they ensure the supply. "Seek and ye shall find" is not a divine promise made to us in this sphere. Nor is it true that mankind never set themselves a problem they cannot solve.

Tocqueville said that, as equality and the passion for it grow, there grows with them the power of the state. About this assertion there is nothing paradoxical, for it puts the state to one side over against private citizens. Public authority is exercised, of course, by individuals who are more powerful than the persons subject to their authority, but their power belongs to them by virtue of their office. Tocqueville did not mean, literally, that where the state is strong, there is in general less inequality; he meant rather that, where it is strong, there is less inequality among private citizens. But he was mistaken, even if this was his meaning. There is little evidence, even in the West, that inequality among private citizens has diminished with the growth of state power; the evidence rather is that it has changed in character, that new kinds of inequality have replaced the old. Yet it was natural enough in Tocqueville's day that men should be struck more by the decay of old forms of inequality than by the rise of new ones, for it was the old forms that the reformers wanted to get rid of as obstacles to progress, whereas the new forms were, at least to some extent, effects of their reforms.

In the West in the last two centuries, and increasingly outside the West as Western influences have spread through the world, there have arisen two different attitudes to the modern state. Ever greater demands have been made on it in the name of freedom, and its growing activities and powers have been attacked, above all in the liberal democracies, as threats to freedom. These two apparently contradictory attitudes are often to be found in the same persons. No doubt, to take up one in some contexts and the other in others is not to contradict oneself, for in some spheres state intervention may enlarge freedom while in others it curtails it. Nevertheless, there is in practice a good deal of confusion of thought, and even self-contradiction, both among people who take up these attitudes and among those who discuss them.

Suspicion of the powerful and centralized state has been strong in the West among all classes ever since that state emerged. Though the wealthy have looked upon it as the defender of institutions on which their wealth and its attendant privileges depend, they have also seen it as a threat; and the poor, though they have looked to it for great benefits, have also denounced it as the instrument or ally of the privileged and wealthy. These suspicions and hopes have all, to some extent, been well founded. But to the liberal there are three questions about the state in relation to freedom that are supremely important: To what extent does securing the essential freedoms to everyone require the control by public authority of what men do? To what extent must this control, to be effective, be centralized over large areas and populations? How can it be contrived that the great inequalities of power inseparable from a centralized and many-sided control of the activities of vast numbers of people do not curtail the freedoms the control is meant to secure? Yet these questions, important though they are to everyone who cares about freedom, are rarely put, and there have been few attempts to answer them.

In the early days of socialism, most socialists, reformers as well as revolutionaries, disliked vast accumulations of power exercised over large communities. Before there were socialists, or before the word *socialist* came into use, there had been philosophers who advocated common ownership of land and other resources, public control of production and distribution, and authoritarian government on a large scale. But the socialists of the early industrial era were most of them liberals in the broad sense of the word; for, though they did not call themselves by that name, and sometimes despised the persons who did, they wanted everyone to have what, in the eyes of the liberal, are the essential liberties. Not all of them wanted this, and some of them wanted it much less than others did; and yet even the least liberal of them, the disciples of Saint-Simon, though they wanted hierarchy and cen-

57

tralized control of credit and ridiculed the idea that authority must be acquired by popular election, looked forward to the eventual disappearance of organized force to maintain social discipline.

Many of the early socialists ignored the state or paid little attention to it. They imagined small self-governing communities whose members would be well off materially, would be able to do work attractive to them, could marry whom they pleased, could cultivate their minds and educate and indulge their tastes. In their communities the three liberal principles that we spoke of earlier would be realized. And though these early socialists were not concerned, as the liberals were, to define the rights of the individual, this was because the communities they imagined were so small that their members did not need carefully defined legal rights to secure their freedom. For example, Charles Fourier, whose ideal community, the phalanx, was to number some 1600 souls, felt no need to discuss, in the manner of Benjamin Constant, the judicial and political procedures required to secure his essential rights to everyone in a country the size of France. There are, to be sure, some important differences between the conceptions of freedom of Fourier and Constant; and yet the two men were both, in the broad sense, liberals.

The indifference to the state of many of the early socialists meant that they took little notice of two questions of great concern to liberals: What legal rights must the citizen have, if he is to be free, and how can the rulers of large communities be made responsible to their subjects? But from this we must not conclude that they cared little for freedom or for the principle that authority should be exercised either by all who are subject to it or else by persons responsible to them. And yet, where indifference to the state turned to hostility, it often brought with it contempt for the legal rights that meant so much to the liberal. The socialist who looks upon the state as an "organ of class rule" or an "instrument of class oppression" and denies that giving the vote to everyone can change its essential character must argue that the rights and procedures, supposed to secure freedom within the state and to make governments responsible to the governed, are · delusions.

Socialist and anarchist hostility to the state feeds on two beliefs that are different from one another though often confused: that the state is an instrument for the oppression of some classes by others, and that any vast and highly centralized structure of authority is incompatible with individual freedom and genuine democracy. Though these beliefs differ and have different implications, there is one conclusion to be drawn from both of them: that the state, as we now have it, must be abolished, if there is to be either freedom or author-

ity exercised by the people or their true representatives.

Not all socialists have been anarchists, or close to being so; many have believed that in developed commercial and industrial societies, the vast and centralized structure of authority that we call the state is indispensable. It can be oppressive, and can be used by some groups to exploit others; but it can also be used to enlarge and extend freedom. It can be either oppressive or liberating, and the problem is to ensure, as far as possible, that it is the second and not the first.

Socialists have often, in practice, alternated between denouncing the state as oppressive and calling upon it to enlarge freedom. Suspicion of the state and faith in it have been, and still are, socialist, just as they have been and still are liberal. And this is only to be expected, for up to some fifty years ago most socialists—with the partial exception of the disciples of Saint-Simon and a few other sects—believed in freedom, as the liberal conceives of it. They condemned established institutions, social and political, largely on the ground that they denied freedom to the individual, especially if he belonged to the poorer classes. They accepted, as fervently as anyone, what we have called the three liberal principles, or ideas equivalent to them; and if they were more concerned than liberals were with social as distinct from political rights, this was because their suspicion of the bourgeois state went deeper and they were keener to establish small self-governing communities or associations of producers.

Before the Bolshevik revolution, Marxists were no less concerned than were other socialists for the essential liberties of the individual, though, like the anarchists, they were also contemptuous of "bourgeois liberalism." Since that revolution, their devotion to freedom (except for those among them who became Social Democrats in opposition to Moscow), has dwindled rapidly. They do not reject the liberal principles, nor do they say that it matters little whether the individual has the rights and opportunities that both liberals and socialists claimed for him long before there were Marxists in power anywhere. On the contrary, they boast that they are doing more than anyone to liberate mankind. In the countries they dominate they have abolished or have failed to establish political freedom; but they either deny that this is so, or else justify their actions by saying that "counter-revolutionaries" or "enemies of the people" would abuse this freedom to prevent their carrying out reforms needed to establish the social conditions of freedom for everyone. They are, so they say (or, rather, suggest, for in this matter they are prone to indirection of speech), doing without some freedoms for the time being in order that freedom should be achieved more fully in the end.

While as yet there were none of them in control of society anywhere, Marxists could launch on "bourgeois liberalism" a kind of attack to which they were themselves still immune. Challenged to explain what institutions they would put in the place of the ones they denounced as bourgeois shams, they could say that this was a problem to be solved after the revolution. But now that they control two of the largest countries in the world and several smaller ones, they are much more open to criticism. Or at least they would be, if they did not silence it where they are in control, and turn a deaf ear to it where they are not.

They admit that the countries they rule are not *liberal* democracies, but they claim that they are democracies nonetheless because those who govern are supported by the great majority of the people, the manual working classes. They even claim that they are responsible to the workers, having the right to govern only because they enjoy their confidence. It is difficult to believe that they take this last claim seriously. For, if they did, they would ensure that the classes they say they speak for could repudiate them, if they so wished. Leaders who contrive that their "followers" cannot get rid of them or express lack of confidence in them cannot be supposed to be sincere when they claim to speak for them. And yet, sincere or not, they still pay a kind of lip service, loud and ambiguous, to the political liberties they in practice repudiate. They deny that the elections they hold are not free, and yet admit that they do not allow "enemies of the people" to put up candidates; they claim that the people, or at least the workers, are free to associate to promote their interests and express their aspirations, and yet boast of silencing their "enemies." They divide society into "the people" and "the enemies of the people," and deny that they deprive the people of essential liberties, while allowing that social conditions surviving from the past to some extent diminish them; and they say that the enemies of the people are deprived of freedom only because they would use it to impede the great work of liberation.

The denial and the assertion are both sophistical; for it is the rulers (or the ruling party) who decide who the "enemies of the people" are. These "enemies" are those who oppose them in their work of "liberation," and so the "people" are those who do not oppose them. In other words, there is freedom to agree with them, or at least not to disagree, about matters which they choose to regard as important.

Today, almost everywhere, political leaders claim to be concerned for freedom, for the "essential" liberties of the individual understood broadly in the sense we have tried to define. Nobody rejects freedom in this sense, just as scarcely anybody rejects democracy in the sense of government (or administration, where the word *government* is avoided) by the people or by persons responsible to them. The enemies of liberalism do not say that freedom is willing submission to beneficent authority, any more than they say that democracy is government *for* the people rather than *by* the people. They are not idolators of the state. On the contrary, they claim to be more concerned than the liberal that the individual should be free, and that decisions affecting the people should be taken either by them or by agents answerable to them. They outbid liberalism; they claim to offer—even though only in the fullness of time—a larger freedom and a more genuine democracy. They deny that the rights and procedures evolved in the West really do secure to everyone the essential liberties. The Western liberal, as they see him, either deludes himself into believing what is false, or else pretends to believe it. The institutions sacred to him are parts of a social order in which only a minority can have much freedom or influence on government.

The liberal who is really concerned for freedom has good reason to regret that so many of the attacks on the democracies of the West should come from where they do. For the attackers are mostly Communists or sympathizers with Communism, and their attacks, judged at the intellectual level, are weak. When the attackers live in Communist countries, their attacks are too often abusive, ignorant, or crude; they are presumably for domestic consumption and not meant to be taken seriously abroad. When the attackers are Communists or sympathizers living in the West, the attacks are better informed and intellectually more formidable. If the vitality of a theory is to be measured by the quality of the thinking of its adherents, Marxism is today much more alive in the West than in other parts of the world. But even in the West, its quality is not high. (We speak of the thinking of avowed Marxists and not of theories deeply influenced by Marx or assessments of his doctrines by admirers.) The Western Marxist too often wastes his ingenuity in defending what is done in the name of Marx outside the West. Not that what he defends is altogether indefensible, but much of it is difficult to reconcile with Marxism, if Marxism is taken to be what Marx himself taught together with accretions compatible with his teachings. The Western Marxist is too respectful of crude versions of Marxism produced outside the West, or too reluctant to reject them openly, to be able to examine the doctrines he holds critically and to refashion them, so as to make them more clear and more relevant. Though

Marxists speak of Marxism as of a theory that is always developing, assimilating the teachings of experience, of history, of the social studies, the claims they make for it are not true. Admittedly, it has changed greatly, and is no longer what it was when it left the hands of Marx; but it has changed above all to meet the needs of political leaders. Intellectually, it is poorer than it was, and nowhere more so than in the countries where it is the ideology of a ruling party. Intellectually, the social and political creed which is still the great rival of Western liberalism is a blunt instrument.

"Marxist" parties are, of course, very powerful in the countries they rule, and have considerable power in other countries. Politically, they are formidable. Their arguments in many parts of the world have been as attractive, or more attractive, to the people they were addressed to as those of their liberal opponents. At the business of ideological warfare they are as adept as their rivals, but this kind of warfare is not rational argument. On the ideological front, liberal democracy still has opponents who stretch its resources to the full; on the intellectual front it has not.

This is to be regretted. For in the Western countries there is dissatisfaction in plenty, and frustration also. There is a widespread feeling that liberal democracy is falling too far short of its own ideals. There is no lack of criticism, and there are opportunities as large as ever there were for giving vent to disaffection. Yet the criticism is often blind and unrealistic. Many of the faults pointed to are there, but there is almost no enquiry into how they arose and how they can be removed. The two ideals that everyone subscribes to, freedom and democracy, are not rigorously analyzed, and there is little attempt to discover how they could be more fully achieved in vast industrial societies. There is plentiful discussion of legal rights and procedures by lawyers and students of law, and there are many accounts of how institutions and systems of institutions function.

These accounts do more than just describe how people behave; they also examine the rules that govern their behavior, suggesting improvements. There is a great deal of theorizing that is prescriptive as well as explanatory. But the rules and practices examined and assessed relate mostly to particular institutions; as, for example, rules of procedure in legislative assemblies, rules of evidence in courts of law, or electoral rules. It is at this level that normative theory is precise, subtle, and realistic. When it goes beyond this, when it seeks to define the rights and opportunities that everyone should have or what democracy essentially is, and to explain what rules and practices, what institutions, are needed to realize them, it soon becomes

looser, cruder, and less clearly related to the real world.

The need, at the level of political theory or philosophy, as distinct from politics and propaganda, is not really to defend liberal democracy against the attacks of people who do not believe in it, for their attacks were never more inept than they are now; it is rather to criticize the Western democracies in the light of their own ideals.

BIBLIOGRAPHY

Pierre Bayle, *Commentaire philosophique sur ces paroles de Jésus-Christ, "Contrains-les d'entrer"* (1686), in *Oeuvres diverses,* 4 vols. (The Hague, 1727), photoreproduction, Hildesheim. S. Castellion, *De haereticis, an sint persequendi* (1554). Benjamin Constant, *De l'esprit de conquête . . .* (1814), and *Principes de politique applicables à tous les gouvernements représentatifs* (1815), in *Oeuvres* (Paris, 1957). T. H. Green, *Lectures on the Principles of Political Obligation,* in *Complete Works,* Vol. II (London, 1889–90; rev. ed. 1941); idem, *Prolegomena to Ethics* (Oxford, 1883). G. W. F. Hegel, *Phänomenologie des Geistes* (1807), trans. J. B. Baillie as *Phenomenology of Mind* (London, 1910; 2nd ed. 1931); idem, *The Philosophy of Right,* trans. and ed. T. M. Knox (Oxford, 1942). W. von Humboldt, *Ideen zu einem Versuch die Grenzen der Wirksamkeit des Staats zu bestimmen* (1791), *Gesammelte Schriften,* Royal Prussian Academy, 17 vols. (Berlin, 1903–36). Immanuel Kant, *Critique of Practical Reason and Other Works on the Theory of Ethics,* trans. T. K. Abbott (Mystic, Conn., 1909). John Locke, *Epistola de Tolerantia* (Gouda, 1689), trans. William Popple as *Letter Concerning Toleration* (London, 1689); idem, *Two Treatises of Government* (1690), ed. Peter Laslett (Cambridge, 1960). J. S. Mill, *On Liberty* (London, 1859; many reprints). Charles-Louis de Secondat de Montesquieu, *De l'esprit des lois,* ed. G. Truc, 2 vols. (Paris, 1945; many earlier editions); reprint of early trans. by Thomas Nugent as *Spirit of the Laws* (New York, 1949). Jean Jacques Rousseau, *Émile* (1762), trans. B. Foxley (London, 1948); idem, *Political Writings,* ed. C. E. Vaughan, 2 vols. (Cambridge, 1915; reprint Oxford and New York, 1962). Benedict Spinoza, *Tractatus theologico-politicus* (1670), in *The Chief Works of Spinoza,* trans. R. H. M. Elwes, 2 vols. (London, 1883; New York, 1955–56). R. H. Tawney, *The Acquisitive Society* (London, 1921; reprint New York, 1946). Alexis de Tocqueville, *De la démocratie en Amérique* (1835), trans. as *Democracy in America,* ed. H. S. Commager, trans. Henry Reeve (New York, 1947).

Selected additional references: Isaiah Berlin, *Four Essays on Liberty* (Oxford and New York, 1968). R. D. Cumming, *Human Nature and History: A Study of the Development of Liberal Political Thought,* 2 vols. (Chicago, 1969). M. Cranston, *Freedom: A New Analysis* (London, 1953). H. L. A. Hart, *Law, Liberty and Morality* (Stanford and London, 1963). A. D. Lindsay, *The Modern Democratic State* (Oxford and New York, 1943). D. D. Raphael, ed., *Political Theory and the Rights of Man* (London and Bloomington, 1967).

D. G. Ritchie, *Principles of State Interference* (London, 1902). G. de Ruggiero, *The History of European Liberalism*, trans. R. G. Collingwood (Oxford, 1927; Boston, 1959).

JOHN PLAMENATZ

[See also Education; **Equality;** Hegelian Political and Religious Ideas; Heresy; **Individualism;** Law, Natural, and Natural Rights; Marxism; Religious Toleration; **Social Contract;** Socialism; **State.**]

LINGUISTICS

FOR THE purposes of this article, and to avoid overlapping with the article on Language, the history of linguistics will here be viewed as concerned with those studies and activities in which one's language is considered as *a* language rather than as language pure and simple. This accommodates a good many quite disparate attitudes; to use modern terms, these might be said to range from the most extreme structural relativism under which it is implied that there are no substantive limits to language diversity to the position taken by some generative grammarians in whose eyes languages differ only in surface structure but share the fundamental oneness of language.

Thus the idea of distinguishing the study of language from the study of languages is in itself a possible touchstone for what is important and for what has changed in intellectual emphasis. The nineteenth century, for instance, would have thought in terms of a division of labor—frequently a hostile division at that—between philosophy and linguistics. At other times, both before and after, this particular borderline has existed in a far less sharp form.

Multilingualism has been a pervasive fact of life, far more so than participants in modern technological civilization and members of large and dominant speech communities are inclined to think. Besides, far more than other facets of language (for instance, the internal properties of one's own principal language, dialect, or style), language diversification emerges above the threshold of awareness. Hence mythical and theological ways of accounting for language diversification are widespread. They center around such questions as how languages were created or invented, how "things" got their names and, indeed, why languages are many.

Among the oldest extant examples of this must be a Sumerian text (Kramer, 1968) which bespeaks a legendary past in which "the whole universe, the people in unison(?) To Enlil in one tongue spoke . . . Then

Enki . . . changed the speech in their mouths, [brought (?)] contention into it, into the speech of man that (until then) had been one." The idea of a monolingual golden age crops up again and again. Its biblical version is, of course, the story of the great dispersal after the abandonment of the tower of Babel. The familiarity and authority of this story remained one of the two controlling influences on linguistic thought in the Western world.

The other influence was one which allied itself naturally with the first, although its basis lies in a very different intellectual region. This was Greco-Roman secular thought. Greek historians frequently use what they call "resemblance" (however recognized) in speech as an argument for the descent of one population from another. The realities of Greek life supported this, of course: the ties which linked colonies to their mother cities and the affinity that existed between the dialects of the cities so linked were too obvious to escape notice. It is worth remembering that the standard (and only half-appropriate) classification of Greeks into Ionians, Aeolians, and Dorians had its chief application among the Greek settlers in Asia Minor and was at least in part a linguistic one.

When extended beyond the Greek world the argument became essentially speculative and impressionistic. Considering the deep philosophical interest of the Greeks in the nature of language, in "etymology," and in logic; and considering further the peripatetic penchant for discovery and taxonomy which sent along naturalists of all kinds on Alexander's campaign, it remains remarkable that languages in their diversification went without systematic attention, one may say, throughout antiquity. Only glosses, i.e., isolated foreign words, were collected (to serve us now, incidentally, as scant and uncertain sources of information on otherwise lost languages). And this was so despite constant contact with a variety of populations and the widespread bilingualism and multilingualism of the Hellenistic-Roman world; despite the demand for (and supply of) translations from literary foreign languages like Etruscan and Punic; and also despite the never-ceasing literary and rhetorical confrontation between Greek and Latin with the attendant stereotyped value-judgments (about the "poverty" of the Latin language; Lucretius, *De rerum natura*, I, 139). Foreigners appear on the Greek and Roman comedy stage speaking some amusing gibberish (Persian, Punic, even, it seems, Kannada of South India). But the only evidence of philosophical concern seems to be Plato's casual and irrelevant remark, in *Cratylus* (409–10), that Greek words ("names") may have been borrowed from barbarian languages (e.g., from Phrygian). If it is really true that it was the Phoenician background of the Stoic philosopher Zeno of Kition (ca. 300 B.C.) which prompted him to introduce certain novel categories into Greek grammar (Pohlenz, 1926), nothing could be more characteristic than that the circumstance was not made explicit. Both Aristotle and the Hellenistic poet and scholar Callimachus wrote on "Non-Greek Customs" (Pfeiffer [1968], p. 200), and both appear to have left language out of the picture. It is also remarkable that there survive bilingual composition books (e.g., the so-called *Hermeneumata Pseudo-Dositheana*) but no learners' grammars of either imperial language written specifically in, and for the use of speakers of, the other. Translations of grammatical works were made, to be sure. When the Greek-written Greek grammar of Dionysius "the Thracian" (first century B.C.) was translated into certain languages (for instance, Armenian) the aim was, however, not to teach Greek but to create a grammar (however awkward) of the target language.

When the argument leading from resemblance to descent was applied to "barbarian" languages it intersected, in ways which are not clearly understood, with at least one other principle, namely that of explaining language differences (or differences between types of languages, as we would say) through climate. This begins at least with the Ionian physicians who, to be sure, may have had no more than the timbre of voice in mind when they spoke of a division into "clear-voiced" and "heavy-voiced" people according to the zones which they inhabit. But as the notion recurs in the Stoic thinker Posidonius (ca. 135 B.C.–ca. 55 B.C.) it becomes part of a general and influential system of ethnography. In the end it enters into that well-known body of semi-learned linguistic folklore from which metaphors and ad hoc explanations are available. Not unfittingly, climate figures in nineteenth-century scholarship as a potential "cause of change" (see the amazingly respectful, if critical, discussion in Prokosch [1939], pp. 55–56).

With regard to the inference from language resemblance to prehistoric descent, posterity has tended to be equally uncritical. It is not reasonable, for instance, to expect the judgment of the rhetorician and historiographer Dionysius of Halicarnassus (beginning of the Christian era) about the Etruscans being "unlike any other nation in language" to mean what we mean when we say that Etruscan (or Basque, or Burushaski) is genealogically isolated. To place such ancient pronouncements exactly is both a more specific and a more comprehensive task. Its solution depends on our ability to reconstruct the preconceptions as well as the practices inherent in entire lines of lost scholarship.

If languages at large were not much touched by empirical study or even only by speculation, the same is not quite true of the dialects of Greek including, in the ancient view, Latin (on which Philoxenus wrote at the beginning of the first century B.C.; Pfeiffer [1968], p. 274). The stimulus consisted in the fact that local dialects, in stylized form, had literary uses (the Aeolic of Alcaeus and Sappho, the Doric of choral lyric poetry, etc.). But this was not all: the great Alexandrian librarian Aristophanes of Byzantium, as others before and after him, studied the spoken vernacular in detail. And it was in connection with domestic observation of this kind that at least occasional glimpses occur in the direction of a chronological interpretation of dialect differences. Already Plato's Socrates (in the *Cratylus*) recognizes change as a normal property of language, although it is true that he does not emphasize the point. A more widespread view (and one which had great persistence in later history) is represented in Herodotus' famous story (hardly a specimen of *Egyptian* linguistic thinking) of King Psammetichus' experiment in wishing to discover the "oldest" language: when two children reared in isolation cried *"bekos"* and it turned out that the Phrygian word for bread was *bekos* the answer was simple. Clearly, this inference is incompatible with the idea that all languages change constantly and that all are equally "old."

For the Middle Ages our knowledge is still limited. In particular, it is difficult to assess the extent to which the enormous intellectual effort spent on points of grammatical and semantic theory was matched by efforts to collect and explain data having to do with variety. In the West, the theology of dispersal to which we have alluded, and the corresponding popular assumption that the pre-Babel *lingua Adamica* was Hebrew, held dominant sway (see A. Borst's magnificent work on the subject, *Der Turmbau von Babel*). Islamic thinking, it seems, was very greatly concerned with the primacy of Arabic over other languages. The two Western European figures standing out from this general background are, not too surprisingly, two of the greatest universal thinkers of the high Middle Ages, namely Roger Bacon and Dante. To Roger Bacon belongs the both very medieval (essentially Aristotelian) and very modern-sounding formulation that grammar "is the same in all languages in its substance, and that surface differences between them are merely accidental variations" (Robins [1967], pp. 76–77). What distinguishes Roger Bacon from countless others making similar remarks is that he, as a writer of a Greek grammar and as a student of Arabic and Hebrew looked upon this as a concrete problem, to which there was an empirical side: there is clear evidence that he saw the analogy between interlanguage differences of the grosser kind, on one hand, and the much subtler relationship between one standard and the various dialectical forms of a language, on the other, and that he attached central importance to it. In this he was akin to Dante. The views set forth in Dante's treatise *De vulgari eloquentia* (shortly after 1300) must be seen against the backdrop provided by the influential *modistae* and by the equally popular *Doctrinale* of Alexander of Villedieu (1199; a versification of traditional Latin grammar and syntax) to have their originality appreciated. Dante faces the contradictions which arise when observation of living language (in his case local types of Italian which he classifies with great acumen) and formulated Latin grammar clash. His interpretation, to be sure, is unhistorical: to him authoritarian, "dead" Latin grammar was created, and always was a "secondary" and artificial language such as some but not all people possess. But all people, since the Dispersal, speak their vernacular; each man receives his "without any rules," from his nurse. The vernaculars are more "noble" than (Latin) *grammatica*. Their variability and instability is a consequence of the Dispersal. Before it, all men spoke divine and unchanging Hebrew (a position from which Dante himself deviated later in *Paradiso* XXVI). What is so remarkable (and what no doubt accounts for the insignificant effect which the work had in its time) is not only the preference given to the vernaculars "without rules" but even more the concrete realization that change is slow but all-pervasive, and that variety is a function of it; its extent is proportionate to distance in time and space. ("Here we are investigating something in which we are not supported by any authority.") This gives Dante an opportunity to set forth his grandiose genealogical classification of the languages of the known world. Here we also find the artifice, so common later on, of using certain key-words (such as the word for "yes") as convenient shibboleths.

Symbolically speaking at least, it was the fall of Constantinople in 1453, with the ensuing migration of Byzantine men of letters to western Europe which opened up a period of feverish activity in the new medium of print: Lascaris' Greek grammar appeared in 1476, and thereafter dictionaries and grammars were produced ceaselessly. Represented are not only literary languages with their own internal grammatical tradition like Arabic and Hebrew, but vernaculars of every kind: Dutch (1475), Breton (1499), Welsh (1511), Polish (1564), Basque (1587). And shortly after the middle of the sixteenth century the first "missionary" grammars of Central and South American Indian languages make their appearance. Superficially, these works follow a traditional Latin model. But the assumptions and procedures involved in fitting newly observed material into

those conventional categories still need to be analyzed and understood.

Special mention must be made of a particular genre of scholarly production which begins as early as 1427, with Schildberger's *Pater Noster* in Armenian and Tartar: collection after collection, for an ever-widening circle of languages, of the Lord's Prayer, with appropriate commentary, geographic information, attempts at classification, and so on. It is perhaps sufficient to mention two of the most famous works in this chain which bear the same title: Conrad Gesner's *Mithridates* of 1555 (with the Lord's Prayer in twenty-two languages) and J.-C. Adelung's *Mithridates* in four volumes, of 1806–17), with the Lord's Prayer "in almost five hundred languages and dialects" (W. von Humboldt took part in this effort). In a sense, the British and Foreign Bible Society's *Gospel in many Tongues* (e.g., 1950), is a present-day sample. These works may be only compilations, but they occupy a pivotal position in the history of linguistic ideas. They are the main link between observation and speculation (since speculative writers had a way of relying on them in large part and often exclusively), and at the same time they reflect, in their commentary, contemporary interpretation with considerable faithfulness.

In the course of the sixteenth century the older Dantean notions assert themselves in one form or another. Joseph Justus (the younger) Scaliger (1540–1609) takes up the classification of the European languages by *matrices linguae* or "mother languages" (in a technical sense) of which there are, according to him, eleven. None of the eleven are related to each other. With this, the idea of common, monolingual descent, whether from Hebrew or otherwise, is abandoned as unprovable at the very least. Each *matrix lingua* is identified by shibboleth (see above). The criterion for classification under a *matrix lingua* is by vocabulary, and proceeds by inspection for "common characteristics." There is as yet (to make this anachronistic comment) no hint at a more detailed analysis of the change processes which make the descendants different from their *matrix lingua*, and consequently no discussion of how to evaluate common characteristics in borderline instances.

This would not be worth remarking on but for the fact that a few decades earlier an important step in that direction had already been taken, quite inconspicuously, by Claudio Tolomei (1492–1555; quoted by R. A. Hall, Jr. [1964], p. 301, with appropriate comment) who for the first time (so far as our knowledge of such priority goes) not only notes the difference between (Latin) *grammatica* and (Italian) vernacular but interprets it historically; he does so in a methodologically impeccable fashion through a confrontation

63

of doublets, within Italian, such as arise from a Latin word as it has come down to "the middle of the town square of Tuscany" (e.g., *pieve* from Lat. *plebem*) and then again as the same word is "set up . . . by someone who wished to enrich the language, preferring to use [it] in the form in which he found [it] written in Latin" (e.g., *plebe*).

The seventeenth century saw a good deal of theoretical debate on grammar. It has been remarked that the thinkers of Port-Royal wrote as though *Mithridates* did not exist: no reference is made to languages at large (Mounin [1967], p. 129), perhaps because, for their purposes, none needed to be made. But in any event this is not true of one of the greatest intellects of that century, G. W. Leibniz. His function in the history of linguistics is twofold: he continues the tradition of language classification into families (though he entertains the notion of a possible common descent for all); an important aspect of this classification is its chronological-historical interpretation (he dwells on the importance of such studies as a tool for the writing of history). And secondly, in this field as in others, one of his claims to fame is that of having been an organizer of research. He tried to interest Peter the Great in making a highly sophisticated language survey of his dominions in Europe and Asia. The task was taken up in earnest in the reign of Catherine II on an even wider basis: word lists were obtained from governors, diplomats, and scholars from all over the world and published without delay in 1786 by the German traveler P. S. Pallas under the title *Comparative Vocabularies*. The work made a deep impression. We may be particularly grateful that it prompted a review by the Koenigsberg political economist, Chr. J. Kraus (Arens [1955], pp. 118–27). This review is the voice of a well-informed man who, incidentally, had had some practical experience in data-gathering. He sympathizes with the curiously antispeculative, positivistic frame of mind which characterizes the whole Russian effort in the first place: he pleads for more careful elicitation ("if there are mistakes in the material, no conceivable reasoning is available to correct them") and for a more accurately planned, cartographic presentation of the results. He also uses the term "comparison" almost like a technical term (more so than others, e.g., Leibniz, before him). Comparison, he says, has two aspects. In part it is philosophical and teaches us how men think and how differently they think: relativity in matters of both sound and meaning is stressed as never before. On the other hand, comparison is also a tool of history. Just because structural differences can be so great, an agreement or similarity between two languages proves historical connection. In this respect we can appreciate how the general outlook had changed, partly through the enormous increase in empirical breadth, since the days of Scaliger. What is still missing in this view of languages is their role in history as objects (or agents) of change rather than as mere witnesses towards the establishment of historical truth. In this, Kraus was a spokesman for his age.

The age, to be sure, was more varied than that. It was also rife with controversy over the origin of language, on the nontheological basis which the Enlightenment had provided. Thus, Rousseau and Lord Monboddo, to select these two figures somewhat arbitrarily, were preceded—though apparently not influenced—by G. B. Vico (1668–1744) and followed by J. G. von Herder (1744–1803). The importance of men like these lies in the fact that they were historians (or philosophers of history) by temperament and thus had, in the light of later events, something decisive to offer. But the gap was great. Their influence was therefore not always palpable and certainly not steady. It took time and a personality and career like Jacob Grimm's to weld Herder's feeling for universal and national history to the substantive tradition. On the surface the observer has the impression that the French Revolution and the age of Napoleon, with the academic reforms that followed, simply put an absolute end to all that "prescientific" theorizing—an impression which was allowed to harden into the familiar myth of the sudden emergence of serious linguistics around the year 1800.

Pallas' collection, mentioned above, as well as the one made largely from missions material by Lorenzo Hervas in 1800–05, had the incomparable merit of overwhelming the scholarly community with data which were fresh and not encumbered with literary history and artificial tradition. In the best style of the doctrine of the Noble Savage this new knowledge helped to gain a new perspective on more familiar materials. For the same reason, the knowledge which then existed of the more marginal European and Near Eastern areas was especially instructive. Already in Leibniz' time, the Semitist Job Ludolf (1624–1704) had formulated a rather clear view of how to recognize a "family" of languages (namely, not merely by words— an allusion to the traditional fascination with vocabulary lists—but by *grammaticae ratio*). Presumably he was aided in this by his familiarity with an especially close-knit and superficially diversified (as well as, of course, literarily accessible) stock. Even more impressive was the technical excellence with which the Finno-Ugric family of languages had been explored, by Scandinavians, like Ph. Strahlenberg in 1730, then in 1770 by the Hungarian J. Sajnovics, in Danish service, in his *Demonstratio,* of the identity of the Hungarian with the Lapp language, and finally by his far better known compatriot S. Gyarmathi (1751–1830). Gyarmathi's treatise on the relation between Hungarian and Finnish appeared, under the aegis of the historian A. L. von Schlözer (1735–1809) of Göttingen, and previously of Saint Petersburg, the influential champion of the Slavs and their East and North European neighbors.

Novelty of a different, and, as a matter of fact, very ancient sort, was provided by the celebrated spread of the knowledge of Sanskrit in the West. Sir William Jones (1746–94) and other Englishmen studied Sanskrit in India, that is, in natural conformity with the imposing national tradition of the Hindu grammarians. Sir William's enthusiasm was born in the general cultural climate in which that distinguished man had spent his earlier life, and was fed not only by the intellectual excellence of Indian grammar but also by the attitude of religious reverence with which it approaches its subject, the "accomplished" (*saṁskṛta*) language. "The Sanscrit language," said Jones in 1786 "is of a wonderful structure; more perfect than the Greek, more copious than the Latin." Comparisons of this sort were indeed very much part of the eighteenth-century outlook, except insofar as the new knowledge of indigenous languages had exerted a dampening effect. Such comparisons remained in vogue much later (and are, of course, still with us in folklore); thus W. von Humboldt, writes, casually, in 1822: "Sanskrit is among the oldest and first to possess a true edifice of grammatical forms . . . , but it is Greek which has undoubtedly attained the highest perfection of structure."

It must, however, not be overlooked that Jones's observation, conventional as it was, carried a special force (likewise conventional in nature). Perfection and copiousness were much-discussed properties with which to place languages in the scheme of things. The argumentation has theological roots, although these were not necessarily visible under the eighteenth-century guise of early evolutionism. A typical writer of a hundred years earlier, Daniel Morhof, had put it as follows: "It is most credible that the first language was not one of the languages now known (which owe most to art), but rather some language different from them." He was, then, one of those (like the Dante of the *Paradiso*) who did not believe that man first spoke Hebrew—because Hebrew is too "perfect" and not (as we might now say) "primitive" enough. Clearly this is why Jones goes on to say that the "first language" from which the three perfect languages are descended must be "a common source which perhaps no longer exists." Furthermore, when he states that the (later so-called) Indo-European languages have a "stronger affinity" than could be produced by accident, he takes sides in another popular controversy, namely that of possible polygenesis. Not only was it possible to doubt that the language of Adam had been Hebrew, but

many, Lord Monboddo and Adam Smith among them, were quite satisfied that more than one primeval language could have existed. Like so many of the earlier authors these men accepted the idea of an irreducible number of separate families, each one with a primitive ancestor. It was, therefore, important to Jones to declare that in his opinion those languages had "a stronger affinity" than could have been produced by "accident" (when a more obvious source would have been monogenesis!). Later in the nineteenth century, such a statement would have carried the implication that there exists a statable method for excluding accident, or that the proof of common descent lies in the performance, in detail, of a consistent reconstruction. It is excusable that such thoughts were also read into Jones a hundred years later; but unless one takes a fanciful view of preformation and premonition in the history of scholarship this remains a distortion. This is not to say that Jones was not interested in thinking about what the "common source" may have been like. Indeed, his inclinations went in that direction; he also believed that "Pythagoras and Plato derived their sublime theories from the same fountain with the sages of India" (Edgerton [1946], p. 236)—an idea which, by itself, should warn us against facile linear interpretations of simple precursorship. Jones' enormous scholarly distinction lay elsewhere; in matters of language he shared the view of the best of his older as well as younger contemporaries who, in turn, differed less radically from one another than it appeared in retrospect.

Nor should the position of F. Schlegel (1772–1829) and his dithyrambic *Sprache und Weisheit der Indier* (*Language and Wisdom of the Indians*), published in 1808, be oversimplified. Interestingly, the title contains echos of "Pythagoras and Plato," but this is less important than the new turn given, apparently, to the concept of comparison which, as we have seen, had slowly come into prominence, at least since Leibniz. F. Schlegel calls for a "comparative grammar" which will furnish "completely novel insights into the genealogy of languages," on the express analogy of the then much admired field of comparative anatomy. It must be remembered that G. Cuvier's *Leçons d'anatomie comparée* had just appeared (1801–05) and that Schlegel was one of those who found themselves in Paris during the first years of the century, in contact with the rising school of French Oriental scholars, but also with similarly stranded Anglo-Indians like Alexander Hamilton (1762–1824), the British orientalist. It is most intriguing, also, to realize that it is precisely in the names of those two disciplines, comparative anatomy and comparative (grammar or) linguistics that the word "comparative" carries, to this day, a technical meaning which is no longer self-descriptive and indeed quite often misunderstood. "Comparison" is here not comparison for comparison's sake (i.e., what in linguistics is usually called typology or typological comparison) but for the sake of retrieving a past, linguistic or evolutionary as the case may be.

It is not for nothing, however, that Schlegel speaks of comparative "grammar"; the term was not (as it later became) simply a synonym for comparative linguistics. His thinking about grammar is akin to that of Ludolf and Gyarmathi. The choice is, in a sense, a negative one. It stems from a dissatisfaction with arbitrary, lexical etymology. Words travel easily, or come to "resemble" one another by accident. Grammatical structure goes deeper. Besides, Schlegel believed in qualitative criteria both for classification and for the determination of antiquity; to his mind languages retain traits that are characteristically archaic and acquire traits that are characteristically innovative. At the same time, there are two classes of languages: the inflected Indo-European ones which are born and have developed "organically" (Mounin [1967], pp. 160–62), and all others. For the above-named typological reasons he is convinced (unlike Jones; and, of course, in our view, "wrongly") that Sanskrit is "the oldest" of the Indo-European languages and that the others are descended from Sanskrit, but (still, it appears, in deference to the idea that perfection is the result of growth) Sanskrit is said to go back, in turn, to an older form of speech. Language contact has produced "mixed" idioms; non-inflected languages have thereby improved their nature—the term is applied even though Schlegel takes great romanticist care to disavow value-judgments put forward too explicitly.

Schlegel can be a textbook case of the pitfalls of "presentism" (Stocking [1965], p. 211)—so much so that it is useful to stop and ponder some of the detail by way of looking ahead. "Comparative" refers to a typological comparison (in the ordinary sense of the term) which enables the investigator to reconstruct because he possesses qualitative knowledge to tell the old from the new. At a later period, the term will become entirely technical and will refer to a non-qualitative, essentially formal, binary matching procedure through which some features which, taken severally, might be retentions as well as innovations, are shown to be either one or the other. Those features, as we shall discover, are precisely *not* "grammatical" ones in the ordinary (and still familiar) sense of the word, but they are, more often than not, phonological and can be discovered within the lexical material itself. Hence the twofold quaintness of the term "comparative grammar" as it is retained later on, or rather, as it will have been transferred to activities of which

Schlegel knew and could know nothing. The typological comparison, on the other hand, which for Schlegel is fraught with chronological and classificatory meaning, will lose its intimate connection with chronology as well as with the so-called comparative method of the later nineteenth century. It will be found that genealogical classification and typological taxonomy can intersect, and besides it will be clear not only that the "inflected" sort of some of the better known and older Indo-European languages is not typologically unique, and also that the noninflected types one might almost say, to the naked eye are as different from one another as they are from what seemed the acme of human perfection to Schlegel. In other words, if Jones differed less than is thought from some of his contemporaries, so did Schlegel, although the forces that impinged on the young German, writing fourteen years after Jones' death, were naturally not the same.

One of the best-studied figures of that great period is the Dane Rasmus Rask (1787–1832). The somewhat grotesque and even tragic circumstances of his life are not merely anecdotal. Apparently Rask was the man he was because he went through an intellectual crisis of an interesting sort; in Mounin's words: "In order to understand [his career] in all its complexity one must realize that while he started out as a romantic in the German fashion and immersed himself in Scandinavian antiquities for the same reasons, no doubt, as did his contemporaries, he changes his vision rapidly and ceases to be interested in text philology and in history in order to turn to the problem of describing the system of languages—a notion to which he is led by his eighteenth-century education and by his personal bent" (Mounin [1967], pp. 166–67). Rask was an admirer of the botanist and classifier, Linnaeus. Thus, he became a typologist *avant la lettre*, quite unlike some of his deeply historical and romanticist contemporaries in the heart of continental Europe. Hence perhaps some of his more surprising "aberrations" such as his initial refusal to recognize Celtic as an Indo-European subfamily: Celtic, though demonstrably a descendant of the common Indo-European ancestor, is typologically one of its most deviant descendants. And, most intriguing of all: Rask's famous "anticipation" of "Grimm's Law," which from the point of view of cumulative knowledge was an epoch-making accomplishment indeed, and one that figures rightfully in the subsequent, linear histories of the profession, was probably intended as a taxonomic observation. As Rask compares Greek and Icelandic he finds (1) that both languages when pronounced "correctly" have the same "letters," i.e., sounds, (2) that they obey the same "euphonic" rules whereby sounds alternate within paradigms in each language, and (3) that certain transitions from sound to sound and from language to language, such as between Greek *p* and Icelandic *f* in *patér: faðir* "father," appear very frequently. His biographer says: "It is characteristic of Rask that he adduces all these 'identities' as equally valid proof of relationship" (Diderichsen [1960], p. 236). A later generation would have regarded the first two as either merely universal or typological, while according full status to the third as an argument in favor of the specific historical connection called common descent or "relatedness." To Rask, the sound correspondences (in the recognition of which he was guided by J. G. Wachter's *Glossarium germanicum* of 1737) stood as regular and recurrent characters rather than as the result of events in time. Nevertheless, it was the discovery of the recurrence "set forth for the first time completely, and without heterogeneous admixtures" (Diderichsen [1960], p. 236), that made all the difference.

If there was a man who was responsible for the feeling of continuity with which the practitioners of the discipline have looked back over the nineteenth century (but not beyond it!) it was Jacob Grimm (1785–1863). His and his brother's labors for the cause of Teutonic antiquities—legal, folklore, and mythological as well as linguistic—characterize him as the paragon of the new romantic attitude. His *Deutsche Grammatik* (*German*, i.e., Germanic, *Grammar*) is a "historical grammar," perhaps the first of the many works explicitly so named. Grimm's theoretical utterances have been called vague, and so they seem at first blush. But the impression disappears once an effort is made to read them in the light of the accompanying positive work. For once there is harmony between the two. For all his metaphorical style, Grimm was averse to speculation. He was taken with the concreteness and individuality of language phenomena, and hence with history. He combatted "general logic" and prescriptiveness; he insisted on the primary importance of dialects. The lexical aspect of language, with its irrational abundance of life, fascinated him increasingly as he matured. It was towards the end of his life that he began to plan his famous German dictionary. Consequently, he turned to etymology, conceived in the modern sense as *histoire des mots* rather than as the recovery of "real" meaning, as the literal (the "etymological"!) implication of the term has it. This emphasis, combined with a characteristic desire to embrace all the phenomena and see the typical while at the same time keeping an eye out for aberrancy explains a new and growing interest in matters of sound. The first edition (1819) of the *German Grammar* does not deal with phonology. The second (1822) contains 595 pages of it where Rask's observation about the consonant shift is not only incorporated but given the appropriate

chronological interpretation. Nor was this an isolated instance; Grimm paid the same kind of attention to the characteristic vowel alternations of Germanic (those of the types *sing: sang: sung*, and *foot: feet, mouse: mice*) which still bear their Grimmian names, *ablaut* and *umlaut*.

Wilhelm von Humboldt (1767–1835), most of whose linguistic writings come from the years after his retirement from politics in 1820, is the author of two lengthy works both (1827–29 and 1830–35) concerned with the "differences in language structure." These highly literary treatises are difficult to evaluate because Humboldt can so rarely be observed dealing systematically with the language data to the collection of which he devoted such vast time and energy. We notice at once, however, how thoroughly Grimm had impinged on Humboldt's thinking. There are references, in the spare manner of the period. More important, unacknowledged pieces like the important passage at the end of the chapter, "Language and Nations" (in the 1827–29 work) show how quickly innovation had spread. "In order to establish anything firm with regard to relationship between languages it is necessary to . . . separate the similarities which may be found among them. . . . I have used historical connection as my main criterion. . . . As the only proof of historical connection I have recognized sound . . ." (*Werke* [1963], III, 357). This is not to say that Humboldt does not contain other types of theorizing, both traditional and original, as well. In a sense, he was as much of a typologist as he was a historian; "the development of languages interested him only insofar as it allows us . . . to go back to their origin," that is, to the point in time at which their typological complexion was set (Mounin [1967], p. 189). What is most remarkable of all, however, is the degree to which Humboldt can be considered, legitimately or deceptively, to be the precursor of later linguists. It is a tribute to his suggestive style, though it is also more than that, that both the Whorfian relativists and the deep-structure universalists of the twentieth century have been able to claim Humboldt as their intellectual sponsor: the former by quoting him to the effect that a language will condition the speaker's understanding of the world, and the latter by an appeal to the many passages in which all language is admired for its recursive *energeia* ("process") rather than stationary *ergon* ("accomplished act") properties.

As Grimm's *German Grammar* had been epoch-making by aiming at the mastery of massive rather than intuitively (and conveniently) selected data, so did the writings of Franz Bopp (1791–1867), especially his 1839 *Vergleichende Grammatik* (*Comparative Grammar*), aim at "comparing and summarizing all that is related" in the major Indo-European languages. A.

Meillet thought that Bopp "went out to explain Indo-European [e.g., in terms of reducing affixation to compounding with old, formerly independent roots, in a way that was quite reminiscent of Platonic *etymologia*] and ended up by finding comparative linguistics [in the modern sense] just as Columbus had gone out to travel to India and had discovered America" (Meillet [1937], p. 458). To recognize obvious similarites is not enough; the task, says Bopp, is rather to reduce "the more or less extensive differences between them to the laws to which they are due" (quoted after Arens [1955], p. 199), that is, to discover those laws. And rather like Rask, but very much unlike the majority of his contemporaries, Bopp turns his back on the idea that the study of language is but a tool. "In this book, the languages with which it deals are treated for their own sake, that is as an object, rather than as a means, of knowledge" (Arens [1955], p. 198).

Yet Bopp was centrally concerned with declension and conjugation, that is, with what was still comparative *grammar* in the narrower sense, and not, as Grimm was, with the vocabulary as well. It fell to one of the more peculiar figures of the period, the long-lived, individualistic, and difficult A. F. Pott (1802–87), to develop this side of things, and with it the heart, as it were, of the coming "comparative method." He began in 1833, simultaneously with Bopp's work, to publish his *Etymologische Forschungen* which contains many of the etymologies that are still considered central. Nor are statements of principle missing, some quite running counter to ordinary cant; "the letter [i.e., the sound] is a surer guide in the labyrinth of etymology than is meaning which is so often subject to sudden leaps." He is conscious of his intellectual kinship with Grimm as he lauds him for "his historical exposition of the sound changes in the Germanic languages [which] has more value than many a philosophical grammar full of one-sided and futile abstractions," and for "restoring 'letters' to their rightful place."

A. Schleicher (1821–68) was younger than Pott by a decisive nineteen years. Both were trained as classical scholars but only Schleicher studied with F. Ritschl, a contemporary of Pott. Ritschl's influence was enormous; he presided over a school in which the art of textual criticism by formal method was cultivated and, as the younger generation came to feel, ultimately mechanized and well run into the ground. Schleicher's relations with Ritschl were close, and there is no doubt that among his first intellectual experiences must have been the exposure to such doctrines as the principle of the shared error. If two or more manuscripts exhibit some gaps or copying mistakes in common and to the exclusion of other manuscripts (and if certain other conditions are fulfilled), they are thereby proved to be direct or indirect copies from one (sub-)archetype. The established device to represent such dependencies was, of course, the genealogical tree, or stemma. Schleicher also had an early interest in the biology of the day with its pre-Darwinistic evolutionism. His linguistic work includes a number of intriguing, rather abstract typological studies. He was also the first Indo-Europeanist to abandon the traditional concentration on the great literary languages as they appear in the earliest texts. During a sojourn in the Baltic region he collected texts of spoken Lithuanian and organized them into a grammar and chrestomathy. By this he added decisively to the knowledge of Indo-European sources, and incidentally raised problems of a theoretical sort for the discussion of which there had been no real opportunity since the days of Pallas. In 1861 he published, in its first edition, his most famous work, known in English as the *Compendium of Comparative Grammar of the Indo-European Sanskrit, Greek, and Latin Languages* (2 vols., 1874–77).

To understand Schleicher one must note that he had two preoccupations, one with phonology (his Lithuanian grammar had a large section on this subject), and one with the scheme of the tree to represent relationships within a language family. The two are closely related in an operational sense for the following reason. It was a consequence of the work of Grimm and Pott that the nonrandom nature of sound correspondences between "sister" languages was more and more seen as the result of original sound differences having been either retained or blurred in one but not in the other of two descendant languages. In the simplest case this means that when, say, a *t* in language I is in some words answered by a *t*, but in other words (in essentially similar kinds of syllables) by a *d* in language II, the difference must be ascribed to the common source, with the proviso that a sound change has eliminated it in language I. Language I has innovated (by merging) where language II has retained a feature. True, not all innovations are phonetic; in fact those occurring in other areas such as grammar and meaning are more varied and in many ways more significant. But only in the realm of sound is there a procedure of matching which by itself determines which is retention and which innovation.

Schleicher, in effect, represented innovating languages, that is, descendant languages sharing at least one common innovation, on a separate branch of his genealogical tree. In conformity with the prevailing climate and with his own avowed interests he put an evolutionist interpretation on the matter; first a pre-Darwinian one, and then, when his attention was called to Darwin's work, one in which he hailed Darwin as a kindred spirit. Naturally both his followers and his detractors followed suit. But it may be argued that the real basis lies deeper and that Schleicher had, in fact, acted on the logical analogy between phonemic innovation (in languages) and scribal error (in manuscript copying). There is a lesson, then, in the manner in which objective and biographical factors are interwoven in his story.

Like the oversimplified manuscript histories produced by Ritschl's students, the oversimplified language families of Schleicher's trees do not allow subfamilies to intersect; if A shares an error (a sound law) with B to the exclusion of C, then it cannot significantly share another error (another sound law) with C to the exclusion of B. If it appears to do so nevertheless, this must be a matter of independent duplication by accident or by a factor of intrinsic probability for that particular error (or sound change) to occur more than once—or else there was collation between sister manuscripts (contact between sister languages). To guard against these possibilities it is therefore necessary to amass all the correspondences and even subject them to some qualitative judgment. Thus everything must be accounted for: all the errors (sound changes) must be explained. The goal, in any event, is clear. It is the reconstruction of all the features of what is in one case the archetype manuscript and in the other the proto-language. In Schleicher's ideal view, the very act of reconstituting the complete history of a phonology from the descendants upward in time is identical with the act of determining the distribution of the languages among subfamilies. Hence his concern with the "asterisked" proto-forms which he introduced into scholarly use, and hence, quite naturally, even his much-derided attempt at setting down on paper a complete proto-Indo-European fable.

Thus Schlegel's comparative grammar, even while retaining its name, was replaced by a powerful if technically limited triangulation procedure. The limitation was to the phonemic shape of dictionary items, a concern that had not been particularly strong with many earlier linguists. The power rested on the fact that this limited reconstruction can be used as a sure means, or so it was claimed, to resolve questions of ancestry and descent, complete with subfamilial relationships, in a unique fashion. What was more, such a claim necessarily went beyond the narrow confines of linguistics; it was bound to interest historians and archaeologists as well. There developed, in fact, a borderline field of research devoted to the extralinguistic exploitation of schemes of language relationship, and the old romanticist attempts at reconstructing the religion and mythology of the ancestral Indo-Europeans were taken up again under the new auspices and this time in subordination (not parallelism) to language,

especially by A. Kuhn (1812–81). As other aspects of culture were added, however, and as the need to reconcile "linguistic palaeontology" with regular archaeological work increased, it became painfully clear that the Comparative Method as outlined above did not primarily aim at the reconstruction of meanings. Still, the Words-and-Things technique, as one particular side of that special effort came to be called, was extended to fields other than Indo-European and led to valid results.

But the principal results were intradisciplinary. Now that reconstituted proto-forms were something concrete, the "uniformitarian" nature of knowable language history was beyond the slightest doubt: proto-languages were different from their descendants, but no more so, necessarily, than the descendants were from each other. They were "just languages," and any idea that fundamental alterations in the history of the species had occurred during the shallow interval accessible even to the newly refined method was plainly wrong. It was in this vein that a good many of the once familiar topics were discouraged, and that the question of the origin of language, in particular, was banned by statute from the proceedings of the Société de Linguistique of Paris. The profession turned in on itself, and a period of Victorian sobriety, marked by indefatigable collection of data and by the testing of the now orthodox procedures, set in.

One must, of course, distinguish between the actual working principles and their formulation. The fact that Schleicher himself did not and could not see his own position clearly does not detract from his contribution, nor from the fact that the changes that had come to a head in the sixties were indeed great. The great "neo-grammarian" debate came a decade later, and it was little more than a somewhat murky expression of what had already occurred. The total accountability principle which had won the day in matters of phonology did indeed make it necessary for the researchers to distinguish replacements (from older to later stage) which may be stated without reference to specific word lists (e.g., all *kn-* is replaced, in spoken southern and standard English by *n-* at a certain time in history; hence (*k*)*not* (*k*)*night* (*k*)*now* (*k*)*nee*) from others requiring such listing (*inwit* yields to *conscience; rooves,* in some styles of speech, to *roofs,* while *knives* retains its *-v-*). In a somewhat misleading way, the former may be labeled "regular." Alternatively, they were also labeled with the technical term "sound change." Taken in this way, the regularity of sound change, or as A. Leskien (1840–1916) put it in 1876, the exceptionlessness of sound laws, is only a tautology. The fact that it became and remained a battle cry for the next sixty years of theoretical debate was unfortunate because it clouded the real issue which was important enough and which had to do with the typical historical and demographic settings in which sound changes are likely to take place. But the problem could not be clearly stated until the advent of synchronic phonemic analysis. Thus it is worth remarking in passing that Leskien had more reason than his classicist and Sanskritist colleagues to worry about the nature of sound replacement; he stands in the Schleicher tradition of East European studies, where alphabetic representation is not always a philological datum but part of the scholar's work—and a theretofore unformulated part at that.

However that may be, some of the important new discoveries were being made by men who did not recognize Leskien's dogma but who nevertheless adhered to the notion of reconstruction underlying that dogma. Karl Verner (1846–96) discovered the hidden "regularity" of "exceptions" to Grimm's Law (in the very same year, 1876) and it became one of the most potent arguments in favor of exceptionlessness. Yet Verner remained pointedly aloof himself. Others were more belligerent in their attacks and pointed to situations in which the tree model had important factual weaknesses. Subsequent contact between descendants may be extensive; there may be no clear cleavage. This does not invalidate the comparative method, but it may pose serious problems to its application. After Johannes Schmidt (1843–1901) had pointed this out, Schmidt's "wave theory" was long regarded as a kind of antidote to Schleicher's tree. More interesting than Schmidt's opposition was that of Hugo Schuchardt (1842–1927), who was not an Indo-Europeanist but more specifically a Romance scholar. The injection of fresh and different material into the theoretical debate had great importance. It was primarily in the Romance and the Germanic fields in which the graded nature of dialect areas was investigated, and men like Jost Winteler (1846–1929) and Jules Gilliéron (1854–1926), the initiator of the French Linguistic Atlas, contributed decisively to the theory of change in ways which, on mature reflection, turn out to be far less destructive to the real core underlying the "neo-grammarian" position than is sometimes thought (Bloomfield [1932], p. 231).

The precariousness of a methodological discussion which was not always relevant to the real scholarly issues was most keenly felt by some of the most brilliant pragmatic workers. The clearest cases in point were perhaps the Italian Graziadio I. Ascoli (1829–1907) and, a generation later, the Swiss scholar Ferdinand de Saussure (1857–1913). Both had made decisive technical contributions to what was then the center of the field (in 1870 and 1879, respectively), both were dissatisfied with the theory, as it was then stated, of what they were doing, and both, being physically somewhat removed from the center of things in the German universities, found original and effective ways of speaking out. Ascoli's strength was that he controlled Semitic and Romance materials in addition to being in the mainstream of the Indo-European work. He wrote with a detachment and self-knowledge that are almost without parallel at the time. The concept which has made him famous is that of the ethnic substratum as a "cause" of linguistic change. By asking, in effect, "How must we picture the genesis of different languages on the soil of the Roman empire?" (Arens [1955], p. 333), he took an important step toward filling the theoretical gap which had been left since Humboldt by the increasing neglect of the synchronic study of speech communities and of language contact.

Hermann Paul (1846–1921), the great and conscientious theorist of the neo-grammarians, still held, in his *Principles of the History of Language* that only a historical study of language had scholarly and scientific value when a new interest in nonhistorical questions began to stir. In part this interest seemed innocuous because it was clearly limited to an area which, it seemed, could safely be relinquished to specialists. This was phonetics. There was some overlapping, especially in the persons of E. Sievers (1850–1932) and Henry Sweet (1845–1912); but especially in England, with Sweet's successors, phonetics became indeed a discipline by itself. The reason why this was possible lay in the fact that the gap between synchrony and diachrony (history) remained to be bridged: it was not clear just how the physical description of speech sounds related to the entities which had somehow come to be represented in the (syllabic or) alphabetic records in which the various well-studied literary languages were recorded. Alphabetic representation was obviously a simplification of endless physical fact, yet it was just as obviously an appropriate and congenial simplification. The old confusion between letter and sound was, for some reason, not all that destructive.

The problem had come to the special attention of those few leading linguists who had combined historical-comparative studies with "field" activities. This was true of Schleicher, Leskien, and Winteler, as was pointed out before; it also held for O. Böhtlingk (1815–1904) with his fascinating combination of achievements in Sanskrit lexicography, Hindu grammar, and, the Russian ethnographic-linguistic tradition, with his expert description of Yakut, a Turkic language of Siberia. Students of European dialects were less troubled by it, since many of them were more interested in confounding the neo-grammarian enemy by judicious use of phonetic detail than in clarifying the issue. Some extra-Indo-European fields, however, suffered considerable damage; Finno-Ugric studies, for example, were seriously hampered by the deliberate and perverse introduction of phonetic raw material into comparative problems.

Characteristically, the problem was first seen in all its depth on East European soil, by J. Baudoin de Courtenay (1845–1929) and his collaborator N. Kruszewski, both Poles. By defining the role of oppositions or contrasts between classes of sounds they laid the groundwork of phonemic theory and suggested, among many other things, that alphabetic records of the familiar sort do not, in the ideal case, falsify language just because the phonetic detail is simplified, since the phonetic detail can be classified into functionally unimportant and functionally important ("phonemic") fact. It turned out that those who had worked with literary languages had in reality always had an implicit analysis performed for them by the orthographic tradition. It was on the basis of this understanding that de Saussure proceeded in his lectures (published by his students as the famous *Course in General Linguistics* in 1916) to explain the relation between synchrony and history. Out of this pair he made, partly for pedagogical reasons, a rather rigid dichotomy. In this sense de Saussure is hailed as the originator of structuralism in linguistics. The particular phonemic facets of the movement were hammered out with great vigor, especially by N. Trubetskoy (1890–1938), with strong attention being paid to nonliterary languages (Trubetskoy had a deep knowledge of the languages of the Caucasus) and, in general, to synchronic description as much as to the analysis of change.

The impact of this work was very great, not only on the philosophical view of language, but on typology which it helped to come to new life. On the whole, the study of nonliterary and "primitive" languages had languished since Humboldt. Outside of the occasional activities mentioned earlier the only major figure to approach such material from a linguistic point of view was F. N. Finck (1867–1910). His amazing *Haupttypen des Sprachbaues* (1910) stood, to all intents and purposes, alone, and it is quite unjust to go on blaming philosophers from W. Wundt to Ernst Cassirer for building on poor empirical foundations when nothing better was being offered. The change came, partly with Trubetskoy's Prague School, and partly when F. Boas (1858–1942), then professor of anthropology at Columbia University and also Honorary Philologist at the Bureau of American Ethnology, began his prodigious work on American Indian languages, both in the *Handbook of American Indian Languages* (2 vols., 1911–12) and elsewhere. Building on very respectable domestic traditions he became the founder of a highly successful school of American descriptive linguistics dedicated to careful phonetic recording and to an objective and strictly relativistic conception of grammar and semantics in which as little as possible was taken for granted, and any analogies with language categories familiar from traditional (i.e., European) language structure were suspect. E. Sapir (1884–1939) and L. Bloomfield (1887–1949) had been closer than Boas to academic linguistics of the conventional kind; both brilliant field workers, they spent considerable effort on problems of genealogical as well as typological classification. All three were considerable thinkers on the nature of language as a faculty and as an institution, and all three had their outlook profoundly determined by their widened typological knowledge. Some of the implications of all this were formulated in the highly stimulating writings of B. L. Whorf (1897–1941). In a manner reminiscent of Humboldt's ideas on the relation between language structure and world view, Whorf propounded the primacy of the semantic structure of the language, with its formal properties, over much that passes in ordinary, and not so ordinary, philosophy as content such as is amenable to expression in any language but in itself preexistent. Considering the observations made along the line, and the value of the ensuing debate (Hoijer, 1954), Whorf's innocence of the prehistory of this old philosophical problem did little damage.

The need to catch up, as it were, with "classical" comparative linguistics, and to give it the theoretical foundation it had not had, had other aspects, too. On one of them we have touched already. It was one thing to classify change processes, even successfully so far as methodological goals were concerned—this had been accomplished in the 1860's or shortly thereafter; it was another thing to interpret the classification, again in synchronic terms, by preserving historical concreteness. Ascoli had pointed the way, and others followed. Among them were a number of distinguished Frenchmen who knew Durkheim's sociology, like Antoine Meillet (1866–1936), whose famous essay on *How Words Change Their Meaning* (1958, pp. 230–71) shows him at his best on generalized topic, although his strength lay on the whole in his finesse on individual points and his ability to synthesize vast fields of factual knowledge—his *Introduction to Indo-European Comparative Linguistics,* while dependent on the gigantic neo-grammarian achievement of K. Brugmann (1849–1919) and B. Delbrück (1842–1922), is nevertheless the one enduring interpretive work on this classical subject. In time this line of endeavor was to develop into the field of sociolinguistics in which the structure of speech communities is studied in such a way as to enclose within itself as a special case as it were, the study of linguistic change. This is especially easy to illustrate with instances of borrowing; that is, with certain consequences of contact between language communities—the phenomenon to which U. Weinreich (1926–67), in particular, directed his attention. But there is no doubt that the point of view is far broader. Here, too, very old concepts are coming to the fore again: language mixture, for one, as reinterpreted in the light of such seemingly marginal phenomena as the pidgin and creolized languages which captivated the original and unorthodox mind of O. Jespersen (1860–1943).

It would be strange if the discipline of linguistics with its constant thrust toward greater and greater formalization had remained untouched by developments in mathematics and in logic. Much of this (especially what belongs with the much-discussed relation between linguistic and philosophical semantics) has, almost by definition, little to do with language *diversity*. Statistical methods have, of course, been tentatively applied to problems of linguistic change—most spectacularly perhaps, in the effort of M. Swadesh (1909–67) to calculate the degree of time depth behind divergent members of a family or of an area through glottochronology, that is, by assuming constancy for the rate with which "basic" vocabulary is replaced. The demand for content analysis or translation by machine has had very little direct effect on the theory of natural languages, although it has led indirectly to the asking of novel questions on the subject.

Transformational syntax as developed in the 1950's and 1960's is, however, a development of such general importance that it is inevitable that it should bear on the theory of language diversity. The claims vary greatly, but in the view of those who prefer a "generative" formulation it is evident that the relativity of natural language structure has receded into the background or rather gone to the level of "surface structure"; all languages share much or all of their deep structure which is often regarded as genetically given. In an older, slightly ambiguous, terminology the deep structure is a "universal," but not quite in the sense in which the tag has been applied to empirically widespread surface features or, especially, their concatenation. This relegates both typological and historical diversification to a low station in the hierarchy of concepts and, for that matter, of grammatical statement. But just because of that, manners of changing genealogical relationship, and the grading of typological areas created by diffusion ("contact") processes must be reformulated. What intrigues the historian of methodology is the fact that in addition to sound change, the other varieties of linguistic change may find a more solid berth in this framework than they have had in the past. It is an almost traditional complaint in the literature that neither historical syntax nor semantic change had had any really systematic treatment and that even a classical work of J. Wackernagel (1853–1938), *Vorlesungen über Syntax*, or of C. D. Buck (1866–1955), *Dictionary of Selected Synonyms*, mainly serves to show the lack of proper concepts.

Linguistics is a self-conscious field. Throughout its existence it has not only developed working theories about its subject, language (or, in our special cases, languages); it has also theorized about itself. More so, perhaps, than in some other areas of knowledge, the results have tended to be unhappy. Self-description, of which there is a good deal in the form of forewords, popularizations, and polemics must of course be taken with a grain of salt always; much the same is true of historiography. The tendency to look upon the people of the past with the simple question, what did they know, or fail to know, that we, now, consider true, is all too frequent. The alternative attitude, that is, one in which past error becomes as important as anticipated truth, is of no immediate apologetic value, and yet it alone guarantees an understanding of how truth is found. Some of the pitfalls are only verbal, but others are more subtle: few things, for example, are as instructive as the manner in which the biblical and classical notion of ancestry and descent, amenable as it is to the metaphor of the tree with its successive bifurcations, is filled, almost unbeknownst to the writer, with a fresh content; or how the concept of "comparison" (which is of course not limited to concern with languages) changes so decisively.

BIBLIOGRAPHY

H. Arens, *Sprachwissenschaft* (Freiburg and Munich, 1955). A. Borst, *Der Turmbau von Babel* (Stuttgart, 1957–63). B. Delbrück, *Einleitung in das Studium der indogermanischen Sprachen*, 6th ed. (Leipzig, 1919). P. Diderichsen, *Rasmus Rask og den grammatiske tradition*, Hist. Filos. Medd. Dan. Vid. Selsk. **38**, no. 2 (Copenhagen, 1960). F. Edgerton, "Sir William Jones: 1746–1794," *Journal of the American Oriental Society*, **66** (1946), 230–39; reprinted in *Portraits of Linguists*, ed. T. A. Sebeok (Bloomington and London, 1966), I, 1–18. R. A. Hall, Jr., *Introductory Linguistics* (Philadelphia and New York, 1964). Harry Hoijer, ed., *Language in Culture* (Chicago, 1954). Also published as Memoir No. 79 of the American Anthropological Association. S. N. Kramer, "The Babel of Tongues: A Sumerian Version," *Journal of the American Oriental Society*, **88** (1968), 108–11. A. Meillet, *La méthode comparative en linguistique historique* (Paris, 1924); trans. G. B. Ford as *The Comparative Method in Historical Linguistics* (Paris, 1967); idem, *Introduction à l'étude comparative des langues indo-européennes*, 8th ed. (Paris, 1937); idem, *Linguistique historique et linguistique générale*, latest ed. (Paris, 1958).

G. Mounin, *Histoire de la linguistique des origines au XXe siècle* (Paris, 1967). H. Pedersen, *Sprogvidenskaben i det nittende aarhundrede* (Copenhagen, 1924); trans. J. W. Spargo, as *Linguistic Science in the Nineteenth Century* (Cambridge, Mass., 1931); reissued as *The Discovery of Language* (Bloomington, 1962). R. Pfeiffer, *History of Classical Scholarship* (Oxford, 1968). M. Pohlenz, "Zeno von Kition und die Tempora," *Neue Jahrbücher für Wissenschaft und Jugendbildung,* **2** (1926), 259–60. E. Prokosch, *A Comparative Germanic Grammar* (Philadelphia, 1939). R. H. Robins, *A Short History of Linguistics* (Bloomington and London, 1967, 1968). T. A. Sebeok, ed., *Portraits of Linguists* (Bloomington and London, 1966). H. Steinthal, *Geschichte der Sprachwissenschaft bei den Griechen und Römern,* 2nd ed. (Berlin, 1890, 1891). G. W. Stocking, Jr., "On the Limits of 'Presentism' and 'Historicism' in the Historiography of the Behavioral Sciences," *Journal of the History of the Behavioral Sciences,* **1** (1965), 211–18. V. Thomsen, *Sprogvidenskabens historie* (Copenhagen, 1902); trans. H. Pollak, as *Geschichte der Sprachwissenschaft* (Halle, 1927). W. von Humboldt, *Werke in fünf Bänden,* ed. A. Flitner and K. Giel (Darmstadt, 1960, 1961, 1963, 1964, ——).

Several of the works cited make good introductory reading, especially those by Meillet (*Introduction,* Appendix I), Mounin, Pedersen, Robins, Sebeok, Steinthal, and Thomsen.

HENRY M. HOENIGSWALD

[See also Evolutionism; **Language**; **Linguistic Theories**; Myth; Primitivism; Romanticism; **Structure**; Uniformitarianism.]

LINGUISTIC THEORIES IN BRITISH SEVENTEENTH-CENTURY PHILOSOPHY

ENGLISH LINGUISTIC speculation from Francis Bacon to John Locke ranges of course over a variety of very disparate interests and problems: problems of semantic logic and historical semantics; pedagogical interests; discussions of the means of scientific communication, of the reform of style, of the function and technique of the comparative study of languages. Two themes, however, seem constantly to recur, insuring the unity of these inquiries and in a way constituting their guideline; the critique of ordinary language, and the gradual formation of the idea of the arbitrariness of the linguistic sign.

I. EMPIRICISM AND CRITIQUE OF LANGUAGE IN FRANCIS BACON

The problem of language is, we know, not a primary problem for Bacon, but is part of the more general subject of a reform of scientific method. Despite this, the Baconian encyclopedia of the sciences surely constitutes, even on the level of linguistic reflection, the best review of the linguistic problems transmitted by tradition and the best point of departure for their discussion in the seventeenth century. In fact, besides an inventory of the traditional linguistic problems, the English seventeenth century inherited from Bacon that kind of linguistic skepticism which will repeatedly call for justification and reform of language, or outright invention of language *ex novo,* to adapt it to the authentic aims of communication. English thought seems in short to find in the works of Bacon not only an encyclopedia of the natural and human sciences, but also a catalogue of the superstitions and prejudices which obstruct the communication of knowledge.

A first aspect of this critique of language is to be found in the examination Bacon makes of the arts of communication, and in particular of the traditional dialectics, inadequate and incompetent before the obscurity and profundity of nature, which escapes its grasp—whereas induction stimulates sense, imposes itself upon nature, and almost identifies itself with nature's works (*Cogitata et visa* [1607–09], *Instauratio magna* [1620], in *Works,* ed. J. Spedding, R. L. Ellis, D. D. Heath, London [1857–59], III, 606–08; *Novum organum* [1620], *De augmentis scientiarum* [1623]; *Works,* I, 135–39, 151–54, 161, 614ff.). Nevertheless dialectics still has a function, not however in respect of the increase of knowledge but only of its transmission. And it retains a privileged place in rhetoric, thanks to its objectivity, to its power to appeal to the intellect without the intervention of fancy or imagination. But its objectivity is not, all the same, the objectivity of science. The true discourse of science is not reasoning but experiment: to communicate scientific knowledge means to exhibit the operations of science. The ultimate objectivity of scientific discourse is given not by its incontrovertibility on the plane of argument but by its conformity to the facts, which is not rational evidence but sensible evidence, the possibility of repeated experimental verification.

From this arises the second aspect of the Baconian critique of language. Precisely because reasoning is no longer endowed with self-evidence and demonstrative rigor, the need arises of delivering scientific method from the looseness and uncertainty of the common language, in which errors and prejudices are deeply imbedded. These prejudices and errors are a class of the idols or false images of things which vitiate the operations of science, and are among the most troublesome and most dangerous since they are implicit in the very conferring of names: in the very learning of their mother tongue children are forced to swallow this *infoelicem errorum cabala* (*Cogitata et visa* and *Advancement of Learning* [1605], *Works,* III, 396–97,

599; *Novum organum* and *De augmentis scientiarum*, *Works*, I, 164, 170–72, 645–46).

The linguistic skepticism implicit in the doctrine of the *idola fori* is confirmed by Bacon's occasional reference to the ideal of Adamic language (whose names are endowed with immediate congruency with the nature of things) as mythical limit of human language, always conditioned by the nature of the human intellect and reflecting distortedly the images of things (*Instauratio magna* and *De augmentis scientiarum*, *Works*, I, 132, 434, 465–66). The opposing of Adamic language to conventional human language—a traditional theme, beginning with patristic philosophy —assumes in Bacon the value of a hypostasis of opposition between the immaculate science of the first days and human science since the Fall, between the natural language of the first human knowledge and the conventional language of recovered science. One might in fact apply to Bacon the observation Basil Willey makes (*The Seventeenth Century Background*, London [1934], p. 174) touching Glanvill: the figure of Adam becomes a sort of "wish-fulfillment" of the philosopher, conscious of the limits of human science and language.

The conformity of word to thing, which scientific communication must at any rate aim at, will therefore never be the immediate congruency of the Adamic naming. It will be rather a pragmatic conformity, so to speak, the fruit of true induction, that is of the new method of the interpretation of nature. Helpful in this will be the science of grammar, and in particular philosophical grammar, which has the double task of subjecting current linguistic usage to analysis and of studying the influence the "genius," that is to say the character, of different peoples has upon their respective languages (*De augmentis scientiarum*, *Works*, I, 476a, 654).

Since it is in the last analysis the trustworthiness of sensory intuition that guarantees semantic congruity, this congruity becomes the more precarious and compromised the more words depart from sensory evidence. Hence the linguistic value attributed to gesture, emblem, symbol, hieroglyph, all immediately endowed with sensible analogy to the thing or idea they signify, and all signifying without recourse to the mediation of words. The mediation of imagination also guarantees the sensible evidence of metaphor, which is not therefore merely an embellishment of discourse, but has an essential function as an instrument of communication.

II. THE CRITIQUE OF LINGUISTIC INNATISM

The debt to Bacon of seventeenth-century linguistic speculation has been stressed by Richard Foster Jones,

who has shown how from the Baconian "distrust of language" there descends that opposition of word to thing, of philological science to experimental science, which is amply documented in the scientific and didactic writings of the time. Within this general framework, with this general posture of mind, linguistic speculation addresses itself to its particular problems. Unquestionably the root problem is the problem of the origin and nature of language. The conventionalist thesis, generally accepted in entirety, manifests itself in the first half of the century as confutation of linguistic innatism, as confutation of the idea of a natural language, innate, created by and in the logos, which reveals itself both in the primordial language of humanity and in the astrological signs, and is the common cipher of macrocosm and microcosm. This idea of a "language of nature" had been strengthened, doubtless, by the wide diffusion (following perhaps in the wake of the magical Platonism of Robert Fludd) of typical expositions of the mysticism of the Logos: the *Philosophia occulta* of Cornelius Agrippa (translated into English in 1650) and the writings of Jacob Boehme (all of them translated into English between 1623 and 1661). The most devoted interpreter of this idea, in England, is John Webster, author of an *Academiarum examen* (London, 1654), a criticism of academic learning in which Baconian themes interlace with themes drawn from Renaissance Platonism and from Rosicrucian doctrine. Unlike institutional language, which is "acquisitive," says Webster, the language of nature is "dative"; it is the "mystical Idiome" which reveals itself in "heavenly Magick" and is understood by all creatures save "sinfull man who hath now lost, defac't and forgotten it" and has superimposed upon it his institutional languages (pp. 26–32).

This idea of a language of nature is challenged in *Vindiciae academiarum* (Oxford, 1654), Seth Ward's reply to Webster. Condemning in general the "Rosycrucian Rodomontados" of his adversary, Ward says among other things that the universal language, which Cabalists and Rosicrucians—these "credulous Fanatick Reformers"—have vainly sought in Hebrew and in the mythical language of Adam, will be rather the outcome of science, which will make possible the construction of a language—conventional, even artificial—founded on an analysis of ideas and capable therefore of an exact mirroring of them (pp. 18–23). The idea of an innate language had already been confuted by John Wilkins (*Mercury* [1641], in *The Mathematical and Philosophical Works*, London [1708], I, 1–2) with an argument that was to be picked up by other authors, for example by George Sibscota (*The Deaf and Dumb Mans Discourse*, London [1670], pp. 23–25):

. . . as Nature made Man without Knowledge that he may be capable of all the Arts, . . . she created him without any Language, that he may learn them all.

But the most radical challenge of the idea of an original privileged language is to be found in Thomas Hobbes (*Leviathan* [1651], *English Works*, ed. W. Molesworth, III, 18–19; *Logic* [1655], *English Works*, I, 16). It may be that Adam learned a few names directly from God; but for the Adamic language in general the rule holds, as for all human languages, where the act of naming proceeds *pari passu* with experience and the need to communicate. The Adamic language too, accordingly, must have been arbitrary.

The denial of an innate and privileged character of the Adamic language does not, however, mean denial of the doctrine of the monogenesis of languages. The idea of a primordial linguistic unity of the human race is universally accepted. But almost all writers agree on the impossibility of recovering or reconstructing the primeval language with the tools of philology (etymological research, comparative study of languages, etc.). This is the thesis of Wilkins (*An Essay towards a Real Character and a Philosophical Language*, London [1668], pp. 2–5); of Matthew Hale (*The Primitive Origination of Mankind*, London [1677], pp. 163–65); of William Wotton (*Discourse concerning the Confusion of Languages* [1713], London [1730], pp. 6–15), to mention only a few examples.

III. THE ARBITRARINESS OF LINGUISTIC SIGN

The epistemological premiss of linguistic conventionalism, for all the authors thus far recalled, is the explanation of the semantic relation given by Aristotle at the beginning of *De interpretatione*: names are the conventional signs of ideas, but ideas are the natural signs of things. The semantic relation is accordingly validated by the natural sign's mediation between name and thing. This is the premiss for numerous projects of an artificial language, the best known being the *Ars signorum* of George Dalgarno (1661) and the *Essay towards a Real Character and a Philosophical Language* of John Wilkins. Analyzing the mind's contents, drawing up tables of categories of all simple and complex ideas, then assigning a symbol to each of these, one could, it was thought, obtain a language which, eliminating the mediation of words, would be free of the ambiguity and uncertainty of human languages.

Contemporary epistemological inquiries, however, were working in the direction of a criticism of the Aristotelian view of the relation between name and thing, and in general of a criticism of the idea of

language as the mirroring, the phonetic translation, of a scheme of natural signs. The semantic investigations of Hobbes (*Human Nature* [1650], Chs. 5, 13; *Leviathan* [1651], Chs. 4–7; *Logic* [1655]) concern rather the theory of truth than the nature and function of language. Nevertheless, at least two aspects of Hobbes's doctrine contributed to the subversion of the Aristotelian conception of the semantic relation. In the first place, the idea of reasoning as "computation," in which signs are the essential things: in this perspective it is no longer thought that conditions speech, but on the contrary it is the use of signs that conditions thought. In the second place, the idea that universality pertains not to things or to ideas but only to names: with the consequence that the universalizing function is a function not of thought but of language.

The development of this second theme is one of the fundamental motives of Lockean semiotic (*Essay on Human Understanding* [1690], III). The meaning of words is the ideas they stand for. But the collections of ideas are the product of an abstractive function which is itself arbitrary. It is arbitrary because it forms collections of simple ideas which have no real pattern; this is the case with the names of mixed modes. Or else it is arbitrary because the collection of simple ideas, though it have a real pattern, yet never expresses this pattern but only the nominal essence, that is to say a pattern, determined by the choice of the speakers, which never reaches to the real essence of the thing and does not even exhaust its properties. The semantic relation, therefore, is never stable and exhaustive: the choice made in the linguistic act never rests on the real essence of the thing; and the determination and the range of significance vary from time to time, according to the needs of communication, and the state of knowledge, and current linguistic usage. Through this dynamic conception of meaning, Lockean semiotic constitutes the crisis of Aristotelian conventionalism, anchored in the theory of the idea as natural sign of the thing; and becomes the first radical affirmation of the arbitrariness of linguistic sign.

BIBLIOGRAPHY

General studies of English linguistics of the seventeenth century are: D. C. Allen, "Some Theories of the Growth and Origin of Language in Milton's Age," *Philosophical Quarterly*, **28**, 2 (1949), 5–16, and L. Formigari, *Linguistica ed empirismo nel Seicento inglese* (Bari, 1970). Important references are also contained in L. Rosiello, *Linguistica illuminista* (Bologna, 1967).

On the linguistic doctrines of Francis Bacon see: O. Funke, *Sprachphilosophische Probleme bei Francis Bacon* (1929), in *Gesammelte Aufsätze zur Anglistik und zur*

Sprachphilosophie (Bern, 1965); R. Wallace, *Francis Bacon on Communication and Rhetoric* (Chapel Hill, 1943); W. S. Howell, *Logic and Rhetoric in England: 1500–1700* (Princeton, 1956; 2nd ed. New York, 1961), pp. 365–76; P. Rossi, *Francesco Bacone, Dalla magia alla scienza* (Bari, 1957), Chs. IV–VI; E. De Mas, "La filosofia linguistica e poetica di Francesco Bacone," *Filosofia,* 14 (1963), 495–542. On the influence of Bacon the studies of R. F. Jones, reprinted in *The Seventeenth Century* (Stanford and London, 1951), are essential.

On proposals for an artificial language: O. Funke, *Zum Weltsprachenproblem in England im 17. Jahrhundert* (Heidelberg, 1929); J. Cohen, "On the Project of a Universal Character," *Mind,* 63 (1954), 49–63; B. DeMott, "Comenius and the Real Character in England," *P.M.L.A.,* 70, 5 (1955); idem, "Science versus Mnemonics," *Isis,* 48 (1957), 3–12; P. Rossi, *Clavis universalis* (Milan and Naples, 1960); V. Salmon, "Language-Planning in Seventeenth-Century England: Its Context and Aims," in *In Memory of J. R. Firth,* eds. C. E. Bazell, J. Catford, M. A. K. Halliday (London, 1966), 370–97.

On Hobbes: R. M. Martin, "On the Semantics of Hobbes," *Philosophy and Phenomenological Research,* 14 (1953–54), 205–11; M. Robbe, "Zu Problemen der Sprachphilosophie bei Thomas Hobbes," *Deutsche Zeitschrift für Philosophie,* 8, 4 (1960), 433–650; D. Krook, "Thomas Hobbes' Doctrine of Meaning and Truth," *Philosophy,* 31 (1956), 3–22; H. Törnebohm, "A Study in Hobbes' Theory of Denotation and Truth," *Theoria,* 26 (1960), 53–70; A. G. Gargani, "Idea, mondo, e linguaggio in T. Hobbes e J. Locke," *Annali della Scuola Normale Superiore di Pisa,* 2nd series, 35 (1966), 251–92.

On Locke: R. I. Aaron, *John Locke* (1937; reprint Oxford, 1965), Ch. VI; idem, *The Theory of Universals* (1952; 2nd ed. Oxford, 1967), Ch. II; J. W. Yolton, "Locke and the Seventeenth-Century Logic of Ideas," *Journal of the History of Ideas,* 16 (1955), 431–52; D. A. Givner, "Scientific Preconceptions in Locke's Philosophy of Language," *Journal of the History of Ideas,* 23 (1962), 340–54; R. I. Armstrong, "John Locke's 'Doctrine of Signs': A New Metaphysics," *Journal of the History of Ideas,* 26 (1965), 369–82; C. A. Viano, *John Locke, Dal razionalismo all'illuminismo* (Turin, 1960), 469–76.

LIA FORMIGARI

[See also Baconianism; **Language;** Macrocosm and Microcosm; Metaphor; Myth; **Nature; Structuralism.**]

LITERARY PARADOX

PERHAPS because of its origins in the rhetorical and dialectical training of young academicians, the literary paradox is a belle-lettristic form particularly hospitable to "ideas." The rhetorical paradox was a standard epideictic type, a praise of something commonly regarded as unpraiseworthy (a nut, an ass, tyranny or a given tyrant, Thersites, Helen), a defense of something contrary to received opinion or to the audience's expectations of the orator (folly, "nothing," "nobody," a new theory of motion, a new astronomical model). Such assignments were evidently set the young dialectician as tests of his control over logic and rhetoric; the *dissoi logoi* and various *aporia* are likely the "impossible" or indeterminate problems serving as exercises in mental agility. Of logical paradoxes, renowned from antiquity, Zeno's "Achilles and the Tortoise" and "the Arrow," both on the problem of infinite series and infinitesimals, are classic examples; these paradoxes were designed to demonstrate the limits of mathematical descriptions of motion; they were foils in the disputes of the Eleatics with the Pythagoreans and atomists. One of the most famous of all logical paradoxes is "the Cretan" or "the Liar": "Epimenides the Cretan says, 'All Cretans are liars.'" This particular paradox has an impressive history; referred to by Saint Paul, it is a self-contradictory formulation recurrent in belles-lettres as well as in logic. Montaigne used the paradox in his paradoxical *Apologie de Raymond de Sebond;* Sancho Panza was faced with it, in *Don Quixote,* I. li.

Paradoxical formulations test certain rational limits —the limits of grammar, rhetoric, and logic, chiefly— and test those limits by means of the very conventions they test: that is, paradoxical formulations are methodologically self-critical. Zeno's paradoxes and the self-referential paradoxes, "the Liar" in particular, raise the problem of "matching" verbal utterance to perceived reality and to conceptions, a topic also explored, with due attention to verbal and logical paradox, in the *Sophist,* the *Theaetetus,* and the *Parmenides,* investigations into the limits of discourse and discursive thinking. Further, though precisely formulated according to given rules, paradoxes nonetheless tend to indeterminacy: Achilles never catches the tortoise, and the tortoise, presumably, never crosses the finish line either; the Cretan by lying does not lie—or, in telling the truth, he lies. We cannot decide once and for all how few hairs a man must have to be "bald," nor which grain makes the noise when corn is tipped from a container.

Though they are carefully constructed, usually dialectically (in the Renaissance phrase, as "defenses of contraries"), paradoxes tend toward relativism. By its curious tautology, the self-referential paradox abolishes the possibility of external measuring-rods; praise of the conventionally unpraiseworthy, however, is itself a measuring rod, of the standards by which values are established. Why is a nut intrinsically less praiseworthy than a garden, an ass than a horse,

Thersites than Agamemnon? Paradoxes imply, though they rarely refer directly to, a double or multiple standard. They do so by operating at the limits of the technical conventions by which knowledge is organized and expressed—the conventions of grammar ("the Liar"), of logic (again "the Liar"), of discursive thought (the *Parmenides*), of intellectual formulation ("the Arrow," the Copernican paradox). By their literalist insistence on "correctness" and "rules," paradoxes manage to bring into question precisely that correctness and precisely those rules. Their precision is balanced by an indeterminacy designed to make audience and readers uneasy, for paradoxes oscillate between dialectical extremes, equivocate by their words and in their structure, reach a tenuous transparency of meaning maintained largely by control of technical skills in logical and rhetorical expression.

It is difficult to identify a purely "literary" paradox in antiquity, since the paradoxical orations, like their unparadoxical counterparts, were always designed as works of literary art as well as of functional rhetoric. Both Gorgias and Isocrates excelled at paradoxical as well as at "conventional" oratory: their defense of the conventionally indefensible or unworthy is one reason for Plato's attack on the relativism inherent in the Sophists' method. The association of formal paradox with both epideixis and play suggests that it was early regarded as an artistic, or at the very least a leisure-time, activity. This playfulness has as necessary pre-conditions considerable skill in the arts of the trivium (grammar, rhetoric, logic), a groundwork of conventional values familiar to both paradoxist and his audience, and an intellectual atmosphere in which values and value-systems competed for attention and adherence. So Cicero could write out the Stoic axioms of his *Paradoxa Stoicorum* with ironic intent, knowing that his audience recognized their official moral value and knew that the axioms ran counter to current morality in Rome. The life history of a "paradox" is often interesting: as Hamlet said to Ophelia, "This was sometime a paradox, but now the time gives it proof"— that is, a formulation introduced contrary to contemporary orthodoxy (as, for instance, the stern Stoic axioms were) is at first regarded as paradoxical, but later that same axiom may turn out to be "true" or may harden into orthodoxy. The "Copernican paradox," at first merely a schema introduced against the prevalent Ptolemaic system of the universe, subsequently became astronomical orthodoxy. Paradoxes have been considered chiefly to occur in periods in which competing value-systems strengthen philosophical pluralism and relativism; certainly the literary paradox occurs in periods marked by considerable disturbance of intellectual patterns. The Renaissance

is, partly for this reason, rich in paradoxy, although another reason for the form's popularity in the period is simply the humanist recovery of classical literary models, among them the paradox. Ancient paradoxes were recovered, studied, imitated, and adapted to new conditions. Indeed, in the late Renaissance the great anthologies of ancient and modern paradoxes were put together; at the same time, similar joco-serious collections of mathematical and scientific anomalies were gathered as "mathematical recreations," a near-literary genre of its own.

But paradoxy is by no means limited to the Renaissance, though most of this article's typical examples will be drawn from that period; in the Western tradition, epistemologically inquisitive authors (Mandeville, Swift, Sterne, Diderot, for instance) tended to formulate paradoxes. Paradoxy has always had its associations with nonsense, and the highly intellectual work of Lewis Carroll and Christian Morgenstern offers both the classical paradoxical topics and major contributions to literary paradox. In the modern period, such diverse authors as G. K. Chesterton, Joyce, Sartre, Queneau, Borges, and Heller, as well as Zen-influenced poets and detective story writers such as Nicholas Freeling, have prolonged the tradition of Western literary paradox in their work. Freud's study of the antithetical sense of "primal words" as well as his contributions to the theory of word-play have given new dimensions to paradoxy, important in literature as well as in psychological method. For the American school of literary critics still called after forty years the "New Critics," whose method of scrupulous close reading is current pedagogical orthodoxy, paradox was one major measure of the "richness" of a given text.

Basically, a paradox is a word-play, a pun, expressed in rhetorical and logical form. Any verbal test of skill is likely to develop into an art form, so that one need not be surprised that one major ancient writer wrote in praise of the nut (Ovid), and that a poem on the gnat was attributed to another (Vergil). This sort of subject proliferated in the Renaissance: Jean Passerat wrote on nothing; Rémy Belleau on an oyster, a shadow, a tortoise; Pierre de Ronsard on a cat, a salad; John Donne on a shadow, a flea; Giambattista Marino on a firefly; Richard Lovelace on a snail; Saint-Amant on a melon. Such topics may seem trivial, but they offered fine opportunities for the "playing wit" mentioned by Sir Philip Sidney in his rhetorical defense of poetics, which "can prayse the discretion of an Asse, the comfortablenes of being in debt, and the iolly commoditie of being sick of the plague." Nor were they all nugatory: Synesius' praise of baldness, for instance, calls into question the basis for a socially important aesthetic preference. The "low things"

77

which paradoxists praise often turned out to be thematically more elevated than their audience at first took them to be. For instance, when Erasmus constructed his fine self-referential mock-oration in which Folly praises folly, we discover, by working through the rhetorically ingenious travesty of logical argument, that folly turns out to be the highest spiritual state to which a man may aspire. Again, Sir John Harington's *The Metamorphosis of Ajax* (1596) is about a flushing water-closet; this paradox, though it certainly praises what in received opinion is the repository of "lowest" things, argues for standards of personal cleanliness which, when adopted three centuries after this facetious plea, caused a social as well as a hygienic revolution.

Because of its canonical opposition to received opinion (social, moral, intellectual cliché), paradoxy often dealt with material "new" in any given intellectual context. Montaigne's longest essay, his *Apologie de Raymond de Sebond*, is an example of a paradox operating consistently paradoxically: the essay begins by apparently defending the notion of an hierarchical universe, but actually adduces "evidence" from many different ranges of experience and authority to refute the validity of that notion. Montaigne's defense is in fact a censure: his apologia apologizes for the book his title appears to praise. Most examples of paradoxical novelty are less grand than this great essay in skepticism. In his *Paradossi* (1542), the first vernacular collection of paradoxes in Europe, Ortensio Lando argued for various disagreeable and officially low conditions, such as imprisonment, exile, debt, cuckoldry, and bastardy; all these are made to seem, however the paradoxist must reach for his instances, in some context or other preferable to their dialectical opposites: Shakespeare's *King Lear* is, among much else, a demonstration of the "truth" of several of Lando's paradoxes. Debt was a widespread topic for Renaissance paradoxists, trying to cope with the new situations arising from a cash economy. Ridiculous though Lando's arguments for debt were in terms of medieval economic theory and current morality, they turned out to be normal enough in an era of extensive credit. Both Rabelais and Bodin dealt, of course very differently, with the paradoxes in economic behavior perceived as new modes of economics massively altered the old: Panurge's praise of debt in *Gargantua et Pantagruel* is humorous enough, but it touches on the real anomalies of a new commercial age.

By the sheer multitude of paradoxical formulations in his *Gargantua et Pantagruel*, particularly clustered in the *Tiers livre*, Rabelais offers a wonderful anthology of Renaissance paradoxy. He praises many unpraiseworthy things besides debt: his praise of the codpiece is a considered essay on generation, as well as an ironic commentary on that segment of a man's trousers. Panurge's debate on whether or not he should marry makes us aware of the Renaissance's oscillations in sexual relations, most noticeable in the fact that clerics might marry, according to the new dispensation; obvious as well, though, in education, in religious, social, and business life. Rabelais does not specifically write a paradoxical praise of women, but other humanists did, and throughout his book he accords them, especially in his utopian section, a remarkable degree of freedom and responsibility. Lando's paradox on bastardy, thematically very close to Rabelais' on the codpiece, points toward a related social change, as patterns of inheritance altered under the impact of the new commercialism. Paradoxes on marriage, cuckoldry, and bastardy all have to do with social matters and with social change: another related paradoxical topic was virginity. The young John Donne and Parolles in *All's Well that Ends Well* speak of that particularly valued and disvalued condition in almost the same ironical terms. Falstaff's discourse on honor in *I Henry IV* is a paradoxical redefinition of an aristocratic value long unquestioned but, after the decline of active feudalism, a topic for the anti-idealist paradoxists of the Renaissance.

Falstaff himself embodies a Renaissance social paradox, *le chevalier sans cheval*, the knight unhorsed, or deprived of his feudal function, a figure who was also the subject of one of Erasmus' *Colloquia*. Falstaff has strong affinities with another figure for paradox, the literary Fool. Privileged to speak out, usually on behalf of a satirical view of actuality, against received opinion, convention, and social cliché, the Fool (in literature at least) was a rich source for paradoxical utterance. From Socrates, who alleged that his only knowledge was the limitation of his own knowledge, via Saint Paul and the Pseudo-Dionysius to Nicholas of Cusa and Erasmus, *docta ignorantia* was attributed to the gifted fool. Alcibiades' image from the *Symposium*, of Socrates as an ugly Silenus-box containing the sweetest perfume, was explicated by Erasmus in the *Adagia*, exploited in the *Moriae encomium*, adapted by Rabelais in the Preface to *Gargantua*, and referred to by a host of other paradoxists as a visual emblem of the functions of the formal paradox, evidently ugly but with a sweet truth within. Falstaff belongs in this company of wise fools, though he has none of the spirituality of Erasmus' "Saint Socrates"; Lear's fool is wisely ignorant, speaks in grammatical paradoxes and touches on many paradoxical topics (nothing, shadow, folly, codpiece, world-upside-down); Lear himself is schooled to the piercing accuracy of moral and social judgment characteristic of the highest forms of Renaissance folly.

Another principle book of the period, itself a paradoxical essay, Henry Cornelius Agrippa's *De vanitate scientiarum* (1530), rejected the academic and occult disciplines (practiced and publicized by the author in other works) to argue for a pious nescience; in a curious sequel, Agrippa retracted much of what he had written in the *De vanitate*, but since he also defended the book against its calumniators, it is difficult to tell what he "really" thought about his paradox. Whatever else the book is, it is a demonstration of its author's command of contemporary learning; like Folly's discourse and Montaigne's *Apologie*, Agrippa's book illustrated the paradoxical *sine qua non* of technical control which the paradox existed to reject. For the paradoxist anyway, *ignorantia* had to be *docta* to count: for that reason, the literary paradox can claim its place in an encyclopedia of philosophy.

From the many examples here cited, one can see how the paradox doubles back on itself, acts out the self-negation of which "the Liar" is so economical an example. The subject of negations was an old philosophical topic, for instance in the *Sophist*. The initial formulations of the *Parmenides*, cast in negative syntax, were apparently preserved through the Middle Ages and seem to have been the models for such elaborations of the negative theology as those of Dionysius the Areopagite (the Pseudo-Dionysius), by which the transcendent God is "defined" by negative terms— infinite, eternal, immutable. The great extender of this tradition into the Renaissance was Nicholas of Cusa, important also for his comprehensive formulation of *docta ignorantia*; Giordano Bruno also specialized in marvellous negative formulations in metaphysics and ontology. A literary by-product of the concentration on negative statements, grammatically "safer" or more protected than positive statements, by definition subject to challenge or refutation, was a spate of secular paradoxes on "nothing," "nobody," and "nowhere." "Nothing can come of nothing; speak again," said King Lear to his youngest daughter; later in the same play, his Fool reminds him of the same truism from Aristotelian physics. Passerat's Latin poem, "Nihil," provided a model for many other paradoxical poems and essays on nothing, as well as others on "Aliquid" and on the zero-shaped "Ovum." If Homer did not, in making Odysseus say his name was "Nobody," then Ulrich von Hutten wrote the classic "Nemo" paradox. More important than these was the imaginary commonwealth described by Sir Thomas More and given the paradoxical title *Utopia*, "nowhere." Such no-

wheres abound, through *Erewhon* to *1984* ("This was sometime a paradox, but now the time gives it truth"), organized in dialectical opposition to what their authors recognized as their own local somewhere. And they offer an interesting case-history in paradoxy: utopian commonwealths often proved so persuasive that their paradoxical character gave way before their didactic function. Irony faded away as the paradox turned into a model.

An exception to this generalization is Rabelais' utopian Abbey of Thélème, so topsy-turvy a rendition of community life that its readers always took it as an ironic counterpart to reality, a defense by contraries. This utopian paradigm has its analogue in an ancient paradoxical encomium on Helen, who as the cause of civilization's ruin was manifestly an unworthy and a low thing, not worth praising. Isocrates' oration seems to have been ironic, and recognized as such; subsequently, audience reaction altered the paradoxical quality of orations on Helen, so that *topoi* used in ironic praise of the most beautiful woman in the world became the magniloquent response to female loveliness familiar to us from the lips of Marlowe's Faustus and Goethe's Faust. So with utopias: the ideals they codify were too precious for an ironic context and their paradoxicality was ultimately rejected.

More's *Utopia* however classically demonstrates the form's remarkable balancing, merely by its manipulation of elements from utterly different philosophical programs; both its Epicureanism and its Stoicism have been fully documented. Folly is an even more astonishing manipulator of traditions—Epicureanism and Stoicism are certainly identifiable components of her oration, both for good and for bad; so are skepticism and Christian fideism, modulated with immense skill into one composition. Compared with his fairly consistent Stoic stance in other essays, Montaigne's skeptical *Apologie* offers yet another manifestation of paradoxy, as this longest of his essays makes its extraordinary plea for a suspiciously Christian Pyrrhonism. The tightrope-walking paradoxist took as his task, quite literally, equivocation, as part of his loyalty to indeterminacy and inclusiveness.

Other sorts of literary paradox should be mentioned— the play on words: *Le coeur a ses raisons, que la raison ne connaît pas;* or, in a pleasant self-reference, *Diseur de bons mots, mauvais caractère* (Pascal); *L'hypocrisie est un hommage que le vice rend à la vertu* (La Rochefoucauld); "Until I labour, I in labour lie" (Donne); all these have the sharp wit with which epigrammatists make their point. Religious poetry draws heavily on both the epigrammatic tendency to verbal paradox and the theological tendency to adapt 79 the paradoxes of the infinite to the deity. So Shakespeare can paraphrase Saint Paul one way, in a secular sonnet:

> So shalt thou feed on Death, that feeds on men,
> And, Death once dead, there's no more dying then

and John Donne another, in a Holy Sonnet:

> One short sleep past, wee wake eternally,
> And death shall be no more; Death, thou shalt die.

Angelus Silesius exploits the negative theology in his epigrammatic formulation of God's immanence and man's perception of it:

> *Die zarte Gottheit ist ein Nichts und Übernichts:*
> *Wer nichts in allem sieht, Mensch, glaube, dieser sichts.*

Other efforts to invoke the indescribable and ineffable may result in verbal paradoxy—"Dark with excessive bright thy skirts appear," wrote Milton of God's ambiance, and of Satan's, "darkness visible." Literary efforts to render intense feeling, either of sacred or of secular love, exploited that grammatical figure for paradox, the oxymoron, so that readers became accustomed to Petrarchan lovers' burning in a sea of ice and drowning amidst a fire; accustomed also to the the painful pleasure of religious experience, exemplified in Saint Theresa's ecstatic apprehension of God, and in Donne's invocation to the Deity:

> for I
> Except you'enthrall me, never shall be free,
> Nor ever chast, except you ravish me.

Even the oxymoron's contradictoriness returns us to the self-referential, self-cancelling quality inherent in paradoxical formulations; it is not surprising that suicide, or individual self-cancellation, self-annihilation, became a recurrent topic of paradox. Certainly the Stoics, whose rigorous morality was expressed in axioms apparently paradoxical because they ran so counter to man's natural self-indulgence, advocated suicide as a preservation of individual integrity against intolerable pressure. By Stoic standards, it was paradoxical that Nero, who drove the Stoic Seneca to his suicide, should be the subject of paradoxical encomia—but just because Nero was a proper subject for paradox, he naturally became so. Seneca, apparently, did not become a paradoxical topic, but suicide did: suicide, the archsin of Christianity, was defended by several paradoxists, none more complexly than John Donne in his *Biathanatos*. Metaphorically, it had been taken for granted that man was his own executioner (Donne's phrase), his own assassin (Sir Thomas Browne's), his own Atropos (Browne once more)—but this was metaphor, and its reverse was also metaphor, the notion underlying much

of Folly's praise of folly and of Castiglione's *Cortegiano*, that a man also "makes" himself. In received opinion, however, man was made by his parents' endeavors and inspirited by God; his death, too, normally came to him, and should always have come to him, by some outside instrumentality. A man could connive at his own death, as in fencing (Hamlet, Montaigne, and Donne all regarded fencing as tantamount to self-homicide); he could also connive at his death by seeking martyrdom and blessedness (a problem faced by Saint Augustine much earlier). One can see how paradoxical Donne is in his *Biathanatos*, when he adduces not only the Christian martyrs but also Christ Himself as evidence for the legitimacy of suicide. In this formal paradox, Donne worked against received opinion in many ways.

That paradox, like most paradoxes, ends equivocally. Though his witty and sympathetic forces seem to sanction suicide, in special cases anyway, Donne never passes overt judgment for or against that sin. In this, he obeys the paradox's decorum. Either because of their self-referential formulation or because their author refuses to come to an overt conclusion, paradoxes tend not to end, to be indeterminate in both form and "message." We do not know, for instance, whether Panurge does or doesn't marry—the subject is simply left unsettled, though we witness Panurge in other activities later in the book. Folly backs away from her conclusions about folly and in her last words denies the continuity of human culture which her oration has relied on throughout—"I hate a man that remembers," even what she has said in her encomium: self-denial, self-cancellation. At the end of the *Apologie*, Montaigne turns from nescience to fideism, a topic formally unprepared for throughout the essay; and so he ends, with the God whom he has not elsewhere invoked in the essay.

A remarkably paradoxical work, Robert Burton's *Anatomy of Melancholy*, may serve to illustrate some of the workings of the paradoxical method. To begin with, a total assertion is made, such as those of Lando's *Paradossi*—"It is better to live in a cottage than in a great palace"; "It is better to have no servants than a great retinue." Or Folly: "All men are foolish"; or Montaigne: "Man can know nothing." Burton: "All men are melancholy," and he shows how anything can cause melancholy and anything (or nothing) can cure it. He stresses the contradictions in the disease, since all men, whatever their natures and qualities, are melancholy, all possible types of behavior are merely symptoms of melancholy. Burton offers many "cures" for the condition—but the cures he gives us cancel each other out, and anyway are all too often identical with the causes of melancholy. Within his huge book, as encyclopedic as its title suggests, he has many passages, some very long, on standard paradoxical topics—exile, imprisonment, virginity, nescience, self-love, suicide. He wrote a systematic utopia into his book, and used many tricks of self-reference, to himself and to his book. *The Anatomy* ends inconclusively, though it ends as it began, exhorting the melancholy man to be thankful for whatever respite from melancholy he can find—in this case, by a fine self-reference, having been so long busy with Burton's book. *The Anatomy* is, further, an argument for the vanity of the arts and the sciences, a highly learned book, chock-a-block with quotations from authors of every sort, a book which nonetheless rejects the comforts and remedies offered by those authors. Finally, it is a paradox concealed (or not so concealed): by seeming to assert the preeminence of melancholy, Burton calls into question the whole humoral psychology, shows its conceptual bankruptcy, and turns away from his subject without offering any new solution to the cosmic problem. Burton's massive book is, besides much else, an indeterminate exercise in received opinions, mocked by their methodical juxtaposition designed to show their inadequacies. It is, then, as paradoxes should be, an epistemological study, an examination of the nature of human thought by means of human thought, a knowing consideration of human knowledge which shows how powerful is human unknowing.

BIBLIOGRAPHY

B. Bolzano, *Paradoxieri der Undendlichen* (Leipzig, 1851), trans. as *Paradoxes of the Infinite* (London, 1950). Theodore C. Burgess, *Epideictic Literature* (Chicago, 1902). Greta Calman, "The Picture of Nobody," *Journal of the Warburg and Courtauld Institutes*, **23** (1960), 60–104. Rosalie L. Colie, *Paradoxia Epidemica: The Renaissance Tradition of Paradox* (Princeton, 1966). Augustus De Morgan, *A Budget of Paradoxes* (London, 1872). Sister M. Geraldine, C.S.J., "Erasmus and the Tradition of Paradox," *Studies in Philology*, **61** (1964), 41–63. E. H. Gombrich, *Art and Illusion* (London and New York, 1960). Walter Kaiser, *Praisers of Folly* (Cambridge, Mass., 1963). William and Martha Kneale, *The Development of Logic* (Oxford, 1962). Alexandre Koyré, *Epiménide le menteur* (Paris, 1946). A. E. Malloch, "The Technique and Function of the Renaissance Paradox," *Studies in Philology*, **52** (1956), 191–203. Henry Knight Miller, "The Paradoxical Encomium . . . ," *Modern Philology*, **53** (1956), 145–78. Karl Popper, "Self-Reference and Meaning in Ordinary Language," in *Conjectures and Refutations* (London, 1965). W. V. Quine, "Paradox," *Scientific American* (April 1962), 84–96. Warner G. Rice, "The *Paradossi* of Ortensio Lando," *Michigan Essays in Comparative Literature*, **8** (1932), 59–74. Alexander Rüstow, *Der Lügner* (Leipzig, 1910). Alexander Sackton, "The Paradoxical Encomium in Elizabethan Drama," University of Texas, *Studies in English*, **28** (1949), 83–104.

ROSALIE L. COLIE

[See also **Ambiguity**; Satire; **Style; Wisdom of the Fool.**]

LITERATURE AND ITS COGNATES

THE TERM "literature" is derived from the Latin *litteratura* which, in turn comes from the root *littera*, letter. According to Quintilian (*Institutiones*, lib. 2., cap. 1) it is a translation of the Greek *grammatikē*. It meant thus simply a knowledge of writing and reading. Other passages refer to the alphabet or an inscription (Wölfflin, 1885). Cicero speaks of Caesar as having *literatura* in a list of qualities which includes "good sense, memory, reflection, diligence." It must here mean something like "erudition, literary culture." We have to go to Tertullian (*De spectaculis*) and Cassian, in the second century A.D., to find the term used for a body of writing. They contrast secular literature with scriptural, pagan with Christian, *litteratura* with *scriptura*.

The term, in this form, seems to have disappeared during the Middle Ages and the Renaissance. It emerges late in the seventeenth century meaning "knowledge of literature," "literary culture." Thus J. de La Bruyère, in his *Caractères* (1688), speaks of *gens d'un bel esprit et d'une agréable littérature*.

Examples of this usage can be found all through the eighteenth century. Voltaire, in *Le Siècle de Louis XIV* (1751, Ch. XXV), speaks of Chapelain as having *une littérature immense*. In the unfinished article on "Littérature" for his *Dictionnaire philosophique* (1764–72) Voltaire defines literature as "a knowledge of the works of taste, a smattering of history, poetry, eloquence, and criticism." Voltaire's follower, Jean-François Marmontel, who wrote the literary articles for the great *Encyclopédie*, which were collected as *Eléments de littérature* (1787), defines "littérature" as a "knowledge of belles lettres" in contrast with erudition. "With wit, talent, and taste," he promises, "one can produce ingenious works, without any erudition, and with little literature."

In England, the antiquary John Selden was, in 1691, called a "person of infinite literature," and Boswell, late in the eighteenth century, refers to the writer Giuseppe Baretti as an "Italian of considerable literature." Dr. Samuel Johnson in his *Dictionary* defines 81

"Literature" simply as "learning; skill in letters." The *Tatler* (No. 197, July 13, 1710) implies that it meant mainly a knowledge of Latin and Greek: "It is in vain for folly to attempt to conceal itself by the refuge of learned languages. Literature does but make a man more eminently the thing that nature made him." This use of the term survived in the nineteenth century when James Ingram gave a lecture "On the Utility of Anglo-Saxon Literature" (1807) meaning the utility of knowing or studying Anglo-Saxon, or when John Petherham wrote *An Historical Sketch of the Progress and Present State of Anglo-Saxon Literature in England* (1840) where literature means the study of literature.

Apparently not later than the thirties of the eighteenth century the term began to be used as a designation for a body of writing. François Granet's series, *Réflexions sur les ouvrages de littérature* (1736–40) is an early example. Voltaire in *Le Siècle de Louis XIV* (1751) speaks of *littérature légère* and *les genres de littérature* cultivated in Italy. L'Abbé Sabatier de Castres seems to have been the first to put the term on the title-page of a French book: *Les Siècles de littérature française* (1772), the year in which Tiraboschi's multivolumed *Storia della letteratura italiana* began to appear in Italy. In Germany this use seems to be established slightly earlier in prominent texts. Lessing's *Briefe die neueste Litteratur betreffend* (1759ff.) applies clearly to a body of writing, and so does Herder's *Über die neuere deutsche Litteratur* (1767). Still, the term must have been felt as strange and new as Nicolas Trublet's *Essais sur divers sujets de littérature et morale* (1735–54) were translated as *Versuche über verschiedene Gegenstände der Sittenlehre und Gelehrsamkeit* (1776).

In English the same process took place. Sometimes it is difficult to distinguish between the old meaning of literature as literary culture and the new reference to a body of writing. The *New English Dictionary* quotes its first example for "body of writing" from 1822. In 1761 George Colman, the elder, however, thought that "Shakespeare and Milton seem to stand alone, like first-rate authors, amid the general wreck of old English literature." In 1767 Adam Ferguson included a chapter, "Of the History of Literature," in his *Essay on the History of Civil Society*. In 1774 Dr. Johnson, in a letter, wished that "what is undeservedly forgotten of our antiquated literature might be revived" and John Berkenhout in 1777 subtitled his *Biographia Literaria, A Biographical History of Literature*, in which he proposed to give a "concise view of the rise and progress of literature." Examples from the late eighteenth century could be multiplied. Still, the first book in English called *A History of English Language*

and Literature by Robert Chambers dates from as late as 1836.

In all of these examples literature is used very inclusively. It obviously refers to all kinds of writings including those of an erudite nature, history, philosophy, theology, etc. Only very slowly was the term narrowed down to what we today call "imaginative literature," and imaginative, fictive prose. An early conscious declaration of this new use is in the Preface to Carlo Denina's *Discorso sopra le vicende della letteratura* (1760), a book which was soon translated into English and French. Denina professes "not to speak of the progress of the sciences and arts, which are not properly a part of literature"; he will speak of works of learning only when they belong to "good taste, to eloquence, that is to say, to literature." That literature was used in this new aesthetic sense at that time may be illustrated by A. de Giorgi-Bertòla's *Idea della letteratura alemanna* (Lucca, 1784) which is an expanded edition of the earlier *Idea della poesia alemanna* (Naples, 1779) where the change of title was forced by the inclusion of a report on German novels.

Two comments by important nineteenth-century writers may show that the term "literature" was felt to be new and even objectionable, at least in France. Philarète Chasles comments in 1847: "I have little esteem for the word literature; it seems to me meaningless." It is "something which is neither philosophy, nor history, nor erudition, nor criticism—something I know not what: vague, impalpable, and elusive." Ernest Renan in *Questions contemporaines* (1868) still felt the novelty of the term: He speaks of *L'ensemble des productions qu'on appelait autrefois les "ouvrages de l'esprit" et qu'on désigne maintenant du nom de littérature* ("The group of works that used to be called 'works of the mind' and are now designated as 'literature'").

Literature was a new or alternate term for what in antiquity was usually called *litterae*. In Cicero we find *Graecae litterae, historia litteris nostris,* and *studium litterarum*. A Christian writer, Cassiodorus, wrote *Institutiones divinarum litterarum* in the sixth century. In the Middle Ages, with the establishment of the seven liberal arts and the trivium, the term *litterae* was used rarely. Poetry was assigned to grammar or rhetoric. *Litteratus* occurs, but does not mean a writer but anybody acquainted with the art of writing and reading. With the Renaissance a consciousness of a new secular literature opposed to scripture and theological writing or to the writing of schoolmen and pedants emerges and with it the terms *litterae humanae, lettres humains,* and *bonnes lettres*. They are used widely by Rabelais, Du Bellay, Montaigne, and other French writers of the sixteenth century often in contrast to *saintes lettres.* The term *litterae humaniores* survives in Oxford as one of the honors schools.

The term *belles lettres* emerges only in the seventeenth century. In 1666 Charles Perrault proposed to Colbert, the minister of finance of Louis XIV an Academy with a section *belles lettres* which was to include grammar, eloquence, and poetry (*Lettres,* ed. P. Clement, Paris [1868], V, 512f.). The term must have been felt to be identical with *lettres humains,* as the *Dictionnaire de Trévoux* (1704) says: *on appelle les lettres humaines ou les belles lettres, la grammaire, l'éloquence, la poésie.* This common French term spread then early in the eighteenth century to England and Scotland. At Marischal College, in Aberdeen, "the principles of criticism and *belles lettres*" were taught in 1753 (A. Morgan, *Scottish University Studies* [1933], p. 73); and Hugh Blair became Professor of Rhetoric and *Belles Lettres* at the University of Edinburgh in 1762. His *Lectures on Rhetoric and Belles Lettres* (1783) was a popular textbook even in the United States far into the nineteenth century. Today *belles lettres* both in French and English, is used rather rarely and the noun "belletrist" and the adjective "belletristic" have assumed a faintly derisive shade of frivolity and inconsequence. Thomas De Quincey in 1837 refers to William Roscoe as "a mere belletrist" (Masson, XI, 127). Vernon Louis Parrington in *Main Currents of American Thought* (1927–30), assigns the problem of Poe to the "belletrist." A. L. Guérard is quoted as saying "The *belles lettres* fragrance that clings to the humanities repelled the social scientists."

Literature in the eighteenth century began to be felt as a particular national possession, as an expression of the national mind, as a means toward the nation's self-definition. The Germans were particularly conscious of their nationality and in German the term "Nationalliteratur" began to be used widely. Leonhard Meister's *Beyträge zur Geschichte der teutschen Sprache und Nationallitteratur* (1777) is an early example. Most of the best known literary histories carry the term in their title: those of Ernst Wachler, August Koberstein, G. G. Gervinus in 1835, and later the popular August Vilmar and Rudolf Gottschall.

The emphasis on nationality and locality elicited the need for contrary qualifications. "Comparative literature," "world literature," and "general literature" are rival terms emerging in the nineteenth century. "Comparative literature" in English is of very late occurrence. A letter by Matthew Arnold from 1848 is not really relevant. He says "how plain it is now, though an attention to the comparative literatures for the last fifty years might have instructed anyone of it, that England is in a certain sense far behind the Continent" (*Letters,* ed. Russell, London [1895], I, 8). Here the term

"comparative" means merely "comparable." The decisive use was that of Hutchison Macaulay Posnett, an Irish barrister who later became Professor of Classics and English Literature at University College, Auckland, New Zealand, who put the term on the title of a book in 1886. Posnett in a later article "The Science of Comparative Literature" (*Contemporary Review,* 1901) claimed "to have first stated the method and principles of the new science, and to have been the first to do so not only in the British Empire but in the world." But of course this is entirely untrue. French and German use of the term preceded the English. The lateness of the English use of the term must be in part explained by the fact that "comparative literature" preserves the older meaning of the term as "study of literature" which had fallen into oblivion. It raised objections such as those of Lane Cooper who refused to call the department at Cornell University, of which he became Chairman in 1927, "Comparative Literature," insisting on "The Comparative Study of Literature." He considered "Comparative Literature" a "bogus term" that "makes neither sense nor syntax. . . . You might as well permit yourself to say 'comparative potatoes' or 'comparative husks'" (*Experiments in Education,* Ithaca [1942], p. 75). Today the ellipsis seems generally understood, and the term is accepted also in English.

The French were more fortunate; *Littérature comparée* makes good syntax and sense. The term was apparently suggested by G. Cuvier's *Anatomie comparée* (1800) or J. M. Degérando's *Histoire comparée des systèmes de philosophie* (1804). In 1816 two compilers, F. J. M. Noël and Guisbain F. M. J. de Laplace, published a series of anthologies from French, classical, and English literature with the otherwise unused and unexplained title page: *Cours de littérature comparée.* Charles Pougens in *Lettres philosophiques à Madame XXX sur divers sujets de morale et littérature* (1826) complained that there is no work on the principles of literature he can recommend: *un cours de littérature comme je l'entends, c'est-à-dire, un cours de littérature comparée.*

The man, however, who gave the term currency in France was undoubtedly Abel-François Villemain, whose course on eighteenth-century literature was a tremendous success at the Sorbonne in the late twenties. It was published in 1828–1829 as *Tableau de la littérature française au XVIIIe siècle* in four volumes, with even the flattering reactions of the audience inserted: *Vifs applaudissements. On rit* ("Lively applause. Laughter"). There he uses several times *tableau comparé, études comparées, histoire comparée,* but also *littérature comparée* in praising the Chancelier d'Aguesseau for his *vastes études de philosophie, d'his-*

toire, de littérature comparée. In the second lecture series, *Tableau de la littérature au moyen âge en France, en Italie, en Espagne et en Angleterre* (2 vols., 1830), he speaks again of *amateurs de la littérature comparée,* and in the Preface to the new edition in 1840, Villemain, not incorrectly, boasts that here for the first time in a French university an attempt at an *analyse comparée* of several modern literatures was made.

After Villemain the term was used fairly frequently. Philarète Chasles delivered an inaugural lecture at the Athenée in 1835: in the printed version in the *Revue de Paris,* the course is called *Littérature étrangère comparée.* Adolphe-Louis de Puibusque wrote a two-volume *Histoire comparée de la littérature française et espagnole* (1843) where he quotes Villemain, the perpetual Secretary of the French Academy, as settling the question. The term "comparative," however, seems to have for a time competed with *comparée.* J.-J. Ampère, in his *Discours sur l'histoire de la poésie* (1830), speaks of *l'histoire comparative des arts et de la littérature* but later also uses the other term in the title of his *Histoire de la littérature française au moyen âge comparée aux littératures étrangères* (1841). The decisive text in favor of the term *littérature comparée* is C. A. Sainte-Beuve's very late article, an obituary of Ampère, in the *Revue des Deux Mondes* in 1868.

In Germany the word "comparative" was translated *vergleichend* in scientific contexts. Goethe in 1795 wrote "Erster Entwurf einer allgemeinen Einleitung in die vergleichende Anatomie" ("First Draft of a General Introduction to Comparative Anatomy"). *Vergleichende Grammatik* was used by August Wilhelm Schlegel in a review in 1803, and Friedrich Schlegel's pioneering book, *Über Sprache und Weisheit der Inder* (1808), used *vergleichende Grammatik* prominently as a program of a new science expressly recalling the model of *vergleichende Anatomie.* The adjective became common in Germany for ethnology, and later psychology, historiography, and poetics. But for the very same reason as in English, it had difficulty making its way with the word "literature." Moriz Carriere in 1854, in *Das Wesen und die Formen der Poesie,* probably used *vergleichende Literaturgeschichte* for the first time. *Vergleichende Literatur* occurs surprisingly as the title of a forgotten periodical edited by Hugo von Meltzl in the remote city of Klausenburg (now Cluj, in Rumania): his *Zeitschrift für vergleichende Literatur* ran from 1877 to 1888. In 1886 Max Koch, at the University of Breslau, founded a *Zeitschrift für vergleichende Literaturgeschichte,* which survived till 1910. Von Meltzl emphasized that his conception of comparative literature was not confined to history and, in the last numbers of his periodical he changed the

title to *Zeitschrift für vergleichende Literaturwissenschaft.* A fairly new term in German, *Literaturwissenschaft,* was adopted early in the twentieth century for what we usually call "literary criticism" or "theory of literature." The new German periodical *Arcadia* (1966–   ) is called *Zeitschrift für vergleichende Literaturwissenschaft.*

There is no need to enter into a history of the terms elsewhere: In Italian, *letteratura comparata* is clearly and easily formed on the French model. The great critic Francesco De Sanctis occupied a chair called *della letteratura comparata* at Naples, from 1872 till his death in 1883. Arturo Graf became the holder of such a chair at Turin in 1876. In Spanish the term *literatura comparada* seems even more recent.

In Russian, Alexander Veselovsky, the greatest Russian *comparatiste* did not use the term in his inaugural lecture as Professor of General Literature at St. Petersburg in 1870, but he reviewed Koch's new periodical in 1887 and there used the term *sravitelnoe literaturovedenie,* which is closely modeled on *vergleichende Literaturwissenschaft.*

The term "world literature," *Weltliteratur,* was used in 1827 by Goethe commenting on a translation of his drama *Tasso* into French, and then several times, sometimes in slightly different senses: he thought mainly of a single unified world literature in which differences between the individual literatures would disappear, though he knew that this would be quite remote. In a draft, Goethe equates "European" with "world literature," surely provisionally. There is a well-known poem by Goethe, "Weltliteratur" (1827), which rehearses rather the delights of folk poetry and actually got its title erroneously from the editor of the 1840 posthumous edition. Today world literature may mean simply all literature, as in the title of many books, or it may mean a canon of excellent works from many languages, as when we say that this or that book or author belongs to world literature: Ibsen belongs to world literature, while Jonas Lie does not. Swift belongs to world literature, while Thomas Hardy does not.

"General literature" exists in English; e.g., James Montgomery gave Lectures on *General Literature, Poetry,* etc. (1833), where "general literature" means what we would call "theory of literature" or "principles of criticism." The Rev. Thomas Dale in 1831 became Professor of English Literature and History in the Department of General Literature and Science at King's College, London. In Germany J. G. Eichhorn edited a whole series of books called *Allgemeine Geschichte der Literatur* (1788ff.). There were similar compilations: Johann David Hartmann, *Versuch einer allgemeinen Geschichte der Poesie,* in two volumes

(1797 and 1798), and Ludwig Wachler, *Versuch einer allgemeinen Geschichte der Literatur,* in four volumes, (1793–1801), and Johann Georg Grässe's *Lehrbuch einer allgemeinen Literärgeschichte* (1837–57), an enormous bibliographical compilation.

In the 1960's Paul Van Tieghem tried to make a distinction between "comparative literature" which studies only the relations between literatures taken two at a time and "general literature" which concerns "the facts common to several literatures." It seems an artificial distinction as it would, for instance, be impossible to draw a line between the influence of Walter Scott and the rise of the historical novel. In American practice comparative literature is used to include what Van Tieghem calls general literature. The limitations of comparative literature to "relations of facts" between two literatures is a narrow conception which makes comparative literature a mere auxiliary discipline of literary history with a fragmentary, scattered subject matter. Outside of the French academic establishment comparative literature has flourished largely because it has been interpreted as a study of all literature from an international perspective independent of linguistic, ethnic, and political boundaries. It is not confined to a single method. Description, characterization, interpretation, explanation, evaluation are used in its discourse as much as comparison.

The concept of "literature," independently of its formulation in specific terms still awaits its historian. Speaking sweepingly one can say with some confidence that in older times literature or letters was understood to include all writing of any pretence and permanence. Poetry, however, was set apart, mainly due to the clear distinction made by verse and the special craft required in its practice. Prose forms as far as they were recognized were usually incorporated in rhetoric: the sermon, the didactic or philosophical treatise, historiography, and even fictional narratives. The view that there is a peculiar art of literature, a verbal art which includes poetry and prose as far as it is imaginative and thus excludes the informative statement, scientific information, and even rhetorical persuasion emerged very slowly as did the whole modern system of the arts. Such a view is manifestly impossible before the central problem of aesthetics was posed, even before the invention of the term by Baumgarten in 1735, in the discussions of taste, *je ne sais quoi, virtù,* imagination, genius and in the very term "belles lettres." It took almost a century to prepare for Kant's *Critique of Judgment* (1790), which clearly distinguished the good, the true, and the useful from the beautiful. Slowly the purely didactic and mimetic conception of poetry receded: the ancient view—as expressed, for example, in Bacon's *Advancement of Learning* (1603)

which recognized only drama and epic and ignored or slighted the lyric—yielded to a new conception in which the lyric or the song assumed the center of poetry. The shift is accomplished in different countries with diverse authors: with J. G. von Herder in Germany, G. Leopardi in Italy, and J. S. Mill in England. All these three critics disparage drama and epic in favor of lyrical poetry, often in extravagant terms. The slow rise in the prestige of the novel, long frowned upon as frivolous, collaborated in establishing a concept of literature as an art parallel to the plastic arts and music, which in former centuries had been often set apart as menial crafts.

Today three distinct meanings of "literature" prevail, if we ignore such phrases as the "literature of the subject" (i.e., the books and articles about a subject) or "campaign literature" (pamphlets). First, literature signifies the totality of literary production: everything in print; secondly, literature refers to great books, books of whatever subject, of historical impact; thirdly, literature may be more or less rigidly limited to imaginative writing. These distinctions are of considerable practical importance for writing on as well as teaching of literature and literary history. The first or widest conception allows us to study everything in print as a source for cultural history. Edwin Greenlaw argued in favor of a concept of literary history which states that "nothing related to the history of civilization is beyond our province and that we are not limited to *belles lettres* or even to printed or manuscript records in our effort to understand a period or civilization." Literary study becomes simply identical with the history of civilization or intellectual history, in which printed sources play the main part (though not the only one) as documentary evidence.

The second conception of literature defines it in terms of great books which, whatever their subject, are "notable for literary form or expression." Here the criterion is either aesthetic value alone or aesthetic value in combination with general intellectual distinction and historical impact. This is the conception of literature underlying much literary history, which may include the discussion of eminent historians, philosophers, and even scientists. This view, however, by limiting the history of imaginative literature to great books, obscures the continuity of literary tradition, the development of literary genres often from anonymous sources, and indeed the very nature of the literary process. In history, philosophy, and similar subjects, it introduces an excessively aesthetic point of view. Scientists, historians, and philosophers are singled out for their expository style or their skill in organization, with the result that the literary historian will have to prefer popularizers to the great original minds.

85

In its practical consequences the concept of literature advocated by the so-called New French critics is not so very different. They emphasize that anything is literature which challenges close interpretation, subtle reading, and rereading. Criticism and philosophy are included in the term *écriture* (Roland Barthes), a purposely inclusive term which allows the distinction between creative and critical work to disappear.

Increasingly a coherently aesthetic point of view has prevailed: the concept of literature as imaginative literature, which includes poetry and the prose forms such as the novel, and which share with poetry the basic element of fictionality and aesthetic effect. Literature in this sense corresponds to the German term *Dichtung* which is often used so broadly. Dostoevsky, who never wrote verse, is referred to as *Dichter*. In recent decades in Germany terms such as *Wortkunst* emphasize the art of literature. In Russian the term *slovesnost* (from *slovo*, "word") has this meaning of literature including what in English has been recently referred to as "oral literature." This is a *contradictio in adjecto*, in view of the derivation of literature from *littera*, but is a needed term since the oral tradition is a necessary component of any meaningful history of the verbal forms of art.

If we recognize fictionality, invention, or imagination as the distinguishing trait of literature, we think thus of literature in terms of Homer, Dante, Shakespeare, Balzac, Keats rather than of Cicero or Montaigne, Bossuet, or Emerson. Admittedly, there will be "boundary" cases, works like Plato's *Republic* to which it would be difficult to deny, at least in the great myths, passages of "invention" and "fictionality," while they are at the same time primarily works of philosophy. This conception of literature is descriptive, not evaluative. No wrong is done to a great and influential work by relegating it to rhetoric, to philosophy, to political pamphleteering, though doing so may pose problems of aesthetic analysis, of stylistics and composition, similar or identical to those presented by literature, except for the absence of the central quality of fictionality. This descriptive conception of literature will thus include in it all kinds of fiction, even the worst novel, the worst poem, the worst drama. To classify a work as belonging to literature should be distinguished from evaluation.

The distinction between literature and other forms of writing has increasingly been made in terms of the particular use made of language in literature. The main distinctions to be drawn are between the literary, the everyday, and the scientific uses of language. A discussion of this point by Thomas Clark Pollock, *The Nature of Literature* (1942), though true as far as it goes, seems not entirely satisfactory, especially in defining the distinction between literary and everyday language. The problem is crucial and by no means simple in practice, since literature, in distinction from the other arts has no medium of its own and since many mixed forms and subtle transitions undoubtedly exist. It is fairly easy to distinguish between the language of science and the language of literature. The mere contrast between "thought" and "emotion" or "feeling" is, however, not sufficient. Literature does contain thought, while emotional language is by no means confined to literature: witness a lovers' conversation or an ordinary quarrel. Still, most scientific language is primarily "denotative" insofar as it aims at a one-to-one correspondence between sign and referent. The sign is completely arbitrary, hence can be replaced by equivalent signs. The accurately defined scientific sign is also transparent; that is, without drawing attention to itself, it directs us unequivocally to its referent.

Thus scientific language tends toward an increasing use of a system of signs provided by mathematics or symbolic logic. The rationalistic philosophers' ideal is such a universal language as the *characteristica universalis* which Leibniz had begun to plan as early as the late seventeenth century. Compared to scientific language, literary language will appear to many rationalists to be in some ways deficient. It abounds in ambiguities; it is, like every other historical language, full of homonyms, arbitrary or irrational categories such as grammatical gender; it is permeated with historical accidents, memories, and associations. In a word, it is highly "connotative." Moreover, literary language is far from merely referential. It has its expressive side; it conveys the tone and attitude of the speaker or writer. And it does not merely state and express what it says; it also wants to influence the attitude of the reader, persuade him, and ultimately change him. There is a further important distinction between literary and scientific language: in the former, the sign itself, the sound symbolism of the word, is stressed. All kinds of techniques have been invented to draw attention to it, such as meter, alliteration, and patterns of sound.

These differentia of literary from scientific language may be made in different degrees by various works of literary art: for example, the sound pattern will be less important in a novel than in certain lyrical poems, impossible of adequate translation. The expressive element will be far less in an "objective novel," which may disguise and almost conceal the attitude of the writer, than in a "personal" lyric. The pragmatic element, slight in "pure" poetry, may be large in a novel with a purpose or in a satirical or didactic poem. Furthermore, the degree to which the language is intellectualized may vary considerably: there are philosophical and didactic poems and problem novels which approximate, at least occasionally, the scientific use of language. Still, whatever the mixed modes apparent upon an examination of concrete literary works of art, the distinctions between the literary use and the scientific use seem clear: literary language is far more deeply involved in the historical structure of the language; it stresses the awareness of the sign itself; it has its expressive and pragmatic side which scientific language will always want so far as possible to minimize.

More difficult to establish is the distinction between everyday and literary language. Everyday language is not a uniform concept: it includes such wide variants as colloquial language, the language of commerce, official language, the language of religion, the slang of students, and others. But obviously much that has been said about literary language holds also for the other uses of language excepting the scientific. Everyday language also has its expressive function, though this varies from a colorless official announcement to the passionate plea aroused by a moment of emotional crisis. Everyday language is full of the irrationalities and contextual changes of historical language, though there are moments when it aims at almost the precision of scientific description. Only occasionally is there awareness of the signs themselves in everyday speech. Yet such awareness does appear—in the sound symbolism of names and actions. No doubt, everyday language wants most frequently to achieve results to influence actions and attitudes. But it would be false to limit it merely to communication. A child's talking for hours without a listener and an adult's almost meaningless social chatter show that there are many uses of language which are not strictly, or at least primarily, communicative.

It is thus quantitatively that literary language is first of all to be differentiated from the varied uses of everyday discourse. The resources of language are exploited much more deliberately and systematically in literary language. In the work of a subjective poet, we have manifest a "personality" far more coherent and all-pervasive than persons as we see them in everyday situations. Certain types of poetry will use paradox, ambiguity, the contextual change of meaning, even the irrational association of grammatical categories such as gender or tense, quite deliberately. Poetic language organizes, tightens, the resources of everyday language, and sometimes does even violence to them, in an effort to force us into awareness and attention. Many of these resources a writer will find formed, and preformed, by the silent and anonymous workings of many generations. In certain highly developed literatures, and especially in certain epochs, the poet merely

uses an established convention: the language, so to speak, poeticizes for him. Still, every work of art imposes an order, an organization, a unity on its materials. This unity sometimes seems very loose, as in many sketches or adventure stories; but it increases to the complex, close-knit organization of certain poems, in which it may be almost impossible to change a word or the position of a word without impairing its total effect.

The pragmatic distinction between literary language and everyday language is much clearer. We exclude from poetry, or label as mere rhetoric, everything which persuades us to a definite outward action. Genuine poetry affects us more subtly. Art imposes some kind of framework which takes the statement of the work out of the world of everyday reality. Into our semantic analysis we thus can reintroduce some of the common conceptions of aesthetics: "disinterested contemplation," "aesthetic distance," "framing." Again, however, we must realize that the distinction between art and nonart, between literature and the nonliterary linguistic utterance, is fluid. The aesthetic function may extend to linguistic pronouncements of the most various sort. It would be a narrow conception of literature to exclude all propaganda art or didactic and satirical poetry. We have to recognize transitional or intermediate forms like the essay, biography, and much rhetorical literature. In different periods of history the realm of the aesthetic function seems to expand or to contract: the personal letter, at times, was an art form, as was the sermon, while today, in agreement with the contemporary tendency against the confusion of genres, there appears a narrowing of the aesthetic function, a marked stress on purity of art, a reaction against pan-aestheticism and its claims as voiced by the aesthetics of the late nineteenth century. It seems, however, best to consider as literature only works in which the aesthetic function is dominant, while we can recognize that there are aesthetic elements, such as style and composition, in works which have a completely different, nonaesthetic purpose, such as scientific treatises, philosophical dissertations, political pamphlets, sermons.

But the nature of literature emerges most clearly under the referential aspect. The center of literary art is obviously to be found in the traditional genres of the lyric, the epic, the drama. In all of them, the reference is to a world of fiction, of imagination. The statements in a novel, in a poem, or in a drama are not literally true; they are not logical propositions. There is a central and important difference between a statement, even in a historical novel or a novel by Balzac which seems to convey "information" about actual happenings, and the same information appearing in a book of history or sociology. Even in the subjective lyric, the "I" of the poet is a fictional, dramatic "I."

Other concepts of literature rather emphasize the difference from poetry. In Croce's *La Poesia* (1936) such a contrast is elaborated with *letteratura* signifying writing in its civilizing function, immersed in history, rhetorical, didactic, or instructive, while poetry which is not only in verse but rather corresponds to what was described above as the third meaning of literature. Imaginative literature of high quality is said to be exempt from history, timeless, without overt purpose, open only to aesthetic contemplation. Croce's conception isolates the great poets and denies literary history except as cultural history or mere annals.

Sartre's *Qu'est-ce que la littérature?* (1946) does not answer the question of the title but pleads impassionately for the didactic and rhetorical function of literature, for *littérature engagée* but allows, with some condescension, for the existence of poetry remote from social concern. The dividing line between literature and poetry is drawn in very similar terms to Croce's, even though the pathos and emphasis is directly opposite to Croce's.

In recent discussions, mainly by linguists, attempts have been made to arrive at a definition of literature which would avoid traditional aesthetic criteria such as "fictionality," "invention," "imagination." Permanence, repetition, a certain length of utterance, structural regularities not required by grammar and even "nonbanality," or what in Chomsky's terms is called "ungrammaticalness," have been suggested as the distinguishing characteristics of "literature." But not one of these criteria can withstand closer examination. Permanence can be ascribed to myths or legal documents, and the other criteria would fit many oral utterances. The problem is shifted to that of style which cannot be the single criterion distinguishing literature from nonliterary forms of discourse. The old aesthetic criteria seem still satisfactory.

Still, one should realize that the very notion of literature (and art) has been increasingly questioned in recent decades. This has to do with the breakup of aesthetics begun in the late nineteenth century, when the German aesthetics of empathy (*Einfühlung*) reduced aesthetic experience to physiological processes of inner mimicry, of feeling into the object. It is implicit in Croce's theory of intuition, in which aesthetic experience becomes identified with every act of perception of individual quality. John Dewey's *Art as Experience* (1934) denies all qualitative distinction between the aesthetic and the intellectual, in favor of a unity of experience which is simply heightened vitality. In the writings of I. A. Richards the distinction between aesthetic and other emotions is abolished and

art and poetry are reduced to means of "patterning our impulses," to tools in mental therapy. Similarly, Kenneth Burke and Richard P. Blackmur dissolve the concept of literature into action and gesture.

More recently has come an onslaught on aesthetics by some analytical philosophers who dismiss as "nonsense" the traditional problems of aesthetics (W. Elton, *Aesthetics and Language,* Oxford, 1954). In practice, in the arts, particularly in Pop-art, but also in concrete music, a deliberate attempt is being made to abolish the differences between art and nonart. Objects such as grocery boxes or water pitchers are accumulated or noises of machines, or of the streets, are produced. One hears, for example, Ihab Hassan speak of the "self-destructive element of literature, its need of self-annulment." "Perhaps the function of literature, is not to clarify the world but to help create a world in which literature becomes superfluous" (*Comparative Literature Studies,* 1 [1964], 266). Hassan quotes D. H. Lawrence against the "evil-smelling logos" and invokes his saying "Come in silence and say nothing." In France a similar questioning has become common. But there, in Maurice Blanchot's *Le Livre à venir* (1959), the appeal is rather to Hegel's saying that "art is for us something past" and to the negative aesthetics of Mallarmé, than to the ferocious antirationalism of D. H. Lawrence. Literature is supposed to have reached its "zero point," some final impasse depicted in Beckett's *Endgame.* "The death of the last writer" is envisaged with some horror and sadness, while it seems welcomed in the paradoxical celebrations of silence indulged in by the loquacious George Steiner, Susan Sontag, and Ihab Hassan. The prophecies of Marshall McLuhan sounding the knell of the Gutenberg era, parallels these moods prevalent at this moment (1970). Still, a humanist with a sense of history will doubt that literature can ever disappear as long as man wants to speak, and hence to commemorate his speech in writing and print.

BIBLIOGRAPHY

No treatment of the history of the concept of literature is known. For the term, besides dictionaries, see: Robert Escarpit, "La Définition du terme 'Littérature,'" *Actes du IIIe Congrès de l'Association Internationale de Littérature Comparée* (The Hague, 1962), 77–89. A. Archibald Hill, "A Program for the Definition of Literature," *The University of Texas Studies in English,* 37 (1958), 46–52. F. W. Householder, et al., comments in *Style in Language,* ed. Thomas A. Sebeok (New York, 1960), pp. 339–40, etc. Roman Ingarden, *Das literarische Kunstwerk* (Halle, 1931). Paul Oskar Kristeller, "The Modern System of the Arts," *Journal of the History of Ideas,* 12 (1951), 496–527, and 13 (1952), 17–46; also in *Ideas in Cultural Perspective,* eds. Philip P. Wiener and A. Noland (New Brunswick, N.J., 1962), 145–206, and in *Renaissance Thought II* (New York, 1965), pp. 163–227. Thomas C. Pollock, *The Nature of Literature* (Princeton, 1942). René Wellek, "The Name and Nature of Comparative Literature," *Comparatists at Work*, eds. Stephen G. Nichols, Jr. and Richard B. Vowles (Waltham, Mass., 1968), pp. 3–27; idem with Austin Warren, *Theory of Literature* (New York, 1949), with bibliographies. Eduard Wölfflin, "Litteratura," *Zeitschrift für lateinische Lexikographie und Grammatik*, **5** (1885), 49ff.

RENÉ WELLEK

[See also Ambiguity; Classification of the Arts; **Criticism; Motif**; Myth; **Periodization**; Style; *Ut pictura poesis*.]

LONGEVITY

1. Problems of longevity play a central part in modern debate about the human condition. This concern stems from the decline since the Renaissance of faith in supernatural salvation from death; concern with the worth of individual identity and experience has shifted from an otherworldly realm to the "here and now," with intensification of earthly expectations. One current of thought is the belief that the length of life can be extended significantly by increasing human control over natural forces, i.e., through biomedical science. In 1956, Gruman termed this concept "prolongevity." Prolongevity is a subsidiary variant of meliorism, the belief that human effort should be applied to improving the world. The antonym to meliorism is apologism, which condemns attempts to alter earthly conditions; in this essay apologism stands for the idea that prolongevity is neither possible nor desirable.

"Length of life" (or longevity) may refer to either of two different concepts. "Life expectancy" is the average expectation of life at birth (or at any specified later age), and, during the course of history, the mean expectation of life at birth has increased greatly, especially since 1800. Increased life expectancy reflects advances in controlling infectious and food-deficiency diseases, and the rate of increase seems to have reached a plateau as biomedical science operates in the area of cardiovascular diseases, cancer, and "aging."

The other meaning of length of life is "life span," the extreme limit of longevity. Statisticians estimate the maximum human life span at about 110 years; this has not increased during the course of history. The concept is valuable in challenging complacent optimism that foresees an automatic increase in longevity as a by-product of social and scientific progress. But the concept of life span is not absolute; statisticians acknowledge numerous assumptions involved in their analyses (Spiegelman, 1968), and some gerontologists believe the slope of the Gompertz curve can be changed (Strehler, 1967).

What constitutes a "significant" extension of longevity? It is helpful to take into account the scientific and philosophical background of the time. In the present era, the question focuses on the nature of the life span: the issue concerns the possibility of some medical or scientific breakthrough in the field of aging, and an increase in the healthful and productive period of life, not merely an extension of time per se.

2. It is useful first to examine apologism. Apologist thought is based not only on assumptions as to the *possible* but also includes value judgments concerning the desirable. A statement that, at the present time old age and death are inevitable, almost always goes on to make a virtue of necessity. In a curious way, this concern provides a basis for the optimism of prolongevity. Indifference to aging and death would be much more subversive to prolongevitism. In contemporary Western culture, a crisis concerning death occurs about the age of five; later the problem is suppressed from consciousness. Of pertinence is the concept of "cognitive dissonance": after reaching an uncomfortable decision, an individual will subconsciously refashion his beliefs to support its "reasonableness."

In myth and legend, Gilgamesh exemplifies recurrent apologist ideas; rebellion against mortal fate is futile, and man should concentrate on immediate enjoyments of this life. Hellenic apologist themes are provided in Hesiod: Prometheus is punished directly, and mankind is chastised by Pandora, who brings a "jar" with old age and death. Hesiod also presents the legend of Tithonus, one condemned to suffer the infirmities of age forever. This theme appears frequently (Juvenal, Swift, Tennyson, Wilde, A. Huxley). According to Frazer, comparative folklore indicates the Hebrew Eden myth originally revolved entirely on immortality, but the written version is more apologist and concerned with salvation from evil.

In Greco-Roman philosophy, Epicureanism and Stoicism emphasize attainment of serenity by developing a proper attitude towards death. Lucretius argues that it is childish to believe that the dead suffer. The key to Epicurean apologism is the "fullness of pleasure"; without belief in progress, there is nothing to look forward to, and prolongevity is not desirable. Marcus Aurelius carries Stoicism to an ascetic position, advising one to think often about death and despise the body.

The gerontological thought of Aristotle, Galen, and Avicenna is apologist in tendency. "Innate moisture" (like the oil of a lamp) burns out, and the body becomes cold and dry. The cold-dry hypothesis of senescence is not, of itself, apologist. But in Aristotle's cosmology, the contrast between decay on earth (four elements) and the eternal celestial bodies (fifth element) is too great, so that Galen recoils from the "impiety" of prolongevitism. Also the teleological bent of Aristotle leads to the precept that nature does everything for the best; therefore, Galen asserts old age cannot be a "disease." Avicenna's theological commitments incline him to state the physician's role is "not the art of . . . securing the utmost longevity possible."

In religion, Buddhism seems thoroughly apologist, but there are bases for prolongevity, e.g., Tantrism. As to Hinduism, Vedanta, and Yoga, most scholars focus on apologist interpretations, but another can assert India provides "the best Oriental example of prolongevitism." Apologist statements in Taoist religion and philosophy did not prevent the flourishing of a prolongevity school. The Bible is predominantly apologist, but the Old Testament does value long life on earth as a reward to the righteous (Job 42:16–17).

Thomas Aquinas' explanation of death blends Aristotelianism with Christianity (*Summa theologica* 1. 3, qu. 97, art. 1 and 2. 2, qu. 164, art. 1). A supernatural power bestowed on Adam's soul by divine grace kept the opposing elements in harmony. After original sin, the body is abandoned to sexual lust, old age, and death. Later, some proponents of prolongevity seek to reassert the rule of mind over body (Godwin, G. B. Shaw). Also significant for prolongevity is Augustine's theory of history (*The City of God*, Book 12, sec. 13–17) as a meaningful process which involves salvation from death: "The last enemy to be destroyed is death" (I Corinthians 15:26).

3. Prolongevity legends may be divided into three groups. First is the "antediluvian": that people lived much longer in the past. In Genesis 5, 9:29 are spans as high as 969 years (Methuselah). Antediluvian traditions are subsidiary variants of primitivism.

The "hyperborean" theme is based on Greek legends of long-lived people in the North. The Greeks also had Isles of the Blest, usually in the Atlantic. "Hyperborean" legends are significant in China, because they strengthened Taoist prolongevitism. The most vivid hyperborean-type legends were Celtic: a land of youth in Western islands, and a "magic cauldron" (the medieval Holy Grail). Such legends stimulated exploration; e.g., Columbus' search for a new route to the East.

The "fountain" theme is typified by the Fountain of Youth. This story has been traced to the Hindu legend of Cyavana (before 700 B.C.) which blended with Hebrew legends, the Christian Fountain of Life, and Greek legends of Glaukus, who became immortal by eating a marvelous herb. Alexander the Great's search for a fountain in the East, in Arabic legend, features el Khidr, "the Green One," modeled on Glaukus (Koran, Sura 18:61–95). The Alexander legend attained finest expression in twelfth-century French romance, and, by the time of Ponce de León, Spanish explorers certainly might think of a fountain of youth in "the Indies." Aside from the waters of a fountain, there are mentioned in folklore a multitude of other substances with the power of prolonging life because of divine, magical, or empirical properties.

Miscellaneous prolongevity themes include the challenging phoenix theme that there exist animals enjoying greater length of life than man, and the Endymion theme that youth might be preserved by trance-like sleep.

4. In regard to prolongevity, there is a striking contrast between China and the West. In ancient Western civilization, there are religious and magic forms of prolongevity and examples of natural prolongevity: but these tendencies remain fragmentary, while in China they occupy a central position. As Max Weber observed, Taoism for the first time in history fashioned the vagaries of prolongevity magic and folklore into a rationalized and disciplined system.

Lao Tzu, Chuang Tzu, and Lieh Tzu provided an intellectual framework for Chinese prolongevity (350–250 B.C.). First, the *tao* (the basic natural process) is a single force. Distinctions between various phenomena remain blurred; this supports "transformation"; a human can change into an immortal *hsien*. Second, "naturalistic pantheism" (Needham) endows every individual with a spark of the divine. Third, mysticism urges communion with the vivifying *tao*. Fourth, "effortless action" conserves vital forces and bestows remarkable powers over nature. Fifth, primitivism glorifies primeval sages, immune to aging.

Institutional forms for prolongevitism were contributed by the Taoist religion (A.D. 184). The priesthood tried to lead every member into the practice of prolongevity techniques—a gigantic health cult. As the techniques became more complex, the pursuit of immortality became restricted to monasteries. This breakdown in communication between adept and lay members caused the decline of religious Taoism. The adepts underwent a sort of indirect apotheosis ("deliverance of the corpse"); prolongevity techniques change the body to imperishable substance, and the *hsien* abandons the "cocoon." Another analogy is to the development of an embryo in the womb.

There were four major physiological techniques for prolongevity. Respiratory techniques are central because of the possibility of contact with the heavens. The long-term goal is to get enough nourishment from the spirit-like air to dispense with grains, the products of earth. It was believed the stomach extracts an essence or "breath" from foods, and this food-breath can be replaced by the more spiritual airbreath. Dietary techniques are associated with respiratory ones; grains and many other foods are prohibited. Drama is added by an enemy inside the vital centers: the "Three Worms" explain conflicts and dreams. Anoxia is complicated by malnutrition, and it is necessary to use *hsien* medicines. The adept tries to ingest substances richest in *tao*-like essence. Taoist gymnastics definitely influenced Western medicine. The purposes of the exercises are to aid the circulation of the breath and "essence" (respiratory and sexual techniques).

Taoists encouraged controlled sexual activity to increase yet conserve the *ching*, identified with semen and menstruum but ethereal. Observing that these become scanty in the aged, Taoists assumed that retention of the *ching* is revivifying. It is necessary to bring many partners to orgasm, while the adept himself "returns the *ching* to the brain" (manually blocking the urethra). Despite the secular semblance of such techniques, adepts usually were religious and believed material transformation must be accompanied by moral and spiritual improvement.

Historians are coming to recognize the significance of Chinese contributions to Western science and technology, and these achievements owe much to Taoism motivated by the desire for prolongevity.

5. Chinese alchemy was tied to Taoism: about ten percent of the titles in the Taoist scriptures refer to alchemy. Characteristic of Chinese alchemy is its dedication to prolongevity, seen in Ko Hung (ca. A.D. 320) who assumes everyone agrees on the *desirability* of longer life. His concern is the *possibility* of prolongevity, and he edges toward an idea of progress. Everything includes some vital spirit, and alchemy prepares substances rich in "essence" for increasing the life-force. Cinnabar (mercuric sulphide) has reactions which can suggest survival powers. Instead of "dead" ashes, the application of heat produces a shuttling from a "living" (red) mineral to a "living" (fluid) metal. Ko Hung details the preparation of "sublime" cinnabar which can cause immortality.

The first systematic alchemy in the West (Alexandria, ca. fourth century) evolved in a way somewhat similar to the Chinese; instead of Taoism, there is Neo-Platonism. But Owsei Temkin finds little significant association between Hellenistic alchemy and medicine. The first medical alchemy in the West appears in Arabic writings, especially those ascribed to Jabir (eighth century). Indeed, the literature of Arabic alchemy includes such vivid biomedical imagery that the lack of explicit concern with prolongevity poses an intriguing problem for students of comparative history.

Latin alchemy, personified by Roger Bacon, is the first systematic prolongevitism in Western civilization. Bacon consciously opposes the traditional regimen of Galen and Avicenna which aimed to "protect" the aged; Bacon desires to "free" them. He suggests one might attain 150 years, and later generations might reach three to five centuries. His explanation of aging is similar to that of Avicenna (decay of "innate" moisture), but the process can be reversed.

Paracelsus is the last of the great alchemists; deeply concerned with the prolongation of life, he organizes iatrochemistry and directs it towards chemotherapy.

6. Luigi Cornaro's *Discorsi della vita sobria* (1558) represents a Renaissance combination of Cicero's idealization of senescence and a simplified Galenic regimen. *Anyone* can expect a span of 100 to 120 years of healthy, happy life. The *Discorsi* are suffused with a *joie de vivre* unknown in comparable Greco-Roman writings.

Cornaro's *Discorsi* serve as the prototype of "prolongevity hygiene": the belief that longevity can be extended significantly by simple reforms in the individual's habits of life. The primitivist assumption that man is long-lived "by nature" was reinforced by credulity about supercentenarians; e.g., Harvey's autopsy report on Thomas Parr (d. 1635), who, according to the physiologist, had attained nearly 153 years. The romantic physician Christoph Wilhelm Hufeland (*Art of Prolonging Life*, 1796) aims at 200 years via preservation of a "vital power" (analogous to electromagnetism); also he cites the "law" of comparative biology of Albrecht von Haller that an animal lives eight times as long as its period of growth.

The individualism and simplistic pathology underlying prolongevity hygiene were eroded by the rise of social hygiene and the development of sophisticated etiological concepts and powerful therapeutic methods (Shryock, 1936). And William J. Thoms (*Human Longevity*, 1873) established criteria which effectively challenged the validity of traditional cases of supercentenarianism.

7. With the idea of progress, prolongevity makes its way to the center of the stage in Western civilization. According to Becker (*Heavenly City* . . . , pp. 119ff.), the great ideas of the Enlightenment are based on a secularization of the Christian drama of salvation, its transformation into advance towards a "heaven" on earth. No sooner does man's confidence in supernatural salvation begin to weaken than energies are diverted to an intensified effort to lengthen life.

Although Descartes differs from Bacon on methodology, he holds similar views in favor of meliorism, including prolongevity. In the concluding section of the *Discourse on Method* (1637), he pledges his talent to finding ways of retarding or overcoming senescence. Buoyed by confidence in his philosophic method, he has an intense desire to lengthen his life, and there is evidence that at times he hopes to gain for himself 100 to 500 years (Gruman [1966], pp. 77–80). At other times, he is torn by deep religious conflicts and favors apologist ideas.

With the triumph of Newtonian science, the writings of Francis Bacon took on a sort of prophetic sanctity which gave new prestige to prolongevity, the "most noble" goal of medicine. In the *Advancement of Learning* (1605) he admonishes physicians to cherish this part of their work, and in the *New Atlantis* (1624) he depicts his savants adding to longevity, experimenting in resuscitation of persons "dead in appearance," and replacing vital organs. By comparison, his *History of Life and Death* (1623) is disappointingly unoriginal.

Esteemed by Condorcet as "the modern Prometheus," Benjamin Franklin witnessed so many "advances" that he felt a strong desire for greater longevity and expected science to prolong life *beyond* the patriarchal 969 years. Franklin speculated about anabiosis (as did the surgeon John Hunter who attempted to preserve animals by freezing them), and he encouraged research into resuscitation of persons apparently dead (Gruman [1966], pp. 83–84). The Enlightenment movement for resuscitation attained institutional form in the Humane Societies, pioneers of artificial respiration and other "heroic measures" of modern medicine.

The *Enquiry Concerning Political Justice* (1793) of William Godwin includes the idea that a "free" individual can exert the supremacy of mind over matter and bring bodily processes under conscious, rational control. Life will be lengthened by one's cultivating benevolent and optimistic attitudes and a clear, well-ordered state of mind (cf. Aristotelian "harmony"). Bodily processes increasingly can be made subject to the will until sleep, aging, and death are banished. In reply, Malthus' *Essay on the Principle of Population* (1798) not only disparages the possibility of significant control of body by mind but also raises the spectre of overpopulation.

In his *History of the Progress of the Human Mind* (1795) and his unpublished commentaries on Bacon's *New Atlantis*, M. J. de Condorcet envisions an almost limitless extension of longevity through improvement of the environment, inheritance of acquired characteristics, and a comprehensive program of scientific research supported by the government. The last proposition is the most important, for Condorcet realizes the limitations of eighteenth-century medicine and looks to the future for the reliable data needed for prolongevity. Malthus (*Essay . . .* , 1798) criticizes all

three points and attacks Condorcet's advocacy of birth control. Also Malthus points out (as Becker does later) that the *philosophes* are not skeptics but men of faith, and he attacks (as neo-orthodox writers still do) the injustice of progress which benefits only some future generation of supermen. But the essentials of modern beliefs about prolongevity had become widespread by the time of Condorcet; Napoleon could state in 1817 that, viewing the progress of science, a way will be "found to prolong life indefinitely."

8. Most utopian works include at least a brief reference to prolongevity; however, such remarks are limited. One might think utopians would be the most radical of prolongevitists, but this is not the case, nor should it be if one defines utopianism as the belief that a near-perfect society can be introduced *quickly* by means which are already *available*. By accepting these conditions, utopians focus attention more on changing internal attitudes than external conditions. Inhabitants of utopian communities are depicted as not *suffering* from infirmities of age, but this often is due to their acceptance of the "inevitable." However, there also are utopian writers who are strongly prolongevitist: e.g., J. A. Etzler, *The Paradise Within the Reach of All Men* (1833).

If utopians are not as prolongevitist as usually thought, the romantics have undergone an opposite distortion by intellectual historians who associate romanticism with the cult of death. There are inclinations toward prolongevity in romantic writings by Goethe, Shelley, E. Darwin, C. W. Hufeland, and even Novalis, and there are romantic tendencies in the prolongevitist thought of Kirk, Reade, Metchnikoff, and Stephens. The most far-reaching romantic prolongevitist is Nicholas F. Fyodorov (1828–1903)—his writings began to circulate about 1868 and a collection was published posthumously as *The Philosophy of the Common Task* (1906). Fyodorov calls for a fusion of Christian ethics and scientific methods to bring about complete salvation from death (including resurrection): recent philosophers consider it possible that "future science will recognize Fyodorov as a 'prophet' of its own achievements" (Edie, et al., 1965).

The idea of progress was given renewed vigor by Darwinism, and the cautious Darwin himself pictures a future "progress towards perfection." However, just as Social Darwinists divide into apologists and meliorists, so also in biomedicine there is a division. The apologist spokesman August Weismann, who claims senescence is essential to the evolution of higher species, influenced the psychoanalytic concept of a "death instinct" (see Freud, *Beyond the Pleasure Principle*, Sec. 6). The best known meliorist was Élie Metchnikoff who argues that man can overcome "premature" aging by cell-stimulating sera and by combatting "toxic" intestinal bacteria. Others in the prolongevity group included William Sweetser (*Human Life*, 1867); Wynnewood Reade (*The Martyrdom of Man*, 1872), who faces the ethical problem of "expendable" generations in progress towards a super-race; Hyland Kirk (*The Possibility of Not Dying*, 1883); and C. A. Stephens (*Natural Salvation*, 1903), who states clearly the religious origins of his prolongevitism and attempted to establish the first institute of gerontology.

Prolongevity is a standard theme in Marxist literature. The Soviet government has encouraged prolongevitism, and the first international gerontology conference was held at Kiev in 1938. However, in communist thought there appears also a subordination of the individual to the collective, and the longevity of a person (or even a generation) may be sacrificed.

No school of prolongevity thought has been so controversial as the one which attempts to secure a return to youth by repairing deficiencies in sex-gland function. Already in Taoism (see above) there had been efforts to retain sexual fluids. More specific to mid-nineteenth-century France was the Comtean (positivist) doctrine that conservation of a sexual substance would strengthen body and mind. A biomedical basis for this was provided by experimental investigations by Claude Bernard and his successor Brown-Séquard whose announcement (1889) that he had injected himself with testicular extracts caused a phenomenal increase of interest in internal secretions and established a basis for modern endocrinology (Olmsted, 1946). Serge Voronoff in 1922 caused a new sensation with his claims for successful grafting of ape and monkey testes; the idea of organ transplants has continued.

In the twentieth century, the most important developments are the rapid creation of the specialties of geriatrics and gerontology, the accelerating rate of research on all aspects of aging, and the increasing private and public support for this research. Some developments in biomedical research relevant to prolongevity are: "immortality" of tissue cultures, prolongation of life by underfeeding or cooling, studies of atherosclerosis, isolation of "status quo" hormones, discovery of protective action of glycerol and dimethyl sulphoxide in freezing (the "cryonics" movement and the first interment at ultra-low temperature in 1967).

In the modern dilemma about longevity, P. B. Medawar (1960) points out that nature is "indifferent" with regard to aging. The "worth" of the individual is not so much a fact as a goal; i.e., a product of meliorism. And social scientists find that meliorism is an essential part of modern culture. This meliorism is causing an "aging population" (which, in turn, causes increased biomedical research). In 1900 in the United States there were 3 million persons over sixty-five years of age, 4 per cent of the population. By 1975 it is estimated the number of the aged will be 21 million, about 10 per cent of the population (U.S. Bureau of Census, 1967). In a "welfare state," society, of necessity, is committed to prolongevity. Indeed, it may be argued (A. Harrington), that such a society risks spiritual disintegration if it wavers in the struggle against suffering and death.

BIBLIOGRAPHY

The most comprehensive historical study is G. J. Gruman, *A History of Ideas About the Prolongation of Life: The Evolution of Prolongevity Hypotheses to 1800* (Philadelphia, 1966), with documentation and bibliographical lists; in most libraries this work will be listed under "American Philosophical Society," (*Transactions*, N. S. **56**, 9). The best history of gerontology and geriatrics is M. D. Grmek, *On Aging and Old Age* (The Hague, 1958). An exhaustive series is N. W. Shock, ed., *A Classified Bibliography of Gerontology and Geriatrics* (Stanford, 1951ff.). See also G. J. Gruman, "An Introduction to Literature on the History of Gerontology," *Bulletin of the History of Medicine*, **31** (1957), 78–83; and R. L. Grant, "Concepts of Aging: An Historical Review," *Perspectives in Biology and Medicine*, **6** (1963), 443–78. On statistical concepts, see M. Spiegelman, *Introduction to Demography* (Cambridge, Mass., 1968). On theories of aging, see A. Comfort, *Ageing: The Biology of Senescence* (New York, 1964). On prolongevity in China, see J. Needham, *Science and Civilization in China* (Cambridge, 1954ff.). On Arabic medical alchemy, see P. Kraus, *Jabir ibn Hayyan*, 2 vols. (Cairo, 1943); and O. Temkin, "Medicine and Graeco-Arabic Alchemy," *Bulletin of the History of Medicine*, **29** (1955), 134–53. On Latin prolongevity alchemy, see R. P. Multhauf, "John of Rupescissa and the Origin of Medical Chemistry," *Isis*, **45** (1954), 359–67; and W. Pagel, *Paracelsus* (Basel and New York, 1958); and also writings of A. G. Debus. On Enlightenment prolongevity, see C. L. Becker, *The Heavenly City of the Eighteenth-Century Philosophers* (New Haven, 1932); and R. H. Shryock, *The Development of Modern Medicine* (Philadelphia and London, 1936). On Fyodorov and a selection from his writings, see J. M. Edie, et al., ed., *Russian Philosophy*, Vol. 3, (Chicago, 1965), 11–54. On radical prolongevitism, see R. C. W. Ettinger, *The Prospect of Immortality* (New York, 1964); and A. Harrington, *The Immortalist* (New York, 1969). See also J. M. D. Olmsted, *Charles-Édouard Brown-Séquard* (Baltimore, 1946); P. B. Medawar, *The Future of Man* (New York, 1960); and remarks by B. L. Strehler in "Mortality Trends and Projections," *Transactions of the Society of Actuaries*, **19** (1967), D428–D493.

GERALD J. GRUMAN

[See also Alchemy; **Death; Health and Disease;** Primitivism; Progress; Sin and Salvation; Utopia.]

LOVE

Definition. "There are so many sorts of love that one does not know where to seek a definition of it. The name 'love' is given boldly to a caprice of a few days' duration; to a sentiment devoid of esteem; to a casual liaison; to the affectations of a 'cicisbeo'; to a frigid habit; to a romantic fantasy; to relish followed by prompt disrelish; yes, people give this name to a thousand chimeras" (Voltaire, *Encyclopédie*, art. "Amour"; see Schneider, I, 73).

Chimeras or realities, there are five distinguishable groups of ideas here which have been called "love" in Western civilization at various times or simultaneously: (1) the generative principle of the Cosmos, hence the very being of God (creativity); (2) friendship, the attachment to other creatures, the yearning for others (benevolent, educative, transformative, admiring, and exalting) or for concrete or ideal things (an active attitude); (3) the emotional attraction, the effects in man of a power which "possesses him," a physiological, psychological, or mythical force (a passive attitude); (4) the torment of a passion willfully chosen, the artificial devices and "perversions" of eroticism, desire cultivated for its own sake (culture); (5) sexual relations, procreative and generic desire (instinct).

These are the "ideas of love," ranging from the divine to the sexual, which we shall try to distinguish in this article by describing the most typical of their successive manifestations in the history of Western civilization.

The Method of this Article and its Limits. Whatever can be said about love through the ages is based on discourse on love, for what love "really" is must escape us. Surely multitudes have loved without having even dreamed of writing about it. It is, for all that, doubtful that they have "loved" very differently from the way love is spoken of in stone inscriptions, poems, songs, and then the books of their time; or else, they were not aware of it and had no "idea" of love; it will not be possible therefore, to talk about it in such cases.

It is often very difficult to decide whether an author quoted on love (e.g., Plato or the Marquis de Sade) is representative of his time, or whether we picture his time according to our interpretation of the author; we lack nonliterary verifications of the love customs of the times in particular countries and classes. Furthermore, how sure are we that these historico-genetic categories are relevant to our topic? After all, in an article of this kind we are exploring the meaning of an idea "for us" rather than some hypothetical "meaning-in-itself-for-some person or other." The latter meaning would be interesting only by way of contrast or similarity to our own reactions. So much for the first limitation on objectivity.

The second limitation: any definition of love which would not convey the signs of a basic emotion aroused by the mere enunciation of this word would be radically inadequate because it would be ruined by an objectivity fatal to the real meaning of the term.

Ancient Greece provided the sole language which exercises a verifiable influence on all the modes of expression associated with the idea of love in the West. Not only are all the varieties of amorous experience foreshadowed and anticipated in the Greeks—but also a strange unity, that is to say, everything that Western man for twenty-five centuries was able to see or feel as common to what are at times radically heterogeneous experiences, which he designates by the same word.

There are numerous words in Greek which stand for the diverse forms of friendship (*philia* or *philotes*): kindness among creatures of the same race (*physike*); benevolence towards guests (*xenike*); the mutual attachment of friends (*hetairike*); sexual desire (*erotike*). This last form of friendship is close to *Eros*, a love of feeling or passion which ennobles the soul and "makes a poet even of a bumpkin" (Euripides), a love especially appropriate among men, whereas the voluptuous relations between men and women derive from Aphrodite (*aphros*, foam, sperm), the dark, cruel, chthonic (infernal) goddess, very like the Babylonian Ishtar.

The Greeks established very clear distinctions between these diverse natures of *philia* or *eros*, on the one hand, and, on the other, *agapē* or disinterested affection (a term with a promising future in Christianity), *storge* or tenderness, *eunoia* or good will, *charis* or the love of gratitude. Plato placed frenzied or unchained passion on as high a level as *enthousiasmos*, that is, divine possession, while Plutarch, on the contrary, saw in it a form of mental disease: "certain people think it is a madness."

The common denominator of these dozen or more terms is an attraction, in some instances, physical or physiological, in others, more moral or more sentimental. Let us examine the usage made of this very rich lexicon by Greek thinkers.

For Heraclitus (end of the sixth century B.C.) and Empedocles (fifth century B.C.), fathers of our Western philosophy, love is not a sentiment but the physical principle of the universe and its unifying agent. (We must understand "physical" in the modern scientific sense, and not in the banal sense of a purely sexual attraction, said to be "purely physical.") There are two forces in the cosmos: attraction and repulsion. Heraclitus held that *harmonia*, his name for love, results from the tension of opposites: "What is opposed, cooperates, and from conflict arises the most beautiful harmony. Everything is done through discord." Empedocles, on the contrary, held that similars attract similars, but the result of the process of attraction is the same:

Things never cease continually changing places, at one time all uniting in one through Love, at another each borne in different directions by the repulsion of Strife. Thus, it is their nature to grow out of many, and to become many once more when the one is parted asunder . . . (Schneider, I, 23).

This problem of the Same and the Other, of the One and the Many—as fundamental for all Western philosophy as for Hindu wisdom (although they have solved the problem in opposite ways)—is of course located at the center of Plato's thought. In Plato, the problem takes the form of opposition between the Singular and the "infinite Dyad," and of their final reconciliation in an eternal unity: Love is the agent of this dialectic and this unifying function is its very definition.

Though love is the basis of all moral and spiritual progress—as it is for Plato and for his teacher Socrates—and is even the very specific instinct of immortality and universality, it must be qualified by the condition that in and through love the search for the good of the person loved always prevails over the sexual instinct. However, this qualification cannot be applied to marriage which has no other end than to produce children in families for the State. (Aristotle added later that "man does not unite with a woman solely for procreation, but also for seeking what is indispensable to exist. . . . That is why in this sort of affection, the useful is joined to the agreeable" (*Nicomachean Ethics* VIII, 12, 7). The true *eros*, for Plato, is one which drives men and boys to embrace: "This bachelor Plato conceives a love between a man and a woman profound only when it exists outside of and in violation of the laws of marriage" (Flacelière, p. 162).

The theory of a primordial androgynous creature, whose two halves after separation seek each other (Aristophanes' speech in the *Symposium*), is not expressed without Plato's critical comments. He thus has Diotima address herself to Socrates: ". . . to my mind the object of love is neither a half nor a whole." True love tends to "a creation of the beautiful, whether of body or soul. . . . The union of man and woman is a creative art, and in this act there is something of the divine; there is even in this living creature, though mortal, a quality of immortality present in fertility and procreation." However, spiritual and philosophical fertility remains the superior attribute of true *eros*, which can only be the love of boys, extramarital love, or chaste love. Eros had his statue in the temple of Diana, goddess of virginity, and he was especially known as the enemy of Aphrodite—his mother!

In the order of ideas it is very certain that the Platonic conception has dominated the whole development of European civilization, despite some isolated cases of resistance; Plato's idea surely constitutes the main Greek contribution to what may be called "the metaphysics" of love (Flacelière, p. 222).

Assuredly there is little chance that the mind of a genius like Plato should simply answer to the social condition of his people and his time. It took nearly two thousand years for the Florentine Renaissance to make this esoteric philosopher and his doctrine symbolic of Greek thought and the Greek idea of love. "Esoteric" here refers to that essential part of Plato's work which he taught only to the students of the Academy, and which was neither published nor even written; a fact that has been shown by K. Gaiser (1963).

Aristotle's Lyceum, with his "economical" theory of marriage, and Epicurus' Garden, with his theory (expressed so remarkably later by Lucretius' *De rerum natura*, IV) of the dissociation of baneful pain and beneficent pleasure, were both radically opposed to Plato's Academy, but they only the better interpret the moral and emotional facts of daily life in Greek society. The hedonist Aristippus of Cyrene says of his mistress Lais: "She doesn't love me? Why should I care? I don't think that wine or fish have any love for me, and yet I consume them with pleasure."

The fact remains that Plato acts on us as our heredity, a sort of chromosomal "information." Was it not an inborn or hereditary Platonism which came to life again in the love courtship (*cortezia*) of the troubadours, the love which ennobles, which lives in violation of matrimonial rules, and, whether chaste or not, is liberated from the procreative instinct? Plato, who could be read perhaps by one out of a thousand Greeks, is nonetheless one of the detectors (in the chemical sense) or indicators (in the sociological sense) privileged to reveal the condition of Western man. Moreover, as José Ortega y Gasset has said, "It is impossible to tell to what deep levels of the Western mind Platonic notions have penetrated. The simplest sort of person regularly employs expressions and betrays views which are derived from Plato" (*Estudios sobre el amor*, 1939). Illustrating Ortega's remark, we call unwitting or innocent Platonists all those—from German romanticism to recent popular poetry—who speak of "soul brother or sister," "the fusion of souls" in "the ecstasy of love" in which lovers believe they are "joined as One," and those who describe themselves as being loved by their "better half." We may also include those who have proposed an article on the "Idea of Love," and the author who writes the article.

Though the Platonic idea of love is resolutely positive, creative, edifying, and idealistic, it would be wrong to infer that the Greeks did not know the dark and sombre couple Eros-Thanatos, love and death:

Three myths, in fact, show us that the Greeks meditated on the mysterious relations between love and death, well before the courtly Middle Ages and the romance of Tristan and Isolde which contains moreover so many reminiscences of antiquity: Orpheus and Eurydice, Admetus and Alcestis, Protesilaus and Laodamia (Flacelière, p. 54).

Orpheus and Eurydice served as the model for the other two stories. It seems that these three myths illustrate also the dream or the ideal of "love stronger than death," more so than the passion of "the love of death" which is, as we shall see, the secret of Tristan. Or, let us at most admit that in Greek mythology the theme of mortal passion is virtually present, like the black point in the white part of yin and the white point in the black part of yang.

Two Latin poets seem to have had some idea of love such as we experience it, both exalting personal attachment "until death" (but we must insist again that this attachment is not *for* death). Propertius inaugurates a great theme of love rhetoric:

A great love goes beyond the shores of death.

Tibullus, in his Sixth Elegy, expresses a new sentiment for his time, which comes close to matrimonial love, when he addresses his mistress:

Let me gaze upon you when the hour comes for me
That, dying, with my feeble hand I hold thee.

(*Te spectem, suprema mihi cum venerit hora,
Te teneam moriens deficiente manu.*)

Five centuries after Plato, Plutarch praised marriage for love in the highest terms: "The physical union with one's wife is a source of friendship; it is like sharing a great mystery together" (*hierōn megalōn*). A contemporary of Plutarch, Saint Paul, had written on his part that marriage is a "great mystery" (*mysterion mega*).

This meeting of minds, before the Gospels had been composed, is all the more surprising insofar as Saint Paul in his Epistles constantly denounced both Jewish and pagan (especially Hellenistic-Roman) sacrament as coming under the category of law in contrast to the "freedom of the children of God." The key to the mystery, to which he alludes above, does not lie in Delphos (where Plutarch was one of the high priests), for it does not have nor can it have a key at all, because it designates a human condition whose spiritual significance lies "buried with Christ, in God." Saint Paul's revolution is contained in his proclamation that "all things are lawful unto me, but all things are not expedient . . ." (I Corinthians 6:12), referring to the totality

of prohibitions and taboos, the system of sexual taboos being foremost always, and in all religions *except that of Christ*. However, in the same Epistle, Saint Paul again inveighs against lewdness and incontinence, and goes on to write that it is good for man not to have any contact with woman. Sexual relations thus remained taboo for him—though not for the Evangelists; therein is the source of the passionate contradictions into which he fell as soon as he approached the topic, clearly associated with his neurosis. This first "secularization" of ethics came about through a substitution of Grace for the Law, as though God's love permitted one thereafter to dispense with all religious strictures imposed by priest, prince, or custom—the magic of sovereignty, power, and fertility according to the trinity of fundamental Indo-European values, so thoroughly investigated by G. Dumézil (1968). This revolutionary and secular liberation is given complete expression by Saint Augustine's dictum: *dilige et fac quod vis,* or "love and do what you will" (*Super epistulam Johannis,* quoted by Abélard in his *Sic et non*).

The paradox of Christianity is that this religion of love declares that "God is love," yet has no code of love, no sexual rites, and no eroticism either sacred or profane. As distinct from the great Asiatic religions, Christianity gives little or no importance to sexual love or sentimental love, in short, to *eros,* and antithetically bestows the highest rank on active love or *agapē.*

The Gospels never confuse these two terms as twentieth-century Occidentals think it "quite natural" to do. If we wish to recover the true sense of *agapē,* we must first see clearly the radical contrast between Jesus' use of this word and our current use of the word "love" which stands for sexuality as well as for the feeling or action for others' welfare.

If *eros* had been in the eyes of Christ *the* sin above all, as it became for certain Church Fathers, for the more or less Gnostic ascetics, for the medieval clergy, for the puritans of all faiths, and subsequently for the devout bourgeois starting from the first third of the nineteenth century, it would have been logical that some sort of sexual temptation should overshadow all those that Satan made Jesus experience in the desert; but the Evangelists do not say anything about this.

The phrase "she loved exceedingly" does not mean that Mary Magdalene had a great many clients as a prostitute, but refers to the disinterested act—sacrificing a high priced perfume—in favor of a human being in order to honor the Spirit in him. "She will be pardoned for much" means that *agapē* wipes out the prejudice against the profession and socially degraded condition of a prostitute. But this phrase perhaps also implies, when addressed to quasi-Essene disciples, a certain reflection on their asceticism, on their pseudo-

Manichaean conviction that sexuality is equivalent to sinfulness.

The definition of *agapē* occurs in the parable of the Good Samaritan (Luke 10:29–37). To the question, "and who is my neighbor?" Jesus in effect answers, him for whom you can do something in particular and who expects it from you. That *agapē* is an act and not a sentiment is also the result of two sentences (Leviticus 19:8 and Deuteronomy 6:5), united in one by Jesus: "Thou shalt love the Lord thy God and thy neighbor as thyself" (Matthew 22:35–40). For one cannot command or order a feeling, but one can prescribe an act.

Finally, Saint Paul's statement: "Husbands, love your wives, even as Christ also loved the Church . . ." (Ephesians 5:25) raises marriage to the level of highest love (against the general opinion of the Greeks and of religious Asia) and makes matrimonial love in all its aspects—sexual, social, and personal—a form of spiritual existence.

With all that, there is no ethics other than the Beatitudes, in which love does not enter; there is no mystical or practiced ritualistic or pedagogical eroticism, and even less of sexual or matrimonial casuistry.

It is an especially disturbing fact that the Christian doctrine and the doctors of the Church have not remarked the phenomena of love and said nothing about its meaning. All that we find in patristic literature concerning marriage and the family strikes us by its low level. Saint Methodus' treatise *The Feast of the Ten Virgins* is pitifully banal. It amounts to a description of physiological processes and to an exaltation of virginity. But no problem of sex or of marriage is explored by it. As to Saint Augustine's treatise, it is almost unreadable, exhaling as it does so much of bourgeoisdom (N. Berdyaev [1935], p. 300).

Berdyaev explains this last word by adding the following note: "Saint Augustine's attitude towards the woman who was his companion for sixteen years and by whom he had a child witnesses the mediocrity of his ideas of love" (ibid.).

What impresses and scandalizes Berdyaev is the fact that the Church Fathers' treatises on sex and marriage "are treatises on the organization of generic life and remind one singularly of dissertations on child-rearing. Personal destiny and love are completely lacking in their works. Nobody mentions the phenomenon of love which is radically distinct from the physiological phenomenon of sexual satisfaction and from the social phenomenon of the family life of the species." Now though it is true that "love by its essence signifies destruction and choice" and that it "proceeds from a person to a person" (Berdyaev, p. 244)—and that observation should be applied in the first place to matrimonial love—it is nonetheless true that in the course

of the first millennium of the Christianization of the Near East and the West, this form of *personal* love does not seem to have played any practical, legal, or even psychological role. Marriage was certainly a sacrament, but it linked two inheritances and two families, clans, ranks, and procreators, not two persons. It was indeed no more than a social sacrament, a sort of demographic relation, a mystery of fertility, "religious" in the sociological sense of Émile Durkheim, and devised solely for the welfare of the species. From the fourth to the twelfth century, love as antiquity knew it was eclipsed, and the love which we think to be only "natural" and "as old as mankind" does not yet appear, directly or indirectly, in any historical indication or in any documentary proof of its existence in Europe during this period.

With the twelfth century came a complete change. As the witty sally of the French historian, Charles Seignobos, put it: "Love is an invention of the twelfth century!" Love, which for us denotes sentimental feeling or passion, took on this meaning only with the poetry of the troubadours, written and sung, which appeared suddenly in southwest France (Poitou, Limousin, and Languedoc), and spread over the whole continent with surprising rapidity. This love resembled nothing that the ancient or Christianized world knew; it seemed to fall from the sky. *La cortezia*, with its fixed and refined forms and its absolutely novel doctrine, could not possibly have been only the more or less accidental discovery of a few pious musical members of the church at Saint-Martial de Limoges, and/or minstrels with little education, which is the "prudent" thesis of most nineteenth- and twentieth-century specialists of the *Trobar*. But if they are right, how could this poetry have conceivably transformed our ways of feeling, our customs, and our arts for centuries? Would it not be, on the contrary, the sign of a more general revolution operative in the Western mind at this time? Let us try then to draw a general picture of the twelfth century and of its leading intellectual and moral phenomena. Shall we find among these phenomena considered as a whole—heterogeneous and independent of one another as they may be—some system of causal, final, successive, or simultaneous interrelationships?

Since the beginning of the eleventh century, heterodox religious movements proliferated in Italy, the German Rhineland, Flanders, the north and then the center and south of France—Reims, Orléans, Poitou, Périgord, Aquitaine—all these movements being more or less associated with Manichaeism. They confronted the Church with a purified spirituality; all condemned marriage—which Pope Gregory VII had just forbidden to priests—and all declared the soul to be divine, and judged the body to be so vile that nothing it did could be conducive to well-being.

The most powerful of these heresies was Catharism which came from the Armenian sect of Paulines, across Anatolia, the Balkans, Bosnia, and northern Italy, spreading from northern Italy in one direction to the north of France and even to England, and in another direction towards the West where it was firmly installed in the courts and castles of Provence, Aquitaine, and Toulouse, and then among the artisans of the cities of the South. Its teaching was Manichaean: the soul or the part of man created by the true God, is a prisoner of the body, or that part of man created by the Demiurge or the Devil. Hence, the necessity, for the genuinely spiritual, or "Perfect Ones," to abstain from carnal procreation, which would cause the soul to fall more deeply into the body's vileness. Most of the plain "believers," finding it too difficult to obey the requirement of absolute chastity, limited themselves to cursing marriage, that legal fornication (*uirata fornicatio*) devised in the laws of the human species, of inheritance, and of masculine brutishness.

An itinerant preacher, Robert d'Arbrissel (born about 1050), famous for his impassioned diatribes against luxury, founded (in 1101) at Fontevrault a women's convent governed by a woman. It soon became renowned because the highest ranked ladies of Poitou and of France came to seek refuge in it against the gross tyranny of feudal and Catholic marriage. Around Fontevrault there developed an "epithalamic" literature, but it was intended only for the nuns and nurtured by commentaries on the Song of Songs.

Another convent for women, the Paraclete, was founded a little later by Abélard, in a very different spirit and purpose. Pierre Abélard of Brittany, poet, philosopher, theologian, and the greatest "Doctor" of his time, was also the first hero of the love-passion, that is to say, of love frustrated by encountering increasingly tragic obstacles, and exalted in the resulting torment. Abélard and his young pupil, Héloïse, experienced a passion that was both carnal and spiritual, and which ended in the tragedy of their separation. Each of them entered religious orders, Héloïse, obeying her husband, became the Abbess of the Paraclete, but they swore to each other to meet again in death. They had previously exchanged love poems in Latin (all lost) which the young priests of the time knew by heart, and used to sing.

A very new form of sung poetry soon arose in Poitou and Limousin with the first works (of which eleven are extant) of the very high lord William, sixth Count of Poitiers and ninth Duke of Aquitaine. He was immediately followed by hundreds of poets who were called "troubadours" (i.e., inventors, composers). This poetry exalted woman, hitherto neglected and despised, and celebrated her under the name of "Lady" (*Dame* or *domina*)—whence the name "mistress" given later to the beloved female—thus assimilating her to the feudal lord to whom the knight owed allegiance. Against the marriage "of reason," as against gross luxury, arose the cult of love the conqueror, respectful of woman but not of social ties.

At the same time appeared the romance of *Tristan and Isolde* (known in the south of troubadour France even before it was published in the first French version by Béroul around 1150–60). This very ancient Celtic myth, reinterpreted under the influence of the *cortezia* of the Western troubadours—whence the name "romance" given to the work—became the very paradigm of all love-passion, of all love "subjected" to constantly renewed trials and separations, which can only lead lovers to the supreme rendezvous in death.

Against this powerful and widespread rise of a love that was almost religious, and therefore smelling of heresy, and against the cult of idealized woman made into a symbol of the power of salvation, the Church and its monks could not fail to erect a belief and a cult which would answer to the same deep desire emerging from the collective soul. Thus, Saint Bernard of Clairvaux who intended to combat Abélard's doctrines on the one hand, and the Catharist heresy and no doubt the growing exaltation of the troubadours on the other, preached the first mystic "Love of the Divine," the love which is its own end: *Amo ut amem*.

During the same period the canons of Lyon, in 1140, established the holy day of the Immaculate Conception of the Virgin: "Our Lady" (*Notre-Dame*) was the antithesis of the ideal Lady (*Dame*) of the courtier's love. In the same vein the multiplying monastic orders were replies to the knights' orders inspired by the *cortezia* of the South; the Franciscans called themselves "Knights of Mary," and Saint Francis himself preferred to be a disciple of the troubadours, whose verses he sang. He called friar Gilles a "Knight of the Round Table."

A last typical trait of this era seems to be all the more striking in being absolutely independent of all those traits just described. It appeared in the twelfth century: in the game of chess, the Queen (*la Dame* in French) became the principal piece; for some mysterious reason, it was substituted for the four kings which at first dominated the game, originally from India.

The above paragraphs thus present the lively background out of which arose the poetry of the troubadours and its new doctrine of Love (*cortezia*). The twelfth century was really the stage of a fundamental revolution in the European mind, a revolution at once moral and spiritual, the quintessence of which appeared in the lyricism of the Provençal poets.

Once the doctrine of courtly love is placed back in the spiritual complex of the twelfth century, we can see better why the times occasioned the success it had: the troubadours contributed the *language* needed to express the aspirations of the medieval soul, and thereby to confess itself in broad daylight in the purified form of the rhetoric of courtship.

What still remains mysterious is the *origin* of this beautiful rhetoric which was at a given point all ready and formed to respond to these aspirations. Until a generation ago the question was completely enigmatic. Today we know at least two possible solutions, which are moreover in no way mutually exclusive, provided that we place the answers in the *whole* which has just been described "by enumeration" of its aspects.

1. The Count-Duke William IX wrote ribald songs and sang of his sexual prowess. He lodged in a tower of his castle a notorious woman answering to the name of the "Dangereuse de Chatellerault." But then, in 1115, his second wife, Philippa of Aragon, and their daughter left him for the convent of Fontevrault—where, furthermore, they found his first wife, repudiated by him. Thus, they passed into the camp of Robert d'Arbrissel and his spiritualism, which both liberated woman from the servitude of sex and opened to her the "exalted" position of "Superior," even over men (see Reto Bezzola). The Count-Duke's reaction: a polemical parody. Legend has it that he founded an "anti-abbey" of courtisans because the founder of Fontevrault first wished to gather prostitutes converted by his preaching. Then he began to praise woman in songs having the form of monastic hymns, rhythms, stanzas, and systems of rhymes imitating runs and codettas (*sequentiae et conductus*) which were particularly plentiful in the Abbey of Saint Martial of Limoges. Now he became its "lay abbot" as Count of Poitou. However, form gradually gained over content—the medium became the message—and from the sixth fragment (out of the eleven extant) he went on to praise an unknown Lady whom he had never seen and did not know when or where he would find, but of whom he had dreamt while riding. He did not know what difficulties she had in reserve for him, but he was burning to undergo them, so great is her worth! The fragments which follow praise *obedience* to the Lady, the principle of fidelity to one's self and also the law of every community. And, of course, he constantly praises profane love:

> All the world's joy is ours
> Lady, when we love each other.

But he ends with a cry that is stupefying for a theological age:

> Through her alone shall I be saved!

Thus all the rhetoric and metaphysics of the troubadours burst out all at once on the threshold of an era which was to witness the simultaneous blossoming of Catharism and courtly lyricism in the same courts and the same castles.

2. William and his first disciple, the Viscount Eble of Ventadour and Marcabru, seem to have borrowed from Arabic poetry the forms and themes, the rhyming systems, the verse stops, and at times the melodies of their appropriately called "court songs" (*chansons courtoises*). William of Poitiers had sojourned in the Near East during a Crusade, and he was linked to Spain through his second wife, widow of a king of Aragon. He borrowed from the Arab poets of the Cordovan school certain formulas of his art, if not of making love, at least of the expression of love, which is for our purpose just as important.

3. The relationship of Hispano-Arabic poetry to the old Provençal troubadours is known in the world of scholars (see especially A. R. Nykl, 1946). However, not enough importance has been placed on the fact that the love poetry of the Arabs of Andalusia was intimately linked to the mystical school of the Sufis (from Iraq) whose chief representatives were Al-Hallaj of Bagdad, Ruzbehan of Shiraz, Suhrawardī of Aleppo, and later, Ibn-ʿArabī of Murcia in Spain. All these mystics went back to the forms of the poetry of profane love in order to express their ideas of divine love; such poetry appeared heretical enough to lead several of the poets to execution. The parallel between the Arabic poetry of courtship (*muwassaha*)—a popular form of which was called *sadjal*—and the poetry of the Provençal troubadours is duplicated by a very remarkable parallel between the sects of the Sufis and the Cathars.

William of Poitiers arrived at a lyricism exalting the Lady by means of a parody on the convent asceticism and on the poetic forms taken from the liturgy (hymns, runs, and *conductus*). In Islam, the poets inspired by Sufi mysticism exalted the object of their love (often a male) in terms judged blasphemous by the orthodox. Thus the orthodox poet Ibn-Dawoud denounced the great mystic Al-Hallaj, accusing him of Manichaeism. However, Ibn-Dawoud and his Andalusian disciples, in the work entitled *The Dove's Neck-Ring* (trans. A. R. Nykl, Paris, 1931) had recourse to the same rhetoric as the Sufis! The relation between the Cathars and the troubadours seems illumined by these two cases, and would be directly homologous to the relation which contrasts and links Robert d'Arbrissel to William IX,

99

and inversely homologous to the contrast and linkage between the Sufi and the orthodox poets.

Furthermore, was not the asceticism of Robert d'Arbrissel, condemning "the flesh," closer to the doctrine of the Catharite "Perfect Ones" than to evangelical Christianity? And, on the other hand, was not William of Poitiers more Christian in his realism, acceptance of the incarnation, and his humanism than his monastic adversary? Were not poets, found in both camps, in dialectical relation with the religious groups ("heretics" like the Sufis, or the "orthodox" like R. d'Arbrissel) from whom they borrowed their vocabulary and problems, free to arrive at opposite conclusions? Whether they wished and believed themselves to be Sufis, Cathars, or orthodox followers of Islam and of Catholicism, the rhetoric of heresy spoke for them and expressed its message in "courtship" language, which was fundamentally Manichaean.

It is evident that the Catharist doctrine was derived from Manichaeism, which on its side greatly influenced the Sufi mystics. Persian Manichaeism was then the common source of two more or less heretical traditions, one in Christianity and the other in Islam.

The Christian heresy travelled along the northern shores of the Mediterranean, from Iran, the fatherland of Mani, across the Pauline sect in Asia Minor, the Bogomil kingdom of Bulgaria and northern Italy, until it reached France in the north, then the center and the south, remaining triumphant for two centuries under the name "Catharism." The other heresy came out of Bagdad, Aleppo, and Damascus until it reached Arabic Andalusia, following the southern shores of the Mediterranean. And it was in the Catharist south in the twelfth century that appeared one of the most extraordinary convergences of history, viz., a literally congenital union of a rhetoric of love with a religious heresy. The poetry of courtship originated at the confluence of two spiritual currents along the two shores of the sea of civilization; and from that poetry come all our European literatures as well as all the commonplaces of love as we sing of it, as we write about it, and as we live it, even to this day.

But concerning this idea of love, which has become so familiar to us that we imagine that it has always and everywhere existed unchanged, how can anyone explain that this idea remains inconceivable outside the domain defined by the Koran and the Bible?

For the fact is that the Asia of the Brahmins and Buddhists has never known our idea of love and regards it with astonishment mixed with irony and suspicious fear. For the Hindu, the Chinese, the Malayan, the Korean, and the traditional Japanese the relations between the sexes belong to the domain of nature or to social morality. Any kind of romanticism, of ideal-

ization, or quasi-mystical ardor is excluded. Love, such as we understand it since our twelfth century does not even have a name in their languages. In Chinese the nearest approach to our verb "to love" is a word which denotes the relationship between a mother and her son. There is desire and there are the recipes for physical pleasure such as India has codified in the Kama-Sutra or represented in statues of didactic eroticism on the facades of its temples. There are family attachments, conjugal rules, rites of initiation with puberty, liturgies of fertility; but that is all. On the opposite side, ideal passions, moral anxieties, nostalgia, feelings of guilt, problems, and obsessions which fill our novels, tragedies, and operas, and occupy so much time in our thoughts, our dreams, our actions, and the secrecy of our confessionals, all these are simply unknown in Asia. From the viewpoint of the idea of love, there are really two worlds, the Oriental and the Occidental. We have just seen that historically at least, the Arab contribution has become an integral part not of the Orient but indeed of the Occident.

These salient facts about culture and civilization seem ultimately to bring into relief man's religious attitudes and his fundamental religious preferences. The religions of India, or those originally from India, know no personal God, and regard the individual as an illusion.

"There is only one Self for all creatures," we read in the Upanishads. The individual self is destined to disappear and become absorbed in the nameless and formless Absolute of pure spirit. The sooner the individual escapes from the cycle of reincarnations in space and time, the sooner will he cease being an individual self, and the better off he will be, for the self is after all an error: it can only be corrected by its progressive disappearance! In such a world how impossible it is to imagine the importance of personal relations which are the basis of love? If "the idea of Me enters only into the thought of fools," as a Tibetan text says, the idea of Thou is no better. But if our neighbor is an illusion, why love him? We may desire him or her, for that is the natural order of a quite imperfect and provisional creation, but that poses no serious problem, the aim still being to detach oneself from everything and to extinguish the ties.

There is a complete basic and concrete change in a world which was dominated and remains forever shaped by the "Abrahamic" religions of Judaism, Christianity, and Muhammadanism. In these, God is a Person who says "I," and man is a person also, who must answer to God: his eternal welfare depends on the very nature of his answer. The relations of Person to person, between God and man, are relations of obedience or revolt, confidence or doubt, happy agreement or despairing hostility; hence, active and emotional relations, and after all, relations of love. Orientals might thoroughly understand the Gospel's definition "God is Spirit," but not "God is Love."

It follows that in the Asiatic religions the sentiments of human love cannot be the reflection of a spiritual process. Whereas in Christianity, for example (as we have seen), marriage may very well serve as a symbol of the union in spirit between the Lord and his faithful. In like manner, the Christian mystics and the Sufis compare the union of the soul with God to the salutory torment, mild burning, ecstasy, and intoxication of human love. Saint Theresa of Avila borrowed her vocabulary from the love poets of Languedoc and from the romances of court chivalry in the cycle of the Round Table which had delighted her in her youth. Without going so high, there were the canticles sung in the churches, Protestant as well as Catholic, expressing the piety of the faithful in feelings of fervor and ardor, eternal vows, and yearning for union, in short, in terms of love.

But there is more. Love, such as the troubadours or authors of the romance of *Tristan* conceived it, cannot be addressed to the body alone (as animal instinct does), nor surely to the intellect alone; it does address itself to the spiritual and the soul, and tends to deify them. For all love seeks in the beloved that which is most exalting, that which justifies the passion. Love ennobles both the one who loves and the one who is loved, as the troubadours endlessly repeat. However, to desire to the point of creating that which is best in the other, viz., his divine element, is to wish for God through the other. The great Sufi mystic of Andalusia of the twelfth century, Ibn-'Arabī, dared to carry courtly love to an ambitious extreme by writing:

It is God who in each loved one manifests himself to the gaze of each lover . . . for it is impossible to adore a being without imagining the divinity present in that being. . . . Thus it goes for love: a creature really loves no one but his Creator (Corbin, p. 111).

This recalls the golden rule of Christianity: "Thou shalt love the Lord thy God and thy neighbor as thyself." To love God really is to love Him through one's neighbor. But it takes two to be in love, the popular saying goes. Then how can one love one's self except by loving the best in the self, that which in the self reflects the divine, the call recognized as coming from God? To love one's neighbor as one's self is, therefore, to love in the other what is best in him, i.e., *to love his angel.*

Let us then bring out the last fundamental feature which distinguishes all the Oriental religions (Hindu, Chinese, Japanese) from the Islamic and the Christian religions: all the Oriental religions with their impersonal absolute know no angels. The angels, for ancient Persia, for the Muhammadans, Jews, and Christians, are those beings intermediary between the individual and God, that correspond to the divine part of each person. Perfect love is addressed to the angel of the loved one, to what the mystics call his "Divine Name," and which is what will remain of him after death. When lovers call one another "my angel," they repeat an old cliché; they don't know what they are saying, but they are saying something which is the real core of all love of the mystical type and which is more true of themselves than they realize.

Thus the love-passion arose, was avowed, and was developed in a context in which men were able to conceive it as a symbol and reflection of the relations between the soul and its God. Orthodoxy (both Christian and Islamic) condemned it because it was thought that this new passion was going to explode the taboos of morals and reason. But though it is true that heresy cannot survive the death of orthodoxy, it is also quite true that the love-passion is nurtured by the same sources as the Occidental religions and that it is condemned to perish to the extent that these religions will cease to animate it, combat it, and be combatted by it. In short, a culture *indifferent* to religion is the only real danger threatening our passions, for indifference can dry up the very wells of passion.

Only in Europe, therefore, did the love-passion deploy all its powers, both for civilization and for anarchy, and become for centuries not only the great inspiring theme of poetry, the novel, the theater, and music, but also the central problem of individual and social morality. It has, finally, invaded the most diverse domains of civilization, giving its language to mysticism and its rules of art to war. All this has happened in Europe and not elsewhere. How can we explain this new enigma?

The answer is undoubtedly to be found in the evidence of experience that *passion is deepened and releases its energies only in proportion to the resistance it meets.* Europe, in the Catholic and northern regions, was to offer the most persistent and deepest resistance to the spread of *cortezia* from the shores of the Arabic and Latin Mediterranean, where the climate is more cheerful, the customs freer, and sensual pleasure more innocent.

We already see in the poetry of the troubadours that courtly love is distinguishable from simple sexual attraction by the refinement of its expressions, the cultivation of feelings, and the quasi-religious respect for the woman whom they put on a pedestal, and of whom they complained that she was placed "too high above" or that she was even inaccessible, like the distant

101

Princess of Jauffré Rudel. "The Love at a distance," that Rudel sang, the praise of chastity, the strictly codified laws of Love, the rules of chivalry, all indicated the same wish to impose a control over the instincts and to put a *distance* between lovers. This constraint allows natural attraction to rise to exaltation and to become a passion.

Self-control or constraint is the fundamental feature that was to manifest itself in a much more open and dramatic manner when courtly love was to find its romantic expression in northern France (Brittany and Normandy). The living link between the troubadors and the authors of the Romance of Tristan is a very noble woman of strong character, who played a very important role in the history of European ideas and customs: Eleanor (Alienor) of Aquitaine, granddaughter of the first troubadour William of Poitiers, wife of Louis VII, King of France, whom she accompanied on a crusade, then wife of Henry II, Plantagenet King of England, and finally mother of Richard the Lion Hearted (himself a court poet) and of Countess Marie de Champagne, famous for her "court of love." The Countess, in her turn, was the protector and inspiration of poets like Chrétien de Troyes, the principal author of the romances of the Round Table. Out of this impressive constellation of high nobility and genius was to arise the cycle of Breton romances, the Quest of the Grail, the characters of King Arthur, Perceval or Parsifal, Galahad, and finally Tristan.

The story of *Tristan and Isolde* remains the eternal prototype of the love-passion discovered or invented by the poetry of the south of France but transposed in the more somber and tempestuous climate of Brittany, Ireland, and Wales. Analyses of this romance par excellence have led to the following conclusion: *passion is that form of love which is nurtured by the obstacles put in its way.*

Tristan, having conquered Princess Isolde after a great struggle, does not keep her for himself—as custom would like to have it—but gives her to King Mark whom she marries. Then the lovers, resuming their liaison, taken by surprise are driven from the court. They live hidden in a forest, with apparently nothing to oppose their desire. However, Tristan at times deposits the sword of chastity between the Queen and himself and this conventional obstacle is to permit their passion to maintain itself. Nevertheless, after three years of exile, Tristan sends Isolde back to King Mark, for this separation, a new obstacle which he deliberately chooses, cannot but inflame his passion. And finally, love having conquered all the shackles of life—morals, matrimonial and feudal law, physical separation, jealousy, and even the attrition of time—the lovers discover in death the supreme obstacle which transfigures their passion and renders it eternal.

Without obstacles there is no passion. "Happy people have no history," a French proverb says. A happy couple do not make a romance. The history of love in Europe is hence to be the history of love's obstacles and its misfortunes, preferred to plain happiness. But this history begins with a catastrophe.

The civilization of the troubadours was crushed in the beginning of the thirteenth century by the crusade against the Albigenses. This was the first and also the most tragic manifestation of relentless hostility which northern Europe and Catholic orthodoxy were to hurl against the fascinating and tempting *heresy* which the new love represented. But, from the stakes ignited by the Inquisition in the south, the sparks were to jump out far, spreading to all of Europe the ideal of courtly love and the current of religious heresy which favored its birth. It can be assumed that without the bloody repression of the crusades, courtly love would not have known the incredible prestige which it has enjoyed until recently, and which had exhausted its role without any catastrophe as it was soon to do in the Arab world.

The principal avenues for the diffusion of courtly love, its poetry, and its music, correspond in Europe to the avenues for the diffusion of the heresies to England, Flanders, The Rhineland, Hungary, Bohemia, Russia (the Dukhobors). The legend of Tristan was spread from the fifteenth century on. Everywhere the Church and the public powers fought heresy and denounced the literature of love, considered, not without reason, as subversive and as contrary to morality and the marriage sacrament. But the more they fought, the more these heresies proliferated and profoundly contaminated the psyche of the European elite. All European literature was converted to the style of the troubadours.

Dante (a disciple of the Provençal poets) and his associates baptized themselves the "Faithful in Love" (*Fedeli d'Amore*). All the Rhenish, Flemish, Italian, and then Spanish mystics submitted to the secret influence of religious Manichaeism.

In an entirely different sphere the rules of courtesy became the orders of chivalry, and in this indirect way were to transform the art of war: the "Tournament," whose prize was the love of a woman, shows the conventional model of the "battle array," that is to say, a battle conducted according to the customary rites and conventions. Since then, it is possible to observe a constant parallel between the style of wars in Europe and the style of love in the same period: hand to hand combat and the group tournament correspond to courtly love; war in laced costume (*guerre en dentelles*) corresponds to the facile, passionless love of the eighteenth century; the revolutionary battles of Bonaparte and national wars of the nineteenth century to the passionate kind of love let loose again by romanticism. This parallelism came to an end only in the twentieth century with the advent of total war, which no longer has any equivalent kind of love (because total war aims at annihilating whatever it conquers), and thus, perhaps, marks the end of an era in our culture. For until the twentieth century we witnessed the vicissitudes of the constantly renewed duel between the religion of the "Faithful in Love" and the orthodoxy of the Christian churches, between individual passion and the collective morality of the community, between eternal romanticism and the necessities of social order.

Each time that society created new obstacles to the anarchy of the passions, the religion of love with renewed vitality discovered fresh ways of expressing itself and spreading its "contagion."

Thus, when French society—which set the tone for all of Europe in the seventeenth century—was firmly organized under Louis XIV's reign, the anarchy of the Fronde was countered by that quasi-totalitarian order of the state, of religious belief, and of the culture of the so-called "Great Century." Passion contrived the means for expressing itself with all its strength on the stage—the theater being a powerful social force—in the guise of classical forms: Andromaque, Bérénice, and Phèdre owed much less to antiquity (which Racine pretended was what inspired him) than to courtly love and the passion fatal to Tristan. We can thus see how passion became the way to "feel love," which thereafter became the "natural" way for Europeans.

The eighteenth century offered a contrasting example of how passion weakens with the weakening of social and moral obstacles, and is submerged by rationalist criticism or ridiculed by those who set the fashion, such as that great lady of letters, Madame du Deffand, who wrote: "We still find good households among people of the lower classes, but among people of quality, I do not know a single example of reciprocal affection nor of faithfulness." It was the character of Don Juan who at that time was on the stage and triumphed in Mozart's opera. Now Don Juan was the antithesis of Tristan, his complete negation: faithless by definition, a man of endless love affairs, while Tristan was a man of a single fatal love; Don Juan violated all the rules of courtesy and became the hero of a cynical century, indifferent to spiritual values, and hence incapable of passion. Only the rebellious Rousseau who, moreover, came from Switzerland and hated the customs of the century, revived courtly love in the subject and the style of his *Nouvelle Héloïse*—a work with a significant title, since it recalls the passion of Abélard, the first living model resembling the myth of Tristan.

It was Rousseau who indicated the opposite direction which passion was soon to take: romanticism. Even the name of the new movement reveals to us its profound sources: "romanticism" comes from "romance"; the first romance was that of Tristan, and it was called romance because it inspired the troubadours who sang in a romance language, in other words, in the vernacular instead of Latin. Romanticism was a forceful return of the religion of the "Faithful in Love" under its most anarchistic and subversive forms in all spheres: morality, politics, religion, art, and literature. It happened thus because the obstacle against which romanticism revolted and mobilized its strength was none other than the entire bourgeois order, the reign of a new materialism, the daily tyranny of a utilitarian morality, of a new system of taboos; and it was also the beginning of the rise of the masses, of timetables, of work with fixed hours, and of mechanism in its ugliest forms. Against all that, romanticism was going to set up justifications of passion, which at that time were confused with those of liberty. The German poets, like Novalis, rediscovered the secrets of the courtly mystique, singing of the night and of mortal love. They brought back into fashion the troubadours, Héloïse, Petrarch, and Dante's *Vita nuova*.

But here this same romanticism was to mark a fatal turning point in the evolution of passion. By too easily adopting and absorbing certain romantic values, by vulgarizing and making them bourgeois, Western society was to succeed in suppressing in large measure the savage energy of passion. It was to begin little by little to *base marriage itself on love,* that is to say that Western society was going to attempt to reconcile the two sworn enemies of the original drama, passion and marriage.

Considered from the viewpoint of courtly values, marriage for love, which seems so natural to us today, was a scandalous novelty; it was introduced into bourgeois customs in the eighteenth century and has triumphed since the middle of the nineteenth century. The love tribunals of the Middle Ages had condemned it without appeal: "Love cannot extend its laws between husband and wife," clearly proclaims a judgment of the Countess Marie de Champagne, in 1174. Four centuries later Montaigne repeated this judgment, however, with different considerations. "One does not marry for himself, no matter what is said," but for posterity and family, the "love license" has nothing to do with it: "A good marriage, if there be any, dispenses with the companionship and condition of love" (Montaigne, pp. 86, 90).

The classical age made no innovations in this area. "There are good marriages, there are no delightful ones," Rochefoucauld was to state. But the rise to power of the bourgeoisie, especially with the ethical and cultural values characteristic of their class (beginning with Rousseau, Diderot, and Richardson) was to produce a profound transformation in the motivations for marriage and in the idea of marriage that would be given to young people.

The bourgeoisie did not share the cynicism of the nobility with respect to erotic pleasures, and the dowries of their daughters were without prestige: instead of influential names and fiefs, sums of money. The bourgeoisie acceded to social and political power from 1789 to 1830, at the same time that capitalism, individualism, and romanticism began to rise. These three phenomena had the conjoint effect (which was greatly accelerated by the Revolution of 1789 and then by Napoleonic ventures) of dissolving traditional bands, historic rights, and sacred customs, making way for contracts freely agreed to among individuals equal in principle. At the same time romanticism revived the values of passion and ideal love capable of offering to women and young people the elements of dream and poetry which real life suppressed more and more. But passion became diluted in too eloquent outpourings of "sentiment," the tragic style revolved in gloom, and this edulcorated form of *cortezia* modestly concealed, without disturbing, the money interests, while serving the purposes of the human race. Thus economic interests, the new social ethics, and the new cultural style found themselves acting in concert, and as though it were connived, proceeded to mystify the prosaic realities of marriage. The whole Victorian era (to which the Louis-Philippe and the Biedermeyer styles correspond) was to live on these matrimonial conventions, born of these forces, and conjoined and destined to safeguard their equilibrium. More and more they spoke and wrote as though marriage were only an affair of love, and love an affair of feeling. Any allusion to money or to sex was rigorously forbidden at the table of a family whose members respected each other.

It was then, between 1830 and 1848, that expressions such as "eroticism," "sexuality," and "sexual problem," appeared, first in Fourier and his socialist disciples, then in Kierkegaard; that is to say, in the most radical critics of the bourgeoisie and of its system of values which were judged incompatible either with social justice or with Christian duty or liberty.

Baudelaire, sensing profoundly the feelings of his age, expressed an inward and woeful erotic view, as a defense against industrial civilization, thriving on urban spleen and on a nostalgia for a crepuscular sky (romanticism, Baudelaire, and symbolism were to cultivate a lyricism of love, surfeited and weary, and therefore crepuscular, in contrast to the passion of the *dawn* of the troubadours). In his *Journaux intimes*, Baudelaire wrote: "Mysticism is the other pole of the magnet of which Catullus and his crew knew only the pole of sensuality." Entering, in spite of himself, into the bourgeois categories which he wished to combat,

he added that "the sole and supreme pleasure in Love lies in the absolute knowledge of doing evil. And man and woman know, from birth, that in evil is to be found all voluptuousness (*Intimate Journals,* p. 34).

Meanwhile, the English novel (from C. R. Maturin's *Melmoth the Wanderer* to the Brontë sisters and then to Thomas Hardy) betrayed the underlying influence of the myth of Tristan, and reactivated by the taboos of the new society reintroduced the blissful torments of impossible and forbidden love. But it was Richard Wagner who was to reveal its esoteric meaning musically, at the time that bourgeois marriage, sufficiently established, permitted and encouraged a psychological and dramatic form of escape in a dream of passion with its culminating climax in death, beyond the prison of the body, in the ecstasy of the union of souls, the "supreme happiness" of Isolde in agony. Supreme, but at the same time an exemplary unhappy ending.

All this was evolving toward a radical crisis. The hypocrisy of the "marriage of love," repressing economic motives and disguising its sexual motives, was bound to end in a neurotic situation and to create a real social uneasiness. But, above all, sentimental love was precisely the most unstable basis that one could imagine for marriage; as an institution its primary reason for being was to satisfy the need for what is lasting, stronger in mankind than the need for surprise offered by passion and its storms. The young man who only asks of a young girl "Do I love her?"—to the exclusion of all considerations of social milieu, of character, and of level of culture—eliminates the most enduring factors and retains only those most subject to change.

Finally, as Engels saw clearly in *The Origin of the Family, Private Property, and the State* (1884; Eng. trans., 1902), individual rights affirmed against tradition, the economic emancipation of women, and the disappearance of the patriarchate, inasmuch as it was tied up with property, were bound to lead logically to a monogamous union based on "love" alone. But "if only marriages that are based on love are moral, then indeed only those are moral in which love continues." This view leads to suppressing the indissolubility of marriage and practically announces the anarchy which we see today. This results, on the whole, in the rapid erosion of the taboos of the bourgeoisie which were challenged and destroyed by Marx and Freud: money and sex.

The reason why Freud so profoundly shocked the Western bourgeoisie, but at the same time gave to a small number of fanatical disciples (and after a generation spread to a wider public by hearsay) the sudden certainty that his doctrine "explained all," was due to the fact that he explained neuroses and some psychoses by starting with sex, one of the two elements tabooed by the current morality. Not much earlier Marx produced a shocking effect and a conversion of a comparable intensity—and just as exaggerated—in "explaining all" by the action of the other tabooed element, money.

Freud brought nothing new to our idea of love but contributed greatly in removing the mystery by a ruthless reduction of its motivations to sexuality. In the *Vocabulaire de la psychanalyse* by J. Laplanche and J. B. Pontalis (Paris, 1967), we do not find the word *love*, but only the expression of genital love, defined as "the form of love at which the subject would arrive in the attainment of his psychosexual development, which assumes not only access to the genital stage, but going beyond the Oedipus complex." The authors concede that: "We find [in Freud] the idea of a complete form of sexuality and even an 'attitude completely normal in love' where the currents of sensuality and 'tenderness' (*Zärtlichkeit*) come together." This last term (*tendresse*)—placed by the authors between quotation marks, as if to excuse themselves for its strangeness—is defined a little further on in the same work: "In the specific usage which Freud gives to it, . . . designated by opposing it to 'sensuality' (*Sinnlichkeit*) an attitude towards another who perpetuates or reproduces the first mode of the love relation of the infant where sexual pleasure is not found independently, but always in supporting itself on the satisfaction of the impulses of self-preservation." This purely sexual and egoistic interpretation of love, according to Freud, seems not to take account of the opposition, which Freud underlines several times, between "true love" and "purely sexual desire" (cf. *Ueber die allemeine Erniedrigung des Liebeslebens,* and *Essais de psychanalyse,* II, 8). Yet, the Freudian context does not define this love as "true" but strives to show its "exaggerations," "idealizations," "narcissistic detours," projections, introjections, erroneous substitutions, and illusions. Absent from the work of Freud is any idea of love for a fellow creature considered as an act (and not a more or less disguised passion): "The core of what we call *love* is formed naturally by what is commonly recognized as love and about which poets sing, that is to say, it is formed by sexual love whose goal is sexual union." On the other hand, the *illusions* of passionate love are brilliantly exposed.

Sentimental love, "idealized," is reduced to the role of an illusion well adapted to the culture, concealing the fact that the force which drives us is in reality sex, "the beast within," in the eyes of reason. In brief, it can perhaps be said that in the eyes of Freud the love of a fellow creature, disinterested, self-living, friendly, in the last analysis is only a particular case of sexual love, whereas conversely, for a Christian conception of the world and of man, sexual love is only a particular case of that cosmic, spiritual Love "which moves the Sun and the other stars," according to Dante.

Freud's pseudo-Manichaean conception (but he chose the low form and not the high form that the troubadours chose) corresponds to a period of maximum eroticism of the Western psyche in Paris, London, and Berlin, as well as in Vienna, in 1900 and during the *Belle Époque.* Sexuality, denied by the pious or atheistic bourgeoisie, by lay morality, and by the Church, took a double twist, scientific and knavish. The right-thinkers cast in the teeth of Freud a pan-sexuality of which bourgeois art (see the salons of the Third Republic), the theater (a large number of shows in the nude in Paris around 1910), and European literature (very generally masochistic, from Sacher-Masoch to Marcel Proust) illustrated the real condition.

From the early 1930's, vulgarized Freudianism influenced an increasingly wide public which believed that according to Freud it was necessary at any price to avoid "suppressing" the instinctive impulses of infants for fear of "giving them complexes." The partisans—anarchists and romantics—of "the rights of passion" took the occasion to condemn every form of sexual discipline, regarding them as repressive. But from this universal permissiveness, morality was to suffer less than passion; nothing makes passion suffer more than facile access. Let us indeed recall that courtly passion thrived on shackles, resistance, and on natural, sacred, social, or legal obstacles; passion would even invent them if it were necessary. Without accumulated obstacles among the legendary lovers—the principal one being the marriage of Isolde with King Mark—there would be no romance or mortal passion, and therefore no myth. One cannot imagine the old king Mark bowing before "the rights of passion," accepting divorce, and authorizing the queen to marry the knight in a properly arranged wedding. And one recoils in dismay at the idea of Isolde's becoming Mrs. Tristan. However, that is what we would come to as soon as marriage is no longer a sacred, indissoluble bond inimical to anything that is worthy of passion. Such a marriage, far from provoking passion by its uncompromising refusals, pretends to be based on the *love* sentiment itself, that is to say, on a very dilute substitute for passion, taken in a very weak dose, like a *vaccine* one could say, thus completing the suppression of the myth and at the same time the very foundations of the matrimonial institution.

This socialization of passion was antisocial par excellence and perhaps the final profanation of a great myth. Must we now think that the powers of the myth are exhausted, and that we shall have been the last in this generation to submit to its "delightful torment," as Thomas, an author of the primitive legend, said?

As a matter of fact, in this last third of the twentieth century, bourgeois morality is approaching complete decadence. Its taboos no longer hold. Freud and the psychoanalysts have accredited, in spite of themselves, the idea which has become popular, that it is less dangerous for society and for the equilibrium of the individual to free the sexual instinct than to repress it. Consequently, educative disciplines have been relaxed. Censorship of publications is an attempt to open the eyes of the public, though condemning a work reputed to be licentious will simply give the work publicity. Eroticism and nudity are on open display in our streets, on our billboards, in advertisements, in literature, and in the cinema.

This, moreover, does not mean that sexuality is more vigorous and turbulent, nor even more anarchical today than formerly. Who can judge? What is certain is that its expression is no longer repressed, and consequently most of the social, legal, and religious prohibitions have lost their virtue of taboo. Let us consider the case of the novelists. They realize that a true romance (*roman*), taking its name from the romance language of the troubadours and the *trouvères*, is nothing but a revitalized version of the courtly archetype of Tristan and Isolde. They therefore are searching all over for the resistant obstacle and they could hardly find any. *The Man Without Qualities*, by Robert Musil, who describes an incestuous passion between brother and sister, and *Lolita*, by Vladimir Nabokov, which describes the passion of a quadragenarian for a twelve-year-old nymphet, are the last echoes of the myth, revived thanks to the last taboos which the era still respects. But now the hero in *Lolita* is described to us as an anti-hero, that is to say, as a case of mental illness. A psychoanalyst might have cured him, and the novel would not have been written.

And what are the artists of the new generation doing? Anticipating the evolution that would logically lead to the extinction of the passionate or even sentimental element, they are beginning to write descriptions of objects "purified of all psychology," to paint pictures which represent nothing, to compose music which no longer expresses any sentiment of the heart. The new novel, abstract painting, concrete music, therefore, use instruments conceived in such a manner that they can no longer express the passion of love, but only combinations of objects, brute sensations, and mathematical relations. Everything happens as if the young artists of these schools deny themselves in advance, and by the choice of their means of expression, whatever comes from the *soul* and not from the senses or the intellect. It is as if passion itself has become their taboo!

For passion needs not only obstacles and constraints, but leisure, privacy, and distance; it also needs a spiritual background, an anxious and desirous belief in the reality of a world beyond visible and measurable things; a world which has a soul, and not only intellect and sexuality. But we have a technical, scientific, and hygienic civilization which cultivates nothing more than the body and the intellect, and neglects the soul. It is true that our technical advances promise us leisure, and this leisure allows us time to develop our culture. Here is a new hope, or at the very least the potential means for a more harmonious development. But a living, creative culture assumes a spiritual horizon and an elite which scorns fads or, on the other hand, which dictates them in the name of a true intuition or faith. Now we have a conception of the world which is drawn from physics and astronomy, and which leaves no further room for ideas of the world beyond. Its physics describes for us a cosmos made up of a *void*, as Democritus had already anticipated. There is no meaning in that universe, or in God, or even in any justification at all for living. But, at the same time, sociology forecasts a world much too *full* of private individuals leading their individual lives, a world much too crowded for life to remain viable. We are already so crowded in our cities that significant distances between living beings become minimal, at the same time condemning us to physical promiscuity and psychological solitude. And we are calmly told that humanity will double its population in the course of the next forty years. If we continue to grow and multiply at the same rate, in less than three centuries there will be more than seven hundred billion human beings, which means one person for every ten square meters over the entire land surface of the earth. Then by the year 2400 there will be one man for every square meter. A half century later, they will all be touching each other. And there our calculations stop.

Obviously these numbers are absurd, but the fact is that up to now not one sociologist or one moralist has found or made acceptable anything which could prevent the whole thing from becoming true. And even to assume that the means to stop this demographic nightmare is discovered, if we imagine the world of the year 2400, what do we have the right to foresee? Too many people, too crowded without privacy or space, perfectly adapted to the requirements of well-organized mass production, and thereby purged of all individual problems.

It surely seems that passion is condemned, and that we are heading directly towards a society without surprises or drama, therefore without history—disciplined, normalized, immunized, policed, psychoanalyzed. Every man is continually being examined, tested, and repaired with the help of spare parts, like an automobile. It is a world regulated by technology, symmetry, and equal justice. This is a *masculine* world. It considers only the body and the intellect. It therefore tends to frustrate more and more the values of the *soul* which form the intermediary zone between the body and the mind—those emotional sensitive and animating values which feed the arts, love, and passion, and which are *feminine* values. In short, we are approaching a collective *Boredom*.

But it is here that the sociological forecast reverses itself and suddenly changes signals. For it seems improbable that this boredom will not stir up in the depths of our being a thirst for something which is outside the world of order, and that it will not provoke a rebellion of the spirit, a revolt of the unconscious, claiming a new liberty comparable to that which was produced in the collective psyche of the twelfth century: a tremendous *upsurge of the feminine principle* in search of new symbols, new ways of showing themselves and of expressing themselves.

The last works of C. G. Jung foretold this return of powers of the soul symbolized by the eternal wisdom (*Sophia Eterna*) of the gnostic heresies, supreme Wisdom (consubstantial with God), eternal Mother prefiguring the coming of the godly Virgin in popular piety. And C. G. Jung was not afraid to write—in this far from Catholic context!—that the proclamation of the dogma of the Assumption of the Virgin was the greatest date in religious history since the Reformation, meaning by religious history the evolution of the collective psyche.

A social psychologist of religion (in the broadest sense of the term) nowadays could enumerate the symptoms of this revival of soul with its irrational powers and affections. We may mention several odd instances ranging from the lowest to the highest: a widespread eroticism, popularized in published works and in advertisements; informal estimates of the extent of magic—fortune-tellers, medical quacks, and prophetesses—often exceeding scientific research budgets; the sly encroachment of pseudo-oriental esoteric ideas, initiation cults, and their erotic, magical physiological procedures; the surrealist revolt culminating in the cult of the "Woman-Child" as saving man from his enslavement to reason (André Breton, 1944); the "hippie" movement of Western youth; the revival of the cult of the Virgin and the dogmas of Mariology in Catholicism (both Roman and Eastern); the ardent curiosity of a growing public interested in the gnostic writings recovered in Egypt, in Manichaeism, and in Catharist doctrines; finally, the spreading influence of the ideas of two thinkers, viz., C. G. Jung and Teilhard de Chardin, otherwise having little or nothing in common, but converging on this topic. All of this revival recalls the psychical features of twelfth-century Eu-

rope. Certain farfetched analogies arise between the troubadours and surrealist poets, between the mystique of love in Saint Bernard and the new doctrines of the Virgin Mary, even between Jung and Joachim of Floris or between Abélard and Teilhard de Chardin . . . , which all leads to very different, even opposite, roads.

The powers of the soul, frustrated by technology and reclaiming their own, can provoke collective neurotic and anarchic furor, endemic crime, and religious folly. These powers can also be wasted in delirious idealism, whether of the Anabaptists, of the Enlightenment's syncretism, or of the "hippies," in whom everything is confounded with no hope of reconciliation with science or theology. Finally, these same powers of love can fail in their counter-offensive, and the result will be that any idea of love that goes beyond sex will be judged reducible to a neurosis or even to a perverse political idea ("capitalistic," "imperialistic," "liberal," "anti-socialistic," and so forth), and will be cured by chemical therapy controlled by the state.

After this happens, almost inevitably, three attitudes will be redefined, distinguished, and then mixed in variable proportions in the lives of our descendants; that is, among those who will have escaped from the totalitarian process of conditioning anticipated above: a) an eroticism increasingly distinct from any sentimental love; knowing no more taboos and seeking with diminishing success the refinements and stimulation capable of temporarily doing duty for obstacles which are absent, absence being ruinous for pleasure; b) a resurgence of courtly love, for "Love is an incurable malady which can find a remedy only in itself, being a delectable condition and desired pain—he who has not caught it has no desire at all to remain healthy, and he who suffers from love finds no pleasure in being cured." So wrote the Andalusian poet, Ibn-Hazm, in the thirteenth century; c) an *agapē* which will no longer be preoccupied with taboos, rules, toleration, or sin, but with its power to integrate personality in marriage.

BIBLIOGRAPHY

Translations, unless identified otherwise, are by the author of this article.

Charles Baudelaire, *Journaux intimes* (Paris, 1938), Fuzées, III; trans. Christopher Isherwood as *Intimate Journals* (London, 1947). Nicolas Berdyaev, *De la destination de l'homme* (Paris, 1935); trans. as *The Destiny of Man* (London, 1937). Reto Bezzola, *Les origines et la formation de la littérature courtoise en Occident* (Paris, 1944). André Breton, *L'Amour fou* (Paris, 1937); idem, *Arcane 17* (New York, 1944). Henry Corbin, *L'Imagination créatrice dans le soufisme d'Ibn 'Arabī* (Paris, 1958). Georges Dumézil, *Mythe et épopée. L'Idéologie des trois fonctions dans les épopées des peuples indo-européens* (Paris, 1968). Friedrich Engels,

The Origin of the Family, Private Property, and the State (1884; trans., Chicago, 1902). Robert Flacelière, *L'Amour en Grèce* (Paris, 1960). K. Gaiser, *Platons ungeschriebene Lehre* (Stuttgart, 1963). Robert G. Hazo, *The Idea of Love* (New York, 1967). Carl Gustav Jung, *Antwort auf Hiob* (Zurich, 1952). Michel Eyquem de Montaigne, *Essais*, ed. P. Villey (Paris, 1923). René Nelli, *L'Érotique des troubadours* (Toulouse, 1963); a basic work. A. R. Nykl, *Hispano-Arabic Poetry and its Relations with the Old Provençal Troubadours* (Baltimore, 1946). José Ortega y Gasset, *Estudios sobre el amor* (Madrid, 1939); trans. T. Talbot as *On Love* (New York, 1957). Denis de Rougemont, *Love in the Western World* (New York, 1940; 1956); also published as *Passion and Society* (London, 1940; 1956); idem, *Love Declared* (New York, 1963); also published as *The Myths of Love* (London, 1963). Isidor Schneider, ed., *The World of Love*, 2 vols. (New York, 1964), contains the translations from Empedocles and Voltaire. F.-M. A. de Voltaire, articles in *L'Encyclopédie* (Paris, 1751–77).

DENIS DE ROUGEMONT

[See also Dualism; Gnosticism; Heresy; Motif; **Platonism; Romanticism; Women.**]

LOYALTY

LOYALTY is the virtue, state, or quality of being faithful to one's commitments, duties, relations, associations, or values. It is fidelity to a principle, a cause, an idea, an ideal, a religion or an ideology, a nation or government, a party or leader, one's family or friends, a region, one's race—anyone or anything to which one's heart can become attached or devoted. One can be fiercely and consistently loyal, or have the mild and opportunistic loyalty that marks the "summer soldier and the sunshine patriot." One can have an exclusive loyalty or multiple loyalties. Loyalty can be evoked by bad as well as by good causes—the Mafia's code, for example, inculcates absolute loyalty in its members through rituals, customs, rewards, and punishments. One expects loyalty from one's spouse, and also from one's business partners. Loyalty between a superior and a subordinate in a hierarchical order—as in feudalism— may be expected, not as a sentiment but as a matter of institutional custom. In modern times the term has been used chiefly in association with patriotism, in the sense of political allegiance and attachment, involving the obligations, formal and informal, of a citizen to his country, its government, and its institutions.

Through governmental investigation into loyalty, through excessive emphasis on loyalty by patriotic societies, through loyalty oaths, through identification of loyalty with conformism and support of the status quo, and through the demand of one hundred percent patriotism or nationalism as proof of loyalty, the term has achieved a pejorative sense which must be taken into account. A totalitarian regime may demand unqualified, total loyalty; but chauvinistic elements in a free society may make similar demands—"our country, right or wrong."

A consideration of loyalty necessarily involves consideration of disloyalty, which must also be viewed in different and shifting contexts, and in a variety of forms, including treason, sedition, security risk, and subversion, each in gross and in subtle meanings. It also involves the history of political theory and morals, of religious and political persecution and martyrdom, the history of ideologies, philosophies of history, indeed, involves the whole range of the history of civilization and culture. We can point only selectively to some of the chief lines of its meaning, use, and abuse.

I

The roots of the idea of loyalty may be found in the deep religious consciousness of ancient man, where it is interwoven with implicit metaphysical, psychological, moral, and sentimental meanings—a phenomenon which is of more than antiquarian interest.

In the Hebrew Scriptures—and in the Hebraic consciousness—the word for truth (*emet*) often means faithfulness, honesty, trust, fidelity, firmness, steadfastness—all suggesting loyalty in one or another relationship. So, too, the word for grace (*chesed*) often suggests in context what we call loyalty. Thus, for example, when David learned that men of a certain town had given decent burial to Saul, he said: "May you be blessed by the Lord, because you showed this loyalty (*chesed*) to Saul. . . . May the Lord show . . . faithfulness (*emet*) to you" (II Samuel 2:5–6, R.S.V.).

The biblical word for faith, faithful, trust, sureness (*amunah*) often suggests loyalty, for one who has faith will cling to it; he will be loyal to his faith. His loyalty is a test of the sincerity of his faith. Thus Ezra said that the Lord found the heart of Abraham "faithful" before him (Nehemiah 9:8), and Habakkuk said that the righteous shall live by his faith—or by his faithfulness, loyalty, steadfastness (Habakkuk 2:4).

The classical Hebraic model of loyalty is the story of the Akedah, the sacrifice of Isaac by Abraham on Moriah (Genesis 22). As generally interpreted the incident was a "testing" of Abraham's loyalty to God. A widely-read modern commentary states:

There are loyalties which deserve all that a man can give, and in that giving he is blessed. Not only the story of Abraham but history in general witnesses to the instinctive belief that this is true. Consider what men have done and will do for their clan or their country. They give their sons to die in battle, to "make the supreme sacrifice." Though they themselves are bereaved, they trust that their nation may be blessed, because through the dedication of young lives the nation may hear the promise which was spoken to Abraham, "Thy seed shall possess the gate of thy enemies" (*The Interpreter's Bible* 646 [1952], Vol. I).

Exhortation to and defense of martyrdom as the ultimate proof of loyalty to one's religion or God have been common at least since Rome instituted the imperial cult, and Jews and Christians refused, in the face of the threat of death, to perform an act which to them was an expression of idolatry.

The apocryphal book known as *IV Maccabees* (A.D. 37–41) became a popular work among Christian orators and teachers for its treatment of martyrdom, and inspired resistance to Rome. In the book, the young men, threatened with torture and death if they fail to violate the Jewish law, cry out to the tyrant:

Why, tyrant, do you delay? Ready are we to die, rather than transgress our forefathers' commandments. Our forebears we should verily shame if we did not show obedience to the Law. . . . But if old men of the Hebrews have died for religion's sake, and persevering through torture have abided in their religion, it is even more fitting that we who are young should die. . . . Proceed, then, with your trial, tyrant; and if you take our lives and inflict upon us a death for religion's sake, do not think that you are injuring us by your torments. We, by our suffering and endurance, shall obtain the prize of virtue; and we shall be with God, on whose account we suffer . . . (9:1–9, trans. M. Hadas).

This passage shows some of the common themes of martyrology: loyalty to one's origin and forebears, loyalty to God, loyalty in the face of indescribable torment, the identification of such loyalty with virtue, compensation of such loyalty in the certainty that God will know and approve.

Idolatry in its essence is rebellion against God, rejection of God. The Bible speaks often of those who desert God and play the harlot (Ezekiel 16:41). At times the Bible speaks of sin as rebellion, as a breach of loyalty to God. One of the root words for sin (*pesh*) means rebel. Another basic biblical word for sin (*chet*) in some contexts means going astray, missing the way; it suggests that man or his heart is wayward, inconstant, unsteady—disloyal (e.g., I Samuel 19:4; 24:12; 26:21). Often the Bible suggests that the essence of sin is found in breach of the covenant, the people go awhoring after strange gods as an adulterer who has violated his agreement—a supreme act of disloyalty (Hosea 4:12; 9:1; Ezekiel 23:30).

In Job, one of the leading themes is the conviction that, no matter what, a man must be true to himself, must not waver in his loyalty to the truth and the reality as he knows them to be in his innermost heart.

Thus Job holds his ground firmly against the charges and derogatory intimations of his friends; but even more, he remains loyal to himself even against the will of God:

Behold, he will slay me; I have no hope; Yet I will defend my ways to his face (Job 13:15. R.S.V.).

Perhaps the root idea out of which flow the many meanings of loyalty with all their rough and sophisticated shadings can be traced back to the idea of love—

and you shall love your God with all your heart, and with all your soul, and with all your might (Deuteronomy 6:5).

Israel is to have only one loyalty; God is to be loved with the totality of one's devotion. Israel has covenanted to have only one God, as a man covenants to have only one wife—only one love. There is also the law of love which makes oneself and one's fellow men objects of loyalty: "Thou shalt love thy neighbor as thyself" (Leviticus 19:18; cf. Matthew 22:37–40, Luke 10:27–28). One must, therefore, be "true" to God, to one's own soul, and to fellow men. From ancient times to the present, these basic meanings of loyalty—in whatever terms expressed—have persisted.

II

While the ancient Greek philosophers—unlike the writers of the Hebrew Scriptures and of the Apocrypha—consciously sought to achieve intellectual clarity, their moral conceptualizations are by no means clear-cut. While a few concepts attain a high degree of articulation, others, including loyalty, are left largely to suggestion, implication, or myth.

The drama of the trial and death—martyrdom—of Socrates, however, clearly spelled out what loyalty meant to the greatest of Athenian teachers. "The truth of the matter is this, gentlemen," Socrates said to the jury:

Where a man has once taken up his stand, either because it seems best to him or in obedience to his orders, there I believe he is bound to remain and face the danger, taking no account of death or anything else before dishonor (*Apology* 28D, Loeb trans.).

It would be difficult to find anywhere a clearer instance of loyalty to a mission. Were the jury to acquit him on condition that he give up his mission, Socrates said that he would retort to the jury as follows:

Gentlemen, I am your very grateful and devoted servant, but I owe a greater obedience to God than to you. . . . You know that I am not going to alter my conduct, not even if I have to die a hundred deaths (ibid., 30B).

109

In the *Crito* Socrates makes it clear that he considered himself the victim of a miscarriage of justice, for which he blamed not the laws or the state, but his fellow men (*Crito* 54C). Accordingly, he said that he must gladly submit to the legal punishment, and in this way avoid the great sin against the state: violence against its laws.

Socrates is thus a classic paradigm of a man who, even in the face of death, chose to remain loyal to his country, to God, and, above all, to his mission, to his soul.

What came to be accepted as the four cardinal virtues—wisdom, courage, justice, and self-control or temperance—appear in three of Plato's leading dialogues: *Phaedo* (69C), the *Republic* (IV. 427E–433B), and the *Laws* (631C). Loyalty is not explicitly discussed as a virtue, but surely it is an ingredient of each of the cardinal virtues as they are treated by Plato. Courage, the prerogative of the soldiers in the *Republic*, would hardly be possible unless they felt loyalty to the state and its order. Self-control, the dominant virtue of the governed, would be impossible without loyalty to one's neighbors, on whose rights one may not trespass. Justice, the principle of a place for everyone and everyone in his place, assumes loyalty to one's station and its duties. Wisdom, the virtue that peculiarly characterizes the philosopher-kings, who specialized in governance according to their knowledge of good and evil, surely implicates loyalty to Truth, to the Form of the Good, to the city-state, and to the legitimate interests of the other social classes. Indeed, the governing guardians are to have community of wives and children so that they may not be distracted from the public work by domestic loyalties.

Both the *Republic* and the *Laws* are consistent with the Hellenic position that the chief outlet for unselfish loyalty and devotion is the city (*polis*). In the *Laws*, when Plato came to providing for a court for capital offenses (855C), he took as his model the Areopagus, which Solon had invested with the power to punish sedition and treason (856–57). The greatest enemy of the state is he who stirs up civil strife, and next to him is one who, aware of an act of sedition, fails to inform the officials or to prosecute the conspirators (856B–C). Other serious public crimes include failure to report for military duty, desertion from the army, and disloyal conduct by an envoy to a foreign state (941, 943). There is also the serious crime of traffic with the enemy (857).

Certainly Plato's proposals for a strict censorship of the arts is in part motivated by the objective to instill in the masses of citizens, who will have "opinion" and not "knowledge" as their motive power for action, absolute loyalty to a tradition with which they have been imbued by their "social environment" rather than "loyalty to the claims of a *summum bonum* grasped by personal insight" (A. E. Taylor, *Plato*, 2nd ed. [1956], p. 280). Loyalty to tradition is a basic requirement for the control of the polities projected by the *Republic* and the *Laws*.

It is strange, however, that Plato, and the other Greek thinkers as well, hardly discussed the problem of conflicting loyalties—e.g., that the duty to inform on criminal conspirators may conflict with loyalty to one's relatives or friends. Perhaps they assumed, as many do in modern times, that it is sufficient to resolve all such questions to say that the duty to be loyal to the state rises above all other duties. Yet there was always the example of Socrates expressing his loyalty to Athens by his determination to die rather than obey what he considered to be an unlawful state order; also, there was always the theme of Sophocles' *Antigone:* the conflict between loyalty to God or Nature or the Soul and to the state or its historically-conditioned law. But the successors of Socrates refused to see a sharp conflict here. They were more impressed by the insistence of Socrates that while the state's laws and customs are not exempt from critical examination, it is these very laws and customs that make life and the search for the good possible; therefore, one must willingly and unconditionally obey the state. This seems to be the lesson learned by Plato, as developed in the *Republic* and especially in the *Laws*.

Aristotle even more clearly than his teacher, Plato, articulated the belief that it is impossible for man to fulfill his ends—to live as a rational being—outside of a community, to live the moral life outside of the state.

For the moral, virtuous life, man needs to exercise his rational insight to discover the mean between two extreme lines of conduct—e.g., courage is the mean between an excess which is foolhardiness, and a deficiency which is cowardice. Aristotle considers other examples (*Nicomachean Ethics*, Book II, Ch. vii); he does not, however, treat of loyalty as such; but he admits that not every action or emotion admits of the observance of a mean (II, vi, 18); some qualities do not admit of excess or deficiency; it may be that Aristotle would say that loyalty is the mean between fanaticism and perfidy. Nor is the mean—and one would assume that this would be true of every virtue, including loyalty—the same for everyone under all circumstances: "The agents themselves have to consider what is suited to the circumstances on each occasion" (II, ii, 4).

While loyalty is not expressly mentioned in Aristotle's discussion of friendship and love of country, it is clearly implied, as in the following passage:

But it is also true that the virtuous man's conduct is often guided by the interests of his friends and of his country, and that he will if necessary lay down his life in their behalf. For he will surrender wealth and power and all the goods that men struggle to win, if he can secure nobility for himself; since he would prefer an hour of rapture to a long period of mild enjoyment. . . . And this is doubtless the case with those who give their lives for others. . . . Also the virtuous man is ready to forgo money if by that means his friends may gain more money; for thus, though his friend gets money, he himself achieves nobility . . . (IX, viii, 9; Loeb trans.).

Both Plato and Aristotle not only sketched ideal states but also subjected the Greek states, which they knew, to judgment according to ideals and principles. Aristotle's *Politics* also devotes a long section (Book V) to causes of revolution, sedition, and constitutional change. Yet neither of them undertook a philosophic analysis of loyalty and disloyalty, key conceptions involved in the formation, maintenance, and dissolution of societies, states, and governments.

III

As long as the city-state existed and was looked upon as the model form of political organization, loyalty was confined within walls from which even Socrates could not, as we have seen, wholly escape. But after Alexander's conquest of the so-called barbarians, the loss of Greek independence, and the rise and spread of the Stoic philosophy after Zeno (336–264 B.C.), men spoke of the brotherhood of man, of the family of man, of the unity of the race and of nations, of all men as children of one father, of all men as citizens of one world. At the same time the Stoics emphasized their belief that it is the rational quality of men that unites them—it is in sharing rationality and goodness that true kinship is found. "My father is nothing to me," said Epictetus, "but only the good" (*Discourses*, III, iii). But loyalty, fidelity, trustworthiness, according to Epictetus, is as essential to human nature as are rationality, goodness, and justice. In the *Discourses* (II, iv), the following characteristic scene is reported:

As Epictetus was remarking that man is born to fidelity, and that the man who overthrows this is overthrowing the characteristic quality of man, there entered one who had the reputation of being a scholar, and who had once been caught in the city in the act of adultery. But, goes on Epictetus, if we abandon this fidelity to which we are by nature born, and make designs against our neighbor's wife, what are we doing? Why, what but ruining and destroying? Whom? The man of fidelity, of self-respect, of piety. Is that all? Are we not overthrowing also neighborly feeling, friendship, the state? In what position are we placing ourselves? As what am I to treat you, fellow? As a neighbor; as a friend? Of what kind? As a citizen? What confidence am I to place in you? . . . For, assuming that you cannot hold the place of a friend, can you hold that of a slave? And who is going to trust you? (Loeb trans.).

Marcus Aurelius spoke of "the natural law of neighborliness" (*Meditations*, III, 11, Loeb trans.). But all men are neighbors, and all are citizens of the highest state, the Universe, "of which all other states are but as households" (ibid.). There is a law common to all mankind. This, said Marcus Aurelius, means that the law is operative in a state; the Universe must be that state; we are all, therefore, citizens of one state (IV, 4). All things, he said,

are mutually intertwined, and the tie is sacred, and scarcely anything is alien the one to the other. . . . For there is but one Universe, made up of all things, and one God immanent in all things, and one Substance, and one Law, one Reason common to all intelligent creatures, and one Truth . . . (VII, 9).

Man is a citizen of the world-city (XII, 36). What is advantageous to the whole cannot be hurtful to the part (X, 6).

In Hebraic thought, as we have seen, loyalty to God transcended all other duties. To Socrates, loyalty to one's soul, one's true self, transcended all other duties and was identified with loyalty to God. In the Hellenistic philosophy of the Stoics, loyalty to Natural Law, the law of the Universe, to the rational principle, by which man is defined, become merged with loyalty to the true self and loyalty to God. In all these instances parochial loyalties are transcended—and yet, as we have noted in the incident of Epictetus and the man caught in the act of adultery, the closer, narrower loyalties are preserved and validated; for a man will be faithless to humanity and God if he is not trustworthy in his own home and neighborhood. Plato and Aristotle, however, placed their emphases on loyalty to the state—in Plato's ideal polities the emphasis on this loyalty seems over-arching.

At the same time there were philosophers who, by implication, viewed the whole business of political and moral loyalty with considerable skepticism. In Plato's *Republic* (336A–354C) Thrasymachus understands by justice the interest of the stronger, the notion that might is right, or whatever is to the interest of the ruler. He himself then draws the inference that a man ought to try to satisfy his own interest, and not that of another—at least insofar as he can prudently do so. The result of this view may well be nihilism. In the same dialogue (357–367E), Glaucon speaks for the view that justice is purely a matter of convention, grounded in fear, and is the necessary protector of the weaker. In the *Gorgias,* Callicles speaks for the theory of the natural right of might, and for the idea that all law

111

is made by the weak to defraud the strong of their just rights. When justice is to do what one can, and what one can get away with, or is obedience to authority when one must obey but otherwise is to do what one wants, then loyalty is no virtue and has no virtue.

But throughout biblical literature and in the Hellenic and Hellenistic writings, the ideal of loyalty as the soul of friendship is kept alive in poetry, drama, elegy, oratory, and philosophic debate and analysis. Plato's *Lysis* deals with friendship, and Aristotle is deeply concerned with the subject and writes movingly on it in the *Ethics* (IX, viii). Cicero's *De amicitia*, influenced by Aristotle, Xenophon's *Memorabilia*, and a lost treatise on friendship in three volumes by Theophrastus, deal with the subject elaborately and lovingly. It has been suggested that friendship is a topic which plays a much more prominent part in ancient than in modern ethical literature for the reason that conjugal affection and romantic love were given small scope for expression; there were, therefore, two outlets for unselfish loyalty—the city-state and the lifelong friend (Taylor, *Plato*, pp. 64–65).

IV

"Every association," according to Aristotle, "seems to involve justice of some kind and friendship as well" (*Nicomachean Ethics* VIII, i). Thus, holding the city-state in the highest esteem, Aristotle saw its roots in ethical conceptions—justice and loyalty. Indeed, it can be contended with much reason that during the centuries of feudal history in Europe, when often there was no tribal or racial solidarity to weld men together, men were saved from complete political anarchy by the feeling of loyalty to the person of the Emperor (C. H. McIlwain, *Growth of Political Thought in the West* [1932], p. 142). Feudalism with its customs and practices of homage and fealty, and its theory of the feudal contract between lord and vassal, established itself not only on the feelings of personal loyalty, but also on the Hebraic and Stoic notion that society flows out of a covenant—and a covenant, even between God and his people, is worthless if the parties are not committed loyally to fulfill its terms.

In the Middle Ages, when people at times suffered oppression from an evil ruler, a distinction was made between loyalty to his sacred office and loyalty to his person. God, it was said, commanded only the former when the ruler violated his part of the bargain. From this the conclusion was sometimes drawn that loyalty to the king's sacred office did not stand in the way of resistance to the tyranny of the evil ruler.

Chapter 61 of the Magna Carta provides a definite procedure to be followed by the king when barons charge him with delinquency toward anyone or transgression of any article concerning the peace or security. The conclusion that was drawn from this chapter is that when the king does not adhere to his part of the feudal contract, rebellion against him would be legal.

This was a logical consequence of the distinction between the man and the office: loyalty to the latter does not necessarily mean loyalty also to the former. This distinction made it easier for medieval thinkers to move away from the position of Augustine that the evil ruler is sent by God as a punishment for sins, and that it was, therefore, one's duty loyally to submit to him (*De civitate Dei*, Book 5, Chs. 19–21). The distinction between the man and the office naturally led to the distinction between the true king and the tyrant, and to the idea, as we see it—e.g., in Magna Carta—of the right of resistance, and the idea of authority based on covenant or contract, and the right to withdraw allegiance or loyalty when there is a serious breach. In John of Salisbury there is praise of tyrannicide, and of the assassin as the agent of a just, watchful, and avenging God (*Policraticus*, Book VIII). Thomas Aquinas, while stressing that rulership must be limited and must move only within lawful confines, disavows tyrannicide; but he holds that the people as a whole have a right to resist. While he condemns sedition, he denies that justifiable resistance to tyranny is sedition (*De reginiore principum*, Book I, Ch. 6. *Summa Theologica*, 2 a, 2 ae, q. 42, q. 104).

If there is a single dominant theme that one can detect running through all the controversies in medieval writings, it is that the state must serve moral ends and help fulfill God's purposes for man—personal salvation; that there is a common good, to which the ruler must contribute; that the power of the ruler is derived from God; that the power of the ruler is limited by law; that transgression of the lawful limits makes a ruler into a lawless tyrant. Though thinkers may differ as to what may lawfully or morally be done in the face of tyranny, the implication was seen by many that the subject's political loyalty is a conditional one, at least with respect to the man as distinguished from the office. In this way medieval thought synthesized the Hebraic-Hellenic-Hellenistic inheritance: there is accommodation of loyalty to the human community, to God, and to the soul. While there was, of course, substantial disagreement as to the meaning of these terms, there was, nonetheless, basic agreement on the need to transcend loyalty to the state in order to be loyal to God and to the soul accountable to God. The political government of the world must, therefore, be seen under the head of the moral and the divine government of the world, and loyalty must be considered within a philosophy of history which takes into account politics, morals, and religion.

V

As the modern period began, the traditional institutions to which Europeans had been loyal for centuries had decayed and were seen as archaic, and there was widespread religious, moral, and political corruption. Loyalty to ideals, and loyalty itself as an ideal, were scoffed at as childish inventions. Machiavelli's *Prince* (1513) can be taken as the new voice of modern political absolutism. In this treatise there is no concern with religious or moral considerations; the author candidly accepts the view of Thrasymachus that government rests on force, and the view of Callicles that deception is inseparable from rulership. Government is an autonomous art and is not subject to external ideals or guideposts. The only proper loyalty is to the prince, who may be omnipotent and who is certainly outside the law and morality. But Machiavelli was not cynical when it came to national patriotism, for he believed that duty to one's country wiped out all other duties or loyalties (*Discourses on the First Ten Books of Titus Livius* [1513], III, 41). The idea of the omnipotent prince was accorded fuller philosophical treatment in Hobbes' *Leviathan* (1651). This line of thought was coincidental with the rise of the modern national state, which has culminated, in the twentieth century, in the totalitarian states of the fascist, Nazi, and communist varieties, in the democratic, liberal states, and in the various experiments that have been tried in order to transcend and to orchestrate national loyalties and interests—as in the League of Nations, the United Nations, the Council of Europe, and the Organization of American States.

At one extreme is the demand of total, exclusive loyalty—the fanatical national and ideological devotion demanded by Nazi and communist theory and practice, whether ostensibly on behalf of the proletariat class and state, or on behalf of the Fatherland, the *Führer,* and the Aryan "race." But the demand of single-minded loyalty has also been made at times by leaders of democracies. For example, Theodore Roosevelt attacked what he viewed to be the divided loyalties of immigrants to the United States, whom he labeled "hyphenated-Americans" and "the foe within the gates"; both Roosevelt and Woodrow Wilson insisted that if America was indeed a "melting pot," the type into which immigrants were to be melted was the type of American that had been shaped from 1776 to 1789.

The philosophy of loyalty, however, more intimately and more often associated with the democratic process is that of cultural pluralism. As formulated by Horace M. Kallen in articles published in 1915, and in 1924 in *Culture and Democracy in the United States,* cultural pluralism is projected as an ideal multiplicity in union,

the right to be different, the orchestration of differences, the creative interaction of coexisting loyalties— "the union of the different," "a federation of nationalities," a federation "sustained . . . by their equality and by the free trade between these different equals. . . ." This position calls for the legitimacy of pluralistic loyalties. It was expressed in 1943 by Justice Jackson for the United States Supreme Court as follows:

> But freedom to differ is not limited to things that do not matter much. That would be a mere shadow of freedom. The test of its substance is the right to differ as to things that touch the heart of the existing order. If there is any fixed star in our constitutional constellation, it is that no official, high or petty, can prescribe what shall be orthodox in politics, nationalism, religion, or other matters of opinion or force citizens to confess by word or act their faith therein (*W. Va. State Bd. of Education v. Barnette,* 319 U.S. 624).

Multiple loyalties can create personal and national tensions; e.g., John F. Kennedy in the 1960 presidential campaign felt it necessary to say that as President he would act in accordance with what his conscience would say is in the national interest and without regard to "outside [Roman Catholic] religious pressures or dictates." On the other hand, black militants in the United States in the late 1960's took the position that in a conflict between the demands of the black community and the larger community, their loyalty would be with the former. In each instance the tension or conflict was resolved by raising one loyalty above all others, but this was seen as an undesirable forced option and as a process which did not totally annihilate competing loyalties.

VI

The pluralistic approach to loyalty is, however, hardly representative in the world of the twentieth century; and in the United States, it is a fact honored both in the observance and in the breach.

Allegiance was defined by Blackstone as the tie

> which binds every subject to be true and faithful to his sovereign, in return for that protection which is afforded him; and truth and faith to bear of life and limb, and earthly honor; and not to know or hear of any ill intended him, without defending him therefrom (*Commentaries on the Laws of England* [1765–69], Book IV, Ch. 1).

Blackstone noted that treason was a general term used by the law to denote not only offenses against the king or the government but also an act of disloyalty even as between private persons, between whom there is a natural, a civil, or even a spiritual relation. He cited as examples a wife killing her husband, a servant killing his master: "these, being breaches of the lower allegiance, of private and domestic faith, 'were formerly' 113 denominated *petit* treason. But when disloyalty so rears its crest, as to attack even majesty itself, it is called by way of eminent distinction, *high* treason . . ." (ibid.). Blackstone found that the common law knew seven kinds of high treason. One kind was to "compass or imagine" the death of the king, or of his queen, or of their heir. Written or printed words could be compassing the death of the sovereign and constituted an overt act sufficient to be treason. By statute of George III, the use of any words to excite people to hatred and contempt of the king or "government and constitution" was made a high misdemeanor. Laws and prosecutions were especially directed at words which may have a "tendency" to cause disloyalty among men in the armed forces. The "bad tendency" doctrine as applied to publications and speech lingered in Great Britain until 1832.

In the United States the bad tendency doctrine was supposed to have disappeared with the adoption of the First Amendment in 1791. Yet in 1798 Congress enacted the infamous Alien and Sedition Laws, which punished false, scandalous, and malicious writings against the government, Congress, or the President, if published with intent to defame, or to excite hatred against them, or to stir up sedition. Jefferson attacked these laws as unconstitutional, and when he took office as President in 1801, pardoned all who were prisoners under these laws.

The two world wars revived the spirit, if not the letter, of these laws and of the common law doctrines of treason and sedition. The Espionage Act of 1917 made it an offense to attempt to cause "disloyalty" in the armed forces, and the Sedition Act of 1918 made it a crime to utter or publish any disloyal language intended to cause contempt for the American form of government, or the Constitution, or the flag, or the uniform of the Army or Navy. The latter act was officially defended on the ground that without it loyal people would take matters into their own hands and punish persons for making disloyal remarks—men had to be sent to prison for terms of many years in order to protect them from mob violence! Some school boards and state legislatures prohibited the teaching of the German language—in the interests of Americanism and loyalty; and school textbooks were carefully screened by censors charged with the duty to expose disloyal utterances. As Attorney General from 1919 to .1921, Alexander Mitchell Palmer became notorious for the so-called Palmer Raids, which involved zealous prosecutions of persons, especially aliens, suspected of disloyalty. Socialists lost their elected seats in the New York State Legislature during World War I. There was also eager prosecution under state laws—it is estimated that in 1919–20 some three hundred persons were

imprisoned for violation of state sedition and syndicalist statutes (R. K. Murray, p. 234).

The record for the period of World War II was not as grim. Under federal anticommunist laws in effect since 1940, twenty-nine communists went to prison as co-conspirators to violate the Smith Act of 1940, and only one went to prison as a member of the party. Many laws were used against the party, but an equally great armory of legal defenses was used to protect it and its leaders and members.

The most shocking action was taken against 112,000 Japanese-Americans, two-thirds of them American citizens (Nisei), living in the Pacific coast states, who were taken from their homes under an evacuation order in 1942, though no person of Japanese descent had been charged with any disloyal act.

The Korean War (1950–53) was, however, largely coincidental with the so-called McCarthy period (1950–54), when the search for persons suspected of disloyal intentions became a witch-hunt, which seemed to revive the common law idea that it was treasonable merely to "compass or imagine" an act against American interests or institutions, or what Senator Joseph R. McCarthy construed as a disloyal, subversive, communist, or un-American act. In addition to conventional criminal law prosecutions, there were federal and state hearings, employment security checks, loyalty oaths, blacklistings of members of "front" organizations, legislative enactments, administrative proceedings (e.g., by the Subversive Activities Control Board), grand jury investigations, registration requirements, listings of organizations—allegedly subversive— by the Attorney General and the House Un-American Activities Committee, restrictions on the right to passports, and prosecutions for perjury and making false statements or affidavits. The McCarthy period did not generate an intensified patriotic fervor; it generated mutual suspicions which affected obscure men and persons holding the highest positions and rocked churches no less than labor unions.

While relaxation of tensions between the United States and the U.S.S.R. and the introduction of pluralism into the communist world—polycentrism—have greatly reduced pressure for sustaining the spirit of McCarthyism, support for loyalty tests continues, and the forces behind them score occasional successes as, for example, the loyalty requirement in the Medicare Act (1966). Decisions of the Supreme Court of 1966 to 1971 have made enforcement of loyalty oaths and affidavits well-nigh impossible. The Court's decisions in cases involving legislative committee hearings, the Smith Act and other anticommunist statutes, and the Subversive Activities Control Board have greatly narrowed the range of constitutionally valid legislation aimed at exposure or punishment of allegedly disloyal Americans (for cases see Konvitz, *Bill of Rights Reader*, 5th ed., 1972, and *First Amendment Freedoms*, 1963).

VII

It is odd that, despite the important role loyalty has played in the religious, moral, and political life of men over the centuries, only one philosopher has given the concept serious and sustained study; namely, Josiah Royce, one of America's half-dozen leading philosophers, in *The Philosophy of Loyalty* (1908). Royce saw in loyalty "the heart of all the virtues, the central duty amongst all duties." He made "loyalty to loyalty" the categorical imperative, "the central spirit of the moral and reasonable life of man" (p. 118).

Royce defined loyalty loosely as "the willing and practical and thoroughgoing devotion of a person to a cause." His description of loyalty to a cause is reminiscent of the biblical commandment to love God: something that "appears to you worthy to be served with all your might, with all your soul, with all your strength." For the loyal man, his cause provides an answer to the question: "For what do I live?" Loyalty tends "to unify life, to give it centre, fixity, stability." The cause becomes one's conscience, and unifies one's ideals and plans. Against his cause a man can contrast his transient and momentary desires.

Royce recognizes the fact that there may be loyalty to an evil cause, and also that men's loyalties may conflict. The principle of loyalty to loyalty provides a solution, according to Royce: in choosing his cause a man should choose one that will further, rather than frustrate, the loyalties of other men, as well as his own multiple loyalties. Accordingly, "Murder, lying, evil speaking, unkindness, are all . . . simply forms of disloyalty," and a cause is predatory when it lives by overthrowing the loyalties of others; it is an evil cause when it involves "disloyalty to the very cause of loyalty itself." Again reminding us of the biblical view, Royce notes that "speaking the truth is a special instance of loyalty," and that "Justice means, in general, fidelity to human ties in so far as they are ties" (p. 138).

As leading philosopher in the neo-Hegelian school of idealistic thought in the United States, Royce naturally developed his ideas with an eye on the role of loyalty in the spiritual unity or the Absolute in which all values are preserved; but a discussion of this aspect of his thought, which involves also his notion of community as developed in *The Problem of Christianity* (1913), would take us beyond the scope of our undertaking. Let us note, however, that the compulsion of his system of thought to experience ever higher levels of meaning, pushing one's life "to get into unity with the whole universe," points in the direction of the Stoic

belief that in some way the world is a state with a common law that binds all men as fellow men in a common loyalty.

BIBLIOGRAPHY

Aristotle, *Politics*, Loeb Classical Library (London, 1932); idem, *Politics*, trans. Ernest Barker (Oxford, 1948); idem, *Nicomachean Ethics*, Loeb Classical Library (London, 1939). Association of Bar of City of New York, *Report of Special Committee on Federal Loyalty-Security Program* (New York, 1956). Alan Barth, *Government by Investigation* (New York, 1955); idem, *The Loyalty of Free Men* (New York, 1951). Edward L. Barrett, *The Tenney Committee* (Ithaca, 1951). Eleanor Bontecou, *The Federal Loyalty-Security Program* (Ithaca, 1953). Irving Brant, *The Bill of Rights* (Indianapolis, 1965). Ralph S. Brown, Jr., *Loyalty and Security* (New Haven, 1958). William F. Buckley, Jr., *The Committee and Its Critics* (New York, 1962). Robert K. Carr, *The House Committee on Un-American Activities 1945–1950* (Ithaca, 1952). Zechariah Chafee, Jr., *Free Speech in the United States* (Cambridge, Mass., 1941). Lawrence H. Chamberlain, *Loyalty and Legislative Action* (Ithaca, 1951). Cicero, *De senectute, de amicitia, de divinatione*, Loeb Classical Library (London and Cambridge, Mass., 1923; 1959). Vern Countryman, *Un-American Activities in the State of Washington . . .* (Ithaca, 1951). Merle Curti, *The Roots of American Loyalty* (New York, 1946). Charles P. Curtis, *The Oppenheimer Case* (New York, 1955). Epictetus, *Discourses*, 2 vols., Loeb Classical Library (London and Cambridge, Mass., 1925, 1928; 1956). David P. Gardner, *The California Oath Controversy* (Berkeley and Los Angeles, 1967). Walter Gellhorn, *Security, Loyalty, and Science* (Ithaca, 1950). Milton M. Gordon, *Assimilation in American Life* (New York, 1964). Morton Grodzins, *The Loyal and the Disloyal* (Chicago, 1956). Sidney Hook, *Heresy, Yes—Conspiracy, No* (New York, 1953). Harold M. Hyman, *To Try Men's Souls* (Berkeley and Los Angeles, 1959). Oscar Jaszi and John D. Lewis, *Against the Tyrant* (Glencoe, Ill., 1957). The Earl Jowitt, *The Strange Case of Alger Hiss* (London, 1953). Horace M. Kallen, *Culture and Democracy in the United States* (New York, 1924). Milton R. Konvitz, *Bill of Rights Reader*, 5th ed. (Ithaca, 1972); idem, *First Amendment Freedoms* (Ithaca, 1963); idem, *Alien and Asiatic in American Law* (Ithaca, 1946); idem, *Fundamental Liberties of a Free People* (Ithaca, 1957); idem, *Expanding Liberties* (New York, 1966). Niccolò Machiavelli, *The Historical, Political, and Diplomatic Writings*, 4 vols., trans. C. E. Detmold (Boston, 1891). David R. Mayhew, *Party Loyalty among Congressmen* (Cambridge, Mass., 1966). Glenn R. Morrow, *Plato's Cretan City . . .* (Princeton, 1960). Robert K. Murray, *Red Scare* (Minneapolis, 1955). Plato, *Euthyphro, Apology, Crito, Phaedo, Phaedrus*, Loeb Classical Library (London and Cambridge, Mass., 1914; 1960); idem, *Republic*, trans. F. M. Cornford (Oxford, 1945); idem, *Laws*, trans. A. E. Taylor (London, 1960). H. Mark Roelofs, *The Tension of Citizenship* (New York, 1957). Michael P. Rogin, *The Intellectuals and McCarthy . . .* (Cambridge, Mass., 1967). Josiah Royce, *The Philosophy of Loyalty* (New York, 1908); idem, *The Problem* of Christianity, 2 vols. (New York, 1913); reprint in 1 vol. (Chicago, 1967). Samuel A. Stouffer, *Communism, Conformity and Civil Liberties* (New York, 1955). Telford Taylor, *Grand Inquest* (New York, 1955). Rebecca West, *The New Meaning of Treason* (New York, 1964).

MILTON R. KONVITZ

[See also **Civil Disobedience; Democracy;** Ideology; **Justice;** Law, Common; Nationalism; State; Stoicism; *Virtù*.]

MACHIAVELLISM

I. MACHIAVELLI AND THE BEGINNINGS OF MACHIAVELLISM

MACHIAVELLISM has historically come to mean that effectiveness alone counts in politics; political actions should not be restricted by considerations of morality, of good or evil.

In this sense Machiavellism existed before Machiavelli, and is as old as politics itself. The view that the struggle for political power should be excepted from the usual norms of ethical behavior was widely recognized in the ancient world. It was stated in the dialogue between the Athenians and the Melians in the fifth book of Thucydides' *History of the Peloponnesian War* and was given a simple poetic formulation in Euripides' *Phoenician Maidens* (lines 524–25): "If wrong may e'er be right, for a throne's sake were wrong most right:— Be God in all else feared." In these quotations the drive for power appears as almost instinctive, something that cannot be kept in check. Roman writers were more conscious of the problems involved in the transgression of moral laws. Cicero (*De officiis,* Book III, Ch. II), and Tacitus (*Annals,* Book XIV, Ch. XLIV), said that they believed violation of moral law was permissible only if the *utilitas rei publicae* ("public welfare") required it. With this they introduced an idea that would become of great importance in the history of Machiavellism.

Despite recognition of the problem in the ancient world there are good reasons why discussions on the general validity of moral norms in politics are connected with the name of Niccolò Machiavelli. The ancient world and the Renaissance were separated by the Christian Middle Ages in which justice and peace were regarded as the only legitimate purposes of government. Admittedly, even in the Middle Ages rulers had not always acted according to the prescriptions of the Christian religion. Canonists and legalists, aware of this fact, had tried to determine the situations and conditions under which the *ratio publicae utilitatis* or the *ratio status* ("reason of state")—to use some of their

terms—allowed violations of the common law or the moral code. It has been argued therefore that the doctrine of "reason of state" which exerted great influence in the political thought and life of the sixteenth and seventeenth centuries was actually a medieval doctrine. Such a thesis disregards the medieval legal doctrine that violation of law and ethical rules was permitted only in order to protect the community instituted by God and the law of nature as necessary for achieving the social and political ends of man on earth. A lower law could be disregarded for a higher, divine law. In contrast to the doctrine of "reason of state" which was developed in the centuries after Machiavelli, in medieval legal doctrine the government or the ruler remained subordinated to a higher—divine or natural—law.

With the Renaissance the gap between underlying assumptions and the practical conduct of politics widened. Doubts about the general validity of the accepted moral code became a powerful ferment in modern political thought and in this development Machiavelli's writings have been crucial.

However, many of the notions which are connected with the term Machiavellism were not explicitly stated by Machiavelli but only implied in his political writings. Of these Machiavelli's *Istorie Fiorentine* was significant because it contained an attack against the worldly power of the Papacy which weakened the hold of the preachings of the Church. However, the doctrines of Machiavellism were chiefly developed from *Il Principe* and the *Discorsi*. Machiavelli's treatment of virtues and vices in Chs. XV–XIX of the *Principe* was meant to shock and it had this effect. One can see this from the frequency and passion with which its theses were discussed and rejected. There are many vehement refutations of Machiavelli's suggestion that a prince ought not to scorn murder if this serves his purposes, or that in order to be popular and secure in power a prince need not be virtuous, only appear so. It is evident from the frequency with which writers debated the issue that they were puzzled and bothered by Machiavelli's view that princes could be expected to keep promises, commitments, and alliances only as long as these agreements corresponded to their interests.

Of course, the most novel and startling feature in the *Principe* and the *Discorsi* was the open recognition of the role of force in politics. "You must know, then, that there are two methods of fighting, the one by law, the other by force: the first method is that of men; the second that of beasts; but as the first method is often insufficient one must have recourse to the second" (*Il Principe,* Ch. XVIII). The *Discorsi* possessed other features of a startling and upsetting character; they presented a defense of freedom and republicanism. Since republican government was a rarity in these centuries of the rise of monarchical absolutism, Machiavelli's defense of republicanism reinforced the impression that he advocated doctrines which undermined the fundamental tenets of the existing political, social, and moral order.

In 1559 Machiavelli's writings were placed on the Index. Insofar as this measure had any meaning it was limited to Italy and Spain. Manuscripts of Machiavelli's writings, particularly of the *Principe*, circulated widely in France and England, and Machiavelli's works continued to be printed and translated. However, Catholic writers shied away from open acknowledgment of their acquaintance with Machiavelli. Allusions to his theories and writings were made in a somewhat cryptic manner. This secretiveness had its bearing upon the image of Machiavelli and Machiavellism. It was easy to assign to him views and ideas which were only loosely connected with the theories of the great Florentine.

II. MACHIAVELLISM FROM THE SIXTEENTH TO THE EIGHTEENTH CENTURY

From the middle of the sixteenth century until the French Revolution Machiavellism represented a powerful current in intellectual life. In the 1580's Machiavellism was so much acknowledged as a recognizable, distinct attitude that the term Machiavellist appeared in print (1581 in France in Nicolas Froumenteau's *Finances;* 1589 in England in a treatise by Thomas Nash).

Although Machiavelli's exclusive concern had been politics, the mystery which the condemnation of his writings wrapped around him fostered the belief that his teachings were applicable to any kind of human activity. The common denominator of all Machiavellist attitudes was doubt that successful action was compatible with living according to a strictly moral code. Despite agreement on this basic assumption, and despite the fact that the development of Machiavellian attitudes toward life and of a Machiavellian outlook on politics went hand in hand, a historical presentation of the unfolding of Machiavellism might most conveniently separate the story of (1) Machiavelli as teacher of human behavior from that of Machiavelli as political counselor, and in the area of Machiavellian politics it might be advisable to make a distinction between (2) Machiavelli's views on the management of the internal affairs of a society and (3) Machiavelli's notions about the conduct of foreign policy.

(1) The view which in the sixteenth century was formed about Machiavelli's prescriptions for human behavior can be summarized in the simple formula that he was considered to be a teacher of evil. His message was that being evil was more useful and efficient than being good. One might deceive, lie, commit crimes, even murder, if this helped to achieve success. As an advocate of such evil doctrines Machiavelli moved close to the Devil.

An identification of Machiavelli with Satan was made early in the sixteenth century by Reginald Pole in his *Apologia Reginaldi Poli ad Carolum V* (1539), and the acceptance of this view is reflected in the widespread belief that "Old Nick," the name given to the Devil, was an abbreviation of Machiavelli's first name (actually the name "Old Nick" for the Devil is older than the sixteenth century). The French held the same view about those who regarded Machiavelli as their *Évangile* ("Gospel"):

Pour mieux trahir faire la chattemite,
Mentire, piper, deguiser verité,
Couvrir le loup de fainte saincteté,
Sembler devot et n'estre qu'hypocrite.

("To better betray affect an air of benevolence,/ Lie, beguile, disguise the truth,/ Cover the wolf with a pretence of holiness,/ Seem devout and be nothing but a hypocrite.")

Machiavellian doctrines were the instruments by means of which the Devil exerted his influence in the world. Huguenots saw the Satanic character of Machiavelli's advice in the actions of their enemies; they considered the Guises as faithful pupils of Machiavelli. The first systematic attack against Machiavelli—Innocent Gentillet's *Discours sur les moyens de bien gouverner . . . contre Nicolas Machiavel Florentin* (1576)—was composed by a Huguenot and dedicated to the Duc d'Alençon who was in sharp opposition to his mother, Catherine de'Medici. She was said to have Machiavelli's works at her bedside, and the massacre of Saint Bartholomew was viewed as a plot inspired by a study of Machiavelli.

There were particular reasons for the rise of an ardent anti-Machiavellism among Protestants and in Northern Europe. Machiavelli was an Italian, and as such, his ideas were assumed to guide the behavior of two kinds of people who were regarded with distrust and hatred north of the Alps: Italians and Jesuits. The activities and resources of Italian merchants and bankers had given them influence and power at the courts and among the ruling groups of most European countries. Their reputation as leaders in art and scholarship made them much sought after for prominent positions in chancelleries and universities. Papal legates played a determining role in the ecclesiastical affairs of Catholic countries; they were mostly Italians and often brought Italians with them in their suites, and among them, Jesuits. The dominant position of these Italian foreigners naturally aroused the enmity of the natives. Italians were held responsible for misgovernment and 117 corruption, for diverting the rulers from their traditional honest ways of government. It was this anti-Italianism which also fed anti-Machiavellism.

In France, from 1559 to 1574, during fifteen politically crucial years, the Queen Mother, Catherine of Medici, exerted decisive political influence. She showed a great preference for Italians and things Italian, and opposition to her policy was reinforced by strong anti-Italian feelings. Catherine's policy was wavering and tortuous and although this might have been due to weakness rather than to calculation, the impression which she gave was that of deceitfulness and unreliability. Her policy confirmed the equation of Machiavellism and Italianism. François Hotman, the most powerful voice among French anti-Catholic polemicists, identified in a quite crude way Italy, Catherine de'Medici, canon law, and Machiavelli. In England the religious content of the political struggles made the Papacy, and the Jesuits as the Papacy's most effective defenders, the chief target of attack, and Machiavellism and Jesuitism were frequently seen as identical. Even English Catholics regarded the Jesuits as ambitious Italian foreigners who wanted to rule the Church and—to quote from an English Catholic pamphlet of 1601—whose "holy exercise" was "but a meere Machivilean device of pollicie."

Because Machiavelli's doctrines were seen as embodied in personalities with particular characteristics, the author of these doctrines also acquired personal features and became a recognizable individual. As such Machiavelli entered literature and became the prototype of a character which in different forms has appeared in drama and in novels. The imaginative creation of a Machiavelli figure has significance in the history of literature, but the existence of such a concrete image of Machiavelli has also reinforced interest in political Machiavellism and its impact.

Machiavelli's entry on the literary scene took place in the Tudor and Stuart period. In Christopher Marlowe's *Jew of Malta* (ca. 1589) Machiavelli himself comes on the stage as Prologue. His words enunciate in a simplified manner basic features of Machiavelli's political ideas: "Might first made kings, and laws were then most sure,/when like the Dracos they were writ in blood." These notions, however, were only applications of a more general philosophy; Marlowe's Machiavelli is a man who disregards moral bonds in every sphere of life: "I count religion but a childish toy/and hold there is no sin but ignorance." Marlowe's contemporaries and successors quickly recognized the dramatic possibilities inherent in the Machiavellian figure. The literature on this topic is extended and it might be enough here to indicate Shakespeare's use of the Machiavellian prototype. The figure in Shake-

speare's oeuvre that is clearly conceived as a personification of Machiavellian doctrines is Richard III. Shakespeare acknowledged the Machiavellian aspects of his concept of this king openly in the words which in *Henry VI* (Part III, Act III, Scene ii, lines 182–95) he put into the mouth of the young Duke of Gloucester:

> Why, I can smile, and murder whiles I smile;
> And cry content to that which grieves my heart;
> And wet my cheeks with artificial tears,
> And frame my face to all occasions.
> I'll drown more sailors than the mermaid shall;
> I'll slay more gazers than the basilisk;
> I'll play the orator as well as Nestor;
> Deceive more slily than Ulysses could;
> And, like a Sinon, take another Troy;
> I can add colours to the cameleon;
> Change shapes with Proteus for advantages;
> And set the murderous Machiavel to school.
> Can I do this, and cannot get a crown?
> Tut, were it further off, I'll pluck it down!

Richard III is an amoral human being rather than a purposeful politician. Nevertheless, his Machiavellian activities have politics as their center. Shakespeare has created another Machiavellian figure, however, whose evilness is purely personal and has nothing to do with politics: Iago in *Othello*. Iago lies, deceives, intrigues, conspires to reach his own personal ends. By his devilish acts he forces others who stand morally far above him into his nets and destroys them. In Othello's words Iago is a "demi-devil" who has "ensnar'd my soul and body."

Iago demonstrates that the name of Machiavellism could be affixed to any kind of evilness as long as it was evilness on a grand scale. The Machiavellian looked only after his own interests and desires and was willing to lie and to deceive, to use crooked means, in order to obtain them. He concealed his true intentions and masked them behind words of piety or goodwill. He liked to work in the dark and without others knowing it he maneuvered them into doing his bidding.

Because in its broadest sense Machiavellism is assumed to be synonymous with amorality and evilness in general, every class and profession can have Machiavellians. Since Machiavelli made his appearance on the Elizabethan stage literature has been full of figures who are Machiavellists or have some Machiavellian flavor. Certainly figures from the ruling group—court favorites, diplomats, ministers—are most easily presented as Machiavellists. Marinelli in G. E. Lessing's *Emilia Galotti* (1772) is probably the best-known figure of a Machiavellian courtier in dramatic literature. But persons with Machiavellian behavior are to be found also in novels or plays that describe the life of the middle classes or of the bourgeoisie. A favorite figure in eighteenth-century literature is the intriguing evil kin who tries to ruin the naive honest hero. There is in Henry Fielding's *Tom Jones* (1749) Master Blifil "whose affections are solily placed on one single person [himself] whose interest and indulgence alone they consider on every occasion." There is Joseph Surface in Sheridan's *School for Scandal* (1777) who has the "policy" not to deviate "from the direct road of wrong." Admittedly all these figures are variations on the theme of hypocrisy.

But the eighteenth-century notion of Machiavellism patterned the qualities and actions which writers assigned to the hypocrites of their creation. The eighteenth century was a moralist century, however, and usually the honest hero triumphed over his sly antagonist; in this respect the Machiavellism of eighteenth-century writers is somewhat defective. There is one thoroughly Machiavellian eighteenth-century novel, however—Choderlos de Laclos' *Liaisons dangereuses* (1782)—which depicts a world in which goodness and morality unavoidably succumb to the powers of vice, deceit, and egoism. The struggle for domination between men and women which forms the content of this novel is conducted with strategies, ruses, moves, and countermoves like the conflicts of politics and war. It should be added that Julien Sorel in Stendhal's *Le Rouge et le Noir* (1831) is in this tradition. Stendhal actually mentions the Machiavellism of his hero and uses quotations from Machiavelli for chapter headings. Nevertheless, Julien Sorel is an exception in the nineteenth century; pronouncedly Machiavellian characters are becoming rare.

Heroes in the novels by George Meredith (*The Egoist*, 1879) or Henryk Sienkiewicz (*Without Dogma*, 1891) are egoists out of weakness, out of fear of life, not out of strength. In the nineteenth century the belief which gave to Machiavellism its attraction and fascination—namely, that behind evil there was a demonic strength which made evil an equal rival to good—disappeared. The maintenance of evil was not in the plan of providence but right measures would progressively remove it. Goethe's *Faust* (pub. 1808) might be taken as a sign of the change which took place with the nineteenth century. For actually in Goethe's *Faust* God is the Machiavellian. He robs the Devil of Faust's soul by a trick; as a force *die stets das Böse will und stets das Gute schafft* ("which wills evil and yet does good"; I, line 1335) the Devil is an instrument of the divine will. In Hegelian terms nothing is entirely negative because even what might appear so is only a *List der Vernunft* ("the cunning of reason"). Such a unifying and reconciling conception of the process of world history is incompatible with Machiavellism which, at

least as a doctrine bearing on all aspects of human behavior, draws its power from the belief in the ineradicability of evil.

(2) Machiavelli's ideas could form a point of departure for all those who transformed Machiavelli into a devil incarnate recommending evil-doing in all spheres of life. But actually the connection between Machiavelli's views and such recommendations for a general code of human behavior is tenuous. Machiavelli's writings aimed at political action; therefore, only interpretations of his thought concerned with questions of political conduct should be closely linked to his views. In political Machiavellism we find the outgrowth of Machiavelli's own ideas although he might not always have liked the conclusions which were drawn, or approved of the extreme simplifications into which his views were condensed.

Machiavelli's *Principe* was addressed to a man who wanted to found a new state in divided Italy. The slow rise of absolutism in the sixteenth and seventeenth centuries made this advice appropriate and timely for the handling of internal affairs all over Europe. The absolute monarch tried to cut off all outside interference in the affairs of the territory which he was ruling and to make his power independent of the approval of those he was ruling; this involved subordination of the Church, reduction of the power of the estates, disregard of old rights, and infringement of privileges. Because Machiavelli had allowed and recommended violations of legal commitments in the interest of self-preservation and aggrandizement, it was easy to see his spirit behind the actions of the absolute rulers or their ministers.

In France and England the cry "Machiavellist" was raised against all those who tried to enlarge royal power. In France the writers of the *Fronde* claimed that Mazarin, in his attempt to destroy the old French liberties, followed *Maximes Italiennes et Machiavélistes* which he had brought into France from the other side of the Alps (Claude Joly, 1652). In England the opposition to the financial and religious policy of Charles I saw in this Stuart king a disciple of Machiavelli "who counseled his Prince to keepe his subjects low, by taxes and impositions and to foment divisions among them, that he might awe them at his pleasures" (from a pamphlet of 1648).

One issue in particular drew Machiavelli's name into the political discussions of this period, that of religion and the Church. Machiavelli was believed to have been an atheist to whom religion was primarily a useful instrument in the hands of the rulers. When in France a group of politicians suggested the possibility of ending the civil war by tolerating two churches in one state these men (*politiques*) were immediately called **119**

Machiavellists, that is, men who subordinated religion to worldly political interests. When in England dissension developed among the various religious groups about the part of religion and of the Church in the ordering of society each group accused the other of Machiavellism; in particular the Presbyterians were accused of "Jesuitical and Machiavellian policy." The same criticism—that of pursuing politics under the name of religion—was used against Cromwell after he had become Lord Protector; to his opponents Cromwell was also a Machiavellian.

The tone changed somewhat when in the eighteenth century the struggle about the extension of royal power had ended and at least on the continent monarchical absolutism had won out. The critics of the existing regimes—the *philosophes*—were no opponents of monarchy or even absolutism; what they demanded was that the ruler follow the rules of reason and morality, that he carry out his functions in the interest of all. Their fight was directed against despotic arbitrariness which imprisoned people in order to gratify personal wishes and desires, which burdened the subjects with taxes in order to waste money on luxurious buildings, which sacrificed the lives of peoples in wars for prestige and fame, and which maintained the irrational rule of the Church in order to keep people quiet and obedient. Machiavelli was a chief target of the *philosophes* because he preached an amoralistic selfishness which promoted despotic arbitrariness.

Voltaire characterized as the great principles of Machiavellism *ruinez qui pourrait un jour vous ruiner; assassinez votre voisin qui pourrait devenir assez fort pour vous tuer* ("ruin anyone who might someday ruin you; assassinate your neighbor who might become strong enough to kill you"). And Diderot defined Machiavellism briefly as *l'art de tyranniser*. This moralistic view colored also the views which eighteenth-century statesmen held about Machiavelli. Although Bolingbroke, well acquainted with the political literature of the past, had great respect for Machiavelli's understanding of political techniques, his Patriot King (*Idea of a Patriot King*, 1749), faced like Machiavelli's prince by the task of restoring political life in a corrupted society, contained a sharp rejection of Machiavelli because, according to Bolingbroke, he lacked true patriotism which was concerned with the well-being of everyone. The most famous eighteenth-century condemnation of Machiavelli, of course, is the *Anti-Machiavel* (1740) of Frederick the Great in which every one of Machiavelli's maxims is refuted.

Since, in Catholic countries during the sixteenth and seventeenth centuries, Machiavelli was an author whom one was not supposed to know and therefore not to quote exactly, the qualities which in the eyes of the people of these centuries distinguished a man as a Machiavellist, must be deduced primarily from the image which anti-Machiavellists had formed. However, because the defenders of the old rights and privileges saw in Machiavelli an inspirer of the new absolutist policy, their opponents, the advocates of royal power, became anxious to know whether these bitter attacks against Machiavelli meant that the Florentine offered a reasonable justification of absolutist policy, and they took a careful look at his writings. Therefore in the seventeenth century there were not only anti-Machiavellists but also men who defended Machiavelli as a political thinker of insight and understanding.

In Venice, where the long struggle with the Papacy over the boundaries between political and ecclesiastical jurisdiction reached its critical highpoint in the first years of the seventeenth century, Machiavelli was said to enjoy great popularity, and in the writings defending the position of the Venetian government, particularly in those of Paolo Sarpi, echoes of Machiavelli's theories can be found. The first openly positive evaluations of Machiavelli's theories, however, were composed in France and came from the surroundings of the great royal ministers who led the fight against the restricting and inhibiting influence of the French nobility: Richelieu and Mazarin. Gabriel Naudé in his *Considérations politiques sur les coups d'état* (1639) started with the traditional thesis that the *bonum commune* justified actions neglecting legal forms. But he then argued that such justification of violence ought to be extended to sudden *coups d'état* like the assassination of the Duc de Guise; politicians condemned Machiavelli in theory but acted according to him in practice. In Louis Machon's *Apologie pour Machiavelle* (1641) a vehement anti-clericalism was combined with an exaltation of monarchical absolutism resulting in an appreciation of Machiavelli's theories. The climate of the decade in which the German emperor found it necessary to order the murder of his General Wallenstein was certainly conducive to a better understanding of Machiavelli.

The tendency to recognize Machiavelli as an important political thinker received impetus and confirmation from a group of writers whose views on Machiavelli were diametrically opposed to the interpretation given by the anti-Machiavellists. These political writers did not regard Machiavelli as an advocate of despotism or power politics; if Machiavellism is understood as an intellectual attitude which permits amoral actions for political ends, it is questionable whether the views of these admirers of Machiavelli form part of the history of Machiavellism. The thinkers of this group saw in Machiavelli primarily an advocate of republican freedom. The *Principe* was meant as a warning. The book showed what would happen if people became negligent in protecting their liberty. The idea that the *Principe* was meant to put people on guard against the rise of tyrants had been suggested already in the sixteenth century; it can be found, for instance, in Alberico Gentili's *De legationibus* (1585) and it has had adherents ever since, even in the twentieth century, although all the documents bearing on the composition of the *Principe* show that there is no substance behind it. For the history of Machiavelli's reputation, however, the suggestion was important because it directed attention away from the *Principe* to the *Discorsi* as containing Machiavelli's authentic message. Thus Machiavelli began to take on a Janus face. The inspirer of despotism was also the defender of freedom.

The discovery of the republican Machiavelli in the seventeenth century was chiefly the work of a group of English political writers. In England alone a relatively free discussion of political ideas was possible and a radical trend of ideas, generated in the period of the Commonwealth, lived on under the Restoration. The chief representatives of this opposition have been called "classical republicans." They were steeped in the admiration of classical political wisdom and wanted to reorganize English political life according to classical principles. They were attracted by Machiavelli's writings because he was one of the few if not the only republican political theorist in modern times. Moreover, they considered him to be the most important transmitter of classical teachings to the modern world. There were also some more particular reasons for their interest in Machiavelli. His insistence on the necessity of going back to the beginnings, "the principles," was compatible with their plan for rebuilding society on new foundations. And Machiavelli had given some praise to the notion of mixed government which they believed would secure England from another civil war between extremes. Thus James Harrington, the author of the *Commonwealth of Oceana* (1656), called Machiavelli the "prince of polititians" and for Henry Neville, the author of the *Plato Redivivus*, Machiavelli was the "divine Machiavel."

Although the particular emphasis which these writers placed on Machiavelli's ideas was conditioned by the political situation in England, their views indicate that below the surface of criticism and condemnation there were students of politics who recognized that one could learn from Machiavelli because his views were based on acute and realistic observations of political life. This attitude can be traced back to Bacon who in his *De augmentis scientiarum* (*Advancement of Learning* [1623], Book VII, Ch. 2) confessed that "We are much beholden to Machiavelli and other writers of that class who openly and unfeignedly declare or describe what men do, and not what they ought to do."

This aspect of Machiavelli's writings could not fail to impress the great political thinkers of the eighteenth century. To Hume Machiavelli was a "great genius"; Montesquieu frequently referred approvingly to Machiavelli's views. These eighteenth-century thinkers were repulsed by his amoralism but they suggested that the stress on the political effectiveness of amoral actions was the work of later writers. They separated Machiavelli from Machiavellism and emphasized that Machiavelli himself had loved liberty. Diderot, who in the *Encyclopédie* characterized Machiavellism as an *espèce de politique détestable, qu'on peut rendre en deux mots par l'art de tyranniser* ("odious kind of politics, which can be described briefly as the art of tyranny"), also said in his article on Machiavelli that the purpose of the *Principe* was to depict the terrors of despotism: *Voilà la bête féroce, à laquelle vous vous abandonnerez* ("See here the ferocious beast, to whom you abandon yourself"). It was the fault of the reader that he took *un satyre pour un éloge* ("a satire for a eulogy").

By the end of the eighteenth century, therefore, the image of Machiavelli had become rather complex and even contradictory. The contrast between the devilish Machiavelli whom Marlowe had brought on the stage and the sagacious Machiavelli who appears in Goethe's *Egmont* (1788) is instructive. Goethe's Machiavelli knew that people need to lie and to deceive in politics, but he knew also that such measures have little effect if they do not take into account the real feelings of the people. You cannot force religious convictions on them or treat them arrogantly from above. Goethe's Machiavelli implies that Machiavellism is necessary and appropriate only because—and as long as—rulers give no rights to their people. A new time in which the people will have power will make Machiavellian policy superfluous; *Egmont* was written in 1787, two years before the French Revolution.

(3) When Frederick II of Prussia became involved in the struggle for Prussian aggrandizement Rousseau said that it was appropriate for a disciple of Machiavelli to begin his political career with a refutation of Machiavelli. Frederick's *Anti-Machiavel* has frequently been characterized as hypocritical, but this accusation is not quite fair. In his *Anti-Machiavel* Frederick had pointed out that Machiavelli's political experience came from a scene in which princes *ne sont proprement que des Hermafrodites de Souverains, et des Particuliers; ils ne jouent le rôle de grands Seigneurs qu'avec leur domestiques* ("are only in fact hermaphrodites of rulers and individuals; they play the part of great lords only with their servants"). Frederick denied that this

Italian world of small princely states could serve as a model for the conduct of politics. He thought it necessary to distinguish between petty intriguing, characteristic of small states, and the justifiable aims of a great power to expand.

In Frederick's times it had become a widely recognized theory that powerful states had a right to expand and to pursue their interests by all possible means. Machiavelli was certainly the most important influence in the development of these ideas. However, because of the evil repute in which his name was held in the sixteenth and seventeenth centuries it was regarded as inopportune to mention his name, and consequently the name of Machiavelli remained rather detached from that development of thought with which his ideas are most closely linked—the attitudes toward foreign affairs.

A point of departure for the development of new ideas on the nature of foreign policy was Machiavelli's thesis that the decisive factor in politics was power, not justice; and that the attainment of political ends permitted the use of force, violence, even crime. The ensuing discussion centered on the problem of whether there were limits to the application of force in the struggles among states, and if so, what they were. The crucial concept in this development was the notion of *ragione di stato* ("reason of state"), which implied that the relationship among states had its own rules, different from those determining human behavior in other spheres of life. Although some statements made by Italians of Machiavelli's time suggest that they recognized that in affairs of state actions might be necessary that are not permissible in other fields of human activities, the term *ragione di stato* neither occurs in Machiavelli's writings, nor was it used in the early sixteenth century. It came into use in the middle of that century and then soon became immensely popular. It was heard in the marketplace but also in the council room; for instance, as early as 1584, James VI of Scotland declared to his Privy Council "that he married for reasons of state, chiefly to provide his kingdom with an heir."

Originally the meaning of *ragione di stato* was not very different from that of the medieval notion of *ratio status* or *ratio publicae utilitatis* which permitted the ruler to violate positive law if the promotion of the higher spiritual aims of the social order made such action necessary. But the idea of reason of state became strikingly transformed in the modern period. The religious struggles of the sixteenth and seventeenth centuries—or, more precisely, weariness produced by these struggles—gave rise to the view that one state could embrace adherents of different churches and that politics had its own principles independent of those of religion. Politics had its own law, that of the interest of the state. Furthermore, the rise of absolutism resulted in an identification of prince and state. The interest of the ruler became the reason of state. Nevertheless, a line was drawn between those political aims in which the interest of the prince coincided with the interests of the entire political body and those ambitions which arose from personal desires or arbitrary whims. The latter had to be repudiated as signs of tyranny.

From these assumptions there developed an extensive literature on the interests of the state and of the princes. The writers of this school tried to establish criteria for distinguishing between true and false interests and to determine those factors which constituted the true interests of the state. Because the presupposition of these thinkers was that politics was an autonomous field, speculations about the interests of the state were calculations in terms of power politics. They were concerned with those factors which constituted the strength of a state and would make aggrandizement possible: population, geographical position, financial resources, military posture, relation to neighbors. In the seventeenth and eighteenth centuries the writings on reason of state and interests of state amounted to a considerable part of the existing political literature.

The crucial influence of Machiavelli on the development of these ideas is obvious. He had proclaimed that politics ought to be conducted for purely political ends, for increasing the strength of the political body. He was instrumental, therefore, in introducing into the theory of reason of state that element which separated it from the older medieval concept in which the *ratio status* remained subordinated to nonpolitical or suprapolitical values. The emphasis on competition for power as the central factor in political life was thoroughly Machiavellian, although in Machiavelli's writings the word *stato* in the modern sense of embracing territory, ruler and ruled, rarely occurs. Machiavelli's *principe* had only to be interpreted as synonymous with the state in order to find in Machiavelli's writings a serious discussion of the problem of *ragione di stato*.

Although the writers on the interests of state did not acknowledge their debt to Machiavelli, and even concealed it by attacking him, their writings reflect their careful reading of the Florentine's works. Giovanni Botero, whose *Della Ragione di Stato* (1589) is one of the most influential early statements of the problem, accepted Machiavelli's thesis that no reliance could be placed on alliances or treaties. Traiano Boccalini (1556–1613) commented in his *Bilancia politica* on many of Machiavelli's theses and made the very Machiavellian statement that self-interest *è il vero Tiranno dell'Anime de'Tiranni, ed anche de'Principi non Tiranni* ("is the true tyrant of the souls of tyrants as well as of princes who are not tyrants"). Although Paolo Paruta (1540–1598) declared in his *Discorsi politici* that Machiavelli was "buried in perpetual oblivion" he agreed with him on many issues and acknowledged that the operations of a prince should be measured by quite different rules from those of a philosopher.

Two centuries later, in the eighteenth century, discussions of the European political situation, historical works, invented political testaments ascribed to famous rulers and statesmen, and pamphlets—all made use of reason of state and interests of princes in their arguments; at that time Machiavelli's name was no longer to be passed over in silence. However, the connection of his name with the ideas of this school of political thought did not help Machiavelli's reputation among the *philosophes* and the reformers. They were profoundly critical of the manner in which foreign policy was conducted in this period. They saw no sense in wars of aggrandizement and regarded the money spent on the maintenance of a large army as an obstacle to the economic well-being of the masses. These were features of the *ancien régime* that ought to be eliminated. As a master in the arts of *ragione di stato* Machiavelli became associated with the *ancien régime*.

The most characteristic representatives of the abhorred policies of the *ancien régime* were the diplomats—the "ministers" as they were called at this time. They became the particular target of the reform-minded writers of the eighteenth century who, in their descriptions of the activities of the diplomatic profession, endowed ministers with Machiavellian features. Such ministers, according to G. F. Le Trosne, cultivated *art obscure qui s'enveloppe dans les plis et les replis de la dissimulation* ("a dark art wrapping itself up in the folds and cloak of dissimulation"); because they lack frankness they become *compétiteurs en grimaces* (Mirabeau). Machiavellists, as we mentioned before, can be found in all groups and professions. If one profession is particularly identified with this attitude it is the diplomatic profession, and in the popular view it has remained so since the eighteenth century.

In the last year of the eighteenth century a French translation of the works of Machiavelli was published with an introduction by T. Guiraudet who had first served the *ancien régime*, then the Revolution, and was finally a high official in the Foreign Office under the Directorate. With its emphasis on Machiavelli's anti-clericalism and his nationalism Guiraudet alludes to aspects of Machiavelli's thought, one of which had agitated his readers in the past, and the other was to occupy students of Machiavelli in the future, although the prominent place given to these two ideas echoed the ideas of the French Revolution. But the most striking and interesting feature is the attempt of Guiraudet to reconcile those contradictory features of Machiavelli which in the course of the eighteenth century had emerged in sharp contrast:

Machiavel, qui aimait la liberté d'une manière éclairée, savait que les hommes, qui se sont réunis en société, se sont associés éminemment pour être heureux, et non uniquement pour être libres. . . . Ils ont vu que la liberté était un moyen, mais qu'elle n'était pas un but . . . le premier des biens, c'est le salut de l'État, le bonheur et la prospérité de ses membres, auxquels peut nuire momentanément une liberté illimitée; or y laisser instantanément mettre quelque bornes, ce n'est pas être ou un esclave ou un lâche, c'est prouver seulement qu'on n'est pas toujours aussi libre qu'un fou.

("Machiavelli, with his enlightened love of freedom, knew that men, who have united in society, came together primarily to be happy and not simply to be free. . . . They have seen that freedom was a means and not the end . . . that the primary good is the welfare of the State, the happiness and prosperity of its members, who can be hurt for a while by unlimited freedom; now to allow momentarily certain limits to be imposed on their freedom does not mean being a slave or a coward, but only proves that we are not always as free as a madman.")

III. MACHIAVELLISM IN THE MODERN WORLD

It is most doubtful that Machiavellism survived the fall of the *ancien régime*. This statement does not imply that interest in Machiavelli diminished or died; on the contrary, in the nineteenth and twentieth centuries an extended literature concerned with Machiavelli and Machiavelli's thought was produced, but the nature of interest in Machiavelli has changed.

In previous centuries Machiavelli's ideas had been regarded as the nucleus of a system which was of practical significance for every kind of political action and human behavior. With the political and social transformation brought about by the French Revolution Machiavellism lost the environment in which its notions would strike sparks.

A secularized outlook on the world, frequently coupled with an optimistic belief in progress, could regard evil actions as a result of strange, abnormal circumstances or psychology. But that awe for the demonic power of evil that had made Machiavelli's recommendations not only abhorrent but also tempting was lost.

Likewise, after the French Revolution, tyranny and despotism seemed to belong to a discarded past. Even if the march to full democratic rule of the people was slow, even if a written constitution limiting the extent and the forms of government interference and a determination of the rights of man had become accepted features of a civilized political society, much of the advice which Machiavelli had given to his prince and on which Machiavellist writers like Naudé or Machon had enlarged became irrelevant.

Finally, the rise of nationalism stripped the Machiavellist theories on the unlimited use of force in foreign affairs of much of their explosive character. If the nation and the national state embodied the supreme ethical value and the individual could accomplish his own ethical ends only within a strong nation, then application of force to secure the life of the nation was easily justifiable and Machiavelli's views sounded much less extravagant than when they seemed to proclaim the unlimited right of the stronger over the weaker. In this changed political atmosphere people were inclined to minimize the consequences of Machiavelli's thought rather than to face them in their ruthless radicalism. Because of the appeal to liberate Italy from the barbarians in the last chapter of the *Principe*, Machiavelli was transformed into a prophet of the age of nationalism, and the amorality of his doctrines was explained as a result of the hopelessness of the Italian political situation: it was so desperate that Machiavelli was forced to prescribe poison, to use the words of the German historian Leopold von Ranke.

In the changed climate of the nineteenth century, with the development of a new and differentiated outlook on internal politics and foreign affairs, Machiavellism lost the appearance of providing a coherent system. This is reflected in the manner in which the words "Machiavellian" and "Machiavellist" are used in language and literature of the nineteenth and twentieth centuries. Whoever takes mental note of the occurrences of the term "Machiavellist" in modern times will be amused and fascinated by the widely varied and even contradictory applications of the word.

It is logical—and in accordance with the history of Machiavellism—that those features in modern political society which still bear the traces of the *ancien régime* frequently receive the label "Machiavellian." Diplomats are regularly suspected to be Machiavellians and Americans in the times of Woodrow Wilson were inclined to regard the entire European system of foreign policy, based on the assumption of sovereignty, as containing a Machiavellist element. Likewise statesmen proceeding in an authoritarian manner are usually considered as disciples of Machiavelli; in the nineteenth century both Metternich and Bismarck were called Machiavellian.

It is a small step from here to a use of the word that regards every clever political maneuver as Machiavellian. And the reading of political biographies, for instance, the biography of *Huey P. Long* (1967) by T. Harry Williams, or of issues of the *American Historical Review*, will provide many examples of this.

Cleverness, of course, arouses distrust because a clever man is suspected of keeping something back, and of not being entirely frank and open. Briefly, he behaves very much as a Machiavellian would be expected to behave. And indeed, "Machiavellian" and slyly "clever" are often used synonymously. The concept "Machiavellian" has become so vague and ambiguous that every human activity which tries to achieve its ends through exclusion of all extraneous—human or moral—considerations is called "Machiavellian"; a businessman, therefore, might have a Machiavellian strategy. The application of technical devices, because they reduce human or moral qualities to calculable factors, is frequently considered Machiavellian. In the 1960's the labels of Machiavellian or Machiavellistic could be affixed to anything that was considered to be wrong or inhuman.

If the idea of Machiavellism lost in coherence and significance in the nineteenth century, the development of scholarship, and particularly of historical scholarship, maintained and perhaps intensified interest in Machiavelli; however these scholarly concerns separated Machiavelli from Machiavellism and placed Machiavelli in a very new light.

The historical literature on Machiavelli pursued two lines of research. The one was to determine his place in the development of political thought. The other was to see him as a figure of his time, of the Italian Renaissance. In the field of political thought the relation of his thought to classical or medieval political theorists became clarified, and detailed investigations established the influence of his thought on later political thinkers like Montesquieu, or even more recent ones like Gaetano Mosca or Antonio Gramsci. The study of Machiavelli as a figure of the Renaissance resulted in a better understanding of the institutional and social milieu in which he lived and to which his writings were aimed; the difference between his real aims and those ascribed to him by later generations emerged sharply. Because these scholarly efforts described Machiavelli as an Italian of the Renaissance or as a link in the development of political thought, because they "historicized" Machiavelli, they contributed to the decline of Machiavellism as a system of permanent validity and applicability.

On the other hand, the scholarly approach placed Machiavelli at the beginning of a development which has extended into modern times. Machiavelli was shown to have touched upon many questions of political techniques—control of the masses by psychology, the role of an elite—which are recognized as essential factors in every political society and, as such, have become objects of intense study in the development of political science. Moreover, because the Renaissance was believed to have begun the modern period of history, the characterization of Machiavelli as a typical representative of this period made him a forerunner of modern man. Actually it was not so much Machiavelli as his picture of Cesare Borgia which was regarded as characteristically modern—a personality which emancipated itself from the bonds of conventional morality and lived a free life according to its natural instincts. This was Nietzsche's view of Cesare Borgia which he had taken from Machiavelli's *Principe*. Thus, even in the efforts of modern scholarship, Machiavelli has remained—although remotely and tenuously—tied to the concerns of the present day.

This is important because it has its bearing on what might be called the latest, most recent chapter in the history of Machiavellism, the relation of Machiavellism to twentieth-century totalitarianism. Fascist dictators liked to refer to Machiavelli as a master who had understood the true nature of politics; Mussolini professed that he wanted to write a dissertation on Machiavelli. But there is no sign that Hitler or Mussolini had any concrete knowledge of Machiavelli's writings or ideas. They were influenced by social Darwinist ideas of the necessary triumph of the stronger over the weaker. And in the popular mind this was a theory which Machiavelli had already advanced. They pretended to be adherents of Nietzschean philosophy, and thought of Machiavelli's Cesare Borgia as a model of the superman. In the organization of their party and their government system the concept of elite was crucial, and Machiavelli would be mentioned as one of the first political scientists raising this issue.

These were probably the contexts in which they became aware of Machiavelli. They ascribed to him basic ideas of intellectual movements of their own time which had molded their minds, and they found this convenient because they liked to place their policies and systems under the protection of the name of the great Florentine. To maintain the existence of a serious connection between Machiavelli and the ideas and policies of the modern totalitarian dictators is a misunderstanding. It must be added, however, that the history of Machiavellism is quite as much a history of misunderstandings as a history of the impact of Machiavelli's true ideas.

BIBLIOGRAPHY

Machiavelli's principal works—the *Principe*, the *Discorsi*, and the *Istorie Fiorentine*—were first printed in Rome in 1531, but before they were printed, they circulated in manuscript copies, and throughout the sixteenth century, handwritten copies remained as important for the spread of Machiavelli's ideas as printed editions; on this, see Adolf Gerber, *Niccolò Machiavelli. Die Handschriften, Ausgaben und Übersetzungen Seiner Werke im 16. und 17. Jahrhundert* (1913; reprint Turin, 1962), although since the appearance of Gerber's book in 1913, additional handwritten copies of the *Principe* and the *Discorsi* have been discovered.

The classical work on the history of Machiavellism is Friedrich Meinecke, *Die Idee der Staatsräson* (1924; Munich, 1960), trans. D. Scott as *Machiavellism* (New Haven, 1957). The older work of Charles Benoist, *Le Machiavélisme*, 3 vols. (Paris, 1907-36), has now become obsolete although its references to source materials remain valuable. Of a somewhat different character is the book by Giuliano Procacci, *Studi sulla Fortuna del Machiavelli*, Istituto Storico Italiano per l'Età Moderna e Contemporanea (Rome, 1965), which investigates the developments of Machiavelli scholarship rather than the history of the influence of Machiavelli's ideas.

On the intellectual developments in the Middle Ages foreshadowing Machiavellism and the doctrine of reason of state, see Gaines Post, *Studies in Medieval Legal Thought* (Princeton, 1964).

For the developments from the later Middle Ages to the seventeenth century, see Rodolfo de Mattei, *Dal premachiavellismo all'antimachiavellismo*, Biblioteca Storica Sansoni, Nuova serie XLVI (Florence, 1969), and the periodical *Il Pensiero Politico*, I, No. 3 (Florence, 1969); this issue is devoted to Machiavellism and anti-Machiavellism in the sixteenth century.

For the attitude of the eighteenth century to Machiavelli and Machiavellism, see Peter Gay, *The Enlightenment: An Interpretation* (New York, 1966), and Felix Gilbert, "The 'New Diplomacy' of the Eighteenth Century," *World Politics*, 1 (1951), 1–38.

For reason of state and for the change in the views on Machiavelli in the nineteenth century see the article by Albert Elkan, "Die Entdeckung Machiavellis in Deutschland zu Beginn des 19. Jahrhunderts," *Historische Zeitschrift*, 119 (Munich and Berlin, 1919), 429–58; for more recent examples of the application of reason of state, see Alfred Vagts, "Intelligentsia Versus Reason of State," *Political Science Quarterly*, 84 (1969), 80–105.

There are a number of studies on the influence of Machiavelli and on Machiavellism in individual states: for Venice, see William J. Bouwsma, *Venice and the Defense of Republican Liberty* (Berkeley and London, 1968); for France, see the survey by Albert Cherel, *La pensée de Machiavel en France* (Paris, 1935); and for the crucial second half of the sixteenth century, see Vittorio De Caprariis, *Propaganda e pensiero politico in Francia durante le guerre di religione*, Vol. I, *1559-1572* (Naples, 1959), and Donald R. Kelley, *Foundations of Modern Historical Scholarship; Language, Law, and History in the French Renaissance* (New York, 1970); for England, see Felix Raab, *The English Face of Machiavelli* (London and Toronto, 1964); and for detailed investigations of Machiavelli's influence on individual writers, see George L. Mosse, *The Holy Pretence* (Oxford,

1957); H. Butterfield, *The Statecraft of Machiavelli* (London, 1940); and the article by J. G. A. Pocock, "Machiavelli, Harrington, and the English Political Ideologies in the Eighteenth Century," *William and Mary Quarterly*, 3rd series, **22** (1965), 549–83.

For a recent bibliography, see the article by Richard C. Clark, "Machiavelli: Bibliographical Spectrum," *Review of National Literatures*, I (1970), 93–135.

Also of interest is S. E. Hyman, *Iago; Some Approaches to the Illusion of His Motivation* (New York, 1970).

FELIX GILBERT

[See also **Balance of Power**; Constitutionalism; **Nation**; Renaissance Humanism; State.]

MACROCOSM AND MICROCOSM

THE IDEA indicated by the couple, Macrocosm-Microcosm, is the belief that there exists between the universe and the individual human being an identity both anatomical and psychical. The macrocosm is the universe as a whole, whose parts are thought of as parts of a human body and mind. The microcosm is an individual human being whose parts are thought of as analogous to the parts of the larger universe. Thus the idea is similar to all ideas that project human traits into Nature, ideas such as that of creative causation, natural teleology, moral progress as a natural law, and obviously all instances of the pathetic fallacy.

Creative causation is the idea that physical causes produce their effects as an artisan produces his artifacts: the cause of rain, for example, *makes* it rain. By natural teleology is meant the idea that all changes in nature are made for a purpose. But the only purposes we know anything about are human purposes. And when we say that the eye was made for seeing, or that the plant breathes carbon dioxide in order to furnish oxygen for the animals, we are reading into things that are nonhuman traits that are specifically human. And when we say that the course of natural history is towards maximum goodness, we are expressing the idea of moral progress as a natural law.

If we extend such ideas, we find that we are investing the whole of nature with more and more human characters. For instance, the ancient Greeks and Romans saw omens of the human future in the flight of birds, in the shape and markings of the entrails of sacrificed animals, in an eclipse of the sun or moon, or in the appearance of a comet. Behind all this lay the vague notion that man's place in nature was different from that of any other animal. The cosmos existed for his sake and hence anything out of the ordinary must have some special message for him. Some of this has survived in our popular superstitions, superstitions about lucky and unlucky days or numbers, about thunder on the left, about black cats crossing one's road. Modern science has depended upon the abandonment of all such ideas and has seen the universe as a mechanism completely independent of humankind except insofar as mankind modifies it.

That man was a microcosm makes the identification of man and the cosmos almost complete. The element of incompleteness is the perfection of the macrocosm and the imperfections of man. The macrocosm has no imperfection for the simple reason that it is the model of perfection. That is why it is called a cosmos, the primitive meaning of which is "order." But what will be called order will depend on what sort of regularity one is looking for. And there are certain regularities in human individuals as there are in the heavens: the rhythms of sleeping and waking, of hunger, of sexual desire, of menstruation, of fatigue. Curt Richter in his work on "biological clocks" has shown how many illnesses recur at rhythmic intervals.

The projection of human rhythms into the cosmos is only one form of identifying the microcosm and the macrocosm. But classical mythology is full of similar projections. In fact in one of the early Greek philosophers, Empedocles (fifth century B.C.) we find that the two fundamental forces in the universe are identified with the gods of Love and Strife, Aphrodite and Ares. Love brings order into the world, Strife disorder; Love produces harmony, Strife warfare. Thus the cosmos is like an individual torn between conflicting impulses which recur at regular intervals. The manic-depressive would be a modern illustration of this. We should today preserve Empedocles' two gods, but we should depersonalize them and call them attraction and repulsion. Yet even so sophisticated a thinker as Aristotle when he came to explain the action of his Unmoved Mover upon the world which he moved, said that it came about in the same way as the beloved moves the lover. The Unmoved Mover could thus preserve his immobility and yet attract the lower world towards exemplifying the order that is inherent in him.

The literary source of the idea of the microcosm is usually given as Plato's dialogue *Philebus* (29). In that dialogue Socrates says that just as there are four elements in the universe, so there are in us. In us they are weak and mixed, but in the cosmos they are pure and strong and are the source from which we derive our own. So we would say that the hydrogen, oxygen, carbon, and so on that compose our bodies are identical with the same elements in the nonhuman world. But Plato's elements were only four in number, earth, water, air, and fire, and they exist in us as bones, blood and the other liquids, breath, and bodily heat. It is obvious that our earthy parts must come from our solid food, our liquids from the water we drink, our breath from the air about us, and our heat from the sun.

But there is more to a human being than a body. What unifies and holds together the elements in our bodies? Why do we not fall apart? We know that the body acts as a unit, the parts acting "for the sake of" the whole. This can only be explained, as Greek scientists would say, by some agent. And that agent is the soul. But if this is true of the human body, then it must also be true of the universal body, the cosmos. The cosmos, says Socrates, must have a soul just as we have, a soul which in the Middle Ages was called, after Plotinus, a third-century Greek philosopher, the "Soul of the World" (*anima mundi*). Our soul is primarily rational; we are rational animals. The Soul of the World must have a corresponding rationality and the idea of a rational universe was thus launched. And the split between a world in which miracles could happen and one in which all proceeded according to law was definitely made. Plato argued in this same dialogue (30A) that the Soul of the World, like our own, must have wisdom (*sophia*) and intelligence (*nous*). This idea is repeated in another dialogue, of the greatest influence in later times, the *Timaeus* (30), where the cosmos is said to be an image of the Demiurge, endowed with soul and intelligence and thus duplicates the individual human being.

The actual word "microcosm"—the word, not the idea—meaning a little world, was first used by Plato's pupil, Aristotle, in his *Physics* (252b 26). In this passage he assumes that animals can initiate motion; they propel themselves about. If, he says, this is true in the little world, why should it not also be true in the large world? This argument from analogy evidently seemed sound to the inventor of syllogistic logic and it established the habit of referring to the cosmos as if it were alive and self-contained. It was, in fact, later called by the Stoics, who were materialists, a great animal (*mega zoon*).

All such analogies strengthened the idea of man as a microcosm. In Aristotle's psychology, for example, there are three kinds of living beings, plants, animals, and men. The plants feed and reproduce themselves and their souls are said to have the faculty of appetite. The animals have a vegetable soul, but add to it the faculty of sensation. And men have not only vegetable and animal souls, but also reason which is unique in them. Man therefore recapitulates all life and forms a psychic universe parallel to the universe as a whole. Though Aristotle makes no overt use of the microcosm as an idea, it evidently was in the back of his mind.

The microcosm was also used when discussing the state. In Plato's *Republic* we find that there are three kinds of people, the appetitive, the irascible or spirited, and the rational. All men have appetites, some have both appetites and irascibility, and a few have these two faculties plus reason. It is their reason which keeps the other faculties under control. In the state, seen as a large human being, there are three classes of men who correspond to three psychological types. They are the artisans (the appetitive type), the military (the irascible), and the philosophers (the rational). Each serves a legitimate function but trouble arises when one or the other of the two lower classes gets control of the state and usurps the power of reason. The state then becomes like a man who is a lustful glutton or a belligerent captain. Therefore things must be so arranged that the three classes will be kept in their proper places and philosophers will be rulers.

Such ideas only hint at a full-fledged theory of the identity between microcosm and macrocosm, but at least they use the human being as a basic metaphor of something larger and not obviously human. But at the end of the pagan period we find the idea of the microcosm in both the Jewish philosopher, Philo of Alexandria, and in the *Hermetica*. Philo, like so many other theologians, was worried over the biblical verse, "Let us make man in our image, after our likeness" (Genesis 1:26). In *De opificio mundi* (23, 69), he points out that the likeness could not be corporeal and must therefore be psychical. The psychical image of God in man is the intelligence (*nous*), which rules us exactly as God rules the world. He thus takes over from the Platonic tradition that the world is a world of order and reason. This bolsters his use of the allegorical method of interpreting the Bible, for were he to take it literally, he would have to grant the existence of things which would be almost nonrational by definition.

Another Platonic strain comes out in Philo's *Legum allegoria* (I, 29, 91–92), where he says that we may think of God as the soul of the whole. And in the *Migration of Abraham* (*De migratione* 33, 185) he uses the simile of the household for the body, the household in which there is a duality between the master and those subject to him, the living and the lifeless, the rational and the irrational, the immortal and the mortal, the better and the worse. So the cosmos as a whole has God corresponding to the mind, the master, the life, the immortal, the best, the rational, and so on. Just as the mind rules the body, so God rules the universe. And indeed he takes over Aristotle's term, the little world, and says that man is a small world and the cosmos a large man (*Quid rerum?* 29–31, 146–56). In fact the use of the phrase, the human being as a little replica of the universe and of the universe as an enlarged man, is frequent in Philo and is evidence of how commonplace the term and its usage had become by the end of the last pre-Christian century.

Similar metaphors are found in the *Hermetica* which date from the end of the pagan period to the end of the second century A.D., though some of the writings may be earlier and some later. In *Poimandres* (I, 12, 31) we are told that nature is the image of man and that just as eternity is the image of God, so the cosmos is the image of eternity, the sun of the cosmos, and man of the sun (Nous to Hermes, *Poimandres* XI, 15). Man, we also read, is called a cosmos from his divine composition (*Asclepius* 10). How much of this is playing with figures of speech and how much is serious philosophizing can only be determined by one's sympathy with the vagueness of religious writing. But at least it shows, as do the passages from Philo, that the notion of man as a microcosm was common at this time.

In Seneca the earth itself was talked of in terms of the human body. In his *Natural Questions* (III, 15, 1) he says that just as we have veins and arteries, so has the earth. Our veins carry blood and our arteries air; in the earth there are conduits like them that carry water and air. We have various "humors," brain, marrow, mucus, saliva, tears; the earth has other humors which harden into minerals and become gold, silver, bitumen. Just as blood will spurt out if you open a vein, so a spring or river will gush forth if you open one of the veins of the earth. Seneca carries out the correspondence to the point of correlating the periodicities of the body—quartain fever, gout, menstruation, the time of gestation—with the overflowing of springs and their dessication. It was common belief that stones grew in the body of the earth and that the earth as a whole had grown old and its powers of production weakened. It was common practice to speak of the earth in terms of the human body.

Meanwhile the pseudoscience of astrology was developing. In astrology not only are certain planets, including the sun and moon, said to have characters resembling human temperaments, but they, like the signs of the zodiac, have a mysterious control over human life, the kind of control that in primitive science is believed to exist between similars. In Greek thought we find that there must always be an identity between cause and effect and in astrology the saturnine temperament, for instance, is produced in a man born under the sign of Saturn, the jovial in the man born under the sign of Jupiter. Thus the heavens possess psychological traits identical with those of human beings. We preserve this idea in our vocabulary when we speak not only of saturnine and jovial people, but also of lunatics, mercurical people, and venereal diseases. In one of the Hermetic fragments preserved by Stobaeus (fifth century A.D.), we find that the planets are actually

in us. That is why we breathe, shed tears, laugh, grow angry, beget children, sleep, speak, and have desires. For tears come from the Kronos (Saturn) who is within us, generation comes from Zeus, speech from Hermes, anger from Ares, sleep from Luna, desire from Aphrodite, and laughter from the Sun.

The control of the zodiacal signs over our bodies was believed to be even more detailed. For each sign had its particular region of our anatomy under its sway. The list follows.

The Ram (Aries)—the head
The Bull (Taurus)—the neck
The Twins (Gemini)—the arms
The Lion (Leo)—the shoulders
The Crab (Cancer)—the breast
The Maiden (Virgo)—the entrails
The Scales (Libra)—the buttocks
The Scorpion (Scorpio)—the genitals
The Centaur (Sagittarius)—the thighs
The Goat (Capricornus)—the knees
The Water Bearer (Aquarius)—the lower legs
The Fish (Pisces)—the feet

It was thus possible to envision the zodiac as a great man lying in a circle with his head at Aries and his feet at Pisces. And because of the astrological association of planets with the zodiacal signs, the correlation of the heavens with man was both anatomical and psychological. For since the planets had definite temperaments, the zodiacal man had not only control over the various parts of our bodies but the planets influenced our souls as well. Like most figures of speech this one broke down, for the planets were not part of the zodiac and, though lustful desires arise in our genitals controlled by Scorpio, the connection between Scorpio and Venus may be remote.

By the third century the Platonic tradition had developed into Neo-Platonism under Plotinus. According to Plotinus the universe was not created by God but emanated from Him as light emanates from a candle. God is replaced by The One, whose first two emanations are the Intelligence (*nous*) and the Soul of the World (*anima mundi*). From the former emanate all the Platonic ideas and from the latter the individual souls of men, animals, and plants. The importance of this for us lies in its positing two human characteristics at the source of all being. The Intelligence and the Soul of the World can be described only in human terms and therefore at the very heart of reality was a human element. The three persons (*hypostases*) of Plotinus' trinity were analogous to the three elements of a human being, his unity, his intelligence, and his soul. Psychically he is as he was described by Philo, a little world. And since out of an individual's intelligence were believed to flow his most general ideas, and from them his less general, down to sensations, so from the cosmic intelligence flowed all the abstract ideas that were logically possible and from them the less general, down to particulars. The Tree of Porphyry, which can be found in any elementary textbook of logic, illustrates how from the most abstract and general of ideas, that of Being, emanate the species of being until one comes down to the material world.

The process of emanation permitted a philosopher to have a God as a supreme being, immutable and eternal, and yet the source of all beings. But it conflicted with the biblical account of creation. This might have proved a stumbling block to the Jewish philosophers of the Middle Ages but, as the Cabala shows, emanation seemed reconcilable with creation in the eyes of some of them. As early as the *Abot* (eighth or ninth century) we find R. Nathan (Ch. 31) comparing every part of the human body to some feature of the earth, the hair to the forests, the bones to the wood, the lungs to the wind. And in Bahya (eleventh century) the nine spheres correspond to the nine substances of the human body, while the twelve signs of the zodiac correspond to the twelve apertures. There is a complete parallel between the bodies and souls of individuals and the cosmos. A similar but less fantastic point of view was expressed by the tenth-century Jewish Neo-Platonist, Isaac Israeli. Borrowing from Al-Kindi (ninth century), who said that philosophy is self-knowledge, and that self-knowledge expands to knowledge of all things, he says, "For this reason the philosophers called man a microcosm" (Israeli, p. 28). The source of the idea that self-knowledge is cosmic knowledge is probably a treatise by Porphyry, *On Know Thyself*. This exists only in fragments and the following can be found in Stobaeus (Vol. 3, Ch. 21, no. 27, p. 580):

[Those] who say that man is properly called a microcosm say that the term implies knowledge of man. And since man is a microcosm, he is ordered to do nothing other than to philosophize. If then we seriously wish to philosophize without taking a false step, we shall be eager to know ourselves, and we shall acquire a true philosophy from our insight, ascending to the contemplation of the Whole.

That self-knowledge is cosmic knowledge is based upon an identity between the self and the cosmos, an identity of a "spiritual" rather than a corporeal nature. Yet unless one believed in a strict existential duality between mind and body, one was likely to believe that each faculty of the mind corresponded to some faculty of the body. Just as, for example, vision was dependent on the eye, the eye could be, as Schopenhauer was to say in the nineteenth century, a corporeal embodi-

ment of the desire to see. In this manner the whole material world became a symbolic set of desires and thoughts, and parallelism between material and mental existences was developed in detail. Just as any abnormal occurrence was an omen to the pagans, so a comet or earthquake or sudden flash of lightning or, of course, a dream "meant" something to the medieval Christian. Hence there grew up the tradition that the microcosm was of a spiritual nature and the corporeal parallels were not emphasized.

So Godefroy de Saint Victor (d. 1194) said in so many words in his *Microcosmus* (Ch. 18) that man is called a world not because of his body but because of his spirit. In his case the parallelism is based on Saint Augustine's identification of the ages of the world and those of the individual. To this is added a parallel with the six days of creation. In Godefroy the details are all worked out. "In the beginning of nascent time," he says (p. 47), "Moses says that God created heaven and earth." And in the beginning of nascent mankind God created the human spirit capable of celestial and terrestrial things by communicating to him the aptitude of four powers, sensuality, imagination, reason, and intelligence. And as the earth was "without form and void," so the human spirit was created only with the aptitude of exercising these faculties, not with their actualization. Godefroy then takes up each day of creation and explains it as one of the ages of man from infancy on.

In the second chapter of Book I (p. 31) he points out that "most men may be called a world." "Indeed," he continues, "the philosophers call the world generally by the Greek name of *cosmos*, which again they divide as it were into two kinds, one the macrocosmos, the other the microcosmos, meaning by the megacosmos [sic] this visible machine of the world. But by microcosmos they mean man." The parallelism between man and the universe is given in detail in Chapter 12 (p. 39).

Man was created by God stable in body, that is, able to stand upright, able not to lie down, able not to die. Thus he was made superior to all mutable things of this naturally mutable world. For all things in this sublunary world pass away, nor do they remain. All that comes goes, nor can that stand firm which flows with time. Man, however, was so created that he would not flow with flowing things had he wished to stand firm. But he did not so wish and began to flow with the flowing, to fall with the falling, and was thus made by himself similar to this falling world, falling himself. Nor does it pertain to his dignity, but rather to his vileness, that the name of this world was dealt out to him.

Thus the word "microcosm" in Godefroy is not a term of praise. The changes of the world are all in the   129 direction of degeneration, another idea that comes to Godefroy from Saint Augustine. So each age of an individual man is a step towards degeneration and death.

A more proper use of the word *mundus*, we are told, has nothing to do with man's body. It is properly used only in reference to his spirit. There follows (Chs. 21ff.) a discussion of human psychology which develops the parallelism between the four elements and the human body and soul. The body corresponds to the two passive elements and the soul to the two active. The body corresponds to the former and the soul to the latter. Left to himself, man goes steadily downhill, but can be rescued by grace, another Augustinian element. By grace he may come to know the good (*scire bonum*), to will the good (*velle bonum*) and to have the power to do the good (*posse bonum*). *Posse* comes from the Father; *scire* from the Son; *velle* from the Holy Spirit, an order which, says Godefroy, is the exact opposite of the order of things in nature. The details of this account are all worked out and give one a clear idea not only of the microcosm as a spiritual being but also of the medieval imagination. Distinctions are made only to be erased; all interpretations are based on biblical texts; and they are all allegorical. The spiritual microcosm, enlivened by grace, corresponds to the Trinity, and just as the three Persons of the Trinity coalesce into one, so do the three powers of the human spirit.

The use of man as a basic metaphor was also to be found in political treatises, as it was in Plato. To take but the most famous example, John of Salisbury talks of the prince as the head of the body politic—the expression *corpus politicum* is itself of interest—the senate as the heart, the court as the sides, the officers and judges as the eyes, ears, and tongue, executive officials as the unarmed hand, the army as the arms, the financial department as the belly and intestines, and so on (Gierke, p. 131, n. 76). This goes back to Plato's *Republic*, though Plato made no such detailed similes, and it continued at least until our own times, as when people say that the legislature reflects the will of the people, the executive carries out the decisions of Congress, and the judiciary reasons to the conclusions of the law. It is as if the government had sensation (Congress), reason (The Supreme Court), and will (the President).

By the fifteenth and sixteenth centuries the idea of man as a microcosm took a different turn. It is found in "spiritual magic" (Walker) and even in architecture (Wittkower, Yates). These derivatives probably stem from the revival of interest in the Cabala in men of whom Pico della Mirandola and Reuchlin were the most important. Confining ourselves to these two, the idea that interests us is to be found in the former's *Heptaplus* (1491) and the latter's *De arte Cabalistica* (1517).

There are, says Pico, four worlds, but each is a replica of them all. They are the angelic and invisible world, the celestial, the sublunary and corruptible world, and mankind. Since each world reproduces all the others, this must also be true of man. Going back to the Cabala, Pico bases his ideas of the Tree of Sephirot, a representation of the metaphysical universe in which the Spirit of God is at the top and matter at the bottom. In between are the various levels of reality as in Plotinus (Sérouya, p. 259). Just below the Spirit of God comes the Metatron who communicates between the ideas and the corporeal world, called by Reuchlin (p. 773) "the intellectual agent of the First Mover." This corresponds to the Neo-Platonic *nous*. Just below the Metatron is the Soul of the Messiah, "of an essence continuous with both the angelic and divine worlds." Then comes the "Soul of Elba." In spite of these distinctions, there are no gaps between these worlds; all is continuous. Similarly there are no gaps in the microcosm, the Intelligence, the Will, and the Memory being tightly bound together, three functions of one being.

In the *Heptaplus* Pico asserts the existence of only three worlds, the intellectual, which is the realm of the Platonic Ideas, the celestial, consisting of the heavens with the stars and planets, and the corruptible, which is sublunary. In this place he clearly states that these stand for the three parts of a man, "at the top his head, then that which extends from his neck to his navel, third that which extends from his navel to his feet" (p. 61). There is a complete similarity among these three parts of the microcosm and the three realms of the macrocosm. In the head is the brain, the source of knowledge and hence of the ideas. In the chest is the heart, "source of vital motion and heat." And below are the organs of generation. So in the macrocosm there is the level of the angels who know the Ideas directly, the heavens in which is the sun which corresponds to the heart, and below that the moon where corruption and change begin. This correspondence is so exact that magical influences can be brought down from heaven by preparing the soul to receive them (Yates, passim). One of the effects of music is this end (Walker, Ch. 1).

In the sixteenth and seventeenth centuries the correspondences between microcosm and macrocosm were used in a variety of ways; in the perfection of memory (Yates), in medicine, and in divinatory astrology. But the most influential use of the idea is to be found in the *Monadology* of Leibniz (Wiener, p. 533). In this metaphysical treatise the universe is a constellation of centers of force called monads. There is no interaction among the monads; each is self-enclosed, or in Leibniz' words, "windowless." But each monad reflects all the others by a pre-established harmony, and hence, the monad which is the soul of a man represents as in a mirror all the other monads in the universe. The only differences among these beings is the clearness and distinctness of the images. Monads on the sub-human level have less clear reflections of the higher monads but the higher monads have clearer images of those below them as well as of those above them. Thus man is preserved as the image and likeness of God, who is also a monad, but one of infinite clarity. As in Pico, there are no gaps in Leibniz' universe. There is a continuous gradation of clarity and activity running from God down to the most inert level of existence. It was this philosophy which eventuated in the nineteenth century in that system of metaphysics known as personalism.

The rise and rapid progress of the natural sciences proved to be an obstacle to the idea of the microcosm and it became, like astrology, an interest only of historians. No one of the stature of Pico or Leibniz could take it seriously as science, though it may survive in popular beliefs. The zodiacal man can still be found in rural almanacs and is still reproduced in books on astrology (MacNeice, p. 127). It is one of those ideas that go underground and then emerge from time to time as the ideas of self-taught philosophers. But to all intents and purposes it is obsolete except as a figure of speech, sometimes meaning no more than any small independent group of people, a lodge or church or school. When we speak of the head of the state, we do not consciously apply the idea of the microcosm to the state. In fact the idea became so watered down that when Maurice Scève came to write his poem, *Le Microcosme* (1562), he used the term to denote only Adam before the Fall, living in pure innocence, without art or science, without even an articulate language, "knowing only his God."

BIBLIOGRAPHY

Translations, unless otherwise identified, are by George Boas.

George Perrigo Conger, *Theories of Macrocosmos Microcosmos in the History of Philosophy* (New York, 1922). Robert Fludd, *Utriusque cosmi* . . . (1617). Otto Gierke, *Political Theories of the Middle Ages*, trans. F. W. Maitland (Cambridge, 1900). Godefroy de Saint Victor, *Microcosmus*, ed. Philippe Delhaye (Lille and Gemblous, 1951). Louis Ginzberg, article, "Cabala," *Jewish Encyclopedia* (New York, 1902). Louis MacNeice, *Astrology* (Garden City, N.Y., 1964). Pico della Mirandola, *Heptaplus*, in *Opera omnia* (Basel, 1557). Johann Reuchlin, *De arte Cabalistica*, in Pico's *Opera omnia* (Basel, 1557). Curt P. Richter, *Biological Clocks in Medicine and Psychiatry* (Springfield, Ill., 1965). Maurice Scève, *Le Microcosme*, ed. Albert Béguin (Paris, 1947). Henri Sérouya, *La Kabbale* (Paris, 1947). D. P. Walker, *Spiritual and Demonic Magic from Ficino to Campanella* (London, 1958). Rudolf Wittkower, *Architectural Principles in the Age of Humanism* (London, 1949). Frances A. Yates, *The Art of Memory* (Chicago, 1966).

GEORGE BOAS

[See also Allegory; **Analogy in Early Greek Thought; Analogy of the Body Politic;** Anthropomorphism; Astrology; God; **Neo-Platonism;** State.]

MAN-MACHINE FROM THE GREEKS TO THE COMPUTER

THE TERM "man-machine" denotes the idea that the total psychic life of the individual can be properly described and explained as the product of his physical organization viewed as a mechanical system in structure and function. An account of the ramified history of the idea, however, requires a somewhat less rigid definition, which will in several instances pertain to the mechanization of only some, but not all, aspects of mental activity; whereas on other occasions it must be made broad enough to encompass the animal as well as man. Similarly, the notion of "machine," in particular when used as an equivalent of the living organism, cannot be assigned in advance any precise or concrete sense that would hold good over the entire length of this study. The history of the man-machine is in large part that of the relativity of the concept of mechanism, as it has been understood with increasing breadth and refinement, from Greek times to our own day, in those sciences that have had a decisive influence on the shaping and scope of the idea in question, namely, physics, biology, medicine, technology, and (more recently) chemistry and psychophysiology. Moreover, in its relations to philosophy the fortunes of the man-machine may be regarded as having closely conformed, up to and since its first thoroughly consistent exposition by La Mettrie in 1747, to the general curve followed by the growth of materialism. However, it would be historically sounder to eschew an absolute linkage between the man-machine idea and any ultimate materialistic position of a metaphysical kind, despite the strong affinities that persist logically between the two notions.

The man-machine is typically a modern doctrine, but it is necessary to go back to ancient Greece in order to discover both the speculative tendency and the positive elements from which it evolved. Quite early in Greek thought the attempt was made to conceive of the soul as an organized function of matter. Some Pythagoreans spoke of it, for example, as the "harmony of the body," even if such a notion had for them perhaps a more mystical than scientific meaning. In Empedocles (ca. 490–30 B.C.), however, we already find the rudiments of a psychology of sensation based on exclusively physical factors. The external world, viewed as continuous in substance with the organs of sense, was described by him as registering replicas of things (*simulacra*) directly on the senses in the form of perceptions. This precocious empiricism, probably indebted to the medical writings of Alcmeon, remained tied to the error, prevalent in antiquity, that the heart rather than the brain served as the *sensorium commune*. There was, nevertheless, a glimmer of the man-machine in the Empedoclean opinion that the varieties of psychic constitution among men, including their different aptitudes and characters, depend, as decreed by the cardio-sensory theory, on the composition of their blood, that is, on the size, distribution, and combination of the particles assumed to compose it.

Epicureanism carried out to its conclusion, within the technical limits imposed by Greek science, the type of psychophysical explanation initiated by Empedocles, and in so doing came nearest in the classical period to the modern thesis of the man-machine. Because the Epicurean tradition spanned several centuries, its teachings underwent much change from the founding of atomism in the fifth century by Democritus, through its continuation under Epicurus (ca. 341–270 B.C.), to the time of Lucretius (ca. 95–50 B.C.), in whose *De rerum natura* a synthetic presentation of its philosophy has been preserved. As regards the atomistic prefiguration of the man-machine, it will suffice to summarize the Lucretian version. The soul, like all else in the universe, was held to be a corporeal entity consisting of an assemblage of atoms. Those atoms which made up the soul, however, were of an extreme fineness comparable to the intangibility and mobility of air (*pneuma*), fire, or heat; in consequence they permeated the whole body. Soul and body therefore remained constantly in a state of mutual dependence by virtue of physical contact. While the soul-atoms did not separately possess life, consciousness, or sensibility, these attributes of the organism were the outcome of their appropriate combinations. From the Epicurean standpoint, all psychic phenomena were envisaged as the effects of specific (even if as yet ill-defined) atomic structures. The operations of the various senses and the faculty of sensation itself were explained on the same basis. It was supposed that all objects emit *simulacra*

of themselves composed of a subtle grouping of atoms, and that these replicas on entering through the related sense-organs impinge upon the soul as sensations and ideas. It followed that the conscious and thinking principle in man was mortal, and that the age-old belief in personal survival after death was an illusion. The soul temporarily forming with the body a composite in which the role of each was essential to that of the other, this reciprocity ended with the destruction of the body and the dispersal of the soul-atoms. The absolute material unity of man was thus affirmed—a unity which made of death a simple physical event in the cycle of aggregations, dissolutions, and re-aggregations of the eternal atoms. The general picture of man that emerged from Epicurean philosophy was that of a momentarily coherent system of particles, of which both the internal motions and the interactions with a natural environment produced, by fundamentally mechanical means, not only the phenomena of life and sensibility that were common also to animals, but the higher mental functions believed to be peculiarly human.

Atomistic speculation contained within itself, at least virtually, the seeds of modern science, including as an offshoot of the latter the man-machine. When the moment for the birth of that idea was to become ripe many centuries later, the inspirations and precedents offered by Epicureanism were to be put to important use. But it must be admitted that ancient atomism itself fell short of a genuine mechanistic conception of mind. It was prevented primarily by its own abstract postulates about the nature of matter from representing the organism in terms of its observable structures and processes. One detects still in the image of the soul as a diffusion of atoms within the body something of the earliest doctrines that identified the Greek *pneuma* and the Latin *anima* with breath or air, in the naive materialism typical of the origins of thought on the subject. The persistence, however much transformed, of such primordial intuitions in the Epicurean hypothesis of ethereal soul-atoms, which served to exclude in theory a truly physiological approach to the mechanics of vital and psychic phenomena, was a reflection, moreover, of the poverty of anatomical knowledge in antiquity—a situation resulting from the religious ban against dissections of the human body. Not only was medicine of little help here, but what existed as a science of mechanics in the same period was also unable as yet to offer any schematization of the laws of motion which might have led the Epicureans to suppose that the organism was, rather than a vague and fortuitous assemblage of atoms, an actual machine of a definite type.

The handicap of inadequate scientific data was

compounded by the curious fact that classical atomism, although it laid the foundations for the future of physical inquiry, remained itself singularly indifferent to the objective truth or error of the particular theories it framed about the "nature of things." It failed to see in its anticipation of the man-machine a starting point of scientific study. The paramount aim of the atomistic definition of soul, as of all Epicurean physics, was ethical. In furtherance of this, what counted was the type of explanation offered, rather than the detailed form it took. The ethical aim of Epicurean physics being to reassure its followers about the hazards of life, this was believed best attainable by banishing from the world the arbitrary intervention of the Gods. The fatalistic belief in the soul's mortality was comforting because death, or rather the punishments to follow preached by religion, ceased thereby to be a source of dread. To induce the *ataraxia*, or peace of mind, of the sage, one atomistic theory, provided it was credible, was obviously as good as another. Thus the earliest approximation of the man-machine was taught as an antidote for the superstitious terror of the supernatural powers presumed to control human destiny. Its antireligious emphasis accounts for the vigorous suppression of the Epicurean idea of the man-machine, along with the entire philosophy of which it was a facet, once the official triumph of Christianity took place; for the new faith was less tolerant of its critics than many a paganism had been. The idea was not to rise again to the surface and pursue its career until the resurgence of pre-Christian modes of thought in the seventeenth and eighteenth centuries. When that was to happen, the underlying tension between religion and the man-machine conception was also to be revived, until the latter idea was to mature finally into a full-fledged doctrine, a refutation of Christian dogma about the spirituality and immortality of man's soul.

If Epicureanism supplied the materialist world view that later nurtured the man-machine, it was from a different source in Greek thought—from the Hippocratic school and its descendants—that the specifically medical background of the idea first came. The theory of the four humors, which was to enjoy so durable a vogue, attempted to explain the behavior of the mind, particularly as manifested through personality-types, in terms of physiological causes. Indebted, seemingly, to the "four elements" of Empedocles and to the prevalent taste for microcosmic-macrocosmic analogies, the treatise *De natura hominis* of the *Corpus Hippocraticum*, dating probably from the second half of the fifth century B.C., worked out a scheme of correlations between the preponderance in the body of blood, yellow bile, black bile, or phlegm, and the respective predominance of the character-traits of sanguinity,

biliousness, melancholy, or apathy. Gross and fanciful as this system of causes and effects was, the real value of "humoralism" proved to be the scientific method and medical philosophy it exemplified. By assuming that mental states were regularly dependent on bodily conditions, it made this dependency a crucial object of further investigation and therapeutic practice. As an adjunct to its humoral doctrine, the Hippocratic school held also that climatological and other factors in the natural environment acted upon the temperament by way of the body, thereby producing variations of aptitude and mentality among individuals.

In the ultimate impact of ancient medicine on the formation of the man-machine, the role of Galen (129–ca. 199) was no less important than that of Hippocrates. Not only did Galen organize the medical knowledge of his day into a vast *corpus*, but his own contributions to it were such as to strengthen notably the link between humoralism and an incipient man-machine attitude. While retaining and developing the theory of the four temperaments and their related psychic classifications, he laid the groundwork for a physiology of the nervous system by being the first to demonstrate experimentally that the brain was the point of origin of the multitude of nerves which controlled, by specific functions, the various vital, sensory, or motor activities of the body. To explain how this control was effected physically, Galen launched on its long and adventurous career the hypothesis of "animal spirits" composed of that invisibly rarefied fluid supposed to be contained in the imagined tube-like hollow of the nerves. Man was seen, consequently, as an organism regulated in its operations by a definite organ, the brain, which, thanks to the animal-spirits of the nervous network, mechanically received sensory messages from all parts of the body and sent back its voluntary or involuntary commands. In this Galenic model, of which the combined humoral and neurological aspects tend to construe man as a sort of hydraulic-pneumatic machine (reflecting in Greco-Roman times the privileged status of water-technology and the popularity of the *pneuma*-concept of soul), we have already the rudimentary structure that in fact unifies body and mind into an organic entity. On the basis of it, Galenism foreshadowed a materialistic picture of man, even though the philosophical opinions of its founder remained eclectic and, on the particular problem of the soul, loyal to Platonic and Aristotelian assertions of its substantial immateriality. But the soul, in so far as it came under the double dominion of the humors and the brain, was no longer treated as an independent being, but rather as something so fatefully bound up with the body that medical science was held to be the most effective means of regulating the passions, and thereby of remedying character-disorders. By proclaiming the interdependence of corporeal, moral, and mental states in the interests of a therapeutic ideal, Galenic teaching approached the threshold of the man-machine idea during the classical era—a fact that La Mettrie's *l'Homme machine* was going to appreciate. It is important, furthermore, to recall that the Hippocratic and Galenic traditions, in contrast to the ideological suppression of Epicureanism, remained in authority without interruption until the seventeenth century, and were thus able historically to exert, at the right moment, a maximum influence on the maturing of the man-machine, at least to the extent that the latter idea had major roots in medical thought.

It remains, finally, to relate how the man-machine was prefigured in the achievements of ancient technology; that is, to what degree the latter succeeded in simulating animal or human behavior by mechanical means. The inventiveness of antiquity was applied, on the whole, to machines for lifting or pulling heavy weights (pulleys, winches, cranes, levers), engines of war (catapults, siege and defense equipment), pneumatic and hydraulic contrivances (waterclocks, fountains, pumps, water-organs), presses of various kinds, and similar instruments of relatively simple design and operation. Truly automatic devices were rare and, when encountered, belonged mostly to the class of toys and other objects intended for amusement or entertainment, rather than to that of machinery for useful work. Among the reports of such gadgetry that have come down to us, surely the most remarkable deals with the "automatic theatre" of Heron of Alexandria (second half of the first century A.D.), who was perhaps the most versatile mechanist of the Greco-Roman period. The theater in question, as described in his treatise *Peri Automatopoietikes*, featured a five-act tragedy based on the legend of Nauplius; it was performed with the appropriate dramatis personae, scenery changes, sound effects, etc., all of it automatically controlled by a system of strings, reels, cogs, and levers attached to a motor consisting of a counterweight that descended slowly and uniformly. The technological virtuosity of Heron of Alexandria apparently did not, however, have any philosophical meaning for his contemporaries. It may, for one thing, be said to have come too late, when the gift for original speculation had largely spent itself. But in a broader sense, the triumphs of Greek engineering attributed to such figures as Ctesibios, Philo of Byzantium, and Heron remained outside the main stream of science. Even the genius of Archimedes (d. 222 B.C.), whose generalization of certain laws concerning the equilibrium of bodies had intimated the modern synthesis of geometry and physics, proved to be an isolated case, and failed

to inspire the following that his methodology deserved. Because the Greek imagination in science was typically theoretical in temper rather than given to contriving machinery, there was something abortive, or at least markedly premature, in the discoveries of an Archimedes and in the inventions of a Heron of Alexandria, each of whom exhibited in his way a strong techno-mechanical bent.

To make clearer why "machinism" did not become a philosophical perspective in antiquity, it should also be stressed that the mechanical arts and everything pertaining to them were regarded as inherently too base for such a purpose. Philosophy, chiefly aristocratic in outlook from its inception, was concerned primarily with contemplative or ideal pursuits. Nor did the passion for mathematics in the Pythagorean and Platonic schools favor, as it has in modern times, the fusion of philosophical and technological modes of thought, because as a rule the mathematicism of the Greeks remained "pure." Behind these attitudes it is evident that there was in operation a pervasive sociological factor, which would have rendered the man-machine idea "unthinkable" even if (contrary to what was actually true) all of its logical and technical components had already been given. Mechanical devices fell within the department of the artisan, many or most of whom were, in fact, slaves. The introduction of related concepts or criteria into philosophical thinking would have signified to the Greek intellect its own "enslavement"; for the unconscious equivalent of the man-machine, had such an idea been somehow proposed, would have been the slave himself, in the sense that the slave was quite literally man reduced to a machine. By the same token, it is not merely fortuitous that the rise of the man-machine doctrine will coincide, in the eighteenth century, with two causally connected revolutions, the one technological, the other socio-democratic.

To summarize, the man-machine was principally approached in classical thought from three different but converging directions: that of atomistic materialism and its extensions in biology and psychology; that of medical psychophysiology, as best seen in the Hippocratic and Galenic schools; and that of the technology pertaining to automata. These three approaches had not yet found, however, the synthesizing mind capable of bringing them effectually together; for not only were the materials made available by each of them still insufficient to that end, but the sociocultural climate (which participates in the shaping of even the most abstract notions) was such as still to exclude the possibility of man's self-image as a machine.

The man-machine idea remained in abeyance during the period of almost twelve hundred years when the reigning Christian ideology checked or suppressed whatever in the philosophical heritage of the past remained unassimilable to its own position. The mechanistic conception of human nature was, of course, incompatible with theological dogmas affirming the spirituality and immortality of the soul and picturing man as a creature of God endowed with free will. It was not until the sixteenth century, when long repudiated aspects of Greek thought were revived, that a naturalistic view of man was reinstated. This first resulted at Padua from the reinterpretation of Aristotle. Reappraising from a medical standpoint Aristotle's texts in the original, the Paduan criticism, especially Pomponazzi's and Zabarella's, had the double effect of rendering the spiritual permanence of the soul undemonstrable by reason, and of redefining the faculties of the "sensitive" and "intellective" soul as functions of the "material form" of the body. The work of Pomponazzi shows that Aristotelian metaphysics had the potential of yielding an essentially naturalistic psychology, to the extent that its key-concept of *form* could be made to coincide with the structure itself of the organism, that is, with anatomical and physiological data. That such a development was at least a possibility in the career of the man-machine idea is attested by the fact that, when La Mettrie's *Histoire naturelle de l'âme* (1745), inspired by medical materialism, gave a preliminary theory of man, it did so in the context of a scholastic metaphysics suitably construed for the purpose. Nevertheless, the role of Peripateticism in the evolution of the man-machine remained quite modest. The reason was not only that Italian naturalism had relatively little impact beyond the Alps, but also that the imminent revolution in science stemming from the physico-mathematical method was soon to be consummated *against*, and stubbornly resisted by, those claiming to be faithful to Aristotle. Therefore, a new and opposing philosophy, meant to legitimatize a physics concerned with formulating quantitatively the observable laws of motion, would henceforth serve as the conceptual framework for the man-machine. The mechanization of nature, which found its most systematic and far-reaching *rationale* in Cartesian thought, was the decisive step in the intellectual process that led finally to the mechanization of man himself.

That process, however, was strongly helped by several events in science and technology during the sixteenth and early seventeenth centuries. Among the most important was the rebirth of anatomy, particularly under the impetus of Vesalius' epoch-making *De humani corporis fabrica* (1543). The modern mind thereby became familiarized with the image of the human body as a neat and exact assemblage of related structures—an image made all the more incisive by progress in the techniques of anatomical representation. Thus the inevitable analogy between the internal organization of the body and that of, say, a clock was first a common fact of visual experience. Harvey's discovery of the circulation of the blood (ca. 1616) was another occurrence of the same type. It furnished the missing key to the dynamics of what now appeared more than ever to be a hydraulic machine: the organism was not only arranged like a clock, but it "ticked" like one, with its mainspring simply a pump. The task which thereafter devolved on physiology was to explain, consistently with the mechanics of circulation, the subordinate mechanisms of muscular movement and of sensory as well as motor impulses. To these permutations in man's self perception should be added the emergence of a technological ideal no less revolutionary than the rest, already heralded before 1500 by the remarkable vision of Leonardo da Vinci. The resolve to conquer nature and make it serve man—a theme that Bacon and Descartes soon elaborated philosophically—was in time, along with the retreat of occultist schemes of domination, to focus on the machine as the specific weapon of conquest. In the seventeenth century, it is true, the machine was still seen as no more than a means to an end; there was no question yet of a process of assimilation, technologically conditioned, between it and man. But the passionate use of a particular means modifies, in addition to the end it serves, the agent whose destiny becomes inseparable from its use. At the historic moment when technological mastery of nature became a methodically conscious goal, the idea of the man-machine was predictable by a general law of cultural change, according to which man comes eventually to resemble the instrumentality of his ambition and power.

It was Descartes' definition of the animal as an automaton that initiated the modern phase of the man-machine. Although a similar opinion had been voiced as early as 1554 by the Spanish physician Gomez Pereira, it had no noticeable effect until it reappeared as part of the Cartesian philosophical reform. French thought from Descartes to the Enlightenment thereby became the theater in which the concept of automatism was by degrees generalized from the animal to man. The *bête machine* doctrine had resulted from Descartes' metaphysical dualism. Once given the sharp distinction between a thinking and extended being (*res cogitans* and *res extensa*), it was patently less absurd to banish animals collectively from the realm of thinking substance than to have to distribute "rational souls" to them from the ape down to the flea. But more than a case of metaphysical expediency, the animal-automaton served also to illustrate positively the universal mechanism of matter. As the bio- **135** logical counterpart of Cartesian physics, it was a theoretical culmination of the iatromechanical current which had already become widespread in the medical sciences of the first half of the seventeenth century. The meaning of the beast-machine as a physiological postulate can best be understood by viewing it in the light of its human equivalent sketched in the *Traité de l'homme,* where Descartes, as if momentarily forgetting his dualist position, seemed on the verge of recognizing in man, too, an automaton. Historically, the *bête machine* proved to be (contrary, no doubt, to what its author intended) simply a minimal and preliminary version of human automatism. In the long run the animal acted as a mediator between the machine and man—a service which early attested the projection from animal to human nature that has since become a commonplace of biological and psychological research. That the mechanistic emphasis of Descartes' physiology threatened to undermine his metaphysics by inviting a transformation of the beast-machine into the man-machine, can be seen clearly from the description of organic functions given in the *Traité de l'homme* (1664):

... all the operations which I have attributed to this Machine, such as the digesting of food, the beating of the heart and arteries, nourishment and growth, respiration, waking, and sleeping; the reception of light, sounds, odors, tastes, warmth, and other like qualities into the exterior organs of sensation; the impression of the corresponding ideas upon a common sensorium and on the imagination; the retention or imprint of these ideas in the Memory; the internal movements of the Appetites and Passions; and finally, the external motions of all the members of the body ... I wish that you would consider all of these as following altogether naturally in this Machine from the disposition of its organs alone, neither more nor less than do the movements of a clock or other automaton from that of its counterweights and wheels ... (*Oeuvres,* Pléiade ed. [1953], p. 873).

The above passage shows that the technological models with which Descartes equated the "organic machine" were of a rather inept sort. The clock (which Aquinas had long ago compared to the motions produced in animals by instinct and appetite) was to remain, nevertheless, the seventeenth century's favorite example of an automatic device simulating intelligence. Descartes had in mind also analogies offered by the hydraulically operated automata in the royal gardens of Saint-Germain, which the *Traité de l'homme* alluded to in order to explain how sense-perceptions activate the brain:

External objects which ... determine [the corporeal machine] to move in various ways according to how the parts of the brain are disposed, are like strangers who, on entering some of the grottos where those fountains are found, themselves cause without being aware of it the movements that take place before their eyes: for they cannot enter without stepping on paving stones so arranged that, for instance, if they approach a bathing Diana, they will cause her to hide behind some shrubbery; and if they attempt to pursue her, they will cause to come towards them a Neptune brandishing his trident ... (ibid., pp. 814–15).

There is evidence that Descartes, seeking experimental proof of his automatist doctrine, designed a little robot that could perform somersaults on a tightrope. Although such examples might well suggest that his sense of the imitative powers of mechanism was naively exaggerated, it is unlikely that Descartes regarded clock-like automata as reproducing in a literal fashion the far more complex and versatile behavior of animals. Ultimately, his notion of the beast-automaton was deduced from the general mechanism of nature, while the actual models proffered in support of it were merely the best that the technology of the period could provide. Cartesian biology pictured the living organism—not unlike the universe of whirling vortices (*tourbillons*) which enclosed it—as basically a hydraulic machine. The activity of the nervous system, patterned on that of the vascular circulation, was explained by supposing that the nerves contained a rarefied fluid—i.e., the animal spirits (*esprits animaux*), made up of the finest blood-particles—which, propelling itself back and forth between the brain and the periphery of the body, controlled all sensory and motor functions. To this hydraulic scheme Descartes added a thermodynamic feature by assuming that the heart operated on heat; and also, as his most promising contribution, he imagined a primitive form of reflex mechanism to account for involuntary muscular movement.

The modern idea of the man-machine came into being largely as a result of the development that the animal-machine and the physiological science related to it underwent in common. The final outcome had indeed been foreseen in Descartes' own time, and gave rise to objections against his view by various critics, some of whom went so far as to accuse him of heresy and of abetting materialism. In the "Sixth Objection" to the *Méditations métaphysiques,* a group of theologians claimed that the beast-automaton would lead its supporters to conclude that the continuity in intelligence between animals and human beings was attributable simply to machines of differing levels of complexity. This rejoinder was repeated often by opponents of the *bête machine,* who thereby unintentionally bestowed a measure of popularity, and even plausibility, on the very inference that they were eager to avert.

The problem of "animal soul" became the subject of endless controversy, lasting well into the next century, between Cartesians and anti-Cartesians. While in one sense such metaphysical polemics for or against the animal-machine could only have proved futile (for it is impossible to know if any creature other than man is endowed with what we experience inwardly as *res cogitans*), in another sense it helped indirectly to render the automatist thesis more acceptable. This came about in several ways. Those who sought to refute Descartes on the grounds that beasts often exhibit, by their skill and cunning, a degree of intelligence equal and occasionally superior to that of human beings, were in effect citing evidence that could boomerang against them. For when the man-machine philosophy was at last proclaimed, its exponents—with La Mettrie at their head—could argue that if animals, despite their alleged merits, were mere machines, there remained no reason to suppose that human abilities implied a loftier kind of causation. The adversaries of the Cartesian doctrine, relying on scholastic tradition, also proposed a "corporeal soul," situated midway between materiality and spirituality, as the specific principle of feeling and intelligence in animals. But the notion of "corporeal soul," a derivative of the Aristotelian "substantial forms," was logically inconsistent, and in the end, encouraged some to identify it more conveniently with the organic machine itself. That, at any rate, was what La Mettrie did in his *Histoire naturelle de l'âme*, in which Peripateticism, with reminiscences (as noted) of Pomponazzi and the Paduan school, became an ingredient of the materialistic definition of soul. Those Cartesians, moreover, who took up the cudgels for the *bête machine* were obliged to explain, in ever more ingenious detail, how merely mechanical processes could be the source of all the amazing variety of animal actions. In so doing, they freely introduced Descartes' principles of psychophysiology into the subject of animal automatism, with the result that the mechanistic interpretation of psychological phenomena, at least in animals if not yet in man, crystallized as a general practice.

To the above developments should be added the curious vogue that the beast-machine enjoyed in certain religious circles, especially among the Jansenists. Far from regarding it as heretical, the latter, represented by their leading thinker, Arnauld, were fascinated by the automatist concept, discovering in it (as Descartes had intimated) a number of theological advantages. Not only did it set in a brighter light the dogma of a separate and transcendent destiny for the human soul, but it absolved men (and God) of blame for the sufferings erroneously believed to be inflicted on innocent beasts. More important still, it attested to the infinite art and wisdom of God, who had contrived such marvelous automata capable of imitating intelligent behavior. This excursion of the animal-machine into the sphere of natural theology was, in particular, to offer a dubious precedent which played eventually into the hands of the free-thinkers. For it followed that, if God could create such remarkable automata as animals were acknowledged to be, there was no need for him to do anything more, in creating man, than to improve on the mechanical models already in existence. The man-machine idea will thus ironically find theological support in the assertion that it is impious to consider the Supreme Artisan incapable of fashioning a machine as complicated and as admirable as man.

Although the animal-soul debate was concerned mainly with the question whether beasts were or were not pure automata devoid of feeling and thought, Descartes' own position had in reality been more nuanced and even somewhat ambiguous. In denying a soul to animals, he had meant only that they were without *rational* awareness—an opinion confirmed empirically both by the "unreflecting" efficiency of their actions and by their lack of the linguistic means needed for the formation of abstract ideas. This signified that the animal, unlike Descartes, did not perform intellectual operations of the type *cogito, ergo sum;* but its inability to *cogitate* did not necessarily deprive it also of all nonreflective kinds of mental activity, such as simple consciousness, memory, emotion, and perception. Descartes conceded to the beast, in fact, a level of psychic life directly dependent on its physical organization. The extension of the *bête machine* doctrine, so understood, to the behavior of man by those Cartesians, prone to naturalism, who saw in it above all the opportunity to explain psychological phenomena mechanistically, had its initial logic in Descartes' over-restrictive definition of the soul as a purely rational substance distinct from all else in the universal mechanism where it was so tenuously lodged. The proposal to investigate within the machinist context, first in the animal and subsequently in man, such "sub-rational" faculties as sensation, memory, imagination, feeling, and volition, oriented the future program of psychophysiological science and thereby set the stage for the maturing of the man-machine idea.

Among those who notably caused Cartesian thought to evolve in this direction, Henricus Regius, professor of Medicine at Utrecht, gave to the automatist thesis, in his *Fundamenta physices* (1646), an interpretation which, neglecting dualist metaphysics, stressed the conformity of psychic processes with their organic counterparts. Jacques Rohault's *Entretiens sur la philosophie* (1671) followed Descartes in denying to animals a rational soul, but thereupon proceeded to examine the remaining aspects of their conscious life in terms of those mechanical structures assumed to be the basis of the vitality and sensibility which they manifested. 137

In a similar exposition of the *bête machine*, Pierre Sylvain Régis (*Système de philosophie*, 1690) had as his purpose not so much to deprive animals of attributes commonly included under the designation of their "soul," as to demonstrate that those same attributes were owing to "the arrangements of their organic parts alone, and to the heat of their blood and the force of their animal-spirits." In this physiologizing inheritance of Cartesian natural science, the animal-spirits in particular were soon to have a privileged role, namely, as the innervating substance believed to engender and sustain the higher functions of the brain. Some advanced thinkers all but substituted this substance for the soul itself.

Thus the progress of physiology tended to minimize the "ghost" which Descartes had found it metaphysically necessary to introduce into the "human machine" of the *Traité de l'homme*. An inherent contradiction of dualism had been the supposed interaction between a substance that occupied—indeed *was*—space and a substance—thought—that was essentially nonspatial. Given the impossibility of discovering the laws of such an interaction, there could be no *science* of the cause-and-effect relations between body and mind in accordance with Cartesian principles. Descartes' own attempt to solve the problem by assuming that the soul was housed in the pineal gland, where it acted like a brakeman switching the incoming impulses of the animal-spirits in one direction or another, can only be considered futile in view of both the neurological fantasy and logical inconsistency that it displayed. Indeed, dualistic psychology led into a blind alley. The attempts of Leibniz, Malebranche, and Spinoza—each of whom was concerned to overcome within the framework of dualism the dilemma posed by Descartes' unintelligible parallelism of mental and bodily functions—did not in the end forestall the solution of the dilemma that was forthcoming from the man-machine philosophy. If Leibniz' pre-established harmony, Malebranche's occasionalism, and Spinoza's monism vindicated, each in its way, a metaphysical modality of the mind-body correspondence, none of these explanations was of any special use in determining empirically the laws which governed that correspondence.

As it turned out, the *impasse* of dualism seemed to be circumvented best by the increase in knowledge of the central nervous system, and particularly of the cerebral localization of specific functions. The result of such advances in physiology (which by La Mettrie's time had arrived at a rough differentiation of the types of activity peculiar to the cortex, cerebellum, and brain-stem, as well as at the stage of a comparative neuro-anatomy of man and several animal species), was the gradual replacement of the unlocatable soul by the brain itself, which came to be seen as a "machine" producing thought. The long-run sterility of dualism as a psychological hypothesis—for it could only lead either to a gratuitous dichotomization of its human subject, or to the introduction of a nonfunctional soul into the unity of body and mind—caused it at length to be abandoned by certain unorthodox thinkers in favor of the man-machine hypothesis, which by contrast had the advantage of recognizing the concrete nature of man as that of a being in whom mental and physical events were never divorced from one another.

The triumph of mechanistic psychology cannot be understood, however, without taking fully into account the influences exerted on it, often in an eclectic manner, by the overlapping currents of Hobbism, Lockean empiricism, and Epicureanism in the intellectual setting of the early eighteenth century. In the *De homine* (1658) of Hobbes, there was already outlined, contemporaneously with the Cartesian postulate of automatism, a complete *rationale* for the mechanization of mind. Inspired by the new physics, Hobbes was the first to reduce *all* things to nothing but bodies in motion; and since for him only efficient causes were real, psychology and epistemology became branches of mechanics like any other science of nature, except that imperceptibly minute motions were said to be involved in the entry of sense-impressions into the brain. Psychic phenomena were thus conceived essentially as "a motion in the internal substance of the head." The grossness of Hobbesian materialism, coupled with the anti-experimental and deductive method that supported it, limited somewhat the historical importance of its precocious version of the man-machine theme. While there was no hesitancy on its author's part to describe man abstractly as a machine, the scientific motive for imagining specific analogies between mechanism and organism was lacking in Hobbes' reliance on physico-mathematical generalities. Nevertheless, his contribution was valuable especially because of the linkage it effected between the mechanics of sensation and an empirical theory of knowledge. In following to its conclusion this epistemological lead, the materialists of the Enlightenment will succeed in "mechanizing" the *homo duplex* of metaphysical tradition. The immediate ground of this final step, however, proved to be the empiricism of Locke, who far more than Hobbes shaped their thinking. Once the procedure to refer mental and emotive states to the organic dispositions that accompanied them had become well established, it seemed logically and psychologically appropriate to combine this unification with a consistent sensationalism. Approaching Lockean epistemology with a marked materialistic bias, La Mettrie and those who followed him achieved between empiricism and mechanistic biology a synthesis which eliminated all recourse to an immaterial principle in analyzing how the mind acquires its ideas.

In this outcome, the role of Gassendi, who championed an empiricism of Epicurean stamp, paralleled and soon merged with that of Locke. Moreover, Gassendi's revival of the atomistic definition of sensitive soul as a rarefied, fiery substance was easily assimilated to the mechanistic physiology then prevalent, serving to reinforce the opinion that psychic activity resulted from the flow of *esprits animaux* back and forth between the brain and the sensory apparatus. Such a combination of automatism, atomism, and empiricism is well seen in the case of Guillaume Lamy, a professor of the Paris Medical Faculty, who as early as 1678 anticipated the man-machine in his *Explication mécanique et physique des fonctions de l'âme sensitive, ou des sens, des passions et du mouvement volontaire*. But in the trend to materialism which thus drew sustenance from a broad spectrum of sources, the importance of Spinoza as a catalyzing agent should not be neglected. It was mainly in Spinozism that La Mettrie and a number of *philosophes* found, as part of what they took to be a naturalistic and atheistic metaphysics, the key notion of necessity which they consolidated with the man-machine idea, arriving at a doctrine of mental and moral determinism that made of free-will a mere subjective illusion.

All the attitudes and influences discussed above made their least inhibited appearance in the free-thinking literature that circulated privately in France after 1700, and in which different approximations of the man-machine may be said to have enjoyed at first an "underground" existence. The idea was originally propagated, therefore, as a salient feature of the radical *critiques* aimed at the official ideology of the *Ancien Régime*. In this initial phase of its career, the incipient man-machine idea had predominantly an antireligious and subversive meaning, and was regarded rightly, on the whole, as dangerous to social and political institutions by the defenders of tradition and authority, who sought, though ineffectually, to suppress it. Among the many examples of such a use of mechanistic psychology are to be found the revolutionary *Testament* (1729) of the notorious apostate priest, Jean Meslier, and, in the class of anonymous works extant in manuscript, *L'Ame matérielle* and *Essai sur les facultés de l'âme*.

It was not, however, until the publication of La Mettrie's *L'Homme machine* (1747) that the idea provocatively epitomized by its title was at last affirmed as the basis and focus of a coherent philosophical position. From profusely cited evidence of what he took to be an invariable correlation between mental and physical states in the individual, La Mettrie concluded that, in addition to every vital and involuntary function, all the forms of conscious life—such as sensation, the passions, memory, thinking, volition—are regularly contingent upon the "organic machine," and more exactly on the structures and activity of the central nervous system. Characteristic of this viewpoint was the fact that its author, himself a physician who had been a disciple of the leading iatromechanist, Hermann Boerhaave (1668–1738), gave it as the gist of a materialist philosophy that remained closely responsive to the methodology, scope, and aims of the medical sciences. As a result, while his advocacy of the man-machine still retained numerous antireligious, polemical, or propagandist traits, it had the originality of being put forward primarily as a general heuristic hypothesis for the scientific study of behavior. La Mettrie eschewed, as far as possible, its metaphysical implications (whether positive or negative) in regard to the ultimate nature of matter and mind, or of the causality underlying their mechanistic union. He thereby succeeded in harmonizing the experimentalist ideal of modern science, which had only recently come to the fore in France, with his main thesis. The man-machine was held to be a logically valid notion not because it expressed any apriorist truth about human nature, but on the strength of induction from verifiable psychophysical data. Consistently with this, La Mettrie was fond of analogies that pictured the mind as a "thinking and feeling machine" into which ideas, entering as coded symbols, were not merely stored, compared, and combined, but were also continuously colored and modified by emotive and instinctual messages flowing into the same centers of perception. The goal of psychology, according to the man-machine hypothesis, became the gradual clarification in detail of the complexities, admittedly limitless, of this cerebral process—a goal which, La Mettrie believed, held out the best hope of diminishing the enigma that man posed both generically and individually.

Although he stated that his doctrine was simply that of the beast-machine drawn out to its final consequences, actually La Mettrie's use of mechanism as a biological concept represented an important advance over the Cartesian view of the organism as essentially like any man-made, artificially actuated device. In contrast to such a "dead mechanism" approach, La Mettrie sought to describe the vital machine with which man was equated as a dynamical and self-sufficient system typified by an internal finality. "The human body," he wrote, "is a machine that winds its own springs—the living image of perpetual motion"; and more organismically: "man is an assemblage of springs that are activated reciprocally by one another, without it being possible to say at what precise point

139

of this human circle nature has begun." This conception was only in part inspired by technological achievements. The favorite criterion of an "intelligent" machine, in the eighteenth century as in the seventeenth, continued to be the ordinary clock, alongside which La Mettrie placed, however, the harpsichord as a model for the epistemological mechanics of registering, composing, and reproducing ideas like so many musical notes played on the cerebral "chords." Special mention deserves to be made also of Vaucanson's automata, the most ingenious of the period, which had in fact been contrived as practical simulations of different biological processes. There was among others his famous "duck," which could paddle itself about, and "digest" food by means of a stomach that substituted, as might be expected, mechanical for bio-chemical operations. But while the *homme machine* clearly profited from such scientific interests, it rested on more specifically biological grounds. La Mettrie referred the capability of automatic reactions which the organism possessed to the reactive energy manifested in a concrete way by the key-phenomenon of irritability. He thus saw in the property of muscle-tissue irritability, which Haller had recently discovered and illustrated experimentally, the vital force responsible for the purposive dynamism peculiar to physiological, as compared with merely physical, machines.

In most quarters, the man-machine philosophy was angrily denounced as a dangerous paradox, first, because it offended peoples' religious sentiments or deflated their vanity (which La Mettrie fully intended); but it was even more offensive because of certain implied moral conclusions. Claiming in his *Discours sur le bonheur* (1750) that happiness was a mental state dependent essentially on somatic conditions, La Mettrie divorced the "supreme good" of man from the practice of traditional virtues, and redefined it primarily as a medical rather than an ethical question—a reversal which, taken together with his readiness to relieve even criminals of the "disease" of guilt and remorse, struck his contemporaries as an immoralist's cynical defense of vice and anarchy. The usefulness of La Mettrie's deterministic—hence amoral—psychology is, however, far plainer to us now than it was to his own century. The man-machine idea had the merit of bringing to the age-old problem of the moral perfectibility of man a whole new dimension, consisting in the ability of medicine to act upon the mind, emotions, and personality by variously modifying their underlying organic causes. La Mettrie may be said to have introduced into the sphere of general ethics a set of criteria inspired by medical humanitarianism, and supported by the psychiatric evidence that man's behavior is not in fact as free as it is commonly held to be.

Since La Mettrie, almost all materialist philosophy has subscribed in one form or another to the man-machine (even if the term itself, doubtless owing to its shock value, has never been popular). The leading advocate of the idea later in the eighteenth century was Diderot, whose versatile genius provided a nuanced and rich context for its development. He brought out, especially, its organismic potential by differentiating three structural levels in the human machine—that is, the elementary "cellular" units, the individual organs, and the organism as a whole—and by placing at the apex of their integrated operations the various manifestations of psychic life. Assuming, furthermore, that there was in nature an indeterminate number of "molecules," endowed with latent sensibility, which coalesced according to fixed laws, the *Rêve de D'Alembert* (1769)—which would remain unknown until the next century—sought to trace, with a gift for mechanistic analogies that was as much literary as scientific, the emergence of life, consciousness, sensation, the passions, memory, and reflection in terms of the ascending complexity and functional continuity of the related organic structures. More than this radical morphologizing of the man-machine, Diderot was the first to present the latter within the framework of a general transformistic theory embracing the history of all the animal species, with the outcome that man was perceived not merely as a machine, but as one that had been slowly constituted in time by the same universal laws of moving matter that governed his present behavior. The man-machine thereby found a suitable place in the system of evolutionary materialism that Diderot expounded in a largely hypothetical and conjectural vein. It was in his work, moreover, that the modern socioeconomic overtones of the idea first began to appear, although still indirectly, alongside its far more obvious antecedents in biological and medical science. When seen in relation to the enormous importance that Diderot ascribed, in the *Encyclopédie,* to the machinery and techniques of the manufacturing arts, the man-machine idea would appear to have been on the verge of a new significance. In his dual effort to mechanize man and to humanize technology, there was implicit a coextensiveness of the man-machine with the nascent reality of an industrial world, in which man was to be described at length not merely as himself a machine, but as the creator and master of countless other machines that would be objectifications of himself and, as it were, his "offspring." Diderot thus succeeded in evoking the broader implications, both biological and techno-social, of the man-machine; but no less clairvoyant was his sense of the basic contradictions between an impersonally mechanistic and deterministic view of human nature and man's inward awareness of freedom in choosing the moral, artistic, and affective values essential to his experience. The probing treatment, in a fictional work such as *Jacques le fataliste*, of this dilemma posed by Diderot's equally deep commitment to a humanistic and to a scientific vision of things, served in the end to point up a permanent paradox at the core of existence itself.

Among other versions or near-versions of the man-machine in the fertile eighteenth-century milieu, the physiological psychology of David Hartley should be noted. Influenced by Newton's theory of the ether no less than by Newton's reduction of the multiplicity of physical events to a single principle, Hartley's *Observations on Man* (1749) proposed to interpret all mental phenomena as resulting from vibratory motions in the brain and nerves—a hypothesis that had the great advantage, in his eyes, of accounting for the mechanics of the "law of association" by which all ideas were assumed to cohere. Although his associationist psychology, unlike the man-machine doctrine, preserved a formal distinction and parallelism between body and mind, Hartley did not hesitate to apply his vibration-principle in a comprehensive and deterministic fashion; he thereby represented the organism in general on the model of an elastic machine in which the impact of external events generated the specific vibratory responses that were the biological basis of every variety of psychic event.

A different and more limited use of the man-machine idea may be found in the two treatises of Helvétius: *De l'esprit* (1758) and *De l'homme* (1774). Conceding the premiss that "Man is a machine which, once set in motion by physical sensibility, executes all its acts necessarily," Helvétius elaborated a rigidly environmentalist theory of education by way of explaining the enormous variations among individuals. The corrective to this one-sided method came, however, with Diderot's *Réfutation d'Helvétius*, in which it was argued that a psychology aiming to be at once materialistic and sensationistic must consider as a variable, not only the total environment in which each mind develops, but the organism that underlies and informs its development.

In the writings of Holbach, the man-machine took a militantly atheistic turn. His *Système de la nature* (1770) made it the starting point of an intransigeant, rather reductive materialism, which, beyond its vehement anticlericalism, had positive ethical and political goals. The Holbachian man-machine served, more precisely, as the psychological complement of a "natural morality" derived from the pleasure-principle and consistent with the rule of social utility. This he opposed sharply to the "unnatural," spiritualist morality imposed by the Christian religion, and called for a radical reform of the political institutions of the *Ancien Régime* in the name of the felicity to which man, as

a physical being, was logically entitled in this world.

Finally, in the major contribution of Cabanis, *Rapports du physique et du moral de l'homme* (1795), the culmination of eighteenth-century interest in psychophysiology may be witnessed. Convinced no less than La Mettrie, Diderot, or Holbach of the primacy of the organic machine, he combined this approach *in extenso* with the method by which Condillac and Helvétius had already furnished a descriptive analysis of the role of sense-perception in the formation of ideas. In a well-known passage, Cabanis pictured the brain as an organ that produced thinking in the same manner that the stomach digested food, adding: "We conclude that the brain somehow digests sense-impressions, that it effects organically the secretion of thought." Contrary to this rather blunt formula, he worked out the details of his psychophysiology in a methodical and thorough way, laying special stress on such factors as age, sex, temperament, diet, physical exertion, occupational pursuits, pathological conditions, the use of drugs and stimulants, climate, and so forth. As in La Mettrie, the theme of "physiological salvation" loomed large, supported by the broad responsibility that Cabanis granted to medical science in the improvement of the human personality. On the other hand, it must be admitted that Cabanis referred only summarily to the actual mechanistic character of the organism, and, if anything, chose to play down the man-machine equation during the post-Revolutionary years when it was linked in public opinion with the ideological excesses that atheistic materialism was accused of having promoted.

In retrospect, the career of the man-machine idea during the Enlightenment may be said to have consisted of two phases. Up to about 1740, the concept of mechanism with which physiologists remained imbued was too rigid and narrow to offer, except in isolated instances, plausible models for the organic behavior it pretended to interpret. Beginning with the 1740's, however, a profound shift took place in biological speculation, exemplified by such figures as Buffon, La Mettrie, Diderot, and Maupertuis, the effect of which was to bring into sharp focus precisely those qualities of living things that would strike later generations as vitalistic rather than mechanistic in character. This reorientation of interest did not, as might have been expected, bring about the rejection of the established modes of explanation; instead it resulted in a new tendency to conceive of the mechanical with a degree of flexibility and imaginativeness sufficiently great to allow the inclusion of vital phenomena within the compass of loosely mechanistic hypotheses. To be sure, the notion of mechanism, in such a stretching of definitions, no longer corresponded to the rigorously geometrical method of the Cartesian school. By a **141** seemingly paradoxical, but in reality merely transitional step, the mechanistic biology of the second half of the eighteenth century ceased to be mathematical in spirit, and even sought to transcend, with an attitude of deliberate antimathematicism on the part of Diderot and Buffon, the authority of classical mechanics, which was now felt to be, however philosophically valid, futile and stifling in a technical sense. Inevitably, the commitment to mechanistic principles or models among such biological-minded *philosophes* as La Mettrie and Diderot had something vague and suppositional about it; what it gained in suggestive visual power, it lost (at least temporarily) in analytical clarity and quantitative precision. The truth is that the century which invented the man-machine disposed as yet of very modest means for inferring biological, to say nothing of mental, processes from what was reliably known about the behavior of the inanimate world. The meaning of the man-machine idea, as propounded by La Mettrie or Diderot, was therefore above all an affirmation of scientific faith—an appeal addressed to posterity—concerning the ultimate fecundity of the mechanistic method in bridging the gap between the living and nonliving, and between the conscious and unconscious, aspects of a presumably unitary nature.

It was in the Enlightenment that the man-machine idea may be said to have attained optimum expression, aided by the pre-Revolutionary thrust of materialistic and atheistic attitudes. But even then its success extended only feebly beyond the borders of France to countries such as England and Germany, where intellectual loyalties remained conservative. In the first half of the nineteenth century, moreover, the vogue of idealistic philosophy and introspective psychology, under the sway of romanticism, forced a broad retreat of the man-machine thesis. From this temporary eclipse the latter will gradually work its way up again to a new kind of prominence by the end of the century, under the influence of scientific developments favorable to it. Despite its final vindication, the man-machine will never quite regain its past authority as a systematic principle. It has survived since the eighteenth century mainly as an essential element—or often as a basic tendency—present either explicitly or implicitly in various configurations of thought in those disciplines that have contributed most to its growth. Owing to this changed historical status of the question, it would seem unprofitable henceforth to treat the man-machine idea sequentially. Rather, its fortunes will be assessed in relation to pertinent progress in the fields of biology, physiology, psychology, technology, and philosophy. Such a procedure is all the more fitting because of the differentiation that the sciences themselves underwent during the nineteenth century in the course of their

emancipation from "natural" and "mental" (or "moral") philosophy. Following this specialization of the methods and goals of research, the man-machine came to have significantly different applications and meanings for each of the branches of knowledge in which it enjoyed a vested interest.

The advances in neurology proved specially germane to the resurgence of the idea. Charles Bell's (1774–1842) discovery of the dual character of the nervous system served to clarify the distinction between efferent and afferent impulses, thus preparing the ground for a comprehensive and exact investigation of reflex action. The work of Claude Bernard (1813–78) on vascular reflexes and on the regulatory role of the sympathetic system was a forward stride for the man-machine, because it showed experimentally that the viscera, by direct or indirect links to the brain, were able to produce bodily changes affecting memory, perception, emotivity, and thinking. In fact, the general elucidation since the early nineteenth century of the varieties of reflex mechanism, together with the more recent extension of the principle to the Pavlovian conditioned reflex, has demonstrated in detail how far specific forms of conscious activity proceed from the integrated automatic play of the nervous apparatus. The perfecting of "neuron theory" led simultaneously to a better understanding of the nature of neural conduction and of psychophysical dynamics. To these discoveries should be added, of course, the accumulation of data concerning the problem of cerebral localization. From the pseudoscientific "cranioscopy" of Franz Joseph Gall (1758–1828), through the crucial researches of Pierre Flourens (1794–1867) on the behavior of decorticated pigeons, to the tentative brain-topography sketched from clinical observation of various motor and sensory types of aphasia, the nineteenth century offered increasing evidence for the belief that the central nervous system was the adequate and controlling instrument of mental life. Such a conclusion was supported, moreover, by what histological analysis revealed in regard to the association-patterns of fibres and the functional stratification within the brain.

Nineteenth-century philosophy mirrored or confirmed, albeit in a minor key, the standpoint of human machinism. It was favored by Comtean thought to the extent that the latter insisted, as against introspective or speculative approaches, on the value of a positivistic method in psychology which, in the historically given circumstances, could only lead to the primacy of the physiological factor. The current of materialism that came to the fore in Germany around the mid-century, represented by figures such as Feuerbach, Vogt, Moleschott, Czolbe, and Büchner, took for granted the validity of the man-machine conception. In England,

Spencer's "Synthetic Philosophy," although not actually materialistic, did not hesitate to classify "mental science" as one of the natural sciences, with the result that in the Spencerian hierarchy of the sciences, psychology mediated the transition from biology to sociology. G. H. Lewes (1817–78), rejecting the dualist separation of mind and body, held that "sentience" was a mechanical process peculiar to animate beings, out of which, under the appropriate conditions, consciousness in all its degrees developed. Hippolyte Taine (1828–93), who was inclined to view man as a "nervous machine" and to define thoughts and feelings deterministically as products not unlike sugar and vitriol, applied his psychophysical theories to literary criticism; while, under his aegis, Émile Zola and the naturalists sought to illustrate through the medium of fiction that individual fate was the inexorable outcome of hereditary and environmental forces.

Physiological psychology as a special branch of science flourished under the stimulus of the aforementioned interests. In the period roughly from 1830 to 1860, the group of German experimentalists which included J. Müller, Virchow, Helmholtz, Du Bois-Reymond, and others, made remarkable progress in the study of the physiology of sensation and perception. Rudolph Hermann Lotze's (1817–81) *Medizinische Psychologie, oder Physiologie der Seele* (1852), a prototype of many similar treatises, was proof that the viability of the man-machine idea did not narrowly suppose monistic or materialistic convictions; for its author, although a philosophical idealist and occasionalist, regarded the nervous system as a pure mechanism in his discussion of it as the basis of mind. A. Horwicz (*Psychologische Analysen auf physiologischer Grundlage*, 1872–78) studied emotion as the somatically conditioned source of consciousness and of psychic life in general. T. Ziehen's *Leitfaden der physiologischen Psychologie* (1891) affirmed, among other things, that there was no real distinction between voluntary and involuntary thinking, thus echoing the automatist theory propagated by the eighteenth-century materialists. These principles were expanded upon by H. Münsterberg (*Grundzüge der Psychologie*, 1900), who predicted that psychology would become an exact science only in so far as it utilized the unequivocal evidence furnished by neurophysiology. In England, too, there was a parallel tendency to explain the energetics and conduct of the mind in terms of its organic constituents, as attested by the work of A. Bain (*The Senses and the Intellect*, 1855) and by that of such exponents of the same school of psychology as T. Laycock (*Mind and Brain*, 1860), W. B. Carpenter (*Principles of Mental Physiology*, 1874), and Henry Maudsley, who plainly took the view (in *Physiology*

and Pathology of the Mind, 1867) that consciousness was a by-product of brain processes. In America, William James gave a large place to the physiological method in his investigation of behavior, as best seen perhaps in the James-Lange theory of emotion.

A decisive factor in the long-run success of human machinism was Darwinian biology and the new orientations that it provoked in psychology. The hypothesis that man was descended from lower forms of life dramatically weakened whatever presumption was still left that his origins and nature had a spiritual, transcendent dimension; and in the same proportion it reinforced the axiom that all human characteristics were natural phenomena admitting of natural explanations. It was consistent with evolutionist logic to explain the diverse levels of psychic capability in man as direct correlates of the ascending order of complexity and differentiation that the selective struggle for existence had wrought in his organic endowment. The continuity thus established between him and the higher animal species was an invitation to study human beings by the same behavioral criteria, rooted in biologically given instincts and needs, that were appropriate (and indeed inevitable) in the study of animals.

The combined impetus of the developments in science and philosophy that have been briefly summarized was responsible for the reemergence of the man-machine doctrine at the start of the twentieth century with the sort of intellectual respectability that it had clearly lacked in its eighteenth-century version. Its restored vitality involved, of course, several qualifications of its meaning and scope. The new man-machine did not signify any simple or self-apparent equation between human nature and man-made mechanical devices (a fact which indicates why the idea itself caught on much better than La Mettrie's rather offensive sounding name for it). On the contrary, the machinery of the body was now seen as an enormously complex self-adaptive system of a physicochemical type analyzable into molecular structures, for which, moreover, no faithful analogue could be cited among artificial machines. The man-machine therefore affirmed only that the dynamics of organism must ultimately be governed by the same laws that governed mechanical systems—an assumption in methodological agreement with the twin principles of simplicity and the unity of science. In its psychological and philosophical reaches, the idea has come to mean that psychical events, at least in theory, are empirically attributable, according to specific, regular, and determinable patterns, to neural mechanisms, without it being obligatory to define, whether *a priori* or *a posteriori*, the underlying causation or the ontological status of mind.

Since around 1900, the man-machine has been a pervasive idea in the three disciplines—namely, biology, psychology, and philosophy—among which its career and promise continue mainly to be shared. In each case, however, it has come to have a different sort of relevance. In the biological sphere, the ever more exact clarification of the physicochemical processes of the organism—and of the electrochemical properties of its nervous component—has had the cumulative effect of justifying the experimental procedures and theoretical standpoint of the "mechanists." Nevertheless, the status of the man-machine remains contingent upon the centuries-old, still unsettled controversy between vitalism and mechanism. An episode in that debate which might seem pertinent here occurred when E. Rignano published *Man Not a Machine, A Study of the Finalistic Aspects of Life* (1926), and was promptly refuted by J. Needham's *Man A Machine, in Answer to a Romantical and Unscientific Treatise* (1928). The vitalistic contention that the organism, while admittedly a physical system, cannot be understood in terms of the same fundamental laws exemplified by the behavior of inorganic mechanisms, remains tenable as long as living things cannot be synthesized in the laboratory, despite the methodological sterility and diminishing plausibility that may be reproached against it. The thrust of vitalism, at any rate, has been to deny that man is accurately describable as a machine, apart from the question whether his psychic being is or is not a dependency of his body.

Twentieth-century psychology, although it has been largely unconcerned with deciding if the brain works "mechanistically" or "organismically," has in various other ways embodied or corroborated some form of the man-machine idea. The highly specialized interest in animal psychology initiated by John B. Watson and pursued by the behaviorists has lent weight to the man-machine by virtue of the uniformity it supposes between the more mechanical and predictable acts of animals and those, seemingly less so, of human beings. Thus, the comparison of man and animal under a single psychological perspective in our time has been an experimental reenactment of the speculative step which, during the seventeenth and eighteenth centuries, had already transformed the beast-automaton into the man-machine. More broadly, behaviorism has coincided with the standpoint of human mechanism in proportion as it has limited itself to observing the mind nonsubjectively from without, for such happens to be also the only way in which the behavior of a machine can be perceived and explained. Conversely, it is only the external or "public" behavior of a human being that the machine is able to simulate. To insist on a psychology restricted to behavior alone makes

psychology, therefore, the science of machines no less than of animals or men. By excluding from consideration what is least amenable to mechanistic analogies—that is, consciousness and subjective states—behaviorism has given a blanket endorsement to the man-machine. In the case of Freudian psychology, it may be said that the blurring of the ordinary distinction between voluntary and involuntary actions as a result of the role of the unconscious, has corroborated the same idea by suggesting that conscious thoughts and desires are continuations, on a different plane, of those instinctual forces—in particular, the sexual—which manifestly originate in the organism. Psychoanalytic exploration of countless "unconscious mechanisms" has brought to light and catalogued a whole new province of "automatisms" in the life of the psyche. The primacy of instincts (or "drives") arising from the biological makeup of the animal or human being has been the standpoint, similarly, of the purposive psychology associated with the names of McDougall and Tolman. While its various exponents have differed over the degree of physiological determinism involved, the theory of "drive" has generally been useful to the man-machine doctrine by providing a sort of nexus for mechanistic and motivational accounts of psychodynamics. Hull, moreover, has stressed the neurological basis of motivation to the point of asserting the isomorphism of cerebral and mental structures, and of envisaging a science of psychology guided by the homeostatic principle. This science of man would be deducible (at least hypothetically) from physiological postulates about stimuli issuing from the external and internal environment of the organism, and from inherited neural connections between receptors and effectors. Köhler has realized, in the attempt to explain visual perception, a synthesis of Gestaltist and mechanistic hypotheses by the extension of physical field theory to cerebral functioning. No less significant for the man-machine position, however, has been the impressive advance of psychophysiology itself in our era. The role of endocrinological factors, although perhaps overestimated a few decades ago, has, nonetheless, been fitted conspicuously into the overall picture of how the body controls the mind. The importance of glandular determinants is reflected in the human typologies that Kretschmer and Sheldon have worked out by means of statistical correlations between personality and physique. Continuing research, aided by new techniques of localization, has greatly perfected the functional topography of the brain, particularly in regard to the roles of the mid-brain and brain-stem, as well as their patterns of integration with one another and with the cortex. But these technical contributions, while strengthening the presumption in favor of the man-machine, also remain problematical. For example, the investigation of "projection areas" and their interchangeability of function has made it more difficult than before to imagine an exact isomorphism between mind and brain, or to suggest actual mechanical models for how the latter performs its task. At the same time, all of the available psychophysical knowledge can explain no more than the general features and grosser aspects of the organic basis of mind. The infinite diversity that individual thoughts, feelings, and actions exhibit still remains quite unrelated in any verifiable sense to specific neural traces or processes.

In contemporary philosophy, the status of the man-machine is inseparable from the mind-body problem. Many philosophers would now concede both that the organism is reducible to the same laws operative in all nonorganic systems, and that mental events cannot exist except as the consequences of neural events. But the real problem lies elsewhere; because if, in the man-machine formula, biology has been concerned mainly with the term "machine," and psychology with the term "man," the essential concern of recent philosophy has become the hyphen connecting the two terms. The decline of dualistic, monistic, and materialistic doctrines founded on the concept of substance has set the validity of the man-machine thesis in an entirely different key. Logical positivism has led Carnap and Neurath to the view that meaningful statements about the mind are only those which refer to its outwardly observable properties and can therefore be tested. This epistemic form of materialism has in turn promoted, as best seen perhaps in the work of Wittgenstein and Ryle, a behavioristic analysis of mind, the general effect of which has been to construe "mentalistic" propositions as "physicalistic" propositions. Such "reductionist" efforts to circumvent the perennial mind-body dilemma are tantamount to re-articulating the man-machine idea as a program of logical reconciliation between two separate universes of experience and of discourse. More radically consistent with the idea, however, is the "identity theory" of Feigl, Place, and Smart, which assumes a *de facto*, empirical identification of mental states or processes with states or processes of the central nervous system. Nevertheless, certain difficulties persist. That every mental event has its specific causal counterpart in a neuromechanical event remains a merely hypothetical, and probably in practice an unverifiable, principle. As a result, the physicalistic method of analyzing the mind tends to interpret psychic reality in an idiom which, when it refers to neural processes, risks becoming gratuitously indirect and obscure, and, when it refers to public behavior, fails to express what is given phenomenologically in consciousness.

The advent of cybernetic technology has greatly added to the analogical force of the man-machine idea. The construction of numerous mechanical devices with purposive and self-adaptive characteristics has had, first, a decisive impact counter to vitalism, by showing that modes of behavior long held to be peculiar to living systems need not necessarily lie beyond the range of mechanism. Simultaneously, a whole gamut of intellectual capabilities, such as remembering, learning, judging, foreseeing, problem-solving, etc., have been simulated by information-fed machines that are able, among other things, to run mazes, prove theorems, compose music, play chess, translate from one language into another, and calculate with an efficiency unapproachable by the human mind. The design of these auto-regulated devices has suggested various useful hypotheses in neurophysiology and psychophysiology, especially as regards the mechanism of reflex action and the neural mechanics of analogous operations occurring in the brain. Cybernetics has thereby brought to the man-machine thesis a new dimension borrowed from electronic technology: notions such as "conductors," "circuits," "signals," "relays," "electric charges," "thresholds," "feed-back," and the like, have gained currency in attempts to describe the performance of the central nervous apparatus. The corresponding model of man that has emerged is a composite of the earlier physicochemical machine and of a computerized guidance system present within it. While the influence on philosophy of such technological innovations has been obviously to bolster the postulate that mental events are somehow identifiable with neuro-mechanical events, in other respects the contribution of cybernetics has been controversial and confusing. It has led, in particular, to the inverse formulation of the man-machine, that is, to what might be called the "machine-man" idea—a reversal of things which had, in fact, always been implicit in the original. Some philosophers have consequently chosen to deal behavioristically with the "mentality" of machines by an ambivalent or metaphorical use of terms properly descriptive of human beings and animals. But the "thinking" in which machines engage is limited normally to predetermined operations that are, moreover, reducible to mathematical sequences. It is not easy to imagine a mechanical analogue of the brain that could faithfully reproduce the intertexture of all the types of thinking appropriate to all the situations that human beings confront, together with the nonlogical modes through which ideas are associated in the "stream of consciousness." Even if such a feat of simulation were theoretically conceivable, there would be no technological means of imitating subjective reality. A kind of dualism thus attaches to mechanistic philosophy itself as regards the distinction between natural and artificial machines, the former manifesting a techno-logic of which consciousness remains the essential and nonduplicatable trait.

Yet concern about the "mentality" of machines in contemporary thought is symptomatic of the sociocultural meaning that the man-machine has acquired in post-industrial societies on the threshold of automation. The technical superiority of the machine, by transforming mere efficiency into a human ideal, has set in motion a convergence between itself and man which tends, on the one hand, to lift the robot to a sort of sub-human role, and on the other, to assimilate man to the machine not only in the biological or psychophysiological sense, but also in relation to his values and conduct. Such an invasion of man's private world by criteria typical of automata has provoked, understandably, a reaction which raises the problem of how far his nature may be equated with that of the machine. The *golem*, which in sixteenth-century Yiddish folklore was envisaged as a beneficent servant of man, has spawned in our own time a numerous progeny of "mechanical creatures" about whose intentions we are far less confident. The obsessive *leitmotiv*, so popular in science fiction, of human civilization being threatened by a robot takeover, would seem thus to betray symbolically a widespread fear of the automatization of life; for the menacing robot rival is actually man himself perceived in a depersonalized future shape.

In conclusion, the man-machine idea may be said at present to occupy a strategic and fateful position at the confluence of several disciplines and traditions: in neurophysiology and psychology it is above all a fecund empirical hypothesis of indefinite promise to research; in philosophy, it is a speculative option in the attempt to resolve the body-mind problem; in technology, it expresses the demiurgic goal of mastering our environment by the mechanical maximation of our limited powers; and as a theme in sociology and the imaginative arts, it most often conveys the malaise of dehumanization in modern culture, and conjures up fantasies that put in doubt the survival of man's authentic self.

BIBLIOGRAPHY

George S. Brett, *History of Psychology*, ed. R. S. Peters (London, 1962; New York, 1963). John Cohen, *Human Robots in Myth and Science* (London, 1966; South Brunswick, N.J., and New York, 1967). K. Gunderson, *Mentality and Machines* (Garden City, 1971). Heikki Kirkinen, *Les Origines de la conception moderne de l'Homme-Machine* (Helsinki, 1960). F. A. Lange, *The History of Materialism* (New York, 1950; original German edition, 1865). Leonora C. Rosenfeld, *From Beast-Machine to Man-Machine: Animal Soul in French Letters from Descartes to La Mettrie* (New York, 1941). Aram Vartanian, *Diderot and Descartes: A Study of Scientific Naturalism in the Enlightenment* (Princeton, 1953); esp. Ch. IV; idem, *La Mettrie's L'Homme Machine: A Study in the Origins of an Idea*, critical edition with an introductory monograph and notes (Princeton, 1960).

The translations for Descartes are by the author of the article.

ARAM VARTANIAN

[See also **Behaviorism;** Dualism; **Epicureanism and Free Will;** Historical and Dialectical Materialism; Necessity; Organicism; Positivism; **Psychological Ideas in Antiquity;** Pythagorean . . .; Unity of Science.]

MARXISM

MARXISM like Christianity is a term that stands for a family of doctrines attributed to a founder who could not have plausibly subscribed to all of them, since some of these doctrines flatly contradict each other. Consequently any account that professes to do justice to Marxism must be more than an account of the ideas of Karl Marx even if it takes its point of departure from him.

As a set of ideas one of the remarkable things about Marxism is that it is continually being revived despite formidable and sometimes definitive criticisms of its claims and formulations. For this and other reasons, it cannot be conceived as a purely scientific set of ideas designed "to lay bare the economic law of motion of modern society" (Preface to first edition of *Capital*) and to explain all cultural and political developments in terms of it. There is little doubt that Karl Marx himself thought that his contributions were as scientific in the realm of social behavior as Newton's in the field of physics and Darwin's in biology. But there is no such thing as a recurring movement of Newtonianism or Darwinism in physics or biology. The mark of a genuine science is its cumulative development. The contributions of its practitioners are assimilated and there is no return to the original forms of theories or doctrines of the past.

The existence of Marxism as a social and political *movement* inspired by a set of ideas, sometimes in open opposition to other movements, is further evidence that we are dealing with a phenomenon that is not purely scientific. For such a movement obviously goes beyond mere description or the discovery of truth. That its normative goals may in some sense be based upon descriptive truths, i.e., not incompatible with them, may justify using the term "scientific" at best to differentiate these goals from those that are arbitrary or impossible of achievement.

Marxism has often been compared with, and sometimes characterized as, a religion with its sacred books, prophets, authoritative spokesmen, etc. But this is not very illuminating until there is agreement about the nature of religion, a theme which is even more ambiguous and controversial than that of Marxism. Nonetheless there are some important features which Marxism shares with some traditional religions that explain at least in part its recurrent appeal despite its theoretical shortcomings.

Marxism is a monistic theory that offers an explanatory key to everything important that occurs in history and society. This key is the mode of economic production, its functioning, the class divisions and conflicts it generates, its limiting and, in the end, its determining effect upon the outcome of events. It provides a never failing answer to the hunger for explanation among those adversely affected by the social process. That the explanations are mostly ad hoc, that predictions are not fulfilled, like the increasing pauperization of the working class, that important events occur that were not predicted like the rise of Fascism, the emergence of a new service-industry oriented middle class, the discovery of nuclear technology—are not experienced as fatal, or even embarrassing, difficulties. Just as belief that everything happens by the will of God is compatible with whatever occurs, so belief in the explanatory primacy of the mode of economic production and its changes is compatible with any social or political occurrence if sufficient subsidiary hypotheses are introduced. That is why although Marxism as a social and political movement may be affected by the events and conditions it failed to explain (like the latter-day affluence of capitalist society), as a set of vague beliefs it is beyond refutation. In the course of its history, now more than a century old, few, if any, Marxists have been prepared to indicate under what empirical or evidential conditions they were prepared to abandon their doctrines as invalid.

A second reason for the recurrence of Marxism in various guises—there are today existentialist Marxisms and even Catholic Marxisms—is that its theories are an expression of hope. Marxisms of whatever kind all hold out the promise, if not the certainty, of social salvation, or at the very least, relief from the malaise and acute crises of the time. Whether the future is conceived in apocalyptic terms or less dramatically, it is one with a prospect of victory through struggle, a victory that will insure peace, freedom, prosperity, and surcease from whatever evils flow from an improperly organized and unplanned society, dominated by the commodity producing quest for ever renewed profit.

The third reason for the recurrence of Marxism is a whole series of semantic ambiguities that permit Marxists to appeal to individuals and groups of democratic sentiment despite the fact that Marxists often direct savage and unfair criticisms against nonsocialist democracies. The growth of democratic sentiment and the allegiance to the principle of self-determination in all areas of personal and social life are universal phenomena. They are marked by the fact that almost every totalitarian regime seeks to pass itself off as one or another form of democracy. Marxists, for reasons that will be made clearer below, are the most adept and successful in presenting Marxism as a philosophy of the democratic left, despite the existence of ruthless despotisms in the USSR and Red China, and other countries that profess to be both socialist and Marxist. Although the existence of these two dictatorial regimes and of other avowedly Marxist regimes in Eastern Europe creates some embarrassment for those who identify the Marxist movement with the movement towards democracy, the terrorist practices of these regimes are glossed over and explained away. They are represented either as excesses of regimes unfaithful to their own socialist ideals or as temporary measures of defense against enemies of democracy within or without.

Finally there are certain elements of truth in Marxism that, however vague, explain some events and some facets of the social scene that involve the growth of industrial society and its universal spread, the impact of scientific technology, the pressure of conflicting economic class interests and their resolution. Although not exclusively Marxist, these insights and outlooks have been embodied in the Marxist traditions. They function to sustain by association, so to speak, the more specific Marxist doctrines in the belief system of their advocates. Although they are generalized beyond the available evidence, they bestow a certain plausibility on Marxist thought when other conditions further their acceptance.

This brings us to the important and disputed question of what constitutes the nature of Marxism. What are the characteristic doctrines associated with the Marxist outlook upon the world? For present purposes we are distinguishing Marxism and its variants from the question of what Marx and Engels *really* meant. Historically, this question is by far not as significant as what they have been *taken* to mean. Marx like Christ might have disowned all of his disciples: it would not affect how their meaning has been historically interpreted and what was done in the light of that interpretation. It may be that in the future there will be other interpretations of what Marx really meant and that even today there are several esoteric views of his thought different from those to be considered but they obviously cannot be considered as part of intellectual history.

There are three main versions of Marxism identifiable in the history of ideas that have received wide support. The first, oldest, and closest to the lives of Karl Marx and Friedrich Engels in point of time is the Social-Democratic version. The second version which acquired widespread influence after the October 1917 Russian Revolution is the Communist version, sometimes called the Bolshevik-Leninist view. The third version, which emerged after the Second World War, may be called "existentialist." Marxism is regarded from an existentialist view as primarily a theory of human alienation, and of how to overcome it. It is based primarily on Marx's unpublished Paris economic-philosophical manuscripts first made available in 1932. Although these three interpretations of Marxism are not compartmentalized in that they share some common attitudes, values, and beliefs, some of their basic theories are incompatible with each other. It would not be too much to say that if the basic theories of one of these three interpretations are taken to be true they entail the falsity of the corresponding basic theories of the other two.

I

The first version of Marxism is represented mainly by the writings of the later Engels, the early Eduard Bernstein, Karl Kautsky, George Plekhanov, and in the United States by Daniel De Leon. It accepts as literally valid six interrelated complexes of propositions.

1. The fundamental and determining factor in all societies is the mode of economic production. All important changes in the culture of a period—its politics, ethics, religion, philosophy, and art—are ultimately to be explained in terms of changes in the economic substructure.

2. The capitalist mode of economic production is fundamentally unstable. It cannot guarantee, except for very limited periods, continued employment for the masses, a decent standard of living, and sufficient profit for the entrepreneurs to justify continued production. The consequence is growing mass misery culminating in the crisis and breakdown of the system of production. The deficiencies and fate of capitalism are not due to any specific persons or human actions, but flow from the law of value and surplus value in a commodity-producing society. The collapse of capitalism and its replacement by a socialist classless society are inevitable.

3. Classes are defined by the role they play in production. Their conflicting economic interests give rise to economic class struggles that override on crucial occasions and, in the long run, all other kinds of struggle—religious, racial, national, etc. The variations in the intensity of these types of struggle, even their origin, are directly or indirectly a consequence of the "underlying" economic class struggle.

4. The state is an integral part of the political and legal order. It therefore has a class character which must be changed through class struggles, peaceful where possible, violent where not, before the forces of production can be liberated from the quest for ever-renewed profit and utilized for the benefit of the entire community, in which the economic exploitation of men by other men is no longer possible.

5. Capitalism prepares the way for the new socialist society by intensive development and centralization of industry, concentration of capital, and rationalization of the techniques of production. These are necessary presuppositions of a socialized, planning society in which the abolition of private ownership of the social means of production, and its vestment in the community as a whole, abolishes the economic class divisions of the past.

6. The movement towards socialism is a movement towards democracy. *Political* democracy must be defended against all its detractors and enemies but from the point of view of democracy as a way of life, it is necessary but not sufficient. Political democracy must be used to achieve a complete democracy by extending democratic values and principles into economic and social life. Where democracy does not exist the socialist movement must introduce it. (The *Communist Manifesto*, because of the absence of political democracy on the European Continent, advocated revolution by forcible overthrow.) Where democracy already exists, the working class can achieve power by peaceful parliamentary means (cf. Engels' critique of the Erfurt Program in 1891 and also his introduction to the first English translation of *Capital*).

There are many other doctrines that are part of the Marxist position (like equality between the sexes, self-determination for national minorities, the desirability of trade unions and cooperatives) that are easily derivable from the above propositions and some implicit value judgments about the desirability of human dignity, freedom, and creative self-fulfillment, even though they are obviously not uniquely entailed by them.

Marxism, in this its original version, was primarily a social philosophy. Its spokesmen as a rule adopted positions in philosophy and religion only in opposition to those metaphysical or theological doctrines whose suspected impact obstructed the growth of the working class movement and the development of its socialist consciousness. Philosophical and religious freedom of thought were extended to all thinkers who accepted the complex of social and economic propositions enumerated above which defined the theoretical Marxist orthodoxy of the German Social-Democratic Party and the majority of the members of the Second International. Dialectical materialism, for example, despite its espousal by Engels in his *Anti-Dühring* (1878) and *Ludwig Feuerbach* . . . (1888; trans. as *Ludwig Feuerbach and the Outcome of Classical German Philosophy*, 1934), was of peripheral importance in the Marxism that flourished up to 1917. The attack on Eduard Bernstein as a revisionist of Marxism was motivated primarily by his criticism of the first four of the complex of propositions identified above, and of the party programs of the political movement based on Marxism. It was only because he rejected the economic analysis of his party comrades and the political program presumably based on it (he approved its day-by-day activities) that attacks were made on his philosophical views.

The predominant characteristic of Social-Democratic Marxist thought is its determinism, its reliance upon the immanent processes of social development to create the conditions that would impel human beings to rationalize the whole of economic production in the same explicit and formal way in which an efficient industrial plant is organized. Formulated during an era in which the theory of evolution was being extrapolated from the field of biology to all other fields, especially the social and cultural areas of human activity, the laws of social development were considered universal, necessary, and progressive. The vocabulary was not very precise, partly because of the popular audience to which the teachings of Marxism were addressed. But even in *Capital*, as well as in his more popular writings, Marx used the term "inevitable" in describing the laws of economic change in heralding the collapse of capitalism. Engels was particularly addicted to the vocabulary of necessitarianism. Although aware of the differences in the subject matter of the natural and social sciences, and opposed to the reduction of the latter to the former, Marxists regarded the laws in both domains as working themselves out with an ineluctable "iron" necessity.

The concept of social necessity remained unexamined by the Marxist theoreticians and could not be squared, when strictly interpreted, with the recognition of alternatives of development, alternatives of action, and objective possibilities presupposed in the *practical* programs of the Marxist movement of the time. Nonetheless it possessed a rational kernel of great importance. For it stressed the importance of social readiness, preparedness, and maturity as a test and check on proposals for reform and revolution. It served as a brake upon the adventurism and euphoria of action induced by revolutionary rhetoric, and also as a consolation in defeat when objective conditions were proved to be unripe.

On the other hand, belief in the concept of social necessity tended psychologically to inhibit risk-taking actions, especially as the Marxist movement and its political parties increased in influence and acquired a feeling of responsibility. Belief in determinism, and in the heartening conviction that the structure of the socialist society was being built within the shell of the old even by those opposed to socialism, could not obviate the necessity of making choices in economics and politics, whether it was a question of supporting a call for a general strike, or voting for welfare and/or war budgets. But it naturally tended to reinforce in practice, if not in rhetoric, the choice of the moderate course, the one *less* likely to provoke opposition that might eventuate in violence and bloodshed. And why not, if the future, so to speak, was already in the bag?

This attitude of caution and restraint was reinforced by the implicitly teleological interpretation of evolutionary processes. What came later in time was assumed to be "higher" or "better"; setbacks were only temporary, the reverse stroke of an historical spiral that had only one direction—upward to a higher level. This led in practice to a commitment to the *inevitability of gradualism* so that the very pace of reforms tended to slow down as a sense of the urgent, the critical, and the catastrophic in history eased, and became replaced by a feeling of security in the overall development of history. Even the outbreak of the First World War in 1914, which destroyed the belief in the necessarily progressive character of change, failed to dispel the moderation of the Social-Democratic variant of Marxism. It was unprepared not only to take power but to exercise it vigorously when power was thrust upon it—at the close of the first World War in Germany. It moved towards the welfare state very slowly, partly in fear of provoking civil war.

Beginning with the last decade of the nineteenth century, as Social-Democratic movements gained strength in Europe, an enormous literature has been devoted to the exposition, criticism, and evaluation of Marxism. At first neglected, then refuted, then reinterpreted, modified, and qualified, Marxism in all its varieties has become at present perhaps the strongest single intellectual current of modern social thought. It has left a permanent impress upon economic historians like Max Weber and Charles Beard, even as they disavowed belief in its basic ideas. Here we shall offer only a brief review of the principal interpretations of the historical role and validity of the central notions of Marxism.

1. The doctrine of historical materialism is accepted 149

by many historians as a heuristic aid in describing the ways a society functions, its class power relations, and their influence on cultural activities. But it is woefully deficient in clarity with respect to all its basic terms. It is clear enough that it is not an economic determinism of human motives of a Benthamite variety, nor a technological determinism *à la* Veblen. But the connection between "the social relations of production" and "the material forces of production" is left obscure, so that there is some doubt whether the basic motor forces of historical development are tools, techniques, and inventions, especially what Whitehead calls "the invention of the method of invention," all of which express the productive drive of human beings—a drive which would open the door to a psychological, idealistic interpretation—or whether the immanent laws of the social relations of production are the ultimate determinants. Actually although many historians express indebtedness to Marxism for its theory of historical materialism, they mean no more by this doctrine than that "economics," in one of its many different meanings, must always be taken into account in an adequate understanding of history. But so must many other things that are not economic.

There is a further difficulty in ascertaining whether Marxism asserts that "social relations of production" or "the mode of economic production" *determines* the cultural superstructure, and if so to what degree, or merely *conditions* it. If it is taken to mean that it determines culture in all important aspects—historical monism—it is obviously untenable. In the face of evidence to the contrary, Marxists are wont to introduce reference to other factors reserving the determination of these factors by the mode of economic production—"in the last analysis"—despite the fact that scientifically speaking there is no such thing as "the last analysis."

The monistic determinism of Marxism is conspicuous in its treatment of "great men" in history. From Engels to Kautsky to Plekhanov to all lesser lights it is dogmatically assumed that no event-making personality has existed such that in his absence anything very important in history would have been different. With respect to any great event or phase of social development it is assumed that "no man is indispensable." Nonetheless, to cite only one difficulty, the overwhelming evidence seems to show that without Lenin there would in all likelihood have been in 1917 no October Russian Revolution.

Even if all problems of meaning are resolved and every trace of incoherence is removed from the theory of historical materialism, its claims that the mode of economic production determines politics, that "no social order ever perishes before all the productive

forces for which there is room in it have developed," and that no new social order can develop except on the basis of the economic foundations that have been prepared for it—have all been decisively refuted by the origin, rise, and development of the USSR and Communist China. Marxism as a theory of social development has been proved false by the actions of adherents of the Marxism of Bolshevik-Leninism. Lenin and his party seized political power in an industrially backward country and proceeded to do what the theory of historical materialism declared it was impossible to do—build the economic foundations of a new society by the political means of a totalitarian state.

2. The economic theory of Marxism is clearer than the theory of historical materialism, and events have more clearly invalidated it by negating its specific predictions especially the pauperization of the working classes, and the continuous decline in the rate of profit. The theory failed to predict the rise of what has been called the "new middle class" of the service industries as well as the economics of the totalitarian state, on the one hand, and of the welfare state, on the other. Even before events invalidated the Marxist economic assumptions, the theoretical structure of Marxist economics never recovered from Eugen Böhm-Bawerk's searching critique in the 1890's of its inconsistencies. Much more successful were the Marxist predictions about the historical development of capitalism, even though they did not uniquely follow from his theory of value and surplus value. The Marxists foresaw the growth of monopolistic tendencies, the impact of science on industrial technology, the periodic business cycle (although mistaken about its increasing magnitude), and imperialistic expansion in quest for foreign markets. Although Marxists anticipated progressive and cumulative difficulties for the capitalist system, as Joseph Schumpeter and others in the twentieth century have pointed out, they failed to see that these difficulties resulted from the successes of the system rather than from its failures.

3. The Marxist theory of the class struggle differs from all other theories of the class struggle in that it weights the component of economic class membership more heavily than any other theory in relation to other social groupings and associations, and in its expectation that economic class struggles will cease when the social instruments of production are collectivized. Although economic class interests and struggles play a large and indisputable role in political, social, and cultural life, on crucial occasions nationalist and religious ties have exercised greater weight. Although the international Marxist movement was pledged to a general strike against war, when World War I broke out, French workmen, instead of making common cause with

German workmen against their respective ruling classes, joined their "domestic exploiters," the French capitalists, in a common "national front" or "sacred union." The same was true in all major countries. National allegiance almost always proves stronger than class allegiance when national interest and class interest conflict. The union of capitalist Great Britain and United States supporting the socialist USSR against the invasion by capitalist Germany not only constitutes a difficulty for the theory of historical materialism—since the mode of economic production here was not decisive—but also for the theory of the class struggle, since the differences between the economic interests of the capitalist class as a whole and those of the USSR, especially in its opposition to capitalism declared from its very birth, are obviously far greater than the differences among the capitalists themselves. Even within the culture of a single capitalist country the Marxist theory of the class struggle fails to account for the degree and extent of class cooperation. The organized American labor movement seems just as hostile to collectivism as an economy and to communism as a political system as is the National Association of Manufacturers.

With the advent of collectivist economies in the Soviet Union and elsewhere, class struggles have not disappeared but have taken on a new form, sometimes expressed in strikes that are legally forbidden, in widespread pilfering, the use of a private sector to buy and sell, growth of bureaucratic privileges that some observers regard as indicia of a new class, and disparities in income and standards of living that are not too far removed from the upper and lower ranges of earned income in some capitalist countries. V. Pareto and Robert Michels, who agreed with Marxism that class struggles rage in society but disagreed with Marxism in holding that these struggles would continue even after Marxists came to power in what they call a socialist society, seem to have been justified by events.

Very little was done to solve some of the obvious difficulties in using the concept of class consistently with its definition, viz., the role played by individuals in the mode of production. In ordinary discourse, the various meanings of class take their meanings from the varied contexts in which they are used. One would have expected an attempt by Marxists to show that the chief uses of the term "class" that are different are derivative from the central Marxist one. Even more important was the failure to relate the concept of class interest to individual interest. Marxism is not a theory of human motivation, and especially not a theory of self-interest or egoism. The question remains: how does class interest get expressed? Classes are not individuals. They are abstractions. Only individuals act in history. On the

Marxist theory of class, regardless of whether individual members of the class are selfish or unselfish, the interests of their class presumably get expressed. How does this happen and through what mechanisms? Is there an implicit statistical judgment that describes the behavior of most members of a class or are there representative leaders who speak for the class? These are some of the questions that remained unexplored, with the result that the concept of class interest, often invoked, appeared as vague and mystical as "national interest," "the spirit of the times," "the spirit of the people," and similar expressions.

4. The Marxist theory of the state in its simplest form asserts that the state—consisting of the legislature, courts, and armed forces—is nothing but "the executive committee of the dominant economic class." If this were so, it would be hard to explain the character of much of the criminal law or rules of evidence and procedure, which reflect either common ethical norms or professional interests not directly related to economic interests. The Marxist movement soon discovered that its economic power could be wielded in a political way to bring pressure on the state to liberalize and humanize the social relationships of men, and to reduce inequalities in living conditions. It soon discovered that with the extension of the franchise it could use the state power to redistribute social wealth through taxation, subsidies, and price supports. Under such circumstances the state, especially when it functions as a welfare state, does not act as the "executive committee" of the dominant economic class. It may do things that are bitterly opposed by that class. The state, then, becomes the instrument of that class or coalition of classes strong enough to win electoral victory. Allowing for time lags, where the democratic process prevails the state can become more responsive to those groups that wield political power with majority electoral support, than to dominant economic interests.

5. Marxism as a movement became unfaithful to Marxism as a theory because of the success of capitalism in sustaining a relative prosperity—even if uncertain and discontinuous in times of acute crisis. Over the years, the numbers of the unemployed and poverty-stricken decreased instead of increasing. Real wages increased. Nonetheless, in order to achieve and sustain this relative affluence the state or government had to intervene in the economy with controls and plans foreign to the spirit and structure of a free market economy. The result has been a type of mixed economy—a private and public (often hidden) sector, unanticipated by the theorists both of capitalism and socialism. It turns out that the free enterprise economy of capitalism and the fully planned and planning col-

lectivist economy of socialism are neither exclusive nor exhaustive possible social alternatives, and that in the political struggles of democracy the issue was rarely posed as a stark choice between *either* a free economy *or* a planned economy, *either* capitalism *or* socialism, but rather as a choice between *"more or less."*

6. The Marxism of the Social-Democratic movement became transformed into a broad democratic people's front in which socialist measures are the means of extending democracy, providing security, defending human dignity and freedom. It no longer speaks in the name of the working class even when the latter constitutes its mass base but instead in behalf of the common interest and common good. Despite the revolutionary rhetoric, it has become a people's socialism. Marxism is no longer the ideology of the German Social-Democratic Party whose program in broad outline (in the 1960's) barely differs from the liberal wing of the Democratic Party in the USA or the Labor Party in Great Britain. A multiplicity of problems remain to be met in order to make the Welfare State truly devoted to the human welfare of all its citizens. Progress is no longer regarded as automatic but as requiring patience and hard work. But so long as the processes of freely given consent are not abridged in democratic countries and so long as large-scale war is avoided, the prospects of continued improvement are encouraging.

II

Marxism of the Bolshevik-Leninist persuasion is an extreme voluntaristic revision of the Social-Democratic variety that flourished in the period from the death of Marx (1883) to the outbreak of the First World War in 1914. The fact that it claims for itself the orthodoxy of the canonic tradition has about the same significance as the claims of Protestant leaders that they were returning to the orthodoxy of early Christianity. Even before the First World War, in Tsarist Russia the Bolshevik faction of the Russian Social-Democratic movement had taken positions that evoked charges from its opponents that the leaders of the group were disciples of Bakunin and Blanqui, rather than of Marx and Engels. Their voluntarism, especially in its organizational bearings, received a classic expression in Lenin's work *What Is To Be Done?* (1902). But the emergence of Bolshevik-Leninism as a systematic reconstruction of traditional Marxism was stimulated by the failure of the Social-Democratic movement to resist the outbreak of the First World War, and the disregard of the Basel Resolutions (1912) of the Second International to call a general strike; by the Bolshevik seizure of power in the October Russian Revolution of 1917 and the consequent necessity of justifying that and subsequent events in Marxist terms; by the accession

of Stalin to the supreme dictatorial post in the Soviet Union; and, finally, by the adoption of the systematic policy of building socialism in one country (the Soviet Union) marked by the collectivization of agriculture—in some ways a more revolutionary measure, and in all ways a bloodier and more terroristic one, than the October Revolution itself. The chief prophet of Marxist-Leninism was Stalin, and the doctrine bears the stigmata of his power and personality. Until his death in 1953, he played the same role in determining what the correct Marxist line was in politics, as well as in all fields of the arts and sciences, as the Pope of Rome in laying down the Catholic line in the domains of faith and morals. Although Stalin made no claim to theoretical infallibility, he exercised supreme authority to a point where disagreement with him on any controversial matter of moment might spell death.

The Bolshevik-Leninist version of Marxism got a hearing outside Russia, at first not in virtue of its doctrines, but because of its intransigeant opposition to the First World War. The Social-Democratic version of Marxism was attacked as a "rationalization" of political passivity, particularly for its failure to resist the war actively. Actually there was no necessary connection between the deterministic outlook of Social Democracy and political passivity, since its electoral successes were an expression of widespread political activity albeit of a non-revolutionary sort. Further, not only did some Social-Democratic determinists with a belief in the spontaneity of mass action, like Rosa Luxemburg, oppose the war, but even Eduard Bernstein, the non-revolutionary revisionist, who ardently believed that German Social Democracy should transform itself into a party of social reform, took a strong stand against the War. The attitude of Social Democracy to the First World War in most countries was more a tribute to the strength of its nationalism than a corollary of its belief in determinism. Nonetheless, the Bolsheviks on the strength of their anti-war position were able to insinuate doubts among some working-class groups, not only about the courage and loyalty to internationalist ideals of Social-Democratic parties, but about their Marxist faith and socialist convictions.

After the Bolshevik Party seized power in October 1917 and then forcibly dissolved the democratically elected Constituent Assembly, whose delayed convocation had been one of the grounds offered by that Party for the October *putsch*, and in which they were a small minority (19%), it faced the universal condemnation of the Social-Democratic Parties affiliated with the Second Socialist International. In replying to these criticisms Lenin laid down the outlines of a more voluntaristic Marxism, that affected the meaning and emphasis of the complex of doctrines of traditional

Marxism, especially its democratic commitments, in a fundamental way.

Finally with Lenin's death and the destruction of intra-party factions, which had preserved some vestigial traits of democratic dissent, the necessity of controlling public opinion in all fields led to the transformation of Marxism into a state philosophy enforced by the introduction of required courses in dialectical materialism and Marxist-Leninism on appropriate educational levels. Heretical ideas in any field ultimately fell within the purview of interest of the secret police. Censorship, open and veiled, enforced by a variety of carrots and whips, pervaded the whole of cultural life.

As a state philosophy Marxist-Leninism is marked by several important features that for purposes of expository convenience may be contrasted with earlier Social-Democratic forms of Marxist belief.

1. Marxism became an all-inclusive system in which its social philosophy was presented as an application and expression of the ontological laws of a universal and objective dialectic. During the heyday of Social-Democratic Marxism, the larger philosophical implications and presuppositions of its social philosophy were left undeveloped. So long as the specific party program of social action was not attacked, the widest tolerance was extended to philosophical and theological views. There was no objection even to the belief that God was a Social Democrat. Social Democrats, without losing their good standing within their movement, could be positivists, Kantians, Hegelians, mechanistic materialists, even, as in the case of Karl Liebknecht, subjectivists of a sort in their epistemology.

All this changed with the development and spread of Marxist-Leninism. The works of Engels, particularly his *Anti-Dühring* and *Dialectics of Nature*, of Lenin's *Materialism and Empirio-Criticism* and *Notebooks*, and subsequently, those of Stalin, became the sacred texts of a comprehensive system of dialectical materialism, devoted to explaining "the laws of motion in nature, society and mind." The details of the system and its inadequacies need not detain us here (Hook, 1941; 1959), but what it professed to prove was that the laws of dialectic guaranteed the victory of communist society, that no one could consistently subscribe to the ontology of dialectical materialism without being a communist and, more fateful, that no one could be a communist or a believer in communist society without being a dialectical materialist.

The comprehensiveness of this state philosophy resulted in a far flung net of new orthodox dogma being thrown over all fields from astronomy to zoology, the development of what was in effect a two-truth theory, ordinary scientific truth and the higher dialectical truth

which corrected the one-sidedness of the former, and political control of art and science. All communist parties affiliated with the Third Communist International were required to follow the lead of the Russian Communist Party. The literalness of the new orthodoxy is evidenced in the fact that the antiquated anthropological view of Engels and its primitive social evolutionism, based upon the findings of Lewis Morgan's pioneer work, *Ancient Society* (1877; 1959), were revived and aggressively defended against the criticisms of Franz Boas, Alexander Goldenweiser, Robert Lowie, and other investigators who, without any discredit to Morgan's pioneer effort, had cited mountains of evidence to show that social evolution was neither universal, unilinear, automatic, or progressive. Oddly enough the acceptance of the Engels-Morgan theory of social evolution, according to which no country can skip any important phase in its industrial development, would be hard to reconcile with the voluntarism of Bolshevik-Leninism, which transformed Russia from a backward capitalist country with strong feudal vestiges into a highly complex and modern industrial socialist state.

Reasoning from the dubious view that all things were dialectically interrelated, and the still more dubious view that a mistaken view in any field ultimately led to a mistaken view in every other field, including politics, and assuming that the party of Bolshevik-Leninism was in possession of the truth in politics, and that this therefore gave it the authority to judge the truth of any position in the arts and sciences in the light of its alleged political consequences, a continuous purge of ideas and persons, in accordance with the shifting political lines, marks the intellectual history of the Soviet Union. Here, as often elsewhere in the world, theoretical absurdities prepared the way for the moral atrocities whose pervasiveness and horror were officially partly revealed in N. Khrushchev's speech before the XXth Congress of the Russian Communist Party in 1956. Most of what Khrushchev revealed was already known in the West through the publications of escapees and defectors from the Soviet Union, and the publications of Commissions of Inquiry into the Truth of the Moscow Trials, headed by John Dewey.

1. The theory of historical materialism was invoked by all the socialist and Marxist critics of Bolshevik-Leninism since, if it were valid, a *prima facie* case could be made against Lenin and his followers for attempting to skip a stage of industrial development and introduce socialism in a backward country. Lenin and Trotsky in consequence reinterpreted the theory by asserting that the world economy had to be treated as a whole, that the world was already prepared for socialism as a result of modern science, technology, **153** and industry, and that the *political* revolution could break out at the weakest link in the world economic system as a whole. This would serve as a spark that would set the more advanced industrial countries like England, the USA, and Germany into revolutionary motion (places where Marx and Engels had expected socialism originally to come). This meant, of course, that the theory of historical materialism could no longer explain the *specific* political act of revolution, since on the theory of the weakest link, a political revolution by a Marxist party anywhere in the world, even in the Congo, could trigger off the world socialist revolution.

On the theory of the weakest link, after the political revolution successfully took its course and spread to other countries, the world *socialist* revolution, marked by the socialization of affluence, would be initiated by advanced industrial countries, with Russia and China once more bringing up the rear because of their primitive economies. But they would be the last in a socialist world, and only temporarily, until the world socialist economy was established and strategic goods and sources flowed to areas of greatest human need.

When the theory of the "weakest link" led in practice to the fact of a severed or isolated link, in consequence of the failure of the October Russian Revolution to inspire socialist revolutions in the West, the program of "building socialism in one country" was adopted. The attempt to build socialism in one country—and in a bankrupt, war-torn, poverty-stricken country at that—flew in the face of any reasonable interpretation of historical materialism. Nonetheless, by a combination of great courage, and still greater determination and ruthlessness, and aided by the ineptitude of their political opponents, the Bolshevik-Leninists succeeded in doing what the theory of historical materialism declared impossible. There is no doubt but that a new economy had been constructed by political means. Despite this, however, the theory that the economic base determines politics and not vice versa is still canonic doctrine in all communist countries.

2. In expectation of the socialist revolution occurring in the highly industrialized countries of the West, the theorists of Marxist-Leninism have clung to the letter of Marx's critique of capitalism and his predictions. For decades they have painted a picture of mass misery and starvation in the West. They have denied that capitalism has been modified in any significant way and that the Welfare State exploits the workers any less than the more individualistic economies it replaced. On the contrary, their claim is that economically the rich get richer, and the poor become poorer—and the rest is bourgeois propaganda.

3. The concept of "class" has been quite trouble-some to Marxist-Leninism particularly with Stalin's declaration that a "classless" society had been introduced in the Soviet Union with the adoption of its new constitution of 1936. If the concept of "proletariat" or "working class" is a polar one it implies, when concretely used, a "capitalist class." But if capitalism is abolished and all social ownership is vested in the community, who or which is the exploiting class? On a functional conception of property, viz., the legal right or power to *exclude* others from the use of things and services in which property is claimed, critics have argued that the social property of the Soviet Union in effect belongs to the Communist Party considered as a corporate body. And although there is no right to individual testamentary transmission, so long as the Communist Party enjoys the privileged position assigned to it in the Soviet Constitution, in effect, one set of leaders, in the name of the Party, inherits the power over social property from its predecessors, and the differential use and privileges that power bestows. Milovan Djilas, in his *The New Class . . .* (1957), on the basis of his study and experience in Yugoslavia and the Soviet Union argued that in current communist societies the bureaucracy constituted a ruling elite enjoying social privileges which justified calling it a "class." Subsequently other writers claimed that divisions and conflicts within the ruling elite presented a picture of greater class complexity (Albert Parry, *The New Class Divided*, 1966). It is obvious that the Marxist-Leninist concept of class cannot do justice to the Soviet, not to speak of the Chinese experience, in which peasants are often referred to as proletariat in order to give some semblance of sense to the terminological Marxist pieties of the Communist Party.

Actually the position of the worker is unique in the Soviet Union, in that it corresponds neither to the "association of free producers," envisaged by Marx nor to "the Soviet democracy" used by Lenin as a slogan to come to power. Nor is it like the position of the workers in modern capitalist societies, since the Soviet workers cannot organize free trade unions independent of the state, cannot without punitive risk leave their jobs, cannot travel without a passport and official permission, and cannot appeal to an independent judiciary if they run afoul of the authorities. Oscar Lange, the Polish communist economist, before his return to Poland, and while he was still a left-wing Socialist, characterized the Soviet economy as "an industrial serfdom" with the workers in the role of modern serfs. Like the phrases "state capitalism" and "state socialism," which have also been applied to the Soviet Union, this indicates that present-day communist economics and class relationships require a new set of economic and political categories to do justice to them.

Nonetheless, that its economy is distinctive, although sharing some of the features of classical capitalism and classical socialism, is undeniable.

4. Even more embarrassing is the nature of the state in the Marxist-Leninist theory. If the state is by definition "the executive committee of the ruling class," then as classes disappear the state weakens and finally withers away. But since the Soviet Union is declared to be a classless society, how account for the existence of the state, which instead of withering away has become stronger and stronger? The conventional reply under Stalin was that so long as socialism existed within one country, which was encircled by hungry capitalist powers intent upon its dismemberment, the state functioned primarily as the guardian of *national* integrity. This failed to explain the regime of *domestic* terror, and a concentration camp economy, worse than anything that existed in Tsarist days. Furthermore as communism spread, and the Soviet Union became no longer encircled by capitalist nations but emerged as co-equal in nuclear power to the West, more threatening to than threatened by the countries adjoining it, the state showed no signs of weakening. Although the domestic terror abated somewhat under Khrushchev, it still remains, after fifty years of rule, much stronger than it was under Lenin, before the Soviet Union consolidated its power.

Theoretically, the Soviet Union is a federal union of autonomous socialist republics which theoretically possess complete ethnic and national equality and with the right of secession from the Union guaranteed. In fact, it is a monolithic state that can establish or destroy its affiliated republics at will, and in which some ethnic minorities have been persecuted and subjected to severe discrimination.

5. The economy of the Soviet Union has remained a highly centralized, planned, and planning economy, primarily a command economy, functioning best in time of war and largely indifferent to the needs and demands of the consumer. The result has been the transformation within a period of fifty years of an agricultural economy into a great, modern industrial economy. The human costs in bloodshed and suffering of this transformation have been incalculable. The excessive centralization has led to inefficiency and waste, the development of a hidden market, and other abuses. To supplement the controlled economy's efforts to take care of consumers' needs, the state has tolerated a private sector in which goods and services are sold or exchanged for profit. Under the influence of E. G. Liberman and other economic reformers, some tentative steps have been taken to decentralize, and to introduce the concept of net profit in state enterprises in order to provide incentives and increase efficiency.

Greeted as a return to capitalistic principles, it overlooks the limited function of profit as conceived in a socialist economy, in which prices are still controlled by the central planning authority.

What these and similar reforms do that is difficult to square with the theory of Marxist-Leninism is to increase the power of the plant manager over the workers, and to differentiate even further the incomes received. Because of differences created by advances in technology, comparisons in standards of living are difficult to make between different historical periods. With respect to per capita consumption of the material necessities of life, the workers in most of the advanced industrial economies today seem to enjoy, without the sacrifice of their freedoms, a substantially higher standard of living than the workers of the Soviet Union. But there is nothing in the structure of the socialist economy which makes it impossible to equal and even surpass the standards of living of workers in capitalist countries. An economy that can put a Sputnik in the sky before other industrial societies, can probably outproduce them, if the decision is made to do so, in the production of refrigerators or television sets. The major differences lie not in what and how much is produced, but in the freedom to choose the system of production under which to live.

6. This brings us to the major Bolshevik-Leninist revision of the Marxism of the Social-Democratic variety—viz., the abandonment of its commitment to democracy as a system of social organization, as a theory of the political process including political organization, and, finally, as the high road to socialism.

Until the October Russian Revolution, the phrase "the dictatorship of the proletariat" was rarely used in Marxist literature. Marx himself used the term very infrequently, and Engels pointed to the Paris Commune of 1871, in which Marx's group was a tiny minority, as an illustration of what the phrase meant. Even those who spoke of the "dictatorship of the proletariat" meant by it the class rule of the workers, presumably the majority of the population, which would democratically enact laws introducing the socialist society. That is what Engels meant when he wrote in 1891 that the democratic republic was "the *specific* form for the dictatorship of the proletariat" (Marx and Engels, *Correspondence 1846–1895*, New York [1936], p. 486). Marx and Engels also anticipated that the transition to socialism would be peaceful where democratic political institutions had developed that gave the workers the franchise. Force would be employed only to suppress armed rebellion of unreconciled *minorities* against the mandate of the majority.

The Marxist-Leninist version of "the dictatorship of the proletariat" is that it is substantially "the dictatorship of the Communist Party," which means not only a dictatorship over the bourgeoisie but *over* the proletariat as well. The Paris Commune on this view is not really a "dictatorship of the proletariat." The dictatorship of the Communist Party entailed that no other political parties, not even other working-class parties, would be tolerated if they did not accept the Leninist line. It meant that there could be no legally recognized opposition of any kind. For as Lenin put it, "Dictatorship is power based directly upon force, and unrestricted by any laws," and again "dictatorship means neither more nor less than unlimited power, resting directly on force, not limited by anything, not restricted by any laws, nor any absolute rules" (*Selected Works*, VII, 123).

This whole conception is based frankly on the assumption that armed by the insights of Marxist-Leninism, the Communist Party knows better what the true interests of the working class are than the workers know themselves; that it cannot give the workers their head but must, if necessary, restrain or compel them for their own good. Thus Lenin proclaimed "All power to the Soviets," the organs of the Russian workers and peasants after 1917, when he anticipated that they would follow the Communist (Bolshevik) Party line, but this slogan was abandoned and even opposed when there was fear the Soviets would not accept the Communist Party dictatorship. This view of the dictatorship of the Party is central to all Marxist-Leninist parties. Thus the Hungarian communist premier, Jan Kadar, in his speech before the Hungarian National Assembly on May 11, 1957, justifying the suppression by the Red Army of the Hungarian workers in the Budapest uprising of 1956, makes a distinction between "the *wishes* and *will* of the working masses" and "the *interests*" of the workers. The Communist Party, knowing the true *interests* of the workers and having these interests at heart, is therefore justified in opposing the *wishes* and *will* of the masses. This is the Leninist version of Rousseau's doctrine that the people "must be forced to be free."

The antidemocratic conception of the political party actually preceded the transformation of the dictatorship of the proletariat into the dictatorship of the party over the proletariat. Logically the two ideas are independent, since a hierarchically organized party could accept the democratic process as providing an opportunity for coming to power legitimately. The Social-Democratic conception of party organization made it a very loose-jointed affair. Marx and Engels actually assumed that in the course of its economic struggles, the working class spontaneously would develop the organizational instrumentalities necessary to win the battle. Lenin, on the other hand, thought of the politi-

cal party as an *engineer* of revolution, spurring on, teaching, even lashing the working class into revolutionary political consciousness.

The political party structure devised by Lenin owes more probably to the fact that the socialist parties were underground and had to work illegally in Russia than it does to Marxist theory. The theory of "democratic centralism" was really better adapted for a resistance movement than for political democratic process. Nonetheless all of the many Communist Parties associated with the Communist International were compelled to adopt that theory as a condition for affiliation. The Central Committee of the Party was the chief organizing center, the final link in a chain of command that extended down to the party cells. The Central Committee had the power to co-opt and reject delegates to the Party Congress which nominally was the source of authority for the Central Committee. Because of its access to party funds, lists, periodicals, and control of organizers, the leadership of the "democratic centralized" party tended to be self-perpetuating. Certain maneuvers or *coups* from the top would bring one faction or another to the fore, but no broad-based movement of member opposition was possible. Until Stalin's death changes in the leadership of Communist Parties outside of the Soviet Union occurred only as a consequence of the intervention of the Russian Communist Party acting through representatives of the Communist International. Thus, to cite a typical example, the leadership of the American Communist Party which claimed to have the support of 93% of the rank and file was dismissed by Stalin in 1928, and the new leadership of W. Z. Foster and Earl Browder appointed. The processes of "democratic centralism" then legitimized the change. After the Second World War, Browder, based on the ostensibly unanimous support of the party membership, was unceremoniously cashiered as leader by signals communicated by Jacques Duclos of the French Communist Party at the instigation of the Kremlin.

There have been some developments in the theory and practice of Marxist-Leninism of the first political importance. Lenin and Stalin both believed that the capitalist countries were doomed to break down in a universal crisis; that because of their system of production they must expand or die, and that before they died, they would resort to all-out war against the Soviet Union. The classic statement of this view was Lenin's declaration of November 20, 1920, repeated in subsequent editions of his and Stalin's writings:

"As long as capitalism and socialism exist, we cannot live in peace; in the end one or the other will triumph—a funeral dirge will be sung over the Soviet Republic or over World Capitalism" (*Selected Works*,

VIII, 297). Despite the hypothetical possibility of a capitalist triumph, the victory of communism was declared to be inevitable in consequence of the inevitable war for which it was preparing. The Soviet Union and all its communist allies must consider itself to be in a state of undeclared defensive war against the aggression being hatched against it; Communist Parties abroad must have as their first political priority "The defence of the Soviet Union"—which sometimes led to difficulties with workers who struck industrial plants in capitalist countries manufacturing goods and munitions for the use of the Soviet Union.

The doctrine of the inevitability of armed conflict between the democratic countries of the West and the Soviet Union undoubtedly played an important role in Stalin's war and postwar policy. Even though Great Britain and the United States were loyal allies in the struggle against Hitler, the war had to be fought with an eye on their capacity for the subsequent struggle against the Soviet Union. This led to an extensive development of Soviet espionage in allied countries during, and especially after, the war; the expansion of Soviet frontiers; the establishment of a communist regime by the Red Army in adjoining territories; and a political strategy designed to split the Western alliance. Although aware of the development of nuclear weapons, Stalin was skeptical about their capacity for wholesale destruction, and remained steadfast in his belief in the inevitable victory of communism through inevitable war.

Nikita Khrushchev, who by outmaneuvering Bulganin, Malenkov, and Beria, succeeded Stalin, had a far greater respect for the potential holocaust involved in nuclear war. Although he spurred on the development of Soviet nuclear power, he revived the notion of "peaceful coexistence," a theme originally propounded by Lenin in an interview with an American journalist in 1920, and periodically revived for propaganda purposes since. But what was highly significant in Khrushchev's emendation of the doctrine, was his declaration that although the final victory of world communism is inevitable, world war was not inevitable; that it was possible for communism to succeed without an international civil war. This recognized the relatively independent influence of technological factors on politics, and created an additional difficulty for the theory of historical materialism.

The second important political development since the death of Stalin has been the growth of communist polycentrism, and the emergence of Communist China as a challenge to Soviet hegemony over the world communist movement. Communist "polycentrism" meant the weakening of the centralized control of the Russian Communist Party over other Communist Parties, and the gradual assertion of political independence in some respects by hitherto Communist Party satellites. For the first and only time in its history the American Communist Party officially declared itself in opposition to Soviet anti-Semitism. After Khrushchev's speech exposing Stalin's terrorism, it has become impossible for Communist Parties to resume the attitude of total compliance to Kremlin demands. The degree of independence, however, varies from country to country—the Italian Communist Party manifesting the most independence and the Bulgarian Communist Party the least.

The strained relations between Communist Yugoslavia and the Soviet Union and especially between Communist China and the Soviet Union—all invoking the theory of Marxist-Leninism—are eloquent and ironical evidence that some important social phenomena cannot be understood through the simple, explanatory categories of Marxism. After all, war was explained by Marxists as caused by economic factors directly related to the mode of economic production. That one communist power finds itself not only engaged in military border skirmishes with another, but actually threatens, if provoked, a war of nuclear annihilation against its communist brother-nation, as spokesmen of the Soviet Union did in the summer of 1969, is something that obviously cannot be explained in terms of their *common* modes of economic production. Once more nationalism is proving to be triumphant over Marxism.

III

The third interpretation of Marxism may be called for purposes of identification, "the existentialist view" according to which Marxism is not primarily a system of sociology or economics, but a philosophy of human liberation. It seeks to overcome human alienation, to emancipate man from repressive social institutions, especially economic institutions that frustrate his true nature, and to bring him into harmony with himself, his fellow men, and the world around him so that he can both overcome his estrangements and express his true essence through creative freedom. This view developed as a result of two things; first, the publication in 1932 of Marx's manuscripts written in 1844 before Marx had become a Marxist (on the other two views), which the editors entitled *Economic and Philosophic Manuscripts*, and second, the revolt against Stalinism in Eastern Europe at the end of World War II among some communists who opposed the theory and practice of Marxist-Leninism. Aware that they could only get a hearing or exercise influence if they spoke in the name of Marxism, they seized upon several formulations in these manuscripts of Marx in which he glorifies the nature of man as a freedom-loving creature—a nature that has been distorted, cramped, and twisted by the capitalist mode of production. They were then able to protest in the name of Marxist humanism against the stifling dictatorship of Stalin and his lieutenants in their own countries, and even against the apotheosis of Lenin.

Independently of this political motivation in the reinterpretation of Marx, some socialist and nonsocialist scholars in the West have maintained that the conception of man and alienation in the early writings of Marx is the main theme of Marx's view of socialism, the aim of which is "the spiritual emancipation of man." For example, Eric Fromm writes that "it is impossible to understand Marx's concept of socialism and his criticism of capitalism as developed except on the basis of his concept of man which he developed in his early writings" (*Marx's Concept of Man* [1961], p. 79). This entails that Marx's thought was understood by no one before 1932 when the manuscripts were published, unless they had independently developed the theory of alienation. Robert Tucker's influential book, *Philosophy and Myth in Karl Marx* (Cambridge, 1961), asserts that the significant ideas of Marx are to be found in what he calls Marx's "original Marxism" which turns out to be ethical, existentialist, anticipatory of Buber and Tillich, and profoundly different from the Marxism of Marx's immediate disciples. How far the new interpretation is prepared to go in discarding traditional Marxism, with its emphasis on scientific sociology and economics as superfluous theoretical baggage alien to the true Marx, is apparent in this typical passage from Tucker:

Capital, the product of twenty years of hard labor to which, as he [Marx] said, he sacrificed his health, his happiness in life and his family, is an intellectual museum piece for us now, whereas the sixteen page manuscript of 1844 on the future of aesthetics, which he probably wrote in a day and never even saw fit to publish, contains much that is still significant (p. 235).

Another source of the growth of this new version of Marxism flows from the writings of Jean-Paul Sartre and Maurice Merleau-Ponty, especially the former's *Critique de la raison dialectique* (Vol. I, 1960) in which despite his rejection of materialism and his exaggerated voluntarism, Sartre seeks to present his existentialist idealism as ancillary to Marxism, which he hails as "the unsurpassable philosophy of our time" (p. 9).

For various reasons, detailed elsewhere, this third version of Marxism is making great headway among radical and revolutionary youth that have disparaged or repudiated specific political programs as inhibiting action. Among those who wish to bring Marx in line with newer developments in psychology, and especially among socialists and communists who have based their critiques of the existing social order on ethical principles, the existentialist version of Marx has a strong appeal.

The theoretical difficulties this interpretation of Marxism must face are very formidable. They are external, derived from certain methodological principles of interpretation and from textual difficulties; and internal, derived from the flat incompatibility of the key notions of existential Marxism with other published doctrines of Marx, for which Marx took public responsibility. Of the many external difficulties with the interpretation of Marxism as a philosophy of alienation, three may be mentioned.

1. The theory of alienation according to which man is a victim of the products of his own creation in an industrial society he does not consciously control, is a view that was common coin among the "true" socialists like Moses Hess, Karl Grün, and others. It was not a distinctively Marxist view. Even Ralph Waldo Emerson and Thomas Carlyle expressed similar sentiments when they complained that things were in the saddle and riding man to an end foreign to his nature and intention.

2. In the *Communist Manifesto* Marx explicitly disavows the theory of alienation as "metaphysical rubbish," as a linguistic Germanic mystification of social phenomena described by French social critics. Thus as an example of "metaphysical rubbish," Marx says, "Underneath the French critique of money and its functions, they wrote, 'alienation of the essence of mankind,' and underneath the French critique of the bourgeois State they wrote 'overthrow of the supremacy of the abstract universal' and so on" (Riazanov edition; English trans. London [1930], p. 59).

3. If Marxism is a theory of human alienation under all forms and expressions of capitalism, it becomes unintelligible why, having proclaimed the fact of human alienation at the outset of his studies, Marx should have devoted himself for almost twenty years to the systematic analysis of the mechanics of capitalist production. The existence of alienation was already established on the basis of phenomena observable whenever the free market system was introduced. Nothing in *Capital* throws any further light on the phenomenon. The section on the "Fetishism of Commodities" (*Capital*, Vol. I, Ch. I, Sec. 4) is a *sociological* analysis of commodities where private ownership of the social means of production exists, and dispenses completely with all reference to the true essence of man and his alienations of that essence. What Marx calls "the enigmatic character" of the product of labor when it assumes the form of a commodity is the result of the fact that *social* relationships among men are experienced directly by the unreflective consciousness as a *natural* property of things. The economic "value" of products that are exchanged is assumed to be of the same existential order as "the weight" of the products.

This results in the fetishism of commodities which is compared to the fetishism of objects in primitive religion in which men fail to see that the divinity attributed to the objects is their own creation. Or to use another analogy, just as what makes an object "food" ultimately depends upon the biological relationships of the digestive system, and not *merely* upon the physical-chemical properties of the object, so what makes a thing a "commodity" depends upon social relationships between men, and not merely on the physical characteristics of what objects are bought and sold. Marx's analysis here is designed to further his contention that men can control their economic and social life and should not resign themselves to be ruled by economic processes as if they were like natural forces beyond the possibility of human control. The Marxist analysis is used here to argue for the feasibility of a shorter working day and better conditions of work.

The "internal" difficulties that confront the existentialist interpretation of Marx are grave enough to be considered fatal in the absence of a politically inspired will to believe.

1. The doctrine of "alienation" runs counter to Marx's scientific materialism. Its religious origins are obvious in the idealistic tradition from Plotinus to Hegel. It is inherently dualistic since it distinguishes an original "nature" of man separate from its alienated manifestations to which men will someday return.

2. It even more obviously violates the entire historical approach of Marxism which denies that man has a natural or real or true self from which he can be alienated. Marx maintained that by acting upon the external world, nature, and society, man continually modifies his own nature (*Capital*, Eng. trans., I, 198), that history may be regarded as "the progressive modification" of human nature, and that to argue that socialism and its institutional reforms are against human nature—one of the oldest and strongest objections to the Marxist program—is to overlook the extent to which the individual with his psychological nature is a social and therefore historical creature. Many of the difficulties of the view that Marxism is a theory of alienation and a social program liberating man from his alienation are apparent as soon as we ask: *From* what self or nature is man alienated?, and then compare the implications and presuppositions of the response with other explicitly avowed doctrines of Marx. The attempt by Tucker to distinguish in Marx between

a constant human nature—productive, free, and self-fulfilling—and a variable human nature—alienated in class societies—attempting to save the doctrine of alienation, fails to explain how it is possible that man's constant nature should come into existence, according to Marx, only at the end of prehistory, only when the classless society emerges. In addition, Marx like Hegel repudiates the dualism between a constant and variable human nature to the point of denying that even man's biological nature is constant.

3. In Marx's published writing, where psychological phenomena are mentioned that have been cited as evidence of Marx's belief in the importance of the doctrine of alienation, despite his refusal to use the early language of alienation, Marx explains these phenomena as a *consequence* of private property in the instruments of production. But in his early *Economic-Philosophical Manuscripts* (written before 1847), he asserts that alienation is the *cause* of private property. This would make a psychological phenomenon responsible for the distinctive social processes of capitalism whose developments the mature Marx regarded as having causal priority in explaining social psychological change.

4. The concept of man as alienated in the early manuscripts implies that alienated man is unhappy, maladjusted, truncated, psychologically if not physically unhealthy. It does not explain the phenomenon of alienation which is active and voluntary rather than passive and coerced. Marx himself was alienated from his society but hardly from his "true" self, for he undoubtedly found fulfillment in his role as critic and social prophet. From this point of view to be alienated from a society may be a condition for the achievement of the serenity, interest, and creative effort and fulfillment that are the defining characteristics of the psychologically unalienated man. Marx's early theory of alienation could hardly do justice, aside from its inherent incoherences, to Marx's mature behavior as an integrated person alienated from his own society.

5. The existentialist interpretation of Marxism makes it primarily an ethical philosophy of life and society, very much akin to the ethical philosophies of social life that Marx and Engels scorned during most of their political career. Nonetheless this ethical dimension of social judgment and criticism constitutes a perennial source of the appeal of Marxism to generations of the young, all the more so because of the tendencies both in the Social-Democratic and, especially, in the Bolshevik-Leninist versions of Marxism to play down, if not to suppress, the ethical moment of socialism. In the canonic writings of these interpretations of Marxism, socialism is pictured as the irreversible and inescapable fulfillment of an *historical* development and moral judgments are explained, where they are recognized, as reflections of class interest, devoid of universal and objective validity. The doctrinal writings of both Marx and Engels lend color to this view—despite the fact that everything else they wrote, and even the works purportedly of a technical and analytical character, like *Capital* itself, are pervaded by a passionate moral concern and a denunciation of social injustices in tones that sound like echoes of the Hebrew social prophets. The very word *Ausbeutung,* or "exploitation," which is central to Marx's economic analysis, is implicitly ethical although Marx seeks to disavow its ethical connotations. Even critics of Marx's economic theories and historicism, like Karl Popper, who reject his contentions, recognize the ethical motivation of Marx's thought. Capitalism is condemned not only because it is unstable and generates suffering, but because uncontrolled power over the social instruments of production gives arbitrary power over the lives of those who must live by their use.

Nonetheless, despite its ethical reinterpretation of Marxism, existentialist Marxism fails to make ends meet theoretically. Either it ends up with a pale sort of humanism, a conception of the good and the good society derived from the essential nature of man and his basic needs—a lapse into the Feuerbachianisms rejected by Marx—or it denies the possibility of a universally valid norm of conduct for man or society, stresses the uniqueness of the individual moral act, makes every situation in which two or more individuals are involved an antinomic one in which right conflicts with right and self with self. If the first version generates a universalism of love or duty and brotherhood of man which Marx (and Hegel) reject as unhistorical, the second points to a Hobbesianism in which "the other" far from being "a brother" is potentially an enemy. Marx conceals from himself the necessity of developing an *explicit* positive ethics over and above his condemnations of unnecessary human cruelty and injustice. The closest he comes to such an ethic is in his utopian conception of a classless society whose institutions will be such that the freedom of each person will find in the freedom of every other person "not its limitation but its fulfillment." Many critics find this expectation an astonishingly naive conception of man and society, which does not even hold for traditional versions of the Kingdom of Heaven. But even this utopian construction can hardly absolve Marxists from the necessity of making and justifying specific ethical judgments for the City of Man.

The periodical revivals of Marxism in our age reflect moral and political interests in search of a respectable revolutionary tradition. The discovery of the social problem by phenomenologists, Neo-Thomists, positivists, and even linguistic analysts usually results in an attempted synthesis between Marx and some outstanding philosophical figure who has very little in common with him (Hook, in Drachkovitch, 1966).

From the point of view of sociological and economic theories claiming objective truth, Marxism has contributed many insights that have been absorbed and developed by scholars who either do not share or are hostile to the perspective of social reform or revolution. Scientifically there is no more warrant for speaking of Marxism today in sociology than there is for speaking of Newtonianism in physics or Darwinism in biology. The fact that Marxism has become the state doctrine of industrially underdeveloped countries in Asia and Africa is testimony to the fact that his system of thought proved to be inapplicable to the Western world whose development it sought to explain. There is also a certain irony in the fact that the contemporary movements of sensualism, immediatism, anarchism, and romantic violence among the young in Western Europe and America which invoke Marx's name are, allowing only for slight changes in idiom, the very movements he criticized and rejected during the forties of the nineteenth century—the period in which Marx was developing his distinctive ideas. Some modes of consciousness and modes of being that are the concern of New Left thought and activity today Marx scornfully rejected as characteristic of the *Lumpenproletariat.*

At this stage in the development of Marxism it may seem as fruitless a task to determine which, if any, version of Marxism comes closest to Marx's own doctrinal intent as to ask which conception of Christianity, if any, is closest to the vision and teachings of its founder. Nonetheless, although difficult, it is not impossible in principle to reach reliable conclusions if the inquiry is undertaken in a scientific spirit. Even if he was in some respects self-deceived, Marx after all did conceive himself as a scientific economist and sociologist. Allowing for the ambiguities and imprecision of Marx's published writings, there is greater warrant for believing that those who seek to provide scientific grounds for his conclusions are closer to his own intent and belief than are those who, whether on the basis of Marx's unpublished juvenilia or Sartre's metaphysical fantasies, would convert him to existentialism. The scientific versions of Marxism have an additional advantage: they permit of the possibility of empirical refutation, and so facilitate the winning of new and more reliable scientific truths which Marx as a scientist presumably would have been willing to accept. Existentialist versions of Marxism, where they are not purely historical, are willful and arbitrary interpretations of social and political phenomena.

"Marxism," declares Sartre, "is the unsurpassable philosophy of our time," but only because he interprets it in such a way as to make it immune to empirical test. Holding to it, today, therefore, is not a test of one's fidelity to truth in the service of a liberal and humane civilization, but only a measure of tenacity of one's faith.

BIBLIOGRAPHY

R. N. Carew-Hunt, *Marxism—Past and Present* (New York, 1954). Milovan Djilas, *The New Class* (New York, 1957). Eric Fromm, *Marx's Concept of Man* (New York, 1961). Sidney Hook, *Towards the Understanding of Karl Marx* (New York and London, 1933). Karl Kautsky, *Die Materialistische Geschichtsauffassung* (Berlin, 1927). V. I. Lenin, *Collected Works* (New York, 1927); idem, *Selected Works* (Moscow, 1932). Karl Marx and Friedrich Engels, *Historisch-kritische Gesamtausgabe* (Frankfurt and Berlin, 1927); idem, *Selected Works* (Moscow, 1950). Karl Popper, *The Open Society* (London, 1945): Jean-Paul Sartre, *Critique de la raison dialectique* (Paris, 1960). Joseph Schumpeter, *Capitalism, Socialism and Democracy* (New York and London, 1942). Joseph Stalin, *Works* (Moscow, 1948). Robert Tucker, *Philosophy and Myth in Karl Marx* (Cambridge, 1961).

Three books on Marxism, written from different points of view, well worth reading, are: George Lichtheim, *Marxism: An Historical and Critical Study* (New York and London, 1961); John Plamenatz, *German Marxism and Russian Communism* (London and New York, 1954); Bertram Wolfe, *Marxism: One Hundred Years in the Life of a Doctrine* (New York, 1965). Two useful collections of essays on Marxism are Milorad Drachkovitch, ed., *Marxism and the Modern World* (Stanford, 1965); idem, *Marxist Ideology in the Contemporary World. Its Appeals and Paradoxes* (New York, 1966).

SIDNEY HOOK

[See also Alienation; Existentialism; **Historical and Dialectical Materialism; Ideology of Soviet Communism;** Nationalism; Social Democracy; **Socialism;** State; Totalitarianism; Welfare State.]

MARXIST REVISIONISM: FROM BERNSTEIN TO MODERN FORMS

HISTORICALLY, "Revisionism" was the name given to the main heresy which arose in European, and particularly German, Marxism and Social Democracy in the time of the Second International (1889–1914). Its originator was Eduard Bernstein, who also gave the most systematic exposition of its theoretical content. The main thesis of this theory was that the catastrophic collapse of capitalist society, predicted by Marx, was unlikely to take place; from this it followed that Social Democrats should alter their political strategy away from revolutionary and towards evolutionary methods. After the October Revolution and the emergence of Moscow as the center of World Communism, Revisionism lost most of its original content, degenerated into a term of abuse, and was largely superseded by other pejorative labels. Only after the Second World War, with the appearance of new divisions in the World Communist Movement, did Revisionism regain any consistent meaning. Still remaining a term of abuse, it was used by the *soi-disant* "orthodox" Marxists to qualify those of their opponents who could at all plausibly (if sometimes unjustly) be embarrassed by the accusation of accommodation with bourgeois society or its extension, imperialism. Even here, however, consistency was not long maintained. With the emergence of Sino-Soviet differences into a full-scale political and ideological dispute, not only did the Chinese accuse the Russians of "Revisionism" on the grounds of compromise with imperialism, but Soviet ideologists, who normally accepted this meaning of the word (without, of course, admitting that it could apply to themselves), also described the doctrines of Mao Tse-tung and his followers as "left" Revisionism.

By the 1890's German Social Democracy was in a position to offer both the institutional stability and the ideological rigidity which are the necessary soil on which any heresy must be bred. These two aspects of German Social Democracy were closely linked. As an institution, it had grown inside, but isolated from, German society of the time; the revolutionary ideology maintained and justified the isolation. Bernstein's perception that certain points of the analysis of society contained in the ideology were apparently at variance with reality therefore had serious implications for the German Party as a whole. In 1890 the adoption of the Erfurt Program by the SPD (*Sozialdemokratische Partei Deutschlands*) crystallized its ideology as revolutionary Marxism, and provided a canon of theoretical orthodoxy. At the same time the Party's organizational success in a generally prosperous economy enabled its leaders to forget the contradiction between their revolutionary doctrine and their increasingly reformist practice. It took a man as uncomfortably honest and persistent as Eduard Bernstein to remind them of this contradiction. His views first reached the public in a series of articles in the *Neue Zeit* in 1896–98, and were presented in book form under the title *Die Voraussetzungen des Sozialismus und die Aufgaben der Sozialdemokratie* in 1899 (trans. as *Evolutionary Socialism,* 1909). Although the systematization of these views possibly owes more to Bernstein's critics than to himself, they may conveniently be considered under the headings of social development, economics, philosophy, and politics.

Social Development. The Erfurt Program had faithfully reflected the classic Marxist belief that capitalist society was moving towards an even greater polarization between the propertied and propertyless classes. Capital was becoming concentrated in fewer and fewer hands; the middle class was disappearing; the proletariat, and its recruits from the impoverished middle class, faced "misery, oppression, servitude, degradation and exploitation." The whole process was furthered by periodic industrial crises, and would culminate in the "collapse" of the capitalist system and a violent revolution. Very soon after the Erfurt Congress, however, academic economists such as F. G. Schulze-Gävernitz and Julius Wolf began to observe that this prospect was unlikely to be fulfilled. At first Bernstein tried to refute their arguments, but a few years later found himself forced to agree with much of what they said. Was the Marxist view correct? "Well," said Bernstein, "yes and no" (Bernstein [1909], p. 41). The growth of concentration and monopoly could be accepted "as a tendency"—indeed many of Marx's theses, such as the falling rate of profit, overproduction, and crises, etc., were empirically observable facts; but strong social forces existed which falsified Marx's general picture of society polarized into two bitterly embattled classes. Bernstein pointed out, with a wealth of statistics from Germany and England, that although large-sized enterprises were increasing in numbers faster than others, the numbers of small and medium-sized enterprises were not decreasing but increasing also. There was no tendency for the middle class to disappear; indeed the number of propertied persons was actually growing. Similarly, when it came to the theory of crises and collapse—the other main plank in Marx's prediction of revolution—Bernstein agreed that crises were an inherent feature of capitalism, but noted that they had become rarer, shorter, and milder.

Moreover, as with the development of class relationships, Bernstein attributed this phenomenon to the emergence in capitalism of certain counter-trends—the growth of the world market, improvements in transportation and communication, more flexible credit systems, and the rise of cartels—which made it unlikely, in his view, that "at least for a long time, general commercial crises similar to the earlier ones" would occur (ibid., p. 80).

Economics. These criticisms of Marxist theory were based mainly on empirical data, and their validity depended in good part on the time scale to which the theory was related. But Bernstein also tackled what many regarded as the central doctrine of Marxist economics—the labor theory of value and surplus value. Bernstein's discussion of this theory did little more than hint at a synthesis of the Marxist and increasingly accepted marginalist versions of value theory, and he concluded by treating the concept of value more as an abstract tool of analysis than a fact of the real world. Surplus value, however, he regarded as "a fact demonstrated in experience"; while denying that the rate of exploitation was directly related to the rate of surplus value, Bernstein emphasized that exploitation was indeed a feature of capitalism (ibid., pp. 28–40).

Philosophy. Bernstein's treatment of value theory removed one of the central "scientific" tenets of Marxism from the picture; to replace it he called in ethics and empiricism. This ethical and empirical bent in Bernstein is most clearly visible in his philosophical views. Instead of the Hegelian dialectic (which Marx claimed to have "stood on its feet") with its revolutionary implications, Bernstein believed that the true philosophical kernel of Marxism was evolution. The dialectic he described as a "snare" (Gay [1952], p. 135), which had led Marx into "historical self-deception." Overemphasis on the dialectical struggle of opposites had, in Bernstein's view, resulted in an unwarranted insistence on violent revolution. Class antagonisms would persist, but would diminish; the transition to socialism would come as a result of work within the State, rather than by intransigeant opposition to it (ibid., p. 137). A further departure from the "scientific" spirit of Marxism is found in Bernstein's attempt to modify Marx's determinism—an attempt which did little more than suggest that Marx had been in some way too determinist, and that Engels had later departed from the previous extremism of his and Marx's earlier definition. Bernstein did not question that the economic factor—the forces and relations of production—were "an ever recurring decisive force, the cardinal point of the great movements of history" (Bernstein [1909], p. 17), and indeed proposed to replace the term "materialist conception of history" by "economic interpretation of history"; but he tried to restore to ideology, and hence to idealistic and ethical motives in men, some of the independence of which they had been deprived by Marxism. This meant no less than the reintroduction of ethics into the causal chain leading to socialism.

When Rosa Luxemburg, one of Bernstein's chief critics in the SPD, accused him of surrendering the "immanent economic necessity of the victory of socialism" Bernstein accepted the charge: "I regard it as neither possible nor desirable to give the triumph of socialism a purely materialistic foundation" (Gay, p. 141). Where, then, did Bernstein seek a basis for his ethics? This was the time of the Neo-Kantian revival in Germany, and some of the leading Neo-Kantians, particularly F. A. Lange and Hermann Cohen, were sympathetic to the political Left. Inevitably, the Revisionists looked to Kant. Bernstein's immediate inspiration came from Lange, with Conrad Schmidt and Ludwig Woltmann—philosophers on the fringe of the SPD—also contributing. But Bernstein's Kantianism was of a strictly limited nature. It provided a sanction for his reintroduction of morality into Social-Democratic ideology; but his use of it was mainly instrumental, to justify his criticism of established dogmas. Setting the device "Kant against Cant" at the head of the last chapter of his *Voraussetzungen*, Bernstein appealed to ". . . the spirit of the great Königsberg philosopher . . . against the cant which sought to get a hold on the working-class movement and to which the Hegelian dialectic offers a comfortable refuge" (Bernstein [1909], pp. 222f.). The cant to which Bernstein referred was the "scientific"prediction of the inevitable achievement of socialism through revolution. "That which is generally called 'the final goal of socialism' . . . is nothing to me *but the movement is everything*," said Bernstein in a phrase much quoted against him (Bernstein [1901], p. 234).

Socialism, for Bernstein, was not inevitable, but desirable, based not on "science" but on demands, interests, and desires—indeed he held that "no -ism is a science" (Gay, p. 149). Further than this, or deeper than this, Bernstein's Kantianism did not go. He used it to buttress his skepticism, but he remained a "common-sense philosopher" (ibid., p. 151), and for him—though not, as will be seen, for all later Revisionists—philosophy was an afterthought, more illustrative than formative in his general outlook.

Politics. In economics, Bernstein tested the received schemata of Marxism against empirical fact, and found them wanting; in philosophy he proved equally skeptical of the sweeping claims of Marxian "science." Either way, theory yielded some ground to praxis. In politics, even more so, Bernstein invited the SPD to discard its revolutionary phrases and admit openly that it had become a democratic reformist party. The politics of German Revisionism were the politics of Social Democracy called by their real name. Bernstein's aim was that the party should encourage and extrapolate recent trends; it should proceed by linear evolution rather than dialectical conflicts. Electoral and parliamentary success was worth having, he thought, not merely as a school of revolution (the radical Marxist view) but as a means towards the achievement of political power. The development of "socialism-in-capitalism" (an idea of which Marx's *Vergesellschaftung* ["socialization"] is one forerunner, but which Bernstein took most directly from the English Fabians) seemed to promise increasing

state intervention in the economy; the formation of trusts and cartels, and the growth of municipal democratic institutions, seemed to portend "the piecemeal realization of socialism" (Bernstein [1901], p. 233). For Social Democrats, this strategy entailed the tactics of alliance—alliance with trade unions, cooperatives, and occasionally nonsocialist bodies. The trade unions, with their built-in interest in partial, practical gains, were natural allies for the Revisionists, though lacking any bent for theory; and Bernstein, though a theorist of praxis, was still a theorist. He therefore worked to shift the SPD from its traditional view of the trade unions as little more than recruiting-grounds for socialists, with no prospect of contributing independently to the achievement of socialism, and to persuade it that they were worthy allies. Cooperatives, according to Bernstein, were also instruments of piecemeal progress to socialism: not producer cooperatives—and here Bernstein parted company with Marx and joined Beatrice Webb—but consumer cooperatives, which he saw as fundamentally democratic and potentially socialistic (Bernstein [1909], p. 118).

More important, and more controversial was the Revisionist view of relations with nonsocialist organizations. Whether to legitimize the South German provincial SPD's practice of parliamentary deals with local nonsocialist parties; whether the Social Democrats should claim, in 1903, the Vice-Presidency of the Reichstag which was their due at the price of a formal call on the Kaiser (wearing knee-breeches, no less!); whether to allow Social Democrats to vote for a (bourgeois) budget containing desirable concessions to the labor movement; in each of these party controversies, Bernstein fought for the obvious advantages of reformist practice against the inhibitions of revolutionary theory.

Summary and Critique. The main elements of German Revisionist thought may now clearly be seen: in economics, a confrontation of the Marxist theory of social development by dialectical struggle and revolution with the facts as Bernstein saw them; the assertion that these facts belied the Marxist analysis and the predictions based on it; in economic theory, the relegation of the labor theory of value to the status of an abstract tool of analysis, and as such compatible with marginalist theories; in philosophy, the substitution of the principle of "organic evolution" for the dialectic, and of ethics for determinism; in politics, reformism instead of revolution. What is the common thread in these different strands? More than anything, it is a shift from the remote to the proximate, a shortening of the time-scale, not indeed the time-scale for the achievement of socialism, but, on the one hand, the scale against which predictive theory should be tested and, 163 on the other, the scale within which constructive social and political action was possible; a shift, that is, from the remoteness of theory to the immediacy of praxis. It was this shift which enabled Bernstein's opponents to accuse him of opportunism, and which led Karl Johann Kautsky, the orthodox "center" ideologist, to characterize both Bernstein's Revisionism and Luxemburg's revolutionary radicalism as different forms of "impatience."

We need not here pursue in any detail the impact and aftermath of the Revisionist controversy within the SPD. For some years, after the electoral setback of 1907 prompted the leadership to adopt and justify Revisionist attitudes to Parliament, it seemed that Revisionism might gradually prevail. But two major events extrinsic to the main lines of debate, the First World War and the Russian Revolution, so altered the terms of discussion that not only Bernstein but later also Kautsky became largely irrelevant. On these two issues, in fact, Bernstein and Kautsky saw eye to eye. Old alignments were swept away: most Revisionists, and some radicals, supported the war, but Bernstein soon came out against it. The splitting of the Social Democratic body by the formation first of the antiwar Independent Party (USPD, *Unabhängige Sozialdemokratische Partei Deutschlands*) and later of the German Communist Party altered the conditions necessary for the existence of a substantial Revisionist heresy. The SPD became what Bernstein had urged it should become—an admittedly reformist party; and Revisionism ceased to have any raison d'être.

These major changes make it less easy to judge Bernstein's Revisionism on its merits. In many ways it proved over-optimistic. If his contention that the middle classes did not disappear was broadly justified, the Great Depression of the 1930's disproved his belief that the era of major crises was past. In politics it is, to say the least, unlikely that the class and legal structure of the German Empire would ever have permitted the peaceful parliamentary transition to socialism which Bernstein envisaged, however relevant such ideas may be in countries with genuine parliamentary institutions. Nor is it certain that, even if the Social Democrats had adopted a reformist program (as they did—too late—at Görlitz in 1921) the radical-liberal bourgeoisie would have agreed to the alliance with them that Bernstein's strategy required. In a speech of 1925, which smacks of special pleading, Bernstein argued Weimar Germany could not be called a "capitalist republic" (Bernstein archives, quoted by Gay, p. 215). But events were soon to prove that Weimar's road away from capitalism led not to socialism but to something else. Although the aged Bernstein, loved and respected but quite uninfluential, warned repeatedly

against the danger of right-wing subversion of the Republic, the middle classes failed to be the allies of the proletariat which he hoped they would be, and even the proletariat turned readily enough to Nazism as a creed of salvation. Paradoxically, perhaps, in philosophy, where Bernstein was least serious and profound, Revisionist ideas have proved most durable. Ethical socialism, as an opposition movement, whether reformist or revolutionary, never amounted to anything; but the injection of ethics (of a different kind: existentialist as much as Kantian) into socialism in power has, as will be seen, played a major part in Revisionist thought in eastern Europe after World War II.

Revisionism in Other Countries. In no other country were the basic conditions for the emergence of Revisionism reproduced as they existed in Germany. What was needed was a single democratic mass labor party, doctrinally committed to revolutionary Marxism, but faced with a prima facie increasingly viable capitalist society in which it had to exist. What emerges therefore is not so much parallel manifestations of Revisionism as refractions of the German controversy, which did indeed echo through the Second International. The nearest approach to the German situation came in Austria, but the Austrian party was much preoccupied with the problems of national groups within the Habsburg Empire, and soon adopted a quasi-federal structure. Moreover, although Karl Renner and Max Adler, both leaders of the Austro-Marxist school, adopted Revisionist positions on such issues as gradualism and Kantianism respectively, the coincidental impact of serious academic criticism of Marxism, in the person of Eugen Böhm-Bawerk, shifted the lines of demarcation to the right and prevented the development of a Revisionist debate or a Revisionist movement in the Austrian party (Lichtheim [1964], pp. 278–306).

Otherwise only in Russia had Marxism become, or was becoming, the accepted doctrine of the Social-Democratic movement; and in Russia there was no mass party, nor was it a question of explaining the unexpected viability of mature capitalism. On the contrary, Russian Marxism appeared in the 1890's almost simultaneously with Russian capitalism, and the concern of its early protagonists was to win adherents from the Populists by stressing the extent and persistence of capitalism, and indeed its ultimate beneficence. But Russian Revisionism also appeared at the same time as Russian Marxism. It was not a revolt against an established and institutionalized orthodoxy, but an initial acceptance of Marxism only with reservations. Indeed, as befitted a movement confined to the intelligentsia and represented by a pleiad of outstanding intellectuals, philosophical doubt played a greater part in Russian than in German Revisionism; several years before Bernstein, Peter Struve, the most prominent and versatile of the Russian Revisionists, considered it necessary to "supplement Marxism" with Neo-Kantian philosophy, which was then becoming popular in Russia as elsewhere (Kindersley [1962], pp. 48, 112f.). For the most part, however, German Revisionism affected the Russian Social-Democratic movement by providing an object lesson for Lenin and other radicals to point to, and a pejorative label to attach to party opponents even when there was no close parallel to the German situation.

In Italy, as in Russia, there was an important intellectual Marxist movement, headed by Antonio Labriola and an equally powerful movement of criticism of Marxism, of which Vilfredo Pareto and Benedetto Croce were the most distinguished representatives. But the Italian Socialist Party was never fully committed to Marxist ideology; nor was it a mass party such as the SPD, aiming de facto at mobilizing an enfranchised membership for the parliamentary conquest of power. The German Revisionist controversy was observed with interest in the Italian socialist press, but it had little relevance to Italian conditions.

Lastly, neither in Britain nor in France was there a serious Revisionist controversy. In British Socialism, the ascendancy of the Fabians meant that Marxism never became the dominant ideology; it was not until 1917, or even later, that Marxism was taken at all seriously by British socialists. In France, the party situation was far more fluid and complex than in Germany: a united French Socialist party was formed only in 1905. The issue of reformism versus revolutionism was debated in France not within a single Marxist party but between rival socialist parties. Precipitated in the extreme form of "ministerialism" when the socialist Alexandre Millerand accepted a post in the Radical cabinet of 1899, the discussion was narrowed to the political question of cooperation with bourgeois organizations, and avoided ideological confrontation. The Marxist Jules Guesde's resolution condemning French Revisionism in orthodox German terms, at the Amsterdam Congress of the International in 1904, was a tactical move aimed at the ideologically eclectic leader, Jean Jaurès, not against a dissident Marxist like Bernstein, for whom there was no French equivalent. In any event, French socialism remained under Jaurès' domination until his death in 1914. There was no ruling orthodoxy, and therefore no Revisionism.

The Soviet Period to the Death of Stalin. The Bolshevik Revolution of 1917 and the establishment of the Communist International in 1919–20 introduced an entirely new situation. The Bolsheviks' seizure and maintenance of power in Russia created a new institu-

tion of orthodoxy, markedly to the left of Kautsky's, with the evidence of success as proof of its validity. The Second Congress of the Comintern forcibly internationalized this orthodoxy and split the European labor movement. But those parties which remained outside the Comintern now became in Soviet eyes not heretics but complete apostates, renegades, or infidels; Moscow could not admit that they had any part of Marxism, and soon many of them did not claim it. In the few Social Democratic parties that did profess Marxism, theory was—in spite of a few works such as Henri de Man's *Au delà du Marxisme* (Paris, 1927), written in a revisionist spirit—submerged in that reformist praxis which was the cause or effect of Revisionism rather than Revisionism itself. In the words of the Program of the Communist International adopted at the Sixth World Congress in August 1928, "social-democracy has completely abandoned Marxism. . . . Having traversed the stage of Revisionism, it has reached that of bourgeois liberal social reform and overt social imperialism" (J. Degras [1960], p. 515).

Nor did the major new heresies, which sprang up in the Soviet Union and the World Communist movement itself, qualify for the label Revisionist. For some ten years after the Revolution, these heresies were on the Left, the products either of doctrinaire adherence to Communist principle where the self-defining orthodoxy of those in power saw the political need for compromise, or of a factional struggle centered round the figure of Leon Trotsky. For a brief spell in the mid-twenties, solitary figures such as Georg Lukács (see below) might be condemned as Revisionist, as a term of opprobrium with little meaning. But by the time that a Right Opposition, led by Bukharin, Rykov, and Tomsky, emerged in the Soviet Union, the label Revisionist was, as has been seen, already considered obsolete. Bernstein had not even been expelled from the German Social Democratic Party, and to call a man Revisionist was something less than calling him a traitor; but in the circumstances of Stalin's emergent dictatorship, collectivization and the first Five-Year-Plan, the lines of loyalty were so harshly drawn that any divergence quickly became treachery. Revisionism is incompatible with a totalitarian system. Thus, with orthodoxy disintegrated on the one side, and totally imposed on the other, the idea of Revisionism virtually disappeared from the international labor movement for some forty years. It was not until new divisions in the World Communist system came to light after the death of Stalin that Revisionism reappeared in any definable form.

Modern Forms of Revisionism. If the original German Revisionism was the result of one Marxist's efforts to produce a coherent statement of his views on economics and politics, modern forms of Revisionism have fallen broadly into two distinct but related types, political and philosophical. Neither type originated in a single mind: each was rather the product of multiple circumstances.

1. Political Revisionism. Perhaps the first sign that Revisionism might be due for a revival came in 1948, when, in the increasingly angry exchange of correspondence between the Soviet and Yugoslav Central Committees, Stalin accused the Yugoslav Party of "being hoodwinked by the degenerate and opportunist theory of peaceful absorption of capitalist elements by a socialist system, borrowed from Bernstein, Vollmar and Bukharin" (R.I.I.A. [1948], p. 16). The Yugoslav challenge to Stalin's authority may be taken as the first postwar manifestation of political Revisionism, of which the chief characteristic was the rejection of Soviet authority, rather than any specific program which might justify the name of Revisionist. Not only were the political circumstances so changed since Bernstein's time—parties in power concerned with the maintenance and development of socialist states in contrast to a party in opposition aiming at the attainment of power by revolution or otherwise—that a close analogy would be hard to find; but in Yugoslavia at least there was, at the time of the break with Stalin, little to justify the accusation of deviation from the Soviet "model" of socialism and nothing to support that of leanings towards bourgeois society. In any event, the Soviet-Yugoslav dispute escalated so quickly that within a year the Russians were calling the Yugoslavs "Fascists." Revisionist thus hardly seemed a useful epithet, although the Yugoslavs subsequently developed certain policies (notably the abandonment of agricultural collectivization, the introduction of "workers' self-management," and the redefinition of the role of the Party in society) with theoretical implications which could plausibly have been called Revisionist; so could their view that neither pure capitalism nor pure socialism exists, but only a spectrum of mixed social forms.

Paradoxically, it was the Yugoslav ideologist Edvard Kardelj who revived the label Revisionist in 1953–54 so that he might condemn Milovan Djilas' "social-democratic" heresy within the Yugoslav Party. But it was not until after the Soviet-Yugoslav reconciliation of 1955–56 that it became an appropriate term for the Russians to use for the official Yugoslav leadership. By then the Twentieth Congress of the CPSU, with Khrushchev's denunciation of Stalin, had set in motion a process which brought the "national Communists" to power: Imre Nagy briefly and tragically in Hungary, Gomułka more enduringly in Poland. Insofar as they rejected Soviet leadership, in the name of their own

country's interests, these men could be called political Revisionists: but the fact that Gomułka, after a struggle, gained Soviet approval for his leadership, enabled him to avoid stigmatization as such. Meanwhile, *Pravda* revived the term revisionism in criticism of Kardelj's failure to support the Soviet view of the Hungarian revolution (Yu. Pavlov in *Pravda*, 18 December 1956); Mao Tse-tung, concerned at the possible disintegration of the socialist bloc, judiciously contrasted "dogmatism," defined as blind imitation of Soviet experience, with Revisionism, defined as "revising Marxism under the pretext of fighting dogmatism" (Mao Tse-tung, 1956).

By 1957 the struggle against Revisionism had become a convenient rallying-cry for all those who feared that the principle of "separate roads to socialism" had been interpreted in such a way that some of the roads might diverge from socialism altogether. These included not only the Soviet leaders, but some others: Gomułka in Poland—for all his challenge to Soviet authority and his rejection of Soviet example in such matters as agricultural and Church policy—was concerned at the appearance within his own Party of philosophical revisionism (see below); Ulbricht in East Germany was faced with a program for the democratization of the régime elaborated by Wolfgang Harich, an intellectual Party member, which included elements from Yugoslav and Polish practice and far-reaching suggestions for rapprochement with the West German SPD. In these circumstances the Soviet leaders, with Chinese encouragement, began an international campaign against Revisionism, which would have the effects of ensuring the bloc against disintegration from the virus of Titoism, and also stabilizing those régimes which were under pressure from Westernizing intellectual dissidents in the Party ranks.

Early in 1957, the Soviet ideologist Boris Ponomarev defined the seven sins of Revisionism in terms which illustrate this double purpose: (1) minimization of imperialist aggression; (2) denial of CPSU leadership; (3) rejection of class struggle and collaborationism between classes; (4) social-democratism; (5) denial of Leninist dictatorship of the proletariat; (6) rejection of a centralized, disciplined Party; and (7) adoption of national Communism (Brzezinski [1962], p. 305). In October 1957 Gomułka complained of Revisionists and Liquidationists "of various sorts . . . [who] offer no positive program . . . [but] act by negation and fruitless criticism" in the Polish Party (*Pravda*, 31 October 1957; trans. R. K. Kindersley). Shortly afterwards, at the meeting of twelve Ruling Parties in Moscow in November, Revisionism was declared to be "the main danger" in the international workers' movement, the Yugoslavs refusing to subscribe.

The Yugoslavs' retort took the form of a new Party Program in the spring of 1958, which was at once recognized as the epitome of political Revisionism, much as the Erfurt Program had been the epitome of orthodoxy. This program was a major document, the length of a small book, and embodied, from the orthodox, i.e., Soviet and Chinese, point of view, five serious transgressions: it exaggerated positive developments in the capitalist world, notably the social effects of the extension of state intervention in the economy; it failed adequately to distinguish between the aggressive nature of the imperialist and the defensive nature of the socialist camp; it underestimated the value of Soviet experience (e.g., collectivization) for other Socialist countries; it spoke prematurely of the withering-away of the State as a practical policy; and it reduced the role of the Party in a socialist country to one of ideological education instead of active leadership. It will be seen that all these are specifications of one or other of the sins of Revisionism listed by Ponomarev in 1957.

In the antirevisionist campaign which followed (and which involved the execution of Imre Nagy and his associates), the Chinese took the lead; and within the next two years their attacks on "modern revisionism" began to be aimed at the Soviet Union rather than the Yugoslavs. The main Chinese argument in support of their accusation has been that the Soviet leaders have compromised with imperialism. In 1968 a Soviet spokesman, prompted by the Maoist inspiration of some of the French student rebels of May 1968, referred to the struggle against the revision of Marxism-Leninism both from the Left and from the Right (*Pravda*, 19 June 1968), and the term "left revisionism" has appeared since on occasion (see, e.g., Chesnokov [1968], p. 3). Like medieval schismatics, each side has called the other heretic, using the terms appropriate to convey *odium theologicum* in a secular movement.

The Czechoslovak Communist reform movement of 1968 represents a further instance of political Revisionism. (The term was used by the Soviet leader Leonid Brezhnev with the Czechs in mind in March 1968.) Mindful of the experience of their Hungarian predecessors in 1956, the Czechoslovak leaders carefully attempted to reassure the Russians on the two points on which the Hungarian Revisionists overstepped the bounds: the Czechs repeatedly affirmed first that they remained loyal allies of the Soviet Union in the Warsaw Pact, and secondly, that they had no intention of allowing the revival of a multi-party system in such a form as would jeopardize the leading role of the Communist Party.

The reasons why these assurances were not accepted fall outside the scope of this article. But two points may be noted in conclusion: Soviet speakers used the terms "revisionism" and "nationalism" repeatedly in close conjunction during their criticisms of the Czechoslovak movement during 1968, almost as if they were two different aspects of the same phenomenon. Secondly, the Chinese took the view that the Czech crisis was the action of one "revisionist renegade clique" against another. These two instances, among many, illustrate the decline of "Revisionism" into an emotive term of political vituperation.

2. *Philosophical Revisionism.* Philosophy was, as we have seen, the weakest side of Bernstein's doctrine but it may well prove to be the most important form of latter-day Revisionism. Modern philosophical Revisionism is the product of numerous philosophers, more or less isolated, working under various conditions, mainly in Poland, Yugoslavia, and Czechoslovakia, but also in the Communist movements of certain Western countries, particularly France and Italy. The term is, nevertheless, used not only by Soviet ideologists to describe certain philosophical trends with which they disagree, but also by non-Marxist scholars in the West (Z. A. Jordan, G. L. Kline) when discussing the same trends from a more sympathetic point of view. It has therefore sufficient currency, if not precision, to justify consideration.

Whereas Bernstein rebelled against Marxist orthodoxy in the name of existing practice, modern Revisionist philosophers have rebelled against Marxist-Leninist—and residually Stalinist—orthodoxy in the name not of reality, of which they are also more or less critical, but of a social ideal. It is for them no longer a question of achievement of power by one or another means—revolution or evolution—but of using the power possessed by ruling Communist parties (of which they have generally been members, at least initially) to create the good society. As philosophers, they have attempted to define the principles relevant to this task in their most general form. Their efforts in this respect have led them from the "Marxism" of Engels, Lenin, and Stalin back to that of Marx himself. They have tended to reject such features of Marxist philosophy (more closely associated with Engels and Lenin than with Marx) as the epistemological theory of reflection, the dialectic of nature, and ontological materialism, while accepting Marx's historical materialism and his critique of capitalism and religion. But they have moved away from impersonal historical determinism to the reassertion of the responsibility and freedom of the individual; from the primacy of society to the primacy of Man; from socialism as a means of material abundance to socialism as an ethical ideal.

The Revisionists and Marxism. Faced as they were with Marxism converted into a justification for Stalinist tyranny, Revisionist philosophers were concerned with **167** reaffirming the validity of the humanist side of Marx's doctrine. This humanism was, in their view, to be found most clearly expressed in Marx's early works; it had been overshadowed, but not erased, in the later works, and even more so by Engels, Lenin, and Stalin.

In spite of this appeal to Marx against his successors, contemporary philosophical Revisionism is not a fundamentalist doctrine. Not all would go as far as the Polish philosopher Leszek Kołakowski, for whom Marxism will cease to exist as a separate doctrine as its valid tenets are sifted and absorbed into the general storehouse of human thought, "just as there is no 'Newtonism' in physics, no 'Linnaeism' in Botany, no 'Harveyism' in physiology and no 'Gaussism' in mathematics" (Kołakowski [1969], p. 206). Others such as Adam Schaff were ready to extend the scope of Marxism to tackle problems hitherto avoided by Marxist philosophers, such as semantics and existentialism (here a direct stimulus came from Sartre), but did not free themselves from the instrumentalist tradition of Marxism, and still retained a basically political motivation. They were willing to revise Marxism in order to defend it. They retained, that is, a certain methodological dogmatism: recognizing that there are definite limits which no one could transgress if he did not wish to sever his connections with Marxism-Leninism, they accepted these limitations (Jordan [1962], **6**, 15). Others again were less concerned to define their attitude to Marxism in general than to select such parts of Marxist doctrine as could be useful to them in developing a philosophy of socialist humanism. In this, their main inspiration has come from the young Marx, but they have also adapted elements of existentialism and Kantianism. They have regarded Marxism as the legitimate harvester of the fruits of other philosophies. They have thus recognized a dialogue between Marxism and contemporary continental philosophy—a dialogue denied by Soviet philosophers, who still insist on the dichotomies of "Marxist" and "bourgeois," "materialist" and "idealist" philosophy.

Determinism, Freedom, and Ethics. Where the orthodox tradition is cosmocentric, contemporary Revisionists have been anthropocentric. Social determinism (seen as a justification of Marxism institutionalized in the rule of a Stalinist party and defined from moment to moment by that Party in response to political needs) has been questioned and diluted with elements of individual responsibility; in this Kołakowski led the way in 1957 with a statement of what amounts to "statistical" but not individual determinism (Kołakowski [1969], pp. 160f.; cf. also Marković, 1963.); others, apparently forsaking rigorous philosophical statement, have opted for "moderate determinism" (Stojanović, in Lobkowicz [1967], p. 171). This

reaction against determinism, together with its ethical consequences, is one of the few features common to Bernstein and to Revisionist philosophers today.

Antideterminism was naturally linked with the rehabilitation of individual moral autonomy: no longer could *Das Sollen* ("the ought") be derived from *Das Sein* ("the is"). Kołakowski insisted that men could not avoid moral judgments of political reality; Mihailo Marković, a prominent member of the *Praxis* group in Yugoslavia, has argued that science can only offer alternative probabilities, from which we choose according to our moral values. Svetozar Stojanović has urged that Marxism should develop a system of normative ethics of its own.

Man and Society: Alienation. Much attention has been devoted to the relations between Man and Society. In this connection, a key concept, derived from the young Marx, has been that of alienation. Though the term is much older, it was first "discovered" by Georg Lukács in the early 1920's, then revealed by the publication of Marx's "Paris" manuscripts in 1932, but only brought to the fore by Western Marxists in the 1940's and 1950's. Alienation has been an important tool of Marxist criticism of existing socialist societies. Marx said that man suffers alienation under capitalism. The contemporary Revisionists' main contribution has been to assert that alienation persists under socialism, particularly in the form of bureaucracy. Just as it was Yugoslav ideologists who first in Eastern Europe produced a critique of Stalinism as a bureaucratic degeneration of socialism (there is perhaps an unconscious echo of Trotsky here), so it is Yugoslav philosophers who have devoted most energy to discussion of alienation in socialist society. It is, moreover, the Yugoslavs who profess to see a possible solution to the problem in their own system of social and workers' self-management. They sharply distinguish the ideal of socialism from affluence based on technology (e.g., Danilo Pejović, in Fromm [1965], pp. 181ff.): for them the socialist ideal is defined in the Communist Manifesto as a society "in which the free development of each is the condition for the free development of all."

The Dialectic. Unlike Bernstein, most contemporary Revisionist philosophers retain the dialectic view not of Nature but of Man and Society. Here again, Lukács, the Neo-Hegelian Revisionist of the 1920's, was their predecessor. For some, such as Karel Kosík and Milan Prúcha in Czechoslovakia, to accept the dialectic is to see Man in the totality of his relationships; for others such as Marković, it is a pledge of permanent social criticism. In either case it is an expression of philosophical radicalism: in Marx's words, *de omnibus dubitandum.*

National Traits of Revisionism. We have seen that

Revisionism and nationalism are closely associated in the orthodox mind: one of the characteristics of political Revisionism is an excessive emphasis on national peculiarities. Insofar as political Revisionism sprang from the rejection of a single (Soviet) model of socialism, this is an understandable judgment, borne out by the rehabilitation of national traditions which has accompanied the manifestations of Revisionism in Eastern Europe. But national circumstances have also left their stamp on philosophical Revisionism.

One reason why Polish philosophers took the lead in Revisionism was the existence in prewar Poland of a distinguished school of analytical philosophers, some of whom were still active after 1948. A. Schaff was a product of this school; in 1951, when Kołakowski was still orthodox, Schaff used its ideas in a critical examination of the Marxist theory of truth (Jordan [1963], pp. 88ff.).

In Yugoslavia, on the contrary, with no philosophical tradition, official political Revisionism removed for some years the stimulus of orthodoxy, and thus delayed the development of philosophical Revisionism. Liberation from the initial dominance of Russian Marxism in its Leninist-Stalinist form was followed by a period of Marxist fundamentalism, characterized by close study of texts, with little application to current social problems. It was not until about 1962, and particularly since the foundation of *Praxis* in 1964, that serious efforts were made to judge social reality by developing the criteria of Marxist humanism. In Czechoslovakia, there was a brief onslaught on philosophical Revisionism, defined as philosophy divorced from politics, in 1959. Among those attacked were Karel Kosík, representative of a dialectic view of totality akin to that of Lukács, and Ivan Sviták, a more typical Marxist humanist, both of whom were prominent in the political reform movement of 1967–68.

Revisionism: Right or Left? In the sense that he could be regarded as advocating a compromise with bourgeois capitalist reality, Bernstein was correctly seen as the originator of a right-wing heresy in Social Democracy. Subsequent forms of political Revisionism were also to the right of orthodoxy, at least until Soviet ideologists began to apply the term to the Chinese: for all except the Chinese (and Albanians) showed a tendency to move not only away from exclusive allegiance to Moscow but towards a position less sharply opposed to "imperialism." But on the philosophical plane the position is far less clear-cut. The Revisionists' interest in, and openness to, Western philosophy (including Thomism and nineteenth-century phenomenology) might seem to place them on the Right; but their emergence has always betokened a radical revolt against dogmatic, conservative, or ossified features of

socialist régimes. Kołakowski, analyzing the concept of the Left, ascribed to it "a position of permanent revisionism toward reality"—meaning socialist as well as capitalist reality (Kołakowski, p. 96). "Criticism of all that exists" was the text from Marx under which *Praxis* originally launched its campaign against "Stalinist positivism," and the heritage which Marković, Petrović, and others claim from Marx is not (as with Bernstein) evolutionary, but revolutionary. Kołakowski has even touched on the possible use of force by the Left under socialism (loc. cit.). In Yugoslavia, Marković has consistently criticized bureaucratic privilege in socialist society; and when political Revisionism, already institutionalized in the Party, espoused economic liberalization, many Revisionist philosophers took up a position of radical opposition. In Czechoslovakia in 1967–68 on the other hand, faced with a régime both dogmatic and conservative, political and philosophical Revisionism joined hands: philosophers such as Karel Kosík and Ivan Sviták were prominent supporters of Dubček's reform movement. Revisionism is the product and antithesis of orthodoxy; it cannot be classified as Right or Left without prior classification of the particular orthodoxy to which it is opposed.

BIBLIOGRAPHY

E. Bernstein, *Die Voraussetzung des Sozialismus und die Aufgaben der Sozialdemokratie* (Stuttgart, 1899), trans. as *Evolutionary Socialism* (London, 1909); idem, *Zur Geschichte und Theorie des Sozialismus* (Berlin, 1901). J. M. Bochenski, "The Great Split," *Studies in Soviet Thought,* No. 1 (1968), 1–15, a study of philosophical developments in Eastern Europe which argues that what is called "Revisionism" amounts to a complete break with Marxism-Leninism. Z. K. Brzezinski, *The Soviet Bloc,* revised ed. (New York, 1961), a ground-breaking study of the political basis of ideological formulae, including Revisionism, since the Second World War. D. I. Chesnokov, "Obostrenie ideyno-politicheskoy bor'by i sovremenny revizionizm," *Voprosy filosofii,* No. 12 (1968), 3–14, a polemical sally against Revisionist philosophers mainly in Eastern Europe. E. Fromm, ed., *Socialist Humanism: an International Symposium* (New York, 1965), contains contributions from most of the leading Marxist humanist philosophers in Poland, Czechoslovakia, and Yugoslavia. P. Gay, *The Dilemma of Democratic Socialism* (New York, 1952), a study of Bernstein's ideas and career. Z. A. Jordan, *Philosophy and Ideology* (Dordrecht, 1963), a good study of the impact of Marxism on Polish philosophy since 1945; idem, "The Philosophical Background of Revisionism in Poland," *East Europe,* **11,** No. 6 (1962), 11–17, 26–29, and No. 7, 14–23. R. Kindersley, *The First Russian Revisionists* (Oxford, 1962), deals with the so-called "Legal Marxists" in Russia up to about 1902. L. Kołakowski, *Marxism and Beyond* (London, 1969), contains crucial articles by the leading Polish Revisionist philosopher. G. L. Kline, ed., *European Philosophy Today* (Chicago,

1965), contains a contribution by the editor on "Leszek Kołakowski and the Revision of Marxism." The opening section of this study of Kołakowski gives an interesting classification of the various brands of Revisionist philosophy today. Karel Kosík, *Dialektika Konkretního* (Prague, 1963), Kosík's major work; German trans., *Die Dialektik des Konkreten* (Frankfurt a. M., 1967). G. Lichtheim, *Marxism*, 2nd ed. (London, 1964), contains a chapter devoted to Revisionism. N. Lobkowicz, ed., *Marx and the Western World* (Notre Dame, 1967), a symposium, including contributions by Gajo Petrović, Svetozar Stojanović, and Karel Kosík. Mao Tsetung, *More on the Historical Experience of the Dictatorship of the Proletariat* (New China News Agency, 29 December 1956). M. Marković, *Dialektik der Praxis* (Frankfurt a. M., 1968), the fullest statement in a Western language of the position of one of the leading Yugoslav Marxist humanists; idem, "Marxist Humanism and Ethics," *Inquiry,* **6** (1963), 18–34. G. Petrović, *Marx in the Mid-twentieth Century* (New York, 1967). Royal Institute of International Affairs (RIIA), *The Soviet-Yugoslav Dispute* [Documents] (London, 1948). A. Schaff, *A Philosophy of Man* (New York, 1963). S. Stojanovic, "Contemporary Yugoslav Philosophy," *Ethics,* **76,** No. 4 (1966), 297–301.

In addition, the following periodicals may be consulted with advantage: *Survey* (London); *Studies in Soviet Thought* (Fribourg); *Problems of Communism* (Washington, D.C.); *Praxis,* (Zagreb, has an International Edition with the main articles translated into English, French, or German; contributors are drawn from a wide range of countries).

R. K. KINDERSLEY

[See also Alienation in Hegel and Marx; **Historical and Dialectical Materialism;** Ideology of Soviet Communism; Marxism; Nationalism; **Social Democracy in Germany; Socialism from Antiquity to Marx.**]

RELATIVITY OF STANDARDS OF MATHEMATICAL RIGOR

FROM A BROAD standpoint, rigor in any field of endeavor and particularly in scientific fields, means the adherence to procedures that have been generally accepted as leading to correct conclusions. Thus the statement, "It has been rigorously established that Norsemen reached the shores of North America before Columbus," can be taken to mean that documentary, archaeological, or other evidence has been produced which conforms to the standards of acceptance set by the group to which the statement is addressed. Such a group might be a society of professional historians, in which case the term "rigorously established" implies that the evidence offered as a basis for the assertion conforms to the standards set by professional historians; for example, the evidence might be documentary materials whose validity is considered acceptable by such a group. If addressed to a group of anthropologists, the evidence might consist of archaeological materials whose authenticity meets the standards recognized as acceptable by this group.

Moreover, it is possible that the statement is acceptable to a group of historians, but not to professional anthropologists; or even to one group of historians and not to another. An example of the latter kind could concern the validity of a certain alleged miracle, which might be established quite rigorously according to the standards of a group of church historians, but not to those of a lay historical group.

Furthermore, rigor is not just a function of the group involved, but of time. Standards of rigor notoriously change with the passage of time. What would have been considered rigorous by scientists of the year 1800 would certainly not meet the standards set by the professional scientists of 1900. On the other hand, standards of rigor do not necessarily become more stringent with time, since cultures rise and fall, and standards set by one culture may be forgotten and have to be recreated or replaced by succeeding cultures. The classical case of this kind may be found in connection with the decay of the Hellenic culture and the gradual ascendency of its successors.

It may be expected, too, that standards of rigor will sometimes become the subject of profound discussion amongst members of a group concerned. Examples of this kind are frequently brought to public attention in connection with the marketing of new drugs, where the standards of rigor governing pretesting are frequently bitterly debated between manufacturer's chemists and those of government agencies. It is probably not generally realized that similar instances occur even in mathematics, a field popularly known as the "most exact" of the sciences; and in which no motives of a pecuniary nature becloud the issues as is often the case when commercial interests are involved. A classic story in mathematical circles relates that one of the contemporaries of David Hilbert, late professor of mathematics at the University of Göttingen, Germany, exclaimed upon reading a short and elegant proof that Hilbert had given, "This is theology, not mathematics!"—indicating an opinion that the proof did not conform to accepted mathematical standards. And this same Hilbert, who was one of the leading mathematicians of the first third of the twentieth century, became engaged in a prolonged debate with the famous Dutch mathematician, L. E. J. Brouwer, over what constitutes rigorous methods of proof in mathematics (see below). Such debates are not of rare occurrence, and have occurred frequently throughout the history of mathematics.

The development of the concept of rigor in mathematics provides a most instructive and revealing story, which can be told without becoming involved in esoteric technicalities and which has meaningful parallels in other fields of learning. As one of the oldest sciences, and especially one in which the concept of rigor has achieved mature formulations, mathematics has traditionally been most concerned with standards of rigor; and the stages through which mathematical rigor has passed, with attention to cultural influences (internal and external), give a superb example of the evolution of a concept (rigor), which in spite of the paucity of ancient documents, can be observed virtually from its inception to the present.

Presumably such a concept as rigor was at first only intuitive, not a consciously realized ideal. The Sumerian-Babylonian mathematics was the earliest for which historical records have been found, although it was not a separate "discipline" such as it became in the later European cultures. In it a number of mathematical formulas and procedures which later became standard were developed, as well as a system of numerals almost as sophisticated as our present-day decimal system. Methods for solving algebraic equations had also been developed along with a number of geometric formulas. Most surprising among the latter was the famous "Pythagorean theorem," relating the square on the hypotenuse of a right triangle to the squares on the other two sides—traditionally attributed to the Pythagorean school which flourished over a millennium later in the Greek culture. Such materials presumably imply the development of some kind of standards according to which these algebraic and geometric ideas became admissible for those uses (usually commercial) to which they were put. The nature of these standards is unknown, but there is no evidence as yet available that they were as advanced as the methods that developed in the later Hellenic civilization. They were probably of an intuitive, traditional nature, although they could also have embraced certain pragmatic and diagrammatic tests. For example, if an ancient Sumerian "Einstein" were faced with a problem involving the determination of the quantity of material needed to erect a certain structure, he might have found a formula for the purpose. Then presumably this formula would not have gained acceptance by his contemporaries without his first convincing them in some way of its validity. It can be surmised that this would have been accomplished merely by showing that the method "worked"—that is, that it gave the desired amount of material, or a reasonable approximation thereto. Or, if the problem were of a geometric character, demonstration of the validity of the formula might have been accomplished by certain visual methods consisting of counting pebble arrangements, or of geometric patterns displaying "obvious" properties. This is conjecture of course; but since the earliest methods used by their Greek successors consisted of just such tests for validity, and since there were cultural contacts between the later Babylonians and the early Greeks, it seems a not improbable hypothesis (Neugebauer [1957], Ch. II).

The course of Greek mathematics, thanks to the extant traces of the unusual intellectual atmosphere in which it developed, is somewhat less conjectural. Specifically, its development within a philosophical milieu influential in both the Greek and succeeding cultures resulted in the preservation of more important written records. Moreover, the circumstances of its evolution contain suggestions of the manner in which cultural influences, both environmental and intrinsic, promoted its development toward increased rigor. This first becomes noticeable in the Pythagorean school of the sixth and fifth centuries B.C. The geographical location of this school was Croton, in the southeastern section of Italy. In nearby Elea, the Eleatic school of philosophy was centered, and one of its foremost exponents, Parmenides, was apparently associated for a time with the Pythagorean school of mathematics. Usually, when two cultural entities meet and mingle, diffusion of ideas from each to the other occurs. In this case, the cultural entities were the Pythagorean school of mathematics and the Eleatic system of philosophy. The cosmological system conceived by Parmenides was evidently influenced by Pythagorean points of view; on the other hand, the Pythagoreans could have become acquainted with the dialectic of the Eleatics, one of whose features was indirect argument (Szabó, 1964).

If such was the case, we have here one of the earliest examples of concepts external to mathematics combining with intrinsic mathematical needs to produce a method promoting greater rigor of proof. Up to this time, Pythagorean methods of proof had not advanced much further than the primitive diagrammatic methods termed "visual." By arranging objects, such as pebbles, in simple geometrical arrays, a number of elementary formulas had been discovered by direct observation. In other instances, the use of superposition—moving one geometric configuration into coincidence with another—was employed. Some have conjectured that the first proofs of the Pythagorean Theorem were accomplished in this way. While such methods were well adapted to the discovery of simple arithmetic and geometric facts, they were not as conclusive as the deductive methods which came into use and which were possibly influenced by adaptation of the Eleatic dialectic to mathematical proofs. The previous primitive methods could never have sufficed to prove certain geometric facts which are completely inaccessible to visual methods, as, for example, the existence of incommensurable line segments; i.e., line segments for which there exists no common unit of measurement, such as the side and diagonal of a square. We can conjecture that the Pythagoreans began to suspect the existence of incommensurable segments and realized the inadequacy of their traditional proof methods. If such was the case, there was thereby set up an intrinsic motivation to find a more rigorous type of reasoning.

It appears likely that the proof of incommensurability of the side of a square with its diagonal was one of the earliest, if not the earliest, to make appeal to the dialectic method. For this proof, it was necessary to show that there cannot exist any unit of length, no matter how small, that will exactly measure both the side of a square and its diagonal. A geometric fact of this kind cannot be handled by visual methods, since the stipulation "no matter how small" places it beyond the range of human perception. However, if the assumption that by using some sufficiently small unit of length, both the side and diagonal of a square can be exactly measured, can be shown to lead to contradiction, then one may conclude that such a unit of length cannot possibly exist; i.e., that the side and diagonal are incommensurable. (Later, the basis for this type of argument was formulated by Aristotle in the Law of Contradiction: "Contradiction is impossible" or more explicitly, "No proposition can be both true and false"; and the Law of the Excluded Middle: "Every proposition is either true or false." Thus, the proposition that there exists a common unit of measure for the side and diagonal of a square is either true or false; and since its truth is untenable, having been shown to imply contradiction, it must be false.)

Such arguments are called "indirect" forms of proof—later called "reductio ad absurdum." They produce a conviction not attainable by visual arguments, which are always open to the objection that they cover only particular cases and may be the result of illusory perceptions. Consequently they soon became standard in Greek mathematics, not to be matched in quality of rigor by visual methods. Indeed, it soon became the rule that no longer was a mathematical formula or method to be accepted because it always seemed to work in particular cases (in Plato's dialogues, Socrates frequently rejects a definition of a concept like justice by enumeration of particular cases falling under it, and demands an essential or universal property); it must be proved by a logical argument such as that of the indirect type. Rigorous proof came to be synonymous with proof by logic.

Although not all historians agree on the details of the above interpretation of the available historical literature, the evidence strongly implies that as a result of a need internal to mathematics combined with the existence of a philosophical dialectic in the culture external to mathematics, greater rigor was achieved in Greek mathematics. Moreover, this was possibly not the only case in which mathematical rigor was indebted to influences external to mathematics. For example, Zeno of Elea, a pupil of Parmenides, had been led by his work on the extension of his master's philosophy to a series of paradoxes which were ultimately recognized to be of fundamental importance to mathematics, in that they raised questions concerning the continuous character of the straight line. For instance, if the line is made up of points, and a point has no length, then how can a line have length? Zeno also argued that motion in a straight line would be impossible since an object could never get from one point to another. Again, historians differ in their opinions regarding whether Zeno's work was influential or not in the development of ancient mathematical thought, but it may have been in the effort to get around such difficulties that mathematicians came to realize that the vague intuitive conceptions on which geometry had been based must be replaced by an explicit set of assumptions which embodied the intuitive "facts" on which proofs could be based. The fourth-century (B.C.) mathematician Eudoxus was most prominently identified with this accomplishment, and it is generally agreed that a considerable part of Euclid's *Elements* stems directly from Eudoxus' work. In the *Elements* the basic assumptions are called "axioms" and "postulates," and the proofs display the mature form of which the indirect method was the first example. These proofs, ultimately called proofs by logical deduction, demonstrate that by "taking thought" alone, one can establish the validity of an assertion covering infinitely many special cases. Another type of reasoning, important heuristically (as a method of discovery), by "analysis," used the device of first assuming the truth of the assertion to be proved in order to ascertain its consequences; if these consequences consisted of basic assumptions (axioms or postulates) or previously proved assertions, then it was sometimes possible to reverse the process by showing that the consequences had the desired assertion as one of their consequences.

The Greek philosopher Aristotle made a noteworthy study of logical deduction, arriving at general frameworks for the methods involved which were applicable to all fields of study, not just to geometry. He proposed a general definition of a demonstrative science which became a model for centuries of later scientific work. According to this definition, a demonstrative science should consist of a collection of basic assumptions, and of the theorems which these assumptions imply (Beth,

1959). The process of implication should utilize the various forms of logical deduction set forth in Aristotle's study of argumentative methods.

So far as rigor is concerned, little further significant progress was made until the nineteenth century, when a combination of circumstances, bearing a curious resemblance to those which seem to have brought about an increase in rigor during the Greek era came into play. These circumstances developed in the following manner.

During the period which followed the Greek decline, mathematics underwent an extensive development and evolution in both symbolic and conceptual content. In arithmetic, the remarkable number system of the Sumerian-Babylonian culture evolved essentially into the decimal system used today. Although the numerals used by the Babylonians were cumbersome (due, perhaps, to the necessity of having to adapt them to the use of the stylus and baked clay media), their place value system in which the "value" of a single digit depended on its position ("place") within the numeral was the same as that used in the decimal system. (It lacked a true zero, but this was clearly evolving by the end of the Babylonian era.) However, the symbolic algebra which we now use was a product of the later European cultures. And (in the seventeenth century) it was the imposition of this algebra on the geometry bequeathed by the Greeks which resulted in analytic geometry, and enabled Newton and Leibniz to crystallize their ideas on the calculus. Although Newton and Leibniz are popularly credited with creating the calculus, what they essentially did was to synthesize, in symbolic form, concepts that had been developed by a host of predecessors going back to the Greeks (Boyer, 1949; Rosenthal, 1951; Bochner, 1966). This achievement was a breakthrough whose motivation lay at least as much in the search for a medium in which to express natural laws as in the desire to bolster the purely symbolic aspects of mathematics: in short, in a combination of cultural and intrinsic mathematical stresses.

However, the success of the symbolic machinery set up by Newton and Leibniz was so great that it went beyond the conceptual background; symbols and operations with them were created for which no one could give a satisfactory meaning, although results achieved with them generally justified their invention. They passed the pragmatic test but flunked the conceptual. As a result, that vaunted rigor for which mathematics had been praised from the time of the Greeks was now lacking, and there ensued a field day for philosophical critics (such as the renowned Bishop Berkeley, who called Newton's infinitesimals "the ghosts of departed quantities"), not to mention the uncomfortable feeling that the mathematical defenders of the new calculus could not escape.

Actually, this lack of conceptual justification was not a new phenomenon in mathematics in those areas where the conditions laid down by Aristotle for a demonstrative science had not been met. Consider the ordinary arithmetic of the integers, for example; no satisfactory conceptual background had ever been furnished for it. But this caused little concern and there is little evidence that anyone was aware of the lack until quite recent times. True, some qualms were experienced by the introduction of negative numbers, which for centuries had been toyed with but rejected as "fictitious," even after their use became common in the seventeenth century. The conceptual basis for the nonnegative integers was purely intuitive, but they had been in use for untold centuries and had achieved cultural acceptability—that is, as meeting the demands of the rigor of the day. But the extension to negative numbers was purely formal—a symbolic achievement embodying such operational rules as the laws of signs, but otherwise having no conceptual justification. Moreover, no axiomatic basis satisfying Aristotle's conditions was given for them until the late nineteenth and early twentieth centuries (Landau, 1951).

A similar situation prevailed concerning complex numbers of the form $a + bi$ (where i stands for the "imaginary" $\sqrt{-1}$) encountered in elementary problems such as the solution of quadratic and cubic equations (a and b being "real" numbers). These numbers and arithmetical operations with them were successfully carried out for several centuries, although a satisfactory conceptual background was not provided until the twentieth century. Intuitive bases of a geometric nature did develop for them much earlier, but by that time geometry was coming to be no longer accepted as a basis for numerical theories.

Thus the introduction of a new symbolic apparatus like the calculus should "logically" not have caused such concern, so long as it passed the pragmatic test—which it certainly did. Of course it lacked the long traditional background possessed by the natural numbers, but this was also true, possibly to a lesser extent, in the case of the negative integers and the complex numbers. However, an idea had become prominent which, although not strictly new in mathematics, had nevertheless not caused much concern since Eudoxus devised his theory of proportion. This was the concept of the infinite. It intruded into all the basic conceptions offered as an explanation of the new calculus, and occurred in two opposing forms; the "infinitely small" and the "infinitely great." Attempts at clarifying the basic concepts of the calculus, such as that of the derivative of a function, made appeal

173

to the "infinitely small," or "little zeroes," and were quite unconvincing (even, one sometimes suspects, to those who devised them). And although the axiomatic method of the Greeks enjoyed quite a vogue at the time (Leibniz had used it in arguments of a political and military nature), notably in social and philosophical theories (as, for instance, by Spinoza), there seems to have been little effort to use it as a means for giving the calculus a firm basis.

Although appeal to the axiomatic method had to await the latter part of the nineteenth century, certain notable contributions to the rigorous development of the calculus were made earlier. Chief among these was that of A. Cauchy, whose *Cours d'analyse . . .* (1821) gave the basic ideas of the calculus a quite rigorous treatment, making no appeal to such vague notions as "little zeroes." In other fields of mathematics, the realization was growing that the axiomatic method offered an acceptable path to greater rigor. This was helped by the accompanying realization that the number systems which had achieved mathematical acceptance either through tradition or by special needs were not the only ones that could be devised. Similarly, the geometry of Euclid was not the only type of geometry that provided a consistent description of physical space. The result of such considerations was the inception of new algebras and geometries, all rigorously defined by means of the axiomatic method in the Aristotelian tradition. Although these developments had many consequences, the one of greatest importance for present purposes was the casting into prominence of the problem of consistency. How could one be assured that all these algebraic and geometric systems, frequently mutually incompatible (as, e.g., Euclidean and non-Euclidean geometries), were within themselves consistent systems? For certainly if a mathematical system harbored contradiction, then it could not have been rigorously developed. In this way, rigor and consistency began to be associated; that which is rigorously structured ought not to be inconsistent, and systems that turn out to be consistent must ipso facto be the result of rigorous formulation.

In contrast, the calculus was still based on fuzzy notions of a number system which, in addition to the ordinary integers and fractions, contained irrationals such as $\sqrt{2}$, π, etc. This number system, known technically as the real number system, had grown as new accretions were needed. With the introduction of analytic geometry, it had been given a more satisfactory intuitive background through association with the straight line. By selecting an arbitrary point P on some fixed line L as a representative of zero, the points to one side of P were associated with the positive real numbers in increasing order, and those to the other

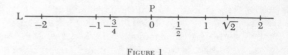

FIGURE 1

side with negative numbers, each negative number being the same distance from P as its positive counterpart on the other side of P (Figure 1). It became intuitively evident that to each point of L corresponded a unique real number in this manner, and that in problems of the calculus appeal could be made to this linear structure, considered as equivalent to the system of real numbers. Proofs were given which made use of this geometric concept and it gradually became clear that the amount of geometric intuition employed in the proofs of theorems of the calculus was exceeding the limits imposed by new standards of rigor. This was made all the more evident by the fact that many of the geometric facts used to substantiate numerical statements were frequently the same "facts" that had seemed so evident to the Greeks that they had never been adequately established in geometry. In short, they had no firm basis either numerically or geometrically.

This unsatisfactory state of affairs became all the more pronounced as the calculus gradually grew into what is now termed classical analysis, which embodied not only the advanced ideas owing to the successors of Leibniz and Newton, but also a theory whose foundation was the system of complex numbers geometrically represented by the points of a Euclidean plane. This growth of analysis was not just an internal evolution, influenced only by mathematical considerations, but was in large measure due to the needs of physical theories (Bochner, 1966). Of great importance was the work of a French mathematical physicist Baron Joseph Fourier (1768–1830), who was not a professional "pure" mathematician—but was one who, in the opinion of one historian (Bell [1945], p. 292), "had almost a contempt for mathematics except as a drudge of the sciences." Being quite uninhibited by such qualms as would have (and did—see Bell [1937], pp. 197–98) beset a pure mathematician, he proceeded to set up mathematical tools whose chief virtue was apparently that they were suited to the needs of such studies as the theory of heat. In particular they involved infinite processes which had little rigorous foundation and which stretched to its limits that geometric intuition upon which mathematical analysts were wont to rely.

As so often happens, mathematicians found themselves confronted, much as in the case of the basic notions of the calculus (which had by now been essentially cleared up by Cauchy), with new symbolic and operational apparatuses which could not be ignored. It was not just that they seemed to prove their worth in applications to physical theories—if this were their only compensating feature, they might well have been left to the whimsies of physics—but they rapidly offered ways in which to treat purely mathematical problems as well as suggestions for new concepts or expansions of already existing concepts (such as that of function). And to accept them meant, again, to find a rigorous foundation for them.

Thus the growth of mathematical analysis brought mathematics to face much the same types of problems as had confronted the ancient Greeks and which were solved by such innovations as Eudoxus' theory of proportion. In particular, it was necessary to replace the largely intuitive conception of the structure of the real number system by a precisely formulated axiomatic system which would serve as a satisfactory base upon which to found analysis. Such a foundation would, one hoped, not only settle once and for all whether the types of series, and functions related thereto, "worked" in applications because of accidental circumstances or whether they could be shown, by logical deduction from the new foundation, to be mathematically sound.

The solution of the latter problem was found, as anyone familiar with the way in which mathematics evolved would expect, by several independent investigators (Meray, Dedekind, Weierstrass, G. Cantor). Although their solutions were not precisely the same, they turned out to be equivalent (in the sense that each could be derived from the others). And one now rejoiced in the feeling that the one apparently remaining insecure part of mathematics had been given a secure foundation; and mathematics could resume its course presumably assured of having once again achieved a rigor safe from all criticism.

But this feeling of security was not to last long. As usually happens when mathematics makes a great advance, new insights are achieved regarding concepts which had long been taken for granted. A mathematician of ancient Greece, for instance, knew perfectly well that a line joining a point exterior to a circle to a point interior to the circle would have to intersect the periphery of the circle; it was self-evident, and needed no justification. Nevertheless, the time arrived (during the nineteenth century) when it was forced upon one that justification really was necessary if the demands of modern rigor were to be met. Similarly, one had no qualms in speaking of a "collection" of numbers or geometric entities; for instance, no one would object to speaking of the collection—the term "set" is more in vogue today—of numbers that were solutions of an algebraic equation. Correspondingly, one might speak of the set of all even numbers, or the set of all odd numbers. True, the latter sets each contain infinitely many numbers, whereas the number

of solutions of an algebraic equation is finite. Nevertheless, the use of the words "set" and "collection" was felt to be the same as their use in the physical world. To speak of a collection of people or a set of chairs is an ordinary usage of the natural language. And although mathematics had become increasingly symbolized over the centuries, employment of the natural language (as in the statements of the axioms and theorems of Euclidean geometry) continued to be acceptable.

However, this apparently innocent use of the notion of a collection turned out to be another case of a concept borrowed from the general culture and put to use in mathematics in ways never before dreamed of. Not only was it used to define such a basic notion as number (theretofore taken for granted, but whose extension to numbers for infinite sets plainly demanded definition), but it lay at the heart of the foundation of mathematical analysis. It was inevitable that a study of the concept for its own sake would become necessary, and this was finally undertaken by the German mathematician Georg Cantor during the latter half of the nineteenth century. Symptomatic of the lack of interest or concern generally felt by mathematicians of his time, however, was the fact that most of Cantor's contemporaries at first considered his researches as neither mathematically justified nor even "good" mathematics. Some of his colleagues considered that Cantor was transgressing the bounds of what could be called "mathematics." Fortunately Cantor persisted in his researches, and not only did they lead to a full-blown theory of great inherent interest, but its applications to such problems as those bequeathed by Fourier proved unexpectedly fruitful. By the end of the century, his ideas were coming to be generally accepted, and the Theory of Sets was well on the way to becoming an established mathematical discipline.

About the same time, the German mathematician and logician G. Frege was turning his attention to the problem of furnishing a rigorous foundation for the arithmetic of integers. He was convinced that all mathematics could be derived from logic and thus rendered free of all criticism regarding its lack of rigor. In showing this, he did not hesitate to use the notion of set, which he apparently felt to be itself rooted in logic. From a somewhat different point of view, both Dedekind and the Italian logician Peano (ca. 1890) gave an axiomatic foundation for the system of natural numbers from which, again using set theory, the real number system could be derived.

As a result of these researches, the mathematical world came to consider, around the turn of the century, that mathematics had at last been placed on a rigorous foundation, and that all criticism of the foundations of analysis had been met. Symptomatic of the general feeling were the words of the renowned French mathematician, Henri Poincaré, in an address at the International Congress of Mathematicians of 1900: "We believe that we no longer appeal to intuition in our reasoning. . . . Now, in analysis today, if we take the pains to be rigorous, there are only syllogisms or appeals to the intuition of pure number that could possibly deceive us. It may be said that today absolute rigor is attained" (Bell [1945], Ch. 13; also see Poincaré [1946], pp. 210–22).

It is doubtful if Poincaré could have been aware, at the time he uttered these words, that contradiction had already been discovered in the theory of sets (communication between various national mathematical groups was rather poor at that time). In the unrestricted use of set-theoretic methods in the realm of the infinite, contradiction had been, and was being found.

The earliest attempt to meet the situation was to call again upon the axiomatic method for help. The first set of axioms for the theory of sets was given in 1908 by the German mathematician Ernst Zermelo. Thus the apparently innocent notion of set, universally used in common discourse, and having come into mathematics because of the use of the natural language, became the central concept of a mature mathematical theory, deserving of axiomatic foundation in the same way that geometry had been axiomatized by the Greeks. And much as the Greeks succeeded in avoiding the difficulties posed by the discovery of incommensurable magnitudes, so did the axiom system of Zermelo promise to avoid the contradictions to which the unrestricted notion of set had led. Unfortunately there was no guarantee that it would suffice to avoid all possible contradictions; that is, there appeared no way of proving Zermelo's system consistent, even though the axioms in themselves seemed to restrict the theory of sets sufficiently to avoid contradiction. One could no longer assert, consequently, that mathematics had attained that absolute rigor which Poincaré had cited.

Concurrently with the axiomatization of the theory of sets, other approaches were made to the problem of giving mathematics a rigorous foundation, and for a time three distinct "schools of thought" emerged (Wilder [1965], Chs. 8–11). One of these, associated with the name of Bertrand Russell, but actually presented in the monumental *Principia Mathematica* (1910–13) of A. N. Whitehead and B. Russell, followed a path based conceptually on Frege's ideas and symbolically upon Peano's work. The central thesis of the Whitehead-Russell doctrine was again that mathematics could be founded on logic. But it developed that in order to build a secure theory of number, free from contradiction, axioms had to be introduced which

had not only never been part of classical logic, but were obviously framed solely to suit the needs of mathematics. Moreover, they did not have the character of universality that one might expect of an axiom of logic, but were clearly manufactured to meet a special situation. Consequently, although the Whitehead-Russell "school" acquired a sizable following for a time, it had only a limited life. Nevertheless, the central theme—that mathematics is derivable from logic—persisted, and the *Principia Mathematica* has continued to be a source of both inspiration and symbolic modes for workers in the foundations of mathematics and logic.

In particular, the so-called "Formalist School," starting under the leadership of the great German mathematician David Hilbert, adopted a symbolism obviously inspired by that of the *Principia Mathematica*. However, the motivating philosophy of this school was not that mathematics is derivable from logic, but that all of mathematics could be formulated in a symbolic framework which, although formally meaningless, could be interpreted by mathematical concepts and shown to be consistent. More specifically, it was Hilbert's idea to set up certain axioms using symbols alone and no words from the natural language, along with a set of rules which, although not an intrinsic part of the symbolic system and couched in the natural language, would specify how theorems could be derived from the axioms. The object of this program was to show that a symbolic system could be set up which would, when interpreted by mathematical concepts, give all of mathematics, and which could be shown would never give the formula for a contradiction. In this way, it was hoped that absolute rigor could be established.

Meanwhile a distinctly different and radical approach to the problem of rigor was being promoted by the Dutch mathematician L. E. J. Brouwer (who was influenced by the ideas of the nineteenth-century mathematician L. Kronecker). Brouwer maintained that mathematical concepts are intuitively given and that language and symbolism are necessary only for communicating these concepts. The intuition basic to mathematics, according to Brouwer, is that of stepwise progression as in the passage of time, conceived as one instant following another; for mathematics, the basic intuition gives the sequence of natural numbers: 1, 2, 3, ... All mathematics must be constructed on the basis of this sequence. In particular, "existence" of a mathematical concept depends upon such a construction; appeal to the logical Law of the Excluded Middle to prove the existence of a mathematical entity, involving showing that assumption of nonexistence leads to contradiction, is not acceptable, for example. Brouwer called the resulting philosophy "Intuitionism." According to its tenets the complete set of real numbers does not exist, since it cannot be built up from the natural numbers without using certain axioms of the theory of sets which are not constructive and hence are not admissible to the Intuitionist. The contradictions encountered in the "orthodox" mathematics are due not to the use of the infinite per se, but to the "unjustified" extension of the laws of logic from the finite to the infinite. By using constructive methods only, these contradictions are avoided.

While the Intuitionist contention that their methods yielded an absolutely rigorous mathematics was apparently correct, unfortunately only a portion of the mathematics which had been built up during the preceding three centuries was attainable by these methods. Acceptance of the Intuitionist path to absolute rigor meant, then, giving up concepts which had not only proved their usefulness but had become firmly imbedded in the culture. It is not surprising, therefore, that Intuitionism attracted few converts, and that the major part of the mathematical community looked for another way out of the difficulties posed by the contradictions.

Later attempts to establish an absolutely rigorous mathematics, employing chiefly the methods of formal axiomatics, have revealed that such a concept as absolute rigor is apparently an ideal toward which to strive, but one that is in practice unattainable except in certain limited domains. It is in much the same category as such an intuitively conceived abstraction as absolutely perfect linear measurement; no matter how much more precise measuring instruments are made, it is in practice unattainable. This does not imply that certain restricted portions of mathematics are not rigorously founded; quite the contrary. It applies chiefly to those parts of mathematics in which the (infinite) theory of sets is employed. Moreover, logic itself has been revealed as only an intuitive cultural construct which gives rise to the same kind of problems and variations as mathematics when subjected to formal symbolic analysis (Beth, 1959).

In the natural sciences such as physics, chemistry, and zoology, at least in their experimental aspects, the amount of rigor attainable is dependent upon technical factors such as measuring devices, and will increase as the related technology becomes more precise. Similar conclusions hold in the social sciences. Both categories of science—natural and social—tend toward greater mathematization as they develop; and so long as the portions of mathematics which they employ can be shown to be rigorous, they will not be affected by the types of difficulty still encountered in the parts of mathematics dependent upon general set theory.

It must be recognized, too, that a sizable group of mathematicians of Platonistic persuasion take the view that mathematics simply has not yet advanced far enough to be able to cope with such vexing questions as arise in modern set theory; that the "truth" concerning these is still a matter for investigation and that their rigorous solutions are still attainable. The situation is much like that of a natural scientist who believes that the "laws" of nature as presently formulated are only an approximation to the true situation which exists. Whether this "true" situation will ever be discovered, or even whether it can be formulated in linguistic or mathematical terms if it does exist, he cannot say. Similarly, the mathematician who feels that rigorous mathematical truth does exist must admit, in the present state of knowledge, that it may never be possible to attain it.

BIBLIOGRAPHY

E. T. Bell, *The Development of Mathematics* (New York, 1945); idem, *Men of Mathematics* (New York, 1937). E. W. Beth, *The Foundations of Mathematics* (Amsterdam, 1959). S. Bochner, *The Role of Mathematics in the Rise of Science* (Princeton, 1966). C. B. Boyer, *The History of the Calculus and its Conceptual Development* (New York, 1949). E. G. H. Landau, *Foundations of Analysis* (New York, 1951). O. Neugebauer, *The Exact Sciences in Antiquity* (Providence, 1957). H. Poincaré, *The Foundations of Science* (Lancaster, Pa., 1946). A. Rosenthal, "The History of Calculus," *American Mathematical Monthly*, **58** (1951), 75–86. A. Szabo, "The Transformation of Mathematics into Deductive Science and the Beginnings of its Foundation on Definitions and Axioms," *Scripta Mathematica*, **27** (1964), Part I, 24–48A, Part II, 113–39. R. L. Wilder, *Introduction to the Foundations of Mathematics*, 2nd ed. (New York, 1965).

RAYMOND L. WILDER

[See also **Axiomatization**; Continuity; Infinity; **Number**; Pythagorean . . . ; Relativity.]

MATHEMATICS IN CULTURAL HISTORY

THE HISTORY of mathematics is but a thin ribbon across the fabric of general history, that is, of the cultural history of events, insights, and ideas. Yet there are major problems of general history that are meaningfully refracted in the history of mathematics, and one such problem, on which we shall concentrate, is the problem of explaining the decline of ancient civilization in the West. On the other hand, it may happen that mathematics is materially involved in a problem in general history, and yet cannot contribute to its illumination; one such problem, on which we intend to comment, is the problem of the rise and spread of phonetic writing. Finally, there are intriguing situations in which the judgment of mathematics on the eminence of an era is different from that of other fields of knowledge, even of physics proper, and in several brief preliminary sections we shall rapidly review a few problems of this kind from periods beginning with and following upon the Renaissance.

But before beginning our reviews we wish to state that the problems to be encountered will be formulated in broad, summary, and even simplistic terms. This is to be expected. As a mode of rational cognition mathematics appears rather early and is quite central, but as a mode of intellectual activity it is rather primitive. For this reason mathematics is effective because of its strength rather than its delicacy, even when involved in sensibilities. Therefore, when participating in the analysis of problems from general history, the history of mathematics is at its best when the problems are stated in large, manifest, even crude fashion rather than in a localized, esoteric, and delicate manner.

The Renaissance. There is a much-studied problem whether and in what sense there indeed was a Renaissance—in the fifteenth and sixteenth centuries, say—as institutionalized by Jacob Burckhardt; that is, whether there is a marked-off era which interposes itself between medieval and modern times. (For a history of the problems see W. K. Ferguson, K. H. Dannenfeldt, T. Helton, also E. Panofsky.) George Sarton, the leading historian of science, once made the statement (which he later greatly modified) that "from the scientific point of view, the Renaissance was *not* a renaissance" (quoted in Dannenfeldt, p. 115). Of course, nobody would deny that there was a Copernicus in the sixteenth century or that the introduction of printing created a great spurt in many compartments of knowledge, scientific or other; but the question, which Sarton's statement was intended to answer, is whether during the era of the Renaissance, disciplines like physics, chemistry, biology, geology, economics, history, philosophy, etc., were developed in a manner which sets these two centuries off from both the Middle Ages and the seventeenth century.

Now, with regard to mathematics no such doubts need, or even can arise. There was indeed a mathematics of the Renaissance that was original and distinctive in its drives and characteristics. Firstly, there was a school, mainly, but not exclusively, represented by Germans (Peurbach, Regiomontanus, and others), that sharply advanced the use of symbols and notations in arithmetic and algebra. Secondly, and strikingly, an Italian school sharply advanced the cause of the algebra of polynomial equations when it solved equations of the third and fourth degree in terms of radicals (Scipione del Ferro, Ludovico Ferrari, Nicolo Tartag-

lia, Geronimo Cardano). Thirdly, a French school, mainly represented by François Viète, achieved a synthesis of these two developments. And finally, an "international" school laid the foundation for the eventual rise of analysis by introducing and studying two special classes of functions, trigonometric functions and logarithms. Regiomontanus, Rheticus, Johann Werner, and later Viète gradually made trigonometry an independent part of mathematics, and Henry Briggs and John Napier (and perhaps also Jost Bürger) created the logarithmic (and hence also exponential) functions. After that, for over three centuries trigonometric and logarithmic functions were the stepping-stones leading to the realm of analysis, for students of mathematics on all levels.

There is a near-consensus among social historians that the rise of arithmetic and algebra during the Renaissance was motivated "preponderantly by the rise of commerce in the later Middle Ages; so that the challenges to which the rise of algebra was the response were predominantly the very unlofty and utilitarian demands of counting houses of bankers and merchants in Lombardy, Northern Europe and the Levant" (Bochner, *Role . . .* , p. 38). On this explanation, the socioeconomic needs that were thus satisfied were not those of the "industrialist" but those of the merchant, in keeping with the fact that in the late Middle Ages, and soon after, the general economy was dominated not by the producer but by the trader (ibid.).

The Seventeenth Century. There was one thing that the mathematics of the Renaissance era did not achieve. It did not continue creatively the mathematics of Euclid, Archimedes, and Apollonius, even if it did begin to translate and study their works. The exploitation in depth of Greek mathematics was achieved only in the seventeenth century, in the era of the Scientific Revolution. It is this development that created the infinitesimal calculus, and thus molded the world image which we have inherited today. For instance, Johannes Kepler anticipated the infinitesimal calculus in two ways; by his approach to Archimedean calculations of volumes, and also by his manner of reasoning which led him to conclude that planetary orbits are not circles but ellipses; and without his intimate knowledge of Apollonius this conclusion would have hardly come about. Next, René Descartes' avowed aim in his *La Géométrie* was to solve or re-solve geometrical problems of the great Greek commentator Pappus (third century A.D.) who was groping for topics and attitudes in geometry that were beyond his pale. Now, Descartes' technical equipment was the operational apparatus of Viète, and it was this fusion of Viète with Pappus that created our coordinate and algebraic geometry. Next, Isaac Barrow, the teacher of Isaac

Newton, perceived the importance of Euclid's 5th book (theory of proportion in lieu of our theory of positive real numbers) for the eventual unfolding of analysis. And, finally, Newton himself, by an extraordinary tour-de-force, pressed his forward-directed *Principia* (*Principles of Natural Philosophy*) into the obstructive mold of backward-directed but powerful Archimedism. That this impressment was even harder on Newton's readers than on Newton is attested to by a memorable statement (in the nineteenth century) of William Whewell:

The ponderous instrument of synthesis [meaning Archimedism], so effective in his hands, has never since been grasped by one who could use it for such purposes; and we gaze at it with admiring curiosity, as on some gigantic implement of war, which stands idle among the memorials of ancient days, and makes us wonder what manner of man he was who could wield as a weapon what we can hardly lift as a burden (Whewell, I, 408).

To sum it up, it was not the Renaissance proper of the fifteenth and sixteenth centuries that saw the "rebirth" of antiquity as much as it was the succeeding Scientific Revolution of the seventeenth century. What the Renaissance did was to contribute a prerequisite algebraic symbolism, and this was something that, from our retrospect, antiquity might have additionally produced out of itself but did not.

The Age of Enlightenment. The merits and achievements of this age are subject to most diverse and divergent interpretations. For instance, Carl Becker, in a small but unforgettable book, *The Heavenly City of the Eighteenth-century Philosophers* (1932), proposed that, on the whole, the intellectual attitudes of the age were medieval rather than modern, Voltaire or no Voltaire. Notwithstanding assertions by some historians of science, the advancement in physical science was rather circumscribed. For instance, the eighteenth century did not achieve much in the theory of electricity, at any rate not before Henry Cavendish and C. A. Coulomb, who were active towards the end of the century after the sheen of the Enlightenment had already been dimmed. Also, optics virtually stood still for over a century. After the lustrous works of Newton, Christiaan Huygens, and others in the seventeenth century almost nothing memorable happened in optics till the early part of the nineteenth century when Thomas Young, Étienne-Louis Malus, Augustin Fresnel, William Hyde Wollaston, and Joseph von Fraunhofer began to crowd the field. Furthermore, Immanuel Kant's famous *Critiques* came toward the end of the eighteenth century, after the "true" Enlightenment had begun to fade; and Kant's predecessors in metaphysics earlier in the century had been not a whit better than Kant had depicted them.

But the eminence of mathematics in the era of Enlightenment is clear-cut. It was a very great century. Mathematicians like G. W. Leibniz, Jacob and John Bernoulli, A. C. Clairaut, L. Euler, J. le R. D'Alembert, P. L. M. de Maupertuis, J. L. Lagrange, and P. S. de Laplace made it as distinctive a century as any since Pythagoras among the Greeks, or even since the age of Hammurabi in Mesopotamia. Also the age had one feature that made it simply unique. It fused mathematics and mechanics in a manner and to a degree that were unparalleled in any other era, before or after. Also, in mathematics, far from being a "medieval" age as in Carl Becker's conception of the eighteenth century, it was a very "modern" age. Monumental as Newton's *Principia* (1686) may have been, it is Lagrange's *Mécanique analytique* (1786) that became the basic textbook of our later physical theory. Lagrange's treatise is old-fashioned, but *readable*, Newton's treatise is "immortal," but antiquarian, and very difficult.

It is not easy to follow in depth the growth of this mathematics in relation to other developments of the era. Socioeconomic motivations do not account for its high level, and there are no explanations from general philosophy that are convincing. Immanuel Kant, for instance, shows no familiarity at all with the advanced mathematics of his times.

The Nineteenth Century. In the history of knowledge, even more complex than the era of Enlightenment is an era following it. It is, schematically, the half-century centered in the year 1800, that is the half-century 1776–1825, which has been called the Age of Eclosion by Bochner. During this era there was a great and sudden outburst of knowledge in all academic disciplines; and in historical studies of various kinds, there emerged a "critical" approach to the evaluation of source material, which is sometimes called "higher criticism." In mathematics there was no such sudden increase of activity, but an analogue to the "higher criticism" did begin to manifest itself. A critical approach to so-called foundations of mathematics began to spread, and even novel patterns of insight were emerging. Thus, C. F. Gauss in his *Disquisitiones arithmeticae*, which appeared in 1801, explicitly formulated the statement that any integer can be represented as a product of prime numbers, and uniquely so. Implicitly the statement is already contained, between the lines, in Book 7 of Euclid's *Elements*. But explicitly the statement is a kind of "existence" and "uniqueness" theorem, for which even number theorists like Fermat, Wallis, Euler, and Lagrange were "not ready" yet.

Afterwards, in the course of the nineteenth century, mathematics filled all those "gaps" in Greek mathematics, which the Greeks themselves could not or would not close. Thus, the nineteenth century finally elucidated the role of Euclid's axiom on parallels, and the role of axioms in general, as well as in geometry; and it finally constructed a "Euclidean" space as a background space for (Greek) mathematical figures and astronomical orbits. In a peculiar logical sense, Greek mathematics was "completed" only around 1900, but by the developments which brought this about, it was also rendered "antiquarian" by them. On the other hand, "humanistic" Greek works like those of Homer and Aeschylus, Herodotus and Thucydides, and Plato and Aristotle were not "completed" in a similar sense, but they have, on the other hand, not been rendered "antiquarian," as shelves full of reissues of these works in paperback can attest.

This completes our preliminary observations, and we now turn to two topics from antiquity for a somewhat less summary analysis.

Phonetic Writing. We are taking it for granted that within the history of civilization there is a correlation, an important one, between the rise of organized knowledge and the emergence of adequate writing, the degree of adequacy being measured by the degree of phonetic articulation. With a suitable definition of "phonetic," we may say that Chinese writing is a fully developed phonetic system, and has been so since its appearance about the middle of the second millennium B.C. (Gelb, p. 85). Now, mathematics is the oldest organized knowledge there is, or nearly so, and our problem is the task of assessing the role of mathematics in this correlation between knowledge and writing.

On hard evidence, the presence of organized mathematics is first attested around 1800 B.C. Now, our first intricacy is the fact that this first evidence for organized mathematics appears in two separate areas simultaneously, in Mesopotamia and in Egypt (Neugebauer, Chs. 1–3). This simultaneity of appearance cannot be readily explained by invoking a "cultural diffusion" or only a "stimulus diffusion" because by intent and content these two mathematics are very different from each other (Neugebauer, loc. cit.; van der Waerden, Chs. 1–3). Both these systems of mathematics are documented by writing that is highly organized (see Gelb, pp. 168ff., for Egypt, and Kramer, p. 306, for Mesopotamia), but of seemingly different provenance. In both geographical areas the mathematics in use appears to be a full part of organized knowledge in general. Also, from our retrospect, the Mesopotamian mathematics even gives the impression of having been in the very vanguard of organized knowledge, although to an "average Mesopotamian" of the era, the code of Hammurabi may have been more important, and, above all, much more familiar.

At this point it might be expected that if writing and knowledge reach a certain stage of organization conjointly, then organized mathematics would do so too. But this would be a very hasty expectation, as can be seen from the development in an area that geographically and intellectually was very proximate to both Mesopotamia and Egypt, namely, the land of the Bible, where writing of various modes was organizing itself in the latter half of the second millennium B.C., and in this area it was even advancing towards its ultimate stage, namely, to the stage of becoming entirely alphabetical (Gelb, pp. 134–53). At the same time, juridical, ethical, and sacerdotal knowledge was organizing itself too, and much of it became ultimately knowledge for the ages. Yet, the history of mathematics knows absolutely nothing about an indigenous mathematics also springing up in this area at the same time. This is our most serious intricacy.

A different problem arises—and it is a research task rather than a conundrum—when we take into account Greek achievements, from the first millennium B.C. It is a fact that the Greeks made writing fully alphabetical. They thus created "a writing which expresses the single sounds of a language" (Gelb, p. 197), and their script was undoubtedly more advanced than Babylonian script from around 1800 B.C. Similarly, the mathematics which the Greeks began shaping within their own thought patterns in the sixth century B.C. was, even from the first, undoubtedly more advanced than the Babylonian mathematics from around 1800 B.C. Now, the research task arising is to determine whether these two advances are commensurate in extent. Greek mathematics drew, as heavily as it could, on all the accumulated mathematics that preceded it. Nevertheless, it is immediately clear that the Greek intellectual innovation in organized mathematics—as also in organized knowledge of any kind—was far greater than the parallel advance in the phonetic quality of writing. An analysis in depth might counteract this impression. But such an analysis could not be an easy one, because it would also have to account for the fact that modern mathematics is immeasurably superior to the Greek creation, although "from the Greek period up to the present nothing has happened in the inner structural development of writing" (Gelb, p. 184).

Finally, we wish to observe that both for organized mathematics and organized writing it is equally difficult to decide whether in China either came into being independently of the West, or in direct dependence on the West, or by a combination of the two possibilities at different times. For organized mathematics the problem of its geographic propagation in Asia was already known, more or less, in the nineteenth century, perhaps under the impact of the corresponding problem for language as it is spoken. In the twentieth century the problem for mathematics has received less attention than the corresponding problem for writing, early or organized, probably because for mathematics the problem has been less able to exploit achievements in archeology than those in writing. For instance, for writing there is a balanced account of the problem in Gelb, Ch. VIII, but there seems to be no analogous account for mathematics.

Dissolution of Ancient Civilization. By "ancient civilization" we mean, as usual, the large conglomeration of component civilizations of so-called antiquity that severally came into being in and around the Mediterranean Littoral. In the last centuries B.C. and first centuries A.D., the conglomeration merged into one compound civilization, creating "one civilized world," the self-styled *oikouméne*. The passing-away of this civilization constitutes one of history's greatest problems. The central part of this problem is the seemingly "formal" question of determining when ancient civilization terminated, if indeed it did "terminate"; or, rather, since the termination was probably a process of some duration, when the process of termination began and when it ended.

It is widely accepted that the process ended towards the close of the fifth century A.D., as symbolized by the fact that in 476 A.D. "the last claimant to the Roman throne in the West was deposed" (Kagan, p. viii). An almost lone dissenter among historians, but a leading one, is Henri Pirenne, who maintains that ancient civilization was brought to an end—and then rather violently so—only in the seventh century A.D., by the widespread militancy of Islam. Ancient civilization was then not actually "killed," but rather pushed away from its Mediterranean habitat into more northern parts of Europe, where it became isolated and immobilized for centuries (Havighurst, 1958).

Another kind of dissent, a qualified one, is caused inevitably by the fact that there was an Eastern Roman Empire which lasted very long, until 1453 A.D. Most Byzantinists of today find that this empire was very viable in 476 A.D. and beyond, until the onset of the Crusades at any rate. They do not deny that there was a ruin of the Western Empire in the fifth century, but most of them do not allow that this ruin came about, to a meaningful degree, by decay from within. They argue that the causes for decay from within would have been present also in the Eastern half of the Empire, and should have had the same destructive effect at the time (Jones, Ch. 24; J. B. Bury, quoted in Kagan, pp. 7–10), so that, in their view, only military and other external causes remain. A very outspoken champion of this view is Lynn White, Jr., and he is severely critical of the details, attitudes, and emphases in Edward Gibbon's key work, *Decline and Fall of the Roman Empire* (White, pp. 291–311).

With regard to the beginning of the process of the decline of ancient civilization widely spaced dates have been proposed, explicitly or by implication. F. W. Walbank finds ". . . the germs of the illness of antiquity already present in the Athens of the fifth century B.C." (Kagan, p. viii). This is a very early date indeed. Less extreme is the finding of M. I. Rostovtzeff that "decline began as early as the second century B.C." (Kagan, p. 2). Finally "according to Gibbon, the Roman Empire reached its zenith in the age of the Antonines [second century A.D.] after which the decline set in" (White, p. 25). Thus, by implication, in the view of Gibbon the decline set in around 200 A.D., after the era of the "Five Good Emperors" (90–180 A.D.).

We proceed now to review the cogency of the above dates in the light of the history of mathematics.

The history of mathematics fully corroborates the familiar textbook assertion that around 500 A.D. a large-scale decline occurred. Mathematics as an intellectual activity—as an academic discipline, so to speak—was suddenly lost from sight, as if swallowed up by a wave of a flood, or buried by a sandstorm. In the Latinized West there had been a mathematics bearing the telltale mark of a Greek heritage even when dealing with non-Greek or extra-Greek topics of the mathematical corpus. It was this kind of mathematics that suddenly disappeared. Also in the West, this kind of mathematics came fully to surface only after seven centuries or so, in the famous *Liber abaci* of Leonardo of Pisa (Fibonacci) around 1200 A.D. This is not to say that in the intervening centuries mathematics was unknown in the West. A mathematics of a kind was of course included in school curricula. There were some translations from the Arabic, especially during the so-called twelfth-century Renaissance. There was also a certain pursuit of "utilitarian" mathematics, even during the so-called Carolingian Renaissance (Smith, I, 175–220). But, before the work of Fibonacci, this pursuit did not evince a quest for the kind of originality, if only on a modest scale, with which mathematics had been imbued since the sixth century B.C., when the Greeks had begun to weave mathematics into the texture of their rationality.

This decay of Greek mathematics did not spare the Eastern Roman empire, which, by an official reckoning, lasted from 529 to 1453, from Justinian to the fall of Constantinople. As far as mathematics is concerned this Empire might have never been. There is an encyclopedic treatise which lists the extant Byzantine writings, including works on mathematics and cognate subjects (Krumbacher, pp. 620–26). The mathematical works of the collection bespeak sterility and stagnation, and only in the art of warfare were there some elements of originality (Taton, p. 446).

Finally, we note that, in the judgment of a leading student of chronological innovations (Ginzel, III, 178ff.), at the beginning of the sixth century A.D. the Roman Canonist Dionysius Exiguus founded our present-day system of designating years by A.D. and B.C. This event, even if conceived very modestly by its author, was, from our retrospect, mathematically tinged, and it took place in Rome, after its "official" fall, even if not long after it. Thus, this may be viewed as a mathematical corroboration of the fact—which was stressed, from very different approaches, by Henri Pirenne, Lynn White, and probably others—that the political fall of Rome in 476 A.D. was not, instantly, also a social and intellectual disintegration.

This achievement of the Roman Canonist, modest as it may appear to be when viewed in isolation, cannot be overestimated as a determinant of history. The Greeks never quite succeeded in introducing a comparable dating of years. Mathematically this would have amounted to introducing a coordinate system on the time axis, and the Greeks never achieved this. Furthermore, it is remarkable that the "Christian" era of Dionysius not only became a "common" era but has turned out to be the most durable era ever. The French Revolution of 1793, the Russian Revolution of 1917, the Italian Revolution of 1922, and the German Revolution of 1933, each attempted to introduce a new era beginning with itself, but none really succeeded or even made the attempt in earnest. Our "common" era, however "Christian" by origin, has become a standard institution that cannot be tampered with.

We now turn to the question of mathematical evidence for the beginning of the decline of ancient civilization. Firstly, mathematics clearly concurs with the assertion of Rostovtzeff that a general decay began in the second century B.C. Secondly, mathematics can offer no tangible corroboration of the fact, known from general history, that life in the Greco-Roman world was much bleaker in the third century A.D. than in the preceding one. Thirdly, and finally, mathematics can even corroborate the thesis of Walbank that germs of some of the illnesses of antiquity can already be found in the Athens of the fifth century B.C.; namely, by a tour-de-force, we may elicit from the nature of Greek mathematics some peculiar comment of the thesis, which can be interpreted as a corroboration of it, in a sense.

Greek mathematics built on a considerable body of mathematics that had preceded it, but it was nevertheless a singular achievement of ancient civilization as a whole, and a hallmark of its Hellenic aspect in particular. Naively or boldly, the Greeks made a fresh start. They were inspired to begin from a new beginning and they succeeded. They erected an edifice of mathematics that was a veritable "system" in our present-day sense of the word. The bricks and stones in the edifice may have been Egyptian, Babylonian, or other, but the structure was Greek. This Greek mathematics attained its intellectual acme in the achievements of Archimedes. Isaac Newton even composed his *Principia* in an Archimedean *mise-en-scène*, but he acknowledged no indebtedness to an Egyptian calculus of fractions, or even a Babylonian calculus of quadratic equations, even if he knew anything about them at all.

From what is known, this Greek mathematics showed the first signs of being itself around 600 B.C. It then grew and kept unfolding for about four centuries, that is, till about 200 B.C., and the last of these four centuries, that is the era from 300 B.C. to 200 B.C., was a culminating one. In fact, around 300 B.C. Euclid composed his *Elements*, Archimedes flourished around 250 B.C., and around 200 B.C., Apollonius produced his monumental *Conics.*

But after that, in the second century B.C., unexpectedly and inexplicably, as if on a signal, the development of this mathematics came almost to a halt. After 200 B.C. it began to level off, to loose its impetus, and then to falter, bringing to the fore only such works as those of a Nicomedes, Dioclos, and Hypsicles. The phenomenon was no passing setback but a permanent recession, the beginning of a decline. It was, for mathematics, the beginning of the end in the conception of Rostovtzeff, even if the true end itself, that is the final extinction of Greek mathematics in its own phase, came only considerably later, around 500 A.D., that is, around the time of the fall of Rome.

It is noteworthy though, that the second century B.C., as if to almost show that it was not entirely down and out, produced the astronomer Hipparchus, famed discoverer of the precession of the equinoxes; and that the second century A.D., as if to lay claim to being indeed a "good" century, brought forth his great "successor" Claudius Ptolemy, author of the majestic *Almagest,* and of a *Geography.* It must be stated however, emphatically, that in "basic" mathematics Ptolemy was in no wise farther along than Archimedes, even if the *Almagest,* as an astronomical text, was a live text still for Copernicus in the first half of the sixteenth century and began to become antiquarian only half a century later in consequence of the mathematically articulated innovations of Kepler.

Limitations of Greek Mathematics. The reasons that have been variously adduced for the dissolution of ancient civilization—the overextension of the *oikouméne* so that "the stupendous fabric yielded to the pressure of its own weight"; inadequacy of industrialization and too much involvement with slave labor;

declining manpower; loss of economic freedom; "the gradual absorption of the educated classes by the masses"; "the pitiful poverty of Western Rome"; etc. (Kagan, pp. xi and xii)—may all help to account for the *ultimate* extinction of Greek mathematics, around 500 A.D., after a gradual decline of long duration. One may even add the view of J. B. Bury that "the gradual collapse . . . was the consequence of *a series of contigent events.* No general cause can be assigned that made it inevitable" (ibid.).

But, in the case of mathematics there is one peculiar fact which no such reasons from general history can really account for. It is the fact that in the second century B.C., much before the ultimate extinction, the decline of mathematics from the heights which it had attained in the preceding century was seemingly too large, too brusque, and too unmotivated by internal developments to be satisfactorily explained by general reasons of this kind. By standard criteria of advancement, mathematics in the third century B.C. was in a state of upward development, and it suggests itself that the rather sudden break in the development after 200 B.C. may have been due, at least in part, to some particular reasons applying to mathematics only. This is indeed our suggestion, and we shall attempt to formulate it.

In the third century B.C., Greek mathematics was not only very good, but it also reached a climax. By this we mean that it reached a level of development that was maximal relative to the intellectual base, mathematical and philosophical, on which it had been erected and on which it rested. Therefore, mathematics could have continued to develop in the second century B.C. and later only if the overall intellectual base on which it rested could also have been broadened in the process. But of this kind of broadening of the total intellectual setting of mathematics, Greek civilization in the second century B.C. was no longer capable. The general intellectual basis for Greek mathematics, which in a sense never broadened or deepened, was laid in the sixth and fifth centuries B.C., especially the latter, and in this peculiarly conceived sense it can be said that, as far as mathematics is concerned the decline of Greek civilization reaches back even into the fifth century B.C. (Walbank).

In order to demonstrate that the mathematics of Archimedes and Apollonius was overripe relative to its intellectual basis we shall compare the conceptual setting in Archimedes and Apollonius with the corresponding setting in Newton's *Principia* (1686), even if Newton's work came nineteen centuries later. A comparison of the works of Archimedes and Apollonius (and Pappus) with *La Géométrie* (1637) of Descartes, which was published half a century before the *Prin-*

cipia, would not serve our present purpose, because Descartes does not retain the setting of antiquity. On the contrary, he radically changed the technical setting by a full recourse to the apparatus of algebraic symbolism as made ready for him by Viète. Not so Newton. He was most expert in the handling of this apparatus, and on occasions he employed it more penetratingly than Descartes and others; but, for reasons best known to himself he elected to cast the *Principia* in a mold of Archimedean technicalities, outwardly, that is. In the *Principia* there are hardly any analytical formulas; but there are circumlocutions and verbalized formulae which, at times, seem to be as condensed and sterotyped as in Archimedes. This makes for hard reading nowadays, but it makes it easy to isolate differences of approach and setting. The differences are enormous, and we list the following ones.

Newton prominently introduced an underlying overall space, his absolute space, as a background space for both mathematics and mechanics. The Greeks achieved nothing like it. They certainly did not introduce a space for mechanics and mathematics jointly. They did introduce a "place" for events in nature which perhaps served as a space of mechanics, but they most certainly did not ever introduce a space of mathematics, or any kind of space of perception, physical, logical, or ontological. In mathematics, they had "loci" for individual figures when constructed, but not a space for such figures before being constructed. In short, the Greeks did not have any kind of space in the sense of Descartes, or Newton, or John Locke.

Newton expressly introduced in his mechanics a *translational momentum* (quantity of motion), defining it, for a mass particle moving on a straight line, as the product $m \cdot v$ in which the factor m is the constant amount of mass of the particle and v is its instantaneous velocity. Archimedes, in his theory of the lever, ought to have introduced the conception of a rotational momentum, defining it as the product $l \cdot p$ in which the factor l is the length of an arm of the lever and p is the weight suspended from this arm. But Archimedes did not introduce such a concept, nor did Greek mathematical thought ever conceptualize a product like $l \cdot p$; and mechanics went on marking time for almost 2000 years.

Even more significantly, Newton had the concept of a function constantly in his thinking, however covertly. Altogether since the seventeenth century the concept of a function kept on occurring in many facets and contexts, in mathematics as well as in other areas of cognition. Greek cognition, however, never had the notion of function, anywhere. Even the absence of products like $l \cdot p$ from Greek thinking was part of the absence of functions, inasmuch as in mathematics of today a product $l \cdot p$ for variable values of l and p, is a function on the set of pairs (l,p). More centrally, in cognition today the most important component of the concept of function is the notion of *relation*, however elusive it may be, to define or even describe what a relation is. Aristotle, the creator of the academic discipline of logic, did not anticipate the importance of *relation* (which he terms *pros ti*), nor did the Stoic logicians after him. But in modern developments, the creation of an algebra or logic by the American philosopher-logician Charles Sanders Peirce was his most outstanding logical achievement.

Operationally, functions occur in Newton's *Principia* in the following way. If a mass particle moves on the x-axis and t denotes the time variable, then Newton covertly assumes that there is a function $x(t)$ which is the instantaneous distance of the particle from a fixed origin. He forms the derivative dx/dt for variable t, which is a new function $v = v(t)$. It is the instantaneous velocity of the motion. He multiplies this by the constant value m of the mass, thus introducing the instantaneous quantity of motion $m \cdot v(t)$, which is again a function in the variable t. Newton then crowns these covert assumptions with the hypothesis, which is apparently due to himself, that the force F which brings about the motion is, at every instant, equal to the rate of change of the quantity of motion, $F = d(mv)/dt$.

This hypothesis, coupled with Newton's specific law of gravitation, created our exact science of today. The Greeks did not conceive of any part of this entire context of assumptions and hypothesis, not because they were unable to form a derivative of a function, but because they did not have in their thinking the concept of a function that is a prerequisite to forming the various derivatives involved. By maturity of insight, Archimedes was better equipped than Newton to carry out the limit process that is involved in the formation of a derivative, if only the concept of function and the entire prerequisite setting had been given to him.

The Greek lack of familiarity with the concept of function does not manifest itself only in mathematical mechanics, which, to the Greeks was a relatively esoteric topic, but also in the entire area of geometry, which, by a common conception, was a stronghold of Greek rationality. There is a purely geometrical context, common to Archimedes and Newton, in which Newton does, and Archimedes does not have functions in his thinking. Namely, Newton views the tangent to a curve at a point of the curve as the limiting position of a secant through the fixed point and a variable point of the curve, so that, in effect, he performs the operation of differentiation on "hidden" coordinate functions. Greek mathematics, however, never broke through to this all-important view, but persisted in the

view, known from Euclid, that a tangent to a curve is a straight line which in its entire extent coincides with the curve at one point only. Archimedes tries to adhere to this Euclidean definition even in his essay on (Archimedean) spirals, in spite of the complication, of which he is apparently aware, that any straight line in the plane of the spiral intersects it in more than one point. Without putting it into words, Archimedes overcomes the complication by a simple adjustment, but he does not advance towards the modern conception of a tangent as in Newton.

Epilogue. In modern mathematics the Greek limitations which we have adduced were overcome mainly by conceptual innovations, namely by the creation of abstractions, and of escalations of abstractions, which do not conform with the cognitive texture of Greek classical philosophy and general knowledge. There is an all-pervading difference between modern mathematical abstractions and, say, Platonic ideas; reductions of the one to the other, as frequently attempted in philosophy of mathematics, are forced and unconvincing. There are analogies and parallels between the two, but not assimilations and subordinations. The Greeks could form the (Platonic) idea of a "general" triangle, quadrangle, pentagon, and even of a "general" polygon, but the conception of a background space for Euclid's geometry was somehow no longer such an idea and eluded them. A Platonic idea, even in its most "idealistic" form, was still somehow object-bound, which a background space for mathematics no longer is. Nor could the Greeks form the "idea" of a rotational momentum, for it simply is no longer an "idea," and cannot be pressed into the mold of one. It is, quantitatively, a product $l \cdot p$ in which l and p represent "ideally" heterogenous objects, but are nevertheless measured by the same kind of positive real number; and real numbers themselves are already abstractions pressing beyond the confines of mere "ideas." Such fusion of several abstractions into one was more than the Greek could cope with; and the formation of (Newton's) translational momentum, as presented skeletally above, was even farther beyond their intellectual horizon.

If it is granted that Greek mathematics has been thus circumscribed, it becomes a major task of the history of ideas—and not only of the history of mathematics—to determine by what stages of medieval development, gradual or spontaneous—the inherited mathematics was eventually made receptive to symbolic and conceptual innovations during the Renaissance and after.

This task is inseparable from the task of determining the originality and effectiveness of medieval Arabic knowledge, mathematical and other, and its durable influence on the Latinized West. Only within this kind of setting will it be possible to comprehend the course of mathematics in its conceptual and cultural aspects.

BIBLIOGRAPHY

Carl Becker, *The Heavenly City of the Eighteenth-Century Philosophers* (New Haven, 1932). Salomon Bochner, *Eclosion and Synthesis, Perspectives on the History of Knowledge* (New York, 1969); idem, *The Role of Mathematics in the Rise of Science* (Princeton, 1966). Carl Boyer, *History of Mathematics* (New York, 1968). Karl H. Dannenfeldt, ed., *The Renaissance; Medieval or Modern?* (Boston, 1959). Wallace K. Ferguson, *The Renaissance in Historical Thought: Five Centuries of Interpretation* (Boston, 1948). I. J. Gelb, *A Study of Writing* (Chicago, 1952). F. K. Cinzel, *Handbuch der mathematischen und technischen Chronologie*, 3 vols. (Leipzig, 1914). Alfred F. Havighurst, ed., *The Pirenne Thesis: Analysis, Criticism, and Revision* (Boston, 1958). Tinsley Helton, ed., *The Renaissance: A Reconsideration of the Theories and Interpretations of the Age* (Madison, 1961). Donald Kagan, ed., *Decline and Fall of the Roman Empire: Why Did It Collapse?* (Boston, 1962). Samuel Noah Kramer, *The Sumerians: Their History, Culture, and Character* (Chicago, 1963). Karl Krumbacher, *Geschichte der byzantinischen Litteratur von Justinian bis zum Ende des oströmischen Reiches: (527–1453)*, 2nd ed. (Munich, 1897). Otto Neugebauer, *The Exact Sciences in Antiquity*, 2nd ed. (Providence, 1957). Isaac Newton, *Mathematical Principles of Natural Philosophy*, trans. A. Motte (Berkeley, 1946; rev. F. Cajori, 1962). Erwin Panofsky, *Renaissance and Renascences in Western Art* (Stockholm, 1960). David Eugene Smith, *History of Mathematics*, 2 vols. (Boston, 1923), esp. Vol. I. René Taton, ed., *A History of Science*, trans. A. F. Pomerans, 4 vols. (New York, 1963), Vol. I, *Ancient and Medieval Science*. B. L. van der Waerden, *Science Awakening* (Groningen, 1954). William Whewell, *History of the Inductive Sciences from the Earliest to the Present Time*, 3 vols. (London, 1837), 3rd ed. (New York, 1869), esp. Vol. I. Lynn White, Jr., *The Transformation of the Roman World: Gibbon's Problem after Two Centuries* (Berkeley and Los Angeles, 1966).

SALOMON BOCHNER

[See also **Infinity; Mathematical Rigor; Newton on Method;** Relativity; Renaissance Humanism; **Space;** Symmetry.]

CHANGING CONCEPTS OF MATTER FROM ANTIQUITY TO NEWTON

THE CONCEPTS of matter in the Western tradition exhibit bewildering confusion. Matter has been held to be essentially inert (ancient atomism) and inseparable from motion and action (L. Büchner; Marxism); essen-tially extended in space (Descartes) and composed of extensionless centers of energy (Leibniz, R. Boscovich); essentially unintelligible or unknowable (Plato, Berkeley, Kant) and the only perspicuous foundation for systematic philosophy (Hobbes); essentially and eternally actual (Democritus) and a form of being which is never more than potential (Plato, Hegel). Any effort to articulate a common focus of these concepts runs the risk of ignoring a formidable array of counter-instances and the certainty of accommodating some historical concepts far more awkwardly than others. Fortunately, one focus does not necessarily exhaust all other possibilities.

The term "matter" or its near synonyms has been used to designate: (1) the stuff of which something is constituted as contrasted with the structure or proportions according to which the stuff is organized. The structure is held to be what can be representatively expressed in ideas and words, if indeed the so-called structure in things is not considered the product of structures of thought or language; but the "material" aspect is precisely that whose existence is most radically other than such formulae.

(2) Matter therefore can only be indicated ostensively and this implies that it can occasion sensory effects. It is through these that it is first encountered in almost all accounts; in most accounts it is tangible in sufficient concentrations. Even when matter is subsequently defined, the definition may be based on an admitted hypothesis (e.g., the cause of sensations in Hobbes), or on an innate idea (e.g., the idea of extension in Descartes), rather than on any self-disclosure of matter itself. "Matter," therefore, has also connoted what confronts us but, at least initially, as unintelligible.

(3) This identification with "brute fact" seems also to account for the role of "matter" as a principle of individuation: formulae can migrate over the instances but the instances are sedentary. Even in many theories where such material facticity is held to be a philosophically inadequate basis for individuation it seems rather because these philosophies "dematerialize matter" than because the empirical connection of "matter" with individuals has been abandoned.

(4) Since the things which a given stuff can go to compose are transient, matter is identified with something that persists through change. The changing things are its appearances, actualizations, or emergents: matter is the more primitive and permanent substratum.

(5) The characterizations of interests as "material," of individuals and societies as "materialistic," and of interpretations of history as "materialist" illustrate usages, favorable or unfavorable, arising from practical concerns. While they obviously represent meaning

185

components additional to, and not always entirely inclusive of, those previously listed, it would be an error to ignore them. Ideas about matter in this sense have rarely developed in complete independence of the value-judgments of those who, on the one hand, found in "matter" a rubric for what they regarded as base and degrading, and those on the other, who liked to invoke it as assurance of their honest practicality.

I. ANCIENT CONCEPTS OF MATTER

1. Before Philosophy. Primitive cultures often possess techniques for transforming matter that are surprising anticipations of scientific methods. By 3,000 B.C. specially designed heating pots were being used in Mesopotamia for distillation of liquids and sublimation of ores, and not much later arts of alloy-making, glass-manufacture, and perfumery were widespread around the Eastern Mediterranean. Primitive cultures also develop elaborate accounts of the processes of material nature, principally in myths where the processes are translated into personal relations of natural deities and semi-deities. Technique and myth are heterogeneously mixed in ritual and magical practices. Such ritual concerns were surely reflected in a relatively sophisticated Babylonian theory of seven chief heavenly bodies, seven metals, seven principal parts of the human body, seven colors, seven days of the week, and seven stages of the soul's enlightenment—a theory which can, incidentally, remind us that progress towards a scientific theory of matter has consisted almost as much in the discovery of disillusioning disorder as of unanticipated order. In spite of the facts that beliefs and attitudes of enormous subsequent influence were formed at this mythological stage of intellectual development, it is difficult to speak of concepts of matter: matter had not yet been distinguished from other elements or aspects of experience.

The two ancient cultures that have had the most direct influence on the development of the Western world are the Hebraic and Greek, and even in the case of a concept so philosophical and scientific as that of matter it might be difficult to say which had had the greater. Both cultures moved away from cosmogonies where, as Thales is reported to have said, "All things are full of gods" and, where as might equally be said, all gods are full of natural forces. By the time of the eighth-century prophets, the Jews were sharply distinguishing Yahweh, the personal, ethical, and absolute lord of history, from the material world. The world correspondingly lost its divine immanence, a development illustrated by prophetic attacks on magic and soothsaying employed to cajole divine compliance, in favor of miracle and revelation, the uncoerced grace of Yahweh to those who served his moral and historical

ends (cf. Numbers 22–24, esp. 23:23; Deuteronomy 18:14–16). It is illustrated above all by the doctrine of creation: in Genesis 1 all the natural order (and no other order so much as entered into the account) was manipulable stuff from and in the hands of the creator. While there was no developed theory of God's immateriality, and in earlier Old Testament accounts God had appeared in bodily form and acted creatively through his breath, he was clearly now conceived in such a manner that the material world could not react reciprocally upon him. If the account was anthropocentric, it was not because man was not part of material creation but because he shared a moral personality with Yahweh.

2. The Pre-Socratics 600–400 B.C. It was with the Greeks that "matter" first emerged as a cosmological concept systematically distinguished from such contrasting notions as those of change, form, void, or mind. The fact that some of these distinctions are currently more vague than they have often previously appeared should not blind us to the enormous intellectual advance such distinctions represented. Of course, the conceptual clarifications came gradually: with the *physiologoi* of the sixth and fifth centuries B.C., the so-called Pre-Socratics, the interpreter is often unsure whether suggestive insights arise from profundities, or merely from the fragmentary character and ambiguities of the texts. The *archai* or "principles" which were the common quest of Ionian inquiry might be historical "origins," "units" composing the material world, or "axioms" of scientific theory.

Nevertheless these Ionian ventures beyond *mythos* and towards *sophia* exhibit progressions. (1) The sequence of material constituents, from Thales' water through Anaximenes' air to Heraclitus' fire, seems to reflect a growing concern that the basic stuff of nature be sufficiently active and refined to account for all its phenomena, including especially those of life, consciousness, and thought. (2) It has also been suggested by C. Lejewski (McMullin, pp. 25–36) that while Thales' water was that *from which* all things first came, Anaximander's *apeiron* ("the unlimited" or "unqualified") was also that *to which* they would eventually return, while the air of Anaximenes (and then the fire of Heraclitus) was in addition that *of which* all things presently consisted. If the fragmentary textual hints are reliable, they would represent an expansion from merely historical to properly metaphysical cosmology. (3) As to the forces effecting these transformations, in Anaximander there was an alternate *separating out* of variously qualified things from neutral stuff creating inequalities within it, and then the compensatory *return*. Anaximenes was concerned to account for the world's unity: its varieties were only products of con-

densation and rarefaction of the all-embracing *pneuma.*

Finally in Empedocles, and then in his successors, it was the *mixture* of separate and different elements (for Empedocles, earth, water, air, and fire) under varying influences (for Empedocles, love and hate) that explained change. This combination of material pluralism and structural monism has been called (Toulmin and Goodfield) "the first appearance in our scientific tradition of an important intellectual model." The general character of that model was preserved in the theory of "homeomerous seeds" statistically distributed under the action of *Nous* ("Mind," "Reason") in the theory of Anaxagoras.

The challenge which came to these Ionian "river gods" from the "patrons of Being," the Pythagoreans and the Eleatics—Parmenides, Melissus, and Zeno—could be described as an attack on "material" explanations of the world. Of course, just as Ionian hylozoism (animated matter) had introduced vitality as an immanent property of the material stuff, so Pythagorean and Eleatic "formalisms" were not entirely abstracted from a material base. Still the judgment of Parmenides that "only that can really exist which can also be thought" (Diels, 3, 8, 34) meant that shapes, patterns, and proportions could be assigned a metaphysical status equal to that of stuff. Indeed Pythagorean acoustic theory played a seminal role in the mathematization of matter and the origin of mathematical physics. Parmenides and Heraclitus provide at their sharpest the contrasts which had developed between the two traditions: permanent Being as against fluent becoming, unity as against plurality, and the requirements of conceptual thought as against the reports of sensory experience. Probably the sharpness of contrasts on questions of such ultimacy stimulated the remarkable outburst of ingenuity on the problem of matter that followed.

The "systematic period" of Greek philosophy, the century from 400 to 300 B.C., embracing the active careers of Democritus, Socrates, Plato, and Aristotle, produced a set of rival theories the contrasts among which foreshadowed many of the broad outlines that subsequent debate has followed. Francis Bacon suggested that these works survived in less fragmentary form than those of the Pre-Socratics only because they were less solid and so did not sink in the flood of barbarism terminating classical civilization. (*Novum Organum*, lxvii). The earlier theories no doubt had the advantage of a more intimate connection with the craft tradition, but craftsmen are not always boldly experimental, and Bacon's regret perhaps underestimates the importance to inquiry of clear and coherently organized concepts. At any rate Democritean atomism, Platonic organicism, and Aristotelian hylomorphism

have been recurrent ideas and pervasive influences in the development of the sciences of matter.

3. The Atomic Theory. The devices by which Democritus (ca. 460–367 B.C.) sought to resolve the conflict between Heraclitean change (witnessed by the senses) and Parmenidean permanence (required by logical thought) were (1) the perpetuation of Parmenides' distinction between appearance and reality, but (2) the differentiation within reality of permanent and immutable least parts of matter—"atoms"—on the one hand, from their perpetual changes of place on the other. All atoms were spatially extended, internally homogeneous, qualityless, solid, rigid, and indivisible; they differed in shape, size, characteristic positions in relation to one another, and consequent velocities. If there were many atoms of the same kind it was not because nature came in species but because, given a finite number of possible quantitative variations of an infinite number of atoms, "chance" must run to duplications. The permanent actuality of the atoms was postulated to avoid deriving being from non-being, but, in defiance of Parmenides, the existence of non-being was asserted in the form of the void to permit atomic motion. Atom and void differed solely as the full (or "well-kneaded") from the empty, but this one real distinction in the nature of things was the source of all others and indeed of all qualitative determinations found in sensory appearance. Time, for example, enjoyed no such ontological status as space (or void), but was the consequence of redistributions of full and empty, "an appearance under the forms of day and night" (Diels, 72). The impenetrability of matter, the total penetrability of space, and their shared dimensions determined natural processes with total and mathematical necessity.

Phenomena were clearly radically in excess of what the universe actually contained. Indeed Democritus probably and his Epicurean followers certainly conceived of philosophy precisely as an emancipation from the deceptions of the senses and emotions. Thus superstitious fear was, characteristically, the product of an overestimation of the capacity of the universe to inflict pain. The cure was provided in the all-inclusive science of the atom, the admittedly inferred but ultimately real least part; sensory (and *a fortiori* imaginary) appearance, by which "man is severed from the world" was a sort of amalgam, or at least product, of the juxtaposition of the atom with its conceptual opposite, the infinitely extended void. The theory, from its development by Leucippus and Democritus, and popularization (cum modifications) by Epicurus and Lucretius has since exercised an abiding attraction: on scientists because of the quantitative character of its model; on humanist reformers because of its antisepsis of religious beliefs and practices; and on all because of its simplicity, clarity, and obvious correspondence to significant mechanical aspects of macroscopic experience.

4. *Plato's Theory of Matter*. In Plato the permanent Being insisted upon by Parmenides and the Pythagoreans found its place in the real and eternal Ideas (forms, essences), while the flux of Heraclitus was represented in the becoming, opinion, and appearance of the empirical realm, matter providing the crucial relation between the two. But matter was not permanently actual as in Democritus: the material thing was "always in a process of becoming and never really is" (*Timaeus* 27e–28a). Nor was material change mere locomotion, but a radical generation and destruction of temporal existents (cf. *Laws* X, 894a). Again, whereas for Democritus matter and space were opposites, for Plato they were identified, for the Receptacle, that "hardly real" principle of which we can form only a "spurious conception" (*Timaeus* 52b) at once provided an occupiable space and yet also was the Mother, impregnated by the immaterial essences and providing the very stuff of the Offspring. The Offspring was the changing empirical object, a "moving image" of eternal Forms, and its essentially temporal character again was the product of the Receptacle. For Plato, then, unlike Democritus, temporal dimensions were as constitutive of material objects as spatial ones and it was impossible neatly to distinguish the two. Even when the verbal formulae sound quite similar, meanings are opposed, for when Plato spoke of "necessity" it was not of something following ineluctably from formal properties, but, contrarily, of resistance to the action of form. "The creation is mixed, being made of necessity and mind" and it was produced when "Mind, the ruling power, persuaded," and thus "got the better of [,] necessity" (*Timaeus* 47e–48a). Indeed such necessity was what was most essential to matter as Plato conceived it. Persuaded by the logical considerations that had earlier impressed Parmenides that changing empirical objects could not be real, he posited eternal and totally intelligible archtypes. But if these were the real, whence the disparity of their sensible appearances from them? Here Plato felt the need to introduce "a third thing" (*Timaeus* 48e–49a) and, like Democritus, to assert that in a certain sense non-being is (*Sophist* 241e); for both thinkers the argument seemed to require a principle contrary to full being. The "third thing" for Plato was the obscurely known Receptacle; it enabled him to account for imperfections in the earthly and mortal spheres because the very function he assigned to it was that of a principle of privation. Forms were universal, absolute, eternal, omnipresent, intelligible, harmonious, and perfect; their images in matter were particular, relative, temporal, localized,

confused, discordant, and defective. For Plato, therefore, matter was precisely what resisted and debilitated Form.

The foregoing account has deliberately emphasized methodological parallels between Democritus and Plato. It could be added that in both instances of accounting for the experienced as a mixture of contraries one of the contraries was matter. The functions assigned to it, however, as we have seen varied as radically as "being" and "non-being." Further, sharing Democritus' judgment of the deceptiveness of sense experience, Plato also saw philosophy as an emancipation from that illusion, but the contrast is more interesting; for while by appearance Democritus meant the surplus by which the epistemologically given exceeded what was ontologically there, Plato meant the deficiency by which it fell short. What distressed him was the "very melancholy" possibility that men would continue to live among diluted shadows and echoes and never reach "truth and the knowledge of realities" (*Phaedo* 90d).

In view of the foregoing contrasts it may seem surprising that Plato nonetheless sketched out a hypothesis of atomic structures (*Timaeus* 53c–58c). Certainly the dialectical method and the doctrine of hierarchically ordered Forms, to say nothing of his specific teachings on the "world-soul" (*Timaeus* 34–37), indicated an "organismic" disposition to explain parts in terms of the whole rather than the reverse. His theory of atomic elements was in fact a confirmation of his identification of matter with spatiality and his preference for geometrical structure over stuff as a principle of explanation. He equated Empedocles' four elements with four of the five regular convex solids Theaetetus had identified. He conceived of these solids as volumes bounded by two sorts of plane triangles, the half (diagonally cut) square and half equilateral triangle (cut from apex to base) which could be recombined according to various possible equations (Figure 1): for example, one liquid atom (an icosahedron with one hundred twenty triangles making up its surfaces) might be broken by the action of fire or air into two atoms of air (octahedrons with forty-eight surface triangles each, for a sum of ninety-six) plus one atom of fire (a tetrahedron with twenty-four surface triangles). Clearly so geometrical a hypothesis of ordered kinds of bodies must be seen as already an instance of Mind's "getting the better of necessity."

What remained most central to the Platonic view of matter, however, was the principle of non-being, the capacity of which to impede the teleology and intelligibility of full Being nevertheless obliges us to concede it a certain existence. It is almost an irony that Max Jammer in his search for the origins of the

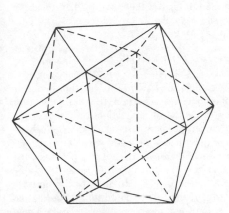
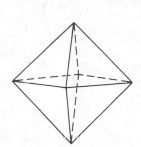
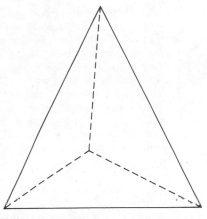

FIGURE 1.   1 liquid atom   2 air atoms   +1 fire atom
              (icosahedron: 20 sides,   (octahedron: 8 sides,   (tetrahedron: 4 sides,
              120 triangles)   48 triangles each)   24 triangles)

concept of mass—that most irreducible of material characteristics—should uncover a trail to the Neo-Platonic conception of the inertial passivity of matter. Johannes Kepler, a millennium and a half later, still found it appropriate to characterize as a "vice" the property of matter: "plump and clumsy to move itself."

5. *Aristotle's Theory of Matter.* Aristotle, like his two famous predecessors, hoped to synthesize the valid insights of rival predecessors, but the rivalry now more immediately felt was between (Platonic) "dialecticians" and (Democritean) "physicists." In his hylomorphism matter ceases to be one of the conceptual extremes whose mixture produces the experienced world and becomes rather the neutral substratum in which contrary properties succeed one another: "For my definition of matter is just this—the primary substratum of each thing, from which it comes to be without qualification and which persists in the result" (*Physics* 192a 31–32). The property of matter, therefore, was potentiality, the indeterminate capacity for receiving alternative actualizing forms. Whatever was in the world must be actual, and existent matter, therefore, was always under some form, e.g., that of an element, plant, or animal, but it was called "matter" by virtue of its continuing and further potentialities. Form involved at once a certain proportion of material parts and an eduction of previously unactualized properties from (or in) them.

The altered role for matter entailed modifications in the concepts of space and time. For both Democritus and Plato space had been a constitutive principle of the empirical world—as the independently existing arena for matter or as identical with it—but for Aristotle the form-matter substance was ontologically pri-

mary, and space was relativized into the sum total of its "places" (*Physics* iv. 1–5), a network of relations of containing and being contained among material substances. Similarly time had now to be conceived neither as an accident of eternal atoms nor as the ingredient of becoming in images (since Aristotle's material substances were neither all eternal nor all perishable), but again relationally in the "before's" and "after's" of given "now's." Finally the sense in which Aristotle found "necessity" in material change was neither that of mathematical determinism nor of resistance to the aspirations of Mind; it designated rather the potentialities without which a given actualization could not take place (e.g., growth without food, a saw without metal) on the *hypothesis* that nature or art were tending towards such actualization.

These contrasts can be traced to those of method. Aristotle is disposed to begin his analyses with the *proximate* stuff of *this* object, in *this* place, *now*, seemingly tending towards *this* end, because of his conviction that the objects of sensory experience are those most knowable to us. Sense neither radically embroiders upon nor radically impoverishes the actual constitution of such objects: the empirical world is part of actuality and the part to whose potential for producing form our cognitive potential for reproducing it most closely corresponds. Prime Mover and prime matter intrigued Aristotle as they have certainly intrigued his interpreters, but scientific or philosophic method was not conceived as mediation between them: they were conceptual extremes to which expanding sciences had finally come and they were conceivable only by analogy with the more familiar concepts of what lay between (*Posterior Analytics* 1. 2. 71b 32–72a 6; 12. 78a

13–21). The plurality of Aristotelian sciences is a consequence of conceiving philosophy as something other than emancipation from sensory deception: different sciences were pursued for different kinds of useful or interesting knowledge and at many formal levels. Matter *qua* matter was unintelligible at the level of abstraction of that of which it is the matter (e.g., bone is not itself an anthropological concept), but its own formal properties might be investigated at a more elementary level (e.g., in physiology or medicine). Of course Aristotle's particular pride was that by means of the actuality-potentiality distinction he thought he had given a consistent account of change, i.e., one in which nonbeing did not have to be invoked as an explanatory principle.

These three rival fourth-century cosmological theories have historically provided paradigm conceptual schemes for the centuries that have followed. The sharpness and pervasiveness of the contrasts almost tempt one to think them, in broadest outline, exhaustive. However the mixing of features in subsequent theories, to say nothing of new concrete knowledge discovered by the sciences and the modification of the conceptual elements which these discoveries make necessary, limit at least somewhat the extent to which it is helpful to characterize a theory as "Platonic" or "Aristotelian."

6. The Stoic Idea of Matter. At least one prominent theory of antiquity is related to the foregoing systems in so complex a way as to deserve separate treatment. The Stoic theory is particularly remarkable in assigning to matter many properties which were in contrast to those defined elsewhere. The theory was in a sense as insistent as the contemporary Epicurean atomism on grounding all quality and action in a material base, but this was matter that could act pervasively and simultaneously throughout an organically structured universe; matter the structures of which were not so much productive of, as concomitant with, its modes of action; matter that acted of necessity indeed, but in the realization of rational and moral ends. The "physics" of the school, whose greatest cosmologist was Chrysippus (ca. 280–206 B.C.), was inspired by that of Heraclitus: all the other three elements were ultimately reducible to fire, the breath of life or soul (*pneuma*), and their respective qualities followed from the diminished degree of their activity. The development of this protean theory of the *pneuma* into an elaborate and long-surviving theory of "nutritional," "vital," and "animal spirits" might incline one to think it scientifically unfortunate, but its modes of explanation have some affinities with contemporary ones in terms of "fields," "waves," and "energy." Toulmin and Goodfield credit the Stoics with "recognizing" and "tackling" "questions in matter-theory which have come to the fore again only in the twentieth century" (*The Architecture of Matter,* p. 108).

II. THE CONCEPT OF MATTER IN THE MIDDLE AGES

The medieval period was one of sometimes enlightening elaborations of inherited theories of matter rather than of significant innovations.

As philosophers became increasingly theological and the pagan Empire increasingly Christian, the dominant metaphysical paradigm was that of Plato. In fact one finds in the Neo-Platonists, the Gnostics, and the Manichaeans more radical statements of the hostility of matter to perfection, intelligibility, and order, and of its derivation from non-being than are to be found in Plato himself. In one respect, however, patristic thought can perhaps be said to be rather Aristotelian, though historically the origins lie in Judaism. Jews, Christians, and, later, Muslims were bound by biblical revelation to a doctrine of creation *ex nihilo,* a creation including that of matter and pronounced by God to be good. This left a generous but still limited latitude for variations. For one thing, if there was to be intellectual accommodation for both God and the world, organism must not be emphasized so far as to swallow up the creature, nor the independence of parts emphasized, as it was in atomism, to the extent that it would obviate the need of a Creator. Again, the Platonic characterization of the material world as "insubstantial appearance" might, if overstressed, undermine the genuineness of the creation; on the other hand the fully actual substances of atomism neither would need to be nor could be created. Finally, though there was no explicit theory of creation in Aristotle, his plurality of substances would at least permit an independently actual Creator and a dependently actual creation. Still, however much this may have impressed later medieval thinkers, the Patristics more immediately felt the tension of two inspirations: the *Timaeus* tradition of the artist-God achieving levels of order with materials that were not good, and the Judaic heritage in which all hierarchy in the material world (like Aristotle's between celestial and terrestrial spheres) was thrown in the shade by its universal creatureliness.

Alchemy, intrigued by the frequently dramatic transformations of matter and dedicated to redeeming it from its baser states, must probably be credited with the most sustained program of empirical investigation and with enough concrete discoveries so that both Newton and Boyle paid it the compliment of serious study. As to its theory alchemy represented a persisting tradition of interpreting the physical and chemical behavior of matter through biological, psychological, and even theological models: matter could be "begotten" in different species, induced to be more "noble," and "spiritualized" into its "essences." But its principal contributions to techniques and apparatus for fermentation, sublimation, distillation, and the like were matched by a multitude of scientifically advantageous technological advances in such fields as engineering, optics, metallurgy, and navigation, and historians have had increasingly to recognize the extent and sophistication of scientific inquiry within the universities from the thirteenth century onwards.

Although Robert Grosseteste's brief treatise *De luce* is of the mid-thirteenth century it illustrates impressively the "light metaphysics" that was a special form of the Neo-Platonic emanation-doctrine of the earlier Middle Ages. The first material substance created (after the "separate substances" which were pure forms) was light. It enjoyed this priority because of, in one direction, its kinship with intelligibility and, in the other, its tendency to uniform, instantaneous, and infinite self-plurification. It thus engendered a three-dimensional, spherical mass rarified at the periphery, condensed at the center, and within it the nine celestial spheres took form, each inner ring being related to the next outer as matter to form. The ninth, lowest, and sub-lunar sphere was that of the four elements: their differential weight behaviors sprang respectively from the "self-assembling virtue" prevalent in earth and water, and the "self-dispersing virtue" prevalent in air and fire. Grosseteste found anticipations of this cosmological system in pagan myth, speculating, for example that "Cybele" was etymologically derived from *cubus* and symbolized solidity. The theory also had its quantitative (or numerological) aspect: light, in which all other bodies were virtual, contained 4 basic constituents, and since the sum of its factors (1, 2, 3, 4) was 10, "it is clear that 10 is the full number of the universe."

The advent in the twelfth and thirteenth centuries of texts of Greek science, including predominantly the physical, astronomical, biological, and metaphysical texts of Aristotle, brought both a great upsurge in scientific interests and the beginnings of a new scientific orthodoxy. While sheer intellectual inertia no doubt played its role in the authority that Aristotle came to enjoy, the medievals were probably initially well advised to adopt a body of science far in advance of anything with which they had been previously acquainted, and thereafter the staying power of the theory was to a considerable extent the result of its range of use and success. But there also were developments within, and departures from, the imported doctrines.

(1) The controversy over the plurality or unicity of substantial forms which ranged Augustinian Platonists like Saint Bonaventura against more radical Aristotelians like Aquinas involved questions of matter both as principle of individuation and as proximate and pure potentiality. Against the Thomistic doctrine that there might be numerically distinct instances of things specifically identical in different "designated (ostensible) matters," the Platonists insisted that individuality was a function of a unique intersection of formal properties. Thomas' contention that with respect to man, for example, "soul is not another form than that through which three dimensions could be designated in the thing" (*De ente et essentia* ii), combined with the traditional Aristotelian teaching that substantial change involves a reduction to "prime matter" or "pure potentiality" seemed to deprive levels of form like "corporeity," "organism," and "animality" of their functions in nature. The dilemma in which the Aristotelians found themselves was that if existing substances could enter into a new substance (e.g., a child) without modification, the new substance was only a mechanical combination; but if there was a reduction of all incorporated substances to prime matter, it would seem that one ought to be able to produce any given substance from any given combination of proximate matters. To meet this difficulty they developed, beyond anything found explicitly in Aristotle, a theory of *virtutes*, or powers. These powers bore close resemblance to the substantial forms of the proximate matter prior to its ingredience in the new substance; they nevertheless represented some modifications by the new environment within the substance; and they were potentially restorable to their original states on the dissolution of the substance.

(2) There was also increasingly from the thirteenth century on a tendency towards more atomistic conceptions of matter. Augustine was typical of the early Middle Ages in maintaining its infinite divisibility: the diffuseness of matter thus stood at the opposite extreme from the total unity of God. Aquinas sharpened the Aristotelian distinction between the potentially infinite divisibility of the "intellectual matter" of mathematicals and the determinate quantities required in actual physical substances, including the elements (*Physicorum* lect. ix. 9–10). William of Ockham's reservation of "absolute existence" to substance and quality alone of the traditional ten categories meant that the view of nature as a network involving connective quantities, relations, and acts was yielding to a view of localized centers of formed matter. But in addition to this very general evolution of medieval thought from enthusiastic system towards critical, and even iconoclastic, analysis, there was specifically a doctrine of elementary minima being elaborated during the Renaissance within the Aristotelian tradition by such

natural philosophers as J. C. Scaliger and Daniel Sennert, so that the adoption of atomistic theories in the seventeenth century was not exclusively a matter of revival.

(3) Finally there seem to have been some anticipations during the latter Middle Ages of modern theories of force and mass. Jean Buridan (ca. 1299–ca. 1358), from whose rejection of Intelligences as movers of the heavenly spheres Duhem dated the beginning of modern science (*Etudes sur Léonard de Vinci* [1955], III, ix) helped to develop a theory of the preservation of motion by an originally impressed impetus which acted without diminution so long as it met no resistance. As for mass, Jammer finds significant the use by Giles of Rome, in his *Theoremata de corpore Christi* (1276), of the phrase *quantitas materiae* in a meaning exclusive of both volume and weight. Prior to the conceptualization of inertial mass by Kepler, natural philosophers like Buridan, Albert of Saxony, Nicole Oresme, and Richard Swineshead were identifying quantity of matter with a product of volume times density. In spite of the greater specificity with which questions about matter were being put, thanks to awakened interest, suspicion of traditional answers, and improved techniques, the late medievals had, of course, no way of determining quantity of matter and density independently.

THE EARLY MODERN PERIOD

It would perhaps be appropriate that a study of the concept of matter in modern times should be forced to consider the indispensable role of the relatively non-conceptual factors of technique and apparatus, for in terms of connotations of matter as they have been laid out these would represent the more material aspects of science. The principal concern here, however, must be with conceptual factors.

1. Changes in the Concept of Matter. Given the range of materials on concepts of matter from, say, Nicolas of Cusa (1401–64) to Isaac Newton (1640–1727) it is useful to try to summarize, roughly, while recognizing the inevitability of exceptions, what distinguishes the modern view from that of the preceding period. The chronological account that follows thereafter can then be selective and merely illustrative.

The medieval universe, whether described by Platonists or Aristotelians, was hierarchically ordered, e.g., in the astronomical distinction between celestial and terrestrial spheres, the biological order of rational, animal, and vegetable souls, and the alchemical division of nobler and baser materials; and almost universally the greater the material component of any nature, the lower in the hierarchy it fell. This view was sup-

planted by an effort to account for all of physical nature by one homogeneous matter operating throughout by one set of mechanical laws. There were no doubt some elements of coincidence in the mutual reinforcement given to this rejection of hierarchy by the growing success of Copernicus, Gilbert, Kepler, Descartes, and Newton in applying the principles of terrestrial mechanics to celestial movement on the one hand, and the emphasis of the Protestant Reformers on the absolute and unmediated sovereignty of God over every creature on the other. Perhaps a majority of the working "natural philosophers" of the early modern period felt that double motivation.

It is relatively easy to detect in the Middle Ages a pattern of transition from the early Platonic syntheses (patristics), to an Aristotelian system of sciences (thirteenth century onwards), to late medieval analysis and critique (especially from the fourteenth century onwards); and the increasingly "atomistic" modes of thought even went so far in Nicolas of Autrecourt (fl. 1340), a philosopher-theologian of the Ockhamist school, as the claim that the hypothesis of Lucretius was preferable to that of Aristotle. The Church was able to repress heretical speculation in Nicolas, but increasingly in the Renaissance the whole range of ancient methods and systems (Platonic corpus by Ficino's translation, 1463–69; Lucretius by 1417) was again available—the Platonic conception of parts as dependent aspects of wholes, the Democritean understanding of wholes as collections of independent parts, and the Aristotelian distinction of essential from accidental in the experientially given. All these resources were exploited by various thinkers and in various mixtures, but it was the long-neglected possibilities of atomism that were most revolutionary. As the "closed world," centered first on the earth and then on the sun, became observationally and conceptually untenable, atomism's postulate of an "infinite universe" seemed scientifically confirmed.

The enthusiasm for "corpuscular philosophy," found in some guise or other in all the most productive thinkers of the time, meant that quantitative or "primary" properties such as extension, duration, and velocity—properties the mathematical statement of which corresponded in fairly direct fashion to what was actually experienced—became the basis of causal explanations. The old "substantial forms" and "sensible species," which were incapable of such equivalent mathematical statement, were rejected as "occult qualities," unverifiable and redundant, and as "secondary" properties resulting from the action of the "primary" ones but having no status other than that of "appearance" in the mind. It further followed that teleological explanations, certainly in terms of the ends inherent in the natures of particular macroscopic species, and, more cautiously, in terms of the general welfare of nature as a whole, were increasingly rejected as unphilosophical. The "great book" of the universe, said Galileo, "is written in the mathematical language—triangles, circles, and other geometrical figures, without whose help it is impossible to comprehend a single word of it . . ." (*Il saggiatore*, sec. 6).

What substituted for patterns of behavior immanent in the forms of a hierarchy of beings from enmattered elements, plants, and animals to immaterial "Intelligences" and God were "laws of nature," usually conceived as externally imposed upon matter at its creation by God. Descartes in some ways carried this tendency further than anyone else. He first correctly formulated the principle of inertia in terms of rest or uniform rectilinear motion. Making sheer geometrical extension the essence of material body, and postulating a law of the conservation of motion (whatever the directional variations), he found it necessary to introduce force or causal agency (as contrasted with inertial transfer of motion) at only one point, God's creative and sustaining fiat. Thinkers such as Spinoza, Malebranche, Leibniz, and Newton were unwilling to centralize physical causality in exactly the Cartesian way, but the occasionalism of Malebranche, the preestablished harmony of Leibniz, and even the monism of Spinoza show Descartes' influence or the same influences that persuaded him. *Cum deus calculat fit mundus* ("As God calculates so the world happens"), and the confidence that the laws of nature would be relatively few and rationally ordered was sustained by the belief in their origin in one supremely rational mind.

While, therefore, there was a revival of atomistic and mechanistic modes of thought in the sixteenth and seventeenth centuries, there was a difference, and it also helps to account for their wider influence in modern times. Given the sociological position of the institutional churches, early science would certainly have had a far more stormy reception if it had not been disposed to use God as the ready-to-hand *deus ex machina* in many a difficulty, or supposed difficulty, where it turned out to be convenient to think of the *machina ex deo*. Thus most—not all—of the champions of corpuscular philosophy held that God had first created the atoms; that the laws by which they were governed, however mechanical, were directed to providential ends; and that human consciousness represented a substance as real as, though radically different from, physical matter.

In metaphysical terms this very often meant that materialistic themes were combined with Platonic as in Descartes, Spinoza, and Leibniz. An interesting case

in point is on the question of the infinite divisibility of matter, denied by ancient atomism, maintained by Descartes and his active school. This was a traditional Platonist doctrine, for such diffuseness at the lower extremity of the "chain of being" was the appropriate dialectical contrary to the absolute and spiritual Unity at its head. It seems clear that Descartes could ignore the atomists' argument that *existence must* finally have its irreducible units, because his matter or extension was an imperfect grade of substance (less perfect than thinking substance, for example) which existed only on the continuing sufferance of God. When Leibniz revived the argument that there could be no *plura entia* without the final *unum ens* ("no multitude without units"), but this time on behalf of the psychical monads of which he conceived matter to be composed, he was as he himself realized, both more atomistic and more scholastic.

These generalizations may now be supplemented with a fuller description of the theories of matter of two thinkers, one of the sixteenth, one of the seventeenth century, illustrative, though something more than typical, of their ages: Giordano Bruno and Isaac Newton.

2. A Renaissance Theory of Matter: Bruno. It has already been suggested that the Renaissance does not conveniently mark an epoch in the history of Western concepts of matter. It was a period of accelerating scientific advance, but so were the later Middle Ages and, even more certainly, the Enlightenment which followed. In its early stages the literary and humanistic preoccupations and the conviction of the vast superiority of antiquity to anything offered by the medievals no doubt led to the neglect of some interesting medieval inquiries e.g., those into "uniform difform" (uniformly accelerated) motions just as the logical, cosmological, and theological preoccupations of the thirteenth century had probably retarded a literary renascence. But the scientific value of a more accurate and complete translation of Archimedes (1543), for example, which humanistic scholarship had made possible, should not be underrated. By the middle of the sixteenth century the most prominent names in philosophy were not primarily humanists but natural philosophers—Telesio, Patrizi, Bruno. What does distinguish the theories of matter of the Renaissance from those of the Middle Ages and the seventeenth century is that it is far more difficult to discover anything like a consensus. Perhaps for that very reason the embattled but commanding figure of Bruno is especially revealing.

Poet, moralist, logician (the "Lullian art"), cosmologist; Catholic, Lutheran, Calvinist; inspired by Plotinus and Nicolas of Cusa in metaphysics and by Lucretius and Copernicus in cosmology, Giordano

Bruno was a wide-ranging dissolvent of the Aristotelian orthodoxies lodged in the universities and, though to a far lesser degree, a prophet of systems to come. He found the sort of philosophical significance in Copernicus that Spencer found in Darwin: the geocentric and anthropocentric theories had been exploded; nothing but an infinite (and thus centerless) universe was compatible with an infinite God. Similarly biological hierarchies with man regularly at the apex were mere pretension—for one thing other heavenly bodies were probably populated as well. His theory of matter appears to have undergone an evolution from inherited Aristotelian hylomorphism towards pantheism. The ephemeral individuals of ordinary experience became accidents rather than substances, accidents of either matter or form which as more permanent features of the universe, he later dealt with as substances. Yet in the final analysis matter and form were one in God, who thus became the only substance and (apparently the final position) identical with nature. (No direct influence on Spinoza has been traced.) The first efficient cause was the World Soul or Universal Intellect immanent in its own matter; at the more local level likewise all future forms were virtually—i.e., incipiently, not merely potentially—present in the matter (cf. *logoi spermatikoi* of Stoics, *rationes seminales* of Augustine). Yet, paradoxically, Bruno seems to have clung to the Aristotelian distinction between elements subject respectively to gravity and levity, in spite of the facts that this seemed to comport awkwardly with his infinite, and therefore directionless, universe (cf., however, Lucretius' absolute "down"), and that Copernicus, Gilbert, and Kepler were already thinking of multiple heavenly bodies as exercising gravitational attraction. Very far from the observational and mathematically-armed scientist, Bruno nevertheless probably deserves to be considered a scientific martyr—for his unsparing exposure of inconsistencies in existing theories, his eclectic independence, his imaginativeness in attempted syntheses, and his courage in finally refusing to recant before he was burned by the Inquisition in 1600.

3. *A Seventeenth-Century Theory of Matter: Isaac Newton.* A. N. Whitehead's characterization of the seventeenth as the "century of genius" seems eminently fitting. To the men whose collective intellectual achievement he regarded as perhaps unparalleled—Galileo, Descartes, Huygens, and Newton—the student of matter might well wish to add the indefatigable and resourceful figure of Robert Boyle. But admitting his great indebtedness to his predecessors and contemporaries, even on specific achievements with which his name is connected, Isaac Newton must stand preeminent for the magnitude of his achievements and their impact upon modes of thought. If, through some barely conceivable quirk of intellectual history, he had been unable to effect his observationally and mathematically fortified synthesis of dynamics and astronomy, the scientific revolution might possibly have faltered and even faded.

Once Newton's success in deriving Kepler's laws of planetary motion—and explanations of a vast range of other phenomena as well—from a unified mechanics of gravitational and inertial forces had been appreciated, the optimism and methodological confidence of the natural philosophers were irresistible. From the hither side of this achievement, particularly when historically we observe the selective accumulation of what were to become parts of the synthesis, it seems inevitable, and it may be worthwhile to consider one conceptual complication relevant to the ideas of matter. On the one hand Newton's system required that one should conceive every particle of matter in the universe as gravitationally attracting every other according to the law of inverse squares; on the other hand the counterbalancing centrifugal forces operated inertially, i.e., as if no external forces whatever affected the mobile. The final equation for planetary motion, therefore, involved combining the maintenance of the universal interaction of all matter with the hypothesis of how it would behave on the contrary assumption that there was no other matter with which the mobile in question could interact.

This was a pitch of abstraction of which a rather ossified Aristotelianism—and some successor doctrines as well—showed themselves quite incapable. This point may also serve to illustrate the ambiguous sense in which Newton's system triumphed through its "simplicity": as Butterfield remarks, it was simple in requiring relatively few *ad hoc* assumptions about the sort of forces involved; it was the reverse of simple in the mathematics necessary to compute the concrete resultant of forces.

In regard to his evolving concepts of matter, Newton never called himself an atomist though he did hypothesize that "God in the beginning formed matter in solid, massey, hard, impenetrable, moveable particles" with varying "sizes . . . figures, and . . . other properties" and in varying "proportions to space" (*Opticks* iii.1). He was closer to the ancient theory than Boyle in one respect: whereas Boyle had thought of atoms as flexible even to the point of actual division, Newton insisted on their indivisibility, "that Nature may be lasting," arguing that substances, including compounds, would not be stable if the component atoms could, with continued friction, be eroded. He also preserved from traditional atomism the absolute mathematical character of space and extended it to time, but he made space and time something more than geometrically ordered non-being by conceiving space as the "sensorium of God." Increasingly he also came to think that space could not be merely "void" but was filled with a fluid "aether"—to convey radiant heat, to account for the optical phenomena of reflection and refraction, to transmit light corpuscles, and perhaps to help explain gravitation. His major departure from ancient atomism (and from Descartes), however, was his rejection of the concept of matter as essentially geometrical and inert. First in gravitational theory, then in his speculations on the nature of matter in the appendix to his *Opticks,* he concluded that matter must be held together by various and variously intense attractive and repulsive forces.

To a considerable number of the more enthusiastic mechanical philosophers, followers, for example, of Descartes or Thomas Hobbes, the invocation of attractions and repulsions acting "at a distance" without immediate bodily contact, entanglement, or impact seemed a retreat to unintelligible explanation by "occult qualities." Although he did in fact "feign hypotheses" to account for some forces, Newton never did so without simultaneously assuming others. (Thus he wondered whether his postulated fluid aether might not account for gravitation through pressure by being more rare in the vicinity of solid bodies, but accounted for that distribution of aether by a mutual affinity of its parts.) His main reply to objections was that these assumptions enabled one to account for such phenomena as gravitation, magnetism, electricity, the varying stabilities and combining properties of chemical substances, deliquescence, internal cohesion of material particles, and capillary action, and that he was more concerned with fidelity to the undoubted fact than with the transparent intelligibility of the explanation—a reply which, incidentally, helps us better to understand the philosophical point involved in the controversy over "occult qualities." Molière was quite right to ridicule as an *explanation* (e.g., a "dormitive faculty" in the case of sleep) something that might possibly function (as it generally seemed to Aristotle) as a cautious and minimal registry of fact, whether or not further causal analysis were possible. If Newton perhaps avoided dogmatism by reason of his willingness to admit active potentialities the mechanics of which he did not purport to understand, it needs also to be added that he avoided obscurantism by his patience and resource to measure, calculate, and verify. Toulmin and Goodfield say that in his synthesis he combined "the atoms of Democritus into coherent order by tensions and forces like those of the Stoics" (*The Architecture of Matter*).

4. Matter in Metaphysical Thought: Locke and

Leibniz. By the time of Newton the progressive specialization that has distinguished physicists, chemists, and other empirical students of matter from the philosophers and metaphysicians was fairly well advanced. The history of the concepts of matter becomes correspondingly complex. On the one hand as the scientists have achieved greater determinacy regarding particular properties of kinds of matter, they have on the whole been more content to leave indeterminate the question of its ultimate generic nature: by the end of the eighteenth century Lavoisier was insisting on that exclusive concentration of his interests. On the other hand, while philosophers have not ceased their effort to excogitate what matter must be and cosmologies have still been produced, more interestingly perhaps, because cosmology has not been the *center* of philosophical interest, theories of matter have been derived from, or even only implied by, disciplines that were—epistemology, semantics, theories of action. Neither Karl Marx's revolutionary program of action nor A. J. Ayer's positivist theory of meaning were indefinitely flexible as to how matter, or "the physical world," were conceived. Both would find some features of some theories of matter we have considered incompatible with their views, and that is to say that their pragmatic and semantic theories have implications for a theory of matter. We may illustrate by the roles matter plays in two contemporaries of Newton, John Locke and G. W. Leibniz when the principal preoccupations of philosophy tended, after the revolution of Descartes, to be epistemological.

Locke and Leibniz are often cited as paradigm instances of (British) "empiricism" and (Continental) "rationalism," but these commitments, and their own curiosity, pushed them to fairly explicit concepts of matter, even though it was the primary concern of neither. Consider contrasting definitions of "substance." Locke says that ". . . substance is supposed always [to be] *something* besides the extension, figure, solidity, motion, thinking [in the mental substances which he also recognizes], or other observable ideas, *though we know not what it is*" (*Essay Concerning Human Understanding* II. 23. 3). Since, we know only that there must be something capable of causing these ideas of itself in us, "Powers therefore justly make a great part of our complex ideas of substances" (ibid., 10; cf. Mill's "permanent possibility of sensation"; Mach's phenomenalism). In terms of the criteria that have here been employed to distinguish concepts of matter, Locke's procedure might be described as the "materialization" of all substance, for he made it stuff, underlying and persisting through our experience, concrete and ostensible but itself defying any representative formulation.

But for Leibniz ". . . this is the nature of an individual substance or of a complete being, namely, to afford a conception so complete that the concept shall be sufficient for the understanding of it and for the deduction of all the predicates of which the substance is or may become the subject . . ." (*Discourse on Metaphysics* VIII). Of course Leibniz was speaking of his monads, psychic substances, each of which mirrored the entire universe from a unique angle of observation. Even that expression is misleading for the orders of space, time, and phenomenal matter were derivative from the internal structure of individual concepts rather than vice versa. Leibniz has identified substance wholly with what is formal, defining, structural, and intelligible. Material substance has become, for Leibniz, only a *phenomenon bene fundatum*, a conceptually useful matrix for ordering phenomena.

There are many ways, by no means all of them touched on here, in which Locke is "Democritean" and Leibniz is "Platonic" though a just account would have to include very significant differences as well. The "Aristotelian" alternative of finding in objects of inquiry both actual and knowable aspects ("form") and also as their ground, still mysterious potentialities and powers ("matter"), was certainly also present in the seventeenth century—to some extent in Newton's confidence that he had discovered real forces operative in the world combined with his uncertainty as to what their precise nature was.

There seems little doubt that awareness of different historical concepts of matter can be a factor in further inquiry into matter itself. The history of the astonishing progress that has been made in that direction finds the same or similar conceptual schemes now opening the way for, now obstructing, particular insights and discoveries. But so long as we continue to be confronted—through highly sophisticated devices of detection, or through ordinary gross observation—by something sensibly and convincingly there, additional to and unexhausted by our ideas and formulae, something like the concept of matter will have work to do.

BIBLIOGRAPHY

The secondary sources listed below are no substitute for the original works of the thinkers discussed in this article, but they can help in the interpretation of the original works.

General. M. Jammer, *Concepts of Force* . . . (Cambridge, Mass., 1957); idem, *Concepts of Mass* . . . (Cambridge, Mass., 1961); idem, *Concepts of Space* . . . (Cambridge, Mass., 1954); sometimes technical, but comprehensive and scholarly. E. McMullin, ed., *The Concept of Matter* . . . (Notre Dame, Ind., 1963; reprint, 1965), consists of papers from a conference on matter. S. Toulmin and J. Goodfield, *The Architecture of Matter* (London, 1962), a generally nontechnical but comprehensive historical survey.

Special Studies and Histories. C. Bailey, *The Greek Atomists and Epicurus* (Oxford, 1928). E. A. Burtt, *The Metaphysical Foundations of Modern Science* (London, 1925). H. Butterfield, *The Origins of Modern Science, 1300–1800* (London, 1957; reprint New York, 1962), pp. 7, 167 of reprint. F. M. Cornford, *Plato's Cosmology* (London, 1937). A. C. Crombie, *Medieval and Early Modern Science* (New York, 1954); idem, *Robert Grosseteste and the Origins of Experimental Science, 1100–1700* (Oxford, 1953). H. Diels and W. Kranz, *Die Fragmente der Vorsokratiker*, 6th ed., 2 vols (Berlin, 1951–52). P. Duhem, *Le système du monde: histoire des doctrines cosmologiques de Platon à Copernic*, 10 vols. (Paris, 1913–59), a study extending into the Hellenic and early modern periods, but principally concentrating on the medieval, of which more than any other work it has forced a reassessment. See also his *Études sur Léonard de Vinci*, 3 vols. (Paris, 1906–13), for late medieval and early modern periods. A. R. and M. B. Hall, *A Brief History of Science* (New York, 1964). E. J. Holmyard, *Alchemy* (Harmondsworth, 1957). G. S. Kirk and J. E. Raven, *The Pre-Socratic Philosophers* (Cambridge, 1962). F. A. Lange, *Geschichte des Materialismus* (1865), trans. as *The History of Materialism* (London, 1926; New York, 1957). E. Mach, *Die Mechanik in ihrer Entwicklung historisch-kritisch dargestellt* (1883), trans. T. J. McCormack as *The Science of Mechanics* (Chicago, 1893; 6th ed. La Salle, Ill., 1960). A. Mansion, *Introduction à la physique aristotélicienne* (Paris, 1913; Louvain, 1946). S. F. Mason, *A History of the Sciences* (London, 1953). S. Sambursky, *The Physical World of the Greeks* (London, 1956); idem, *The Physics of the Stoics* (London, 1959); idem, *The Physical World of Late Antiquity* (London, 1962). R. Taton, ed., *Histoire générale des sciences* (Paris, 1957–64), trans. as *The General History of the Sciences* (London, 1963–66), is a monumental history with the great advantages of combining the expertise and enthusiasm of many specialists. Volumes I and II (of four) carry through the eighteenth century. A. N. Whitehead, *Science and the Modern World* (New York and London, 1925). A. Wolf, *A History of Science, Technology and Philosophy in the 16th and 17th Century*, 2 vols. (London, 1935).

HAROLD J. JOHNSON

[See also **Atomism; Cosmology;** Historical and Dialectical Materialism; **Newton on Method;** Unity of Science.]

METAPHOR IN PHILOSOPHY

1. Special Use of Metaphor in Philosophy. Metaphor in philosophy may be distinguished from metaphor in poetry by being primarily an explanatory rather than an aesthetic device. Its explanatory function is to aid in conceptual clarification, comprehension, or insight regarding a mode of philosophical thought, a problem or an area of philosophical subject matter, or even a total philosophical system. However, the boundary between the aesthetic and the explanatory use of metaphor is admittedly vague. A philosopher may even deliberately select a metaphor for its aesthetic vividness and impact (as with Bergson's *élan vital* or William James's stream of consciousness; and notoriously the Mystics), but the question of the metaphor's having philosophical relevance depends on its explanatory function. Does it contribute to an understanding of the philosophy?

There are relatively superficial uses of metaphor in philosophy, and there are permeating uses. The superficial uses occur when figures of speech are scattered along the written pages to vivify some other unusual conception, and drop out when the conception is grasped. But when the metaphor's use is permeating, it may never completely disappear even after it gets ritualized and deadened under an accepted technical vocabulary within a philosophical school.

It has been frequently noticed that a new mode of thinking or a new school of philosophy as it is emerging and finding itself tends to be expressed in figurative language. This is inevitable before a technical vocabulary is developed with clear definitions and specific designations. Generally, this preliminary tendency is to be regarded as a superficial use of metaphor in philosophy. It is the more permeating use that deserves most attention.

In this connection the term "metaphor" should not be taken in too literal accordance with a definition often found in elementary books on prosody. It is not just a simile with the preposition "like" left out. It is rather the use of one part of experience to illuminate another—to help us understand, comprehend, even to intuit, or enter into the other. The metaphorical element may ultimately be absorbed completely into what it is a metaphor of. The one element, as frequently explained, is "reduced" to the other. The paradox of a metaphor is that it seems to affirm an identity while also half denying it. "All things are water," Thales seems to say. In so saying he would be affirming an identity and yet acknowledging that it is not obvious, and that what is more obvious is the difference. He claims an insight beyond the conventional view of things. It becomes incumbent on him to show how the identity can be justified. The same is true of Lucretius' identifying all things with atoms and the void, and of many other philosophers' modes of identification of the whole of reality with some general aspect of it.

2. The Root Metaphor Theory. The thought was bound to arise sooner or later that metaphor in the above sense was the characteristic mode of developing philosophic theories. Perhaps the first emphatic expression of this thought is in Francis Bacon's discussion of the "idols," in particular the "idol of the theater"

which he described as man's tendency to develop comprehensive systems in the language of myth and fantasy far beyond the data of observation. He was pleading for a method of solid empirical cognition in terms of collecting diverse instances of a subject to lift out the "form" that held them together. His intention was to disparage the use of metaphors, and he virtually excluded their use in hypotheses as means of cognition, although he did recognize them as "anticipations of nature."

However, in recent times with a more generous conception of the use of hypotheses as constructive instruments for both scientific and philosophical thinking, the metaphorical conception of the origin and development of philosophical thinking has been revived without any pejorative connotations.

In *World Hypotheses* (1942), this view is called "the root metaphor theory." It is itself an hypothesis about the origin and development of schools of philosophy or, more specifically, of world hypotheses. World hypotheses are distinguished from the more limited hypotheses of the special sciences by being "unrestricted" in their subject matter or in the scope of the evidence the hypotheses are expected to cover. An hypothesis in optics can reject as irrelevant any items that do not bear on optical phenomena or laws, as would be the case for so many observations in acoustics, geology, astronomy, linguistics, or social psychology. But a world hypothesis cannot be exclusive in this manner, for it cannot evade a group of items that do not seem to fit nicely into its system by declaring them outside its field and so irrelevant. Everything is relevant to a world hypothesis.

The root metaphor theory gains a good deal of credibility if one is persuaded that methods of deriving philosophical systems from claims of certainty (such as those of infallibility, self-evidence, or indubitable and incorrigible data) have proved unreliable. Once such methods of philosophizing from supposedly certain bases of knowledge have been given up, methods for seeking probable knowledge by way of hypotheses and their confirmation become acceptable. And this is the point of departure for the root metaphor theory of philosophic thought.

The problem then arises as to what are the sources of world hypotheses. The suggestion is that world hypotheses get started like any man's everyday hypothesis framed to solve some puzzling practical problem. The man looks back over his past experience for some analogous situation which might be applicable to his present problem. Similarly, a philosopher, puzzled about the nature of the universe, looks about for some pregnant experience that appears to be a good sample of the nature of things. This is his root meta-

197

phor. He analyzes his sample, selects its structural elements, and generalizes them as guiding concepts for a world hypothesis of unlimited scope. This set of concepts becomes the set of categories of his world hypothesis.

If the world hypothesis proves fruitful in its application to the varied items of the world, it will be adopted by other men, and a school of philosophy comes into being, dedicated to the development of this world theory (*Weltanschauung*). Its categories will be refined and modified to render them as adaptable as possible to the total range of the world's facts to which they are applied. The root metaphor itself becomes refined by this process. There evolves a give-and-take between the categories and the facts to which they are applied. The categories are modified to fit the facts, and the facts are interpreted in terms of the categories. The philosophers of the school will then perceive the facts as they are structured by their categories, and the ultimate facts in terms of their categories will come to appear to these philosophers as indubitable. Then it can become almost impossible to disabuse them of the certainty of the foundations of their philosophy except by introducing them to an alternative but equally justifiable world theory constructed with another set of categories yielding a different interpretation of the facts and a different group of apparent indubitables.

Only a limited number of categorial sets, however, according to this root metaphor theory, have proved fruitful enough to acquire a relatively adequate interpretation of the full scope of the world's facts. The position held in *World Hypotheses* was, up to the time of its publication, that the fruitful root metaphors could be reduced to four: (1) *formism*, based on the root metaphor of similarity, or the identity of a single form in a multiplicity of particular exemplifications; (2) *mechanism*, based on the root metaphor of material push and pull, or attraction and repulsion culminating in the conception of a machine or an electromagnetic-gravitational field; (3) *organicism*, based on the root metaphor of a dynamic organic whole as elaborated by Hegel and his followers; and (4) *contextualism*, based on the root metaphor of a transitory historical situation and its biological tensions as exhibited by Dewey and his followers. None of these is fully adequate. There are also several less adequate root metaphors, and in *World Hypotheses* it is suggested that still more adequate ones may appear in the future.

3. The Extensiveness of Metaphor in Philosophy. One corollary of the root metaphor theory is that any treatment of the topic of metaphor in philosophy would spread over the whole history of the subject. Not only are the great traditional systems caught up

in the action of metaphorical interpretations, but the cultural concepts and institutions dominating the beliefs and values of ordinary men are impregnated with them. Common sense and ordinary language have long been saturated with the presuppositions of Platonic, Aristotelian, and Cartesian metaphysics, and lately in many cultures with the Hegelian dialectic and contextualistic operationalism. If to these relatively adequate philosophies are added the metaphorical presuppositions of a number of humanly fascinating inadequate philosophies such as animism and mysticism, the spread of the influence of philosophic metaphors in the cultural thought and practices of men is enormously extended.

The mention of animism leads one inevitably to think of mythology. Here metaphor runs rampant—and with cosmic references also. Its intent is apparently to be as philosophically explanatory as Aristotle's categories of form and matter or A. S. Eddington's Space-Time and Gravitation. This close relation of primitive myth to the relatively adequate philosophies named above in respect to the explanatory use of metaphor should not prejudice one against the relatively adequate world hypotheses or their presuppositions incorporated in modern common sense and in modern science and logic. As long as men must make hypotheses to solve their problems, they will seek analogies to stimulate their invention, and when these analogies generate explanatory categories, these immediately function as explanatory metaphors. The important thing is to find explanatory hypotheses that are widely confirmable, and here is where the difference lies between primitive myth and adequate hypothesis.

4. Categories and Metaphors in Philosophy. The close connection brought out above between a set of categories for a world hypothesis and their generating root metaphor raises the question as to how the metaphorical basis of a set of categories could ever come to light. For the categories are inevitably conceived by the indoctrinated exponents of the philosophy as the actual structural framework of nature. The metaphor is amalgamated with what it is a metaphor of. To a philosopher fully immersed in his system, other interpretations of the world than his are treated simply as errors or meaningless or, perhaps charitably, as partial approximations to the truth. To become aware of the metaphorical nature of one's philosophical interpretations, there is need of a certain amount of cognitive "distance" like the "aesthetic distance" required in the arts to appreciate the realism of a play or a novel or a picture. Yet the distance must not be so great as to convert the object into pure fantasy and absurdity. In art one must recognize the conventions which support and sustain the aesthetic realism. So in philosophy one must recognize the categories that maintain the truth or interpretive adequacy of the world theory. The categories must be taken seriously as constructive instruments serving, like glasses to astigmatic eyes, to reveal reality truly or effectively in ways we have not previously seen. Bacon completely missed the significance of comprehensive philosophy through his lack of recognition of this cognitive distance. He noticed correctly the metaphorical interpretive action of the traditional philosophies, but failed to appreciate the revelatory power of the great systems and the fruitfulness of their metaphors.

At what point in the history of philosophy did an appreciation of the metaphorical action of categories emerge? The ground was laid by Kant when, in his *Critique of Pure Reason*, he argued that the structures of space, time, causality, etc. attributed to nature in scientific cognition were provided by the mind and should not be taken as the intrinsic structures of things-in-themselves. He introduced a little "distance" between phenomena and the interpretive action of his categories (and also space and time which he distinguished as *a priori* forms of intuition). But he regarded his categories as *a priori*, and inescapable, and incorrigible in cognition. As C. I. Lewis later pointed out in his *Mind and the World Order* (1929) there was more than a paradox implicit in Kant's view. There was a self-contradiction—that of being at the same time real and not real operations among cosmic events. For how could a thinker distinguish his interpretive categories from the structure of nature itself unless he had at least one other set of categories with divergent interpretations with which to compare them. In short, the categories must be regarded as corrigible. They must be open to error and correction. They cannot be posited as wholly *a priori* and inescapable in human cognition. They must be allowed enough "distance" between themselves and what they are interpreting to permit of alternatives and judgments of their adequacy. They must be treated in some degree as explanatory hypotheses, or metaphors.

That Kant had some awareness of this dilemma is obvious from his treatment of moral and aesthetic experience as distinct from that of scientific experience. In moral experience particularly he found he could bypass the categorial restrictions of scientific cognition and obtain some authoritative disclosures about the non-perceptual world. He accepted in a questionable way the ideas of God, freedom, and immortality for the moral life and its justification. Here, in a way, were the two sets of categories which revealed to him that the deterministic scientific categories clearly could not be attributed to such structural features of things-in-themselves as God, freedom, and immortality.

It should be acknowledged that there were many earlier premonitions of some sort of mental projections upon external things. Descartes' mind-matter dualism had already raised the issue, and Spinoza's theory of "attributes," Locke's stress on the distinction between primary and secondary qualities (a distinction that can be traced as far back as Democritus), and finally Hume's analysis of impressions, causality, and habit, and his reluctant admission that he just could not help believing in an external world although he could not understand how he could justify any belief in it.

Following Kant, Hegel's dialectic can be viewed as a proliferation of Kantian categories ordered according to their increasing degree of scope and adequacy till they culminated in the total synthesis of the Absolute. But still the categories were not entirely shaken loose from the actual structure of things they categorized. The dialectic was not only a history of increasingly adequate cognition but also a history of a kind of cosmic growth.

It was not till pragmatic or contextualistic modes of thought began to be influential that enough "distance" was introduced between the instruments of cognition and what they cognized for sets of categories to be viewed as metaphors. It was the typical pragmatic theory of concepts as instruments that made this possible. The pragmatic analysis of categories by C. I. Lewis has been mentioned. And Hans Vaihinger's *Philosophy of As If* (*Die Philosophie des Als-Ob*, 1911) may have helped too, though his doctrine of fictions was cognitively ambiguous in leaving one in doubt as to their cognitive function. If the "useful" concepts are rendered too fictional, the sense of metaphor may be almost totally lost. In order to maintain the metaphorical character of a set of guiding concepts, the structure of the concepts must in some degree be identified with what the concepts are applied to. A committed contextualist may accordingly be as unaware of the metaphorical relations of the categorial presuppositions of his own philosophical view as any of the traditional philosophers of the earlier schools. The service of contextualism in revealing the explanatory use of metaphor in philosophy is due solely to its theory of the instrumental role of concepts in knowledge. Emphasis on this role revealed just the degree of cognitive "distance" that has to be recognized before the metaphorical character of a set of categories can be consciously realized.

Once this is realized, a set of categories acquires the role of a useful hypothesis and a philosopher becomes wary of regarding the categories as *a priori* or incorrigible features of the world or of the mind's way of looking at the world. Yet one is aware that the categories direct one's view of the world and one can become critical of the adequacy of the view, and can deliberately seek out other sets of categories offering other views. Then it is possible for one to see that these views are functioning as cognitive metaphors. And if one seeks out the core and origin of these world metaphors, he reaches what may be called their root metaphors.

5. Cognitive Metaphors of Restricted Scope. The term "root metaphor" seems to have entered the language of philosophy in other ways than that of the source of the categories of world hypotheses. It has come often to refer to any central idea about which any complex problem can be organized. It becomes then the point of reference for a restricted or special hypothesis. When so used it overlaps the function lately assigned by extending it over what has come to be known as the "paradigm case."

The term "paradigm case" acquired importance in philosophy mainly through an analysis by Ludwig Wittgenstein of the meaning in ordinary language of such terms as "chair," "leaf," "game." He found that such terms are used to refer to a group of objects which as a group are not characterized by a set of common characteristics. But as a group they have "family resemblances." During childhood men learn the range of application of these family resemblance concepts, which become perfectly well understood by all who speak that ordinary language. Such a concept can be identified or pivoted on any one of its typical objects from which the family resemblances can be traced out to the other members of the group. Such a conveniently selected member would be the "paradigm case" for the group. The paradigm case furnishes the analogy from which the family resemblances of the other members can be traced. It could be called the root metaphor of a family resemblance concept. Some writers appear to be using the term "root metaphor" in much this way. It is one important way of using metaphor in philosophy. It is clearly an explanatory, not an aesthetic, use of metaphor, and falls well within the topic of this article.

It can even be argued that the root metaphors of world hypotheses should better be described as paradigm cases of groups of world hypotheses making up the various schools of philosophy. Thus the world hypotheses of Plato, Aristotle, Aquinas, and many others are easily recognized as having family resemblances pivoting on the relation of form and matter. When one type of formism is presented as representative of the group, this might be offered as a paradigm case for the group.

The chief difference between this interpretation and the root metaphor theory is that in this view a philo-

sophical school exhibits a development of a root metaphor towards a more nearly adequate structure for a comprehensive view of the world. The Wittgensteinian family resemblance concept does not suggest any such developmental process, or allow that the paradigm case which might be selected possesses any special explanatory superiority in respect to the precision and scope of the application of the concept to what may be called its field of application. Indeed the case is quite the reverse. All members of a family resemblance group are on a par, and there is no presumption of the group yielding any special explanatory insight beyond the fact of the family resemblances which the concept records in the usage of ordinary language.

However, some recent writers have spread the use of "paradigm" so as to include the progressive degrees of adequacy exhibited by the paradigm to its field of application. Thomas S. Kuhn in particular has developed this conception in his *The Structure of Scientific Revolutions* (1962). According to his exposition there is practically no difference between the function of the paradigm as a guiding conceptual pattern in scientific procedure and that of the root metaphor as a guiding conceptual pattern in world hypotheses except the restricted scope of the former.

A paradigm for Kuhn is a model or pattern accepted in science like a "judicial decision in the common law . . . an object for further articulation and specification under new or more stringent conditions." At the time of its first appearance it is "very limited in both scope and precision." The survival and endurance of a paradigm depends upon its success in solving problems which the practitioners in the field regard as acute. "The success of a paradigm . . . is at the start largely a promise of success discoverable in selected and still incomplete examples. Normal science consists in the actualization of that promise, an actualization achieved by extending the knowledge of those facts that the paradigm displays as particularly revealing, by increasing the extent of the match between those facts and the paradigm's predictions and by further articulation of the paradigm itself" (pp. 23–24).

According to Kuhn's description, the history of science can be almost equated with the history of the metaphors of limited scope in their pursuit of adequacy through their predictions and articulations in revealing the facts of their special fields. To what extent Kuhn's philosophy of science pivoting on the paradigm will be found acceptable, remains to be seen. It has the virtue of putting emphasis on the practicing scientists' use of "models," which no treatment of scientific method in the philosophy of science can safely ignore. For if on Kuhn's view a scientific model is not quite equated with a paradigm, it must be regarded as at least a material or conceptual embodiment of one.

If some form of the root metaphor theory for unrestricted hypotheses is combined with a form of paradigm theory like Kuhn's for restricted hypotheses, it would suggest that the basis of all productive empirical theory is in principle metaphorical. This would be no disparagement of it. It comes down simply to being realistic about what theories are as products of human creativity.

There is, of course, also the formal logical and mathematical aspect of theory which is perhaps properly regarded as the ideal terminal formulation of any empirical theory whether in science or philosophy. But however contrasted the formal approach may be to the metaphorical, there seems to be no necessary incompatibility between the two in their joint pursuit of some control and understanding of our world. If there is an issue, it lies beyond the scope of this article.

BIBLIOGRAPHY

The root metaphor theory of the basis of metaphysical thinking was developed by S. C. Pepper in his *World Hypotheses* (Berkeley, 1942) and later exemplified by a deliberately chosen new root metaphor in his *Concept and Quality* (La Salle, Ill., 1967). A somewhat similar theory was developed independently by Dorothy Emmet in *The Nature of Metaphysical Thinking* (London, 1945), extending the analogical principle also to myth, religion, and theology. *The Compass of Philosophy* (New York, 1954) by Newton P. Stallknecht and Robert S. Brumbaugh carry on much the same idea by their stress on "key concepts" in metaphysics. And Charles Morris' *Paths of Life* (New York, 1942) is also relevant for a sort of statistical confirmation of the influence of "key concepts" in the attitudes of ordinary men.

C. I. Lewis' *Mind and the World Order* (New York, 1929) has already been mentioned for stimulating the metaphorical conception of metaphysics. Hans Vaihinger in his *Die Philosophie des Als-Ob* (Berlin, 1911), trans. C. K. Ogden as *Philosophy of As If* (New York, 1924) was influential by distinguishing between scientific hypotheses, which could be true, and fictions (As If's), which could not be true but had useful semi-cognitive functions. And metaphysical systems fell in the latter category. Philip Wheelright in his *The Burning Fountain* (Bloomington, Ind., 1954) and *Metaphor and Reality* (Bloomington, Ind., 1962) speaks of the language of metaphor and the language of science as two equally legitimate ways of gaining cognitive insight into two different aspects of the world. Max Black, on the other hand, in his *Models and Metaphors* (Ithaca, N.Y., 1954) makes no such cognitive division but regards metaphors and models as valuable explanatory devices whether in the special sciences or in comprehensive metaphysics. This leads to Thomas Kuhn's still stronger view in *The Structure of Scientific Revolutions* (Chicago, 1962), which, as pointed out

already, regards models and paradigms (virtually in the role of root metaphors) as central explanatory instruments in science. For an exceptionally intensive and original treatment of metaphor in metaphysics and science (and poetry too) the two articles by D. Berggram on "The Use and Abuse of Metaphor" in the *Review of Metaphysics*, **16** (1962/1963) are recommended.

STEPHEN C. PEPPER

[See also Ambiguity; **Analogy;** Antinomy; Form; Literary Paradox; **Metaphor in Religious Discourse;** Myth; Pragmatism; Symbol.]

METAPHOR IN RELIGIOUS DISCOURSE

METAPHOR, which is to be taken here inclusively as any representation of one subject matter in terms literally appropriate not to it but to some different subject matter, has been pervasively present within religious discourse from earliest known times. The explicit recognition of metaphor as metaphor, however, logically presupposes some structured beliefs or theory about what may and may not be considered "literally appropriate" modes of representation when applied to religious subject matter. This additional sophistication, first met explicitly in ancient Greek thought, brings with it the need for exegesis and therefore provides a stimulus for rival theological theories. Consequently, the history of the idea of metaphor in Western religious discourse, involving not only the vital transition to self-consciousness about the "literal-nonliteral" distinction in religion but also the long development of various approaches to religious uses of nonliteral expressions, may illuminate aspects of the theological situation in recent years.

I. PRIMARY IMAGES IN RELIGION

The Bible, as Western civilization's principal religious book, illustrates the pervasiveness of unselfconscious imagery—only later to be distinguished as metaphor—in primary or nontheoretical religious discourse. There can be no fixed boundaries delineating what is "image" from what is not, as we shall see, since various theories of religious metaphor will make these demarcations at very different points, but a few obvious examples drawn from various contexts of religious usage will give at least preliminary substance to this concept.

Prophetic speech, first, is rich with imagery, often of great power. Even the comparatively straightforward threats and denunciations of the first great prophet, Amos, are mingled with such images as the personification of Israel as a prostrate young woman:

> Fallen, no more to rise,
>   is the virgin Israel;
> forsaken on her land,
>   with none to raise her up
>   (Amos 5:2; RSV).

His immediate successor, Hosea, used imagery of various kinds to express God's agonized love for a faithless people. God is depicted as a father and (in a mixed image) as a compassionate herdsman.

> When Israel was a child, I loved him,
>   and out of Egypt I called my son.
> The more I called them,
>   the more they went from me;
> they kept sacrificing to the Baals,
>   and burning incense to idols.
> Yet it was I who taught Ephraim to walk,
>   I took them up in my arms;
>   but they did not know that I healed them.
> I led them with cords of compassion,
>   with the hands of love,
> and I became to them as one
>   who eases the yoke on their jaws,
>   and I bent down to them and fed them
>   (Hosea 11:1–4; RSV).

Hosea is still better known for his image of God as righteously angered but nonetheless loving husband of the adulterous wife, Israel:

> Plead with your mother, plead—
>   for she is not my wife,
>   and I am not her husband—
> that she put away her harlotry from her face,
>   and her adultery from between her breasts;
> lest I strip her naked
>   and make her as in the day she was born,
> and make her like a wilderness,
>   and set her like a parched land,
>   and slay her with thirst
>   (Hosea 2:2–3; RSV).

Not only in speech, but also in significant action, a prophet could express his images. Hosea may have actually married a whore as living enactment of his central image, though scholarly opinion is divided on this question. Certainly other prophets did communicate in part through nonverbal imagery, however, as is illustrated by Jeremiah who publicly broke a potter's vessel after proclaiming "O house of Israel, can I not do with you as the potter has done? says the Lord. Behold, like the clay in the potter's hand, so are you in my hand, O house of Israel" (Jeremiah 18:6). Jeremiah, indeed, is an especially fertile source of image in speech and action. God is represented as a fountain of living waters (Jeremiah 2:13), a planter of good seed (2:21), a husband (3:1), a father (3:22), a lion (4:7), and so on. Other later prophets, like Ezekiel, Deutero-Isaiah, Haggai, Zechariah, and Malachi continue to create and employ imagery in the service of the prophetic ministry.

Devotional literature, despite its very different context of use, is no less crowded with imagery. To take a few obvious examples, one finds God pictured in many of the Psalms as a rock, a shield, a fortress, a horn, besides being represented anthropomorphically, as in the familiar pastoral:

> The Lord is my shepherd, I shall not want;
> he makes me to lie down in green pastures.
> He leads me beside still waters;
> he restores my soul
>   (Psalms 23; RSV).

Not all even of devotional images are so idyllic, of course, nor so concerned as those above with security and protection, but they are typical. A rather startling contrast is presented by the discourse of *apocalyptic* literature. The imagery of apocalypse, as in Daniel, is far more removed from ordinary experience:

> And four great beasts came up out of the sea, different from one another. The first was like a lion and had eagles' wings. Then as I looked its wings were plucked off, and it was lifted up from the ground and made to stand upon two feet like a man; and the mind of a man was given to it
>   (Daniel 7:3–4; RSV).

With the discourse of apocalypse, however, we have come to the end of what deserves the title of primary or unself-conscious religious imagery. The images are consciously constructed with an esoteric significance known only to the initiates. This phenomenon of encoded imagery itself is widely encountered in various religious and cultural traditions, which justifies to some extent the inclusion of apocalyptic imagery, as a primary religious expression, within the present section; but by the time Daniel was being written (ca. 166 B.C.) in Hellenized Palestine, the conscious distinction between levels of religious meaning had clearly been made. We must go back to examine how this occurred.

II. THE DISCOVERY OF METAPHOR IN RELIGION

Explicit awareness of the distinction between would-be literal uses of religious language and "metaphor," as we have here broadly defined it, arose in a significantly different cultural context from the biblical one. Greek religion, like the Hebrew, was shot through with vivid imagery, but at least two significant social differences distinguish their histories. First, Greek religion from the sixth century B.C. was obliged to coexist with a lively independent philosophical movement, as Hebrew religion was not. Second, Greek religion of this period, unlike the Hebrew, lacked an institutionalized priesthood of specialists in the defense, exposition, and transmission of inherited belief. These two differences doubtless worked together in Greece to reinforce the rise of critical consciousness of non-literal religious discourse, both by placing the latter in a competitive situation with alternative accounts of ultimate matters and by giving greater freedom of interpretation to those inclined to amend or reconcile the inherited imagery of religion with reference to those alternatives. That such freedom was not absolute is quite clear from the prosecution of occasional philosophers on grounds of unorthodoxy, notably in the cases of Anaxagoras, who was banished by the outraged citizens of conservative Athens about 432 B.C., and of Socrates, who took the hemlock in order to teach the Athenians a lesson (*Apology* 38C) after they tried and condemned him publicly in 399 B.C. on charges of impiety. Still, such incidents, however noteworthy, were the exception in a normal context of considerable latitude of belief and interpretation.

It is probably not wise to lay heavy emphasis on the famous assertion attributed to Thales, "All things are full of gods" as marking, in itself, a clear break with previous religious imagery; but it remains an instance, from such an ancient philosopher, of reinterpreted philosophical use of traditional religious discourse, inasmuch as Thales was in all likelihood referring here to the behavior of natural magnets and the like. He was, even more important, at the start of a long train of thinkers whose efforts were bent towards constructing naturalistic explanations of the whole of things, a universal domain which had hitherto been the exclusive preserve of mythic images. It would be false, of course, to suppose that these thinkers dispensed with imagery—their bold speculations were, on the contrary, deeply involved in imaginative models of various sorts—but philosophical accounts of things after Thales differed in key ways from the religious imagery of inherited Homeric religion. First, philosophical explanations were constructed rather than inherited; secondly, and consequently, they relied for their acceptability on intrinsic plausibility rather than on extrinsic cultural authority; and thus, thirdly, they were relevant to evidence and open to argument on grounds of consistency, inclusiveness, and the like, on which their plausibility depended. In sum, the aim of the philosophic movement in Greek culture was to provide rational and (in intention, at least) literal theory for the understanding of the universe.

Such an aim and such an intention (no matter the degree of success) is, as we noted earlier, the logical prerequisite for the discovery of metaphor in religious discourse. Only when there is a theory about what is "literally so" can there be explicit recognition of oblique, allegorical, symbolic—in a word, metaphorical—alternative uses of significant forms. What is taken to be the case "literally," of course, is entirely relative to the theories believed, and in consequence the specific content covered by the "nonliteral," or the metaphorical, shifts with shifting beliefs.

Given an intellectual standing place outside traditional religious discourse, Greek thinkers divided on the question of how to assess the inherited Homeric tapestry of images. Some, for example, Xenophanes, Heraclitus, and the Pythagoreans, chose to stand uncompromisingly against the religious tradition. Others, however, were prepared to give the venerated images a reinterpretation to bring them—with their "real" meaning—more into line with what the commentators variously believed to be the literal truth. The usual method of interpretation was through "allegory" (ὑπόνοια), which term (originally derived from Greek rhetoric) simply meant a series of metaphors or a sustained metaphor. Perhaps the first to have introduced this metaphorical interpretation of Homer was a somewhat shadowy figure, Theagenes of Rhegium (fl. 530?), who wrote an "Apology" for Homeric poetry; following Theagenes, a distinguished list of thinkers took up the method. The above-mentioned Anaxagoras, for example, gave a purely ethical metaphorical reduction to the orthodoxy of his day, while his pupil, Metrodorus of Lampsacus (d. 464 B.C.), offered a quasi-scientific account in which Demeter stands for the liver, Dionysus for the spleen, Apollo for the gall, Hector for the moon, Achilles for the sun, and so on. Likewise, the philosopher Diogenes of Apollonia (fl. 440–430 B.C.), who supported the view that air was the fundamental substance of the universe, took Zeus as a metaphor, naturally, for air. Democritus, the great atomist philosopher, was also an enthusiastic allegorizer of Homeric religion.

Plato, on the other hand, was of the opinion that such allegorizing of the traditional religion is greatly overgenerous to the poets. He showed Socrates making delightful nonsense of the attempt to allegorize etymologies of the names of the gods (*Cratylus* 406–08); he also had Socrates dismiss the effort as follows:

Now I quite acknowledge that these allegories are very nice, but he is not to be envied who has to invent them; much labor and ingenuity will be required of him; and when he has once begun, he must go on and rehabilitate Hippocentaurs and chimeras dire. Gorgons and winged steeds flow in apace, and numberless other inconceivable and portentous natures. And if he is sceptical about them, and would

203

fain reduce them one after another to the rules of probability, this sort of crude philosophy will take up a great deal of time (*Phaedrus* 229C).

But the most profound of Plato's objections to this attempt to save the imagery of traditional religion by treating it as metaphorical is that the imagery itself, if allowed to be taken this seriously by the uncritical, has the dangerous power to corrupt truth and morals.

Neither, if we mean our future guardians to regard the habit of quarrelling among themselves as of all things the basest, should any word be said to them of the wars in heaven, and of the plots and fightings of the gods against one another, for they are not true. . . . These tales must not be admitted into our State, whether they are supposed to have an allegorical meaning or not. For a young person cannot judge what is allegorical and what is literal; anything that he receives into his mind at that age is likely to become indelible and unalterable; and therefore it is most important that the tales which the young first hear should be models of virtuous thoughts (*Republic* II 378D).

Plato, here, is clearly not condemning all use of allegory, image, or metaphorical discourse. He himself used such forms of language to excellent effect on a number of crucial occasions (e.g., *Phaedo* 107–15; *Phaedrus* 246A–247C); he knew and respected the power of such discourse. Indeed, precisely because of this great respect for its potency, he wanted to keep it under firm control of literal truth.

There is no need to continue examining the rise to explicit consciousness of the literal and its opposite in religious speech. The distinction is quite clear even before Plato; and we have further seen that different evaluations of how the concepts should be deployed have come to the surface. Metaphor in religious discourse having been discovered, what are its consequences?

III. THEOLOGICAL APPROACHES TO METAPHOR

The confluence of the Hebrew and the Greek cultural traditions, which occurred in the Hellenistic period, is vividly exemplified by the Jewish philosopher Philo of Alexandria. Although the metaphorical exegesis of biblical imagery had been known before him, it was Philo who first turned allegorical interpretation of scripture into a system based on a coherent philosophical position. Ironically, in view of Plato's own attitude toward the allegorizing of religious imagery, Philo's primary philosophical resource was Platonic, though he drew much in addition from current Stoic thought, which tended strongly to support metaphorical methods of approaching religious tradition. The substance of Philo's views need not concern us here; of greater significance is his approach and his

justification for it. Above all one must remember that Philo was both a convinced Jew and, at the same time, a determined philosopher. Truth, he argued, cannot be divided into compartments. If Moses wrote something, it must be true in some sense; if, on the other hand, good reasoning shows something to be the case, it must somehow be compatible with all other truth. Therefore, when there are apparent conflicts between sacred scripture and good reasoning, these putative conflicts cannot be final. In general, Philo thought, wherever the literal meaning of the Bible leads either to absurdity or to impiety, there it is both right and necessary to discover the allegorical meaning behind the metaphor, since metaphor it must be.

Philo was fortunately situated, philosophically, for deploying his distinction of literal-metaphorical in this way because of his thorough acceptance of the Platonic distinction between the visible world of imperfect, changing particulars, on the one hand, and the purely "intelligible world" of perfect, eternal Archetypes, on the other. Such a distinction makes it easy to interpret literal descriptions of events or objects in the empirical world as belonging to an inferior order of reality, knowledge, and value, while also participating—by virtue of the Forms—in a higher order of perfection in all respects. Given such a distinction and such a method, indeed, the dimensions of what could be taken as metaphorical were open to vast enlargement. All things visible, not just a few obvious items like rocks or shields, on this view, refer beyond themselves to the world of eternal Archetypes. If the lion image of Jeremiah had to be given a nonliteral meaning to avoid absurdity or impiety when applied to God, so, too, the mention of the "face" of God, or his "walking" in the Garden of Eden—and the Tree in the Garden, and the Garden itself—must be given metaphorical meaning in any systematic account of scriptural truth. This Philo set out to do, interpreting the Bible as carrying throughout more than its literal significance. The story of Joseph and his coat of many colors, for instance, he treated as a metaphor in which Joseph stood for the Ideal Form of the Statesman and in which his many-hued garment signified the complexity of his political policies.

It is interesting to note that Philo, though profoundly immersed in the allegorizing of his own scriptures, had no use whatever (like Plato) for the allegorizing of the pagan sacred writings in the manner of the contemporary Stoics. This trait, a direct reflection of Philo's Jewish piety, is of course typical of the theological employment of allegorical interpretations: where there is absence of respect for the religious literature in question, there is correspondingly little motivation to "save" it by appeal to metaphor. Where, on the other hand, there is both veneration of inherited material and an explicit theory of what constitutes "absurdity" and "impiety" in it, the recourse to distinctions between literal and metaphorical meanings may be tempting. Here, in fact, we find one of the crucial differences, among many similarities, between Philo and Plato. Both, we recall, objected to whatever might corrupt truth or morals: Plato, on these grounds, urged the censoring of any poetic images which might have this effect; Philo, on the same grounds, urged the very process of allegorizing that Plato condemns. The obvious difference between them is that Plato is free from allegiance to the traditional religious forms while Philo is committed to his.

This difference in commitments is reflected in another way important to the tradition of which Philo was to be the source. Even the Greek philosophers who, unlike Plato, were ready to see metaphorical truths in the religion of their ancestors were not prepared to place primacy on the latter. If in Greece the myths of old were able to be viewed by some as still having intellectual value in terms of more adequate theory, it was only as groping approximations. The literal truths of reason, by which the metaphors alone could be recognized as such, were firmly in the primary place. Philo, however, took the opposite view. The Bible was God's revelation through Moses. There can ultimately be no conflict between the truth given directly by God and the truth discovered by philosophy, but there can be no doubt, for Philo, which must come first. Therefore it was a problem for him and for his Christian successors to explain how the Greeks came by their truth. Different solutions were given—including hypotheses of Greek plagiarism from Moses and the prophets—all, however, leaving no doubt about the priority of God's revelation over man's discovery. In this emphasis we find the root of the famous "handmaiden" theory of the relationship between philosophy and revelation. Revealed truth, given through the tradition to which one is committed, must be the ruling mistress; philosophy, through which the metaphors of scripture are harmonized with each other and with other systematic knowledge, must be ancillary (from *ancilla*, the Latin word for serving girl).

Christian adoption of metaphorical interpretation of their authoritative religious discourse was soon to follow, deeply indebted to Philo, particularly after the second century, and carrying with it the various theological overtones we have just noted. This process was encouraged by a certain amount of allegorizing in the New Testament itself. Saint Paul, for example, takes the statement from Deuteronomy "You shall not muzzle an ox when it treads out the grain" (Deuteronomy 25:4) as a metaphorical justification for his own

financial support (I Corinthians 9:9); and elsewhere he uses allegory explicitly to argue his position (Galatians 4:21). The author of the Gospel of John, too, clearly makes conscious use of metaphor throughout. Jesus' parables, furthermore, whether they were uttered self-consciously or in the primary mode of simple religious speech, lend themselves obviously to allegorical interpretation, sometimes as simple metaphor (e.g., the cursing of the fig tree), and sometimes, when extended, as allegory (e.g., the Sower, the Laborers in the Vineyard).

Enthusiastic use of metaphor of various sorts, primarily allegory, was characteristic of the early Church Fathers both in the Latin-speaking West and in the Greek-speaking East despite the disapproval of Irenaeus (fl. 177) and Tertullian (160?–?230) in East and West respectively. Both of these authors were disturbed by dangerous similarities between allegorized Christian doctrine and the always luxuriantly metaphorical thought of Gnosticism. The tide, however, was too strong in Hellenistic times to be resisted, and one finds the greatest names among the supporters of metaphorical exposition: Clement of Alexandria (150?–?220) and Origen (185?–?254), both of the Greek church, continued to be strong influences in favor of the method despite the multi-volumed polemics of Theodore of Mopsuestia (350?–?428), who argued that without a literal, historical base the excesses of metaphorical hermeneutics could have no check at all. Likewise, in the Latin church, Saint Jerome used metaphor, for example, to justify Jacob's polygamy and favoritism by letting Leah stand for Judaism and Rachel for Christianity. Saint Augustine, too, found metaphorical interpretation useful, especially in apologetics, and justifies it scripturally by an appeal to Saint Paul's distinction between the letter, which "kills," and the spirit, which "gives life" (II Corinthians 3:6). Given such authority, it is not surprising that the approach to religious discourse by means of metaphorical interpretation was widespread in medieval times, though for many centuries the substructure of explicit philosophy—certainly present in Fathers like Saint Augustine—was in little evidence. Instead, as exemplified by the theologians associated with the Abbey of Saint-Victor during the twelfth century, a devotional concern reinforced by a mystic sense of the levels of meaning and of reality, led sensitive thinkers to contemplate the various senses—literal, allegorical, moral, anagogical—in which Scripture could enrich spirituality.

With the rediscovery of Aristotle's thought in the twelfth and thirteenth centuries, the efforts of Saint Thomas Aquinas to unite the truths of Christian revelation with the truths of "the Philosopher" inevitably included a prominent discussion of the place of meta-

205

phor in religious discourse. Aquinas predictably came to the defense of controlled metaphorical interpretation via an appeal to Aristotelian epistemological principle:

It is befitting Holy Scripture to put forward divine and spiritual truths by means of comparisons with material things. For God provides for everything according to the capacity of its nature. Now it is natural to man to attain to intellectual truths through sensible things, because all our knowledge originates from sense. Hence in Holy Scripture spiritual truths are fittingly taught under the likeness of material things (*Summa theologica*, Q. I, Art. 9).

In answer to the charge that it is somehow unfitting to represent higher things by lower, he pointed out that since God is not knowable directly by any sensible concepts, we are saved from erroneously supposing that we have literal understanding by the very incongruity of the metaphors employed in what we have called primary religious imagery. Besides, such metaphors have the virtue of being readily available to "the simple who are unable by themselves to grasp intellectual things" while simultaneously being the means whereby "divine truths are the better hidden from the unworthy" (loc. cit.). Elsewhere Aquinas laid foundations for the important doctrine of analogy, whereby technical theological theory when applied to God could be held to avoid the dual threats of literal anthropomorphism, on the one hand, and vacuous equivocation, on the other. This doctrine, although related to the idea of metaphor in religious discourse, has its primary bearing on other philosophical matters and will not be pursued here.

IV. METAPHOR IN MODERN
RELIGIOUS THOUGHT

The first serious break in Christian attitudes toward the metaphorical interpretation of primary religious discourse (one which was never equally duplicated within Jewish thought) came with the Reformation in the sixteenth century. Martin Luther was by no means an absolute opponent of metaphor and allegory—he used it himself from time to time, especially in interpreting such biblical sources as the Song of Solomon—but his emphasis (and that of the weight of Protestantism after him) was on the sharp reduction of the boundaries, once again, of what could legitimately be considered figurative in scripture. Just as the Protestant movement broke away from the authority of the institutional church of Rome, so it rejected the authority of much within church tradition and interpretation that had over the centuries come to share the sanctity of the Bible. If the Bible was to be the one basic authority for faith, then the Bible, Luther argued, should be permitted as far as possible to speak for itself as liter-

ally as possible. Any other attitude, he saw, would be to elevate human critical standards above the Word of God.

This position, we should note, is not quite identical with that of the Fundamentalism of the nineteenth and twentieth centuries. The latter movement grew in a context of scientific biblical criticism and as a reaction against it—a context which Luther and other early Protestants never knew. In a sense, it can be argued that the history of higher criticism, which parallels the history of science itself, is just as much an opponent of runaway metaphorical interpretation as was Luther, though from different motives. It can also be argued (though it is speculative to do so) that Luther might have welcomed neutral scientific biblical scholarship as providing the best means through which the original biblical texts could be permitted to "speak for themselves." It would have required considerable revision of Luther's rather contemptuous attitudes toward the powers and prerogatives of human reason for him to have taken this attitude, of course, since scientific biblical criticism is emphatically based on certain fundamental beliefs regarding what is literally the case— they are the pervasive presumptions underlying the scientific attitudes of the modern Western world—but since Luther was a man of his time and not of ours it is fruitless to examine this point further. The Fundamentalists, however, were in the historical position of being required to make the choice, and their choice was to hew to the literal language of scripture rather than either to accept the allegorizing of the mainly Catholic past, or to welcome the scientific discovery of biblical history and literature by the Modernists.

In this literalism, of course, there were many degrees. Some metaphors were allowed by most Fundamentalists, although there was little consistent theory to systematize where the literal line could appropriately be drawn. The Song of Solomon, for a prime example, was seldom interpreted by Fundamentalists at face value, which would make of it a rather erotic collection of ancient wedding poetry. But while Philo's warning against "impiety" was carefully followed, his equal emphasis against "absurdity" was not. More accurately, the Fundamentalists would not grant to their opponents that there was anything absurd about the sun standing still in the sky on command (Joshua 10:12), about an iron axe head floating on water (II Kings 6:5), or, especially, about certain "fundamentals" (hence the name) like the virgin birth of Jesus or his bodily resurrection from the dead. All such accounts, indeed, are only absurd relative to a set of beliefs about what is and is not possible. If those beliefs are rejected, then the choice between metaphorical treatment and disbelief is not forced.

Rejection of the set of beliefs in question, however, is inconceivable for most modern men. These are the beliefs that underlie the common sense and the common life of contemporary civilization as well as the intellectual possibility of science. There are today, therefore, comparatively few outright Fundamentalists; but there are still many Christians whose primary religious discourse is full of much that is incompatible with their basic beliefs about reality. This creates a severe problem for contemporary non-Fundamentalist theology, since the footloose freedoms of allegorical interpretation have been blocked by the rise of modern critical consciousness—for Catholics, today, as well as Protestants—and the alternative of sheer disbelief, in the manner of Plato against the Homeric poetry, is unattractive to those who continue to venerate the inherited religious tradition of their culture.

Several attempted solutions have recently been under debate, all recognizing the nonliteral but somehow valuable character of primary religious discourse. One attempt has been made following the German theologian Rudolf Bultmann, to "demythologize" the biblical world-picture, interpreting scriptural stories couched in primary religious discourse in terms of the existential philosophy of Martin Heidegger. Another effort to challenge the underlying philosophical premises on which Christian theology has traditionally rested is based on the process philosophy of Alfred North Whitehead: if the absolutes of the Platonic and Aristotelian philosophies, especially in their bearing on the nature of God, can be replaced with a new relativistic and dynamic theoretical matrix, like Whitehead's, capable of accommodating science and contemporary consciousness as well as of giving a coherent meaning to the traditional religious images, then, it is argued, both religion and intellectual integrity can be saved. Still other positions draw variously on the philosophical views of Ludwig Wittgenstein, of John Dewey, of Edmund Husserl, of Henri Bergson, or on still other theoretical bases found either in philosophy or inherent in the Christian tradition itself.

What is in common to all these efforts, the details of which remain beyond the scope of this article, is the insistence on retaining, so far as possible, primary religious discourse while refusing to allow it to claim literal truth. Its literal interpretation is to be found in some further system of beliefs which, functioning in a way similar to the way a theory articulates and deploys a model in science, relates the vivid imagery of primary religious discourse to what may be responsibly believed relative to current knowledge. In the extended sense of metaphor employed above, therefore, we are witnessing in theology a return to metaphorical interpretation of religious discourse; but it is a meta-phorical hermeneutic of a highly sophisticated form. There are many, of course, who share the hostility of Plato to this entire enterprise, however guarded the method and refined the analysis. Still, as long as the theories which interpret the inherited metaphors of religious discourse are fashioned with integrity and measured with rigor against the appropriate standards of intellectual adequacy, the enterprise can do little harm; and as long as there are many who find rich values in preserving attachment to the primary imagery of their religious tradition, the enterprise will (despite Plato) be doubtless considered worth all the "labor and ingenuity" required.

BIBLIOGRAPHY

A standard American edition of *The Holy Bible*, from which all biblical quotations above have been taken, is The Revised Standard Version (New York, 1952). Since, when discussing metaphor in religious discourse, the element of imagery must be kept distinct from the element of old-fashioned English speech, which makes everything sound vaguely figurative to many, the Revised Standard rather than the King James Version of the Bible has been used throughout the article. The early philosophic sources are reliably examined, with extensive Greek fragments and good English translations, in G. S. Kirk and J. E. Raven, *The Presocratic Philosophers* (Cambridge and New York, 1957). A distinguished translation of Plato's works is available in *The Dialogues of Plato* by B. Jowett (New York, 1937), from which the above excerpts have been taken.

Philo's thought has been treated in depth by H. A. Wolfson in the two-volume work *Philo* (Cambridge, Mass., 1948), which contains excellent notes and further bibliography; and H. A. Wolfson's *The Philosophy of the Church Fathers* (Cambridge, Mass., 1956) is a valuable source for a study of the extension of the philonic tradition of metaphorical exegesis into early Christian thought. Later developments, including the Victorines, are examined in B. Smalley, *The Study of the Bible in the Middle Ages*, 2nd ed. (New York, 1952).

Various editions of the *Summa theologica* of Saint Thomas Aquinas are available; and for a brief systematic critique of the extension of Saint Thomas' theory of religious discourse into the traditional doctrine of analogy, see "Analogy in Theology" by Frederick Ferré in *The Encyclopedia of Philosophy*, 8 vols. (New York and London, 1967), I, 94–97.

Martin Luther's exegetical works are contained in the first thirty volumes of *Luther's Works*, edited and translated by J. Pelikan and W. Hansen (Saint Louis, 1958–67); in addition, a valuable companion volume in the set, *Luther the Expositor*, has been appended by J. Pelikan (Saint Louis, 1959). Another seminal Protestant view is found in Jean Calvin's *Commentaries*, translated and edited by Joseph Haroutunian (Philadelphia, 1958). A useful series of general articles on the Bible and the principles of critical biblical scholarship, including three excellent articles on the history of the interpretation of the Bible, are found in *The Interpreter's Bible*, 12 vols. (New York, 1952), Vol. I.

Some works in English by modern interpreters of religious discourse who believe that it requires fresh articulation in terms of a more literal philosophical theory include the following. Defending exegesis in terms of the thought of Martin Heidegger are R. Bultmann in *Kerygma and Myth*, edited by H. W. Bartsch (New York, 1961) and John Macquarrie in *Principles of Christian Theology* (New York, 1966). Attempting a similar exposition in terms of the philosophy of A. N. Whitehead are John B. Cobb, Jr., in *A Christian Natural Theology* (Philadelphia, 1965), Charles Hartshorne in *Man's Vision of God* (New York, 1941), and Schubert M. Ogden, who combines an interest in both Whitehead and Heidegger, in *Christ Without Myth* (New York, 1961). Working toward analogous ends in terms of the position of John Dewey is Henry Nelson Wieman in *The Source of Human Good* (New York, 1947). And arguing for the articulation of religious discourse in terms of the analyses of Ludwig Wittgenstein are Dallas M. High in *Language, Persons, and Belief* (New York, 1967) and Paul M. van Buren in *The Secular Meaning of the Gospel* (New York, 1963).

FREDERICK FERRÉ

[See also Allegory; Ambiguity; Church, Modernism in; Gnosticism; **God;** Hierarchy; **Literary Paradox; Myth in Biblical Times; Prophecy;** Rhetoric; Symbol.]

METAPHYSICAL IMAGINATION

IN HIS NOVEL *Si le grain ne meurt*, André Gide clearly pinpoints one recurrent source of metaphysical thinking. He writes there of a vague, ill-defined belief that "something else exists alongside the acknowledged, aboveboard reality of everyday life." This "desire to give life more thickness," he suggests, elicits "a sort of propensity to imagine a clandestine side to things." Gide's notion of giving life more "thickness" is reminiscent of a celebrated definition of metaphysics: "the effort to comprehend the universe not simply piecemeal or by fragments, but somehow as a whole" (Bradley, Introduction); and perhaps one could say the "propensity" Gide so graphically describes affords as good an indication as any of what could be meant by "metaphysical imagination." At any rate, in everyday language the phrase could hardly be used more vaguely. If it certainly makes sense today to talk of the "metaphysical imagination" of Plato or of Schopenhauer, of William Blake or of Franz Kafka, and it is not quite unheard of to find critics and others employing the expression when discussing the paintings of Braque or attempting to characterize the music of Bach or of Webern, the slightest reflection shows how very

little specific meaning accrues to the phrase in such contexts. Nor has it been given any special meaning by scholars.

Wilhelm Dilthey, for example, speaks not of "metaphysical imagination" but of "metaphysical consciousness" (*das metaphysische Bewusstsein*), by which he means an awareness of "the riddle of life." According to Dilthey, a thinker's or an artist's *Weltanschauung* is not really his imaginative "vision of the world"; it is his comprehensive answer to the question "What is the meaning of life?" Dilthey thinks that every *Weltanschauung* has three constituents: factual beliefs, value-judgments, and a set of ultimate goals. And in line with his general psychological theory, Dilthey directly relates these constituents not to any special uses of imagination but rather to what he takes to be the three more basic attitudes or aspects of personality: thought, feeling, and will. "In the typical *Weltanschauung* of philosophy," he writes, "a powerful philosophical personality makes one of the general attitudes toward the world dominant over the others, and its categories over theirs" (Dilthey p. 66). So Dilthey takes his main task to be the construction of a systematic theory of philosophical outlooks (a *Weltanschauungslehre*) which will analyze the "metaphysical consciousness" and the way different philosophical outlooks arise from it, classifying them under their most frequent types. In this way, he thinks, it will be possible, first, to expose the conceptual "illusions" on which metaphysicians rely in attempting to give rational support to their outlooks, and ultimately to display the true significance these outlooks have as historically conditioned "interpretations of life." In fact, Dilthey was particularly interested in the concept of imagination and he returned to it again and again throughout his career. Yet he nowhere devoted attention to something that could very precisely be called "metaphysical imagination." This is equally true of most other important writers on the nature of metaphysics, many of whom have been influenced by Dilthey, such as E. Spranger, K. Jaspers, R. G. Collingwood, and E. Cassirer. The phrase scarcely occurs in the relevant scholarly literature.

This is one reason why we shall not attempt here to provide a panoramic review of the various types of "metaphysical imagination" that might loosely be said to have existed from Parmenides to Jean-Paul Sartre, or even, perhaps, from Aeschylus to Luigi Pirandello. And there is also another reason. Under different headings, such monolithic accounts are often produced today. But practically all of them suffer from a methodological defect which seriously detracts from any claims they may have to be genuine contributions to the history of ideas.

One of the more distinguished performances in this genre is Jean Wahl's recent *L'Expérience métaphysique*, a work on a topic nominally very close to our own. Wahl owes much to Dilthey's approach to metaphysics and also to Bergson's belief that every philosophy results from a more fundamental, nondiscursive "intuition." For Wahl, as for Dilthey, the logic of the metaphysician's argument is not his essential characteristic; what is essential is his particular "interrogative experience." All great philosophy is "founded on intuitions, on experiences" of a deeply questioning kind. As a modern example, Wahl quotes André Breton: "There exists a point where life and death, the real and the imaginary, the past and the future, the knowable and unknowable, the high and the low, coincide" (Wahl, p. 86). To discover if this point can be attained is, says Wahl, *une interrogation vraiment métaphysique*. Wahl thinks there is in fact a multitude of "metaphysical experiences" and he tries to locate some of the more fundamental ones through a selective survey of the history of philosophy. Yet near the end of his book Wahl makes a telling revelation about his overall method of enquiry. He still insists that metaphysics is, above all else, a form of "questioning and interrogation," but by now his own survey forces him to go on to say that "the particular form given to the interrogation is, in the last resort, unimportant." For, after all, despite the great variety of "experiences" Wahl has detected even in the history of philosophy alone, his basic program has really committed him to the view that metaphysics is not confined to metaphysicians in the narrow sense.

If one studies Van Gogh's *Letters*, if one reads *Les Illuminations* by Rimbaud, Blake's *Songs of Innocence and Experience*, or the English "metaphysical" poets of the seventeenth century, then also, Wahl hastens to explain, one will find oneself confronted by *efforts métaphysiques* in so far as metaphysics is a deeply interrogative experience dealing in analogies and antitheses, fusion and coincidence. Now in a sense, of course, this is all perfectly true. It is difficult indeed to think of a great metaphysician of whom it could not be safely said that he is profoundly questioning, or even a little more concretely, that he is concerned, somehow or other, with the "reconciliation of opposites." That such a view could be maintained about the works (and even the personalities) of many creative artists also, need hardly be questioned. The main criticism one is bound to level at Wahl's book, however, serves very well to underline the problem that would be involved in writing about metaphysical imagination in analogous fashion. Taken as they are, these highly general categories of experience, interrogation, coincidence, and so forth are far too imprecise for the more empirically-minded historian to operate with. By a rhetorically persuasive use of them, a writer as brilliant as Jean Wahl could make almost any thesis seem plausible. And in this we shall not try to imitate him. A history of metaphysical imagination cannot be written in the same way as a history of classical mechanics or a history of post-Kantian idealism. For the concept of metaphysical imagination does not even begin to have any comparably circumscribed boundaries; if anything, its extension is broader, its horizon more widely and perplexingly fluctuating, than that of philosophy or of metaphysics *tout court*.

We are confronted with two highly complex words. In modern times "metaphysics" has come to mean very different things to different writers; while throughout its long history the term "imagination" (φαντασία, *imaginatio, immaginazione, Phantasie, Einbildungskraft*, etc.) has rarely retained for long one simple, easily identifiable use. This last point alone is, however, of considerable historical interest. One of the most significant linguistic events since the second half of the eighteenth century is precisely the manner in which "imagination" has increasingly come to be used in ways far removed from its root etymological sense of recalling or rearranging sense-data. Today, even for philosophers, to "imagine" is no longer just to "see" inwardly, to entertain mental "images," either of the "productive" or of the "reproductive" kinds, as Aristotle and even J. S. Mill ostensibly taught. It is not necessarily a process of "visualization" at all. To "imagine" can be to think in the sense of to suppose or believe; to simulate, make-believe, pretend; to invent or create; not least, to anticipate. For some contemporary writers it may be any combination of these things and even something more.

"Imagination," according to Gaston Bachelard, "is not the faculty of forming images of reality, it is the faculty of forming images which go beyond reality, which turn reality into song. It is a superhuman quality" (Bachelard, p. 43). Then is imagination perhaps essentially "metaphysical"? Bachelard, for one, would not shy from this formulation; nor, it seems, would Sartre. In his influential phenomenological study *L'Imaginaire*, Sartre attributes to imagination the truly herculean task of a "nihilation of the world in its essential structure." The basic function of consciousness is the creation of a substitute world, a "world of unrealities," "the imaginary"; and to imagine, says Sartre, is to exercise that uniquely human power which overcomes the nauseating disgust inseparable from all consciousness of physical reality (of the *en-soi*, in the terminology of *L'Etre et le néant*). In effect, Sartre relates imagination to the "negating function of consciousness" which, in turn, he equates with man's essential "freedom." The distancing power of imagination demonstrates that the true nature of human consciousness (of the *pour-soi*) is not to be solely in-the-midst-of-the-world; and conversely, "it is because he is transcendentally free that man can imagine." Outside the somewhat narrow confines of the English-speaking philosophical orthodoxies, pronouncements like these of Bachelard and Sartre can by no means be regarded as wildly eccentric. Leaving aside for a moment the high assessments of imagination still made by many contemporary poets and critics, one need only remember that unquestionably sober philosophers like Ernst Cassirer and Susanne Langer have also argued that the use of imagination can be seen to be man's distinguishing characteristic. Moreover, while no one seems to have developed any specific concept or theory of metaphysical imagination as such, many thinkers have held important views not only about what might be called the "metaphysical" (or "anthropological") significance of imagination, but also *about the role of imagination in metaphysical thinking*. It is with these latter views that this article will be primarily concerned. We shall treat the concept of "metaphysical imagination" in a piecemeal and historical fashion by examining what in fact it actually meant, or could have meant, to some of the main thinkers in the Western tradition. This will involve a review of what these thinkers understood by "imagination," and of what they took the role of imagination in metaphysics to be.

The attempt to understand philosophy in what J. H. Randall has called its "imaginative and poetic as distinguished from its critical function" (Randall, p. 100) has become a widespread scholarly preoccupation only in the twentieth century. Of course, all the manifold cultural and intellectual forces that made this attempt possible have their own history, some of the bare outlines of which will be sketched here. But we must take as our starting point the striking fact that before the Renaissance no serious scholar would have thought it even particularly intelligible, let alone valuable, to characterize the work of a great metaphysician by reference to some peculiar exercise of "imagination" on that metaphysician's part. In the Greek of Plato and Aristotle, in the Latin of Augustine or Aquinas an attempted translation of our richly evocative contemporary phrase "metaphysical imagination" would result in a virtually meaningless expression, lacking as much in connotation as in denotation, and amounting almost to a *contradictio in adjecto*. How did this change in terminology, and the very different understanding of the nature and function of metaphysics which it reflects, come about?

Plato would have found the expression "metaphysical imagination" deeply puzzling. He did not, of course, possess the word "metaphysics," which was later fabricated from the Greek τὰ μετὰ τὰ φυσικά, i.e., "the [books of Aristotle] after the *Physics*," but if someone had suggested to him that there was a form of ultimate philosophical insight to be gained primarily through "imagination" (φαντασία, or more commonly in Plato, εἰκασία), he would have dismissed such a suggestion with scorn. For imagining (εἰκασία) is, according to Plato's celebrated simile of the Line, simply a kind of conjecturing; its objects are shadows, reflections, or "likenesses," i.e., those images (εἰκόνες) of visible things which Socrates firmly places at the lowest level of being in the world of appearances. The recommended path of philosophical thinking is a linear progression away from this shadowy level of apprehension, through common-sense belief (πίστις), to mathematical and conceptual thinking (διάνοια); and finally to a knowledge (νόησις or επιστήμη) of the ideal Forms. Furthermore, Plato is so far from taking εἰκασία to be the special faculty of the philosopher that he attributes it, with the clearest of derogatory intentions, to the pseudo-philosopher, the sophist, whose essential characteristic is shown to be the "art of image making," consisting of the making of likenesses (εἰκαστική) and the making of appearances (φανταστική; *Sophist* 236f.). Plato similarly reprimands the artist because he produces a representation twice removed from the reality of the Forms, a mere μίμησις φαντάσματος, which because of its origin in the sensible world may well work on the emotions, but can scarcely be considered a source of philosophical knowledge.

So, on the face of it, this would be Plato's opinion about the cognitive significance of imagination: for him, as in one way or another, for the greater part of ancient and medieval thought, and even for most thinkers up to the middle of the eighteenth century, imagining is a mental reproduction or rearranging of sensible appearances, "a movement [in the mind]," said Aristotle, "which results upon an actual sensation" (*De anima* III. 3. 429a 1); at best, imagination (φαντασία, *phantasia, imaginatio*) acts as a kind of intermediary between sensation and thought, and to this extent its exercise is a necessary condition of our gaining ordinary empirical knowledge. But for Plato, as for the main Western metaphysical tradition that followed him, *this* kind of knowledge relates only to the "visible" or phenomenal, as opposed to the "intelligible," real world; and the philosophic apprehension of the latter is considered to be the function, not of imagination, but, in some sense of the word, of *reason*. To this extent therefore, those scholars seem to be right who see Plato as the initiator of that long tradition of philosophic distrust of imagination that can be clearly traced from Aristotle and the Stoics, through the Church Fathers and Schoolmen, to thinkers like Hobbes, the seventeenth-century rationalists, and beyond. Yet, as any close acquaintance with the Platonic *Dialogues* would immediately suggest, this view of Plato's assessment of imagination must be regarded as only superficially correct. In fact, it depends on too narrow a preoccupation with verbal equivalences; and it well illustrates the difficulties presented by the term "imagination" as a concept in the history of thought. For when one turns from Plato's specific pronouncements on the nature of $\epsilon\dot{\iota}\kappa\alpha\sigma\dot{\iota}\alpha$ and $\phi\alpha\nu\tau\alpha\sigma\dot{\iota}\alpha$ to certain more pervasive features of his philosophy, it soon becomes apparent that historically he also provided a powerful impetus in a direction very different, almost diametrically opposed, to that most often attributed to him.

The English romantic poet William Blake was undoubtedly thinking as a Platonist, or at any rate a Neo-Platonist, when he wrote in 1809: "Vision, or Imagination, is a Representation of what Eternally Exists Really, and Unchangeably" (Blake, p. 145). And Blake's use of "Imagination" in this somewhat mystical sense was, as we shall see, by no means a personal idiosyncrasy, devoid of historical precedent. The crucial point is that Plato himself simply did not possess a word (or a single concept) containing the very wide complex of connotations we have found to be inherent in the modern term "imagination." By examining solely his use of, say, $\epsilon\dot{\iota}\kappa\alpha\sigma\dot{\iota}\alpha$, therefore, we cannot hope to discover whether he thought imagination, in one or more of its richer *modern* senses, could legitimately be used to name a cognitive faculty or mode of metaphysical insight. And in fact a broader look at Plato's thought strongly suggests that Plato would have taken no exception to Blake's use of "Imagination" could it have been translated for him. For "insight" in the sense of an "intellectual vision"—something certainly covered by the modern word "imagination" as its meaning was modified and handed down to us by the romantics—is central to Plato's whole conception of philosophical knowledge. A movement from darkness to light is everywhere used by him to convey the true path from ignorance to wisdom, unconsciousness to consciousness, from error and illusion to truth and reality; it recurs not only in his use of myth and symbol, but even permeates his technical vocabulary. A familiar instance is Plato's word for the ideal Forms ($\epsilon\dot{\iota}\delta os$) which is related to a verb ($\epsilon\dot{\iota}\delta\omega$) meaning "to see," so that it becomes natural for Plato to speak of the world of Forms, or ultimate reality, as something essentially intellectually "perceptible," seen, suffused with light, like the sun in the visible world. What is more, according to the famous passage in the *Seventh Letter* (341C ff.), philosophic knowledge is not to be achieved solely by discursive, dialectical means but by a kind of vision.

There the ascending path towards wisdom moves from the name or word ($\dot{o}\nu o\mu\alpha$) and definition ($\lambda\dot{o}\gamma os$), to intellectual "image, views, and perceptions" ($\epsilon\dot{\iota}\delta\omega\lambda o\nu$; $\dot{o}\psi\epsilon\iota s\ \tau\epsilon\ \kappa\alpha\dot{\iota}\ \alpha\dot{\iota}\sigma\theta\dot{\eta}\sigma\epsilon\iota s$) through which, after many repetitions, the highest form of knowledge is experienced as a sudden "spark transmitted" and "fire kindled" in the disciple's soul, whereupon he is overwhelmed with a feeling of blessedness and fulfillment ($\epsilon\dot{v}\delta\alpha\iota\mu o\nu\dot{\iota}\alpha$).

We cannot enter here into the details of how this conception of the highest form of philosophical knowledge was adapted from Plato by the classical Neo-Platonists during the second to the fifth centuries A.D.; nor how similar views about the significance of imagination reappear in the elaborate doctrines of "illumination" and ecstasy propounded by very many Neo-Platonic and Christian writers throughout the Middle Ages. Perhaps it will be sufficient to note that Plotinus' theory of emanations led him explicitly to single out $\phi\alpha\nu\tau\alpha\sigma\dot{\iota}\alpha$, in its highest sense, as a function of the rational soul and capable of reflecting Forms or Ideas (see Bundy, Ch. 6); and, to mention only one later instance, that Dante's conception of poetico-mystical vision as a form of *alta fantasia*, a sensuous intuition of spiritual reality made possible through the medium of divine grace (see, e.g., *Purgatorio*, Canto xvii, 13–18; *Paradiso*, Canto xxxiii), can be traced back, in part, to Plotinus' use of $\phi\alpha\nu\tau\alpha\sigma\dot{\iota}\alpha$, and hence to Plato's final statements about the nature of ultimate philosophical insight. Instead, we must move directly to the Renaissance. For it is really only then that the relation between imagination and metaphysical thinking was expressly singled out as a topic for detailed investigation and first began to be considered, along with so many other things, in a genuinely empirical spirit.

From the time of the founding of the Platonic Academy at Florence in 1462 to the appearance of Bacon's *Novum Organum* (1620) almost every major thinker discussed the question of the function of imagination in philosophical, theological, and magical knowledge. The variety and complexity of these views is truly remarkable and cannot be reproduced in a short space. (Material suggestive of this complexity, together with a preliminary bibliography, may be found in the fascinating chapter on imagination in Burton's *Anatomy of Melancholy* [1652], Part I, Sec. 2, ii.) Still, the views of Paracelsus and Giordano Bruno, on the one hand, and those of Francis Bacon, on the other, deserve special mention because of their very divergent but highly important impact on later thought.

In their assessment of imagination, both Paracelsus and Bruno strikingly dissent from the main stream of Aristotelian scholasticism. They develop ideas derived from hermeticism and Neo-Platonism, from, for exam-

211

ple, the Alexandrian Neo-Platonist Synesius of Cyrene, whose treatise *De somniis* contained a defense of imagination on the grounds that it was used by divine powers to communicate with man in dreams. Paracelsus sometimes seems to write as if he thinks *magia* and *imaginatio* are etymologically related terms. According to him, it is through use of imagination, "the inner sense of the soul," that things inaccessible to the physical senses can be perceived. Sense perception and reason are the cognitive organs of the physical body; imagination that of the sidereal body. Through imagination the soul intuits the inner powers and virtues of physical things, recognizing their signature or seal (*signatum*). Like Paracelsus, Bruno is deeply impressed by the ancient idea of a correspondence between the macrocosm of the universe and the microcosm of man. He believes that cosmic effects pass through us by means of an imaginative force (*vis imaginativa*) which has its foundation in man's imaginative soul (*spiritus phantasticus*). Although Bruno distinguishes four grades of knowing on a Neo-Platonic model—sense, imagination, reason, intellect—he refuses to see these as compartmentalized, and tries to envisage the whole process of cognition as somehow governed by imagination. Thus, for him, imagination is not merely reproductive and combinatory, as it is for the scholastics, but the living source of original forms, what he otherwise calls the *sinus inexplebilis formarum et specierum*. In his theory of mnemonics, he claims that the practiced confrontation of the mind with significant images can magically excite the imagination in such a way as to bring to consciousness the forms of an intelligible world beyond the world of the senses; whereupon the mind recovers, so to speak, its fundamental organization and unity with the cosmos. In this sense he calls the magically activated *imaginatio* "the sole gate to all internal affections and the link of links." (For a discussion of these views of Paracelsus and Bruno see Pagel, pp. 121–25; Yates [1964], passim., [1966], pp. 228f., 257.)

Such ideas are not easy to state with any convincing show of conceptual precision, and they still remain for the most part unassimilated by the main tradition of Western philosophical thought as this is understood in the English-speaking world. Nevertheless their cultural, and even their philosophical, impact has been very great. As Jean Starobinski points out, from Paracelsus to van Helmont, to Fludd and Digby, to Böhme, to Stahl and Mesmer, right through to the romantic poets and philosophers (via the medical school of Montpellier), such ideas about the cognitive—and spiritually therapeutic—significance of imagination continue unabated. If one were to extend this list to the present day, it would have to further include the symbolist poets in France (thus Baudelaire's panegyrics on imagination in his *Salon de 1859*, where he calls it the "queen of all faculties" which "creates a new world," something "intimately related to the infinite," etc., repeats many of the Neo-Platonic and hermetic formulae), and hence a large part of modern poetic theory. It would also have to include surrealism, the pronouncements of writers like Carl Jung, Bachelard, and Sartre, and, as we shall see, the epistemologies of major Continental philosophers, such as Bergson, Heidegger, and Jaspers—many of whom, thinkers and artists alike, have found it necessary to return to the sources of these ideas in the original writings of Paracelsus and Bruno. Such is one, doubtless the predominant, facet of Renaissance thought about the significance of imagination for metaphysics. It was revived, elaborated, and applied more specifically to the processes of artistic creation at the time of the romantic movement. The Renaissance closed, however, with one of the most devastating attacks upon this whole way of thinking.

Francis Bacon is particularly interesting because in him we first find an extremely clear and surprisingly well-developed account of the role of imagination in metaphysics which has since become something like received doctrine amongst certain kinds of empiricist philosophers. Bacon is fully aware that imagination operates, perfectly legitimately, not only in rhetoric and poetry but in many other areas of human life. As a means of gaining *knowledge*, however, he considers that the use of imagination is strictly limited. While it may be true that in religious experience "our imagination raises itself above our reason" this is not because "divine illumination" resides in imagination; *knowledge* of God can only exist in the understanding. What can happen in religious experiences is that "divine grace uses the motions of the imagination as an instrument of illumination . . . which is the reason why religion ever sought access to the mind by similitudes, types, parables, visions, dreams" (*De augmentis*, Book IV, Chs. 1–3; Book V, Ch. 1). Bacon's recognition of the suggestive and metaphorical power of imagination, its close association with visions, dreams, and with what we would today call "fantasies," is carried over into his influential account of the *idola mentis*.

The "idols of the mind" are those deeply-rooted psychological (and linguistic) "habits" through which are produced premature "anticipations" of nature as opposed to truly scientific "interpretations." Nature will be properly understood and controlled only when the natural but distorting tendencies of the unaided human mind itself are held in check. A radical *humiliatio* of the intellect is needed; a new, regular, systematic (even, Bacon seems to suggest, a mechanical) method of induction must take the place of the hitherto arbitrary, subjective methodologies of philosophers and natural scientists alike. In Book I of the *Novum Organum* Bacon distinguishes four principal types of *idola* each of which he then proceeds to attack. Here we need only note the close connection he makes between speculative thinking in both philosophy and science and the uses of imagination.

Anticipations of nature "being deduced from a few instances, and these principally of familiar occurrence, immediately strike the understanding and satisfy the imagination"; while genuinely scientific *interpretations,* being more complex and less familiarly derived, do not (ibid., Sec. 28). "The human mind," he says in a characteristic image, "resembles those uneven mirrors, which impart their own properties to different objects, from which rays are emitted, and distort and disfigure them" (Sec. 41). Indeed "all the systems of philosophy hitherto received" are both imaginary and imaginative products: "so many plays brought out and performed, creating fictitious and theatrical worlds." And like actual plots invented for the stage, these philosophical productions "are more consistent, elegant, and pleasurable than those taken from real history" (Secs. 44 and 42). Instead of employing what has come to be known today as a method of "falsification," where "in establishing any true axiom [theory, hypothesis], the negative instance is the most powerful," the human mind, left to itself, naturally takes a different course. The speculative philosopher "forces everything to add fresh support and confirmation" to his theory, or rejects clear counter-instances "with violent and injurious prejudice, rather than sacrifice the authority of his first conclusion." A dominant reason for this is that the mind "is most excited by whatever strikes and enters it at once and suddenly, and by which imagination is immediately filled and inflated" (Secs. 46 and 47). An excessive reliance on imagination is also evident in the way philosophers elaborate closed systems of thought according to which the whole nature of the universe is hastily conceived in terms of a single principle, or on the analogy of a small group of phenomena. Gilbert's attempt to erect a complete system of natural philosophy on the basis of his magnetic studies is one of Bacon's favorite whipping horses in this respect. Thinkers of this sort suffer from a kind of *idée fixe* which precipitates them into seeking imaginary "shadows of resemblance" even in the face of the most manifest differences and distinctions (Secs. 53f.). Bacon lays special emphasis on the fact that such "fictions," "preconceived fancies," or "fantastical" philosophies are not infrequently the result of a thinker's subjective desires. A philosopher's feelings often "imbue and corrupt his understanding in innumerable and sometimes imperceptible ways." For "the human understanding resembles not a dry light, but admits a tincture of the will and passions," and a man "always believes more readily that which he prefers." Hence the typically metaphysical search for formal and final causes, the latter being clearly "more allied to man's own nature" (Secs. 49 and 48; cf., e.g., *Advancement of Learning,* Book I, Part 5, Sec. 11, and Book II, Part 7, Sec. 5).

It is then, according to Bacon, through following the natural, undirected propensities of his mind that the metaphysician falls into error. Not least his imagination—that "Janus-like" faculty which has equal relation to "will, appetite and affection" as to "understanding and reason" (*Advancement,* II, 12, 1)—leads him to construe the nature of things *a priori* and anthropomorphically, *ex analogia hominis,* rather than empirically and objectively, *ex analogia universi.*

The originality and historical importance of Bacon's *Novum Organum* does not depend on his having produced any new logical refutation of the arguments metaphysicians use to defend their theories; nor does it rest on his own positive recommendations about the logic of scientific discovery, which proved in the event to be of little practical value. It would, of course, be possible to trace all the ingredients of Bacon's analysis of metaphysical thinking to earlier writers. Here, as elsewhere, he owes much to contemporaries and near contemporaries like Machiavelli, Telesio, and Montaigne. He has learned from the materialistic realism of the ancient atomists, Democritus and Lucretius. One of his favorite quotations is from Fragment 2 of Heraclitus, which might be read as a prefiguration of Bacon's whole skeptical approach to speculative philosophy: "Although the Logos is common, the many live as if they had a private understanding." Nevertheless, in terms of synthesis and unsurpassed virtuosity of expression, Bacon marks a turning point in the history of antimetaphysical thinking. He is the first great pathologist of philosophical thought. It is not so much the logic, but the psychological origin and utility of ideas that concerns him: the hidden motives, subjective dispositions, and emotional needs out of which so many "specious meditations, speculations, and theories of mankind" have been engendered, collectively constituting, he says, "a kind of insanity" (op. cit., Sec. 10).

Outside England, Bacon's critique of speculative thinking did not at first have any great effect upon philosophers. It is true that the great Continental thinkers in the seventeenth century were all preoccupied with the problem of finding, as Descartes put it, a "new method of rightly conducting the reason and seeking for truth in the sciences," and nominally, at any rate, this problem might seem to be the very one that preoccupied Bacon. Like Bacon also, Descartes and Malebranche, for example, often show un-

213

mitigated contempt for the philosophical methods of the scholastics; while, again, on the face of it they share with Bacon the conviction that in metaphysics and natural philosophy "the entire labour of the understanding [must] be commenced afresh, and the mind itself be . . . not left to take its own course, but guided at every step" (*Novum Organum*, Preface). Compare, and contrast, the program of Descartes' *Regulae ad directionem ingenii* (apparently written in 1628). But in fact Bacon's strictures on metaphysics are very much more radical than the *intellectus emendatio* demanded by the Continental rationalists.

When Descartes said a set of rules was needed to help the human mind arrive at truth in the sciences, he did not mean to imply that the mind was, as it were, intrinsically at odds with the real world and in need of external aids to achieve knowledge. Descartes certainly thought observation and experiment played a crucial role in science, but his conception of this role differed significantly from Bacon's. For, like Plato, Descartes believed that the human mind and whatever else was real outside it were essentially commensurate, that they were, perhaps one could say, of the same order of being. It is true that he considered mind and matter to be different "substances," the essence of mind being "thinking" and the essence of matter geometrical "extension." And this celebrated dualism having been set up, it became one of the great problems of seventeenth-century thought to provide a coherent account of psychophysical interaction.

Yet for all this the Cartesian dualism was in no way designed to create an insoluble problem about how the mind could know the real world. For, according to Descartes, not only is the essence of mind "thinking," but the most perfect sort of thinking is the kind that goes on in logic and mathematics. Moreover, the criterion of truth in logic and mathematics is "that which can be clearly and distinctly conceived," and this is also the criterion of truth that must be appealed to, Descartes believed, when one comes to establish the fundamental principles of the natural sciences. The crucial point is that with Descartes, very much as with Plato, a criterion for determining truth (above all, mathematical truth) is made to serve as the criterion for determining what is *real*. The more clearly and distinctly conceivable something is, in particular the more its nature can be expressed in the formal language of mathematics, the more it is a part of "reality" as opposed to appearance or illusion. Simple observation may suggest otherwise, but reflection puts it beyond all doubt that the true world consists of mathematical forms. Hence by its own most innate capacities and natural light, the human mind is perfectly fitted to comprehend reality. Only because this clear intellec-

tual vision is so often clouded by the senses—and by passion, prejudice, the influence of bad education, and so on, all of which distorting factors issue from, or act upon us via, the senses—do misapprehension and error occur. If only the mind can be cleansed of all sensuous distortions the intelligible, mathematical order of God's creation will be revealed. One of these distorting factors is the imagination, which Descartes conceives as a sensuous power of visualization.

In fact, Descartes is not quite so scathing about the philosophical dangers of imagination as Malebranche or Spinoza were and he would probably have considered Pascal's famous diatribe against imagination as *cette partie décevante dans l'homme, cette maîtresse d'erreur et de fausseté* (Pascal, 562–63) to be an exaggeration. Descartes saw that imagination can sometimes be an aid even in mathematics, for instance, in geometrical representations of relations between quantities. But true to the Platonico-Augustinian tradition, Descartes thought of such sensuous representations as only an imperfect aid for finite human understanding. Above all, the sensuous origin of imagination, its close relation to the body, is what worries Descartes. This is why imagination is to be banished from metaphysics and *reason,* a process of clear and distinct conception and deduction, put in its place. For it was from his mathematical studies, Descartes declared in the *Discourse on Method* (1637), that he had been led to believe that all the possible objects of human knowledge were linked together like the series of propositions in an Euclidean demonstration, and that if, in our empirical as well as our conceptual inquiries, we accepted nothing as true that was not self-evidently so "and kept to the right order in deducing one truth from the other," then "there was nothing so remote that it could not be reached, nothing so hidden that it could not be discovered" (op. cit., Part II). What are needed are certain simple "rules for the direction of the mind" which lay down what this "right order" of thinking shall be, how the impediments presented, not by the mind itself in its own inner purity, but by the senses, are to be overcome. Here, imagination is worse than useless. Insofar as it is an affection of the body, imagination "is more of a hindrance than a help in metaphysical speculations" (Descartes, II, 622). The upshot of all this is that Descartes—and on this fundamental point he was followed by Malebranche, Spinoza, and Leibniz—believed reality to be a rational, interconnected, intelligible whole, the general structure of which corresponds very closely to some of the most characteristic forms of human cognition.

Now it was precisely this assumption, that there exists a kind of pre-established harmony between the mind's innermost, *a priori* modes of conception and reasoning and the true structure of the world, that Bacon called in question. Bacon's suspicions about attempts to construe nature on models derived from mathematics run exactly parallel with his skepticism about the use of models derived from Aristotelian logic. The true interpreter of nature begins, not with self-evident truths, "clear and distinct ideas," but with the collection of observed instances, from which he proceeds, by a strict method of *empirical* inference, to make whatever inductions are possible. This is how laws of nature are established. No doubt mathematics will often be used in the practical process of induction, for instance, in weighing, measuring lengths, and so on. And the scientist may sometimes be able to hit upon a mathematical equation which would exhibit the Form of the phenomena he is investigating. But laws of nature need not necessarily be expressed, nor be expressible, mathematically. There is no sufficient reason to believe, as the Pythagoreans did, that "the nature of things consists of numbers" (*De augmentis*, Book III, Ch. 5). Pythagoras was "a mystic," and those modern thinkers who, like Copernicus, follow Pythagoras in approaching nature with preconceived notions of its harmonious mathematical structure commit the cardinal sin of "anticipation." Their theories are little more than "the speculations of one who cares not what fictions he introduces into nature, provided his calculations answer" (Bacon, *Descriptio globi intellectualis*, Ch. 6).

Thus despite their superficial similarities of aim in producing new methods of enquiry, in both philosophy and science, there is in fact a crucial disagreement between Bacon and Descartes, a disagreement which was to be of great significance in the subsequent history of metaphysics. As a guide to the true understanding of nature, Bacon distrusts not so much the senses (or the "sensuous" imagination) but the human mind itself. And really, for him, the role of "reason" is just as suspect as the role of "imagination" in metaphysics. Three of the four general types of idols Bacon enumerates he describes as *ratio humana nativa*, inherent in human reason. Unlike Descartes' *Regulae* then, the *Novum Organum* was not meant to expound a method through which the mind could be cleansed of the allegedly obfuscating influences of the senses, and so be led to apprehend an intelligible world which somehow corresponds to the *a priori* structures of logical and mathematical thought. Rather, Bacon's intention was to provide a method which, if adopted, would lead to a proper use of the senses, and hence to "a true model of the world, such as it is in fact, not such as a man's own reason would have it to be" (*Novum Organum*, I, Sec. 74). Here "reason" (*ratio*) or "understanding" (*intellectus*) is meant to cover also the

vagaries of philosophic imagination. Both reason and imagination are seen to be equally culpable, equally productive of spurious anthropomorphic fantasies which stand in the way of genuine knowledge. "For the world is not to be narrowed down until it will go into the understanding . . . but the understanding is to be expanded and opened up until it can take in the image of the world, as it actually is" (*Parasceve*, Sec. 4).

The full significance of Bacon's perspective on metaphysical thinking was first appreciated on a European scale only during the Enlightenment. For our purposes, however, the most important fact about the eighteenth century is the way Bacon's position underwent an important series of modifications. Most notably, it was first of all much further elaborated by the Abbé de Condillac, and then dramatically transformed and surpassed in the writings of Denis Diderot and Immanuel Kant.

Consciously following Bacon, Condillac gave a psychological analysis of the *préjugés* at the root of what he called *l'esprit des systèmes* (Condillac, *Traité des systèmes*, 1749; revised 1771). An overactive imagination is responsible, says Condillac, for most of the errors of philosophers. Whatever they imagine they believe to have a counterpart in reality, and their systems are elaborated accordingly. No doubt we can admire the architectonic structure of these systems aesthetically, as we would *un chef-d'oeuvre de l'art*. But we are bound to feel the artist himself was suffering from mental derangement (*la plus insigne folie*) in producing it. For how else would he have come to place so superb an edifice on such epistemologically feeble foundations? The truth is that through the demands of their particular temperaments and, more generally, in order to make external reality seem concordant with human desires, metaphysicians *donnent leurs rêves pour des interprétations de la nature*. In metaphysics as elsewhere the order of our ideas ultimately depends on some need or interest. Consequently the surest means of being on guard against metaphysical systems is to study the needs that led them to be created. "Such is the touchstone of error and truth: go back to the origin of both, see how they entered the mind and you will distinguish them perfectly. It is a method with which the philosophers I condemn are little acquainted" (Condillac, op. cit., Chs. 1–3, 19; *Traité des animaux*, Chs. 1–2; *La Logique*, II, Sec. 1; and compare further on the role of imagination Condillac's first major work, *Essai sur l'origine des connaissances humaines*, 1746).

Condillac's argument may need more careful handling than he managed to give it, but needless to say, with the widespread adoption of Locke's sensationalist theory of knowledge, such a genetic psychological method had come to be applied to the whole field of the "science of human nature" in the eighteenth century. The specific criticism of metaphysics, however, originated with Bacon. And one may say that from Bacon and Condillac to the *idéologues* Destutt de Tracy and Cabanis, from early nineteenth-century positivism to writers like F. A. Lange and, above all, Friederich Nietzsche—whose *Götzen-Dämmerung* (1889) was so styled with an intentional reference to Bacon's *idola*—this particular psychological weapon became directed against all forms of speculative thought with increasing severity and sophistication. Freud himself was writing firmly within the Baconian tradition when he described religion as a "universal neurosis," lacking all rational foundation, and largely resulting from "wish-fulfillment" (*The Future of an Illusion*, 1927). As we shall see, due largely to the prestige of science and to the persistence of certain views about the nature of science, the Baconian perspective on metaphysical imagination has reappeared, in one form or another, right down to the present day. Yet already during the Enlightenment its limitations were becoming apparent.

Diderot's *Pensées sur l'interprétation de la nature* (1753–54) was undoubtedly inspired by Bacon; in style and polemical intention it was partly modelled on the *Novum Organum*. And it is impossible to miss the analogy between Diderot's central distinction between *la philosophie rationnelle* and *la philosophie expérimentale*, and Bacon's distinction between the "anticipatory" and "interpretive" approaches to nature. But, despite many such points of connection, Diderot's *Pensées* marks a critical stage of transition in Enlightenment thinking about the nature of science, a stage after which there could be little belief left in Bacon's theory of induction. In the history of modern thought current evaluations of metaphysics have frequently been linked to prevailing ideas about the nature of science. Since the time of Bacon, scientific knowledge has increasingly been taken as the paradigm for *all* knowledge, and it is generally understood that scientific knowledge can be obtained only if certain methodological procedures are adhered to. Opinions about just what these procedures are, or should be, vary significantly from period to period. But at times when there is thought to exist an unbridgeable gulf between genuine scientific investigation, on the one hand, and metaphysical speculation, on the other, the metaphysician's cognitive pretensions may well seem to be wholly illusory. However, at other times the contrast between science and metaphysics is drawn far less sharply or at least in ways far less damaging to metaphysics. Then it is easier for metaphysics to be viewed in a more favorable light. Compared with Bacon's *Novum Organum*, Diderot's *Pensées* represents just such a change of outlook.

For all his warnings about the "anticipatory" nature of *la philosophie rationnelle*, Diderot lays strong and very un-Baconian emphasis on the use of "conjecture" in science. He doubts whether scientific theories are ever arrived at by any kind of rational *inference* from phenomena and laws; rather, he thinks they are the result of *intuition*. In effect, Diderot substitutes this notion of scientific intuition for Bacon's methods of induction. It is not methodic induction, but an inspired conjecture that enables the scientist to relate a given body of facts or elementary laws in such a way as to lead to the progress of knowledge. The greatest experimenters eventually come to possess, as Newton did, says Diderot, "a facility for supposing or perceiving oppositions or analogies." Their close familiarity with nature leads to their developing a sort of *pressentiment qui a le caractère d'inspiration*—an "instinct," "feeling," or *esprit de divination* for the fruitful conjecture. So there is, according to Diderot, an important (and hitherto largely neglected) place for imagination and genius in science (Diderot, op. cit., Secs. 30–31, 14–15). But on this issue Diderot had to conduct a long debate with some of his contemporaries.

Helvétius, in his *De l'homme* (1773), maintained that theory must always advance behind experimentation and never precede it. He cited Descartes as a classic violator of this empiricist maxim. In his *Réfutation d'Helvétius* (1773–74), Diderot reaffirmed his own convictions. "Are experiments made haphazardly?," he asks. "Is not experimentation often preceded by a supposition, an analogy, a systematic idea which experiment will either confirm or destroy? I pardon Descartes for having imagined his laws of motion, but what I do not excuse him for is his failure to verify by experiment whether or not they were, in nature, such as he had supposed them to be" (*Oeuvres philosophiques*, p. 598). The position of Helvétius on scientific method was, of course, nominally the official position of the Newtonian school in eighteenth-century France. Newton's proclamation, *hypotheses non fingo*—"hypotheses whether metaphysical or physical . . . have no place in experimental philosophy"—had been taken very literally by Helvétius, Condillac, Voltaire, and by the majority of practicing scientists. "Particular propositions are [to be] inferr'd from the phenomena, and afterwards render'd general by induction," Newton had insisted, with no reference to the role of imagination in science (Newton, II, 547). *Il faut se conduire,* wrote Voltaire, Newton's most powerful protagonist in France, *comme les Boyle, les Galilée, les Newton; examiner, peser, calculer et mesurer, mais jamais deviner* (Voltaire, XLVI, 202). And in this article on "Imagination," written for Diderot's *Encyclopédie*, Voltaire had refrained from giving imagination any constructive place in scientific thought. Needless to say,

Diderot himself recommends *divination* in science only at a certain point, only after facts have been collected and when *interprétation* of nature begins. But here imagination is vital, as it is, according to Diderot, in so many other areas of human endeavor. For, indeed, "imagination is the quality without which one is neither a poet, a philosopher, a wit, a rational being, nor a man" (*Oeuvres esthétiques*, p. 218).

What were the intellectual origins of this stress on imagination in Diderot's theory of science? Leaving aside the promptings of his own extraordinarily creative personality, there seem to have been two major influences. First, both as editor of the great *Encyclopédie* and as a speculative biologist in his own right, Diderot had become thoroughly acquainted with contemporary scientific work. In particular, Diderot knew the views about scientific method expounded by a series of eminent Dutch physicists, from Christiaan Huygens to s'Gravesande, who authoritatively drew attention to the heuristic and pragmatic nature of scientific principles and theories, and who could find little use for Baconian induction (see Cassirer [1951], pp. 60f.; and for a broader historical discussion Medawar [1967], pp. 131–55, and idem [1969], pp. 42f.). Secondly, these new perspectives on scientific method became fused in Diderot's mind with certain ideas about the nature of creativity in the fine arts. Diderot's enthusiasm for science was at least equalled by his knowledge of the advances in aesthetic theory that had occurred since the beginning of the eighteenth century, and to which he himself had made important contributions. In his *Encyclopédie* article "Beau" (1752), where he surveys some of these ideas, and elsewhere, Diderot developed a concept of genius which was meant to apply to scientific theorizing as well as to creation in the arts. Whether artist, scientist, or philosopher, Diderot's man of genius possesses *l'esprit observateur*. Yet there is also a sense in which he "imagines rather than sees; produces rather than finds; seduces rather than guides" (*Oeuvres esthétiques*, p. 15). And like the fictional D'Alembert in Diderot's dramatic dialogue, *Le Rêve de D'Alembert* (written in 1769), the scientific genius may well suffer from a *délire philosophique*, the dream being for Diderot a suitable medium for the intuitive act of biological speculation. Hence, in the *Pensées sur l'interprétation de la nature*, Diderot's own fascination for the evolutionary hypotheses of Maupertuis and Buffon. Theories of this kind, he believes, depend on a close acquaintance with the known facts of experience. But they do not issue from the rigorous application of "method," inductive or deductive, Baconian or Cartesian. They spring from the free insight of genius which imaginatively seizes upon *les liaisons singulières, délicates, fugitives de quelques idées voisines, ou leur opposition et leur contraste* (ibid., p. 13).

Thus Diderot exposed the arbitrariness of certain current attempts to keep "reason" and "imagination" in separate compartments. It seems appropriate that the work where Diderot most fully unfolds his idea of genius, *Le Neveu de Rameau*, should have been first published by Goethe in 1805, just in time for Hegel to make substantial use of it in the *Phänomenologie des Geistes* (see, e.g., pp. 516 and 534f. in Baillie's translation). At any rate, after Diderot especially, it became clear that the distinction between science and metaphysics had often been drawn too sharply, and hardly even in the right place. This problem preoccupied Kant.

Kant characterized all traditional metaphysical thinking as "transcendent," in the sense that it attempted, he thought, to pass beyond the limits of possible experience. By means of rational argument, the metaphysician tries to come to a conclusion about the *totality* of things and events; unlike the specialized natural scientist, he seeks a complete explanation of the whole of reality. Conceived in this way, however, the metaphysician's task is always bound to fail. Not only is this suggested by the history of metaphysics where, from the time of the Greeks onwards, one system has given way to another without any convincing sign of the sort of progress we have come to expect in the natural sciences, but there are also decisive conceptual reasons for regarding the metaphysician as inevitably doomed to frustration. For, even in principle, we can have knowledge only about the limited and conditioned objects of actual and possible experience. If we attempt to transcend these limitations, if we seek to ask whether, for example, the Universe as a whole is finite or infinite, or whether there is a First Cause, or some overall cosmic plan within which our own role might possibly be discerned—if, more generally, we wish to know whether there exist such things as God, Freedom, and Immortality—then in all these and similar characteristically metaphysical questions, we are raising issues whose solution lies outside the field of possible experience. Answers to such questions may be, and indeed often are, given. But, even in principle, Kant argued, none of these answers can be demonstrated to be true any more than they can conclusively be shown to be false. Hence metaphysics as a science (*Wissenschaft*), in the sense of an established body of systematically ordered and certain knowledge, is impossible. At best metaphysical beliefs can only be dogmatically, rather than demonstratively, maintained, as were in fact, Kant held, the beliefs of his immediate rationalist predecessors of the Wolffian school in Germany. Yet having thus exposed the cognitive pretensions of (at any rate much) traditional metaphysics, Kant did not simply go on to reject all metaphysical thinking, and propose,

217

like Bacon and modern positivism, that philosophical speculation should be dismissed in favor of scientific empiricism. For Kant firmly believed that the "*natural* and inevitable *illusion*" of metaphysics could never be eradicated from the human mind. Even when men are in fact convinced they cannot obtain genuine knowledge through metaphysics, they will still be "impetuously driven on by an inward need to questions such as cannot be answered by any empirical employment of reason, or by principles thence derived." In all men "as soon as their reason has become ripe for speculation, there has always existed and will always continue to exist some kind of metaphysics" (*Kritik der reinen Vernunft*, B 21). And this leads Kant to consider the question "How is metaphysics, as a natural disposition, possible?" It is here, in his diagnosis of man's natural urge towards metaphysics, that we meet some of Kant's most characteristic and historically important ideas; here also, the radical shift in general epistemological perspective that had taken place since the time of Bacon becomes very obvious.

In the Preface to the second edition of the *Critique of Pure Reason* Kant praises Bacon's call for controlled experimentation in the sciences. But he considers Bacon's account of the nature of scientific discovery to be fundamentally mistaken. It was not the philosopher Bacon, but, says Kant, practicing scientists, men like Galileo, Torricelli, and Stahl, who realized "that reason has insight only into that which it produces after a plan of its own." The actual founders of modern science developed theoretical procedures and constructs by means of which nature was effectively constrained "to answer questions of reason's own determining," and to that extent these scientists exhibited a much greater degree of creativity than was ever allowed for in Bacon's mechanical methods of induction. Kant agrees with Bacon that the mind "must approach nature [empirically] in order to be taught by her," yet he thinks the sort of approach made has not only never in fact been, but cannot in principle ever be, so humble and childlike as Bacon's favorite images suggest. For, according to Kant, in scientific investigation the mind can never confront nature "in the character of a pupil who listens to everything the teacher chooses to say," but only "in that of an appointed judge who compels the witnesses to answer questions he has himself formulated" (B, xiii). Bacon wrote as if he thought the *structure* of reality was something existing in an external world independently of the human mind. As we saw, the object of the critique of idols was to effect a "purification" of the mind, a removal of all internal obstacles to unprejudiced vision, so that the real external, and independently existing structure (*forma*) of nature can be

perceived. Baconian induction is simply a methodic instrument with which to free the human mind of its natural obscuring tendencies, of the wayward exercise of both "imagination" and "reason." Kant's whole theory of knowledge was specifically directed against this form of realism.

This is not the place to discuss Kant's intellectual development, but it is worth noting that it had one thing in common with Diderot's. In arriving at the details of his own concept of mind Kant was affected, in clearly traceable ways, on the one hand by eighteenth-century discussions about the nature of scientific discovery (above all by certain accounts given by natural scientists themselves), and on the other hand, by those aestheticians, from Shaftesbury to the Scottish philosophers, and also Diderot himself, who had broken new ground in their analysis of concepts like beauty, taste, genius, and, of course, imagination. Kant's specific discussions of imagination (*Einbildungskraft*) occur in fairly narrow epistemological contexts and he never uses a phrase corresponding to "metaphysical imagination." Yet for our purpose, Kant's uses of *Einbildungskraft* is not the most important thing. What is important is that Kant's conception of the mind's essentially *active* cognitive powers, his conception, that is, of Understanding (*Verstand*), of Judgment (*Urteilskraft*), and of Reason (*Vernunft*)—particularly of the latter in its transcendent, or metaphysical, use—was developed in the context of current discussions about imagination and about creative activity in general. Thus Hume, for example, had assigned a crucial role to imagination in his account of the foundations of empirical knowledge, and he had even found it possible to refer to "the Understanding" as "the general and more established properties of the imagination" (*Treatise* [1739], Book I, Part IV, Sec. 7); while Kant's contemporary, J. N. Tetens, himself a student of the Scottish psychological school, had given an analysis of *Dichtkraft*, or "productive imagination," which helped Kant to determine the part the mind's own synthetic activity plays in the constitution of objective knowledge (on Tetens and Kant see Vleeschauwer, pp. 82f.).

For Kant, the very possibility of human knowledge could be explained only on the supposition that the mind makes an essential contribution to our experience of the external world. Space and time, cause and effect, substance and accident, unity and plurality, indeed all the general formal concepts and categories we tacitly employ in describing our ordinary experience are, according to Kant, "constitutive" of that experience. There can be no experience and no "nature" without them. Far from our being able to discover a ready-made structure in the universe, in order to experience nature at all the human mind is impelled to prescribe a structure to it. Thus, while Kant agreed that in the natural sciences we must approach nature empirically and not "fictitiously ascribe to it" (in any of the more blatant ways of Bacon's "anticipations"), nevertheless he argued that we must inevitably be guided in our research by something we have ourselves "put into nature." And, according to Kant, the mind prescribes to nature at two levels of conceptual organization. The fundamental "forms of sensibility," space and time, and the "categories of the understanding," such as the causal relation, are "constituents" of our very concept of nature in general and we cannot think of nature without them. But in order to make any overall sense of the empirical world we need a further set of organizing concepts.

For example, our study of living things seems to demand that we introduce a new principle in order to understand organic phenomena. Here the concepts of Newtonian mechanics need supplementing by a teleological principle, i.e., by the idea that "an organized product of nature is one in which everything is reciprocally end and means." Ideas of this kind Kant called "principles of reflective judgment." And in certain respects these "principles" are similar to what he calls, in a different context, "transcendental Ideas." Kant considered the principles of reflective judgment and the transcendental Ideas as playing a rather special role in human knowledge. He thought of them not like the "forms of sensibility" and "categories of the Understanding," as "constitutive" of experience, but rather as having a "regulative" function. We cannot *prove* that any objects actually correspond to these Ideas and principles; indeed, the basic error of traditional metaphysics was precisely the futile attempt to provide such proofs. Nevertheless the "transcendental Ideas are just as natural to Reason (*Vernunft*) as are the categories to the Understanding (*Verstand*)" (B670). Not only are they *natural* to the human mind, but, in one form or another, their use is *necessary* if we are to achieve systematic order among our cognitions. Thus the Idea of Freedom is something we need in order to make sense of our moral experience; while principles of reflective judgment often serve as indispensable heuristic devices in the sciences, indefinitely urging us to seek wider unifications among empirical phenomena. So principles like that of the purposiveness in nature are not, according to Kant, inductive generalizations; rather, they are "rules" or "maxims" for gaining knowledge, "prescriptive" means of taking cognizance of nature which, as a matter of fact, we find nature "favors." In the use of all such principles our reflective judgment follows the natural unificatory tendency of the mind and acts, says Kant, *"with art."* (See First Introduction to the *Critique of Judgment*).

Kant saw that there are fundamental differences between the activities of the scientist, the metaphysician, and the poet. But in a much more epistemologically sophisticated manner than any thinker before him, Kant also saw that these activities have something in common. They all result from the mind's natural synthetic power, a power which typically creates, says Kant (echoing Shaftesbury), "another nature, as it were, out of the material that actual nature gives it." For, just as the poet's imagination "emulates the play of Reason in its quest for a maximum," so the metaphysician—and in certain respects even the scientist—goes beyond the limits of experience in his search for "a completeness of which there is no example in nature" (op. cit., Sec. 49). Whether exhibited in art, in science, in moral and religious aspiration, or in metaphysics, this creation of form, totality, structural completeness is the characteristic function of the human mind; it can never be eliminated but only, at best, held in check through rational criticism and empirical verification.

At the level of conceptual analysis, Kant's contribution to our modern understanding of the nature of metaphysics is still the most outstanding. But these historical notes would be radically incomplete if we failed to mention one further contribution. This came from those historians and proto-sociologists, from Vico and Herder in the eighteenth century, to Dilthey and Meinecke in the early twentieth century, whose work is now usually considered under the ambiguous label of *Historismus* or "Historicism." We have already mentioned the aims of Dilthey's *Weltanschauungslehre*; and Dilthey may be taken as the culmination of this line of thinkers, insofar as they have specifically concerned themselves with the nature of metaphysics. Considered as a series of perspectives on historical method, historicism is important from our point of view because of its emphasis on the affective and social functions of speculative thought. In other words, because of its stress on the way different styles of philosophizing issue, not from intellectual considerations alone, but from different styles of life (or of *Erlebnisse*, "lived experiences," as Dilthey would say); and because of its tendency to see metaphysics as a more conceptualized form of what Herder had already called a nation's imaginative "mythology": "a philosophical attempt of the human mind [to understand its place in nature], which dreams ere it awakes, and willingly retains its infant state" (Herder, pp. 47f.). Such views, conjoined with a basically Kantian notion of the mind's "synthetic" propensities, were employed with great power by Hegel in the first notable attempt to write a history of philosophy. Not unlike Herder, Hegel retained the uncritical belief that each philosophy forms "a link in the whole chain" of allegedly purposeful historical development. But Hegel's *Lectures on the History of Philosophy* (first delivered in Jena in 1805) were important for the way they repudiated the idea that the history of philosophy is largely a history of intellectual errors. "Every philosophy is the philosophy of its own day," said Hegel, "and thus can only find satisfaction for the interests belonging to its own particular time" (op. cit., I, 45).

In our own time few thinkers would deny that the practice of metaphysics is, in some sense, an essentially *imaginative* activity. But there is far from a consensus about what is to be meant here either by "metaphysics" or by "imagination." Even a philosopher so basically ill-disposed towards metaphysics as Rudolf Carnap admits that imagination plays a large part in metaphysical thinking. From one point of view indeed, this is precisely why he and thinkers like him have wished to exclude "metaphysics" from the serious concerns of "philosophy" properly so-called. For as they see it metaphysics is a pretentious, conceptually misguided form of myth-making, a "pseudo-science" masquerading as a genuine source of knowledge. The metaphysician seems neither to have contributed to the stock of empirical knowledge provided by the particular sciences, nor has he, at any rate typically and exclusively, concerned himself with the logical analysis of concepts at a formal level. Instead, the perennial efforts of metaphysicians to answer large-scale questions about the "nature of reality as a whole" or about the "meaning of life" have for the most part issued in seemingly arbitrary, empirically untestable visions of the world removed from any close relation with ordinary experience. No doubt these metaphysical visions are often remarkable for the ingenious webs of rationalization with which they are accompanied; sometimes metaphysical theories historically prefigure, or stimulate the growth of, genuine scientific theories. But apart from this, metaphysical thinking possesses little cognitive value or "theoretical content," to use Carnap's phrase. The products of the metaphysician must therefore be seen to be "imaginary" first and foremost in a pejorative sense. For all its show of logical and empirical justification, a metaphysical vision is not a replica of true, objective reality—which, Carnap implies, can be obtained only through some combination of science and common sense—but a fictitious supposition, a subjective fabrication or waking dream whose significance lies outside the verifiable realm of public experience.

Yet there is a second and less objectionable sense in which metaphysicians can be said to exercise imagination. They are imaginative simply in being creative. Metaphysical utterances possess no "theoretical content" (or "representative function") because they are primarily "expressive." And to this extent a metaphysician may be compared to a lyric poet or musician. His utterances "lie completely outside the field of knowledge," yet they frequently have positive value as expressions of feeling, especially as expressions of "permanent emotional or volitional dispositions." So, according to Carnap, a metaphysical system of monism may be an expression of an even and harmonious mode of life; a dualistic system may result from a personal experience of the world as a place of eternal struggle; ethical rigorism may be indicative of an over-developed sense of duty; perhaps realism springs from the type of disposition psychologists call "extroverted," idealism from "introversion," and so on (Carnap, esp. Ch. 1). Carnap's interests do not lead him to develop further this somewhat crude typology of philosophical outlooks, and he seems unaware of the very much more sophisticated accounts given, notably, by Dilthey and K. Jaspers (whose *Psychologie der Weltanschauungen* had already appeared in 1919).

Nevertheless, the idea that certain general kinds of metaphysical outlook can be directly related to supposed psychological—more often allegedly pathological—dispositions of the metaphysicians themselves, is a belief that has appeared again and again in the English-speaking world in recent decades. Particular versions of it figure prominently in both the early and the later Wittgenstein, in influential works like John Wisdom's *Philosophy and Psycho-analysis*, and in the writings of a host of other Anglo-Saxon philosophers who have discussed the nature of metaphysics. Among these writers hardly ever has this belief been accompanied by even the most rudimentary display of biographical evidence or other necessary psychological, sociological, and historical data which would be essential for such a diagnosis of the metaphysician's predicament to attain some semblance of plausibility.

But however that may be, psychological considerations of the sort clearly hinted at by Carnap and elaborated by others have given rise, in the English-speaking world, to a particular perspective on the role of imagination in metaphysical thinking, and to what one might call a further specific nuance in our current use of "metaphysical imagination." Insofar as the metaphysician can be considered to have typically turned away from the "reality principle" inherent in science, in naive realism, in "ordinary language," or in some combination of these, the philosophical outlook expressed in his works is often said to constitute a *fantasy* in a more or less technical psychoanalytical sense. Like the paranoic whose delusive fears can never be subdued by contrary evidence, however strong, so the metaphysician's theory is phrased in such a way as to be compatible with any possible state of affairs; like the advanced neurotic who fails to adjust to objective social reality and lives instead in a compensatory inner world of fantasy, so the metaphysician's atavistic distinctions between appearance and reality, phenomena and noumena, becoming and being, contingency and necessity, and so on, are symptomatic of his own maladjustments. Partly under the influence of the species of logical empiricism disseminated by Carnap and his disciples, and partly, no doubt, through the tremendous impact of Freud's own writings in the 1920's and 1930's, views of this kind, though rarely adequately supported, have become so common as to be almost taken for granted in a large number of articles and books on metaphysics written in English. On the European continent, however, the situation has been very different.

Bergson, Jaspers, and Heidegger, for example, have all written at length on the nature of metaphysics, and they unanimously regard the metaphysician as fulfilling a vital, even a humanly indispensable, role. They are aware that there are connections between metaphysical outlooks and personal temperament and feelings, but, unlike Carnap, they refuse to regard the function of metaphysics as "expressive" in any purely emotive or subjectivist sense. Moreover, they make no critical distinction between metaphysics and philosophy. For them metaphysical or philosophical enquiry leads to *knowledge* of a fundamentally important kind: either the metaphysician attempts to formulate and answer certain basic ontological questions—such as the Heideggerian question "Why is there something and not nothing?"—or, in a less exclusively discursive manner, he seeks to disclose profound orders of experience (Bergson's *durée*, Jaspers' *das Umgreifende*). Neither of these tasks can be accomplished, they believe, through the methods of the empirical sciences, nor through "logical analysis" in any of the ways this is understood in Anglo-Saxon countries. Far from philosophy (or metaphysics) being parasitic upon science, or simply serving as a clarificatory tool for solving conceptual problems in the sciences and in everyday life, it is in fact concerned, says Martin Heidegger, with a quite different level of experience. "Philosophy and its [mode of] thinking," he asserts, "belong to the same order as poetry" (Heidegger [1953], p. 20). With this statement both Bergson and Jaspers are in substantial agreement; and, of course, as we have seen, Carnap would also have agreed, provided Heidegger had been speaking of "metaphysics" rather than of "philosophy." But here the extraordinary gulf between contemporary philosophical traditions widens far beyond any purely terminological dispute. With his poeticizing of philosophy, it is not surprising to find in Heidegger a corre-

sponding upgrading of *imagination* almost to the level of a faculty of metaphysical cognition (this is best seen in his discussion of *Kant und das Problem der Metaphysik* and in his interpretations of the lyric poet Hölderlin). Similarly in the works of Bergson and Jaspers, imagination often appears as the primary *organum* of philosophical insight. *Phantasie*, for Jaspers, *ist die positive Bedingung für die Verwirklichung der Existenz* (*Philosophie*, II, 282–84); while Bergson's *intuition*, that sympathetic *dilatation de l'esprit* through which alone the metaphysician is able "to investigate what is essential and unique . . . to attain to fluid concepts" and so follow reality "in all its sinuosities," might just as well have been called "imagination," as Bergson himself virtually admits (Bergson, IV and VI).

So here, in the discussions of recent philosophers who may fairly be said to represent between them a wide range of contemporary opinion, we have found, in effect, four closely related ways in which imagination is commonly considered in relation to metaphysics. Metaphysicians are often said to characteristically produce *imaginary* worlds; and in doing so they are no doubt *imaginative*, in the sense of inventive, like other creators; but perhaps like the products of artists also, metaphysical creations are substitutes for reality, serving a similar function to the *fantasies* of which psychoanalysts speak; finally, for those thinkers who see imagination as a special source of knowledge, or, like Sartre, as a means of reconstituting the world, metaphysical imagination would be understood as the highest form of *intuition into the true nature of being or reality*. The most obvious and historically immediate source of this last perspective on the importance of imagination for metaphysics is romanticism; but, as we saw, this position is in fact very much older and is quite explicit in the Neo-Platonism and hermeticism of the Renaissance. And, broadly speaking, one may say that the apparently bewildering variety of recent opinion about the place of imagination, not only in metaphysical thinking, but also in artistic creation, in historical understanding, and in scientific discovery, basically reflects—and often tries to combine in a variety of uneasy ways—two quite distinct conceptions about the cognitive significance of imagination. On the one hand, there is what we have identified as the Baconian position. This takes a moderate, sometimes pessimistic, and at any rate always a cautionary view, and considers the use of imagination to be a necessary condition for the growth of human knowledge, but also a customary source of illusion and wish-fulfillment when not held in check by objective criticism. And then, on the other hand, there is a more extreme position which has re-emerged in many forms since the end of the eighteenth century. According to this, imagination—though it is sometimes called by another name: *intuition* by Schelling and Bergson; *Vernunft*, in its allegedly synthesizing, "concrete" role, by Hegel, F. Schlegel, and Coleridge; the process of *Nacherleben*, i.e., the historian's "reliving of past experience," by Dilthey—is conceived to be the primary faculty through which alone nature or God or ultimate reality can be truly located and understood.

The epistemological gulf between these two perspectives on imagination is still very wide. Just as during the Renaissance, with Paracelsus and Bruno on one side, and Francis Bacon on the other, so for the most part the modern proponents of these very different standpoints are hardly on speaking terms, let alone about to effect a reconciliation. But largely through the medium of Kant's theory of knowledge, some degree of rapprochement has in fact occurred. As regards a better understanding of metaphysics, probably Ernst Cassirer's *Philosophy of Symbolic Forms* (*Die Philosophie der symbolischen Formen*, 1923–29) is the most significant work in this respect.

Cassirer sees the activity of the metaphysician as "symbolic" in a special sense. Metaphysics is one of the typical and recurrent ways in which the human mind attempts by means of symbols, linguistic and nonlinguistic, to stabilize the chaos of sensory impressions by shaping these impressions into an intelligible enduring unity. Metaphysics is, therefore, in effect, what Cassirer calls a "symbolic form," like the structures presented by language, myth, art, religion, the study of history, and science. Taken together these constructions make up the human world. For man is not so much an *animal rationale*, as classical thought would have it, but an *animal symbolicum:* he builds up a cultural world of his own, an "ideal" world over and against the purely natural, stimulus-response world of animal life. Each symbolic form is autonomous in the sense that each has its own distinctive mode of synthetic construction; and it is a serious mistake to believe that one form can be reduced to another without loss (as, for instance, positivists of all periods have attempted to reduce mythology, and metaphysics conceived as a species of mythology, to the level of pre- or pseudo-scientific thought). Cassirer believes that our awareness of physical reality as such has in fact receded as man's imaginative, symbolic activity has advanced. "Instead of dealing [solely] with the things themselves, man . . . has so enveloped himself in linguistic forms, in artistic images, in mythical symbols or religious rites that he cannot see or know anything except by the interposition of this artificial medium" (Cassirer [1944], p. 25).

But this does not mean that the constructions of mythology, art, religion, and speculative philosophy,

any more than those of science itself, are pure fabrications without cognitive significance. On a very much more ambitious scale than Kant himself ever envisaged, Cassirer reasserts the Kantian doctrine that the very nature of human consciousness is to seek for "unity in the manifold," to identify the "parts" of experience as elements of a "whole" of which the mind is already in possession as a "regulative Idea." So, for Cassirer, while symbolic forms other than science may not function in the same cognitive way that science does, nevertheless, insofar as they perform a definite task in the construction and organization of experience, they may be said to provide for knowledge. For they offer equally indispensable universes of discourse through which the world of experience may be articulated and revealed, and "our perspectives widen, if we consider that [scientific] cognition . . . is only one of the forms in which the mind can apprehend and interpret being" (Cassirer [1953–57], I, 77; compare, e.g., idem [1944] pp. 169–70). Cassirer considers man's symbolic rendering of experience in the various cultural forms to be essentially an imaginative process. He emphasizes the fact that imagination is not only *reproductive* and *productive*, but also *anticipatory:* it enables us to shape future expectations which may or may not be confirmed by events, but may sometimes influence the course of events. From the making of simple tools to the construction of philosophical utopias this "pre-presentation" of the future underlies all human action. "We must set before ourselves in 'images' something not yet existing, in order, then, to proceed from this 'possibility' to the 'reality', from potency to act" (Cassirer [1960], pp. 75–76). Whether in science, art, or metaphysics, this is one of the most important ways in which the stimulus-response world of animal life is transformed in the "image-world" (*Bildwelt*) of man.

BIBLIOGRAPHY

Aristotle, *Basic Works*, ed. R. McKeon (New York, 1941). F. Bacon, *Philosophical Works*, ed. J. M. Robertson (London, 1905). G. Bachelard, *L'Eau et les rêves* (Paris, 1942). C. Baudelaire, *Oeuvres complètes*, ed. Y.-G. Le Dantec (Paris, 1954). H. Bergson, *La Pensée et le mouvant* (Paris, 1934). W. Blake, *Poetry and Prose*, ed. G. Keynes (London, 1946). F. H. Bradley, *Appearance and Reality* (London and New York, 1893). M. W. Bundy, "The Theory of Imagination in Classical and Medieval Thought," University of Illinois, *Studies in Language and Literature*, **12**, Nos. 2, 3 (May–Aug., 1927). R. Burton, *Anatomy of Melancholy* (London, 1652). R. Carnap, *Philosophy and Logical Syntax* (London and New York, 1935). E. Cassirer, *An Essay on Man* (New Haven and London, 1944); idem, *The Philosophy of the Enlightenment* (Boston, 1951); idem, *The Philosophy of Symbolic Forms*, 3 vols. (New Haven and London, 1953–57); idem, *The Logic of the Humanities* (New Haven and London, 1960). E. B.

de Condillac, *Oeuvres philosophiques*, ed. G. Le Roy, 3 vols. (Paris, 1947–51). R. Descartes, *Oeuvres*, ed. C. Adam and P. Tannery, 13 vols. (Paris, 1897–1913). D. Diderot, *Oeuvres philosophiques*, ed. P. Vernière (Paris, 1964); idem, *Oeuvres esthétiques*, ed. P. Vernière (Paris, 1968). W. Dilthey, *The Essence of Philosophy*, trans. S. A. and W. T. Emery (Chapel Hill, 1955). S. Freud, *The Future of an Illusion*, Eng. trans. W. D. Robson-Scott, rev. and ed. by J. Strachey (London, 1962). G. W. F. Hegel, *Phenomenology of Mind*, trans. J. Baillie, 2nd ed. (London, 1931); idem, *Lectures on the History of Philosophy*, trans. E. S. Haldane and F. H. Simson, 3 vols. (London, 1892–96). M. Heidegger, "Hölderlin and the Essence of Poetry," trans. D. Scott in *Existence and Being*, ed. W. Brock (Chicago, 1949); idem, *Kant und das Problem der Metaphysik*, 2nd ed. (Frankfurt, 1951); idem, *Einführing in die Metaphysik* (Tübingen, 1953). J. G. von Herder, *Reflections on the Philosophy of the History of Mankind*, ed. F. E. Manuel (Chicago and London, 1968). D. Hume, *A Treatise of Human Nature*, ed. L. A. Selby-Bigge (Oxford, 1888). K. Jaspers, *Psychologie der Weltanschauungen* (Berlin, 1919); idem, *Philosophie*, 3rd ed., 3 vols. (Berlin, 1956). I. Kant, *Werke*, ed. E. Cassirer, 10 vols. (Berlin, 1912–22). P. B. Medawar, *The Art of the Soluble* (London and New York, 1967); idem, *Induction and Intuition in Scientific Thought* (London and New York, 1969). I. Newton, *Principia Mathematica*, trans. A. Motte, rev. and ed. by F. Cajori, 2 vols. (Berkeley and Los Angeles, 1962). F. Nietzsche, *Götzen-Dämmerung* (1889) in *Werke*, 3 vols., ed. K. Schlechta, Vol. II, 2nd ed. (Munich, 1960). W. Pagel, *Paracelsus* (Basel, 1958). B. Pascal, *Pensées et opuscules*, ed. L. Brunschvicg (Paris, 1934). Plato, *Dialogues*, trans. B. Jowett, rev. 4th ed. (Oxford, 1953). J. H. Randall, Jr., *How Philosophy Uses Its Past* (New York and London, 1963). J.-P. Sartre, *L'Imaginaire* (Paris, 1940); idem, *L'Etre et le néant* (Paris, 1943). J. Starobinski, "Imagination," in F. Jost, ed., *Proceedings of IVth Congress of the International Comparative Literature Association* (The Hague and Paris, 1966), II, 952–63. H.-J. de Vleeschauwer, *The Development of Kantian Thought* (London, 1962). F. M. de Voltaire, *Oeuvres complètes*, ed. L. Moland, 52 vols. (Paris, 1877–85). J. Wahl, *L'Expérience métaphysique* (Paris, 1965). J. Wisdom, *Philosophy and Psychoanalysis* (Oxford, 1953). F. A. Yates, *Giordano Bruno and the Hermetic Tradition* (London and Chicago, 1964); idem, *The Art of Memory* (London and Chicago, 1966).

MICHAEL MORAN

[See also Baconianism; **Cosmic Images**; Enlightenment; **Existentialism**; **Myth**; Platonism; Positivism; **Romanticism**.]

MILLENARIANISM

MILLENARIANISM, in the strict sense, is the belief that, before the final judgment of all mankind, Christ will return to the earth and, together with resurrected saints, will reign over a glorious kingdom which will last a thousand years. The authority for this belief is Revelation 20:1–5, which relates how the cosmic battles between the divine and the Satanic powers will in part end with the fall of the latter's stronghold, "Babylon." An angel will come down from heaven and imprison the "dragon" for a thousand years (*Revised Standard Version*). After this millennium Satan is to be loosed once more. He will gather the nations of the earth for one grand last stand, at "Armageddon," but he will be defeated. Then he will be thrown into the "lake of fire" and the universal judgment will occur, followed by the establishment of the eternal heavenly state. Events often incorrectly associated with the millennium, such as the coming of a "new heaven and a new earth," are to occur only *after* this final victory of God.

Thus the millennium is only an interval in the war of good and evil which the Christian revelation, following the tradition of Hebrew apocalyptic, sees as the pattern of all history. It utilizes Jewish predictions that a Messianic Deliverer will lead the armies of the chosen people and will annihilate their enemies. In the later Jewish tradition, the messianic leader is to reign over the whole world. He comes to combine qualities of wisdom and benevolence with those of the warrior. The Son of Man of the Book of Revelation, identified with the Christos, exhibits this combination. The chosen people, originally only Israel, is, in Christian teaching, the whole body of the saved. Although the idea of the millennium is found specifically only in the Revelation, it came to incorporate Daniel's vision of the four images and the ten horns, and the mystical numbers of Daniel were utilized in attempts to foretell the exact date of the Parousia (Second Coming).

Christian teaching took over the basic rationale of Jewish apocalyptic. The messianic hope solves the great dilemma of the Jewish prophets: although the righteous, chosen people were promised temporal prosperity and happiness, most of the time they were persecuted or in captivity. Since there was in the Old Testament little anticipation of immortality, with heavenly rewards, a deferred earthly happiness was the logical explanation of the great incongruity between the promises of Yahweh and the facts of history. Daniel, thus, predicts a resurrection of saints to reign in "an everlasting kingdom" (Daniel 12:2).

The decades immediately preceding and succeeding the founding of the Christian church were permeated, in the Jewish world, by expectation of the imminent appearance of the Messiah. Various claimants to this office appeared during the Roman occupation of Israel (beginning in 63 B.C.). Many books of apocalyptic nature were composed. *The Secrets of Enoch*, first half of the first century A.D., is particularly close to the Christian Apocalypse. The creation is to last for seven "days" (each representing a millennium). There is, logically, to be a Sabbatical seventh day, a messianic age. After the end of the temporal "week," as in the Revelation, the "great day of the Lord" and the transformation of the earth into heaven will occur. The *Ezra Apocalypse,* of the same period, distinguishes between a temporary and a permanent messianic kingdom. The former will last 400 years, compensating exactly for the four centuries of Egyptian captivity. The idea of this earthly kingdom resembles that of the Revelation, in that the righteous dead are to be raised in a first resurrection and will not suffer death again.

The idea of the messianic kingdom has a potentially revolutionary character. The established, all-powerful rulers of this world are, ordinarily, evil and tyrannical oppressors in prophecy. They are, however, doomed to be overthrown in a great, decisive revolutionary struggle. The kingdom is to be a kind of holy utopia, not a heavenly state; the inhabitants are to be human beings in the flesh, on this earth, and living in a society. This utopia, moreover, is brought about only by violent conflict in which the decisive factor is a divinely appointed, mysterious general-king. Against him is ranged another mysterious but apparently at least partly human figure, the "Antichrist."

There is throughout history a class division, where social, political, and religious qualities are sharply distinguished. The whole atmosphere of Jewish prophecy implies an association between evil rulers and riches, luxury, and what we should call exploitation; and the oppressed, of course, are the opposite—poor, virtuous, and just. There is here, then, a kind of scenario for revolution with a blank cast which can easily be filled by individuals and groups drawn from contemporaneous circumstances. It can even be secularized, as in Marxism, where the proprietary class is "Babylon" and the workers are the people of the promise. There is, in Marxist practice, usually also a heroic leader who strongly recalls the messianic hero. The great and lasting appeal of the millenarian idea thus may be attributed in large measure to two elements: its promise of a utopian age, when the positions of oppressed and oppressors are reversed, as the culmination of history; and its suggestive outline of a revolution and a redeemer who will be able to break down the seemingly impregnable fortress of power and injustice.

Early Christians embellished the prediction of the millennium with vivid descriptions of a lush paradise from late Jewish apocryphal apocalyptic. Cerinthus, Papias, the Ebionites, Saint Justin Martyr, Lactantius, and Commodianus expected an imminent return of the Lord. Saint Irenaeus, the Greek Church Father (second century), referring to the persecuted Christians, explains the enduring rationale of the Millennium: ". . . in that Creation wherein they laboured, or were afflicted . . . in that same it is meet for them to receive the fruits of Suffering: . . . and in what creation they endured slavery, in the same they should reign" (*Adversus haereses,* trans. John Keble, V:32:1). Commentators on the Revelation have throughout the centuries emphasized the same point: that a heavenly reward is not logically the true end of creation; the world must be restored to its Edenic condition, and the just should be vindicated on this earth.

Millenarian ideas have been effective, also, in that they have been conflated with many kinds of other historical theories. The result has been many apocalyptic works interpreting and prophesying the course of events in many periods. The *Sibylline Books* (ca. 350), is one; another, the *Pseudo-Methodius.* The latter, which is the basis of many subsequent apocalypses, predicts that an emperor is to rise from the grave and defeat the powers of darkness; after a time of peace and happiness, the Antichrist will appear, and Christ will descend to kill him. Here two redeemers are postulated, one of whom is a mortal, even though superhuman. This apocalypse combines, probably, with folklore to produce such legends as those of Emperor Frederick Barbarossa and King Arthur, in that they are sleeping, awaiting their summons to save their people.

By the time of Saint Augustine, the failure of the millennium to arrive had encouraged a new interpretation. The millennium, Augustine explains, is to be considered as only allegorical—of the last stage of the redemption, which began with Christ. The "thousand years" is only a round number signifying a long time. Satan, the head of the City of Man, which is always at war with the City of God in the human community, is even now "bound" in that his power of deceiving men is restricted (Augustine, *The City of God,* 20, 8). The "first resurrection" is of course an allegory of the revival from spiritual death through grace.

With Augustine—whose doctrine became official in the medieval Church—there are completed two opposing attitudes towards the prophecy. One, known as *pre-millennialism,* holds that, after a long period of sorrows, Christ will return to inaugurate the millennial age. The *post-millennialist* opinion regards the millennium as some form of allegory, and expects the Advent only after it is completed. Augustine certainly did not think of the millennium as a temporal utopia, but it was possible to believe that some kind of kingdom in which Christian principles would be triumphant would crown the advance of Christianity.

During the Middle Ages, however, minority groups reverted to the pre-millennialist faith to explain injustice and the puzzling problems of social change.

Almost always there was a revolutionary character to these movements. The Jacquerie revolt (1358) and the Peasant revolt (1381) had a chiliastic background. The eschatological hope was joined, in the "Free Spirit" movement, with the exaltation of "Holy Poverty." *Piers Plowman* envisions a millennial age in which, the world having been freed of avarice and pride, true spiritual and social equality will be realized. The very influential *Book of a Hundred Chapters*, in the early sixteenth century, tells how the "Emperor from the Black Forest," the resurrected Frederick, is the messianic hero. The Jews are no longer the chosen people, but the Germans are: a source of Germanic anti-Semitism. The primitive chiliastic drama was finally enacted in the revolution inaugurated by a group of Anabaptists in Münster in 1525. But the rule of the saints turned into a reign of terror that was overthrown with great cruelty.

Despite the ensuing fears of millenarianism, the idea that the Book of Revelation must be interpreted literally took root among Protestants, who emphasized the importance of plain reading of Scripture to correct the "errors" introduced by the "false Church." The revolutionary potential of the idea was made real again during and after the Great Rebellion in England (1642–60). The very title of these groups—"Fifth Monarchy Men"—shows their inspiration; for the "fifth monarchy" was the final kingdom of God which, according to Daniel's vision of the five images, would end history (Daniel 2). This is a political and economic movement, but the deliverance is to be miraculous and "Lord Jesus" is to rule.

There were many predictions of an exact time for the Parousia. In the nineteenth century many millenarian but nonrevolutionary sects, such as the Millerites, were founded. Fundamentalist Protestants in general, including the Mormons and the Southern Baptists Conference, are millenarian; thus a very large segment of Protestantism today is of this persuasion. The version of millenarianism most common among Fundamentalists is part of "dispensationalism," a new form of the seven-day theory of the history of creation.

Post-millennialism also has had a great influence on recent centuries. In the seventeenth and eighteenth centuries, English-speaking Protestants, both of the Establishment and Dissent, widely accepted a theory that the course of all history is predicted. The Antichrist is the Papacy (or the Papacy and feudalism in conspiracy) which has prevented true Christianity from being preached throughout the world. The "pouring out of the seven vials" (Revelation 15–17) prefigures progressive defeats of the false Church. The high point, of course, is the Reformation. When the last "vial" was poured out, it was believed, the spirit of true Christianity would be able to dominate the world and the triumph of Christian principles would produce a utopian age.

Jonathan Edwards (1703–58) is an important exponent of this idea. This is a version of the concept of progress; such events as the advance of science and technology are seen as preparations for the millennial utopia, although there would also have to be bloody confrontations before the entrenched powers of falsehood and privilege were finally put down. The American Civil War was seen, by many preachers, as a pouring out of one vial; and a common belief in the United States then was that the Anglo-Saxons, and the Americans in particular, are the new chosen nation, called to complete the foreordained plan for the coming of the kingdom of God.

The millennial idea has exercised a greatly diversified effect on modern times—even on persons and groups far from orthodox. Mary Baker Eddy's *Science and Health* (1875), expressed a confidence that the great hope is soon to become fact. The resemblances of the Marxist pattern of history to millennial ideas are too striking to be entirely coincidental. The idea of inevitable progress was certainly encouraged and probably in part inspired by the ancient belief that God will crown his plan for mankind with the millennium.

BIBLIOGRAPHY

On the biblical background of the idea, see R. H. Charles, *Eschatology* (1899; reprint New York, 1963); F. E. Hamilton, *The Basis of Millennial Faith* (Grand Rapids, 1942); and H. Schoeps, *Theologie und Geschichte des Judenschristentums* (Tübingen, 1949). On medieval millenarianism: N. Cohn, *The Pursuit of the Millennium* (Fairlawn, N.J., 1957). On post-Reformation aspects of the history of the idea, see E. Tuveson, *Millennium and Utopia* (Berkeley, 1949) and idem, *Redeemer Nation, The Idea of America's Millennial Role* (Chicago, 1968). For social implications of ideas originating from millenarianism, see *Millennial Dreams in Action*, ed. Sylvia Thrupp (The Hague, 1962). On the transformations of the idea among non-Western peoples, see V. Lanternari, *The Religions of the Oppressed, A Study of Modern Messianic Cults* (New York, 1963). Most of these works contain extensive bibliographies of the vast literature on the subject.

ERNEST TUVESON

[See also **Christianity in History**; Marxism; Progress; **Prophecy**; Reformation; Utopia.]

MIMESIS

I

IMITATION was called *mimesis* in Greek and *imitatio* in Latin: it is the same term in different languages. The term exists since antiquity; the concept however, has changed. Today imitation means more or less the same as copying; in Greece its earliest meaning was quite different.

The word "mimesis" is post-Homeric: it does not occur in either Homer or Hesiod. Its etymology, as linguists maintain, is obscure. Most probably it originated with the rituals and mysteries of the Dionysian cult; in its first (quite different from the present) meaning the mimesis-imitation stood for the acts of cult performed by the priest—dancing, music, and singing. This is confirmed by Plato as well as by Strabo. The word which later came to denote the reproducing of reality in sculpture and theater arts had been, at that time, applied to *dance, mimicry,* and *music* exclusively. In Delian hymns, as well as in Pindar, this term was applied to music. Imitation did not signify reproducing external reality but expressing the inner one. It had no application then in visual arts.

In the fifth century B.C. the term "imitation" moved from the terminology of cult into philosophy and started to mean reproducing the *external* world. The meaning changed so much that Socrates had some qualms about calling the art of painting "mimesis" and used words close to it such as "ek-mimesis" and "apo-mimesis." But Democritus and Plato had no such scruples and used the word "mimesis" to denote imitation of nature. To each of them, however, it was a different kind of imitation.

For Democritus mimesis was an imitation of *the way nature functions.* He wrote that in art we imitate nature: in weaving we imitate the spider, in building the swallow, in singing the swan or nightingale (Plutarch, *De Sollert. anim.* 20, 974A). This concept was applicable chiefly to *industrial arts.*

Another concept of imitation, which acquired greater popularity, was also formed in the fifth century in Athens but by a different group of philosophers: it was first introduced by Socrates and further developed by Plato and Aristotle. To them "imitation" meant the copying of the *appearances of things.*

This concept of imitation originated as a result of reflection upon *painting* and *sculpture.* For example, Socrates asked himself in what way do these arts differ from the others. His answer was: in this, that they repeat and imitate things which we see (Xenophon's *Comm.* III, 10, 1). So he conceived a new concept of imitation; he also did something more: he formulated the theory of imitation, the contention that imitation is the basic function of the arts (such as painting and sculpture). It was an important event in the history of thinking on art. The fact that Plato and Aristotle accepted this theory was equally important: thanks to them it became for centuries to come the leading theory of the arts. Each of them, however, assigned

a different meaning to the theory and, consequently, two variants of the theory, or rather two theories originated under the same name.

Plato's Variant. In his early writings Plato was rather vague in his use of the term "imitation": he applied it to music and dance (*Laws* 798D) or confined it to painting and sculpture (*Republic* 597D); at first he called "imitative" only poetry in which, as in tragedy, the heroes speak for themselves (epic poetry describes and does not imitate, he said). Finally, however, he accepted Socrates' broad concept which embraced almost the entire art of painting, sculpture, and poetry.

Later, beginning with Book X of the *Republic,* his conception of art as imitating reality grew very extreme: he saw it as a passive and faithful act of copying the outer world. This particular conception was induced primarily by the then contemporary illusionist art of painting. Plato's idea was similar to what was in the nineteenth century advanced under the name of "naturalism." His theory was descriptive and not normative; on the contrary, it disapproved of the imitation of reality by art on the basis that imitation is not the proper road to truth (*Republic* 603A, 605A; *Sophist* 235D–236C).

Aristotle's Variant. Aristotle, seemingly faithful to Plato, transformed his concept and theory of imitation; he maintained that artistic imitation may present things either more or less beautiful than they are; it also may present them such as they could or ought to be; it can and ought to limit itself to their characteristics which are general, typical, and essential (*Poetics* 1448a 1; 1451b 27; 1460b 13). Aristotle preserved the thesis that art imitates reality but imitation meant to him not faithful copying but a free and easy approach to reality; the artist who imitates can present reality in his own way. Aristotelian "imitation" was, in fact, the result of a fusion of two conceptions: the ritualistic and the Socratic. The idea of imitation, therefore, was just as applicable to music as to sculpture and theater.

Later theoreticians of art referred more often to Aristotle, but tended to uphold the simpler and more attractive conception of Plato's. Due to Aristotle's personal interests the theory of imitation was for centuries more concerned with poetry than with visual arts. To Aristotle "imitation" was, in the first place, imitation of human actions; however, it gradually became the imitation of *nature,* which was to be regarded as the source of its perfection.

In summary, the classic period of the fourth century B.C. used four different concepts of imitation: the ritualistic concept (expression), the concept of Democritus (imitation of natural processes), Platonic (copying of nature), Aristotelian (free creation of the work of art based on elements of nature). While the original concept was gradually falling into eclipse and the ideas of Democritus were recognized only by a few thinkers (e.g., Hippocrates and Lucretius), both the Platonic and Aristotelian conceptions proved to be basic enduring concepts in art; they were often fused into one and the awareness that they were different concepts was frequently lost.

II

When several centuries later Cicero *contrasted* imitation with truth (*vincit imitationem veritas; De Orat.* II, 57, 215) he of course understood it as a free expression of the artist and upheld the Aristotelian doctrine. Nevertheless, in Hellenistic and Roman days the interpretation of imitation as the copying of reality prevailed. Such an oversimplified interpretation of the arts could not but evoke dissent. Imitation was then contrasted with and replaced by such ideas as *imagination* (e.g., Maximus Tyrius, *Or.* XI, 3; Pseudo-Longinus, XV, 1), *expression* and an *inner model* (Callistratus, *Deser.* 7, 1; Dio Chrys., *Or.* XII, 71; Seneca, *Epist.* 65, 7), *freedom* of the creator (Horatius *De arte poet.;* Lucian, *Historia quo modo conscr.* 9), *inspiration* (Callistratus, *Deser.* 2, 1; Lucian, *Demosth. encom.* 5), *invention* (Sextus Emp., *Adv. math.* I, 297). Philostratus Flavius regarded imagination (*fantasia*) as wiser and more creative than imitation, because the latter confines itself only to what it has actually seen while the former represents also things it has not seen.

The theory of imitation was a product of the classical era of Greece. The Hellenistic and Roman epochs, although preserving the doctrine in principle, brought out reservations and counter-proposals: this, in fact, was their contribution to the doctrine's history.

III

The ancient theory of imitation was founded on typically Greek premises: that the human mind is passive and, therefore, able to perceive only what exists. Secondly, even if it were able to invent something which does not exist, it would be ill-advised to use this ability because the existing world is perfect and nothing more perfect can be conceived.

In the Middle Ages other premises were advanced, formulated early by Dionysius the Areopagite and by Saint Augustine. If art is to imitate, let it concentrate on the *invisible* world which is more perfect. And if art is to limit itself to the visible world, let it search in that world for *traces of eternal beauty*. This may be better achieved by means of symbols than by imitating reality.

Early and radical thinkers like Tertullian went even so far as to believe that God does not permit any imitation of this world (*omnem similitudinem vetat*

fieri; De spectaculis, XXIII); the iconoclasts thought the same; Scholastics, although free from such extreme views, believed that only spiritual representations are important. At the height of the Middle Ages Bonaventura was to say of painters and sculptors that they only show externally what they have thought internally (III, *Sent.* D 37 dub). Painting which faithfully imitates reality was derisively labelled the "aping of truth" (*simia veri*, e.g., Alain of Lille, *Anticlaudianus*, I, 4).

As the result of such predilections the theory of imitation was pushed aside in the Middle Ages and the term *imitatio* rarely used. However, it did not disappear completely; it survived in the twelfth-century humanists, like John of Salisbury. His definition of painting was the same as that of the ancients: it is an imitation (*imago est cuius generatio per imitationem fit; Metalogicon*, III, 8). Above all, Thomas Aquinas, the great Aristotelian philosopher of the Middle Ages, repeated the classical definition without any reservations "art imitates nature" (*ars imitatur naturam; Phys.* II, 4).

IV

With the Renaissance the theory of imitation became again the basic theory of art and poetry, and only then reached its apogee. Saved from oblivion, it appeared as a revelation and made the most of privileges enjoyed by new ideas.

Modern theory took the term *imitatio* from the Romans: *imitazione* in Italian, *imitation* in French and English (while the Slavs and Germans coined their own equivalents). The translator of Averroës in 1481 used the word *assimilatio*; G. Fracastoro wrote in 1555 that it is irrelevant *sive imitari, sive representare dicamus*. Nevertheless the term *imitatio* won an easy and complete victory.

At the very beginning of the fifteenth century, the doctrine of imitation was accepted earliest of all in the plastic arts. It appeared clearly in L. Ghiberti's *Commentaries* (1436), where he spoke of having tried to imitate nature (*imitare la natura*) "as well as it was possible for him" (*I Com.*, ed. Morisani, II, 22). L. B. Alberti adhered to the same theory; he maintained that there is no better way to beauty than by imitating nature (*Della pittura* [1435], part III). Leonardo da Vinci had even more radical views. According to him the more faithfully the painting depicts its object—(*conformità co'la cosa imitata; Tratt.* frag. 411)—the more praiseworthy it is. These were the pioneers who were followed by other Renaissance writers.

The concept and the theory of imitation did not enter Renaissance poetics until the middle of the sixteenth century, that is, only after Aristotle's *Poetics* had been fully accepted; from that time on it became the most essential element of poetics. F. Sassetti (1575) explained in an Aristotelian way that imitation is one of the four causes of poetry, namely, the "formal" one, the poet himself being the "efficient" cause, the poem the "material" one, and the pleasure produced by poetry the "final" one (Weinberg, p. 48).

The Italian theory of imitation penetrated into Germany attracting Dürer (*Aesth. Excurs.* [1528], ed. Heindrich, p. 277), then to France where it was taken up by Poussin (Letter to Fréart, 1, 3 [1966]) and many others. Even in the days of baroque and academism the Italian theory remained in all countries the basic theory of art. In the beginning of the eighteenth century it was still regarded as an important principle of aesthetics even by such innovators as Abbé Dubos and Vico; it was Vico who declared in *Scienza nuova* ([1774], I, 90) that poetry was nothing else than imitation (*non essendo altro la poesia che imitazione*).

On the whole, the modern theory of imitation held its position of strength in the theory of art for at least three centuries. It was not during that period a uniform theory however. Various meanings were assigned to it in the theory of visual arts and different ones in poetics. Some understood it in the Aristotelian way and others in accordance with Plato and the popular conception of faithful imitation. Hence there was more agreement in terminology than in matters of fact; controversies abounded.

Various thinkers tried to overcome in many different ways the obstacles which "imitation" encountered. Some Renaissance writers stressed the point that not all imitations serve art but only those that are "good" (G. B. Guarini, 1601), "artistic" (B. Varchi, 1546), "beautiful" (Alberti), "imaginative" (Comanini's *imitatio fantastica*, 1591). Other theoreticians tried to interpret imitation more accurately and in doing so they departed in various ways from the concept of literal copying of nature. Imitation ought to be "original," bluntly wrote Pelletier du Mans. In Alberti's interpretation art imitates the laws of nature rather than its appearances; according to Scaliger (1561) art imitates nature's norms. According to some, art ought to imitate nature's beauty; according to Shakespeare (Hamlet, III ii)

Let your own discretion be your tutor: . . .
With this special observance that you o'erstep not
The modesty of nature.

The followers of Aristotle (e.g., the Polish poet and theoretician of poetry, M. K. Sarbiewski, *De perfecta poesi* [ca. 1625, 1954 ed.], 1, 4) maintained that nature should be imitated as it could and ought to be. Michelangelo assigned a religious meaning to the doctrine of imitation; it is God in nature which should be imitated. Torquato Tasso (1587), concerned with imitation in poetry, realized what a complicated process it is: words (*parole*) imitate concepts (*concetti*) and these, in turn, imitate things (*cose*).

Particularly important was the following: many writers thought that art should not imitate nature in its rough state but after its faults have been corrected and a selection has been made. This view was held mainly by the French classicists. Other theoreticians stressed the fact that imitation is not a passive act; first nature has to be "de-coded" and its beauty has to be extracted (*herausreissen,* as Dürer said). Some writers assigned to imitation such a broad meaning that it embraced not only imitation of nature but also of *ideas* (Fracastoro, 1555). Others included in imitation even *allegories* (as Petrarch had done) and *metaphors* (E. Tesauro: *metafora altro non è che poetica imitatione;* see *Cannocchiale Aristotelico* [1655], p. 369). Eventually Varchi (*Lessioni* [1590], p. 576) thought that (if correctly understood) imitation is indeed nothing else but spinning of fiction (*fingere*). G. Del Bene (1574) was of a similar opinion; *imitatio* is the same as *finzione*. Those writers might have seemed revolutionary but in fact they were close to Aristotle. Some, like T. Correa (1587) differentiated two kinds of imitation; one is literal, the other one free, *imitatio simulata et ficta*. Similarly, when R. de Piles separated two kinds of truth: the simple and the ideal, he had in view two imitations, i.e., one that is faithful copying and the other which is preceded by selection and which synthesizes the elements of perfection scattered about in nature (*Cours de peinture* [1708], pp. 30–32).

However, many Renaissance and baroque writers reached the conclusion that it is pointless to stick stubbornly to the old theory instead of producing a new and a more accurate one. They were prompted by two entirely different reasons. A minority maintained that imitation is a task too difficult for art because imitation can never equal the model. A majority thought the opposite; imitation is a task too insignificant and too passive. The term *imitatio* was gradually being replaced—not by *creatio* however which belonged to theology—but by *inventio*. Ronsard offered a compromise; *imiter et inventer,* one should "imitate and invent." In V. Danti's view the aim of art was not *imitare* but to portray, *ritrarre* (*Trattato* [1567], II, 11). F. Patrizi said (*Della poetica* [1586], p. 135) that the poet is not an imitator but a "factior" (which, after all, was a literal translation of the Greek "poet"— *poietēs*). Danti maintained that the poet produces new wholes, if not new things. F. Robortello was bolder; art presents things such as they are *not* (*Explicationes* [1548], p. 226). In the next century the great Bernini was to say "painting shows that which does not exist"

(F. Baldinucci, *Vita di Berríini* [1st ed. 1682; 1948 ed.], p. 146). And G. P. Capriano in his poetics said: Poetry is an invention out of nothing (*Della vera poetica* [1555]; cf. Weinberg, p. 733). If that is so, then art indeed *does not* imitate.

The new idea was that art may be more perfect than the object of its imitation, i.e., nature. M. Ficino called art "wiser than nature" (*Theol. plat.* [1482], 1, XIII, *Opere* [1561], p. 296). Michelangelo professed that he makes nature more beautiful (*più bella*); Dolce wrote that the duty of a painter is to surpass (*superar*) nature, and G. Vasari (1550) stated that nature was conquered by art (*natura vinta dall'arte; Vite*, VII, 448).

The Renaissance introduced a new thesis which although of doubtful value was, nevertheless, rich in consequences; the object of imitation should be not only nature but also, and foremost, those who were its best imitators, that is, the Ancients. The watchword of *imitating antiquity* appeared as early as the fifteenth century and by the end of the seventeenth century it supplanted almost completely the idea of *imitating nature*. This was the greatest revolution in the history of the concept of imitation. It changed the classical theory of art into an academic one. A compromise formula was devised for the principle of imitation; nature should be imitated but in the way it was imitated by the Ancients. This meant that sculpture ought to be modelled on Apollo Belvedere and writing on Cicero. The fifteenth and sixteenth centuries called for more imitation of Antiquity in poetry, and the seventeenth and the eighteenth centuries asked for the same in the visual arts. However, dissenting voices were sometimes raised. During the Renaissance at least three protests against the imitation of Antiquity took place: Poliziano (1491) against Cortesi said that "only he writes well who has the courage to break the rules"; Giovanni Francesco Pico della Mirandola (1512) maintained against Cardinal Bembo that *aemulator veterum verius quam imitator;* and finally Desiderius Erasmus (1518) argued that he acts truly in Cicero's spirit who, in keeping with the changing times, *departs* from Cicero.

To give a very general outline of the development from the sixteenth to the eighteenth century we may say that some theoreticians defended the principle of imitation at the expense of some concessions, while others abandoned it completely. It was abandoned by those who adhered to the radical (Platonic) concept of imitation and maintained by those who voiced the moderate (Aristotelian) concept.

All in all, between the fifteenth and the eighteenth centuries there was no principle more commonly applied than *imitatio*. And it is hard to understand how Ch. Batteux could announce in his *Les beaux arts réduits à un seul principe*, (1747), that he had discovered the principle for all the arts, namely, imitation. The point of it is that countless earlier treatises applied the principle of imitation but only to a particular group of arts—some to poetry, others to painting and sculpture. Batteux generalized this principle for *all* arts. He could manage to make such a generalization because he had a vague idea of imitation; he regarded it as a faithful *copying* of nature. He was apparently the first to say: *Imiter c'est* copier *un modèle*, and on the other hand, is a *selection* from nature, is imitation of a *beautiful* nature.

V

The idea of imitation having been thoroughly discussed and analyzed nothing much was left to be done. The eighteenth century inherited and accepted this idea but ceased to be preoccupied with it. These sentiments were best voiced by an aesthetician who was typical of his century, Edmund Burke: "Aristotle has spoken so much and so solidly upon the force of imitation in his poetics, that it makes any further discourse upon this subject the less necessary." This appeared in *A Philosophical Enquiry into the Origin of Our Ideas on the Sublime and the Beautiful* ([1757], Part I, Sec. XVI). However, Burke himself did not interpret imitation in the Aristotelian way, as he demanded faithful copying.

At the end of the eighteenth century after the discovery of Herculaneum and Pompeii and the archeologists' travels in Greece, it became more popular than ever to imitate antiquity. It was the era of Mengs and Winckelmann, Adam and Flaxman, Canova and Thorwaldsen. However, the concern was a matter of practical application; the theory of imitation did not advance farther.

The nineteenth century laid the greatest stress on being faithful to nature (not to antiquity). Nevertheless, the term "imitation," which for ages played the leading part in the theory of art, disappeared suddenly; it acquired a pejorative meaning and was used to denote something unauthentic, faked—imitations of diamonds, marble, furs, etc., and could no longer be applied to art. Which other terms have taken its place? Mainly "realism" and "naturalism." Those were the watchwords of writers like G. Planche (1816), J. H. Champfleury (1857) and É. Zola (about 1870) and artists, beginning with G. Courbet (1855). The theory of naturalism was, in fact, a continuation of the theory of imitation but with a certain difference; it was concerned not so much with art reproducing things but—like science—exploring them.

The twentieth-century theorists of art abandoned not only the term "imitation" but also its principle.

229

Our age does not deny that art relies on nature—even Picasso says that it could not be possible otherwise—but it does not maintain that art imitates nature. For some art is construction, for others expression; for none is it imitation. We indeed agree with the Greek "mimesis" in its original sense of expression and the Democritian sense of being guided by the laws of nature. "We do *not* wish to *copy* nor to reproduce nature," writes Mondrian, "we want to *shape* it as nature shapes the fruit." On the other hand, our times do not wish to imitate in the sense of copying the appearance of things, the idea which was in the foreground for so many centuries after Plato. The majority of contemporaries would rather agree with Girolamo Savonarola in his *De simplicitate vitae humanae* (ed. Lyon [1638], III, 1, 87) who asserted that what in fact belongs to art is only that which *does not* imitate nature (*ea sunt proprie artis, quae* non *vere naturam imitantur*).

BIBLIOGRAPHY

The newest interpretation of the idea of imitation in Greek and especially in Aristotelian thought has been developed by R. Ingarden in his paper on Aristotelian Poetics (*Proceedings of the Polish Academy of Learning,* 1945) and in four books: H. Koller, *Mimesis in der Antike* (Bern, 1954); G. F. Else, *Aristotle's Poetics: The Argument* (Cambridge, Mass., 1957); G. Sörbom, *Mimesis and Art* (Uppsala, 1966); and W. Tatarkiewicz, *The History of Aesthetics,* 3 vols., (Polish ed., Wroclaw, 1960–68; English ed., The Hague, 1970). The three volumes of the present writer follow the development of the idea of imitation from antiquity until 1700. B. Weinberg, *A History of Literary Criticism in the Italian Renaissance* (Chicago, 1961) makes available the variety of opinions of the seventeenth century on imitation. The earlier book of B. Weinberg, *French Realism: a Critical Reaction* (New York and London, 1937) discusses the point of view of the nineteenth century.

W. TATARKIEWICZ

[See also Baroque; **Classification of the Arts;** Form; Iconography; Naturalism in Art; **Religion, Ritual in;** *Ut pictura poesis.*]

MORAL SENSE

I

THE MORAL SENSE is a distinctive conception of moral judgment formulated by Francis Hutcheson and followed, with some modification, by David Hume. By the word "sense" they meant *feeling;* the moral sense is the capacity to experience feelings of approval and disapproval, and the theory of the moral sense is to be contrasted with the view that moral distinctions are perceived by reason. The expression "moral sense" has been used by other philosophers with less precision. An explicit theory of a moral sense can be attributed only to Hutcheson and Hume, and is to be understood within the context of an empiricist epistemology and as standing opposed to rationalist theories of ethics.

1. Shaftesbury. The actual term "moral sense" was first used by Anthony Ashley Cooper, Third Earl of Shaftesbury, in *An Inquiry concerning Virtue* (unauthorized edition, London, 1699; corrected version included in *Characteristics of Men, Manners, Opinions, Times,* London, 1711). In Shaftesbury the expression is purely casual and has no more special significance than the phrase of ordinary language, "sense of right and wrong," which Shaftesbury uses much more frequently. It would be going too far to say of Shaftesbury, as one can say of Samuel Clarke, that the use of the word "sense" for moral discrimination is not to be taken seriously at all. Clarke is a firm advocate of rationalist ethics but is nevertheless able to write, like Shaftesbury, of the "sense men naturally have" of the difference between right and wrong. Shaftesbury's use of the term means more than that—but not much more, for Shaftesbury feels no difficulty in accepting also the phraseology of the rationalists, when he speaks of "knowledge" of right and wrong, of the use of "reason" in moral judgment, and of "eternal" and "immutable" virtue. Hutcheson took the expression "moral sense" from Shaftesbury and used it as a definite name for a definite theory, but the detail of that theory itself owes little to Shaftesbury.

This is not to say that Hutcheson's ethical thought owes little to Shaftesbury. The most important feature of Shaftesbury's moral philosophy is the linking of ethical and aesthetic judgment. That link remains an important feature of the moral philosophy of both Hutcheson and Hume, and in Hutcheson's first book it is, as in Shaftesbury, the central feature. There is, however, no intrinsic connection between a comparison of virtue with beauty and a theory of moral sense. The former goes back to Plato and continues in many philosophers, both rationalist and empiricist.

Shaftesbury influenced Hutcheson in one other respect that is more relevant to the moral sense, namely in the notion that reflection upon motives is a necessary condition of moral approbation. Hutcheson makes some use of this idea, but not a great deal. It was emphasized more by Bishop Butler in his account of conscience, which is emphatically not a theory of moral sense.

Shaftesbury, then, contributed the name of "moral sense" and the general background of an analogy between moral and aesthetic judgment, but little of the actual content of the moral sense theory.

2. Hutcheson. The moral sense theory proper is best seen in the first two books of Francis Hutcheson, *An Inquiry into the original of our Ideas of Beauty and Virtue* (London, 1725), and *An Essay on the Nature and Conduct of the Passions and Affections. With Illustrations on the Moral Sense* (London, 1728). In Hutcheson's later work, notably the final version of his lectures as Professor of Moral Philosophy at Glasgow (posthumously published as *A System of Moral Philosophy*, Glasgow and London, 1755), his original distinctive views are overlaid with ideas derived from Butler.

The primary aim of Hutcheson's initial thoughts in moral philosophy was one which he shared with Butler but which he pursued in his own way. It was to refute an egoistic interpretation of ethics, recently revived by Bernard Mandeville. Hutcheson presents arguments for the view (1) that men can have disinterested motives, i.e., that they can act for the sake of the good of others and not merely for their own advantage, and (2) that they can make disinterested practical judgments, i.e., that they can think an action good for reasons other than that it will serve their own advantage. The disinterested motive with which Hutcheson is chiefly concerned is benevolence, and the disinterested form of judgment that is relevant to ethical theory is the expression of approval and disapproval. Hutcheson's view is that a feeling of approval is the natural reaction of a spectator when he sees a man act from the motive of benevolence. This feeling of approval is what Hutcheson calls the moral sense. A contrary feeling of disapproval would arise naturally towards the motive of malevolence, but disinterested malice, Hutcheson believes, is hardly possible for human nature; hatred is usually the effect of self-love, and in such circumstances self-love is disapproved, though self-love in itself is neither approved nor disapproved, neither virtuous nor vicious. Virtue for Hutcheson is the motive of benevolence approved by the moral sense, and vice is a motive (usually partial to self or to a narrow circle) that overcomes benevolence and is accordingly disapproved by the moral sense.

According to Hutcheson, the reactions of the moral sense are akin to the kind of love or admiration that naturally arises towards beauty. Virtue therefore is a sort of beauty, moral beauty; and to say this is simply to express the thought that our warm reaction to benevolence is like our warm reaction to physical beauty in being natural, immediate, and a species of love.

As Hutcheson's theory developed, however, it turned into the first explicit statement of utilitarian ethics in the following way. Benevolence aims at the happiness of others; a wide benevolence is approved more than a narrow one, and a universal benevolence is approved most of all. Therefore "that action is best which procures the greatest happiness for the greatest numbers." Strictly speaking, this conclusion departs from the original moral sense theory, for it makes ethical judgment, the judgment of what is best, depend on the thought of consequences and not on an immediate reaction of love for the motive of benevolence.

Hutcheson speaks of a moral "sense" because he accepts the empiricist theory of knowledge. John Locke had said that all ideas come from sensation and reflection. Hutcheson thinks the word "reflection" can mislead in suggesting only reflection upon ideas that come to us originally from the external senses, and so he prefers Locke's alternative expression, "internal sense," which clearly means a source of ideas that is additional to the external senses. In his second book Hutcheson distinguishes several internal senses. They are all different species of pleasant and painful feeling: the sense of beauty (or "the pleasures of the imagination"), the public sense (sympathetic pleasure and pain with the happiness and misery of others), the moral sense (the pleasant feeling of approval and the unpleasant one of disapproval), the sense of honor and shame (pleasure at the approval of our actions by others and pain at their disapproval), and perhaps a sense of decency or dignity (a nonmoral esteem or approval of some pleasures over others). While in his first book Hutcheson had been arguing chiefly against egoistic theory in order to establish the disinterested character of moral action and moral judgment, in the second book he defends the empiricist assumptions of his account against the views of rationalists. He argues that justifying reasons are concerned with means to presupposed ends and that the approval of ultimate ends must be a function of "sense," i.e., feeling.

3. Hume. Hutcheson's argument against rationalist ethics gave David Hume the initial impetus to develop the implications of empiricism not only in ethics but over the whole range of philosophy. Hume's contribution to the theory of moral sense was made in Book III of *A Treatise of Human Nature* (London, 1740) and in *An Enquiry concerning the Principles of Morals* (London, 1751). In both works Hume uses the word "sentiment" more commonly than "sense," but the meaning is the same. In the *Treatise* the titles of the first two sections of Book III state that moral distinctions are not derived from reason but are derived from a moral sense. Here the expression "moral sense" is retained from Hutcheson, and the issue raised in these sections is probably the point from which the whole of Hume's philosophy originated.

Hume continues but does not add significantly to the analogy between ethical and aesthetic judgment that had been drawn by Shaftesbury and Hutcheson. The importance of Hume's contribution to the moral sense theory lies in three things. First, he works out an extraordinarily powerful development of Hutcheson's criticism of rationalist ethics. Secondly, where Hutcheson had taken the moral sense or sentiment of approval to be simply an original datum of human nature, Hume explains it as being the result of sympathy and thereby makes it seem less mysterious and more clearly connected with a utilitarian approach to ethics. Thirdly, while Hutcheson had supposed that the object of moral approval is always a species or consequence of benevolence, Hume distinguishes between benevolence and justice as "natural" and "artificial" virtue respectively, and recognizes that the approval of justice by the moral sense cannot be so simple and straightforward as the approval of benevolence.

Hume's view of the respective functions of reason and feeling in moral judgment is essentially that of Hutcheson: reason shows us means, sentiment selects ends. But Hume supports the position with a battery of arguments which together constitute as damaging an assault as can be found anywhere in the history of philosophy. In the *Treatise* they are all the more memorable for being stated with trenchant epigram and wit. "Reason is and ought only to be the slave of the passions"; "an active principle can never be founded on an inactive"; if immorality were telling a lie in action, as one rationalist contends, then immorality could be avoided merely by concealment, e.g., by closing the shutters when seducing a neighbor's wife; a "small attention" to the difficulty of deducing *ought* from *is* "would subvert all the vulgar systems of morality." Hume's chief argument is that reason cannot move to action, as passion can, and since moral judgment is a motive to action it cannot be an expression of reason. This argument is supplemented by taking in turn each of the functions that can be attributed to reason and showing that none of them can suffice for moral judgment. As in aesthetics, when reason has done all that it can do to ascertain the facts, sentiment or taste must supervene to produce an idea of value, which is nothing objective but the expression of a spectator's reaction to the objective facts.

The reaction of the moral sense or sentiment, however, need not be left unexplained as an ultimate instinct of human nature. It is the effect of sympathy with the feelings of those who are affected by an action. Benevolence aims at giving happiness or removing pain, and usually it succeeds in its aim. A spectator of a benevolent action feels a sympathetic pleasure with the pleasure of the person benefited, and this gives rise to the particular kind of pleasant feeling that constitutes moral approval. Similarly disapproval is a particular kind of unpleasant feeling arising from sympathetic pain with the pain of those who are harmed by actions termed vicious or morally bad. Hutcheson had connected the moral sense with the sense of honor by saying that the latter is a form of pleasant feeling which results from the observation that we are approved by the moral sense of others, but he had left the moral sense and the public sense (sympathy) as two independent and ultimate features of human nature. Hume connects them in the sort of way in which Hutcheson had connected the moral sense with the sense of honor, and in consequence there is now a chain of causation for all three; sympathy causes approval, and the knowledge that one is approved causes pride (Hutcheson's sense of honor). A further advantage of Hume's supplement to the theory of moral sense is that the connection between approval and utility becomes more evident. Approval is not simply a quasi-aesthetic reaction to the beauty of benevolence; it is the result of sympathetic pleasure with the effect of benevolence, namely the happiness of one's neighbors, and so it can be generalized into pleasure at the happiness of mankind. In Hume's view, approval is directed both at the immediately agreeable and at the useful.

So much for the approval of "natural" virtue, benevolence, and its usual consequences. The approval of justice is more puzzling, for the stern countenance of justice lacks the beauty of benevolence, and yet the rules of justice are approved even when, in particular instances, they oppose utility. Hume treats justice as "artificial" virtue; approval of it does not depend on human nature alone, as does the approval of benevolence. The rules of justice are a man-made device, necessary because a feature of human nature, selfishness and limited generosity, is combined with a feature of the human situation, the scarcity of goods in relation to men's wants. The rules of justice give men protection for their share of scarce goods. Self-interest leads each man to support the rules, and sympathy with the general interest adds moral approval. The feeling of approval, which was originally directed towards the utility of the rules, becomes attached by association to the rules themselves and remains even in instances where the application of the rules is not useful. Thus a sense of duty can lose contact with sympathy, the original natural basis of approval, and can become an inflexible approval of rules as such.

In this way Hume takes account of a feature of morality that had impressed rationalist or natural law theorists. He also allows that moral and aesthetic judgments are made from a general point of view. They do not express actual feelings, which vary with varying circumstances. As in his theory of knowledge, Hume attributes to the imagination the generalizing activity that others would attribute to reason. In the end, therefore, his theory shares certain insights of the rationalists, though undoubtedly explaining them in a different spirit, within a different framework of ideas.

II

Among other philosophers of the eighteenth century the moral sense theory met both with criticism and with support. Several of the critics understood better than the supporters what was at issue, and their observations are therefore more instructive.

1. Critics. Contemporary criticism of the idea of a moral sense came from more than one direction. John Balguy and Richard Price attacked it in the course of defending and improving the position of rationalist ethics. John Gay did so while reviving egoistic theory under the aegis of associationist psychology. Adam Smith should be regarded as the natural successor of Hume in the history of empiricist ethics, but he quite rightly distinguished his own theory from doctrines of a moral sense.

Balguy criticizes Shaftesbury in *A Letter to a Deist, concerning the beauty and excellence of moral virtue* (1726), and Hutcheson in *The Foundation of Moral Goodness* (1728). Price criticizes Hutcheson and Hume in *A Review of the Principal Questions and Difficulties in Morals* (1758). Both Balguy and Price argue that the beauty or attractiveness of virtue needs to be distinguished from its moral character proper. Price allows that aesthetic judgments express feeling; Balguy thinks, after some hesitation, that aesthetic, like moral, judgments can represent an intellectual grasp of objective truth. Both, however, agree that the moral sense theorists were misled by concentrating their attention on the "moral beauty" of virtue and by neglecting the notions of duty and rightness. They also both insist upon the universality and law-like character of moral principles, and point out that feelings are particular and variable. Price was not alone in failing to see that Hume had anticipated the latter criticism; but then Hume's account of moral judgment as taking a general point of view is a serious departure from the original theory of moral sense or moral feeling, since Hume brings in the imagination to perform the generalizing function that the rationalists ascribe to reason.

Gay refers briefly to Hutcheson's moral sense in *A Dissertation concerning the Fundamental Principle of Virtue or Morality* (1731). Gay reverts to the egoistic psychology which Hutcheson had criticized. He admits that moral approval is not made with a conscious regard to self-interest, but he argues that this is because pleasure has become associated with what was at first merely a means to pleasure, just as men may come to take pleasure in money. One might as well speak of a pecuniary sense, says Gay, as of a moral sense and a sense of honor.

The moral philosophy of Adam Smith, set out in *The Theory of Moral Sentiments* (1759), is a fruitful development of the empiricist approach of Hutcheson and Hume. Its most striking features are a complex account of sympathy (in relation to the motives of agents as well as to the feelings of persons affected by action) and a theory of conscience as a reflection of the views of an impartial spectator. In both these matters Smith is building upon elements of the positive side of Hume's ethical thought. Nevertheless, Smith is a critic of the theory of moral sense, both as it was expounded by his admired teacher Hutcheson and as it was modified by his beloved friend Hume. Smith objects to the idea that there is a single peculiar feeling of moral approval. He follows Hume in taking approval and disapproval to be the expression of sympathy and antipathy, but he points out that since we can sympathize with all manner of feelings, our sympathetic sharing of feelings can itself be of different kinds. Furthermore, the sense of propriety is not the same as the sense of virtue, the sense of merit, or the sense of duty. The sense of propriety is straightforward sympathy with the motive of the agent as being one that any normal man would have in the circumstances. The sense of virtue, however, is a feeling of admiration for a motive that goes beyond what is merely proper. The sense of merit is a double sympathy, with the motive of the agent and with the gratitude of the beneficiary of his action. The sense of duty is a reflected idea of the judgments of propriety that we imagine would be made by an impartial spectator of our conduct. There are therefore several moral sentiments, not just one. That is why the title of Smith's book speaks of "moral sentiments" in the plural.

Later criticism too was not confined to a single point of view. Thomas Reid and Immanuel Kant were both critics of empiricism, in epistemology and ethics alike, but neither simply continued the usual rationalist tradition. They both perceived that there was partial truth on each side in the dispute between rationalism and empiricism, and they tried to effect a synthesis, Kant with more rigor and deeper insight than Reid. Meanwhile Jeremy Bentham had his little fling at the idea of a moral sense along with other theories, whether empiricist or rationalist, on the ground that they were all cloaks for prejudice.

Reid is the chief exponent of the philosophy of "common sense," and he often appeals to the evidence of ordinary language. In his theory of knowledge Reid holds that perception cannot simply be the receipt of impressions but must include a rational judgment. He is prepared to speak of perceptual judgment as the work of the senses because this is in accordance with ordinary usage. Similarly he is ready to speak of a moral sense because in ordinary language we talk of a sense of duty; but he is quite clear that what he means by the moral sense is not at all what Hume means. Reid means a rational judgment that has feeling as its consequence. His arguments against the idea of the moral sense as a feeling consist largely in showing that it is inconsistent with our usual ways of speaking about morals. Reid's views on ethics are in his *Essays on the Active Powers of Man* (1788).

Kant was influenced by the moral sense theory during his earlier years, but in his mature critical philosophy he classed it together with hedonism as a radically mistaken conception of morality. Kant refers briefly to the moral sense both in the *Grundlegung zur Metaphysik der Sitten* (1785) and in the *Kritik der Praktischen Vernunft* (1788). The detail of his compressed criticism is similar to points made by Price and Reid: moral principles have the character of universal law, while feeling varies and applies only to the individual experiencing it; the specifically moral feeling of reverence is a consequence, not the cause, of moral judgment. Kant nevertheless pays tribute to the moral sense theory for recognizing the disinterested character of morality.

One need not take with equal seriousness the equally brief reference to the moral sense theory by Bentham in *An Introduction to the Principles of Morals and Legislation* (printed 1780, published 1789). Bentham throws together in one basket the doctrines of moral sense, common sense, and all the different varieties of rationalist and natural law theory. Each of them, he thinks, is simply a way of trying to foist one's own opinions upon other people, unlike the objective principle of utility. Bentham obviously has no notion that Hutcheson elicited the principle of utility from his theory of moral sense, or that Hume (from whom Bentham first learned of the principle of utility) was also an advocate of the moral sense.

2. Supporters. Nothing of great moment was added to the moral sense theory by writers subsequent to Hume who gave it their support. This may be illustrated by a glance at Hartley and Kames.

David Hartley's *Observations on Man* (1749) is important for working out in detail a scheme of psychology based on the association of ideas. Hartley's thoughts on the subject were first stimulated by the remarks of Gay in the *Dissertation* mentioned above, but Hartley does not follow Gay in reducing morality to self-interest. He regards the moral sense as the effect of associating pleasure with virtue, and pain with vice,

from several different sources: education, self-interest, sympathy, aesthetic feeling, and religious doctrine. Hartley therefore disagrees with Hutcheson's notion of the moral sense as an original "instinct," but his account of its formation is too vague to be enlightening.

Hume's kinsman, Henry Home, Lord Kames, presents himself as a supporter of the moral sense theory in his *Essays on the Principles of Morality and Natural Religion* (1751). He follows Shaftesbury, Hutcheson, and Hume in comparing the moral sense with aesthetic feeling, but criticizes all three of them for giving inadequate attention to the ideas of duty and obligation, which he, like the rationalists, regards as the central concepts of morality. When Kames enlarges upon the "perception" of duty and justice, he writes more in the vein of traditional natural law doctrine than of the empiricist approach to ethics.

III

The eighteenth-century dispute between the advocates of reason and those of moral sense or sentiment as the basis of moral judgment was a reflection of the rift between rationalism and empiricism in the theory of knowledge. In the nineteenth century the focus of interest moved away from epistemological questions in ethics as in general philosophy. The ethical theory of the nineteenth century was more concerned with the criterion and end of moral action than with the nature of moral judgment.

Moral philosophy in the twentieth century, however, has seen a return of the interests (and arguments) of the eighteenth. Rationalist ethics of the kind found in Richard Price and in Kant was revived by the Oxford intuitionists or deontologists, H. A. Prichard, Sir David Ross, and E. F. Carritt. The intuitionism of G. E. Moore, which went along with a form of utilitarianism and a scale of values that recalls Plato rather than Kant, was of a different character, not clearly rationalist, though certainly not empiricist either. It is a mistake to think of Moore's *Principia Ethica* (1903) as upholding a moral sense theory on the ground that Moore compares good with yellow in being, as he thinks, a simple indefinable quality. Moore does not imply that we perceive the quality of goodness through a sense analogous to sight, and in any event this was not suggested by the moral sense theory either.

A twentieth-century revival of the moral sense is to be found rather in the emotive theory of ethics put forward by A. J. Ayer in *Language, Truth and Logic* (1936). As in Hutcheson and Hume, moral and aesthetic judgments are coupled, and the theory arises from empiricist epistemology. The emotive theory holds that moral judgments express or evince, but do not describe, the speaker's emotions of approval and disapproval;

their logical character is that of exclamations, not of statements. The purpose of the theory is to accommodate moral and aesthetic judgments within a framework of empiricism, while avoiding familiar criticisms of the view that these judgments are autobiographical descriptions of subjective feeling. The emotive theory of ethics is an adjunct of logical positivism or logical empiricism, which avowedly owes its inspiration to Hume. No philosopher is more acute than Hume in discerning and pursuing logical subtleties; but his contribution to ethics is enhanced by the comparable subtlety of his psychology. The emotive theory, which confines itself to logical questions, is a crude thing when set beside the moral sense theory of Hume.

BIBLIOGRAPHY

Selections from the relevant eighteenth-century texts are in L. A. Selby-Bigge, *British Moralists*, 2 vols. (Oxford, 1897), and D. D. Raphael, *British Moralists 1650–1800*, 2 vols. (Oxford, 1969). The former does not include Hume, Hartley, or Reid; the latter does not include Kames. For commentary on the development of the idea of a moral sense in Shaftesbury, Hutcheson, and Hume, see especially: Thomas Fowler, *Shaftesbury and Hutcheson* (London, 1882); William Robert Scott, *Francis Hutcheson* (Cambridge, 1900); Norman Kemp Smith, *The Philosophy of David Hume* (London, 1941). James Bonar, *Moral Sense* (London, 1930), surveys the history of the notion from Shaftesbury to Kant. D. D. Raphael, *The Moral Sense* (London, 1947), discusses Hutcheson, Hume, Price, and Reid.

D. D. RAPHAEL

[See also Law, Natural; Rationality; **Right and Good.**].

MOTIF

I. SEMANTICS

THIS IDEA has had so many uses, and has figured so variously in different terminologies, particularly during the modern period, that it can best be approached by way of its semantic history and lexical record. At the outset we must note that "motif" is a gallicism, thereby set apart from the broader implications of its English cognate "motive." Ruskin always used the anglicized expression; but, unlike later writers on the plastic arts, he broadened and blurred its meaning: "the leading idea of a composition," "a leading emotional purpose, technically called its motive" (*Modern Painters*, 1843–60). Others have complained that the term "motif" sounds pedantic (Krappe, 1930); but folklorists especially have preferred it, perhaps for that very

reason, because they have come to employ it in so technical a sense. Etymologically, the word is derived from the Latin verb *movere* ("to move") in its past participial form, *motus*. This, as Ducange indicates, formed the basis of the late Latin adjective *motivus* ("susceptible to movement"), and hence of the medieval noun *motivum* ("cause" or "incitement"). Thus "motive" and its related forms in Western languages originally meant a stimulus or source of movement. Gradually their connotations shifted from the physical to the psychological sphere, in effect from motion to emotion.

That shift is well illustrated by the *Oxford English Dictionary*, when it points out that until the nineteenth century Englishmen habitually spoke of "acting on a motive" rather than of "acting from a motive." To internalize the reason or reasons for any given action was to open the way for what Coleridge called "motive-hunting," and to make the concept of motivation more widely available for psychology as well as ethics. Here the German *motivieren* seems to have adumbrated the verbal form, leading on to the English "motivate" largely through the influence of Gustav Freytag's well-known analysis of dramatic techniques, *Das Technik des Dramas* (1863). La Rochefoucauld had been concerned with internal springs of behavior, as usual, when he observed that a motive was not an excuse (*Un motif n'est pas une excuse*). This remark maintains a sharp French distinction between psychological awareness and moral justification, which would be neutralized by the purport of the more popular maxim, "To understand everything is to forgive everything" (*Tout comprendre, c'est tout pardonner*). What might be termed the traditional definition of *motif*, which stands alone in the *Dictionnaire de l'Académie Française* through the fifth edition (1798), emphasizes moving in both senses: "That which moves and leads to doing something" (*Ce qui meut et porte à faire quelque chose*).

It was not until the sixth edition of its dictionary (1835) that the French Academy was willing to recognize a more specialized use of *motif* in relation to music: "the melodic phrase, the original idea that dominates the whole piece" (*la phrase de chant, l'idée primitive qui domine tout le morceau*). This follows by two generations the *Encyclopédie* (1765), which of course was more advanced in its outlook. It had devoted a substantial article, written by Baron Grimm, to a wholly musical definition oriented toward eighteenth-century opera—going so far as to declare that *motif*, "the main idea of the aria" (*l'idée principale de l'air*), was "what constitute[d] musical genius most particularly" (*ce qui constitue le plus particulièrement le génie musical*). This usage had its natural birthplace in Italy, where *motivo* long had signified the basic segment of a melody. Music, because of its quasi-abstract character, offers the clearest examples of motifs as structural elements, which are built up into finished compositions through sundry devices of repetition, modulation, variation, and orchestral elaboration. Therefore it has frequently served as a model for other arts. The systematic employment of such devices to convey associated ideas, and consequently to provide a sort of choric comment on the action of a music drama or symphonic poem, has been the Wagnerian *Leitmotiv*.

Now Wagner, though an eloquent exponent of his own methods, made no mention of that word; his personal term was *Grundthema* ("basic theme"). *Leitmotiv* seems to have been coined and popularized by his critical apostle, Hans von Wolzogen, whose book, *Die Nibelungenmythos in Sage und Litteratur*, was published at Berlin in 1876—the year that saw the completion and Bayreuth premiere of Wagner's tetralogy, *Der Ring des Nibelungen*. In spite of the farflung reverberations to this event, it cannot be claimed for Wagner himself that he originated his most characteristic device. Mozart had occasionally repeated musical themes to bring out dramatic situations, notably with the Statue in *Don Giovanni*, and Berlioz had lately dramatized his orchestrations by interweaving certain phrases which he referred to as his *idées fixes*. However, Wagner became the most influential exemplar, not only for musicians but also for men of letters, of the creative artist who utilizes motif as the unifying feature of his work. It can be argued, and will later be amplified, that motif has a place of its own in literary structure which goes all the way back to oral literature. Nonetheless it is true that many leading writers of the earlier twentieth century, deeply immersed as they were in time-consciousness and a state of synaesthesia, have made conscious efforts to echo and emulate Wagner.

Thomas Mann indeed has distinguished between the early phase of his own stylistic development, which was more rhetorical in its reiterations, and the thematic musicality of his more mature style ("Lebensabriss," 1930). He has often acknowledged his debt to Wagner, as in the story *Das Wälsungenblut*, where a decadent incest of contemporary Munich finds its mythic parallel in the sibling love between Siegmund and Sieglinde. Similarly, in *The Waste Land*, T. S. Eliot quotes from *Tristan und Isolde*, while Joyce's Stephen Dedalus—wielding his ashplant—self-consciously cries out "Nothung," the name and the *Leitmotiv* of Siegfried's sword. More eclectically, the streams of consciousness in *Ulysses* sometimes flow through *Leitmotive* from other composers: e.g., the duet from *Don Giovanni*,

which is sounded at the threat of impending adultery. But the echoes that make up so much of *Ulysses*, though they range from Stephen's scholastic reading to the advertising copy of Mr. Bloom, come primarily from printed sources; the most poignant of them is the remembered title of a monastic tract on remorse of conscience, *Agenbite of Inwit*. Proust, though he was likewise an enthusiastic Wagnerite, invented a composer of his own, the long neglected and suddenly discovered master Vinteuil. A "little phrase" from Vinteuil's imaginary sonata furnished the accompaniment to Swann's love for Odette, even as Marcel's for Albertine is orchestrated by a posthumous septet.

When Proust created a synaesthetic frame of reference for his great novel, he alluded even more to painting than to music. In both modes of artistic composition, the spatial along with the temporal, rhythm is imposed by the recurrence of some distinctive kind of figuration. Motif is thus equally germane to the plastic arts, where it is most obviously discernible in architectural design and stylized decoration. Some of the older definitions, stressing the formal component, allow for this dual application. But there is a larger conception, as Ruskin sensed, in which an overtone of "motive" is still present: i.e., underlying idea or final cause, insofar as it applies to the intentions of the artist, be he a musician or a painter. Such an enlargement seems to have been reinforced by the subjective nuances and the individualistic viewpoints of the impressionist movement. It is significant that F. W. Fairholt's *Dictionary of Terms in Art* (London, 1854) characterizes *Motif* as "a term lately introduced into the vocabulary of Art," whereas it is altogether omitted from James Elmes's earlier *Dictionary of the Fine Arts* (London, 1826). When the emphasis falls on pictorial representation, critics have shown a tendency to locate the motif in the subject represented. This is all the truer of iconology, the study of art history that interprets visual images in the light of the ideas they symbolize.

II. POETICS

Motif, considered as a critical concept, seems to have enjoyed its longest and fullest relationship with German literature. That may be attributable, in part, to the strategic significance of the rich treasury of household tales collected and edited by the brothers Grimm. Their *Kinder- und Hausmärchen* (Berlin, 1812–15) constituted both a major landmark in the newly developed science of philology and—as augmented and systematized by the wide-ranging commentaries of Bolte and Polívka (1913–32)—an indispensable instrument for analytic inquiry into the world's repertory of narrative. Appropriately, looking far beyond the boundaries of romantic nationalism, it was the cosmopolitan Goethe who first brought motif within the purview of literary criticism, during his conversations with Eckermann on 18 January 1825. It may strike us as peculiarly prescient that this conversation should have dwelt on Serbian poetry, in view of the affinities that Milman Parry and others have more recently established between the Homeric epic and Serbo-Croatian oral literature. Here, as not infrequently elsewhere, Goethe was expressing certain friendly reservations with regard to Schiller, who did not—his friend felt—take sufficient pains over his motifs. "The true power and effect of a poem consists in the situation," Goethe affirmed, "—in the *motifs*" (. . . *aber die Wahre Kraft und Wirkung eines Gedichts in der Situation, in den Motiven besteht* . . .). The apposition would seem to reflect the interrelationship between the formative and the responsive conception.

Goethe's enormous prestige was bound to prevail with those among his compatriots who addressed themselves to the problem. The most determined of these was Wilhelm Scherer, whose solid and serious contributions to literary history were rounded out by a posthumously published outline of his poetic theory (*Poetik*, 1888), wherein he accorded due attention to the general study of motifs (*Allgemeine Motivenlehre*). "What is a motif?" (*Was ist ein Motiv?*) he asked, and answered: "An elementary, unitary part of a poetic matter" (*Ein elementarer, in sich einheitlicher Theil eines poetischen Stoffs*). Scherer speaks more generally and more vaguely when he equates motif with idea or ethos, or when he calls for a canvass of motifs as "a full portrayal of human thought and deed" (*eine volle Schilderung menschlicher Denkens und Thuns*). His practical attempts to enumerate or classify *Die Stoffe* boil down to a handful of rudimentary instances from the Bible or classical mythology: the fratricide of Cain, the matricide of Orestes. Goethe's famous lyric about the land of lemons and oranges (*Kennst du das Land*) is naively categorized, not under its nostalgic theme of longing for the south (*Sehnsucht nach Italien*), but within the academic pigeonhole of botany. Something like a unitary reduction is proposed, however, and some concern is manifested for the difference between a principal motif (*Hauptmotiv*) and a subordinate one (*Nebenmotif*).

Less mechanical and more suggestive were the aesthetic speculations of the *geistesgeschichtliche* philosopher Wilhelm Dilthey, who was deeply interested in the impact of experience on the growth of the poet's mind. His approach, like that of so many thinkers following Goethe, focussed on the organic growth of the individual psyche rather than on the tools and materials of the poet's craft. Yet, when he came to formulate his notions about the creative imagina-

tion—his own foundations for a poetics, according to the subtitle, *Bausteine für eine Poetik*—he was ready to acknowledge the importance of the stuff with which the poet actually worked. Under the heading of *Stoff* he gave first consideration to *Motiv*, recognizing that its function could not fully be understood until it had been collectively examined. "The number of possible motifs is limited, and it is a task for comparative literature to trace the development of single motifs" (*Die Zahl möglicher Motive ist begrenzt, und es ist eine Aufgabe der vergleichende Litteraturgeschichte, die Entwicklung der einzelnen Motive darzustellen* [Dilthey, 1887]). The statement that limits motifs to a finite number opens up the possibility that they might be usefully surveyed, enumerated, and classified. The invitation to trace them individually is one to which comparatists have responded somewhat literally at first, then with a more skeptical reaction, and since the mid-twentieth century with a heightened degree of commitment.

The need was for a methodology which could bridge the gap between invention and tradition, between the personal talent of the imaginative writer and the inherited store of material that he has drawn upon and reshaped. A well-informed and stimulating effort to face that need was made by the Russian scholar, A. N. Veselovsky, through what he termed "Historical Poetics." In a course of lectures, "Poetics of the Subject" (*Poetika sujetov*), delivered in 1897 and published just after his death in 1906, he addressed himself to a central aspect of literature which is usually either taken for granted or else ignored. Subject has too often been identified with the amorphous notion of content, only to be impaled upon the dilemma of its false opposition to form, and consequently neglected by form-minded critics. Veselovsky demonstrated the formal properties of *sujet* (the Russian term is borrowed from the French) by showing how it could be broken down into structural units. In short, it was "a complex of motifs," while motif was defined as "the simplest narrative unit that responds with an image to the different demands of the primitive mind or of everyday observation." The originality of the insight lay, not in its application to the primitive mind, but in its suggestion that the proclaimed results of everyday observation—such as the realistic novel—could be reduced to the simple constituents of the fairy tale.

It would be a long time, however, before there was wide acknowledgment of the fact that Balzac and Dickens were mythmakers as well as social observers. And, if realists balked at the implication that their firsthand human documents somehow managed to fall within a storied pattern, romantics were in no mood to accept the assumption that the potentialities of human experience came to something less than infinity. Veselovsky's formulations were eked out by a massive sequence of citations from philology, anthropology, folklore, and comparative religion; but it has taken about two generations for literary history to catch up with him. To be sure, the notion of subject matter (*sujetnost*) is formalized whenever we speak of plot: not just the story or situation but the links in the chain of events, what is known in Hollywood as "the story line." Now a plot in England had originally denoted a piece of ground; then it became a chart or layout of that ground; thence it was generalized into any plan for construction or design for action—not infrequently villainous, a complot. It enters into the critical vocabulary as a ground plan for drama or narration. There are meaningful contrasts in the Greek word for plot, *mythos,* or the Latin *fabula,* which seems much more didactic, or the French *intrigue,* which has sexual or conspiratorial echoes, or the German *Handlung,* which sounds so businesslike.

The dramatic medium, because it depends so overtly on construction, has always lent itself most readily to analysis in terms of structure. Comedy, most self-evidently, from Menander through the *Commedia dell'arte* to Molière and onward, has gained its effects through standard plots, stock characters, and set gags or *lazzi*—a bag of tricks which might otherwise be described as a collection of motifs. It was asseverated by Count Gozzi, whose own plays were influenced both by fairy tales and by the Italian *scenarii,* that there were no more than thirty-six elemental situations for the stage. Schiller protested against this reductionism, but, on Goethe's challenge, found himself unable to count as many (Eckermann, 1836). A handbook for would-be playwrights by Georges Polti circulated widely under the title *The Thirty-Six Dramatic Situations* (1912). A more searching exploration of this question, by the Sorbonne aesthetician Étienne Souriau, has produced a sober monograph entitled *Les Deux Cent Mille Situations dramatiques* (Paris, 1950). Round numbers are suspicious, and the exact figure is not important. The point is that, numerous as the components of storytelling may be, they are not innumerable—even with a liberal allowance for modification and recombination. The Victorian governess in *The Importance of Being Earnest* differs almost totally from the Nutrix of Plautus or Terence, yet functionally both exist to act out the same motif: the identification of a long-lost infant.

III. FOLKLORE

Literary historians were more used to dealing with chronological than with thematic relationships; literary critics were more preoccupied with the peculiar characteristics of individual writers than with the common body of narrative effects; hence they were both slow in meeting the challenge to develop a *Motivenlehre.* The philological quest for sources and analogues, the researches of medievalists in registering the cycles of romance helped to make an academic pursuit of *Stoffgeschichte*—the German compound seems more appropriate than the endeavor to translate it into "thematology." The Italian comparatist, Arturo Graf, traced such legendary themes as the earthly paradise and the devil; but this direction ran counter to the principles of Croce, whose opposition to comparative methods was grounded in his ideals of organic expression. The Francocentric school that had its organ in the *Revue de littérature comparée* made much less of parallels than of influences, and reserved its friendliest scrutiny for the tracing of synchronic currents and international movements. The programmatic survey of Wellek and Warren, *Theory of Literature* (1949), summed up a widespread reaction: "*Stoffgeschichte* is the least literary of histories." That dictum has worn thin because it stemmed from the narrowly formalistic assumptions that the stuff of art is mere content, that subject matter is somehow less relevant than technique, and that disparities are somehow less revealing than similarities.

Meanwhile scholars had learned to look toward fiction that was anonymous, traditional, and preliterary for a clearer paradigm of the elements involved. Classicists like Sir James Frazer and some of his Cambridge colleagues turned to anthropologists for the light that ritual had to cast upon mythology. Early collectors of folklore had been antiquarian hobbyists, recording local survivals, or travelling amateurs, reporting home from primitivistic explorations. But, as collections accumulated from all over the world, more scientific approaches were devised for comparing the lore, for taking note of its ethnical permutations, and for charting its geographical diffusion. Those investigations found their polyglot center in Helsinki, whence an authoritative series of communications has been issued under the imprint of the Folklore Fellows. The original German version of the pioneering classification and bibliography by Antti Aarne, *The Types of the Folktale,* was first brought out in 1910; twice revised, translated and enlarged by Stith Thompson, in 1961 it contained some 2340 entries. These are ordered into five major categories, and subdivided further into a total of thirty-two lesser ones: e.g., Animal Tales: The Clever Fox. Aarne's scheme, arrived at by an empirical sifting of northern European material, fits in equally well with a wider range of Anglo-American data, as his reviser affirms. Motifs, in their singleness, tend to be more universal than the tales they constitute, which are more closely identified with their respective regions.

On revision, some motifs have been raised to the

status of types, where a tale may hinge upon one salient trait or underlying situation. Where its subjects overlap, it may prove hard to classify. Consequently, the distinction had to be sharpened between the theme, wherein motifs are brought together, and the motif itself as an indivisible unit. Here the Finnish systematization and the tentative insights of Veselovsky were pushed further by the Russian folklorist Vladimir Propp in his *Morphology of the Folktale* (*Morfologia skazki*, 1928). Based on the standard collection of Russian popular tales by A. N. Afanasyev (1855–64), even as the commentaries of Bolte and Polívka were based on the compilation of the Grimms, it was more selective and rigorously analytic, rather an organon than a compendium. Propp was able to atomize motifs with precision and objectivity by redefining them as functions (e.g., interdiction, violation, gift, test) of the dramatis personae (hero, villain, donor, helper). These were identifiable by sigla, which could be simply arranged to tabulate the composition of any given fairy tale, and thereby to demonstrate a basic uniformity in the process and the elements of construction. Propp's techniques, though they have had wide impact, did not receive much recognition in Soviet Russia until recently because, at a time when Socialist Realism drew the strictest ideological lines, they savored of Formalism—an ironic circumstance, in view of the formalistic objections lodged against *Stoffgeschichte*. But the notion of motif had meanwhile been critically refined by one of the Formalists, Boris Tomashevsky.

The past generation has seen the emergence of a *Motif-Index of Folk-Literature*, an exhaustive inventory which lists and classifies incidents drawn from over 40,000 tales, myths, fables, romances, ballads, jestbooks, exempla, and other modes of narration. This has been the monumental work of Stith Thompson, an American scholar trained in medieval English philology, who prepared himself by studying the lore of the Amerindians and by translating and supplementing the more limited monograph of Aarne. Thompson uses the Western alphabet as the outer framework for his listings, which allows him twenty-three classes (*I, O*, and *Y* being omitted to avoid confusion). These are ordered in a spectrum which ranges "from the mythological and the supernatural toward the realistic and sometimes the humorous" (1955). Lest it be inferred that imagination can conceive no more than twenty-three kinds of activity, the terminal letter *Z* is left to stand for miscellaneous addenda. Logically enough, the inaugural letter *A* stands for accounts of the Creation, along with the gods, the cosmos, etc. *B* covers animals, including totemism; then *C* moves on to tabu; and *D*, the largest category, is consecrated to magic. The sequence is filled out through *E*, the dead; *F*, other marvels; *G*, ogres and witches; *H*, tests and recogni-

tions; *J*, wisdom and folly; *K*, deceptions; *L*, reversals of fortune; *M*, judgments, bargains, promises, oaths; *N*, luck; *P*, social; *Q*, rewards and punishments; *R*, captives and fugitives; *S*, cruelty; *T*, sex; *U*, homiletic; *V*, religious; *W*, traits of character; and *X*, humorous.

This adds up to a conspectus of diverse fortunes and attitudes which, in the contrasting perspective of Dickens or Balzac, might help to distinguish the variables from the constants of human nature. The way in which the digits fall into place behind the letters indicates the relation between genera and species. Thus the siglum *D 1420* has to do with all cases where "Magic object draws person (thing) to it," and there are about sixty items in the following decade, plus cross-references. *D 1421.16* states an elementary case where "Magic ring summons genie"; *D 1421.5.1*, where "magic horn summons army for rescue," is slightly more complex; examples may be sought in the *Arabian Nights* or in Grimm. Varying the motif of musical conjuration, *D 1427.1* ("Magic pipe compels one to follow") has its famous exemplification in the story of the Pied Piper, while *D 1426.0.1* ("Magic objects help hero win princess") is exemplified by an Indian tale—as it also might have been by Mozart's *Magic Flute*. One primary subdivision, *X 700–99*, "Humor Concerning Sex," is left virtually blank, with suggested numberings near the middle for jokes concerning courtship and old maids, as well as a note that obscenity is beyond the scope of the undertaking at hand. This itself would seem to be a somewhat old-maidish evasion. In his *Rationale of the Dirty Joke* the pornographologist G. Legman has undertaken to fill in the lacunae; but, significantly, he finds that the space allotted is insufficient for the missing decades.

Yet the *Motif-Index*, on the whole, is impressive in its comprehensiveness, and especially in its linkages of evidence from East and West, exotic and familiar. Its taxonomy has already been extended to more literary spheres, such as that of the novella. In the labelling and the ordering of topics, it could well be refined upon by the stricter analysis of Propp. Moreover, with the motif as with the atom, there is always bound to be a certain methodological doubt as to the ultimate point at which the least common denominator may or may not have been reached. On the analogy of "phoneme" or "morpheme" as units of sound or verbal structure, terms like "mytheme" or "narreme" have been proposed to designate the primary segments of myth or narration. If the suggested term "motifeme" wins acceptance, despite its ungainliness, the inference may be drawn that motif itself is not finally an irreducible element, that it can be further decomposed into what might be regarded as a motif of motifs (Dundes, 1965). At all events, it expresses its fullest significance not in a disjunctive catalogue but in a structural context.

The latter has ordinarily been supplied by the flow of events as narrated, a procedure which has lately been labelled "syntagmatic." The alternative that has been introduced by Claude Lévi-Strauss, which he calls "paradigmatic," is more speculative or intuitive. It seeks an internal pattern which is often a polarity, a folkloristic version of "the figure in the carpet."

IV. MYTHOLOGY

Proceeding by collection and induction, patiently heaping up and sorting out enormous quantities of specific instances, folklorists have developed their analytic tools: a taxonomy and a morphology. Synthesis was bound to be more problematic, and not less so because most of it has been attempted within the speculative realm of mythography, a borderland for many other fields rather than a discipline in its own right. Rather than the pursuit of particulars, it has engaged in sweeping hypotheses, such as the derivation of all mythology from solar myths or vegetation rites or—more subjectively—from a racial memory or a collective unconscious. The object lesson of Mr. Casaubon in George Eliot's *Middlemarch*, who so vainly promised to give the world *A Key to All Mythologies*, has not acted as a deterrent to would-be mythographers. Some of them have sought to incorporate the totality of mythical episodes into the life-cycle of one syncretic hero or heroine: Robert Graves in *The White Goddess* (London, 1948), Joseph Campbell in *The Hero with a Thousand Faces* (New York, 1956). Joyce constructed a "monomyth" of his own in *Finnegans Wake*, but that remains a unique literary contrivance. Frazer had gathered his mythological parallels from diverse cultural contexts, and functional anthropologists have criticized him for his eclecticism. Yet, though his Dying God may be a blurred composite, Frazer retained a comparative awareness of the differences between Balder and Osiris.

The incidence of themes has provided arguments *pro* and *contra* in the long debate concerning the universals of human nature. A secondary topic of debate, among those who accepted the principle of universality, was the question whether its patterns were naturally inherent or had been diffused through transmigration from a common origin. Answers today would be qualified by an increment of pluralism and relativism. For example, an anthropological study of fifty differing cultures has shown that thirty-four of them tell an analogous tale of the Flood (Kluckhohn, 1960). A two-thirds majority is not quite the same thing as a universal manifestation, but it is as high a degree of penetration as any single motif is likely to reach. In a survey designed to illustrate the dependence of myth upon ritual, *The Hero,* Lord Raglan put together a kind of conglomerate model for a heroic career, which consists of twenty-two crises, turning points, or motifs (e.g., exile and return). By this scorecard he proceeded to reckon with a sequence of mythical heroes, ranking them by the extent to which they fulfil his enumerated conditions. Oedipus gets the highest grade with twenty-one, which may lend statistical corroboration to the primacy he was accorded by Freud. Moses and Theseus score twenty, Dionysos and King Arthur nineteen, and so on. The fact that Hamlet would score five confirms a general impression that the scale is inversely relevant to the more sophisticated figures.

Jung expectably favored the concept of a universalized *Heldenleben*, which was recapitulated in the development of the individual personality; each stage had its rite of initiation, but came under the patronage of a different hero. Folklore, on the assumption that an act presupposed an agent or an event a protagonist, had recognized that a motif could be viewed as characteristic of a *persona*. Literature is full of dramatis personae who, often by retrospective simplification, have come to be identified with some outstanding trait, such as the quixotry of Cervantes' knight. Falstaff has become the exemplary glutton, Shylock the extortioner par excellence. Romeo is the eponymous patron of every young lover, Benedick of every married man. A person who brings bad luck is labelled a Jonah, one who laments a Jeremiah. Victor Hugo (1864) seems to have had in mind this habit of typification when he described a hero as "a myth with a human face" (*un mythe à face humaine*). If a rounded characterization can be reduced to a one-dimensional type, it is also possible for one particular figure to typify various things to varying men. The actions of Prometheus, his relations with the gods and with mankind, may present a more or less unchanging outline from Hesiod to André Gide. But the very distance between those authors suggests a vast alteration of meaning under altered circumstances. To consider what others have written about Prometheus—Aeschylus, Tertullian, Calderón, Shaftesbury, Voltaire, Goethe, Shelley—is to retraverse the history of Western thought (Trousson, 1964).

Literary variations on a given theme tend, of course, to go beyond its more traditional versions. Yet the elementary types, insofar as they continue to exist, are destined to undergo renewal and change. Their polyvalence is most strikingly evident in the rich body of documentation surrounding the myth—which perhaps, because it claims some historical roots, should be termed a legend—of Faust. Here a highly elaborate group of motifs is accumulated, recombined, and subjected to displacements. As a rebel seeking forbidden knowledge, Faust shares the Titanism of Prometheus, not to mention the hubris of Lucifer or the curiosity of Adam. If Faust is primarily a magus, that can be an ambiguous role, for it embodies both the reverend sage and the wily trickster. As the latter he has something in common with Odysseus, who was likewise a restless wanderer, along with the Wandering Jew and the Flying Dutchman. That restlessness, which led to Faust's damnation in the Lutheran chapbook and Marlowe's tragedy, furnished the very grounds for his salvation in Goethe's philosophical drama. Changes of the intellectual climate, between the Reformation and the romantic movement, explain the displacement. Faustianism, in the modern sense of endless questing, had come to be regarded as a virtue. Hence the eternal voyager of Tennyson's "Ulysses" stands closer to Goethe's Faust than to his Odyssean prototype, who ended happily in his own kingdom. The thematic charge has been transposed from homecoming to wanderlust.

The legend of Don Juan, almost contemporaneous with that of Faust, has had more than five hundred reincarnations. The title of the original play by Tirso de Molina makes explicit how the two principal motifs were joined together: *The Trickster of Seville and the Guest of Stone* (*El Burlador de Sevilla y Convivado de Piedra*). Don Juan was originally more of a practical joker than an incarnate philanderer, and his libertinism had as much to do with freethinking as with free love. His unrepentant blasphemies propelled him to Faust's destination, hell; but there are belated and romanticized reinterpretations where, like Goethe's protagonist, he is redeemed by womanly love. Redemption of this sort is a motif, applicable in both cases and describable in anonymous terms, whereas myth or legend always has a proper name or at least a local habitation which it gains from the identity of a hero or concrete situation. Thus Jean Giraudoux's *Amphitryon 38* implies that it has been preceded by thirty-seven earlier dramatizations of the same myth, whereas the motif known as "the bed-trick"—also involving the covert substitution of a sexual partner—is differently handled by Boccaccio in *The Decameron* and by Shakespeare in *Measure for Measure* and *All's Well That Ends Well*. The sad story of Pyramus and Thisbe is a myth, whether celebrated by Ovid or burlesqued by Shakespeare. Its motif is the lovers' tryst in the tomb, to which Shakespeare has given such poignant treatment in *Romeo and Juliet*.

Most erotic motifs are triangular, though the dilemmas vary from the *fabliaux* of cuckoldry to Paolo and Francesca (or Tristan and Yseult). The reduplication of personae, in the external shape of twins or mistaken identities, produces farcical situations for reasons which Bergson has probed. Internalized within

the psyche, it takes on the somber guise of the Double or *Doppelgänger*, whose shadow falls so memorably on the pages of E. T. A. Hoffmann, Poe, Dostoevsky, and Stevenson. Such avatars can easily be traced, since criticism has already found them a category. But motifs are not invariably manifested through plot and character; they can be connected with place or time: a haunted house, a flashback to childhood. Further questions may arise over the interrelation of motif and theme. Croce's usage is loosely synonymous, as when he refers to the *motivi* of Shakespearean drama (1920). Critics and historians of art, who speak of motif with regard to the choice of subject (e.g., a hillside in Provence), use theme to indicate the manner of treatment (as it would differ between Cézanne and Van Gogh). Ernst Robert Curtius (1950) seems to follow the artistic rather than the literary practice, taking *Motiv* as the objective factor but making *Thema* the personal coloration. Clearly there is wider agreement on the more technical term. It might be a prudent compromise to save "motif" for the more precise applications, while employing "theme" as the generic conception, the catchword for the critical approach.

V. THEMATICS

The stuff of folklore and of mythology resides in collective tradition, where the actual medium of communication is incidental. They can therefore be considered in the aggregate, through Thompson's index or Roscher's lexicon. Sights and sounds and words, on the other hand, are things in themselves, so that artistic composition must be approached on a concretely individual basis. In music and the visual arts, as noted, the elements of design are apparent to ear and eye. Literature, however, offers signs or signals to be decoded before significant patterns emerge. Yet, just as soon as it presents a text, it invites a scrutiny of the internal arrangements. A motif can be as slight as a single word, so long as that word is repeated in meaningful contexts. Shakespeare, as a concordance will help to show, made effective use of key words in many of his plays. Consider the strategic importance of "grief" in *Richard II*, "space" in *Antony and Cleopatra*, "nature" in *King Lear*, or "art" in *The Tempest*. Key phrases, applied more formally by the Homeric epithet or the Anglo-Saxon kenning, have been a feature of the epic from its earliest manifestation. Parry has demonstrated the functional part that was played by these formulae under the conditions of oral delivery. Many of them were metaphors, such as the Old English *hronrād* ("whale-road") for sea, and they enlarged the literal narration by projecting it onto a figurative plane.

Classical rhetoric had included various figures of verbal repetition: e.g., anaphora, where the same word introduces a series of sentences. An acute practitioner of modern stylistics, Leo Spitzer, in *Motiv und Wort* and numerous subsequent studies, looked for psychological clues to the styles of particular writers in unconscious rather than deliberate repetitions. Psychoanalysis meanwhile was generating motifs of its own, the Freudian complexes and the Jungian archetypes. The Freudians, through their journal *Imago*, and particularly through the monographs of Otto Rank, brought their apparatus to bear upon literature. But most of them were primarily concerned with bringing out the idiosyncrasies of a writer's personality, whereas the Jungians sought to probe more deeply into the common sources of imaginative expression. The English critic, Maud Bodkin, has exemplified this method by disclosing the archetypal pattern of Paradise/ Hades in such poetic creations as *Kubla Khan*. Jung himself (1964) virtually equated motifs ("single symbols") with archetypes ("primordial images"), asserting that it was characteristic of either to remain unchanged while its representations varied. Such conceptions are brought back into a more formally aesthetic sphere by Northrop Frye in his updated poetics, *Anatomy of Criticism* (1957), where motif is defined as "a symbol in its aspect as a verbal unit in a literary work of art," and a poem itself as a "structure of interlocking motifs."

The current interest in symbolism, converging from many viewpoints and from different disciplines, has conferred a new and central significance on motif. Poetry has always relied upon it, to be sure, in controlling its metaphorical structures—an implicit tendency which became explicit through the international influence of the *Symbolistes* and their recent descendants. Since metaphor attains its extra dimension by the projection of images, poets of the past could now be fruitfully restudied by retracing their characteristic trains of imagery. It is revealing to note that the title of a pioneering essay in this field by Caroline Spurgeon, *Leading Motives in the Imagery of Shakespeare's Tragedies* (1930), finds its operative phrase in the English equivalent for the German *Leitmotiv*. Professor Spurgeon's book, *Shakespeare's Imagery and What It Tells Us* (1935), is comprehensive in its tabulations, charts, and statistics; but it utilizes that rich material to sketch a conjectural portrait of Shakespeare himself, rather than to illuminate his artistry as others have done, notably Wilson Knight and Wolfgang Clemen. The continual interplay of brightness and darkness in the language of *Romeo and Juliet,* the morbid tropes of appetite and disease throughout *Hamlet* and *Troilus and Cressida,* the allusions to horses and serpents respectively attached to the hero and heroine of *Antony and Cleopatra*—in each case the image takes up the theme and thereby orchestrates the dramatic action.

Readers of prose narrative are less inclined to perceive symbolic implications in its free flow and manifest content. Yet the early Christian readers of the Old Testament reconciled it to the New by the device of typology, finding prototypical precedents, and by the doctrine of *figura:* e.g., the prefiguration of Christ in the paschal lamb. Though the trend of the novel has been predominantly realistic, it has been occasionally faced with countermovements toward the allegorical and the emblematic, as in the "romances" of Hawthorne. During the present century, indeed, the trend has been all but reversed, under the impact of Joyce's many-levelled narrations and Kafka's enigmatic parables. But retrospectively it can be seen that the so-called naturalists had their symbolistic side, most strikingly Zola. Mario Praz has studied the sophisticated fiction of the *fin du siècle* much as a folklorist might study ballads, and has discerned the visage of *La Belle Dame sans merci* in the heroines of the eighteen-nineties. Looking farther backward, to the heyday of the realists, one could test the validity of Mircea Eliade's remark that, despite its positivistic pretensions, the nineteenth-century novel has remained "the great repository of degraded myths" (1952). Thus the novels of Dickens could be regarded as fairy tales about the babes in the wood, encountering wicked witches in protean disguises, while the focal point of Balzac's work would be the motif of the youngest son who sets out to seek his worldly fortune.

Recently a group of critics writing in French, several of them living in Switzerland, has been addressing itself to the reinterpretation of literature from a point of view which is sometimes designated as phenomenological, but which is also oriented to psychoanalytic and surrealistic theories of dreams and the subconscious. Their forerunner was Gaston Bachelard, the philosopher who moved from science to poetry, endeavoring to explore the workings of "the material imagination" through a sequence of volumes on the four elements (fire, water, earth, air) as these have been poetically apprehended and expressed. The *chef d'école* would seem to be Georges Poulet, who has expended both subtlety and ingenuity in an effort to reveal how various writers have been affected by their preconceptions of time and space. He and his colleagues frequently talk about structure, yet they seem practically more interested in texture—and in inner depth, so far as it is accessible. Deliberately disregarding the formal aspect or the artistic intention of the individual work, they seek to bring out the latent configurations of the author's mind. The key they search for may be conceived as a motif of sorts, albeit one which other readers may find too elusive or subliminal. Here, as elsewhere, much depends upon the tact and discernment of the critic. The psychocritical contributions of Jean Starobinski, further enriched by his background in medicine and the fine arts, might be cited as effective examples.

There have been some occasions when a genre has been shaped by a theme (the *voyage imaginaire*, the Gothic novel, the detective story). This has happened more rarely with a motif, yet a striking instance is afforded by the song of lovers parting at dawn. A collaborative survey of such songs in fifty languages, published under the auspices of UNESCO, well attests the universality of the situation (Hatto, 1965). Within one single tradition of special relevance, that of Latinity through the Middle Ages into the modern world, Curtius has magisterially shown how cultural continuities have been sustained by means of *topoi* (1948). Now a *topos* is a motif which takes the form of a literary commonplace or rhetorical set-piece: e.g., the comparison between nature and a book or between the world and the theater. Hence the idea that it conveys has verbally crystallized. But the history of ideas in themselves, in spite of their fluid nature, also has its paradigms, which are inherent in Arthur Lovejoy's method of tracing the unitary or key idea through a body of literary documentation which registers the metamorphoses. Within the intellectual pattern outlined by *The Great Chain of Being* (1936), an evolution is accomplished which reaches from the spiritual hierarchy of the Neo-Platonists to the Darwinian struggle for existence. "Yes," as Alexander Herzen wrote in his preface to *My Past and Thoughts* (1876), "in life there is a predilection for a recurring rhythm, for the repetition of a *motif*."

BIBLIOGRAPHY

Translations are by the author of this article unless otherwise identified.

Antti Aarne, *Verzeichnis der Märchentypen*, Folklore Fellows Communications 3 (Helsinki, 1910); *The Types of the Folktale*, trans. and enlarged by Stith Thompson, 2nd revision, Folklore Fellows Communications 75 (Helsinki, 1961). Sven Armens, *Archetypes of the Family in Literature* (Seattle, 1966). Erich Auerbach, "Figura," *Archivum Romanicum* XXII (1938); trans. Ralph Manheim in *Scenes from the Drama of European Literature* (New York, 1959).

Gaston Bachelard, *La Psychanalyse du feu* (Paris, 1938); idem, *L'Eau et les rêves: essai sur l'imagination de la matière* (Paris, 1942); idem, *l'Air et les songes: essai sur l'imagination du mouvement* (Paris, 1943); idem, *La Terre et les rêveries de la volonté: essai sur l'imagination des forces* (Paris, 1948); idem, *La Terre et les rêveries du repos* (Paris, 1948). Fernand Baldensperger and W. P. Friederich, *Bibliography of Comparative Literature* (Chapel Hill, 1950). Manfred Beller, "Von der Stoffgeschichte zur Thematologie," *Arcadia*, **5**, 1

(1970). Maud Bodkin, *Archetypal Patterns in Poetry: Psychological Studies of Imagination* (London, 1934). Johannes Bolte and Georg Polívka, eds., *Anmerkungen zu den Kinder- und Hausmärchen den brüder Grimm*, 5 vols. (Leipzig, 1913–32).

Arthur Christensen, *Motif et thème: plan d'un dictionnaire des motifs, des contes populaires, des légendes et des fables*, Folklore Fellows Communications 59 (Helsinki, 1925). Wolfgang Clemen, *Shakespeares Bilder, ihre Entwicklung und ihren Funktionen im dramatischen Werk* (Bonn, 1936); idem, *The Development of Shakespeare's Imagery* (London, 1951). Benedetto Croce, *Ariosto, Shakespeare e Corneille* (Bari, 1920), p. 105. E. R. Curtius, *Europäische Literatur und lateinisches Mittelalter* (Bern, 1948), trans. W. R. Trask as *European Literature and the Latin Middle Ages* (New York, 1953); idem, *Kritische Essays zur europäischer Literatur* (Bern, 1950), p. 219.

Wilhelm Dilthey, *Die Einbildungskraft des Dichters: Bausteine für eine Poetik* (1887), in *Gesammelte Schriften*, VI (Stuttgart, 1958), 216; idem, *Das Erlebnis und die Dichtung: Lessing, Goethe, Novalis, Hölderlin* (Leipzig, 1906). Eugene Dorfman, *The Narreme in the Medieval Romance Epic: An Introduction to Narrative Structures* (Toronto, 1970). Alan Dundes, ed., *The Study of Folklore* (New York, 1965), p. 208.

J. P. Eckermann, *Gespräche mit Goethe in den letzten Jahren seines Lebens*, Vols. I, II (Leipzig, 1836), Vol III (Magdeburg, 1844), trans. John Oxenford as *Conversations with Goethe* (London, 1930), pp. 81, 85, 350. Mircea Eliade, *Images et symboles: essais sur le symbolisme magico-religieux* (Paris, 1952), trans. Philip Mairet as *Images and Symbols: Studies in Religious Symbolism* (New York, 1961), p. 11.

E. H. Falk, *Types of Thematic Structure: The Nature and Function of Motifs in Gide, Camus, and Sartre* (Chicago, 1967). Elisabeth Frenzel, *Stoffe der Weltliteratur: ein Lexikon dichtungsgeschichtlicher Längschnitte* (Stuttgart, 1962; revised ed. 1963); idem, *Stoff-, Motiv- und Symbolforschung* (Stuttgart, 1963); idem, *Stoff- und Motivgeschichte* (Berlin, 1966). Northrop Frye, *Anatomy of Criticism: Four Essays* (Princeton, 1957), pp. 366, 77.

Arturo Graf, *Il Diavolo* (Milan, 1889); idem, *Miti, leggende e superstizioni del medio evo*, 2 vols. (Turin, 1892–93).

A. T. Hatto, ed., *Eos: an Enquiry into the Theme of Lovers' Meetings and Partings at Dawn in Poetry* (London, 1965). A. I. Herzen, *Byloe i dumy*, first published 1876; first complete edition, 5 vols. (Berlin, 1921); *My Past and Thoughts*, trans. Constance Garnett and revised by Humphrey Higgens (New York, 1968), I, xliv. Victor Hugo, *William Shakespeare* (Paris, 1964), p. 299.

C. G. Jung, ed., *Man and His Symbols* (New York, 1964), pp. 53, 67; *Wandlungen und Symbolen der Libido: Beiträge zur Entwicklungs geschichte des Denkens* (Leipzig, 1912); trans. as *Modern Man in Search of a Soul* by W. S. Dell and C. F. Baynes (New York, 1934).

Clyde Kluckhohn, "Recurrent Themes in Myth and Mythmaking," in *Myth and Mythmaking*, ed. H. A. Murray (New York, 1960). G. W. Knight, *The Wheel of Fire: Essays in Interpretation of Shakespeare's Sombre Tragedies* (London,

243

1937). A. H. Krappe, *The Science of Folklore* (London, 1930), p. 1.

S. N. Lawall, *Critics of Consciousness: The Existential Structures of Literature* (Cambridge, Mass., 1968). G[ershon] Legman, *Rationale of the Dirty Joke: An Analysis of Sexual Humor* (New York, 1968). Claude Lévi-Strauss, *Mythologiques: Le Cru et le cuit* (Paris, 1964); idem, "The Structural Study of Myth," *Journal of American Folklore*, **68** (1955). Harry Levin, "Thematics and Criticism," in *The Disciplines of Criticism: Essays in Literary Theory, Interpretation, and History Honoring René Wellek on the Occasion of his Sixty-fifth Birthday*, eds. Peter Demetz, Thomas Greene, and Lowry Nelson Jr. (New Haven, 1968). A. B. Lord, *The Singer of Tales*, Harvard Studies in Comparative Literature 24 (Cambridge, 1964). A. O. Lovejoy, *Essays in the History of Ideas* (Baltimore, 1948); idem, *The Great Chain of Being: A Study of the History of an Idea* (Cambridge, Mass., 1936).

Thomas Mann, "Lebensabriss," *Die Neue Rundschau*, **41** (1930); trans. H. T. Lowe-Porter as *A Sketch of My Life* (Paris, 1930), pp. 30, 31.

Milman Parry, *L'Epithète traditionelle dans Homère: essai sur un problème de style homérique* (Paris, 1928). Georges Polti, *Les Trente-six Situations dramatiques*, 2nd ed. (Paris, 1912), trans. as *The Thirty-Six Dramatic Situations* (Ridgewood, N.J., 1917). Georges Poulet, *Études sur le temps humain* (Edinburgh, 1949), trans. Elliott Coleman as *Studies in Human Time* (Baltimore, 1956); idem, *La Distance intérieure* (Paris, 1952), trans. Elliott Coleman as *The Interior Distance* (Baltimore, 1959); idem, *Les Métamorphoses du cercle* (Paris, 1961), trans. Carley Dawson and Elliott Coleman in collaboration with the author as *Metamorphoses of the Circle* (Baltimore, 1967). Mario Praz, *La Carne, la morte e il diavolo nella letteratura romantica* (Milan, 1930), trans. Angus Davidson as *The Romantic Agony* (London, 1933). Vladimir Propp, *Morfologia skazki* (Leningrad, 1938); *Morphology of the Folktale*, Publications of the American Folklore Society, Bibliographical and Special Series 9, trans. Laurence Scott and revised by L. A. Wagner (Austin, 1968).

F. R. Somerset, Baron Raglan, *The Hero: A Study in Tradition, Myth, and Drama* (London, 1936). Otto Rank, *Der Doppelgänger: ein psychoanalytische Studie* (Leipzig, 1925); idem, *Der Inzest-Motiv in Dichtung und Sage: Grundzüge einer Psychologie des dichterischen Schaffens* (Leipzig, 1912; 1926). W. H. Roscher, *Ausführliches Lexikon der griechischen und römischen mythologies*, 6 vols. (Leipzig, 1884–1937). D. P. Rotunda, *Motif-Index of the Italian Novella in Prose*, Indiana University Publications, Folklore Series 2 (Bloomington, 1942). John Ruskin, *Modern Painters* (1843–1860), in *The Complete Works of John Ruskin*, eds. E. T. Cook and Alexander Wedderburn, 39 vols. (London, 1903–12), VII, 217; III, 170.

Wilhelm Scherer, *Poetik*, ed. R. M. Meyer (Berlin, 1888), pp. 212, 213. Étienne Souriau, *Les Deux Cent Mille Situations dramatiques* (Paris, 1950). Hans Sperber and Leo Spitzer, *Motiv und Wort: Studien zur Literatur- und Sprachpsychologie* (Leipzig, 1918). Caroline Spurgeon, *Leading Motives in the Imagery of Shakespeare's Tragedies* (London, 1930); idem, *Shakespeare's Imagery and What It Tells Us* (London, 1935). Jean Starobinski, *L'Oeil vivant: essai* (Paris,

1961); idem, *Jean-Jacques Rousseau: la transparence et l'obstacle* (Paris, 1957); idem, *Portrait de l'artiste en saltimbanque* (Geneva, 1970).

Stith Thompson, *The Folktale* (New York, 1946); *Motif-Index of Folk-Literature: a Classification of Narrative Elements in Folk-tales, Ballads, Myths, Fables, Mediaeval Romances, Exempla, Fabliaux, Jest-books, and Local Legends*, 6 vols., Indiana University Studies, Folklore series 108–10, 111, 112 (Bloomington, 1932–36); Folklore Fellows Communications, 106–09 (Helsinki, 1932–36); revised and enlarged edition, 6 vols. (Bloomington, 1955–58), I, 20, 21. Boris Tomashevsky, "Thematics," in *Russian Formalist Criticism: Four Essays*, trans. and ed. L. T. Lemon and M. J. Reis (Lincoln, 1965); idem, *Teoriya literatury* (Moscow and Leningrad, 1928). Raymond Trousson, *Le Thème de Prométhée dans la littérature européenne*, 2 vols. (Geneva, 1964); idem, *Un Problème de littérature comparée: les études de thèmes: essai de méthodologie* (Paris, 1965).

V. N. Veselovsky, "Poetika sujetov," in *Istoricheskaya poetika*, ed. V. M. Zhirmunsky (Leningrad, 1940), pp. 494, 500.

Leo Weinstein, *The Metamorphoses of Don Juan* (Stanford, 1959). René Wellek and Austin Warren, *Theory of Literature* (New York, 1949), p. 272.

HARRY LEVIN

[See also Allegory; Ambiguity; Analogy; Criticism, Literary; Harmony or Rapture in Music; Iconography; **Literature and Its Cognates; Motif in Literature: The Faust Theme; Myth; Poetry and Poetics;** Style in Literature; **Symbol and Symbolism in Literature.**]

MOTIF IN LITERATURE: THE FAUST THEME

How FAUST has become a mythic figure for modern man, and "Faustian" (German: *faustisch*) an accepted synonym for "insatiable," "Promethean," "dynamic," etc., is the theme of this article.

I. THE HISTORICAL FIGURE

Various documents of the first decades of the sixteenth century mention a contemporary necromancer calling himself Faust. In 1507 the abbot J. Tritheim wrote in reply to an inquiry:

Georg Sabellicus . . . is a worthless fellow . . . who should be castigated to stop his proclaiming of abominable and sacrilegious doctrines. . . . He has chosen to call himself *Magister Georgius Sabellicus, Faustus junior, fons necromanticorum, astrologus, magus secundus, chiromanticus, aëromanticus, pyromanticus, in hydra arte secundus* ([*Epistolae*] *ad diversos*, Hagen [1536], p. 312; see A. Tille, *Faustsplitter*, Berlin [1900], no. 1).

"Sabellicus" and "Faustus" may be humanist latinizations of a German place name and a German family name (or of two family names), but both "the Sabine"—for ancient Rome the Sabine Hills were the country of witchcraft—and "the Fortunate" are traditional epithets of magicians.

Tritheim reports having been in Gelnhausen the year before at the same time as Faust and hearing from clerics there Faust's boast that, "if all the works of Plato and Aristotle . . . had been lost, he through his genius would, like a second Esra, restore them entire and better than before." In Würzburg, Tritheim continues, Faust even claimed that he could perform all the miracles of Christ; subsequently he was appointed schoolmaster at Kreuznach because of his vaunted alchemical learning, but had to flee when his debauchery of his pupils was discovered.

In 1509 a Johann Faust from Simmern (a principality incorporated into Württemberg in 1504) received the A.B. at Heidelberg; if he was Tritheim's Faust, later tradition was right in claiming that the astrologer was born at Knittlingen (the chief town of Simmern) in the early 1480's. In 1513 Conrad Mudt (Mutianus Rufus, supporter of Reuchlin and friend of Melanchthon) saw and heard Georg Faust at Erfurt; he wrote to a fellow humanist that this "immoderate and Foolish braggart," calling himself the "demigod from Heidelberg," before astonished listeners "talked nonsense at the inn." The accounts of the bishopric of Bamberg record a payment in 1520 to "Doctor Faustus" for casting the Prince-Bishop's horoscope; in 1528 the town council of Ingolstadt forbade the soothsayer Jörg (i.e., Georg) Faust to remain in their city; and in 1532 the junior burgomaster of Nuremberg recorded denial of entry to "Dr. Faust, the great sodomite and necromancer." From 1532 to 1536 the same "philosophus" practiced medical alchemy and soothsaying in the Rhineland and Lower Franconia with some success; he is reported to have died in 1540 or 1541 at a village in Württemberg.

II. THE LEGEND AND ITS SOURCES

During Faust's earlier years, i.e., before the Reformation, humanists and theologians gave little or no credence to the pretensions of the shabby exploiter of contemporary interest in magic. In the course of time, however, some successes—and, obviously, unflagging self-advertisement—established his reputation as a soothsayer and necromancer, and various Protestant theologians, among them Luther and Melanchthon, alluded seriously to his diabolical powers. Soon after his death it was said that he had been destroyed by the Devil, with whose demons he claimed to have consorted, and many traditional tales of the supernatural became attached to his name. Some were collected, ca. 1575, by Christoph Rosshirt in an illustrated manuscript still preserved, by which time there was possibly in circulation a Latin or German manuscript account of his life. From this hypothetical work may derive the story-line of the earliest published work exclusively devoted to the Faust legend:

Historia von D. Johann Fausten . . . Gedruckt zu Franckfurt am Mayn, durch Johann Spies. M.D.LXXXVII (The History of Dr. Johann Faust, the notorious magus and nigromancer: how he indentured himself to the Devil for a stated period, what strange things he therein saw and himself instigated and performed, until he finally received his just deserts. Chiefly compiled from his own posthumous writings and published as a horrid example, frightful instance and well-meant warning to all arrogant, cocksure and godless men. [Motto:] James 4:[7.] "Submit yourselves to God. Resist the devil, and he will flee from you." Printed at Frankfurt by Johann Spies. 1587).

This first Faust-book, the work of an anonymous Protestant with theological training, immediately became a best seller. There were several printings of it, including an unauthorized edition with additional material, in 1587; by 1600 it existed in English, Danish, French, and Dutch translations, as well as in further modified and augmented German versions. The last lengthy Faust-book (1674) was reprinted as late as 1726, only to be replaced in popular favor by a shorter chapbook (1725) whose anonymous author (*ein Christlich Meynender*, "a man of Christian principles") interpreted the legend as a demonstration of the harmful consequences of pre-Lutheran superstition.

Popular interest in Faust thus coincided almost exactly with the heyday of general belief in witchcraft as a punishable heresy. The story of the Renaissance charlatan (or self-deluding magus) became a conflation of folkloristic motifs of greater and lesser antiquity, all now attached to a recently contemporary exemplar of man damned for using forbidden powers. In many societies tales have been told of sorcerers and magi who, if not deified, came to terrible ends because they failed to control the natural forces they unleashed (legend of Pope Sylvester II; Frankenstein motif), or because they insufficiently propitiated the supernatural beings who enabled them to control these forces. Fear and envy of a successful elite well explain the universal fondness for myths of this type, although conservative piety and a deepfelt human need of religious mystery may also underlie them.

Faust's vagrant life made him an elusive and mysterious figure whose supernatural attainments could neither be verified nor disproved, and he quickly became the protagonist of a modern magus myth—its hero insofar as he represented the thirst of an age of geographical and scientific discovery for new knowledge and power, its villain insofar as these threatened accepted religious and theological assumptions. For although some men thought of magic as applied science (H. C. Agrippa, *De occulta philosophia* [1531], Ch. 42: "Natural magic is . . . nothing but the chief power of all the natural sciences . . . —perfection of Natural Philosophy and . . . the active part of the same"; Giordano Bruno: *Magus significat hominem sapientem cum virtute agendi*, "A magician signifies a man of wisdom with the power to act"), science itself seemed frightening for many more, so that even the most reputable alchemist or other scientist could arouse ambivalent feelings.

Magic, though widely practiced in later antiquity, had been regarded by intellectuals as vulgar superstition (cf. Theocritus' and Vergil's Thessalian eclogues, and Lucian's *Philopseudos*, §14) and was used as a serious literary motif chiefly to heighten the depiction of mythical and historical horrors (plays of Seneca; Lucanus' *Pharsalia*). As oriental religions permeated the Greco-Roman world, however, and their exponents vied for influence, a literature of theological propaganda developed in which rival magics occupied a central place. The most important of these religions was Christianity, which claimed exclusive rightness for its own magic, labeling all other "illicit" (Augustine, *De civitate Dei* xii, 14).

Like the theologians of Faust's century, that of the Reformation and Counter-Reformation, the early Church Fathers used great learning and subtlety to demonstrate either the illusory or the evil nature of alien divinities, and there were soon many stories vividly illustrating the greater efficacy of the true faith. The New Testament tells how the newly converted Simon Magus vainly attempted to buy from Peter the gift of the Holy Spirit and then immediately repented his error (Acts 8:9–24), but soon an apocryphal gospel (and Clement of Alexandria) reported Simon's ignominious failure to demonstrate his boasted power of flight. This new story presumably reflects confusion of the earlier Simon with Simon the Gnostic, in his turn denigrated by an account of putative sexual relations with Helen of Troy, who was credited with the birth of his child. Gnosticism, moreover, introduced forms of dualistic thought that continued into Manichaeism, a still greater threat to Christian orthodoxy, and various Saints' legends illustrate the dangers of regarding any power of darkness as the equal of the one God. A fourth-century story tells how, despite recourse to demons, including the Prince of Hell himself, a magician named Cyprian fails to win for a pagan lover the pious Justina, a simple girl with many counterparts in the Apocryphal Acts of Apostles and Saints, and how he is subsequently converted to Christianity. There were also legends of another Cyprian (of Antioch—later confused with the Carthaginian martyr) who repents his vain use of illicit magic to achieve knowledge and love and later dies a bishop-martyr. (The version of this story in which the demon who has promised the Christian girl's love is constrained to offer a quickly unmasked demon-substitute ["Egyptian Helen" motif] is the ultimate plot-source of Calderón's martyr drama *El mágico prodigioso*.)

Toward the end of the fifth century a new motif appears: the pact with a single demon or devil. The "Life of Basil of Caesarea" tells how he redeems a slave who through the services of a magus had assigned his soul to a devil in order to marry his master's pious daughter. As his wife, she notices his avoidance of church and seeks Basil's conversive help; discovering the truth, the saint prescribes effective penance and after some effort routs the devil and his minions. (The struggle between good and evil forces for a soul, later so important in art and literature, is here subordinate to the theme of the need of atonement and the power of grace; the urgency of countering Manichaeism explains the new stature of the single devil-figure.) In later legends still higher intercession is required: Theophilus of Cilicia, repenting of his recourse to magic, is saved only by the Virgin Mary. Until after the Reformation, however, the repentant mortal regularly found redemption through contrition, penance, and good works even if he had signed away his soul in blood (a motif introduced in the thirteenth century) and even though, from Saint Thomas Aquinas on, witchcraft was more and more often officially considered heresy.

If Faust was less fortunate than his precursors, the blame must be placed not on him but on the religious schism that began with Luther. For those who obdurately clung to "false" doctrine there was now no alternative to eternal damnation. Copernican astronomy cast doubts on a traditional cosmogony, humanism glorified pagan moral philosophers and much morally dubious pagan literature, Neo-Platonic and Pansophic mysticisms taught "natural" revelation and even the possibility of man's unaided achievement of salvation, Trinitarianism was openly repudiated—leaders of the Unitarian movement were Laelius Socinus and his nephew Faustus (1539–1604)—and advocates of libertinism and atheism were beginning to be less cautious than in the later Middle Ages. With so many rival beliefs urging irreconcilable claims, witchcraft could exert a more powerful spell than ever before over the minds of persons of all social and intellectual classes. The Council of Trent might reaffirm Saint Thomas' doctrine that neither charms nor conjuring can have effect on the free will, but Protestants accepted

Luther's denial of absolute human freedom at the very time they were deprived of all effective external intercession with their God. For them, Faust's eternal damnation was only too real a possibility: significantly, sixteenth-century legend associated Faust with Wittenberg, where Luther had taught the reality of the Devil and where Giordano Bruno was allowed to lecture (1586ff.) after having been denied that privilege at the theologically stricter university of Marburg. Faust represented many things that were anathema to good Christians, but above all a new and challenging secular intellectualism. (The long identification of Faust with Johann Fust, Gutenberg's collaborator, first found in a Dutch chronicle of 1531, was an unconscious euhemeristic recognition of printing's revolutionary importance for the dissemination of new ideas.)

In the *Historia*, although he is an "Epicurean" or sensual materialist, Faust's greatest fault is "speculation"—scientific theorizing and skeptical philosophizing that make him intellectually and spiritually incapable of faith; he may fear Hell (Catholic-theological *attritio*) but will prove incapable of contrition as preached by Luther. His story falls into three large sections. The first tells how, having studied theology, he turns to magic and medicine (cf. Paracelsus). Soon, however, magic completely engrosses him, and through his conjurings he makes contact with emissaries of Hell. After various quasi-theological disputations he abjures Christianity, signing a blood pact that barters his soul for twenty-four years of magical powers and the services of the devil Mephostophiles [sic], who provides both high living and copious lore about Hell and its torments. The second section describes Faust's successes as astrologer and soothsayer, a visionary visit to Hell, and magical flights to various parts of the earth. (At Rome he plays pranks on the Pope, from the Caucasus he surveys paradise and its four rivers—the large place occupied by travel motifs reflects an important interest of the Age of Discovery and, perhaps, the unsettling effect that glimpses of dissimilar civilizations had on sixteenth-century man.) It concludes with accounts of astronomical, meteorological, and spirit lore.

The final and longest section recounts Faust's last eight years. He performs many feats formerly attributed to earlier magicians, especially during a stay at the court of the emperor Charles V: he conjures up Alexander the Great and one of his wives, causes horns to grow out of a courtier's head, makes a haywain and its horse vanish, furnishes aerial transportation, builds a castle in an inaccessible place, and shows a group of students Helen of Troy. Defying the warning of a mysterious old man to turn again to God, he renews his pact with Hell. His life now becomes more pro-fligate than ever. When but two years remain to him, he takes as paramour Helen of Troy; she bears him a son with precocious prophetic gifts who vanishes with his mother at Faust's death. In his final days Faust vainly laments his evil ways and the imminent torments of Hell; in the last hours before he is horribly killed by supernatural powers he urges student companions from Wittenberg to resist the Devil and lead godly lives with faith in Christ.

III. THE MORALITY FIGURE

The *Historia* is a prose morality largely compiled from sixteenth-century books of travel description, magic, demonology, theological discussion, religious-moral edification, proverb lore, and humorous anecdote. Its central action, more concentrated on a single protagonist (and a single antagonist) than earlier magus stories, had dramatic possibilities that Christopher Marlowe and others immediately recognized and exploited. (A late fifteenth-century Faust play performed at Liège is mentioned in the article "Jesuit Drama," *Oxford Companion to the Theatre*, ed. P. Hartnoll, p. 416; the account of a Nuremberg carnival procession of 1588 reports that Venus was attended by the girl "whom Doctor Faust in the play abducted.") In his *Tragical History of Doctor Faustus* (ca. 1590; 1st ed., 1604; 2nd ed., with important textual variants, 1616), Marlowe largely follows the morality-play tradition, though treating his hero, who is certainly a glorious, at times gloriously lyrical, Renaissance malefactor, with an empathy lacking in the Faust-book. (V. Errante has suggested that Faustus has traits of Giordano Bruno, who was well received in London in the early 1580's.)

More wilfully wicked than his German model, Marlowe's Faustus rebels with obviously youthful arrogance against conventional modes of thought and feeling. Sated with traditional learning and having turned to necromancy as the potential source "Of power, of honor, of omnipotence," he offers his soul through Mephistophilis [sic]—appearing at his summons only because it has involved blasphemy—to Lucifer "So he will spare him four and twenty years,/ Letting him live in all voluptuousness." Mephistophilis is thus the agent of the sin of Luciferian pride that, together with insufficient faith in divine mercy, will ensure Faustus' ultimate damnation, despite repeated warnings from Mephistophilis and the morality figures of his Good and Evil Angels, and despite a repulsive masque-like parade of the Seven Deadly Sins shown him as a "pastime" by Lucifer, Belzebub [sic], Mephistophilis. Unlike the protagonist of the *Historia*, Faustus shows no intellectual curiosity once he has signed his blood-pact, chiefly occupying himself with demonstrations of his magical powers (largely pranks) that

247

culminate in the showing of Helen of Troy to student admirers. A last warning to repent momentarily reduces him to the thought of suicide, but despairing of mercy he reaffirms the blood-pact on condition he have Helen as paramour, and soon he is borne off by Devils through the hell-mouth of medieval art and stage. (In the 1616—perhaps partly earlier—text, his mangled limbs are returned to his chambers so that they may be discovered, as in the *Historia*, by the horrified students.)

Through traveling actors Marlowe's play soon reached Germany and became the source of a long series of sensational dramas (including, with the eighteenth century, puppet shows). It thus directly or indirectly inspired both English and German popular stage spectacles (harlequinades, operettas, ballets) until well into the later eighteenth century. Broadsides from the seventeenth and eighteenth centuries (including English sheet music) generously testify to the continuing familiarity of the story of the heretic or villain who is damned because he has preferred evil to good.

In the age of Enlightenment, however, damnation was no longer a matter of wide vital concern. Evil, for Luther the instrument of God, had become an obscuring of truth by passion (Descartes) or even, with Leibniz, a sensed deprival of perfection grounded in awareness of a discrepancy between any part and the whole. (Ugliness and incongruity were to be integral to the visual and literary arts in G. E. Lessing's aesthetics, and the essential function of dissonance had long been recognized by musical theorists.) To relativistic and materialistic thinkers, evil was but a necessary concomitant of the good; an obdurate sinner like the traditional Faust no longer seemed to have serious human significance.

In the 1750's Lessing, seeking indigenous themes that might aid the liberation of German drama from a stifling French neo-classicism, began a "Faust"—its central action apparently was to be a dream—whose hero gains redemption because a genuine thirst for knowledge and truth cancel out ambition and self-seeking. Lessing later repudiated the conception of drama as a moral-didactic medium, and the play was never completed.

IV. GOETHE

The transmutation of morality play into symbolic drama was Goethe's achievement. He began *Faust*, in the spirit of Storm-and-Stress primitivism, as a loosely constructed play in what was in his youth considered the Shakespearean manner (numerous short scenes in verse and prose). It was to be "popular" in tone, although the theme of an intellectual hero's full self-realization demanded representation of levels of thought and experience irreconcilable with this intention. The so-called Urfaust (a manuscript comprising parts and groups of scenes written in the 1770's) briefly introduces Faust as he turns to magic in the hope of transcending sterile intellectuality through intuitive understanding, then shows him in the company of Mephistopheles as he woos, wins, and causes the death of Margarete (Gretchen) even as through love he begins to intuit the full complexity of life.

In subsequent decades Goethe completed *The First Part of the Tragedy* (false-title in 1808 ed.), reconciling the obligatory folkloristic elements of the legend with his conception of Faust as the symbol of man seeking the meaning of life and the maximal realization of its possibilities. He replaced the traditional—and theologically unsound—pact with Hell by a challenge: if Faust, who regards himself as representative of all men, is ever satisfied by shallow pleasures or by a sense of having achieved all he would and could, he will gladly renounce this life, the only meaningful existence he can conceive of. Mephistopheles, now defined in a prologue in heaven as the spirit of negation, embodies all inner and outer forces hostile to human aspiration and achievement, and functions as the machinery allowing Faust a wide variety of representative human experiences. The Lord (God, the Good) is also anticipatorily defined—in terms that reflect the historical-genetic interests of the Enlightenment and the increasing importance of evolutionary biology in the later eighteenth century (Buffon; Lamarck; Goethe's own theories of metamorphosis)—as creativity, becoming (*Werden*), and love, the potentialities of self-realization on every level of being to which man has access by virtue of his innate impulse to strive and aspire. The dramatic action has become Faust's achievement of a symbolic totality of experience, and the poem as a whole shows his ever increasing understanding of the order of Nature and of Man as immanently meaningful.

By 1800 Goethe had begun the second and final part of *Faust*, most of which was written 1825–31. Like Part I, it is loosely structured and composed in a variety of dramatic and poetic styles. Ideologically, its function is to show Faust's involvement in less narrowly private or personal spheres of human concern than those of Part I. Faust interests himself in the German Emperor's state affairs (finance in Act I, war in Act IV), but like his legendary prototype he is constrained to provide court entertainments. These include magical feats, but they are primarily important as attempts at artistic self-expression and artistic communication. In Act I he stages first an allegorical masque, the chief theme of which is prudent distinction between tangible and intangible wealth or values, then a stately dumbshow of the Rape of Helen at which he himself confuses illusion with reality; his attempt to "rescue" Helen—or Beauty—from Paris produces an explosion that volatilizes the two figures and paralyzes him for an indeterminate period. The central action of Part II thus takes place outside the normal world of time and successively represents—possibly as two dream plays of Faust in a trancelike state—the realms of myth and history.

Myth—in the Classical Walpurgisnight of Act II—includes not only the legends of gods and heroes, of animal and human creatures symbolic of hostile or friendly natural forces, but also (early) philosophy, science, and art as modes of expressing man's intuition of a meaningful cosmic order. Faust, the would-be winner of Helen, is the spokesman of the heroic, but he plays a minor role in this Aristophanic comedy. Mephistopheles is also of secondary importance, being chiefly the dupe of his own lusts and of illusion and superstition. The main interest shifts to a mythopoeic symbol of potential life, their companion Homunculus (an artificial synthesis of organic substances achieved by the successor to Faust's professorship), and to the eager aspiration of this miniature Faust for normal physical existence and constructive activity.

History—in Act III, "Helen"—is represented with radical syncopation as the unbroken continuum of Western culture from the Greek heroic age to the Greek Wars of Independence. Helen, to escape the vengeance of Menelaus, takes refuge with northern invaders (the Migration of the Peoples merges into the medieval establishment of Near Eastern kingdoms) whose leader Faust, ceding her suzerainty over Greece—and, as Beauty, over all the world—woos and wins her. When military threats presage far-reaching political changes (the rise of national states, but also the restructuring of Europe in the Napoleonic era), Faust and Helen withdraw to a timeless Arcadia where a son is born to them. Faust briefly enjoys family happiness, but his son Euphorion, a Byron-like poet-hero, escapes into life to fight and die for his country's freedom. The idyll ends abruptly, Helen vanishes, and Faust returns to Germany (to historical reality) again attended by Mephistopheles.

The episode of Helen has been an "aesthetic education" in Schiller's sense, has revitalized Faust's resolve, made after Margarete's death, to seek a worthy outlet for his energies. Envisioning a state or society unfettered by the past, with Mephistopheles' assistance he crushes a rebellion against the Emperor in return for the privilege of winning from the sea new land that he can colonize. (The past is inescapable, however, for the Church immediately secures its right to traditional levies—Goethe was less optimistic than many of his contemporaries about the realizability of socialistic utopias.) The final act shows Faust outwardly successful and prosperous, but inwardly dissatisfied with an achievement that cannot be entirely credited to his own finite powers. His irritation is momentarily directed against pious Christian neighbors, whose destruction he causes by his impatient eagerness to resettle them elsewhere; although not directly guilty of their death—the agents of his will are Mephistopheles and (men of) violence—he now abjures further recourse to supernatural assistance and again accepts human mortality. Faust, suddenly a blind and dying old man, still hopes to complete his grandiose reclamation project, but he dies even as he envisions its benefits enjoyed by future generations of self-reliant men, like himself free from subservience to a purely speculative-transcendental or a merely primitive magical system of belief. His formulation of a social-religious humanistic faith is his supreme insight, but the conclusion of the drama insists that it be recognized as an expression of *faith* (rooted in the feeling that men can know the divine only as immanence). After Mephistopheles has logically pointed out that all achievement is transitory and death the empty end of any life, Faust's "immortal part" is snatched away from eagerly expectant devils, and we are granted a final vision (Faust's?) of a world of saints and angels, of Margarete and the Virgin Mother, in which Faust is vouchsafed further striving, activity, and spiritual growth.

In its cautious optimism Goethe's *Faust* is still a work of the late Enlightenment, but in its communication of the sense of the unfathomable complexity of human experience it is also an expression of European romanticism. Goethe was not, however, consciously a romantic, and so he sought to represent a totality of critical, emotional, aesthetic, and ethical experiences not as a romantic infinitude, but as a symbolically comprehensive finitude (German Classicism). He imbued the Faust legend with broad mythical significance: magic is no longer mere wish-fulfilment or make-believe, nor simply a convenient poetic device serving to create atmosphere or to further a plot, but the legitimate though paradoxical symbol both of man's religious intuitions and of his ever limited freedom. If Goethe presents Faust sympathetically as an aspiring idealist, he also makes clear that idealism and aspiration can be the expressions of dangerous subjectivity, of alienation from reality: only Faust's insight into his own finiteness, his recognition that lofty intentions do not guarantee the avoidance of error, seems to be represented without dramatic—or other ironical—ambivalence. Man is redeemed by insight, not by achievement, and only through consciously directed activity, wise or foolish, successful or unsuccessful, can this insight be gained.

Faust is thus a tragedy of being—and hence perhaps

of "divine discontent"—but not of the will to power or knowledge, or of mere aspiration and romantic longing. Its parts may be loosely connected and some even potentially discrete, but all illustrate facets of this central theme, which as the paradoxical failure of high aspiration appears in every important action or sub-action of the poem. Faust's will—or that of some analogous figure (Homunculus, Euphorion, even Mephistopheles)—is repeatedly frustrated. Not success, however, but the power of self-regeneration that he shares with all life (a point more than once made explicit) is his salvation. If this was not clear to Goethe as he began *Faust*, he nevertheless knew it intuitively, for the larger part of the "Urfaust" concerns itself with the tragedy of Margarete, a motif for which the Faust legend to all intents and purposes offered no source: a destructive seduction by love is a more universal experience than seduction by learning or magic, by wealth or power, and Gretchen, whose Christian faith is transparently naive, through instinct rather than reason finally achieves full moral autonomy when she refuses to evade her responsibility, her atonement of guilt, by fleeing with Faust. In the end, Faust heroically accepts finitude too.

V. THE NINETEENTH-CENTURY HERO

Surveying subsequent treatments of the Faust theme, in 1910 W. A. Phillips declared:

. . . [Goethe's] *Faust* remains for the modern world the final form of the legend out of which it grew, the magnificent expression of the broad humanism which, even in spheres accounted orthodox, has tended to replace the peculiar *studium theologicum* which inspired the early Faust-books (*Encyclopaedia Britannica*, 11th ed., art. "Faust").

Other "Fausts" appeared during the composition and publication of Goethe's drama or shortly thereafter, notably dramatic works by Friedrich Müller (1778), J. H. von Soden (1797), J. F. Schink (1804), C. D. Grabbe (1829), a novel by F. M. Klinger (1791), a lyric scene by Pushkin (1826), and a verse story by Nikolaus Lenau (1835f.), but none can be said to add important new dimensions to the legend.

Publication in 1790 of *Faust, ein Fragment*—somewhat less than half the text of Part I—established the preeminence of Goethe's poem, which the speculative philosopher F. W. von Schelling immediately hailed as Germany's "characteristic poetic work," as an expression of the ambivalent feelings arising from a peculiarly German *Begier nach Erkenntnis der Dinge* ("thirst for cognition"). (In *Faust II* Goethe satirized the hunger for spiritual infinitude attributed to his protagonist in Schelling's *Philosophie der Kunst* [1802].) Thanks to romantic philosophy, by its very nature "mythic" (glorification of the Absolute without any strict theological frame of reference; speculative indifference to the evidence of empirical science), Goethe's *Faust* was soon to become itself a myth. Mme de Staël's response to *Faust I* (*De l'Allemagne*, Part 2, Ch. 23) is cooler than that of the German romantics and her mentor A. W. Schlegel, but despite an obviously neo-classical literary bias she concludes her influential discussion of the work and its author with the words:

. . . when a genius such as Goethe's rids itself of all trammels, its host of thoughts is so great that on every side they go beyond and subvert the limits of art.

Goethe's *Faust*, regarded as a work both uniquely German and *sui generis,* was thus long admired (as by Shelley and Byron) or condemned (chiefly by Christian moralists) according to the worth attached to secular German thought and culture. The Faust of Grabbe's *Don Juan und Faust* is not only a "profound" thinker, but also a German nationalist and a scientific positivist, and even Nikolaus Lenau's romantic-philosophical hero derives his stature in the first instance from his preeminence in research (*Forschen*). As Germany, especially after the establishment of the Second Empire, ceased to be "the land of poets and thinkers" only, Goethe's poem was read ever more frequently as a glorification of action, which alone could permit full realization of individual and social values; if Faust still symbolized all mankind, mankind's best interests were facilely equated with those of Germany, Elsewhere Faust still stood for German romanticism's "mystical faith in will and action" (the formulation is that of Santayana, frankly hostile to idealistic and vitalistic systems of German philosophy from Fichte on, in *Three Philosophical Poets,* 1900).

Faust was also to stand for the power of modern science and technology to create a better world (Élie Metchnikoff, *Goethe et Faust,* 1907), or—this was closest to the spirit of Goethe, except when equated with the cult of the Superman (*Übermensch* is used in Goethe's text only with pejorative irony)—for a fruitful religious or ethical liberalism. German artists depicted Faust as a Teutonic hero, while in France— and for musicians—he chiefly remained a symbol of human frailty or spirituality.

VI. FAUSTIAN AMBIVALENCES IN THE TWENTIETH CENTURY

Few nineteenth-century interpreters of Goethe's work shared Kierkegaard's view that Faust's (to him: also Goethe's) unqualified glorification of activity was compensation for a sickness of the soul. In the twentieth century, however, both the positive values long attached to the "Faust myth" (Jakob Burkhardt, 1855) and the propriety of regarding Goethe's *Faust* as its supreme artistic expression have been seriously questioned. Adulation of Faust's ruthlessness as an empire builder was condemned even when not recognized as contrary to the tenor of Goethe's text. The benefits of science and technology that Faust long symbolized—G. W. Hertz even interpreted the work as natural-scientific myth (*Goethes Naturphilosophie im Faust*, 1912)—began to seem ever more uncertain. And a theological resurgence made doubtful even the heroic stature of so self-concerned, or at least so strong-willed, a figure. (Only esoteric and theosophic interpretations, notably those offered by the anthroposophist Rudolf Steiner from 1902 on, now minimized the theme of ethical choice in Goethe's drama.) "Faustian" could thus variously mean "Promethean," "superhuman" (Hermann Hesse lectured on "Faust and Zarathustra" in 1909), "dualistically torn between (or simultaneously impelled by) pleasure principle and cognitive desire," "mystically monistic," "socialistically progressive" (cf. A. V. Lunacharsky's play *Faust i gorod* [*Faust and the City*], 1918), as well as "German in its best—or, at the height of World War I, worst—sense."

With the publication of Oswald Spengler's *The Decline of the West* (1918 and 1922) "Faustian" acquired a new meaning. In his morphology of civilizations (*Kulturen*) Spengler opposed the Faustian culture-soul of the West to the Apollonian (or Euclidian) and Magical souls of Greco-Roman and Arabian culture. His Faustian soul knows the lure of infinitude and transcendence, has an ethic of instinct or voluntarism rather than of reason, and its heroes are men of action with Nietzsche's morality of masters. (If Goethe's Faust translates *logos* as *Tat* ["deed," "action"] rather than, say *Ordnung* ["order"—for Goethe a highest value], he does not do so in a moment of supreme insight!) Although the importance that Spengler's concept of the Faustian attributes to practical achievement is that of later historicism and scientism, romantic elements predominate in his thought, which is thus more German than Western (Dabezies, p. 152). For H. Trevor-Roper (*Historical Essays*, London, 1957), Burckhardt is a "Faustian historian."

Simultaneous with the explanation of history in symbolic and mythic terms was an ever more frequent reading—and even creating (Thomas Mann)—of literary works as forms of symbolic and mythic expression. Beginning with his *Psychologische Typen* (1921), C. G. Jung encouraged the interpretation of Goethe's *Faust* as a visionary work, i.e., not as mere poetic invention, but as the expression of archetypal truths (Faust variously as hysteric, as magus-magician, as savior-sage, and—after World War II—as subhumanly ignorant of

ethical emotion, the protagonist of a work revealing a characteristically "German" alienation from all concrete realities). Following both Freud and the earlier Jung, Maud Bodkin (*Archetypal Patterns in Poetry: Psychological Studies of Imagination*, Oxford, 1934) could still recognize that Goethe's poem "is not wholly removed in spirit from such tragedy as that of Shakespeare," deriving its strength from such archetypal figures—"expressions of the sense of self in relation to forces that appear under the names of God, or Fate, and of the devil"—as Margarete (woman as symbol of a transmutation of sentiment or feeling into spiritual values) and Mephistopheles ("an apt embodiment of forces that threaten the ideals of the more concrete persons of the drama"). Her interpretation of Faust's final "ascension" as the archetype of human "feigning for individual lives, after bodily death, the renewal that we know [to be] true of the life-force within them" is particularly apt, since this was the meaning Goethe seems *consciously* to have attached to it.

Under National Socialism Faust could conveniently symbolize service to the state and humanity (Alfred Rosenberg), the supreme value of action (Hitler), and of course the German genius and Führer-principle. The irony of this did not go unappreciated abroad, and in Dorothy Sayers' morality *The Devil to Pay* (premiere: 1939) Faust's worst crime is having tried to play god. Paul Valéry's *Mon Faust* (1941; 1944f.), comprising *Lust, ou la Demoiselle de Cristal* and *Le Solitaire, féerie dramatique* (both uncompleted), transposes Goethe's "chief figures"—for Valéry these are Faust and Mephistopheles, the extremes of the human-humane and the inhuman—into a modern world. In *Lust* (the name is that of Faust's attractive secretary) the uncreative impotence of reason (science? rationalization?) is accepted as bitter reality, although Faust—poet, thinker, and "member of the Academy of Dead Sciences"—brilliantly displays reason's power in his discussions with Mephistopheles, who contracts not to serve him, but to receive his services. Mephistopheles cannot even tempt one of Faust's young admirers ("the Disciple," whom Faust has cautioned against emotionalism) with offers of knowledge and power, or of love. Yet Faust himself seems capable of something like love or affection, although Valéry chooses—this is clearly a corrective to vitalistic interpretations of the Faust figure—to emphasize the centrality of thought and memory to human awareness, even to that of immediate experience.

In *Le Solitaire*—the figure is a nihilistic philosopher who, scorning Faust's, and any, intellectualism, consistently destroys himself—the central theme is even more Goethean: awareness of the potentiality of regeneration (although its Faust is too wise to accept the chance to relive life). The dispute for Faust's soul which was to conclude this play was never written, but what exists of *Mon Faust* is a timeless challenge—there is no mention of purely contemporary events—to perversely irrational and pretentious interpretations of the Faust myth.

In contrast to Valéry's "Faust," that of Thomas Mann concerns itself directly with the ideological and political forces that, producing Nazism and the cultural debasement of Germany, culminated in the catastrophe of World War II. Mann's title, *Doctor Faustus: The Life of the German Composer Adrian Leverkühn as Told by a Friend* (1943–46, published 1947), refers to the *Historia* of 1587, which is the inspiration of his protagonist's German style and final musical composition, and from which derive the main "traditional" motifs that structure his novel. (Goethe's *Faust* was insufficiently apocalyptic to serve Mann's thematic needs; a writer long devoted to interpreting mythic archetypes, Mann may have shared the regret—occasionally expressed earlier, as by Heine in notes to his Faust ballet [1851]—at Goethe's failure to adhere closely to the original Faust legend.) Leverkühn's pact with the devil is his fantasy that syphilitic infection is the price of heightened creative powers. (Mann had long thought to discern a connection between disease and artistic creativity, and had first conceived in 1901 the idea of portraying a syphilitic artist as a Faust figure.) *Doctor Faustus* repudiates nationalistic and nihilistic interpretations of Faust and the Faustian; parallels in it to recent developments in historical, philosophical, theological, psychological, and scientific speculation insist that the cultivation of musical abstraction by its coldly intellectual hero also symbolizes a general alienation from humane values that only a spiritual breakthrough may possibly overcome.

Mann's return to the Faust-book form of the legend coincides with a widespread trend to doubt the exemplary significance of Goethe's *Faust*. Some theologically-minded critics, still reading it as a glorification of ruthless activity, condemned it as an expression of humanistic amoralism, while others interpreted it as a morality play warning against the destructive consequences of human effort unredeemed by theological grace. Although Marxists largely continued to see in it a paean to progress and secular human values, and although there seems to be a positive connotation in F. R. Stannard's use of "faustian" to characterize a mirror- or reverse-time universe (*Nature* [August 13, 1966], 693ff.), pessimistic interpretations of the poem prevailed immediately after World War II—hence the frequently expressed subjective preference (e.g., E. M. Butler, A. Dabezies) for pre-Goethean forms of the legend in which the "existential" distinction between good and evil is made with (naive) clarity. Goethe, however, interpreted the Faust story in a tragedy, not in a morality play, and the lasting significance of the Faust legend will surely again be recognized as deriving not from the theme of existential despair (which it shares with many other tales and myths), but from the paradox of self-limiting and even self-destroying aspiration which, as Goethe knew, the legend symbolizes with apparently unique distinction.

BIBLIOGRAPHY

Translations, unless otherwise noted, are by the author of this article.

The fullest bibliography, to contain some 13,000 entries, is Hans Henning, *Faust-Bibliographie* (Berlin and Weimar, 1966–). *Teil I: Allgemeines. Grundlagen. Gesamtdarstellungen.—Das Faust-Thema vom 16. Jahrhundert bis 1790* records earlier bibliographies, collections of texts and documents, works about or containing references to the historical and legendary Fausts (including works of art and music), and discussions of such parallel figures as Ahasuerus, Prometheus, Simon Magus, Cyprian, Twardowski, and Don Juan. *Teil II (Goethes Faust)*, 2 vols., and *Teil III (1790 bis zur Gegenwart. Namen- und Sachregister)* are in preparation.

Most accounts of Faust as a literary figure (see below) also treat the historical and legendary Fausts and their prototypes. P. M. Palmer and R. P. More, *The Sources of the Faust Tradition from Simon Magus to Lessing* (New York, 1936; reprint 1965), cites or summarizes in English translation the major documents. Specialized discussions are: E. M. Butler, *The Myth of the Magus* (Cambridge, 1948), and *Ritual Magic* (Cambridge, 1949); H. G. Meek, *Johann Faust, the Man and the Myth* (London, 1930).

H. Henning has edited the first Spies Faust-book (Halle, 1963), and William Rose the English translation of 1592 (London, n.d., in the series "Broadway Translations"). H. G. Haile, *Das Faustbuch nach der Wolfenbüttler Handschrift* (Berlin, 1963), reproduces a manuscript possibly antedating Spies; he indicates by typographical devices the parts that may derive from an earlier Latin or German life of Faust.

Recent surveys of Faust as a figure or theme in literary or other art forms and of interpretations of the legend include: E. M. Butler, *The Fortunes of Faust* (Cambridge, 1952); Vincenzo Errante, *Il Mito di Faust;* Vol. I, *Dal personaggio storico alla tragedia di Gœthe* (Florence, 1951); Geneviève Bianquis, *Faust à travers quatre siècles* (Paris, 1955); Charles Dédéyan, *Le Thème de Faust dans la littérature européenne,* 4 vols. in 6 parts (Paris, 1956–65); André Dabezies, *Visages de Faust au XXe siècle: Littérature, idéologie et mythes* (Paris, 1967); J. W. Kelly, *The Faust Legend in Music* (Evanston, Ill., 1960); Wolfgang Wegner, *Die Faustdarstellung vom 16. Jahrhundert bis zur Gegenwart* (Amsterdam, 1962), which may be supplemented by Franz Neubert, *Vom Doctor Faust zu Goethes Faust, mit 595 Abbildungen* (Leipzig, 1932).

An excellent selective bibliography (updated in each new printing) for Goethe's *Faust* and the secondary literature relevant to it is that in *Goethes Werke*, Band III, ed. Erich Trunz (Hamburg, 1949), available separately as *Goethes Faust;* the edition includes the text of the "Urfaust." *Goethe's Faust*, ed. R-M. S. Heffner, et al., 2 vols. (Boston, 1954–55), has an introduction and notes in English. The classic English translation is that of Bayard Taylor; there is a modernized version of it by S. Atkins, 2 vols. (New York, 1965–67). The interpretation in the foregoing article is largely that of S. Atkins, *Goethe's Faust: A Literary Analysis* (Cambridge, Mass., 1969).

STUART ATKINS

[See also Alchemy; Astrology; Demonology; Enlightenment; Evil; Gnosticism; Love; **Motif;** Myth; Romanticism; Sin and Salvation; Tragic; Witchcraft.]

LITERARY ATTITUDES TOWARD MOUNTAINS

I

"EARTH's DUGS, Wens, Warts, Imposthumes"—such are some of the epithets applied to mountains in a seventeenth-century phrase book, which also lists among appropriate descriptive adjectives, "insolent, ambitious, uncouth, inhospitable, sky-threatening, forsaken, pathless." In both biblical and classical attitudes toward mountains there was interesting dualism. Phrases from the Old Testament echo in our memories: "I will lift up mine eyes unto the hills, from whence cometh my help." There are various such passages in the Psalmist. But in the same book we find prophecy of an attitude that is to echo in the New Testament: "Every valley shall be exalted, and every mountain and hill shall be laid low." In spite of the Sermon on the Mount, there is almost no description of mountains in the New Testament, but the general impression is adverse. The social philosophy seems to be that the "high" is suspect, the "low" much preferable. As the seventeenth-century theologian Laurence Clarkson said: "If you would understand the Scriptures, you shall read it calleth rich men wicked Mountains, and poor believing men Valleys."

A similar basic contradiction is felt in classical literature. The Greeks seldom described mountains, but when they did, inclined to such adjectives as "stately, cloud-touching, star-brushing." They worshipped their gods on Mount Olympus and invoked the Muses on Helicon. Gilbert Murray described the Greek attitude thus: "They did not describe forests or mountains; they worshipped them and built temples in them. Their love for nature was that of the mountaineer and the seaman, who does not talk much about the sea and mountains, but who sickens and pines if he is taken away from

them." With the exception of Lucretius, who experienced among mountains the exultation described by romantic English poets, attitudes of classical Latin poets were usually adverse. Catullus, Vergil, and Horace seldom described mountains, and, when they did, felt them dangerous, desolate, hostile and used such adjectives as *ocris, asperus, arduus, horridus.*

Since the mountain-attitudes of Elizabethan and seventeenth-century poets go back almost entirely to the Bible and the classics, we shall not pause over those of the Middle Ages except for one comparison. Dante knew mountains well enough, as his realistic account of Bismantova shows, but, whether influenced by his own experience or by Latin and New Testament forbears, he did not like them. The Mount of Purgatorio is as allegorical as Bunyan's Hill Difficulty. On the other hand, Petrarch ascended Mount Ventoux in April 1335 for his own pleasure and so exulted in the experience that his words have been repeated in anthologies for mountain-climbers. Modern scholarship has shown that his experience was not unique. But for the most part, medieval men climbed mountains only through necessity.

Allegorization, abstraction, and personification so overshadow realism that the mountain-imagery of the Renaissance is largely stereotyped. Shakespeare probably never saw a mountain or a really high hill. Mountains are infrequent in his nature-imagery and a purely literary heritage: ". . . jocund day/ Stands tip-toe on the misty mountain tops"; "new lighted on a heaven-kissing hill"; "make Ossa like a wart"—such phrases had a literary origin. The "mountains on whose barren breast/ The labouring clouds do often rest" of *L'Allegro* were not seen by Milton from Horton or Cambridge. Bunyan's "Delectable Mountains" and his "Hill Difficulty" are simple biblical moralizings. Equally traditional were attitudes Andrew Marvell crowded into a stanza of "Upon the Hill and Grove at Billborow":

> Here learn ye Mountains more unjust
> Which to abrupter greatness thrust,
> That do with your hook-shoulder's height
> The Earth deform and Heaven fright,
> For whose excrescence ill-design'd,
> Nature must a new Center find,
> Learn here those humble steps to tread
> Which to securer glory lead.

Many travellers of the seventeenth century were so conditioned by their Latin or New Testament heritage that they felt little except terror when on the Grand Tour they were forced to cross mountains. Thomas Coryate, attempting a record-breaking journey, described in *Coryats Crudities* (1611), tried to make

253

the ascent on foot from Aiguebelle, because, as he confessed, he was afraid to go on horseback. Finally, he hired natives to carry him in a chair and, when he came to precipices, he kept his eyes closed. James Howell described his mountain-experience in his *Familiar Letters* (1650). He crossed the Alps from Italy after having crossed the Pyrenees, which he found "not so high and hideous as the Alps; but for our mountains in Wales . . . they are but Molehills in comparison of these; they are but Pigmies compared to Giants, but Blisters to Imposthumes, or Pimples to Warts." John Evelyn, an experienced traveller, showed only momentary appreciation of Alpine scenery, largely stressing in his *Diary* dangers and discomforts. His basic preference for plains may be seen in an entry on the sight of the Alps from Mergozzo. The mountains rose suddenly, "after some hundreds of miles of the most even country in the World, and where there is hardly a stone to be found, as if nature had here swept up the rubbish of the Earth in the Alps, to forme and cleare the Plaines of Lombardy."

"The rubbish of the Earth," said Evelyn, and Charles Cotton completed his condemnation of the "Peak district" in *The Wonders of the Peak* with a couplet:

> And such a face the new-born Nature took
> When out of Chaos by the Fiat strook.

Hovering in both minds was something more profound than the literary heritage from Roman and New Testament ancestors, a theological dilemma that was revived in the seventeenth century to become one of the early modern clashes between science and religion.

II

"Hear, O ye mountains, the Lord's controversy!" (Micah 6:2). For many years a controversy continued among Jewish and Christian Fathers which had to do with the appearance of the earth at the time of creation. Involved in this was the question, whether mountains had been original or whether they had arisen later, and, if so, for what cause. Insofar as most of us have ever considered the matter we have probably taken for granted that the world appearing after the Creation-scene in Genesis was in configuration basically like the world we know, with heights and depths and seas. If we again turn to literature as a guide to attitudes of the seventeenth century, we find that Milton in *Paradise Lost* (VII, 282–87) followed the convention many then subconsciously accepted:

> God said,
> "Be gathered now, ye waters under Heaven,
> Into one place, and let dry land appear!"
> Immediately the mountains huge appear
> Emergent, and their broad bare backs upheave
> Into the clouds; their tops ascend the sky.

This, however, is not the implication of Marvell in "Upon Appleton House," (stanza lxxxvi):

> 'Tis not what once it was, the World;
> But a rude heap together hurl'd;
> All negligently overthrown,
> Gulfs, Deserts, Precipices, Stone.

John Donne in *The First Anniversary* (lines 284–301) is even more specific on the fact that the world has lost its original form:

> But keepes the earth her round proportion still?
> Doth not a Tenarif, or higher Hill
> Rise so high like a Rocke, that one might thinke
> The floating Moon would shipwrack there, and sinke? . . .
> Are these but warts and pock-holes in the face
> Of th' earth? thinke so: but yet confesse, in this
> The worlds proportion disfigured is.

The most conventional theory arising from Genesis is, then, that when the original earth emerged from chaos it was in general the world we know, with mountains and depths. However, among classical as well as Jewish and Christian Fathers, there was another tradition, that the earth had once been smoothly rounded, a "Mundane Egg," as it was sometimes called. Mountains had appeared at some later time and were considered blemishes on the fair face of Nature, because they were evidences of the sin of man. One theory that seems to have been peculiar to Jewish legend was that they arose as a result of the sin of Cain. More pervasive than this, and common to Christians and Jews, was a belief that the various distortions of the earth resulted from sins of Adam and Eve. As the poet Henry Vaughan said in "Corruption," man drew "the Curse upon the world, and Crackt the whole frame with his fall." According to the *Midrash Rabbah* (1512), "*three* entered for judgment, yet *four* came out guilty. Adam and Eve and the serpent entered for judgment, whereas the *earth* was punished with them." A chief problem here is the interpretation of the word "earth," ambiguous in other languages as in English. In Christian theology, part of the trouble went back to a mistranslation of a phrase in the Vulgate (Genesis 3:17), as "maledicta *terra* in opere tuo," rather than "maledicta *humus* propter te." The Jerome reading became the accepted interpretation of most Roman Catholics both before and after the Douay edition. If the curse was merely upon the *humus*, or soil, so that Adam was forced to earn his living by the sweat of his brow, the topography of the world was not necessarily altered, but if the curse of God extended from man to *terra*, Nature was cursed and earth may have changed as much as man.

In spite of arguments *pro* and *con* on this matter, there was widespread agreement among Jewish and

Christian Fathers that a later catastrophe, sent because of the continual sinning for two millennia on the part of man, must have had a profound effect upon external Nature. A majority of those who considered that the original earth must have been round and smooth attributed the emergence of mountains to Noah's Flood. Biblical exegetes have always used negative as well as positive evidence, and many stressed the fact that a mountain is not mentioned in Genesis until the ark landed on Ararat, and also that, though Moses described the four rivers, he did not mention mountains. Even those theologians who held that mountains had been original with the creation of the world agreed with the Augustinian theory that the Flood must have had a profound effect upon the configuration of earth, causing mountains to be higher and more jagged than had been the original hills. So the debate continued during the Middle Ages well into the Renaissance, the theory of mountain-origin sometimes primary, sometimes involved with other issues.

On the question of mountain-origin and the place of hills in the scheme of things, the two greatest Reformation thinkers stood opposed. Their dual attitudes were in part a result of psychological factors (as indeed may have been true of various of their predecessors) since Calvin spent many years among Swiss mountains, while Luther was a lowlander whose one journey over mountains filled him with terror. Calvin would never agree that Nature was other than beautiful. He did not believe that God had cursed the earth. Ugliness read into her was the result of man's lapsed condition. Nature, created by God, was beautiful; Calvin's belief that original Nature included mountains is shown by his map of Paradise in the Geneva Bible (1560). With Augustine he acknowledged that some of the original earth had been damaged by the Flood, yet beauty remained even though the wilfully blinded eyes of man could not behold it.

So far as such matters were concerned, Luther's theology was consistently pessimistic. In his commentary on Genesis he went further than most predecessors in his gloom. Adam and Eve, Cain and multitudes of men had sinned before God sent the Flood to wipe out most of mankind. Luther specifically mentioned the emergence of diluvian mountains where fields and fruitful plains had once flourished. Since the Deluge, man has continued to sin; in the not too distant future Luther anticipated the destruction of all mankind and the death of the world. Following in general Augustine's conception of the seven ages of man, Luther insisted that the world would not complete its sixth age. He dated the end of the world as approximately 1560. "The last day is already breaking. . . . The world will perish shortly." The earth, in itself innocent, has been forced to bear man's curse. The world degenerates and grows worse every day. Luther's is an intensely pessimistic picture.

III

There is nothing in the geology of the seventeenth century to correspond to the spectacular discoveries of astronomy. Geology was only part of "natural Philosophy," and not an important part. It is true that Agricola had done important work on stratification, on ores, minerals, and metals, and that the basic principles of modern stratigraphy were formulated by Nicholaus Steno in 1669. But geology, in the modern sense, marked time, indeed lagged behind other sciences. More than most of the others, geology was retarded by Genesis. A new astronomy could readily emerge, since Moses had committed himself only upon the creation of the sun and moon but had said nothing about their nature. Our modern idea of "geological time" was impossible to ages of men who believed in the miraculous creation of the world in time, and divine order in inorganic and organic species. Earth sciences and human sciences were handicapped by the tendency of generations to read cosmic processes into earth and man, and to find inevitable similarities between the body of earth and the body of man. It was not that all our ancestors were "fundamentalists." Scholars read the Bible in various languages and interpreted it broadly. There were ethical, allegorical, analogical, cabbalistical expositions. Yet the fact remained that the earth had been created in time and called into existence by miracle.

The problems they encountered may be seen in their theories of fossils, a subject closely associated with that of the origin of mountains. Unhampered by Genesis, the Greeks had surmised that marine fossils were remains of animals, indicating immense age and showing the vicissitudes of sea and land. Our orthodox ancestors could not accept this, since Moses taught that sea and land had been separated on the third day, animal life not produced until the fourth. Fossils, men argued, were not organic but *lusus naturae*, or results of the influence of the planets, twisting stones into grotesque shapes. This remained the orthodox theory until well into the seventeenth century. Tertullian had suggested the influence of the Flood; marine remains had been deposited as the waters receded. This too was widely accepted and remained orthodox. Both before and after Leonardo da Vinci and Girolamo Fracastoro suggested the true explanation, orthodox thought remained consistent with the Mosaic account.

In the "Digression of Air" in the *Anatomy of Melancholy* (1621), Robert Burton wished that he could determine "whether Mount Athos, Pelion, Olympus, Ossa,

Caucasus, Atlas, be so huge as Pliny, Solinus, Mela relate. . . . The pike of Teneriffe how high it is. . . . Are they 1250 paces high . . . or seventy-eight miles perpendicularly high?" Actually the highest peak of Teneriffe is 12,190 feet, but as late as the seventeenth century it was "a hill whose head touched heaven," from which poets coined grand figures. The adherents of a smooth round earth had little trouble in explaining monstrosities resulting from the various sins of man. Traditionalists largely followed one of two schools of thought, a classical idea that there had been vicissitudes of sea and land, which had changed places; or a collateral belief, implied by Milton in his account of the Creation in *Paradise Lost* (VII, 288–90):

> So high as heav'd the tumid hills, so low
> Down sunk a hollow bottom broad and deep,
> Capacious bed of waters.

Here again we find the ancient belief that the work of the Great Geometer had been based upon symmetry and proportion.

Change in what we now consider geological attitudes was slow. With the exception of a few such men as Agricola and Steno, there were few major geological figures. Compared with astronomy, geology marked time. This becomes clear to anyone who has combed English literature seeking scientific allusions and found almost no reference to geology until the later seventeenth century, with the exception of the broad basic concepts that have been mentioned, all implicit in classical or early patristic thinking. A "new astronomy" had been heralded by dramatic moments, such as the appearance of *novae*, which disproved the belief, held for centuries, that the heavens were eternal and immutable. As John Donne put it in a poem to the Countess of Huntingdon:

> Who vagrant transitory Comets sees,
> Wonders, because they'are rare; But a new starre
> Whose motion with the firmament agrees,
> Is miracle; for there no new things are.

Galileo had announced in the *Sidereus Nuncius* (1610) the discovery of myriads of stars, of the nature of the Milky Way, of the moon and of what he at first believed to be four new planets. These discoveries were spectacular, unexpected. From them imagination took fire. But not yet did imagination respond, as in the eighteenth century, to the idea of long, leisurely processes of earth-development.

In England, until well into the seventeenth century, when men read works about geological ideas, they read books written on the continent, not at home. *A Collection of Discourses of the Virtuosi of France,* published in 1664 and 1665, was originally French but much at home in England in both the original and in translation. One discourse (Conference CLXXXIX) was particularly concerned with mountains. In form this is a conference among six speakers who upheld various points of view. One speaker, who insisted that mountains were original, based his belief less upon Moses than upon Galileo, who had observed mountains not only in the moon but in Mars. Throughout the dialogue we find a concern less with metaphysics than with an implicit aesthetics. Since God created the world in perfection, we should expect "agreeable variety" as "its principal ornament." Another speaker, upholding the diluvian theory, believed that the original earth had been a Circle of Perfection. " 'Tis certain that God gave the Earth that Spherical Form" and that it remained smooth and round until the Flood. The speakers in *A Collection of Discourses* had much to say of the Bible but they were also aware of discoveries of Kepler, Gilbert, and Galileo. A shift was occurring to what came to be known as "physico-theology."

The most widely used book treating the ideas we have been considering was the *Geographia generalis* of Bernhardus Varenius, published in England in 1650 and 1664, revised by Newton in 1672, then appearing as *Cosmography and Geography* in 1682. For nearly a century it was consulted in Latin and in translation, and its science kept up to date. Literary historians have pointed out that it was a handbook of poets from Milton to James Thomson. In his lengthy treatment of the original earth, Varenius followed the *Sphaera mundi* (1620) of Joseph Blancanus, though he also introduced ideas that had come into thinking during the intervening decades. Few writers had been as consistent as Blancanus in their belief in the symmetry and proportion God had given the earth, in which the highest mountain exactly corresponded to the lowest depth of the sea. The original earth had emerged on the third day as a smooth sphere. Had it been affected only by natural law, it would have remained in that form, but the miraculous hand of God had scooped out the channel of the sea and created the Alps and other mountains. If left to its own nature, the world would perish as it had begun, in water. But God would not permit such natural metamorphosis: the world would perish by fire. Following Blancanus, but improving upon him in various ways, Varenius found the origin of terrestrial mountains in water. To the general reader, particularly the poet, the most impressive parts of the *Geographia generalis* were sections in which Varenius sent his imagination over the globe, calling a catalogue of the ranges and peaks in every continent, as they rise, sometimes in majesty, sometimes in terror. Theology still clouded Varenius' eyes to some extent in his mountain-passages, though even the three decades since Blancanus had made him basically more scientific.

There was one seventeenth-century creator of a new world, however, who feared neither God nor man. In his *Principles of Philosophy* (1644), René Descartes momentarily paid tribute to a divine Mechanic who had set in motion a mechanical universe, but, genuflection over, his great clock ticked on, and we see what Blancanus had vaguely surmised, a cosmos emerging by natural principles. The irregularities of the Cartesian world and universe, however, were not results of emergence from water. Descartes posited a theory of the origin of planets from fiery matter cast off by the sun, a universe of cosmical vortices. From the "luminous dust" of the "first element," and the heat and light of the "second element" was produced a "third element" of earth and water-particles. As the planet cooled, a layer of liquid was contained within the crust, the elements in the order of specific gravity. The sun's heat caused cracks in the crust so that the earth was ruptured and collapsed upon the inner globe. A result of the collapse was great irregularities, some rising above the liquid, some falling below: mountains, earth hollows, the bed of the sea. At the center still remained fire, causing earthquakes and volcanoes. Such was the self-consistent Cartesian world-scheme, a mechanistic world in a mechanistic universe. Complex enough to satisfy scientists, its vortices were simple and graphic enough to be grasped by an amateur such as Fontenelle's Marchioness in the *Plurality of Worlds* (1686), who thanked God for the vortex in which she had been placed. Most of all, so far as literary influence was concerned, here was a world-scheme with the drama earlier schemes had lacked, a universe offering imagination the spectacular that had been found in the "new astronomy," so far lacking in a "new geology."

IV

The "mountain controversy" came to a climax in the 1680's with the publication of a work that appeared first in Latin as *Telluris theoria sacra* (1681), then in English as *The Sacred Theory of the Earth* (1684), again in Latin in 1689 with the addition of two more books. This edition was republished in English in 1690–91. There were various other editions during the eighteenth century and at least one in the nineteenth. The author was Thomas Burnet, Master of the Charterhouse and Chaplain to King William, who would probably have become Archbishop of Canterbury had he not published this work. Here was one of the most provocative and influential works of the century, widely read and eliciting many replies.

Burnet's book aroused various issues, several of which have been discussed in *Mountain Gloom and Mountain Glory*. Here only Burnet's views concerning mountain-attitudes will be stressed. Basically Burnet's attempt was to reconcile the new science and the old religion, which he realized were drifting apart. He went back to Scriptural exegesis and considered particularly those Fathers who in his opinion believed that the world and sea were not the originals created by God for Adam and Eve, but that the physical, like the moral, world shows marked steps in degeneration. External Nature, as man had known it since the Flood, is "a broken and confused Heap of Bodies, plac'd in no Order to one another, nor with any Correspondency or Regularity of Parts," and, like the moon seen through a telescope, "rude and ragged." Both moon and earth are images of "a great Ruin. . . . A World lying in its Rubbish." Before the Flood the face of earth was "smooth, regular, and uniform, without Mountains and without a Sea . . . you will not meet with a Mountain or a Rock." In this smooth world with "not a Wrinkle, Scar or Fracture in all its Body" lived our original parents. The first great climax occurred when, after generations of sins, God sent the Deluge to wipe out all mankind, with the exception of one faithful man and his family. Burnet's description of the coming of the Flood is music, if sombre music. We hear the raging waters and the broken waves coming to their height, "so as Nature seem'd to be in a second Chaos." The wild abyss destroyed everything in its path, except "A Ship, whose Cargo was no less than a whole World; that carry'd the Fortunes and Hopes of all Posterity." When the Flood abated and Noah descended upon Ararat, he saw only a great ruin of "wild, vast and indigested Heaps of Stone and Earth." As the Flood receded, there stood the mountains we know today, "the Ruines of a broken World."

No previous writer had felt or shown anything approaching Burnet's mountain-paradoxes. A majority of preceding writers had been uninterested in hills or mountains, some had actively disliked them, a few had shown momentary response to "Mountain Glory," but among all previous writers interest in mountains had been secondary. In Burnet it was primary. His theory had developed as a result of his experience in 1671 of making the Grand Tour with the Earl of Wiltshire, to whom he dedicated the first edition of *Telluris theoria sacra*. When he crossed the Alps and Apennines, "the Sight of those wild, vast and indigested Heaps of Stones and Earth did so deeply stir my Fancy, that I was not easy until I could give my self some tolerable Account how that Confusion came in Nature."

Burnet had grown up with traditional ideas of symmetry and proportion. In his atlases mountain ranges had seemed neat, pleasing, and decorous. Even when he saw the Alps from a distance, he could still believe in proportion and symmetry, but not when he stood among them. He saw "vast Bodies thrown together in Confusion. . . . Rocks standing naked round about him; and the hollow Valleys gaping under him," black clouds above, heaps of snow in mid-summer, and a noise of thunder below him. Burnet's mountain-experience does not seem to have been identical with that of Thomas Coryate who had no head for heights. He was less frightened than appalled at the "incredible Confusion" that broke down all his ideals of symmetry and proportion. Mountains, he found by experience, were placed in no order implying either use or beauty. "There is nothing in Nature more shapeless and ill-figur'd than an old Rock or Mountain, and all the variety that is among them, is but the many various Modes of Irregularity . . . they are of all Forms and Figures except regular. . . . They are the greatest Examples of Confusion that we know in Nature; no Tempest or Earthquake puts things into more Disorder." That chaos and confusion he had found among mountains, he discovered also on his travels when he saw earth's entrails in caves and caverns, when in some districts he discovered the effects of volcano and earthquake. On his journey Burnet faced what he believed was a religious crisis. Actually his theological beliefs did not waver. His ethics was threatened and even more his aesthetics.

Burnet has been deliberately quoted in such a way that he seems the most consistent of men in his repulsion from grand Nature, even more than Luther, beating his breast when he looked upon the ruins caused by man's sin. But, reading Burnet's long descriptive passages on natural scenery, we find that he is the most paradoxical writer up to this time. His stress on formlessness and lack of design in external Nature was an intellectual condemnation more than offset by his emotional response to the grand and the vast. At the same time that he condemned irregularity, he responded to the majesty of mountains and oceans as had no English traveller before him. "Places that are strange and solemn strike an Awe into us," he wrote. The mountains are ruins, "but such as shew a certain Magnificence in Nature." The chapter in which he most drastically condemned the gross disproportion of mountains begins with a tribute to their majesty:

The greatest Objects of Nature are, methinks, the most pleasing to behold; and next to the Great Concave of the Heavens, and those boundless Regions where the Stars inhabit, there is nothing that I looke upon with more Pleasure than the wide Sea and the Mountains of the Earth. There is something august and stately in the Air of those things, that inspires the Mind with great Thoughts and Passions; we do naturally, upon such Occasions, think of God and his Greatness: and whatsoever hath but the Shadow

and Appearance of INFINITE, as all Things have that are too big for our Comprehension, they fill and overbear the Mind with their Excess, and cast it into a pleasing kind of Stupor and Admiration (*Sacred Theory* . . . , I, 188–89).

Burnet was "ravished" by the grand and majestic in Nature. Before the vastness of mountains and ocean, he experienced awe and wonder which he had previously associated only with God. He did not understand his own emotional response, which he realized was not to Beauty. The vast and irregular could not be beautiful, but nothing except the night skies had ever so moved him to thoughts of God and infinity as did the mountains and the sea. As yet he had no vocabulary in which to express the fact that he had discovered the Sublime in external Nature. The development of this part of the story is traced elsewhere in this *Dictionary.* [See Sublime in External Nature.]

V

References of English men of letters to the *Sacred Theory* began to appear in the year of its publication. On June 8, 1684, John Evelyn returned a copy of the translation to Samuel Pepys with flattering remarks. Both diarists were enthusiastic about the work, as at first was Sir William Temple who read it at the same time as a volume by Fontenelle. He thought highly of both until he came to sections in which the writers praised modern literature and learning above ancient. As a result he wrote his essay on ancient and modern learning which led him into the Battle of the Books. Burnet was attacked or defended by nearly every important writer on theology, physico-theology, and science, with the exception of Newton, to whom one volume in the controversy was dedicated. Most of these books and papers have been discussed in *Mountain Gloom and Mountain Glory.* Only a few of the more important will be mentioned here. Burnet made England "mountain conscious" to an extent not hitherto known. John Ray, father of English natural history, published in 1691 his *Wisdom of God*, which went through many editions. His defense of mountains was conventional, the old pragmatic and utilitarian argument. Some, he says, have considered mountains "Warts and superfluous Excrescences." He will devote his energies to proving "the great Use, Benefit and Necessity of them." Much of what Ray said was old convention—a reply to Lucretius as well as Burnet—but on occasion he developed movingly the place of mountains in a universe created by a God of overflowing benignity who had expressed himself in the world with all possible diversity.

In 1692 Richard Bentley delivered the first Boyle Lecture, *The Folly and Unreasonableness of Atheism*

Demonstrated from the Origin and Frame of the World. Men like Burnet, he says in effect, think that mountain, valley, ocean are deformity, ruin or fortuitous concourse of atoms rather than what they are—works of Divine artifice. "They would have the vast body of a planet to be as elegent as a factitious globe represents it."

Interest in the *Sacred Theory* continued well into the eighteenth century. Addison, discovering Burnet in youth, addressed a poem to him and later showed his influence in *The Pleasures of the Imagination.* Steele devoted *Spectator* 146 to the work, quoting several passages, particularly what he called Burnet's "Funeral Oration over this Globe," and his farewell to the "mountains and Rocks of the Earth." Burnet's theory continued to dwell on the minds of travellers to the continent. The mountain-experiences of John Dennis and Lord Shaftesbury, were based to a large extent on Burnet. James Thompson added to "Spring" a passage describing the Deluge in Burnetian mood, and he and David Mallett in their companion-poems showed Burnetian influence. A climax of the enthusiasm for Burnet as a prose-poet came with Wordsworth and Coleridge. The former read the *Sacred Theory* after he had finished *The Excursion* and copied parts of the Latin version to publish with his notes. References to Burnet's work occur frequently in Coleridge's Note Book. He proposed to turn the *Telluris theoria sacra* into blank verse. He classed Plato and Burnet together to show that "poetry of the highest order may exist without metre." The lines prefixed to *The Ancient Mariner* were taken from a later work of Burnet.

The *Sacred Theory* was well known on the continent. Buffon thought it a fine historical romance. Voltaire satirized the work but the Encyclopedists took it very seriously. It has been shown that Burnet was quoted more often than any other English writer by Diderot, Boulanger, Formey, and Jaucourt; Jaucourt classed him with Descartes and Newton. The greatest philosopher among Burnet's admirers was Leibniz, though the *Protogaea*, in which Burnet was discussed, appeared posthumously. Indeed, Burnet's work lived for nearly a century after it was published.

VI

As stated in *Mountain Gloom and Mountain Glory* (p. 345): "If the 'Mountain Glory' did not shine full splendor in the earlier eighteenth century, the 'Mountain Gloom' was gone. We find nothing to parallel Marvell's 'unjust' and 'hook-shouldered' mountains that deform earth, nothing (except conventional hymns) of the early Christian strain of abasing the hills in order to exalt the valleys. Mountains had ceased to be monstrosities and had become an integral part of varied and diversified Nature." Even in a poem like Richard

Blackmore's *Creation* (1713), basically intended as a reply to Lucretius, the author went further than the old utilitarian argument, showing himself aware of the growing interest in geology by introducing passages on the stratification of the earth, the part played by mountains in production of minerals and gems, and the relationship of mountains to the origins of rivers and springs.

The extent to which consciousness of geological theories of mountains developed among laymen may be seen in James Thomson's *Seasons* (1744), individual parts of which began to appear from 1726 to 1730. Thompson had an important prerequisite for his interest in mountains—he was a Scot. As he wrote of the Laplanders, many Scots

> . . . ask no more than simple Nature gives;
> They love their mountains, and enjoy their storms.

When he made the Grand Tour, he felt little of the alarm and distaste of many earlier travellers among the Alps. In *Liberty* (1734–36), he described the mountains as they appeared to him in a passage beginning:

> . . . their shaggy mountains charm
> More than or Gallic or Italian plains;
> And sickening fancy oft, when absent long,
> Pines to behold their Alpine views again.

Alan Dugald McKillop has studied various of Thomson's mountain-passages in *The Background of Thomson's Seasons*, particularly in Chapter II, "Description and Science." He has analyzed in detail an extended mountain-passage in "Autumn" (lines 700–30) as it developed from the quarto edition of 1730 to the complete *Seasons*, fourteen years later. Turning from one scientific authority to another, Thomson considered in turn theories of "attraction," "distillation," "percolation" in relation to the development of mountains. The passage becomes more and more technical as the author proceeds, showing his interest in geological theories which frequently threaten the poetic emphasis of the original passage. But while overemphasis on scientific verisimilitude mars the effect of some particular passages, there is no question that James Thomson was the finest English mountain-poet before William Wordsworth.

Every reader of "Tintern Abbey" or *The Prelude* is aware that in youth Wordsworth had vacillated between fear and exaltation so far as grand Nature was concerned. Terror was often in the ascendency as he remembered himself "more like a man flying from something that he dreads than one who sought the thing he loved."

> While yet a child, and long before his time,
> Had he perceived the presence of the power

Of greatness; and deep feelings had impressed
So vividly great objects that they lay
Upon his soul like substances
        (*The Excursion*, I, 132–38).

"In the mountains did he *feel* his faith." Surrounded by lesser English hills, Wordsworth felt "a sense of stability and permanence," but among the Alps he was always conscious of "the fury of the gigantic torrents," and their "almost irresistible violence," "Havoc, and ruin, and desolation." Among the snow-capped Alps, it was almost impossible to escape from the "depressing sensation" that the whole was in a rapid process of dissolution. The savagery of the terror of Nature echoes through his early acquaintance with Alpine mountains, "winds thwarting winds, bewildered and forlorn," "rocks that muttered close upon our ears," "black drizzling crags," "the sick sight and giddy prospect of the raging storm," "huge fragments of primeval mountain spread/ In powerless ruin." But this is not Wordsworth's mature conclusion of the power of mountains upon human imagination. To comprehend that, we must include with "Mountain-Attitudes" the sense of "The Sublime in Natural Scenery" that accompanied the human discovery of the vast in external Nature.

BIBLIOGRAPHY

Frank Dawson Adams, *The Birth and Development of the Geological Sciences* (Baltimore, 1938). B. Sprague Allen, *Tides in English Taste* (Cambridge, Mass., 1937). Robert Arnold Aubin, *Topographical Poetry in XVIII-Century England* (New York, 1936). Edwin A. Burtt, *Metaphysical Foundations of Modern Physical Science* (London, 1925; other eds.). Douglas Bush, *Science and English Poetry: A Historical Study* (New York, 1950). Katherine Brownell Collier, *Cosmogonies of our Fathers* (New York, 1934). R. G. Collingwood, *The Idea of Nature* (Oxford, 1945). Clair-Éliane Engel, *La Littérature Alpestre en France et en Angleterre aux 18ᵉ et 19ᵉ siècles* (Chambéry, 1930). Christopher Hussey, *The Picturesque: Studies in a Point of View* (London, 1927). Arthur O. Lovejoy, *Essays in the History of Ideas* (Baltimore, 1948). Elizabeth Manwaring, *Italian Landscape in Eighteenth Century England* (New York, 1925). Marjorie Hope Nicolson, *Mountain Gloom and Mountain Glory: The Development of the Aesthetics of the Infinite* (Ithaca, 1959). H. V. S. and Margaret Ogden, *English Taste in Landscape in the Seventeenth Century* (Ann Arbor, 1955). Hedley Howell Rhys, ed., *Seventeenth Century Sciences and the Arts* (Princeton, 1961). Clarence Dewitt Thorpe, *The Aesthetic Theory of Thomas Hobbes* (London, 1940). Ernest Lee Tuveson, *Millennium and Utopia: A Study in the Background of the Idea of Progress* (Berkeley, 1949). Alfred North Whitehead, *Science and the Modern World* (New York, 1926; other eds.).

MARJORIE HOPE NICOLSON

[See also **Ancients and Moderns; Beauty;** Creation; God; **Sublime;** Symmetry; **Uniformitarianism.**]

MUSIC AND SCIENCE

OF ALL the arts, music has had most to rely upon a scientific and mathematical analysis of its materials. Both the relations between pitches and between durations are best defined by numbers and ratios. To construct even the simplest instruments out of strings or pipes, musicians had to derive as best they could the laws of sound production. The most elementary fact, generally accredited to the Pythagoreans but probably known to the ancient Babylonians and Egyptians, is that if a string is stopped in the middle, each of the two halves sounds an octave higher than the whole; if divided into three parts, two-thirds of the string will sound a fifth above the whole; and so on.

Because it relies on precise measurement, music was considered until fairly modern times, indeed until around 1650, a branch of science. In late antiquity it began to be included in the four mathematical disciplines of the quadrivium along with arithmetic, geometry, and astronomy. But actually only theoretical music was accorded this place. No singing or playing was included in this curriculum. Practical music making went its own way, maintaining only limited contact with theoretical music, drifting farthest from it in the Middle Ages and approaching nearer during the Renaissance. The musical component of the mathematical curriculum in the universities never went beyond the heritage of Greek music theory. Only the Renaissance humanists succeeded in making this relevant to Western musical art.

Because of this alliance with mathematics, music figured prominently in cosmology, astrology, and number mysticism. Speculations about the harmony of the universe were often inspired by musical facts, as in Plato's *Timaeus* (31–39), or as in the theory that the planets were governed in their motions by ratios of the consonances and therefore produced an unheard music (*Republic* X). These ideas were attacked by Aristotle (*On the Heavens* II. 8–9), but the musical world generally believed them until the end of the fifteenth century, and Kepler much later was still seeking to prove universal harmony when he discovered the third law of planetary motion (the cube of any planet's distance from the sun varies directly with the square of the planet's period or time of revolution).

Greek writers credited Pythagoras (ca. 582–07 B.C.) with the earliest acoustical observations. He is said to have discovered the ratios of the octave (2:1), fifth

(3:2), octave plus fifth (3:1), fourth (4:3), and double octave (4:1). These were the only consonances recognized by Greek theory. Great metaphysical significance was attached to the fact that the set of numbers from 1 to 4 was the source of all harmony.

It was assumed that these ratios produced the same consonances whether the numbers applied to string lengths, bore of pipes, weights stretching strings, weights of disks, or volumes of air in vessels such as bells or water-filled glasses. Theon of Smyrna (second century A.D.) claimed that Pythagoras had verified these ratios in all these circumstances. Boethius (fifth century A.D.) reported that Pythagoras heard the consonances also issuing from a blacksmith's hammers whose weights were in the same ratios as the string lengths. Actually, as Vincenzo Galilei, father of Galileo, was to demonstrate in 1589 (Palisca, 1961), the ratios are not the same in these cases as in the division of the string. Throughout the Middle Ages and early Renaissance, from Boethius to Gaffurio (Figure 1), almost every author on music recounts the experiments of Pythagoras without realizing their improbability.

The canonization of the octave, fifth, and fourth in their natural ratios as the cornerstones of the harmonic system had a deeper influence on music theory and composition than on instrument building or playing. Musicians tended to tune their instruments by ear, tempering the ratios of the fourths and fifths, because it was discovered early that if one tuned up a cycle of twelve fifths from any note until that note was reached again, this note was higher than that reached through a cycle of seven octaves by

$$\left(\frac{3}{2}\right)^{12} : \left(\frac{2}{1}\right)^{7} \quad \text{or} \quad \frac{531,441}{524,288},$$

approximately 24% of a semitone. According to the theorists, the only acceptable tuning was that which maintained the fifth and fourth at their proper ratios of 3:2 and 4:3. This tuning was called by Ptolemy Diatonic *ditoniaion*, and it is also known as the Pythagorean tuning. In this scheme the tetrachord or modular fourth is composed of two tones and a semitone in the ratios 9:8, 9:8, 256:243. The fifth and fourth, favored by this tuning, were the most prominent consonances in written polyphony from the ninth through the thirteenth centuries, particularly at points of rhythmic or structural emphasis. The thirds and sixths, which were not recognized as consonances by Greek or orthodox medieval theory, were harsh-sounding in the Pythagorean tuning. Nevertheless, they were employed increasingly in polyphony, particularly during the fourteenth and fifteenth centuries.

Renaissance humanism had a somewhat delayed effect on musical theory as compared to other disciplines. Only in the last quarter of the fifteenth century did the ancient Greek treatises begin to be read first-hand and translated; for example, Ptolemy's *Harmonics*, Aristotle's *Problems*, the short introductions of Cleonides and Euclid, and eventually the *Harmonics* of Aristoxenus. At about the same time an antitheoretical movement began among composer-theorists. The first writer to break with the Boethian-Pythagorean doctrine of consonances was Bartolomé Ramos de Pareja. In his *Musica practica* (Bologna, 1482) he proposed a tuning system that allowed for sweetly tuned thirds in the simple ratios of 5:4 and 6:5, as against the Pythagorean 81:64 and 32:27. Ramos' innovations met resistance among conservatives like Franchino Gaffurio. But soon Lodovico Fogliano (1529), Gioseffo Zarlino (1588), and Francisco de Salinas (1577) joined Ramos in dethroning for all times the Pythagorean tuning system. All three leaned upon the recently rediscovered *Harmonics* of Claudius Ptolemy in which a tuning very similar to Ramos' was described under the name Diatonic *syntonon*. Zarlino was convinced

FIGURE 1. This illustration in Gaffurio's *Theorica musice* (Milan, 1492) was intended to show that the same numbers, 16, 12, 9, 8, 6, 4, will always produce the same intervals, as in the series A E a b e a', and that the proportion 2:1 (here 16:8) will always give an octave. But only in the pipes at the lower left will this actually be the case, as Vincenzo Galilei showed in 1589.

that it was the perfect tuning, because both perfect and imperfect consonances were in simple ratios of the class $n + 1/n$, known as superparticular. Zarlino modernized the pre-Ramos number mysticism by replacing the number four by the set of numbers from 1 to 6, the *numero senario*.

A growing use of thirds and sixths paralleled theoretical recognition of a sweet-third tuning. However, if there is a causal connection, it is that the theorists saw the anachronism of standing by a theoretical harsh-third tuning.

The astronomer Ptolemy was known to the Renaissance as the theorist who took the middle road between the rationalist position of the Pythagoreans and the empiricist method of Aristoxenus. Zarlino was attracted to Ptolemy because he too was inclined to worship number while aiming to satisfy the ear. Aristoxenus, on the other hand, rejected ratios as irrelevant to music. He preferred to divide pitch-space directly, if somewhat subjectively. Of his tuning systems the one that most appealed to sixteenth-century musicians was that in which each whole tone contained 12 units of pitch-space and each semitone 6 units. Sixteenth-century interpreters assumed this meant the division of the octave into an equal temperament of twelve equal semitones, as in the tuning of the lute. Such a tuning would permit a melody to sound equally well in any key, something that could not be accomplished with any other tuning. Aristoxenus began to find apostles in the last quarter of the sixteenth century, notably Vincenzo Galilei and Ercole Bottrigari.

Meanwhile no scientific discovery had yet deprived the simple ratios of the consonances of their priority. But in 1589–90 Vincenzo Galilei drafted a treatise that reported some new·experiments with sounding bodies. He discovered that the ratios usually associated with the consonances are obtained only when they represent pipe or string lengths, other factors being equal. When weights were attached to strings, the ratio had to be 4:1, not 2:1 to produce an octave. The volumes of concave bodies had to be in the ratio of 8:1 to produce the octave. Since, in terms of weights, the fifth and fourth were 9:4 and 16:9 respectively, Galilei saw no reason to prefer simple ratios within the numbers of the *senario*.

The bastion of the simple ratios was besieged also by another line of research. In a letter to the composer Cipriano de Rore of around 1563 the scientist Giambattista Benedetti proposed a new theory of the cause of consonance. Benedetti argued that since sound consists of air waves or vibrations, in the more consonant intervals the shorter more frequent waves concurred with the longer less frequent waves at regular intervals. In the less consonant intervals, on the other hand,

concurrence was infrequent and the two sounds did not blend in the ear pleasantly. He showed that in a fifth, for example, the two vibrations will meet every two cycles of the lower note and every three of the higher. He went on to show that in terms of frequency of concurrence the hierarchy of ratios within the octave would be 2:1, 3:2, 4:3, 5:3, 5:4, 6:5, 7:5, 8:5, which challenges both the superiority of superparticular ratios and the sanctity of the *senario*. There could be no abrupt break from consonance to dissonance but only a continuum of intervals, some more, some less consonant. Benedetti's theory was espoused in the next century by Isaac Beeckman and Marin Mersenne, who sought René Descartes' opinion of it. Descartes declined to judge the goodness of consonances by such a rational method, protesting that the ear prefers one or another according to the musical context rather than because of any concordance of vibrations.

The philologist and student of ancient music Girolamo Mei summed up this emancipation of music from scientific determinism in a letter to Vincenzo Galilei of 1572:

The true end of science is altogether different from that of art. . . . The science of music goes about diligently investigating and considering all the qualities and properties of the existing constitution and ordering of musical tones, whether these are simple qualities or comparative, like the consonances, and this for no other aim than to come to know the truth itself, the perfect goal of all speculation, and as a by-product the false. It then lets art exploit as it sees fit, without any limitation, those tones about which science has learned the truth (Palisca [1960], p. 65).

The revolution in musical thought encouraged experimentation in composition, in which a search for new musical resources had already spontaneously begun. Composers found a new harmonic richness; and even in the old tunings they braved modulations to distant keys and ventured melodic motion by semitone. The Aristoxenian "equal temperament," which would have made these things easier, was demanded even by some conservative musicians like Giovanni Maria Artusi, a loyal disciple of Zarlino. Dissonances—seconds, sevenths, and diminished and augmented intervals—were introduced more and more freely into compositions.

If scientific discovery stimulated musical change, the opposite is also true: musical problems stimulated scientific investigation. Benedetti and Vincenzo Galilei were moved by musical problems to inquire into the mechanics of sound production. The most notable case is that of Galileo, who was disturbed by the very problem that stumped his father: Is there a stable connection between consonance and ratio? He made perhaps the most fundamental discovery in acoustics when he proved that there is: ratios between the frequencies of vibration are the inverse of the ratios of string lengths.

The most difficult challenge that music presented to science in the seventeenth century was to explain the multiple pitches that could be heard when a single string vibrated. Aristotle noted that he could hear the octave above (*Problems* 919b 24; 921b 42) and observed the related phenomenon of hearing a string respond sympathetically to one tuned an octave higher. It took Mersenne's acute musical ear to hear from a single vibrating string not only the upper octave but the octave plus fifth, double octave, double octave plus major third, and the double octave plus major sixth. Neither he nor Descartes, nor any of the other scientists of their circle could explain why this happened. In 1673 two Oxford scientists, William Noble and Thomas Pigot, showed that strings tuned to the octave, octave plus fifth, and octave plus major third below a plucked string sounded sympathetically at the unison to the plucked string by vibrating in aliquot parts. They demonstrated this by placing paper riders on the sympathetic strings at the points where, if the string were stopped, unisons would be produced. In 1677 John Wallis reported that multiple sounds would occur in a vibrating string only if it was not plucked at the points that marked off the aliquot parts. This showed that a single string simultaneously vibrated as a whole and in its aliquot parts. Thus harmonic vibration, which was important also for mechanics and optics, was established as a fact.

Of all the laws of acoustics that of harmonic vibration exercised most the imagination of theorists of music. The first to utilize the information was Jean-Philippe Rameau. In his *Traité de l'harmonie* (1722), he had constructed a new system of harmony on the ratios of the divisions of the string. When he learned rather belatedly of harmonic vibration from an exhaustive paper by Joseph Sauveur (1701), Rameau decided that this was the original principle he had been looking for. In his opinion it firmly established his theory of fundamental bass, as he called the bottom note of a triad whose notes are arranged in thirds, for the first six notes of the harmonic series arranged as a chord is equivalent to a major triad over a fundamental bass. Thus his system was a copy of nature. The fundamental bass, in his view, determines the progress of the harmony, as when it leaps down a fifth from the dominant (fifth note) to the tonic (first note) of a key. But Rameau did not stop at this. He made of the harmonic series a Cartesian first principle from which he built up, by manipulating the numbers of its ratios, a system of

theory that embraced every aspect of music. Unfortunately, his numerical operations were often faulty and drew severe criticism from the geometer Jean d'Alembert and the mathematician Leonhard Euler.

The concept of fundamental bass received further support when the celebrated violinist and composer Giuseppe Tartini in 1754 announced his discovery of "the third sound." This is a subjective sensation now known as "difference tone" that is believed to occur because of the presence of nonlinear resonance in the ear. When two pitches are sounded, a third lower one seems to resound. Tartini found it by listening carefully to double-stops played on a violin. Actually, unknown to Tartini, Georg Andreas Sorge had noted the same phenomenon nine years previously (1745). The "third sound" usually reinforced the note of a chord that Rameau identified as the fundamental bass, which Tartini too accepted as a keystone of his system. Like Rameau, he indulged in sweeping mathematical and geometric speculations, which, however, did not withstand the scrutiny of mathematicians such as Benjamin Stillingfleet and Antonio Eximeno.

Both Tartini and Rameau were pioneers in musical composition, at the forefront in technique, style, and structure. But as thinkers they were anachronistic. In the midst of the Enlightenment, which was skeptical of systems and the deductive process, they spun webs of numbers in blissful isolation, only to become hopelessly entangled in them.

Musicians have continued to search for a natural basis for music theory. In the twentieth century, Paul Hindemith extended the idea of fundamental bass to all kinds of dissonant chords. Like his predecessors he based the theory on the harmonic series and on difference tones. He believed, like Rameau, that all harmonic movement depends on the progress of roots of chords, but he freed this process from the simple cadence-like successions of Rameau. Hindemith's theory has been challenged because its premises are fully valid only in a system of just intonation, and because, while exploiting difference tones, he ignored combination tones that are sometimes more audible.

Lately, scientific facts and theories outside the realm of acoustics have inspired philosophies of music. From thermodynamics the concepts of entropy and indeterminacy have been seized upon as a justification for music to copy nature by following laws of chance rather than willful combinations. From information theory and physics composers have borrowed the concept of the stochastic process, in which events are interconnected through a succession of probabilities. It is also possible by analogy to defend as expressive of the contemporary view of reality the modular structures of serial compositions, which are constructed like crystals, multiplying the same cell in successive and simultaneous juxtapositions. Meanwhile the entire corpus of acoustical science is called into play by electronic and computer music, in which art merges indissolubly with engineering. Music may be on the road to becoming once again a branch of science, or at least of technology.

BIBLIOGRAPHY

For references concerning Beeckman, Benedetti, Descartes, Fogliano, V. Galilei, G. Galilei, Gaffurio, Kepler, Mersenne, Mei, B. R. de Pareja, Rameau, Salinas, and Sauveur, see C. V. Palisca, "Scientific Empiricism in Musical Thought," in H. H. Rhys, ed., *Seventeenth-Century Science and the Arts* (Princeton, 1961), pp. 91–137. See also Jean Le Rond d'Alembert, *Élémens de musique, théorique et pratique* (Lyon, 1762); J. M. Barbour, *Tuning and Temperament* (East Lansing, Mich., 1953); E. Bottrigari, *Il Desiderio* (Venice, 1594); M. R. Cohen and I. E. Drabkin, *A Source Book in Greek Science* (New York, 1948), pp. 286–310; R. L. Crocker, "Pythagorean Mathematics and Music," *The Journal of Aesthetics and Art Criticism,* **22** (1963–64), 189–98, 325–35; Signalia Dostrovsky, "The Origins of Vibration Theory: The Scientific Revolution and the Nature of Music" (Ph.D. dissertation, Princeton University, 1969, unpubl.); Stillman Drake, "Renaissance Music and Experimental Science," *Journal of the History of Ideas,* **30** (1969), 483–500; L. Euler, *Tentamen novae theoriae musicae* (Petropoli [Saint Petersburg], 1739); A. Eximeno, *Dell'origine delle regole* (Rome, 1774); E. E. Helm, "The Vibrating String of the Pythagoreans," *Scientific American,* **217** (1967), 92–103; H. Helmholtz, *On the Sensations of Tone* (New York, 1964); P. Hindemith, *Craft of Musical Composition* (New York, 1942); E. Lippman, *Musical Thought in Ancient Greece* (New York, 1964); C. V. Palisca, *Girolamo Mei* (Rome, 1960); idem, "The Interaction of the Sciences and the Arts: A Historical View," *Proceedings of the Fourth National Conference on the Arts in Education* (Philadelphia, 1965), pp. 19–25; idem, "Fogliano," "Galilei," "Gogava," "Mei," "Ramos," "Salinas," "Valla," "Zarlino," *Die Musik in Geschichte und Gegenwart* (Kassel, 1955–68); G. A. Sorge, *Vorgemach der musikalischen Composition,* Erster Theil (Lobenstein, 1745), Ch. 5; B. Stillingfleet, *Principles and Power of Harmony* (London, 1771); G. Tartini, *Trattato di musica* (Padua, 1754).

CLAUDE V. PALISCA

[See also Astrology; Cosmology; Number; **Pythagorean Harmony;** Renaissance Humanism.]

MUSIC AS A DEMONIC ART

THE IDEA of music as a demonic art implies that music is not considered on its merits alone, but points beyond itself and man to the demonic. Thus music can be understood as an invention and inspiration of demons, indeed almost as a demonic possession. It may be interpreted as an imitation or image of demonic prototypes. The musician may be conceived of as a servant or assistant of demons. Demonic music may seduce or destroy human beings. Conversely, however, demons can be influenced, conjured up, or exorcised by means of music. These notions are intimately related, although mostly antithetically, to those of music as a divine art [see next article]. Here too there is a characteristic connection with religion and the history of religion. Of course, a precise definition of the demonic, e.g., by opposition to the divine, is not possible for all epochs. There are fluctuations in many areas. And only in cases where some antecedent division between (good) divinities and (evil) demons is already established can a corresponding dualism arise likewise in musical perspectives. Such conceptions had already been encountered quite early. Like the ideas of music as a divine art, they extend from magical, via mythological, down to theological and philosophical, forms of thought and remain active at least into the baroque period. Thereafter they fall victim in the course of a general process of secularization to an increasingly rational skepticism.

1. Primitive Peoples. The sounds of nature (thunder, water, wind, echo) seem to early man to be the voices of demonic beings, and a spirit is locked within the sounding instrument. The narcotic ecstasy induced by music and dance is seen as superhumanly and demonically inspired. It leads to union with the demon world, or to participation in it, or may serve as protection against it. Different kinds of music correspond respectively to different kinds of demon. Certain demons have a special music pertaining to them, by which they may be influenced. At all events, music and dance play an altogether central part in all activities of magic and witchcraft. The power of shamans and medicine men depends on knowledge and mastery of the musical devices in this connection. Similar magical-demonic elements survive in music, often more slightly modified, well into historical times. They may be recognized without difficulty even today in the concerted pealing of church bells, in the blowing of alphorns at the onset of darkness to frighten off evil demons, or even as a romantic evocation of atmosphere in advanced music, as, for example, in the Wolves' Ravine scene in Carl Maria von Weber's *Der Freischütz.*

2. Civilized Cultures. In the ancient Mesopotamian cultures distinct indications are found of a discrimination between light and dark, beneficial and ruinous demons. Thus in the Babylonian-Assyrian religion a documented existence of apotropaic (evil-averting) rites has shown that music served to rescue man from the activities of destructive demons. Iranian influence is primarily responsible for the emphasis on a dualism between good and evil spirits. This is also encountered in the Old Testament. Jahweh orders his high priest, Aaron, to wear a ceremonial robe with little bells when he enters the Holy of Holies. Belonging to the same context is the scene of David playing the harp to drive with his music the evil spirit of melancholy from the soul of king Saul. To the Greeks all demons are intermediaries in the order of the cosmos. They know nothing of a battle between light and dark powers and acknowledge no devils. Only the syncretist period of later antiquity conceives of the world as governed by good and evil demons. Each has its appropriate music. According to Porphyry (died A.D. 304), good and evil (specialized) demons are intermediaries in the songs of men. They can be invoked only by the song-forms proper to them.

3. Christian Middle Ages. For Christianity Satan is the enemy and opponent of Christ. Over against the kingdom of God stands the realm of the devils and demons. These latter have their own musical perspective, characterized by cacophony and disharmony. Demonic and devilish music are, however, at the same time, antithetically related to celestial music, and virtually presuppose it. They thus equally belong to the order of creation and, after their own fashion, take part in praise of creation, confirming it by contraries. It is for this reason that the realm of Hell together with its music can find a meaningful place in the sculptural decoration of medieval cathedrals. In Dante's *Divina Commedia* the "music" of the Inferno is thus consciously assigned its place.

The specifics of demonic music are taken by the Middle Ages partly from ancient representations of Hades, while others are specifically Christian. They are encountered in literary visions of the other world and in legends, in morality plays, and in art. Typical of "Pandemonium" is its consistently contrasting character: overwhelming volume, eery shrieks, mocking laughter, groans, snarls, rattling of chains, cracking of whips, thunder, howling wind. Instead of playing on tuned instruments the devils prefer noisemakers belonging to a prehistoric and magical world, now discredited and denounced as devilish. They beat on cymbals and pots, ring cowbells, or blow steer horns or animal bones. It bears the same significance when, according to a German folk tradition, the devil plays out-of-tune trombones on the death of witches. Whoever hears such music falls prey to madness. A major role is recurrently played by animal cries and sounds, like the barking of dogs, braying of donkeys, snakes' hissing, and pigs' grunting. Whether explicitly or implicitly, this tonal pandemonium is in the last analysis taken best in contrast to angelic music, to the music of the blessed, of heaven, of paradise.

In the Middle Ages the devil is seen virtually as the ape (*simia*) of God and of the angels. Hence he imitates "apelike" the heavenly and earthly liturgy. He parodies the Latin liturgical songs in order to lead the faithful astray. In some of the morality plays regular parliamentary assemblies in hell were enacted, including dances, acclamations, and chants of praise by the devils before Lucifer enthroned on a barrel, the whole a caricature of the liturgy before God's throne. The themes of angelic music reappear in inverted form in the music of Hell and the devils: from the concord of *una voce* ("unison") is derived discord and disorder; the *sine fine* ("without end") of the jubilus becomes a ceaseless plaint, harmony is made to correspond to discord. The orderly and measured circles of the angelic choruses become a disordered, immoderate leaping and springing (the Devil limps!). The angels move to the right, but the devils to the left, a motion based on the ancient (Orphic) belief that the left is the wrong side.

The devils are as active as the angels as soul-guides, as they conduct the damned to Hell with mocking laughter, howls, contemptuous chants, tuneless music, and grotesque dances. Many representations of the Last Judgment as well as scenes in morality plays display this accompaniment, in which angelic and devilish music are simultaneously heard and seen. The notion of dances of death is undoubtedly related to these conceptions. As minister and deputy of the Devil, Death is made to accompany the living, or those of the dead who have died unprepared and unrepentant on the Day of Judgment, and in the shape and after the manner of a medieval minstrel intones a demonically fascinating music. The inescapable compulsion with which it induces one to dance is an image of the inescapability of death. The dance and play of death, according to medieval convictions, likewise belong to the left, demonic side of music and, like it, are related *e contrario* to music as a divine art.

Not only Hell and the road to it are the scene of demonic-devilish music, but also, and primarily, the mundane world in its concrete actuality. Depending on the viewpoint of the observer and judge, music was repeatedly accounted devilish. Over against spiritual "true" and "good" music, unsatisfactory music was set in opposition as worldly, "false," and "evil." Even Plato, in connection with the Greek doctrine of the "ethos" of different modes and instruments, had distinguished between good music, leading to manliness, and bad, leading to effeminacy and luxury. In Christian times it was not so much certain melodies, modes, or instruments that were accounted demonic or devilish, but rather all heathen religious music altogether, and then came secular and, above all, instrumental music.

To the Church Fathers the devilish nature of heathen cult music was a really outstanding issue. They de- **265** clared it to be a work of demonic deception, chants of the Devil, and contrasted it with the divine and angelic music of Christian psalms and hymns. Clement of Alexandria about A.D. 215 characterized the pagan singers Amphion, Arion, and Orpheus as frauds, for Christ alone was the true Orpheus. The sound of the aulos, the cithara, and the syrinx belong to the Devil's pomp, said John Chrysostom around A.D. 400. Ephraem Syrus (died A.D. 373) says: "Where the chant of psalms resounds in deep contrition, there God is present with His angels. Where the playing of the cithara and dancing occurs, there is a feast of the Devil."

The denunciation of musical instruments as works of the devil, and their rejection for liturgical music led, up to the later Middle Ages, to a difficult problem arising out of the fact that musical instruments are mentioned in Scripture in a wholly favorable light. Above all in the psalms musical instruments are mentioned frequently as tools for praise of God. A few Church Fathers therefore declare that the instruments were once (under the old dispensation) holy but, because of devilish machinations, they had become blasphemous objects. Most authors, however, interpret the instruments mentioned in Psalms allegorically or emblematically by giving them a different meaning (see article "Music as a Divine Art"). They thus liberate them from the offensive character of physically sounding instruments.

Dance and dance music were accused with particular bitterness of diabolism. "The Devil is where the dance is," "the Devil is the patron of the dance," "the dance is the Devil's leap," "the dance is a circle whose center is the Devil." These and similar stereotyped assertions derive from the age of the Fathers until the late Middle Ages and beyond. Their very polemical sharpness is evidence, by the way, of an immense love of dancing that, as we know, did not stop even at the church doors.

Instrument-playing and dance music were in the hands of musicians, who were also called *mimi, joculatores*, or minstrels. They were thus regarded virtually as *ministri Satanae* and were excluded from the stratified societal structure of the Middle Ages. According to the preacher Berthold of Regensburg (thirteenth century) the hierarchy of earthly society corresponds to the celestial hierarchy of the nine choirs of angels. And just as the renegade fallen angels became the choir of devils and went to Hell, so the minstrels are the choir of renegade men. In legends and fairy tales the connection between the devil and minstrel was preserved for a long time as a favorite theme. It is very clearly expressed in Hieronymus Bosch's depictions of Hell. Here musical instruments all but assume the character of torture implements on which the damned

are stretched ("crucified"), or with which they are tormented in other ways. This is pursued undoubtedly in accordance with the old idea that the punishment should be commensurate with the sin and bear a symbolic relationship to it; those succumbing to vanity and sensuous lust, and with them their seducers, the minstrels, are punished with the instruments of their sins.

A distinctive feature of minstrel music and at the same time one of the leading objections to it, is its purely pragmatic character, directed only to practical application. The minstrel lacked real knowledge. He did not understand the speculative aspects of *musica*, its theological context, or the rational and theoretical principles of order that lay at its roots. In contrast to the true *musicus* he is therefore to be compared rather with an irrational animal: *nam qui facit, quod non sapit, diffinitur bestia* (Guido of Arezzo, about 1025).

The interrelated significance that emerges here between Devil, animal, and minstrel, is strikingly characteristic of the Middle Ages. Thus the innumerable representations of music-making animals, demons, and monsters in art are not only manifestations of archetypal conceptions in which recollections of music-making animal divinities in pre-Christian religions surely play a role; nor are they merely an expression of playful fantasy; rather they display in the first place the inverted, demonic-diabolical minstrel aspect of the Christian order in general and of music in particular. The very locus of their appearance outside cathedrals and churches typifies this meaning. Most often they appear outside the west wall, since night and with it most of the demons come from the west; also at the pedestal of the choir, on the cornice, the eaves, the windowsills; and finally, within the church, on the capitals of pillars and the choir pews. The favorite animal musicians are the ape, donkey, bear, dog, hare, and pig; further, compound beings of various animal, and also human, shapes. To these belong also the sirens of Greek legend as the emblem of seductive and diabolical sensuous lust. The most important literary source for all these figures is the Physiologus (or Bestiary) which had appeared in late antiquity. Its medieval versions treated also of the symbolic classification of the partly real, partly fantastic animal figures. In miniatures in books we find representations of dance processions and masquerades in which can be seen music-making minstrels wearing animal masks or skins. In this connection it is also worth recalling that from earliest times down to the modern period valuable musical instruments are found with carved animal figures as decoration. In this too survives the old association of ideas concerning instruments, minstrels, and demonism.

4. Post-medieval Period. The idea of the demonic

power of music reaches well into modern times. It belongs to the *effectus musicae.* Popular traditions preserve it in fairy tales and legends and in customs still surviving today, such as the south German and Swiss Shrovetide celebration with its magical orchestration of rattles, whipcracking, bells, and pigs' bladders. Many tales recount how the Devil enters his victim so as then to be able to shout or sing or cry from within him. This was how the ecstasy of witches was explained; also the so-called St. Vitus' dance, a pathological compulsion to dance that could afflict not only individuals but, like an epidemic, whole groups. More subtly such possession could take the form of melancholy, as had previously been shown by the Bible in its account of David's harp-playing before Saul, a theme that, particularly during the baroque period, was often favored, e.g., in two of Rembrandt's paintings.

The exorcism of demons, devils, or of melancholy by the power of music is based, as we know, on primeval magical conceptions that survive uninterrupted, even though modified, below the surface of the musical perspectives of various periods. Martin Luther, for example, accepts as perfectly real the exorcism of devils by the aid of (spiritual) music: "Should the Devil come again and heap you with care or sad thoughts, defend yourself and say: 'Out, devil, I must now sing and play to my Lord Christ'."

The antithetical polarity of ideas about music as a divine or demonic art respectively survives particularly in the circle of German Protestant musicians of the seventeenth and eighteenth centuries, for example, Michael Praetorius (ca. 1620), Johann Kuhnau, and Andreas Werckmeister (ca. 1700). It still forms part of the basis of Johann Sebastian Bach's thought and oeuvre, while in Italy and France musicians and writers had been for a long time dedicated to more modern and enlightened ideas. The affirmative background of a divine, ordered, and erudite music was long confronted in Germany by a negative evaluation of and attribution of diabolism to minstrels and their baser descendents, the "beer-fiddlers," the "atheists," the "Devil's musicians." Their music was accounted no better than the howling of dogs and wolves, their music was without order, they could "give no *rationes* concerning their own patchwork *harmoniam*," which consisted rather of "a mess, chaos, muddled notions, the whole quite irrational" (Werckmeister). Johann Sebastian Bach's definition of thoroughbass as the foundation of music is well known (1738):

Thoroughbass is the most perfect foundation of music. The left hand plays the prescribed notes while the right hand supplies consonances and dissonances so that a pleasing harmony is produced to the honor of God and a proper delight for the spirit. Like all other music the end and object

of thoroughbass is only for the honor of God and recreation of the spirit. If this is not heeded it is no real music but a devilish howling and tinkling (cf. Ph. Spitta, *Johann Sebastian Bach*, 3rd ed., Leipzig [1921], II, 915).

In the post-baroque period the preconditions of the old metaphysical ideas disappear everywhere, including Germany. Music is henceforth based solely on this-worldly principles, its origin lies in the human heart or within itself. It is the expression of human feelings or cherished for its own sake, a purely aesthetic phenomenon. The idea of music as a demonic art now becomes an empty form, at best a metaphor in which, however, no one any longer believes.

BIBLIOGRAPHY

No comprehensive treatment of this topic exists. However, there are a few works covering particular periods and problems, and these often only skirt the topic.

H. Abert, *Die Musikanschauung des Mittelalters und ihre Grundlagen* (Halle, 1905). R. Dammann, *Der Musikbegriff im deutschen Barock* (Cologne, 1968). Th. Gérold, *Les pères de l'église et la musique* (Paris, 1931). R. Hammerstein, *Die Musik der Engel: Untersuchungen zur Musikanschauung des Mittelalters;* esp. chapter on "Die Musik der Hölle" (Berne and Munich, 1962); idem, "Die Musik in Dantes *Divina Commedia*," *Deutsches Dante-Jahrbuch* 41/42 (Weimar, 1964). E. Langton, *Satan: A Portrait* (London, 1945). J. Quasten, *Musik und Gesang in den Kulten der heidnischen Antike und der christlichen Frühzeit* (Münster, 1930). K. Meyer-Baer, *Music of the Spheres and the Dance of Death. Studies in Musical Iconology* (Princeton, 1970). C. Sachs, *Geist und Werden der Musikinstrumente* (Berlin, 1929); trans. as *History of Musical Instruments* (New York, 1940). H. Schade, *Dämonen und Monstren, Gestaltungen des Bösen in der Kunst des frühen Mittelalters* (Regensburg, 1962). M. Schneider, "Primitive Music," *New Oxford History of Music*, Vol. I (London and New York, 1960). H. Sedlmayr, *Die Entstehung der Kathedrale* (Zurich, 1950).

REINHOLD HAMMERSTEIN

[See also **Demonology;** Dualism; Evil; **Hierarchy; Music as a Divine Art;** Primitivism; **Witchcraft.**]

MUSIC AS A DIVINE ART

THE IDEA of music as a divine art implies that music is not considered on its merits alone, but points beyond itself and man to the divine. Thus music can be understood as an invention of divinities or as a general principle of divine creation. It may be interpreted as an image, imitation, or anticipation of divine or heavenly music. It can be understood as a means of influencing divinities. And, finally, the meaning and mission of music can be realized in cultic praise of the divinity.

Such conceptions are encountered both in magical and in mythical eras, throughout cosmological and theological-metaphysical forms of thought, indeed well into structured philosophical systems. They possess a strongly thematic character, so that their "history" is broadly developed in variations of the same or similar conceptions and perspectives. Nonetheless, shades of meaning may be differentiated in various periods. The idea of music as a divine art is active from the earliest times at least down to the age of baroque in Europe. Thereafter it increasingly becomes a victim of rationalistic skepticism and, after a brief revival in the romantic period, finally yields to a purely this-worldly concept of music. Closely connected with this idea, dependent upon it in many ways, or antithetically presupposed by it, is the idea of music as a demonic art.

1. Primitive Peoples. To the primitive mind the sounds of nature are the voices of spirits, demons, and gods. Their imitation establishes a magical connection with them. Disguising the human voice becomes a tonal "mask" in order to imitate demons or gods in the shape of animals. The same purpose is served by musical instruments. A demon is enclosed within the sounding instrument. The shaman or medicine man who makes use of such sounds is possessed of divine powers, by means of which he can magically conjure up or exorcise evil spirits or demons. With his "music" he can guide the dead (the soul) into another world. Such notions persist well into civilized cultures.

2. Civilized Cultures. The idea of music as a divine art is common to all civilized cultures. Whether this idea developed independently in each of the cultures or arose by reciprocal influences is difficult to say.

Sumerian representations of music-making animals, dating from about 3000 B.C. in Ur, undoubtedly possess a divine and sacred meaning; they probably represent animal gods or at least display their survival in memories of older rites and conceptions. The terms "song" and "religious festival" were represented in Sumerian by the same cuneiform character, the stylized picture of a pagoda-like temple, thus clearly displaying the affinity of meaning.

A connection between music and the divine is quite clear in Egyptian beliefs. The god Thoth divided the world into spheres with his sevenfold "laughter," from which the seven basic sounds (vowels) and the seven strings of the lyre derive. Thoth is also credited as the "inventor" of music and of divine song. Osiris is denominated the god of the sistrum and Hathor the goddess of music and of the dance. Many representations of music-making animals or animal gods point also to divine connections or ancient totemistic

origins. In China music was regarded from antiquity as a transcendent power. The belief in the connection of musical tones with the universe is certainly very old here, even though it can only be documented about 500 B.C. In the idea of a universal harmony primeval notions of the magical power of sounds survive in transformed and spiritualized form. Music, especially ritual music, serves as an indicator of the macro-microcosmic order. "Proper" music sustains the stability of the cosmos as of the state, while the "wrong" music disturbs it. In Indian civilization music is likewise no isolated phenomenon, but is intimately connected with religion, cosmology, and philosophy. A torso of a dancing god dates from the third millennium B.C. In Sanskrit "singing" is called *gangharavidya* (the art of higher beings). According to the Vedic writings (about 1500 B.C.) sound and tone are identical with divine principles of the universe. The primeval musical rhythms of the world are the font of all cosmic energies. The Rigveda says that all things are called into existence by the song of praise composed by the gods. The creator god Pragápati creates the waters with his voice. As a world principle of creation sound is symbolized in post-Vedic times in the syllable OM. It dwells in the divinity (Shiva) as well as in the human heart. One can be guided by music to the divine principles of the cosmos.

3. Greek Culture. In Greek the very name of music (= the art of the Muses) points to its divine origin. From Homer to an advanced period the Muses were regarded as divine beings sprung from the union of Zeus and Mnemosyne (= memory, recollection). They belong to Zeus' Olympian domain and sing of the origins of things, of the lives of the gods, and of the fate of men. Their leader is Apollo (Musagetes), a god in human (not animal) shape bearing a lyre, inventor of music. Those touched by Apollo and the Muses compose and sing praise of the gods. Sons of Apollo by a Muse are Linos and Orpheus. Other divinities also bear a relationship to music. Hermes invented the lyre and gave it to Apollo, retaining the syrinx for himself and his son Pan as shepherd gods. Dionysos' connection with music is less specific than Apollo's, but still he is ranked as inventor of the dithyramb. Music is more important among his followers, the satyrs and maenads; it was the latter who tore to pieces the unfortunate Apollonian singer Orpheus. Among the Greeks the dance of gods, Muses, nereids, and nymphs is often mentioned and depicted along with music. Particular importance is attributed to the singing or instrument-playing sirens as the "Muses of the other world." Their home is thought of as located in Hades, as well as in space. In their role as singing guides of souls they are associated with death. Originally in the form of animals (birds), they came to assume human shape. A related notion is documented in Book XII of the *Odyssey:* the sirens as death-bringing singing monsters. Their function as musical soul-guides is transferred to the angels in Christianity.

The idea of a correspondence between macro- and microcosmic music, which had already been familiar to the ancient oriental cultures, appears to have been developed first by the Greeks into a more rationally structured system. Plato adopts something of a middle position between mythos and logos (*Republic* 616–17): the music of the heavenly bodies (harmony of the spheres) arises because on each of the eight spheres a siren is sitting who produces a particular note. But above all, scientific cosmological speculation is associated with the name of Pythagoras, according to whom the divine world order is maintained by harmonic numbers. They correspond to the fundamental relationships in music (1:2 = an octave; 2:3 = a fifth; 3:4 = a fourth) and determine both the harmony of the spheres and musical assonance, the balance of the seasons, the elements, body and soul as well as spiritual powers, temperaments, and human ethos. By means of the numerical proportions in music the analogical character of everything that exists can be known and demonstrated. Music thus attains philosophical status, revealing knowledge of the world. The whole world appears to the Greek as a harmonious cosmos held together by musical number. At the apex stands the orderly rotation of the stars sounding in spherical orbit, which are the prototype and model for all existence and therewith for human music and dance.

In the hands of Neo-Pythagoreans and Neo-Platonists these ideas become symbolic and mystical in later antiquity. The harmonic numbers are taken to be supernatural beings. Different sounds, numbers, and songs pertain to different gods, who can be reached by these means (Iamblichos). Music can lead to unity with the divine and establishes the connection with the divine intercessors. A network of musical and symbolic numerical relationships is drawn about the visible and invisible, the sensuous and spiritual, world: the number One, for example, signifies the beginning and fundament of harmony; Two is opposition, the manifold, division, the source of all consonance; Three is perfection, beginning, middle, and end, the true regulator of music; Four is the four elements, the seasons, all perfect assonances; Seven is the foundation of all manifestations of sound in the cosmos, the planets, the strings of the lyre, etc. In addition to the harmonic numbers, musical instruments are symbolically interpreted. The cosmos is seen as the instrument of god, as is the individual human being on whom divinity plays. Before birth the soul has heard the divine harmonies, and recognizes them by contemplation of perfect numerical relationships. The musician ($\mu o \upsilon \sigma \iota \kappa \acute{o} \varsigma$)

is elevated by this knowledge from sensuous to spiritual beauty.

4. Christian Middle Ages. The Old Testament visions of Isaiah and Ezekiel display the one Jahweh, worshipped by seraphim and cherubim in service and praise. This praise is not perceived as "beautiful" music, but as numinous sounding and ringing of overpowering volume. The singing of the Gloria by the angels on the birth of Christ allowed the heavenly chant to be heard on earth. Revelation contains the description of an entire liturgy in heaven undoubtedly containing elements of Jewish and early Christian liturgies. The performers of this heavenly music are the four "beasts" (throne bearers), the twenty-four Elders, and above all the angels. They sing the threefold "Holy," the "new song," Amen and Alleluia. The instruments are the cithara and the tuba, the latter in its magical function of heralding plagues.

What is new and characteristic of Christian thought is the idea of the celestial liturgy. Its significance and therewith the significance of all Christian music is praise of the Creator. Its climax is the singing angel. For the whole of the Middle Ages the angel is the origin, prototype, and eternal goal of all earthly liturgical music. Its divinity, its dignity, and its power are all founded in the angel.

The angels sing *alter ad alterum* ("to one another"), *sine fine* ("without end"), *una voce* ("unison"). These labels became central themes, repeatedly employed down to the baroque era and realized again and again in the liturgical music of the Church. Of the liturgical chants the ones that were assimilated repeatedly to the angelic music were preferably the Gloria, the Sanctus (in which, according to the preceding text of the Preface, the praise of the faithful is united with that of the angels), but also psalms and hymns. From time immemorial similar treatment was accorded to the wordless Jubilus, the melismatic Alleluia, and together with these the related musical forms dating from Carolingian times and later: sequence, tropus, polyphony, all regarded as particularly closely related to the angelic song. In addition to the intimate connection with the liturgical music of the Church, the function of the angels, singing, playing, and dancing as they guide the soul to the other world, was of great importance for the entire Middle Ages.

The ideas of angelic music, its themes and motifs are, owing to the Bible, the Fathers, and the liturgical texts, in their essence of extraordinarily stable, and all but invariable, continuity. About this essence an illimitably varied range of developments and ornamentation appears in literature and art.

Visions and otherworldly migrations describe the heavenly music in ever-new variations. Here there is a combination of ancient (Elysium) and Irish-Celtic fairy tale traditional themes (singing trees, sounding pillars and rocks, self-playing instruments, etc.) with the liturgical themes. Dante's *Divina Commedia*, that great compendium of such traditions, contains a systematic array of many such liturgical and nonliturgical motifs. In the rich literature of legend the theme of guide to the soul is frequently encountered. Sometimes, in addition to the singing angels, Christ also appears as a minstrel or dancer to receive and guide the soul with music. In the liturgical drama springing directly from the liturgy, angelic music is brought to the eye and ear. With their Latin chants the angels survive even in the later vernacular morality plays down to the sixteenth century as representatives of liturgical and therewith of celestial music.

In art the representations of the celestial liturgy, or of the singing angels, begin at the altar zone (mosaics or frescos), i.e., at the point in the church building where the connection between the heavenly and the earthly liturgy is established. They are to be found in increasing numbers in illustrations of liturgical books (miniatures), in Romanesque and Gothic cathedral sculpture, in stained glass and frescos, and finally in panel paintings. Whether represented with scrolls, books, or (increasingly from the thirteenth century on) with musical instruments, angelic music is always understood to be song, with the exception of the tuba, canonized by the Bible in the representation of the Day of Judgment. In the course of a general development of style from the fourteenth century on, the realistic nature of the depictions becomes more emphatic. Representations of celestial music increasingly resemble the earthly music, even though the liturgical sense long remains constant. However, the music-making angel increasingly becomes, beginning with the Italian Renaissance, a freely available theme, ornament, and decorative motif. In baroque painting (panel paintings, dome and ceiling frescos, organ fronts) the ancient theme rises once again to a significant level before completely declining.

The theological symbolism of the Middle Ages was concerned with particular intensity since patristic times with musical instruments. This is undoubtedly connected with the contradiction that arose from the circumstance that on the one hand the Bible, particularly Psalms, seemed to have canonized and approved musical instruments as tools of divine praise, while on the other hand they had been rigorously excluded from the church liturgy since the days of early Christianity. Thus they were given an allegorical or symbolic meaning derived either from their names, shapes, material, or sound. For example, the psalter instruments were taken in their totality as symbols of Christianity, the tuba as God's Word, the psaltery as God's tongue or

as the body of Christ, its triangular shape as symbol of the Trinity, the cithara as Christ's Cross or as a symbol of the *vita activa*, the tympanum as mortification of the flesh, cymbals as lips in praise of God. Even the innumerable depictions of king David playing the harp do not possess the nature of a realistic portrayal as much as a symbolic and attributive significance.

The specifically Christian conceptions are frequently in reference to, but also in competition with, the ideas deriving from ancient thought concerning the numerically ordered harmonious cosmos as transmitted to the Middle Ages, above all in the classification of music by Boethius (died A.D. 524): uppermost stands the *musica mundana* of the heavenly bodies, below that comes *musica humana* primarily displayed in the harmonious balance of body and soul, and finally *musica instrumentalis*, actual music, produced with the help of "tools" (*instrumenta!*)—the voice and musical instruments, and in which the same numerical proportions prevail as in the foregoing higher levels of music. The dualism of ancient and Christian ideas is unmistakable: on the one hand the music of the universe with the harmony of the spheres; on the other the celestial-earthly liturgy with the music of the angels at its peak. The ancient cosmological concept of music retained even in the Middle Ages its theoretical and philosophical orientation—music was classed in the system of *artes liberales* as the science of tonal numbers in the quadrivium along with arithmetic, astronomy, and geometry, whereas the theological concept of liturgical music was tied more to practice. Not until the later Middle Ages was the attempt made to conceive of both sides systematically as one (Jacobus of Liège) or poetically as one (Dante): Jacobus in his *Speculum musicae* (before 1330) by expanding Boethius' tripartite division by a further (higher) level, *musica coelestis vel divina;* Dante, in his *Divina Commedia* (ca. 1310) by harmonizing the song of angels, celestial liturgy, harmony of the spheres, and actual earthly music. Toward the end of the Middle Ages the numerical musical speculation of quadrivium is increasingly abandoned—the numerical structural principles of concrete composition were of greater interest to musicians than the laws of the harmony of the spheres—while the ideas of the celestial liturgy and its connection with the earthly liturgy being closer to actual practice survived longer.

5. Reformation. To Martin Luther music is God's creation implanted in the world from the beginning. Its purpose is praise of God. Thus it is most intimately related to theology. A characteristic of Luther's attitude towards music in opposition to the medieval tradition is a strongly eschatological tendency. The relationship of heavenly and earthly music does not appear to him as it did then in the sense of becoming one (as, for example, in the Sanctus of the Mass) or of participation, but rather at most as a hint or foretaste of the heavenly chorus in which the faithful join after death. Calvin likewise emphasizes the divine origin of music as a gift of God, but is at the same time suspicious of it. In clearly purist tones he warns against its dangers, above all those of sensual lust and vanity. It is useful only where it is employed in fear of God for praise and thanks.

6. The Baroque. Ancient and medieval ideas undergo a powerful revival, albeit with characteristic transformations, in the baroque era, especially in the circles of theoreticians, cantors, and organists of German Protestantism. Once again cosmology and theology are combined. God appears as the initiator of a numerically ordered Creation. The whole world is allegorically represented as a monumental organ played upon by the Creator Himself (cf. Athanasius Kircher, 1650). Robert Fludd (1574–1637) describes the harmony of the world as *monochordum mundanum.* The great astronomer, Johann Kepler still strongly believed in a universal harmony of the world and tried to demonstrate it scientifically. In the third and fifth books of his *Harmonices mundi* (1619) he associates the planetary orbits with musical harmonics and presents them in musical notation. Like Pythagoras he also uses the monochord as an instrument of proof. He furthermore calculates by transposition of the numerical values of planetary orbits tonic notes and scales for music theory. The over-all harmony of all the planets virtually serves him as a proof of the existence of God.

As with Kepler, other authors likewise assimilate the preexistent numerical order and its "sound" not only generally to all creation, but also make it the foundation of all music theory, indeed even of every proper musical fabric, of every composition. Thus the totality of intervals is thought of as a graduated structure leading from *unitas* via the perfect and imperfect assonances to the dissonances and nonharmonic relationships. A particular role is played in this by the *trinitas* or *trias harmonica* (= triad) as a fundamental musical phenomenon whose trinitarian theological symbolic meaning is constantly being referred to. Symbolic theological perspectives penetrate even into details of stylistic and performance practice. Michael Praetorius, for example, esteems the employment of several alternating choruses "because the method of singing *per choros* is in truth the proper heavenly way of making music." Polychoral music-making is thus "at the same time an anticipation and taste of heavenly joys." This is simply a highly contemporary interpretation of the old *alter ad alterum.* At the same time

one recognizes once again the typical eschatological feature of Protestant musical perspective: that earthly music furnishes only a premonition of the heavenly, for only after a blessed death will the faithful pass utterly into the "heavenly chorus."

In Germany such ideas, along with the cosmological thought of the quadrivium, remained alive as late as the milieu and work of Johann Sebastian Bach. But the Italians and also the French turned away earlier and more logically from them to more modern musical concepts which saw the significance of music and of the musical work of art not so much in its transcendence and symbolic character but rather in its this-worldly quality, as an aesthetic object, as *absoluta cantilena,* serving the expression of human emotions. In a polemical play on the well-known motto *ad majorem Dei gloriam,* the Italian composer Marco Scacchi (born 1602), for example, proposes, in a letter, that the composer should rather write *ad majorem Musicae artis gloriam.*

7. Post-baroque. With the Enlightenment, Storm and Stress, and classicism, the preconditions for the metaphysic of music finally disappeared, even in Germany. Only romanticism still bears, if only in a markedly secularized, poetic, or mystically colored form, a late reverberation of the old ideas—when music, for example, is taken to be a mere symbol of infinity, as an "expression of endless longing" (E. T. A. Hoffman), as a "sonorous world-Idea" (Schopenhauer). On the other hand romanticism and late romanticism completely dissolved the religious and universalistic ties by placing music, along with art generally, virtually in the place occupied by religion and metaphysics, as in the case of Richard Wagner and others. Post-baroque musical thought conceives of its subject-matter only as a this-worldly phenomenon, as an aesthetic object, whether it is henceforth thought of as the expression of human feelings, as something autonomous, as "sonorous motile form" (Hanslick), or as a product of societal structures and processes. The spiritual reference of music has experienced in the history of ideas a good many vicissitudes of consciousness from magic via cosmology, theology, philosophy of Nature, to aesthetics and sociology. Today the old ideas of music as a divine art have disappeared, and can at best be completely grasped in the course of an historical understanding of older music and musical perspectives.

BIBLIOGRAPHY

There is no previous monograph on the subject of this article. Only in the case of particular periods or problems are there a few specialized accounts which, however, are often only remotely connected with the topic.

H. Abert, *Die Musikanschauung des Mittelalters und ihre Grundlagen* (Halle, 1905). E. Buschor, *Die Musen des Jenseits* (Munich, 1944). R. Dammann, *Der Musikbegriff im deutschen Barock* (Cologne, 1968). H. G. Farmer, "The Music of Ancient Mesopotamia," "The Music of Ancient Egypt," *The New Oxford History of Music*, Vol. I (London and New York, 1960). Th. Gérold, *Les pères de l'église et la musique* (Paris, 1931). R. Hammerstein, *Die Musik der Engel. Untersuchungen zur Musikanschauung des Mittelalters* (Berne and Munich, 1962); idem, "Die Musik in Dantes *Divina Commedia*," *Deutsches Dante-Jahrbuch*, **41/42** (Weimar, 1964). K. Meyer-Baer, *Music of the Spheres and the Dance of Death. Studies in Musical Iconology* (Princeton, 1970). W. F. Otto, *Die Musen und der göttliche Ursprung des Singens und Sagens* (Düsseldorf and Cologne, 1955). L. Picken, "The Music of Far Eastern Asia," "The Music of India," *The New Oxford History of Music*, Vol. I (London and New York, 1960). J. Quasten, *Musik und Gesang in den Kulten der heidnischen Antike und der christlichen Frühzeit* (Münster, 1930). C. Sachs, *Geist und Werden der Musikinstrumente* (Berlin, 1929); trans. as *History of Musical Instruments* (New York, 1940); idem, *The Rise of Music in the Ancient World, East and West* (New York, 1943). R. Schäfke, *Geschichte der Musikästhetik* (Berlin, 1934). M. Schneider, "Primitive Music," *The New Oxford History of Music*, Vol. I (London and New York, 1960). M. Wegner, *Das Musikleben der Griechen* (Berlin, 1949). W. Wiora, *The Four Ages of Music* (New York, 1965).

REINHOLD HAMMERSTEIN

[See also Baroque in Literature; Dualism; **God;** Hierarchy; **Holy;** Macrocosm and Microcosm; **Music as a Demonic Art;** Neo-Platonism; Pythagorean . . .; Religion, Origins, Ritual.]

MYTH IN ANTIQUITY

IMAGINATION plays a large part in all thought as myth does in all civilization. Although abstract thought developed much later than myth, it never completely excludes mythical thought.

Every civilization, even of a very elementary kind, has its myths, which the members of the group share in common; these myths enter into their lives, feeding their emotional reactions and their intelligence (Lévy-Bruhl, Lévi-Strauss, Cazeneuve).

Myths have flourished throughout the ancient world, from India to Egypt, passing on to Chaldea and Crete. The Hebrews had a very remarkable way of refining mythical thought. However, it was Greece that offered one of the most characteristic types of an elaborately structured and organized mythology (Ramnoux). Although Plato speaks about myth with a certain amount of irony, nevertheless mythology along with Greek religion nourished the arts, literature, and many philo-

sophical expository texts; among the most outstanding were those written by the Master of the Academy.

We are in a better position today to understand how classical mythology grew so rich through the juxtaposition and fusion of diverse elements and traditions stemming from prehistorical migrations.

First to be discerned is a distinctively Greek element of an agnatic type associated with certain essentially masculine aspects of deities: Zeus (cf. Cook), Poseidon, and Hades; of complex figures like Hermes (cf. Vernant). In the second place, Cretan and Asiatic influences introduced various representatives of the Great Goddess of Fertility (cf. Przyluski), accompanied by a male creature, a young God who is born and dies. We recognize here not only Hyacinthus but also certain traits of Zeus born on Mount Ida. Diverse representations of the Great Goddess with slightly different characteristics appear juxtaposed, such as Artemis the Huntress, Guardian of wild beasts, and Hecate the Terrible, Ilithyia the Goddess of Childbirth; also Aphrodite, undoubtedly Helen, and Demeter embodying so many different features. Athena is the Guardian of Athens as Hera is Lady of Argos, and many other examples can be cited.

Finally, a third element should be added, namely, the great deities of Oriental origin, who came a little later; these include Apollo and especially Dionysus in certain respects.

Herodotus tells us (*Historiae* II, 53) that Homer and Hesiod created the genealogy and organization of these deities. Indeed Olympus is a world similar to the one in which the epic poets sing to their lords. These Olympians are young, as Aeschylus' *Prometheus* reminds us. Younger still is the cult of Dionysus, who is hardly mentioned by Homer but whose exploits are so well depicted in the *Bacchantes* of Euripides. The mystical growth of this cult revived and enhanced some very old tendencies and certain features crop up again in the mysteries of Eleusis.

In recent years the role played by social factors, ritual, and often simply gestures is recognizable in the beginnings of such representations. The spinning act of Clotho, for example, has been shown to give birth to the legend of Ariadne and Theseus who was guided by a thread through the labyrinth of Daedalus (in order to escape after killing the Minotaur), and then in the myth of Anankē (Necessity) which appears even in Plato's *Republic*. This mythic theme calls for further research and promises some new and interesting results. Although an act, including the ritual act, often illustrates and makes concrete the meaning of a myth, it is also true that a myth is sometimes grafted on an act or a gesture which is no longer understood; the myth serves as a commentary or explanation which may present a rather novel interpretation of it (Schuhl, *Fabulation platonicienne* [1968], pp. 70f.; *L'imagination* . . . [1969], pp. 151f., 155f.).

Mythology provides a simple explanation of many psychological phenomena, for example, of aspirations attributed to divine suggestion; it also furnishes explanations of physical or meteorological phenomena and of cosmology in general. Thunder is explained as caused by Zeus shaking his aegis in anger.

For this type of interpretation the philosophers of Miletus substituted a different one, also simple but of an exclusively physical order: thunder is due to the wind escaping from the clouds, and elementary mechanisms explain the cosmic system. In order to explain the movement of heavenly bodies, the Milesian philosophers resort to analogical models of a mechanical sort. Anaximenes evokes the motion of a cap that a man causes to turn around his head; Anaximander imagines the earth surrounded by moving wheels, hollow and full of fire. This sort of thinking is, of course, still imaginative and analogical, but it is quite different from that of the poets.

The pre-Socratic philosophers were not the only ones to produce a new type of explanation (although an Empedocles often appears to come very close to myth making). There were also those who criticized very sharply classical types of mythical representation. The case of Xenophanes is most striking; himself an epic poet, he criticized violently the immorality of the Homeric gods who indulge in adultery, deception, theft, and so many other iniquitous acts. Against these imaginary creatures he envisages a quite different type of deity, extremely abstract and pure, entirely free from anthropomorphism (Schuhl, *Essai* . . . [1934], p. 275). Pythagoras, for his part, would have the souls of Homer and of Hesiod chastized in Hell as a punishment for what they had said about the gods (Pépin, pp. 93–94).

Plato takes up his share of this criticism, accentuates and sharpens it with unusual vigor, especially in the *Republic*. For an author of so many famous myths Plato's criticism is paradoxical, but the paradoxical appearance may be explained. There is no doubt in Plato's philosophy that ideal realities are intelligible and invisible whereas the sensory world is visible and unintelligible (*Republic* 507b). Though myth possesses an incantational force which undoubtedly makes it dangerous, it is also useful and effective when employed for the good (Boyancé). When thus employed myth can help one grasp certain abstract relations even though it cannot cause one to understand the highest truths, for such understanding is impossible so long as one is in the domain of the senses (*Statesman* 285e).

Thus it is possible to show the role played by a scheme of proportions in some myths of the type $a:b::c:x$, which directs one towards the unknown fourth term (Schuhl, 1968). Above all, myth opens the door to suggestive representations which though not true offer analogies with the truth, at least when presumed. A particular illustration of this point is seen in all the myths relating to the soul and its survival after death, notably in Plato's *Gorgias*, *Phaedo*, *Laws* (X, 904a) *Republic* (Book X), and *Phaedrus* (246a). Plato remarks that it is very difficult to explain the nature of the soul but that it is possible to give an image of it in the myth of the winged horses and their charioteer, symbolizing the soul and its parts. More generally, everything concerning the physical is, for Plato, of a mythical order, as is shown by the *Timaeus*.

As for Aristotle, we find him remarking at the beginning of his *Metaphysics* (A2, 982b 18) that the lover of myths is a philosopher of a sort (Schuhl [1969], p. 7; Pépin, p. 21). In fact, myth through its wondrous nature thrives on the sense of wonder which is the beginning of all philosophy. Myths have been too prolific undoubtedly but they may serve to convey certain valuable suggestions which need to be interpreted and scanned critically in some manner. One instance is the pre-Socratic belief in the divine nature of primary substances, a belief which was later submerged by developments which gave the gods a human or animal form (Aristotle, *Metaphysics* Λ, 8, 1074b 1; Pépin, pp. 121–22). In a similar fashion Aristotle offers a symbolic interpretation of the myth of Uranus and Gaia (*Generation of Animals* 1, 2, 716a 13) as well as of the myth of the Golden Chain. He recognizes in the first myth an image of Heaven fertilized by Earth. As for the Golden Chain, in the eighth book of the *Iliad* Zeus reveals his strength by pulling the chain up towards himself even though all the other gods are suspended from the chain; and Aristotle sees in this myth a symbol of the prime mover, the unmoved cause of all motion (*On the Motion of Animals*, IV, 699b 32; Pépin, pp. 121, 123).

Returning to other disciples of Socrates, we find Antisthenes the Cynic had taken to interpreting, for the sake of illustrating his own moral ideas, myths like that of Heracles and the centaur Chiron, as well as that of Ulysses in his resistance to the charms of the sorceresses Circe and Calypso. Antisthenes in poetic language discriminated meanings in accord with opinion in favor of hidden meanings in accord with truth. He was followed by his disciple Diogenes who in his turn interpreted the legend of Circe trying in vain to seduce Ulysses; the companions of Ulysses were transformed into beasts, thus symbolizing the soul enslaved by pleasure and unable to liberate itself. Diogenes also interpreted the myth of Medea in whom he saw a magical benefactor skilled in the art of rejuvenating her patients (Pépin, pp. 107–11); Diogenes' acceptable interpretation is derived mainly from Dio Chrysostom, *Discourses* (8, 21); Xenophon's *Memorabilia* (I, 3, 7) attributes such interpretations to Socrates.

We find analogous ideas about myth among the Stoics. Zeno adopts anew the distinction between expressions of meaning conforming to truth and those conforming to opinion. He tries, for example, to furnish an interpretation of the names of the Titans. Cleanthes and Chrysippus in turn and in their own respective ways, interpret the name of Apollo; Chrysippus goes on to interpret the names of the Fates (Moerae) and of Destiny. In the second book of Cicero's *De natura deorum*, Balbus in expounding the Stoic view, explains that products like wheat and wine have been deified (Ceres and Liber); but so also have been benefactors like Hercules and Aesculapius as well as the more or less moral qualities or virtues, physical realities, and natural forces (Pépin, pp. 125, 127f.). The study of etymology (often quite capricious, especially in the above interpretations of Zeno, Cleanthes, and Chrysippus) enables us to recognize in these interpretations symbols of the forces of nature, of psychological and moral attitudes, and also to see in the elements of nature some of the greater realities.

In the small *Manual of Theology* of Cornutus, the teacher of the poet Persius (first century of the Christian era), we find many examples of these physical and moral interpretations: Kronos (κρόνος) is time (χρόνος), etc. (Pépin, pp. 156f., 159f. deals with the physical and psychological interpretations through the allegorical road of the myths of Homer, even the most scabrous.)

Epicurus distrusted myths in general, especially those about life after death, which frighten and upset the soul. The Epicurean Colotes reproached Plato and the philosophers employing fictions which amounted to lies (Macrobius, *Commentarium in somnium Scipionis*, I, II, 1–3 in Pépin, pp. 131f., 134f.). Proclus also mentions this criticism and tries to refute it (Kroll, II, 96–109; Pépin, 138).

In Book I of *De natura deorum* Cicero has Velleius summarize the Epicurean criticism of myth, which scolds the Stoics for transforming mythology into physics (Pépin, pp. 125–27). And, in the excavations of Herculaneum were found chapters of the treatise on piety by Philodemus (first century B.C.) reproaching the Stoics for abandoning anthropocentrism and polytheism (*De pietate* 17–18; Pépin, pp. 133–34). Epicurus contrasts the Gods of popular theology with the sage's own refined and purified view of them (Letter to Meneclus, Diogenes Laërtius 123–24; cf. Festugière, 1946).

The New Academy, on the other hand, criticizes the Stoics for seeking to save an untenable religion. And so, in the third book of Cicero's *De natura deorum*, Cotta (the spokesman for Carneades) attacks the arguments of Balbus in Book II, and opposes the proliferation of so many deities, so many deifications of men and foods, of values and desires; he underscores the artificial nature of Balbus' arguments. About the end of the second century A.D. the skeptic Sextus Empiricus continued this criticism (Pépin, 141–43).

Finally, Plotinus often uses myths as a medium for the expression of his thought. He was well aware of what Plato had said in the *Timaeus*, namely, that myth exhibits in a temporal order factors coexistent in reality (*Enneads* III 5, 9, 24–29; Pépin, p. 191). He also insists that the highest reality is ineffable (*Enneads* V 5, 6, 11–13, VI 9, 4; Pépin, p. 190). Among the myths utilized by Plotinus we find that the birth of Eros, in Plato's *Symposium*, figures prominently; but also the myth of Lethe and the Fates, in Plato's *Republic*, without counting various myths like that of Narcissus (the soul attracted to its reflection in matter) and those of Cybele, Prometheus, Pandora, and Heracles. The horrible story of Uranus, Kronos, and Zeus plays the role of symbolizing the three hypostases of Plotinus!

The foregoing is a brief sketch of the manner in which Greek myths provided philosophers with ample material. The creative period of mythology is being only gradually understood, thanks to the researches of various specialists and scholars in comparative studies, archeologists, historians, and sociologists whose findings converge gradually on the truth. Among the continuing investigations of the 1960's the works of J. P. Vernant are outstanding; he has been able to utilize social psychology and the history of thought, illuminating archeology and philology.

We have not reached the creative period of new myths; we have before us myths that have already been elaborated. The further evolution of myth will have its affiliation with the evolution of the arts and of literature (Schuhl, *L'imagination . . .*, pp. 35ff.). To the great classical sculptors even the infant is beautiful. To Praxiteles the Apollo Sauroctonos is a graceful Ephebus and the monster is only a lizard. And so in Homer the libidousness of the gods presents a scene similar in kind to the life of the libertines of the seventeenth century. And for the philosophers myth serves as a means for suggesting ideas. The greatest artists and thinkers have learned how to create masterpieces by means of myths, thus proving that the imagination can be useful in assisting the intellect.

BIBLIOGRAPHY

Pierre Boyancé, *Le culte des muses chez les philosophes grecs* (Paris, 1937). Victor Brochard, *Les mythes dans la philosophie de Platon,* Études de philosophie ancienne et moderne (Paris, 1912). Jean Cazeneuve, *Les rites et la condition humaine* (Paris, 1957); idem, *La mentalité archaïque* (Paris, 1961). A. B. Cook, *Zeus, A Study in Ancient Religion,* 3 vols. (Cambridge, I, 1914; II, 1925; III, 1940). Jean Festugière, *Épicure et ses dieux* (Paris, 1946). Perceval Frutiger, *Les mythes de Platon* (Paris, 1930). Claude Lévi-Strauss, *Les structures élémentaires de la parenté* (Paris, 1949); idem, *Tristes tropiques* (Paris, 1955); idem, *Anthropologie structurale* (Paris, 1958); idem, *La pensée sauvage* (Paris, 1962); idem, *Mythologiques,* I, *Le cru et le cuit* (Paris, 1964); II, *Du miel aux cendres* (Paris, 1967); III, *L'origine des manières de table* (Paris, 1968). Lucien Lévy-Bruhl, *Les fonctions mentales dans les sociétés inférieures* (Paris, 1910); idem, *La mentalité primitive* (Paris, 1922); idem, *L'âme primitive* (Paris, 1927); idem, *Le surnaturel et la nature dans la mentalité primitive* (Paris, 1931); idem, *La mythologie primitive* (Paris, 1935). Jean Pépin, *Mythe et allégorie* (Paris, 1958). Clémence Ramnoux, *Mythologie, la famille olympienne* (Paris, 1962); idem, *La nuit et les enfants de la nuit dans la tradition grecque* (Paris, 1958); idem, *Études présocratiques* (Paris, 1970). Pierre-Maxime Schuhl, *Essai sur la formation de la pensée grecque* (Paris, 1934; 2nd ed. 1949); idem, *La fabulation platonicienne,* 2nd ed. (Paris, 1968); idem, *L'imagination et le merveilleux* (Paris, 1969). J.-P Vernant, *Mythe et pensée chez les Grecs, études de psychologie* (Paris, 1965); idem, *Les origines de la pensée grecque* (Paris, 1962).

PIERRE-MAXIME SCHUHL

[See also **Analogy;** Chain of Being; Cosmic Images; **Myth;** Platonism.]

MYTH IN BIBLICAL TIMES

The Forms of Folk Narrative. Myth has a broad and a narrow sense: the transcendent sense of its total ambience and meaning, and the tangible sense of the documents in which it is studied. Only by beginning with the narrow sense can we move securely to the broad. Tangibly considered, myth is only one form of folk narrative, an oral tale written down. Viewed from outside the sphere of belief as pure fiction, it is often confused with the wider sphere of folktale, or said to be the ancestor of all other folktales.

Folk narrative, however, contains many genres. Halliday (1933) found many varieties in the Greek mythic texts, and Gunkel (1901) long before did the same for Genesis. Folklorists speak of animal tale, proverb, riddle, *Märchen,* novella, jest, local legend, saint's legend, and saga. Ancient Mediterranean culture contains them all: animal tale in Aesop, Noah's dove and raven, an Egyptian text on the origin of unclean animals (Pritchard [1950], p. 10); proverbs in Ecclesi-

astes and Proverbs and Ecclesiasticus, in Heraclitus, the Egyptian Ani, the Aramaic Ahiqar (Pritchard, pp. 412–30); riddles in the stories of Samson (Judges 14:8), Oedipus and the Sphinx, Solomon and Sheba (II Chronicles 9 and a Muslim version in the *Arabian Nights*); the novella or realistic tale in the Egyptian Two Brothers (Pritchard, p. 23) and Joseph and Potiphar's Wife or the Egyptian Rhampsinitus in Herodotus (ii, 21); the *Märchen* or fairy tale in other parts of the Two Brothers, the Greek Perseus story, the Babylonian *Gilgamesh* and *Etana* (Pritchard, pp. 72, 114), the poison maiden (*vagina dentata*) and Grateful Dead Man of the apocryphal Book of Tobit; the jests of Aesop, Aristophanes and the parables of Jesus, the Ugaritic tale of Aqhat (Pritchard, p. 149) and Jacob's tricks with Laban; the local legends describing the origin of places in Jacob's wrestling with the angel at Bethel, Lot's Wife and the Destruction of Sodom, Theseus and the Minotaur in the Cretan labyrinths, Marduk and the building of Babylon in the Akkadian Creation epic *Enuma Elish* (Pritchard, p. 68) and the Tower of Babel; the saints' legends of Elijah, the Acts of the Apostles, the Seven Sleepers, the apocryphal *Martyrdom of Isaiah* (Charles [1913], II, 159); and the sagas or linked hero-tales of Hercules, Theseus, Jason and the Argonauts, Samson, David, Abraham, Moses and Gilgamesh. Gunkel and Mowinckel (Gunkel, 1901; Rowley [1951], p. 162) have shed great light on the Old Testament, especially the lyrical Psalms, with the approach known as "form-criticism." Seen in its folkloristic and literary aspects the Bible has vastly different meaning than when its books were thought to have been composed all of a piece by a Moses, a David, or a Solomon.

Though all these forms are in the Bible and in other Mediterranean narrative collections, as well as in modern oral tales and what we call the Bible of the Folk (pseudepigrapha, Muslim and Mandaean writings, Rabbinical and patristic legend), the crucial question of myth is best understood if we concentrate on three types: myth, *Märchen,* legend. Regarded not by the "neutral" scholar but by the participating believer myth is sacred truth, legend adorned history, and *Märchen* plain fiction. Only to the alien or the too-late born is myth fiction. Regarded in the light of function and purpose myth and ritual are religious reinforcements of the social bond; legend, which informs us of our ancestry and of the migration of peoples, is instructive; *Märchen* is purely for entertainment. To say that the Bible is rich in all of these is not to impugn its contents, for all are true to man as myth is true to the God or gods in whom he believes.

The Problem of Myth in the Bible. Since myth is sacred tradition, not fiction, the word can be applied to the biblical story by devout Jew or Christian with no loss of faith or respect. Chadwick ([1932–40], II, 629–77) said we rarely go to the Bible for myth because there is so much saga and history in it. To claim it all as sober history would be to destroy its poetry, yet there is much history or "metahistory" there, for the Creation and Flood are about beginnings which certainly did begin, the Crucifixion refers to a historical event whatever one might say of the Incarnation and Virgin Birth, and to the Last Judgment we would deny the name of "future history" to our peril. In myth the most profound history is that of the psyche of the men who made it, of the societies which it strengthened, of the religious power it has always commanded. Bultmann, Tillich, and other de-mythologizers of the New Testament do not destroy the "kerygma" or preaching of the gospel of Christ (Throckmorton [1960], p. 115); the Wellhausen analyses of the books of the Old Testament into Jehovist, Elohist, and Priestly documents merely bring the myths back a stage or two without destroying their force of mythic thought (Wellhausen, 1878; Pfeiffer, 1941). Each man sees Jesus in the way he needs: Matthew (27:46) saw him in his human qual-

ity ("My God, why hast thou forsaken me?"), Luke (23:34) in his mercy as judge ("Father forgive them; for they know not what they do"); Saint Paul and Saint Augustine as the incarnate junction between flesh and spirit; the early Catacomb paintings as the good shepherd who leaves "the ninety and nine, and goeth into the mountains, and seeketh that which hath gone astray" (Matthew 18:12); the Byzantine tympanum frescoes and mosaics heralded by Henry Adams turn the shepherd into the stern judge of Doomsday; Ezra Pound's *Ballad of the Goodly Fere* views him through the eyes of Simon Zelotes as a strong hero who drives the money changers out of the Temple and eats of the honeycomb; Bruce Barton sees him as the first advertising man; Piero della Francesca's *Resurrection* and the Old English *Dream of the Rood* make him the warrior who overcomes the sleeping soldiers (Figure 1); the sentimental nineteenth century sees him as a beardless boy and Michelangelo's *Pietà* as a corpse converted to the bambino in Mary's arms; Woody Guthrie sings a ballad to the tune of Jesse James in which he is an outlaw who loves the poor and who was killed by the landlords and a dirty little coward called Judas Iscariot. By itself each of these is a reduction of the myth; together they are holistic. Thus the strength of myth lies not in doctrine but in its perpetual re-creation. Myth is "that haunting awareness of transcendental forces peering through the cracks of the visible universe" (Philip Wheelwright, *Daedalus* [1959], p. 360).

As S. H. Hooke says (1963, pp. 11–16) "Myth is a product of human imagination arising out of a definite situation and intended to do something. Hence the right question . . . is not 'Is it true?' but 'What is it intended to do?'" He subdivides myths into five: ritual myths like the Divine King, the slain and resurrected God; origin myths like the invention of music and civilization by Tubal and Jubal; cult myths like Exodus and Passover; prestige myths which "invest the birth and exploits of a popular hero with an aura of mystery and wonder" (Moses, Samson, Jesus); eschatological myths like Armageddon and Antichrist. Such classifications heed origin and function, and their elaboration and adornment from further pagan sources is signalized by Clement of Alexandria (150?–220): "I will give ye understanding of the mysteries of the Logos by means of images with which you are familiar" (Rahner [1963], p. 12). In all cultures myth reinforces the community, but in the great salvation religions like Judaism, Islam, and Christianity it extends the community by conversion.

The Chain of History. We must distinguish between myths in the Bible and myths about the Bible. For every theorist there is something: sky-gods, fertility

FIGURE 1. Piero della Francesca, *The Resurrection*. ca. 1460–70. MUNICIPAL PALACE, SANSEPOLCRO. PHOTO ALINARI–ART REFERENCE BUREAU

ritual, Jungian archetypes. Myth and ritual, eloquently defended by Frazer and Hooke, have under attack been modified somewhat from their original reductionism (Utley, 1960; Fontenrose, 1966); seen now in perspective they have done much to place Old and New Testament in the Mediterranean and Asia Minor religious milieu. But the divine kingship of these historians is fundamentally a matter of origins alone, and though Israel and Christianity were perpetually subject to new injections of the pagan patterns, to stress them as the only aspect of Myth in the Bible is to fall into the genetic fallacy, admired in the nineteenth century but deplored in the configurational and "structural" twentieth. Though we shall not scant its insights, we shall find the rival theory of *Heilsgeschichte*, Salvation-history, or the Chain of History a better scheme by which to present the Bible's variety. Its plenitude, or making of significance in each event in the Bible, is parallel to that plenitude in the universe which Lovejoy called the Chain of Being. The center of the Hebrew Torah and its Christian sequel is the history of God's chosen people and of those who chose to be with Christ. The Christian scheme, so brilliantly outlined in Augustine's *City of God* (413–25 A.D.), is Creation, Fall, Incarnation, Passion, Crucifixion, Atonement, Resurrection, and Last Judgment. This pattern leaves its mark on medieval drama, *Piers Plowman*, and possibly *King Lear, Beowulf*, and William Faulkner's novels.

Less clearly realized is that the same kind of historical philosophy lies behind the sacred books of the Jews, who like the Christians had a religion of development rather than stasis, a "before and after" rather than a mere annalistic account. "The Lord of Creation is also the Lord of History," no local cult god but One bringing victory over all nations (Robinson, I, 406). In the Law and the Prophets we find Creation, Fall, Redemption through Moses, Lawgiving and the Exodus to the Promised Land, the Suffering Servants of Job and the Prophets, the Messianic Hope and the Apocalypse (for the last see Charles, 1913, and above all the Book of Daniel). The Old Testament is a series of the Covenants with God's People. Though the covenanting is eternal, it is dramatized by Noah and his dietary precepts, by Abraham and circumcision, by Moses and the Decalogue, by that travelling shrine, the Ark of the Covenant, which was often believed to contain Yahweh himself, by Aaron and David and the priesthood and the kingship, and by the prophets Jeremiah and Ezekiel, who are unconscious witnesses to the Christian scheme and the Son of Man.

Hundreds of rabbinical legends testify as well to the Chain of History (Ginzberg, 1912–38). Adam's garments, made of light and given him by God before

the Fall or made of the serpent's skin thereafter, descended to Noah through Enoch and Methuselah, were stolen from the Ark of Noah by Ham, were secreted by Ham's son Cush and thence passed to Nimrod. When he wore them he was invincible and irresistible, and man and beast fell down before him (Ginzberg, I, 79–80; V, 102–04). Aaron's rod, which blossomed with ripe almonds and was created by God before the first Sabbath, was inscribed with the Ineffable Name; Moses conserved it with the Ark of Covenant, and the Judean kings used it unto the destruction of the Temple, when it disappeared. Elijah will recover it and hand it to the Messiah (Ginzberg, II, 335–36; VI, 106–07).

The same idea of plenitude is found in the medieval Christian legend of the Cross. Instructed by Adam on his deathbed and by the angel who guarded Paradise, Seth sets out to find the Oil of Mercy, sees a vision where Tree of Life and Fall are one, in which a dry tree gives way to the Child (Oil of Mercy) in its branches. The angel gives him three apple seeds, which he plants under Adam's tongue, and which grow into a trinity of trees, the high cedar or Father, the sweet cypress or Son, and the fruitful pine or Holy Ghost. Moses draws forth the twigs and they become his miraculous rod; he replants them and David finds them growing as one tree; Solomon trims it to a beam which will not fit the Temple since it has another destiny. Told by Sheba to preserve the beam, he throws it as a bridge across a fish-pool; it floats on a healing well which springs forth and there the enemies of Christ find it and manufacture the Holy Rood. This complex legend is vivid typology become literal history, just as Adam's skull, carried by Noah's ark to Calvary, causes the place to be called Golgotha and rests beneath the Cross, where it is baptized by the Savior's blood (Quinn, 1962).

Given this tendency to fill history to proportions worthy of the Almighty, we shall arrange the Bible's myths in an order which allows them both their individual, archetypal significance and their place in the chain.

From Jewish eschatology, transformed in the mind and by the experience of Jesus, Christianity has inherited a moral interpretation of history and of human destiny, a sense of the profound moral crisis arising from the antinomy between the "present age" and the "age to come," and a conviction that God will not rest until the antinomy has been resolved and the creation has been redeemed (Hooke [1956], p. 201).

Prefiguration is no mere rhetorical device or interpretational method: "The Lamb is slain before the tragedies of history ever begin, and the whole of history is viewed at a glance" in God's Eternal Present (Throckmorton, p. 172).

FIGURE 2. Michelangelo, *The Creation*. ca. 1510. SISTINE CHAPEL, VATICAN. PHOTO ALINARI–ART REFERENCE BUREAU

Creation. All the Mediterranean cultures have anthropomorphized Creation as history become myth: Hesiod and Ovid, the Egyptian masturbatory Atum ("thou didst spit out what was Shu, thou didst sputter out what was Tefnut"—Pritchard, p. 3), the Akkadian *Enuma Elish* with ritual combat and copulation between Apsu and Tiamat (Pritchard, p. 60), the accounts of creation in Genesis 1 and 2, *Fiat lux* climaxed with the Sabbath and reinforced by the philosophic *In principio* of the Gospel of John: "In the beginning was the Word, and the Word was with God, and the Word was God. . . . In him was life, and the life was the light of men." It is found in the great tragedy or divine comedy of Job: "Then the Lord answered Job out of the whirlwind, and said . . . Where wast thou when I laid the foundations of the earth? . . . When the morning stars sang together, and all the sons of God shouted for joy?" In Genesis 1, God made sun and moon to rule over the universe, and man to rule over the beasts and whales and cattle (Figure 2); in Genesis 2, He once more created man and planted the primitivistic Eden and let man name them, and "then he made him Eve." Critics speak of these two stories as a priestly ritual account (P) climaxed with the Sabbath, and a more anthropomorphic account (J) of Yahweh, man-centered (Pfeiffer, pp. 129–209; Skinner, pp. 1–70; Speiser, 1924). Yet the subsequent mythic history can treat them as one.

The Fall of Man, Cain and Abel. To the man and woman, naked and unashamed, came the serpent to tempt them to eat the Forbidden Fruit. They fell, both for the sake of pleasure and of wisdom: "And the eyes of them both were opened, and they knew that they were naked; and they sewed fig leaves together, and made themselves aprons." In true oriental fashion the Lord, "walking in the garden in the cool of the day," in his own desert oasis, comes to cross-examine them and show them the folly of their abandoning Innocence for Experience, to use Blakean and Rousseauistic terms. The serpent (not yet clearly Satan) is cursed: "upon thy belly shalt thou go, and dust shalt thou eat all the days of thy life"; the "seed of man shall bruise thy head, and thou shalt bruise his heel." Woman is condemned to pain and sorrow in childbirth and subjection to man; Man, exiled in a land of thorns and thistles must earn his bread "in the sweat of his face" and must return to the dust from which he was created. Fearing that "the man is become as one of us, to know good and evil . . . lest he put forth his hand and take also of the tree of life, and eat, and live forever," Yahweh drove Adam out of the garden and placed Cherubim with a flaming sword "to keep the way of the tree of life." And Adam knew his wife and she conceived and bore Cain, "a man from the Lord."

With all its man-centered naiveté, the story reflects brilliant speculation. At base a simple origin tale or "just-so" story, it goes to the heart of the problem of evil and the loss of immortality. In Greece Prometheus had made man from clay, and after the Flood his fellow-Titan Deucalion had made him once more by throwing stones over his shoulder; such stories are widespread (Frazer [1919], I, 3–44). The Fall, found in Greece as Pandora's Box, in Assyria forms part of the myth of Adapa, who broke the wing of the South Wind and created dissension among the gods, and though deeply repentant, was cursed by death and disease (Pritchard, p. 101). In the epic *Gilgamesh* the hero seeks Utnapishtim, hero of the Flood, to obtain the secret of immortality, which lies in a thorny plant. "Gilgamesh saw a well whose water was cool. He went down to bathe in the water. A serpent snuffed the fragrance of the plant; it came up from the water and carried off the plant. Going back it shed its slough." Thus, despite the ritual cleansing, all was lost to man. According to Frazer ([1919], I, 45–77) this is the widespread folktale of the perverted message and the cast skin, in which the snake, immortal because of his annual sloughing off, steals immortality from his rival man (see Krappe, 1927 and 1928). The Tree of Life itself is a massive concept, akin to the World-trees of Siberian and Norse mythology (Harva, 1938 and 1952). The Fall of Man finds resonance in the fall of the King of Tyre, "Thou" who "hast been in Eden the garden of God" (Ezekiel 28:13) and that of the King of Babylon, who became identified with Lucifer (Isaiah 14:12): "How art thou fallen from heaven, O Lucifer, son of the morning!" (Bamberger, 1952; Graves, p. 57). Yet Adam's tragic calamity is a *felix culpa*, a blessed sin which leads to the Atonement:

> Ne hadde the appil take ben, the appil taken ben,
> ne hadde neuer our lady a ben heuene quen;
> Blyssid be the tyme that appil take was,
> Ther-fore we mown syngyn, 'deo gracias!'
> (Lovejoy, 1948, p. 277; Weisinger, 1953; fifteenth-
> century poem).

Once the primitive oasis with trees and living waters was violated by the noble savages (Lovejoy and Boas, 1935) the wickedness of man increased, and the first brother slew his sibling rival. The Hebrews saw this as a feud between farmer and shepherd, the settled agriculturalist of Canaan and the wandering Semitic nomad (Graves, p. 85). A modern structural anthropologist sees it as a homosexual incest myth, paralleling the fall of Adam and Eve (Leach, in Middleton [1967], pp. 8–13, 65). External exegesis has explained where Cain's wife came from, why God was so harsh as to refuse Cain's vegetable sacrifice and so kind as to provide him with a protective mark, and how he was slain by Lamech (Frazer [1918], I, 78–104). A notable parallel is the Sumerian Dispute between Shepherd-God and Farmer-God (Pritchard, p. 41). Fratricidal quarrels continue with Isaac and Ishmael, Jacob and Esau, Joseph and his brethren. We still kill our brothers.

Flood and Second Creation. Murder may be a relic of primitive violence or the gruesome beginning of civilization. The nine patriarchs after Adam, with both Cainite and Sethite forms, are climaxed by the Cainite Lamech (Genesis 4) who invents bigamy, kills his ancestor Cain, and sings the ancient fragment of a Bedouin Sword Song to his wives. Fittingly his sons were culture-heroes: Jabal the tentsman, Jubal the inventor of harp and organ, and Tubal-Cain the metalworker. Their sister was Naamah, the lovely one, whom the Middle Ages made the wife of Noah and inventor of clothmaking. Such accounts of the inception of culture, which recall the Greek Prometheus and the American Indian Coyote, are greatly elaborated in the Books of Enoch and Jubilees (Charles [1913], II) and in one of the Dead Sea Scrolls. There is also a good Lamech (Genesis 5), who gives birth to Noah "saying, This son shall comfort us concerning the work and toil of our hands, because of the ground which the Lord hath cursed." Probably this passage reflects the later Noah who brought the vine, Noah the agricultural hero. There follows an undoubted fragment of polytheistic myth, of how "the sons of God saw the daughters of men that they were fair; and they took them wives of all which they chose. . . . There were giants in the earth in those days; and also after that, when the sons of God came in unto the daughters of men, and they bare children to them, the same became mighty men which were of old, men of renown."

God repents that he has made man and punishes him with the catastrophic Flood, which has probably caused more exegesis and expansion in the Bible of the Folk than any other story in Genesis (Figure 3). Merging as the Bible does the ritualistic priestly account, concerned with the seasons, and the earlier Yahwist writing, we may recall that the righteous Noah and his three sons and all their wives were saved along with two or seven of each animal, while those outside the Ark were drowned, that the Ark landed on Ararat after an episode with bird messengers, and that Noah sacrificed on an altar newly built, whereupon God spoke to him the first great Covenant, a set of precepts promising no further flood, demanding an end to murder and to eating meat without proper bloodletting, and setting the rainbow (the sky-god's weapon?) in the clouds as token of the bargain. Thus the world was brought once more to order in a Second Creation.

This story is the inspiration for hundreds of further patristic, Jewish, Muslim, and European accessions to the Bible of the Folk (Dähnhardt, 1907–12; Ginzberg, Gaer, 1951; Allen, 1949; Utley, 1960, 1961, 1968). Apart from these Bible-derived legends it has countless parallels all over the world, which Frazer thinks are local flood stories, only occasionally reflecting the Bible tale ([1919], I, 105–361). The biblical accounts are themselves based on some form of the *Gilgamesh* epic: 279

Sumerian, Babylonian, or Assyrian, either brought in by Abraham from Ur of the Chaldees or experienced in Jewish exile in Babylonia (Pritchard, pp. 42, 72, 109). In the Middle Ages Noah is a type of Christ, with the wood of the Ark prefiguring the Cross, his saving Remnant, his waters of baptism. To the peasants of the Balkans his ark is destroyed by the devil, inventor of brandy and seducer of Noah's wife; it is rebuilt by angels, entered by the proper eight and also by the devil, who hides in the skirts of Noah's wife; as a mouse the devil gnaws a hole, which is plugged by the snake's tail for the price of a man per day after the flood; the snake is burnt and his ashes turn into the lice, fleas, and other vermin which still exact the price (Utley, 1961).

In the narrow sense the Flood is legend, and not myth, since it owes something to a Mesopotamian flood or series of floods; yet its firm place in the Chain of History, as a demonstration of God's mastery over the wicked and his mercy for the righteous and a reinforcement of the tribal laws, make it as powerful a myth as the Bible contains. In their art Michelangelo, Poussin, Benozzo Gozzoli, Marc Chagall, and the great creator of the Ghiberti doors in Florence have made its force apparent. The visual power of the mighty ark on the waters, the pathos and shame of drowning men and animals, the rainbow as a sign of order in the skies, the altar and sacrifice, and the Canaanite fragment of a Dionysian myth in which Noah, unconscious inventor of wine, awakes to his shame, is derided by Ham or Canaan as Christ was by his tormentors, and curses his wicked progeny, has in his massive undraped body given inspiration to hundreds of artists, as well as to racists attempting to defend black slavery—all of these reveal the potent social, artistic, and religious myth (Altmann [1966], pp. 113–34).

The Great Migrations. Almost every race in its "oral history" has its own migration myths, biased in favor of the chosen tribes but bearing marks of earthly reality as well. The cursing of Canaan was one of these, and Noah, second father of mankind, is natural begetter of all races. The divine blasting of the presumptuous Tower of Babel, an iconic legend based on the sight of some Babylonian ziggurat in ruins, is the classic account of the Confusion of Tongues, in which the Hebrew spoken by our first fathers gave way to the three thousand languages of present time (the biblical commentators would call them seventy-two) (Graves and Patai [1964], pp. 120–33; Frazer [1918], I, 362–90). The Noachian genealogies which lead to Abraham, with their shadowy tribes and eponymous name-giving heroes, the wars of Isaac with Ishmael and Jacob with Esau, are topped by the Exodus, in which Moses leads his people through the miraculously divided Red Sea to Sinai. There we have the epiphany of Yahweh in the burning bush and the pillar of cloud, the tablets of the Law, the destruction of the Golden Calf, and the death of Moses on Mount Nebo in sight of the Promised Land (Ginzberg, III, 1–48; VI, 1–168). The conquest is left to Joshua, who made the sun stand still. Such wanderings, which recur in the historical Babylonian Exile and in the later history of the Jews, lie

280 FIGURE 3. Michelangelo, *The Deluge.* ca. 1510. SISTINE CHAPEL, VATICAN. PHOTO ALINARI–ART REFERENCE BUREAU

subtly behind the Christian story of the Wandering Jew (Anderson, 1965). Whether Moses invented monotheism or got it from the Pharaoh Aknahton, as Freud (1939) thought he did, he is the classic hero, from his divine childbirth (his name means "drawn out of the water"—see Jung and Kerényi, 1949) to his mysterious death and lost sepulchre (Raglan, 1949; Rank, 1959). His Yahweh, Lord of Horeb and Sinai and the high places, is a new god, whatever his Semitic and Canaanite origins (Peters [1914], pp. 89–91; Rowley, p. 289). Judaism is Moses' religion and the Torah his record; we shall meet him again as the great Lawgiver.

King and Tyrant. Though Moses lived among the Mediterranean cultures which created the pattern of divine kingship, Moses was never the King. At the outset of Israel's chain of history the king was a tyrant, in the shape of Nimrod, idolater and enemy of Abraham, mighty hunter before the Lord who built Babel and founded cities—symbol of the tyranny of the mighty East to the simple nomads and farmers of Israel (Rappaport [1928], I, 223–45). Israel had its petty kings, the Judges; it had its later monarchy with Saul and David and Solomon and the epigones who came after them (Gaer [1951], pp. 207–50); and the idea of kingship continues in the Messiah whose conception, literal and figurative, gave to Christianity its crucified King of the Jews. Whether the myth-ritual pattern is universal or not, it is certainly part of the perpetual ambience of the Jewish commonwealth, the domains of Attis and Adonis and Osiris of which Frazer writes so alluringly in his *Golden Bough*. Hooke finds it in Egypt and Babylonia and Canaan, in the temple at Jerusalem and in Hebrew ritual and festival (1933); and yet "the most fundamental idea, that of the dying and rising god, was . . . so completely incompatible with the prophetic conception of Jahveh, that it could not, at least in the early stages of the prophetic movement, be transformed or spiritualized" (Hooke [1956], pp. 108–11, 250–57). The Akkadian New Year's Festival of Bel and Marduk, with the death and resurrection of the god in the ritual form of priest-king, with sacred marriage and the keeping of the destinies, was always neighbor to Israel, and often intruded upon it (Pritchard, p. 331). Jeremiah and Ezekiel, leading a pre-Christian enlightenment against priestcraft and monarchy, inveigh against such contaminations of the pure faith of Yahweh, and have set the tone for social conscience among Jews and Christians ever since.

Yahweh and Canaan. Yet Yahweh himself was the Divine King.

For God is my king of old, working salvation in the midst of the earth. Thou didst divide the sea by thy strength: thou brakest the heads of the dragons in the waters. Thou brakest the heads of leviathan in pieces, and gavest him to be meat to the people inhabiting the wilderness. . . . The day is thine, the night also is thine; thou hast prepared the light and the sun. Thou hast set all the borders of the earth: thou hast made summer and winter (Psalm 74:12–17).

Such a poem reflects the seasonal rituals, the sacred dramas of the Canaanite Baal and Aquhat, whose divine bow reminds of the bow Yahweh placed in the clouds for Noah; "While the earth remaineth, seedtime and harvest, and cold and heat, and summer and winter, and day and night shall not cease." The dragon recalls the Hittite slaying of the dragon in the Puruli festival. Gaster finds further parallels in Egypt, Greece, and elsewhere in the Psalms (*Thespis*, 1950). Though Mowinckel has perhaps urged the case too strongly, the Babylonian New Year's festival is surely reflected in the Psalms as much as Canaan is; Hooke sees it reflected in the ritual flight of Cain after his murder of Abel (1963, p. 121).

Ritual Combats. The confrontations of gods, heroes, and monsters thus affect Yahweh worship in spite of monotheism, and live on until the Harrowing of Hell, the battle of Christ and Satan (M. R. James [1924], pp. 1–41). Satan himself, adversary of the suffering Job, is viewed in the Old Testament variously as the emissary of Yahweh, the opponent of such emissaries (in the Balaam episode), and as one of the sons of God (Kluger, 1967). The primeval monsters are personifications of chaos, against which Yahweh strives for order: Leviathan and Rahab come from Canaan, Tehom of the Creation story from the Babylonian combats of Marduk and Tiamat the sea-monster; Jonah's Great Whale is half cosmological; and dragons breed in Egypt as well as Assyria (Altmann, pp. 1–30; Pritchard, pp. 11, 14). The tormentors of Christ's passion reduce the struggle to the human level, as does the strong man Peter when he cuts off Malchus' ear at the Betrayal. When Christ was crucified the veil of the Temple was rent, and "the earth shook and the rocks were split; and the tombs were opened" (Matthew 27:51; Throckmorton, pp. 154–55). Thus chaos threatens at Creation and at the Atonement; at Doomsday it will do so once more. But as in Zoroastrianism, to which both later Judaism and Christianity are indebted for their dualistic developments, the combat always ends in the victory of the Lord. Such mythic combats reflect real antagonisms: El against Baal in Canaan; Elijah's routing of Melkart and Baal in a massive combat on Mount Carmel, with two bullocks as contesting sacrifices and the Lord's epiphany in fire and cloud as once before on Sinai (I Kings 18:21–46; Robinson [1932], I, 300–07; Oldenburg, 1969). Paulinus of Nola (A.D. 353–431) uses classical imagery for the Hero of Easter morning: *Salvem O Apollo vero, Paean inclyte,/ Pulsor draconis* *inferi!* ("Hail, O true Apollo! Renowned Healer! Victor over the dragon of hell!")

The myth of the Harrowing of Hell grew out of the deep necessity of reconciling Old and New Testament heroes, finding an equivalent for baptism of the patriarchs and prophets, and explaining the three days between Resurrection and Crucifixion. It is a clear reflex from Psalms (24:7–10); the Gospel of Nicodemus says:

And again there was a cry without; Lift up, ye princes, your gates, and be ye lift up, ye everlasting doors, and the King of glory shall come in. And again at that clear voice Hell and Satan inquired, saying: Who is this King of Glory? and it was said unto them by that marvellous voice: The Lord of Hosts, he is the King of Glory. And lo, suddenly Hell did quake, and the gates of death and the locks were broken small, and the bars of iron broken, and fell to the ground, and all things were laid open. And Satan remained in the midst and stood put to confusion and cast down, and bound with a fetter about his feet (M. R. James [1924], pp. 133–35; Kroll, *Gott und Hölle*, 1932).

The martial climax of Yahweh's war with the monsters is fought in Revelation (Chs. 12–16) at Armageddon, with the red dragon, now clearly the Old Serpent and Satan, attendant beasts, and the Whore of Babylon and another figure, a kind of anti-Madonna: ". . . a woman clothed with the sun, and the moon under her feet, and upon her head a crown of twelve stars" who "brought forth a man child, who was to rule all nations with a rod of iron." Yahweh, storm god of high places, warrior god and king, giver of victory, enemy of the agricultural gods or Baals of the land, the ethical god whose etymon is unknown (*Temenos* [1969], p. 107), the faceless god of Sinai who once had snake and bull form but became the enemy of graven images, the cult god who would tolerate no rivals in the neighboring cultures, gave rise ultimately to the anointed Christ, warrior god of Armageddon whose greatest mark was mercy and meekness, and whose disciples preached the Gospels everywhere, but whose righteous indignation led to a Church which triumphed over the Western World.

Mother Goddess and Divine Child. In that Church the vessel of mercy inevitably became the Blessed Virgin, mother and intercessor, who resembles the many virgin mothers of the heroes (Raglan, 1949; Throckmorton, pp. 176–81; Hooke [1963], pp. 168–73). She was Christianity's unique contribution to the universal Mother who lives in all religions, and whose nature is sometimes benevolent and sometimes malevolent (Neumann, 1955). The dark mothers are well-represented in Jezebel, Delilah, and the Whore of Babylon. Hebraism has usually been characterized as lacking female goddesses, as rejecting the sacred marriage (*hieros gamos*) of the Divine King, with its temple prostitutes and obscene rituals (Peters, p. 121). Patai (1967) has recently amassed controversial but impressive evidence for Judaic parallels to Allah and Allat, Baal and Baalat, the Canaanite Asherah, Astarte, and Anath (see the important Ras Shamra poem in Pritchard, pp. 129–42) in the Cherubim, the Shekhina, cabbalistic pairings, Matronit, Lilith, and even "the Sabbath—Virgin, Bride, Queen and Goddess." Much of this may be metaphor, but the line between living metaphor and myth will never be securely drawn. Another mystery is how the beautiful series of love poems known as the Song of Songs ever got attached to the biblical canon. Soon, however, it was allegorized by the Jews as a poem about God's love for Israel, and Christianity kept it as the inspiration for monastic poetry by interpreting it as the love of Christ for his Church.

As the offspring of numinous marriages, the Divine Child who is Apollo, Hermes, Zeus, Dionysos, or Herakles appears in the Bible as Moses, Samson, David, and as one who lay in a manger, worshipped by the lowly shepherds and by the lordly Magi alike (Jung and Kerényi, 1949; Frazer [1918], II, 437–54). The Virgin or mysterious birth is paralleled by miraculous adventures and by a mysterious death (Raglan, 1949; Rank, 1959; Utley, 1965). Here too the metaphors continue, as in the parable of the ten virgins (Matthew 25:6): "And at midnight there was a cry made, Behold, the bridegroom cometh; go ye out to meet him. Then all those virgins arose, and trimmed their lamps." In Revelations (21:9) one of the seven angels with seven vials says: "Come hither, I will shew thee the bride, the Lamb's wife." The moon-goddess of ancient Semitic belief is reflected in Passover ritual (Hooke [1933], p. 190; Reik [1964], pp. 69, 93) and in Christmas and Easter rite (Rahner, p. 160), where Christ is *Sol invictus,* "The Conquering Sun." Maria Stella Maris may have pagan antecedents (Krappe, 1948).

Magic, Miracle, and Morality. Most early religions show a faith in mana, the divine spirit power owned by gods and heroes, shamans, and prophets. Samson bore his in his hair and Delilah cut it off, just as the Norse Loki found out Baldur's vulnerability. Solomon ruled the demons, who are scarce in the early Old Testament, but become common in the Apocrypha (Tobit) and in the Pseudepigrapha (Enoch and Jubilees; for all these see Charles, I and II). Joshua's power stops the sun so that he can better fight the battle of Jericho; the Magi bring gifts to Christ. Moses and Aaron battle the Egyptian sorcerers in a typical Magus conflict; they cross the Red Sea between walls of water and draw refreshing water from the rocks in the wilderness. So Jesus turns water into wine, multiplies the loaves and fishes, exorcizes demons from men into swine, walks on water, is transfigured, rends the veil of the Temple, and appears after his death to his disciples. The miracles are often for a clear and universal ethical end (as opposed to manic mystery): Sodom is destroyed to punish an inhospitable people (like the reward for Philemon and Baucis and the punishment of their neighbors in Ovid); Daniel and his three companions are saved in the lion's den because they refuse to eat nonkosher food (Hooke [1963], p. 151); Moses' mountain miracles are climaxed by the Decalogue and the Torah (Figure 4); and Christ's greatest preaching is the ethical Sermon on the Mount.

Though there are other "Religions of a Book" (Islam and Hinduism), no other two great world religions share the same book. On the discovery of Deuteronomy, one portion of the Law, Josiah in 621 B.C. cleared the temple of altars, asherah, and prostitutes (Peters, p. 259). The function of priests is to give Torah, "the decision" (Peters, p. 136), and Moses is the hero of lawgivers as David and Solomon are of brilliant judicial verdicts (Conway; Gaer, pp. 230–50). The role passes to Christ: "For the Father judgeth no man, but hath committed all judgment unto the Son" (John 5:22; II Timothy 4:1). Though the Bible from Philo Judaeus and Augustine on needs exegetical glossing, it remains the Word of God, the Old linked to the New through prefigurative typology. Noah like Christ saves men by wood and water; Abraham's sacrifice of Isaac prefigures the Crucifixion; the Prophets speak of the Son of Man, the Messiah, the great days of judgment to come. Saint Paul rejects the binding nature of the external Law, and for it substitutes conscience and the Spirit of Christ, yet ". . . the law is holy, and the commandment holy, and just, and good" (Romans 7:12; Moore [1932], II, 131). It was dualists like Marcion who heretically rejected the Law and kept only the Gospel (Moore [1932], II, 155).

Priest and Prophet. The priest was guardian of the shrine in Temple and in the Ark of the Covenant, that extraordinary moving shrine which formed the perfect antithesis to the sanctuaries of the local gods who were driven out by Yahweh. Early in Genesis the myth of the priesthood forms itself around the meeting between Abraham and Melchizedek, king of Salem, who ". . . brought forth bread and wine: and he was the priest of the most high God" (Genesis 14:18). Christ himself was subject to the priestly rites of circumcision and baptism, and Melchizedek remained the model of the medieval cleric.

Most religions make some distinction between the ordained priest and the rapt prophet, with his more direct communion with heaven. The Hebraic prophets are the most famous form of the shaman who exists in all religions (Eliade, 1951; Jensen [1963], p. 214). In Salvation-history the Prophets are the link between the Law and the Gospel, and their trance-like visions, part history and part prediction, make way for the apocalypses of Daniel, Enoch, and John the Divine. Jeremiah (Ch. 24) observed the two baskets of figs at the gate of the Temple: one with rich and one with rotten fruit, the first the good Jews who had accepted exile, the other the renegades under Zedekiah who had remained behind. Ezekiel saw the wheels within wheels of Cherubim (Chs. 1 and 10); the multifoliate rose of Dante's Paradise and the rose-wheels of Chartres stained glass, with their still-point at the center of which is God, are Ezekiel's heirs. Isaiah, recounting his own awakening, reveals the spirit power of the shaman: "Then flew one of the seraphims unto me, having a live coal in his hand, which he had taken with the tongs from off the altar: and he laid it upon my mouth and said, Lo, this hath touched thy lips; and thine iniquity is taken away, and thy sin purged" (6:6–7). Elijah and Elisha are the dramatic heroes of the prophetic writers, enemies of Baal (Bronner, 1968);

FIGURE 4. Michelangelo, *Moses.* ca. 1513–16. TOMB OF JULIUS II, SAN PIETRO IN VINCOLI, ROME. PHOTO ALINARI–ART REFERENCE BUREAU

the Christian Carmelites made them the first anchorites, their own predecessors.

The Last Judgment. We cannot trace the intricate lines which join the Jewish Messiah, Son of Man, Healing Remnant and Suffering Servant to Christ's ministry and passion, or the various adaptations to real history of the idea of the millennium. Christ the Healer also brought suffering, as Paul said (Romans 6:4): "Are ye ignorant that all who have been baptized unto Christ Jesus have been baptized unto his death?" Like the circumcision of Abraham and the Jews, baptism is an initiation, a rebirth, to what Paul calls "newness of life" (Eliade, 1958; Hooke [1956], p. 95). By substitution ritual, as with the Old Testament scapegoat Azazel, Christ attracts the sins of all men (Hooke [1956], p. 204). His Resurrection promises a resurrection to us all, if we follow the holy pattern. Yet his own message was often simpler: "The kingdom of God is at hand: repent ye, and believe the Gospel" and "Thou art not far from the kingdom of God" (Mark 1:15, 12:34). Driven by the Pharisees' questioning he says: "The kingdom of God cometh not with observation . . . for behold, the kingdom of God is within you" (Luke 17:20).

Yet as time elapsed and Christ died, to be resurrected as were Adonis and Orpheus and the Phoenix and Psyche, to walk with God as Enoch and Noah and Elijah did, new speculation arose (Throckmorton, pp. 40, 57, 199). The mystery cults of Asia and of Greece, so vigorously warred against and perpetually revived in Judaism, brought new strength to Judaea's child, Christianity. The Fourth Gospel (A.D. 90–110) begins Creation not with a bird-like Spirit of God on the waters, but with the Word, the Logos. Jewish and Christian apocalyptic catch the spirit of the mysteries (Hooke [1956], pp. 102–43). Nearly contemporary with the Fourth Gospel is the Book of Revelation (80–96?), by a John who was probably neither the Beloved Disciple nor the writer of the Fourth Gospel (on the dates see Peake [1919], pp. 744, 926).

Revelation is the last link in the Chain of History. The Revealer sees many visions, among them a Lamb surrounded by four beasts "full of eyes before and behind," like his own great poem. These beasts, like a lion, a calf, an eagle, and a man, are either the four Gospellers or a tetrad of cherubim (Ezekiel 1:10). The Book with seven seals is opened because "the Lion of the tribe of Juda" hath prevailed. The Four Horsemen of war, bloodshed, famine, and death precede the Lamb, who leads the saints and martyrs to "living fountains of waters," in the face of a plague of locusts from the bottomless pit, led by the king Abaddon or Apollyon (the abyss of *tehom,* the primeval chaos of

Creation once more—see Charles [1920], I, 240). Like Ezekiel (3:3) the Revealer eats a scroll which tastes like honey; but this latter-day pessimist finds the after-taste bitter. Moses and Elijah prophesy in sackcloth and ashes, but the Beast from the pit destroys them. In heaven the temple is opened and there appears the ark of God's testament which Jeremiah had hidden in an earthly cavern (Peake, p. 935). There follow the woman with the child, Michael in ritual combat with the dragon, the Lamb on Sion and "the great winepress of the wrath of God, the Scarlet Woman of "Babylon the Great, the Mother of Harlots and Abominations of the earth" who is drunk with the blood of the saints, then the rejoicing of the saints, the marriage of the Lamb, the binding of the old serpent Satan for a thousand years, his revival, the battle with Gog and Magog, and the Judgment. In the great hymn of the Franciscan Thomas of Celano (ca. 1200–ca. 1255): *Dies irae, dies illa,/ Solvet saeclum in favilla,/ Teste David cum Sibylla* ("The day of wrath, that day will dissolve the world into ashes, as David and the Sibyl testify") we find not a Second Flood, but Fire Next Time. As the Revealer's apocalyptic predecessor, the Book of Enoch (ca. 161–64 B.C.—Charles [1913], II, 280–81) has it: "their names shall be blotted out of the book of life . . . and their seed shall be destroyed for ever . . . and they shall cry and make lamentation in a place that is a chaotic wilderness, and in the fire shall they burn. . . . And I will bring forth in shining light those who have loved My holy name, and I will seat each on the throne of his honour" (Figure 5). Turning once more to the Revealer: "And I saw a new heaven and a new earth," a New Jerusalem but without a temple now, "for the Lord God Almighty and the Lamb are the temple of it . . . [and] a pure river of water of life, clear as crystal . . . [with] the trees of life, which bare twelve manner of fruits . . . and the leaves of the tree were for the healing of the nations. . . . And if any man shall take away from the words of the book of this prophecy, God shall take away his part out of the book of life, and out of the holy city, and from the things which are written in this book." So the last book of the Great Book ends, and the Chain of Salvation is complete, with imagery of Fall and Water, Tree and Salvation, Fire and War and Sacred Marriage, the Father's Creation and the Mother's Child, Paradise Lost and Paradise Regained. The Lost Eden of Genesis was primitivistic. But with Christ and the Kingdom of God within us Eden returned, the mysterious Fortunate Fall is fulfilled. The Chain is cyclic now, and the return will be as described in Revelation, a rebirth for the saints by the Man who won us immortality instead of losing it.

Figure 5. Jan Van Eyck, *The Adoration of the Lamb*. 1432. st. bavo, ghent. photo bulloz–art reference bureau

BIBLIOGRAPHY

For biblical quotations the Authorized (King James) Version is used.

D. C. Allen, *The Legend of Noah* (Urbana, 1949). A. Altmann, ed., *Biblical Motifs* (Cambridge, Mass., 1966). G. K. Anderson, *The Legend of the Wandering Jew* (Providence, 1965). B. J. Bamberger, *Fallen Angels* (Philadelphia, 1952). L. Bronner, *The Stories of Elijah and Elishah as Polemics against Baal Worship* (Leiden, 1968). H. M. and N. K. Chadwick, *The Growth of Literature* (Cambridge, 1932–40). R. H. Charles, ed., *The Apocrypha and Pseudepigrapha of the Old Testament in English* (Oxford, 1913). R. H. Charles, *A Critical and Exegetical Commentary on The Revelation of St. John* (Edinburgh, 1920). M. D. Conway, *Solomon and Solomonic Literature* (Chicago, 1899). O. Dähnhardt, *Natursagen* (Leipzig, 1907–12). M. Eliade, *Le Chamanisme et les techniques archaïques de l'extase* (Paris, 1951); trans. W. E. Trask as *Shamanism: . . .* (Princeton, 1964). J. G. Frazer, *Folk-Lore in the Old Testament* (London, 1918); idem, *The Golden Bough* (London, 1935). J. Fontenrose, *The Ritual Theory of Myth* (Berkeley, 1966). S. Freud, *Moses and Monotheism* (New York, 1939). J. Gaer, *The Lore of the Old Testament* (Boston, 1951); idem, *The Lore of the New Testament* (Boston, 1952). L. Ginzberg, *The Legends of the Jews* (Philadelphia, 1912–38). R. Graves and R. Patai, *Hebrew Myths* (Garden City, 1964). H. Gunkel, *The Legends of Genesis* (New York, 1901; reprint 1964). W. R. Halliday, *Indo-European Folk-Tales and Greek Legend* (Cambridge, 1933). S. H. Hooke, ed., *The Labyrinth* (London, 1935); idem, *Middle Eastern Mythology* (Harmondsworth, 1963); idem, *The Siege Perilous* (London, 1956); idem, ed., *Myth and Ritual* (London, 1933). E. O. James, *Prehistoric Religion* (New York, 1962). M. R. James, *The Apocryphal New Testament* (Oxford, 1924). A. E. Jensen, *Myth and Cult among Primitive Peoples* (Chicago, 1963). C. G. Jung and C. Kerényi, *Essays on a Science of Mythology* (New York, 1949). R. S. Kluger, *Satan in the Old Testament* (Evanston, 1967). A. H. Krappe, "Maria Stella Maris," *The Review of Religion*, **13** (May, 1948), pp. 375–81. J. Kroll, *Gott und Hölle, Studien der Bibliothek Warburg* **20** (Leipzig and Berlin, 1932). A. O. Lovejoy, *Essays in the History of Ideas* (Baltimore, 1948); idem and G. Boas, *Primitivism . . . in Antiquity* (Baltimore, 1935). J. Middleton, ed., *Myth and Cosmos* (Garden City, 1967). Edmund Leach provides "structural charts" describing the various versions of Creation, Fall, and First Murder in accordance with the ideas of Claude Lévi-Strauss. G. F. Moore, *History of Religions*, 2 vols. (New York, 1913–1919; reprint 1932). Henry A. Murray, "Myth and Mythmaking," *Daedalus* (Spring 1959), 211–380. E. Neumann, *The Great Mother* (London, 1955). U. Oldenburg, *The Conflict between El and Ba'al in Canaanite Religion* (Leiden, 1969). W. O. E. Oesterley and T. H. Robinson, *A History of Israel*, 2 vols. (Oxford, 1932), I by Robinson. R. Patai, *The Hebrew Goddess* (New York, 1967); idem, *Man and Temple* (Toronto, 1947). A. S. Peake, ed., *Peake's Commentary on the Bible* (New

285

York, 1919). J. P. Peters, *The Religion of the Hebrews* (Boston, 1914). R. H. Pfeiffer, *Introduction to the Old Testament* (New York, 1941). J. B. Pritchard, *Ancient Near Eastern Texts Relating to the Old Testament* (Princeton, 1950). E. C. Quinn, *The Quest of Seth for the Oil of Life* (Chicago, 1962). Lord Raglan, *The Hero* (London, 1936; 1949; reprint, 1963). Reference is to the 1949 edition. H. Rahner, *Greek Myths and Christian Mystery* (New York, 1963). O. Rank, *The Myth of the Birth of the Hero* (New York, 1959). A. S. Rappaport, *Myth and Legend in Ancient Israel* (London, 1928). T. Reik, *Pagan Rites in Judaism* (New York, 1963). T. H. Robinson, see Oesterley. H. H. Rowley, ed., *The Old Testament and Modern Study* (Oxford, 1951). John Skinner, *A Critical and Exegetical Commentary on Genesis* (New York, 1910). E. A. Speiser, ed., *Genesis,* The Anchor Bible (Garden City, 1964). *Temenos: Studies in Comparative Religion,* 4 (1969). B. H. Throckmorton, *The New Testament and Mythology* (London, 1960). A. J. Toynbee, *A Study of History,* Vol. VI (London, 1939). F. L. Utley, "The Devil in the Ark," Internationaler Kongress der Volkserzählungsforscher, *Vorträge und Referate* (Berlin, 1961), pp. 446–63; idem, "Folklore, Myth, and Ritual," *Critical Approaches to Medieval Literature,* ed. D. Bethurum (New York, 1960); idem, "Noah, His Wife, and the Devil," *Studies in Biblical and Jewish Folklore,* eds. R. Patai, D. Noy, and F. L. Utley (Bloomington, 1960), pp. 59–91; F. L. Utley, "Rabghuzi—Fourteenth-Century Turkic Folklorist," *Volksuberlieferung: Festschrift für Kurt Ranke* (Göttingen, 1968), pp. 373–400. H. Weisinger, *Tragedy and the Paradise of the Fortunate Fall* (London, 1953). J. Wellhausen, *Prolegomena to the History of Ancient Israel* (New York, 1878; 1957).

FRANCIS LEE UTLEY

[See also **Christianity in History;** Cycles; God; **Myth; Prophecy in Hebrew Scripture;** Religion, Origins of, Ritual in; Sin and Salvation.]

MYTH IN THE MIDDLE AGES AND THE RENAISSANCE

THE SURVIVAL of pagan mythology in a Christian world is one of the most complex chapters in the history of Western culture. The object here is simply to sketch the main aspects of that tradition, and to trace its major ramifications through the Middle Ages and the Renaissance.

The tradition is twofold: textual and figurative. These two aspects can hardly be dissociated, as most of the time they supplement and illuminate each other. This was already the case in antiquity. The parallelism of a legend, and of its illustration, was established long ago by such students of Greek vase paintings as Carl Robert in his *Bild und Lied* (1881) and Charles Dugas in *Tradition littéraire et tradition graphique dans*

l'antiquité grecque (1937). In J. D. Beazley's and P. Jacobstahl's monographs, *Bilder griechischer Vasen,* paintings are classified stylistically; but they provide invaluable means of comparing the texts and the iconography. These are not always complementary; they may be in competition, or even in opposition, because a myth is primarily made of images rather than ideas; and the image itself possesses an autonomous power of evocation and proliferation. In the medieval and Renaissance periods, figurative mythology sometimes simply reflects the textual tradition; it may also supply its missing links or reveal its strange detours; and it occasionally generates a tradition of its own.

This raises the general question: Through which channels has the knowledge of the Fable been perpetuated and renovated? They have not always been the most immediate. Sometimes a basic text such as Ovid's *Metamorphoses* is known through intermediaries; all sorts of compilations, handbooks, or dictionaries have, so to speak, "predigested" the stories of the gods. Conversely, a famous antique work of art may very well inspire a medieval or Renaissance artist only through a reproduction, a description, or even a reconstitution. Finally, between artist and writer, there is constant exchange. A mythological theme is thus altered, enriched, or diversified. Not only is the vision of antiquity modified with the changing perspective of time, but the myth is subjected to a never ending process of re-creation.

The essential question, however, is not how but why did the legends and figures of the gods continue to obsess men's minds and imaginations since the end of the pagan era. The cause is to be found in the interpretations which antiquity itself had proposed on their origin and on their nature. These interpretations can roughly be reduced to three.

The first, and the most prosaic, is euhemerism: the gods were only men, famous or powerful men, who had been deified after their death through the adulation of their contemporaries. This theory is eagerly seized upon by the Christian apologists, who use it as a weapon against paganism; but it is a double-edged weapon. While it debases the gods by setting them on a level with mortal beings, it also confirms their past existence: it makes them part of history. What Orosius, Isidore of Seville, and their followers—such as Petrus Comestor in the twelfth century—attempt to do is to assign to the gods a place in time, in relation with the great figures of the Bible; the result of these synchronisms is to restore their prestige, by placing them on the same footing as the Patriarchs. And indeed they seem to deserve this rehabilitation, if they had been deified, to start with, for their virtues, their wisdom, or their services to mankind. Cicero observed in the *De natura deorum:*

Many divinities have with good reason been recognized and named both by the wisest men of Greece and by our ancestors from the great benefits that they bestow. For it was thought that whatever confers utility on the human race must be due to the operation of divine benevolence towards men. Thus sometimes a thing sprung from a god was called by the name of the god itself, as when we speak of corn as Ceres, or wine as Liber. . . . Human experience moreover and general custom have made it a practice to confer the deification of renown and gratitude upon distinguished benefactors. This is the origin of Hercules and Aesculapius. These were duly deemed divine as being supremely good and immortal because their souls survived and enjoyed eternal life (*De natura deorum*, trans. H. Rackham, Loeb Classical Library, 1933, 1967).

The Middle Ages, too, proclaim the gratitude of humanity towards those "men" on whom antiquity had conferred apotheosis; they even feel themselves related, as well as indebted, to them, as civilization is a treasure which has been handed down through the centuries, and no further distinction is made between the sacred and profane precursors of Christianity, who first forged that treasure.

There is another side to euhemerism, and another consequence. Racial pride inspires medieval clerks to look back into fabulous antiquity for founders of their own peoples; just as the Romans boasted the Trojan Aeneas as their ancestor, the Franks claim another Trojan, Francus, as their eponymous hero. The prodigious fortune of the *Roman de Troie* should be explained, at least partly, by its ethnogenic character. Not only do mythological figures become "patrons" of some national group; they also initiate dynasties. Princes glory in having at least a demi-god as the head of their lineage. In this way, medieval chronicles and world histories become the vehicle of a mythographical tradition which blossoms during the Renaissance.

An entirely different tradition is perpetuated by the "physical" interpretation, according to which the gods are cosmic powers. Again it is neatly summed up by Cicero.

We must assign . . . divinity to the stars, which are formed from the most mobile and the purest part of the aether. . . . The consciousness and intelligence of the stars is most clearly evinced by their order and regularity; . . . the eternal order of the constellations indicates neither a process of nature, for it is highly rational, nor chance, for chance loves variation and abhors regularity; it follows therefore that the stars move on their own free will, and because of their divinity (ibid.).

The mythological names given to heavenly bodies achieved the identification; the fusion between gods and stars was fully accomplished by the end of the pagan era. But by the third century A.D., what had started with the Stoics as a "rationalist" explanation of the movements of the spheres had become, mainly through the spreading of Oriental cults, an intensely superstitious creed: astral gods preside over the destiny of men. Thus, the old Olympians, who were hardly more than phantoms on earth, had now become masters in heaven, and to conciliate these dangerous masters, everyone had recourse to soothsayers, amulets, and talismans.

Here again, Christian controversy succeeds in confirming what it was expected to destroy. The general reason may be that the idea of "two worlds" was part of the religious topography of man in late antiquity. For pagans and Christians alike, the "other world" was the seat of a supreme God, infinitely remote from the human world; hostile powers had come increasingly to pour in the gap between men and God. In an "age of anxiety," men had an acute sense of being subjected to the malign influence of these mediating demons: hence the popular appeal of the magic practices which were supposed to placate them. Even those among the Church Fathers, such as Saint Augustine, who claim that stellar domination can be overcome by man's free will and by the grace of God, leave untouched the underlying belief in demons, in which astrology is rooted. Meanwhile, the last champions of paganism such as Macrobius attempt a purgation of astral mythology: all gods are but the manifestation of the Sun, the *numen multiplex* of a paramount deity.

Astrology, however, remains ingrained in medieval culture. Not only is the planetary week retained, but so also is the whole system of concordances which made both the planets and the zodiacal signs serve as the basis for the classification of seasons, elements, and humors; they are set in relation with the virtues and the liberal arts. Thus all forms of knowledge—not astronomy alone, but mineralogy, botany, zoology, physiology, medicine—fall ultimately under the sway of the cosmic powers. From the twelfth century on, the penetration of Arabic science in the Western world makes their tyranny even more oppressive and universal. The *Ghaya*, a handbook of magic arts made up of oriental and Hellenistic materials, is translated into Spanish at the court of Alfonso X under the title of *Picatrix*. One can learn from it the invocations and the instruments which make Jupiter, Mars, Venus, and Saturn favorable; their images are engraved on gems which capture their influence. The pagan gods appear in lapidaries, just as they appear in chronicles.

Even the great minds do not entirely repudiate the astrological theory of causation. Dante places Michael Scot, Frederic II's astrologer, in the abyss reserved for sorcerers; but he admits, reflecting the views of Saint Thomas Aquinas, that the stars have the power, if not to determine human fate, at least to "initiate" or to "incline" human will and passions. Dante's use of mythology in the *Divina Commedia*, however, is most original. He deals gravely with the *dei falsi e bugiardi*, false and mendacious in appearance only; for these supernatural beings were invested once, before the advent of Christ, with a beneficent authority. Like the Old Testament prophets, they castigated pride and rebellion against Divinity; they kept order on earth. The demi-gods themselves—heroes such as Theseus and Hercules—acted, through their good works, as auxiliaries of the true God. Only the *inferi* were Lucifer's accomplices: hence their permanent functions in Hell. We are back to the notion of the pagan gods as "mediating" demons, filling this time not only the gap between men and God, but the interval between the Fall and the Redemption.

The third system of interpretation consists in detecting in the figures of the gods a spiritual significance—they are personified virtues and passions—and, in their adventures, a moral teaching. This allegorical method, applied by the Stoics concurrently with the physical one, to explain away the seeming absurdity or immorality of the myths, became in the hands of the Neo-Platonists a means of sanctifying them: mythology is now scrutinized as a sacred text, and even the most shocking legend is given a pious or philosophical meaning. For instance, the story of Attis and Cybele is understood as the trials of the soul in its search for God. It is in fact for the last pagans—Emperor Julian among them—an ultimate expedient for salvaging the gods. For this very reason, the Church should have been hostile to allegory; but the Fathers themselves, some of whom, like Saint Ambrose, are deeply imbued with New-Platonism, apply the same method to the Holy Scriptures; also, since they retain profane classical literature in education, they find it necessary to expurgate it through moralization.

In the sixth century, the biblical allegories (*Moralia*) of Gregory the Great have as a counterpart Fulgentius' edifying *Mythologiae*, where, for instance, the three goddesses between whom Paris must choose become the symbols of the active, the contemplative, and the amorous life. The whole of the pagan Fable is turned into a *philosophia moralis*; after the eleventh century, this kind of exegesis assumes astounding proportions. This is the time when Ovid is rehabilitated not only as *Ethicus*, but as *Theologus*. The *Metamorphoses* are dealt with in Arnulph of Orleans' prose commentary, and in John of Garland's *Integumenta*. They can now be read safely by the nuns themselves, as well as the *Remedia amoris*. The fourteenth century sees the tri-umph of these *Ovides moralisés*. Yet the most extravagant monument of Christian allegory applied to mythology is, in the following century, the work of a Franciscan monk, John Ridewall, *Fulgentius metaforalis*.

The three traditional frameworks within which the gods survived were not, in fact, separate; the historical, physical, and moral interpretations were not mutually exclusive. They had sometimes been proposed simultaneously by the philosophical schools of antiquity; in the same way, we find medieval scholars applying the three methods to a single mythical personage, or episode; and one should, of course, take into account the polyvalent character of the myths themselves: the story of Narcissus, for instance, assumes through the ages a bewildering variety of meanings. This in turn explains its successive, and sometimes simultaneous integration into different literary genres. Furthermore, there were points of contact or overlappings between the various spheres: for instance, the notion of temperaments supposedly determined by the stars facilitates the transition from the planetary gods to the virtues. There is an *Ovidius scientificus* as well as an *Ovidius ethicus*. History and ethics could also interpenetrate: Boccaccio, composing his *De casibus virorum et feminarum illustrium*, goes to mythological heroes for edifying anecdotes.

Finally, the encyclopedic character of medieval culture, obvious in both learned and popular compilations, made it easy to introduce mythology into an all-embracing system of knowledge: whatever their disguise, the gods were sure to be enmeshed, since they belonged at the same time to the *Speculum historiale*, the *Speculum naturale*, and the *Speculum morale*. Indeed, we meet them in miniatures illustrating encyclopedias such as Isidore's *Etymologiae* or Rabanus Maurus' *De rerum naturis*; and in the porches of the cathedrals the zodiacal signs are associated with the labors of the months, the virtues, and the liberal arts.

Mythology, therefore, had remained alive in men's thoughts since antiquity; the Renaissance did not, properly speaking, bring out its "rebirth." The continuity of the tradition has been obscured simply because the Middle Ages, while keeping the ideas embodied in the gods, had lost their classical form, or let it deteriorate. One can follow, from the Carolingian period down to the sixteenth century, the astonishing story of their metamorphoses; this is possible mainly through the very rich iconography provided by the miniatures of astrological or allegorical manuscripts. These miniatures fall into two groups, according to their origin, which can be either a plastic or graphic model, or a descriptive text. The first of these groups, in turn, is divided into families, some still purely occidental (such as the figures of the constellations in the *Aratea*), some oriental (such as the same figure in the Arabic manuscripts, or again the illustrations of Michael Scot's treatise which go back to Babylonian prototypes). The classical types, in these last series, are altered beyond recognition; but the figures issued from the literary tradition are just as bizarre. They are to be found, mainly, in moralizing works; there the gods are literally "reconstructed" from texts borrowed from late antique mythographers. Starting from these texts, the illustrators of Rémi d'Auxerre's *Commentary on Martianus Capella*, for instance, or of Ridewall's *Fulgentius metaforalis*, have generated monsters, or caricatures; furthermore, in the absence of any antique model, the Romanesque or Gothic miniaturist naturally adapts mythology to the fashion of the day: the gods are dressed in contemporary garb, Mars as a knight in armor, Apollo with a furred mantle.

Of special interest in this group is a *Liber imaginum deorum*, whose author, "Albricus," has been identified with the Mythographus Tertius, who might be Alexander Neckham (1157–1217); after all sorts of vicissitudes, it is abridged into a *Libellus de imaginibus deorum*, and illustrated, at last, around 1420. To sum up, both the "plastic" and the "literary" traditions result, by the end of the medieval period, in a very mixed Olympus. Whether a Hellenistic model was distorted by an Arabic copyist—ignorant, of course, of mythology; or whether Juno or Jupiter was painstakingly fabricated by a conscientious miniaturist from a mosaic of descriptive texts—the outcome is always a set of barbaric figures.

These metamorphoses, however, are highly instructive: they reveal the unexpected channels and circuitous routes through which antique culture was transmitted; they also provide the key to puzzling problems of late medieval and early Renaissance art. The reliefs in Giotto's campanile, the capitals in the Ducal Palace in Venice, the frescoes in the Cappella degli Spagnuoli, become fully intelligible only by reference to Arabic or Babylonian inspirations. As for the *Libellus*, which was designed as a handbook for artists, it is the source of a whole series of French, Flemish, and Italian miniatures, sculptures, and tapestries. It will serve, even beyond the fifteenth century, as a pictorial code of mythology.

The true Renaissance, in that field, begins only when the gods have resumed their classical form; but this is a gradual process, which is delayed, unexpectedly, by the invention of printing. This is because (apart from Cicero's *De natura deorum*) the first mythographic texts to come out in print are those which were known to the Middle Ages, or the medieval compilations themselves. Albricus' *Liber* . . . , for instance, has ten edi-

tions, starting in 1480. Boccaccio's *Genealogia deorum* is largely a medieval legacy; yet it remains the essential repertory of myths through the first half of the sixteenth century, whereas Apollodorus' *Bibliotheca*, a classical authority, will appear only in 1555.

The illustrated books have played a still more important part in disseminating an "impure" mythological tradition. The great mythological incunabula are Boccaccio's *De casis* (Ulm, 1473), and his *De la Ruyne des nobles hommes et femmes* (Bruges, 1476); during the same period Antwerp and Paris publish the *Recueil des histoires de Troie*, the *Faits et prouesses de Jason*, the *Destruction de Troie la grant*. The woodcuts, most of which reproduce the spurious types of the *Libellus*, have a distinctly Nordic flavor, and might as well illustrate romances of chivalry. Yet they are responsible for the graphic diffusion of some of the favorite themes of the Renaissance: the Rape of Europa, the Rape of Proserpina, etc. Courtly society feeds on them; by the end of the fifteenth century this "Gothic" vision of the Greco-Roman world has captured the imagination of civilized Europe; not, of course, the minds of the humanists, who reject all "vulgar" imagery, but the imagination of women who want to read even the classical fables in translation, and with pictures: for instance, *Le Epistole d'Ovidio* (Naples, 1478) and the *Metamorphoses* in the version of Giovanni di Bonsignori (Venice, 1483).

Such productions appear quite remote from the aesthetic ideal of the Renaissance, and from its concern for archaeological accuracy. Now the discovery of genuine antiquity had started in Italy and elsewhere. Collectors, typical of whom is Ciriaco d'Ancona, have filled their notebooks with copies of medals, inscriptions, fragments of statues. This "antiquarian" trend is combined with the "courtly" one in a strange and splendid book published by Aldus in 1499. The *Hypnerotomachia Polyphili* combines a love story—with enigmatic overtones—and a repertory of classical archaeology. Besides that hybrid work, one should recall another graphic masterpiece, no less influential: Petrarch's *Trionfi*, edited several times before 1500.

Still another category of illustrated books generates a lasting tradition, namely the Emblems. Their main roots are archaeological: the antique medals, and the hieroglyphs, which are supposed to be decipherable since Cristoforo de' Buondelmonti brought back from Andros, in 1419, the manuscript of Horus Apollo's *Hieroglyphica*. Their influence is already obvious in the *Hypnerotomachia*. Aldus prints them in 1505, and Pierio Valeriano publishes in 1556 his monumental commentary. Meanwhile, the humanists, who believe that they have found the key to a sacred language, fabricate cryptograms of their own, drawing their material from various sources besides Horus, particularly from the Greek Anthology. The first collection of Emblems is that of Andrea Alciati (1531). Mythology of course plays a major role: the gods, their figures, and their attributes are interpreted as signs covering moral truths, or wise maxims. These so-called hieroglyphs will play a special part at the end of the sixteenth century, at the time when it will be necessary to reconcile pagan Fable with Christian teaching; the Emblems then will provide a perfect medium of compromise.

Around 1550 mythology seems ubiquitous. In Italy it has invaded public and private palaces, and even at times churches; fountains and gardens, domestic furniture, processions, and masquerades. Its role, however, is not simply decorative: this imagery frequently betrays various currents of thought. It is significant that it reappears, very often, within the medieval frameworks; the Renaissance, indeed, holds on to the traditional interpretations, and develops them still further. Minerva and Ceres had been placed by Boccaccio among famous women, benefactresses of mankind; Jacopo da Bergamo and Polydore Virgil celebrate the gods, inventors of arts and crafts. Jean Lemaire de Belges, in his *Illustrations de Gaule et singularités de Troie*, assigns mythical founders to various places, including cities and nations; the Burgundians are made to descend from "the great Lybian Hercules"; the Golden Fleece is placed, of course, under Jason's patronage; Jupiter and Hercules are shown on tapestries, bringing the alphabet to the Gauls; and Pierre de Ronsard's *Franciade* (1572) connects King Charles IX and the French dynasty with a fabulous Trojan origin.

Again, astrological beliefs spread more widely during the Renaissance, and gain more impetus; never since antiquity have the stars played a greater role in the lives of states and individuals. Their ascendancy over men's bodies is still illustrated by the astro-medical theme of the microcosm; their moral and intellectual influence by the theme of the "planets' children." Some great decorative cycles are but the translation in visual terms of a concept of the universe in which pagan powers have regained the place of sovereign masters. The mythological figures in the vault of the Farnesina, which might appear purely ornamental, are the precise transcription of Agostino Chigi's horoscope, whereas in Santa Maria del Popolo, the planetary gods are hovering over his tomb, in the cupola designed by Raphael. This time, however, they are dominated by God the Father: they are but the agents and auxiliaries of His supreme will, as in G. Pontano's *Urania* (1480; published 1505).

Imbued as they are with the literature and philosophy of late antiquity, the humanists still adhere to the belief in demons; even when they reject the tyranny of the stars, at least over the soul, they remain, like Marsilio Ficino, obsessed with the fear of cosmic bodies, inhabited by mysterious intelligences. That fear, of course, persists among the common people, who turn to magic practices and rely on images and formulas such as the ones prescribed by the author of *Picatrix* or by Cornelius Agrippa to protect themselves against baleful influences. Attempts may be made to "Christianize" the veneration of the skies, to bring it in line with theology: it still bears the imprint of mythological powers.

Albrecht Dürer's famous print, *Melencholia I*, is a sort of confluence of traditions and contemporary attitudes; it also exemplifies the profound renewal of a theme by a meditative genius. In an exhaustive study, Saxl, Panofsky, and Klibansky have disentangled *Melencholia's* complicated ancestry; by analyzing the features of this strange figure and its heterogeneous attributes, they have shown that it results from the fusion of two traditional types: a temperament, the saturnine one; and a liberal art, geometry. Dürer's originality was to bring together these two types, one embodying a creative mental faculty, the other a destructive state of mind, thereby giving a new twist to an ancient allegory. The old Melancholy was idle because she had fallen asleep, out of sloth and acedia; the new one is idle because her mind is preoccupied with interior visions. She is surrounded by the instruments of work, but darkly aware of the inadequacy of the powers of knowledge. The thoughts which underpin the whole composition can be traced back to a scholastic philosopher, Henry of Ghent; but Melancholia's brooding mood and discouraged posture also reflect the astrological apprehensions of Marsilio Ficino.

Finally, the "moral" tradition lives on, as the vogue of the Emblems has just reminded us. It is evidenced, again, by a copious iconography. The sequels to the mythological miniatures of the *Roman de la Rose* and of the *Echecs amoureux* are the psychomachies painted for Isabella d'Este by Perugino and Mantegna: the *Battle between Chastity and Lust*, the former represented by Pallas and Diana, the latter by Venus and Cupido with the edifying stories of Europa, Daphne, Glaucera . . . in the background; the *Triumph of Wisdom over Vice*, where Wisdom appears in the guise of Minerva who puts to rout Venus, mother of Dalliance and Sloth. Under this cover, the gods again are found in unexpected places: Correggio introduces Diana with her nymphs and the naked Juno in a convent in Parma, to remind the nuns of the duties of monastic life.

There are, of course, interferences and correlations between these various sectors where mythology continues to proliferate; they overlap, as they did in the Middle Ages. Planetary gods, for instance, are brought together on the same monument with heroes deified as precursors of civilization. This was already the case of Giotto's campanile; but there are countless examples of mythical figures appearing in encyclopedic programs of decoration, where, moreover, the Fable and the Scriptures are often brought into parallel. In the Tempio Malatestiano in Rimini, the Muses, the Sybils and the Prophets, the planets and the signs of the zodiac concur in Sigismund's apotheosis, he himself being figured as the Sun. All this imagery clothes a philosophy: the doctrine of the immortality of the soul, as exposed by Macrobius in his commentary on Cicero's *Somnium Scipionis*. The encyclopedic spirit breathes in the Camera della Segnatura, which indeed may be considered the supreme Renaissance monument to concordance and conciliation. Each part can be fully understood only as a fragment of a whole: not only does Poetry, personified by the Parnassian Apollo, combine with Theology, Law, and Philosophy to make up the sum of human learning; the Elements, too, are symbolized by episodes arranged in four pairs, where a mythological scene is coupled with a historical one. Furthermore, these various cycles are interwoven; the Elements are connected with the Liberal Arts through the mediation of Virtues, according to a pattern which reveals, at the same time, the interconnection of the Arts: Theology and Philosophy stand in the same relation to each other as Fire to Water; Law and Poetry, in the same relation as Earth to Heaven.

In short, Renaissance mythology largely retains and develops, both in contents and treatment, the medieval tradition. It is, however, deeply original in several respects. For one thing, it mixes more closely with political life. Decorative programs elaborated by the humanists contain, besides their conventional meaning and their edifying purpose, all sorts of intentions or allusions, to contemporary events or persons. Giulio Romano's frescoes at the Palazzo del Te, for instance, are made of heterogeneous elements: they combine erotic scenes with emblems related to Federico Gonzaga's personality and to his dynasty; they recall, after Raphael, the story of Psyche, as told by Apuleius, remoralized by Lactantius Placidus, and Neo-Platonized by Equicola; they illustrate the astrological systems of Manilius and Firmicus Maternus. Jupiter crushing the Giants is a warning to those who rebel against divine authority, but also a tribute to Charles V trying to reestablish imperial power in Italy. In the same way, in the Ducal palace in Venice, Tintoretto's Mercury, Graces, Ariadne, and Bacchus are meant to praise the Republic and its government. In the mythological ballets danced in the French court before Catherine de' Medici, Circe represents the horrors of civil strife, Minerva the restoration of order and peace. In Elizabethan England, the symbolism of the Virgin—Diana or Astraea—is exploited for the purposes of propaganda.

How does this process of "paganization" affect religion itself? The question can be raised, since Christian themes also are treated sometimes very boldly in pagan terms, in art as well as in poetry. What are we to make of Herculean or Olympian Christs? It would be wrong to conclude from these substitutions of forms that Renaissance culture was deeply secularized, for they work both ways. The sacrifice of the Paschal Lamb may well be represented according to the purest pagan ritual; but a sacrifice to Priapus follows the pattern of a Presentation to the Temple, and the scheme of a baptism is discernible even in Botticelli's *Birth of Venus*. These interversions seem rather to manifest a sense of continuity, or of concordance: while Giovanni Bellini's Redemptor pours his blood into a chalice, a scene of libation takes place in the background on a bas-relief. Also, one should remember that the Renaissance uses classical patterns not only in a different context, but with a different meaning—witness the frantic Maenad transfigured into a Holy Woman, crying in despair at the foot of the Cross (in the drawing by Bandinelli, École des Beaux-Arts, Paris).

Nor should the omnipresence of the gods be viewed as the expression of the unbridled enjoyment of life; they certainly did recover, along with their beauty, their sensuous or heroic appeal; but they reconquered at the same time a striking degree of dignity. The restoring of their classical shape was also, in a sense, a reconsecration: the Renaissance is aware that mythology was a theology, as well as a poetry, and that, for men of antiquity to whom Christ had not been revealed, it was the true religion; a religion all the more fascinating for having wrapped divine things in mysterious symbols. Hence the praise of paganism by an Augustinian preacher, Egidio da Viterbo; hence, also, the humanists' attitude towards pagan beliefs: their mythological erudition is, like their fervid interest in philology and archaeology, a form of piety, *docta pietas*. They even revive the dream of a syncretic and esoteric doctrine, with Platonism as a gospel.

This ambition is made manifest by the great mythological paintings and sculptures of the Renaissance, many of which are deliberate riddles: such as Botticelli's *Primavera* and the *Birth of Venus*, Piero di Cosimo's *Mars and Venus*, Michelangelo's *Leda* and *Bacchus*, Titian's *Sacred and Profane Love*. To elucidate the meaning of these works, it is not enough to point out their immediate sources; one must recreate the climate and the mood of those humanistic circles,

291

where they were originally conceived. E. Panofsky's iconological researches, and E. Wind's capital study, *Pagan Mysteries in the Renaissance*, have established the validity of such a method. Wind demonstrates that the Neo-Platonists of the Quattrocento, who saw Plato through the eyes of the last exponents of paganism, Jamblichus, Porphyry, Proclus, Plotinus, and Plutarch, had borrowed from them a particular notion of the mysteries, and of the initiation rituals; as a result, they had worked out a theory of cryptic expression applied to the visual arts, in the belief that beauty is achieved only by adumbration. Under their influence, the artists themselves obscured the ultimate significance of their works, which become intelligible only when their doctrinal intentions are detected. In this way, the Renaissance reanimates at once a philosophical and an aesthetic tradition; for precedents could be found in antiquity: as Franz Cumont's work, *Recherches sur le symbolisme funéraire des Romains* (1942), has revealed, mythological characters, episodes, and emblems, reproduced by marble cutters on Roman sarcophagi of the imperial era, were selected for their symbolic and not only for their decorative value: these figures had been "spiritualized" in the schools of philosophy, whose esoteric interpretations had infiltrated the artists' workshops.

One of the keys to Renaissance mythologies is the so-called Orphic theology, which Plato, according to Proclus, had inherited. It is a triadic system, a philosophy of transmutation. Development of the One into three; coincidence of the opposites within the unity; *discordia concors*—these formulas provide the solution to seemingly hermetic works of art; they uncover, in fact, their hidden structure: for mythology, too, has its triads of Graces and Fates, illustrating procession, conversion, and return. Under Paris' eyes perfection resolves itself into three goddesses. Furthermore, each of the gods is an ambiguous one: he contains both extremes. Mercury is at once the eloquent and the silent god; Apollo inspires both frenzy and moderation; Minerva is peaceful and warlike; Pan is hidden into Proteus. This duplicity generates inexhaustible combinations, as the divinities are alternately divided and conjoined through a dialectic movement. As for Marsyas and Psyche, their story conveys essentially the same lesson: purification through trial. The earthly Marsyas suffers torture in order that the celestial Apollo should be crowned; Psyche's misfortunes are but the stages of a mystical initiation, ending up in redemption.

This Orphic revival coincides with a rehabilitation of Epicureanism, whose teachings are now reconciled with those of Plotinus: pleasure is deemed valuable, and sensual delight exalted as a noble passion. This hedonism with its spiritual overtones also finds its radiant expression in Titian's masterpieces. Finally, other aspects of humanism and art remain obscure, until one takes into account paradoxical or ironical intentions: the Neo-Platonists had learned from Plato himself the way of dealing playfully with sacred subjects; Apuleius and Lucian had taught them the *serio ludere*, "art of playing seriously." The facetious note is perceptible in Giovanni Bellini's *Feast of the Gods;* and the mood in Mantegna's *Parnassus* is humorous rather than heroic. The unique appeal of the great mythological compositions of the Renaissance results ultimately from the fact that, whether they smile or vaticinate, they are shining through veils: *Vela faciunt honorem secreti.*

In France and Germany as well, an analysis of mythological representations would reveal how deeply they are impregnated with humanistic thought; and again, in the greatest works "the hidden depth comes to the surface." Dürer's gods, for instance, should be reviewed in their context which is the circle of Peutinger, Schedel, Pirkheimer, and Celtes. Tracing the origins and the fortunes of a particular figure, such as *Hercules gallicus*, means roaming over several fields and several countries. This unwonted type of Hercules, first described by Lucian, shows the hero dragging a troop of prisoners, chained to his tongue by their ears. We meet him again in Dürer, in Holbein, and Geoffroy Tory. Quite naturally this figure which to the humanists was the flattering symbol of eloquence, also serves as an emblem to the French Kings: we meet it again in the decorations designed by Jean Goujon in 1549 for the stately entry of Henri II in Paris. The mythological programs of such festivities originated in the French Academies (the first model of which was the Neo-Platonist Academy in Florence); in France also, poets and scholars were called upon to provide the themes for monumental decorations: Pontus de Tyard suggests for Anet "twelve fables dealing with rivers and fountains, all drawn from Greek and Egyptian mythology."

Such learned suggestions carry a danger of pedanticism. The greater artists retain a freshness of feeling, but mythology is gradually codified in bookish form. Leaving aside the editions of the *Metamorphoses*, which multiply in the whole of Europe, the main authorities used in the first half of the sixteenth century were still, as we have seen, either those which had been used by the Middle Ages or the medieval collections themselves: Boccaccio's *Genealogia deorum* had remained without a rival. Towards the middle of the century, a series of handbooks appear: G. B. Gyraldi's *De Deis gentium varia et multiplex Historia*, Natale Conti's *Mythologiae*, Vincenzo Cartari's *Immagini degli dei degli antichi*. The first one, the work of a philologist, seems to have been destined for a scholarly circle; the other two cater to a larger public: from the number of their editions and of their translations one may conjecture that for a century or more they were to be found in every cultivated man's library.

Cartari's main purpose, however, is iconographical, and his handbook is illustrated from 1571 onwards. The illustration, as the text itself, is largely nonclassical. It gathers together a bizarre Pantheon where oriental, Celtic, and Germanic divinities mix with the Greco-Roman ones. Yet it is this miscellaneous mythology that the late Pléiade poets and the Elizabethans feed on; its elements and its spirit pervade the English *masques* as well as the great pictorial cycles of G. Vasari, J. Zucchi, and F. Zuccari. These productions rest on such erudite and complex arguments that they need detailed commentaries, or *ragionamenti*, to be understood at all. By the end of the century, it is clear that mythology has become a science. In their dogmatic treatises on painting, G. B. Armenini and G. P. Lomazzo proclaim the necessity for the artists to consult learned authorities on the subject; and the study of the Fable becomes part of the syllabus in the academies of Fine Arts.

At the same time when pagan imagery is strictly codified and widely diffused (mythological texts, including Ovid, are presented more and more in the form of dictionaries), the Counter-Reformation has been taking place; the Catholic Reformation transforms the world of literature and art. It should have started a reaction, and indeed the Fable is banned as profane and lascivious; yet it cannot be eradicated from culture: churchmen themselves cannot repudiate, as humanists, a tradition which they condemn as theologians. Furthermore, they possess a convenient justification for the use of mythology: like the Fathers of the Church, they offer allegory as an antidote to pagan venom. The allegorical monument of the period is Cesare Ripa's *Iconologia*, first published in 1593. It digests the mythological knowledge accumulated by the Renaissance, and turns it into a dictionary of symbols: every image is converted into an abstraction.

The great masters of allegory, however, are the Jesuits. Their educational program integrated pagan letters into the scheme of Christian instruction; in circumstances not unlike those in which the Fathers had found themselves—face to face, that is, with a culture which they knew to be contrary to their faith, but which enjoyed immense traditional prestige—they adopted a similar attitude. They, too, recall the example of the Jews taking away the Egyptians' jewels; and they, once more, accept and transmit the pagan heritage—but they turn it to good purpose. Mythology occupies a place of honor in Jesuit colleges: not only are the gods consecrated as elements of rhetoric and ornaments of formal discourse; their stories, again, are presented as a body of moral precepts, cunningly hidden under the mask of fiction. Along with mythology, the Jesuits teach their pupils the science of "emblematics": Does not that science consist precisely in imparting instruction through figures drawn from the Fable? The Emblems, in fact, were perfectly adapted to the Jesuits' pedagogical principle: to combine the useful and the pleasurable. More generally, the persistence of the humanistic tradition in education makes the gods, more than ever, a part of the mental furniture of civilized Europeans. True, they are now reduced to tutorial, or ceremonial, functions; but for that very reason the *merveilleux païen* is all the more readily accepted: mythology has acquired the authority of a convention. To the baroque age, fond of decorative and theatrical splendor, it will offer an inexhaustible wealth of imagery.

Its absorption into Western culture from late antiquity on has been, therefore, a continuous process. Saved from oblivion and protected from hostility by the systems devised by the ancients themselves about its nature and significance, it could not be excluded from either art, poetry, or education. A tenacious tradition gathers up all that had survived of the fabulous world of paganism and hands it on, as common currency, down through the ages.

It is legitimate, as pointed out above, to speak of the "resurrection" of the gods during the Renaissance insofar as they recovered in that period their classical form and their full prestige. It is legitimate, also, to speak of their decline at the end of the Renaissance insofar as mythology from then on becomes increasingly erudite and diminishingly alive, less and less felt and more and more conventional. Poetic sentiment seems to be drying up. Yet, the gods are still to experience astonishing revivals, even after they have been relegated to the schoolroom, or to the stage machinery of opera: the names of Rubens and Poussin suffice to remind us that genius can always give them back their blood and their soul.

BIBLIOGRAPHY

J. Seznec's *The Survival of the Pagan Gods* (New York, 1953) brings bibliographical information up to that date. R. R. Bolgar's *The Classical Heritage and its Beneficiaries* (New York, 1954) gives a survey of the transmission and absorption of ancient culture up to the end of the Renaissance. H. Hunger's *Lexikon der griechischen und römischen Mythologie, mit Hinweisen auf das Fortwirken antiker Stoffe und Motive in der bildenden Kunst, Literatur und Musik des Abendlandes bis zur Gegenwart* (Vienna, 1953) provides a useful repertory.

Especially important among recent studies are: for late antiquity, A. Momigliano, ed., *Conflict Between Paganism* and Christianity in the Fourth Century (New York, 1963). For the medieval period: F. Munari, *Ovid im Mittelalter* (Zurich and Stuttgart, 1960); P. Renucci, *Dante disciple et juge du monde gréco-latin* (Clermont-Ferrand, 1954); S. Viarre, *La survie d'Ovide dans la littérature scientifique du 12e et 13e siècles* (Paris, 1966). For the Renaissance period: A. Chastel, *Marsile Ficin et l'art*, Travaux d'Humanisme et Renaissance, XIV (Lille and Geneva, 1954); E. Garin, with M. Brini, C. Vasoli, and C. Zambelli, *Testi umanistici su l'ermetismo* (Rome, 1955); E. Iversen, *The Myth of Egypt and its Hieroglyphs in European Tradition* (New York, 1961); R. Klibansky, E. Panofsky, and F. Saxl, *Saturn and Melancholy* (New York, 1964); DeW. T. Starnes and E. W. Talbert, *Classical Myth and Legend in Renaissance Dictionaries* (Durham, N.C., 1956); E. Wind, *Pagan Mysteries in the Renaissance* (New York, 1958).

Monographs have been dedicated to individual myths, such as: A. Buck, *Der Orpheus Mythos in der italienischen Renaissance* (Krefeld, 1961); R. Trousson, *Le thème de Prométhée dans la littérature européenne* (Geneva, 1964); L. Vinge, *The Narcissus Theme in Western European Literature up to the XIXth Century* (Lund, 1967).

JEAN SEZNEC

[See also **Allegory;** Astrology; Christianity in History; Demonology; **Hermeticism;** Iconography; **Neo-Platonism.**]

MYTH IN ENGLISH LITERATURE: SEVENTEENTH AND EIGHTEENTH CENTURIES

OF THE SEVERAL generally recognized theories of the interpretation of myth: the historical, or euhemeristic; the physical, or cosmographical; the allegorical; and the allegorical-theological, the writers of the seventeenth century seem to have been chiefly occupied with the latter two, and it is interesting that each of these theories finds respective support from two of the most eminent literary figures who lived at the turn of the century. Sir Francis Bacon in *De sapientia veterum* (1608; translated in 1619 by Sir Arthur Gorges as *The Wisdome of the Ancients*) interprets allegorically some thirty-one classical myths, treating them as "elegant and instructive fables." Sir Walter Raleigh declares in his *History of the World* (1614) that "Jubal, Tubal, and Tubal-Cain were Mercury, Vulcan, and Apollo, inventors of pasturage, smithing, and music. The dragon which kept the golden apples was the serpent that beguiled Eve. Nimrod's tower was the attempt of the giants against heaven" (C. M. Gayley, *Classic Myths . . .*, Waltham, Mass. [1939], pp. 439–40).

Among writers who introduced other varieties and combinations of interpretations during the period George Chapman (d. 1634) is one of the most perplexing and eccentric. He was both a belated Elizabethan and a harbinger of the later sophistications of the seventeenth century. As Douglas Bush says, Chapman was "at once an orthodox and a notably individual exemplar of Renaissance humanism. His contempt for the unlettered crowd and his faith in culture and poetry are proclaimed with more than normal fervor" (Bush, a, p. 223). Notwithstanding his "completion" of Marlowe's *Hero and Leander*, he is nearer to John Donne, Ben Jonson, and Fulke Greville than to Marlowe and Spenser. As early as 1595 Chapman defends a deliberate obscurity of composition and style on moral and ethical grounds. In a dedicatory epistle to his friend Matthew Roydon, the learned mathematician, he wrote,

The profane multitude I hate, and only consecrate my strange poems to those searching spirits whom learning hath made noble, and nobility sacred . . . varying in some rare fiction from popular custom, even for the pure sakes of ornament and utility. . . .

But that Poesy should be as pervial as oratory and plainness her special ornament, were the plain way to barbarism, and to make the ass run proud of his ears, to take away strength from lions, and give camels horns.

The argument continues with an illustration from the art of painting, that was to become one of the most popular conventions of the seventeenth century:

It serves not a skilful painter's turn to draw the figure of a face only to make known who it represents; but he must limn, give lustre, shadow, and heightening; which though ignorants will esteem spiced, and too curious, yet such as have the judicial perspective will see it hath motion, spirit, and life . . . (*Poems*, ed. Swinburne [1875], pp. 21–22).

Chapman published one of the most extraordinarily mythological poems of the period, the *Andromeda liberata* (1614), which allegorically portrays the Earl of Somerset as Perseus and the Countess of Essex as Andromeda. The scandals in which this couple were involved stand in great contrast to their virtues in the poem as extolled by the author, who rallies to defend them against "the monstrous beast, the ravenous multitude." It is with no surprise that we learn that the poem was not well received, or that Chapman was impelled shortly to publish a prose tract in "justification" of the work, which concludes with a dialogue in verse between Pheme (Rumor) and Theodines (divinely-inspired Chapman himself).

Our special interest in the *Andromeda* lies, however, in the indebtedness that even so learned and enthusiastic a classical scholar as Chapman owed to the mythographers and to other continental sources, ancient and recent. Thanks to the original and extensive researches of M. Schoell (1926) it is clear that much of the poem derives in part from Natalis Comes, in part from Xylander's Plutarch, and in part from Pausanias by way of Ficino (Schoell, pp. 3, 14, 32, 40, 195, 234–35; it is shown that the prose Argument, prefixed to the poem, is an exact translation of passages in Comes' *Mythologiae*. See also Phyllis Bartlett's edition of Chapman's poems, Introduction, p. 10, and Notes, p. 462). In this eclecticism, coupled with his fervid dedication to the Homeric ideals and to the principles of Renaissance Platonism, Chapman is a strikingly representative, as well as an oddly individual, transitional figure.

In pursuing our examination of typical attitudes toward myth, we should bear in mind that the full impact of Renaissance influence took effect considerably later in England than in Italy or France, with the result that many motifs, themes, and forms of expression which had been vigorous and popular in continental Europe for decades became naturalized in England more slowly and gradually.

Rosemund Tuve, in her study of *Elizabethan and Metaphysical Imagery* (1947), observed that because of their long inheritance and continuous practice, Elizabethan writers and their audience could accommodate readily even to extremes of indulgence in allegorical, metaphorical, and symbolic imagery. She pointed out that both writers and readers had long been accustomed to "allegorizing" myth, that is, to considering myths, not as toys nor as part of history, but as sets of symbols embodying universally meaningful notions— an attitude that became "related to rooted habits of thought" (p. 161). This habit of easy comprehension of double meanings, or even of more complex relationships, persists at least to the beginning of the "age of reason," and attests to the vigor of the mythological tradition in England.

In some respects the seventeenth century differed greatly from the Renaissance, of course, and these differences were ultimately to have the effect of dampening the enthusiasm for mythology that had earlier amounted almost to rapture. Yet the roots of Renaissance culture were deep, and the death of the gods was far from a sudden expiration. If John Milton, the Puritan, felt occasionally uncomfortable in the presence of the pagan deities with which his Christian poetry abounds, yet his expert use of mythological themes, motifs, and personages certainly does not suffer by comparison with that of Spenser. It seems clear that it was owing, in part, to the survival of Spenserianism, through such writers as Michael Drayton, Giles Fletcher (1585–1623) and his brother Phineas (1582– 1650)—both sons of Giles Fletcher, the elder (1548–

1611)—and William Browne of Tavistock, author of *Britannia's Pastorals* (1613–16), that the use of myth for natural and moral allegory continued for some years to find a congenial audience. Certain non-Spenserians as well, like Ben Jonson and his "sons"; the metaphysical poets; and the later Andrew Marvell (e.g., his *Daphnis and Chloe*) illustrate the persistence and variety of the allegorical-mythological strain.

Drayton's treatment, which owes much to the Elizabethan decorative and pastoral mode, continues for some time as an attractive fashion, in contrast to Chapman's muscular, recondite, and obscure style; but toward and beyond the middle of the century the difference between the later poets and translators and their Elizabethan prototypes becomes more apparent and more influential.

Nevertheless, the Elizabethan character is still strong in poems like Shakerley Marmion's *Legend of Cupid and Psyche* (1637) and in Sir Richard Fanshawe's translation, *The Fourth Book of Virgil's Aeneid on the Loves of Dido and Aeneas* (1648). Bush comments particularly upon the value and significance of the latter work and cites an enthusiastic passage from an essay on Fanshawe by J. W. Mackail in praise of the translation and its civilizing influence (Bush, a, p. 246).

But before such a "civilized" objective could be completely achieved many things were to happen that would effectively postpone the advent of neo-classicism in England. Within the year King Charles was executed, and shortly thereafter John Milton was to give up his muse for the mighty pen of controversial prose.

In the meantime certain forces continued to operate effectively in England after they had lost some of their momentum in continental Europe. One of these was the remarkable popularity of the emblem book. Another was the progressive transit of ideas which related poetry to the graphic and plastic arts. This phenomenon stemmed mainly from dogmatic treatises like those of Armenini and Lomazzo. As Jean Seznec has shown, the influence of these writers was important in establishing the notion that artists should consult learned authorities on the subject of mythological representation (pp. 257–58). Before pursuing this point let us look into the vogue of the emblem book.

In the encyclopedic *Anatomy of Melancholy* (1621) Robert Burton devotes a section to the pangs and effects of love. Having anatomized all the symptoms, and having cited dozens of examples of infatuated lovers in literature all the way from Homer to Spenser, the author concludes with the following paragraph:

The major part of lovers are carried headlong like so many brute beasts, reason counsels one way, thy friends, fortunes, shame, disgrace, danger, and an ocean of cares that will certainly follow; yet this furious lust precipitates, counterpoiseth, weighs down on the other; though it be their utter undoing, perpetual infamy, loss, yet they will do it, and become at last *insensati*, void of sense; degenerate into dogs, hogs, asses, brutes; as *Jupiter* into a Bull, *Apuleius* an Ass, *Lycaon* a Wolf, *Tereus* a Lap-wing, *Callisto* a Bear, *Elpenor* and *Gryllus* into Swine by *Circe*. For what else may we think those ingenious Poets to have shadowed in their witty fictions and Poems, but that a man once given over to his lust (as Fulgentius interprets that of *Apuleius, Alciat.* of *Tereus*) is no better than a beast (*The Anatomy of Melancholy*, The Third Partition, Sec. II, Subsec. I, p. 177).

Burton's reference to "Alciat." directs our attention to that ubiquitous and durable form of expression, the emblem book, that is often a deliberate combination of the literary and the figurative, the moral and the decorative, the aristocratic and the homely, the "pervial" and the obscure, the secular and the sacred. Relatively a latecomer in the Renaissance, its pioneer author was Andrea Alciati, a learned jurist, whose *Emblematum liber* was published at least as early as 1531 and frequently thereafter. It became the inspiration and chief source for a host of emblem writers and collectors throughout Europe.

The connection of Spenser (the "new poet" of the English Renaissance) with this development is found in van der Noodt's *Theatre for Worldlings* (1569) containing translated canzoni of Petrarch illustrated by woodcuts, but still more abundantly in the *Shepheardes Calendar*, with its numerous emblems, devices, and mottoes. Contemporary readers of the *Faerie Queene* could easily recognize characteristics of the genre in detailed descriptive attributes of many an allegorical personage which were related in one way or another to the emblem literature. The first English anthology of emblems was Geoffrey Whitney's *A Choice of Emblems* (1586), which contains a wide variety of emblematic material and was evidently widely popular.

In 1605 William Camden, a much respected historian and courtier of both Queen Elizabeth and King James, inserts a passage in his learned *Remaines . . . concerning Britaine* that takes the trouble to distinguish between the *impresa* and the *emblem* (this is quoted in full by Chew, pp. 275–76). And Francis Quarles, whose *Emblemes* appeared in 1635 and in innumerable editions thereafter, stated that "An emblem is but a silent parable"—an unsatisfactory definition because it both oversimplifies and confuses. Mario Praz has provided what is perhaps the most accurate and useful definition of this complicated species: "An emblem is a symbolic figure accompanied by a motto, an explication in verse, and sometimes a prose commentary" ("Embleme," *Enciclopedia Italiana*, 18, 861, quoted by Chew, p. 395).

It is generally agreed that Henry Peacham's *Minerva*

Britanna or a Garden of Heroical Devices (1612) is the most representative of the emblem books in English, although the later publications of Wither and Quarles enjoyed a longer popularity. In other respects Peacham deserves our attention, and especially for his treatises on drawing and painting, *Graphice* (1606) and the *Gentleman's Exercise* (1612), comprising material subsequently included in the *Compleat Gentleman* (1st ed. 1622). It is worth noting that Peacham composed other emblem books: *Basilicon doron* and *Emblemata varia*, several manuscripts of which are extant in the British Museum. In the *Minerva* Peacham rather wistfully regrets that his own countrymen have not been very fertile in the production of emblem books.

Peacham's teaching in the *Compleat Gentleman* is consistent with Elizabethan and Renaissance doctrine generally as seen in various courtesy books, but he devotes special attention to the arts, including drawing and painting, architecture, music, sculpture, and heraldry, as well as to the criticism of poetry. In the latter his indebtedness to Scaliger is very evident. For our purpose, the importance of Peacham is his recognition of the interrelationship between poetry and the other arts, with considerable attention to mythology. In his chapter "Of Poetry" he naturally devotes most attention to Vergil, whom he calls the "King of Latine Poets," and to Ovid, whom he declares to be next in rank because of "the sweetnesse and smooth current of his stile, every where seasoned with profound and antique learning . . . every where embellished with excellent and wise Sentences." Peacham raises an eyebrow slightly when he refers to the "wanton" passages; but he adds, "Concerning his bookes *Amorum* and *De arte amandi*, the wit with the truely ingenuous and learned will beare out the wantonnesse: for with the weeds there are delicate flowers in those walkes of Venus" (*Compleat Gentleman*, p. 88).

Thus we see in Peacham a popular illustration of the two main streams of influence in the handling of mythology: the literary and the figurative; and we note that the taste for pictorial representation of the myths of the gods, so evident in the sixteenth century, continues into the next.

The kind of tapestry portrayals in which Spenser delighted were repeated quite as elaborately by Drayton, who provided, in addition, an extensive description of mythological scenes as rendered by a painter upon wall panels. Just as Christopher Sly in the *Taming of the Shrew* had been regaled by the servants with a showing of pictures representing Venus and Adonis, Jupiter and Io, and Apollo and Daphne, so the reader of Drayton's *Barons' Wars* (1603) is treated to a gallery of similar paintings, to which the poet devotes a whole series of seven-line stanzas of vivid Ovidian description (*Works*, ed. Hebel, II, 110–13). In his own marginal notes on the passage Drayton expounds the mythological figures, events, and settings, making use of technical terms from the arts— terms that were relatively new in England: *landskip, cornice, pilaster*. He notes that "a steady and pure Light giveth much grace to Painting" (ibid., p. 113).

That such descriptions were not mere figments of the imagination is shown in a variety of ways; for example, a number of extant inventories testify to the abundance and gorgeousness of this kind of decoration, both in the Elizabethan and in the Stuart periods. The inventory of Leicester House, 1588, lists over 150 items of tapestry. Although the inventories do not list all titles of tapestries or paintings in detail, there can be no mistaking items like "Cupid and Venus," "Diana bathyng hirselfe with hir nymphes," and "A picture of Diana and Acteon." An inventory of the Earl of Somerset's effects, made in 1615, lists, along with other rich furnishings, tapestry, hangings representing the wars of Troy, two of "Roman Story, thirteen feet deep," and besides a variety of paintings of biblical subjects, the following familiar, and obviously Ovidian themes: "Venus and Cupid," "Bacchus, Ceres, and Venus," and "Venus and Adonis."

During the first half of the century there was a considerable amount of activity in the importation of works of art from abroad, many of them certainly of mythological subjects. Courtiers like Arundel, Salisbury, and Buckingham vied with each other and even with King James and King Charles in the splendor of their collections. The royal galleries at Hampton Court, Richmond, Nonesuch, and Whitehall were so magnificent as to call forth admiration by a number of visitors from the continent (W. B. Rye, *England as Seen by Foreigners . . .* , pp. 200, 242–43).

At the same time that Inigo Jones was introducing Palladian architecture into England, he was designing elaborate mythological settings for the masques for Ben Jonson, Chapman, and their fellows. It was to Jones that Chapman dedicated his translation of Musaeus (1616). The Stuart taste for courtly display, ceremonies, and "triumphs," with their frequent figures from myth, was no less lively than that of the Elizabethans.

Sir Henry Wotton, during his ambassadorship to Venice, which extended over a period of twenty years, collected Italian paintings for Salisbury and Buckingham, and for James I and Charles I. Logan Pearsall Smith wrote of Wotton that he was "the most accomplished connoisseur of the time—a time when there was in England a truer love of beauty, and a juster appreciation of art, than there had been before, or indeed, than there has ever been since" (*Life and Letters of Sir Henry Wotton*, I, 194–95).

Against such a background Andrew Marvell's poem *The Gallery* becomes perhaps more meaningful, especially in the light of its pictorial and emblematic qualities. Here the gallery is the lover's soul, with the great arras hangings laid away, and only the portrait of his mistress Clora remaining in his mind. The poem proceeds with two pairs of contrasting (portrait) stanzas: the first, of the murthress with tormenting instruments versus Aurora in the dawn; the second, the enchantress vexing her lover's ghost versus the picture of Venus in her pearly boat. There follow two stanzas, in the first of which the poet declares that besides the pictures already described there are a thousand more, either to please or torment, indeed a "num'rous Colony" of a collection "choicer far/ then or Whitehall's or Mantua's were." This is an allusion to Charles I's great collection at Whitehall to which was added that of the Duke of Mantua, which was finally dispersed by act of Parliament in July, 1650 (*Social England*, IV, 107). In the conclusion the poet declares that of all these wonderful pictures the one "at the Entrance," which portrays Clora as her lover first saw her, pleases him the most, for its simple, pastoral charm:

> A tender Shepherdess, whose Hair
> Hangs loosely playing in the Air,
> Transplanting Flow'rs from the green Hill,
> To crown her Head, and Bosome fill.

Another current of influence from the continent found its way into the stream of ideas—a variation on the conventional *ut pictura* theme which relates the painter to the poet. This notion continued to flourish in England for a considerable period of time after the translation of Giovanni Paolo Lomazzo's *Trattato dell'arte della pittura* by an odd scholar of Oxford, Richard Haydocke, student of Physic, which was published in 1598. Nicholas Hilliard, the miniaturist, read and applauded the work which appears to have inspired his own treatise on the art of limning (published by the Walpole Society, ed. Norman [1912], I, 1–50).

From the point of view of this survey it is significant that several seventeenth-century writers on painting helped themselves to Haydocke's translation, usually without acknowledgment, and promulgated its notions, dogmas, and conventions to their succeeding audiences. Perhaps the most flagrant of these plagiarists was Alexander Browne, a mid-century painter, engraver, and teacher of London, one of whose pupils was Mrs. Samuel Pepys. He published in 1660 *The Whole Art of Drawing*. This was followed in 1669, by *Ars Pictoria: or an Academy treating of Drawing, Painting, Limning, Etching*. A second edition, "corrected and enlarged," was printed in 1675. The whole book is a complex of borrowings from Haydocke's translation. It is practically a verbatim reprint, except that Browne has tried to conceal his pilferings by juggling the order of the chapters; but the attempt at deception would be immediately discovered by any reader familiar with Haydocke's Lomazzo.

Lomazzo devotes almost a whole book (VII) to the iconography of the gods. As Seznec has shown, Lomazzo owes practically all of his text in this section to Vincenzo Cartari's *Genealogia,* which he reproduces in abridged form (p. 258). This is another instance of the indirect influence of the mythographers in successive periods, and further testimony of the relatively late inflow of continental commentary on literature and the arts into England. Lomazzo's advice to painters that they should read the poets for information and inspiration is emphasized in Haydocke's book, especially in the sections on "The Passions of the Mind" and "Actions and Gestures." Here the author calls attention to the poets, who in similes and examples deal with men or animals in vigorous action, such, he says, "as we may find in Homer, Virgil, Ovid, Horace, Catullus, etc., all of which the worthy Ariosto hath imitated in that his incomparabel Furioso." On this passage Haydocke comments, in a note printed in the margin, as follows: "Our English Painters may reade Sir Philip Sidney, Spencer [sic], Daniel, etc."

This theme is taken up again in another work which looks backward to the sixteenth and forward to the eighteenth century—*The Painting of the Ancients* by Franciscus Junius (François du Jon) the Huguenot scholar who lived in England for a considerable number of years, and for whom the Junius Manuscript is named. He was librarian of the Earl of Arundel, whose magnificent collection of art was intact at the time. In 1637 Junius published, in Amsterdam, *De pictura veterum.* This work was declared by Roland Fréart, Sieur de Chambray, to be so valuable that it would have rendered unnecessary the writing of his own book (*Idée de la perfection de la peinture,* 1662) if the painters for whom he wrote had been able to read Latin. The same impediment had deprived the Countess of Arundel of enjoying the work, so Junius tells us, and she commanded an English translation, which Junius made and published in London in 1683. Junius owes something to Haydocke's Lomazzo for his plan and chapter organization, and in Book III, Chapter VI he pays respect to Spenser and Sidney by quotation, and indeed, here and elsewhere, he is under marked obligations to E. K.'s commentary on the *Shepheardes Calender.*

Other contributions to this collocation of ideas would include Sir William Sanderson's *Graphice* (1668), the anonymous treatise called *The Excellency of the Pen and Pencil* (1668), and the exceedingly popular *Poly-*

graphice of William Salmon, which went through eight editions between 1672 and 1701. The eighth edition of this *omnium gatherum* consists of 475 pages of text, embellished with twenty-five copper-plate engravings of a kind usual in manuals of drawing and painting, all preceded by an engraved portrait of Salmon himself and a fulsome dedicatory epistle addressed to Sir Godfrey Kneller. In a preface Salmon says "In this Eighth Edition we have inserted above five hundred several additions of singular use to the matter in hand . . . ," and he points particularly to chapters on the portrayal of abstract figures and allegorical personages according to ancient authority; for example Book iv, Ch. xv shows "How the Ancients depicted Neptune, and the Sea Gods," and there are over fifteen sections on similar topics. He says that these "various depictings of the Ancients, according to the Customs of several Nations, [are] drawn from the best, most experienced Authors, whether English, Italian or Latin: together with the Original Advancement and Perfection of these Arts." It is no surprise to find that the author has helped himself freely to the words of his predecessors (there are five or six pages lifted bodily from Franciscus Junius), and that so derivative and miscellaneous a text is mainly useful in showing, first, the wide diffusion of the combined pictorial and literary ideas in the allegorical tradition; secondly, the extraordinary multiplicity and variety of sources; and lastly, the apparent demand by a wide public for such composite treatises. On this last point it is worth remarking that in examining examples of these handbooks of the seventeenth century, one is struck by the evident attention with which many of them were read by their original or other owners, who frequently inscribed heavy underscorings or elaborate marginalia, often pictorial as well as written.

In mentioning his foreign sources Salmon restricts himself to the authors who wrote in Latin or Italian, omitting the French.

The influence of French manual writers upon the English can be illustrated by such books as Roland Fréart's *Parallèle de l'architecture antique avec la moderne* (Paris, 1650), translated by John Evelyn in 1664; and, more importantly, the Latin treatise of Charles Alphonse du Fresnoy (1611–65), and the work of Roger de Piles, who translated du Fresnoy's *De arte graphica* into French (Paris, 1684), and was in turn translated by John Dryden. The latter's English version was first published in 1695. Towards the end of the eighteenth century du Fresnoy's work was again translated by William Mason, with annotations by Sir Joshua Reynolds and a catalogue of eminent painters by Thomas Gray.

In de Piles's "Observations" on du Fresnoy's text,

included as a kind of appendix, the translator urges the painter to furnish himself sufficiently with good reading, for "Learning is necessary to animate his Genius and to complete it." The list of recommended reading includes Homer, Vergil, Ovid, Philostratus, Plutarch, and Pausanias. Lack of proficiency in the ancient tongues is no excuse, for "translations being made of the best authors, there is not any Painter who is not capable, in some sort, of understanding those books of Humanity which are comprehended under the name of *belles Lettres*" (1716 ed., p. 111). Especially commended are Spenser's *Faerie Queene*, the *Paradise Lost* of Milton, Fairfax's translation of Tasso, and the History of Polybius, by Sir Henry Shere (p. 112). The mythographers, like Boccaccio, Cartari, and Natalis Comes are not neglected, for we find (p. 113) "The *Mythology* of the Gods," "The *Images* of the Gods," and "The *Iconology*." De Piles commends two other of his compatriots: André Félibien and Roland Fréart. Regarding the latter author's *Parallèle*, he recommends the Preface rather than the book itself. He says of Félibien's treatises on history, architecture, and painting, that their foundations are "wonderfully solid" (p. 115). Finally, he completes this "Library of a Painter" with three works which, as we have already seen, were widely used by handbook writers, emblem book writers, and painters, namely, those of Armenini, Lomazzo, and Franciscus Junius.

As can be observed in the researches of Franck L. Schoell and Charles W. Lemmi, the works of Chapman, Bacon, and a number of their contemporaries relied heavily upon the manuals of Renaissance mythographers for their handling of myth, allegory, and symbol. Information on these and other widely used secondary source manuals has been extended more recently by De Witt T. Starnes and Ernest William Talbert in their book, *Classical Myth and Legend in Renaissance Dictionaries* (1955). Beginning with the *Elucidarius* of the Dutch scholar Herman Torrentinus (1498) the authors trace the enormous popularity of this work through its various versions, especially the *Dictionarium* by the Stephanus brothers, Robert and Charles. Of this there were at least nine editions before 1600; and throughout the seventeenth century the book appeared to be "especially cherished by English poets and dramatists." Ultimately it became the basis of Louis Moreri's encyclopedic *Grand Dictionnaire Historique*, published in Lyons in 1674. This is only one of a number of dictionaries, lexicons, and other manuals whose effect on literary history has been established by Starnes and Talbert. The particular bearing of such works of reference has been treated in separate chapters of their work, relating respectively to the minor Elizabethan writers, to Spenser, Shake-

speare, Ben Jonson, Thomas Heywood, and John Milton. There is an important appendix devoted to the second edition of George Sandys' translation of Ovid's *Metamorphoses* (1632).

The full title of this last-named work is *Ovid's Metamorphoses Englished Mythologiz'd and Represented in figures by G. S.* Bush calls Sandys' commentary "the greatest repository of allegorized myth in English," and mentions its attraction for John Keats (Bush, a, pp. 254–55). A hint of its prodigious range can be given in a partial list of authorities whom Sandys cites. They include Plato, Plutarch, Raphael Regius, Jacobus Micyllus, Muretus, Stephanus, Hyginus, Diodorus, Saint Augustine, Macrobius, Fulgentius, Lactantius, Vives, Comes, Copernicus, Galileo, Tycho Brahe, and Francis Bacon.

We have already noticed Bacon's redaction of myths in his *Wisdom of Ancients*. Two brief references to his preface to that work will show Bacon's main view of mythological interpretation. He believes that from the beginning there lay beneath the fables of the ancient poets "a mystery and an allegory"; and he concedes that perhaps his reverence for the primitive times may have carried him too far. Yet he is convinced of the truth that:

In some of these fables, as well as in the very frame and texture of the story as in the propriety of the names by which the persons that figure in it are distinguished, I find a conformity and a connexion with the thing signified, so close and so evident, that one cannot help believing such a significance to have been designed and meditated from the first, and purposely shadowed out. . . .

After giving several illustrations of this point he proceeds next to an argument from the very absurdity of mythical narrative itself, which points to the need for mythological interpretation:

. . . for a fable that is probable may be thought to have been composed merely for pleasure, in imitation of history. But when a story is told which could never have entered any man's head either to conceive or relate on its own account, we must presume that it had some further reach.

He gives as an instance the myth of Jupiter and Metis:

Jupiter took Metis to wife: as soon as he saw that she was with child, he ate her up; whereupon he grew to be with child himself; and so brought forth out of his head Pallas in armour! Surely I think no man had ever a dream so monstrous and extravagant, and out of all natural ways of thinking. . . .

Following some further reflections upon "all kinds of fables, and enigmas, and parables, and similitudes," Bacon reaches the conclusion that the wisdom of the primitive ages was either great or lucky:

. . . great, if they knew what they were doing and invented the figure to shadow the meaning; lucky, if without meaning or intending it they fell upon matter which gives occasion to such worthy contemplations. My own pains, if there be any help in them, I shall think well bestowed either way: I shall be throwing light either upon antiquity or upon nature itself . . . (*The Wisdome of the Ancients, Works*, VI, 695–99).

There can be small doubt that Bacon's treatment of myth was attractive to his seventeenth-century readers, many of whom would have been familiar also with the commentary of Sandys that testified to the great man's authority.

Although the variegated literary and pictorial forms of expression continued more or less sporadically for some years, it is apparent that significant artistic use of mythology is gradually on the wane after the last and greatest of its English exponents, John Milton, completed his work.

From this point onwards in the seventeenth and eighteenth centuries mythological literature is treated facetiously, and consists mainly of innumerable and unedifying examples of mock-heroics, burlesques, political satires, or other kinds of travesty.

Bush explains the eclipse of a serious concern with mythology at this time as resulting from a number of causes, including the rise of Puritanism, the new philosophies which had their seeds in Bacon and Descartes, and an increasingly skeptical rationalism manifested by a "cool Anglicanism and a cooler Deism;" and he concludes that "our great classical age is the age of sterility" as regards the importance of its use of classical mythology, whatever its other undeniable virtues may be." He clinches this observation with the remark, "Milton is a poet; Dryden is a man of letters" (Bush, a, p. 309).

Doctor Johnson was impatient with Milton's use of myth (see his *Life* of Milton, especially the strictures on the mythological allusions in *Lycidas*); and Joseph Addison condemned mythology generally and Milton's use of it in particular, allowing its use only for mock-heroic poems like the *Rape of the Lock* (*Spectator*, No. 297). In alluding to Thomas Tickell's poem "The Prospect of Peace" (1712) Addison announced in the *Spectator*, No. 523, "I was particularly well pleased to find that the Author had not amused himself with Fables out of the Pagan Theology, and that when he hints of any thing of this nature, he alludes to it only as a fable." And later in the same issue he declares:

When we are at School it is necessary for us to be acquainted with the System of Pagan Theology, and may be allowed to enliven a Theme, or point an Epigram with an Heathen God; but when we would write a manly Panegyrick, that should carry in it all the Colours of Truth, nothing can be more ridiculous than to have recourse to

our *Jupiter's* and *Juno's* (*Spectator*, ed. Donald F. Bond, II, 361–62).

These views may be taken to represent an era that was preoccupied with common sense, reason, universal truth, and reality. There was small room in that *milieu* for the "heathen gods"; consequently they remained almost completely neglected until their restoration in the romantic revival.

BIBLIOGRAPHY

Robert Burton, *The Anatomy of Melancholy*, ed. A. R. Shilleto (London, 1920). Douglas Bush, (a) *Mythology and the Renaissance Tradition in English Poetry*, rev. ed. (New York, 1963); idem, (b) *Mythology and the Romantic Tradition in English Poetry* (Cambridge, Mass., 1937); both of these volumes contain excellent bibliographies. George Chapman, *Poems*, ed. Phyllis B. Bartlett (New York, 1941). Samuel C. Chew, *The Pilgrimage of Life* (New Haven, 1962). Michael Drayton, *Complete Works*, eds. J. W. Hebel, K. Tillotson, and B. Newdigate, 5 vols. (Oxford, 1931–41). Rosemary Freeman, *English Emblem Books* (London, 1948). Frederick Hard, "Ideas from Bacon and Wotton in William Sanderson's *Graphice*," *Studies in Philology*, **36** (1939), 227–34; idem, "Some Interrelationships Between the Literary and Plastic Arts in Sixteenth and Seventeenth Century England," *College Art Journal*, **10** (1951), 233–43. Charles W. Lemmi, *The Classic Deities in Bacon* (Baltimore, 1933). Henry Peacham, *The Compleat Gentleman*, facsimile of 1634 ed. by G. S. Gordon (Oxford, 1906). Mario Praz, *Studies in Seventeenth Century Imagery* (Rome, 1964); contains an extensive bibliography. Franck L. Schoell, *Études sur l'humanisme continental en Angleterre* (Paris, 1926). Jean Seznec, *The Survival of the Pagan Gods* (New York, 1953). J. E. Spingarn, *Seventeenth Century Critical Essays*, 3 vols. (Oxford, 1908–09). De W. T. Starnes and E. W. Talbert, *Classical Myth and Legend in Renaissance Dictionaries* (Chapel Hill, 1955). Rosemond Tuve, *Allegorical Imagery* (Princeton, 1966); idem, *Elizabethan and Metaphysical Imagery* (Chicago, 1947). Enid Welsford, *The Court Masque* (Cambridge, 1927).

FREDERICK HARD

[See also Baconianism; **Iconography**; **Metaphor**; **Myth**; Renaissance Humanism; **Symbol and Symbolism**; *Ut pictura poesis*.]

MYTH IN THE EIGHTEENTH AND EARLY NINETEENTH CENTURIES

AN IMPORTANT aspect of mythology from 1700 to 1850 is the conscious sense that the true meaning and value of myth is first being rediscovered or even revealed.

The achievement but also the dilemma of mythic thought in this period is to move the problem of myth into ever larger realms. Mythic thought gradually frees itself from the biblical-Christian context, and frees the idea of myth from confinement to the past. The subject of myth broadens first to include non-Christian, non-European religions and histories; but soon broadens still further to include the origins of the "irrational," of civilization, and of art. By 1800, theorists of progress can see myth as almost equivalent with the pre-enlightened human past. Under romantic aegis, myth begins to refer to what is "highest" in man, creatively, and philosophically.

Rationalist Mythology. By 1700, three different views of myth appear. First, the orthodox Christian mythology which sees pagan religion as a corruption or prefiguring of revealed truth; the methods include etymology and comparison of rites and dogmas. Deism, a new approach, explains myth as natural monotheism corrupted into idolatry. Rationalism newly explains myth in terms of secular progress. These new positions emerge distinctly first with Charles Blount's deistic *Great is Diana of the Ephesians* (1680), Bernard de Fontenelle's *Histoire des oracles* (1686), and his *L'Origine des fables* (written 1690–99, published 1724).

Why these approaches may be called new is inseparable from the question why such changes in ideas about myths occurred when they did. The answer lies only partly in new non-Christian or non-European sources of myths. This material had accumulated since the sixteenth century; the early eighteenth century adds little genuinely new—such an exception is W. Bosman's report on African fetishism (1704). The Jesuit Joseph François Lafitau's comparison of American Indian and ancient Greek *moeurs* (1724) is the most influential and detailed inventory of such "conformities" of the period; but it is the culmination of a century of such comparisons of savage or enlightened heathenism with the customs of ancient Israel and Greece. What changes most significantly are the new methods and purposes applied to this comparative material. Confined to internal Christian disputes, myth had been of importance primarily as negative evidence for or against scriptural authority or various doctrines. *Philosophes* and deists use mythic pluralism or analogies to embarrass orthodox Christianity. But a major innovation lies in their hope to reconstruct religious and human history in radically rational terms.

The renewed study of ancient religions served two broad, enduring eighteenth-century purposes: first, to discern the rational principles underlying religion, morality, and history, as achieved earlier for physics; next, to combat intolerance, *l'infâme,* and all irrationality by diagnosing their origins and thus helping to foster a cure. A leading conviction here is that religious and historical origins can indeed be grasped and explained outside revelation; and that with such secure starting-points, the past can be rationally reconstituted. The effect here is to approach ancient religion freshly; recovery of the "true" origins means studying history precisely to be able to criticize and reinterpret it.

In this spirit, Pierre Bayle rereads mythic history via psychology. He corrosively dissolves the half-truths of religious history to penetrate to what really happened there: myth springs from human ignorance or gullibility. But his *pyrrhonisme de l'histoire* seemingly has only negative aims. Bernard Le Bovier de Fontenelle is the first who uses such destructive criticism to seek "certain" knowledge of mythic origins, in order then to reconstruct "true" laws of religious beginnings. With similar assumptions about the right method, deism begins to redefine Christianity in terms of evidence sought outside revealed history. Myth becomes newly important as the main source of such evidence. First, as the epitome of historical unreliability, pagan myth may be safely and boldly analyzed where Christianity must still remain immune. More important, mythic history begins—though only gradually—to stand for earliest nonbiblical history itself.

Euhemerist, psychological, and political explanations of myth are revived naturalistic theories. The three views are connected: myth becomes one or another kind of history. A constant motive here is to discredit any claim by myth to higher meaning. Pagan or Christian allegorism of myth is dismissed or degraded as wrongly dignifying myth or else ignoring history in favor of mystery. The most widespread of these revived views is euhemerism—the doctrine of Euhemerus that the gods are simply idealizations of famous mortals—and the most influential euhemerist treatise of the period is A. Banier's *La Mythologie et les fables expliquées par l'histoire* (1711; revised 1715, and extensively, 1738–40). As an orthodox mythologist, Banier finds euhemerism useful: as merely falsified or mistaken history, myth can be corrected and fitted back into biblical chronology and sacred history. Isaac Newton (1728), Samuel Shuckford (1728), and Dom Calmet (1735) pursue a severe euhemerism. But Banier more typically is also the eclectic *philosophe;* he notes sixteen possible origins for myth and is also interested in myth for its literary value.

Euhemerism is usually blended with other views. Deists primarily exploit the political-moral explanation. Concerned to explain why natural monotheism was succeeded by idolatry, they see myth as utilitarian religion, rising from political and moral purposes. In John Toland's *Letters to Serena* (1704)—an assertive, reductive, typical deist mythology—idolatry begins when men start to worship the dead. This error results from the "Craft and Ambition" of priests and leaders who profit by misleading the multitude; as much blame, however, is due the vulgar multitude's demand for superstitious ritual and dogma—described by Toland with an eye to Catholic practice. Toland's mythology is, in fact, an early, crude version of a thesis elaborated endlessly through the century: that early societies had one religion for the elite, one for the people. The Abbé Noël-Antoine Pluche (1739), David Hume, C. G. Heyne, and Charles François Dupuis repeat the accusation of "priestcraft," while Thomas Blackwell (1735) and Bishop Warburton (1738) defend the priests as civilizers of brutish mankind.

The psychological interpretation of myth is at once the subtlest and finally most important. It is carried forward by Giambattista Vico, David Hume, Charles de Brosses, and Paul-Henri, baron d'Holbach among others; and then, is transmuted from religious enthusiasm to creative imagination and affirmed by romanticism. Fontenelle's *L'Origine des fables* asks why such a strange phenomenon as religion should occur at all in the human mind. His answer is that earliest man reasoned like modern man, explaining the unknown in terms of the known and reacting strongly to nature. But, ignorant of "true philosophy" and *bon sens,* primitive man personified natural causes; myth thus mirrors the weakness and poverty of the savage mind. But as such, myth is crude philosophizing. Thus, too, the natural final goal of mythic thought is not revelation but reason. Myth yields the origins not of idolatry but of civilization: if human nature is unchanging, the American Indian will in time thus become like the ancient Greek. Fontenelle is the first to place myth clearly within a rational theory of progress.

But these early confident analyses and reconstructions of myth also show another and uneasy side. Deism is always confronted by a disparity between Nature and the savagely "natural." This is reflected in the disparity between the European exalting of the noble, innocent savage and European self-justification for conquering, exploiting, and converting these peoples. As Frank Manuel's study (1959) of rationalist myth shows, the inner problem that myth presents to the *philosophes* is strikingly expressed in how their psychology of religious origins turns obsessively on the emotion of fear or even terror. As superstitious ignorance of a superseded past, myth may be dismissed. But rationalist mythology begins to demonstrate the depth of human irrationality in the past, and also in the present.

Although the new mythic approaches rise in the name of new historical evaluation and nontraditional evidence, the practice does not measure up to the program. A. Momigliano (1950) makes clear how "antiquarian" history diverges from "philosophic" history from about 1700. Cartesian and Pyrrhonic attacks

on historical knowledge had a vivifying effect when they were carried over into mythic study, a new bold spirit of inquiry. But the larger result is a widening gap or hostility between the *érudit* and *philosophe.* In Fontenelle or Voltaire, an impatience with *les érudits* is manifest. Mythologizing becomes speculative, even deductive, seeking for principles more than for exact, empirical detail. The antiquarian collections from Ezechiel Spanheim (1671), Jean LeClerc (1697), or Bernard de Montfaucon (1719) to Joseph Spence (1747), A.-C. P. de Caylus (1752), or J. D. Michaelis (1753) later, are much less influential than they might have been. One reason is narrow antiquarianism. A prime example is the general flaccidity of theorizing shown by the prestigiously erudite Académie des Inscriptions et Belles-Lettres. Though Fontenelle, Nicolas Fréret, and de Brosses were members, they were exceptions; more typical is Étienne Fourmont, fluent in several oriental languages, who placidly accepted the biblical diffusion theory to account for Chinese religion and civilization. The dominant rationalist mythic method through the period may be described by Dugald Stewart's phrase (1794) as "Conjectural History": a search for the true causes of historical development as against merely empirical history.

These *a priori* explanations of myth slide easily into claiming themselves to be genuine historical reconstructions. A further refinement of mythology emerges as these rationalist historiographic difficulties come under criticism. Fréret, from within the Académie, begins as a euhemerist but by his death in 1749 is an important voice against *a priori* mythicizing: he argues against mere fact-finding, facile reductions, and pleads instead for recognition of the enormous historical problems involved in studying myth.

Both the historiographic and philosophic problems are raised most profoundly by Vico, who remains the greatest critic of rationalist mythology but also the most original rationalist mythologist. One key to his thought lies in his emphasis on Providence guiding man's development through secondary causes. Myths are poetic truths, poetic truth is metaphysical truth—but only for those lacking Christian revelation. Humanity begins in religious fear, not of men but of the divine. The first religion is idolatry, but it is a "true" idolatry, a providential step towards a "rational civil theology." In the first age, man sees all only in terms of the gods; in the next, in mixed divine-human terms; finally, in human terms wholly. "Homer" is thus not one of the true ancients, but looks back to an age of gods. Vico's exegesis anticipates the romantic affirmation of the wisdom of the mythic origins; but Vico himself remains decisively in the rationalist camp.

By about 1750, rationalist and deist mythology reaches both a stabilization and crisis. On one side, the earlier approaches become widespread and enjoy a certain acceptance. The *Encyclopédie* in its article on mythology simply reprints without acknowledgment a text by Fréret to which the "author," Louis de Jaucourt, adds an introductory paragraph and conclusion, together with a fragment from Banier. The young Edward Gibbon is absorbed in myth. But popular handbooks remain conventional. F. A. Pomey, in *Tooke's Pantheon* (1698), Pierre Chompre (1727), or Benjamin Hederich (1724) present myth as idolatry, lean to euhemerism and nod mechanically toward Christian allegorism. Deist mythology may be said to reach its consummation—and impasse—in Voltaire's *Essai sur les moeurs* (1756). This universal secular history shows a daringly wide use of comparative religion as a deist weapon against Christianity and classical paganism alike. Greece, Israel, and Rome shrink to small, late moments in the world's historical-religious development. But if Voltaire stresses man's religious pluralism to confute orthodoxy, as a deist he praises only those sides of Chinese, Indian, or Arabian religion akin to natural religion.

Between 1750 and 1760, three works appear which drastically revalue rationalist mythic thought: Hume's *Natural History of Religion* (written 1749–51, published 1757); Turgot's discourses on the theory of progress (1750); and Charles de Brosses' *Du culte des dieux fétiches* (1760). By redefining the scope and goal of reason, Hume and Turgot naturally redefine how myth must be understood; and both thinkers make clear the inner problem which myth poses to rationality.

Hume has the scorn of a *philosophe* for mythic barbarism and fear-founded religion. But his real challenge is in fact to earlier rationalist mythology. Reason reveals itself unexpectedly as limited in its ability to explain either faith or religious origins with any certainty. The original religion was not monotheistic, since monotheism presupposes some developed degree of reason; all primal religion must therefore have been polytheistic. Hume frees myth from ultimate judgment by reason. What myth then purports remains skeptically open, and problematic. Though Hume suggests that human thought rises with civilization to higher levels, he keeps this historical tendency apart from any theory of progress which would make an upward movement necessary. In this, he is partially seconded by Holbach (1770) and N. A. Boulanger (1761) who see the move from original awareness of nature into a "higher" religion as hardly an advance. For Holbach, once nature becomes intellectually hypostatized into gods or God, a dangerous error is committed and perpetuated; for Boulanger, religion is myth enduringly infecting man's dignity.

In Hume, the suggestion is made clear that mythic and rational thought differ radically; and he declares that myth historically preceded reason. But Hume left unexplained how the simple, concrete, and experientially limited mind of the savage could rise to reason. This now becomes a central problem. Turgot and later theorists of progress suggest an answer. The progress of reason is transferred to the historical process, characterized now by invariable laws of development. With Turgot, mythic thought shifts from emphasis on what happened in the beginnings to what must happen at the end of history. The savage mythic past is superseded by a Christian universality and charity moving constantly into secular improvement. Myth exists only as the barbaric first stage in this great movement. In M. J. de Condorcet (1793–94), the stages of progress occur in ten stages, with myth confined to the first. As he is more optimistic than Turgot about the inevitability of perfectibility, so Condorcet rejects myth even more. And yet, in Condorcet too, myth retains a modicum of dignity and importance: certain prejudices had to arise at each step of progress. In Auguste Comte (1826–29), the periodization of rational progress is elaborated and codified. The earliest stage of myth is now identified with fetishism; the source for this is in de Brosses. De Brosses' work had raised again the enduring problem for eighteenth-century thought of how to explain the discomforting evidence for Egyptian animal-worship or worse, African fetish-worship. De Brosses' explanation is uncompromisingly blunt and simple: drawing on material from African religion, he sees the savage worshipping the mere object utterly; no higher meaning or thought can be intruded into this plain idolatry. De Brosses locates this level of fetishism as the first and universal stage of all religion.

A late, important rationalist mythology is Dupuis' *Origine de tous les cultes* (1795), explaining all myth as "allegories" celebrating the sun's diurnal passage. Dupuis also stressed the primitive worship of natural fertility, as did R. P. Knight (1781).

Romantic Mythology. Romantic mythic thought may be fairly described first as breaking with all derogation of myth as ignorance or idolatry. For romantics, myth now appears as an inexhaustible mode of truth or even power. This conviction is central to the remarkable enthusiasm and vitality, but also to the inner perplexities, of romantic myth. Myth seems irreducible to familiar Christian or rationalist explanations. Instead, myth reflects or expresses a different, deeper wisdom, sublime feeling, a primal unity and totality. Myth thus implies, and romantic mythology generally undertakes, an ambitious syncretic program: spirituality, knowledge, and creative energy are to be reconciled and revitalized. Indeed, romantic mythic theorizing stimulates a profoundly original artistic use of myth, seemingly vindicating and demonstrating myth's claim to speak vitally from all "wise and

303

beautiful" depths to the present. But while these themes unify and animate, the inner history of romantic mythology remains most complex. In part, there remains the great problem of clarifying the nature of the truth which myth offers. In part, also, while German, English, and French romantics share in developing this movement, they develop at different times and with important national distinctions.

Beyond the general romantic attack on rationalist assumptions, new mythic views emerge more specifically as the origins of history and poetry are radically reassessed; these are anciently intimate with myth, and what is newly claimed of one transfers easily to the other. A first such change is found in the new importance placed on historical "particulars" in forming nations and art. One result is that the "oldest" mythic sources are now seen as created under special historical conditions: climate, laws, customs, and language. Thus, Blackwell (1735) seats Homer necessarily in his semi-savage Greek epoch; Robert Lowth (1753) analyzes the Old Testament as poetry depending on special Hebrew religious, linguistic conditions; J. J. Winckelmann (1755) stresses the totality of the Greek spirit and age for understanding Greek art. Poetry and art become living entrances to history and religion. However intended, such historicizing also undermines classical or biblical claims to supreme universality, so that a new dignity accrues to "modern" poetry but also to savage or folk epics, songs, and national lore. Since similar conditions occur in the history of every people, the "barbarian" Homer may have his rivals or even superiors among, say, the Iroquois or early Nordics. Moreover, as history modifies art, so art can seem an expression of a whole people or era. With Vico, Fréret, Blackwell, and Montesquieu a sense of independent and organic national genius emerges; with E. Young and J. G. Hamann "original" genius is praised. Robert Wood (1769) draws even more extreme conclusions that Homer perfectly reflected only the oral traditions of his naïve age; the way is open to F. A. Wolf's scholarly dissolution (1795) of the "poet" Homer into earlier folk-oral traditions.

Genuinely new nonclassic mythic documents cause important changes with Paul Henri Mallet's texts of the *Eddas* (1755–56); material from India arrives in force only after 1780, with full impact on mythology after 1800. Mallet saw European civilization deriving from Scandinavian, not classical, sources. In Mallet's time the *Chanson de Roland*, *Nibelungenlied*, *Kalevala*, and *Beowulf* were unknown. The *Eddas*' myths thus become decisively important to understanding the origins of central and northern Europe. Mallet, also, however, claimed the myths of Odin and apocalyptic destruction to be a corruption of an earlier,

gentler natural religion—but he gave no evidence. Confirmation seemed to arrive with James Macpherson's alleged Ossianic fragments (1760–62). This "ancient" Nordic epic breathes a spiritual refinement different from or even purer than Homer's. Ossian, "Homer of the North," could fulfill Rousseauistic, deistic, and preromantic visions of a pre-Christian society unspoiled by institutions and filled with love, melancholy, and nature.

The first and finally most powerful development of these ideas for myth occurs in Germany by 1765 to 1770, with J. G. von Herder's early characteristic formulations. His work absorbs and culminates the swift maturing successively of preromanticism, Pietism, romantic Hellenism, German nationalism, and the *Sturm und Drang* movements. With Winckelmann and the philologist C. G. Heyne, especially, the German study of Greek art and myth aims consciously at revivifying contemporaneous art and mythology. Winckelmann's praise of Greek artistic superiority also teaches that Greek art developed in historical stages. Further, he sees that Greek myth imaged truth sensuously, and his views point ahead to myth as an autonomous symbol.

Heyne's is perhaps the first important scholarly effort to separate myth from poetry on a rigorous philologic basis. He argues that myth can be understood rightly only by seeing things as the wondering, insecure, frightened primitive did. But mythic thought comes to us always indirectly, in recorded or poetic form. Lowth had earlier shown how Hebrew poetic forms necessarily sprang from and led back to revealed content. By philologically analyzing how poetry develops progressively from simple to complex, Heyne seeks a way back to the conditions surrounding myth before poetry intervened. An end point of Heyne's method is D. F. Strauss' *Das Leben Jesu* (1835–36), which uses mythic analysis to analyze the Bible.

Herder is the greatest innovator and influence in German romantic mythologizing. He is certainly the first major figure since Vico to make myth central to his whole position. He reargues the case for the richness and primal unity of myth in new terms. Christians, deists, and *philosophes* saw myth as either failing to attain the universal or else as falling from it to limited or false beliefs and knowledge. Herder defends mythic wisdom precisely by appealing to such differentiation. The separate cultural values and growth of peoples become proof of culturally relativistic original harmony. He holds that such primal unity can nowhere be found as such; no single absolute revelation or timeless cultural ideal has been given to man. But the innumerable languages, poetries, histories, and religions all arise from and preserve such original human totality. As he rejects any separation between reason and imagination or between thought and action as artificial, so Herder rejects allegorizing myth. All myth is a sensuous symbolic truth, at once poetry, theology, philosophy, and energy. Myth is creative: by projecting himself into his surroundings, mythic man finds truth. The natural goal towards which myth strives now is *Humanität*. But all myth, like all language, is necessarily national—an expression of each people's spirit (*Volksgeist*). Each myth is the authentic single form taken by a nation's *genetische Kraft* ("genetic power") as it shapes its culture out of cosmic-natural energy. Mythopoesis remains communal, and as long as the culture lives, goes on perpetually, as in folk poetry. Comparative mythology is thus the way to study mankind, but only our own mythology can lead us to know ourselves.

Herder's influence on mythology accompanies his pervasive influence on poetry, criticism, philosophy of history, social history, and nationalism. In his own generation, his impact on Goethe is well-known. Goethe early achieved a profound originality and freedom in using mythic themes. His poetic use of myth is too great to be summarized here: it runs from 1770 with such lyrics as *Prometheus* through the mythic panorama of *Faust*. Goethe also provides new emphasis on myth as an aesthetic symbol springing from nature rather than from any *Volk*. The statues of the gods "are really what they represent." "Jupiter" is the image of divine majesty, but an image which such majesty itself would assume could it become plastic. Karl Philipp Moritz' *Die Götterlehre* (1790), perhaps with Goethe's collaboration, develops these Plotinian-romantic ideas.

German mythic thought enters a new productive period beginning about 1797, with younger romantics like Novalis, Friedrich Hölderlin, and the Schlegels; with F. W. J. Schelling, and with the symbolist mythology of F. Creuzer and Joseph von Görres. After 1810, the impetus here dissipates, although Schelling's new, important, but isolated mythic theorizing continues to his death in 1854. In contrast to Herder's and Goethe's emphasis on a perfected differentiated form, the romantics seek to recover the undifferentiated primordial mythic moment before human totality fell and sundered. In contrast, too, the romantics have deep Christian and philosophical idealist commitments. Thus, they see myth less as organic growth or natural type than as a reconciling of polarities between necessity and freedom, infinite and finite, sensuous and spiritual. Related to this is the new conviction that modern poets not only will use myth, but may perhaps create new myths. Primal unity once occurred in spontaneity and innocence, and can now be regained only by a self-conscious effort at reconciliation. Such self-con-

sciousness, however, fulfills rather than falsifies the true meaning of myth. Especially important here is the poet Schiller's teaching that the modern soul yearns for the infinite, the undetermined; what was only partly shadowed forth in "finite" pagan myth or even Christianity must now be freely raised to a higher and fully universal power. New importance is thus placed on the all-embodying, endlessly expanding but self-referring symbol. The true fulfillment of myth will come only when all contradictions are synthesized, all spiritual potentialities are realized, all religions and philosophies merge in oneness. This hope pervades romantic myth: in Novalis' "magic idealism," transforming the world into a waking dream and *Totalwissenschaft* ("total knowledge"); in Hölderlin's gods whose return heralds the Golden Age again; in F. Schlegel's call for a truly romantic "universal and progressive poetry"; in Schelling's "Odyssey of the Spirit" which seeks itself through nature, to return self-possessed and fulfilled, to God.

To achieve this redemptive mythic oneness, the romantics offer two main approaches. First, a hope to create a radically modern myth from wholly modern materials such as modern science or idealism. Romantic mythopoesis is most powerfully and early proposed in F. Schlegel's *Rede über die Mythologie* (1800). Without a mythic center of its own, modern poetry and life must remain inwardly fragmented; with it, the moderns may surpass the ancients. A corollary here is F. Schlegel's and other romantics' exaltation of the Asiatic and ecstatic god Dionysus against Apollonian classicism.

Another main romantic approach looks back to India as having a mythic past entirely consonant with its own aspirations. Here, for the first time, India decisively supplants Greece as the prime mythic source and image. The European image of India begins to form after mid-century with historical reports by Joseph de Guignes or J. Z. Holwell. Sanskrit philology revives in a major way only around 1780, with translations by Sir Charles Wilkins and especially Sir William Jones. The early impact of this material is wide, stimulating, but the mythic implications remain problematic. In his *On the Gods of Greece, Italy and India* (1784), the greatest early Sanskritist, Sir William Jones, suggests the Indians as a new source for Egyptian religion; but he is careful to set Genesis apart from the Vedas, which he places as written after the time of the flood. Beyond his translations, Jones's main contribution is in suggesting a modern comparative philology based on the common descent of Sanskrit, Greek, and Latin. From Jones on, however, English and French Indology remains conventional in its study of myth. But with Herder, India becomes a catalyst for romanticism. As

305

A. L. Willson's study (1964) of German romantic Indism shows, Herder is the chief contributor to the enthusiasm for India as the homeland and cradle of religion and civilization, of mythic innocence. The Schlegels' *Athenäum* (1798) exalts and codifies India as the very source and model of romantic yearning for the infinite. Though he knew no Sanskrit, Friedrich Majer becomes the encyclopedist for this literary interest (1803–10).

From 1810, the philologic-historical approach begins its rise to dominance, again first in Germany. Romanticism contributes importantly to this change, first by stimulating philologic research, and next by revealing its own assumptions as vulnerable to philological criticism. Both sides appear in F. Schlegel's effort to corroborate romantic views of Indian sublimity by direct study of Sanskrit from 1802, resulting in his *Über Sprache und Weisheit der Indier* (1808). But the work shows him disillusioned by Hindu fatalism and dualism; Hinduism remains higher than Greek myth but inferior to Christianity. After Schlegel, the romantic mythic image of India finally breaks. A major result in part is to make all myth the preserve of special philologic disciplines: the first Sanskrit chair is founded in 1814 in the Collège de France, Franz Bopp's comparative grammar appears in 1833–52, and Eugène Burnouf advances Persian (Avestan) and Buddhist study (1832; 1845). On the other side, "Orientalism" passes into literary or speculative use—sometimes greatly as in Goethe's *Divan* or Schopenhauer's Buddhist interest, but mostly in merely modish pseudo-Oriental styles and subjects.

The further ascendancy of the philological school is marked by F. Creuzer's romantic *cause célèbre*, his *Symbolik und Mythologie der Alten Völker* (1810). This work provokes damaging rebuttal from unsympathetic historians. Christian August Lobeck's *Aglaophamus* (1829) massively refutes Creuzer's attempt to derive all Greek religion from migrating Indian priests who lowered the high, pure Indian religion to popular Greek mythic form, while concealing the true doctrines in symbolic Mysteries. Lobeck's attack on Creuzer's claim that these Mystery doctrines were essentially Orphic and Neo-Platonic derogated as well similar Mystery views held by Novalis, or Görres. K. O. Müller (1825), perhaps the most influential classicist of his age, accuses Creuzer of wrongly explaining Greek myth as imported or invented, rather than as rising integrally from within a slowly evolving Greek context. Müller's work heralds a "scientific" return to Herder's stress on local, national myth. The work of the Grimms in Germanic folklore is similarly Herderian in spirit.

The most expansive philosophizing on myth in the period is in Schelling's "last" phase. His *Philosophie*

der Mythologie (1857) subsumes history under a metaphysical system proving myth "objective." Creuzer had separated the primal symbol from later, vulgarized myth. Schelling rejoins symbol and myth, now calling myth "tautegory" to avoid reducing mythic unity to allegory. Myth is a "history of the gods." But contradicting euhemerist apotheosis, myth represents how the gods become human, i.e., incarnate. Each theogony is a "moment" in both the self-unfolding of the Divine and the human religious consciousness. Time and history occur as myth appears, for myth is nothing but a first revelation, though still unfree when compared to the fuller, wholly free Christian revelation.

In the nineteenth century, the German joining of mythology, literary criticism, philosophy, and mythopoesis is not duplicated elsewhere—an example is Richard Wagner's ambitious synthesis of myth, literature, theater, music, and mythic theory in his operas and essays toward the middle of the century. In England, there is no comparable body of theoretic innovation or speculative depth: Jacob Bryant (1774–76) mixes fanciful etymologizing with the theories of French *philosophes;* Captain Wilford (1804) or H. T. Colebrooke (1824–27) are antiquarian Indic enthusiasts; the Druidic mythologists—from William Stukeley (1740) through Edward Davies (1809)—furnish mystically patriotic speculation. But English poetry produces an incomparable body of work using myth. From 1790, William Blake's remarkable series of mythic poems culminates in the "Prophetic" books, *Milton* and *Jerusalem*. Wordsworth and Keats look back to John Milton and English poetic tradition more than to mythic theory of their age or before. In France, mythic theory emerges partly under positivist influence, with much interest in Charles François Dupuis' solar views; but also partly under the impact of German ideas, as Edgar Quinet's interest in Herder shows, or indirectly, Jules Michelet's interest in Vico. But this French mythic theorizing, from about 1820, remains somewhat apart from the creative use of myth in Gérard de Nerval, Victor Hugo, or Eugène Delacroix. The last great literary achievement in myth in our period occurs around mid-century in America, with Herman Melville, Henry David Thoreau, and Walt Whitman; these writers look back to English literature, but are also surprisingly versed in German romantic mythology.

BIBLIOGRAPHY

B. Feldman and R. Richardson, *The Rise of Modern Mythology 1700–1850* (Bloomington, Ind., 1971) provides texts and a comprehensive bibliography. Otto Gruppe, *Geschichte der Klassischen Mythologie und Religions-geschichte* (Leipzig, 1921) surveys mythic theory, as does

Jan de Vries, *Forschungsgeschichte der Mythologie* (Munich, 1961) with useful texts. See also: Frank Manuel, *The Eighteenth Century Confronts the Gods* (Cambridge, Mass., 1959; reprint, 1967), which illuminatingly analyzes Enlightenment mythology; Fritz Strich, *Die Mythologie in der deutschen Literatur von Klopstock bis Wagner* (Halle, 1910); A. L. Willson, *A Mythical Image: The Ideal of India in German Romanticism* (Durham, N.C., 1964); Raymond Schwab, *La Renaissance orientale* (Paris, 1950); A. Momigliano, "Ancient History and the Antiquarian," in *Studies in Historiography* (London, 1966).

BURTON FELDMAN

[See also Christianity in History; Deism; **Dualism; Enlightenment;** Historiography; Irrationalism; **Perfectibility;** Primitivism; Romanticism; *Volksgeist.*]

MYTH IN THE NINETEENTH AND TWENTIETH CENTURIES

IT IS NOT an easy task to present the important theories of myth from the late nineteenth century to the present day. Most of the authors who dealt with the meaning and function of myths were investigating problems considerably broader in implication—for example, the origin, meaning, and function of religion (Tylor, Lang, et al.); the origin and structure of society (Durkheim, Freud, et al.); the meaning and destiny of culture (Frobenius, Lévi-Strauss, et al.); or the origins of drama and epic poetry (G. Murray, F. M. Cornford, T. Gaster, et al.). To discuss conveniently their views on myth, a summary of their respective theories would have been indispensable, but the structure of this article did not always permit it. Furthermore, a number of theories were proposed by folklorists who usually insisted on the similarities between myths and folk tales, and considered them as species of a single family known as the folk narrative. Understandably, we had to limit ourselves by alluding only to such folkloristic theories.

Finally, there is another difficulty of presentation, which becomes more embarrassing as we approach the second half of the twentieth century—namely, the varying preconceptions concerning the nature of the documents which different scholars brought to their analysis and evaluation of myth. Indeed, until about 1920 (and following the traditions of both Greek philosophy and Judeo-Christianity) myth was understood as "fable," "invention," or "fiction." As a matter of fact, the triumph of scientific and historicistic ideologies in the last quarter of the nineteenth century restated the problem in almost the same terms as those given at the end of antiquity when, contrasted with both *logos* and later with *historia, mythos* came to denote "what cannot really exist."

But with the deepening of our understanding of the "primitive," i.e., archaic societies, a new meaning of myth became apparent. For the "primitives," what we call "myth"—that is, a narrative having as its actors supernatural or miraculous beings—means a "true story" and, moreover, a story that is sacred, exemplary, and significant. This new semantic value given to the term "myth" makes its use in contemporary parlance somewhat equivocal. Today the word is employed in both the older sense of "fiction" or "illusion" and in the sense of "sacred tradition, primordial revelation, and exemplary model." For example, when Bultmann and other theologians speak of "de-mythologizing" the Christian religious experience, they understand the term "myth" in the Greek sense of "fable" or "fiction." When, on the other hand, an historian of religions such as Pettazzoni speaks of the "Truth of Myth," he is referring to "primitive" and traditional societies where myth is "living" and supplies models for human behavior and, by that very fact, gives meaning and value to life.

MAX MÜLLER AND THE NATURE-MYTHOLOGY

The wide interest in Indo-European mythologies, religions, and folklore which characterizes the second half of the nineteenth century is in great measure an outgrowth of Max Müller's literary activity. From the brilliant essay on "Comparative Mythology," published in *Oxford Essays* (1856) to his two-volume work, *Contributions to the Science of Mythology* (1897), the learned Vedic scholar untiringly explained, defended, and restated his conception of the origin, meaning, and function of myths. According to Müller, mythology is the result of a "disease of language." The fact that an object can have many names (polynomy) and, conversely, that the same name can be applied to several objects (homonymy) produced a confusion of names. This gave rise to the combination of several gods into one and the separation of one god into many. *Nomina-numina:* what was at the beginning a name, *nomen,* became a divinity, *numen.* Moreover, the use of endings denoting grammatical gender led to the personification of the gods.

According to Müller, the ancient Aryans constructed their pantheon around the sun, the dawn, and the sky. The solar myths played the foremost role. "I look upon the sunrise and sunset, on the daily return of day and night, on battle between light and darkness, on the whole solar drama in all its details that is acted every day, every month, every year, in heaven and in earth, as the principle subject of early mythology" (1869, p. 537). Therefore, Cronus swallowing and later disgorging his children is only the "mythopoeic" expression of a meteorological phenomenon—namely, the sky devouring and later releasing the clouds. Likewise, the Baltic tales with the golden boat that sinks in the sea, or the apple that falls from the tree, actually refer to the setting sun.

Müller also found that the solar myths among the non-Aryan races are the result of the "disease of language." The myths of the Polynesian hero Maui reveal their meaning when we discover that this name signifies the sun, or fire, of the day; the Hottentot god Tsui-goab, now understood as "Broken-knee," originally meant "the dawn" or "rising sun" (Dorson in Sebeok, p. 26).

In his old age, Max Müller witnessed the collapse of the solar-mythology. The discrediting of this once popular method of interpretation was partially due to the devastating criticism of Andrew Lang, but also was due to the consequence of the wild exaggerations of some of Müller's disciples. Thus George William Cox reduced all Indo-European mythologies and folklores to the contest between light and darkness. While Müller endeavored to establish the identity of certain Greek and Indian gods through etymology, Cox compared the epic elements present in the different myths. As a result, all the Greek heroes, from Heracles and Achilles to Odysseus and Paris, and even King Arthur, the Frog Prince, and Cinderella, revealed themselves to be impersonators of the same solar deity. "The story of the sun starting in weakness and ending in victory, waging a long warfare against darkness, clouds, and storms, and scattering them all in the end is the story of all patient self-sacrifice, of all Christian devotion" (Cox, I, 168).

TYLOR AND THE ANIMISTIC THEORY OF MYTH

Edward Burnett Tylor did not directly attack Müller's theories, but the appearance of his *Primitive Culture* (1871) represented a decisive blow to the *nomina-numina* doctrine. As an anthropologist, Tylor observed in *Primitive Culture* that the primitives are still living in the myth-making stage of the mind. His general thesis is that "Myth arose in the savage condition prevalent in remote ages among the whole race" and that it remained comparatively unchanged among the contemporary primitive tribes; and that, moreover, even higher and later stages of civilization retained parts of mythical traditions (2nd ed. [1873], I, 284). Mythical thinking being specific "to the human intellect in its early childlike state," the study of myth must begin "at the beginning," that is, among the less civilized peoples, "the nearest representatives of primeval

culture" (I, 287). This was, of course, directed against Müller's exaggerated emphasis on the archaism of the Vedic culture. As a matter of fact, a few years later, the great French Sanskrit scholar, Abel Bergaigne, proved that the Vedic hymns, far from being the spontaneous and naive expression of a primeval naturalistic religion, were the rather recent product of a highly sophisticated class of ritualistic priests.

As could be expected from the originator of the doctrine of animism, Tylor found the principal cause of the transfiguration of daily experience into myths in the belief that all nature is *animated* and, as such, susceptible to *personification*. "To the lower tribes of man, sun and stars, trees and rivers, winds and clouds, become personal animate creatures, leading lives conformed to human or animal analogies" (I, 285). But, Tylor hastened to add, again rejecting Müller's doctrine, that "the basis on which such ideas are built is not to be narrowed down to poetic fancy and transformed metaphor." It is rather a crude philosophy of nature, "thoughtful, consistent, and quite really and seriously meant." Tylor agreed that language has had a great share in the formation of myth, but he felt that "the great expansion of verbal metaphor into myth belongs to more advanced periods of civilization" (I, 299). As for the Müllerian emphasis on solar-myths, Tylor pointed out that a great number of historical characters—such as Cortés or Julius Caesar—can be shown to embody solar episodes in their lives (I, 319).

Compared with the rather monolithic doctrine of Max Müller, Tylor's understanding of myth is notably more subtle. He carefully analyzes the various stages of the mythical process and separates the morphologically distinct mythological creations. He delineates, for example, the difference between a myth engendered by the animation and personification of Nature, on the one hand, and the formation of legends, either by the stiffening of metaphor caused by semantic errors, or by the introduction of fiction into events held to be traditional. Ultimately Tylor distinguishes what he calls "two principles of mythologic science." The first concerns the universality and the regularity of mythical creations: whatever may be the individual, national, or even racial distinctions, myth reveals itself "as an organic product of mankind at large," expressing the "universal qualities of the human mind." The second principle concerns the relation of myth to history. Tylor argues that, although the traditions of real events are disfigured through mythopoeic processes, their historicity is not completely destroyed. Unconsciously, and as it were in spite of themselves, the authors and transmitters of sagas have preserved "masses of sound historical evidence." They molded into mythological adventures of gods and heroes their own cultural heritage; "they placed on record the arts and manners, the philosophy and religion of their own times, times of which formal history has often lost the very memory" (I, 415–16).

Consequently, for Tylor, the mythopoeic process is active at all phases of human culture. But, while among the primitives mythical creations are essentially related to the understanding of natural phenomena, at later stages myths reflect historical events and cultural traditions as well. This second principle of Tylor's— "mythologic science"—knew a certain popularity at the beginning of the twentieth century when many scholars tried to decipher and reconstruct the historical data supposedly embedded in the sagas and the epic poetry of ancient medieval peoples.

ANDREW LANG AND THE MAKING OF RELIGION

For more than twenty years, Andrew Lang attacked Müller's doctrine, mainly with arguments inspired by Tylor's anthropological interpretation of mythology and religion. He pointed out that myths reflect actions, ideas, and institutions which were actual at some time in the past. For instance, the myth of Cronus dates from an epoch in which cannibalism was practiced, and in the mythology of Zeus one can decipher a primitive medicine man. But after reading Alfred William Howitt's reports on the "High Beings" of the Australians and other data on the Andamanese, Lang rejected Tylor's theory that animism was the first stage of religion. Tylor held that animism was followed by polytheism, and finally by monotheism. A belief in "High Gods" could not, therefore, possibly be original among the primitive peoples, for, according to Tylor, the idea of God developed from the belief in nature-spirits and the cult of ancestor ghosts. But among the Australians and Andamanese, Andrew Lang found neither ancestor-worship nor nature cults.

This discovery of the priority of "High Beings" marks the beginning of a long controversy over the origins of religion and "primeval monotheism," in which Lang's evaluation of myth plays an important role. Lang was convinced that the mythopoeic processes can explain the apparently paradoxical fact that the belief in "High Gods" is found among the most archaic tribes, while it fades away or disappears completely in more advanced primitive societies. Lang thought that mythical creativity was somehow a sign of degeneration. Because he had discovered very few myths associated with the Australian "High Beings," he thought that myth was secondary and ultimately disruptive of the highly ethical religious values. "Among the lowest known tribes we usually find, just as in Ancient Greece, the belief in a deathless 'Father',

'Master', 'Maker', and also the crowd of humorous, obscene, fanciful myths which are in flagrant contradiction with the religious character of that belief. That belief is what we call rational, and even elevated. The myths, on the other hand, are what we call irrational and debasing." And he adds: "the religious conception rises up from the human intellect, in one mood, that of earnest contemplation and submission; while the mythical ideas rise up from another mood, that of playful and erratic fancy" (I, 4–5).

Basically myth is irrational and, as such, is a product of animism, while the belief in High Gods or Supreme Beings, which is the real substance of religion, is rational. Lang argues, however, that the "pure" religion of the beginnings degenerates because of the growing influence of animism; for man is more attracted to ghosts and fetishes, which he can invoke for help or use for his egoistic interests, than to the noble and moral Creator who is indifferent to gifts and opposed to lust and mischief (*The Making of Religion*, pp. 257–58).

Lang's theory of the radical difference between myth and religion, and its corollary of the priority of the idea of God with regard to mythological creation, was taken over, corrected, and systematized by Wilhelm Schmidt in his massive twelve-volume work, *Der Ursprung der Gottesidee* (1912–55). One of Schmidt's main theses was that the idea of a Supreme Being, without mythology and devoid of any anthropomorphic traits, belongs to a religious stage preceding any mythological formulation. We must add that such an assumption is in contradiction to everything that we know of *homo religiosus* in general and of primitive man in particular. A Supreme Being is always a *primordial* and *creative* Being, and "primordiality" and "creativity" are mythical thought structures *par excellence*. If, almost everywhere in the world, the mythologies of the Supreme Beings are not as rich as the mythologies of the other types of divine figures, it is not because such Supreme Beings belong to a premythological epoch, but simply because their activity is somehow exhausted in the works that they do in the beginning, i.e., cosmogony, the creation of man, and the foundation of the principal religious and social institutions.

Lang and Schmidt slighted the mythical creations because they considered them irrational and immoral. Beginning with the early twentieth century, a number of scholars insisted upon the irrational character of myth, but not all of them necessarily considered irrationality in negative terms. They related mythical creations to the very processes of life, the unconscious or social structures. Directly or indirectly, most of these authors are influenced by Bergson, Freud, or Durkheim. But a few years before the ascendancy of such interpretations, a new naturistic-rationalistic evaluation of mythology came suddenly into prominence.

THE ASTRAL-MYTHOLOGICAL AND PAN-BABYLONIAN SCHOOLS

At the beginning of this century the so-called astral-mythological and Pan-Babylonian schools became popular in Germany. Although originally representing two independent approaches, their basic presuppositions were similar, and in 1906 the partisans of both schools founded the *Gesellschaft für vergleichende Mythenforschung* (Society for the Study of Comparative Mythology) in Berlin. The first volume published by the society was E. Siecke's *Drachenkämpfe: Untersuchungen zur indogermanischen Sagenkunde* (1907). This passionate and prolific author can be considered the founder and the leader of the new school of thought. For Siecke, myths must be understood literally because their contents always refer to some specific celestial phenomena, namely, the forms and movements of the planets and stars. Consequently, for Siecke myths do not reflect animistic experiences and conceptions; they have nothing to do with belief in souls, or with dreams and nightmares. The most important mythical figures are the sun and especially the moon. As a matter of fact, Siecke, Böcklen, and Hüsing emphasized so strongly the role of the moon in the mythical process that their doctrine could be called "pan-lunarism" (Schmidt, *Origin* . . . , p. 94).

One of the most distinguished followers of the astral-mythology school, P. Ehrenreich, reacted against these excesses. In his book *Die allgemeine Mythologie und ihre ethnologischen Grundlagen* (1910), he pointed out the importance of the sun and other heavenly bodies in the mythologies of a considerable number of primitive and archaic peoples. In the last analysis the study of moon-myths revealed that early man was relating astral phenomena to the mystery of death and resurrection. The dying moon became an image of the mythical ancestor, and the lunar rhythms were considered as somehow being the paradigm of human existence (birth, growth, death, resurrection).

Pan-Babylonianism was represented principally by H. Winckler, A. Jeremias, and E. Stucken. Despite their copious productivity, very little of their work has retained any lasting significance. In his three-volume work *Astralmythen* (1901–07), Stucken tried to prove the direct or indirect Mesopotamian origin of all the mythologies of the world. For the Pan-Babylonianists, all myths are concerned with the movements of the sun, the moon, and the planet Venus. Celestial revolutions were regarded by the Mesopotamians as the expression of the power, will, and intelligence of the deities. As early as 3000 B.C. this system was completely developed in Mesopotamia, whence it was then diffused over the whole earth, being found even today in the myths of the "primitives." The Pan-Babylonianists saw evidence of this diffusion in the astronomical knowledge implied in mythological systems. Such scientific observations, they argued, were certainly impossible for the archaic peoples. Thus the Pan-Babylonianists link the *naturistic* origin of myths with their *historical* diffusion. Against the supporters of animism and of the theory of "elementary ideas" of Bastian who explained the similarity of myths by the basic unity of the human mind, the Pan-Babylonianists emphasized the highly elevated, "scientific" origin of mythology, and its diffusion even among the most primitive tribes.

The Pan-Babylonian school declined as a consequence of its own extravagant generalizations and excesses. It was easy to prove, for example, that the primitive myths concerning the Pleiades have nothing to do with the passage of the sun through the zodiac (Schmidt, *Origin* . . . , pp. 101ff.). But some of the Pan-Babylonianists' presuppositions were reasserted by other schools—although in different contexts. For instance, a quarter of a century later, "diffusionism" became extremely popular in England under the influence of G. Elliot Smith's Pan-Egyptianism. This Pan-Egyptianist school tried to explain the totality of myths, rituals, and social institutions (with the exceptions of those of the hunters and food-gatherers) as ultimately deriving from Egypt. The British Myth and Ritual School also conceded an exceptional place to the Babylonian documents.

THE PRIORITY OF RITUAL

Already by the end of the nineteenth century, W. Robertson-Smith considered myth the explanation of ritual, and, as such, altogether secondary. "The myth was derived from the ritual, and not the ritual from the myth; for the ritual was fixed and the myth was variable, the ritual was obligatory and faith in the myth was at the discretion of the worshipper" (*Lectures on the Religion of the Semites* [1894], p. 18). He goes on to say that since myth is the explanation of a religious usage, in many cases it could not have arisen until the original meaning of the usage had fallen into oblivion.

For the following half-century, similar ideas were expressed by a great number of scholars and specialists in different areas of study. One may distinguish at least three important groups: the classical scholars, the anthropologists, and the Old Testament specialists. The most articulate among the classicists was Jane Harrison. She argued that *mythos* was, for the ancient Greeks, primarily "just a thing spoken, uttered by the *mouth*."

Its correlative is "the thing done, enacted, the *ergon* or work" (*Themis*, Cambridge [1912], p. 328). But while Robertson-Smith considered mythology inessential "for it had no sacred sanction and no binding force on the worshippers" (op. cit., p. 17), Jane Harrison aptly pointed out the religious value of myth. Indeed, a myth is not merely a word spoken; it is a re-utterance, recited collectively—or at least with collective sanction. When it is related to the ritual, myth becomes a narrative charged with magical intent and potency (op. cit., p. 330).

A number of outstanding classical scholars from Cambridge applied Jane Harrison's "ritualist" model to other Greek creations. F. M. Cornford traced the ritual origins of Attic comedy and of some philosophical ideas, and Gilbert Murray reconstructed the ritual pattern of Greek tragedy. This new approach opened the way to further study of the ritual origins and implications of other literatures (S. E. Hyman in Sebeok [1955], pp. 87ff.; Wayne Shumaker [1960], pp. 157ff.). The Danish scholar W. Grønbech applied, in *The Culture of the Teutons,* a similar method in the study of old-Germanic myths; he understood them as organically interrelated to festivals. And for Grønbech, the festivals represented a "creation or new birth outside time" (1931, II, 222ff.).

The British anthropologists A. M. Hocart and Lord Raglan generalized the ritualist approach and proclaimed the priority of ritual as the most important element in the understanding of human culture. "If we turn to the living myth, that is, the myth that is believed in, we find that it has no existence apart from the ritual" (Hocart [1933], p. 223). Hocart claimed that myth is only the verbal explanation and justification of ritual: the actors impersonate the supposed inventors of the ritual, and this impersonation has to be expressed verbally. Thus for Hocart *all* myths *must* have had a ritual origin; to prove this principle, he was compelled to explain the cosmogonic myths as the verbal commentary of a ritual renewal of the world, and he derives the myths of flying through the air from some climbing rituals, neglecting the fact that the myths of flying are archaic and universally distributed, whereas the rites are rare and limited to certain areas. In 1936 in his *The Hero,* Lord Raglan insisted on the nonhistoricity of the heroic myths and sagas. He explained the similarity of the myths by the similar rites with which they are related.

In the preface of *Themis* Jane Harrison acknowledged her debt to Durkheim's sociological interpretation of religious experience. As a matter of fact, Durkheim, in his *Elementary Forms of Religious Life,* did not elaborate on the structure and function of myth, partly because he considered it a "work of art" and,

as such, beyond the "jurisdiction of the simple science of religion" (Durkheim, pp. 121–22). As to the origin of myth, Durkheim was somewhat hesitant to offer an explanation: in principle, he writes, the cult is derived from religious beliefs and their mythological expressions, but it also reacts upon them. The myth is therefore modelled after the ritual in order to account for it, especially when its meaning is no longer apparent (ibid., p. 121). But in a later chapter he limits the function of myth to the interpretation of rites (p. 152).

BRITISH AND SCANDINAVIAN MYTH AND RITUAL SCHOOLS

Two famous Old Testament scholars, H. Gunkel and H. Gressmann, explicated the cultic background of the Psalms. In his *Psalmenstudien* (Vols. I–III, 1921–29) S. Mowinckel went even further: he deciphered the structure of the ancient Israelite New Year Festival. One of the principal themes of the festival was the symbolic reenactment of Jahweh's victory against his enemies and his enthronement as king of the world. The *myth*—Jahweh's combat and victory—was thus the expression of existential experiences acted out in the cult. The mythological aura of the king, in Israel as well as elsewhere in the ancient Near East, was closely connected with the cult.

Independently of Mowinckel's investigations, a group of English Orientalists and biblical scholars launched, with their contributions to the two volumes edited by S. H. Hooke, *Myth and Ritual* (1933) and *The Labyrinth* (1935), the movement known as the "Myth and Ritual School" or "Patternism." Taking for granted the precedence of ritual over myth, the authors emphasized the cultic role of the king and especially the basic pattern of all the religions of the Ancient Near East, including Israel. A few years later, the Swedish scholars Ivan Engnell, in *Studies in Divine Kingship in the Ancient Near East* (1943)—and G. Widengren, *King and Savior* (Vols. I–VI, 1945–55)—developed in greater detail and, at times, overstated the main thesis of the British School.

In his Frazer Lecture for 1951, *The Problem of Similarity in Ancient Near Eastern Religions*, H. Frankfort attacked the presuppositions of the "Myth and Ritual" school, pointing out that differences are more important than similarities and that, consequently, the myths and rituals of the Egyptians, Babylonians, and of neighboring countries cannot be described as a "pattern." Frankfort's criticism was answered by Hooke (1958, pp. 1–25) and by G. Widengren (*inter alia,* ibid., pp. 149–203).

The impassioned debate which took place around the "Myth and Ritual" School reveals a confusion of methodological issues. We do not refer here to the exaggerations of some Scandinavian authors, nor to their philological imprudences and historical distortions. What is at stake is the legitimacy of comparing the historically related and structurally analogous religious phenomena of the Ancient Near East. It is true that if there is one area in which comparisons can be rightfully applied, it is the Ancient Near East. We know that agriculture, Neolithic village culture, and finally urban civilization start from a Near Eastern center with many radii.

Working with the same documents as the "Myth and Ritual" School, Theodor H. Gaster proposed a rather different theory. For him myth is not, as for Robertson-Smith and Jane Harrison, a mere outgrowth of ritual or the spoken correlative of "things done." It is the expression of a parallel aspect of real and ideal inherent in ritual from the beginning. Its function "is to translate the real into the terms of the ideal, the functional into terms of the durative and transcendental" (*Thespis*, 2nd ed. rev. [1961], p. 24).

There is something common to all those authors who considered myth secondary, i.e., only a verbalization, interpretation, or validation of ritual. All of them tacitly take for granted that the primary and fundamental element of religion, and hence of human culture, is the *act* done by man, not the *story* of divine activity. Freud accepted these presuppositions, but he tended to push them much further. He identified the primordial, unique *act* which established the human condition, and consequently opened the way to mythical and religious creations.

FREUD AND THE PSYCHOANALYTIC INTERPRETATIONS OF MYTH

Freud's interpretation of myth was a part of a more ambitious endeavor which sought the origins of human culture, i.e., the origins of religious and ethical ideas and social institutions. Briefly stated, Freud's theory was that the mythopoeic process emerged, together with the first religious ideas and social institutions, as a result of a primordial parricide. Freud accepted Atkinson's view that the earliest communities consisted of older and stronger males, together with a number of females and children; the head of the horde kept the females for himself and drove out his sons as they became adults. The expelled sons finally killed their father, ate him, and appropriated the females. In *Totem and Taboo* Freud writes:

The violent primal father had doubtless been the feared and envied model of each one of the company of brothers: and in the act of devouring him they accomplished their identification with him, and each one of them acquired a portion of his strength. The totem meal, which is perhaps mankind's earliest festival, would thus be a repetition and a commemoration of this memorable and criminal deed, which was the beginning of so many things—of social organization, of moral restrictions, and of religion (1950, pp. 141–42).

This primordial parricide was either a unique event, perpetually (though unconsciously) remembered, or was repeated many times, as a result of the conflict between sons and fathers in the primeval horde.

We shall not discuss this interpretation of the origins of religion, culture, and society, since it has been rejected by most anthropologists. Suffice it to add that Freud interprets myths as substitutive gratifications through fantasy, comparable to dreams and other fantasy creations. He insists that the beginnings of religion, morals, society, and art converge in the Oedipus complex (ibid., p. 156). Understandably, myths are for him the reveries of the race, the imaginary realization of repressed desire, i.e., of the Oedipal impulse. As in dreams, the hero of the myth undergoes a division into several figures. These mythological duplicates can be traced to the relationship between child and parents. In sum, myth is, for Freud, a *fantasy repetition* of a *real act*, the primordial parricide.

A number of psychoanalysts have attempted to interpret mythological and folkloristic personages using the Freudian pan-sexual symbolism. Ferenczi, for instance, sees in Oedipus the phallus, and in his blinding himself, an act of castration brought about by his horror of mother-incest. In *The Myth of the Birth of the Hero* (1909), Otto Rank found in the repudiation of the father the desire to replace the real father by a more distinguished one, which is only the child's longing for the happy time when the father appeared to be the strongest and greatest man, and the mother seemed the most beautiful woman. But, says Rank, this is a delusion specific to paranoia; thus, he concludes that the myth of the hero reveals a paranoid structure.

JUNG AND THE ARCHETYPES

C. G. Jung's interpretation of myth is interdependent with his theory of the collective unconscious. Indeed, it was mainly the striking similarities between the myths, symbols, and mythological figures of widely separated peoples and civilizations that led Jung to postulate the existence of a collective unconscious. He noticed that the images and structures of this collective unconscious manifest themselves through what he called "archetypes," and he regarded them as somehow similar to Bastian's *Elementargedanken* or Burckhardt's "primordial images." The archetypes appear not only in myths and fairy tales, but also in dreams and the products of fantasy. Like Freud, Jung considers myths, dreams, and fantasies to be the indifferent products of the unconscious. But departing from Freud, Jung does not consider the unconscious as a reservoir of repressed personal libido. Consequently, the fantasy images and mythical figures are not the "wish-fulfillment" of the repressed libido, for they were never conscious and thus could never have been repressed. These mythical images belong to the structures of the collective unconscious and are an impersonal possession. "The primitive mentality," writes Jung, "does not *invent* myths, it *experiences* them" (Jung and Kerényi [1949], p. 101). In other words, myths precede any type of culture, even the most primitive, though of course their verbal expressions are molded according to the different cultural styles.

For Jung, religious life is essentially a vital link with those deep psychic processes which are independent of and beyond consciousness. Since the archetypes do not refer to anything that is or has been conscious, but to something fundamentally unconscious, it is, in the last analysis, impossible to say what they refer to. Consequently, it is useless to specify that a myth refers to the sun or the moon, the father or mother, sexuality, fire, or water; "all we can do is to circumscribe and give an approximate description of an *unconscious core of meaning*. The ultimate meaning of this nucleus was never conscious, and never will be" (ibid., p. 104). In contrast to Freud's insistence on the primacy of the *deed* (the first parricide), myths are for Jung the expressions of a primordial psychic process that may even precede the advent of the human race. Together with symbols, myths are the most archaic structures of the psychic life. They did not need rituals, "things done," to emerge from the deep layers of the collective unconscious.

Though he published a book in collaboration with Jung, the classical scholar Kerényi has more of a personal understanding of myth, nearer to the ideas of Frobenius and Walter Otto. For Kerényi, mythology lays the foundation for a meaningful world. Myths are always unfolded in a primordial time. "The teller of myths steps back into primordiality in order to tell us what 'originally was'" (ibid., p. 10). Joseph Campbell also began with a psychological interpretation of myths which utilized the Jungian approach, as in *The Hero With a Thousand Faces* (1949); but in his later work, *The Masks of Gods* (4 vols., 1959–68), he tried to elucidate the meaning and function of mythology, utilizing the findings both of depth psychology and the history of early cultures.

FROM BACHOFEN TO
CULTURAL MORPHOLOGY

Jung, Kerényi, and Campbell were familiar with the works of Bachofen and Frobenius; and Kerényi and Campbell were directly influenced by them. Bachofen, almost ignored during his life, became quite popular after World War I, especially for his theory of the antecedence of matriarchy. But it was also his interpretation of myths and symbols that struck a singular note in the middle of the nineteenth century. Bachofen emphasized the spiritual and historical values of myths and symbols. For him, as for Frobenius and Kerényi, myths were not only psychological and sociological documents; they also had a spiritual meaning and hence a perennial value.

Bachofen considered myth as the exegesis of symbol. A myth unfolds in a series of actions what the symbol embodies in a unity (*Gräbersymbolik*, 1855). Later on, in *Die Sage von Tanaquil* (1870), Bachofen emphasized the value of myth for understanding the specific genius of an ancient people. "Myth is nothing other than a picture of the national experience in the light of religious faith" (*The Myth of Tanaquil*, in *Myth, Religions, and Mother Right*, p. 213). Therefore, he would see the presence of similarities of ideas and forms in mythologies of countries far removed from one another as a proof of migration. Studying the myth of Tanaquil, Bachofen noticed that the "Letaeric King-woman of Asiatic dynasties" was transformed in Rome from a *religious* to a *historical* figure. The historicization of myths, argues Bachofen, is a characteristic of Roman genius (ibid., pp. 236ff.)—an idea which was to be developed by Georges Dumézil in the 1940's.

If Bachofen's manner of interpreting the archaic symbols, myths, and institutions of the Eastern Mediterranean was highly significant in the German-speaking world between the wars, no less important was the influence of Frobenius. Analyzing the genius of African cultures, Frobenius strongly emphasized the irrational character of spiritual creativity—coining the term *Ergriffenheit* (literally, "seizure") to describe the mystery of cultural creation. In any creation, argued Frobenius, man is seized by the very essence of things; he receives from the realities that surround him a deeper knowledge, a kind of revelation of the inner order and meaning of nature. Ultimately man is "seized" by that which is divine in things, and this experience is the source of all creations—religious and mythological, as well as artistic and social.

Frobenius' disciple, Adolf E. Jensen, worked in the same direction, especially in his *Myth and Cult Among Primitive Peoples* (1951; Eng. trans., 1963). For Jensen the recitation of a myth represents an act of a cultic nature, and the basis for any cult is the activity of a Supernatural Being in primordial times. But Jensen distinguishes "real" myths from the etiological, i.e., explanatory ones, which are seen as only degenerate forms of genuine myths. In the authentic, solemn, and majestic myths we witness a true expression of mythic experience, because the nature of the world is brought to life, made vivid, clarified (ibid., p. 65).

In the same year that Frobenius published his most important work, *Kulturgeschichte Afrikas*, the noted Greek scholar, Walter Otto, brought out *Dionysus* (1933) in which he set forth at length his views on myth and cult. For Otto any cult presupposes a myth, even if the myth is not evident. Otto's originality consists in his highly personal understanding of Greek religion, and of the non-Christian religions in general. He emphatically denies in *Dionysus* that myths and rituals arose as idle tales and as actions with a utilitarian purpose; they are cultural creations of a monumental nature, like buildings and sculptures (trans. 1965, p. 24). To become creative, however, the human mind has to be "touched and inspired by a wonderful otherness." At the beginning, that is, at the center of all religions, stands the appearance of a God. It is only such a divine epiphany that gives meaning and life to all primordial forms of religion. Rejecting all the modern explanations of the origin of ritual and myth, Otto writes: "Let us finally be convinced that it is foolish to trace what is most productive back to the unproductive: to wishes, to anxieties, to yearnings; that it is foolish to trace living ideas, which first made rational thought possible, back to rational processes; or the understanding of the essential, which first gives purposeful aspirations their scope and direction, to a concept of utility" (ibid., pp. 29–30).

What characterizes the interpretations of Jung, Frobenius, Otto, and Jensen is their tacit admiration and nostalgia for mythical thought. For this reason their theories were criticized as encouraging the dark tendencies of German irrationalism. Despite this criticism, their contributions are of lasting value; indeed, they opened new worlds of meaning for modern Western culture. Otto, followed to a certain extent by Kerényi, tried to recapture the value of Greek *mythos* as it was before its demythicization. Frobenius and Jensen endeavored to make accessible to Western man the archaic type of creativity, illustrated mainly by the myths and cults of Africa and Melanesia. All three of them emphasized the permanent *spiritual value* of the cultures they studied and, without overtly admitting such a goal, they nevertheless presented other worlds of meaning that were comparable to those of the Western tradition of Judeo-Christianity and the more recent secular, scientific spirit of the Enlightenment.

RECENT TRENDS IN
HISTORY OF RELIGIONS

Such a sympathetic understanding of the meaning and function of myth, although without the implicit

nostalgia which can be seen in the work of Frobenius and Walter Otto, was not exceptional during the interbellum period. After living some years among the Trobriand Islanders, Bronislaw Malinowski was convinced of the fundamental importance of myth for primitive and traditional societies. "Myth," wrote Malinowski in 1926, "fulfills in primitive culture an indispensable function: it expresses, enhances, and codifies belief; it safeguards and enforces morality; it vouches for the efficiency of ritual and contains practical rules for the guidance of man" (repr. in *Magic, Science and Religion* [1955], p. 101). Myth is not an idle tale; nor is it an intellectual explanation or an artistic imagery, "but a pragmatic charter of primitive faith and moral wisdom." The myth reveals a primeval, greater, and more relevant reality, which determines the present life and the activities of men; the knowledge of myth not only discloses the motive for ritual and moral actions, but also supplies indications as to how to perform them (ibid., p. 108).

Especially after World War II a number of historians and phenomenologists of religion insisted on the positive aspects of mythical thought. Gerardus van der Leeuw emphasized the relation of myth to sacred power and sacred time. Raffaele Pettazzoni pointed out the distinction made by many tribal societies between "true stories"—i.e., real myths—and "false stories" or folktales. The first cannot be recited except within the cult and with the exclusion of noninitiates, while the "false stories" are recited any time and can be heard by everyone. According to Pettazzoni, the "true story" is sacred because it recounts the beginnings of things (cosmogony, etc.). Through their reactualization in the ritual, myths assure the preservation and increase of life (1954, pp. 11–24).

For M. Eliade as well, myth represents the most important element in archaic or traditional cultures. Myth narrates a sacred history; it relates an event that took place in primordial time, the fabulous time of the "beginnings." But myth is always an account of a "creation"; it tells how something came into being. The actors are supernatural Beings; and myths disclose their creative activity and reveal the sacredness (or simply the "supernaturalness") of their work. Thus, the history of this activity is considered to be absolutely *true* (because it is concerned with realities) and *sacred* (because it is the work of supernatural Beings). Since the myth is always related to a "creation" (the world, man, an institution, etc.), it constitutes the paradigm for all significant human acts. By knowing it, one knows the "origin" of things, and hence can control and manipulate them at will; it is a knowledge that one "experiences" ritually, either by ceremonially recounting the myth or by performing the ritual for which it is both a model and a justification. In the traditional societies, one "lives" the myth in the sense that one is seized by the sacred, exalting power of the events which are recollected or reenacted (Eliade, 1963).

Although he did not elaborate a general theory of myth, Georges Dumézil made important contributions through his studies on the Indo-European tripartite ideology (Littleton, 1966). The originality of Dumézil's approach is that he conveniently utilizes a historical and structural analysis. Victor W. Turner has recently proposed a new interpretation of myths as "liminal phenomena." According to him, the various types of myth refer to critical situations, the paradoxical interval between two modalities of being—"death" and "rebirth," chaos and cosmos, "nature" and "culture."

PHILOSOPHERS AND MYTH

For more than half a century philosophers ignored the problems raised by mythical thought. In his three-volume work *Mythus und Religion* (1905–09), Wilhelm Wundt still followed Tylor's theory of animism, although he criticized some minor points. Wundt's ambition was to relate the different species of mythologies to the cultural evolution of mankind. But he emphatically asserted that the mythical mentality was transcended in the age of reason.

Of the modern philosophers, it was Ernst Cassirer who rediscovered the significance for philosophy of the mythical processes. For Cassirer, "in mythical imagination is always implied an act of *belief*. Without the belief in the reality of its objects, myth would lose its ground" (*An Essay on Man* [trans. 1956], p. 101). Myth has a double face: it has both a conceptual and a perceptual structure. Myth and religion have their origin in feeling, and they promote a feeling of solidarity and unity of all forms of life. "To mythical and religious feeling nature becomes one great society, the *society of life*" (ibid., p. 110). Cassirer follows both Robertson-Smith and Durkheim in asserting that society is the true model of myth and that one cannot understand myth without studying ritual. While ritual is the *dramatic* element in religious life, myth represents the *epic* element. Since myth rationalizes and validates the ritual, religion remains indissolubly connected and infused with mythical elements throughout its history.

Although a disciple of Cassirer, Susanne K. Langer takes another view toward the origin and function of myths. For Langer myth is a product of fantasy, as are dreams; but through the process of recounting, the dream-narratives become stories (the animal fable, the trickster story, the ghost story), and these develop ultimately into the fairy tale. But myths do not represent a new modification of folktales. They are, rather, the result of a mutation: instead of the wishful thinking reflected in fairy tales, myths reflect the quest for an understanding of nature and the meaning of life. Thus, although both folktales and myths originate in fantasy, myths are related to the tragic awareness of the human condition and, as such, may be considered as a primitive philosophy. (A similar distinction between folktale and saga was elaborated by the Dutch folklorist Jan de Vries; cf. Eliade [1963], pp. 195–202).

In the mid-twentieth century, the investigation of mythical thought has attracted a great number of continental philosophers, especially in France, Italy, and Germany. But the majority of these authors approached the problem of myth in a larger perspective: that of the study of language, or of symbol, or that of the analysis of imagination. For Georges Gusdorf, instinct and mythical thinking represent two successive stages before the "age of philosophy." In both cases, we are confronted with "ritual behavior," i.e., with definitive adaptations to a series of given situations. Myth constitutes, in fact, the first "culture," but one which has still retained the consistency of Nature. The world revealed by myth is a global determination of reality, the same for every member of the respective ethnic group. The human life ruled by myth looks like an immense liturgy of repetitions. Mythical consciousness, wrote Gusdorf, is not astonished at anything. The myth justifies the present by throwing it back to an ontological precedent. The birth of philosophy depicts the awakening from the sleep of mythical immobility. Escaping from the "captivity of participation," the individual becomes aware of a truth for which he feels himself responsible. And thus begins the adventure of human freedom (Gusdorf, 1952).

Paul Ricoeur discusses the problem of myth in relation to his studies on the symbolism of evil. Consequently he does not undertake an analysis of the living myth in archaic societies, but limits his investigation to the religions of the Ancient Near East. He begins his analysis with the symbolism of defilement and sin—symbols which precede, in his opinion, the myths of the fall and of exile. From symbol to myth, writes Ricoeur in *The Symbolism of Evil* (1967), one passes from a "hidden time" to an "exhausted time." Gilbert Durand holds the contrary view that mythical thought is primordial, and precedes any other type of thinking. For this reason, Durand rejects Ronald Barthes' opinion that myth is a "secondary semiological system" with regard to language (cf. *Les structures anthropologiques de l'imaginaire*, 1960). A similar justification of the priority and the irreducibility of myth was brilliantly elaborated by Gillo Dorfles in *Nuovi riti, nuovi miti* (1965, pp. 49ff.).

315

MYTHS AND FOLKTALES: THE FOLKLORISTIC APPROACH

For some time, a number of anthropologists and folklorists have considered myth as a special form of the folktale, i.e., as a traditional, dramatic, oral narrative. For these authors, folktale "includes serious myths dealing with the supernatural, as well as tales told primarily for entertainment: purportedly factual accounts of historical events; moralistic fables; and other varieties of narrative which may be distinguished on varying grounds of classification" (Fischer [1963], p. 236). The investigations followed mainly two orientations: historical, and morphological or structural. According to W. E. Peuckert, the folktale originated in the eastern Mediterranean during the Neolithic period. C. W. von Sydow proposed, at first, an Indo-European origin of the folktale, and later, an origin in the pre-Indo-European megalithic culture. In a book on the "historical roots of the folktale" (*Istoričéskie korni volšebnoj skazki*, 1946), the Russian folklorist Vladimir Propp, developed P. Saintyves' ritualistic hypothesis: he argued that the folktale conserved the memory of totemic initiation rites. The extensive and meticulous work of the "Finnish School" can equally be considered to follow a historical orientation. Through an exhaustive study of the variants, these scholars thought that they could arrive at a "primordial form" (*Urform*) of a tale (Eliade [1963], pp. 196ff.).

This historical orientation, popular also in the United States, thanks primarily to Franz Boas and his disciples, has recently lost prominence. In the 1950's and 1960's, a number of important contributions exemplified in various ways nonhistorical, morphological, or structuralist approaches. The reasons for this new orientation are multiple, but the most important seem to be the following: the prodigious development of Saussurean linguistics and of phonology; the prominence of "formalism"; the discovery by Western scholars of Propp's morphological study of folktales; and especially the general vogue of structuralism in anthropology and philosophy, particularly the brilliant use of the structuralist method by Claude Lévi-Strauss (see Sebeok). It must be added that a quarter of a century before his "historical" work, Propp elaborated a morphological analysis of folktales, which became accessible rather late in English and Italian translations (Propp, 1928; 1958; 1966). Propp's method was applied by Alan Dundes, *The Morphology of North-American Indian Folktales* (1964), and it was sympathetically received by Lévi-Strauss, who saw in it an anticipation of his own structural analysis of myth and tales (*L'analyse . . .*, 1960; Italian trans. in Propp [1966], pp. 165–99). However, Lévi-Strauss finally rejected Propp's approach as being "formalistic."

In his reply to Lévi-Strauss' article, Propp defended his method, insisting especially on the following points: it is not "formalistic" but empirical, being inspired by Goethe's morphological researches; his "historical" researches, far from indicating a surrender of morphology, represent an effort toward a total understanding of the folkloristic creations; Lévi-Strauss is not interested in the folktale and does not try to know folktales, but is satisfied with logical operations and abstractions (Propp [1946], pp. 203–37). In short, Propp defends the organic character of his morphology, and the possibility of reconstructing the history of folkloristic creations, against the logico-mathematical structuralism of Lévi-Strauss. He also points out that many structuralists have followed his method and criticized Lévi-Strauss' approach, and he quotes Dundes' book (cited above) as an example.

The controversy between Propp and Lévi-Strauss is only one example of the disagreements which exist among the scholars following a morphological or structuralist interpretation of myths and folktales. In spite of their differences, all these authors do have common elements. First, they all consider the myths as *narratives*, i.e., as an oral literary genre. Moreover, they concentrate on studying the forms or structures of the documents, and are less interested in deciphering their religious meaning. For that reason, as we have already remarked, most of these authors (with some exceptions, e.g., Propp), ignore the differences between myths, saga, fairy tales, and other folkloristic narratives. The models of their investigations are borrowed from structural linguistics, and there is a tendency to apply mathematical devices and to utilize electronic computers in order to classify and analyze the documents.

THE STRUCTURAL ANTHROPOLOGY OF LÉVI-STRAUSS

By far the most important contribution to the structuralist interpretation of myths is that of Claude Lévi-Strauss. In linguistics and ethnology, a structure is a combinatory game independent of consciousness. Consequently, Lévi-Strauss does not look for the "meaning" of myth on the level of consciousness. Following the example of the phonologists, he analyzes the infrastructures of primitive thought, identifying the basic logical process in "binary opposition" (in Sebeok [1955], p. 62). Myth being an expression par excellence of primitive thought, its purpose is "to provide a logical model capable of overcoming a contradiction" (ibid., p. 65). One of the most striking results of Lévi-Strauss' first attempt to analyze myth is the awareness that the "kind of logic which is used in mythical thought is as rigorous as that of modern science, and that the difference lies not in the quality of the intellectual process, but in the nature of the things to which it is applied" (p. 66).

Lévi-Strauss concluded his 1955 essay by asserting that "man has always been thinking equally well." His *La pensée sauvage* (1962; *The Savage Mind*, 1966), abundantly illustrates and enlarges this thesis. Neolithic man, writes Lévi-Strauss, was the heir of a long scientific tradition. Mythical thought and modern scientific thought represent "two strategic levels at which nature is accessible to scientific enquiry" (*The Savage Mind*, p. 15). The basic characteristic of mythical thought consists in its concreteness: it works with signs, which have the peculiar character of lying *between* images and concepts. That is, signs resemble images in that they are concrete, as concepts are not; however, their power of reference also likens them to concepts. Mythical thought is a kind of intellectual *bricolage* in the sense that it works with all sorts of heterogeneous material which is available. While science, thanks to its structures (its hypotheses and theories), creates its means and results in the form of events, mythical thought "builds up structures by fitting together events" (p. 22). For that reason, mythical thought "is imprisoned in the events and experiences which it never tires of ordering and re-ordering in its search to find a meaning" (p. 22).

Lévi-Strauss returns to the problem of mythical thought in a projected four-volume series on South and North American mythologies, of which the first two have been published thus far, *Le cru et le cuit* (1964) and *Du miel aux cendres* (1966). This considerable work is difficult reading, because of the technicalities and the intricate analysis of a great number of myths, but at the same time it represents a new and more personal evaluation of mythical thought. Here Lévi-Strauss goes beyond the linguistic models and recognizes that the structure of myths is closer to music than to language. This fresh approach permits him a series of brilliant observations on time and suppression of time, on the ability of music and mythology to achieve a "hyper-mediation" between nature and culture, operating simultaneously on the mind and on the senses, stimulating both ideas and emotion.

Lévi-Strauss' method and interpretation have made a notable impact on the cultivated public in Europe. Nevertheless, the majority of anthropologists, in spite of their admiration for his brilliance, maintain a more or less polite reserve. But the significance of Lévi-Strauss' contribution is only partially dependent upon its acceptance or rejection by his colleagues. Thanks to the depth and originality of his writings, mythical thought and the primitive mind have become a subject of interest to a growing number of philosophers, as well as literary critics and artists. In other words, primitive thought and the primitive mode of existing

in the world are coming to be considered part and parcel of the history of the human mind, which history has been assumed by so many Western authors to have begun only with the pre-Socratics.

Thus after being declared a disease of language, a naïve animistic creation, a playful and debasing fancy, a projection of astral phenomena, a verbalization of ritual, or a fantasy related to a primordial parricide or to the collective unconscious—myth has begun to be understood in a more positive way. That is, myth has been seen either as a sacred story, model, and justification of a meaningful and creative human life; or as the expression of "primitive" but no less valid logical processes. The first group, in this more recent and positive form of interpretation, insists on the *religious values* of myth; the second group, and particularly Lévi-Strauss' interpretation, emphasizes the *logical structures* of mythical thought.

BIBLIOGRAPHY

J. J. Bachofen, *Versuch über die Gräbersymbolik der Alten* (Basel, 1859); idem, *Die Sage von Tanaquil* (Heidelberg, 1870), trans. R. Manheim as *The Myth of Tanaquil*, in *Myth, Religion, and Mother Right . . .* (Princeton, 1967). S. G. F. Brandon, "The Myth and Ritual Position Critically Considered," in *Myth, Ritual and Kingship*, ed. S. H. Hooke (Oxford, 1958), pp. 261–91. E. Buess, *Geschichte des mythischen Erkenntnis* (Munich, 1953). Joseph Campbell, *The Hero With a Thousand Faces* (Princeton, 1949; 1968; reprint New York); idem, *The Masks of God*, 4 vols. (New York, 1959–68). Ernst Cassirer, *An Essay on Man* (New Haven, 1944; New York, 1953). Giuseppe Cocchiara, *Storia del Folklore in Europa* (Turin, 1952). G. W. Cox, *The Mythology of the Aryan Nations*, 2 vols. (1870; reprint Port Washington, N.Y.). Jan de Vries, *Forschungsgeschichte der Mythologie* (Freiburg and Munich, 1961), contains a critical review of interpretations of myth from antiquity to the present. Gilbert Dorfles, *Nuovi riti, nuovi miti* (Turin, 1965). Richard M. Dorson, "The Eclipse of Solar Mythology," in *Myth. A Symposium*, ed. Thomas A. Sebeok (Bloomington, Ind., 1955), pp. 15–38; idem, "Current Folklore Theories," *Current Anthropology*, 4 (1963), 93–112. Gilbert Durand, *Les structures anthropologiques de l'imaginaire* (Paris, 1960). É. Durkheim, *The Elementary Forms of the Religious Life*, trans. Joseph Ward Swain (New York, 1961). P. Ehrenreich, *Die allgemeine Mythologie und ihre ethnologischen Grundlagen* (Berlin, 1910). M. Eliade, *Myth and Reality* (New York, 1963). Ivan Engnell, *Studies in Divine Kingship in the Ancient Near East* (Uppsala, 1943). J. L. Fischer, "The Sociopsychological Analysis of Folk Tales," *Current Anthropology*, 4 (1963). S. Freud, *Totem and Taboo*, trans. James Strachey (London, 1950). Theodore H. Gaster, *Thespis*, 2nd ed. rev. (New York, 1961). W. Grønbech, *The Culture of the Teutons*, 2 vols. (London and Copenhagen, 1931). G. Gusdorf, *Mythe et métaphysique* (Paris, 1952). A. M. Hocart, *The Progress of Man* (London, 1933). S. H. Hooke, *The*

Labyrinth (London, 1935); idem, ed., *Myth and Ritual* (1933); idem, ed., *Myth, Ritual and Kingship* (Oxford, 1958), esp. pp. 1–21. Stanley Edgar Hyman, "The Ritual View of Myth and the Mythic," in *Myth. A Symposium*, op. cit., pp. 84–94. Adolf E. Jensen, *Mythos und Kult bei Naturvölkern* (Wiesbaden, 1951), trans. Marianna Choldin and Wolfgang Wiessleder as *Myth and Cult Among Primitive Peoples* (Chicago, 1963). C. G. Jung and C. Kerényi, *Essays on a Science of Mythology*, trans. R. F. C. Hull (New York, 1949). Clyde Kluckhohn, "Myths and Rituals: A General Theory," *Harvard Theological Review*, **35** (1942), 45–79. Andrew Lang, *The Making of Religion* (1898), 3rd ed. (London, 1909); idem, *Myth, Ritual and Religion*, 3rd ed. (London, 1901). Claude Lévi-Strauss, "L'analyse morphologique des contes russes," in *Journal of Slavic Linguistics and Poetics*, **3** (1960); idem, *La pensée sauvage* (1962), trans. as *The Savage Mind* (Chicago, 1966); idem, *Du miel aux cendres* (Paris, 1966); idem, *Le cru et le cuit* (1964), trans. John and Doreen Wightman as *The Raw and the Cooked* (New York, 1969); idem, "The Structural Study of Myth," in *Myth. A Symposium*, op. cit., pp. 50–66, presents a structuralist interpretation. C. Scott Littleton, *The New Comparative Mythology: An Anthropological Assessment of the Theories of Georges Dumézil* (Berkeley and Los Angeles, 1966). Bronislaw Malinowski, "Myth in Primitive Psychology" (1926), reprinted in *Magic, Science and Religion* (New York, 1954). J. Melville and Frances S. Herskowitz, "A Cross-Cultural Approach to Myth," in *Dahomean Narrative* (Evanston, 1958), pp. 81–122, presents current theories of myth. F. M. Müller, *Contributions to the Science of Mythology* (London, 1897); idem, *Lectures on the Science of Language, Second Series* (London and New York, 1869). Wilhelm Wundt, *Mythus und Religion*, 3 vols. (Leipzig, 1905–09). Walter Otto, *Dionysus* (1933), trans. R. B. Palmer (Bloomington, Ind., 1965). R. Pettazzoni, *Essays on the History of Religions* (Leyden, 1954), pp. 11–36. Vladimir Propp, *Istoričeskie korni volšebnoj skazki* (Leningrad, 1946); idem, *Morfologija skazi* (Leningrad, 1928), trans. Laurence Scott as *Morphology of the Folktale* (Bloomington, Ind., 1958), and as *Morfologia della Fiabba* (Turin, 1966). Otto Rank, *The Myth of the Birth of the Hero* (Leipzig, 1909). Paul Ricoeur, *The Symbolism of Evil* (New York, 1967). W. Robertson-Smith, *Lectures on the Religion of the Semites*, new ed. (London, 1894). Wilhelm Schmidt, *The Origin and Growth of Religion*, trans. H. J. Rose (New York, 1931), presents different methodological approaches. T. A. Sebeok, ed., *Myth. A Symposium* (Bloomington, Ind., 1955). Josef L. Seifert, *Sinndeutung des Mythos* (Munich, 1954). Wayne Shumaker, *Literature and the Irrational* (New York, 1960). E. Siecke, *Drachenkämpfe: Untersuchungen zur indogermanischen Sagenkunde* (Leipzig, 1907). E. Stucken, *Astralmythen* (Leipzig, 1901–07). Edward B. Tylor, *Primitive Culture*, 2nd ed. (1873; reprint New York, 1958). George Widengren, *King and Savior*, 6 vols. (Uppsala, 1945–55).

MIRCEA ELIADE

[See also Astrology; **Creation;** Death; God; Nature; Primitivism; Structuralism.]

MEDIEVAL AND RENAISSANCE IDEAS OF NATION

IT IS A common assumption that nation, state, and nationalism are partly ancient but chiefly modern phenomena both in fact and in thought. Whether they arose to importance in the Middle Ages must therefore be judged in comparison mainly with modern concepts.

Even now nation, state, and nationalism bear so many connotations in relation to human society that definitions vary almost as much as their historical manifestations. It is really better to offer presumptions than definitions. So in recent times it has been normally presumed that a fully existent nation is a state, and the state a nation. (At times, however, when such a people as the Irish or the Jews did not have a territorial state, each was viewed as a kind of nation aspiring to national statehood.) The nation-state is sovereign, for it is independent, legally subject to no superior authority in all the world. It is the object of what is called nationalism including patriotism, the ideal of loyalty to nation or state as the common fatherland which exists to assure the well-being of the people, and the safety of which is approved by God.

The state in itself is the essential bearer of the ideas of nation and nationalism. But what is the state? Essentially it is an abstraction deduced in varying degree from people, social organization, the constitutional order or government, and sovereign independence. Above members who govern and above members who are governed, an end superior to that of any and all individuals within its territory, the state is thus an abstract entity. In other words, while not a corporation, it is a supreme corporate body, by fiction acting as a person, yet actually acting through its agents, the ruler or rulers, with or without the consent of the people. As such a body the state enjoys the attribute also of territoriality, although at times boundaries have been poorly defined.

Of greater importance is the attribute of public law. The state itself is the highest object of public law; and at the same time it is the only community which possesses that true public law by which all lesser communities and all the people within it are its subjects. This is because by the public law the state is not only independent but is also "sovereign above all," sovereign even above the sovereign power that represents and acts for it. For the public law is the supreme law of the state, dealing with its public welfare and safety and with all the means necessary for assuring its ends. Therefore while the public law aims also at the common welfare of the people, lest the state itself be endangered by confusion and anarchy, the public law is superior to the private law just as the right of state is superior to private rights and interests. In other words, the public law, because it is the law of the state, deals more with the constitutional order or government by which the sovereignty of the state is maintained than with individual members of the state. Yet it should also assure the orderly working of the private law by which the common welfare is assured for the sake of the state itself.

Are these presumptions to be found in medieval legal and political ideas? Since they are based on ancient Roman as well as modern definitions and concepts, it should not be surprising that, as the result of the great revival of the Latin classics and of the Roman law in the twelfth and thirteenth centuries, we find them abundantly expressed by medieval jurists and political writers. In fact, at the very time when kings were overcoming the extreme individualism and private rights of feudalism, and when a new economic life was furnishing the financial means, legal ideas found in the Roman law greatly aided them, as they aided Italian communes, in the work of creating states. Feudal personal relations and proprietary rights began to yield to ideas of public law and the state; localism and provincialism also gradually felt the impact of a renewed concept of a central, public authority. Moreover, ideas that had pertained to the public law of the universal state of the Roman Empire were attached to rising kingdoms each of which was the more rapidly looked upon as a common fatherland (*patria communis*) or nation, and became the object of ideals of nationalism.

The process began, however, in the early Middle Ages. Barbarian invaders destroyed the unity and universalism of the Roman Empire. Yet the idea of Rome, and some memory of Roman public law, survived in England, Visigothic Spain, and Merovingian and Carolingian France. With the dissolution of the Carolingian Empire in the ninth century and the rise of feudalism, and with the destruction of the Visigothic kingdom by the Moors, only Anglo-Saxon England existed in the tenth and eleventh centuries as a kind of state. In Germany, despite the efforts of the Ottonian and Salian kings, feudalism began to take hold and frustrate efforts to create a German state. In France feudal princes until the twelfth century triumphed over the old idea of the public authority of the king in the realm as a whole. Nevertheless, even in France the idea of the state and its public law vaguely survived in ideas of kingship and enjoyed a revival in the twelfth century.

Francia was still essentially the limited region of the Île-de-France. But French kings began to use feudal principles in recalling that even the greatest fiefs held by counts and dukes were within the realm and owed services to the king as suzerain. The Duke of Normandy himself, though now the king of England, should do homage and fealty to the king of France. In England the idea of a unified realm became more effective as a result of the Norman conquest. From William the Conqueror on, the Norman-Angevin kings increasingly centralized the public authority and thus, especially in the reign of Henry II, established England as a state. In the mid-twelfth century John of Salisbury, the learned classical humanist, thought of England as a sovereign state under a sovereign king, a state of which the king as head and his subjects were all members. In the same period the Christian reconquest of most of the Iberian peninsula was accompanied by the revival of the tradition of the Visigothic kingdom and the concept of the unity of Spain. From the twelfth century on, poets and chroniclers and jurists glorified the independent realm of Spain, regardless of the actual development of the separate kingdoms of Portugal, Castile, and Aragon.

This tendency to look upon the early medieval kingdom as an inheritor of the Roman idea of the state received considerable support from the Church, or rather from the prelates in each realm—but also at times from the papacy. Bishops favored a strong monarchy and the ideal of a unified royal authority over the whole realm so long as the king could defend their rights and privileges from local lords who were trying to seize control of ecclesiastical lands and wealth. There was a close cooperation of Anglo-Saxon prelates and kings, the bishops serving in royal councils. William the Conqueror and his successors continued this close relationship; and in the twelfth century Anglo-Norman bishops, with the exception of Thomas Becket and a few others, continued to serve the king in the interest of the general welfare of the community of the realm. Bishops and lesser ecclesiastics were often administrators and advisers in the royal government—so Nigel, Bishop of Ely, Richard Fitzneale, and Gilbert Foliot, Bishop of London, in the reign of Henry II. Still in the thirteenth century ecclesiastics like Bracton, the famous jurist, served as royal justices and counsellors, until by the end of the century educated laymen began to take their place. A similar cooperation of the clergy with the secular royal governments of France and Spain was common. One can speak neither of Anglicanism nor of Gallicanism; yet ecclesiastics in each kingdom aided the king in his efforts to make the realm into a state. For example, the scholastic theologian, Vincent of Beauvais, writing on the subject of French kingship about 1260, associated the public estate of the king and the royal court with "the administration of the republic and the government of the whole realm" (Schneider, p. 218, n. 39). Long since, popes themselves, while demanding that kings subordinate themselves to their superior spiritual authority, had been recognizing the *regnum* of France as a valuable ally and support of the Church.

In the twelfth and thirteenth centuries, moreover, a relatively new concept of the Church began to affect the theory of the state. Defined already as the whole body of the faithful, the Church was defined also as a mystical body. This concept was soon applied to the kingdom, the *regnum*. As a mystical body, the kingdom was more than ever an entity that embraced king and people and could not be completely identified either with king and crown or with the people living within it. More than ever the idea of the *regnum* was that of a sovereign community which was sanctioned by God and the law of nature as a supreme necessity for the common welfare and safety of all its members, ruler and subjects alike.

Important as the concept of the mystical body was, beneath it lay a more practical, legal concept of the corporation. The legal theory of the corporation was chiefly a contribution of the revived Roman law in the twelfth and following centuries, and was applied to guilds of merchants and artisans, to the rising communes and cities of Italy and France, to cathedral chapters, and to the rising universities. Each corporation was a subject of private law, and by legal fiction was a kind of person as well as a collectivity of individual members. It could sue and be sued in the courts. Its head, whether the mayor of a commune or the rector of a university, and its members could choose agents or representatives to act for it. Although it existed for the protection of the individual members, the corporation in legal thought was itself an entity the general welfare of which was more important than the welfare of head and members viewed as individuals.

Such a corporation or body, however, was a lesser community within the general *universitas* or community of Empire, Church, or independent kingdom. It was subject, in theory, to the private law of the state as interpreted by the ruler. But the state itself, whether kingdom or Church, was the subject of public law, and therefore strictly speaking could not be a corporation. Nor could a province or county within the state be a corporation. Nevertheless, in the thirteenth century, jurists and royal governments began to apply the legal theory of the corporation not only to the English shire but also to the kingdom itself. The *regnum* or realm, an organism with head and members according to John of Salisbury, was now a public corporation. If it was a mystical body, it was now also, as it were, a super-corporation which through its head, the king, could act as an "artificial" person in international relations, could send agent-ambassadors to other heads of corpo-

rate realms, and could all the better assume to itself a public welfare and safety that were sovereign and independent. So in 1302 and 1303, in the name of the realm of France, the king, Philip the Fair, could appeal to a General Council of the Church against Pope Boniface VIII. In legal theory it was the corporate, mystical body of France that acted in defense of its public welfare, which the pope, allegedly, was endangering. If the king could speak of the realm as if it belonged to him ("our kingdom"), nonetheless the corporate body of the realm was more than king and subjects. Its safety knew no law. As Philip the Fair said in 1305, individually and collectively all the clergy and laity, "as members of our realm truly living together in one body, are bound to the preservation, defense, and care of the unity of this realm." In this case the king was the *ex officio* representative of the corporate realm of the state; but he was not the state itself, nor above the state; he acted for the state.

Such a kingdom, a mystical, corporate body approved by God, was becoming an empire in itself, sovereignly independent of the Holy Roman Empire. To be sure, Dante, in his *De monarchia* could still dream of a restoration of the glory of the universal Roman Empire, with Rome and Italy its vital center as in the great classical age; and some canonists and popes continued to look upon the Church as the true universal, unifying institution of all Christendom, with the pope acting as the true emperor. By the twelfth century, however, what the Norman-Angevin kings had built on the foundation of Anglo-Saxon England, namely, a strong, fairly well centralized realm, received the learned John of Salisbury's concept of the realm as an independent state. Soon, as if to denigrate the Holy Roman Empire under Frederick Barbarossa and his Hohenstaufen successors, and as if to enhance the authority of the pope and the Roman Church over the Empire, canon lawyers added emphasis to the idea of the sovereignty of England, France, and Spain. Some canonists who were loyal to the German emperors spoke only of the *de facto* independence of such kingdoms from the emperor and Empire. Others, however, perhaps influenced by their "national" origins, talked in terms of rightful, legal independence. So about 1200 Alan the Englishman declared that every king who was subject to no one had the same jurisdiction in his own realm as the emperor had in the Empire. Vincent of Spain in the early thirteenth century emotionally boasted of Spanish superiority over the French and the Germans; and he stated that Spanish kings were *de jure* as well as *de facto* sovereigns in their realms. Pope Innocent III about 1200 strengthened this attitude: the French king, he said, recognized no superior in temporal affairs (but, of course, the great pope was sure that by reason of sin such a king was subject to the papal jurisdiction). The Latin formula, *rex superiorem non recognoscens*, led to a new formula, that the king who recognized no superior was emperor in his own realm (*rex imperator in regno suo*).

If the pope and canonists nonetheless granted no sovereignty to kings and their realms with respect to the universal claims of the spiritual authority of the pope and the Church, in fact English kings were preventing appeals from their clergy to the papal court; and in France Louis IX, of saintly fame, tolerated no interference of popes in properly French affairs. The ideas of English and French jurists encouraged and supported the royal policy. So in England Bracton, an expert in the common law and acquainted with the Roman and canon laws, and also a royal justice, held that the king of England was "under no man, but under God and the law." In France, almost at the same time (ca. 1250–60), Jean de Blanot, trained in the Roman law at Bologna, literally stated that the king of France was emperor (*princeps*) in his realm. Some years later, Beaumanoir, who wrote a famous treatise on the customary law of the region of Beauvais, said that the French monarch was sovereign over all in the realm, having the supreme jurisdiction over the people whether dukes, counts, and barons, or ordinary men. The result was that Philip the Fair could defy Pope Boniface VIII, declaring that he had the right to tax the French clergy, in case of the necessity of a just war of defense of the realm, without getting the permission of the pope, and to try a bishop accused of treason when according to the law of the Church such a case should be judged by the pope. Edward I of England was assuming similar rights over the English clergy.

Not yet, however, would a sovereign king or state declare independence of the Christian faith as interpreted by the Roman Church. Nonetheless, in the thirteenth century legal ideas of the sovereignty of the state were preparing the way for Henry VIII's declaration of independence from Rome in 1533: Henry proclaimed that the realm of England was an Empire; that the king had the "dignity and royal estate of the imperial crown"; and that, in effect, even in purely spiritual matters the pope and the Roman Church no longer possessed any authority over the completely sovereign imperial realm.

Meanwhile, in the late twelfth and thirteenth centuries the greater north Italian communes such as Florence, Milan, and Siena, were becoming city-states (Venice had in fact achieved its independence much earlier). While some acknowledgement of a kind of social superiority of the German emperor of the Holy Roman Empire endured, the commune was arrogating to itself the independent, sovereign right to tax even the clergy within its territory in times of great danger or necessity; it claimed for itself all the powers necessary for its public welfare. Popes enjoyed no real success in declaring that without their consent no commune could tax its clergy. (As we have noted, kings also defied this principle of papal consent.) It was but a logical consequence of these developments in theories of the "right of state" as well as in political fact, that in the 1320's Marsiglio of Padua, in his remarkable treatise, *Defensor pacis*, should defend against the papal authority the idea that every city-state, and every kingdom, was sovereign, for it had no superior (*superiore carens*). And Marsiglio anticipated, and perhaps furnished, ideas of the government of Henry VIII by denying that the pope had any authority over the city-state. For even in purely spiritual and religious matters the city acknowledged not the papal authority but the authority of a General Council which represented not only the clergy but also the laity in their separate states. (Thus Henry VIII was to go beyond the Marsiglian theory of sovereignty, for he did not acknowledge any superiority of a General Council of the Church.) Bartolus of Sassoferrata, the greatest Italian jurist of the fourteenth century, succinctly stated the concept of the factual sovereignty of the Italian commune when he called the city its own prince (*civitas sibi princeps*).

Indispensable to any concept of the sovereign state is the attribute of its own "constitutional" or public law, of that law which regulates the powers of the government and its relations with the people, and which deals directly with the overriding public welfare and safety of the state, and deals indirectly with the common welfare of all members whether viewed as individuals or as a collectivity. In the feudal age, to repeat, ideas of the public law became so feeble in France and in Western Europe as a whole that they almost disappeared. But from the twelfth century on, the revival of the Roman law and Roman legal theories of the public law greatly aided kings and their counsellors and justices in the process of overcoming the private and proprietary rights of the feudal ordering of society. The Roman law revealed anew the principle that the public law was concerned with the state of the realm as a whole, that it was the law of the public welfare as it was the law of the government or magistracy which was necessary for the maintenance of law and justice and of the public order. The public law was also that law by which religion, churches, and priests were considered as indispensable to the public and common welfare alike (for it was to the public and common interest that religion and priests help men save their souls for the life eternal), and could ultimately be subordinated to the state rather than to the papacy and the universal Church. It sanctioned the public right of kings, by right of their supreme public office, not only to govern all the people in the state, but also to encroach, as we have seen, on the rights of clergy and churches, and even on the authority, in matters of the faith, of the Roman Church. In a word, as in the ancient Roman Empire, religion again became a primary concern of the state—not, as in the early Middle Ages, in the sense that the state should defend the Church while remaining subordinate to it. So in the thirteenth century the state, instead of being within the Church, was beginning to absorb and nationalize the Church. Again this is a part of the background of the ideas of Henry VIII and the English Church. At the same time, the gradual "laicization" of society was substituting laymen learned in the newer legal science for ecclesiastics in the role of justices and administrators, who aided kings in governing more effectively in the name of the new state and its public welfare.

Feudalism and feudal society also began to yield to the public law of the state. Increasingly the supreme public authority of the king and the royal jurisdiction prevailed over feudal immunities or liberties. In England, Bracton, reflecting both the centralization accomplished by the monarchy from the Conquest to the mid-thirteenth century and the influence of the Roman law, in his theories of kingship and the public law held that great feudal immunities or liberties were delegations of the royal jurisdiction, hence subject to those rights of the crown which pertained to the welfare and safety of the realm. Like Bracton, but still more under the influence of the Roman law, French jurists were asserting that no prescriptive rights could prevail against the public authority; and they encouraged the royal government to claim that the king's highest court (the *Parlement* of Paris) possessed the final *ressortum* or the supreme jurisdiction in cases of appeals from the feudal courts of the greatest counts and dukes (after 1259, indeed, even from the ducal court of the king of England in Gascony).

From the public law, too, came those ultimate public rights of the sovereignty of the state which in general can be called "reason of state." Experts in the Roman law taught that when the ruler used "right reason" his will was not arbitrary, like that of a tyrant, but was in accordance both with the public law and the public welfare. John of Salisbury had spoken of the king's reasoning for the public welfare. In the thirteenth century the jurists maintained that all or any reasoning was right which resulted in acts for the safety of the state in times of emergency or great danger, as in cases

of just wars of defense. "Reason of state," *ratio status* or *ratio publicae utilitatis,* was already modern in its implication. To be sure, the king's use of it should not violate the moral commands of God. Yet, since the realm or state was a mystical body approved by God, and the necessity of its safety knew no law, already the state as a higher moral entity amply justified in the eyes of God the public right of the government to indulge in "reason of state." In claiming for themselves the public law belonging to each city, the Italian communes were likewise practicing the ideas belonging to what we call "reason of state." The principle and practice were not invented by Machiavelli. Now we can understand why, according to the rules of public law, the government, whether royal or communal, was, as Beaumanoir said (ca. 1280) about the king, "sovereign above all" in the state.

Nevertheless the public right of the kings of England and France to make use of the public law in terms of eminent domain, the public welfare clause, and reason of state, did not constitute the modern idea of absolutism. The whole medieval tradition, enhanced by feudalism, insisted that the ruler in all important actions (whether in legislating, in judging, or in waging war or establishing peace) should consult with the great men of the realm. If it was a question either of a just war or of extraordinary taxation to raise money for waging the war, it was the legal duty of the king to hold an assembly in order to consult with all those who were bound by feudal custom to furnish military service or whose rights were touched by the proposed subsidy. True, the "right of state" and the right of its public welfare and safety were in the newer theories superior to all private rights. Nonetheless, private rights were fundamental, and the possessors must at least be consulted in times of emergency. We can now understand, then, that in assemblies summoned by the king those who had rights affected by the king's claim that the state was in danger, might well argue before the king and his court, in his council and assembly or parliament, that there was no real necessity or emergency, that the "public welfare clause" or "right of state" was not involved, and that the king was unjustified in demanding their consent. If the king, according to theories of the public law, had the final right to make the decision after hearing all arguments or pleas, nevertheless it was a political necessity, based on feudal custom and on the weight of private rights, that he heed complaints. After all, the greater men of the realm could and did at times argue that the king was wrong, that he accepted poor advice, and that they knew better than the king when the war was just or unjust, and when the public welfare was at stake. They could therefore limit the king's appeal to the public welfare and "reason of state." They could appeal from the king poorly informed to the king better informed.

In such circumstances, what could the king and his government do in order to overcome overt resistance, in order to convince the assembly of great men and, by 1300, representatives of communities of lesser men, that the royal reasoning was right, and that all members of the kingdom should aid the king in its defense? The answer is that the government could resort to propaganda, to appeals for general support based on an adjunct principle of public law, namely, the principle that when the state was in danger all men in its territory should either fight for the common fatherland or pay extraordinary subsidies to meet the costs of war. In other words, kings and their legally trained counsellors began to make full use of the ideas and ideals of nationalism and patriotism.

To be sure, the word *natio* still designated a more local area than the state; normally it meant either the locality in which one was born, or an organization of students in the University who came from the same general region. It was exceptional indeed when the barons, in 1259, complaining to the king about his favoring the French, spoke of the *natio regni Angliae*. The usual designation for what we call the state, was, as has been indicated, *res publica, regnum,* or *civitas* ("republic or commonwealth, kingdom, or city"). What then was the medieval equivalent of nation as state? It was, given the connotation of patriotic loyalty and nationalism, the *communis patria,* the common fatherland. *Patria* by itself had usually meant, almost like *natio,* a locality, or a county or province. The revival of the Roman law, however, introduced the ancient Roman jurists' designation of Rome and the Empire as the *patria communis*—every lesser city or province in the Empire was simply a local *patria.* The idea that each kingdom had a capital city, such as London or Paris, as the *caput regni,* appeared by the late twelfth century. By the later thirteenth century French jurists were beginning to say that Paris as the capital of the French realm was another Rome. At the same time they seized upon the Roman idea of the common fatherland and transferred it to the kingdom as a whole—again a part of the concept of the *regnum* as an empire in itself, independent of the traditional Holy Roman Empire. Logically, it followed that, inspired by the Latin classics (Cicero above all) and by the Roman law, the lawyers and political writers stressed patriotism, or patriotic devotion to the king and the realm, in ancient-modern terms of nationalism. Scholastic philosophers, for example, Thomas Aquinas and Henry of Ghent, justified patriotism. Legists, quoting the classical jurists, declared that it was glorious, if need be, to die for the fatherland. But dying for the fatherland naturally presupposes fighting in its defense. So the lawyers repeated over and over again the Roman maxim attributed to Cato the Censor, "Fight for the Fatherland!" A son, they said, who in battle unavoidably killed his father among the enemy, was guilty of no crime. The pious duty of loving the fatherland was superior to that of the love (in Christian charity) of the poor, superior indeed to the love of one's children. This legalistic reasoning was accepted by William of Ockham in the fourteenth century (Post, *Studies* . . . , pp. 451f.) when he argued that for the defense of England Edward III need pay no attention to the plea of the clergy, that their money should be used for feeding the poor rather than for the payment of subsidies. (The "Great Society" must yield to "reason of state.")

Such ideas of patriotic loyalty to the state, however, scarcely touched the people as a whole. Privileged nobles and towns and provinces often resisted, either openly or by legal subterfuges, the appeal of the royal government to patriotism. Modern, mass-patriotism was to come with the French Revolution. Yet the medieval expression of the ideal of nationalistic devotion to the state was important. Skillfully used by able kings, appeals to patriotism strengthened their authority, and hastened the development of the early modern nation-state. The modern state, shall we say, has the great advantage of being able to command patriotism more generally and effectively than was possible in the Middle Ages.

In the Middle Ages, in sum, the most important concepts that define the state and the nation as state appeared. The practical attributes of the nation-state (efficient, well centralized government, with an adequate police power and a civil service, and universal military conscription) were poorly developed. But the ideas of the state and its public law, and the ideas of nationalism and patriotism, were all expressed. These ideas survived and became simply more effective in the modern age.

The Italian renaissance added little to the ideas and ideals of state and nation. The reason is that Italian humanists and political thinkers devoted their patriotic sentiments not to Italy as a kingdom or state, but to particular city-states. Machiavelli's *ragione di stato* belonged more to Florence than to Italy. It was in the medieval kingdoms' becoming modern in the sixteenth century and later that ideas of the national state were more fully developed. We merely glorify the word "nation" as state more than was done in the Middle Ages. The ideas and ideals are the same. (And today we find that many people in the state are as little converted to patriotic devotion as ordinary people were in the thirteenth and fourteenth centuries. What is a just war of defense? What justifies fighting and dying for the common fatherland?)

BIBLIOGRAPHY ·

For modern theories of the state, public law, and the nation the following books are good: Hans Kelsen, *General Theory of Law and State* (Cambridge, Mass., 1945); R. M. MacIver, *The Modern State* (London, 1926); F. H. Hinsley, *Sovereignty* (London, 1966); Hans Kohn, *The Idea of Nationalism* (New York, 1946); and Boyd S. Shafer, *Nationalism: Myth and Reality* (New York, 1946).

Medieval ideas on the same subjects are treated by Ernst Kantorowicz, *The King's Two Bodies* (Princeton, 1957), esp. Ch. V; and by G. Post, *Studies in Medieval Legal Thought* (Princeton, 1964), Introduction and Chs. V, X, XI for a detailed account of ideas of public law, "reason of state," and nationalism. For the development of these ideas in France, see Joseph R. Strayer, "Defense of the Realm and Royal Power in France," *Studi in onore di Gino Luzzato* (Milan, 1949), pp. 289–96. Fritz Kern, *Kingship and Law in the Middle Ages*, trans. S. B. Chrimes (Oxford, 1948), while valuable, has nothing on the rise of ideas of public law and the state. For similar ideas in the Renaissance see Friedrich Meinecke, *Machiavellism: The Doctrine of Raison d'État and Its Place in Modern History*, trans. Douglas Scott (London, 1957; New York, 1965); Hans Baron, *The Crisis of the Early Italian Renaissance* (Princeton, 1966); and Vincent Ilardi, "'Italianità' among Some Italian Intellectuals in the Early Sixteenth Century," *Traditio*, **12** (1956), 339–67. Finally, for a quotation given above, see Robert J. Schneider, "A 'Mirror for Princes' by Vincent de Beauvais," in *Studium Generale. Studies Offered to Astrik L. Gabriel* (Notre Dame, Ind., 1968), pp. 207–23.

GAINES POST

[See also Church; Constitutionalism; Law, Ancient Roman, Natural; Machiavellism; **Nationalism;** Renaissance Humanism; **State;** War and Militarism.]

NATIONALISM

NATIONALISM has been the *idée force* in the political, cultural, and economic life of Western Europe and the Western hemisphere since the late eighteenth century. In 1848 it spread to central Europe, in the late nineteenth century to eastern Europe and Asia, and finally in the mid-twentieth century to Africa; thus it can be regarded as the first universal *idée force,* or motivating force, which acts to organize all peoples (who once lived in dynastic or religious states, tribal agglomerations or supranational empires) into nation-states. In each of these states nationalism provides the foremost and predominantly emotional incentive for the integration of various traditions, religions, and classes into a single entity, to which man can give his supreme loyalty. In this sense we can speak, in the second third of the twentieth century, of the age of pan-nationalism. Nationalism has become one of the dominant pivotal ideas of the modern age.

Generally the rise of nationalism has gone hand-in-hand with the rise of the at least presupposed general participation of all members of the nation (citizens) in the affairs of the state and their activization as subjects; the people cease to be mere passive objects of history. Thus nationalism is closely linked with the self-determination of the life of the group, with the introduction of modern science and technology in the service of the nation, with the exaltation of the national language and traditions above the formerly frequent use of universal languages (in Europe Latin and later French) and universal traditions (Christianity or Islam). Thus nationalism has "democratized" culture and, through general education, has aspired to endow the nations with a common background of a sometimes legendary past. From this background is deduced the nation's claim to greatness and to a mission of its own. In spite of the close connection of nationalist self-assertion with different religions (Judaism among Jews; Roman Catholicism among Irish or Poles, the *regnum Marianum;* the autokephalos patriarchates among Orthodox Christians; Islam among Arabs or Pakistanis; Buddhism among Singhalese or Burmese), nationalism has tended towards the secularization of political and cultural life and frequently towards becoming in itself a kind of religion. It dissipated the cultural unity predominant in Europe in the Middle Ages and in the Enlightenment and in Islam, in favor of the distinctive national cultures and languages of each ethnic nation. It was on the strength of this "cultural" nationalism, that in the nineteenth century, chairs of "national" literature and history were for the first time established in European universities; that doctoral dissertations were no longer written in Latin; and that the study of Greek, Latin, and Hebrew ceased to represent in Europe and America the core of higher education.

Some of the principal ideas often encountered in modern nationalism have their forerunners in antiquity. The Hebrews and the Greeks, though far removed from the desire of forming a nation-state in the modern sense of the word, nevertheless subscribed to the idea, responsible for so many excesses of modern nationalism, of being a fundamentally different people from all others—the Gentiles (*goyim*) or the barbarians—basing this difference upon the Will of God (in the case of the Hebrews) or upon Nature (in the case of Aristotle).

The idea of being a people chosen by God, a people to whom God had promised a specific land whose original inhabitants lost their right to the land—though it was truly the land of their ancestors—and of God fighting on the side of "his" people, has been one of the most dangerous elements of nationalism inherited from Old Testament times and the history of the conquest of Canaan.

But modern nationalism represents much more than a revival of tribalism, even a tribalism sanctioned by a tribal religion. It is true that the awakening of nationalism in the eighteenth century was influenced by the revival of classicism. The "father" of modern political nationalism, Jean Jacques Rousseau, wished to restore the exclusive togetherness of the Greek city-state, and founded his *volonté générale* on this close togetherness. In the age of reason, nationalism demanded a rational organization, unknown in the antiquity of tribe or polis. The absolutist state in early modern Europe created the centralizing structure or form into which, in many cases, nationalism entered later as the integrating and vivifying force, drawing all classes of the population into a commonwealth and politico-cultural partnership.

Nationalism and the modern nation-state presupposed for their actualization certain social and technological conditions which hardly existed even in western Europe (with the exception of England) before the French Revolution—improved communications and the beginning of geographic and social mobility; a government based upon the not only passive but active "consent of the governed," a consent sought today even by "dictatorial" governments through the promotion of education and indoctrination; the growth of religious toleration and this-worldliness, which included the obligation of the nation-state to care for the welfare of the people; the lessening of ancient local traditions and loyalties; and growing urbanization and industrialization. Thus nationalism as an idea was dominant among the intellectual classes, and as a movement (though not necessarily as a sentiment) was born, so far as historical trends or movements can be measured by precise dates, in the second half of the eighteenth century. But that century was also the time of a conscious cosmopolitanism (*Weltbürgertum*) among the educated classes in the Western world.

The same eighteenth century which emphasized in its educated classes an internationalist consciousness—the masses still thought and felt within a purely local context—also witnessed among the educated classes the first expressions of modern nationalism. Yet the later antagonism between nationalism and internationalism was widely unknown. They formed two aspects of the same movement; both were manifestations of the great moral and intellectual crisis through which the Western world passed in the second half of the eighteenth century, a crisis which represented a search for regeneration, for better foundations of social life, for new concepts of public and private morality. The French Revolution was only the terminal focal point of a general movement which can be broadly called "nationalism" or "democracy," implying a struggle against the existing traditional, and by now obsolete, forms of government and hierarchical social order.

Government and society, state and people were aligned in the eighteenth century against each other; the movement of renovation strove to fuse them in the name of liberty. The concept of political liberty and human dignity united internationalists and nationalists alike. As H. N. Brailsford pointed out, Benjamin Franklin's epigram, "Where liberty is, there is my country," and Thomas Paine's crusading retort, "Where liberty is not, there is mine," sum up the spirit of the new cosmopolitan patriotism of the later eighteenth century. It was the same spirit which is basic to Kant's essay, "Zum ewigen Frieden" ("Perpetual Peace"). Cosmopolitanism or internationalism and patriotism or awakening nationalism intermingled in that age of promise and hope under the aegis of liberty and peace.

The "fathers" of modern nationalism, Jean Jacques Rousseau and Johann Gottfried von Herder, were at the same time cosmopolitans or internationalists. Deeply attached to their *patrie*, or their native language and tradition, and to their *amour de la patrie*, they regarded at the same time the whole of mankind as a greater and higher fatherland and thus were attached also to *l'amour de la liberté* and *de la paix*. Rousseau followed the example of Plato and of Sparta in regarding the love of the *patrie* as the most heroic of all passions and in stressing the distinctive self-being and self-centeredness of each people. But veering from Plato and Sparta's example, Rousseau extolled the rural population, the common man of his time, not the educated classes or philosophers or warrior noblemen, as the matrix of national life and genius. In 1765 and in 1771, he appealed in his projects for the Constitutions of Corsica and Poland to the need of a fervent nationalism as the essential basis of the moral and democratic regeneration of a people and of the age. He called upon the Corsicans to take an oath of devotion to "liberty and justice and the Republic of the Corsicans"—in that order, it should be noted. Rousseau insisted on universal military service for patriotic and moral reasons, even though his ideal nation was also to renounce all thought of military glory or expansion. The true nation, according to Rousseau, will prefer happiness to greatness (*ne sera point illustre, mais elle sera heureuse*).

Herder, a nonpolitical thinker in the nonpolitical German world of his time, was at heart a humanitarian democrat and cosmopolitan pacifist, as Rousseau was, despite the presence of contradictions in their rich and often unsystematic thought. With greater moral indignation than ever even appeared in Rousseau, Herder saw in Roman pride and lust and in the glorification of the sword and war the evil historical inheritance of Western civilization. He discovered the *Volk*—the national community based upon the so-called "lower classes"—as a genetic, developing, and creative unit. With this discovery he gave a new perspective to our understanding of history, of civilization, of arts and letters. However, he never endowed the *Volk* with absolute value or with ultimate sovereignty. He viewed the peoples of northern Europe with remarkable objectivity, not followed by his imitators. His description of the Slavs and Latvians, among whom he grew up and liked to live, has become famous. Peaceful, charitable, and industrious, the Slavs and Latvians "have been sinned against by many nations, most of all by those of the German family." Herder was convinced that with the progress of civilization, the peaceful cultural intercourse of people, these "submerged peoples" would come into their own. The historian of mankind must not favor one nationality to the exclusion or slighting of others deprived by circumstances of opportunity and glory. Like Kant, Herder castigated the colonial expansion of the white race of his time. "The human race is one; we work and suffer, sow and reap for one another" (*Das Menschengeschlecht ist ein Ganzes; wie arbeiten und dulden, säen und ernten für einander*). Rousseau, Kant, and Herder were conscious of the dangers contained in a nationalism that does not treat all other peoples, whatever their power or their degree of development, as possessing equal status and equal rights.

Rousseau and Herder influenced the development of nationalism in different ways: Rousseau, the political nationalism of the French Revolution; Herder, the romantic nationalism of central and eastern Europe. Rousseau expressed the convictions which (after the preludes of the English and North American revolutions) inspired the French Revolution: that sovereignty and government are not the King's but the people's; that the common men form the nation, that their consent legitimizes government, and that they have the aptitude and the right to take national destiny into their hands. Nationalism was thus in its beginning part of that general movement of emancipation which started in England and Holland in the seventeenth century. This nationalism marked, to use Kant's defini-

tion of the Enlightenment, the people's growth to maturity and its release from tutelage. It was part of the democratic movement for individual liberty—the *Déclaration des droits de l'homme et du citoyen* (1789) emphasized universal individual rights—and a movement of integration of all people on the basis of equality, whatever their class, descent, or religion.

The new nation-state born in the French Revolution was, as it was in the English-speaking countries, primarily a political-territorial concept, based upon common law and citizenship, a *Gesellschaft* to use the term of Ferdinand Tönnies from his *Gemeinschaft und Gesellschaft* (1887). *Qu'est-ce qu'une nation?*, Sieyès asked, and he answered: *un corps d'associés vivant sous une loi commune et répresenté par la même législature* (*Qu'est-ce que le tiers état?*, 1789). The laws had to be just and wise, promising happiness to all the citizens and promoting their virtue. At the festival of federation at Dijon on May 18, 1790 the Abbé Volfius, the future Constitutional Bishop of the Côte d'Or, defined "fatherland" as being "not at all this soil on which we live, these walls which have seen our birth. The true fatherland is that political community where all citizens, protected by the same laws, united by the same interests, enjoy the natural rights of man and participate in the common cause." This fatherland could identify itself, as it did in the case of Milton, Locke, or Jefferson, with the new message of individual liberty. It aimed to reform an existing state on the basis of liberty, to vitalize and strengthen it by the new dynamic forces of the new age. It was neither narrow nor backward looking.

The new nation-state preserved at its beginning the cosmopolitan pathos of the Enlightenment. The French revolutionaries acted on behalf of the *genre humain;* their doctrines claimed universal validity; through their action Paris became the new Zion, the new Rome, from which issued the new gospel. In article 4 of his *Essai de Constitution* (April 24, 1793), Saint-Just stressed the internationalism, the open society of the free fatherland. All peoples were brothers; all "tyrants"—one's own as well as alien—were enemies.

This early French nationalism found hardly an echo among other peoples on the European continent: some intellectuals sympathized with it, the masses remained indifferent or hostile. Only the campaigns of the French armies over two decades carried the seed of the new nationalism abroad and stirred other peoples, or at least their educated classes, into a mood receptive to it. But it was no longer the cosmopolitan nationalism which had incorporated into its constitution the promise "never to use force against the liberty of any people." Nationalism became militant. The French began to think of themselves as warriors; the fatherland became a divinity. Soon after the outbreak of the revolutionary wars France promised help to all peoples who wished to "recover" their liberty. The republican army not only brought "liberty" to the peoples against whose governments it fought; it also saved the Revolution and France. It seemed to endow France with a new strength and authority, for the people's army achieved more glorious victories than the royal armies ever had. The revolutionary transformation of French society and the appeal of nationalism apparently regenerated the nation. Only few saw then that, by their excesses, the revolutionary wars would leave France exhausted, and that it would take some time to bring her back to the rational tradition of measure and moderation. From the wars of the revolution there emerged in France the highly centralized, sovereign, continental nation-state, conscious of a civilizing mission, *la grande nation*, which set a pattern for nineteenth-century continental Europe, as the court of Versailles had done in the seventeenth century. Yet in the concept of the nation-state formulated after 1789, the sovereignty of the state was not unlimited; for the state, in the long run and in spite of many vicissitudes, remained respectful of individual rights and of a rational political order, conceived in liberty and equality.

Herder's influence on the development of nationalism in central and eastern Europe was different. Nationalism in Britain, France, or Scandinavia could fit itself into a historical area and pattern. It continued a political development, revitalizing and grounding it in firmer foundations. Nationalism in central and eastern Europe did not fit into existing state patterns. At the onset of the age of nationalism such political molds were lacking among Germans and Italians, among western and southern Slavs. Herder and the romanticists directed attention to prepolitical, prerational foundations—the mother tongue, ancient folk traditions, common descent, or the "national spirit." These nonpolitical criteria created an ethnic-linguistic nationalism, which differed from the territorial state-nationalism in the West. This more intimate and more unconscious nationalism corresponded to the "spontaneous" or instinctive ancestral community, the *Gemeinschaft* as defined by Tönnies. Subordinating political criteria to the ties of inheritance and tradition, Germans, Italians, and Slavs in their efforts to build their nation-states insisted that people speaking the same tongue or claiming a common ancestry should form one political state. A similar insistence was hardly known in France regarding French-speaking Swiss or Belgians, or in the Netherlands regarding the Flemish.

This nationalism which based itself upon the vague and semimystical concept of folk and folk culture made its most significant contribution to the development of nationalism in German romanticism, and, under its influence, in Russian Slavophilism. Both rejected the Enlightenment and French rationalism in favor of a transfigured national past with ancient traditions and beliefs. Both envisaged a perfect national community, in which the individual would be fully himself only as an integral part of the nation; in such a case individual and society were no longer in need of legal or constitutional guarantees. They became two sides of one perfect life which would be all in all, beyond and above rational or universally valid laws. This nationalism rejected individual liberty as its foundation; it stressed the belief that every individual was determined by the organic national or ancestral past, fundamentally unaltered and unalterable, forward into the future. The national past set the model, which was no longer universally valid, but valid only for all individual members of the national community. The concept of an organic and unique personality was transferred from the individual to the nation. The latter was no longer primarily a legal society of individuals entering into union according to general principles and for mutual benefits; it was now an original phenomenon of nature and history, following its own laws. This natural personality, alive, striving, and growing, often stirred by desires for power and expansion, appeared as a manifestation of the divine, entitled and called upon to explore all its dynamic potentialities without much consideration for the rights of other nations.

This concept of nationalism became characteristic above all of politically and socially underdeveloped societies which faced the challenge of the new dynamic age. It was promoted and guided by intellectuals and writers rather than by statesmen or legislators. Fighting against the preponderance of French civilization, the intellectuals extolled the beauty of their own language and literature in contrast to that of the French. Out of the myths of the past and out of dreams of the future, they constructed an ideal fatherland, long before an actual fatherland, often very different from the dream, became a reality. To these writers and intellectuals nationality appeared as "sacred," as the source of morality and creativeness. But with these nationalist intellectual leaders, nationality remained, in the first half of the nineteenth century subordinated, at least in theory, to the good of humanity as a whole; even if a nationality—or rather its spokesmen—arrogated to itself a messianic mission, a primacy among the nations of Europe or the world, it was a mission in the service of mankind. In the 1840's the intellectuals often felt in many cases no antagonism between their nationalism and the claims of internationalism.

The majority of the peoples themselves in central and eastern Europe were then still untouched by

327

nationalism; the overwhelmingly rural populations remained loyal to their hereditary princes, and their interests were confined to a narrow local outlook. Communications were still slow, travel was largely unknown, the literacy rate very low. The literate population, men with a wider horizon, felt definite international responsibilities. The ruling classes of the period of the Holy Alliance distrusted nationalism, for a nationalist or patriot meant to them a potential revolutionary, a democrat, a friend of the common man. Though the nationalist movement—Carbonari, Decembrists, Young Europe—were loose organizations without clearly defined goals or structured cooperation, they easily appeared as an international conspiracy. Because they fought domestic or foreign "tyrants" on behalf of the people, these early nationalists felt a fundamental affinity across national boundaries.

The concept of nationalism as it changed between 1840 and 1890 is striking: by 1890 nationalism ceased to be regarded as a democratic-revolutionary movement of the people; it had become a predominantly conservative or reactionary movement, frequently representing the upper classes against the people, and it was strongly opposed to all internationalism. Its ideal was, by the end of the century, an exclusive, self-centered, closed society. That was generally not the case before 1848. The nationalists of that period, men like Michelet in France, Mazzini in Italy, or Adam Mickiewicz in Poland, saw nationalism as a ubiquitous movement. However enthusiastically they might extol their own nationality and its mission, they welcomed others. They professed, as the meaning of the national mission, not separation and domination, but cooperation and service. In his *Le peuple* (1846) Michelet called all classes and peoples, especially the backward ones, into the great association, which, according to him, France had started in 1789. In a lecture at the Collège de France, on February 8, 1849, Michelet defended the growth of national cultures by urging the preservation of diverse races: "To each people or race we shall say: Be yourself. Then they will come to us with open hearts." This generous and utopian nationalism of the 1840's changed in character after the defeat of the democratic revolution of 1848–49.

The two types of nationalism which emerged in Europe in the early part of the nineteenth century—territorial-political and romantic-ethnic nationalism, representing two kinds of society, an open and a closed one—are "ideal types"; no actual nationalism represented them in pure form. In reality there were and are innumerable transitional stages between the historical passage from one to the other of the two types; yet at all times and in each individual case one or the other type prevails. In some cases we find that a terri-

torial nationalism is replaced in the course of history by an ethnic-linguistic nationalism or by the conflict of two or several of such nationalisms within the framework of the former territorial nationalism. Such a development can lead to bitter enmity among groups which formerly cooperated. Such was the case with the Czech and German linguistic nationalism which in 1848 replaced the formerly strong Bohemian territorial patriotism. Finland, too, changed from a territorial nationalism (*Staatsnation*) to an ethnic-linguistic nationalism. But Finland, in contrast to Bohemia, was able to achieve a synthesis between ethnic-linguistic nationalism and territorial-political nationalism which allowed two ethnic or linguistic groups to live as equals within one political nation.

In his essay on "Nationality" (1862), Lord Acton insisted that in the interests of human liberty, multi-ethnic states which guaranteed the equality and the autonomous free development of several ethnic groups within one political nation were most desirable. However, European history between 1848 and 1945 did not follow the course recommended by Acton. Though after 1848 several polyethnic states did exist (e.g., Germany, Russia, and Austria-Hungary before 1914; Poland, Czechoslovakia, and Yugoslavia after 1918), these states regarded themselves as essentially mono-ethnic nation-states, and identified the state with the domination or superior position of one of the several ethnic (linguistic or religious) groups. After 1918 many constitutions, under the influence of the League of Nations, provided a theoretically "good" treatment for the "minorities," but the minority considered itself an underprivileged group, because it was not accepted as an equal partner in the common state. For a polyethnic state will prosper on the national (state) and international level, if psychologically the feeling of a "majority" and "minority" relationship does not exist. Such an attitude implies that none of the ethnic, linguistic, or religious groups suffers from the impression that the state identifies itself with one of them at the expense of others. The Italians in Switzerland are numerically a small minority, only 10 percent against 70 percent German-speaking Swiss; but psychologically they do consider themselves not a minority but an equal partner in a polyethnic nation.

The principle of an equal partnership, irrespective of numbers, wealth, or influence, is the "ideal" foundation for a "nation of many nations" in the United States. It is because of this background that since World War II the Americans of African descent have sought equality with the help of the federal government in this nation of many nations. The majority does not consider itself anything but American, which it truly is. Its cultural and political home is the United States;

its loyalty belongs to it. The vast majority does not wish to emigrate to some "historical" African "homeland" nor to form an autonomous ethnic entity within the United States, but to work together with Americans of all other descents in full equality for the better future of all.

This demand is not only morally and politically justified from the point of view of democracy; it corresponds also to the founding principles of the American nation. For the United States, as a nation, has from the beginning not been based on common descent or common ancestral traditions, on a common religion or a rootedness in ancestral soil, but on a common "idea" which, rather than looking to the past which separates and divides the various groups, looks to a common future. The "idea" is the tradition of liberty, of a moderate and mild government, which has developed in English history and which has become, as a result of two seventeenth-century revolutions there, the "birthright" of Englishmen. Under the influence of the Enlightenment, the nation builders in the North American colonies reinterpreted this historical "idea" without cutting it off from its traditional basis, as a universal "idea," not a historical right but a "natural" human right, valid for every citizen of the United States whatever his ancestry, and valid ultimately for all human beings. The assimilative power of the United States, which transformed many millions of the most diverse immigrants into a "new race of men" was made possible by this "universality" of American nationalism, which a nationalist like Walt Whitman recognized.

Switzerland is another example of a polyethnic state. Three ethnic and linguistic groups, which outside Switzerland were bitter enemies and jealous of each other, have lived together for centuries in peace on the basis of equality and federal autonomy. But the Swiss nation with its much older roots is more firmly based on historical principles than the United States, though it was the Enlightenment and the spirit of 1848 which flowed from it, that helped Switzerland to achieve its polyethnic and multilingual nationhood.

Switzerland does not assimilate as the United States does. It preserves within one nation the various ethnic groups, and it does this successfully because the numerical majority there forgoes prerogatives in favor of the "minorities." Fundamental for the solution of the problems of duo- or polyethnic states is not primarily the attitude of the minority or minorities but that of the majority. The weaker groups in the population must receive a greater consideration than would be proportional to their numerical strength. They must have a greater share in the benefits of the state than is their "due." Then they will know that the state is their homeland, too, and the natural privilege inherent

in greater numbers or greater wealth will be compensated by "favors" extended to the "minority." But so far, in the age of nationalism, most polyethnic states have used the state power to strengthen the "majority," which has claimed to "own" and to represent the state. For these reasons the polyethnic states which can be found on all continents, have often not become a blessing for all citizens, as Lord Acton believed, but a burden on its weaker members.

The three decades from 1848 to 1878 were decisive in the history of European nationalism. Federation was then much discussed, for the various regions and even for Europe as a whole. With the exception of Switzerland these vague plans to create polyethnic states on a democratic basis of equality came nowhere near success. Some enlightened Greek patriots in the early nineteenth century tried to federalize the Balkan peoples and thus to prevent the creation of bitterly antagonistic nation-states. But soon the Greeks themselves became ultra-nationalistic and the Balkans, from 1821 to 1945, became a scene of violent struggles among nationalities.

This development in the Balkans, however, was not unique; the wars of independence and mutual jealousies there set a pattern for most of central and eastern Europe. The hopes of the liberal nationalists of 1848 were defeated, partly because the new ethnic-linguistic nationalism proved a stronger emotional force than liberalism with its rational-cosmopolitan tradition. The number of those who, when the chips were down, subordinated aspirations for national power and glory to concern for individual liberty and international solidarity was astonishingly small: one of them was Carlo Cattaneo, who tried to overcome national egoism and to integrate nationality into the great movement of the European democratic revolution. At a time when Italian nationalist passion was aroused in the struggle against Austria, this Milanese patriot regarded the incorporation of Lombardo-Venetia into a democratic Austrian federation as equally acceptable as incorporating it into a democratic Italian federation. He emphasized democratic federalism, not nationalist self-assertion, as the trend of the future, and envisaged a federated Austria and a federated Italy as partners in a European federation, in which the nationalism of the various nationalities would lose its absolutist claim. Such a development might have precluded the struggle for nationalist prestige and power which led to the wars of 1870, 1914, and 1939. But Cattaneo and his few fellow-thinkers in other nationalities were quite alone. Nationalist passions paid no heed to them.

On the European continent this new passionate nationalism, which insisted first and foremost on national interest, unity, and power, frustrated the hopes for European federation of the 1830's and 1840's. When in the two decades of 1848 and 1878 the national aspirations of Germany, Italy, the Magyars, and the Christian Balkan peoples were, at least partially, realized, their success was no longer due to the revolutionary idealism of the 1840's. Nationalism no longer formed part of the popular democratic European movement, which started in the late eighteenth century; instead, it relied on the means and methods of the new *Macht-* and *Realpolitik,* and gratefully acknowledged and accepted their success. After the middle of the century nationalism abandoned its hope and aspiration to create a new popular political and social order; it willingly made its peace with the traditional power structure. The peace-loving idealism was replaced by slightly Machiavellian politics; the temper of the *Communist Manifesto* (1848) and of Darwin's *On the Origin of Species by Means of Natural Selection, or the Preservation of Favoured Races in the Struggle for Life* (1859) stimulated a view of history as incessant war, with conflict as a vehicle of progress. Struggle for power seemed to be inherent in society and history, among individuals, classes, races, and above all, nations.

Economy and biology entered the conceptual arsenal of nationalism, which until then had been political and cultural. The economic orientation of nationalism stemmed from an emphasis on national power and independence. This emphasis ran counter to the late eighteenth-century concept of a worldwide economy, of free trade. It started, interestingly enough, in the United States, when an immigrant having come in 1784 from Ireland, Mathew Carey, who hated England—which then supplied manufactured goods to the former colony—fought in his *Pennsylvania Herald* (1785) against imports and for the promotion of domestic manufactures. Otherwise, he warned, the United States would again become a dependency, in what is called today "neo-colonialism."

Georg Friedrich List, the German nationalist and economist who came to the United States in 1825, was deeply impressed by this economic nationalism and became its propagandist in Germany. In his *The National System of Political Economy* (1841) he objected to the then accepted political economy because "it took no account of nations, but simply of the entire human race, on the one hand, or of single individuals, on the other." He described "nationality" as the distinguishing character of his system. As a man of the pre-1848 era, he still favored the idea of a "universal union or confederation of all nations" commended by common sense and religion. Then the principle of free trade would be "perfectly justified." But such a union could come about, he believed, only when the nations attained as nearly as possible the same degree of civilization and industry. Until then, he urged, it is necessary that "the governments and peoples of Germany be more and more convinced that national unity is the rock on which the edifice of their honor, their power, their present security and future greatness must be founded."

The German governments and peoples were then in no way willing to accept List's advice. Five years later he committed suicide. But in his book he not only emphasized the fundamental importance of a nationalistic economy for national existence, but suggested that a united Germany, which would include Holland, Belgium, and Switzerland, would form the nucleus of a durable continental alliance, opposed to English maritime supremacy, and that finally Britain would be forced to join a European coalition against the supremacy of America.

The biological element in nationalism was introduced a decade later by Arthur, Comte de Gobineau, who in contrast to Herder, proclaimed the inequality of human races. To him the highest race was the Teutonic race, of which he claimed the French aristocracy of Frankish origin, to which he belonged, as the noblest specimen; furthermore, racial ability depended upon "purity of blood." Gobineau's theories of biological nationalism were not widely accepted in his day. Leading French historians like Michelet and Renan stressed racial intermingling as the fertile basis of French nationalism and as the foundation of a liberal policy. Louis Joly wrote in his *Du principe des nationalités* (1863) that emphasizing ancestors was contrary to the principles of 1789.

The association of men which is not constituted by the sympathies and hatreds stemming from common descent is superior to one based upon the recognition of these 'natural' [feelings]. The fusion of races, as it happened in France, Britain, and the United States, is one of the great beneficial factors of mankind. The leading powers in the world are the very ones where the various nationalities and racial strains which entered into their formation have been extinguished and have left few traces.

Alexis, Comte de Tocqueville wrote Gobineau that his biological nationalism was hostile to individual liberty, and added that his ideas had a chance in France only if they were imported from abroad, especially from Germany. There Richard Wagner, Gobineau's contemporary, began at about the same time, to extol race and blood as the foundation of all intellectual and moral life and of a sound national existence. Racialism in German nationalism grew with the opposition to the principles of 1789. Biological nationalism endowed cultural differences among nations with a "moral" or metaphysical sanction at the same time that political antagonism between nations was deepened by the emphasis on economic conflicts and competition. In the second half of the nineteenth century nationalism became an all-inclusive concept.

This new attitude led to a disregard for the rights and interests of other nationalities; it set each nationality against other, especially neighboring, nationalities. The consequences were worst where nationalities were intermingled, or where, with the new emphasis upon their national past, they recalled the fact that formerly they had settled or dominated lands which, though long "lost," were now reclaimed on the strength of what was called "historical rights." In April 1849, John Stuart Mill wrote in *The Westminster Review* an article vindicating the French Revolution of February 1848:

It is far from our intention to defend or apologize for the feelings which make men reckless of, or at least indifferent to, the rights and interests of any portion of the human species, save that which is called by the same name and speaks the same language as themselves. These feelings are characteristic of barbarians; in proportion as a nation is nearer to barbarism it has them in a greater degree: and no one has seen with deeper regret, not to say disgust, than ourselves, the evidence which recent events have afforded, that in the backward parts of Europe and even (where better things might have been expected) in Germany, the sentiment of nationality so far outweighs the love of liberty, that the people are willing to abet their rulers in crushing the liberty and independence of any people not of their own race and language.

Similar sentiments, hostile to mass-urbanization, to "uprooted" cosmopolitanism, to humanitarian considerations, became more and more characteristic of certain trends of nationalism, as Europe approached the fateful year of 1914. In his *National Life and Character* (1893) Charles Henry Pearson, formerly a highly efficient minister of education in the Australian state of Victoria, wrote that a nation was "an organized whole . . . kept up to a high pitch of external efficiency by contest, chiefly by way of war with inferior races, and with equal races by the struggle for trade routes and for the sources of raw material and of food supply." The same feeling of an assertive and aggressive nationalism was expressed in the United States by the Republican Senator from Indiana, Albert Jeremiah Beveridge, who in his speech on January 9, 1900, pressed for the annexation of the Philippines by the United States.

Yet another historian, a student of English seventeenth-century history, Samuel Rawson Gardiner, warned at about the same time with regard to England that "Too much power is never good for man or nation." On the whole, moderation has prevailed over extremism in British and American nationalism; the

heritage of the Enlightenment proved stronger there than the newer forces of irrationalism and activism. In these and other democratic nations the consciousness of the interdependence of nations in a balanced system of mutual responsibilities survived more strongly than in some of the "younger" nations of central and eastern Europe, where liberalism, in the Western sense of the word, had weaker roots and less staying power. After a brief period of growth liberalism gave way to a more radical self-assertion from the right and the left.

The industrial transformation of these societies proceeded in the political and social framework of a pre-industrial society. Tensions and discontent resulted which led on the one hand to a rejection of the liberal nationalism of the West and on the other hand to a spiritual superiority complex of the "younger" nations, who found in it a compensation for their actual retardation, which encouraged them to combat the liberal nations.

The character of European nationalism between 1860 and 1914 differed from what it had been before 1848. The new nationalism was opposed to internationalism and put no emphasis on the common people as the foundation of the nation. It became the political doctrine of the upper classes, of the "rightists" in the political spectrum of the day. It stood in sharp opposition to socialism, an "international" movement that included industrial workers and peasants, who, in most respects, felt excluded from the national society.

The emergence of the new internationalism of the postwar period was opposed between 1918 and 1945 by a specially violent form of nationalism which rejected all international obligations and stressed and glorified the need for a hierarchical and authoritarian structure of the nation. Though this fascist nationalism took various forms in different countries, according to their national traditions and social structure, it represented in all its forms a total repudiation of the liberal ideas of the seventeenth- and eighteenth-century revolutions, of the rights of the individual, and of the desirability of a rational international order based upon the equality of men and nations. Fascism was not, as it was sometimes believed, the last stage of capitalism, but a defence of largely precapitalist, premodern social hierarchies. Capitalism has survived fascism and seems, though of course different from what it was in 1840 or 1900, more strongly established in the 1960's than in the 1930's, when fascism, proud of its alleged moral superiority and higher efficiency, believed that nonfascist capitalism, called "plutocracy," would crumble under the blows of fascist aggressiveness.

Fascism in its various forms had its roots in certain pre-1914 nationalist trends in the various countries—especially, but not only, in Germany—and though it was in no way the inevitable outcome of late nineteenth-century national ideas, it was their extreme consequence. Nationalism in its fascist period—motivated partly by the fear of social change, and partly by the impact of modern civilization in countries insufficiently modernized in their social structure and overly traditional in their attitude—assumed far beyond anything known in the period before 1914 an absolutist and extremist self-assertiveness, glorifying war between nations or races. Fascism, therefore, helped to dismantle the League of Nations, which represented the first attempt to institutionalize an international order based upon the victory of the Western democracies. The League conformed in some respects to the concept of nationalism which predominated before 1848; its proponents believed in a modus vivendi of nationalism and internationalism and in the resumption of the modern trend toward peace, equality, and moderation. Only the complete defeat of fascism in 1945 allowed the United Nations to resume the institutionalization of internationalism.

The Great European War of 1914 originated in nationalist struggles, and primarily in a conflict of Germanism and Slavism. As far as Europe was concerned the war ended the dynastic state: the great monarchies which in 1815 controlled the whole of central and eastern Europe—the Romanovs, Habsburgs, Hohenzollern, and the Ottoman Sultans—were suddenly replaced by republics that, at least originally, followed the pattern of parliamentary constitutionalism which the dynasties had long combatted.

From a global point of view, the year 1917—the entrance of the United States into the war and the November revolution which, at least temporarily, took Russia out of Europe—transformed the war for European hegemony into a war for a world balance of power. The era of European preponderance had lasted from the early eighteenth century, the time of the rollback of the Ottoman Empire by Austria and Russia and the rise of a more efficient and dynamic political and social order, based upon the new public morality of the Enlightenment, until 1917. From then on, to a growing degree, European policy (in both West and East) has become intelligible only in a global framework. Yet this beginning of interdependence coincided in 1918 with the triumph of the nationalities in Europe, a triumph which seemed a belated justification of the revolution of 1848. Again, as in 1848, this triumph was short-lived: quarrels, jealousies, mutual suspicions, resentments, and contradictory historical claims of the various nationalities endangered not only peace and constitutional liberties, but their very existence.

At the same time nationalism was spreading, as a result of the impact of Western civilization and of the war itself, to Asia, Africa, and Latin America. This was little noticed by the European statesmen, peoples, and historians in 1918. Yet even before the war, the revolution in Mexico in 1910, the Turkish revolution in 1908–09, the Chinese revolution in 1911–12, and the revolutionary unrest in India and Egypt in 1905–07 were unmistakable indications of the fact that nationalism had come to the underdeveloped countries in order to stay and to develop them.

Modern civilization, which originated in the West in the eighteenth century, exercised its worldwide dynamic impact because, though classic and Christian in its roots, it was a rational, postclassic, and post-Christian civilization which potentially appealed to all men and could be accepted by them. Half a century after writing the Declaration of Independence and a short time before his death, Thomas Jefferson wrote about the Declaration: "May it be to the world, what I believe it will be—to some parts sooner, to others later, but finally to all—the signal of arousing men to burst the chains under which monkish ignorance and superstition has persuaded them to bind themselves, and to assure the blessings and security of self-government." Almost a quarter of a century after Jefferson's letter, the *Communist Manifesto* prophetically anticipated that

In place of the old local and national seclusion and self-sufficiency, we have intercourse in every direction, universal interdependence of nations. And as in material, so also in intellectual production. The intellectual creations of individual nations become common property. . . . The bourgeoisie, by the rapid improvement of all instruments of production, by the immensely facilitated means of communication, draws all, even the most barbarian nations into civilization. . . . It compels all nations . . . to introduce what it calls civilization into their midst. . . . In a word, it creates a world after its own image (Part I, trans. Samuel Moore).

This process had hardly started in the fall of 1847; the overwhelming majority of mankind was still far removed from universal intercourse; major portions of the globe were uncharted or completely secluded; yet by 1965 the predictions of Jefferson and Marx had to a large extent come true.

The nationalism of the post-1945 era is in many ways different from that of 1900. It regards itself again as compatible with international or supranational organizations; it knows of the interdependence brought about by recent technological changes. Above all, nationalism has become a people's movement to a considerably larger degree than before 1848. Nationalism in most countries and socialism in its various forms are no longer opposite and conflicting trends. Nationalism has become "socialist" and socialism has become fundamentally patriotic or nationalist, caring and assuming the responsibility for the welfare and future of the people at large.

As a result socialist or workers' parties entered or formed the government in many European countries after 1918, above all in the long-established and industrially advanced democracies, e.g., Britain and Scandinavia. After 1945 Catholic Conservative parties and Marxist Social Democratic parties cooperated in national governments as members of an often long-lasting coalition, e.g., in Austria and in Italy, a coalition which in 1935 would have been unacceptable to both sides. Most newly established nations in Asia and Africa call themselves "socialist" and find therein no contradiction to their strongly emphasized nationalism. On the contrary, they regard socialism as the indispensable foundation of nationalism. Socialism may mean many things but it always involves the claim of caring for the welfare and equality of the people and for their active participation in national life. This new populist nationalism is concerned with the education of the masses, with guiding them from their traditionalist way of life to meeting the challenge of modern society. Thus socialism in the underdeveloped countries has become the generally accepted term for the modernization of the administrative and economic structure and of social and cultural life, for the fight against traditional corruption of public life and the apathy and fatalism of the masses.

In most cases it is still undecided whether this socialism stands for one of its Western forms—democratic or Marxist—or for a neo-traditionalism. In all probability, it represents, to a varying degree, an amalgam of all these trends. In 1924 the Chinese Nationalist leader Sun Yat-sen in his *The Three Principles of the People* (*San min chu'i*) named socialism as one of these principles, a socialism which stressed national solidarity and was supported by the Confucian saying that "All under heaven will work for the common good." Prince Norodom Sihanouk of Cambodia called on November 22, 1963, for a "Buddhist national socialism." A report on recent developments in the Himalayan Kingdom of Sikkim in the *Neue Zürcher Zeitung* of October 3, 1963 described them under the apt title "Vom Feudalstaat zum Sozialstaat." Today, nationalism in most of the "new" states and also in a growing number of "old" nations is no longer, and does not intend to be, a movement of upper-class elites but has become "people-based." At the same time this new nationalism realizes, as it did before 1848, that it can fulfill itself only in the framework of a wider supranational interdependence.

In 1917 Marxist communism was generally seen as the negation of nationalism. Realities of life and historical traditions proved stronger than ideologies. The Marxist historian Michail Pokrovsky an uncompromising internationalist, thought that Russian Tsarist imperialism was worse than West-European imperialism. He rejected the patriotic legends of other Russian historians and writers. "In the past we Russians—and I am a most pure-blooded Great Russian—were the biggest robbers imaginable," he said at the first All-Soviet Conference of Marxist historians. In 1934, two years after Pokrovsky's death, his school was declared out of favor with the Russian communist government. On March 28, 1937 *Pravda* took Pokrovsky to task for having asserted that "the conquest of Russia by the Tartars was not the invasion, as Solovyov thought, of an agrarian country by the savages of the steppe, but the encounter of two equal civilizations, of which it would be difficult to say which of the two was superior to the other." In the same year A. V. Shestakov wrote in the introduction to his officially approved and used textbook "History of the USSR, Brief Course" (*Istoriya USSR, Kratky kurs*): "We love our motherland and you must know well her wonderful history. Whoever knows history will better understand the present, will better fight the enemies of our country, and will consolidate socialism." In the Great Patriotic War a fervent faith "in our Russian, our native folk" animated the official proclamations and the popular poetry. The general slogan was not for socialism and world revolution, but for the motherland and Stalin, *za rodinu, za Stalina*. All that does not mean that Soviet Russian nationalism is identical with the Russian nationalism of before 1917. There are great differences, just as there was a very great difference between the France before and the France after 1789. Yet in both cases the continuity of certain ideological and political trends is obvious. It can even be argued that 1917 meant the birth of Russian nationalism in the modern sense of the word, the integration of the masses into the national life and culture, as 1789 meant in France. Under Lenin the treatment of the non-Great Russian nationalities of the former Russian empire improved compared with the treatment of Tsarist times. Though Party and Army deepened the unitarian character of the former empire, the federal structure of the Union of formally equal Soviet Socialist Republics afforded an outlet for the development of national languages and folkloristic traditions. But even in Lenin's time it was difficult to strike the right balance which would avoid Great Russian chauvinism on the one hand and local "bourgeois" nationalism on the other hand. In Stalin's later years the balance was abandoned in favor of Great Russian chauvinism; the post-Stalinist regime has tried to restore the balance. But there can be no doubt that nationalism in the Soviet Union is very strong, both among the Great Russians and among the other nationalities. Under the surface of a uniform communist ideology and of a rapid urbanization and industrialization, older traditions live on and enter into combinations with the dominant international ideology.

The fusion of communism and nationalism plays a great role not only in the Soviet Union but in all the communist countries. The conflict which broke out in 1948 between Communist Russia and Communist Yugoslavia was not caused by one or the other being more or less communist, but by the conflict of national interests. The same has happened since in other communist countries—in Hungary, in Poland, in Albania, and later in Rumania. Each one is asserting its national character. Originally the constitution of the USSR was drawn up to include, at least potentially, all people. In 1945 many expected that the new communist "satellites" would ultimately become republics within the USSR. However, this happened only to the Baltic countries which had formed part of the Russian empire for over two centuries and which, because of their relatively small size, seemed "digestible." The other satellites have developed a growing independence, and among them Albania, the smallest, is most vociferous in its opposition to the USSR.

Communist parties in noncommunist countries have proclaimed their patriotism. In *Fils du peuple*, the communist leader, Maurice Thorez declared that French communists denounce and attack those who compromise their national heritage (*le patrimoine national*). Love of country and its glorious traditions should make one willing to regard his nation as a torch-bearer of destiny (*Notre amour du pays, c'est la volonté de le rendre à sa destinée de porteur de flambeau*).

Chinese communism interprets Marxism-Leninism differently from post-Stalinist Soviet ideology, but at the same time it stresses its relationship to the Chinese philosophical moral traditions. In 1940 Mao announced that the Chinese Communist Party would continue the national watchword of Sun Yat-sen: "Nationalization of Marxism." Sung Wu, in his *Philosophy of the New Democracy* advocated the union of dialectical materialism with Chinese native philosophy. In his Program Statement, "On the Party" (1954), Liu Shau-tze said: "Mao-tze Tung's theory is as thoroughly Marxist as it is thoroughly Chinese."

Mao-tze Tung himself defined the relationship of communism to nationalism in his speech on "The New Democracy" in January 1940. He declared that the culture of the nation was the basis of its new democracy, because it was opposed to imperial aggression that threatened the national dignity and independence of China. He did not recommend the wholesale

Westernization which had hurt China in the past, and the same should hold true of the way in which Chinese communists should apply Marxism to China. They should combine the universal truth of Marxism-Leninism with China's national traits, for Chinese culture must have its own national form.

Thus communism has adapted itself to nationalism. With all due differences, there is some similarity to the way, for example, the Roman Catholic Church has tried as a supranational organization to identify itself with, and to shape, the nationalism and national life in Quebec or in Ireland. There can be no doubt that many individual communists are sincerely devoted to the national cause which they try to promote while fervently believing in the philosophy of history and salvation taught by Marx. Nationalism and socialism are no longer, as they were around 1900, in opposition to each other.

Everywhere this process of "modernization" comprises the introduction of social and geographic mobility, the impact of scientific and rationalist thought, the rationalization and greater efficiency of the administrative apparatus, the application of science and technology to economic production in the industrial and agrarian sectors, the opening up of opportunities to all classes of the population, the growing intercourse among castes and religions, the spread of general education of both sexes, and the struggle against illiteracy. Yet this global similarity of trends does not produce a uniformity of attitudes. Older ideological traditions persist everywhere. Modernization—the *aggiornamento* of which Pope John XXIII spoke—is the inevitable and worldwide process of the twentieth century, to which even the most traditionalist society must adapt. It is not primarily economic or social in the narrow sense of the word; it is as much intellectual and moral, and reaches to the innermost depth of personal existence and interpersonal relationships. It has to accommodate itself everywhere to the ideological traditions of existing national, religious, or social groups. It does not destroy them but transforms them so that these groups can enter the modern age. This process is complex and diversified to the utmost degree. Its understanding will be made easier by a comparative approach which not only compares the diverse developments in the various regions and peoples but does so at their various stages and epochs. The universal historian in this first global epoch of history is perhaps better able to understand this general process in its concrete and individual variety than can either an historian who takes a regional or national approach or who follows an a-historically thinking school of social science. This comparative view is especially true of the new nationalism which has so rapidly come to fruition since 1945 in Asia, Africa, and Latin America.

Political scientists frequently question whether the new nationalism in the underdeveloped countries can be regarded as fundamentally similar to European nationalism. Nationalism in early nineteenth-century Europe represented, with all due differences, what nationalism represents today in Latin America, in Asia, and in Africa: the repudiation of a traditional social and political order that served poorly the large majority of the people involved, and the assertion of the people's right to be subjects not only objects of history. A few decades ago, nations hardly existed in Asia or Africa where today nations exist or are being formed out of ethnographical material, with all the difficulties inherent in transitional stages. Similar conditions were found formerly in Europe, and in eastern and southeastern Europe hardly more than a century ago. The Arab nation today is groping for its unity as the Italians did 120 years ago and the southern Slavs, 60 years ago.

The new nations in southeast Asia, in the Middle East, in Africa, and in Latin America have, with few exceptions, not followed the democratic pattern of parliamentary representative government. But this again does not differentiate them from many older nations on the European continent. Europeans and North Americans tend to overlook the fact that in many European nation-states created or enlarged in 1918— from Lithuania and Poland to Yugoslavia and Greece —parliamentary democracy hardly survived for a few years and that even in more consolidated nations— Germany and Italy, France and Spain—parliamentary democracy and the liberal tradition were not generally accepted. What most peoples—old and new—wanted or want is to be governed by men whom they do not regard as alien, to acquire a sense of dignity and participation, to be able to expect economic betterment, and to catch up with and, among the more powerful and aggressive ones, to overtake more advanced nations.

Lately it has been stressed that the new nations in Africa are formed within "artificial" boundaries, inherited from colonial times. The same situation has existed for now almost 150 years in Latin America. In spite of the fact that a vague sense of Latin American solidarity, a *conciencia americana*, exists, and in spite of a unity of language, religion, and past history, surpassing by far any unifying elements to be found in Africa or Europe, Latin America has made no real progress toward creating more "natural" units above and beyond the existing state borders. Yet the leaders of the movements for national independence, Simón Bolívar and José de San Martín, had a vision of Latin American unity and strove for its realization. And it is interesting to note that the theme of Latin American unification in a nationalist sense was taken up by an Argentinian Trotzkyite, Jorge Abelardo Ramos, in his *America Latina: un país* (1949), in which he invoked both Bolívar and Lenin as his sources of inspiration. His book bears testimony to the nationalist character of Argentinian communism, which is sometimes called *socialismo gauchesco* or *marxismo vernáculo* ("cowboy socialism or vernacular Marxism").

The largest Latin American nation, Brazil, was the only one that withstood the process of disintegration which befell the larger Spanish-American units, Gran Columbia, Central America, and the vice-royalty of the Rio de la Plata in the early stages of their independence. Brazil, too, has experienced in the middle of the twentieth century social transformation under the banner of nationalism. Nelson Werneck Sodré in his inaugural lecture in 1959 at the Instituto Superior de Estudos Brasiléiros saw the roots of Brazilian nationalism in "the process of change which our country is going through, in her effort to surmount the deficiencies inherited from her colonial past, and in the absence of a bourgeois revolution in her historical development." Sodré regarded the politico-military revolution of 1930, led by Getúlio Vargas, as the most important date of contemporary Brazilian history, corresponding in some respects to the Mexican revolution of 1910.

This process of change to a modern nationalism began in Brazil (according to João Cruz Costa of the University of São Paulo) with the publication in 1902 of the book *Os Sertões* (*Rebellion in the Backlands*) by Euclides da Cunha (1866–1909). Like many Middle Western populists in the United States or Frederick Jackson Turner in his glorification of the Western frontier as the true home of American democracy and vitality, da Cunha accused the intellectual leadership in the large eastern coastal cities of being captives of their fascination with Europe, bemused by a longing for spiritual values to which they had not contributed and of which they were merely consumers. He made himself the spokesman for the forgotten and neglected peasants of the interior and demanded on behalf of those men coming out of the jungle, a change in the Brazilian mind. A similar opposition on behalf of the "West," the pioneer lands of the interior, developed in Argentina against the *porteños*, the residents of Buenos Aires, who were accused of "selling out their country" (*vendepatria*) to succumb to "alien" civilizations and foreign capital.

Cruz Costa put the new passionate Latin American nationalism into its worldwide context: "After the wars of our century, so indicative of the deep changes undergone by all peoples; after the awakening of Asia followed by that of Africa, it dawned on us that our destiny in America must go beyond the role of mere cordial spectators of the universal drama." The new Brazilian nationalism has not only become conscious of its being part of a worldwide transformation; under Vargas it adopted some typical practices of the non-liberal nationalism of the new era, limitations on the employment of foreigners in business and of their part in the liberal professions, exclusion of those not born in Brazil from public office, and the demand for the progressive nationalization of key economic areas.

Twentieth-century forms of nationalism in Asia, Africa, and Latin America incline toward "socialism," the word being used mostly in a vague sense. The reason for this has often been pointed out: there are exceptions in the three continents, but as a general rule, these areas lack a strong middle class comparable to that which has transformed northwestern Europe and North America in the eighteenth and nineteenth centuries with their ethos of dedication to work, their entrepreneurial initiative and willingness to take risks. The human resources of higher skills and administrative efficiency are so scanty that by necessity the new governments must assume a much greater responsibility for the economic and social modernization of the country than did governments in northwestern Europe or in North America. Edward Shils, speaking of the political development in the new states, regards as their chief sociological characteristic the gap between a small group of active, aspiring, relatively well-off, educated, and influential people in the large cities, and an inert or indifferent, impoverished, uneducated, and relatively powerless peasantry. A situation similar to that which prevails in many parts of Asia, Africa, and Latin America today could be found a century ago among the people in the Balkan and Iberian peninsulas, in southern Italy, and in Russia.

Governmental direction of economic and social transformation is regarded in the less developed countries as necessary to speed up the formation of a modern cohesive nation. This process took many virtually undisturbed decades or centuries in the West; now, under the much less favorable conditions of an immensely accelerated process of worldwide change, the non-Western nations wish to catch up with the West as speedily as possible. Impatience has become a characteristic quality of the twentieth-century mind; it is especially understandable in the developing nations. The rapid progress of scientific technology and the population explosion add to the feeling of frustration and the demand for government action. This "socialism" does not mark the nationalism of the developing nations as being necessarily "leftist." The nineteenth-century categories of left and right have lost much of their significance in our time. Nationalism and

socialism are both means of integrating the nation into a cohesive whole, willing to work for the political, economic, and cultural strength and distinctiveness of the group, a process which involves also the struggle against the economic and cultural influence of more developed countries. This trend is a noticeable one in Latin America as it is in Asia and Africa; it exists as well among the communist countries, as Rumania's recent attitude in favor of her own industrialization and against close reliance on the Soviet Union proves. A young Brazilian scholar, Candido Antonio Mendes, a left-wing Roman Catholic, stressed this point in his *Nacionalismo e desenvolvimento* (*Nationalism and Development*) which was published in 1963 by the Instituto Brasiléiro de Estudos Afro-Asiaticos. The book treats the problems of nationalism and economic development from a global point of view, counselling for all developing nations in Latin America as in Asia and Africa a policy of "positive neutralism."

The new nations, many of them without any previous history of nation-state existence, have aimed at national unity and integration of various tribal, ethnic, or linguistic groups rather than at the secure establishment of individual rights. Capitalism seemed to favor emphasis on individualism and private or personal goals; like the existence of political parties it seemed a divisive element. Socialism, on the other hand, appeared to stress communal efforts and the subordination of individual or group interests to the common good. Thus "socialism" was claimed as the morally better principle of economic and political organization; the guidance by the state, originally accepted out of necessity, was now welcomed as the "morally higher" instrument for achieving a more efficient and satisfactory economy. What was a perhaps unavoidable consequence of economic and social backwardness was now dignified with the virtue of a spiritual halo.

Such a spiritual halo has been an important defense mechanism of the less developed nations when they felt the impact of socially and economically more advanced nations. This assumption of cultural superiority, either based upon an alleged depth of religious sentiment or on a heightened aesthetic sensitivity, has in no way been confined to the new nations. Italian nationalists like Alfieri or Mazzini felt toward France as German nationalists felt toward the West in general. Some Germans distinguished *Kultur* and *Zivilisation*, the latter supposedly characteristically Western in its superficial adoration of technical and material achievements. The Russian Slavophiles praised the depth, purity, and originality of the Slavic folk-soul as against the ruthless power drive and utilitarian tinsel of the West in which, though they themselves were under the influence of German romanticism, they included the Germans. The consciousness of a higher civilization apparently also inspired General de Gaulle's aversion to the "Anglo-Saxons" whom he felt had usurped the place of cultural leadership rightfully belonging to France.

The same attitude could be found in the United States. The citizens of the Confederacy in the middle of the nineteenth century regarded their life of civilized leisure and social beauty as superior to the material progress and dollar-mindedness of the "Yankees." In all cases, of which we have cited only a few examples, spiritual superiority was to "compensate" for "backwardness" in the political, social, and economic structure.

Everywhere among the "new" nations we find trends and movements similar to those existing among European nations. Thus the problem of establishing a national language creates difficulties in many cases. The government of Malaya promoted a campaign under the slogan *Bahasa Jiwa Bangsa*—"Language is the soul of the nation," introduces a national language month, and through its Language and Literature Agency is trying to modernize and enrich the Malay language. Amidst a population of mixed origin, using several languages, a national language is intended to form a uniting bond.

Similar language problems have beset many nations in Asia and Africa. The racial and minority problems, too, are no less frequent or bitter than they were or are in the Western world. The large Hindu-Tamil minority in Ceylon has complained about discrimination on the part of the Singhalese-Buddhist majority, who wish to create a Singhalese nation-state. Koreans feel as bitter about the Japanese as ever an African people did about European rulers. Indonesia and Burma have their difficult minority problems, and in India the Nagas fought many years for independence or autonomy. The Chinese in southeast Asia and the Indians in Burma and in East Africa appear as foreigners who show neither great eagerness nor capacity for integration into the majority native race. In southern India the Dravida Munnetra Karagam demanded the establishment of an independent Dravidian state. Briefly, nationalism in the new nations has given rise to ethnic, racial, and religious tensions and problems familiar in the history of nationalism in Europe.

Asian, African, and Latin-American nations incline to intellectual attitudes not so different from those found among some European nations. In the reconstruction of a "glorious" past and in the expectation of an exalted future there are many similarities. Under Kamal Atatürk (1880–1938) Turkish writers discovered a heroic pre-Islamic past of the Turkish nation. A beautifully produced volume called *New Africa*, pub-

lished by the Secretariat of State for cultural affairs and information of the Tunisian government confidently states that Africa's rejuvenating and renewing influence will spread to every level of thought, backed by the rapidly growing African population with its youth and vigor, and that African thought will enable Western thought to rediscover those universal values which European philosophy seems to have forgotten. The insistence on peculiar uniqueness (*Eigenart* or *Samobytnost*) by some German or Russian nineteenth-century nationalists is matched by the quest for African identity today. What Edward Blyden, who became the first President of the University of Liberia, said in an address on "The Idea of an African Personality" has been said previously by many nationalists in other continents: "We are held in bondage by our indiscriminate and injudicious use of foreign literature. . . . The African must advance by methods of his own. . . . It has been proved that he knows how to take advantage of European culture and that he can be benefited by it. . . . We must show that we are able to go it alone, to carve out our own way. . . . We must not suppose that Anglo-Saxon methods are final, that there is nothing for us to find out for our guidance, and that we have nothing to teach the world." He concluded the address with a clear challenge to the African to improve his condition. "The suspicions disparaging to us will be dissipated only by the exhibition of the indisputable realities of a lofty manhood as they may be illustrated in successful efforts to build up a nation, to wrest from nature her secrets, to lead the vanguard of progress in this country and to regenerate a continent."

The present emphasis on folkloristic art in Africa and on a revival and reinterpretation of the history of ancient kingdoms went on in Europe a few decades ago. Again, as happened in many European countries in the early stages of nationalism, religious or messianic movements seem to create a bridge between traditionalism and incipient nationalism. In some cases nationalist, racialist, messianic, and socialist elements enter into a strange and new amalgam. Through these declarations of African nationalism the historian will find parallels in the nationalist utterances from other continents. Yet everywhere nationalists frequently regard their situation, attitudes, and aspirations as unique. They easily overlook the difficulties which a complex reality presents to the realization of their goals.

Nor are these goals static. Nationalism as a historical phenomenon is everywhere in flux. Some nationalism loses itself in the course of time in a more encompassing one as did the Egyptian-Pharaonic nationalism of the 1920's and 1930's in the Arab nationalism of the 1960's.

On the other hand, subnationalisms can develop into full-fledged nationalisms. Religion and nationalism can influence each other in various ways. Religion created in Pakistan a "new" nation, the emergence of which seemed improbable in 1900 or 1920. The "grand old man" of India's Muslim awakening, Sir Sayyad Ahmad Khan (1817-98), lecturing in Persian on nationalism in Calcutta (1872), praised above all love of mankind, quoting the Persian poet Shaikh Sa'di Shirazi:

> People are organically related to each other,
> Since their creation is from the same soul.
> When a limb throbs with pain,
> All other organs share this pain.

Beneath this love of mankind Khan placed Muslim nationalism, for the sake of which he founded his monthly *Muslim National Reformer,* in which he declared that "love of one's nation is the essence of faith." Of his successors in the twentieth century Muhammad Iqbal and Muhammad Ali Jinnah started as Indian nationalists before becoming Muslim nationalists and the fathers of Pakistan, whereas Abu'l Kalam Azad started as a Muslim nationalist, and even as a Pan-Islamist, and founded the weekly *al-Hilal* ("The Crescent"); but after 1920 he accepted the principle of secular and territorial nationalism, following therein the Turkish and Arab examples. In 1940, when the overwhelming majority of Indian Muslims decided for Pakistan, Azad separated from his co-religionists and presided over the All-India National Congress. Before this predominantly Hindu body he declared: "I am part of the indivisible unity that is Indian nationality. I am indispensable to this noble edifice and without me this splendid structure of India is incomplete. I am an essential element which has gone to build India. I can never surrender this claim."

In the 1960's we face in Asia, Africa, and Latin America an awakening nationalism in a great variety and complexity of manifestations. One element, however, is common today to all these diverse movements: they are revolutionary movements, "people-based" movements, which, as did European nationalism in the early nineteenth century, are directed towards a new political and social order. Within the framework of this situation, anticommunist nationalism has as revolutionary a content as has communist nationalism. The army ruled Burmese revolutionary government under General Ne Win created in 1963 its Burma Socialist Program Party. Its socialist nationalization policy was intended to win popular backing for the military government from peasants and workers.

A similar revolutionary trend dominates Egypt and Iraq, Algeria and Syria, Ceylon and Guinea. At the same time a new nationalism, revolutionary in essence, is in communist and in noncommunist countries a quest for roots in the past. Such a quest has led the Philippinos, for example, to the growing assertion of their Asian-Malay identity instead of their Spanish-Catholic character. The Filipino administration under Macapagal was the driving element behind the creation of Maphilindo, the short-lived Pan-Malaysian grouping of the three Malay nations—Malaya, the Philippines, Indonesia—which was formed in Manila in June 1963.

Though the student of nationalism in the present world will concentrate on Asia, Africa, and Latin America, he will not overlook the fact that nationalist passions are in no way confined today to the underdeveloped or to the communist countries. The Western world knows them too. In France General de Gaulle appealed to French nationalism and, like Napoleon III, stressed Pan-Latin sentiments. In Belgium there has been antagonism between the Flemish and the Walloon segments of the population; in South Tyrol and in Quebec the demands for autonomy or independence have led to terrorist acts. Even in Switzerland with its firm tradition of civic moderation the French-speaking, Catholic, and agricultural districts in the Jura mountains—which in 1815 became part of the German-speaking, Protestant, and economically more highly developed canton of Bern—demanded autonomy or the constitution of their own canton, and though acts of terror were very few and the number of the activists much smaller than in Canada or South Tyrol, the *Rassemblement Jurassien* dedicated itself to "a determined struggle for the defense of its country and to the achievement of its independence." Thus we are living in the age of pan-nationalism on all continents.

Yet the very existence of pan-nationalism has made the first universal intercourse of nations and civilizations possible. The structuring of societies everywhere along similar lines, the fact that popular aspirations have become more alike everywhere, has made possible the first global epoch of human history.

BIBLIOGRAPHY

See Koppel S. Pinson, A *Bibliographical Introduction to Nationalism* (New York, 1935), and Karl W. Deutsch, *An Interdisciplinary Bibliography on Nationalism, 1935–1953,* (Cambridge, Mass., 1956). Special Studies are Carlton J. H. Hayes, *The Historical Evolution of Modern Nationalism* (New York, 1931); Hans Kohn, *The Idea of Nationalism* (New York, 1944), until the French Revolution, idem, *Prelude to Nation-States* (Princeton, 1967), for the decisive period 1789–1815, and idem, *The Age of Nationalism* (New York, 1962) since the French Revolution; L. L. Snyder, *The Meaning of Nationalism* (New Brunswick, N.J., 1954); Boyd C. Shafer, *Myth and Reality* (New York, 1955); R. Wittram,

Das Nationale als Europäisches Problem (Göttingen, 1954); Eugen Lemberg, *Nationalismus*, 2 vols. (Reinbek bei Hamburg, 1964); Benjamin Akzin, *State and Nation* (London, 1964); Georges Weil, *L'Europe du XIX siècle et l'idée de nationalité* (Paris, 1938); Félix Ponteil, *L'éveil des nationalités et le mouvement libéral* (Paris, 1960); Rupert Emerson, *From Empire to Nation* (Cambridge, Mass., 1960).

HANS KOHN

[See also Balance of Power; Democracy; Ideology; **Liberalism**; Marxism; **Nation**; Socialism; Totalitarianism.]

NATURALISM IN ART

TAKEN IN a historical sense, "naturalism in art" designates certain fairly obvious features to be met with in the fine arts and in the literature of various periods. Taken in a more reflective sense, however, the expression raises fundamental questions as to basic artistic elements and the development of art.

In ordinary usage, as found in dictionary definitions, "naturalism" denotes a theory or doctrine of art that specifies "conformity to nature" as the primary criterion of a work of art. The trouble with all such general definitions is that they are too vague: "conformity with nature's external appearances" would be more exact. Another vagueness is the way "naturalism" is used interchangeably with "realism," especially in French and Italian. (In art history neither term has much of a connection with philosophers' usage of the same terms.) In modern German, this vagueness is somewhat mitigated using "realism" for the more general meaning of any sort of fidelity to nature—including the subject matter of works of art—reserving "naturalism" for works in which "realism" is carried to extreme, for example, in the treatment of detail. In German, *Verismus* (from the Italian *verismo*) denotes a still more extreme fidelity to the actual appearance of the subject as found in nature.

As a term designating a recognized stylistic movement, "naturalism" is only used in connection with literature, not with the visual arts. It refers to a type of narrative and dramatic writing that appeared in the second half of the nineteenth century, primarily in Germany (Gerhart Hauptmann, Arno Holz, Johannes Schlaf), in France (Émile Zola), and occasionally also in Russian and Scandinavian literature. This is the earliest use of this term to designate a style, although it was occasionally used before then in a purely descriptive sense, perhaps most strikingly in Bellori's major work, *L'Idea del pittore, dello scultore e dell'architetto* (1664). Here the author emphatically rejects "naturalists" of the Caravaggio sort. (Bellori's attitude has been examined in detail by Erwin Panofsky in his basic study *Idea*, in which the problem of "naturalism" is treated from the epistomological point of view.) Used in this derogatory sense, the term still turns up in the mid-nineteenth century, e.g., in the most important of Ferdinand Georg Waldmüller's programmatic writings. In his *Andeutungen zur Belebung der vaterländischen bildenden Kunst* (Vienna, 1857), this painter admits proudly to being a "naturalist," in reply to critics who had called him just that. Also in a positive sense, the term was used by the art critic Castagnary who referred to the painters of early French impressionism as the "school of naturalism" (*école naturaliste*) and described their works as "naturalistic," thereby winning Zola's approval. (See Castagnary's reviews of the Salons from 1863 on; Zola's article "Le Naturalisme au Salon, I," in *Le Voltaire* of June 18, 1880; and John Rewald, *The History of Impressionism*, New York [1946], esp. pp. 126ff.)

At the turn of the century, which also marked a turning point in art—namely, a period when naturalism was beginning to be rejected—we find the same attitude in major art historical writings. In *Die Wiener Genesis* (Vienna, 1895), Franz Wickhoff analyzed a decidedly naturalistic period of art, namely, the "official" art of imperial Rome, describing it as an "imitative naturalistic style," and occasionally referring to it as an "arid naturalism"; however, what he had primarily meant was a specific genre which he called "illusionistic style." Alois Riegl—in his major work *Spätrömische Kunstindustrie* (1901) and also in his *Stilfragen* (1893)—has practically excluded the concept of naturalism, because he was essentially interested in the analysis of form and the autonomy of the creative components it implies. A similar line was taken by Heinrich Wölfflin, according to whom the subject of naturalism has nothing to do with his inquiries into the history and psychology of form, as can be seen from the very title of his major work, *Kunstgeschichtliche Grundbegriffe: Das Problem der Stilentwicklung in der neueren Kunst* (1915). In his essay *Idealismus und Naturalismus in der gotischen Skulptur und Malerei* (1918), the art historian Max Dvořák supplied no definition of naturalism although it was a key term in his inquiry. This hardly helped remedy the all too common vagueness prevailing in its usage.

Obviously, without a more exact definition, the term is of limited value; it has advantages as well as disadvantages. The principal value of "naturalistic" as a cursory description of a work of art is that it evokes comparisons with some model in nature. So far as it goes, this usage offers a useful basis for comparison, though it is a purely quantitative one. The trouble is,

FIGURE 1. Jan Van Eyck, *The Annunciation* (detail). 1432. ST. BAVO, GHENT. COPYRIGHT A. C. L. BRUSSELS

structure, surfaces, and textures of living and inanimate things alike. "Partial" naturalism is far commoner in the history of art than "total" naturalism. The latter appears to be a very late development within any artistic tradition.

So much, then, for the relatively short history of the term's usage. We have now to go on to the much lengthier and more involved matter of what the term designates, whether within a given artistic period, a given style, a given artistic genre, or a given single work of art. This must lead to the question of where "naturalism" stands in relation to other artistic elements.

One of the most striking observations to be made, even in the most cursory survey, is how often naturalism turns up cheek-by-jowl with other artistic practices, even of the seemingly most unrelated or opposed sorts. We have already mentioned Egyptian and Assyrian reliefs. In them, the naturalism or closeness to nature, is in the treatment of the figures, whereas everything else, including their overall rhythmic organization, derives entirely from other sources or traditions. The figures are set in the void, and there is no equivalent striving for perceptual accuracy anywhere else in these works. We find something very similar in the art of the late Middle Ages in Europe, as for example in the manuscript illustrations of ca. 1400, as well as in the painting from the Van Eycks on (Figure 1). Here the richest naturalism in the treatment of visual detail is combined with age-old obedience to general principles of symmetry and compositional organization profoundly at odds with naturalism, although to some extent a nascent concern for perspective begins to make itself felt. Perhaps the next most important effort at a strict naturalism occurs in the portraits of Hans Holbein the Younger (Figure 2). Here, too, painstaking naturalism in the representation of the human body—as well as of inanimate objects—is linked with compositional schemes of an entirely different inspiration; yet the gulf between the two grows narrower. At least where the pictorial scene represents rooms within houses, the perspective employed is closer to our habitual ways of seeing.

In naturalism of the baroque era, the compositional scheme is altered to accommodate lifelike, true-to-nature figures and details. We see this in Caravaggio, who also contributes a new element to the "naturalistic" repertory: the representation of light and dark. By and large, however, baroque painting as a whole is not characterized by so extreme a pursuit of naturalistic effects. Another example is the art of Vermeer van Delft. What is so special about Vermeer's naturalism, as also about Caravaggio's, is the way fresh attention to light as found in nature leads to further modifications of the general compositional scheme, within which the

no one can state clearly where the presumed "closeness to nature" exactly begins or ends. In extreme cases, there is no argument, but within these rather wide limits (of exact fidelity to and unmistakable departure from the model in nature), "naturalistic" suffers the same shortcomings as all designations of quantity or degree. Moreover, it is possible to make a rough yet decisive distinction between a partial naturalism that refers only to portions of a representation, and a thoroughgoing or total naturalism. This total naturalism, in contrast to partial naturalism, includes the principal elements of visual reality, such as the illusionistic treatment of space (whether linear or aerial perspective) and of light. Therefore total naturalism does not appear until relatively late in the history of painting, whereas a partial naturalism can be found in so-called "pre-perspective" representations, as for example, in ancient Egyptian and Assyrian reliefs. It is clear that it is possible to single out certain comparatively naturalistic features. We find greater or lesser care in rendering anatomy and physiognomy, the naturalistic elements seem more at home than in the Netherlandish primitives or in the Renaissance masters. The secret of this mode of composition is its adaptability to perspective as perceived in nature. Vermeer's naturalism could almost be called a "total" (rather than a "partial") naturalism, were it not for the extraordinary stillness and splendor of his predominant forms. Like the older modes of composition that survived down to the Middle Ages and into the Renaissance, Vermeer's naturalism has its source in a kind of creative aim other than in a mere striving for fidelity to nature in the individual figure. And there is something more, the peculiar contribution to the baroque: painterly illusionism. The latter will be discussed below, in reference to the sort of baroque naturalism most importantly represented by Velázquez and Frans Hals.

We encounter much the same combination of naturalism, in the treatment of certain details and certain forms, with an essentially antithetical ("idealistic") structure, in some classicist works of the late eighteenth century in France. One of the most striking of these is Jacques-Louis David's *Death of Marat*, the whole point of which lies in its attempted synthesis of naturalistic detail with a grander sort of formal conception. This work influenced artists for a long time and produced important results, above all, in French painting, e.g., Géricault's *Raft of the "Medusa"* and the work of Ingres. The few examples we give here—it being understood that in some cases one great name stands for a group—show how a naturalism of detail was subordinated to a conception of pictorial form, and how the two were more or less fully and adequately blended.

In the treatment of landscape and human figure in the romantic movement of the early nineteenth century, the attempted synthesis was often successful, especially in the landscapes of Caspar David Friedrich and Ferdinand Olivier. Their assiduous pursuit of naturalism proved not incompatible with the "idealistic" character of their approach to the subject.

At the same time, however, such success as was achieved along this line was destined not to be perpetuated indefinitely. In particular, the relationship between the general composition and "partial" naturalism began to change, and the moment of balance passed. The successful synthesis lasted longer, however, in the explicitly naturalistic landscape painting of the Biedermeier period, one of the high points in nineteenth-century naturalism in art. The most striking examples are the landscapes and townscapes by Waldmüller and Rudolf von Alt in Austria, Eduard Gärtner's city-scapes in Germany, and the landscapes by Wilhelm Eckersberg and Christen Købke in Denmark. In Biedermeier genre painting, on the other hand,

a considerable conventionalism becomes apparent in the composition, as also in the historical painting around mid-century. The artistic unity of the pictorial whole appears most clearly threatened, however, wherever naturalism is put at the service of a programmatically "idealistic" figurative painting, e.g., in the art of an Anselm Feuerbach. This development occurred concomitantly with the growing importance of realism and naturalism in the arts, at the expense of such more "intellectual," perhaps even idealistic "intellectual" painting as that of the Pre-Raphaelites and the first stirrings of "Jugendstil" (Art Nouveau). Such movements represented a reaction to naturalism: a more symbolic treatment of nature and history, a new formalism in composition. The art of Fernand Khnopff supplies an especially revealing case in point. Gradually a basic antagonism was beginning to take shape between naturalistic modes of representation and a new attention to the super- or extra-natural properties of a subject, an antagonism that had not arisen at earlier stages in the history of art. Occasionally in the painting of the second half of the nineteenth century, there are to be found individual instances of an unmistakable, seemingly naive, yet amazingly vigorous naturalism of the older, more poised variety, especially evident in Wilhelm Leibl's works (those of his so-called "Holbein period") and in works by Edgar Degas and Adolf Menzel.

FIGURE 2. Hans Holbein, the Younger, *Portrait of the Merchant Georg Gisze*. 1532. STAATLICHE MUSEEN PREUSSISCHER KULTURBESITZ, GEMALDEGALERIE, BERLIN (WEST)

341

Throughout the nineteenth century, however, a type of naturalism makes its appearance in painting that can hardly be mentioned in the same breath with what we have been describing so far. This is what has come to be known as impressionism, i.e., a painterly illusionism that turns up in very different forms and in very different degrees. Its earliest, "classical" manifestation is found in the art of Constable and Corot (again, we are letting single names stand for larger groups), and its final stages extend well beyond the impressionist movement proper into the twentieth century. It will not do to speak of "illusionistic naturalism," however, for the naturalism we have so far mentioned is also quite illusionistic, and intended to be so. The difference is that the new illusionism is characterized by a loosening of pictorial forms, and so is illusionistic in a twofold sense, in two layers, so to speak. The mode of representation with compact, closed forms and tightly modeled bodies of course implies a certain negation, an attempt to make us forget the picture plane, whereas in the more "open" treatment with the brush-strokes showing, a further process of optical projection is added; the viewer is expected continuously to combine the tiny "microstructures" into an illusion of bodies and space. Here we cannot, of course, go into much detail, but the difference can also be defined as that between a relatively simple or naive illusionism, corresponding to the way we actually see the world around us, and a more complicated illusionism. This is not intended to be taken as a value judgment; only insofar as nineteenth-century impressionism represents the most radical type of illusionism does it have historical validity. In principle, naturalistic illusionism has a long history, the main stages are to be found in late antique art, progressively diminishing in the painting of the early Middle Ages and then, after a long interruption, emerging in the centuries of baroque painting.

To the extent that illusionism may be equated with naturalism, we discover still another duality—besides what we earlier called "partial" and "total" naturalism —namely, a direct and an indirect naturalism, the latter characterized by the kind of optical projection practiced by the impressionists.

Naturalism makes its appearance in sculpture at the same time as it does in the two-dimensional arts of painting and drawing, taking into consideration the limitations of the medium. That is, there were naturalistic sculptures in the antique period, in the Hellenistic era, in the art of the Roman Empire, in the late Middle Ages, in the early and the high Renaissance, to a lesser extent in baroque and neo-classical art, but becoming increasingly widespread in the nineteenth century, especially in its final phase. The distinction between "partial" and "total" naturalism, which strictly speaking is applicable only to two-dimensional art, in a broader sense can be applied to naturalistic sculpture in the round, in that the latter incorporates the real space in which it stands.

Even such a very rough classification and enumeration casts some light on the part played by naturalism in the history of art, at least of its outward aspects. Above all, it enables us to see more clearly how partial naturalism developed historically into total naturalism, how painting gradually broadened its horizons, going beyond representation of individual beings to recognition of a supra-individual nature, giving ever more to the dominating elements of space and light. The result was incontestably a broadening of knowledge, but of course it can be so evaluated only in terms of a nature-oriented theory of art. It was the attempt to achieve an ever closer rendering of the phenomena of nature as externally visible that led to a supra-individual conception of nature.

At the same time, ever since the classical age and continuing down through the Middle Ages, there had been a non-naturalistic, "idealistic" strain in Western art, which had no room for individuality as such, due either to obedience to religion or to theological preoccupations with the cosmos, the "whole." Even after the late Middle Ages, when Western art became increasingly concerned with individual things as such and with the external appearance of nature for their own sakes, so that what we have called "partial" naturalism began to come to the fore, the ultimately transcendental strain in Christian thought still held sway, by no means to the detriment of creativity. Only with the development of a "total" naturalism in the course of the nineteenth century was Western art at last secularized, and antagonism expressed in quarrels between "idealists" and "realists"—ultimately between "idealists" and "naturalists." And yet the "profane" (as opposed to the "divine") view of the world, the "earthly" sort of naturalism, held its own for a comparatively short time only. It soon gave rise to a worldly view that subordinated individual man and particular nonhuman phenomena to general laws. And recently, when a type of naturalism once again appeared on the scene, namely the surrealist art of our century, it was again a "partial" naturalism, this time bound within the limits of the spheres of fantasy.

The foregoing rapid survey of naturalism's ups and downs in the evolution of art—of European art, for there is no parallel current in the art of extra-European cultures—has told us next to nothing about the essence of naturalism in art, nor about its function in the process of artistic creation. All we have done is to view it externally, noting that it reached a sort of culmination in all the arts in the course of the nineteenth century beyond anything hitherto seen. The nineteenth century was "realistic" and "naturalistic" par excellence.

Accordingly it is reasonable to suppose that we shall get at what is essential in naturalism most readily by concentrating on nineteenth-century art and theories of art. Looking back over the long conflict between the antithetic ideologies of idealism and naturalism—irresolvable because involving basic differences concerning the nature of creative activity—we can see that idealism (taking this term in its broadest sense) has kept its dominant position, whereas naturalism has been put on the defensive. Nonetheless, it has to be pointed out that most of modern Western art's significant achievements were conceived of as being "on the side of" naturalism, that is, enlisted under its banner. Realism and naturalism forged ahead in all the arts in self-conscious opposition to whatever was the prevailing "idealistic" art, penetrating first neo-classicism, then romanticism. It is instructive to examine the record here, to discover just how this state of affairs came about. During the so-called Age of Enlightenment, the era of Winckelmann, Lessing, Kant, Schiller, and Goethe, more firmly constructed theories of art were produced than any that had been attempted since the Renaissance. These theories gave explicit recognition to the autonomy of art as a human activity. As never before, attention was drawn to creative capacities as such in this particular sphere, and to actual works of art explicitly distinguished from the world of reality. In its expression, however, this insight was greatly influenced by the prevailing neo-classicism of the late eighteenth and early nineteenth centuries, a rather simplifying aesthetic program. In reaction to it, champions of naturalism could attempt only an even simpler program, following the slogan "be true to nature," "be true to life." However, this implies that the ultimate or essential source of creativity lies in the artist's experience with nature. Thus the program of the naturalists was much less pretentious and more primitive than that of their adversaries.

One among many passages that might be cited is Courbet's argument of his *réalisme: L'art en peinture ne saurait consister que dans la représentation des objets visibles et tangibles pour l'artiste. . . . Je tiens aussi que la peinture est un art essentiellement* concret *et ne peut consister que dans la représentation des choses* réelles *et* existantes . . . ("In painting, the art comes to no more than the representation of those objects that the artist himself sees and touches. . . . I also take the line that painting is essentially a *concrete* art; there is no more to it than the representation of *real, actually existing* things"). This down-to-earth,

plain man's attitude is not so remote as then seemed from the classical philosophic conception of *mimesis* or imitation of nature—a conception that antedates all subsequent reflection on the visual arts. A number of nineteenth-century thinkers—Schopenhauer, among others—were not overwhelmed by this sort of "strict realism," which Plato had long since questioned. The question arose: What, then, is the purpose of adding an image of nature or reality to what we are already in full enjoyment of? As Panofsky pointed out, the theory of art now reached an antinomy: aesthetics was at loggerheads with itself. Throughout the nineteenth century, the long controversy was softened by remembering how the thinkers of the Enlightenment had assured artists of "being on their own," and in the late nineteenth century theories of art were formulated by Konrad Fiedler and Alois Riegl who stressed the artist's specific functions with respect to imagination and formal structure. However, theoretical justifications of this type are as valid for one kind of work of art as another: the naturalistic vision is merely one kind of vision, naturalistic art merely an art "like any other."

At present we can view nineteenth-century naturalism in perspective, so that it is possible to look at the works themselves and ask just what sets them off from the other kinds of art; in just what does their particular contribution consist. Let us assume, not unreasonably, that the true criteria of a work of art lie in its basic conception, in its overall construction, in a *Kunstwollen* (as Riegl put it) on the part of the working artist. On the basis of such criteria, however, how can the extreme naturalistic work hope to rate very high? In a really thoroughgoing piece of naturalism, what room is left for the artist's ordering will, in any truly creative sense? Applying such criteria we are confronted with the question: Is naturalism just indifferent to the more inventive aspects of art, or is it actively hostile to them? Following this line of reflection, we may perhaps reduce all such questions to one: What makes an extreme naturalistic work, presented as such, a full-fledged work of art "despite everything"? Here we might recall Théophile Gautier's famous exclamation when he stood in front of that great picture, Velázquez's *Las Meninas,* one of the masterpieces of naturalism: *Où est donc le tableau?* ("But where's the picture?") In relation to the above questions, his exclamation must be regarded as a criticism.

Needless to say, there is an answer to the question: What makes a naturalistic work a work of art? Why, its quality, of course! There is a good deal of truth in this, but also a certain glibness: as is well known, "quality" evades precise definition. It is not the ultimate answer, in any case not a full one. Moreover, though the discrimination of quality is fundamental in

NATURALISM IN ART

FIGURE 3. Frans Hals, *Portrait of an Officer* (*"The Laughing Cavalier"*). 1624. REPRODUCED BY PERMISSION OF THE TRUSTEES OF THE WALLACE COLLECTION, LONDON

all art appreciation, it is not a discrimination that sheds much light upon naturalistic works as opposed to other kinds of work: some abstract or fantastic works, for example, are also incontestably better than others in the same category. Obviously, to grasp the specific character of naturalistic art, we have to descend from the theoretical heights to the actual works themselves.

Paintings like the *Laughing Cavalier* by Frans Hals (1624) in the Wallace Collection, London, and Wilhelm Leibl's *Three Women in Church* (1878–82) in the Hamburg Kunsthalle are of remarkable artistic intensity and stand out as leading examples of pictorial naturalism (Figures 3, 4). At first glance they look about even on the score of attention to external physical appearances—logically speaking, all outspokenly naturalistic works *should* be at the same level—yet closer examination reveals basic differences. Seemingly, in its entirety as in every single one of its parts, Leibl's picture exhibits a masterly attention to detail, a "literalness" in the rendering of substances and surfaces, without the slightest lapse into a painterly technique, which attracts the viewers' attention. In his main works of this period Leibl was consciously going back to such a model of late-medieval, Netherlandish naturalism as well as Holbein. The Hals portrait shows the same type

of naturalism especially in the rendering of the head, but in other parts, especially the clothing, he had recourse to an "indirect" naturalism of the more painterly, illusionistic sort. The difference is most apparent when the two works are viewed up close; stand back a bit from the Hals and the treatment of the clothing blends perfectly with that of the head. (In his early group paintings, above all the two officer's banquets of 1627, Hals had employed the "illusionistic" technique throughout with virtuoso skill to create a breathtaking "lifelike" effect. His other technique, for achieving a more "direct" sort of naturalism is much rarer in the works by him that have come down to us; the face of the *Laughing Cavalier* is the most notable example of it.)

As for the compositional elements of these two pictures that prove decisive from the strictly formal point of view, one of these is quite obvious. Both pictures are very emphatically composed to contrast figures portrayed in depth against an absolutely flat background. The contrast may be a trifle less marked in the Hals portrait simply because the motif is a less complex one. Nonetheless, the cavalier's pose is so aggressively striking that it is quite as effective compositionally as the arrangement of three figures in Leibl's painting. Though more complex, the latter is easy to grasp, and we are in no doubt about the careful planning that went into it (one painted sketch survives, as evidence of this point, though only two of the figures appear in it). There are any number of carefully thought-out parallels, interlockings, and other interrelationships in the way the rather constricted picture space has been filled; for example, the curves at the ends of the pew reflect curves in the female figures—especially the figure in the middle, or the way the three figures gradually turn their bodies towards us, accentuating the development in depth. At the same time there is one departure from correct perspective, as has frequently been pointed out. The figure of the young peasant woman in the foreground is disproportionately large, especially her hands in relation to her face. It is hardly surprising that a representation of such fidelity to natural models should be criticized for something less than accuracy on the score of perspective. This might then be the appropriate place to ask: Just how is the naturalistic accuracy here related to the overall artistic effect? The painter himself does not seem to have been bothered by the exaggerated size of the one figure nor by the inaccuracy of the perspective (although a little later, when he painted the group of figures entitled "Poachers" he was so dissatisfied that he cut up the picture into individual portraits). The latter-day viewer is not disturbed by these inaccuracies, either; they do not detract from his experience of the picture as a work of art. Rather he accepts them as part of the distortions of any close-up view, which here actually enhance the effect of depth.

Thus, in this composition based on large silhouettes, the role of the formal pattern, i.e., one purely artistic element of form, is perfectly clear. Furthermore it is quite strong enough to suffice of itself to make this picture a work of art. And yet there still remains the question raised earlier, which we have not yet answered: What is the role of the "microstructures" in such a work; how do they contribute to the overall pictorial naturalism? This is by no means easy to say, because where all the details are rendered with all but "photographic" precision, the carefully painted detail work is swallowed up in the total effect. Here we should note the difference of the Leibl from the key passage in the Hals portrait, where unprecedentedly impressionistic technique is so conspicuously at odds with the more traditional illusionistic naturalism. The Leibl is so remarkable for the way the intellectual ordering power of the picture as a whole is combined with something like a higher power in the capturing of visual detail. The result ought not to be so perfectly homogeneous, but it is. (It is pertinent here to recall the somewhat different example of David's *Death of Marat*. The clarity is classic—a clarity beyond that of classicist painting generally, much less cold and bloodless, much more vivid. But beyond the clarity there is a naturalism of detail which, because less literal than Leibl's, demands less in the way of explanation to account for the picture's perfection. Ingres' so-called "classicist naturalism" ought also to be evoked in this connection.) More to the point, notice in the Leibl picture that one area is much more stylistically rendered than the rest: the peasant girl's apron, especially the folds and pleats at the bottom. You nearly always find especially carefully worked out details of this sort in German painting of the Renaissance period—in Dürer and Holbein, most notably.

The point may be trifling, but let us focus on it; it may help us eventually to get down to the matter of even less conspicuous details of brushwork, namely, the differences, however, "trifling," which do in fact turn up on more or less microscopic examination. Is it, in fact, a leading trait or characteristic of naturalistic art that quantitative, mathematical consistency really has nothing to do with it, because artistically speaking, really tiny things do not exist in naturalistic painting, or, at least, that in naturalistic art such matters are not to be judged by the usual standards? Perhaps this is one of the solutions to the question. In all naturalistic art this microstructure, which influences the character of the painting as a work of art, is something specifically unnaturalistic. From this point of view naturalis-

tic works of art would be works of art like any others, except insofar as they persuade us to search out tiny deviations or departures from their models in nature. Yet trying to grasp the artistic content of a naturalistic work solely by isolating what is *not* naturalistic in it must surely be unsatisfactory. No doubt naturalistic works of art project "ideal" values, whether in terms of symbolic significance or mere mood, but neither individual *oeuvres* nor the art of such an epoch as, for example, seventeenth-century Holland (as Seymour Slive has pointed out) would be well served by such an approach.

Something remains to be said about what inspires the creation of naturalistic works. In various periods of artistic development, inner vision was variably combined with the power of perception. This power of perception need not be a dominant element of creativity, however it would be arbitrary and one-sided to ignore it. Where a naturalistic work is concerned, we should never ignore the experience of nature in the life of the artist, which the picture revives. The

FIGURE 4. Wilhelm Leibl, *Three Women in the Church*. ca. 1878–82. HAMBURG KUNSTHALLE

345

important thing, perhaps, is not so much the more or less exact reproduction of nature, but the artist's capacity for making us share his experience with him. To mention another famous case in point, consider Brueghel's winter landscape with hunters trudging through the snow (1565), in the Kunsthistorisches Museum in Vienna. It is only naturalistic, really, in comparison with all other landscape paintings of the sixteenth century, but it *is* naturalistic in details like the black blackbird against the winter twilight sky and the snow-covered hills. It is also "naturalistic" in that formal analysis alone cannot do justice to it; some remotely comparable experience has to be brought to it.

What has made it so hard to be fair to naturalistic art is this: that in it the material or content always threatens to overpower our sense of the artist's mastery of it. Ought not the painter to do something utterly un- or non-naturalistic, give us lessons in drawing, color, and composition? Naturalistic works of art seemingly or actually distract attention from the artistic accomplishment as such; but surely, so to distract us, the artist must have managed some especially subtle or skillful reshuffling between what we think of as the "materials of art" and their "spiritualization." Great naturalistic works are perhaps the most mysterious of all.

In conclusion, we may attempt to give answers in defense of naturalism to some questions raised earlier. Is the naturalistic work somehow of a lower rank than other kinds of art? No, and certainly not necessarily. Where are we to look, in naturalistic works, for the traditional criteria of a work of art? Well, by the way they have been hidden away, or the viewer's eye distracted from them. Does the artist's tendency to naturalism impair his own imagination and his other creative qualities or has it no bearing on them? The latter, surely, not the former; indeed, it has been claimed that there is no such thing as naturalism in art; naturalism can go too far, as in excessive pursuit of the *trompe-l'oeil*, but then so can every kind of art. And one last question, the one that sums up all others: How can an explicitly, extremely naturalistic work nevertheless be a work of art in the full sense of the term? The answers to the preceding questions may have provided at least the beginning of an explanation.

BIBLIOGRAPHY

Rudolf Arnheim, *Art and Visual Perception: A Psychology of the Creative Eye* (Berkeley and Los Angeles, 1954; 1960). Johannes Dobai, *Die Kunsttheorien des 18. Jahrhunderts in England* (Vienna, in print). Max Dvořák, *Idealismus und Naturalismus in der gotischen Skulptur und Malerei* (Munich and Berlin, 1918). K. Fiedler, *Gesammelte Schriften über Kunst* (Leipzig, 1896; 1971). Hanns-Conon von der Gabelentz-Altenburg, "Zum Begriff 'Naturalismus' in der bildenden Kunst, Versuch einer Klärung," in *Anschauung und Deutung—Willy Kurth zum 80. Geburtstag* (Berlin, 1964). Etienne Gilson, The A. W. Mellon Lectures in Fine Arts (1955), *Painting and Reality*, 2nd ed. (London and Princeton, 1957). Ernst Gombrich, *Art and Illusion: A Study in the Psychology of Pictorial Representation* (New York, 1960). René Huyghe, *Dialogue avec le visible* (Paris, 1955). Ernst Kris and Otto Kurz, *Die Legende vom Künstler: Ein geschichtlicher Versuch* (Vienna, 1934). Erwin Panofsky, *Idea. Ein Beitrag zur Begriffsgeschichte der älteren Kunsttheorie*. Studien der Bibliothek Warburg, Vol. 5 (Berlin, 1924); trans. Joseph Peake as *Idea: A Concept in Art Theory* (Los Angeles, 1968). Alois Riegl, *Die spätrömische Kunstindustrie* (Vienna, 1901; 1927); idem, *Stilfragen* (Berlin, 1893). Georg Schmidt, "Naturalismus und Realismus. Ein Beitrag zur kunstgeschichtlichen Begriffsbildung," *Festschrift für Martin Heidegger zum siebzigsten Geburtstag* (Pfullingen, 1959). Seymour Slive, "Realism and Symbolism in Seventeenth-Century Dutch Painting," *Daedalus*, **91**, 3 (Summer, 1962). Franz Wickhoff, *Die Wiener Genesis* (Vienna, 1895). Heinrich Wölfflin, *Kunstgeschichtliche Grundbegriffe. Das Problem der Stilentwicklung in der neueren Kunst* (Munich, 1925); trans. as *Principles of Art History, The Problem of the Development of Style in Later Art* (reprint Gloucester, Mass., no date).

FRITZ NOVOTNY

[See also Art and Play; Baroque in Literature; Form; Impressionism; Mimesis; **Nature;** Romanticism; Style; *Ut pictura poesis.*]

NATURE

NATURE, AS NORM, is the idea that "nature" and "natural" in one or more of their many senses set the standard for the good life, both of the individual and of society. The words themselves have at least sixty-six senses, distinguished by A. O. Lovejoy, and each of them has been the basis for praise and dispraise. But the multivalence of the word "nature" comes out very clearly when we think of some of those ideas to which it is antithetical: the supernatural, art, custom, the post-primitive as contrasted with the primitive. The natural is held by some to be better than the artificial, the customary, the contemporary. Of these four terms, only the supernatural is usually considered to be better than the natural.

When the natural is opposed to the supernatural, the latter in ancient and medieval times was believed to be inherently better than the former. Along with the notion of gods and angels, went the connotation of spirituality, immortality, ideality, immutability, all of which in the minds of many authors implied moral and aesthetic superiority. The Greeks, for instance, used the words, "the Immortals," as a synonym for the gods and each of the Olympian gods, though not the demigods, nymphs, and local divinities, was characterized by some outstanding quality—wisdom, military bravery, artistry, beauty—which was his or her "nature," in the sense of fundamental quality. When the pagan gods became Christian demons, clearly admiration for them turned to horror and there was no longer any possibility of equating the supernatural exclusively with the good.

The natural meanwhile was the material, in the sense of the tangible, the perceptible, the "real" in the popular sense of that term. It was probably Plato more than any other individual who removed the real from the material world to the world of ideals, by pointing out that the ideals (universals, Forms) were immutable, eternal, or timeless, whereas the so-called real things (particulars) were constantly changing and obviously temporal. Just why value was associated with the timeless and immutable has never been explained, if indeed any explanation of it is possible. The association seems to be spontaneous and it is probable that value and duration form a couple which seems to many men to require no explanation. For in the dominant tradition of European philosophy change is to be lamented and the Sage will reject the mutable in his search for the permanent. His search, like Faust's, will end when he can say, *Verweile doch du bist so schön!*

Meanwhile it had become clear to such Greek philosophers as Heraclitus, Empedocles, and perhaps the Pythagoreans, that though nature as the perceptual world did indeed change, it changed in accordance with fixed, universal, and rational laws. This made itself felt even outside the circle of science, where both the Greeks and the Romans relied on omens as a basis for decisions both military and civil. The augur must have believed that certain signs in, for instance, the liver of an animal that had just been sacrificed, were infallible portents of the future. The fixity of natural law was transferred to the supernatural and just as the law which explained the transformations of fire in Heraclitus was immutable, so was that binding the omen to its reference. But the idea of the pervasiveness of immutable law was also seen in some Greek tragedies where a decision of the protagonist leads to an inevitable consequence.

This too, like everything else, was modified by Christianity. The best evidence of the supernatural, according to some exegetes, was the violation of fixed law. Not only did Jesus raise the dead, but so did some of the Apostles and later the saints. Whereas the pagans had identified the immutable with the divine, the Christians maintained that one proof of divinity was the ability to break the immutability of the laws of nature and to accomplish the impossible, the *adynaton*. God Himself was immutable but at the same time He was omnipotent. In fact the fixed laws of nature, according to Newton in the General Scholium of the *Principia*, were an edict promulgated by God. Yet He was able and apparently willing to break the immutable laws which He had issued. Consequently Christian writers now emphasized the regularity of the supernatural decrees and at other times their intermittence.

From the cosmic point of view the nature in which we all live is the sublunary world, a world of change, corruption, diversity. It is in the superlunary world that the everlasting, the incorruptible, the unified is to be found. This fact attracted the admiration for the timeless into astrology, and in the Renaissance a man like Pico della Mirandola, in his *Heptaplus*, argued that man's "real" nature was to be found in his identification with some parts of the superlunary world, and by "real" here he meant "spiritual" or that which responds to the divine. Man's nature in Christian writings is peculiar in that it is halfway between that of the angels and that of the beasts. In one sense of the word "nature" man is akin to the animals; in another he is only a little lower than the angels. He is consequently in a paradoxical situation. If he was to be a good Christian, he would turn against his animal nature and cultivate his angelic nature. Hence he was likely to look down upon the "life according to nature" as it was interpreted in the pagan tradition.

In Greece of the fourth century B.C. the great contrast was that between nature and custom. "Nature" in this context meant the world unmodified by man. To the Christian this was interpreted as the world freshly created and, as far as human life was concerned, man before the Fall. Custom thus became that which was added to nature and hence if one was to live a life in accordance with nature, one would have to abandon everything that human intelligence had invented or discovered. The followers of Diogenes of Sinope, the Cynics, were the most extreme believers in such a program. Houses, clothing, cooked foods, social organization were not natural and hence Diogenes lived in a wine jar, wrapped a single strip of cloth around his body in lieu of fur, feathers, or scales, lapped up water like a dog, and withdrew from all social duties. The behavior of the Cynics, though not their motivation, was taken over by the solitary monks, and the tradition of rejecting social claims and the pleasures of civilization is still alive in certain areas in the twentieth century.

In the United States an approach to Cynical isolation and self-dependence could be seen in Thoreau, though

347

he was never completely consistent in this respect. In American fiction Leatherstocking might exemplify the rejection of tradition, society, and dependence on others. Life in the primeval forests seemed the life according to nature, though, unlike Diogenes, Leatherstocking had weapons with which to kill his game and knew how to light a fire. Diogenes is said to have eaten his food raw.

To live the life according to nature demanded a knowledge of just what nature was. One technique of finding out was to look for those standards which did not vary from people to people and could thus be called universal. This gave rise to the idea of something called "human nature." In antiquity this was specially emphasized by the Stoics, who were so convinced of the "rightness" of that which is universal that they even identified the true with that which is universally believed. The *consensus gentium* is truth as rooted in human nature. It developed into the medieval notion of the *lumen naturale*, the "natural light." It reappeared in Descartes, and was analogous to Pascal's heart which had reasons which the reason knew not, and was found again in Rousseau's "Profession of Faith of the Savoyard Vicar." In the Scottish philosophy of Thomas Reid it was called common sense and was taken over in Restoration France by Royer-Collard and Jouffroy. Its interest for us is that it was implanted in the human mind, as the innate ideas were, and was thus a stock of thoughts known by all men "by nature."

Many such ideas were mathematical or logical but some, such as the ideas of God or of right and wrong were ethical and religious. There could therefore be a religion and an ethics independent of Revelation, a Natural religion. In the seventeenth and eighteenth centuries in the works of such men as Lord Herbert of Cherbury, Toland, Shaftesbury, Voltaire, and Rousseau were to be discovered the sources of this natural religion which in Lord Herbert was based on the inner light, in Shaftesbury on sentiment, in Voltaire on reasoning, and in Rousseau on "the heart." Along with these elaborated philosophical doctrines there developed, particularly after the Reformation, a variety of religious sects to which the testimony of the natural light was omnicompetent.

But the inferences drawn from this type of innate knowledge were very different from one another. The one point of similarity in these views lay in their authors' denying the need for authority other than an individual's own private means of information. One might say that all of these men believed in God but each had his own God. Presumably no indoctrination was necessary. One simply relied on his own form of illumination. One knew "naturally." To some this knowledge was the voice of God; to others it was human nature made articulate. As a source of knowledge it was analogous to C. G. Jung's conception of the archetypal knowledge which emerges from the "collective unconscious" into the individual's mind.

The basic distinction here is that between nature and art, where art means those concerns in which the human being consciously and deliberately changes the raw material of experience. To one who prefers nature to art all learning, all education, and, to a man like Rousseau, in his *Discourse on the Sciences and the Arts,* all intellectual constructions whatsoever, should be rejected. Just as Diogenes turned to the animals for his exemplars, so the anti-intellectualist relies on some power which he will probably call instinct to guide him. The beasts follow nature; why should not man do the same? The difficulty was to find a human being whose nature was as yet unspoiled by art. The closest approach to the natural man was the savage "whose untutored mind"

> Sees God in clouds, or hears him in the wind;
> His soul proud Science never taught to stray
> Far as the solar walk or milky way;
> Yet simple nature to his hope has giv'n,
> Behind the cloud-topped hill, an
> humbler Heav'n, . . .
> (Pope, *Essay on Man,* Book I, lines 90–95).

"Proud Science" in these verses of Pope is exemplified by astronomy, an idea that goes back to Socrates.

That the savage had an idea of a God and a code of ethics was corroborated by some explorers. But it was the European essayist, the Greek ruminating on Anacharsis, or the Roman like Seneca, criticizing the luxury of his contemporaries and exclaiming, "That was a happy age when there were no architects and no builders," who created the Noble Savage. This mythical natural man seems to have arisen in Scythia, but soon appeared in various other exotic countries and imaginary habitats. The land of the Hyperboreans is a good example of the latter, and various islands of the Atlantic, both real and imaginary, of the former. A distinction must be made, however, between people like East Indians and the Chinese, who were exotic but far from savage, and the inhabitants of the West Indies or Polynesia, who were supposedly living in "a state of nature." Both types of people were highly admired for one reason or the other but what one might call exoticism is very different from primitivism. The Noble Savage might have virtues like those of the Spartan, who could do without the comforts of civilization, or those of the Sybarite to whom Mother Nature had freely given the delights of food, love, and leisure. The savage, however, was not the only model for the natural life.

We have already mentioned the animals. By the middle of the sixteenth century a new candidate appeared, the child. Cicero had called the child a *speculum naturae*, a mirror of nature, and in the Gospel of Matthew (18:3) Christ was reported to have said, ". . . except ye be converted, and become as little children, ye shall not enter into the kingdom of heaven." These phrases became a double root for the cult of childhood as the paradigm of the natural human being. It was obvious that the child was innocent of art, at least at birth, but it was impossible to find a child who had preserved the innocence of the newly born. This seemed to be understood by most writers. Yet, oddly enough, even the infant Jesus was not reverenced until the beginning of the Renaissance, roughly the fourteenth century. But, perhaps because of the charm of infancy, perhaps because the Renaissance was thought of as a time of rejuvenation, the child began to take on an air of authority as the period drew to a close.

With the coming of Protestantism the inner light came into its own and no one had the power to deprive anyone of its possession. Childhood in its purity and innocence became a symbol of the soul who has innate knowledge, as if in Wordsworth's words he had just come from Heaven. By the nineteenth century the child had become recognized as the source of all congenital, almost magical, wisdom. One sees such children in some of the novels of Dickens, but perhaps the best example is little Effie in *Silas Marner*. By the twentieth century, which Ellen Key, the famous feminist, called "the century of the child," the children had become the heroes of novels. Novels were even written for children and no less an artist than Henry James had written some from the child's point of view. By the middle of the century, however, children had lost something of their glamor and some authors, of whom William Golding is typical, were able to portray them in their naked depravity.

If searchers for the natural man did not find him in either the savage or the child, he was likely to turn to the peasant. The cult of the peasant has yet to be fully studied. By a man like Michelet he is seen as the embodiment of the nation. In Wordsworth even his plain speech is adopted for poetic use, though Wordsworth omitted his oddities of grammar and pronunciation. Innate honesty, sincerity, simplicity, were the peasant's outstanding virtues and only a few writers, of whom Zola is a good example, undertook to divest him of such trappings. The intimacy with nature, in the sense of the "unspoiled" landscape, was believed to give him superiority over both the country gentleman and the urban dweller. Wordsworth again is our best example of the man who thinks that "One impulse from a vernal wood may teach [you] more of man,/ of moral evil and of good, than all the sages can." But when Wordsworth wrote these lines in "The Tables Turned," he was in such a decidedly anti-intellectualistic mood that he was willing to toss away his books to listen to the linnet's song. The peasant did not have to sacrifice his books, for he owned none and could "let Nature be [his] teacher." Just what one learned from the linnet and the throstle was never disclosed by Wordsworth but that was probably because their lessons were ineffable, like the Beatific Vision.

The admiration for the out-of-doors was fully expressed in landscape painting. Though occasional landscapes had been painted as early as Giorgione and later by Salvator Rosa, Claude, and Gainsborough, they usually contained human figures also, bandits, shepherds, nymphs, carters, or, as in Watteau and Pater, ladies and gentlemen dancing or at similar pastimes. The nineteenth century saw the landscape without figures come into its own. The cause of this relatively new theme is unknown. It may have been a reaction from the spread of industrialism and a nostalgia for rural scenery but, whatever its source, it did express a love for nature in the sense of the environment untouched by man. When people in the nineteenth century spoke of nature, they usually meant nonhuman nature. This comes out brilliantly in such an essay as Emerson's "Nature." The touch of the vernal wood is here expanded to include the hills, the streams, and the meadows, and it is interesting to observe that Emerson never seems to include a human being as part of nature. In poetry it had been the custom to address some bird or other animal, or in the case of Emerson some flower and derive from looking at it some moral lesson. Thus Emerson seeing the rhodora also saw "that beauty is its own excuse for being," and Bryant seeing a water fowl was induced to pray that God would guide him as He guided the bird. But in the later nineteenth century the spectacle of untouched nature sufficed not only for painters but also for poets. Like the Imagists, they wanted "no deep thoughts."

Observation detached from theological and ethical preoccupations had made its start in the work of a man like Galileo, though like everyone else he had his predecessors. In Newton's *Principia* the theorems simply state what happens and, as is commonly known, the purpose of all this is not mentioned. Science as it developed from the seventeenth to the twentieth century became more and more a precise description of events limited by the methodological rules of experimentation and inference. The ideal was complete objectivity and, as far as possible, the elimination of the human equation.

One of the meanings of "nature" which has had

increasing vogue is the individual's special disposition, constitution, bent, or temperament. Just as people spoke of human nature as the special character of the whole human race, so they spoke of an individual's nature which might in certain cases be different from that of most other people. The result was twofold: first, some writers urged men to be true to the common nature of their fellowmen; second, that in the words of Polonius they must above all be true to themselves. Along with this went the feeling that people who were true to themselves and disdained the common traits of human nature, were guilty of Adam's sin of pride (*superbia*), that their individuality was abnormal, as it obviously was by definition, and monstrous because unnatural. On the other hand those whom we might call individualists felt that conformity to the general human nature was abnegation, self-destruction, psychic suicide. The second point of view gained wide approval in the early nineteenth century as part of the romantic program. Deviance from the statistical norm was rooted in individuality. Peter was bound to be more or less different from Paul and this could not be avoided.

But besides such innate differences, there were acquired tastes and manners. The romanticist not only accepted, as he had to, the innate peculiarities but added to them ways of accentuating his individuality. Such ways might be no more than wearing a red waistcoat or, as in the aesthetic movement, carrying a lily or sunflower in one's hand. Such manners were trivial. But on a more serious plane, whereas up to the middle of the twentieth century homosexual relations were called crimes against nature, after that time they were called deviance and the matter was dropped. Again, whereas in educational situations the child had been taught to be true to the school spirit in costume, speech, and general behavior, later the school boasted of encouraging self-expression and individuality. So up to the romantic period one could find manuals of painting, analogous to Fux's *Gradus ad Parnassum* (1715), in which the rules for "historical" painting, portraiture, and landscape were outlined; after that period the rules, perspective, "correct" drawing, color harmony, were gradually abandoned until in the second quarter of the twentieth century some artists, both pictorial and musical, expressed themselves so freely that they let chance determine their work. Instead of art's being an imitation of nature, it became an expression of an individual's nature. It is worth noting that the adjective "creative" became a eulogistic term, entailing novelty and above all individuality.

Nature in the sense of the whole physical world was sometimes thought of as the height of regularity, but at other times as irregular, and people who took nature as their model emphasized now the one now the other of these aspects. The pre-Socratic scientists, like their modern analogues, based their research on the assumption that nature is regular in all its changes and that universal laws can be framed to express that regularity. This tradition, broken by the importance given to miracles, obtained for centuries and still obtains in scientific circles. Also, the "geometry" of nature was used as the basis and vindication of rational ethics and neo-classical aesthetics. The good man had a consistent character and his acts were based on reason. One of the evils of the passionate life was precisely its incoherence and unreliability. In art, as John Dennis wrote in 1704, "the work of every reasonable creature must derive its beauty from regularity, for Reason is rule and order" (Lovejoy, "The Chinese Origin of a Romanticism," *Essays* . . . , p. 99).

In accordance with this men turned to Greek architecture for exemplars of perfect beauty and for two centuries the Greek temple was reproduced in churches, schools, banks, and even houses. But as A. O. Lovejoy showed in his essay, "The Chinese Origin of a Romanticism," the winds of doctrine shifted their orientation in the eighteenth century and admiration for irregularity became the mode. The taste for Gothic architecture, the unfinished and sometimes ruined state of which concealed its original regularity, the *goût chinois*, the picturesque, were all blended together and by the nineteenth century produced the man whose passions, and particularly the passion of love, became the paradigm. Lord Byron and other windblown poets and painters were typical instances. The most extreme case found voice in *Lucinde* in the phrase, "longing for the sake of longing." The legend of Don Juan was interpreted as the soul's search for the ideal which by its very nature eludes him. As late as Auguste Renoir (1884) we find a painter writing that great artists are ". . . careful to proceed like nature. They are always respectful pupils, and are on their guard never to transgress [her] fundamental law of irregularity" (Gauss, pp. 36f.). These two notions of nature subsisted side by side and have remained equally popular.

There was, however, a possible basis for reconciliation in the astrological thesis that perfect regularity existed in the superlunary world and disorder in the sublunary. That the upper heavens were incorruptible is a belief that goes back to Aristotle at least, and however the word "incorruptible" is defined, it must qualify something that is beyond the perceptible limits of spatial vision. For all about us is change, birth, decay, and death. The idea that what comes into being inevitably comes to an end is pronounced in Plato's

Timaeus, the cosmological Bible of the first twelve Christian centuries. Thus on the authority of the two most influential scientists it could be asserted that the universe or nature in the grandest sense of the word was twofold, one part being immutable and divine, the other subject to decay and human. The person who reflected on this was not likely to preach that men should live in accordance with the laws of the sublunary world even though it was his only habitat. His problem was to find some escape from it, and he found his escape in religion. The classic ascent to the incorruptible world was through the Mystic Way, the closest approach to which was of course virtue.

It was a common postulate up to the seventeenth century that nothing would change of its own accord. If then the sublunary world was in a constant state of change, there must be some active cause producing this effect. This cause was also called Nature, personified in the Middle Ages as the Goddess Natura, "queen of the mundane region." The cause of all sublunary change became in the later Middle Ages, in the *Roman de la Rose,* the sponsor of what might be called the marital state of nature, anticipated in the verse of Lucretius (Book V, line 962), *et Venus in silvis iungebat corpora amantum,* "and in the woods Venus united the bodies of lovers." There was then a minimum of two Natures, one an active force which determined what changes were to take place, and one a passive object of that force. The former was called as early as the twelfth century, according to W. Windelband, *natura naturans* and the latter *natura naturata.* But the distinction, though not the terms, was made by John Scotus Erigena in the ninth century when he spoke of that which creates and is uncreated as contrasted with that which is uncreating and created. In Nicholas of Cusa, Giordano Bruno, and Spinoza, the two natures were fused in God.

To feel the presence of *natura naturans* is at the heart of romantic nature-worship. It was perhaps in a spirit akin to Wordsworth's that the ancients saw nymphs in springs and trees and even in the ocean as Shakespeare found tongues in trees, books in the running brooks, sermons in stones, and good in everything. The animation of the landscape led to the pathetic fallacy, pretty well avoided by the middle of the twentieth century. This might have led to the recognition of man's being himself a part of the natural world and that all his traits, even when abnormal, are to be attributed to nature. Such a point of view became more and more acceptable in the second half of the twentieth century when adjectival expressions derived from "nature" seem to have lost their eulogistic tone. The thesis that everything men do is natural could easily be defended if the unnatural were to be defined statistically. The normative use of "natural" and "nature" would then disappear and only their descriptive meanings would remain.

BIBLIOGRAPHY

For the sixty-six senses of "nature" and its derivatives see A. O. Lovejoy and G. Boas, *Primitivism and Related Ideas in Antiquity* (Baltimore, 1935), appendix, pp. 447–56, and A. O. Lovejoy, "Nature as Aesthetic Norm," in *Essays in the History of Ideas* (Baltimore, 1948), pp. 69–78. For the admiration of the childlike, see G. Boas, *The Cult of Childhood,* Studies of the Warburg Institute, **29** (London, 1966). For William Wordsworth's admiration of the peasant, see especially his preface to *Lyrical Ballads.* Auguste Renoir on the irregularity of nature can be most conveniently found in C. E. Gauss, *The Aesthetic Theories of French Artists* (Baltimore, 1949), pp. 36f. For the origin of *natura naturans* see W. Windelband, *A History of Philosophy,* trans. James H. Tufts (New York, 1893), pp. 336, 338, 368, 409. In addition to these works, one should consult also the bibliographies under articles "Primitivism" and "Theriophily." The *Roman de la Rose* exists in a variety of editions. It should be supplemented by the *De planctu naturae* of Alain of Lille (Alanus de Insulis) in Migne, *Patrologia Latina,* Vol. 210.

GEORGE BOAS

[See also Cosmology; Cycles; Cynicism; Law, Natural; Naturalism in Art; **Newton on Method; Pre-Platonic Conceptions; Primitivism;** Stoicism.]

NECESSITY

1. Introduction. Necessity and Explanation. In trying to view the development of the notions of philosophical and historical necessity and of their interrelations in the light of successive dominant modes of explanation, it will be convenient to distinguish between the following periods: the beginnings of Greek science and philosophy, the age of Plato and Aristotle, the dominance of theology, the emergence of modern science, the age of rationalist epistemology, the period of empiricism and Kantianism, the age of Hegel and Marx, the struggle between positivism and the doctrine of historical empathy, twentieth-century views of the historical process, and recent views on natural and historical necessity. The periods overlap, and more attention will be given to the ideas than to the chronological order of their first appearance.

Necessity is either logical or nonlogical. Logical necessity is a characteristic of propositions or of their linguistic expressions. It is the subject matter of formal logic. Nonlogical or substantive necessity—e.g., metaphysical, natural, historical—is a characteristic of relations between parts or aspects of reality which may, but need not, be temporally separate. The statement that a part or aspect of reality, say α, necessitates another part or aspect of reality, say β, means in its weakest (and least tenable) sense no more than that whenever α exists then, as a matter of fact, β coexists with it, or that whenever α occurs then, as a matter of fact, it is succeeded by β. In its stronger senses the statement means in addition that the coexistence or succession is grounded in some deeper feature of reality which is accessible to introspection, observation, or reflection of a special kind.

What a person or society means by its concept of necessity cannot be understood in isolation from the whole conceptual system in which this concept is embedded. It cannot, in particular, be isolated from the manner in which the system serves the differentiation of experience into individual phenomena and categories of such, the predictive connection of phenomena, and the explanation of phenomena in an intellectually satisfactory manner. A person's concept of necessitation clearly depends on the manner in which he individuates phenomena (e.g., whether he places them into unidirectional or cyclical time) and on the categories of phenomena which he acknowledges (e.g., supernatural events). It depends on the concepts which he uses for prediction (which may include concepts of pure chance or randomness and thus limit the applicability of "regular succession" and consequently of "necessitation"). Lastly, a person's concept of necessitation is closely related to his general view of a satisfactory explanation (which may lead to the assessment of certain kinds of necessitation as blind or unintelligible). The explanatory power of a conceptual system does not lie in any of its specific concepts, such as a particular concept of necessitation. It resides rather in the conceptual system as a whole, insofar as the person who uses it in his reflections is satisfied with it or, at least, prefers it to alternatives which are available or conceivable to him. Thus a conceptual system of great predictive power, the application of whose concepts excludes the existence of a worshipped Deity, will give less intellectual satisfaction to a theist than a conceptual system with little predictive power, which does justice to his religious beliefs and emotions.

The explanatory power and general intellectual appeal of conceptual systems, whatever their specific content, depends to a considerable extent on the degree of their systematic unity, in particular on their capacity to serve the description and prediction of the course of events in a uniform way. Western thought has from its very beginnings shown a marked tendency to extend modes of description and prediction which have given intellectual satisfaction in one field of reflection to others, in particular to conceive of phenomena as being "ultimately" of one type only (physical, mental, spiritual, etc.), and of predictive connections as also being "ultimately" one (teleological efficacy, mechanical causation, probabilistic connection, etc.). The historical development of conceptual systems is characterized by fairly long periods in which one mode of description and prediction is dominant in the sense that it constitutes the archetype and standard of intelligibility and explanation. There have also been comparatively brief periods in which two or more modes of description and prediction had a more or less equally intellectual appeal or vied for superiority.

2. The Beginnings of Greek Science and Philosophy. The predecessor of both natural and historical explanation is mythical thinking. Looked at from the outside a myth is a story which, among other things, functions as a metaphorical description and predictive connection of natural or social phenomena, regarding them as manifestations of supernatural agencies. This characterization, although sufficient here, suffers from the obvious defect that it uses concepts which are not only unavailable to mythological thinking, but quite alien to it. Mythological thinking makes no sharp distinction between metaphor and plain description, or between the orders of nature and history on the one hand and the supernatural on the other. A proper appreciation of mythological explanation would have to proceed by means of some anthropological theory which regards thinking in terms of myths and thinking in terms of a nonmythical, conceptual system as species of the same genus and employs a suitable apparatus for investigating the whole genus. (For an attempt in this direction and further literature see C. Lévi-Strauss, *Structural Anthropology* [1963], especially Chapter XI.) It seems worth emphasizing the difference between total mythical thinking and the employment of myth in order to indicate and fill gaps in nonmythical explanations. The latter kind of mythologizing, which has affinities with the expression of an intellectual message by a work of art, is occasionally and with great effect employed by Plato, for example in the tenth book of the *Republic*.

The beginnings of a conscious opposition between myth and reality, and the conscious working out of conceptions of metaphysical, natural, and historical necessity are found in the philosophers of Miletus of the seventh century B.C. It is likely that the metaphysical speculations of Thales and his successors were stimulated by the mathematical and physical discoveries of their 'neighbors. Mathematical truth and the logical necessity which connects the axioms of geometry with its theorems became the archetype of every kind of necessary connection. It was then that the idea of the book of nature being written in the language of mathematics first took hold of metaphysicians and scientists. Pythagoras of Samos (ca. 540–500 B.C.) is reported to have expressed it by the dictum that things are numbers.

The main philosophical effort of the pre-Socratic thinkers is devoted to an understanding of the physical universe, i.e., of its real nature or *Physis* (φύσις)—a term with different, though closely related, meanings. It means in particular the ultimate constituents or elements of natural phenomena, their real essence and the laws underlying their genesis or growth out of each other. *Physis* in all these senses is opposed to *Tyche* (τύχη) or chance, which is often conceived as mere appearance. *Physis* is also, especially, in the sense of conformity to permanent, unalterable laws of nature opposed to *Nomos* (νόμος) in the sense of accidental, man-made, social convention. The pre-Socratics were, particularly through the atomistic theories of Leucippus and Democritus, more successful in proposing fruitful concepts and classifications of ultimate physical elements than in formulating laws of the regular or necessary connection of phenomena. They expressed the need for such laws rather than the laws themselves.

3. The Age of Plato and Aristotle. The interest in a scientific, as opposed to a mythological, understanding of social and historical phenomena starts, on the one hand, with the attempts by Herodotus and Thucydides to report the remembered (rather than the mythically conjectured) past, and on the other hand with Socrates' criticism of the moral conventionalism and relativism of his contemporaries, a relativism which is a consequence of the opposition between physical necessity and human convention. For the Greeks there was no essential difference between individual and social morality, so that for them ethical inquiry leads naturally into an examination of the structure of political life and of the genesis, growth, and decay of societies. The philosophy of Plato presents us with an explicitly formulated conceptual framework by whose application not only the physical, but also the social universe is to become intelligible and which is to reveal the reality behind the changing natural and social phenomena.

Plato's conception of natural and historical necessity is in many ways a synthesis of his predecessors' theories, although it is fair to say that the dominant Platonic mode of explanation is the Pythagorean mathematization of the physical universe, i.e., the attempt to understand physical reality in terms of an underlying mathematical structure. The reason for this is that while geometry and astronomy were highly developed sciences, Herodotus, Thucydides, and the Greek historians generally were content with rather modest inductive generalizations and marginal comments on the role of chance and necessity in history.

Plato's central doctrine, which he developed throughout his life and which scholars find difficult to disentangle from the oral teachings of his master Socrates, is an attempt to understand the ever-changing physical and social world by relating it to an unchanging reality. This reality he conceives as mind-independent Ideas or Forms which stand in unchangeable relations to each other. The Forms are, as it were, eternal models of which the changing phenomena are imperfect copies. It seems that in its final version the Platonic metaphysics rests on mathematical Forms, such as the Forms of the One and the Many, of the perfect straight line or the circle; and ethico-political Forms such as the Form of perfect courage or of the perfect social community.

To explain the phenomena in their necessary relations to each other is to grasp the ideal structure—the Form or the relationship between Forms—to which they approximate or in which they "partake," and the degree of this approximation. Thus a mathematical physicist understands the necessary connections in the movement of physical bodies as close approximations to mathematically expressed relations between mathematical Forms; and thus a social philosopher (in Plato's aristocratic tradition) understands the Athenian society of the fourth century B.C. as a very poor approximation to a perfectly just city-community. Plato's conception of the connection of natural phenomena as a fairly close reflection of the necessary connection between Forms is one of the seminal ideas in Western scientific thought and has—as is almost universally agreed by experts—helped to shape the methodology of Galileo Galilei and his successors.

In the philosophy of history, and in historical thinking generally, Plato's approach has proved less influential, although his *Republic* has been the model for the construction of many utopias and has thus indirectly influenced political thought and action. The comparative lack of Platonic influences on later theories of history might be explained on two counts. First, the projection of permanent, especially mathematical, structures into temporal processes fits on the whole repetitive processes better than unrepetitive ones, and sets strict limits to the emergence of novel features as opposed to mere recombinations of preexisting elements. Second, Plato's theory of the mind as independent of nature conflicts with the conception that man can change nature by his actions in accordance with ideas which are not so much his discovery as his invention.

When Plato tries to apply his theory of Forms to historical change, it loses the inner completeness which it possesses as a philosophy of mathematics and the natural sciences. He has to draw not only on rudimentary psychological and biological theories but also heavily on myth. The myth of the universe developing in ever-repeating cycles, which is found in most oriental religions, helps him to explain social change as a gradual decay of a community from the golden age of a just aristocracy to the state of almost complete political injustice in a tyranny. The decay is brought about by biological deterioration through intermarriage of the guardians of the state with members of the lower social orders and is ultimately (perhaps only ironically) explained in astrological terms.

Just as Plato's way of classifying and connecting of phenomena is mainly inspired by the mathematics and physics of his time, so Aristotle's mode of explanation is modelled on biological and anthropological descriptions and predictions in terms of purposes. Very roughly speaking, Aristotle extends the manner in which a person plans and acts, in order to achieve his purpose or purposes, to the objective phenomena of the physical and of the social universe: whatever exists has a purpose and every change is a stage in the realization of a purpose. Necessary connections in the real world, as opposed to logical connections between propositions, are teleological. The principles of any scientific inquiry whatsoever are mainly developed in his first philosophy or "metaphysics" which he conceives as the science of being *qua* being, in opposition to the special sciences which "divide off some portion of being and study the attributes of this portion, as do for example the mathematical sciences" (*Metaphysics* IV, 1003a ff.). The nature of material things, including men, is understood in terms of his doctrine of the four causes of which "one is the essence or essential nature of the thing . . . , the second is the matter or substratum; the third is the source of motion; and the fourth is the cause which is opposite to this, namely the purpose or 'good'; for this is the end of every generative or motive process" (*Metaphysics* I, 983a 20ff.).

To ask for an explanation is thus always to ask for a purpose. This mode of explanation is applied by Aristotle throughout—in ethics and politics as well as in physics. But whereas teleological explanations—at least in the attenuated form where the purpose of an organism is replaced by the totality of its functions—have been kept alive in the biological and social sciences and in history, a wholly antiteleological manner of explanation has dominated the natural sciences since the times of Galileo.

Although Aristotle's conception of teleological connection with its strong tendency to differentiate the world into organic units was to influence many later philosophers of history, his own interest in history was negligible and his assessment of its intellectual content almost contemptuous. Even poetry "is something more philosophical and of more serious import than history since its statements are of the nature of universals, whereas those of history are singulars" (*Poetics* 1451b 5). This statement foreshadows the view that the historian cannot discover, and should not search for, general laws governing the events whose sequence he records in their concrete and unrepeatable singularity.

Neither Platonism, with its predominant mathematical orientation, nor Aristotelianism, with its antihistorical bias, could provide Greek historians with any explicitly formulated philosophical or scientific concept of historical necessity. They had to link their theorizing either with the traditional myths or develop their own theoretical understanding while grappling with their subject matter. Roman culture did not greatly increase the store of metaphysical, scientific, or historical modes of explanation. But it confronted the historian with the unprecedented success of Roman political, legal, and military organization and, consequently, with the specific problem of explaining it.

"Whoever," asks Polybius, "is so obtuse and indifferent that he would not like to know, how and by which kind of constitution the whole inhabited earth has in not quite fifty-three years fallen under the rule of one people, namely the Romans—something that never happened before . . . ?" (*Historiae*, Book I, Ch. I). The question is based on the assumption that an understanding of political structures and of the laws governing their development contains the key to historical understanding. This assumption is combined with a methodological principle which anticipates the later theories of Dilthey and Collingwood, namely that historical explanation is closely allied to introspection. Paraphrasing the well-known Platonic remark about philosophers and kings, Polybius asserts that historical writing will be in a satisfactory state "only when statesmen will undertake the writing of history" or when historians will "regard political activity as indispensable to historical writing" (ibid., XII, III).

4. The Dominance of Theology. The rise of Christianity and the importance which it assumed in the lives of men concentrated the intellectual energies of the early Christians and of most medieval thinkers on the formulation and elaboration of the teachings of the New and the Old Testament in the forms of dogma and theology. Greek modes of philosophical and scientific thinking were used in the interpretation of the Scriptures, but were subordinated to them. The result is a unified view of the universe, created and governed by the God of Christian (as well as of the Jewish and Muhammadan) religion, and otherwise conceived after the fashion of Platonism or Aristotelianism. The conflict between these two philosophies continues also within the new theological framework. The dominance of theology and of theological explanation implies that all understanding of natural and social phenomena, and of their connections, must ultimately be an understanding, however imperfect, of the nature of God. All natural and historical necessity is ultimately theological.

Christian religious doctrine and its theoretical elaboration through theology contains comparatively few ideas which have any bearing on the development of the natural sciences. This does not mean that the period between the fall of Rome and the so-called Renaissance was without influence on the development of the natural sciences. Medieval thought was not all theology and we have learned to distrust the older view that there is no continuous development leading from later medieval thought to modern science. Yet the specifically religious doctrines of Christianity profoundly influenced the Western conception of historical necessity. The central ideas of a Christian philosophy of history were expressed with great clarity by Saint Augustine in his *De civitate Dei*. They constitute the theoretical basis of most Christian historical writing and recur in recognizable variants in many later philosophies of history.

Neither Plato's conception of necessity, based on mathematics and physics, nor Aristotle's conception of necessity, based on (nonevolutionary) biology, excluded the doctrine of a cyclical history as expressed in some Greek myths. Augustine insists that this conception is incompatible with Christian dogma, since "Christ died only once because of our sins and since having risen from the dead He does not die again . . ." (*De civitate Dei*, Book XII, Ch. XIV). If there exists one sequence of events which is not repeatable, then any doctrine of the eternal repetition of all events must be rejected. Moreover the world and time—for Augustine, like Leibniz, regards the concept of an empty time as spurious—have one beginning in being created by God and one end, the Last Judgment.

Since history is the manifestation of the will of God, who created man after His own image, it is meaningful to inquire into the purpose or sense of history. Just as Aristotle explained the course of nature in terms of purposes conceived after the analogy of man's purposes, so it is possible to conceive God's purpose in history after the analogy of human ends. God's purpose in history is a moral purpose, which we cannot fully grasp, except at the end of history, which will also reveal it as the true theodicy, i.e., as the vindication of the divine providence in spite of the existence of evil and wickedness.

The working of the divine providence cannot be explained by any purely philosophical or scientific theory. It must be explained with the help of the Christian moral insight that mankind is divided into two kinds: "such as live according to man, and such as live according to God." Augustine calls them the "two cities" of "which one is predestinated to reign eternally with God, the other condemned to perpetual torment with the devil" (ibid., Book XIII, Ch. I). He calls the distinction "mystical," an expression which might suggest a remote similarity to the explanatory use of myths by Plato. Indeed the relation between the two cities is explained by reference to the story of Cain and Abel according to which "Cain built a city, but Abel was a pilgrim and built none. For the city of the saints is above, though it have citizens here on earth. . . ." The working of divine providence in the conflicts between the two cities anticipates later patterns of historical explanations, e.g., the working of Hegel's or Marx's dialectics of history in the conflicts between nations and social classes.

5. The Emergence of Modern Science. The Renaissance was not so much a period of the wholesale rejection of medieval thought, as of the critical reassessment of medieval and classical theories in an atmosphere in which theology was no longer the predominant mode of explanation. This atmosphere not only gave rise to the impression of novel theories but favored the emergence of real novelty. The thinkers of this period were right—though not all to the same degree—in calling their theories "new" sciences opposing them to old and often useless ones. The *Novum Organum* (1620) of Francis Bacon was to put a new inductive logic beside the old deductive logic of Aristotle. The *Two New Sciences* (1638) of Galileo "pertaining to mechanics and local movements" were to replace the Aristotelian physics and by implication much of the Aristotelian and Thomistic metaphysics. The *Discourse on Method* (1637) by Descartes was to be a new methodology of science in the sense that "while comprising the advantages" of the logic and analysis of the ancients and the algebra of the moderns it was to be "exempt from their faults" and applicable in all inquiries (*Discourse* . . . , Parts I, II). The *Principles of a New Science* (1725) by G. B. Vico was to lay the foundation of a science of the historical—as opposed to the natural—world.

According to Bacon the connection between phenomena is discoverable by classification, inductive generalization, and experimental testing, provided that the procedure of the inquirer is governed by the proper method. Bacon's importance lies more in his insistence on the need to test theories and on the pragmatic and technological aspects of science, than on any clear methodological achievement. His method, which depends among other things on the assumption that every natural phenomenon consists of a finite number of "Forms," is not the method of Galileo and his successors. The reason for this and for Bacon's lack of understanding of the physics of Copernicus and Galileo is Bacon's neglect of the role of mathematics in physics.

Galileo's conception of natural necessity, which he explains by occasional remarks in his *Dialogues,* combines the Platonic conviction that the structure of the universe is expressible in mathematical language, with the Baconian conviction that the truth of any scientific law or theory must be established by experiment and observation. Galileo claims that the combined use of mathematical theorizing and empirical testing may reveal necessities in the course of nature and not merely "hypotheses," i.e., provisional, predictively useful assumptions. (The issue between the Inquisition and Galileo concerns this philosophical point about the nature of the Copernican astronomy—even though Galileo's treatment at the hands of Cardinal Bellarmine does not appear any different for being based on philosophical rather than scientific heterodoxy.)

If Bacon's nonmathematical, inductive, and pragmatic methodology corresponds only very imperfectly to Galilean physics, it expresses the practice of the Renaissance historians much more closely. Their attention is fully devoted to descriptions, predictions, and practical precepts based on the observation of a secular society apart from any relations which it may have to the Augustinian society of God. Historical writing in the Renaissance differs less from that of a Thucydides, Polybius, Livy, or Tacitus, than does scientific theorizing from its classical predecessors. This was recognized by most historians of that age who follow Machiavelli in paying sincere tribute to the Greek and Roman historians.

6. The Age of Rationalist Epistemology. Galileo's scientific achievement and the absence of any similarly spectacular success in the understanding of social and historical phenomena play a large role in shaping the modern epistemological approach to mathematics, the natural sciences, and history. This approach is based on the assumption that the conditions for the truth or necessity of all kinds of propositions are found not only in the structure of a mind-independent reality but also in the constitution of the mind which apprehends this reality. Although the assumption is not new (it is, for example, found in Neo-Platonism) it becomes dominant in the thought of Descartes and Vico.

Descartes opposes his own conceptions of necessary connection and deduction to those of formal logic. Logical deduction—e.g., the deduction of Pythagoras' theorem from the axioms of Euclidean geometry—only exhibits the content of the premises without enlarging it. The syllogisms and most other rules of logic "serve on the whole the purpose of explaining to others what one already knows" (*Discourse on Method,* Part II). Cartesian deduction is intended to be ampliative like induction, which leads beyond the content of the premises. But it is intended also to be certain like formal deduction, so that if we start with self-evident axioms we arrive at genuinely (as opposed to merely psychologically) new knowledge. It is, as it were, meant to combine the merits of empirical induction and logical deduction.

Descartes' view of deduction is based on the alleged recognition of necessary connections—a connection "between things" being necessary "when one is so implied in the other in a confused manner that we cannot conceive either of them distinctly if we judge them as separate from each other" (*Regulae ad directionem ingenii,* comments on rule XII). The apprehension of necessary connections among phenomena may be aided by experiments and observations, but consists ultimately in our apprehending the connections among our ideas. Descartes believed that it is possible to start with one indubitable idea and to reveal in successive deductive steps the whole coherent network of all ideas; and that to do so is to reveal the whole of reality. His own application of this method, to which he ascribed his immortal discovery of analytical geometry, yields among other things a fallacious proof of the existence of God. His influence on later thinkers is enormous. Almost any later theory which employs a conception of a nonlogical necessity or of nonlogical, but certain, inference can be traced back to Descartes' ideas of "necessary connection" and "deduction." To mention only the most obvious examples, the Hegelian (and therefore also the Marxist) conception of dialectical necessity and dialectical reasoning, and all so-called coherence theories of truth are heavily indebted to Descartes.

Since history and social phenomena are intimately connected with human motives, designs, and reasoning, one would expect Descartes' introspective epistemological approach to be particularly fruitful in the philosophy of history. Many historians, such as Polybius or Machiavelli, try to understand political events and their connections by entering into the minds of statesmen—minds which apart from their special training and character are like the minds of all other men. They share Descartes' assumption that *the* human mind is capable of apprehending reality and that "the power of forming a good judgment and of distinguishing the true from the false . . . is by nature equal in all men" (*Discourse on Method,* Part I). Yet the affinity between Descartes' epistemology and the historians' approach is obscured by his almost exclusive interest in mathematics and the natural sciences, whose "mechanistic" assumptions, simplifications, and terminology are alien to historical description and explanations as practiced by working historians.

Giambattista Vico attacks Cartesianism for its one-sidedness and neglect of historical knowledge which is different from, independent of, and superior to natural knowledge. According to Vico in his *Principi di una scienza nuova* (1725) the philosophers have failed to reflect on the "world of nations or the historical world" which is accessible to human knowledge "because men have created it," whereas nature as the creation of God is known only to Him (3rd ed., Naples, 1744). History is a branch of "philology"—the genetic science of man's creations such as "languages and the deeds of the nations, the internal deeds such as morals and laws as well as the external deeds such as war, peace, treaties, travels, commerce" (ibid., Book III, sec. 3, §139). Just as Plato, Galileo, and successive generations of theoretical physicists have explained the course of nature in terms of ideal, mathematical structures, so the new science of philology and more especially of history is to explain the course of history in terms of "an eternal ideal history traversed in time by the histories of all nations" (ibid., Book II, sec. 1, §393). Whoever reflects on this science is, "in so far as he is telling himself this eternal ideal history," apprehending historically necessary connections because "he who creates the things is talking about his own creation."

Vico compares the necessities of history to the necessities of geometry. He proposes principles of historical understanding and the evaluation of historical evidence among which he includes, in particular, myth and language. He revives the Augustinian doctrine of divine providence which "men without noticing it and often contrary to their plans" help to realize. This doctrine is very like Hegel's "cunning of the Absolute."

Vico's necessary connections are, like the Cartesian ones, nonlogical and yet certain because both are derived from allegedly self-evident principles by allegedly self-evident steps. And just as Descartes proceeds by way of allegedly necessary connections to unprovable metaphysical dogmas and obsolete physical hypotheses, so Vico proceeds in similar manner to unprovable dogmas of an Augustinian theology and to obsolete anthropological hypotheses. Although the necessary connections of Descartes and Vico rest on feelings or convictions, which are by no means permanent and characteristic of all generations, they both profoundly influenced their successors. It is rightly said of Vico that he belonged to the nineteenth century rather than his own. His theory of the nature of myth and language might even be said to belong to the twentieth century.

7. The Period of Empiricism and Kantianism.

Descartes' mechanistic and Vico's historical necessitarianism, which explain the connection of phenomena in terms of ideal mathematical systems and ideal genetic sequences, are only one answer to the philosophical problem posed by Galileo's success in creating that unity of observation and mathematical theorizing which is theoretical physics. A diametrically opposite solution of the problem was attempted by the British empiricists Locke, Berkeley, and particularly Hume, whose account of the concept of necessary connection (outside logic and mathematics) is, briefly, that the concept is strictly speaking empty. Men, according to Hume, observe no more than apparently regular repetitions in nature and history. These regularities strengthen, as a matter of fact, our beliefs, expectations, and predictive habits that the observed past will be like the future and was like the unobserved past. The illusion of a (strictly) necessary natural and historical connection or natural and historical causality arises from our mistaking a subjective expectation of a regular sequence for a feature of the objective world. Yet the concept of causal connection *qua* observed and expected regularity in the sequence of phenomena is, according to Hume, indispensable to both science and history. Thus, the ideas of necessity in Descartes' "geometric method" and in Vico's "historical method" are replaced by a contingent psychological determinism of "habit" in Hume.

Descartes' attempt to assimilate the observed regularities in nature to mathematical or quasi-mathematical necessities, and Hume's attempt to exorcise all noncontingent connections from the regularities observed, seem to be one-sided accounts of Galilean physics, and call for a synthesis which does justice to them both. Kant's philosophy was intended to be such a synthesis. Its central idea reminds one of Vico's remarks that man as the maker of his history can know his creation. According to Kant man is to a certain extent, which is capable of clear demarcation, also the maker of his world, namely, of nature as apprehended by him. Kant holds that the manifold of sense-experience is located in space and time, which are forms of human intuition, and organized into objective phenomena by the application of Categories, which are forms of human conceptual organization. The necessity of mathematical propositions is due to their describing the structure of space and time. The necessity of the general principles of science, such as the principle of causality or principle of the conservation of substance, is due to their expressing conditions for organizing the manifold of sense-experience (by the application of the Categories) into the experience of an objective world or a world of public objects.

The details of the Kantian synthesis of empiricism and rationalism—a synthesis deeply influenced by Galilean and Newtonian physics—cannot be described here. Its most important features from our present point of view are the following: first, the human mind does not only apprehend the world passively, but imposes its own perceptual and conceptual form upon it. Second, the principles describing the forms of perceptual and conceptual organization are both synthetic (i.e., not merely truths of logic) and *a priori* (i.e., independent of sense-impressions). Third, the synthetic *a priori* propositions determine the fundamental structure of the natural sciences and of morality. Fourth, the synthetic *a priori* principles are common and indispensable to all human thinkers. Fifth, apart from the synthetic *a priori* principles which express the conditions of an objective experience possible to human beings, the human mind also forms concepts, called "Ideas," which introduce heuristic, aesthetic, teleological, or systematic unity into scientific thinking, but which have no objective content. The conception of a providential design in history is such an Idea.

Both Hume and Kant wrote on historical topics. Hume's *History of Great Britain* (1745–63) is—as might be expected—methodologically no different from the mainly descriptive, cautiously inductive, and mildly moralizing historical writings of, say, a Voltaire; it shows no obvious traces of his philosophical position. Kant's more speculative historical essays, on universal history, and on perpetual peace—*Idee zu einer allgemeinen Geschichte in weltbürgerlicher Absicht*, (1784) and *Zum ewigen Frieden* (1795)—bear the obvious stamp of his theory of Ideas. Thus he says in the first of these works that "one *may regard*" (my emphasis) the history of mankind "as the execution of a hidden plan of nature in order to achieve an internally—and to this purpose also externally—perfect constitution as the only state of affairs in which nature can fully develop all the faculties of mankind" (trans. S. Körner).

In the period from Vico to Hegel there is, on the whole, a lively interaction between the natural sciences and philosophy. In this interaction philosophers for the most part accept the scientific method as an implicit standard of truth and reasoning, which they try to clarify and extend to other fields. There are—unless we confer the status of a philosophical theory on the romantics' worship of personalities and personality—no important new departures in either the philosophy of history or in the writing of history. Montesquieu, Voltaire, and others are eager to find and apply general psychological and sociological laws which are essentially Baconian in form and inspiration.

8. The Age of Hegel and Marx. Kant distinguishes sharply between the empirical self or subject, revealed in self-awareness and introspection, and the transcendental self or subject; the latter, by connecting subjective impressions into objective experience is the source of necessity in mathematics and the natural sciences. Kant's concept of the transcendental self seemed both obscure and unsatisfactory to his immediate idealist successors such as Fichte and Schelling. It seemed to them to hover precariously between mere intersubjectivity and real objectivity and to be too modestly endowed with creative powers, especially the power to create historical reality. The tendency to identify the transcendental self with more familiar ideas such as the spirit of a nation, of a society, or of mankind was strengthened by the emergence of a romantic nationalism in Germany and elsewhere and by the resistance of German philosophical jurists to the ever increasing preponderance of Roman law over the original German law. The leader of the so-called historical school of law was F. C. von Savigny (1779–1861) who taught that the substance of any legal system "is determined by the whole past of a nation—not as the result of arbitrary decisions so that it might be this rather than another, but as emerging from the innermost spirit of the nation and its history" ("Vom Beruf unserer Zeit für Gesetzgebung und Rechtswissenschaft," *Zeitschrift für geschichtliche Rechtswissenschaft* [1815], Vol. 1, No. 1.). Savigny's conception of legal development is essentially one of organic development—the developing organisms being not individuals but nations. In this respect the historical school of law reminds one of Rousseau's social theory and of Burke's reflections on politics, among others.

In Hegel's philosophy the place of the Kantian transcendental self which creates the necessary truths is taken by the spirit or the Idea which *is* reality and reveals itself to itself. Its essence Hegel calls "Logic" or "Dialectics." It expresses itself in space as Nature and in time as History. Hegel identifies the Idea as thought with the Idea as reality, and his philosophy is no longer a mere theory of knowledge but it is also a theory of reality. His grand system has been regarded as a philosophical revelation by some and as pretentious rubbish by others, e.g., Karl Popper, in *The Open Society and its Enemies* (4th ed., 1963). But this is not the place to enter the battlefield as a combatant. To an outside observer the enormous influence of Hegel's conception of dialectics and necessity on the philosophy of history and on historical writing and politics is indubitable. Their influence on the philosophy of science and science itself is comparatively small.

From the point of view of Hegel's *Logic* the Idea (*die Idee* = Spirit = Reality) is a system of necessarily connected Categories which differ from each other in richness of content. In trying to grasp the content of a separate Category one is forced to think of another with which it is necessarily connected. The connection is not that of formal logic, but is synthetic and ampliative, like the Cartesian necessary connection. It is also "dialectical." This means that if a thinker reflects on the most general Category, namely "Being," he is forced to think its antithesis, namely "Nothing," and onwards to think the synthesis of "Being" and "Nothing," namely "Becoming." The new Category is a thesis which again "dialectically implies" its antithesis; thesis and antithesis dialectically imply synthesis and so forth until the absolute Idea is reached, which contains "the truth" of all the poorer Categories. It is not feasible here to show this "logical movement" in detail.

World history is the manifestation of the Idea in time. Its bearer in every phase of history is a people or, more precisely, the spirit of a people (*Volksgeist*). The spirit of a people, however, has only a limited existence and a content which dialectically implies the emergence of another people, whose spirit is different. The passions and actions of men are, as it were, used by the spirit of the people to which they belong and thus by the spirit of history as means for its self-realization. This feature of historical development which Hegel calls "the cunning of history" implies that only the dialectical historian understands the necessities of history which remain obscure to the historian who looks merely at individual plans and actions.

The Marxist philosophy of history owes much to the Hegelian metaphysics. It is the creation of Karl Marx in collaboration with Friedrich Engels, and is to some extent the mirror image of Hegel's philosophy of history. Marx, like Hegel, holds that both nature and history are dialectical in their essence. But he replaces Hegel's "dialectical idealism" by a "dialectical materialism." In his view, "the mental [*das Ideelle*] is nothing but the material as transferred and translated into the human head" (*Das Kapital*, Vol. I, postscript to 2nd ed., Hamburg [1872]). The substance of reality is not spirit, but matter in dialectical movement. History is the temporal manifestation of material reality which is merely reflected in human minds or, more precisely, in human brains. The ultimate stage of the historical process is not a state which "governs persons" but the mere "administration of things and the guidance of processes of production." "The state," which according to Hegel is the highest form of human organization, *"withers away"* (F. Engels, *Herrn Eugen Dührings Umwälzung der Wissenschaft* [*"Herr Eugen Duhring's Revolution in Science"*] Stuttgart, 1894). The vehicles of dialectical, historical progress are not peoples, or the spirit of peoples, but social classes. History in its essence is the history of class struggles. It is these class struggles which are used by the "cunning of history"

to lead through thesis, antithesis, and synthesis to the classless society, i.e., perfect communism in which everybody uses his abilities as best he can and everybody's needs are fully satisfied.

The following often quoted passage—from the preface to *Zur Kritik der politischen Oekonomie* (Berlin, 1859)—conveys the central points of Marx's theory of history:

In the social production which men carry on they enter into definite relations that are indispensable and independent of their will; these relations of production correspond to a definite stage of development of their material forces of production. The sum total of these relations of production constitutes the economic structure of society—the real foundation on which rises a legal and political superstructure and to which corresponds definite forms of social consciousness. The mode of production in material life determines the social, political and intellectual life processes in general. It is not the consciousness of men that determines their being, but, on the contrary, their social being that determines their consciousness. At a certain stage of their development, the material forces of production in society come in conflict with the existing relations of production or—what is but a legal expression for the same thing—with the property relations within which they have been at work before. From forms of development of the forces of production these relations turn into their fetters. Then begins an epoch of social revolution. . . . In broad outlines we can designate the Asiatic, the ancient, the feudal and the modern bourgeois modes of production as so many epochs in the progress of the economic formation of society (trans. S. Körner).

The parallels between this summary of the Marxist philosophy of history and the Hegelian are fairly obvious. The irrefutability of both these philosophies by the actual course of history is guaranteed by the very generality and flexibility of their concepts and theses. There is, however, another way of considering Marx's philosophical pronouncements, namely, not as descriptive but as programmatic or regulative. This is what Marxists seem to mean when they say that Marxism is "not a dogma, but a method." On this interpretation the principles of Marxist philosophy require the construction of testable, predictive theories—in particular economic and sociological theories—implying specific predictions rather than statements which are too comprehensive to be exposed to precise tests. So far the most elaborate theory, conforming to the Marxist philosophical program, is Marx's economic theory.

9. Positivism and Historical Empathy. Insofar as positivism is the rejection of the truth-claims of any theories other than empirical or logico-mathematical, it can be traced at least to Hume. The name "positivism" was coined by Auguste Comte (1798–1857) who claimed to have discovered a law of historical progress of all societies from a stage of theological fiction in which the human mind "supposes all phenomena to be produced by the direct and continual action of supernatural beings" through the metaphysical stage, where the place of supernatural beings is taken by abstract forces, which are really "personified abstractions," to the positive stage where the mind "has given up the search after the origin and destiny of the universe and applies itself to the study of the laws governing the phenomena"—the laws being conceived as describing "their invariable relations of succession and resemblance (*Cours de philosophie positive*, 7th ed., 1877, *première leçon*). The positive stage of physics has been reached rather early, the positive stage of physiology very late. It is the task of Comte's philosophy to prepare the necessary historical ground for "social physics." Comte's law of the three stages and Darwin's theory of evolution were among the main reasons for the rise in the nineteenth century of an optimistic scientism according to which the physical sciences, fashioned in Newtonian style, and the biological and social sciences, subordinated to Darwin's theory of evolution, are capable of answering all meaningful empirical questions; they inevitably produce the material and moral progress of mankind as a necessary consequence of the increase of human knowledge.

Thus J. S. Mill argues that the "order of human progression in all respects will mainly depend on the order of progression in the intellectual convictions of mankind." This view is also held by H. T. Buckle, who bases his *History of Civilization in England* (1857–61) on four "leading propositions." The first asserts "that the progress of mankind depends on the success with which the laws of phenomena are investigated, and on the extent to which a knowledge of those laws is diffused" (*Civilization*, Vol. II, beginning of Ch. I). The Marxist and positivist views of science and history are as much a part of the contemporary scene as are the views of their opponents to which we now turn.

For the positivists history is part of nature and historical necessity is no different from natural necessity. They implicitly reject Vico's distinction between the "philological" and the natural sciences as concerned respectively with two fundamentally different realms of phenomena. This distinction is forcefully revived by W. Dilthey (1833–1911), whose main aim was to lay the foundations of an empirical science of mental phenomena. The means for understanding these phenomena is the empathy by which a person understands another as a spiritual being. Only such understanding (*Verstehen*), from the inside as it were, and not external observation and scientific explanation can reveal the nature of works of art and other human creations and the nature of historical development.

A theory of historical understanding, which is indebted to Dilthey and his predecessors from Hegel to Vico, has been expounded with great clarity by R. G. Collingwood in *The Idea of History* (Oxford, 1946). To understand an historical event and the historical sequence of events is to "reenact" the experience of the people who were involved in them. It has often been pointed out that it is logically impossible to reenact any event or sequence of events, if only because of its spatio-temporal uniqueness; and that it is impossible for one person to reenact the experiences of a crowd of people or any other interacting group of persons, if only because the historian is one person and not many simultaneously interacting persons. Yet the inner experience of different persons may nevertheless have some features in common, to which description and theorizing after the fashion of the natural sciences has no access. In practice almost all historians assume some degree of empathy in their readers and some uniformity in human feelings, desires, motives, and plans.

10. Twentieth-Century Views of History. The philosophy of history of the twentieth century is no longer dominated by the idea of historical progress, which for Christian historians follows from their theology, for Hegelians and Marxists from their dialectical metaphysics, and for positivists from evolutionary biology. By opposing historical and natural necessity, it becomes possible once again to adopt a cyclical conception of historical development, especially if the ultimate subject of historical development is conceived as a kind of organism with a limited time of life. The Darwinian theory of evolution is quite compatible with a nonevolutionary theory of quasi-organisms, such as nations, societies, civilizations which emerge and decay in essentially the same manner. Such a theory was developed by O. Spengler in deliberate opposition to scientific theorizing and in a much attenuated form by A. J. Toynbee. In reading Spengler one may have the impression that he does violence to historical facts in order to fit them into his idiosyncratic vision. In reading Toynbee one may, on the contrary, have the impression that his main theses are formulated in so general, vague, and qualified a manner that no historical fact could ever clearly conflict with them.

Spengler distinguishes between the world as nature and the world as history—each of these worlds being understood in terms of entirely different categories. The category by the application of which all natural change can be predicted and explained is mechanical causality; the category in terms of which all historical change can be predicted and explained is destiny. The bearers of natural change are physical systems; the bearers of destiny are cultures. The causal laws governing the changes of physical systems are formulated by mathematical formulae; the destiny of a culture which it realizes in its historical development is expressed by analogy. The structure of natural time is discovered by physics. The structure of historical time is such that two cultures at the "same" stage of development are to be regarded as contemporary. Thus, for example, the period of the oldest Upanishads in India, of the Orphic religion in Greece, and of Nicholas of Cusa (Cusanus) in Western culture are contemporary. Historical necessity is apprehended by recognizing through analogy the "spring," "summer," "autumn," and "winter" of a culture as it develops its inner essence, expressed by its "prime symbol." The "prime symbol" of the Greco-Roman culture is "the individual body" as the ideal type of the extended, whereas the prime symbol of Western or "Faustian" culture is "pure and infinite space." (See Vol. 1, Ch. III of *Der Untergang des Abendlandes,* Munich [1920]; *The Decline of the West,* 2 vols., New York [1926; 1928].)

Even a much fuller description of Spengler's vision of the necessary realization of the destinies of the various cultures would seem bizarre to some and profound to others. Some methodological remarks however seem in order. First, Spengler's theses are supposed to be intuitively clear so that whoever remains unconvinced can be accused of not having grasped them. Second, since so-called arguments by analogy lack cogency and have merely heuristic value, Spengler's exposition at best suggests a point of view which needs independent justification. Third, Spengler's intuitive understanding of historical development is an extreme, and thus much more vulnerable form of Dilthey's conception of historical understanding, since we are not merely asked to enter the minds of other human beings but the "mind" of a pseudo-organism called "a culture." Yet, if we consider Spengler from the point of view of the history of ideas we must admit that he is firmly rooted in a tradition to which Hegel, Vico, and even Augustine belong or have strong affinities.

A. J. Toynbee's philosophy of history is, as he acknowledges, very closely related to Spengler's although he developed his own ideas independently. He too holds the view of the "philosophical contemporaneity of all civilizations." (See Ch. I of *Civilization on Trial,* Oxford [1948], part of which is reprinted in *Theories of History,* ed. P. Gardiner, Glencoe, Ill. [1959].) But Toynbee rejects Spengler's historical determinism. The genesis, development, and death of civilizations takes the "form of challenge and response" and he sees no reason "why a succession of stimulating challenges should not be met with a succession of victorious responses *ad infinitum.*" But then he also sees no reason why it should be so met. It is a restatement rather than an explanation of the facts, to note that a challenge

does, or does not, elicit a successful response. Yet even if Toynbee's account of challenges and responses in different civilizations has less explanatory value than may perhaps appear at first sight, it may have heuristic value in directing the historian's mind to questions about whole civilizations as units of historical development and to a search for challenges and responses which can be meaningfully and fruitfully ascribed to a whole civilization. The heuristic value of this approach will depend on the historical knowledge and grasp of the historian who adopts it. Toynbee's own monumental *Study of History* in twelve volumes (London, 1934–61) must, as a contribution to history, be judged by other standards than those which have to be applied to his rather meager conception of historical development and necessity.

11. Recent Views. As a result of the rise of modern mathematical logic, recent philosophers of science were provided with new analytical tools which permitted a sharper analysis of the concept of necessity in the natural sciences and of the relation between natural and historical necessity. Though their accounts of the notion of natural necessity differ in many details, they agree in the following point: every fully-developed scientific theory can be expressed as an axiomatic system by adding to the logical and mathematical framework within which its reasoning proceeds, the substantive concepts and postulates of the theory. Thus classical mechanics is axiomatized by adding both the substantive concepts occurring in the three laws of motion and these laws themselves to the logical and mathematical concepts and postulates of classical logic and classical analysis (differential and integral calculus). Let s_1 be the description of a certain state of the universe in terms of the physical theory, and s_2 be the description of another such state. Then to say that the state described by s_1 necessitates s_2 is equivalent to saying that the state-description s_1 together with the substantive (i.e., non-logico-mathematical) axioms of the theory logically imply (by virtue of the underlying logical and mathematical theory) the state-description s_2. In some versions of this analysis, e.g., by K. R. Popper in *Die Logik der Forschung* (*The Logic of Enquiry,* 1935) s_1 and s_2 are regarded as straightforward descriptions of the physical universe, whereas in other versions s_1 and s_2 are regarded as idealizations of physical states which can only in certain contexts and for certain purposes be identified with descriptions (see Körner, 1967).

Some philosophers of science who accept the foregoing account of natural necessity deny its applicability to historical phenomena. Thus according to Popper predictions connecting s_1 and s_2 in the manner explained, presuppose that s_1 and s_2 describe states of systems which are "well-isolated, stationary and recurrent." But "these systems are very rare in nature; and modern society is surely not one of them" ("Prediction and Prophecy in the Social Sciences," in *Theories of History*, ed. Gardiner [1959]). Popper concludes that prediction of anything but the most trivial historical events is impossible. Carl Hempel, on the contrary, holds that historical prediction is substantially no different from scientific prediction.

Just as Vico objected to the application of Descartes' mechanistic philosophy to history, so some recent philosophers protest against regarding historical explanation as a species of scientific explanation. Like Vico they point to other types of activity such as artistic creation or simple storytelling as being more akin to explaining and predicting historical events than, for example, physics. Although admitting the possibility of sociology and anthropology conceived as natural sciences, they deny the reducibility of history to them. The problem of the relation between natural and historical necessity remains an open question.

BIBLIOGRAPHY

Fuller bibliographies are contained in F. Wagner's *Geschichtswissenschaft* (Freiburg, 1951), and P. Gardiner, ed., *Theories of History* (Glencoe, Ill., 1959).

H. B. Acton, *The Illusion of an Epoch* (London, 1955). I. Berlin, *Karl Marx*, 2nd ed. (London, 1948). H. T. Buckle, *History of Civilization in England*, 4 vols. (London, 1857–61). J. Burnet, *Early Greek Philosophy* (London, 1930). H. Butterfield, *The Origins of Modern Science* (London, 1950). I. B. Cohen, *The Birth of a New Physics* (London, 1961). B. Croce, *The Philosophy of Giambattisto Vico*, trans. R. G. Collingwood (New York, 1913). W. Dray, *Laws and Explanation in History* (Oxford, 1957). F. Engels, *Herrn Eugen Dührings Umwälzung der Wissenschaft* (Leipzig, 1878; Stuttgart, 1894), trans. as *Anti-Dühring: Herr Eugen Duhring's Revolution in Science* (New York, 1966). G. C. Field, *The Philosophy of Plato* (Oxford, 1949). J. N. Findlay, *Hegel: A Re-examination* (London, 1958). W. B. Gallie, *Philosophy and the Historical Understanding* (London, 1964). C. G. Hempel, *Aspects of Scientific Explanation . . .* (New York, 1965). S. Hook, *From Hegel to Marx* (London, 1936). S. Körner, *Experience and Theory* (London, 1967). A. Koyré, *Études galiléennes* (Paris, 1939). C. Lévi-Strauss, *Structural Anthropology*, trans. C. Jacobson and B. G. Schoepf (New York, 1963). K. Marx, *Das Kapital*, 2nd ed. (Hamburg, 1872), *Capital* various editions; idem, *Zur Kritik der politischen Oekonomie* (Berlin, 1859), trans. as *A Contribution to the Critique of Political Economy* (New York, 1970). H. J. Paton, *Kant's Metaphysic of Experience* (London, 1951). K. R. Popper, *Die Logik der Forschung* (Vienna, 1935), trans. as *The Logic of Scientific Discovery* by the author, with the assistance of Julius Freed and Lon Freed (London and Toronto, 1959); idem, *The Open Society and its Enemies* (London, 1945); idem, "Prediction and Prophecy in the Social Sciences," in *Theories of History*, ed. P. Gardiner (Glencoe, Ill., 1959). J. E. Raven, *Pythagoreans and Eleatics* (London, 1949). W. D. Ross, *Aristotle*, 5th ed. (London, 1949). A. Roux, *La pensée d'Auguste Comte* (Paris, 1920). N. K. Smith, *Studies in Cartesian Philosophy* (London, 1902); *The Philosophy of David Hume* (London, 1949). P. A. Sorokin, *Social Philosophy of an Age of Crisis* (Boston, 1950). O. Spengler, *Der Untergang des Abendlandes* (Munich, 1918), trans. as *The Decline of the West*, 2 vols. (New York, 1926–28). A. E. Taylor, *Platonism and its Influence* (London, 1932). A. Toynbee, *Civilization on Trial* (Oxford, 1948). Giambattista Vico, *Principi di una scienza nuova*, 1st ed. (Naples, 1725; repr. Bari, 1942), trans. T. Bergin and M. Fisch as *The New Science* (Ithaca, 1948). W. H. Walsh, *An Introduction to the Philosophy of History* (London, 1951). M. de Wulf, *History of Medieval Philosophy*, 3rd ed., trans. P. Coffey (London, 1935–38).

STEPHAN KÖRNER

[See also Axiomatization; Baconianism; Chance; Cycles; **Determinism;** Free Will; Hegelian . . . ; Metaphor in Philosophy; Nationalism; Newton on Method; Organicism; Platonism; Positivism; Progress; Romanticism.]

NEO-CLASSICISM IN ART

I

NEO-CLASSICISM dominated all the arts from about 1750 to about 1840, in architecture, painting, sculpture, and the decorative arts. The style embraced palaces and pottery, grand tombs and intimate portraits; it spread through Europe, and to Russia and the United States.

The word "neo-classical" seems to have been first applied to art in 1881, but not in the same sense as it is found nowadays. The term was first used, however, to describe literature in the time of Dryden and Pope by William Rushton, in *Afternoon Lectures on English Literature* (London [1863], pp. 44, 63, 72). The writer of a review of Old Master paintings in London's Royal Academy exhibition says of one work that "the neo-classic, if not the Italian, mode of design is finely illustrated." The passage, however, is not a comment on an eighteenth-century work but on a Poussin, *St. John on Patmos*. The writer continues by using such adjectives as "noble," "solemn," "austere," and in describing the figures in the composition he talks of "sculpture-like dignity" (*Athenaeum*, no. 2782 [1881]). Such epithets have been frequently applied since to eighteenth-century works which are now labelled neo-classical. The word appears in its present meaning by 1893 when it is noted in a newspaper review that "a man must be a scholar before he can make neo-classicism even tolerable in art" (*The Times* [6 May

1881], p. 17). From the 1920's onwards the word has been in regular use by art historians, and applied to eighteenth- and early nineteenth-century works of art; its meaning has been continually broadened in scope and depth. The result is a wide application of the term neo-classical about which there can now be no one, precise definition.

The term "neo-classical" appears easy to define. The prefix "neo" is used, as it has been commonly used from about 1860 onwards, with the Greek etymological meaning of a new form of some already existing—but possibly long dormant or dead—language, idea, or belief. In its most rudimentary definition neo-classicism thus denotes the renewed forms of classical art that were dominant in the second half of the eighteenth century and the earlier part of the nineteenth. Neo-classical art and architecture resulted from a serious archaeological outlook of the artist, architect, or designer, reacting against the excesses of the baroque and the extravagances of the rococo. Neo-classical artists used forms, details, and subject matter deriving from a wide range of classical antiquity, but with adaptations and alterations that the Greeks, Romans, Egyptians, and Etruscans would not have recognized. But such a definition does not specify which of the many varied aspects of classical art is being revived, how these aspects were interpreted, and what elements in the neo-classical style derive from other, nonclassical sources.

II

The eighteenth and early nineteenth centuries had a more limited knowledge of classical antiquity than is possible today. The great archaeological excavations in Asia Minor and Greece of such men as Heinrich Schliemann had not yet taken place. Not only had some of the now famous original Greek sculptures of the fifth and fourth centuries B.C. not been found, but also little was known of Greek art before the fifth century. Few sixth-century works were available. Nothing was known of Mycenean and Cycladic art: only a few examples became known as late as about 1820. The eighteenth century's firsthand knowledge was therefore confined to Roman art, and Roman copies of Greek originals. Such masterpieces as the original fifth-century friezes from the Parthenon and the Phigaleian temples appeared late in the development of neo-classicism. Although the former were known from a few copies, and from engravings published in the second volume of James Stuart and Nicholas Revett's *Antiquities of Athens* (1787), they did not create an artistic stir until brought to Britain by Lord Elgin in 1808, from whom they were in due course bought by the government for the British Museum. The Phi-

galeian Marbles were to be bought by the same government in 1814. Until these two sets of marbles were removed from Greece, all the countless eulogies of Phidias and his age were based on literary and on secondhand visual evidence (Figure 1).

This visual and literary evidence was considerable, forming a large body of material upon which artists and architects could draw. From the medieval period until the mid-nineteenth century, classical art and literature influenced the creativity of the contemporary European mind, at some times more strongly than at others. Neo-classicism thus belongs to the broad stream of classicism, constructing its own, identifiable version. In addition to the Renaissance, seventeenth-century, and early eighteenth-century literature available, the second half of the eighteenth century witnessed a rapid growth in archaeological publications and classical influence. The knowledge of classical antiquity had been most widely disseminated through gems and cameos, which had often played a more important role than statues and reliefs. Earlier important publications had included Pietro Santi Bartoli's *Admiranda Romanorum antiquitatum* (1685) on sculptural reliefs, Lorenz Beger's *Thesaurus Brandenburgicus selectus* (1696–1701) which had dealt primarily with gems and coins, and Baron Philip von Stosch's famous *Gemmae antiquae* (1724) which was concerned entirely with gems, engraved by Bernard Picart. The most ambitious survey of antique art, with long text and many engravings, was to be found in the folios of Bernard de Montfaucon's *L'Antiquité expliquée représentée en figures* (1719–24).

But unlike archaeological publications before the mid-eighteenth century, which were either without plates or generally inadequately illustrated with inaccurate engravings, those of the later eighteenth century were lavishly and usually accurately illustrated. The wealth of new architectural and archaeological evidence showed more clearly than ever before the diversity of styles in classical art. One of the most important publications of engravings of archaeological discoveries (other than architecture) was the series of folios published by the Accademia Ercolanese from 1755 onwards. The Herculaneum site produced a wealth of major and minor objects from elaborate illusionistic frescoes to simple oil lamps, which were illustrated in these volumes, and which could also be seen in the museum at Portici (subsequently transferred to the Museo Nazionale in Naples, where they still are). The enthusiasm with which artists expressed their feelings for this museum is summed up by one artist when he writes: "The moderns, with all their vapouring, have invented nothing, have improved nothing, not even in the most trifling articles of convenient household uten-

363

FIGURE 1. Great Hall, Syon House, Middlesex, England. Designed by Robert Adam in 1761. In foreground, eighteenth-century bronze copy of antique *Dying Gaul*, purchased in 1773. COURTESY OF DUKE OF NORTHUMBERLAND. PHOTOGRAPH COPYRIGHT *Country Life*, LONDON

sils. . . . Is there anything new in the world?" (James Barry, *Works*, London [1809], I, 110). The year following the publication of the folio containing the Herculaneum *Seller of Cupids*, the French painter Joseph-Marie Vien produced his version of the same subject, based fairly obviously on the engraving (1763, Musée National, Fontainebleau). This painting is one of the best known of the many transpositions of classical patterns into neo-classical works of art. Other important excavations apart from Herculaneum and Pompeii included Ostia, Tor Colombaro, Monte Cagnolo, Castel del Guido, and Gabii, as well as the prolific site of Hadrian's Villa at Tivoli. Among the leading excavators was the British painter and picture-dealer, Gavin Hamilton. Other leading dealers in antiquities were also British, namely James Byres and Thomas Jenkins.

Pioneer archaeologists in Greece itself and in the Middle East were also, very largely, British.

All these excavations contributed a wealth of classical sculptures, frescoes, and minor objects unknown to earlier centuries, providing the eighteenth century, and the neo-classicists in particular, with a quantity of firsthand visual evidence far in excess of that available to men of the Renaissance. The Vatican collections, established in that period, rapidly grew in size to become the most important in Europe. Other collections were expanded, and new ones formed. The young nobleman or gentleman of leisure on his Grand Tour through the continent and down to Italy, inevitably spent a long sojourn in Rome. There he bought Old Masters and classical sculptures and cameos to enrich or start his collection at home.

The predominance of ancient Roman art in these archaeological finds and in contemporary collections led to a more distorted view of classical art than that current today. As Greek art was seen through the intermediary of Roman copies, it was believed that all ancient sculptors generalized their anatomy and omitted facial features. Sir Joshua Reynolds expressed this eighteenth-century misconception when he said in one of his Royal Academy discourses that: "The face bears so very inconsiderable a proportion to the effect of the whole figure, that the ancient sculptors neglected to animate the features, even with the general expression of the passions" (Reynolds, p. 181). Such a description of antique sculpture characterizes much neo-classical art.

Ancient Greece, and to a larger extent Rome, provided the neo-classicists with the major part of their stylistic repertoire. Egypt also contributed its share. The Egyptian Revival in the eighteenth century was a sporadic one, seen at its best in Giambattista Piranesi's pyramids and sphinxes with which he decorated the walls of the English Coffee House in Rome (now lost, but known from Piranesi's engravings). Publications on Egypt, such as Norden's *Egypt* (1741), were few and not very influential. When Anton Raphael Mengs decorated the Sala dei Papiri in the Vatican he chose, logically, Egyptian motifs. However, the full impact of Egypt was not felt until after Napoleon's Egyptian campaign (1798–99). Although in terms of military history the venture was a disaster, archaeologically and artistically it was a triumph. The account and engravings which Baron Denon published, *Voyage dans la Basse et la Haute Égypte* (1802), helped to spread "Egyptomania" throughout Europe. Together with Greek and Roman forms and details, chairs became adorned with sphinxes, clock mounts were decorated with hieroglyphics and doorways designed as if entrances to Egyptian temples. Whereas the mid-eighteenth-century Egyptian Revival was largely confined to wall decoration, by about 1800 it was mainly found in architecture, furniture, and other aspects of the applied arts.

The full extent of neo-classical electicism is to be seen in the engravings in Thomas Hope's *Household Furniture* (1807), the most influential design book in Regency Britain. His Picture Gallery was based on architectural motifs seen in Athens. In the Drawing Room hung paintings of Indian Moorish architecture, under a ceiling based on that of a Turkish palace; the room devoted to Egyptian antiquities was decorated in this style. Most of the furniture throughout the house was Greek, Roman, or Egyptian in inspiration, often with appropriate iconographical details: the dining room sideboard was adorned with appropriate emblems of Bacchus and Ceres.

The development of neo-classicism witnessed both the emergence of an increasingly clear distinction between the characteristics of Greek and Roman art, and hostility between those who, on the one hand, favored Roman superiority and those who, on the other hand, favored Greek. The body of available information was such that a controversy was feasible in a way that it would not have been in previous centuries. The eighteenth century knew both the austerities of the Greek Doric order at Paestum as well as the Roman complexities of Diocletian's Palace at Split (this latter in a work published by Robert Adam in 1764). The neo-classical architects looked directly at antique patterns, unlike the classically inspired architects of the first half of the eighteenth century who looked at antiquity very largely through the eyes of Andrea Palladio.

The Scottish painter Allan Ramsay (not himself a neo-classical artist) helped to start the controversy of Greek versus Roman supremacy with his essay, *Dialogue on Taste* (1755), in which he argued that the canons of Greek art would never be overthrown "unless Europe should become a conquest of the Chinese." Another important advocacy of Greek supremacy is found in Julien David Le Roy's *Ruines des plus beaux monuments de la Grèce* (1758). Against such publications Piranesi launched his *Della magnificenza ed architettura de' Romani* (1761) and his *Parere sull' architettura* (1765), in which he championed the supremacy of Roman architecture and other arts, derived from their predecessors the Etruscans, and debased by the Greeks. Such archaeological nonsense was supported by Piranesi's excellent engravings, which in visual terms were important in promulgating the ornate rather than the austere aspects of antiquity. The time of Hadrian was the finest in antiquity for Piranesi,

and works from this period and their elaborate restorations are seen for example in his *Diverse maniere d'adornare i cammini* (1769) and his *Vasi, candelabri* . . . (1778). In actual interiors, Piranesi's taste is comparable to Robert Adam's decoration, and to some of the designs, later, of Charles Percier and Pierre-François Fontaine.

But the advocates of Greek supremacy had an ever-growing, important body of visual evidence with which to defend their case, and slowly the Greek gained precedence, finally emerging as the Greek Revival: a style which had widespread influence firstly in Europe and then, principally in the nineteenth century, throughout North America. Accurate architectural engravings in Stuart and Revett's *Antiquities of Athens* (1762 onwards), together with the growing interest in Greek temples in Sicily and at Paestum, and their reproduction in such works as Thomas Major's *Ruins of Paestum* (1768), made an increasingly accurate knowledge of the ancient Greek world possible. The isolated examples of Greek Revival architecture and design in the mid-eighteenth century eventually gained momentum. The Greek Doric temple by Stuart at Hagley (1758) and the furniture *à la grecque* made for Lalive de Jully, in the same decade, were to become in due course the rule rather than the exception. The swing towards a Greek taste was also much aided by the writings of Johann Joachim Winckelmann, whose scholarly approach made possible an assessment of Greek art in a way that such a book as George Turnbull's *Treatise on Ancient Painting* (1740) did not. Turnbull had had the presumption to compare the paintings of Raphael with those of Apelles, undeterred by the complete disappearance of the latter's original works.

III

Neo-classicism was generally serious; its architecture was not playful, its painting and sculpture not frivolous. It could be light (e.g., Robert Adam or Angelica Kauffmann) and occasionally erotic (e.g., Vien), but never as hedonistic as rococo or baroque. Architecture was dominated by the sobriety of antique forms; painting and sculpture by a classical morality, often Stoic. In the realm of theory, Shaftesbury had been an important precursor before Winckelmann in elucidating the connection between art and morals, a connection first made by Aristotle. It was argued that it was more important for a work of art to instruct than to delight the spectator. Instruction was nobler than pleasure; the mind ought to be satisfied in preference to the eye. Shaftesbury held this belief, as had Poussin before him. Aristotle in his *Poetics* had written:

"The reason of the delight in seeing the picture is that one is at the same time learning—gathering the meaning of things" (4, p. 29). Winckelmann and the neo-classicists inherited and developed this conviction. Winckelmann analyzed art and morality in the context of the antique; his great contemporary Denis Diderot discussed them more broadly as a general goal to which all arts should aim, namely the love of virtue and hatred of vice.

The painter Greuze came closer than any other artist to Diderot's ideal. Jean Baptiste Greuze interprets his contemporary scene of *The Wicked Boy Punished* (1778, Paris, Louvre) in a similar compositional manner to his earlier *Septimius Severus reproaching Caracalla* (1769, Paris, Louvre): in both a penitent, worthless son stands beside the bed of his father; Caracalla points reprimandingly, whereas the contemporary father has just died. With Greuze, and some of his neo-classical contemporaries, the work of art serves a didactic purpose, namely to teach a lesson in virtue. These lessons culminate in Jacques Louis David's canvases just before and during the French Revolution, starting with his famous *Oath of the Horatii* (1784–85, Paris, Louvre). The three brothers swear allegiance to Rome before going off to battle. David has invented a probable incident in classical history, inspired by plays of Corneille and Voltaire, and turned his theme into a great neo-classical statement of Republican virtue in ancient Rome. The painting was subsequently interpreted as foretelling Revolutionary struggles in contemporary France, and the gestures of allegiance were reenacted in 1794 at a Republican demonstration organized by the artist together with Robespierre. A similar idealistic and moral theme was chosen by David in 1789 in his *Lictors returning to Brutus the Bodies of his Sons* (two versions: Louvre, Paris, and Wadsworth Athenaeum, Hartford, Conn.). Here the theme is more austerely Stoical, as the father has condemned his own sons to death because of their rebellion against him (Figure 2). This example from Roman history of a father's feelings giving precedence to the state's welfare had direct relevance to contemporary French political history, and was interpreted as such at the time. With these paintings by David, French neo-classicism during the Revolution attains a character unique in Europe; nowhere else is there such a fusion between ancient history, contemporary politics and philosophy, and the forms of classical art.

IV

With the notable exception of a few great, progressive architects of form and space, such as Claude Nicolas Ledoux, Étienne-Louis Boullée, and John Soane, the neo-classical style was up to about 1800 essentially one of surface decoration in architecture and in the applied arts. This characteristic was paralleled by a concentration on outline or contour in painting, the graphic arts, and sculpture. While architects looked to the elaborate surface ornamentations of late Roman architecture, including that on the periphery of the Empire (for example, Robert Adam's interest in Palmyra), the painters and sculptors looked at Roman bas-reliefs and particularly at painted Greek vases.

Only a very few Greek—or as they were then erroneously called, Etruscan—vases were known and collected before the eighteenth century. The most important collections put together in the eighteenth century were the two formed by Sir William Hamilton, British plenipotentiary at the Court of Naples. Both collections were lavishly illustrated in folios, the first publication (1766–67) having handsome colored engravings. Soon afterwards Hamilton had to sell his vases to the newly established British Museum to recoup the heavy cost of publication. In the second series of volumes (1791–95) the illustrations were uncolored. The set contained a preface by Hamilton in which he eulogized upon these vases, saying they provided the most important antique pattern available to the modern artist. The line drawings influenced the drawing and compositional style of many artists; their subject matter was freely plundered, and the shapes as well as decorations were crucial to such enterprising businessmen as Josiah Wedgwood, who supplied the fashionable market with chinaware in classical taste. The linear qualities of the painted decoration on these vases, chiefly of the fifth and fourth centuries B.C., had considerable influence on the development of the neo-classical style. The vases intensified the interest already being shown in the two-dimensional qualities of Roman sculptural bas-reliefs. At its most austere, neo-classical art consists only of outline with no modelling or spatial depth; even in more fully modelled paintings and friezes the action is contained within a narrow shelf-like space. Movement is clearly articulated across the surface plane, diametrically opposed to the spatial complexities in depth of the baroque.

The basic tenets of neo-classical theory, including this emphasis on outline, are embodied in the widely read writings of the German scholar Johann Joachim Winckelmann. As librarian to Cardinal Albani in Rome, and also in charge of his antiquities (Albani was one of the leading eighteenth-century collectors in Europe), Winckelmann was one of the principal figures in circles interested in classical antiquity in the city. His first influential essay was written before he arrived in Italy: his *Gedanken über die Nachahmung der Griechischen Werke* (1755) had been inspired mainly by the few pieces of classical sculpture in the royal

FIGURE 2. Jacques Louis David, *Lictors returning to Brutus the Bodies of his Sons.* Salon of 1789. LOUVRE, PARIS. PHOTOGRAPHIE GIRAUDON

collection in Dresden. To this visual evidence, together with gems, he added his wide knowledge of classical literature, and pronounced, in an often-quoted sentence:

The last and most eminent characteristic of the Greek works is a noble simplicity and sedate grandeur beneath the strife and passions in Greek figures (Winckelmann [1765], p. 30).

The fact that he had not seen an original Greek work did not for him, or for his contemporaries, undermine the validity of his argument. To the qualities of simplicity and grandeur, Winckelmann added idealization and stress on outline: for him they summarized the best period in art, namely that of Greece during the fifth-century B.C.

All Winckelmann's subsequent writings are, essentially, an elaboration of his thesis in the 1755 essay. His outstanding publication was the important *Geschichte der Kunst des Alterthums* (1764), in which his classification and dating of ancient art is a major contribution to the language of modern archaeology. His history was an important addition to the already existing large body of literature on the subject, which had tended not to treat ancient art chronologically, but to be either very unscientific, or to group material together according to subject matter and themes. The thematic treatment had been that favored by Montfaucon in his *L'Antiquité expliquée,* still in use in the second half of the eighteenth century. Winckelmann's

other publications included a catalogue of the antique gems owned by Baron Stosch (1760), two essays on ancient architecture (1759 and 1762), studies of the excavations at Herculaneum (1762 and 1764), an attempt at an up-to-date, complete iconography in his *Allegorie* (1766), and two volumes of *Monumenti Antichi Inediti* (1767), his only work to be illustrated in his own lifetime by many fine engravings.

Winckelmann used his scholarship as a tool in the construction of a theory. He argued that a modern artist could become great only by imitating the works of classical Greece, thus acquiring a more perfect knowledge of beauty than was possible by studying nature itself. "The Greeks alone," wrote Winckelmann ecstatically, "seem to have thrown forth beauty as a potter makes his pot" (Winckelmann [1765], p. 264). By imitating the ancients Winckelmann did not mean servile copying, a fault for which he has often been erroneously blamed. Winckelmann meant (as had such theorists before him as Shaftesbury and Jonathan Richardson who had influenced him), that only by imitating the ancients could ideal beauty be discovered, and when discovered should be conveyed in the spirit of the original. Properly understood, therefore, Winckelmann's writings had a very constructive influence on the eighteenth century's interpretation of the antique, and in particular the way in which neo-classical artists looked at their source material.

Winckelmann's theories did, nevertheless, contain

367

flaws and inconsistencies. His descriptions are sometimes highly charged with subjectivity. He was able to write of the *Apollo Belvedere* (in a manner that also reveals his homosexuality):

An eternal spring . . . plays with softness and tenderness about the proud shape of his limbs. . . . Neither bloodvessels nor sinews heat and stir his body, but a heavenly essence, diffusing itself like a gentle stream, seems to fill the whole contour of the figure (Winckelmann [1880], II, 313).

Winckelmann's most fundamental flaw was his divorce of energy and vitality from simplicity and grandeur. His admiration is reserved essentially for those works which convey the spirit of the fifth century B.C., not the "baroque" works of the second and first centuries B.C.: yet he is able to admire the *Laocoön*. There is a dichotomy in his writings between calmness on the one hand and emotion on the other, and a similar dichotomy is found in neo-classical art. Although Winckelmann tried to argue that Laocoön's anguish was restrained, this great sculptural group does not conveniently fit into a theory that was primarily conceived in terms of the *Apollo Belvedere*. Generally in neo-classical paintings and sculpture, gestures and emotions are restrained. Bacchanalian scenes are not exuberant in a Rubensian sense, but are held in check. If Hector is being mourned, Andromache does not show her tears. Even in a scene as potentially violent as that in which the angry Achilles drags the dead body of Hector around the walls of Troy, in full view of the Trojans, artists tended to minimize Achilles' arrogant and rash gesture, and portray few if any horrified spectators.

V

The neo-classical conception of the creation of a work of art is fundamentally that of Renaissance and seventeenth-century idealization, overlaid with an even greater emphasis on antique models. Perfect beauty was not to be found in nature: a servile copying of nature, it was argued, merely led down to the debased still lifes of seventeenth-century Holland. The upward path to higher genres of painting, with history-painting occupying the peak, was attainable only by improving nature's "imperfections," "ugliness," and "disproportions" (words frequently found in idealist theories). Art should create a superior beauty by reflecting on nature, and improve it, just as "bees collect honey from bitter plants" (a metaphor used by André Félibien, author of *Entretiens sur les vies et les ouvrages des plus excellents peintres anciens et modernes* [1666–88], in his tenth *Entretien*, subsequently used by Winckelmann and others). The idealists were familiar with the example of the ancient Greek painter Zeuxis, who selected five women from whose various beauties he could blend his perfect image of Helen. The particular and accidental were eliminated so that a generalized, idealized beauty might be attained.

Anton Raphael Mengs's writings are often cited as an important influence on the development of neo-classicism, but he did not add to Winckelmann's ideas and few pages are devoted to antiquity. In Mengs's best-known work, *Gedanken über die Schönheit und den Geschmack in der Malerei* (1762) he merely elaborates the seventeenth-century concept of "idea," finding true beauty in God. The neo-Platonic element in his ideas may have influenced his friend Winckelmann. Mengs is really more of a neo-classicist in some of his paintings.

The seventeenth-century French and Italian academic tenet of "decorum" remained a dominant factor in the following century, greatly aided by increased archaeological knowledge. Decorum meant the accurate rendering of historical settings and details from architecture to costume and furniture. Nicolas Poussin had expressed concern in a letter for the correct form of pyramids and landscape which he regarded as essential in the background of a painting of the flight into Egypt. The eighteenth-century neo-classicists were to be just as particular on such points. If Hector is saying farewell to Andromache, or the victors at Olympia are being crowned, painters might place Doric temples prominently in the background. Germanicus on his death bed or Hannibal taking his oath are surrounded by correctly draped figures, with helmets, shields, ewers, and statues all indicating knowledge—often firsthand—of antique prototypes. Even when the subject matter was not classical, but medieval, artists would turn to tomb sculpture, stained glass, and seals for their accurate source material.

In painting, so strong was the influence of Poussin on certain neo-classical artists in the 1760's and the 1770's, that an alternative stylistic term has been suggested, namely "Neo-Poussinism." Some of the earliest neo-classical painters distilled their view of antiquity partially through the intermediaries of Raphael and Poussin. Winckelmann said that Raphael was the ideal modern artist to imitate, and Poussin is admired in Winckelmann's letters. Diderot, too, recommended following Poussin's example as an interpreter of classical moral themes. A key early neo-classical work such as Mengs's *Parnassus* (1761, Villa Albani, now Torlonia, Rome) owes much of its inspiration to Raphael and to Poussin. Benjamin West's *Judgement of Hercules* (1764, Victoria and Albert Museum, London) derives directly from Poussin's painting of the same subject. Neo-classical works have a homogeneity of style that makes them as recognizably individual as works of any other style, but underneath this unity lies much disparity. Neo-classicism has often been interpreted, for instance, as a strong reaction against the rococo, but there are rococo elements in early neo-classical works. Neo-classicism has been seen as a counter force to Romanticism, but it can with more validity be interpreted as an early part of the Romantic movement itself. Neo-classicism has been called an embodiment of frigidity, but the style is equally imbued with sentiment and emotion. These, and other, apparently contradictory strands within the one style, make it more complex than the name neo-classicism implies.

In the broad context of the history of art a new style has often been seen as a reaction to the immediately preceding one, and this assessment has been encouraged by the writings of artists themselves. Neo-classicism is no exception. It is easy to interpret its austere and uncompromising aspects as the very antithesis of the elegant and frivolous sides of rococo. But detailed analysis generally reveals the initial reaction to have been exaggerated. The leading neo-classical sculptor of Europe, Antonio Canova, started to carve in a style reminiscent of rococo, gradually emerging as a neo-classicist. Other prominent sculptors such as John Flaxman and Étienne-Maurice Falconet show a comparable development. In painting, the early works of artists as varied as Mengs, Pompeo Girolamo Batoni, Vien, Angelica Kauffmann, Benjamin West, and Gavin Hamilton, reveal rococo tendencies derived from François Boucher and his contemporaries. The intricate surface patterns created by Robert Adam on his ceilings and walls grow out of his youthful rococo works. His Etruscan Room at Osterley Park, although ostensibly recreating motifs from so-called Etruscan vases, employs a compositional arrangement of scrolls reminiscent of rococo interiors.

The word "simplicity" often occurs in neo-classical artists' writings, signifying an outstanding merit to be found in certain periods of art of the past. It occurs as a partial explanation of the neo-classicists' own aims. Simplicity is never precisely defined. However, it tends not to be used of the periods from the High Renaissance onwards, with the exception of its application to Poussin and similar seventeenth-century classicists. The tortuous characteristics of mannerist, baroque, and rococo art were generally, but not consistently, anathema to the neo-classicists. Simplicity embraced both the idealization of Phidias, thirteenth-century tombs in medieval churches, and the elemental quality of Giotto's frescoes. The neo-classicists sought characteristics of economy and precision in the art of the past, but it was a very selective search. Before the Nazarenes and the Pre-Raphaelites, the neo-classicists, in both their art and their writings, were the first group really to rediscover the merits of medieval art, as well as that of the fourteenth and fifteenth centuries in Italy. This admiration for what used to be called the "Primitives" did not extend as far back as Romanesque art and architecture, or to Greek vases of the sixth century B.C.: such art would have been regarded as too crude in an eighteenth-century canon. The Romanesque Revival only came in the mid-nineteenth century. Simplicity was therefore regarded as a reduction to essentials, a purification of all that was "wicked" in post-Raphael art (to use Shaftesbury's neat dismissal of Gian Lorenzo Bernini). The absolute reduction to simplicity in neo-classical works appears at its clearest in outline drawings and engravings, and in the designs of such architects as Friedrich Gilly and Étienne-Louis Boullée. Simplicity, as a somewhat less evident stylistic characteristic, appears in such neo-classical traits as a shelf-like space and the removal of distracting details not essential to the subject matter portrayed.

VI

Although the eighteenth-century Gothic Revival, which was largely confined to Britain and Germany, produced an interest in Gothic architecture and art, this interest was a limited one. The eighteenth century inherited the previous century's academic conviction that Gothic art did not merit serious consideration in its own right, and was certainly inferior when compared to the classical past of Greece and Rome. Charles-Alphonse Dufresnoy had discussed the inadequacy of paintings constantly changed in design through lack of careful preplanning, by comparing them to "those old Gothic castles, made at several times, and which hold together only as it were by rags and patches" (De arte graphica, trans. John Dryden, London [1695], p. 113). One of the important neo-classical contributions to contemporary taste was to reverse this unjust dismissal of the Middle Ages. At the same time some of the neo-classical artists and architects produced a unique fusion of classical with Gothic forms.

In architecture the blending of Gothic with classical was at its most superficial when decorative motifs from the two sources were mixed together in surface decoration. A more fundamental and original understanding of Gothic structure was shown by such neo-classical architects as Jacques-Germain Soufflot, Boullée, Ledoux, and Karl Friedrich Schinkel who combined principles of form and space from the two vocabularies. Soufflot in the interior of his Sainte Geneviève (Panthéon) in Paris (1757) is completely Roman in his vaults, entablatures, capitals, and columns, and in all 369 the decorative details, but the overall spatial concept of the plan, with its transepts and diagonal vistas between columns, is that of a Gothic cathedral. Roman detailing and classical regularity were fused, as the architect himself wrote, with Gothic architectural "lightness."

In neo-classical painting and sculpture the fusion is of a different character, leading to a reassessment of medieval art, and to stylistic characteristics unique to neo-classicism. The typical early eighteenth-century attitude towards Giotto is shown in Jonathan Richardson's comment: "That degree of vigour that served to produce a Dante in writing could rise no higher than a Giotto in painting" (1792, p. 255). The neo-classicists not only produced some fine interpretations of Dante (e.g., Flaxman), but also admired Giotto and many of his contemporaries, as well as the then equally scorned and ignored fifteenth-century Renaissance works of Lorenzo Ghiberti, Fra Angelico, and other artists. The neo-classicists' attitude towards the Middle Ages and early Renaissance was an original contribution to the development of eighteenth-century taste and ideas, more individual than their attitude

towards the antique, towards idealization, and towards other concepts which largely derive from the preceding century. Drawings and sketchbooks by such artists as Flaxman, Canova, and J. A. D. Ingres show copies of Gothic and early Renaissance works. In stylistic terms the classical-gothic synthesis characterizes some of the linear designs of such artists as J. A. Koch, Flaxman, and William Blake. Perugino was much admired by David, who compared the purity of his art and that of other "primitives" of the fifteenth century to similar qualities he found in the art of Polygnotus, a Greek painter of the fifth century B.C.

The neo-classical concern for pre-High Renaissance art represented a quest for fundamental principles of art which had become overlaid and obscured by subsequent developments. The outlook was essentially retrogressive, in a desire to regenerate contemporary art: an outlook expressed at its most extreme by the group of David's pupils self-styled "The Primitives." They dismissed all art of the past except Greek vases and the earliest of antique sculptures, all architecture except the Greek Doric temples of Paestum and Sicily, and all literature except the Bible, Homer, and Ossian. Other artists were not quite so uncompromisingly exclusive.

VII

In one of the posthumous assessments of Canova's work, a contemporary sculptor perceptively noted that "we sometimes seek in vain for the severe chastity of Grecian art" (Flaxman). Greek and Roman principles are indeed difficult to find in some neo-classical works, especially when imbued with the most eighteenth-century of characteristics, sensibility. The cult of sensibility is revealed in the whole pose and facial expression of the classical Muse who leans on the sarcophagus of Alfieri (Figure 3) in Santa Croce, Florence (by Canova, 1810), as well as in the face of the charming figure of the child, Penelope Boothby, reclining on her sarcophagus in Ashbourne Church in Derbyshire, England (by Thomas Banks, 1793). When Canova recreated the *Medici Venus* because it had been taken to Paris as part of the Napoleonic plunder, his marble was imbued with more grace and sentiment than the prototype (1812, Palazzo Pitti, Florence). In neo-classical paintings, Cupid and Psyche are liable to show more sensibility in their relationship than their classical precursors would have admitted. Tombs, and paintings of death, show in particular neo-classical sensibility. Skeletons are banished, anguished baroque death pangs disappear and are replaced by single, pious scenes in which death is an equation of sleep: tranquillity and sensibility reign. Such simple neo-classical statements of death, often devoid of transcendental allusions,

FIGURE 3. Antonio Canova, *Vittorio Alfieri Monument.* 1810. SANTA CROCE, FLORENCE. PHOTO ALINARI-ART REFERENCE BUREAU

paved the way for the masterpiece, the secular pietà by David of the *Death of Marat* (1793, Brussels, Musées Royaux des Beaux-Arts).

Antique art and its principles, concepts of idea and decorum, and other seventeenth-century academic attitudes, indicate clearly that neo-classical art was governed by reason. But such rational ideals embraced, as did the Age of Reason itself, the concept of sentiment. The literature and art of the period also included extremes of emotion, terror, and horror: the period saw the birth of the "Gothick" novel, for instance. It is therefore not surprising to find these contradictory elements within neo-classicism itself. William Blake is a good instance of this inherent contradiction. In his early drawings he is a neo-classicist; neo-classical elements occur, inconsistently, throughout his art, but he is very ambivalent in his attitude towards classical antiquity and could describe himself as a "Mental Prince."

The rule of Imagination, so apparently contradictory to that of Reason, is an equally important characteristic of the eighteenth century. Flaxman's portrayal of the demented rage in his *Fury of Athamas* (1790–93, Ickworth), in which mad Athamas dashes one of his sons onto the rocks whilst his wife Ino clings pleading, takes its violent pose and heavy musculature (of Athamas' body) from the *Laocoön* and the *Torso Belvedere*. The violence of emotion in such a neo-classical marble is exactly comparable to that of Canova's large *Heracles and Lycas* (1796, Galleria Nazionale d'Arte Moderna, Rome). Henry Fuseli, whose subject matter was chosen widely from classical and post-classical history and literature, showed a marked preference for fantasy and terror, a characteristic which he shared with members of William Blake's circle. From classical antiquity Fuseli extracted from Plutarch such a subject as *Dion seeing a Female Spectre sweep his Hall* (etching). Other elements of the supernatural appear in neo-classical works, drawn from Dante, Shakespeare, and Milton. Flaxman's outline engravings of the *Divine Comedy* (before 1799, possibly 1793) were regarded at the time as an outstanding series of plates, and were praised by Goethe for being both "spirited" and "calm": the conflict between these adjectives is symptomatic of the complexities of the neo-classical style. For such reasons neo-classicism has even been called not a style but a "coloration" (Giedion, p. 9).

BIBLIOGRAPHY

For general discussions see R. Rosenblum, *Transformations in Late Eighteenth Century Art* (Princeton, 1967); H. Honour, *Neoclassicism* (Harmondsworth, 1968); C. Justi, *Winckelmann und seine Zeitgenossen*, 5th ed. (Cologne, 1956; first ed. 1866–72); and R. Zeitler, *Klassizismus und Utopia* (Stockholm, 1954). S. Giedion, *Spätbarocker und romantischer Klassizismus* (Munich, 1922), a pioneer book, is still to be read with profit. See also M. Praz, *Gusto neoclassico* (Rome, 1940), trans. as *On Neoclassicism* (London, 1969); J. A. Leith, *The Idea of Art as Propaganda in France 1750–99* (Toronto, 1965); D. Irwin, *Winckelmann: Writings on Art* (London and New York, 1972); L. Bertrand, *La Fin du classicisme et le retour à l'antique* (Paris, 1897); and L. Hautecoeur, *Rome et la Renaissance de l'antiquité à la fin du XVIIIe siècle* (Paris, 1912).

Painting and sculpture are covered by the following: E. L. Delécluze, *Louis David, son école et son temps* (Paris, 1855); J. Locquin, *La Peinture d'histoire en France de 1747 à 1785* (Paris, 1912); D. Irwin, *English Neoclassical Art* (London and Greenwich, Conn., 1966); M. D. Whinney, *Sculpture in Britain 1530–1830* (Harmondsworth, 1964).

Architecture, partially discussed in some of the above items, is best covered by E. Kaufmann, *Architecture in the Age of Reason* (Cambridge, Mass., 1955); L. Hautecoeur, *Histoire de l'architecture classique en France*, 7 vols. in 8 (Paris, 1943–57), Vols. IV and V; J. Summerson, *Architecture in Britain 1530–1830*, 4th ed. (Harmondsworth, 1963); L. V. Meeks. *Italian Architecture 1750–1914* (New Haven, 1966); and Talbot Hamlin, *Greek Revival Architecture in America* (New York, 1944; also reprint).

References have also been made to the following: Aristotle, *Poetics*, trans. Gilbert Murray (Oxford, 1920), 4, p. 29; Sir Joshua Reynolds, Discourse X (1780), *Discourses*, ed. R. Wark (San Marino, Calif., 1959), p. 181; Jonathan Richardson, "Science of a Connoisseur" (1719), *Works* (London, 1792), p. 255; J. J. Winckelmann, "On the Imitation of the Painting and Sculpture of the Greeks," *Reflections on the Painting and Sculpture of the Greeks*, trans. Henry Fuseli (London, 1765), pp. 30, 264; idem, *History of Ancient Art*, trans. G. H. Lodge (Boston, 1880), II, 313.

DAVID IRWIN

[See also **Art and Play;** Classicism in Literature; **Classification of the Arts;** Gothic; **Periodization;** Renaissance; Romanticism; Stoicism.]

NEO-PLATONISM

I

NEO-PLATONISM is the term used by modern scholars to describe the final form taken by the revived Platonism of the Roman Empire. This was the dominant philosophy in the Greco-Roman world from about the end of the third century A.D. to the end of the public teaching of Greek philosophy by pagans in the sixth century A.D. Neo-Platonism had a deep influence on Arabic and Jewish thought, and on Christian thought from the later patristic period till the seventeenth century, and in some cases even till our own times.

The philosophers whom we call Neo-Platonists would not have been pleased with the name. They spoke and thought of themselves simply as Platonists, and believed that their philosophy was an authentic exposition of the ancient masters, Pythagoras and Plato. In their way of thinking the oldest philosophy was the truest. And there was much more continuity in the development of the revived Platonism of the Empire than the rather artificial modern division into Middle Platonism and Neo-Platonism would suggest, and its earlier forms had more continuing influence than is sometimes realized. But nonetheless the philosophy of Plotinus (third century), the first and greatest of the Neo-Platonists, and his successors, is so original and distinctive and has been so deeply and widely influential, that it deserves separate treatment and special attention.

1. As has already been said, Neo-Platonism was the final stage of a continuous development of Platonism. This began with the revival of dogmatic teaching in Plato's school, the Academy, after a skeptical and critical phase which lasted for some two centuries, by Antiochus of Ascalon who was head of the Academy at Athens in 79–78 B.C., when Cicero heard some lectures by him. This revived dogmatic Platonism, of which the general features begin to become clear to us in the first century A.D., was in fact based on a highly selective reading of Plato and on interpretations of his thought which were current among his immediate successors in the Old Academy, before the skeptical period. There was some Stoic influence, though the school carried on a continual polemic against the Stoics, which is very apparent in the writings of Plotinus. Some Platonists also were deeply influenced by the thought of Aristotle, though others (notably Atticus in the second half of the second century A.D.) were strongly anti-Aristotelian. Plotinus, though some aspects of his thought show clearly Aristotelian influence, spends a great deal of time criticizing Aristotle, often very acutely. The revival of Pythagoreanism which seems to have begun at about the same time as the revival of dogmatic Platonism in the first century B.C. contributed a good deal to the development of Neo-Platonism, and especially to its most distinctive doctrine, that of the transcendent One, the source of all reality. There was already a strong Pythagorean element in the thought of Plato himself, and still more in that of his pupils and immediate successors, Speusippus and Xenocrates, and post-Platonic Pythagoreanism was deeply influenced by the later thought of Plato. Thus it was natural that the two schools under the Empire should develop with a great deal of mutual influence and interaction.

The "Middle" Platonists of the period from the late first century A.D. to the early third century were a very varied group, showing widely differing degrees of philosophical knowledge and intelligence. But their thought has enough unity to make possible some general statements about it which will be sufficient to show how it led up to the Neo-Platonism of Plotinus and his successors, and why it had a considerable and persistent influence on contemporary Jewish and Christian thought, although it must be remembered that these large generalizations conceal considerable divergences and inconsistencies. The Middle Platonists were, much more clearly and unmistakably than Plato, monotheists in the sense of believing in a single supreme being, the highest divine Intelligence. They quite often use *Theos* ("God") as a proper name for this supreme being in a way which sounds familiar to those brought up in the Judeo-Christian tradition, but is not in accordance with earlier Greek usage; they of course recognize the existence of many other *theoi* and *daimones*, gods and spirits subordinate to and dependent on the supreme Intelligence. An important distinction made by some of them is that between the supreme Intelligence or God and a Second Intelligence or God inferior to and dependent on the First. In the Neo-Pythagorean Numenius, who in some ways anticipated Plotinus, the First God is purely contemplative and it is the Second who is active in forming and directing the world. His Third God is the World-Soul (all Platonists, following the *Timaeus*, believed that the physical world was an ensouled living being). The Platonic Forms or Ideas are conceived by most Middle Platonists as the thoughts of the supreme God. Their eternal existence is in his mind, and they are often thought of as the plan or pattern on which he makes the world (again an interpretation of the *Timaeus*). This extremely important development goes back at least to before Philo Judaeus (an older contemporary of Saint Paul), but its origins, in spite of much modern speculation, remain obscure. The transcendence of the supreme God is very much stressed, and sometimes there are already traces of the "negative theology," which Plotinus and the later Neo-Platonists developed so fully, in which God is said to be "not this," "not that," to indicate how he is completely other and better than anything we can think or imagine. In the thought of some Neo-Pythagoreans the first principle is already the transcendent One, which became of such great importance in Neo-Platonism. But though the supreme God is the transcendent head of the hierarchy of spiritual being, the Middle Platonists do not always think of him as extremely remote. In Plutarch and Atticus there is a good deal of simple straightforward piety, an affectionate insistence on God's goodness and providential care for men.

When they turn from God and the divine hierarchy to the world and man the Middle Platonists tend to be dualists in two different senses. Their attempted solutions of the problem of evil are in most cases dualistic; evil is due either to the disturbing and polluting influence of a preexisting matter, coeternal with and not created by God, or to an evil soul, again a coeternal independent principle. Their conception of man is dualistic in a different sense, following and developing Plato's doctrine in the *Phaedo*. Man is a spirit, godlike by the possession of intelligence, temporarily resident in and using an earthly body (or a series of earthly bodies) and he can only attain true happiness by escaping from this lower world and returning after purification to his true home in the divine world. The austere (though not inhumanly ascetic) morality which they taught, which derived ultimately from Plato and was often strongly influenced by Stoicism, fitted well with this dualistic view of human nature. But the mention of Stoicism should remind us that in later Greek philosophy asceticism and moral austerity are not necessarily bound up with otherworldliness. The austere Stoics were generally agnostic about a future life, and their God was the wholly immanent principle of life and order in the physical universe: their intense religion and rigorous morality were generally wholly this-worldly. And even the Epicureans, with their dogmatic disbelief in life after death and divine intervention in the world, were austere and even ascetic in their view of how man should live to secure lasting happiness.

2. But though the deepening and intensification of religious concern and the austere morality which are characteristic of Greek philosophy in the first centuries of the Christian era were not necessarily otherworldly, they became more so as time went on, and in the form of philosophy which finally became dominant, Neo-Platonism, the whole object of the good and wise man was to return in spirit to the divine intelligible world to which he really belonged, a world immeasurably superior to that perceived by the senses. The question is therefore worth asking whether and in what sense this intensely religious and otherworldly philosophy was the result of a reaction from the extremely insecure and unpleasant conditions of the society in which it developed, i.e., the society of the later Roman Empire from the end of the second century A.D. onwards, the period which E. R. Dodds calls the "Age of Anxiety." There can be little doubt that the misery and insecurity of this period account to some extent for the way in which religious concerns and activities become more and more important as it goes on, and the best and most serious minds turn away from a hopeless world to the quest for God. It is true that almost everything

which is worth reading in the age from Plotinus to Justinian, and beyond, is centered in some way on the quest for God and written by deeply religious men. But we must not exaggerate the otherworldliness of the period. This world as a whole was by no means ultra-spiritual and most men in it, from emperors to peasants, were much interested in the well-being of their bodies and the accumulation (if they had the chance) of very tangible possessions. Even the religion of most of them, pagans or Christians, was directed to a great extent to securing by divine favor very this-worldly and material ends. The genuinely otherworldly people, then as in most other periods, were a very small minority, and this is particularly true of Neo-Platonists. The description given by Porphyry, the editor and biographer of Plotinus, of the circle of his master at Rome, suggests that the circle was a small and exclusive one: and no later Neo-Platonist attracted any sort of mass following. The Neo-Platonic paganism of the Emperor Julian was not attractive to the mass of his subjects, though comparatively few of them, probably, were very fervent Christians. Nor were the people who turned most enthusiastically to otherworldly philosophical or nonphilosophical religion necessarily or normally those who suffered most from the insecurity, injustice, and cruelty of the late Roman world. Plotinus found his following among the aristocracy of Rome, as later did Saint Jerome; and though most of the Christian ascetics in Egypt and Syria were no doubt peasants, many came from the comfortable classes. Further, if we are not to be grossly unfair to these otherworldly religious men, we must remember that neither Plotinus and other Neo-Platonists nor the great Christian otherworldly ascetics who became bishops, like Saint Basil and Saint Augustine, neglected their duty to their fellow men in this world or thought that it should be neglected. Care for widows and orphans and the poor and the practice of common honesty, decency, and humanity in personal relationships were by no means absent from these small otherworldly circles. But no man of the later Roman Empire ever seems to have thought that anything could be done to change or improve radically the in many ways horrible society in which he lived, though he might do what he could to help its victims. And this sense of powerlessness, this resignation to or disgust with an almost intolerable world, probably had a good deal to do with the turning of the best minds of the age to an interior religious quest, though it cannot be the whole explanation.

II.

1. In the third century A.D. one of the greatest of Greek philosophers, Plotinus, gathered together the speculations of his Middle Platonist and Neo-Pythagorean predecessors and made them into a far stronger, more attractive, and influential philosophy by thinking through them again, correcting and developing them under the pressure of his own living experience of discovery of the divine intelligible world and its transcendent source. The ideas which have been mentioned in the account of Middle Platonism above, of the One beyond being, of the Forms in the Divine Mind, of the universe given life and direction by divine Soul, and of man as an intelligent spirit temporarily resident in an earthly body, whose whole object is to find his way back to the divine world to which he belongs, are presented with a new depth, power, and mutual coherence in the thought of Plotinus. This is the real beginning of Neo-Platonism. Plotinus of course did not think that he was producing a new philosophy but that he was giving the authentic interpretation, with some explication and development where necessary, of the thought of Plato, and so expounding the one true philosophy, whose truth was confirmed both by its evident reasonableness and by ancient authority. Contributing to the Neo-Platonism of Plotinus were—besides Plato (read very selectively) and the Platonist and Neo-Pythagorean commentators on his thought—a constructively critical consideration of Aristotle and his Peripatetic commentators and an influence, deep at some points, of Stoic ideas which Plotinus' conscious and frequently expressed hostility to Stoic corporealism could not overcome. That he was the real founder of Neo-Platonism does not mean that he was regarded by later Neo-Platonists as the supreme philosophical authority. His influence in the Platonic school was deep and decisive. But he was a somewhat isolated figure in the philosophical world of his time, and the Neo-Platonists of later generations never thought of him as the second founder or reformer of the school or hesitated to disagree with him, even on important points, if they thought fit. If his devoted disciple and editor, Porphyry, had not published the great edition of his master's works which we know as the *Enneads* it is possible that Plotinus would have before very long been almost completely forgotten. But the *Enneads* were published and read, and they imposed a distinctive metaphysical pattern on post-Plotinian Platonism which persisted through all later elaborations and variations.

2. Philosophy for Plotinus is, even more than for his predecessors, a way of life, requiring not only an intense intellectual but also an intense moral effort. It is a procedure for discovering who we really are, which eventually carries us beyond our true selves to their origin. In our philosophizing, if it is genuine, we become aware of ourselves as having, beyond ordinary human experience, an eternal existence in a divine world of living intelligence, and we are able to share in the everlasting return of that divine whole to unity with its origin, the One or Good. The fact that Plotinus sees philosophy in this way—as a process of self-discovery and growing awareness of reality—means that though he is capable of intellectual rigor and can argue and criticize powerfully and intelligently, he is not always unduly worried by paradox or careful about consistency. It also means that he would rather be vague, or give accounts in different places which are not easy to reconcile with one another, than leave anything out or fail to do justice to all aspects of the reality which he believes himself to be discovering within himself under the guidance of the ancients and the pressure of his longing to return to union with the Good. The goal of philosophy for the later Neo-Platonists was the same. But it seems for them to have been less a matter of experience and more a matter of tradition and study. They were more scholastic than Plotinus, both in the sense of being more concerned with learned (though often by the standards of modern scholars perverse) exposition of ancient thought and in the sense of being more concerned to attain complete clarity and consistency, to present a logically coherent system of concepts precisely defined (so far as the nature of their understanding of reality would permit).

3. The basic pattern of reality according to Plotinus, which all later Neo-Platonists follow in essentials, is that in which the transcendent source, which is absolutely one, undetermined, and unlimited, produces a series of levels of being which are progressively less unified, more dispersed and separate and multiple, and consequently weaker and more imperfect; though even the last and lowest, the physical universe, is held together and given a certain degree of unity which prevents it from vanishing altogether into nonbeing by the power of the One. Plotinus calls the transcendent source of reality by the traditional names of the One and the Good, though he is well aware that these names, like all others, are inadequate. He very rarely speaks of the One as God (his disciple Porphyry, like some Middle Platonists, uses *theos* [θεός] as a name for the supreme principle more frequently).

The One is beyond the reach of words or thought and is best indicated by negations, or statements that he is other and more than we can conceive. It or he (Plotinus normally uses neuter substantives, but masculine pronouns in speaking of this source of reality) is beyond the reach of thought, and cannot even be said to be, because he is absolutely beyond determination or limitation: being for Plotinus means being something, a particular, describable thing. But the One is certainly not nothing; he is more real than the beings we can know or speak of.

Another negation which is important for Plotinus is the denial that the One can be said to know himself because self-knowledge implies a minimum duality between subject and object and so a kind of internal division and limitation. But again this negation is not meant to imply that the One is unconscious and inert but that when we are directing our minds towards the source of living intelligence the language which we use even of its highest product is no longer applicable. The One, though he can only be reached through thought, is beyond thought. He is the source of all our values and the goal of all our aspirations who lies always beyond the horizons of our minds: that is why he is also the Good.

4. The One or Good produces eternally, completely spontaneously, but also quite inevitably—because for a Platonist a Good which does not diffuse or communicate itself is unthinkable—the first determinate and describable reality, the Divine Intelligence. This springs eternally from the One as a life not yet formed and determinate and, as it springs, turns back upon the One in contemplation, impelled by the love the One gives it in producing it as life. In this contemplation it cannot receive the One in his absolute unity and simplicity (though its love for its source carries it eternally beyond its contemplation so that it is also joined to the One in a mystical union in which we at our highest can share). It determines itself as a one-in-many, a whole of parts as perfectly unified as anything except the One can be, the One-Being which is the Platonic World of Forms or Ideas. This is at once Absolute Being, perfect Intelligence, and Life at its most intense. The Forms in it are, as in Plato, the eternal archetypes of all else that to any degree exists, but they are not just objects of true thought but, being parts of Intelligence and Life, themselves living intelligences, each of which knows and so in a sense is the whole of which it is a part. Since Intelligence is a determinate reality possessing immediate, intuitive, and complete self-knowledge it is a limited reality in the sense that the number of Forms is finite, though Plotinus sometimes speaks of Forms of individuals. But its power is infinite.

5. We at our highest belong in some way to the world of Intellect and can be carried back with it in its eternal self-transcendence to mystical union with the One. But we are properly situated on the next level, that of Soul, which is produced by Intellect as Intellect is produced by the One. Plotinus, developing and sharpening an earlier Platonic distinction, generally distinguishes the spheres of Intellect and Soul very clearly. Intellect is the level of intuitive thought, which

is one with its object in a single act of apprehension; and Soul of discursive thought, which attains its object in a more external way by reasoning from premises to conclusions. It is because Soul has a succession of thoughts and not a single eternal act of thought that time comes into being in it and the material universe which it forms, orders, and animates is subject to time: for in Plotinus, as in all Platonic systems, one of the most important functions of Soul is to be the link between the intelligible and sensible worlds and to form, order, and govern the physical universe on the model of the intelligible Forms. Plotinus distinguishes between a lower phase of Soul, Nature, which is the immanent principle of life and gives form to bodies, and the higher World-Soul which orders and administers the universe spontaneously and without previous planning, deliberation, or choice, in a way which is more like a process of organic growth than the carefully organized action of a human administrator or craftsman. Plotinus strongly opposes the "artisan" conception of divine action, as found in Jewish and Christian thought, in earlier Platonists, and, apparently, in Plato himself, which represents God as making plans and then proceeding to carry them out. The everlasting material universe which is formed and ruled by Soul is the best possible of its kind, the most perfect image on the level of sense-perception of its intelligible archetype, but it is immeasurably inferior to the archetype, both because the Forms in it are the weakest reflections or expressions of the original Forms in Intellect, and because what underlies it, matter, though derived from the spiritual realities which bring the material world into being, is a principle of opposition to them, a negative antireality which imparts something of its negation to material things.

6. Though Plotinus, when considering the order of intelligible reality, distinguishes the spheres of Soul and Intellect very clearly, he does not always maintain the distinction and there is considerable overlapping. Soul at its highest often appears as a permanent inhabitant of the world of Intellect. This overlapping and crossing of frontiers is particularly apparent in Plotinus' account of men, who can live consciously on any level within the wide range of souls, from Intellect's world of light to the ghost-forms which flit through the darkness of matter. Our true higher self, the "man within" lives eternally and unchangingly on the level of Intellect (whether we are conscious of it or not). It does not sin or suffer and remains essentially unhindered in its thinking activities by the body and its world, into which it does not "come down." Plotinus' accounts of this higher self often do not make it clear whether it belongs to the sphere of Soul or Intellect, or both. He does not, sometimes, appear to think it matters very much. But his final conclusion appears to be that we at our highest are souls living on the level of Intellect, illuminated and raised to its level by its continuous action. That in us which is subject of what most people regard as normal human experience is an image or expression of the higher self on a lower level, which "comes down" and joins with the bodily organism to form the "composite" being, the "other man." It is important to notice that "come down" is not a phrase which Plotinus intends to be taken literally. The spiritual world for him is not "up there," remote in space like the heaven of the more naïve pagans and Christians, or distant in time, to be reached only after the end of the present world, like the heaven of early Christian tradition. It is eternally present within us, here and now, immediately accessible if we will make the initially intensely difficult effort to turn to it, to become consciously aware of and live on the level of our true selves. The task of philosophy is to bring about this return to our selves which enables us to rise above them to the final union with their source, the Good. The driving force behind it is the love, the impulse to return which the Good gives to all which it produces. By moral discipline, by recognition of the beauty of the higher world in the images which nature and art provide in the lower, and above all by intense intellectual concentration, we awake to our true nature and return to the goal of our desire. And for Plotinus the way of philosophy is the only way of return. For Iamblichus in the next century, and many of his successors, the actual way of return to the divine was through theurgic ritual rather than philosophy. But in the religion of Plotinus rites and sacraments are of no importance.

III

1. Platonism as expounded by Plotinus provides the foundation and framework for all later Neo-Platonic speculation, that is, for all Greek philosophy for the next three hundred years. The Three Hypostases, the transcendent source of reality, the world of Intellect, real being, and true life, and the sphere of Soul which forms, animates, and governs the material world, are taken for granted by later Neo-Platonists. But there are many developments and variations. Plotinus is, as has already been said, by no means regarded as a decisive authority, and there are other influences at work in the development of later Neo-Platonism which are apparent already in the thought of Plotinus' own pupil and editor, Porphyry. The chief of these are the continuing influence of the earlier type of Platonism described in the first part of this article, and the influence of some very odd writings called the *Chaldaean Oracles*, of which only fragments survive. They were produced as divine revelations probably in the second half of the second century A.D. by the two Julians, father and son, the "Chaldaean" and the "Theurgist," and seem to have been a theosophical farrago in verse containing ideas drawn from popular Platonism, Pythagoreanism, and Stoicism and with affinities with the pagan Gnosticism of the *Hermetica*. Porphyry, their first commentator, gave them only a limited and grudging recognition, but for Iamblichus and his successors they had the status of sacred scripture, and the effort to produce a philosophical exegesis of them had a confusing and complicating affect on later Neo-Platonic thought.

2. Porphyry used to be considered as a transmitter of the thought of Plotinus rather than as a thinker in his own right. But the recent work of a number of scholars, notably P. Hadot (see bibliography), has shown that he developed Neo-Platonism in a manner of his own, distinct from and in some ways opposed to that of later Neo-Platonists who followed Iamblichus. This Porphyrian Neo-Platonism had a considerable influence on fourth-century Christian thinkers, notably Marius Victorinus and Synesius. Its most distinctive characteristic seems to have been its monistic tendency. The One for Porphyry is much closer to and more on a level with Intellect than it is for Plotinus. The horizontal articulation of Intellect into the triad Being, Life, and Intelligence (of which the beginnings are apparent in Plotinus) plays an important part in his thought, as it does in that of all later Neo-Platonists. And the One, it seems, for him was the unknowable and ineffable pure being or activity of which the first self-determination was Intellect. This is the form of Neo-Platonic doctrine which came closest to, and had most influence on, the Trinitarian theology of Post-Nicene Christian thinkers. Porphyry also seems to have regarded Soul in its real nature as practically identical with Intellect.

3. On both these points, for bringing the One down to the level of what comes after it, and for confusing Intellect and Soul, Porphyry was severely criticized by Iamblichus and his successors, whose development of Neo-Platonism early in the fourth century took a different direction, though it owes a good deal in some ways to Porphyry's developments of Plotinus. Iamblichus was the originator of the distinctive type of Neo-Platonism which became dominant in the later schools, and which we know best from the voluminous works of Proclus (fifth century A.D.), who became head of Plato's school at Athens. This, far from showing any tendency to interpret Plotinus in a monistic way, sharpened the distinctions between the hypostases and multiplied the levels of reality. The ineffable source of reality was described in terms more negative than anything in Plotinus; even our negative statements about it have to be negated, and in the end we are reduced to utter silence and ignorance about it. The mystical union, though still regarded as theoretically possible, does not seem to have been a matter of experience for most later Neo-Platonists. Between the ineffable first principle and the first intelligible triad Iamblichus and his successors placed a rather Neo-Pythagorean One before all multiplicity, a One of which we know at least that it is One.

The intelligible world and the sphere of Soul are extremely elaborately subdivided both horizontally and vertically, with continual use of the triadic articulation which appears already in the triad of Being, Life, and Intelligence. The need to provide a precise systematic exegesis of everything in those dialogues of Plato which they thought important (especially the *Parmenides* and the *Timaeus*); the need to take the *Chaldaean Oracles* and other alleged revelations (especially Orphic) seriously; and the need to find a place in the system for every god and spirit of the Hellenic and Near-Eastern pantheons; all these deeply felt necessities contributed to the complication of the later Neo-Platonic systems. For these men, as for Plotinus, the end of human life was to return to the divine. But the return for them could not be accomplished by themselves through the natural love and intelligence which they receive in their origin from the Good. It was brought about by the gracious operation of a descending and generous divine *eros* which is remarkably like Christian *agapē:* and the method of return was through the performance of theurgic rituals revealed by the gods themselves. But they did not confuse theurgy with philosophy, and the amount of attention paid to theurgy varied a good deal from one school or individual to another. They were deeply religious men, utterly committed to the defense of what they regarded as the authentic ancient religious tradition which the world around them had abandoned. But they were also concerned to give a philosophically rigorous, clear, coherent, and systematic account of their beliefs.

4. An important feature of this later Neo-Platonism was the increased attention paid to Aristotle, and especially to his logical theory, which the later Neo-Platonists continually studied, criticized, and adapted in their effort to give their system logical coherence and rigor. This concern with Aristotle's logic begins with Porphyry, and extensive commentary on the works of Aristotle was one of the main activities of the Neo-Platonic school of Alexandria: though it seems that in their metaphysics the Alexandrians were orthodox post-Iamblichean Neo-Platonists, and did not differ as much as has been supposed in the fifth and sixth centuries A.D. from the contemporary school of Athens,

though they were less bitterly hostile to Christianity. It was at Alexandria in the later sixth century that the teaching of philosophy finally passed from pagans to Christians.

IV

In considering the influence of Neo-Platonism on early medieval thought in the East and West of the former Roman world, it is first of all important to remember the continuing influence—especially on Christian thought—of the earlier Platonism described in the first part of this article. The relatively simple and unsophisticated theism of Middle Platonism had a strong attraction for Jewish and Christian minds, and the majority of Christian thinkers in the fourth century and later, even when they are influenced by Neo-Platonism, base their philosophical theology on a conception of God which is Middle Platonist rather than Neo-Platonist in that it presents him as Being and Intelligence. The Christian Origen, whose influence was very great, is immediately pre-Neo-Platonist and not Neo-Platonist in his conception of God. When there is a question of properly Neo-Platonist influence one must distinguish between the limited, though important, influence exercised by the direct reading of pagan Neo-Platonist treatises, and the much more widespread influence exercised by eminent Christian, Muslim, or Jewish thinkers who had assimilated some Neo-Platonic ideas but had adapted and developed them according to their own religious preconceptions and personal casts of mind.

The works of the Greek Neo-Platonists continued to be copied, and to some extent read, in the Byzantine world, from which they eventually reached Renaissance Europe. Marius Victorinus and others read Plotinus and Porphyry in Greek in the West in the fourth century A.D., and Augustine read them in Latin translation. In the sixth century Boethius was well acquainted with Greek Neo-Platonism. In the Muslim East a great collection of translations of works which had been studied in the Neo-Platonist philosophical schools was produced, first in Syriac and after A.D. 800 in Arabic. It was the reading of these translations which inspired the Muslim philosophers, from Al-Kindi to Averroës, to develop their often highly original philosophies which later deeply influenced the medieval West. In the Greek-speaking Byzantine world Neo-Platonic ideas had some influence on Christian thinkers from the fourth century A.D. onwards, which was considerably increased by the work of the anonymous author who wrote probably in the late fifth to early sixth centuries A.D. under the name of Dionysius the Areopagite, and adapted and in many ways transformed fifth-century Neo-Platonism for the purposes

377

of his own very distinctive Christian philosophical theology. The Christian Platonist tradition of "Dionysius," further Christianized by his successors (notably his great seventh-century commentator Saint Maximus, a most original and important theological thinker), eventually reached the West in the Carolingian period through Erigena.

But the most influential of Neo-Platonic Christian thinkers in the West was, of course, Saint Augustine, who was deeply impressed by his reading of Plotinus and Porphyry and produced his own thoroughly Christianized and highly personal kind of Platonic philosophical theology, which left its mark on most later Western Christian thinking. In the sixth century A.D. Boethius, in the book which he wrote in prison before his execution, the *Consolation of Philosophy,* expounded a simple Neo-Platonic theism perfectly compatible with Christian doctrine, though not explicitly Christian, which had a great influence on the thought of the early medieval West.

BIBLIOGRAPHY

The Cambridge History of Later Greek and Early Medi-aeval Philosophy, edited by A. H. Armstrong (Cambridge, 1967; reprint 1970), gives a full account of Neo-Platonism, its development, and its influence on early medieval thought. Part I, by P. Merlan, deals with pre-Plotinian Platonism; Part II, by H. Chadwick, with Philo of Alexandria and the earliest Christian thinkers; Part III, by A. H. Armstrong, with Plotinus; Part IV, by A. C. Lloyd, with the later Neo-Platonists. The remaining four Parts, by R. A. Markus, P. Sheldon-Williams, H. Liebeschütz, and R. Walzer, are very largely concerned with Neo-Platonic influences on Christian patristic and early medieval thought in East and West, and on Muslim philosophy. All parts have extensive bibliographies, including the principal editions and translations of Neo-Platonic texts.

On Plotinus and his predecessors, see also *Les Sources de Plotin,* Entretiens Hardt V (Vandoeuvres and Geneva, 1960); J. M. Rist, *Plotinus: The Road to Reality* (Cambridge, 1967), which includes a good bibliography. On Porphyry see *Porphyre,* Entretiens Hardt XII (Vandoeuvres and Geneva, 1966); and P. Hadot, *Porphyre et Vietorinus,* Vols. I–II (Paris, 1968). On the later Neo-Platonists the most important work in English besides A. C. Lloyd's contribution to the *Cambridge History* referred to above is the commentary of E. R. Dodds on Proclus, *Elements of Theology,* 2nd ed. (Oxford, 1963). See also L. J. Rosàn, *The Philosophy of Proclus* (New York, 1949), with extensive bibliographies; J. Trouillard, *Le Néoplatonisme, Encyclopédie de la Pléiade, Histoire de la Philosophie,* I, *Orient-Antiquité-Moyen Age* (Paris, 1969), pp. 886–935. *Le Néoplatonisme,* ed. P. Hadot (Paris, 1971), is also valuable.

A. HILARY ARMSTRONG

[See also Dualism; **Gnosticism**; God; **Hierarchy; Platonism;** Pythagorean . . . ; Stoicism.]

NEWTON AND THE METHOD OF ANALYSIS

ISAAC NEWTON's disciples in the eighteenth century were impressed not only by his discoveries in optics and celestial mechanics and by his admirably ordered System of the World, but by the method he employed. A variety of writers mention him as the inventor of the only proper way of investigating nature: of a method that d'Alembert called "exact, profound, luminous and new." Laplace found his method "happily applied" in the *Principia* and the *Opticks,* works valuable not just for the discoveries contained in them, but as the best models to be emulated, as the embodiments of this method (Laplace, pp. 430–31). Moreover, Newton's method—as understood by men of letters like Voltaire and Condillac—was thought to be, besides a technique for investigating physical nature, "a new method of philosophizing" applicable to all areas of human knowledge. What Newton called his "Experimental Philosophy" had wide application. It set the bounds to human presumption; it was systematic, yet as Condillac pointed out, was opposed to the *esprit de système;* it rejected unsupported or gratuitous *hypotheses.*

Analysis, the dissection of nature, men in the eighteenth century took to be the key to knowledge, the great and novel intellectual tool, indeed the essence of Newton's method. Yet if we read carefully the important Newtonian passages, or the best of Newton's expositors, we discover that Newton's methodological prescriptions were by no means confined to this "dissection of nature," although he lays great stress upon it. Men who possess Newton's experimental philosophy, wrote Roger Cotes,

. . . proceed in a twofold method, synthetical and analytical. From some select phenomena they deduce by analysis the forces of Nature and the more simple laws of forces; and from thence by synthesis show the constitution of the rest. This is that incomparably best way of philosophizing, which our renowned author most justly embraced in preference to the rest (Newton, *Principia,* ed. F. Cajori, p. 547).

Colin Maclaurin wrote, "In order to proceed with perfect security, and to put an end for ever to disputes, [Newton] proposed that, in our inquiries into nature, the methods of *analysis* and *synthesis* should be both employed in a proper order" (1775, p. 9).

Newton first referred in print to his methodological principles, at least in a major work, in the new Queries added to the Latin version of his *Opticks* which appeared in 1706. In one of these Queries (Q. 20/28) he reproves those "later philosophers" (*physici recentiores*) who invoke mechanical hypotheses to explain all things,

[w]hereas the main Business of natural Philosophy is to argue from Phaenomena without feigning Hypotheses, and to deduce Causes from Effects (*Opticks*, p. 369).

He is even more explicit in a passage towards the close of the last new Query (Q. 23/31), a passage that was greatly expanded when Newton in 1717–18 brought out a second English edition of his *Opticks*. Since this English text is the most familiar, to say nothing of being more complete, and indeed is the *locus classicus* for any study of Newton's method, it deserves to be given here in full, with the passages that had earlier appeared in the much shorter Latin statement of 1706 given in italics:

As in Mathematicks, so in Natural Philosophy, the Investigation of difficult Things by the Method of Analysis, ought ever to precede the Method of Composition. This Analysis consists in making Experiments and Observations, and in drawing general Conclusions from them by Induction, and admitting of no Objections against the Conclusions, but such as are taken from Experiments, or other certain Truths. For Hypotheses are not to be regarded in experimental Philosophy. And although the arguing from Experiments and Observations by Induction be no Demonstration of general Conclusions; yet it is the best way of arguing which the Nature of Things admits of, and may be looked upon as so much the stronger, by how much the Induction is more general. And if no Exception occur from Phaenomena, the Conclusion may be pronounced generally. But if at any time afterwards any Exception shall occur from Experiments, it may then begin to be pronounced with such Exceptions as occur. By this way of Analysis *we may proceed from Compounds to Ingredients, and from Motions to the Forces producing them; and in general, from Effects to their Causes, and from particular Causes to more general ones, till the Argument end in the most general. This is the Method of Analysis: And the Synthesis consists in assuming the Causes discover'd, and establish'd as Principles, and by them explaining the Phaenomena proceeding from them, and proving the Explanations* (*Opticks*, pp. 404–05).

Several points in this text deserve to be noted. First, Newton advocates a single procedure, made up of two "methods" both of which must be employed, but one of which (the analytic) must be carried out before the other (the synthetic or compositional). Second, that although he describes these two methods by terms used for analogous methods in mathematics, by analysis he means the making of observations or the performing of experiments, and deriving conclusions from them by induction. Experiments are among the certain truths, yet inductions from them do not "demonstrate" the conclusions drawn; still this is "the best way of arguing which the nature of things admits of."

If this is Newton's most important statement of his scientific method, what of the famous Rules of Reasoning in Philosophy which Newton placed at the beginning of Book III of the *Principia?* With the single exception of Rule IV, they do not deal with method, at least as the term was commonly used in Newton's day, and will be used in this article. The first two rules—statements of the law of parsimony and of the principle of the analogy and uniformity of nature—can perhaps be described as basic articles of scientific faith, as meta-scientific principles. Rule III, which has been much discussed and variously interpreted, can be characterized, at least in a loose way, as an analogical rule. Its manifest purpose is to justify extending observations and measurements concerning gravity on the earth and in the solar system so as to "allow that all bodies whatsoever are endowed with a principle of mutual gravitation." Rule IV was added to the third edition of the *Principia* (1726) and clearly echoes what he had written some eight years before in the expanded Query 23/31 of the *Opticks*. This Rule reads as follows:

In experimental philosophy we are to look upon propositions inferred by general induction from phenomena as accurately or very nearly true, notwithstanding any contrary hypotheses that may be imagined, till such time as other phenomena occur, by which they may either be made more accurate, or liable to exceptions.

This is clearly a methodological rule which, Newton adds, "we must follow, that the argument of induction may not be evaded by hypotheses" (*Principia*, p. 400). Newton in his *Universal Arithmetick*, a work significantly subtitled "A Treatise of Arithmetical Composition and Resolution," describes arithmetic as synthetic, since we "proceed from given Quantities to the Quantities sought" whereas algebra is analytic because it "proceeds in a retrograde order" assuming the quantities sought "as if they were given." And he comments that "after this Way the most difficult Problems are resolv'd, the Resolutions whereof would be sought in vain from only common Arithmetick" (*Universal Arithmetick*, London [1728], p. 1). These remarks cast light on what Newton had in mind when, in Query 31, he compares the method of investigation in natural philosophy with those in mathematics.

Method vs. Logic. At this point, let us agree to an important distinction: that between logic and method. Both, of course, are concerned with how our mind should operate in order to arrive at reliable knowledge, but there are differences. The word *method* seems to have been a coinage of Plato; it first appears in his *Phaedrus*, where Socrates is advocating an art or technic of rhetoric as opposed to the devices of the Sophists. The word suggests a "path" or "route," being derived from *meta* and *odos*, indicating a movement according to a road.

To think or argue clearly and effectively it is necessary to understand the route along which we conduct our thoughts. He who has such a route, such a direction, possesses method. Logic and method are not the same thing. Logic is, of course, indispensable to method: it is the *inner machinery* conducting us along the path; it provides us with the tactics we employ. If method indicates the grand strategy, the road (or roads) we should follow, logic in turn provides the means of transportation, together with the *code de la route.*

Aristotle was not primarily concerned with the problem of method as the word is defined here. But there are passages in the *Organon* which testify that he believed there were two modes or directions of conducting our reasoning: the deductive or syllogistic and the inductive. Both lead to understanding, and understanding requires knowledge of the reason for the fact. But the deductive or syllogistic mode of demonstration assumes that we know the cause or principle from which the consequences can be drawn. In the jargon of the medieval philosophers, it is demonstration *propter quid* (demonstration *wherefore*) by which we start from what is prior in the order of nature and end up with what is "prior in the order of our knowing," that is, what is directly accessible to us. Some inquiries properly move in the opposite direction: from what is more knowable and obvious to us we proceed to those things that are "more knowable by nature." In the *Physics* Aristotle makes it clear that in this branch of philosophy "we must follow this [inductive] path and advance from what is more obscure by nature, but clearer to us, towards what is more clear and more knowable by nature (*Physics*, I, i, 184a–184b 10).

There is, however, a passage in the *Nicomachean Ethics* (Book III, Ch. 1, 1112a–1113a 14) where Aristotle contrasts men who deliberate with those who analyze in geometry, and men who act upon those deliberations with those who engage in geometrical synthesis. This is perhaps the earliest explicit echo of those two *directional* ways of conducting thought in mathematics to which Newton referred in our chief text (Heath, pp. 270–72). In all likelihood the two mathematical methods were known in the time of Plato and Eudoxus. Nevertheless the classical account is that given much later in the *Mathematical Collections* of Pappus who attributes the elaboration of two methods to the work of Euclid, Apollonius of Perga, and Aristaeus the Elder (M. R. Cohen and I. E. Drabkin, pp. 38–39). In analysis, Pappus writes, the mathematician assumes what is sought as if it were true, and by a succession of operations arrives at something known to be true. Synthesis, on the other hand, reverses the process: the geometer starts with what is known (axioms, definitions, theorems previously proved) and by a series of deductive steps arrives at what he has set out to prove. This synthetic method is, of course, characteristic of the most familiar proofs of Euclid's geometry. The two methods may be thought of as alternative paths to be chosen according to the demands of a particular inquiry. Yet it appears likely that the analytic method is the one used for purposes of investigation and discovery (as Aristotle implies), and that this is then followed, for formal demonstration, by the method of composition or synthesis which, unlike analysis, follows the "normal" direction of logical consequence (Hintikka, 1966).

Pappus' text, unknown to the Middle Ages, was rediscovered in the Renaissance, and it gained currency especially through Commandino's Latin translation of 1589. The two procedures or methods in mathematics were obviously common knowledge by Newton's day. Algebra, in which the sixteenth and the seventeenth centuries made such notable progress, was seen to explore problems analytically, although quite differently from the "geometrical analysis of the ancients." It is in this sense that the two procedures are discussed by Newton's friend Edmund Halley in the preface to his edition of Apollonius. Algebraic analysis Halley describes as *brevissima simul perspicua* ("the shortest and clearest"); synthesis, by contrast, is *concinna et minime operosa* ("elegant and easier").

There is—and it surely deserves mention—a text with which Newton must have been familiar. In his *Mathematical Lectures,* delivered in 1664–65, Newton's friend and teacher, Isaac Barrow, equates the mathematical and philosophical uses of these two terms. Barrow explains why, in enumerating the parts of mathematics he is "wholly silent about that which is called Algebra or the Analytic Art."

I answer, this was not done unadvisedly. Because indeed *Analysis* . . . seems to belong no more to *Mathematics* than to *Physics*, *Ethics* or any other Science. For this is only . . . a certain Manner of using Reason in the Solution of Questions, and the Invention or Probation of Conclusions, which is often made use of in all other Sciences. Wherefore it is not a Part or Species of, but rather an Instrument subservient to the Mathematics: No more is *Synthesis*, which is the manner of demonstrating Theorems in Contradiction to *Analysis* (Barrow, p. 28).

The relation between mathematical procedures and general intellectual method had, we saw, been rather casually invoked by Aristotle. Yet he devoted most of his attention to elaborating his demonstrative logic and his theory of the syllogism. Early in our era—by the second and third centuries A.D.—philosophers and commentators began to use the mathematical terms in writing about method. For example Alexander of Aphrodisias, in his commentaries on Aristotle, mentions geometrical analysis as one of nine different senses of the word analysis used by philosophers.

A most important figure is surely Galen, for he brings the subject out of the realm of pure dialectic into the practical world of the physician. His concern is with method (or perhaps with methods) and with the proper way the doctor should think about and teach his art. Galen, we know, wrote a major work called *Concerning Demonstration*, but it was subsequently lost. Almost certainly it did not deal only with logic in the narrow sense, but with the problem of method, a problem that arose for him because of the different approaches to medicine of the chief rival schools into which his contemporaries and rival physicians were divided: the Empiric and the Dogmatic. What he sought was a middle way between those who relied wholly on accumulated experience, and those who based their procedures upon medical theory. In a treatise called *On Medical Experience* Galen wrote "The art of healing was originally invented and discovered by the logos [reason] in conjunction with experience. And to-day also it can only be practised excellently and done well by one who employs both of these methods" (R. Walzer, p. 85). But how are these methods to be employed?

References to method are scattered through Galen's major works; but his small work, the *Ars parva* (or *Microtegni*)—one of the first Greek medical writings to be made available in Latin—was the chief vehicle for transmitting Galen's thoughts on method. It was translated from an Arabic version into Latin by Constantine the African in the eleventh century, and later by Gerard of Cremona who rendered it along with the remarks of its Arab commentator, Haly Rodohan. In this form it was printed as an early medical incunabulum. Galen's introductory paragraph is very short, yet it provided the basis for much subsequent discussion of method in medicine. Galen says there are three ways of teaching or demonstrating the art of medicine: these are by *analysis*, by *synthesis* and by *definition* (Galen, ed. Kühn, I, 305–07). The use of the mathematicians' terms "analysis" and "synthesis" may have come to Galen from philosophical writings, yet it calls to mind his great admiration for the demonstrative procedures of the Greek geometers.

Perhaps too much has been made of Galen's methodology, but it should be emphasized that he is talking about methods of teaching, of leading the thought of the learner in teaching him medicine. There is nothing to suggest that the two procedures are to be used together, or that they are supplementary aspects of a single method. Rather it is that medicine can be taught analytically, by rising from the facts of observation (as, for example, in anatomy or pathology) to the principles or causes of health and disease. Or it can be presented in reverse fashion by starting with the principles—i.e., with medical theory—descending thence to the observed facts. But Haly in his preface identifies these two methods of teaching with the two directions of reasoning Aristotle presents in the *Posterior Analytics:* reasoning that moves from causes to effects, and that which proceeds from effects up to causes. (For Haly's prologue see A. Crombie, pp. 77–78. The Latin translation gives *conversio* and *solutio* for "analysis" and *compositio* for "synthesis.")

The earliest text in the Latin West involving a discussion of method is not related to medicine, but to philosophy. It is a passage in the commentary of Chalcidius, a fourth-century Christian Neo-Platonist, on Plato's *Timaeus*. Chalcidius is discussing the number and nature of the principles or elements of things; there is, he says, a *duplex probatio* for dealing with such matters, a double method of demonstration, the two parts of which are called *resolutio* and *compositio*, terms which correspond respectively to *analysis* and *synthesis*. *Resolutio* is a method of inquiry that begins with things sensible, prior in the order of understanding (that is, more known to us) from which we infer the principles of things, principles which are prior "in the order of nature." *Compositio* (or synthesis) is the method of syllogistic inference from the principles. The historian of science, Alistair Crombie, asserts that Chalcidius "defined the combined *resolutio-compositio* as the proper method of philosophical research" (ibid., p. 59). But an examination of the Chalcidius text shows that the business is much more complex: the two procedures, while in some sense supplementary, do not seem to form a single method, but are alternative methods. *Resolutio* is the method used in arriving at the material principles of things; *compositio* has a wider application: by means of it we demonstrate the formal relationships (*genera, qualitates, figuras*) from which we are led to grasp God's harmonious order and his providential role (*Platonis Timaeus interprete Chalcidio cum eiusdem commentario*, ed. Iohannis Wrobel, Leipzig [1876], CCCII–CCCV, pp. 330–34).

Chalcidius' commentary was widely read in the early Middle Ages. For example we find the terms *resolutio* and *compositio* used by the ninth-century thinker, John Scotus Erigena, in his mystical *De divisione naturae* where the aim is metaphysical understanding. Clearly, then, *resolutio* need not be an analysis of natural phenomena, but an analysis of thought.

The philosophers of the twelfth century had little interest in problems of method, but rather in logic as they first found it in the old logic (*logica vetus*) of Aristotle. The rationalism, moveover, of an Anselm, a Gilbert de la Porrée, a Richard of St. Victor, even

381

an Abelard, led them to deprecate the evidence of the senses as leading only to "opinion" not truth, and as unsuitable for handling the questions that really interested them. The only appropriate procedure was deduction from necessary and indemonstrable first principles. With the recovery of the later books of Aristotle's *Organon*, the *logica nova*, men of the thirteenth century focussed upon syllogistic logic, and paid little attention to the problem of method. With a single important exception, discussion of method was confined to the medical centers of Italy. And even this remarkable person was almost certainly influenced by what he knew of Galen. The exception, of course, is Robert Grosseteste, to whose role as scientific methodologist and scientist Professor Crombie has devoted a major book. For Grosseteste scientific knowledge is knowledge, as it was for Aristotle, of the causes of things, knowledge *propter quid*. The natural procedure in any science is to proceed from those particulars and whole objects known to us, directly but confusedly through the senses, up to the principles or causes, and then by a deductive chain to show the dependence of the particulars upon the principles or causes. But Grosseteste's method is primarily dialectical; its aim is the discovery of a *definition*, a generalized verbal characterization, and it is perhaps not surprising that he discusses composition before taking up resolution, for in certain sciences (notably mathematics) the synthetic or compositive method is all that seems to be needed in most cases. A different approach is needed in physics which is uncertain, because, as Crombie paraphrases him, there can be only "probable knowledge of changeable natural things" (Crombie, p. 59). Causal definitions in physics could not be arrived at *a priori* (or *simpliciter*) like the axioms of geometry; they had to be reached by analysis or resolution of experimental objects, a process involving first, a dissecting of the object or phenomenon, and then, an inductive leap. But "the special merit" of Grosseteste's methodology, as Crombie points out, was to recognize that the induction is not probative, not a demonstration. What is necessary is verification or falsification of the principles or definitions arrived at by analysis (*resolutio*). The procedure of deducing the consequences of the definition, cause or principle, is of course the *compositio:* it serves to confirm (or falsify) the analytic results. Together both procedures—*resolutio* and *compositio*—constitute a single method. In the study of nature the two procedures must be used together.

Speculations on method never flourished in Paris or Grosseteste's Oxford, but attracted much attention in the universities of northern Italy, in the late fifteenth century and more especially in the sixteenth century.

Two writers had a particularly great influence, Agostino Nifo (ca. 1473–1545) and Jacopo Zabarella (1533–89). Both men, arguing much like Grosseteste, asserted that the object of a science is to discover the causes, the *propter quid*, of observed effects. To discover the causes, one must first proceed *a posteriori*, inferring causes from effects, i.e., using first the method of resolution or analysis; then the demonstrative or compositive method can be used to develop the consequences. The double procedure constitutes the method.

Ernst Cassirer was the first to call attention to Zabarella, to bring him to light once more, and to see him as an influence on Galileo's scientific method, a position taken later, and even more strongly, by J. H. Randall, Jr. (Cassirer, I, 136–44). But Neal Gilbert in a recent book, *Renaissance Concepts of Method* (esp. Ch. 7), casts doubt on this interpretation. As with Grosseteste, the emphasis of these Renaissance philosophers is on the method for its own sake, on method as prescriptive for all areas of knowledge; the concern is not with its application to natural science alone, but to all disciplines, metaphysical, moral, dialectical. The empirical element, as Gilbert has pointed out, is weak. While it is true that in analysis or resolution we pass from what is better known to what is more remote from us, the better known "experiences" may not be observations of scientific fact; they can as well be "clear and distinct ideas" resulting from the analysis of thoughts and concepts, and the principles or causes are verbal definitions. Even if this is somewhat unjust to Zabarella, there is an important difference between his method and that of Galileo, and an even greater gap between Galileo and Newton.

In the *probatio duplex*—the double method of Grosseteste and Zabarella—the really probative element is supplied by the synthetic, deductive arm. The analytic or resolutive procedure is merely suggestive or conjectural. This, it would appear, is also characteristic of Galileo, but with him the empirical element which Gilbert finds lacking in Zabarella is, of course, much more important.

In many passages, notably in the *Letter to the Grand Duchess Christina*, Galileo, in phrases that are reminiscent of Galen's injunctions, insists that the proper approach to natural philosophy is to employ jointly "manifest experiences and necessary proofs"; "direct experience and necessary demonstrations"; "experiments, long observation, and rigorous demonstration" (Galileo, trans. S. Drake, pp. 179, 183–84, 186, 197). In such phrases he seems to be implying a double method of resolution and composition, of analysis and synthesis. But how does one carry this out?

The Third Day of the *Discorsi* throws light on the matter. Galileo opens with the famous statement of purpose: that he intends "to set forth a very new science dealing with a very ancient subject," the subject of motion in nature. Concerning this, he remarks, "I have discovered some properties of it which . . . have not hitherto been either *observed* or *demonstrated*" (Galileo, trans. H. Crew and A. de Salvio, p. 153; emphasis added).

After several pages describing the kinematics of uniform motion, Galileo enters upon the subject of accelerated motion:

And first of all it seems desirable to find and explain a definition best fitting natural phenomena. For anyone may invent an arbitrary type of motion and discuss its properties . . . but we have decided to consider the phenomenon of bodies falling with an acceleration such as actually occurs in nature and to make this definition of accelerated motion exhibit the essential features of observed accelerated motions (ibid., p. 160).

This suggests, if his earlier statement about discovering his results did not satisfy us, that he has observed and perhaps crudely determined the acceleration of falling bodies in order to arrive at his definition. Thus at least a crude *analysis* of experience led him to the rule nature might follow, led "by the hand, as it were, in following the habit and custom of nature herself, in all her various other processes." "And this, at last," he says in the same paragraph, ". . . after repeated efforts we trust we have succeeded in doing. In this belief we are confirmed mainly by the consideration that experimental results are seen to agree with and exactly correspond with those properties which have been, one after another, demonstrated by us" (ibid.). Such an experimental confirmation completes the synthesis, or compositional phase, of Galileo's double method. It is notable that the language used (as later with Newton) is that of mathematics: kinematic descriptions, measurable and representable (as his pages show) by numbers and geometry. Galileo's "definitions" are mathematically symbolized "laws."

A passage in the *Dialogue on the Two Great World Systems* seems to confirm our inference; it contains, also, an explicit reference to the method of resolution:

Simplicio[:] Aristotle first laid the basis of his argument *a priori*, showing the necessity of the inalterability of heaven by means of natural, evident, and clear principles. He afterwards supported the same *a posteriori*, by the senses and by the traditions of the ancients.

Salviati[:] What you refer to is the method he uses in writing his doctrine, but I do not believe it to be that with which he investigated it. Rather, I think it certain that he first obtained it by means of the senses, experiments, and observations, to assure himself as much as possible of his conclusions. *Afterwards* he sought means to make them demon-

strable. This is what is done for the most part in the demonstrative sciences; this comes about because when the conclusion is true, one may by making use of the analytical methods [*methodo resolutivo*] hit upon some proposition which is already demonstrated, or arrive at some axiomatic principle. . . . And you may be sure that Pythagoras, long before he discovered the proof for which he sacrificed a hecatomb, was sure that the square on the side opposite the right angle of a right triangle was equal to the squares on the other two sides. *The certainty of a conclusion assists not a little in the discovery of its proof* . . . (*Dialogue* . . ., trans. S. Drake, pp. 50–51).

What Galileo seems to be saying is that nonrigorous, exploratory methods, based on trial and experiment, can lead to a certain degree of probability in the conclusion. This conclusion can then be *demonstrated*, either because (as in the mathematical analysis) it leads to something already known, or because it leads to something that can be tested experimentally. A point worth emphasizing is the stress that Galileo places on the *analytic* or *resolutive* procedure as strongly suggestive, though falling far short of probative demonstration. The analytic procedure, as he makes clear, is the method of discovery (in natural philosophy the only method of discovery or invention); the synthetic procedure rounds out the process, and is the method of final demonstration and formal presentation. In the seventeenth century the problem of method, as distinct from logic, became of paramount concern. Indeed—as the Kneales point out in their *Development of Logic* (1962)—this led to a neglect or an impoverishment of logical studies in this century. This new concern, an attempt to formulate a doctrine of method in natural science, scientific method, is first encountered in Francis Bacon.

Bacon has suffered at the hands of many historians of science and of philosophy, and he has often been grossly misinterpreted. His self-appointed role was to stress experience and experiment, and to do so with all the rich resources of rhetoric. His aim, as he put it, is to restore "the commerce between the mind of men and the nature of things." In the study of nature we cannot succeed if we rely excessively or exclusively on the human reason, "if we arrogantly search for the sciences in the narrow cells of the human understanding, and not submissively in the wider world" (cited by Basil Willey, p. 36). But any careful reading of Bacon reveals that his goal is the discovery of axioms and principles from which a demonstrative science can be constructed. In any case, these axioms and principles should not be ad hoc or gratuitous; they should not be "hypotheses" in Newton's pejorative sense: they must somehow be rooted in, derived from, Nature herself. What Bacon wrestles with, if not too successfully, is the problem of induction, in other words the problem of increasing the probative value of the analytical arm of the double method; since the synthetic arm had been thoroughly investigated from Aristotle to his own time, it could be momentarily left aside. To arrive at axioms we must learn how to analyze and dissect nature, *dissecare naturam:*

Now what the sciences stand in need of is a form of induction which shall analyze experience and take it to pieces, and by a due process of exclusion and rejection lead to an inevitable conclusion [that is, to axioms and causes] (Bacon, ed. J. M. Robertson, p. 249).

In his effort to strengthen the upward procedure perhaps Bacon helped to distract attention away from the *double* method. Interest in the double method, and an appreciation if its power as a scientific instrument, waned in mid-century. But for this Descartes is perhaps as much at fault as Bacon; at his hands the "method" is distorted in a very interesting way. It is Newton who has the honor of restoring and sharpening it as a tool of what he called "Experimental Philosophy."

It has been claimed that the double method of analysis and synthesis, of resolution and composition, is the central feature of Descartes' famous method. As everyone knows, his doctrine of method is set forth in the readable, but here and there oddly cryptic, *Discourse on Method* (1637). The method is summed up in the famous four rules which Descartes introduces in Part II of his book, but more completely set forth in the twenty-one rules of his posthumous *Regulae ad directionem ingenii* (*Oeuvres* . . . , X, 359, 469).

The *Discourse*, as we commonly encounter it, was only a preface, an introduction, to those illustrations of the "method" which were published in the original book, and which have ever since been generally omitted from modern editions: the *Dioptrique*, the *Météores*, the *Géométrie*, intended together to illustrate the range of application of the method. When one examines the two physical essays as examples of Descartes' method, there is certainly no trace of a double way, a *probatio duplex*. The *Dioptrique* begins with a discussion of the nature of light, and the phenomena of refraction, presented in synthetic fashion. The *Météores* is an even better example of hypothetical reasoning, taking its departure from a purely conjectural picture of the shapes of particles.

It would seem that for Descartes analysis and synthesis are simply two alternative directions in which one can conduct one's thoughts in orderly fashion. Analysis, to be sure, is the road to first principles, leading to the clear and distinct ideas; but it is the analysis of concepts, of thought, not the analysis of sense experience or experiments. In either direction

one follows long chains of reasoning in which the validity of each step involves the spontaneous operation of the *vis cognoscens*, the power of the mind to grasp directly the "simple natures," the "atoms of evidence" which are the links of the chain. This power, or rather the action of the mind at each of these elementary steps, is what Descartes calls *intuitus*.

All reasoning, for Descartes, is thus a series of intuitive steps. And what men need, instead of the rules of formal logic which may be dispensed with, are the practical injunctions of his Four Rules. Method, for Descartes, is merely *order* in thought, order that will permit the natural intellect to operate unimpeded. This order can be insured by observing the simple rules of intellectual behavior which Leibniz found so absurdly obvious yet so vague. Descartes' famous rules are perhaps best described as propaedeutic, or even as prophylactic, injunctions. When they are scrupulously observed, the power of the mind, the *vis cognoscens*, operates reliably and surely. There seems to be little justification for finding in Descartes' method the dual procedure we have been describing. The truth value does not come from the mutual support of the two limbs of a dual method, but from perceiving clear, distinct, and irrefutable ideas.

Whether or not it is adequate to present Descartes' "method" in this fashion, one thing at least is certain: those of his followers who discuss *analysis* and *synthesis* clearly see these as *two* sorts of method, not as jointly constituting, when used one after the other, a single method. Arnauld and Nicolle, the authors of the book called the *Art of Thinking*, a work published in 1662 and often called the *Port Royal Logic*, write as follows:

We distinguish two kinds of method: the one for the discovery of truth is called *analysis* or the *method of resolution* or the *method of invention;* the second, used to make others understand the truth, is called *synthesis* or the *method of composition* or the *method of instruction* (Arnauld and Nicolle, p. 302).

Analysis, they remark farther on, is used "to investigate a specific thing rather than to investigate more general things as is done in the method of instruction [i.e., composition]." And they add that this analysis "consists more of discernment and acumen than of particular procedures," a statement that reminds us, not only of Descartes, but of Bacon's remark that analysis by experiment, which he calls the Chase of Pan, is really a kind of sagacity. And the Port Royal logicians bluntly state that "the more important of the two methods" is the method of composition "in that composition is used for explanation in many disciplines" (ibid., p. 309).

A similar distinction is made by Pierre-Sylvain Régis,

a Cartesian physicist. In his *Système de philosophie*, published in 1690, Régis speaks of *two* methods: "of which one serves to instruct ourselves and is called *analysis,* or the method of division, and the other which is used to instruct others is called *synthesis,* or the method of composition" (cited by Mouy, p. 148).

The same ideas are expressed in W. J. 'sGravesande's *Introductio ad philosophiam, metaphysicam et logicam continens* (Leiden, 1736). Book II is devoted to logic, and the third part of this is called "On Method." The opening words are as follows:

It now remains to indicate the route that the person . . . should follow to reach a true understanding of the things he has set out to examine.

The method should be different, according to the different circumstances.

First I shall treat the method for discovering truth, and then the method that we use to explain to others that which we know.

The first method is called *analytic,* or the method of resolution; the other is *synthesis* or the method of composition.

The general difference between the two methods consists in this: that in the first method one passes from the complex to the simple by resolution; and in the second one goes from the simple to the compounded (trans. from French version, ed. J. N. S. Allamand, Part II, p. 120).

We see how different from Newton's these statements are, which is curious when we recall that 'sGravesande is chiefly remembered for his exposition of the Newtonian philosophy. In his pages on method the Dutch scientist owes much, it would seem, to the later Cartesians and perhaps more immediately to the *Port Royal Logic.*

NEWTON'S SCIENTIFIC METHOD

Before trying to assess Newton's method of analysis and synthesis, comparing it with the twofold scheme so long and so variously elaborated by his predecessors, it might be well to consider a longer and more relaxed exposition that Newton never published, and which is closely related to the famous methodological section of Query 23/31 cited at the beginning of this article:

As Mathematicians have two Methods of doing things w^(ch) they call Composition & Resolution & in all difficulties have recourse to their method of resolution before they compound so in explaining the Phaemoena of nature the like methods are to be used & he that expects success must resolve before he compounds. For the explications of Phaenomena are Problems much harder then [sic] those in Mathematicks. The method of Resolution consists in trying experiments & considering all the Phaenomena of nature relating to the subject in hand & drawing conclusions from them & examining the truth of those conclusions by new experiments & new conclusions (if it may be) from those

experiments & so proceeding alternately from experiments to conclusions & from conclusions to experiments untill you come to the general properties of things, [& by experiments & phaenomena have established the truth of those properties.] Then assuming those properties as Principles of Philosophy you may by them explain the causes of such Phaenomena as follow from them: w^(ch) is the method of Composition. But if without deriving the properties of things from Phaenomena you feign Hypotheses & think by them to explain all nature you may make a plausible systeme of Philosophy for getting your self a name, but your systeme will be little better than a Romance. To explain all nature is too difficult a task for any one man or even for any one age. Tis much better to do a little with certainty & leave the rest for others that come after you then [sic] to explain all things by conjecture without making sure of any thing (Cambridge University Library, MS. Add. 3970 [5]).

Others before Newton used the word "romance" to describe fanciful hypotheses. See, for example, Henry Power in his *Experimental Philosophy* (1664), who speaks on p. 186 of those "that daily stuff our Libraries with their Philosophical Romances."

In contrast to Descartes, the logicians of Port Royal and 'sGravesande, Newton sees the two methods as constituting a single procedure, in which one begins by analysis or resolution, and follows this by a synthetic demonstration. Formally, this is the double way, the *probatio duplex,* of Grosseteste, Nifo, Zabarella, and the other early methodologists. Unlike them, however, Newton—like Galileo—would have us analyze not so much our ideas about things as the *phenomena.* But in turn Newton's double method differs from that of Galileo in a subtle but important way. With Galileo, as we saw, the analysis by experiment and observations is merely suggestive or indicative. The real cogency of the method depends on the demonstration: on synthesis or mathematical deduction. With Newton, however, the stress is on the *analysis* which "consists," as he says in the *Opticks,* "in making experiments and observations and in drawing general Conclusions from them by Induction." For Newton the analytic procedure is independently probative, although falling short of strict demonstration. Indeed (like Bacon before him) he feels it necessary to stress this analytic procedure, as he does in the *Opticks* by devoting more space to it than to the synthetic arm. Like Descartes and the Port Royal Logicians, he too sees analysis as the true method of discovery, of "invention." We must, he wrote, admit of "no Objections against the Conclusions, but such as are taken from Experiments, or other certain Truths. For hypotheses are not to be regarded in Experimental Philosophy." Although this experimental and inductive process does not lead to demonstration, "yet it is the best way of arguing which the Nature of Things admits of" (*Opticks,* 4th ed. [1730], p. 404). 385

If the force of Newton's dual method does not wholly depend (as it seems to have mainly done with Galileo) upon the synthetic procedure, what does this deductive limb of the double method actually contribute? Newton does not restrict it to a confirmatory role; still less does he limit its use to presenting or teaching what has already been discovered. The deductive limb can also be a means of prediction and discovery for, as he points out in the draft from which we have quoted above, one can deduce unexpected consequences. Having discovered "from Phaenomena" the inverse square law of universal gravitational force, and then using this force as a Principle of Philosophy, he writes (in the same unpublished MS cited above):

I derived from it all the motions of the heavenly bodies & the flux & reflux of the sea, shewing by mathematical demonstrations that this force alone was sufficient to produce all those Phaenomena, & deriving from it (a priori) some new motions wch Astronomers had not then observed but since appear to be true, as that Saturn & Jupiter draw one another, that the variation of the Moon is bigger in winter then in summer, that there is an equation of the Moon's meane motion amounting to almost 5 minutes wch depends upon the position of her Apoge to the Sun.

The later history of science has again and again confirmed the power of a well-founded theory to predict new phenomena, and to explicate other facts which had not been considered when the theory was elaborated.

In Query 31, immediately after describing his method, Newton tells us how the two procedures are exemplified in the foregoing books of the *Opticks* (op. cit., p. 405). In the greater part of the First Book, Newton sets forth his classic experiments showing that light is a heterogeneous mixture of rays of different refrangibility, and that rays of different refrangibility differ also in color. Although in this book Newton affects a kind of axiomatic presentation beginning with definitions and axioms, and enunciating a series of propositions, the procedures are really analytic in his sense, as he tells us they are: the propositions are not abstract mathematical statements, but affirmations of physical or experimental fact, and they are justified, not by mathematical deduction, but by what he calls "proofs by experiment." These discoveries being proved, Newton writes, "they may be assumed in the Method of Composition for explaining the Phaenomena arising from them." An example "of which Method I gave at the end of the first Book." He does not specify what propositions he means, but it is clear that he is referring us to those propositions he designates as "problems" rather than as "theorems" and which we encounter in Book I, Part II (ibid., pp. 161–85): to explain the colors produced by a prism (Prop. VIII.

Prob. III); to elucidate the colors of the rainbow; (Prop. IX. Prob. IV); and to explain the permanent colors of natural bodies (Prop. X. Prob. V).

NEWTON AND EXPERIMENT

At first sight it may seem odd to find Newton equating the analytic procedure with experimentation. Yet if we think about it for a moment, Newton's reasons are quite clear. A convincing and well-designed experiment involves a sort of dissection of analysis of nature, an isolation of the phenomenon to be examined, and the elimination of disturbing factors. As Lavoisier wrote long after Newton's time:

One of the principles one should never lose sight of in the art of conducting experiments is to simplify them as much as possible, and to exclude (*écarter*) from them all the circumstances that can complicate their results (Lavoisier [1789], p. 57).

Experiment, indeed, is usually necessary to determine which factors can safely be eliminated or at least must be held constant, and which are those that primarily determine the phenomenon. As W. Stanley Jevons wrote: "The great method of experiment consists in removing one at a time, each of those conditions which may be imagined to have an influence on the result" (Jevons [1905], p. 417). Physical nature does not readily reveal its secrets to the phenomenologist, but only to those who analyze.

Newton, in any event, profoundly altered that conception of experiment which Bacon had advocated and which in his spirit was accepted by so many virtuosi of the early Royal Society. Newton's Experimental Philosophy is not what Thomas Sprat or Henry Power, or even Robert Boyle, called by that name. Newton would not have agreed that experiment merely serves to render plausible the great sweeping "hypotheses" of the mechanical philosophers. Nor, at the other extreme, could he have agreed with Samuel Parker that probably "we must at last rest satisfied with true and exact Histories of Nature" (cited by Van Leeuwen), or with Locke who argued that improving knowledge of substances by "experiences and history . . . is all that the weakness of our faculties in this state of mediocrity which we are in in this world can attain to" (*Essay Concerning Human Understanding,* Book IV, Chs. 12, 10; cf. Chs. 3, 29).

On the title page of his *Experimental Philosophy* (1664), a miscellany of microscopic observations and experiments with the Torricellian Tube and with the magnet, Henry Power described them as providing "some Deductions, and Probable Hypotheses . . . in Avouchment and Illustration of the now famous Atomical Hypothesis." With greater experimental gifts and a richer scientific imagination, Robert Boyle can be said to have guided his own investigation in the same spirit.

For Newton, experiment is essentially a device for problem solving, for determining with precision the properties of things, and rising from these carefully observed "effects" to the "causes." More clearly than Bacon was able to do, Newton showed by his method that experimentation could lead with at least "moral certainty" to axioms, principles, or laws. In two ways Newton's method must be distinguished from that of the majority of his predecessors and nearly all his contemporaries. He insisted upon the cogency of a single, well-contrived experiment to answer a specific question, as opposed to the Baconian procedure of collecting and comparing innumerable "instances" of a phenomenon. Perhaps even more significant, Newton's experiments, whenever it is possible, are quantitative.

Robert Hooke, to be sure, was fully capable of designing and carrying out experiments to test a conjecture or working hypothesis. This he did in his "Noble Experiment" in which, by dissecting away the diaphragm of a dog and blowing air through the immobilized lungs, he showed that the animal could be kept alive, and in this way verified "my own *Hypothesis* of this Matter," namely that it is the air passing into the blood, not the motion of the lungs, that was necessary for life. Yet in his dispute with Newton over the latter's first paper on light and color Hooke's arguments are often Baconian. He argues that Newton's famous prismatic experiment, what Newton called his *experimentum crucis*, being a single isolated experiment, is unpersuasive, compared to "all the experiments and observations," and the "many hundreds of trials" he (Hooke) had made (Newton, *Papers and Letters*, pp. 110–11).

But it was upon this lone experiment, Newton replied, that "I chose to lay the whole stress of my discourse." By the Baconian term *experimentum crucis*—a phrase he borrowed from Hooke's *Micrographia* (1665)—Newton means an experiment designed to decide between two alternative outcomes, in other words an experiment designed (like Hooke's "Noble Experiment") to answer a clearly formulated question posed to Nature. In adopting this point of view, Newton of course had distinguished forerunners in Galileo, William Gilbert, William Harvey, and Blaise Pascal, among others. But it is interesting to cite some words of Isaac Barrow, a man to whom Newton was greatly indebted:

The Truth of Principles [Barrow wrote] does not solely depend on *Induction*, or a perpetual Observation of Particulars, as *Aristotle* seems to have thought; since only one Experiment will suffice (provided it be sufficiently clear and indubitable) to establish a true Hypothesis, to form a true Definition; and consequently to constitute true Principles. I own the Perfection of Sense is in some Measure required to establish the Truth of Hypotheses, but the Universality or Frequency of Observation is not so (Barrow, p. 116).

NEWTON'S MATHEMATICAL WAY

For his notion that scientific investigation should consist in the solving of discrete, well-defined problems Newton surely owed much, as the name of Isaac Barrow suggests, to the mathematical tradition, for that is how mathematicians of necessity proceed. We should remember that among students of physical nature, were men like Galileo, Torricelli, and Pascal—all of them mathematicians more than natural philosophers—who pointed the way and demonstrated by their achievements that this modest, piecemeal approach was the most fruitful way of studying not only mathematical problems but also nature. Few if any of these men would have described what they were doing as "physics," for in the seventeenth century "physics" meant natural philosophy, which was sharply set apart from mathematics, as it had been since the time of Aristotle. Subjects like optics, mechanics, music (acoustics and harmonics), which we now consider branches of physics, were described as belonging to the "mixed or concrete mathematics" (ibid., pp. 16–20; see also Proclus' *Commentary on Euclid's Elements*, in Cohen and Drabkin, pp. 2–5). They were subjects that treated mathematically things perceived by the senses, whereas pure mathematics dealt only with things "conceived by the mind." But they were not parts of physics (Cohen and Drabkin, pp. 90–91).

Physics in Newton's day was exemplified by those all-embracing, all-encompassing systems of nature devised by the so-called mechanical philosophers: Pierre Gassendi, Thomas Hobbes, Descartes, and their lesser followers. These men all shared the view—in opposition to Aristotle with his "substantial forms" and "occult qualities" and to Paracelsus with his spiritual agencies—that the underlying principles of physical nature were to be found in matter and its motions, and they built their different systems on an all-embracing mechanism. Common to all their systems, despite their rejection of Aristotle, was the conviction that the purpose of physics—a science of nature in a sense that is almost Aristotle's—was to explain the visible world in terms of particulate matter: the sizes, shapes, motions, and mechanical interaction of invisible particles, or what Francis Bacon had called "the secret motions of things." Physics; a branch of philosophy, was a dialectical science that imparted knowledge, derived from "first principles," about the whole material universe. As Descartes put it, physics was that second branch of philosophy (the first being metaphysics) "in which, after having found the true principles of material things, one examines in general how the whole universe is composed; then in particular what is the nature of this earth and of all the bodies that are commonly found around her, like air, water, fire, the magnet and other minerals" (Descartes, IX, 14). Even more self-confident and succinct is the definition of Descartes' disciple, Jacques Rohault. Physics, he wrote in his *Traité de physique* (1671), is the science "that teaches us the reasons and causes of all the effects that nature produces" (p. 1).

The logical model for the builders of these systems was mathematics, and their method of presentation was, in general, synthetic and deductive. Yet the language and syntax are verbal, not mathematical. Mathematizable in principle, Descartes' *Principles of Philosophy* has no trace of mathematics. Indeed because of this widely accepted separation between the disciplines of mathematics and physics, a mathematical physics appeared to most men to be a contradiction in terms. But there are important exceptions.

One of the earliest is Galileo, who wrote in his *Saggiatore* a passage that has often been quoted:

Philosophy is written in that great book which ever lies before our eyes—I mean the universe—but we cannot understand it if we do not first learn the language, and grasp the symbols, in which it is written. This book is written in the mathematical language, and the symbols are triangles, circles, and other geometrical figures, without whose help it is impossible to comprehend a single word of it; without which one wanders in vain through a dark labyrinth (Galileo, V, 6, p. 232).

Even more eloquent in opposing the conventional split between mathematics and natural philosophy was Isaac Barrow, one of that small number of Englishmen who had mastered Galileo's work, and from whom, in all likelihood, Newton was led to understand the thought and achievement of the great Italian scientist. Barrow, in discussing those "Sciences termed *Mixed Mathematics*," commented:

I suppose they ought all to be taken as Parts of *Natural Science*, being the same in Number with the Branches of *Physics*. . . . For these mixed Sciences are stiled Mathematical for no other Reason, but because the Consideration of Quantity intervenes with them, and because they require Conclusions to be demonstrated in Geometry, applying them to their own particular Matter. And, according to the same Reason, there is no Branch of natural Science that may not arrogate the Title to itself; since there is really none, from which the Consideration of Quantity is wholly excluded, and consequently to which some Light or Assistance may not be fetched from Geometry.

And he goes on, in what is almost a paraphrase of the famous Galilean passage:

For Magnitude is the common Affection of all physical Things, it is interwoven in the Nature of Bodies, blended with all corporeal Accidents, and well nigh bears the principal Part in the Production of every natural Effect (Barrow, p. 21).

Elsewhere Barrow wrote that no one can expect to understand or unlock the hidden meanings of nature without the "Help of a Mathematical Key":

For who can play well on *Aristotle's* Instrument but with a Mathematical Quill; or not be altogether deaf to the Lessons of Natural *Philosophy*, while ignorant of *Geometry*? (ibid., pp. xxvi–xxvii).

We need hardly stress the essentially mathematical character of Newton's major work, *The Mathematical Principles of Natural Philosophy*. If a glance at the book were not enough to convince us, Newton makes sure that we understand what he is about, and how he has bridged the gulf between mathematics and physics. In his Preface he writes that like "the moderns" he has in his treatise "cultivated mathematics as far as it relates to philosophy" and offers his book . . . as the mathematical principles of philosophy, for the whole burden of philosophy seems to consist in this—from the phenomena of motions to investigate the forces of nature, and then from these forces to demonstrate the other phenomena . . . (*Principia*, ed. F. Cajori, pp. xvii–xviii).

By "philosophy" Newton means, of course, natural philosophy or "physics." And he seems in this passage to refer to the traditional distinction between mathematics and physics. Yet he makes clear that these "principles"—the laws and conditions of certain motions and of powers or forces—are the things "we may build our reasonings upon in philosophical inquiries." One passes indeed without difficulty from one domain to the other:

In mathematics we are to investigate the quantities of forces with their proportions consequent upon any conditions supposed; then, *when we enter into physics,* we compare those proportions with the phenomena of Nature . . . (ibid., p. 192; emphasis added).

One question immediately confronts us: did Newton conceive of the famous method—his double procedure of analysis and synthesis set forth and exemplified in the *Opticks,* and where the analytic arm is identified with experiment and observation—as applying equally well to the *Principia?* This has recently been denied, yet the answer is surely in the affirmative. To be sure, the two works offer a striking contrast; they treat not only different aspects of nature, but at first glance seem to treat them in different ways. The *Principia* is, at least in the first two books, a work of abstract rational mechanics, strictly mathematical and presented in axiomatic fashion. A chain of propositions treat of mass points or idealized spherical bodies subject to certain imagined forces. Yet even when the results are applied to "physics"—to the real bodies of the solar system— these are treated as bodies qualitatively similar, deprived of what John Locke would have called their "secondary qualities" and differing only in such quantifiable properties as mass, extension, impenetrability, and state of rest or motion.

Abstract and mathematical though it appears throughout, the *Principia* was deemed by Newton to be as firmly rooted in observation and experiment as the *Opticks*. In the *Scholium* to the axioms or laws of motion Newton wrote that "I have laid down such principles as have been received by mathematicians, and are confirmed by abundance of experiments" (ibid., p. 21). This, he felt, need not be insisted upon for the first two laws of motion. But his third law, the law of equality of action and reaction, he saw to be a novel assertion requiring further justification. To this end he invoked at some length the experiments on elastic impact carried out some years before independently by Christopher Wren, John Wallis, and Christian Huygens; and he concludes that "so far as it regards percussions and reflections [the third law] is proved by a theory exactly agreeing with experience" (ibid., p. 25). To show further that the law can be extended to attractions, he cites an experiment he has made on the mutual attraction of a lodestone and iron. And elsewhere throughout the work we find scholia serving the same purpose of supporting important propositions by experimental evidence. Many years later, in the unpublished discussion of his method of analysis and composition (the first part of which was quoted above) he wrote:

Thus in the Mathematical Principles of Philosophy I first *shewed from Phaenomena* that all bodies endeavoured by a certain force proportional to their matter to approach one another, that this force in receding from that body grows less & less in reciprocal proportion to the square of the distance from it & that it is equal to gravity & therefore is one and the same force with gravity (loc. cit.).

Having tried to persuade us that the famous principle and law of universal gravitation was discovered through analysis, he describes in the passage quoted earlier his subsequent use of the synthetic method.

Newton's *Opticks*, by contrast, deals with the "secondary qualities" of things: chiefly color and—if we take the famous Queries into consideration—those attributes which differentiate various kinds of bodies:

chemical behavior, phenomena associated with heat, and such physical properties as cohesion, surface tension, and capillary rise (I. B. Cohen [1956], pp. 115–17).

Yet it is wrong to insist, as one scholar has done, that there are two kinds of Newtonianism: the mathematical Newtonianism of the *Principia* and the "experimental Newtonianism" of the *Opticks*. To remove any reasonable doubt as to what Newton himself thought, we may quote from an anonymous review what are generally acknowledged to be his own words:

The Philosophy which Mr. *Newton* in his *Principles* and *Optiques* has pursued is Experimental; and it is not the Business of Experimental Philosophy to teach the Causes of things any further than they can be proved by Experiments (*Philosophical Transactions*, 19, no. 342 [1717], 222).

The *Opticks*, unlike the *Principia*, consists largely of a meticulous account of experiments. Yet it can hardly be called nonmathematical, although little more than some simple geometry and arithmetic is needed to understand it. In spirit it is as good an example of Newton's "mathematical way" as the *Principia*: light is treated as a mathematical entity, as *rays* that can be represented by lines; the axioms with which he begins are the accepted laws of optics; and numbers— the different refrangibilities—serve as precise tags to distinguish the rays of different colors and to compare their behavior in reflection, refraction, and diffraction. Wherever appropriate, and this is most of the time, his language of experimental description is the language of number and measure. It is this which gives Newton's experiments their particular cogency.

Observation is not merely looking and seeing; it is a kind of reporting. We report to ourselves or to others some aspect of an object that arouses our interest. In this broad sense a painting or a poem is a kind of report. Some aspect of visual or auditory or tactile experience is singled out from the flux of nature to be attended to. But not all reports, as we know to our sorrow, are really observations. Any observation deserving the name, certainly any observation we might call "scientific," involves a comparison with something else. And the most precise and unambiguous comparisons are those expressed in the language of number and measure. When we measure we do not simply contrast two objects with one another. We do not just report that object A appears bigger, heavier, brighter, or faster than object B; we report *how much* they differ from each other. What is required is some way of attaching a more precise meaning to "bigger," "heavier," and so on. This we do by comparing both objects with some standard. Just as in counting we compare a set of objects with that abstract standard or scale we call the system of natural numbers, so when we *measure* we physically compare the objects at hand with a unit or standard of measure, which in turn involves comparing both the object and the standard with our abstract numerical scale. When we perform this operation of comparison, using the language of numbers—that is, when we measure—we are reporting this relationship of the objects as *ratios*. This, indeed, is the meaning that Newton attaches to the word "measure."

Newton interprets the numbers themselves as ratios or measures. Thus he writes: "By *Number* we understand not so much a Multitude of Unities, as the abstracted Ratio of any Quantity, to another Quantity of the same Kind, which we take for Unity. And this is threefold; integer, fracted, and surd: An *Integer* is what is measured by Unity, a *Fraction*, that which a submultiple Part of Unity measures, and a *Surd*, to which Unity is incommensurable" (*Universal Arithmetick*, London [1728], p. 2).

An experiment is, of course, only a contrived observation, and all the advantages of precision and lack of ambiguity that accrue to observations by being cast in the language of number and measure must necessarily be found in what we call "quantitative experiments," which Newton's almost always are. There is no better instance of Newton's quantitative approach to his experiments than the following undated manuscript page describing things "To be tryed" to elucidate the phenomenon of diffraction, that is the bending of light, and the production of colored fringes (*fasciae* to Newton), when light passes through a tiny hole or past a knife-edge:

1. *What are the numbers limits and dimensions* of the shadow & fasciae of a hair illuminated from a point at several distances.
2. *How far* a hair in the edge of light casts light into the shadow surrounding the light.
3. Whether in the approach of a hair to the shaddow the fasciae *encreas* & wch fasciae vanish first.
4. *How many* fasciae can be seen through a Prism.
5. *At what distances* each fascia begins to appear.
6. *What alteration* is made by the bluntness & shapness [*sic*] of the edge or by the density of the matter.
7. *How much* the shadow of a pin or slender wiar is broader then that of a hair.
8. Whether one hair behind another make a broader shadow & *how much*.
9. *At what distances* from one another two hairs, two backs or edges of knives or raisors, two wiars or pins & two larger iron cilinders make their fasciae meet.
   How the same or other bodies make their fasciae go into one anothers shadows.
   In what order the fasciae begin to appear or disappear *increase or decreas* [*sic*] in going into or out of any well

defined shadow (Cambridge University Library, MS. Add. 3970 fol. 643; emphasis added).

From a series of observations men habitually are impelled to generalize. To generalize is to report and sum up in some tidy way the results of a series of comparisons. The pitfalls of ordinary language compound the dangers of the generalizations we make in everyday life. But even the murky business of generalizing—of making an inductive inference—gains precision through the use of numbers, of mathematical rather than verbal language. The end product is a mathematically expressed "rule," or "law," or—to employ a favorite word of Newton's day—a "principle." Thus Newton opens the *Opticks* with what he called "Axioms" which are simply the well-established laws of geometrical optics. When, on the other hand, he enunciates a law that he has himself discovered, a generalization that he has reached by an inductive inference and which is quantitatively expressed, he often employs the word "rule." Thus after reporting a series of detailed measurements on the colored rings produced when light passes through thin, transparent bodies, he concludes: "And from these Measures, I seem to gather this Rule: That the thickness of the Air is proportional to the secant of an angle, whose Sine is a certain mean proportional between the Sines of Incidence and Refraction" (*Opticks* [1704], Book II, Part I, p. 12).

Clearly Newton's extreme confidence in his Method of Analysis, in the probative power of inductive inferences from his experiments, depends not a little on the fact that the ascending chain of comparisons by which he reaches these "rules" or "laws" is expressed in the language of mathematics. This use of number, one hardly needs to add, strengthens the deductive, synthetic limb of his double method, for the syntax of mathematical demonstration is at his disposal, in pursuing the downward path from "principles" and "laws" back to the phenomena. It is a syntax well understood and devoid of the ambiguities and traps of purely verbal deduction. E. W. Strong, in his "Newton's Mathematical Way" (in *Roots of Scientific Thought*, eds. Wiener and Noland), summed the matter up when he wrote: "Newton's 'mathematical way' encompasses both experimental investigation and demonstration from principles, that is, from laws or theorems established through investigation" (p. 413), and this procedure "requires measures for the formulation of principles in optics and mechanics—principles that incorporate a rule of measure. Were there not mathematical determinations in the experiment, there would be no subsequent determination in the demonstration" (p. 421).

BIBLIOGRAPHY

Aristotle, *Physics*, Book I; *Nicomachean Ethics*, Book III; cf. Thomas L. Heath, *Mathematics in Aristotle* (Oxford, 1949), pp. 270–72. F. Bacon, *The Philosophical Works of Francis Bacon*, ed. J. M. Robertson (London, 1905), p. 249. Isaac Barrow, *Mathematical Lectures read in the Publick Schools at the University of Cambridge*, trans. John Kirkby (London, 1734); for Barrow's familiarity with Galileo's works see Marie Boas Hall, "Galileo's Influence on Seventeenth-Century English Scientists," in *Galileo, Man of Science*, ed. Ernan McMullin (New York and London, 1967), pp. 411–12. Ernst Cassirer, *Das Erkenntnisproblem*, 3 vols. (Berlin, 1922–23), I, 136–44; for Randall's view, see his well-known paper "Scientific Method in the School of Padua," *Journal of the History of Ideas*, 1 (1940), 177–206, and its revision in his *The School of Padua and the Emergence of Modern Science* (Padua, 1961). Cassirer accepted the results of Randall's inquiry but could not "subscribe to his conclusions," for he believed Galileo's conception of the dual method, despite the identity of the terms used, to be more influenced by the mathematical tradition than by the philosophers of Padua; see his "Galileo's Platonism," in M. P. Ashley Montagu, ed. *Studies and Essays in the History of Science and Learning* (New York, 1946), pp. 279–97. I. B. Cohen, *Franklin and Newton, An Inquiry into Speculative Newtonian Experimental Science . . .* (Philadelphia, 1956). M. R. Cohen and I. Drabkin, eds., *A Source Book in Greek Science* (New York, 1948; Cambridge, Mass. 1959). A. Crombie, *Robert Grosseteste and the Origins of Experimental Science* (Oxford, 1953). Descartes, *Oeuvres de Descartes*, eds. C. Adam and P. Tannery, 13 vols. (Paris, 1891–1912). Galen, *Claudii Galeni Opera omnia*, ed. C. G. Kühn, 20 vols. (Leipzig, 1821–33); idem, *Galen on Medical Experience*, ed. and trans. R. Walzer (London and New York, 1944). Galileo Galilei, "Letter to the Grand Duchess Christina" (1615), in S. Drake, *Discoveries and Opinions of Galileo* (Garden City, N.Y., 1957); idem, *Opere di Galileo Galilei*, ed. A. Favaro, 20 vols. (Florence, 1890–1909; reprint 1929–39); idem, *Dialogues Concerning Two New Sciences*, trans. H. Crew and A. de Salvio (New York, 1914); idem, *Dialogue Concerning the Two Chief World Systems*, trans. S. Drake (Berkeley and Los Angeles, 1953). Neal Gilbert, *Renaissance Concepts of Method* (New York and London, 1960). Thomas L. Hankins, *Jean D'Alembert—Science and the Enlightenment* (Oxford, 1970), passim. Jaako Hintikka, "Kant and the Tradition of Analysis," *Deskription, Analytizität und Existenz*, 3–4 Forschungsgespräch des internationalen Forschungszentrums für Grundfragen der Wissenschaften Salzburg, ed. Paul Weingartner (Pustet-Verlag, Salzburg, and Munich, 1966), pp. 254–72. Robert Hooke, *Micrographia* (London, 1665); Hooke used Bacon's term *instantia crucis* but in one place modified it to read *experimentum crucis*. See Richard S. Westfall, "The Development of Newton's Theory of Color," *Isis*, 53 (1962), 354, and note 46. For a skeptical appraisal of Newton's famous experiment see A. I. Sabra, *Theories of Light from Descartes to Newton* (London, 1967), pp. 294–97. Sabra's argument that only Newton's adherence to a corpuscular doctrine permitted him to infer the heterogeneity of white light from this experiment is inconclusive. W. S. Jevons, *The Principles of Science* (London and New York, 1905). P. S. de Laplace, *Exposition du système du monde*, 6th ed. (Paris, 1835). A. L. Lavoisier, *Traité élémentaire de chimie* (Paris, 1789). Colin Maclaurin, *Account of Sir Isaac Newton's Philosophical Discoveries*, 3rd ed. (London, 1775). Paul Mouy, *Le Développement de la physique cartésienne, 1646–1712* (Paris, 1934). Isaac Newton, *Mathematical Principles of Natural Philosophy*, ed. F. Cajori (Berkeley, 1934); idem, *Opticks*, 4th ed. (1730); idem, *Isaac Newton's Papers and Letters on Natural Philosophy*, ed. I. B. Cohen (Cambridge, Mass., 1958); idem, "Account of the Booke entituled Commercium Epistolicum, etc.," *Philosophical Transactions*, 19, no. 342 (1717); trans. "Recensio," in the second edition (1722) of the *Commercium*; for Newton's authorship of this "Account" see Louis T. More, *Isaac Newton* (New York, 1934), pp. 590–91, note 43; idem, *Universal Arithmetick* (London, 1728). Jacques Rohault, *Traité de physique* (Paris, 1671). W. J. 'sGravesande, *Introductio ad philosophiam, metaphysicam et logicam continens* (Leiden, 1736); trans. into French as *Oeuvres philosophiques et mathématiques de Mr G. J. 'sGravesande*, ed. J. N. S. Allamand, two parts in one vol. (Amsterdam, 1774). E. W. Strong, "Newton's 'Mathematical Way'" in *Roots of Scientific Thought*, eds. Philip P. Wiener and Aaron Noland (New York, 1957); the article is reprinted, somewhat abridged, from the *Journal of the History of Ideas*, 12 (1951), 90–110. Henry G. Van Leeuwen, *The Problem of Certainty in English Thought* (The Hague, 1963). Basil Willey, *The Seventeenth Century Background* (London, 1949).

HENRY GUERLAC

[See also **Baconianism;** Classification of the Sciences; Cosmology; **Experimental Science; Newton's** *Opticks;* Number; Optics; Unity of Science.]

NEWTON'S *OPTICKS* AND EIGHTEENTH-CENTURY IMAGINATION

I

"IN A VERY DARK Chamber at a round Hole, about one third Part of an Inch broad, made in the Shut of a Window, I placed a Glass Prism, whereby the Beam of the Sun's Light, which came in at that Hole, might be refracted upwards toward the opposite Wall of the Chamber, and there form a colour'd Image of the Sun" (*Opticks*, Book I, Part I, Prop. II). So Isaac Newton described the simple apparatus that led to important discoveries about light. The *Opticks*, in which he reported them, was not published until 1704, but many of his theories were known well before that time. "Part of the ensuing Discourse about Light," he noted in his introduction, "was written at the Desire of some Gentlemen of the Royal Society in the Year 1675 and then sent to their Secretary, and read at their Meetings, and the rest were added about twelve Years later." His theories were known, too, from lectures he delivered before his students at Cambridge. John Locke had accepted them before he published his *Essay Concerning Human Understanding* in 1690, as may be seen by comparison between the printed work and a draft of 1672. A letter of Joseph Addison shows that the optical theories were known to Nicolas de Malebranche, whom Addison met while he was making the Grand Tour at the end of the seventeenth century.

Newton said in a letter to Henry Oldenburg, long Secretary of the Royal Society, that he considered his early discoveries about light and color as "the oddest, if not the most considerable deductions which hath hitherto been made in the operations of Nature." Many laymen found them so. The "deductions" of the *Principia* were of course known to men of letters and are widely reflected in both poetry and prose. But men could read the English *Opticks* who could not grasp the Latin *Principia*. I. Bernard Cohen has well expressed the difference in the Preface to his edition of the *Opticks:*

The *Opticks* invites and holds the attention of the non-specialist reader while . . . the *Principia*, is as austere and forbidding as it can possibly be. Of course, the general reader of the *Opticks* would be more interested in the final section of "Queries" than in the rest of the work, just as the general reader of the *Principia* would be drawn to the General Scholium at the end of Book Three; but whereas in the *Opticks* such a reader could enjoy about 70 pages, in the *Principia* there would be but four. The latter would discuss for him the mechanism of universal gravitation and give him a hint of the direction of Newton's thinking about this important problem; but the former would allow the reader to roam, with great Newton as his guide, through the major unresolved problems of science and even the relation of the whole world of nature to Him who had created it.

The publication of the first edition of the *Opticks* aroused a certain amount of interest among men of letters. Addison did not devote a full paper of the *Spectator* to the work, but referred to Newton's optical theories a number of times. Richard Blackmore showed knowledge of theories of the *Opticks* in his *Creation*, published in 1712. Alexander Pope used figures drawn from the prism and Newton's theories of color in *An Essay on Criticism* (1711) and the second version of *The Rape of the Lock* (1714). "False Eloquence," he said, is like a prism, spreading gaudy color everywhere. Colors come from light and return to it:

When the ripe Colours soften and unite,
And sweetly melt into just Shade and Light.
(Essay on Criticism, lines 488–89)

Pope's most charming adaptations are in passages on the "Fays, Faeries, Genii, Elves and Daemons," which he added to the second edition of *The Rape of the Lock*. Among these are some who ordinarily live in the realms of ether, where they are clothed in pure light, but when they descend to earth, light is refracted:

Loose to the Wind their airy Garments flew,
Thin glitt'ring Textures of the filmy Dew;
Dipt in the richest Tinctures of the Skies,
Where Light disports in ever-mingling Dies,
While ev'ry Beam new transient Colours flings,
Colours that change whene'er they wave their Wings.
(II, 63–68)

The most extended poetic treatment of Newton before his death was in *The Ecstasy*, by John Hughes, written shortly before the poet's death in 1717. Hughes seems to have set a pattern for a number of later poets in a passage in which the soul of Newton, "the great Columbus of the skies," is imagined on daily visits to the stars and planets, "in search of knowledge for Mankind below." Ideas from the *Principia* and the *Opticks* were in Hughes's mind when he wrote:

Here let me, thy Companion, stray,
From Orb to Orb, and now behold
Unnumber'd Suns, all Seas of molten Gold;
And trace each Comet's wand'ring Way,
And now descry Light's Fountain-Head,
And measure its descending Speed;
Or Learn how Sun-born Colours rise
In Rays distinct and in the Skies,
Blended in yellow Radiance flow,
Or stain the fleecy Cloud, or streak the Wat'ry Bow;
Or now diffus'd their beauteous Tinctures shed
On ev'ry Planets rising Hills, and ev'ry verdant Mead.

These were only preliminaries to the poetic outburst that followed Newton's death in 1727, when the feeling for "Britain's justest pride" amounted almost to deification. A host of elegies and eulogies poured from the press in 1727 and 1728, none greater than Pope's succinct couplet:

Nature, and Nature's Laws lay hid in Night.
God said, *Let Newton be!* and All was *Light*.

Some of the dedicatory poems were based on Hughes's *Ecstasy* and some upon the ode which Edmund Halley had introduced into the first edition of the *Principia*. Other verses were amorphous, as if as yet the poets had found no pattern. A model was offered by James Thomson, "To the Memory of Sir Isaac Newton," in which he hymned the author of the

Principia and the *Opticks*. Like Halley he praised the discovery of universal gravitation and discussed comets and the effect of the moon on tides. He paid particular attention to Newton's discovery of the relation between light and color:

> Even Light itself, which every thing discloses
> Shone undiscovered, till his brighter mind
> Untwisted all the shining robes of day;
> And, from the whitening undistinguish'd blaze,
> Collecting every ray into his kind,
> To the charmed eye educed the gorgeous train
> Of parent colours (lines 96–102).

In Thomson's elegy, Newtonian poets found a pattern for poems, often beginning with an apostrophe to light, calling the roll of the "parent colours," mentioning the rainbow, and concluding, as did Thomson, with a suggestion that Newton had added new beauty to the world:

> Did ever poet image aught so fair,
> Dreaming in whispering groves by the hoarse brook.
> Or prophet to whose rapture heaven descends!
>   (lines 119–21)

In addition to the model of Thomson's poem, Newtonian poets were stimulated by the publication in 1728 of Henry Pemberton's *A View of Sir Isaac Newton's Philosophy*. This was particularly designed for the layman who, Pemberton said in his Introduction, might better grasp "the Force and Beauty of this great Genius . . . when the simple and genuine Productions of the Philosopher are disengaged from the Problems of the Geometrician." Every gentleman, Pemberton continued, may come to understand the structure of the universe "with the same Ease he now acquires a Taste of the Magnificence of a Plan of Architecture, or the Elegance of a beautiful Plantation; without engaging in the minute and tedious Calculations necessary to their Production." As the *Principia* had been introduced by Halley's poem, Pemberton used as introduction "A Poem on Newton" by Richard Glover, less charming than Thomson's but more technical, dealing with gravitation, light, and color. Here versifiers could find the language they needed.

Other scientific writers of the period, such as J. T. Desaguliers, Colin MacLaurin, Benjamin Martin, James Ferguson, and L'Abbé Pluche, followed Pemberton in popular expositions of the Newtonian theories. William Derham, in the many editions of his *Physico-Theology* and *Astro-Theology*, discussed both the *Principia* and the *Opticks*. With books of popular science pouring from the press, and models like Thomson's and Glover's before them, poets set themselves happily to versify Newtonian theories. We shall first consider some of their expositions of light and color.

II

Until the period shortly after Newton's death, the chief source for descriptions of light among eighteenth-century poets had been Milton. "L'Allegro" and "Il Penseroso" were little studies in light and darkness, but in *Paradise Lost*, in the treatment of Hell, Heaven, and Chaos, darkness and light had become highly symbolic. In part because of his biblical, philosophical, and poetic heritage, in part because of his blindness, Light was to Milton godlike, awful. No single passage from *Paradise Lost* was more familiar to his eighteenth-century followers than the invocation in Book III:

> Hail, holy Light, offspring of Heaven first-born!
> Or of th' Eternal coeternal beam
> May I express thee unblamed? Since God is light,
> And never but in unapproachèd light
> Dwelt from eternity, dwelt then in thee,
> Bright effluence of bright essence increate.

Echoes from that invocation, with phrases from other prologues and Satan's address to the sun, recur frequently among the later poets. Yet the differences are as striking as the similarities. James Thomson, David Mallett, Richard Savage, Christopher Smart did not forget Milton, but they also followed Newton. They remembered that the ultimate source of light is God but they were even more conscious that the immediate source of light is the sun. Newton might say that the "Science of Colours" was a mathematical speculation, based on his prism, but the interest of the descriptive poets in the *Opticks* was not mathematical. Ironically enough, Newton—who had no interest in poetry—gave color and light back to poetry, from which they had almost disappeared during the period of Cartesianism. To the eighteenth-century poets light was magnificent in itself, but it was most beautiful when it was refracted into color. Poets discovered new beauties in individual colors of the prism, at sunrise and sunset, in the succession of colors throughout the day. There entered into poetry a "symbolism of the spectrum," suggested by many, but by none more deftly than Thomson in "To the Memory of Newton." Beginning with the "whitening undistinguished blaze" of light, he introduced the "gorgeous train/ Of parent colours":

> First the flaming red
> Sprung vivid forth; the tawny orange next;
> And next delicious yellow; by whose side
> Fell the kind beams of all-refreshing green.
> Then the pure blue, that swells autumnal skies,
> Ethereal played; and then, of sadder hue,
> Emerged the deepest indigo, as when
> The heavy-skirted evening droops with frost;
> While the last gleamings of refracted light
> Died in the fainting violet away (lines 102–11).

393

Many of the eighteenth-century poets followed Thomson in calling the roll of precious stones. The colors of gems, like those of flowers, had been used as poetic materials for centuries, but the Newtonian poets wore their rue with a difference. Again Thomson outdid all others in a deft passage in "Summer" in which light affects all parts of Nature, animate and inanimate. Diving beneath the surface of the earth into the "embowelled caverns," light wakens the precious stones:

> The unfruitful rock itself, impregned by thee,
> In dark retirement forms the lucid stone.
> The lively diamond drinks thy purest rays,
> Collected light compact. . . .
> At thee the ruby lights its deepening glow,
> And with a waving radiance inward flames.
> From thee the sapphire, solid ether, takes
> Its hue cerulean; and, of evening tint,
> The purple-streaming amethyst is thine.
> With thy own smile the yellow topaz burns;
> Nor deeper verdure dyes the robes of Spring,
> When first she gives it to the southern gale,
> Than the green emerald shows. But, all combined,
> Thick through the whitening opal play thy beams;
> Or flying from its surface, form
> A trembling variance of revolving hue,
> As the site varies in the graver's hand (lines 140–59).

Here are the red, orange, yellow, blue, green, violet of the spectrum, but here also something more subtle —the resolution of light into colors and the return of colors to light. We see first the pure light of the diamond, pass through the prismatic colors, then watch them brought together in the "whitening opal," which reflects them all, and begins to return them to the white light from which they were derived.

Most obviously the prism was associated by poets with "Newton's rainbow." In spite of Newton's own careful statements about his predecessors, the rainbow in English literature became and remained Newton's. A dozen poets described it, but since Thomson was the best among them, we may use a passage that he added to "Spring" a year after his poem to Newton, lines which he rewrote in at least two later versions:

> Meantime, refracted from yon eastern cloud,
> Bestriding earth, the grand ethereal bow
> Shoots up immense; and every hue unfolds,
> In fair proportion running from the red
> To where the violet fades into the sky.
> Here, awful Newton, the dissolving clouds
> Form, fronting on the sun, thy showery prism;
> And to the sage-instructed eye unfold
> The various twines of light, by thee disclosed
> From the white mingling blaze (lines 203–12).

In his description of the rainbow, as in a comet-passage in "Summer," Thomson contrasted the attitude of simple souls who fear the comet and of the swain who runs to catch the rainbow with that of the "enlightened few/ Whose godlike minds philosophy exalts." He was characteristic of many who thought themselves intellectually mature, having outgrown the swain seeking for a pot of gold, or Noah, to whom the rainbow was miracle. Thomson's generation did not feel, as did Keats, that Newton had taken beauty from poetry. He had added new beauty because he had added new truth.

But, like the Newtonian poets, having observed the refraction of light into the colors of the spectrum, let us return these colors to light, and consider the eighteenth-century obsession with the latter. Milton's influence is still there, though, like the moon, he shone by reflected light after "Newton rose, in orient beauty bright." The light that shines so persistently in eighteenth-century poetry is, of course, not entirely Miltonic or Newtonian, but goes back to remote ancestors they shared in common, over whom we shall not pause. Light-figures are persistent in the dedicatory poems. As Newton's soul departed this earth, it rose to light. Allan Ramsay wrote in his "Ode to the Memory of Sir Isaac Newton":

> The god-like man now mounts the sky,
> Exploring all yon radiant spheres;
> And in one view can more descry
> Than here below in eighty years.

Aaron Hill, in his "Epitaph to Sir Isaac Newton," declared:

> when the Suns he lighted up shall fade,
> And all the worlds he found are still decay'd;
> Then void and waste, eternity shall lie,
> And Time, and Newton's name, together die.

Newton, said Christopher Smart, in "On the Omniscience of the Supreme Being,"

> shone supreme, who was himself the light,
> Ere yet Refraction learn'd her skill to paint,
> And bent athwart the clouds her beauteous bow.

Old figures of speech came back in this generation with new significance. Light was "the spark, the light, the lamp, the ray, Essence or Effluence of Essential Day." It was "a bright emanation of the Godhead," a "fountain of living lustre." The sun was the "fountain of light and colour, warmth of life! The king of glory!" It was the "fountain of the golden day," the "ocean of flame." The Deity of the eighteenth century dwelt amidst "the blaze of uncreated light." His creation, Nature, was "a child of heavenly light"; his creature, man, "a beam, a mere effluvium of his majesty." "Science," his creature and evidence for his existence, was "a fair diffusive ray from the great source of mental day" which with "resistless light" dispersed phantoms of night. In various of the "excursion poems" of the century, which tended to subsume the "cosmic voyages" of the preceding period, poets divided their attention between earth and the heavens. Color was largely associated with the terrestrial world and with beauty; light radiates in passages on the heavens, associated less with beauty than with sublimity.

III

Poets like James Thomson were not only descriptive; they prided themselves on also being "scientific" and "philosophic" poets. Mark Akenside was speaking for them when he wrote in his "Hymn to Science":

> Give me to learn each secret cause;
> Let number's, figure's, motion's laws
> Revealed before me stand.

As Edward Young said, they had been "born in an age more curious than devout." Under the influence of Newton sprang up a whole group of "scientific poets," most of them now forgotten. Among the most "scientific" were John Reynolds in various editions of *A View of Death* (1709, 1716, 1725); Moses Browne in his *Essay on the Universe* (1735, 1739); Henry Brooke in *Universal Beauty* (1734, 1736). The works of most of them, widely read in their day, belong less to the history of poetry than to that of the many encyclopedias of science intended for the layman. Indeed, various versifiers included in their so-called poems elaborate series of notes drawn from encyclopedias and from such popularizers of Newton as have been mentioned.

All the versifiers—and many of the descriptive poets—were greatly interested in theories of the speed of light. Indeed, they had every reason to be, since few more spectacular discoveries have been made than that of Olaus Römer [or Roemer (1644–1719)] whose careful astronomical measurements, by proving its movement and velocity, put an end to the scholastic theory that light is instantaneous. Today the layman speaks easily of "millions of light years" but no such association had been made in earlier times. The poets cited Römer, Christian Huygens, Newton, and others. Reynolds quoted Newton in saying that rays of light spend "about seven or eight minutes in coming to us from the sun," and added that it was estimated that light travels 130,000 miles a second. Thomson wrote in his poem on Newton:

> Nor could the darting speed of light immense
> Escape his swift pursuit and measuring eye.

"How distant some of these nocturnal suns," wrote Young in *Night Thoughts* (1742–45):

> So distant (says the sage), 'twere not absurd
> To doubt if beams sent out at Nature's birth,
> Are yet arrived in this so foreign world;
> Though nearly half as rapid as their flight.
> (IX, 1224–28)

If the poets were confused about the propagation of light, they had every reason, since Newton himself had vacillated between a wave and a corpuscular theory, and in his discussion about the "Aethereal Medium" in the *Opticks* had said candidly, "I do not know what this Aether is." Certainly the poets knew much less. Yet they grappled heroically with problems of the nature of ether and air and with theories of the transmission of light and sound.

Even more interesting to the versifiers were questions about the physics of sight, with particular reference to the optics of the eye. Here they found materials in the "Queries" affixed to the *Opticks*, which they seized upon as gospel truth, though Newton himself had phrased them in often hesitant words. As Richard Jago wrote in his long poem *Edge-Hill* (1765, but sections published much earlier), the "vulgar race of men" accepted evidence of their senses without questioning:

> But sage philosophy explains the cause
> Of each phenomenòn of sight, or sound,
> Taste, touch, or smell; each organ's inmost frame,
> And correspondence with external things.

On questions of how we see, philosopher and layman put himself to school to Newton. It is significant that, although this was the great age of English satire, Newton was taken so seriously—even reverently—that he remained largely above and beyond satire. Descartes and Hobbes might be damned with impunity, Locke and Berkeley lead to laughter. But the "godlike Newton" remained aloof.

One of the problems that most interested the layman was the question of a "man born blind," that had been raised by William Molyneux, further developed by Locke, Berkeley, and others. What if such a man should gain sight in years of maturity? Would his visual response to objects prove the same as his earlier tactual response? In his *Essay*, Locke had told of a man born blind who boasted that he knew what colors signified, and upon a friend's "demanding what scarlet was," replied, "It was the sound of a trumpet." Newton's persistent interest in the "harmony" of color and sound afforded important evidence to those who believed that the blind might "see" color in terms of sound, since Newton had frequently drawn mathematical similarities between certain color-rings and the chord. Synesthesia became a matter for comment. Great popular interest was taken in the "clavecin" or "colour-organ" exhibited in London in 1757 by Père Louis Bertrand Castel to prove that the blind might hear the music of the eyes, the deaf see the music of the ears, while normal man might appreciate both music and color better by enjoying them at the same time.

In popular works of the eighteenth century we find many expositions of the physics and physiology of optics and various lists of optical terms which the gentleman, and even the lady, were evidently supposed to know. They referred easily to the "Tunica Cornea" and to the "Tunica Retina," terms which they had learned from Newton. They had much to say of pictures "painted" on the eye; they spoke of the lenslike function of the "crystalline humour." With Henry Needler they asked

> Who form'd the curious texture of the eye,
> And cloath'd it with the various tunicles
> Of texture exquisite; with chrystal juice
> Supply'd it, to transmit the rays of light?

"Pictures" of external objects, Newton had pointed out, which are "lively painted" on the "thinner Coats" of the eye and propagated along the fibres of optic nerves into the brain, are the cause of vision. Why, having two eyes, do we ordinarily see "single" rather than "double"? The layman is always interested in scientific explanations of imperfect vision, which often touch his own experience. Newton had mentioned among causes for "faint" and "confused" vision such diseases as jaundice, the decay of the eye through age, shortsightedness or farsightedness, or, as he put them, the visual limitations of men "whose Eyes are too plump" and others suffering from the defect of "plumpness in the Eye." Berkeley further developed the problems from other points of view. The descriptive and the scientific poets frequently discussed theories of imperfect vision, none more frequently than Thomson who used several of them in the *Seasons*. He too mentioned the effect of jaundice: "The yellow-tinging plague/ Internal vision taints." He introduced into "Autumn" a familiar cause of "double vision," an evening's jollity that went too far:

> Before their maudlin eyes,
> Seen dim and blue, the double tapers dance,
> Like the sun wading through the misty sky.
> (lines 554–56)

His characters experienced "confused vision" in autumn fog, when the sun "sheds weak and blind, his wide refracted ray." One of his best descriptions of "faint vision" occurred on an evening in "Summer":

> A faint erroneous ray,
> Glances from the imperfect surfaces of things,
> Flings half an image on the straining eye;
> While wavering woods, and villages, and streams,
> And rocks, and mountain-tops that long retained
> The ascending gleam are all one swimming scene
> Uncertain if beheld (lines 1687–93).

Indeed the poets of the Age of Newton found theories of optics particularly apt for application to familiar antitheses. For centuries Light had been equated with Reason; old ideas of the passions could be fitted neatly into the new idea of color refracted from light. Light "discolour'd through our Passions" afforded a nice variant for an old idea. The distinction between Reason and Fancy could be expressed in terms of the new optical theories. Fancy responded to "imperfect," "faint," "confused" sight, while Reason always saw clearly.

IV

The poets of the Age of Newton read into their master certain aesthetic implications—largely what might be called an aesthetic of color and light in which the *Opticks* became curiously fused with Addison's *Pleasures of the Imagination*. Light was associated with the Sublime, color with the Beautiful. (This association—although not there specifically with reference to Newton—is treated elsewhere in this *Dictionary* under "The Sublime in External Nature.") It was Newton, many of the poets felt, who gave color back to poetry and flooded the world with light.

When we come to consider what may be called the metaphysical implications read into the *Opticks,* we shall find the poets for the first time beginning to part company and hear occasional dissonance in what has seemed until now a paean of praise. In his "Hymn to Science," Mark Akenside, for all his admiration for Newton, warned

> There, Science! veil thy daring eye,
> Nor dive too deep, nor soar too high.

Pope in *An Essay on Man* went further in criticizing growing tendencies of the generation:

> Go, wond'rous creature! mount where Science guides,
> Go, measure earth, weigh air, and state the tides;
> Instruct the planets in what orbs to run,
> Correct old Time, and regulate the Sun; . . .
> Go, teach Eternal Wisdom how to rule—
> Then drop into thyself, and be a fool!
> Superior beings, when of late they saw
> A mortal Man unfold all Nature's law,
> Admired such Wisdom in an earthly state,
> And shew'd a Newton, as we shew an Ape (II, 19–34).

It was not Newton himself but the Newtonians Pope

castigated. But even Newton, with all his genius, could not solve eternal mysteries:

> Could he, whose rules the rapid Comet bind,
> Describe or fix one movement of his Mind?
> Who saw its fires here rise, and there descend,
> Explain his own beginning, or his end?
> Alas, what wonder! (II, 35–39).

There is a point beyond which neither science nor metaphysics can go. There are limitations to science and to human Reason. "Trace Science, then, with Modesty thy guide." It was to the lavish and unrestrained adulation aroused by Newton that Pope replied in *The Dunciad*, to some extent in the edition of 1728—written when memorial-tributes to Newton were pouring from the press—and much more in the "New" or "Greater" *Dunciad* of 1741–42.

Between the period of the early and the later *Dunciad* the tide was turning. Pope protested the excesses to which poets of the Age of Newton had gone in elevating science and metaphysics above religion and ethics, in believing that ultimate truth was to be found in the works of mathematicians, scientists, philosophers. The metaphysicians were oversubtle in spinning "cobwebs of learning" out of their own substance, absurd in clothing in elaborate philosophical jargon what was obvious to common sense. If intellectual England continued as she seemed to be bound, the sons of "Dulness"—in the *Dunciad* the word connoted not that "Dunces" knew too little but that they prided themselves on knowing too much—would come to worship man rather than God:

> 'Tis yours a Bacon or a Locke to blame,
> A Newton's genius, or a Milton's flame:
> But oh! with One, immortal one dispense;
> The source of Newton's Light, of Bacon's Sense.
> (*Dunciad*, III, 215–18)

But there were various other implications read into the *Opticks*.

In a period when the Cartesian shears seemed to have cut matter "out there" from mind "in here," such problems of vision and perception as have been mentioned seemed more poignant than to us. Plato's man, sitting in his cave, watching the shadows on his wall, became a symbol of the greatest thinkers of the Age of Newton, as Locke's familiar "closet simile" suggests. The same general symbolism could be read into Newton. He who had given color back to the poets and flooded the world with light, "Newton with his prism and silent face," he too had darkened his Cambridge room to see light and color. Light entered that dark chamber only through a pin-prick, light reflected, refracted, inflected. We may let two of our contemporary philosophers speak.

E. A. Burtt wrote in *The Metaphysical Foundations of Modern Physical Science* . . . :

It was of the greatest consequence for succeeding thought that now the great Newton's authority was squarely behind the view of the cosmos which saw in man a puny, irrelevant spectator (so far as a being wholly imprisoned in a dark room can be called such) of the vast mathematical system whose regular motions according to mathematical principles constituted the world of nature. . . . The world that people had thought themselves living in—a world rich with colour and sound, redolent with fragrance, filled with gladness, love and beauty, speaking everywhere of purposive harmony and creative ideals—was crowded now into minute corners in the brains of scattered organic beings. The really important world outside was a world hard, cold, colourless, silent and dead; a world of quantity, a world of mathematically computable motions in mechanical regularity (1932 ed., pp. 236–37).

Let us add some sentences from Alfred North Whitehead, as he discusses the mechanistic in *Science and the Modern World:*

Whatever theory you choose, there is no light or colour as a fact in external nature. There is merely motion of material. Again, when the light enters your eyes and falls on the retina, there is merely motion of material. Then your nerves are affected and your brain is affected, and again this is motion of material. . . . Nature is a dull affair, soundless, scentless, colourless; merely the hurrying of material, endlessly, meaninglessly.

However you disguise it, that is the practical outcome of the characteristic scientific philosophy which closed the seventeenth century (p. 80).

Whence, then, arises that "pleasing delusion" of the beauty of nature long shared by poets and artists? Whitehead replies:

Nature gets credit which should in truth be reserved for ourselves: the rose for its scent; the nightingale for his song; and the sun for his radiance. The poets are entirely mistaken. They should address their lyrics to themselves, and turn them into odes of self-congratulation on the excellency of the human mind (ibid.).

It is probable that the eighteenth-century poets might not have grasped the implications of the Cartesian, Lockean, Newtonian metaphysics as well as they did, had it not been for Addison. In his essays on the pleasures of the imagination, he put before his followers the picture of the new universe we have heard described by Professors Burtt and Whitehead. Let us limit ourselves at present to Addison's *Spectator* 413:

We are everywhere entertained with pleasing shows and apparitions, we discover imaginary glories in the heavens, and in the earth, and see some of this visionary beauty poured out upon the whole creation; but what a rough unsightly sketch of Nature should we be entertained with,

397

did all her colouring disappear, and the several distinctions of light and shade vanish? . . .

I have here supposed that my reader is acquainted with that great modern discovery, which is at present universally acknowledged by all the inquirers into natural philosophy, namely that light and colours, as apprehended by the imagination, are only ideas in the mind and not qualities that have any existence in matter.

Addison made use of a figure of speech which, like many of his analogies, was picked up by his followers:

. . . our souls are at present delightfully lost and bewildered in a pleasing delusion, and we walk about like the enchanted hero in a romance, who sees beautiful castles, woods, and meadows; and at the same time hears the warbling of birds, and the purling of streams; but upon the finishing of some secret spell, the fantastic scene breaks up, and the disconsolate knight finds himself on a barren heath, or in a solitary desert.

Had the eighteenth-century poets been philosophers, they might have felt themselves living in such a world, and poetry would have fallen upon still more evil days. But poets cannot continue long in an abstract world. The school of Pope was carrying abstractions as far as possible. In spite of their reading in philosophy, the poets were not philosophers. Edward Young's *Night Thoughts* (1742–45) is the only long poem of the period that might have been written according to the prescription laid down by Addison in his generation, and by Burtt and Whitehead in ours. Into the camera obscura of perpetual night, Young retired in order that Reason might see light pure, not colored, refracted, inflected. There is no color in the *Night Thoughts;* there is only light streaming down from heaven at night. Mark Akenside was rather a philosophical poet than a poet of Nature. In *The Pleasures of Imagination* (1744) he shows clearly that

Mind, Mind alone, (bear witness, earth and heav'n!)
The living fountains in itself contains
Of beauteous and sublime: . . . (Book I, lines 481–83).

Yet Akenside suggested no blame for the man who, knowing nothing of the New Philosophy, walked happily about, bending his ear "To the full choir of water, air, and earth," responding to a beauty he believed to be in Nature. Pope, Young, Akenside, in their various ways, were indicative of one aspect of this period in that they were largely abstract poets of thought rather than concrete poets of Nature, reflecting ideas of reality rather than reality itself.

Of all the poets who were publishing major poems around 1744, James Thomson seems at first glance the most ambivalent. No poet of the period discussed the New Philosophy at greater length. There are moments in *The Seasons* when we are highly conscious that

Thomson was writing in the age of Locke and Newton and had developed the characteristic self-consciousness about processes of vision and perception. No poet of the period introduced as much discussion of such processes into his work. Yet it was not for his philosophical analyses that his age loved him and we remember him. Responsive though he was to Locke and Newton, he never radically departed from his allegiance to the religious and poetical heritage that had been his before he discovered the philosophers. He never believed himself Addison's "disconsolate knight" on a heath or desert. His soul was not "lost and bewildered in a pleasant delusion"; Nature, to him, was no "rough unsightly sketch." To Thomson beauty really existed in external Nature. He climbed real hills to "See the country, far-diffused around," to describe affectionately scenes with which he was entirely familiar. Walking abroad in Nature, he responded to the impressions of his senses to receive

The whole magnificence of heaven and earth,
And every beauty, delicate or bold.

The influence of Newton upon poetry—which he would never have understood—continued throughout the eighteenth century, though the climactic years were from Newton's death to the mid-century. In the last decade of the century another voice presaging the romantic reaction against science begins to be heard in William Blake. "Art is the Tree of Life," he said in one of his captions, "Science is the Tree of Death." Again and again in his marginalia, annotations, epigrams, and fragments, he introduced Newton's name, often with those of Bacon, Descartes, and Locke, as an enemy of art and poetry.

Reason says "Miracle"; Newton says "Doubt."
Aye! that's the way to make all Nature out.

Bacon's philosophy was the beginning. "Bacon's Philosophy has Ruin'd England," Blake commented:

Newton & Bacon cry, being badly Nurst:
"He is all Experience from last to first."

Newton was expert in mathematics. "God is not a Mathematical Diagram," commented Blake. "The End of Epicurean or Newtonian Philosophy . . . is Atheism." Newton was associated in Blake's mind with all that was anathema. To the earlier poets, Newton had given the world new beauty with new truth. They had glorified until they almost deified him. William Blake presided at the poetic damnation of Sir Isaac Newton.

BIBLIOGRAPHY

Joseph Addison, *The Spectator*, ed. with an introduction and notes by Donald F. Bond, 5 vols. (Oxford, 1965). Mark

Akenside, *The Pleasures of Imagination* (London, 1744). E. A. Burtt, *Metaphysical Foundations of Modern Physical Science: A Historical and Critical Essay* (New York, 1924; 2nd ed. rev. 1932). John Dillenberger, *Protestant Thought and Natural Science: A Historical Interpretation* (Garden City, N.Y., 1960). Hoxie Neale Fairchild, *Religious Trends in English Poetry*, 6 vols. (New York, 1939–68). Elsie C. Graham, *Optics and Vision: The Background of the Metaphysics of Berkeley* . . . (New York, 1929). William Powell Jones, *The Rhetoric of Science: A Study of Scientific Ideas and Imagery in Eighteenth-Century English Poetry* (Berkeley and Los Angeles, 1966). Kenneth MacLean, *John Locke and English Literature of the Eighteenth Century* (New Haven, 1936). John Locke, *An Essay Concerning Human Understanding*, in *Philosophical Works* . . . , with a Preliminary Essay and Notes by J[ames] A[ugustus] St. John, 2 vols. (London, 1889), Vol. I. Isaac Newton, *Opticks, Or a Treatise on the Reflections, Refractions, Inflections & Colours of Light*, preface by I. Bernard Cohen (New York, 1952). Marjorie Nicolson, *Newton Demands the Muse: Newton's Opticks and the Eighteenth Century Poets* (Princeton, 1946). Henry Pemberton, *A View of Sir Isaac Newton's Philosophy* (London, 1728). Alexander Pope, *Poems of Alexander Pope*, Twickenham Edition, 6 vols. in 7 (London, 1939–61). James Thomson, *The Complete Poetical Works of James Thomson*, ed. J. Logie Robertson (Oxford, 1908). Alfred North Whitehead, *Science and the Modern World. Lowell Lectures* (New York, 1925; also reprint). Edward Young, *Night Thoughts* . . . , with Notes by the Rev. C. E. De Coetlogon (London, n.d.)

MARJORIE HOPE NICOLSON

[See also Beauty; **Mountains; Newton on Method;** Optics; Romanticism; **Sublime;** *Ut pictura poesis.*]

NUMBER

FOR MODERN man it is impossible to conceive of a world without numbers. If we were unable to distinguish between 1 and 2, between 10 and 12, between one thousand and one million, our whole culture and civilization would collapse. No policeman could stop us for passing the speed limit, for this limit must be fixed in terms of numbers, provided of course that it would be possible to build automobiles without being able to count the number of wheels or doors to be built into them. Whatever we think about in our daily life and surroundings is in one way or another dependent on our ability to count. In this sense, if in no other, certainly the old Pythagorean saying is true: "All is number."

Considering for a moment the number system in common use today, probably the most remarkable fact about it is that the whole of civilized mankind, with very few exceptions, is using the same kind of system and symbols. Though we speak many languages and write in different scripts, the number of different number systems still in use today all over our planet is far more limited. And for all scientific work there is in fact only one system—the one Westerners have all known since their childhood. Consisting of ten symbols 1, 2, 3, 4, 5, 6, 7, 8, 9 and 0, it is so highly developed that all other numbers are expressible by means of these two handfuls of signs. A remarkable achievement, if one stops to think about it for a moment.

The story of our numbering system has two aspects. It is the story of the names given to numbers, and it is the story of the symbols representing numbers. Both have, in various degrees, contributed to the concept of number itself and the systematic structure of our present number system.

Besides the spoken number sequence, the number words, and the written number sequence, the number symbols, there once existed a third way of communicating the meaning of a number from person to person: the use of gestures. By different positions of the ten fingers one may convey various numbers. Methodically developed, this can be extended to rather large numbers. Thus, medieval manuscripts and early printed books contain pictures indicating how by different positions of the ten fingers it is possible to represent any number up to 9999.

In the eighth century the Venerable Bede, an English monk of the order of Saint Benedict, for the first time in history recorded the gestures for numbers in his work on the ecclesiastical calendar. While Bede described the method in detail, let it be sufficient here to say that the three outer fingers of the left hand had to represent the units from 1 to 9, the index finger and thumb of the same hand the tens from 10 to 90, the same two fingers of the right hand the hundreds, and the outer three fingers of the right hand the thousands. Thus, for the person facing a man who signalized a number this way, the four digits would appear in increasing order from right to left. In fact the meaning of "digit" here is derived from the Latin word for finger: *digitus* (Figure 1).

While it is impossible to say definitely where and when these "finger numbers" were invented for the first time, it seems very likely that they arose from the needs of commerce; they are a language of tradesmen. A similar way of representing numbers by means of fingers can still be observed in certain Arabic and East African marketplaces. Seller and buyer will touch and rub each other's hands under a cloth so that onlookers are unable to find out for what price the bargain is completed. This method works even when the traders do not speak a common language—they

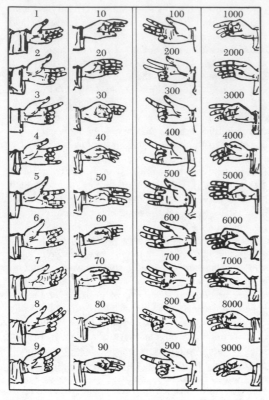

1	10	100	1000
2	20	200	2000
3	30	300	3000
4	40	400	4000
5	50	500	5000
6	60	600	6000
7	70	700	7000
8	80	800	8000
9	90	900	9000

FIGURE 1. Finger Numbers, after chart from L. Pacioli, *Summa de arithmetica*, Venice, 1494

do not need a language as the gestures speak for themselves. Even in our modern industrialized world there still exists a place where finger gestures are used to transmit numbers: at the stock exchange. The system, however, is adapted to the special need of the brokers. In general, finger numbers are no longer a common medium for the conveyance of numbers.

Finger gestures are a mode of silent communication about numbers. They are by nature short-lived and transitory, not suitable for keeping a permanent record. The same holds for the spoken number word, unless it is remembered and thus kept alive in a human mind. For a permanent record, numbers must be written down or stored in some other convenient way. Modern computers, for instance, may store numbers on a magnetic tape which can be "read" again by the computer though not directly by the human eye. Primitive men, too, invented procedures of storing numbers. Some of these do work on a very elementary, and yet, as we shall see, very basic, principle, not needing any signs or script.

The Wedda on the island of Ceylon, when counting coconuts, used to take a bundle of sticks and assigned one stick to each coconut, always saying "this is one." In this way they obtained just as many sticks as there were coconuts; nevertheless they had no number words. But they were able to keep a record: if a coconut was stolen, one stick was left over when the assignment of sticks to coconuts was repeated.

Mathematically speaking, what the Wedda do is establish a *one-to-one correspondence* between the objects to be counted and an auxiliary set of objects. This is the most basic principle of counting of all, here applied in its most elementary way. One coconut—one stick, another coconut—another stick, still another coconut—still another stick; one stick for each coconut, but never more; hence also: one coconut for each stick, and not one less. It may come as a surprise to some that it is possible to count without having numbers, yet, as we just saw, it can be done. It is inconvenient, of course, since the sticks have to be carried and kept, and the process of counting is slow. To inform a fellow about a number, one has to show a set of auxiliary objects of the same number of items.

Awkward as it may seem we do sometimes employ the same elementary process. Think of a teacher who is sent with his pupils into another classroom. If he wants to know whether there is a sufficient number of chairs for his students he need not first count the students, then the chairs; he will just ask the class to sit down and observe if somebody will be left without a chair. The one-to-one correspondence will solve his problem, not a single number word or number symbol being required.

Number systems are nothing else but such *auxiliary sets* of a very special kind. First of all, these sets do not consist of hard objects. The real objects are replaced by symbols written on paper or made visible in some other way. Secondly, the objects or elements of the auxiliary set are not all alike. Both these facts are real advances over the primitive method applied by the Wedda. Both are related to the invention of the art of writing, although the second distinction is not limited to written symbols.

Consider an ancient way of counting soldiers. Passing through a gate in single file, a pebble was dropped into a box as each soldier passed. When ten soldiers had passed, the ten pebbles were taken out of the box and one pebble was put into a second box instead. For each of the following soldiers one pebble was placed in the first box until again ten men had passed. Then the ten pebbles were taken out of this box and another pebble was placed into the second instead. When the second box received its tenth pebble, these ten were interchanged for one pebble in the third box, and so on. After all soldiers had' passed, their total number could be determined almost instantly.

This story exemplifies another principle in counting: the introduction of a *collective unit*. One pebble in the second box represents ten pebbles in the first, one pebble in the third box is valued as much as ten pebbles in the second, etc. Although there is, in this example, only one kind of pebbles, the value assigned to each depends on its position, on its being placed in a certain box. Another way of introducing collective units would have been possible. Using, for instance, small pebbles to count the individual soldiers, medium-sized pebbles to represent ten small ones, and large pebbles to represent ten medium-sized ones, only one box would have been necessary. We see: when collective units are introduced, this can be done in two ways. If there is only one type of objects (or symbols) at hand, the distinction must be made by help of the *position;* if on the other hand different objects (or symbols) are available for the various collective units, position does not matter. As we continue our study of number systems, this will lead to important consequences.

An example of a number system in which collective units are used in regular fashion is the Egyptian hieroglyphic one, dating from about 3000 B.C. Except for the symbol for one, a simple stroke, there are no other symbols but six collective units, for ten and its powers (Figure 2):

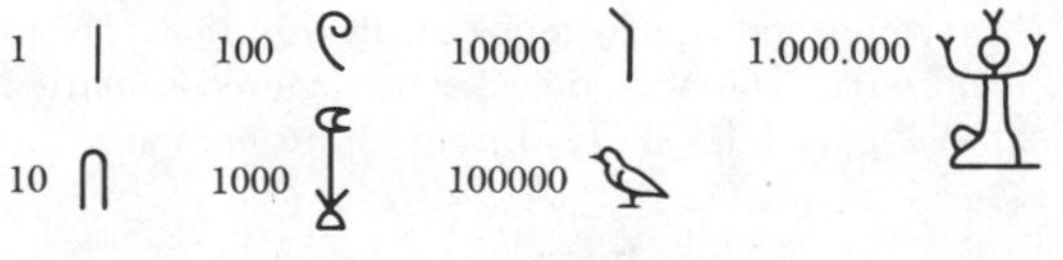

FIGURE 2

In writing a number, these symbols could be repeated, each up to nine times. An example is (Figure 3):

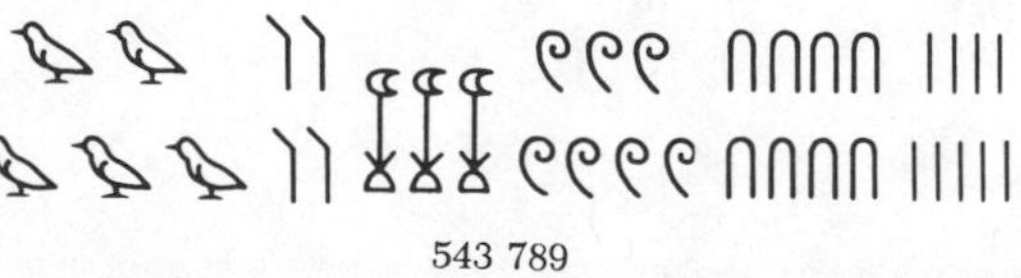

543 789

FIGURE 3

The order of the symbols does not matter, they could be arranged in horizontal as well as in vertical directions. That is, position is irrelevant; each sign carries its meaning in a unique way. We call such a system a *tallying system,* since the individual number symbols are marked or tallied as often as required.

The Roman number system essentially is a tallying system, too. It is distinguished from the old Egyptian one in that it employs collective units not only for the powers of ten (I, X, C, M = 1, 10, 100, 1000 respectively), but also for the quintuples of these (V, L, D = 5, 50, 500). There is no essential difference; the addition of the latter symbols only makes the numbers more readable since at most four symbols of one kind are necessary, against nine in the Egyptian mode of writing numbers:

MMMDCCLXXXVIIII = 3789

(The use of IX for nine, instead VIIII, or XC for LXXXX, etc., is a later development.)

Both the Egyptian and the Roman system are constructed by rule, in that all powers of ten (up to a certain limit) are assigned new symbols as collective units. The number ten therefore is called the *base* of the system. Not all number systems have base ten; in fact, not all have a base at all. In our present time measurement, for example, 60 seconds are equivalent to one minute, 60 minutes to one hour, but 24 hours to one day, 30 days to one month, and 12 months to one year. This system has no base, therefore.

The systems discussed so far operate with relatively few signs which, if required, must be repeated several times. Mankind also invented systems that in principle do not demand any repetition of symbols. Such for instance is the Greek method of taking the letters of the alphabet as number signs (Figure 4):

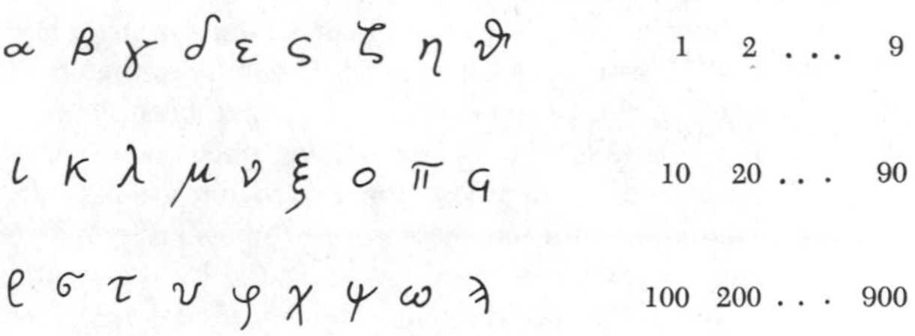

FIGURE 4

While repetition of symbols is eliminated in this Alexandrian system, and hence numbers become much shorter and more easily readable, the disadvantage clearly lies in the fact that a very large number of signs is necessary. Even the Greeks had to add a few Semitic signs to their alphabet in order to have at least 27 symbols (9 for the units, 9 for the tens, and 9 for the hundreds). For thousands, they repeated the signs for the units, distinguishing them by a little stroke. It would have been more consistent to use entirely different characters. There is no tallying in the Alexandrian number system since each number has its own code symbol; we therefore call it a *code system*. Again, order or position of the symbols within a number does not really matter as each sign carries only one value. The handicap lies in the quantity of symbols necessary to extend the system far enough.

Let us summarize our observations. Counting, we saw, is based on the principle of one-to-one correspondence between the objects to be counted and the elements of an auxiliary set. In the simplest case these elements are indistinguishable sticks or strokes. In a more advanced case there are some different kinds of elements in the auxiliary set, e.g., those representing the first powers of ten, or other collective units. In the extreme case each element of the auxiliary set is different from all others; a long alphabet would be an example, in which no two letters were alike. Which of the three cases could serve as an ideal number system? The first has the advantage of providing an infinitely large auxiliary set (stroke after stroke without end), but the elements are not distinguishable, and reading of large numbers becomes cumbersome. The last allows for easy reading as each number has its own character, but the sequence cannot be extended to cover "all" numbers since nobody can remember infinitely many different signs. What is needed for an ideal number system obviously is an arrangement of some, but not too many *code symbols* with repetition after a given pattern. How this pattern can be formed was suggested in the story about counting soldiers: it is the *position* of symbols that must be used in addition to their immediate meaning.

Such a system we have in our *Hindu-Arabic number system*, as it is usually called. It combines the advantages of the various systems that have been discussed in this article: there is no tallying since code symbols for each of the numbers from one to nine are provided. Beginning with ten these code symbols are employed again with a new meaning indicated by the position in which they are standing. This repeated employment is taking place completely regularly: the system has a base ten. Thus, the symbol 3 may stand for three, but also for thirty, three hundred, three thousand, etc.; only its position within the number fixes its value exactly. The base being ten, all collective units are multiples of ten. It is therefore possible to extend the system as far as necessary; even if one should run out of number words, the number symbol for any number however so large can immediately be written down.

Such a *positional system* contains one logical difficulty which does not occur in a tallying system with collective units. Consider the number three hundred and six in Roman numerals: CCCVI. There are no tens in this number, hence the symbol X does not appear. It is very simple. Not so in a positional system. We cannot simply write 36 but need only indicate that the place for the tens is empty, i.e., we need a place-holder as it is sometimes called. This is of course the symbol 0 for zero. Logically this presents an immense difficulty: one writes *something* to indicate that there is *nothing*. That must have sounded queer to many an early student of our positional number system! It was one of the really great steps in the historical development of number systems that such a sign was introduced. Without it, our mode of numeration would be far less perfect.

There does indeed exist a way to evade, so to speak, the invention of zero. As example let us consider the basic numbers of the Chinese; they have several number scripts. A decimal system with base ten, it consists of a mixture of code symbols for the units from 1 to 9 and collective units for the powers of ten (Figure 5).

一二三四五六七八九十百千

| 1 | 2 | 3 | 4 | 5 | 6 | 7 | 8 | 9 | 10 | 100 | 1000 |

FIGURE 5

We may call the collective units "labels" for they serve to label the positions within a number. In other words: the code symbols, taken by themselves, carry the values from one to nine, but when they are combined with a label they multiply the latter's value by their own. No symbol for zero is required. If, e.g., there are no hundreds in a number, the label for hundred is omitted, as in Figure 6 (to be read from top to bottom):

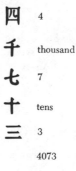

四	4
千	thousand
七	7
十	tens
三	3
	4073

FIGURE 6

This Chinese system therefore is a *positional system with labels*. Its distinction from a positional system without labels—such as ours—is to be found in two points: (1) the suppression of the labels, the meaning of each position being understood as self-evident according to its natural sequence; (2) the introduction of a place holder, i.e., a symbol for zero which then becomes necessary. With these two steps we can construct the singularly efficient positional system without labels. Logically, there only remains the choice of the most convenient base for it. Historically this base came to be the number ten, but from time to time arguments have been aired in favor of twelve which would allow for easier divisibility of numbers into the most common small fractions.

We need not tell the history of our Hindu-Arabic number system in detail, but we may take a glance at the highly essential *concept of zero*. It was not until the seventeenth century that zero was accepted as a "real" number. In the second century B.C. a little circle appeared in Greek astronomical texts as a place holder, most probably an abbreviation of the Greek word *oudén* ("not one," "nothing"). It may well be the same little circle that we meet again in a Hindu inscription (ninth century A.D.) where the number 270 is represented in this form: $= 7_\circ$. The inscription is written in Brahmi script, the very number script which, with some variations, was taken over by the Arabs and by them transmitted into Europe, and named the *Hindu-Arabic number system*. As for the spoken word: the original Indian term for the little circle as place holder was *sunya* ("empty"). It was translated by the Arabs as *aṣ-ṣifr* ("emptiness"), which word was taken over into Latin as *cifra* or *zefirum*. Our *cipher* is derived from the former word; our *zero* from the latter. It is strange to observe that *cipher*, once the name for zero only, became the term for all "ciphers," i.e., for the figures from 1 to 9, too. This is a witness to the great difficulties that were encountered when the strange characters of the present number system were first introduced into Europe. Another Latin name for zero was *nulla figura* ("no figure"), the origin for the German *Null* and identical in meaning with the English *nought* = nothing. In a formal way prescriptions for the handling of zero had been given in late antiquity, but it was not before the sixteenth and seventeenth centuries respectively, that zero was admitted as coefficient or as root of an algebraic equation. Only with A. Girard and R. Descartes did the symbol 0 gain full equality of rights as a number.

Apart from zero *unity* too was for centuries not considered a number. The ancient Pythagoreans (fifth century B.C.) were the first to philosophize about the nature of number. Their statement, "All is number" expresses their belief that numbers are the essence of all existing things. Hence to understand a thing one had to know its number. As Philolaus remarked: "All things which can be known have number; for it is impossible for a thing to be conceived or known without number" (Diels [1934], 47 B 1). Unity itself, however, was not a number but the principle from which all (further) numbers were generated. This view persisted beyond medieval scholasticism, but again, and no later than Descartes, all distinctions between 1 and the rest of the integers had completely vanished. At the same time, and not least by the influence of Descartes, the *modern* mathematical point of view towards numbers was gaining ground. Here numbers are nothing but abstract entities that can be produced according to certain rules and that serve to describe order and quantity. This is the number concept of the mathematician who does not know the difficulties mankind had to overcome before this abstract idea could be formed, before it could be molded into a rigorous logical framework.

The historical process, in large parts not reconstructible and hence for ever open to speculation, nevertheless has left some marks. Use of the names for 0 illustrates an important step in the construction of a written number system. The vast store of names for other numbers, in particular for the first positive integers, in many living and dead languages, makes it possible to draw further conclusions about the history of the idea of number. One of the main insights one gains from a comparative study of number words in various languages, particularly those of primitive people, is the fact that in the early stages of counting numbers have much in common with adjectives. That is to say, numbers are seen in very close relation with the objects they count.

In some cases, the number concept may even merge with the noun to make a special grammatical form, as in Greek, where besides the singular and the plural there exists a special dual:

ho philos the friend   *to philo* the two friends
hoi philoi the friends (more than two)

In other cases, a number word has several forms according to the gender of the noun to which it belongs. Thus, in Latin "one" has three forms, "two" and "three" have two forms, and only from "four" onwards the number words are indeclinable. In still other cases, number words may not be used with any arbitrary object but only in connection with items of a special kind or class. A tribe of American Indians had special number words for living objects, for round objects, for long objects, and for days. Even the English language today contains several expressions for the number 2 which can only be applied with respect to certain situations: a yoke, a pair, a couple, a duet, twins.

While all these examples show the close relationship between early numbers and the things they count, other number names reveal that in many parts of the earth counting began with the help of fingers, and sometimes toes, too. The number words of the Déné-Dindje, a tribe of American Indians, have the following meaning:

1   the end is bent (little finger)
2   it is bent again (ring finger)
3   the center is bent (middle finger)
4   there is one left over
5   my hand is finished

Not often is the relation between the names for the first numbers and the finger gestures so clear as in this example. The following number words are collected from various cultures:

5   whole hand; once my hand
6   one on the other hand; other one
10 both hands; both sides; two hands die (i.e., all ten fingers are bent)
11 one on the foot
16 one on the other foot
20 my hands, my feet; a man; man brought to an end.

Where fingers (and toes) formed the first auxiliary set for counting and provided a ready source for the first number names, a decimal (or vigesimal) system was the natural outcome if the system was later extended in regular pattern. It is therefore not surprising that decimal systems are widespread among the spoken number sequences, or that they are mixed with vigesimal elements, as we see in French:

10	dix
20	vingt
30	trente
40	quarante
50	cinquante
60	soixante
70	soixante-dix
80	quatre-vingts (four times twenty)
90	quatre-vingt-dix
100	cent

Reference to the human body might go beyond the use of fingers and toes as the number sequence of a Papuan tribe demonstrates:

1	anuso	little finger (right)
2	doro	ring finger
3	doro	middle finger
4	doro	index finger
5	ubei	thumb
6	tama	wrist
7	unubo	elbow
8	visa	shoulder
9	denoro	ear
10	diti	eye
11	diti	eye (left)
12	medo	nose
13	bee	mouth
14	denoro	ear (left)
15	visa	shoulder
16	unubo	elbow
17	tama	wrist
18	ubei	thumb
19	doro	index finger
20	doro	middle finger
21	doro	ring finger
22	anuso	little finger

Unfortunately there cannot be given such a simple and instructive explanation for our own number words. They are modifications of the Anglo-Saxon ones, which in turn are of old Germanic origin. All Germanic languages show similarities in their spoken number sequences but the original meaning is not clear. Here we leave historical considerations and turn to the modern mathematical viewpoint.

Formally, if he considers zero and the positive integers $1, 2, 3, \ldots$ to be given, the mathematician may construct further numbers as roots of equations, whose coefficients are taken from these integers. The equation $x + 1 = 0$ for instance will produce the "root" or solution $x = -1$, since $-1 + 1 = 0$. Similarly, all other negative integers may be produced. We may hence assume the general form of an algebraic equation to be

$$a_n x^n + a_{n-1} x^{n-1} + a_{n-2} x^{n-2} + \ldots + a_1 x + a_0 = 0$$

where all coefficients $a_0, a_1, \ldots, a_n$ are positive or negative integers or zero. Let us see how further types of numbers can be constructed by means of such equations.

The simplest type that is contained in the general form above is the so-called linear equation in which the unknown x appears only in the first degree: $a_1 x + a_0 = 0$. This equation may be understood as the definition of the fraction $-a_0/a_1$ for if $x = -a_0/a_1$ it will satisfy the equation. Suppose, e.g., $a_0 = -1$, $a_1 = 2$, then the equation would be $2x - 1 = 0$ with the root $x = 1/2$. Hence we have "generated" the fraction $1/2$. In an obvious way all other fractions, positive or negative, may be thus constructed. It is the task of the mathematician to show that these fractions do obey the common laws to which all numbers have to be subjected, and that in particular the elementary operations (addition, subtraction, multiplication, and division) can be carried out in a meaningful and noncontradictory way.

New types of numbers may occur when equations

of the second degree are studied: $a_2x^2 + a_1x + a_0 = 0$. Supposing for simplicity that $a_1 = 0$, the basic type of such a quadratic equation is $a_2x^2 + a_0 = 0$, whose root we have to write in the form $x = \sqrt{-a_0/a_2}$. If, for instance, $a_0 = 18$, $a_2 = -2$ $(-2x^2 + 18 = 0)$, the numbers $x = 3$ and $x = -3$ will solve the equation, and there is no further problem. If, however, we are given $x^2 - 2 = 0$ $(a_0 = -2, a_2 = 1)$, the root can be written in the form $x = \sqrt{2}$, but it cannot be expressed as an integer or a fraction. Such a number is called *irrational* since it does not form a ratio or fraction (in the sense of $1/2 = 1:2$ or $5 = 5:1$). It was a fundamental discovery of far-reaching consequences, made first by the Pythagoreans, that not all numbers are rational numbers, that is, fractions or integers. As a consequence they had to reconstruct a great deal of their mathematics. It is possible to show that these irrational numbers can be incorporated into the number system without difficulty. In fact, without irrational numbers the number system would be incomplete. By the way, more complicated roots such as $\sqrt[3]{7}$ or $\sqrt[5]{7} + \sqrt[3]{2}$ are not of an essentially different type. Rational and irrational numbers together are called *real numbers* by the mathematicians. For any two unequal real numbers it is possible to decide which one is greater than the other. In consequence, all real numbers may be ordered according to magnitude and represented on the real number line (Figure 7):

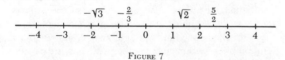

FIGURE 7

There remains one case to be considered: the square root of a negative number. The most simple case would be the solution of the equation $x^2 + 1 = 0$, that is $x = \sqrt{-1}$ which means $x^2 = -1$. Now there is no real number—whether integer, fraction or irrational—whose square is -1. This fact has baffled mathematicians since the sixteenth century; before that time they would simply say that this equation has no root at all. Slowly they learned to accept the new, "imaginary" type of number for the reason that it was possible to operate with it in the usual way. Writing $i = \sqrt{-1}$ for brevity's sake it became clear that *all* numbers which may arise as roots of algebraic equations are either real, or *imaginary,* of the complex form $a + bi$, where a and b are real numbers and $i = \sqrt{-1}$. For instance, the equation $x^4 - 6x^2 + 25 = 0$ has a root $x = 2 + i$ $(a = 2, b = 1)$.

A different problem was how to realize or represent this new type of number which no longer fitted into the linear arrangement on the line of real numbers. It was only about 1800 that independently of one another C. Wessel, C. F. Gauss, and J. R. Argand conceived the possibility of representing these *complex numbers* $(a + bi)$ in a plane, the complex number plane (Figure 8).

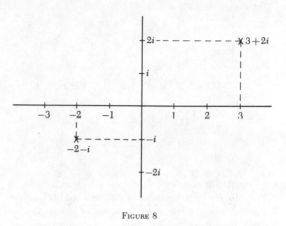

FIGURE 8

Later in the century W. R. Hamilton developed a more abstract introduction of complex numbers as pairs (a, b) of real numbers. He also showed that no further extension of the number system is possible if all the usual laws of the four elementary operations $(+, -, \times, \div)$ are to remain valid.

An extension of the number system of quite another kind was given by G. Cantor in 1874. Galileo had discussed the question whether the number of squares $(1, 4, 9, 16, \ldots)$ is to be reckoned the same as the number of positive integers $(1, 2, 3, 4, \ldots)$. The problem required a quantitative treatment of the *actually infinite;* neither Galileo nor other mathematicians believed such treatment to be possible. Cantor, much against his will, was forced to the following conclusions. If a one-to-one correspondence is taken as the essential principle of counting, the infinite set (or collection) of all positive integers has exactly as many elements as the infinite set of all square numbers. The obvious correspondence is a one-to-one matching of each element of the whole set, to each element of the subset:

set of positive integers:	1	2	3	4	....
set of squares:	1	4	9	16	....

Introducing the concept of "power," mathematicians say with Cantor that two sets have the same power, if they can be matched element for element. For infinite sets there is an immediate consequence: it is no longer true that a subcollection or part is less than the whole set, and the whole may have the same power, as in the example just given.

All infinite sets that can be arranged in one-to-one correspondence with the set of positive integers are said to be *denumerable*. For instance, the set of all positive rational numbers (i.e., fractions) is seen to be denumerable by the following arrangement:

set of positive integers: 1   2   3   4
set of positive rationals: 1/1   1/2   2/1   1/3

     5   6   7   8   9   10
2/2   3/1   1/4   2/3   3/2   4/1   1/5   2/4
1/1   1/2

     11   12   13   14
3/3   4/2   5/1   1/6   2/5   3/4 ....
1/1   2/1

Not all infinite sets, however, are denumerable. If they were so, the concept of power would be useless. Cantor was able to show that the set of all positive "real" numbers—which include irrational numbers, like $\sqrt{2}$—is not denumerable, i.e., it is impossible to match all such reals with the positive integers: there are just "too many" of the former. Hence the set of real numbers has a power greater than that of the integers. It is called the *power of the continuum*. One may construct infinite sets whose power is greater than that of the continuum. Indeed, the sequence of these powers or *transfinite numbers,* which so to speak count the orders of infinity, is itself infinite. This is truly beyond the powers of imagination of any human being; it can only be established by strict logical reasoning.

When one surveys the whole development of the idea of number from its earliest cultural origins to the abstract modern concepts, one becomes aware of the close relations and mutual interdependence between the course of this development and the growth of science and technology that has taken place since the Renaissance. In those days the study of nature turned away from the Aristotelian world view with its emphasis on qualitative change and teleological reasoning. The basic question of the philosopher of old: "Why does this happen?" was replaced by the more restricted question of the modern scientist: "How does this happen?" Galileo recognized that the answer to this last question could only be expressed in the language of quantity, that is, in mathematical form. Geometry and algebra in the time of Galileo and Descartes offered the patterns according to which the new science of mechanics could be modeled. As mechanics grew, new branches of mathematics began to blossom: differential and integral calculus, probability theory and statistics,

differential geometry, the theory of differential equations and the calculus of variations, and a host of other mathematical disciplines. The great success of analytical mechanics and its applications during the seventeenth and eighteenth centuries inaugurated a mathematization of more and more physical, natural, and social sciences during the past two centuries, which seems to be still far from its peak. Thus number in one way or another has conquered our whole culture. As concept, it is everywhere present, materialized in thousands or millions of computers (which begin to become the secret rulers of all our life), it has opened the door to a new scene of our technological civilization.

It is a generally observable fact in the history of human ideas, particularly of ideas capable of development to a high degree of abstraction, that progress towards logical clarification and abstract formulation has to be paid for by loss of the close connection with the original cultural descent of these ideas. While without an abstract and rigorous building-up of the number concept modern science and technology which is based on mathematical theories would be impossible, without the first intuitive steps in numeration made by primitive man in prehistoric time no number system could have been developed. Those finger gestures, spoken number words, and written number symbols of ages long gone by mark the beginning of a development which resulted in the present-day highly sophisticated mathematical number concept. A few of the aspects of the early beginning and of later improvements have been touched upon in the present article, showing how our number system and number concept are rooted in the general cultural soil which nourished the historical growth and unfolding of all human ideas.

BIBLIOGRAPHY

The most complete treatment of the historical development of number systems and elementary arithmetic published in recent years is: K. Menninger, *Zahlwort und Ziffer. Eine Kulturgeschichte der Zahl,* 2 vols., 2nd ed. (Göttingen, 1957–58); trans. P. Broneer as *Number Words and Number Symbols: A Cultural History of Numbers* (Cambridge, Mass. and London, 1969). This outstanding work contains an extensive bibliography of primary literature. The same subject is dealt with on a much more restricted scale in the little book by D. Smeltzer, *Man and Number* (London, 1958). Good introductions are also the following: D. E. Smith, *Number Stories of Long Ago* (Washington, 1919; repr. 1951); D. E. Smith and J. Ginsburg, *Numbers and Numerals* (Washington, 1937); D. E. Smith and L. C. Karpinski, *The Hindu-Arabic Numerals* (Boston, 1911).

T. Dantzig, *Number, the Language of Science,* 4th ed. (New York and London, 1954) emphasizes the mathematical development up to and including the Cantorian transfinite numbers. C. J. Scriba, *The Concept of Number* (Mannheim and Zurich, 1968) was written as a text for a graduate course offered at the Ontario College of Education; it deals with the origins of number systems, the development of elementary arithmetic, algebra, and number theory, and includes nineteenth-century contributions to the number concept.

Also recommended are Carl B. Boyer, *A History of Mathematics* (New York, 1968), and P. E. B. Jourdain, trans. and ed., *Contributions to the Theory of Transfinite Numbers* (Chicago and London, 1915; also reprint). The Diels reference is to H. Diels, *Die Fragmente der Vorsokratiker . . .* , 5th ed. (Berlin, 1934).

CHRISTOPH J. SCRIBA

[See also Axiomatization; **Infinity;** Mathematical Rigor; **Pythagorean. . . .**]

OPTICS AND VISION

I. OPTICS FROM ANTIQUITY TO THE MEDIEVAL ARABIC CONTRIBUTIONS

THE ORIGINS of optics are shrouded in the darkness of time. However, for the purposes of our survey, we shall take our start in the fifth century B.C. with the opinion of Empedocles concerning the nature of light; he believed that light was produced by an effluvium which emanated from bodies and impinged on the organ of sight. The atomist Leucippus of Miletus, a contemporary of Empedocles, expressed some more definite ideas about sensations:

Every change produced by or impressed on things takes place by virtue of a contact; all our perceptions are tactile, and all our senses are varieties of touch. Consequently, since our mind does not proceed from within us to sally forth and touch external objects, it is necessary for these objects to come and touch our mind by passing through our senses. Now we do not see objects approaching us when we perceive them; therefore, they must be sending to our mind something which represents them, some shadow-like images or material likenesses (*simulacra*) which cover these bodies; these images move about on their surfaces, and can detach themselves in order to bring to our mind the shapes, colors, and all the other qualities of the bodies from which they emanate (Leucippus A, 29–31 Diels-Kranz).

Not all the philosophers of that time, however, shared these same opinions. Thus, Democritus, according to Theophrastus' (*De sensibus* 50; in Diels-Kranz, A 135) report, maintained that "the air interposed between the eye and the object receives a kind of impression as a result of the compression exerted upon it by the eye and by the object." Archytas of Tarentum, according to Apuleius, had a still more divergent idea: he held that vision arises as the effect of an invisible "fire" emitted from the eyes so that on encountering objects it may reveal their shapes and colors.

This variety of opinion shows that in the fifth and fourth centuries B.C. the problem of vision was at the center of philosophical speculation; this sort of thinking constituted the "optics" of that time. The word "optics" is obviously of Greek origin, and really signifies "science of vision." It was not merely concerned with an isolated problem, but entered into the great forum of philosophical speculations of that period concerning our "knowledge of the external world." To the question: How can the mind know that which surrounds it?, the answer was quickly given that the sensory mechanism served that function. The inquiry went deeper, however, in order to explain the functioning of each of the senses, and an exhaustive explanation was offered for touch, taste, smell, and hearing. On the other hand, the problem concerning sight presented insurmountable difficulties. To explain how it is possible to see simultaneously so many figures of diverse shapes and colors and located in different places required the investigations and researches of a score of centuries.

Putting aside the difficulty of "action at a distance," a problem which appears in the fragment of Leucippus quoted above, the possible solutions of the problem of vision were very limited; either something from the object arrives at the eye, or something from the eye goes out to the object, or else the intervening medium serves as the connection between the object and the eye. However, all of these solutions invited devastating criticisms; discussion was both intense and violent among the supporters of conflicting opinions. To demolish the ideas of opponents was easy, but no one succeeded in constructing an acceptable theory.

As the result of extended studies speculation rallied around two extreme conceptions: "visual rays" and "replicas."

The theory of visual rays was maintained by mathematicians, and it dominated the philosophical forum for more than a thousand years. It was justified by adopting an idea taken from a tactile experiment: a blind man could know the shape, size, and position of an object by exploring it with his hand; but he could also explore it by means of a stick held in his hand, that is, by an indirect "contact." Since it was believed, following Leucippus' dictum, that "all the senses are varieties of touch," it was not absurd to think that the eye was supplied with something like sticks capable of exploring the external world and of informing the "sensorium," i.e., the sensitive part of the eye, about the world, as the blind man's stick does. It was therefore supposed that every eye emitted rectilinear and slender emanations capable of exploring the external world and of supplying the mind, by way of the eyes, with the elements representing the external world, and thus creating "the world of appearance." This model was very suitable for the study of perspective. A follower of this theory was none other than Euclid who used it in his *Optics* and *Catoptrics*. Claudius Ptolemy, when he wrote his *Optics*, also made use of visual rays.

The theory of "replicas" (also called *simulacra*, or shadowy images) was the idea contained in the fragment of Leucippus, quoted above; but one had to admit that the replicas emitted from a body (in all directions) had to contract along the way, while remaining similar to themselves, until they became small enough to pass through the pupil of an eye wherever it might be.

But the most important event of this period was the contribution of Plato. He was deeply concerned with the problem of the knowledge of the external world, and particularly with that of the sense of sight. Unfortunately, he arrived at conclusions that had a disastrous effect.

There was the very widespread and much discussed opinion that the sensory apparatus generally does not guarantee the information which it transmits to the mind. On the other hand, the Epicurean school considered the senses infallible; all the others without exception were convinced that the senses were more or less deceptive. Still other thinkers found that not all the senses were equally deceptive, and in the studies of this subject came to the conclusion that touch is the one sense in which we could place the greatest confidence (although not completely, because touch might also yield mistakes). Much more important, however, was the conclusion that least deserving of confidence was the sense of sight itself.

Plato's reasoning here was perfectly logical. The external world comes to be known through the representations that the mind makes of it, that is, by means of the world of appearances. Now these mental representations may be produced by the information coming to the mind through the senses, but they may also be spontaneous. Well then, Plato reasoned, those representations which are created in the mind by means of sensory information, especially when it comes by way of the eyes, as a rule merit belief least of all; they do not represent truth. On the other hand, those representations made by the mind on its own initiative do not show any trace of the deceptiveness of the senses, and are therefore perfect, and therefore true.

These perfect and true representations are mathematical; reasoning in this way Plato denied all value to experience and assigned the entire value of speculative thought to mathematical conceptions. In this regard there is a very significant passage in the *Phaedo*, one of the best known of Plato's dialogues:

And thought is best when the mind is gathered into herself and none of these things trouble her—neither sounds, nor sights nor pain nor any pleasure—but when she takes leave of the body, and has as little as possible to do with it, when she has no bodily sense or desire, but is aspiring after true being . . . (*Phaedo* 65B; trans. Jowett).

The repercussions of Plato's philosophy were incalculably far-reaching. Given the authority of Plato, his ideas practically paralyzed experimental activity in the world of science. Sight in particular was condemned as a dangerous sense. A terrible sentence was pronounced upon it: *Non potest fieri scientia per visum solum*—"scientific knowledge cannot be achieved by vision alone." The rule was laid down that seeing is believing only when sight conforms with touch. These instructions entered the curriculum, and were taught from one generation to another for more than twenty centuries.

The evidence on this matter is incredibly vast. It is sufficient to consider the texts on optics in antiquity and in the Middle Ages. In each of these texts a few pages are devoted to the description of a few well-known optical phenomena, but many more pages emphasize optical illusions. Even Lucretius, a convinced Epicurean, in his poem *On the Nature of Things* (*De rerum natura*) did not doubt the deceptiveness of the sense of sight, but instead of putting the blame on the sensory apparatus, he attributed it to the inability of the mind to interpret correctly the information coming to it from the eyes. He concluded his treatment of optics as follows:

Many other things of this sort we may observe with no less wonder, phenomena which would lead us to distrust our senses; all in vain, since most of them deceive us on account of the mind's judgment which we interpolate ourselves, so that we end up believing we have seen things never perceived by the senses. In fact, there is nothing more difficult than distinguishing plain facts from the delusions which the mind straightway adds of itself (Book IV, lines 462–68).

Considering the novelty of these ideas, we may profitably examine other passages. One of them refers to a well-known episode. The doubting apostle Saint Thomas, was not present when Jesus, having risen from the grave, entered the room where the apostles were assembled. Thomas did not believe what the other apostles told him, and he asserted that he would believe only if he had "touched with his hand" the side of the body of the Redeemer. And when Jesus reappeared, he satisfied Thomas accordingly (John 20:24–27).

Another very interesting passage, fifteen centuries later, is an excerpt from the *Treatise on Painting* (*Trattato della Pittura*, ca. 1550) of Leonardo da Vinci:

Masters do not rely on the judgment of the eye, because it always deceives one, as is proven by anyone who wishes to divide a line into two equal parts by judging with the eye, and finds out how often the experiment fails. Wherefore good judges always fear as suspicious similar reports of eye witnesses, reports which ignorant persons accept . . . (Paragraph 32).

II. THE ARABIC CONTRIBUTION

It is well known that as a consequence of the political events in the centuries following the advent of Christianity, the center of gravity of the civilized world was displaced from Greece to the Middle East. So far as optics is concerned, an especially important contribution was made by the school that flourished in Bagdad around the ninth century. The famous philosopher Abu-Yūsuf Ya'qūb ibn-Ishāq (813–80), called Alkindi (or al-Kindi) in the West, asserted in the course of his astrological studies that the action of the stars on terrestrial things came about by means of rectilinear rays emitted by every star in all directions. At another time he advanced the idea that vision also came about through the action on the "sensorium" of rectilinear rays like those from the stars, but emitted by terrestrial sources.

These ideas were taken up by Abu Ali Mohammed ibn al-Hasan ibn al-Hythan, known in the West as Alhazen. Previously, Lucretius had written in the aforementioned work *On the Nature of Things:*

Moreover the eyes shun flaming objects and avoid looking at them. Thus the Sun can blind you if you should continue to look at it steadily, because its force is powerful and its images, vibrating from the sky above across the clear atmosphere, disturb the tissues of the eyes. But any bright splendor sears the eyes for the reason that it possesses seeds of fire which penetrate the eyes and produce pain in them (Book IV, lines 324–31).

Alhazen repeats these observations and adds another of great interest: if anyone, after looking at the Sun or any other intensely bright source, closes his eyes, he continues to see its shape in "after-images" persisting for an appreciable time. Today this phenomenon is called "persistence of retinal images." These phenomena can be explained only by admitting that an external agent acts on the sensorium, and therefore, the theory of visual rays had to be regarded as demolished.

However, Alhazen did not limit himself to advancing new arguments in order to demolish a theory which many had already criticized. To be exact, his most important contribution was to have offered reasons which permitted him to explain how the replicas or "skins" of a body as big as a mountain could pass through the pupil into the eye without having to undergo a contraction along the way. He regarded every object as composed of so many elements, each of which emitted its own tiny replicas in every direction; these can enter the pupil of an eye wherever the eye happens to be, and that can occur without any contraction during their propagation. It is necessary to add that these elemental replicas, while entering the eye, retain their rectilinear path; and this was in agreement with the ideas then current concerning the structure of the eye and the path of refraction. In this way then the eye comes to obtain an impression of shape similar to that of the observed object. Although Alhazen did not make the image reach as far as the retina (because he wished to avoid the inversion of the image itself) and made the hypothesis or simply assumed that the sensitive area was the front surface of the eyeball, he gave the initial ideas of the elements involved which later led to the retinal image, thanks to the studies of Maurolycos and especially to Kepler. This was a definite achievement, even if the optical mechanics on which it was based was only to be perfected in due time. But that is how what we today call the "retinal image" arose.

Although the belief was strengthened that the sensorium received an impression from an external agent, still it was the general opinion that this impression had to be received and elaborated by the mind, and that to the latter belongs the final function of exhibiting the impression in the world of appearances. But then the problem of determining the nature of the external agent assumed major proportions; and in the scientific Latin vocabulary of that time this external agent was designated by the term *lumen* while *lux* was used to indicate its mental representation.

Alhazen's ideas (which were not limited to those mentioned above) penetrated the Occident very slowly; knowledge of these ideas was largely due to the work of Vitellius or Witelo, who wrote an *Optics* in ten books (*Opticae libri decem*). The work was in substance actually a paraphrase of the works of Alhazen, even though his name was not mentioned. Witelo's work enjoyed a widespread diffusion and came to be regarded as a classic, known as Witelo's *Optics*, or simply "Witelo."

In order to understand the variety of contributions that make the history of optics so rich and interesting, it should be made clear that vision is a very complex phenomenon, including as it does physical, physiological, and also psychological elements. Because persons of very diverse backgrounds and points of view have occupied themselves with these elements in the theory of vision, progress was made at different times now in one branch of the subject and then in another. Thus the theory of visual rays led to notable advances in the geometrical treatment of the phenomenon, because mathematicians like Euclid and Ptolemy had been interested in optics. The predominantly physico-physiological bent of the Arabs had advanced the study of the organ of vision. Then, around the thirteenth century, the contribution of ecclesiastical dignitaries consisted in giving special consideration to psychological and philosophical as well as to theological aspects of vision.

In the West the Greek term "optics" was replaced by the word "perspective," of Latin derivation, without any change in content. Thus, the principal cultivators of the science of *perspectiva* in the thirteenth century were Robert Grosseteste, bishop of Lincoln, John Peckham, archbishop of Canterbury, the Franciscan friar Roger Bacon, Saint Bonaventura, and Saint Thomas Aquinas. In their works *perspectiva* came fairly close to being an article of theology, even if they took into serious consideration the principles and contributions of the Arabic school. Henceforth, no one was to doubt any longer that vision was due to the action of a *lumen* on the eye, but for them the central problem was about the nature of the light (*lux*), which some actually regarded as divine. At the same time, however, the nature of the *lumen* was discussed in depth, especially the nature of the *species*, a name which in the Middle Ages denoted a new conception of the replicas, like their Greek prototypes, but much less materialistic. There was a great deal of argument over the suitability of "substance" or "accident" or "quality" to describe the *species* of light, but the discussions, though subtle, were inconclusive.

On the other hand, mathematicians continued to make use of visual rays even if these rays now were no longer needed to represent real entities. Nonetheless they still constituted an excellent working instrument, especially for studies of perspective (in the modern sense of the word), which retained its essentially geometrical content.

In summary, the closing centuries of the Middle Ages witnessed a veritable decay among the theories in this field of optics, in which it was barely possible to distinguish three principal tendencies: the mathematical one of visual rays, the physico-physiological one of the Arabic school, and the metaphysical one. Ideas concerning vision may be summarized as follows: the *lumen*, composed of "solar rays," by illuminating bodies produced an emission of "species" from the bodies; these "species," according to the process described by Alhazen, entered the eyes and by stimulating the sensorium produced a mental picture of the shapes and

colors of the world of appearances, which thus came to be perceived as light (*lux*).

If in that manner one could explain vision when the eye looked directly at an object, the problem became entirely mysterious when the path of the "species" was changed by an optical instrument, as in the case of a plane mirror, and even worse in the case of a curved mirror. There was as yet no idea at all about the true nature of the optical image given by a plane or curved mirror. Everyone was agreed in considering the image an optical deception as the figures were seen where the objects were certainly not to be found.

Some began to study the reflection of rays by concave spherical mirrors, and since they began at first with mirrors of wide angular opening (like those that were entirely hemispherical), they began to construct "caustic curves"—which are epicycloids, as is now well known (Figure 1). Now, at night, by directing a con-

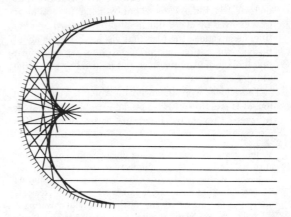

FIGURE 1. Caustic envelope of rays, reflected by a hemispherical mirror, with incident rays parallel to the axis

cave mirror towards a star in the sky, the mathematician who had calculated the caustic saw a luminous point beyond the mirror itself. It was humanly impossible to find a connection between the caustic formed by the rays coming from the star and reflected by the mirror, and the luminous point seen. It was necessary to conceive two distinct entities; the rays constituting the *light* (*lumen*) and the "species" capable of producing vision.

Comparable reasoning had to be applied to the study of rays passing through a glass sphere (*pila crystallina*). Here too caustics like those of spherical mirrors were found, complicated besides by the appearance of colors. In this case, also, there was no way of connecting these caustics with the figures that were seen by looking through the sphere.

III. FROM THE FAILURE OF MEDIEVAL OPTICS TO THE RENAISSANCE ERA

A new development, that was bound to have far-reaching consequences, occurred some time between 1280 and 1285 (the exact year cannot be determined). Some artisans discovered that by placing in front of the eyes of old persons transparent glass disks with upcurved, clear surfaces, these persons saw things at close quarters as well as they had when they were young. These glass disks, having a shape similar to that of a thick lentil, were called "lentils of glass" and also "glass lentils" (later, "lenses").

The proof that this discovery or invention was made by artisans is based on several considerations. Assuming that it was not known at that time what presbyopia (farsightedness) was, and even less was known as to how a lens really functioned (the law of refraction was not formulated until more than three centuries later), no possible reasoning could have led anyone to correct farsightedness with a convergent lens; besides, the fact that the glass disks were named after a vegetable surely excludes the idea that they were fabricated or named by a man of science. But the most convincing proof that the glass lens was not a product of the science of the thirteenth century is shown by the fact that when the mathematicians became acquainted with the lens, they examined it in the light of the science of the time, and pronounced the inevitable verdict: "The glass lenses are deceptive contrivances; don't look through them if you don't wish to be fooled."

This judgment may seem absurd today, but at the time when it was pronounced it constituted the most correct and logical application of the prevailing science; since the figures seen through the lenses are never verified by touch, they therefore are not true but deceptive. For that reason glass lenses were not admitted to the field of science, and no man of science took them seriously. If the lenses survived condemnation, it was owing to the "ignorance" (as Leonardo da Vinci expressed it, in the passage quoted above) of the artisans who had not faced the difficult problems of man's knowledge of the external world.

The improvement of the lenses was likewise due to the fact that the artisans gave the lenses' surfaces different curvatures according to the age of the user; and we also owe to the artisans the invention of concave lenses for the correction of myopia (nearsightedness). Historical search for the inventor of lenses, of the kind to correct either presbyopia or myopia, shows no hope of success; the makers of eyeglasses, who were mostly illiterate, have written nothing about them; men of scientific learning did not take the invention of eyeglasses seriously; consequently, a discovery such as the correction of nearsightedness, which today would be rewarded with the richest international prizes, has remained unhonored and unsung.

The banishment of lenses from science lasted for a full three centuries. The history of lenses and especially of the reversal of the situation, constitutes one of the most significant and most interesting chapters in the history of science. The protagonists in this great turning point, which had repercussions of enormous consequence on scientific progress in general, were Giambattista della Porta, Johannes Kepler, and Galileo Galilei.

Della Porta (more commonly known as Porta) has to be credited with having initiated this chapter of history, but his contribution was not a truly scientific one. Everything published about lenses, before Porta, hardly fills an entire page, and while nearly everything published was written in order to accuse the lenses of deception, Porta in his *Magia naturalis* ("Natural Magic") of 1589, devoted an entire chapter (Book XVII, Ch. X) to the descriptions of the curious effects of lenses. Besides, in the introduction to that chapter he had the courage to write:

... (these wonders) are the same as the effect of lenses (*specillorum*), which are absolutely necessary to the conduct of human life. Nobody has as yet demonstrated either their effects or the reasons [for these effects].

It is noteworthy that lenses were discussed here for the first time in a printed book, and that it was not a scientific book, but a collection of curiosities; also it was not because the author was a man of science, but an autodidact in search of wonders. It is to be noted also that here lenses are called *specilli*, a respectable name not reminiscent of any vegetable like lentils.

The passage quoted above had a remarkable historical importance for two reasons: in the first place because Porta's *Magia naturalis* had an enormous circulation (it was translated into various languages including the Arabic) and hence drew the attention of a very large public to lenses; in the second place, because in the quoted sentence there is implied a direct accusation against science for not even having tried to explain the operation or effects of lenses.

Porta himself thought of filling this serious scientific lacuna by publishing his work on refraction (*De refractione*, 1593). It is a very pretentious work but of less than modest content; nonetheless it is important because in Book VIII Porta makes the very first attempt at a scientifically oriented study of lenses. There are absurd arguments in it, even if Porta declared himself satisfied with them, but they constitute a most important testimonial of the optical knowledge of the time. It is quite obvious to a reader today that it was impossible for the ideas of medieval optics to explain the functioning of lenses. Therefore, either medieval optics

411

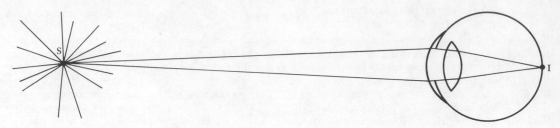

FIGURE 2. Refraction of rays through the eye

or lenses had to disappear from the scientific scene. Since lenses had already had three centuries of experimental success, the fate of medieval optics was sealed.

As a matter of fact medieval optics was replaced very soon by a new optics that is still valid today. The birth of this new optics may be said to have occurred in 1604, the year which saw the publication of Johannes Kepler's work, *Paralipomena ad Vitellionem*. Actually the abbot Francesco Maurolico in several manuscripts, some bearing the date 1521, had already advanced some new ideas such as the assumption that every point of a body emits rectilinear rays in all directions, rays that are neither visual nor solar but simply *geometrical;* they are the rays of the geometrical optics of today. However, since these manuscripts were only first published in 1611, thirty-six years after their author's death, Maurolico must be considered an isolated pioneer who was not understood. Nevertheless, Kepler carried out Maurolico's reasoning to conclusions of fundamental importance.

There is a mine of new ideas in the aforementioned volume of Kepler, but here we shall select two in particular: the key to the mechanism of vision and the conception of the optical image. We are in fact dealing here with two fundamental and definitive achievements.

As for the mechanism of vision, we owe to Kepler the proof of how "retinal images" (as they are called today) are formed on the retina (*Paralipomena ad Vitellionem*, Ch. III, Pro. ix). He demonstrated that a cone of rays emitted from a point source becomes transformed, by refraction through the transparent media of the eyes, into another cone that also has the pupil for its base but has its vertex on the retina. And so, if the object is formed of many points, we obtain on the retina a stimulus arranged in an order corresponding to that of the object (Figure 2).

He went further. He did not limit the process to the formation of the retinal image, but pursued his inquiry as far as the boundaries of the mind, even facing the classical problem of how the mind utilizes the elements of the retinal stimulus in order to create

therefrom its representation of the observed world. The idea was clearly that this representation had to be a figure created by the mind and located in front of the eyes. The problem was to establish criteria for determining the shape and position of this figure.

Taking as his first object a point emitting rays, Kepler quickly came to the conclusion that the stimulated area of the retina defines the dimensions of the figure, so that if this stimulated area is very tiny (as in the case of a point-source of rays), the figure must be a "luminous point." He also inferred that the "position" of the stimulated point on the retina defines the "direction" in which the object-point is located and in which, therefore, the luminous point is to be found (Figure 3).

At this juncture Kepler ran into the greatest difficulty concerning the visual process, namely, how to determine the distance from the object-point to the eye. The solution of this problem was enormously important. Kepler started from the idea that to measure a distance by means of optical data, it is necessary to triangulate, and he showed that this is precisely what happens in binocular vision by virtue of the convergence on the object of the visual rays of both eyes. But he noted further that vision can be accomplished also by one eye alone, and that also under these conditions the mind must have the elements needed to determine the distance from the object to the eye. Moreover, in this case, too, a triangulation is required, and Kepler found the triangle formed by the point-object as its vertex and the diameter of the eye's pupil as its base. He assumed that the observer's mind is able to evaluate the elements of this (telemetric) triangle, and he called the latter "the triangle which measures distance" (*triangulum distantiae mensorium*).

In conclusion, the mechanics of vision, as Kepler conceived it, emerges as follows: the object-point emits rays in straight lines in all directions; from these rays a small cone is formed as they enter the eye of the observer; the cone is refracted and transformed into another cone having its vertex on the retina, which becomes stimulated at a point. From this point signals start along the optic nerve reaching the brain and mind, which thus is informed that the object is a point lying in a certain direction at a certain distance. The mind therefore creates a very tiny figure, a "luminous point"; which it locates at the vertex of the telemetric triangle, where the object-point should be found. The observer then asserts that he is "seeing the object."

Although Kepler did not concern himself with other characteristics of the "luminous point" such as its color and brightness, his achievement is a masterpiece that will never be sufficiently admired. He soon drew from this theory about luminous points consequences that are fundamental for modern optics. The reasoning, outlined above, requires that light rays proceed in straight lines, but that does not always happen; in particular they can be bent by reflection at a mirror or by refraction through one or more surfaces. Kepler first considered the simplest case, that of a plane mirror. The rays coming from an object-point are reflected by the mirror so that their lines of prolongation back of the mirror meet in a point behind the reflecting surface. Therefore they impinge upon the eye of the observer as if they proceeded from that point. Penetrating the eye, the rays stimulate the retina, and consequently by applying the mechanical procedure described above, the observer's mind is bound to locate the luminous point at the vertex of the telemetric triangle. For this reason the observer cannot locate the point on the object but has to locate it at the point symmetrically opposite, behind the mirror. Therefore, a figure can be also seen where the object actually is not situated. Hence the observer cannot say that he "sees the object," but should say he "sees its image."

That is how the current idea of an optical image originated. However, we no longer talk about a telemetric triangle, because since Kepler's time new ideas about optics have arisen which we shall discuss shortly.

But before proceeding, we must point out that Kepler himself asserted that his theory did not always correspond to experience. To be precise, things went well when the images fell on a screen, but did not always turn out so well when the eye looked directly at a mirror or other optical device. Kepler understood that in these two sets of conditions there was something clearly different, and he expressed this conviction by the use of two different names for the figures seen; those seen on the screen he called "pictures" (*picturae*), and the others he called the "images of things" (*imagines rerum*). He advised his scientific readers to concentrate their attention on the pictures.

The fact remains that Kepler was the first to explain in a satisfactory manner why we see the figures of objects placed in front of a mirror as though they were behind it (op. cit., Ch. V, Pro. xviii, Definition).

Among the numerous new and important ideas contained in Kepler's *Paralipomena ad Vitellionem* it is interesting to note an omission, namely, that there are no studies of lenses (op. cit., Ch. III, passim). Despite his competence in optics, even Kepler did not believe in lenses. He did devote one page to explaining the correction of farsightedness by means of convex lenses, and of nearsightedness by means of concave lenses. But he makes a point of writing that he made this inquiry as a result of the insistent pressure, over a three-year period, of a high authority in Prague. It is obvious that Kepler wished to excuse himself before the mathematicians of his day for giving to lenses any consideration at all (op. cit., Ch. V, Pro. xxviii).

Kepler's book did not produce any reaction when it appeared; it was too new and too difficult to understand. The fact that Kepler's work was soon forgotten may be attributed to the extremely conservative tendency of the science of the time, shared by all in that

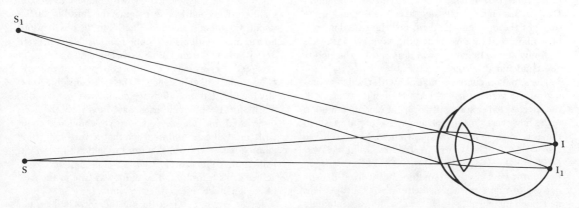

FIGURE 3. How the eye locates the direction from which the point source emanates, as determined by the corresponding position of a stimulus point on the retina

cultural environment. It is incredible that such a rich harvest of new ideas and great accomplishments should have been so neglected that even towards the end of the seventeenth century nearly all scientific men were still talking the language of medieval optics.

However, the arrival on the scene of Galileo Galilei brought about in a much more effective manner the collapse of ancient optics and the renewal of the scientific mentality. It may seem odd that a result of this sort should have been produced by a scientist who had such a very modest competence in optics, a science which was then entirely limited to medieval optics. Galileo was a professor of mechanics and astronomy at the University of Padua.

Galileo's contribution came about in 1604 when some artisans of Middleburg, Holland put into circulation some spyglasses with a diverging eyepiece. These spyglasses were made by copying a model that came from Italy and bore the date 1590. These spyglasses met with no approval. Strange as it may seem today, the fact is that no scientist was interested in the new instrument. But this negative response could not have been different for any instrument that used lenses.

Even though the general public was not imbued with philosophical prejudices, it did not appreciate the new instrument because people considered it useless. This reaction was due to the fact that the spyglasses from Holland were made with the lenses of ordinary eyeglasses and, as today's technical optics can easily explain, such lenses cannot make a worthwhile spyglass. The result, in fact, was that the Dutch did not succeed in getting a magnification of more than three times, and it is known that an instrument magnifying only three times is a poor instrument and serves no useful purpose. This was precisely the conclusion reached by the layman to whom the spectacle-makers of the time tried to sell the new "spyglasses" (occhiali). Despite this fact, in 1608 spyglasses were found in the shops of the opticians in Paris, but the situation may be summarized by saying that the spyglass was made badly by the opticians; it was despised by the public and condemned by the scientists.

The situation changed radically with Galileo's coming on the scene. He had learned of the existence of the spyglass in the spring of 1609, but paid no attention to it; however, during the first week of July he had the new idea that the spyglass could be a valuable instrument (C. De Waard, Jr., De Uitvinding der Verrekijkers, The Hague [1906], pp. vi, 340). He began to build it with his own hands for he realized that he needed to make the lenses better than the opticians had made the eyeglasses. He devoted himself intensely to this task of improving the power of the eyeglass, and in a short time he achieved extraordinary results;

his telescopes within three months attained a power of magnification of thirty times. To the public "Galileo's telescope" was a new instrument which left the spyglass of the spectacle-makers far behind. In reality, it was the same spyglass with a diverging eyepiece, except that Galileo's lenses were much better made.

With this new instrument Galileo made amazing astronomical discoveries, among which the most revolutionary was his discovery of the satellites of Jupiter. When Galileo announced in his Sidereal Messenger (Sidereus nuncius, March 1610), the discovery of four additional "moving bodies" in the sky, besides the mountains of the moon, and the stars of the Milky Way, the learned world launched a campaign of unprecedented violence against him. His discoveries struck a deadly blow at traditional philosophy, astrology, and even medicine, which was then closely linked to astrology. The scientists denied absolutely that these discoveries had any value, seeing that they had been made only by means of the telescope, an instrument notoriously unworthy of confidence.

There ensued a tremendous polemic between the whole scientific world (without any exception) on the one hand, and Galileo all alone, on the other; yet he was firmly convinced that he was right in believing what he saw in his telescope, even though it was not confirmed by the sense of touch.

As we have said, Galileo's competence in optics was very modest. Still his adversaries hurled against him the learning of all the philosophers and astronomers of the twenty preceding centuries. He never chose to fight back on technical grounds, and instead resorted to totally extra-academic tactics by availing himself of the collaboration of the Grand Duke of Tuscany, Cosimo de' Medici. With this purpose in mind, Galileo named the satellites of Jupiter "the Medicean Planets."

Conducting his campaign with superlative skill, Galileo succeeded in overcoming the hostility of the scientists, and in making his "faith" in the observations he had made with his telescope (cannocchiale) prevail. Today this Galilean faith has become so universally accepted that we have even forgotten about the pre-Galilean lack of confidence in the sense of sight. Actually the fact that this diffidence dominated the scientific world for twenty centuries has only recently been discovered, and not everyone is as yet convinced about it. It must also be pointed out that a very long time elapsed before the old skepticism yielded to the Galilean faith in lenses; it took several generations to achieve this transition. The same was true in the case of Kepler's new ideas in astronomy.

Kepler's own conduct during the anti-Galilean polemic over Galileo's telescope was very interesting. For some years Kepler himself showed a lack of confidence in the discoveries made with Galileo's telescope. Kepler did not treat them in his *Paralipomena ad Vitellionem* or in his *Dissertatio cum nuncio siderio*. His initial lack of confidence, in common with the general skepticism of his time, was also evident from the way in which he subjected to very severe tests the telescope built by Galileo, given to him by the Elector of Cologne, as though it was expected that its failings would then appear, as others were trying to show. But after two weeks of all these testings by himself and others, Kepler was thoroughly convinced that Galileo was right, so he became a convert to the new faith about the end of August 1610, and wrote the *Narratio* (published in September 1610).

Now that he was converted, Kepler again took up the optical theory expounded in his *Paralipomena ad Vitellionem,* and in a few weeks wrote the *Dioptrice* (published in January 1611). It was a wonderful little book which for the first time propounded the theory of lenses, and explained the operation of the telescope with a diverging lens as eyepiece, and also laid down the theoretical basis for the telescope with a converging eyepiece as well as for the telephoto lens.

IV. SINCE GALILEO

Even if the great majority of scientific men remained faithful to the principles of classical philosophy, in particular to Platonic ideas, and deeply distrusted anything experimental in character and hence based on the senses, the number of converts to the new faith increased every day. They formed a new class of persons who preferred the direct observation of natural phenomena to the reading of classical texts.

The philosophical line adopted in the behavior of these persons is very interesting. They knew no argument capable of destroying the impeccable reasoning of the classical philosophers and therefore never engaged in debates that would surely end in favor of their opponents. Instead, they simply closed their ears to the classical teachings and ignored the old doubts about the workings of the senses. They forgot the judgment: "Science cannot be achieved by vision alone" (*Non potest fieri scientia per visum solum*) and employed the optical instruments with complete confidence and enthusiasm.

In summary, the contribution made by Galileo to this sector of the subject was both technical and philosophical. From the technical point of view he greatly improved upon the spyglass and made it a usable telescope; from the philosophical point of view he restored confidence in the sense of sight both by direct observation and by means of optical instruments, thus restoring the value of sense experience. Having given mankind a new and powerful instrument and the faith

to use and appreciate it, Galileo may be considered the true and principal founder of modern science. The birth date of modern science may be taken as August 24, 1609, the date of Galileo's letter to the Doge of Venice. That letter was the first written document in which a scientist had the courage to declare solemnly that the telescope was capable of rendering services of "inestimable aid."

A confirmation, that may be called brilliant, of much that has been expounded above is to be found in the new history of the microscope. Many historians of science have studied the history of the compound microscope, believing that the history of the microscope must be based on it. But the facts have to be considered otherwise.

The compound microscope has its own history as an instrument, because it has become a truly scientific instrument after nearly two centuries of efforts by persistent technicians. In reality it had its actual influence on scientific progress after 1840, the time when Giovan Battista Amici placed a hemispherical lens in front of the objective, and put forward "the technique of immersion" (placing the object under scrutiny in a drop of oil, between the front lens and the cover glass). Until that time microscopy was done with the simple (single-lens) microscope which gave better service than the compound microscope did before the above-mentioned innovations. All the great discoveries in the microscopic field of research were made with the simple microscope until the middle of the nineteenth century.

The "father of microscopy" is, by unanimous consensus, Anthony van Leeuwenhoek; during his long life he built hundreds of microscopes, but they were all simple ones, not even one being compound. And with the former simple type he made some stupendous discoveries. His simple microscopes were converging lenses, placed in a small metal mounting with a pair of screws for bringing the object into focus.

Thus the history of microscopy is not that of the compound microscope, which came upon the scene only at a later date. Yet one may wonder whether the simple microscope, consisting optically of a single convergent lens, might not have been put to use before the end of the thirteenth century. Why was it not employed?

But that is not all. A concave mirror is also a microscope, and, as we have already emphasized, the concave mirror had been studied from the time of the Greeks. Euclid in particular dealt with it in his *Catoptrics,* and it was studied intensively in the *Optics* of Claudius Ptolemy; hence, by that time it might have been possible to make microscopic observations. The fact then that as early as 1524 Giovanni Rucellai published a short poem (*L'Ape*, lines 963–95) in which he described the anatomy of a bee as seen in a concave mirror, draws our attention to the behavior of his contemporaries, not a single one of whom followed Rucellai or used his technique of observation. Why?

The answer to this question is very simple; science and philosophy regarded lenses and concave mirrors as being deceptive, because they made one see figures that were false to the sense of touch. The new Galilean faith was needed to overcome this mode of reasoning, and equally needed were new men. It is not without significance that Antony van Leeuwenhoek's profession was that of a sheriff's bailiff in the States-General of Holland, and not that of a college professor. He had learned to use lenses, while a child, for the purpose of counting threads in a textile business.

However, alongside the new men, the numerous and tenacious band of robed philosophers insisted on maintaining the positions formulated in the classical texts. The laws of nature rather than ratiocination and study provided for the liquidation of these texts, but that would take many decades. Only at the end of the seventeenth century was medieval optics practically displaced from the scientific field. Lenses had entered the field of research with flying colors. They constituted a subject of fertile study at the hands of first-rate mathematicians and experimenters. Astronomy especially profited from them in a most conspicuous way.

Optical studies settled down on new sites. The mathematicians who had once been occupied with studying the geometrical behavior of visual rays and then with that of solar rays, now devoted themselves to studying the new geometrical rays. Kepler had demonstrated the utility of these rays as a representative model of *lumen* whether in reflection, refraction, the functioning of lenses, or the mechanism of vision.

Scientists of an experimental and physical orientation came face to face with the great subject of the nature of *lumen* and color, a subject which was of interest not only from the scientific but also from the philosophical point of view. The technical problem finally assumed more importance and interest every day, especially because men doing research were always asking for more powerful instruments free of any defects. Some particulars about the development of research along these new lines will bring us to considerations of noteworthy interest.

The "new men," as we have designated them, were full of enthusiasm for the study of nature, and were inspired by a great faith in observation and experiment, having decided not to take too seriously the preparation and philosophical criticism of their work. Instead of limiting themselves, under the classical rule, to

"describing" natural phenomena, they substituted the claim to "explaining" phenomena by means of "mechanisms." This new way of proceeding produced, on the one hand, an unprecedented progress of science, but, on the other hand, it failed to provide research with a secure and thoroughly scrutinized foundation.

Generally speaking, though an exaggerated and uncontrolled positivism installed itself, it was nonetheless enjoying an illusory position despite its usefulness. The classical and basic distinction between the "world of appearance" and the "world of reality" was forgotten, and the result was to take as true, that is, as physically and objectively real, what was indisputably a subjective creation of the mind of the observer. Thus they succeeded in not realizing, or in taking least into account, the role of the observer in the observation of phenomena; they minimized everything that in classical science had a psychical character, and they ended up by attributing a physical nature to everything, whatever the cost.

An excellent example of the methodology just described is furnished by the evolution of the concept of "optical image." There is no doubt that the images seen with the use of optical instruments—whether it is the simplest plane mirror, the magnifying lens, or the more complex instruments for aiding vision—are psychical entities, as Kepler had so well demonstrated. The importance of the works of this learned scientist can be better appreciated if we take due account of the fact that observations made by different persons have very subtle subjective characteristics, and are therefore as diverse as there are different observers. So long as this difficulty was not overcome, it was not possible to square the optical observations with optical theory. Kepler himself avoided concerning himself too much with the images of things (*imagines rerum*). On the other hand, the "pictures" (*picturae*) corresponded fairly well with the rule of the (telemetric) triangle, and that fact unified the functioning of the eyes of different observers, and permitted the mathematization of the theory of images. This method was a victory of incalculable value, because it made possible the development of geometrical optics.

However, in the new philosophical climate those pursuing mathematical studies forgot that it was necessary to intercept the *picturae* on a screen in order to conform to the rule of the telemetric triangle, and also forgot that the image is actually something "seen," that is, created by the observer's mind. Besides, their thinking became distorted when it followed a line of reasoning of the following sort: according to the rule of the telemetric triangle, the observer "must" see the image at the vertex of the cone of rays emerging from the optical system and entering the eye; it is useless

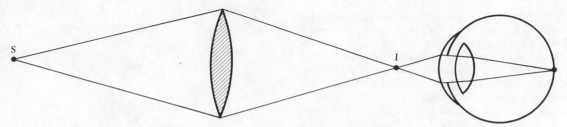

FIGURE 4. Transition from the idea of the image "seen," to that of the mathematical image

to repeat this every time that an image is studied. Thus the vertex of the cone of rays (Figure 4) emerging from the optical system, was considered and called the image, and one ceased to talk about the eye and the telemetric triangle.

Thereupon the optical image lost its mental character and assumed a purely objective and physical character independent of the observer. And that is why Kepler was ignored or forgotten, and without any genuine open discussion or deliberation a geometrical optics was spontaneously installed, based on the hypothesis that the rule of the telemetric triangle is always and exactly verified. This was a clandestine hypothesis that no one was conscious of as such, and that is why it was never discussed and criticized. In fact, the above-mentioned rule was also forgotten, and very rarely it was fleetingly asserted that the image of an object-point is seen at the vertex of the cone of rays that reach the cornea of the observer's eye, as if this were a self-evident truth.

Only recently have Kepler and the rule of the telemetric triangle been exhumed, and the function of the human eye been discussed in the light of modern scientific knowledge of optics. The result has been disastrous: the rule itself is hardly ever verified; it really plays the role of a wonderful "working hypothesis." For that reason geometrical optics is not the general study of images, but is valid only for "pictures" (Kepler's *picturae*), even if this label has been forgotten and replaced by "images." When this criticism was enunciated, it remained surprising to observe how the experimental test of geometrical laws was systematically avoided in the study of optics. The really disturbing fact was that when optical images are observed without projecting them on screens (especially so-called "virtual" images which cannot be assembled on screens), there is an enormous discrepancy between the conclusions of geometrical theory and the experimental data. The fact that the discrepancy was not mentioned by anyone until a much later date shows to what extent a well attested mathematical theory was able to convince and blind so many experimenters.

It is thus evident that in the geometrical treatment of optical images a definition of their nature was avoided. When anyone tried to offer one, the many conceptual difficulties which had been successfully minimized by silence reappeared; and so the mathematical treatment lost much of the value that had been previously attributed to it.

Nowadays the definition of "images" has been thoroughly discussed, with the result that various types of images must be distinguished; some are physical, some mathematical, some mental, some chemical, and some electronic. It has become clear that the images considered in geometrical optics are mathematical abstractions with the aid of which we try to represent experimental images, but they are really very far from doing so.

In the field of research on the nature of *lumen* and of color, positivistic philosophy has exerted an influence analogous to the one just described with respect to optical images. Dismissing the clear distinction between the world of reality and the world of appearances, one has to cease also accepting as clear that the *lumen* (radiation) is in the world of reality and the *lux* (light) in the world of appearances. Just as was done for *picturae* and *imagines rerum*, the distinction between *lumen* and *lux* was eliminated, and the use of a single word light (*luce*) was inaugurated; it was this term also that represented the mental entity. However, though people ceased calling attention to the difference in "nature" between the external agent and the mental representation, they spoke instead of the "nature of light" (*luce*), of the "velocity of light," and of the "action of light" on the eyes. Thus they absolutely avoided making it clear whether they were talking about a physical object or the image that an observer sees. In that way light became a physical entity. The same course was run by the concept of color, a concept which has always followed closely the fortunes of light. Color also ended up by being considered a physical, objective entity, and therefore independent of the observer.

The most salient consequence of the philosophy of 417

physicists from the eighteenth to the twentieth century was the emergence of two new sciences; *photometry* and *colorimetry,* both arising with the evident purpose of measuring light first and color afterward. An aim of this kind could be conceived and pursued only by persons convinced that light and color were physical entities, since mental entities still cannot be measured.

It is of some interest to point out that this unfortunate influence of philosophy on the distortion of the fundamental concepts of optics was exerted despite the fact that the great masters to whom we owe the most important researches concerning the nature of *lumen* and color, like René Descartes, Father Francesco Maria Grimaldi, Isaac Newton, and Christiaan Huygens, and so many others, had made it very clear that light and color were clearly only entities of the mind.

In the seventeenth century the nature of *lumen* was the subject of very animated discussions, which also had repercussions in theological circles. For example, Father F. Grimaldi wrote an impressive work on the nature of *lumen,* color, and the rainbow (*Physico-mathesis de lumine, coloribus, et iride*), published in 1665, two years after his death. Most of the professors were opposed to considering *lumen* as a *substance,* not only because they were Aristotelians but also because of the hostility in their circle towards atomism. The opinion that prevailed among them was that *lumen* was an "accident of the genus quality" (*lumen accidens de genere qualitatum*) or a motion, necessarily of an undulatory nature.

However, for some time there had arisen a minority who were convinced that *lumen* was of a material or corpuscular nature, because only thus could one explain its rectilinear propagation (which no one doubted), for no one had succeeded in explaining how such rectilinear propagation could result from wave motion. On this point René Descartes was particularly explicit in his *Dioptrique* of 1638; even while proposing various models to explain light phenomena, he insisted above all on the corpuscular model, regarding *lumen* as a swarm of spherical corpuscles (Figure 5) endowed with two motions: a very rapid translatory motion and a rotational motion around the center of each corpuscle, which today would be called a "spin." Descartes' opinion was that this rotary motion was the physical cause of the vision of colors in the sense that an observer would see various colors according to the spin with which particles impinged upon the retina. Still using this corpuscular model, Descartes states in his *Dioptrique* the law of refraction, which Willebrord Snell had already formulated but not published. The finding of an exact and definitive law of refraction, after so many centuries of fruitless efforts, gave a fresh impetus to the progress of optics.

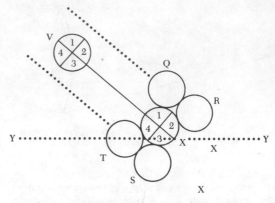

FIGURE 5. Descartes' corpuscular model of light and color

Even Father Grimaldi was on the side of the followers of the material conception of *lumen,* but he also insisted on the subjective nature of light and color. He has been considered a forerunner of the wave theory of color because he attributed vision of the various colors to the innumerably diverse frequencies that the vibration of matter might have along the path that the light-ray followed (Figure 6). He was driven to the point of writing that he suffered an "irritation of the bile" because of the irrational insistence of most philosophers of his time that color was something inherent in bodies while he himself maintained that colors were the subjective effect of the action of rays of *lumen* of diverse frequencies on the retina. And then it should also be remembered that in Father Grimaldi's volume, mentioned above, there was described for the first time a group of phenomena known as "diffraction," and that he coined the term (Pro. XLV, No. 41; Pro. I, passim).

Isaac Newton's contribution profoundly influenced the development of optical theories, especially those concerning color, since for the nature of the *lumen* he simply embraced the corpuscular theory, already followed by many others. Newton began his research activities in this domain when Father Grimaldi's work appeared. Newton's theory was hailed as a great success because he gave an explanation of the phenomenon of refraction whereas no one in so many centuries of studies had succeeded in giving a mechanistic explanation of refraction. Newton's new idea was to explain the deviation of the rays in refraction by means of the force of attraction exerted by the matter of the refractory body on the material corpuscles composing the *lumen.* Admiration for Newton rose to great height when he drew from his theory of universal attraction the explanation of optical dispersion already observed and studied by Marcus Marci of Kronland, who wrote about it in his *Thaumantias* . . . (1648; Theorem XVIII, p. 99; XXI and XXII, p. 101). Newton explained dispersion by imagining that the particles constituting *lumen* possessed diverse masses, and consequently, refraction made them undergo different amounts of deviation, according to their mass. With that idea in mind, he correlated colors with the deviations experienced in refraction and consequently with the mass of the particles. However, in the most explicit and determined manner, he insisted on asserting that colors are subjective phenomena, and that for this reason the rays, or corpuscles of *lumen*, should be called "ruby-like" (producing red) and not red. Newton declared that in his own writings he had used the term "red," not because it was *strictly and philosophically* correct, but only because "the vulgar" would not have been able otherwise to understand the experiments he was prepared to describe (*Opticks*, Book I, Part II, Pro. ii, Definition).

Unfortunately, Newton himself had to remark that his idea of explaining optical phenomena by means of the force of attraction between matter and corpuscles led to conclusions that conflicted irremediably with experience. In fact, he abandoned that idea, explicitly admitting that corpuscles were endowed with natural "dispositions" of the medieval type and that only these "dispositions" and not the material forces of attraction allowed one to explain the new optical phenomena discovered in his time—the coloration of thin sheets (by interference), the phenomenon of diffraction (discovered by Father Grimaldi), and the double refraction of Icelandic spar (discovered in 1669 by Erasmus Bartolinus). In this situation Newton abandoned the universality of the law of material attraction.

The conception of *lumen* as a swarm of colored particles became untenable at the beginning of the nineteenth century, through the works especially of Thomas Young and Augustin Fresnel, when the corpuscular theory, which Isaac Newton had valued so highly and made so famous, collapsed quickly and was replaced by the wave theory of Young and Fresnel.

Besides, by attributing to light an ethereal motion of various frequencies, there was left no way of attributing luminosity to this motion which possessed neither brightness nor color; the reason for color, finally, was found in the frequency of the motion. This way of thinking is still widespread on a vast scale among physicists failing to consider how grotesque and absurd are its logical consequences.

Subsequent researches in this domain formed a branch of the science called "Physical Optics." The name was well justified so long as it was a matter of physical research into the nature of an entity, *lumen*, observable only by the use of the eyes, and hence, a part of optics. But in the early years of the nineteenth century Frederick W. Herschel discovered the infra-red rays; Johann W. Ritter and William H. Wollaston discovered the ultra-violet rays. Then other discoveries, even more sensational, followed, leading to the magnificent synthesis of James Clerk Maxwell; in his theory the waves constituting light were made part of the great series of electromagnetic waves.

As a result the study of the nature of the waves, which had been a typical subject of optics, began to lose its significance insofar as it was absorbed in the study of electromagnetic waves in general. One could deduce from this that optics would become a branch of the science called electromagnetism and thus lose its status as an autonomous science. The situation became all the more complicated and precarious when, in the meantime, new "detectors" were invented, namely, instruments capable of revealing those waves which until the beginning of the nineteenth century had been observable only by means of the eye; specifically, these inventions were the photosensitive emulsions, used in photography, the thermoelectric pile, the bolometer, the radiometer, and still others. To these instruments radio receivers and photoelectric cells can be added even if the latter are not all suited to reveal electromagnetic waves capable of stimulating the human eye also. The net result is that the eye lost its exclusive function of revealing *lumen*, and descended to the modest level of a very selective detector of electromagnetic waves in competition with the others listed above.

Such was the outcome of the extreme positivism that had dominated optics in the eighteenth and nineteenth centuries. As soon as most of the interest and attention became concentrated on the *physical* agency capable of stimulating the eye, and prevailed over research sufficiently to disregard the contribution of the eye in visual phenomena, it was inevitable that optics should lose its significance as an autonomous science and

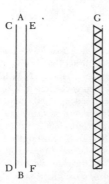

FIGURE 6. Grimaldi's vibrational model of light and color

become absorbed in a more general branch of the science of physics.

In order to avoid such a catastrophic conclusion it was necessary to return to the origins of optics. Instead of considering it as the study of a gamut of electromagnetic waves, limited to frequencies included in the range capable of stimulating the human eye (limits which nobody has as yet succeeded in defining in a way accepted by or acceptable to the civilized world), optics has been regarded as the "science of vision." Accordingly, optics has regained all of its unique and indestructible character as an autonomous science. As such, it is more complex in its constituents: partly physical through the study of the external factor capable of stimulating the human eye; partly physiological through the study of the response of the organ of vision to the external stimulus; and finally, the decisive psychological role played by the mind which is concerned with the representation of the world of appearances resulting from the external stimulation of the eye.

Before concluding this article, we must indicate the importance of the development taken by "technical optics" as a result of the establishment of the telescope and microscope as scientific instruments of extremely great value. Today we witness an extraordinarily delicate and precise technique with scientific foundations of a very distinctive nature. Galileo's initiative in devoting himself to working on lenses as the objectives of telescopes, with a much greater care than that given to the lenses of eyeglasses, was appreciated and followed by several "masters." With admirable persistence and skill they obtained results which made them famous. It suffices to recall the names of Ippolito Mariani (the righthand assistant of Galileo), Francesco Fontana and Eustachio Divini, and also Evangelista Torricelli, successor of Galileo in the high office of Mathematician of the Grand Duke of Tuscany, who worked on objective lenses which are extraordinary for their excellence, approximating the better ones we have today.

Towards the middle of the eighteenth century, S. Klingenstierna, in Sweden, and John Dollond, in England, constructed the first achromatic objectives by combining lenses made of different kinds of glass, thus improving the performance of optical instruments. However, optical technique has become very complicated and could not remain exclusively in the hands of even the most skillful artisans. Hence, it was necessary to have recourse to the collaboration of expert mathematicians to develop the "optical calculus," a new branch of applied mathematics, indispensable for research on the design of systems most suited to provide the best performance. At the same time, it was also necessary to generate the production of new types of glass, called "optical glass," endowed with the particular characteristics of refraction and dispersion without which the designs prepared by the optical calculators cannot be realized.

However, optical systems attained a rational basis only after the wave-theory allowed the precise definition of tolerance in the characteristics of the materials employed in working on them. These tolerances are measured exactly in fractions of an optical wavelength, which, as is well known, is of the order of magnitude of half a micron (a thousandth of a millimeter).

The cooperation of mathematicians specializing in geometrical optics with physicists specializing in wave-theory has brought technical optics to the limits of theoretical possibilities. Today there are optical systems that are called "optically perfect," in the sense that even if they were made with finer tolerances they would not perform any better. The limit of performance is determined by the structure of the radiation employed and not by the excellence of the workmanship.

CONCLUSIONS

Thus optics has returned to having the significance assigned to it by the ancient Greek philosophers when they coined the name which exactly stands for the "science of vision," as we indicated in the beginning. The same definition was adopted by Denis Diderot in the great *Encyclopédie* of the French Academy. After a long detour, the science of vision has returned to the forefront of studies, bringing back order and clarity in a field in which as a result of the great expansion of research, due to the influence of the study of radiation, there has occurred an unprecedented and enormous upheaval. Refusing henceforth to talk about "physical optics" and returning to its awareness of the indisputably mental character of light, colors, and images, "optics, the science of vision" resumes its march towards a bright future.

BIBLIOGRAPHY

Alhazen, *Opticae thesaurus libri septem*, trans. from the Arabic by Friedrich Risner (Basel, 1572). Giambattista della Porta, *Magia naturalis* (Naples, 1593); idem, *De telescopio* (Florence, 1962). George Berkeley, *Essay Towards a New Theory of Vision* (London, 1709). René Descartes, *La Dioptrique*, part of *Discours de la méthode* (Paris, 1637), in *Oeuvres de Descartes*, ed. Charles Adam and Paul Tannery, 13 vols. (Paris, 1897–1913). Euclid, *Optics*, trans. Harry E. Burton, *Journal of the Optical Society of America*, **35** (1945), 357–72; idem, *Catoptrica, Euclidis quae supersunt omnia*, ex Recensione David Gregorii, M.D. (Oxford, 1703). Galileo Galilei, *Siderius nuncius* (Venice, 1610), trans. E. S. Carlos as *The Sidereal Messenger* (1880; reprint London, 1960). F. M.

Grimaldi, *Physico-mathesis de lumine, coloribus, et iride* (Bologna, 1665). Christiaan Huygens, *Traité de la lumière* (Leyden, 1590; Paris, 1694). Johannes Kepler, *Paralipomena ad Vitellionem* (Frankfurt, 1604); idem, *Dioptrice* (Augusta [Augsburg], 1611). Marcus Marci de Kronland, Thaumantias Liber, *De arcu coelesti, deque colorum apparentium natura, ortu et causis* (Prague, 1648). Francesco Maurolico, *Photismi de lumine et umbra, Diaphaneon* (Naples, 1611). Isaac Newton, *Opticks* (London, 1704). V. Ronchi, *Storia della luce*, 2nd ed. (Bologna, 1952), trans. V. Barocas as *The Nature of Light* (London and Cambridge, Mass., 1970); idem, *Galileo e il suo cannocchiale*, 2nd ed. (Turin, 1964); idem, *Optics, the Science of Vision*, trans. Edward Rosen (New York, 1957); idem, *Sui Fondamenti dell'acustica e dell'ottica* (Florence, 1967); idem, *New Optics* (Florence, 1971). E. Rosen, "The Invention of Eyeglasses," *Journal of the History of Medicine and Allied Sciences*, 11 (1956), 13–46, 183–218. Giovanni Rucellai, *L'Ape* (Venice, 1539). Colin M. Turbayne, "Berkeley and Molyneux on Retinal Images," *Journal of the History of Ideas*, 16 (July-Sept. 1955), 339–55. Francesco Sizi, *Dianoia astronomica, ottica, physica* (Venice, 1611), trans. C. Pighetti (Florence, 1964).

VASCO RONCHI

[See also Astrology; **Atomism; Experimental Science;** Newton on Method; Idea; Platonism; Positivism.]

ORGANICISM

AESTHETIC organicism usually refers to the doctrine of organic unity and to its cognates like the idea of organic form or of "inner" form. The designation arises from the assumption that a work of art may be compared to a living organism, so that the relation between the parts of a work is neither arbitrary nor factitious, but as close and intimate as that between the organs of a living body. The classic formula for this relation is double: (1) the parts of the work are in keeping with each other and with the whole, and (2) alteration of a part will bring with it the alteration of the whole. By means of this formula the closest unity between the parts of a work of art is predicated or, alternatively, the formula provides the closest way of conceiving aesthetic unity.

Some critics like John Dewey use the simile to describe the growth of a work from a faint suggestion in the mind of the author to the finished composition, likened to the stages in the growth of a living being from the germ to the embryo to the fully developed organism. Indeed it is almost impossible not to use some organic metaphor in describing this process. But organicism refers to the ultimate result, not to the genesis but to the relation of the parts in the work once the whole process of composition is finished, and this or-

ganic conception has important critical consequences. Organicism may also be embodied in the concept of Organic Form in contrast to Mechanical Form: the latter is imposed from the outside on something which is alien to it, while the former develops spontaneously "from within," i.e., from the subject matter itself and not from external rules or prescribed models, and becomes its appropriate conformation. Sometimes organic form has been termed "inner Form" (Schwinger and Nicolai, 1935), in contrast to external or mechanical form, the latter being an attempt to fashion mechanically a composition from the outside. Hence the historical function of these concepts has been to loosen the rigid rules of traditional poetics and the pedantry of genres, and to foster the free play of the creative imagination that makes up its own rules as it goes along, and sets them according to the nature of the subject and the inspiration of the poet—two things which may be said to constitute a complex unity and are actually vital factors in the act of creation. The structure that the finished work will possess will not be lawless, because of the two conditions of organic unity mentioned above.

In other words, the general effect of the organic conception has been to move away from narrow classicism in the direction of what may be vaguely named romanticism. But the concepts themselves are of classical (i.e., ancient Greek) origin; they were originally formulated by Plato and Aristotle. The clause designated above as (1), the congruence of parts with each other, and with the whole, comes from Plato's *Phaedrus* (264C), and clause (2) from Aristotle's *Poetics* (VIII. 51A 32–35). In modern times they have been supplied with new philosophical foundations, being fully developed in the aesthetics of German idealism. Kant himself powerfully contributed to the trend, applications to aesthetics being due especially to the great romantic thinkers and literary critics, Schelling and Hegel, the Schlegels and Coleridge. Through their use in literary criticism organic concepts have gained wide currency in modern writing of all kinds and may be found in many paraphrases and adaptations, up to the point of becoming almost a cliché; but they are capable of being exactly formulated. They have been so formulated quite recently by John Hospers:

The unified object should contain within itself a large number of diverse elements, each of which in some way contributes to the total integration of the unified whole. . . . everything that is necessary is there, and nothing that is not necessary is there.

. . . in a work of art, if a certain yellow patch were not in a painting, its entire character would be altered, and so would a play if a particular scene were not in it, in just the place where it is (1967).

This makes it clear that in the idea of organic unity, the concept of totality or wholeness is implied. Going one step further back, we find that the basic concepts of the One and the Many are implied. For organic unity consists of a multiplicity of parts which is reduced to unity, and of a unity which is made up of a multiplicity. "How the one can be many, and the many be one" is one of the questions that was argued in Socrates' circle (*Philebus*, 14C).

The problem eventually found a solution of one kind in the Platonic concept of the Idea, which is the unity of a multiplicity, and then received a different solution in Aristotle's sense of composite whole (*synolon*). In more modern times this unity comes under the category of an *a priori* synthesis in the Kantian sense: its components are not conjoined empirically, but belong *originally* to each other. Using the organic metaphor, they may be said to belong "naturally" to each other. For instance, it may be said that Sancho is not an extrinsic addition to Don Quixote, but that the Don belongs to Sancho just as much as vice versa: the great comic situation would not be what it is if one of the two were omitted.

But there is no need to resort to the organic metaphor in order to define such a clear logical unity as the synthesis of parts in a whole. Also, it should be noted that this unity can be affirmed of other mental products besides works of art. A philosophical system or a mathematical demonstration may be said to possess such unity; also, a history or any ratiocinative composition. Hence its already mentioned wide use in all subjects.

In order to be meaningful in aesthetics and in literary criticism, the concept must be integrated by other concepts drawn specifically from the sphere of aesthetics. To be aesthetic, the object defined must be endowed with beauty, and so beauty itself must be defined. In the course of this century, beauty has been defined as *Gestalt* or total image, created by the poetic imagination and expressive of human feeling. The parts discernible in the object are organically (indissolubly) united, so that alteration of one part produces alteration of the whole. Nor can aesthetics really be grounded without a concept of reality, or some type of metaphysics. This means introducing other concepts besides the organic ones and going well beyond the Platonic and Aristotelian sphere of ideas.

Considered however in its abstract generality, as it is in ancient thought, organic unity is susceptible of another formulation: "the whole is more than the sum of its parts," a saying often repeated in modern times, but the author of which is unknown. But Plato said something very close to that when he wrote: "The all is not the whole" (*Theaetetus*, 204B), "the all" being,

as the context shows, the sum of the parts. In aesthetics this means that the work of art is not produced by the mere superaddition of isolated pieces to each other: to join the single parts an essential link is necessary, connecting all of them.

Still more philosophically, Aristotle said that "the whole is prior to the parts" (*Politics*, I. 2. 1253a 20). This is often interpreted to mean that the parts *imply* the whole. Aristotle himself commented that the parts are posterior to the whole because in the whole they exist only potentially: "only when the whole has been dissolved they will attain actuality" (*Metaphysics*, V. 11. 1019a 9–10). Aristotle applied this principle to the theory of the State and it had considerable vogue afterwards. Aestheticians took up the principle: the great representative of organicism in England, Samuel Taylor Coleridge, speaks in *The Friend* (1818) of "the Aristotelian maxim, with respect to all just reasoning, that the whole is of necessity prior to its parts" (Part II, Essay 10). More specifically in his *Philosophical Lectures* (1819) he enjoins: "Depend on it, whatever is truly organic and living, the whole is prior to the parts."

It is the *a priority* of the whole that makes its unity intrinsic, as opposed to the extrinsic aggregation of parts. To quote Coleridge again, "the distinction, or rather the essential difference, betwixt the shaping skill of mechanical talent, and the creative, productive life-power of inspired genius; in the former, each part separately conceived and then by succeeding act put together."

The concept of organic unity raises some basic questions: (1) Is it *possible* to divide an organic work of art into parts? (2) If it is possible, is it *necessary* so to divide it? What purpose is served by the division? (3) If it is both possible and necessary to divide, what procedure should be followed in this division? How do we divide the work into parts that are vital and not artificial?

The first question implies the more general problem of the divisibility of any unit, which has been debated by several philosophers. Into this debate we cannot enter here, but we indicate that there is such a problem. Assuming (1) that the work admits of division, we ask: (2) What purpose is achieved by doing so? Precisely to show the necessary unity of the whole by observing the relation of the parts to each other and to the whole. This can only be done by taking them in succession, one after the other, as A. W. Schlegel did in his analysis of *Romeo and Juliet* (1797), one of the earliest examples of organic criticism: first the characters are considered, then the features of the style. Another exponent of organicism, A. C. Bradley, raised the question: If we believe in the organic unity of the parts, why do we separate them in analysis? To which he gave the answer:

To consider separately the action and the characters of a play, and separately the style and versification, is both legitimate and valuable, so long as we remember what we are doing. But the true critic in speaking of these aspects does not really think of them apart: the whole, the poetic experience, of which they are but aspects, is always in his mind; and he is always aiming at a richer, truer, more intimate repetition of that experience (1909).

As Goethe said, we must first distinguish, and then unite (Gott und Welt: Atmosphäre, 1821). Division of parts is essential also to a criticism that comes to an adverse conclusion on the value of the work, since the worse the work, the greater will be the incongruity between the parts, like Horace's Humano capiti . . . (Ars poetica, 1).

Once the work has been divided into its essential parts, the procedure of the critic will be to evaluate the relation of the parts to each other and to the whole, basing his final judgment on the results thus arrived at. But (3) what is the correct method of dividing a work of art into parts? It may be answered that they should be so divided that each part preserves some meaning of its own. Hence a poem should not be divided into purely verbal units, since such words as articles and conjunctions do not possess a meaning of their own, nor do most single words really. But a complete line of verse or a complete stanza may have a meaning of its own, so that it can stand by itself. The same is true of sections of prose such as paragraphs, chapters, etc., and of plays, such as acts and scenes, so they may all be legitimate divisions.

However, it is a moot point whether the parts of a beautiful object should be beautiful too. Plotinus argued that if the whole is beautiful, the parts also must be beautiful: "the whole cannot be made up of ugly parts; beauty must penetrate everything" (Enneads, I. vi. 1 50). Here it may be enough to say about this division what Plato said, that one must not hack away at the parts of a beautiful whole like a clumsy butcher (Phaedrus, 265C.). The individuality of the work of art is also relevant to this question, since it excludes the so-called rules of composition and the partitions of rhetoric, as Socrates rejected the partitions and rules of contemporary rhetoricians (ibid., 266–67).

In the Poetics, Aristotle applied the principle of organic unity only to the plot of tragedy, but not to the other parts of tragedy, nor to their relation with each other and with the whole. The other parts are enumerated and defined, but even their number is not definite: once five, then three. However, the principle is implicit in the Ars poetica of Horace or the Epistle to the Pisos (ca. 14 B.C.). From its very first line, a poem is compared to a living body, in which it would be incongruous if a human head were joined to a horse's neck (1–13). Unity has been rightly called the governing consideration of the Ars: the poem should be simplex dumtaxat et unum (34), actually a unity of different parts. Cicero, like Philodemus, extended the principle of organic unity to the relation between language and thought in expression: "words do not subsist if you remove the meanings (res), nor can there be light in the meanings if you remove the words" (De oratore, III, 5–6). The principle reappears in pseudo-Longinus, On the Sublime: "Since by nature there are in all things certain parts which are necessarily involved in their matter, it follows that one cause of excellence is the power to choose the most suitable of the constitutive elements and to arrange them so that they form a single living body." For instance, Sappho in her most famous ode selects the most characteristic symptoms of passion, and then proceeds to "bind them one with the other" forming a perfect poem (Ch. X).

Plotinus in his first book (Enneads, I. vi) considers the beautiful object a synthesis of various parts brought together so as to form a coherent whole, the many being reduced to one. He then raises the already quoted question about the beauty of the parts. While he does not use explicitly the organic simile, the human face is his example of living beauty; but he rules out mere symmetry and proportion as the definition of beauty, and introduces the Aristotelian concept of Form, to which we now turn.

Aristotle's hylomorphism assumes certain powers in Form that make it much more than mere shape: it is actuality in antithesis to potentiality, and it confers meaning and purpose on its matter. But it was not extended to literature by Aristotle, who never speaks of Form in the Poetics. However, the concept has been found most fruitful by later criticism, as the Form and Content of literature (French la forme et le fond, German Gestalt und Gehalt or Form und Stoff). In its simplest definition the content of a work is what it is about, and the form is the manner in which it is treated; but the two concepts admit of deeper definition. When they are thought of as the parts of which the work of art is made up, their relation may be defined in terms of organic unity, that is, form must be in keeping with content and content with form, so that if you alter the one, the other is altered too. Taking form in the sense of metrical form, the content of a sonnet must be perfectly adapted to the form of the sonnet, and it cannot be turned into the content of an ode without altering it, and vice versa.

The organic unity of form and content is denied by

423

all theories that make one of the two predominant and the other unessential, conceiving them as separate parts that can be manipulated independently of each other. Such is the meaning of Formalism, which makes Form everything, and reduces content to nothing. This J. C. F. von Schiller does in his *Aesthetic Letters* (1795, letter XXII), followed later by Oscar Wilde's "Form is everything" (1891). The opposite theory (for which we have no name, but it might be called Contentualism) makes content predominant, and form indifferent. But in organicism the two cannot be separated.

Since for Aristotle form is operative not only in artefacts but also in living beings, the latter form may well be defined as organic. But in Aristotle we do not find the phrase, which is characteristic of romantic speculation. For Aristotle, Form is applied to matter by natural forces, as part of the system of the universe; in art, form preexists in the mind of the artist or craftsman and is applied by him to the chosen matter. But for Aristotle, faithful to ancient realism, this form is not produced by the artist, and the whole concept of artistic creation is alien to him.

In recent times the form of the literary genre or type—such as the set form of tragedy or the epic, as defined by rules—has been considered Organic Form. But since it is indifferent to its matter, it is not really organic. The content of all poetry being individual, the form should also be individual, and not set and rigid according to preconceived rules. Few conceptions are so alien to the organic principle as the divisions and subdivisions of rhetoric, especially in its application to poetry. There form is separated from content and defined independently of it, and the unifying power is lost from sight. But the fact that the parts of a sentence are called by rhetoricians "members" (*árthra, kóla*) shows that an echo of the organic simile may still be heard in the babel of rhetorical classifications.

Through the medieval period the rhetorical tradition kept alive these vestiges of organicism, and Horace no doubt helped. The speculations of the scholastics on unity brought them closer to the Platonic tradition, even though the *Phaedrus* was apparently forgotten. It is therefore remarkable that Dante could formulate the organic principle and its simile so definitely in his *Convivio*:

Men call beautiful the things in which the parts fully answer to each other, so that from their harmony pleasure results. Thus a human being appears to be beautiful when the members duly answer each other; and we say a song is beautiful, when its sounds are duly respondent to each other according to art (I, v, 3–15; trans. G. N. G. Orsini).

With the Renaissance and the revival of the *Poetics* (not to speak of Plato), the principle returned into the critical discussion of literature. Aristotle's definition of organic unity in the plot, for instance, reappears in Aristotelian interpreters like Daniel Heinsius, in his *De tragoediae constitutione* (1611). From there it passes into Ben Jonson's *Timber; or Discoveries . . .* (posthumous, 1641), thus becoming a part of neo-classical tradition in England. In the same century Nicolas Boileau was legislating on poetry in France, mainly on the foundation of Horace, as interpreted by strict French intellectualism (1674). Organic precepts reappear, but somewhat less sharply:

> Il faut que chaque chose y soit mise en son lieu,
> Que le début, la fin, répondent au milieu;
> Que d'un art délicat les pièces assorties
> N'y forment qu'un seul tout de diverses parties.
> (I, lines 177–80)

Boileau also translated Longinus, thus making available another source of organic ideas. Twenty years later (1694) he published a commentary on Longinus, mainly disputing Charles Perrault.

In the eighteenth century we may find organic concepts even in the manifesto of English neo-classicism, Alexander Pope's *Essay on Criticism* (1711):

> In wit, as nature, what affects our hearts
> Is not the exactness of peculiar parts;
> 'Tis not a lip or eye we beauty call,
> But the joint force and full result of all.
> (Part II, lines 43–46)

Shaftesbury's share in the formulation of the concept has been made much of by German scholars, but it seems that he just came very near and merely caught a glimpse of it. "Inner form" appears in him, apparently on the foundation of Plotinus, but only once does he ascribe organic unity to the work of art (*Notion of the Tablature*, posthumously published in 1714).

The concept of inner form was transformed by J. Harris (*Hermes*, 1751), and Herder saw it as the spirit within the body of the poem. Herder is the first literary critic to make use of the concept of organic form in practical criticism. In 1771 he applied it to Shakespeare's dramas and in 1776 Goethe, then Herder's disciple, set up the "inner form" of a play as against "the unities, beginning, middle and end the rest of it," the traditional Aristotelian concepts of form.

As science developed the investigation of the physical organism, so philosophy turned to analyze the essence of the living organism. Leibniz gave a mechanical definition of it as "a natural mechanism," i.e., a machine made up of smaller machines (*Principles of nature and grace* [1714], para. 3). His own metaphysical speculations turned on the unity of substance and its division into parts which are posterior to the whole (at least *in idealibus:* letter to Des Bosses, 31 July 1706), thus reaffirming the Aristotelian *a priority* of logical unity.

Goethe's view of nature was fundamentally organic. He condemned the analytical scientist, who murders to dissect, in a famous passage of *Faust:* "The parts in his hand he may hold and class/ But the spiritual link is lost, alas!" (lines 1938–39). A modern scholar states that Goethe took over from Neo-Platonism "the idea of form from a process at work even in the inmost parts of an organism and to fuse it completely with the idea of form as an outward shape. The one is not the cause of the other; they are completely reciprocal. Inner structure determines outward shape and outward shape inner structure" (Wilkinson, 1951).

Kant had already employed organic unity to define the structure of pure reason in the *Critique of Pure Reason* (2nd ed., 1787). The ideal principles of pure reason constitute "a self-subsistent unity, in which as an organized body each member exists for every other, and all for the sake of each" (B xxviii). The idea is more fully developed in the "Dialectic of Pure Reason" and the "Doctrine of Method," the last parts of the *Critique.*

In his aesthetic theory, Kant came very near to defining explicitly the work of art as an organic unity. The idea is implicit in his *Critique of Judgment* (1790, para. 65), where he traces out the "analogy" between a work of art and a living body, and also does something which critics of organicism claim has not been done: he points out the differences between them. These are, first, that in an organism "parts produce one another: it is self-organizing"; second, that an organism that goes out of order "repairs itself"; and third, that a natural organism can reproduce itself. Kant definitely warns that there is no real identity between nature and art, because the art product always involves an "artificer" while nature does not.

Kant also made the sharpest antithesis between the organic and the mechanical by defining the organism teleologically, as a whole in which "every part is reciprocally end and means" (para. 66). In a work of art purposefulness is also apparent, but not real, although the harmony of the parts produces aesthetic pleasure (*Wohlgefallen*).

The powerful impulse of Kant can be felt in all later German speculation. Mere atomistic empiricism, the unconnected sensation or enumeration of the parts of a subject, became anathema; every intellectual production, be it a philosophical treatise or a poem, was to be organically articulated, each part related to the others and to the whole. In Schelling's *System of Transcendental Idealism* (1800) art became the intellectual intuition which reaches the Absolute beyond all contradictions, and in his *Discourse on the Relation between the Fine Arts and Nature* (1807) he formulated the concept of organic form in the arts.

Meanwhile the brothers Schlegel had carried the concept of organic form into literary criticism. In August Schlegel's Lectures of 1801 organic concepts prevail, as well as in the more famous Vienna lectures on the drama (1810). There he gave the final blow to the neo-classical depreciation of Shakespeare, whose tragedies, being devoid of the classical dramatic unities, were claimed to be without form. But the unities, he showed, are a purely mechanical form, applied externally to a subject; while real art possesses organic form which is inborn and develops from within, producing an outward arrangement dictated by the nature of the subject. This was immediately taken up by Coleridge in his English lectures, and became the foundation of a new, positive interpretation of Shakespearean tragedy—an interpretation which has borne fruit ever since.

Coleridge is the main representative of organicism in English criticism. In his most formal definition of Beauty he started from Plotinus: "the indivisible unity which appears in the many" (*Enneads,* I. vi. 3) and then stated that "the sense of beauty consists in the simultaneous intuition of the relation of parts, each to each, and of all to the whole" ("On the Principles of Genial Criticism Concerning the Fine Arts," III [1814]).

"Unity in multiplicity" is Coleridge's favorite aesthetic formula, which he repeats in many guises ("unity in multeity," *il più nell'uno,* etc.). In his definition of the Imagination, this unity becomes a unity of disparates, or even of contraries, thus converging into another speculative doctrine dear to the idealists: the unity of opposites. It may even be suggested that this unity is the only one close enough to act as the unifying power of the Imagination, the "esemplastic" power of which Coleridge theorized (*Biographia Literaria,* Ch. XIII). The use Coleridge made of these concepts in his practical criticism was fully expounded by Gordon MacKenzie (1939).

William Blake also asserted the organic unity of expression: "Ideas cannot be given but in their minutely appropriate parts" (*Prose Address,* ca. 1810); an original invention cannot ". . . exist without execution organized, delineated, and articulated. . . ." As Croce will say, "The poem is as those words, that rhythm, and that metre" (*Essence of Aesthetic* [1912], Ch. II).

After Schelling, Hegel definitely affirmed (in 1838) that organic unity was the basic characteristic of a poem: "Every genuine work of poetry is an essentially infinite organism . . . in which the whole, without any visible intention, is sphered within one rounded and essentially self-enclosed completeness" (*Philosophy of Fine Art*, Part III: "Poetry"). From Germany the idea spread to other European countries where it found support in native traditions.

During the Victorian era the greatest literary representative of organicism was perhaps Walter Pater, as seen in his *Appreciations* (1889). Later in the century the idealistic philosopher B. Bosanquet reaffirmed organicism as his definition of beauty (1892).

Coming to the present century, the definition of organic unity was debated among English philosophers of the twenties and thirties, J. E. McTaggart (1921–27) and C. D. Broad (1933). One of the strongest champions of organic unity in English aesthetics of the mid-twentieth century is Harold Osborne. In his *Theory of Beauty* (1952) he defines beauty as organic unity or *Gestalt*, "a configuration such that the configuration itself is prior in awareness to its component parts and is not explicable by a summation of its parts and their relations according to discursive and additive principles." On this foundation he built up his detailed work, *Aesthetics and Criticism* (1955).

German thought also fertilized Italian criticism. From Hegel Francesco de Sanctis developed his aesthetic, which he applied extensively to the criticism and to the history of Italian literature. The aesthetic form of a work for him is actually generated by its content; it is ". . . the life which the content acquired in the mind of the poet" and the two are organically inseparable (essay on Settembrini, 1869). From De Sanctis, Benedetto Croce developed his own organicism. In his earliest *Aesthetic* (1902; trans. 1909; 1922) he appealed to the principle that ". . . the whole determines the quality of the parts" (Part I, Ch. i) and that the imagination effects ". . . the fusion of all impressions into an organic whole" (ibid., Ch. ii). On the basis of the unity of thought and expression Croce rejected "modes of expression," such as the plain and the ornate, the simple and the elevated, the poetic and the prosaic, as well as "figures of speech" and all other ornamentations (Part I, Ch. ix), thus consolidating his exclusion of rhetoric and the theory of genres from literary criticism. The concept of dynamic form is paramount in every sphere of Croce's thinking (Orsini, 1961). Hence his warning not to take ". . . the metaphorical term 'organism' literally, as was done by linguists like A. Schleicher" (1905). His own criticism generally looks for the form of mental activity prevalent in the individual work—practical or theoretical, conceptual or utilitarian—and distinguishes it from the other forms which may also enter into the work ("poetry and non-poetry").

Organic concepts, or at least organic terms, play a large part in American criticism. In the nineteenth century Coleridge's ideas were largely influential, as shown in the surveys of H. H. Clark and R. H. Fogle (1955). They turn up in writers such as Poe, Emerson, Thoreau, and Whitman. In time the Coleridgian concepts were watered down, and some twentieth-century writers have only a vague notion of them. The term "organic" is prominent in S. Pepper's aesthetics (1945), but his philosophical use of it is his own. He calls "organistic criticism" the kind that conceives aesthetic value as "the integration of feeling," which omits the unity of the parts in the whole. Cleanth Brooks called "organic" his own idea of the poem as a system of actions and reactions, of stresses and balances like the physical pressures in a bridge, which is obviously not organical but mechanical (1941, p. 36). He draws closer to genuine organicism in books written in collaboration with R. P. Warren, especially *Modern Rhetoric* (1949). A faithful presentation of the organic concepts is by R. B. West and R. W. Stallman (1949). M. H. Abrams in *The Mirror and the Lamp* (1953) gave one of the fullest definitions, both historically and critically, of organicism, but he unnecessarily adopted Pepper's classification of kinds of theory. M. Krieger put forward an "organic theory of poetic creation" (1950), but he was diverted from the organic concepts by the Aristotelian theory of language as a medium and not as an organic form.

The distinction between organic unity and organic form may perhaps be defined as that between an earlier and less developed form of theory and a later, more specific form of it—the latter still having a future in front of it. But the concepts are now so widespread that it is impossible to follow out all variations of them. Organic unity is so indispensable a prerequisite of aesthetics that it is often taken for granted and omitted as obvious. But both concepts in their strict form are still capable of development and revision.

There are also critical trends adverse to organic conceptions. The opposition comes mainly from representatives of traditional poetics and rhetoric, with their separation of form and content, thought and expression, and from their prescriptive formulas for composition; also from neo-Aristotelians and others who are opposed to the idealistic philosophy which underlies much of organicism. The latter has been identified by other critics with the idea of unconscious growth, which ignores "the conscious, critical element in composition." But in the idealistic context organic unity applies to the result of the conscious act of composition, to the completed work and not to its genesis. Likewise, the incomplete or fragmentary condition of a work today cannot provide an argument for denying organic character to its original text, nor can the fact that the original text may now be disfigured by textual corruption. More recent critics have denied the idea that a good poem is injured by losing some of its parts (Lord, 1965); others have traced the principle to different philosophical systems, like Leibniz' (Benziger, 1951). The fact that the organic metaphor refers to a biological phenomenon like the human body has been considered a fault, but that can be easily removed by dropping the metaphor and formulating the concept in its logical form as the synthesis of particulars, to be found actually in a work of art as created by the mind, and only analogically in a living body. Nor is the metaphor necessary to provide the name for the principle, since it has been given other designations, such as "esemplastic" or "coadunative unity" by Coleridge, an "intensive manifold" by T. E. Hulme, or a "synthetic configuration" by Osborne.

BIBLIOGRAPHY

Most of the topics in this article are more fully treated in G. N. G. Orsini, "The Organic Concepts in Aesthetics," in *Comparative Literature*, 31 (1969), 1–30. The most notable contributions to the history of the idea were made by the German scholar Oskar Walzel in his *Vom Geistesleben alter und neuer Zeit* (Leipzig, 1922), and other works listed in this article. In English, the fullest historical exposition is in M. H. Abrams, *The Mirror and the Lamp . . .* (New York, 1953), and one of the most perceptive critical expositions is in Sir Herbert Read, *The True Voice of Feeling* (New York, 1953). The works of René Wellek contain much that bears directly on the subject.

The following are references made in the course of the article. W. Blake, *Complete Writings*, ed. G. Keynes (Oxford, 1966), pp. 395–96. B. Bosanquet, *A History of Aesthetic*, 2nd ed. (London, 1904), pp. 32–33. A. C. Bradley, *Oxford Lectures on Poetry* (London, 1909), pp. 257–59. C. D. Broad, *Examination of McTaggart's Philosophy* (Cambridge, 1933), I, 240. C. Brooks, "The Poem as Organism: Modern Critical Procedure," *English Institute Annual 1940* (New York, 1941), pp. 20–41; idem, "Implications of an Organic Theory of Poetry," in M. H. Abrams, ed., *Literature and Belief, English Institute Essays, 1957* (New York, 1958), pp. 53–79; idem and R. P. Warren, *Modern Rhetoric: With Readings* (New York, 1949). H. H. Clark, "Changing Attitudes in Early American Criticism: 1800–1840," in Floyd Stovall, ed., *Development of American Literary Criticism* (Chapel Hill, N.C., 1955). S. T. Coleridge, "On the Principles of Genial Criticism . . ." (1814), in J. Shawcross, ed., *Biographia Literaria*, 2 vols. (London, 1907), II, 238–39; idem, *The Philosophical Lectures, Hitherto Unpublished*, ed. K. Coburn (New York, 1949), p. 196; idem, *Shakespearean Criticism*, ed. T. M. Raysor, new ed., 2 vols. (London, 1960), I, 4–5. B. Croce, *Brevario di estetica*, trans. Douglas Ainslie as "The Breviary of Aesthetics" (Houston, Texas, 1912); book title, *The Essence of Aesthetic* (London, 1921); the original is also in *Nuovi saggi di estetica*, 2nd ed. (Bari, 1920), pp. 39ff;

idem, *Aesthetic as Science of Expression and General Linguistics*, trans. Douglas Ainslie, 2nd ed. (London, 1922), pp. 2, 20; idem, *Problemi di estetica* (Bari, 1910), pp. 192–93. F. De Sanctis, "Settembrini e i suoi critici," in *Saggi critici*, ed. L. Russo, 3 vols. (Bari, 1965), II, 306. J. Dewey, *Art as Experience* (New York, 1934), pp. 192–93. R. H. Fogle, "Organic Form and American Criticism: 1840–1870," in Stovall, op. cit. For J. Harris, see Schwinger, below. G. W. F. Hegel, *Philosophy of Fine Art*, trans. F. P. B. Ormaston, 4 vols. (London, 1920), IV, 51; cf. on "The Beauty of Nature," I, 163–67, 173–75. J. Hospers, "Problems of Aesthetics," in *The Encyclopedia of Philosophy*, ed. P. Edwards, 8 vols. (New York, 1967), I, 43. M. Krieger, *The New Apologists for Poetry* (Minneapolis, 1950); idem, "B. Croce and the Recent Poetics of Organicism," *Comparative Literature*, 7 (1955), 252–58. G. MacKenzie, *Organic Unity in Coleridge* (Berkeley, 1939). J. E. McTaggart, *The Nature of Existence* (Cambridge, 1921), I, 165–66. G. N. G. Orsini, *B. Croce as Philosopher of Art and Literary Critic* (Carbondale, 1961), p. 317, n. 26; idem, "Coleridge and Schlegel Reconsidered," *Comparative Literature*, 16 (1964), 116–18. H. Osborne, *The Theory of Beauty* (London, 1952), p. 124. S. C. Pepper, *The Basis of Criticism in the Arts* (Cambridge, Mass., 1945). R. Schwinger and R. Nicolai, *Innere Form und dichterische Phantasie* (Munich, 1935). R. B. West and R. W. Stallman, *The Art of Modern Fiction* (New York, 1949), esp. "Form," p. 647, and "Structure," p. 651. O. Wilde, *Intentions* (London, 1891), p. 201. E. M. Wilkinson, "Goethe's Conception of Form," *Proceedings of the British Academy*, 37 (1951), 186.

For the identification with unconscious growth see: J. Benziger, "Organic Unity, Leibniz to Coleridge," *PMLA*, 66 (1951), 24–48. The following titles do not discuss "unconscious growth" but the general concept. T. E. Hulme, "The Philosophy of Intensive Manifolds," in his *Speculations*, ed. H. Read (London, 1924), pp. 171–214. C. Lord, "Organic Unity Reconsidered," *Journal of Aesthetics and Art Criticism*, 52 (1964), 263–68. W. Van O'Connor, *An Age of Criticism, 1900–1950* (Chicago, 1952), p. 58.

G. N. G. ORSINI

[See also **Analogy of the Body Politic;** Classicism; Criticism; **Hegelian . . . ;** Literature; **Metaphor in Philosophy;** Platonism; **Romanticism in Post-Kantian Philosophy.**]

ORIENTAL IDEAS IN AMERICAN THOUGHT

I. THE IMPACT OF ORIENTAL IDEAS ON AMERICAN CULTURE IN THE NINETEENTH CENTURY

THE HISTORY of Oriental ideas in America in the nineteenth century is largely a story of discovery and exploration. In 1800 Oriental thought was almost totally unknown, a largely unexplored region in the world of the mind. In 1900 Oriental thought was still a mystery to most Americans, perhaps, but many of its secrets had been revealed and its territory roughly mapped. Though the Eastern exploration never attained the proportions of a major intellectual movement—the thought was both too rich and too alien for rapid assimilation—nevertheless, its impact reached more widely and more deeply than has been appreciated. And unlike many nineteenth-century movements, it has continued to stimulate and influence Americans of the twentieth century: the modern interest in Oriental philosophy, Zen Buddhism, yoga, and Oriental art may all be traced back to nineteenth-century beginnings.

In the following survey we have sought to delineate the high points in the American discovery. This has necessitated certain limitations which may be indicated at the outset. Though the term "Oriental" is vague, it is used here, first, because it was the common generic term used in the nineteenth century, perhaps more suitable here exactly because it suggests the vagueness of the nineteenth-century concept of the East; and second, because no better term has been widely accepted that embraces the diversity of the Eastern cultures. In this survey the term will be confined almost entirely to India, China, and Japan. The ideas traced will be mainly religious ideas. The political, economic, and social ideas of the Eastern cultures were noticed in the nineteenth century, but the major focus was consistently on moral and religious thought. The treatment will be selective: only a few key individuals and movements connected with discovery have been closely analyzed, assuming that a more detailed examination of the most important cases would be more instructive than a comprehensive but superficial listing of all.

Finally, it is to be noted that if the Orient and its thought were practically unknown in America at the beginning of the nineteenth century, the situation was different elsewhere in the West. In Europe, Oriental ideas were already enjoying a vogue in the seventeenth and eighteenth centuries: intellectual leaders such as Quesnay, Voltaire, Leibniz, and Christian Wolff were acclaiming Chinese thought; *chinoiserie* and the cult of Confucius the Sage were stylish among certain elements of European high society; and the first translations of the Oriental classics were appearing from the hands of scholars such as Anquetil Duperron and Sir William Jones. Oriental thought continued to have impact in Europe after 1800; and the European impact in turn influenced the American reaction. While aware of its significance, we shall pass over the European role in the transmission of Oriental ideas to America.

II. FIRST STIRRINGS IN THE EARLY 1800'S

The absence of American interest in Oriental ideas before the nineteenth century is understandable. During the seventeenth century America was still a very primitive society already overburdened by the task of establishing the rudiments of Western civilization; and eighteenth-century America was preoccupied with the pressures of war and revolution. There was neither energy nor time for Oriental explorations. The Oriental tale did, indeed, enjoy a certain popularity in eighteenth-century American periodicals, but it was of only minor significance as the channel of authentic Oriental ideas. The stirrings of change came with a shift in America's economic position in the last decades of the eighteenth century. The Revolutionary War had forced the new American nation to look beyond England for the trade upon which her survival depended; the consequent opening of commercial relations with India and China in the 1780's and 1790's first directed American attention upon the Orient. Though the focus was economic, there were intangible cultural ramifications. In addition to Oriental goods, the Eastern trade stimulated the dispatching of missionaries, interest in the curious customs of distant peoples, and the importation of increasing numbers of books about the Far East. The Oriental bric-a-brac that American sailors brought back from the East undoubtedly quickened the intellectual curiosity of more sedentary Americans. As the major port of the Far Eastern trade, Salem (Massachusetts) figured most prominently in the budding American interest in the East. The "Salem East India Marine Society" was established in 1799, and there the first American collection of Oriental objects was housed. It is significant that both Samuel Johnson, one of the first American students of Oriental religion, and Ernest Fenollosa, the great nineteenth-century American advocate of Oriental art, grew to maturity in Salem.

The Eastern trade undoubtedly quickened general interest in the Orient, but it must be doubted that the American sailors and traders who carried on this commerce concerned themselves deeply with Oriental thought and culture. The first Americans to become interested in Oriental thought had to look elsewhere for information: fortunately, there was a source near at hand. Periodicals, both English and American, seem to have supplied the earliest American knowledge of Oriental ideas. The *Edinburgh Review*, perhaps the most notable in this respect, provided a surprisingly extensive treatment of Oriental affairs and of Oriental ideas in the early 1800's. Of early American periodicals, the most significant was the *North American Re-*

view. From its inception in 1815, this distinguished American periodical published a steady series of articles, extracts, reviews, and travel accounts dealing with the Orient. The second number of the new journal incorporated a brief report of the pioneering work of the French Orientalist, Anquetil Duperron, followed by an account of the criticisms of Duperron made by Sir William Jones, the famous British Oriental scholar. Between 1817 and 1828 the *North American Review* offered its readers such major articles as Edward Tyrrel Channing's "Lalla Rookh, an Oriental Romance"; William Tudor's "Theology of the Hindoos, as Taught by Ram Mohun Roy"; Theophilus Parsons' "Manners and Customs of India"; Alexander Hill Everett's "Remusat's Chinese Grammar" and his "Chinese Manners"; John Chipman Gray's "Cochin China"; and Edward Everett's "Hindu Drama." The first accounts were mainly devoted to description and exposition, with little attempt at analysis; but information was needed before evaluation and assimilation could occur. They did serve to naturalize the strange and alien ideas of the East.

III. TRANSCENDENTALISM AND THE ORIENT

The transcendentalist awakening to Oriental thought in the late 1830's was a decisive event. For the first time Americans representing a major movement turned seriously to the East. And unlike earlier explorers they incorporated and assimilated certain strains of Oriental thought into their intellectual views. The key figures were Emerson and Thoreau, of course; but several of the lesser transcendentalists—including James Freeman Clarke, Samuel Johnson, Moncure Conway, Thomas Wentworth Higginson, Samuel Longfellow, William Henry Channing, and Octavius Brooks Frothingham— were also significant. (Others on the periphery of transcendentalism—in close contact with and influenced by the New England movement, and who also indicated some interest in Oriental ideas—included Francis Ellingwood Abbot, Lydia Maria Child, William Torrey Harris, Oliver Wendell Holmes, John Chadwick, Charles De Berard Mills, and Lewis George Janes.) If Oriental thought was not a dominant preoccupation in any of the transcendentalists, it was a factor in all the individuals mentioned. The major interest was in Hinduism, and to a lesser extent Confucianism; Buddhism, which tended to dominate interest in the later nineteenth century, was at first ignored.

A combination of factors contributed to the favorable transcendentalist response to Oriental thought. Intellectually, its spokesmen were ripe for new ideas. In rebellion against the Calvinistic Christianity, rationalistic Unitarianism, and materialistic Lockean-

ism that then dominated New England intellectual life, leading members of the movement were receptive to the new currents of idealism they found in the Orient. What they sought they could have found, and often did find, in certain strains of Western thought—in Neo-Platonism and in Western mysticism, for example— but they also tapped the East. The deeply spiritual and intuitive quality of Oriental thought struck a responsive chord. The eclecticism of transcendentalism was a second factor. As eclectics, the transcendentalists found little difficulty in incorporating selected Oriental ideas into their view. Had they been more rigorous and consistent in approach, the possibilities of assimilating Oriental thought would have been correspondingly lessened. The method, as much as the trend of their thought, was conducive to a favorable response to the Orient. Again, by the late 1830's the Orient was more accessible than it had been at the beginning of the century. By the late 1830's it became possible for the first time to go beyond the usual English and American periodicals to the fountainhead of Eastern thought. Owing to the labors of the great English Orientalists— Sir William Jones, Charles Wilkins, Horace Wilson, and Brian Hodgson—the first English translations of the classical Oriental works were making their way into America. The timely appearance of the *Laws of Menu* (also called *Manu*), the *Vedas*, the *Bhagavad-Gita*, the *Sakuntala*, and the *Ramayana* in authoritative translation made it possible to approach the Orient more directly and more confidently than before.

1. Emerson. Emerson was the pioneer who scouted the trail that the others were to follow. The major studies agree upon the earliness of his first acquaintance with the Orient: both through his youthful reading in the *Edinburgh Review* and *Christian Register* and through the stimulus of his aunt, Mary Moody Emerson, who drew his attention to the brilliant Indian reformer Rammohun Roy. (The movement Roy created, the Brahmo Samaj, exercised a magnetic attraction upon American and English Unitarians throughout the century. The movement's emphasis upon rationalism, social reform, and a "unitarian" conception of God encouraged Western Unitarians to look upon the Samaj as the Indian expression of a world Unitarianism. American and English Unitarians acclaimed the later Western visits of Roy's successors—first, of Keshub Chunder Sen to England in the 1860's and subsequently of Protap Chunder Mozoomdar to the United States and England in the 1880's and again in the 1890's. The Brahmo Samaj played a significant role in encouraging American Unitarian interest in the Orient.)

Emerson's first reaction was a critical one: his recently rediscovered poem, "Indian Superstition" (1821), written as a senior at Harvard, indicates his many reservations. Indeed, he did not express a positive attitude toward Oriental thought until the later 1830's, after the publication of his first book *Nature* (1836) in which he crystallized the ideas that he would maintain for the rest of his life. His Oriental interest blossomed rapidly after 1837 as indicated by his expanding reading in Oriental literature. By 1845 references to the Orient were everywhere in his journals; henceforth, Oriental quotations would sprinkle his writings until his death. The fruits of this enthusiasm were such major poems as "Brahma" and "Hamatreya"; the "Ethical Scriptures," which he and Thoreau selected from the Oriental classics and published in *The Dial* (1842–43); and such major essays as "Over-Soul," "Illusions," and "Fate." All pointed to his assimilation of Oriental thought.

Indian thought drew Emerson's deepest appreciation. An idealist with profound admiration for Plato and the Neo-Platonists, he was naturally most drawn among the Oriental systems to Hindu philosophy, especially to the nondualistic Advaita Vedanta system. The close resemblances of his concept of the "Over-Soul" to the Hindu concept of Brahman, of his "Compensation" to karma, and of his "Illusions" to maya are striking. Of course, he had already arrived at these concepts before developing a wide and sympathetic interest in the Orient, but it is evident that he quickly assimilated the Hindu formulations into his thought. Hindu philosophy widened and deepened his thought rather than formed it. In his later writings it is practically impossible to separate the Eastern and Western components; Indian monism and Western idealism, the Hindu atman and the Western self, Oriental mysticism and Neo-Platonism transmuted into Emersonian transcendentalism.

After philosophical Hinduism, Emerson was most attracted to Persian poetry and Chinese ethical thought. Coming upon the Persian poets after his other Oriental discoveries, he enthusiastically responded to them, as seen in his essay "Persian Poetry" and his "Preface" for the first American edition of Saadi's *Gulistan* (1865). The beauty and joyfulness of Saadi and Hafiz apparently inspired his approval. He was somewhat more reserved toward Chinese thought, repelled by its materialistic tendencies (he did not know Taoism, which he might have found more attractive); but he often quoted from Confucius and the classic Chinese books. The ethical concern, activism, and common sense of the Chinese thinkers won his admiration. Unlike his Hindu and Persian reading, his reading in the Chinese failed to stimulate major essays or poetry. If a rather curious combination, Emerson's Oriental enthusiasms corresponded to the several facets of his creative life: as an idealist, he was drawn to Hindu philosophy; as artist, to Persian poetry; and as moralist, to Chinese thought.

There was, at the same time, much that Emerson rejected from the Orient. And what he accepted, he altered to suit his own preconceptions. An excellent example of rejection was his hostility to Buddhism, the one major Oriental system that never enjoyed his favor. (In part, this stemmed from nonacquaintance. Like the other early transcendentalists, he had only the haziest idea of Buddhism's teachings: on one occasion, for example, he referred to the *Bhagavad-Gita* as "the much renowned book of Buddhism" [*Letters*, III, 290]. The difficult enterprise of translating and explicating Buddhism to Western audiences was largely carried through in the latter decades of the nineteenth century.) Apparently identifying the concept of an inevitable and irresistible fate with Buddhism, he rejected its implied quietism and pessimism. Though drawn to mysticism, of both the Eastern and Western varieties, Emerson was too much the Yankee to look favorably on any form of withdrawal from the world. It was characteristic that the essay on "Fate" in his *Conduct of Life* (1860) was followed by "Power," and that in both essays he urged the role of freedom in man's life. He frequently expressed critical reservations about the excessive formalism, cruelty, and primitivism of some phases of Oriental thought.

2. Thoreau. Thoreau was for a time as excited by Oriental thought as Emerson. Soon after reading the *Laws of Menu* in 1841 he wrote: "When my imagination travels eastward and backward to those remote years of the gods, I seem to draw near to the habitation of the morning, and the dawn at length has a place." He confided: "I cannot read a sentence in the book of the Hindoos without being elevated as upon the table-land of the Ghauts. It has such a rhythm as the winds of the desert, such a tide as the Ganges, and seems as superior to criticism as the Himmaleh Mounts" (*Journal*, 83, 85). He apparently developed his first serious Oriental interest after a period of residence in the Emerson home in 1841. Though he had some prior acquaintance with the East—revealed by references to Persian writings in one of his college essays and by an 1838 reference to Confucius—his access to Emerson's Oriental library and the simultaneous stimulation of his friend's enthusiasm appear to have been the decisive factors. After 1841 his *Journal* indicates a wide reading in and strong attraction to Oriental thought. Like Emerson, he sprinkled his writings with quotes and references from Eastern sources. He collaborated with Emerson in presenting the "Ethical Scriptures" in *The Dial*, editing the selections published as the "Laws of Menu," the "Sayings of Confucius," the "Chinese Four Books," and the "Teachings of Buddha." Through the generosity of an English friend, Thomas Cholmondeley, he was, after 1855, the proud owner of one of the finest private Oriental libraries in mid-nineteenth-century America: a collection of forty-four of the Oriental classics embracing the work of a generation of Western scholarship. Appropriately, the collection passed on to Emerson after his premature death.

Thoreau's response to Oriental thought differed in important ways from Emerson's. Both, it is true, were attracted to Hindu thought; they both showed appreciation for Persian and Chinese thought. Both approached the Orient eclectically, drawing off those passages and ideas that best suited their literary and intellectual needs. Neither assented unqualifiedly to the message of the Orient. But beyond such agreement their responses diverged. Thoreau's involvement with the Orient was briefer, developing later and closing sooner than Emerson's. Greatly taken with the Eastern writings in the 1840's, his reading and extracting from them had largely ceased by the early 1850's. Emerson reacted to specific doctrines—Brahman, karma, and maya—which he analyzed and discoursed upon philosophically. Thoreau's response was more general and less intellectual. His attraction was to the mystical sweetness and the strange resonance of Oriental thought, to Oriental symbols and images more than to Oriental ideas. The concept of an all-embracing Godhead or of a self-punishing justice, which won Emerson's intellectual appreciation, were largely lost on his younger friend. Thoreau perhaps dived more deeply than Emerson into the waters of Oriental thought, but he revealed less interest in exploring its secrets and surfaced more quickly.

Characteristically, the Oriental concepts of self-discipline and detachment embodied in what Indian philosophy terms "yoga" seemed most to influence Thoreau; here as elsewhere he tended not to the abstract but to the practical dimension. In a tantalizing passage written in 1849, he remarked: "Depend upon it that, rude and careless as I am, I would fain practice the yoga faithfully. . . . To some extent, and at rare intervals, even I am a yogi" (*Writings*, VI, 175). Accepting Thoreau at his word, Arthur Christy has commented (in his *Orient in American Transcendentalism*, pp. 199ff.) that perhaps Thoreau undertook his experiment at Walden in the spirit of Indian asceticism. It may be objected that if Thoreau was drawn toward self-discipline and detachment, he was also the proponent of activism, as he demonstrated in his support of John Brown and in his famous essay on civil disobedience. Further, the question arises: Need one

appeal to the Orient for explanation, when temperamental proclivities and reading in such Western sources as the Stoics provide explanation? There is, however, strong evidence of an Indian influence. In Thoreau's readings of the Eastern classics his most enthusiastic effusions were reserved for the *Laws of Menu* and the *Bhagavad-Gita*—where yogic self-discipline and detachment are emphasized. He repeatedly expressed admiration for the emphasis of Hinduism upon meditation and nonattachment. The yoga he admired was of the philosophical variety that sought the "yoking" of the mind, what Hindus speak of as *jnana yoga*, not the lower form caricatured in the West as the practice of lying upon a bed of spiked nails or gazing steadfastly at the sun. Recent studies by William B. Stein, Winfield E. Nagley, and Sreekrishna Sarma all agree in recognizing Thoreau's acquaintance with and assimilation of yoga; passages both in *Walden* and *A Week on the Concord and Merrimack Rivers*, they argue, are explicable only by reference to the Indian discipline.

If the impact of Oriental ideas upon Emerson and Thoreau was important, it does not follow that their writings contributed significantly to the broader impact of the Orient upon nineteenth-century American culture. Such an implication is unfortunately conveyed in most of the twentieth-century writing that deals with their Oriental interest. Thoreau's literary reputation, of course, was already in eclipse even before he died; thus, the nineteenth century largely escaped the impress of his thought and writings. Emerson's fame never dimmed, but his Oriental interest was until recently neither widely appreciated nor fully understood. Much of his transaction with the Orient was a private one, confided to the secrecy of journals which were not published until after his death. And his response, like Thoreau's was so personal that it did not easily communicate itself to others. None of his writings offered either a systematic or a popular presentation of Oriental thought, and the Oriental concepts he drew upon were so fully integrated into his own modes of thinking that few contemporary readers could have suspected the degree to which he was indebted to the East. Contemporary critics ignored or else dismissed his interest as an idiosyncrasy that flawed his larger accomplishments.

IV. THE LESSER TRANSCENDENTALISTS

1. James Freeman Clarke. The credit for first successfully adapting and presenting Oriental ideas for popular American consumption belongs not to Emerson and Thoreau, but to such lesser transcendentalists as James Freeman Clarke, Samuel Johnson, Thomas Wentworth Higginson, and Moncure Conway. Though stimulated by Emerson to look East, each was to move out along paths of his own. Clarke was most influential; his *Ten Great Religions* stands out as one of the most popular presentations of Oriental thought to appear in nineteenth-century America. An outstanding leader of Boston Unitarianism for nearly fifty years, a fervid worker in the cause of temperance, women's suffrage, and the abolition of slavery, Clarke was also an early transcendentalist. Unlike Emerson, he never found it necessary to abandon the Unitarian ministry; instead he sought the reconciliation of transcendentalism and Christian Unitarianism. Though not a trained Orientalist, he was one of the earliest Americans to achieve some familiarity with the best European Oriental scholarship; his writings on the Oriental religions were consequently more solidly based and more authoritative than earlier American works.

Clarke had arrived much earlier at the views elucidated in his *Ten Great Religions* (1871), as indicated by his article "Comparative Theology of Heathen Religions," published in the Unitarian journal, the *Christian Examiner*, in 1857. An appointment in 1867 as lecturer on non-Christian religions at Harvard apparently enabled him to expand his examination. The *Ten Great Religions* appeared in 1871; in 1883 he further elaborated his ideas in a separate volume entitled *Ten Great Religions, Part II*. The 1871 work achieved immediate acclaim. The chapters on the Western religions were undoubtedly useful and informative, but the chapters on the Eastern religions must have been a revelation—opening as they did a largely unknown world of belief that in age, following, and subtlety challenged comparison with the most highly developed Occidental systems. The clear, readable manner in which Clarke presented the Oriental religions and the evidence he revealed of wide reading in the best English, French, and German Oriental scholarship made his work precisely the one that interested Americans had awaited. Clarke's acceptance of the final superiority of Christianity and his affirmation of its role as the harmonizer of the "ten great religions" guaranteed its favorable reception among all but the most intransigeant Christians. Some nineteen editions of the work were subsequently printed.

One of the major novelties of Clarke's study was its sympathetic attitude toward the Oriental religions. He lamented the fact that earlier writers had always shown the "heathen" religions in their worst aspect, reflecting less concern with a fair presentation of their doctrines than anxiety to bolster the claims of Judaism and Christianity. Such writers, he complained, had "insisted that, while the Jewish and Christian religions were revealed, all other religions were invented; that while

these were from God, those were the work of man; that, while in the true religions there was nothing false, in the false religions there was nothing true" (*Ten Great Religions*, p. 4). He insisted not only that there was more truth than error in the non-Christian religions, but that there were areas in which the Orient might even instruct the West: he cited Buddhist toleration as one example, contrasting it with the Christian Inquisition. While quick to note the limitations of the Eastern religions, he accorded them a respect that had been largely missing in earlier accounts.

Clarke's approach in the *Ten Great Religions* was rather self-consciously modeled on that of the scientist, thus reflecting the rising authority of science in nineteenth-century America. In his "Introduction" he announced that he would treat his subject from the perspective of "comparative theology," pursuing his analysis impartially and in the spirit of a "positive science." The comparative approach that was being widely adopted in the natural sciences would now provide a religious science. His division of the religions of the world into "ethnic" religions and "catholic" religions was meant to convey his use of a scientific, nonnormative approach. He classified the various world religions as a botanist might have classified plants: "ethnic" religions were the nonmissionary religions restricted to a distinct people and a delimited geography; "catholic" religions were those religions that engaged in active missionary labors and that transcended racial and geographical limits. In Clarke's judgment only Christianity qualified as a "catholic" religion; all others were "ethnic" religions. Each of the great Oriental systems was judged to be one-sided: thus Hinduism (he referred to it as "Brahmanism") was "complete on the side of spirit, defective on the side of matter; full as regards the infinite, empty of the finite; recognizing eternity but not time, God but not nature." Buddhism, on the other hand, had "exactly the opposite truths and the opposite defects. . . . It recognizes man, not God; the soul, not the all; the finite, not the infinite; morality, not piety" (*Ten Great Religions*, pp. 21–22). Hinduism was idealistic and pantheistic; Buddhism rationalistic and humanistic. Though not without the usual reservations, Clarke seemed especially appreciative of Buddhism. He compared its revolt against the excessive ritualism, hierarchy, and ecclesiasticism of early Hinduism to that of Protestantism's rebellion against Roman Catholicism; he entitled his chapter, "Buddhism, or the Protestantism of the East." Buddha, it appeared, had been an Oriental Martin Luther. The rationalism and humanism that he discovered in Buddhism were undoubtedly attractions. Clarke's striking but oversimplified formulations quickly won acceptance as the conventional terms for the popular discussion of Oriental religions.

Whatever its improvement over earlier studies, the *Ten Great Religions* was no work of science. Like Emerson and Thoreau, Clarke approached the Orient selectively and normatively. His conclusion that Christianity was the only "catholic" religion was most revealing in this regard. No less than the Christian writers whose special pleading he criticized, he was ultimately an apologist for Christianity, who indeed insisted on the merits of Oriental thought only so that they could be contrasted with the still greater merits of Unitarian Christianity. In his view Christianity had all the positive elements of the Oriental religions and none of their limitations; it offered a "pleroma" or fulfillment of all the other religions. Clarke differed from earlier Christian writers only in advocating Christianity as an "inclusive" rather than an "exclusive" system. Thus, a place was made for the Oriental religions.

2. Samuel Johnson. In 1872, just a year after the publication of Clarke's work, the first volume of Samuel Johnson's *Oriental Religions and their Relation to Universal Religion* appeared. The first of three rather massive volumes on the Oriental religions, Johnson's effort offers an interesting contrast to that of Clarke. Like Clarke, Johnson's roots were in Unitarianism; he also identified himself as a transcendentalist. Unlike Clarke, he gave up the Unitarian ministry after one year, preaching henceforth in a nondenominational church. Departing from Christianity he championed what he called "Universal Religion," which embraced all religions. His approach to the Oriental religions was both more sympathetic and more transcendental than Clarke's. He apparently became a serious student of Oriental thought as early as the 1850's, for he delivered a series of lectures on the Oriental religions in the winter of 1852–53. He commented, in the Introduction of his 1872 volume on India, that the work was the outgrowth of studies pursued for "more than twenty years." Retiring from the ministry after 1870 he dedicated the remaining twelve years of his life to the *Oriental Religions*. The first volume (on India) appeared in 1872 and the second (on China) in 1877. The last volume (on Persia) was nearly finished when he died in 1882; it was subsequently edited by his friend Octavius Frothingham and published in 1884. Though he engaged in a variety of enterprises, writing regularly for the Free Religious Association journals, the *Oriental Religions* was the major work of his creative life.

Johnson's treatment of Oriental thought was inseparable from his transcendental religious philosophy. In this respect he, much more than Clarke, carried on the legacy of Emerson and Thoreau. As a transcendentalist he refused the usual distinctions between the sacred and the profane, between the spiritual and material, or between the divine and the human. God was immanent in nature and man: all creation revealed the presence of an "infinite Mind." Religion was not a matter of creed or organization but the spirit that flowed through such externalities. If a transcendentalist, Johnson was also an evolutionist. He envisioned the history of religion as a process of growth from primitive myth toward "Universal Religion." He rejected the materialistic interpretation of evolution for an evolution of spirit through matter. The culmination of the evolution of spirit would be "Universal Religion"—embodying the essential elements in all past religious development. By combining transcendentalism with evolutionism, Johnson could claim to incorporate both the permanence and the transcience of religion, both its universality and particularity.

Johnson's *Oriental Religions and their Relation to Universal Religion* embodied an enormously detailed demonstration of his transcendental evolutionism. Each of the great religions manifested the evolution of the divine. What distinguished Hinduism or Confucianism from Christianity was not the falsehood of the one or the truth of the other, but the differences in race and environment within which the "infinite Mind" had channeled. Thus the peculiarities of Aryan intellectualism and the enervating climate of the Indian continent had given the Indian religious mind its distinctive mystical dreaminess and antimaterial qualities. Similarly, the utilitarianism of China's thinkers and the geographical isolation of her vast population, locked in by water and mountain barriers, had given the Chinese mind its distinctive Confucian stamp. Each of the great world religions embodied universal elements; but none was free of nonessential and corrupted elements. Johnson envisioned a growing progress in the gradual elimination of the nonessential until the great religions had coalesced into the "Universal Religion." Defining the relationship of the Oriental religions to this ultimate religion, he declared: "Universal Religion, then, cannot be any one, *exclusively*, of the great positive religions of the world. Yet it is really what is best in each and every one of them; purified from baser intermixture and developed in freedom and power. Being the purport of nature, it has been germinating in every vital energy of man; so that its elements exist, *at some stage of evolution*, in every great religion of mankind" (*Oriental Religions: India*, p. 6).

The virtues of Johnson's approach to Oriental thought were its broad universality and freedom from

433

sectarianism. Having rejected Christianity as his angle of vision, he was prepared to see the Eastern religions empathetically, from the inside. Even the most condemned features of Oriental social and religious life were treated as understandable and logical outgrowths of the peculiarities of their environments. Point by point he sought to explain how such practices as widow-burning, ancestor-worship, or the caste system had arisen. Polytheism, which nineteenth-century Americans seemed to hold in peculiar horror, he explained as the natural expression of the spiritual element in primitive form. However unsatisfactorily— and often his explanations were patently fanciful—he sought to relate religious ideas to the social customs and political and economic systems within which they flourished.

The major weakness of Johnson's work was its a priorism: all data were pressed into support of his transcendental evolutionism. His formulations, like Clarke's, were frequently gross oversimplifications. Thus, he characterized the Hindu mind as cerebral and introspective, the Chinese mind as muscular and plodding, and the Persian mind as nervous and mediating. The problems created by such a classification can be seen in the difficulty with which he explained how Buddhism, a product of Indian cerebrality, could have rooted itself in a muscular China. Taoism, he had to claim, was not so mystical as had been believed, but merely another expression of Chinese practicality and concreteness. The immensity of the three volumes, a certain heaviness in style, and an indulgence in frequent anti-Christian barbs prevented Johnson's work from ever enjoying the wide popularity gained by Clarke's book. Nevertheless, his discussion was frequently referred to in writings of the period.

3. Free Religious Association. Clarke and Johnson were not the only lesser transcendentalists to focus on Oriental thought; indeed, practically all the later transcendentalists favored the East with some attention. Many of these were in the disaffected group who broke away from the main body of Unitarianism in 1867 to form the Free Religious Association. A diverse and very independent movement, the Association nevertheless strongly reflected transcendental influence, not least by its attitude toward the Orient. Opposing the residual Christianity espoused by Unitarianism's more conservative members, the Association's members joined Johnson in championing a universal religion. The Oriental religions were granted an importance equal to, if not above, that of Christianity. A perusal of the two major journals of the schismatic group, the *Radical* and *Index*, reveals a steady concern with Oriental thought. Thomas Wentworth Higginson, Moncure Conway, Samuel Longfellow, Charles De

Berard Mills, Lewis George Janes, Francis Ellingwood Abbot, William James Potter, Octavius Brooks Frothingham, and Benjamin Franklin Underwood were among those who contributed articles on the Orient. Seeking to dramatize the universality of religion, the Association sponsored several meetings in which spokesmen were invited to present the various world religions. At their annual meeting in 1870, the Association held a miniature congress of religions at which Samuel Johnson spoke up for "The Natural Sympathy of Religions," Thomas Wentworth Higginson for Islam, William Henry Channing for the religions of China, and William James Potter for the religions of India. Free Religion could claim with some justification to have pioneered the concept of a congress of religions that was later publicized in the Parliament of Religions in 1893.

By the 1870's the transcendentalist stimulus to Oriental discovery had largely ceased. Its leaders had completed their work, died, or else turned their energies to other things. Meanwhile, new currents had arisen which were to dominate the last three decades of the century. The emergence of an American school of Oriental scholarship, the growth of a movement for the comparative and historical study of religion, and the efflorescence of popular and intellectual interest in Buddhism were the most important of these.

V. BEGINNINGS OF AMERICAN ORIENTAL SCHOLARSHIP

The beginnings of serious Oriental scholarship in America may be dated from the founding of the American Oriental Society in 1842 and the publication of the *Journal of the American Oriental Society* in 1843. At first dominated by missionaries and biblical scholars, the Society concentrated in its early years upon Middle Eastern and Old Testament research. By the 1870's, however, it had increasingly shifted its investigations to include the Far East. William Dwight Whitney, who had been made Professor of Sanskrit at Yale in 1854, emerged as America's first great Orientalist. Though the long dependence upon European Orientalists did not end—as seen by the influence during the later nineteenth century of scholars such as F. Max Müller, T. W. Rhys Davids, Cornelius Tiele, Paul Deussen, and Hermann Oldenberg—Americans began to make important contributions to scholarship for the first time. Whitney's *Sanskrit Grammar* (1879), Charles Rockwell Lanman's *Beginnings of Hindu Pantheism* (1890), Henry Clarke Warren's *Buddhism in Translations* (1896), and Edward Washburn Hopkins' *Religions of India* (1895) were among the significant volumes now to appear. In 1891 Lanman and Warren commenced the *Harvard Oriental Series,* which grew over the next forty years to provide popular but authoritative editions of the texts of many formerly obscure Oriental classics. Lanman's stated objective in presenting the *Series* suggests how much the religious question continued to dominate even the most scholarly American writings on the Orient. "It aims," he declared in the preface to the *Series*, "to make available for us people of the West the incomparable lessons which (if we be wise enough to maintain the teachable habit of mind) the Wise Men of the East can teach us—lessons that concern the simple life, moderation of our desires, repose of the spirit, and above all, the search after God and the realization of the divine immanence." Most of the books and articles produced by the early American Orientalists were too technical, too concerned with questions of linguistics and details of scholarship to win a wide audience; nevertheless, the appearance of a school of Oriental scholarship was an important step in the ripening of Oriental thought in America.

VI. MOVEMENT FOR THE COMPARATIVE-HISTORICAL STUDY OF RELIGION

The rise in the 1880's and 1890's of a movement for the comparative and historical study of religions helped transfer consideration of Oriental thought out of the scholar's study and into the university and seminary. Joining the findings of biblical scholarship, Higher Criticism, Darwinistic evolutionism, and Oriental scholarship to the insights of archaeology, anthropology, psychology, and linguistics, the proponents of the new movement sought a "science of religion." Those drawn to historical study concentrated upon the genesis and evolution of religion; the comparative religionists, on the other hand, were more concerned with the similarities and differences in the concepts and forms of the living world religions. In practice, there was a close working alliance between the two groups; both reflected the trend away from the theological and toward the scientific study of religion. Citing Goethe's remark that "He who knows one language knows none," the spokesmen of the movement liked to point out that it was equally true that one who knew only one religion actually knew none. The leaders chiefly centered within departments of religion at the universities and among theologians interested in a modern, more comprehensive foundation for foreign missions. James Freeman Clarke and Samuel Johnson had already pioneered the approach.

The new movement's rapid spread in America in the last decades of the nineteenth century may be traced through the establishment of chairs, lectureships, and journals, partly or wholly, devoted to comparative and historical religious study. As early as 1867 James Freeman Clarke had held a brief appointment as lecturer on the non-Christian religions at Harvard, but the first chair of "Comparative Theology and the History and Philosophy of Religion" was created in 1873 at Boston University with William Fairfield Warren as occupant. By 1900 many colleges and universities had established similar positions, led by the Princeton Theological Seminary, New York University, Cornell University, and the University of Chicago. Louis Henry Jordan, an early student of the movement, commented upon this phenomenon in 1905; ". . . There is no country whose Universities and Theological Schools have done more of late, in providing students with the means of securing a competent acquaintance with Comparative Religion, than have some of the foremost Colleges in the United States" (*Comparative Religion*, p. 383). Paralleling the establishment of chairs in the universities and seminaries, international lectureships were also created. England led the way with the Hibbert Lectures, inaugurated in 1878, and the Gifford Lectures, commenced in 1888; but America followed closely behind with the inauguration of the American Lectures on the History of Religions in 1891 and the Haskell Lectures in Comparative Religion in 1894. Journals such as the *Biblical World, American Journal of Theology, New World*, and *Journal of Speculative Philosophy* devoted much of their space in the 1880's and 1890's to articles and reports in the field. The *Atlantic Monthly, North American Review, Harper's Weekly*, and *Arena* provided more popular outlets. The writings of Charles Carroll Everett, Crawford Howell Toy, Frank Field Ellinwood, Samuel Henry Kellogg, John Henry Barrows, Charles Cuthbert Hall, Edmund Buckley, and William Torrey Harris were deeply permeated with the new approach. Much of the impetus underlying the comparative-historical movement undoubtedly derived from the search for a new Christian apologetics, newly dressed in the garb of scientific methodology; nevertheless, the Oriental religions were beneficiaries. They received both intensive and sympathetic attention. Since the spokesmen for the movement commanded the best periodicals and lecterns in the land, Oriental ideas were disseminated to a wider and more influential audience than ever before.

1. Paul Carus. The activities of Paul Carus indicate how concern for a more comparative, more scientific conception of religion promoted the impact of Oriental thought. Though hardly a typical figure, his approach was very similar to that of the American school of comparative-historical studies. Carus was born and educated in Germany; he immigrated to the United States soon after completing studies in philosophy, philology, and natural science that culminated in the Ph.D. in 1876. It is probable that he gained his first exposure to Oriental ideas in Germany, for Oriental studies were then enjoying a considerable vogue in its universities. Hermann Grassman, the German mathematician whose ideas most influenced Carus' philosophical views, was highly regarded as an Indologist and as a translator of the *Rig-Veda*. In America Carus briefly edited a German-language journal; wrote several articles for the *Index*, the Free Religious Association organ; and finally in 1887 undertook the editorship of the *Open Court*, which would continue under his active direction until his death in 1919. In 1890 he added the *Monist* to his editorial duties.

The *Open Court* and *Monist* centered on philosophy, science, and religion; their contributors included some of America's and Europe's best-known thinkers and scholars. Beginning in late 1893 Carus increasingly featured Oriental thought, with occasional articles from such eminent authorities as Max Müller, Hermann Oldenberg, and Richard Garbe. In 1897 Daisetz Teitaro Suzuki, subsequently a noted proponent of Zen Buddhism and a major figure in the twentieth-century Western impact of Oriental ideas, came to America to serve as his editorial assistant; he worked closely with Carus until his return to Japan in 1908. The two men collaborated on several Chinese translations, and Suzuki published a number of articles and book reviews in the *Open Court* and *Monist*. In the decade after 1893 practically every issue of the *Open Court* included some piece dealing with the Orient: an article on Indian philosophy; a book review of a new volume on Oriental mythology; or again an essay comparing the origins and doctrines of Buddhism and Christianity. No important American journal at the end of the century devoted so much attention to the Orient.

Carus' interest in the Orient was more than an academic one. Many of the journal articles on the East came from his pen. He was especially drawn to Buddhism, contributing a series of articles in the *Open Court* to an analysis of its doctrines and similarities to Western scientific thought. He also wrote or edited a number of books bearing on the subject, including: *The Gospel of Buddha* (1894), a compilation from various translations of the life of Buddha; *Buddhism and its Christian Critics* (1897), an examination of Buddhism's major teachings; *Chinese Thought* (1907), an outline of the major features of intellectual life in China; and several Oriental tales built around key Buddhist doctrines. While criticized by scholars, several of the books, especially *The Gospel of Buddha*, won favor with the public, going through several editions. Beyond his writing, Carus also worked actively for direct contacts between East and West. Greatly impressed by the meeting of Eastern and Western religious leaders at the Parliament of Religions in 1893,

he led in several organized ventures during the late 1890's which sought to increase exchanges between the spokesmen of Oriental religions and American religious leaders. He cultivated friendships with many of the Oriental religious leaders and lecturers who came to America in increasing numbers.

Carus approached Oriental thought from a position he identified philosophically as "Monism." He was strongly convinced that Western thought had fallen into error early in its development when it had accepted distinctions between body and mind and the material and the spiritual. Kant had formalized this dualism in Western philosophy when he had divided the field of knowledge between the phenomenal and the noumenal realms; and Christianity had rooted it in the Western religious viewpoint when it had differentiated between the soul and the body, and the natural and the supernatural. Rejecting such dualisms, Carus looked to science to reestablish the unity of knowledge. The philosophical result he labeled "Monism." He showed special concern at the growing split between science and religion, advocating a scientific religion as the need of the age. Such a religion must combine the highest ethical teachings with the most rigorous empirical procedures; it must, he declared, be both a "Science of Religion" and a "Religion of Science." Drawing upon the increasing evidence of historical and comparative religious studies, he came to believe that Buddhism offered the best hope of reconciliation.

Carus developed the case for Buddhism in a series of articles which he published in the *Open Court* in early 1896. These contained the crux of the argument that he developed in his various books on Buddhism. As a scientific religion, Buddhism merited approval on several grounds. First, it was empirical, approaching the religious question factually and morally rather than abstractly. Both Hinduism and Christianity failed at just this point because they placed theory before facts: "In Buddhism," he asserted, "theory is nothing, and facts are everything" (*Open Court*, X, 4853). He emphasized that unlike the other great religions Buddhism required no belief in miracles or authority. Second, Buddhism was monistic, as was to be seen in its treatment of the body-soul question. While Hinduism and Christianity abstracted the soul from the body, Buddhism, through its doctrine of *anatman*, avoided such separation. Carus rejected the widespread interpretation that Buddha had denied the existence of the soul in his *anatman* doctrine; rather Buddha had denied the separateness of soul or consciousness from its physical vessel. Soul, *atman*, self, or consciousness— which were merely different names for the same thing —were one with the body. He maintained, therefore, that Buddhism was a "consistent Monism." Finally,

Buddhism was universal. It provided a positive faith capable of bringing religious consolation to one and all, as a scientific religion must. It could provide both intellectual satisfaction for the philosophers and comfort for the lowly and afflicted; it offered "the skeleton key which in its abstract simplicity fits all locks" (*Buddhism and Its Christian Critics*, p. 83).

Obviously, insofar as Carus accepted Buddhism—and he advocated it only up to a point—it was a Buddhism made over to his own needs. Critics were quick to point out Carus' error of confusing the age-old Buddhist doctrines with the fundamentals of scientific thought. However, his Buddhism was a "scientific Buddhism" that owed as much to Western thought as to Eastern; he sought not the total assimilation of Oriental thought, but the combination of the best in the Western and Eastern traditions.

VII. VOGUE OF BUDDHISM IN THE LATE NINETEENTH CENTURY

Carus was not the only American of his time to discover the charms of Buddhism. In the last two decades of the century the religion of Buddha enjoyed a brief but rather widespread vogue, stimulated by the American publication in 1879 of the *Light of Asia* by Sir Edwin Arnold. A poetic presentation of Buddha's life, the work placed Buddhism in a most attractive light that did not fail to appeal to Western readers. One of the most popular books ever written on Buddhism, it went through some sixty English and some eighty American editions and sold between one-half and one million copies in Great Britain and the United States. The book was sponsored in America by Franklin B. Sanborn, George Ripley, and Oliver Wendell Holmes, who gave it enthusiastic reviews. Eventually, Arnold exploited the sensation the book created by coming to the United States in 1891 to lecture on Buddhism and to read from the *Light of Asia* before enthusiastic audiences. He made fifty appearances in various American cities and had agreed to one hundred more when the failure of his health forced a halt. Sparked by Arnold's book and lectures, as well as by the rising interest in the comparative and historical study of religion, a spate of articles on Buddhism appeared in contemporary American periodicals.

Paralleling the popular interest, a number of America's writers and intellectuals responded to the appeal of Buddhism. The most noteworthy, besides Carus, were Lafcadio Hearn, Ernest Fenollosa, Sturgis Bigelow, Percival Lowell, and Henry Adams. A diverse group, their responses varied so much that generalization is difficult. Each in his own way was attracted to the religion of Buddha, though the element of interest and degree of impact differed in every case. Perhaps

Lafcadio Hearn will serve to suggest just how deep in some instances Buddhist influence reached. Indeed, his passionate response may be considered the outer limit of the American nineteenth-century cultural interaction with the Orient.

1. Lafcadio Hearn. Hearn was an immigrant, coming to the United States from Great Britain in 1869. During the two decades he resided in America, he engaged in newspaper work in Cincinnati, New Orleans, and the West Indies and wrote several books that established him as one of the country's more promising young writers. His interest in Oriental thought was apparently first stimulated by his reading of Arnold's *Light of Asia* in 1879; he subsequently became interested in Japan through observation of the Japanese exhibit at the New Orleans World Industrial Exposition in 1884. He wrote occasional newspaper articles on Oriental themes during the 1880's; then, in 1890, rather suddenly, he departed for Japan where he was to spend the remainder of his life. In the following years he went far in his effort to blend into his new environment: he traveled extensively throughout the islands, married a Japanese woman, changed his name for a Japanese one, and eventually was buried in his new homeland. No Westerner had gone further toward a full acceptance of Oriental life and belief.

Hearn's discovery of the Orient may be traced in the volumes that now flowed from his pen: *Glimpses of Unfamiliar Japan* (1894); *Out of the East: Reveries and Studies in New Japan* (1895); *Kokoro: Hints and Echoes of Japanese Inner Life* (1896); *Gleanings in Buddha-Fields: Studies of Hand and Soul in the Far East* (1897); *Exotics and Retrospectives* (1898); *In Ghostly Japan* (1899); *Shadowings* (1900); *A Japanese Miscellany* (1901); *Kotto* (1902); and, finally, *Japan: An Attempt at Interpretation* (1904). The titles of the books suggest his intense effort to get behind the externals of Japanese life to its inner soul; their contents reflect an often romantic, idyllic view of their subject. Largely collections of separate essays and stories written for publication in American periodicals, the books were loosely structured and impressionistic. They dealt with nearly every aspect of Japanese culture from folk religion and the life of silkworm cultivation to industrialization and military training. Hearn tended to prefer Japanese ideals to Western norms throughout, though the later works were more qualified because of his rising disillusionment with the modernization of Japan. In time he became the champion of Old Japan against the new. Though he never mastered the Japanese language, the profound sympathy and intimacy he revealed in his treatment of his subject won an authority for his writings that has endured into the twentieth century. The novelty of his report of Japanese life, conveyed in a finely wrought literary style, contributed to his books' wide contemporary appeal in America.

Appreciation for Buddhism pervaded Hearn's writings. In time he came to believe that its force underlay practically every facet of Japanese life and culture. As his own commitment to its doctrines grew, he became convinced that it offered a religious system compatible with the modern scientific view that had much to teach the West. (There were striking parallels with Paul Carus, but some important differences chiefly due to Carus' scientific philosophy in contrast to Hearn's more mystical intuitionism.) The growth of his admiration may be traced in such successive essays as "The Stone Buddha" in *Out of the East,* "The Idea of Pre-existence" in *Kokoro,* and "Nirvana" in *Gleanings in Buddha-Fields*—culminating in "The Higher Buddhism," his final, most revealing, testament in his last book, *Japan: An Attempt at Interpretation* (1904). Though always sympathetic to the peculiarities of Japanese Buddhism, he came to prefer a nonsectarian, philosophical Buddhism, the "Higher Buddhism" of his last essay. In his view philosophical Buddhism was distinguished by its combination of monism and evolutionism. Hearn wrote: "The higher Buddhism is a kind of Monism," noting that "it includes doctrines that accord, in the most surprising manner, with the scientific theories of the German and the English monists" (*Japan,* p. 232). Buddhism was monistic because it held that the only reality was the Absolute; mind and matter, the "I" and the "Not-I" were ultimately unreal. But, he continued, Buddhism "is also a theory of evolution. . . ." Karma was the key to Buddhist evolution. The universe as well as consciousness, Hearn explained, were "aggregates of Karma" undergoing constant evolution through an enormous past. There were, of course, critical differences between Western and Buddhist evolution: where the former was mechanical and materialistic, explaining development as the result of heredity, Buddhism offered a moral and spiritual evolution that explained development as the result of willed action and introspective meditation.

But how could Buddhism be both a monism and an evolutionism? The monistic Absolute suggests stasis, rest, perfection; evolution, on the other hand, movement and incompletion. If the Absolute were truly the only reality, what remained to evolve? How could reality be both an undifferentiated unity and at the same time an unfolding differentiated plurality? Hearn's explanation hinged on the distinction between unconditioned reality and conditioned phenomena, what in his "Higher Buddhism" essay he termed "permanence" and "actuality." "Buddhism," he explained, "does not deny the actuality of phenomena

as phenomena, but denies their permanence and the truth of the appearances which they present to our imperfect senses" (*Japan,* p. 235). Buddhism clearly insisted that the sole reality was the Absolute, but refused to dismiss the phenomenal world as illusion. From the perspective of final, unconditioned reality the "Higher Buddhism" was a monism; but from the phenomenal perspective of conditioned actuality it was an evolutionism. The tension between reality and actuality, between monism and evolutionism, was finally resolved in nirvana, at the point where the evolving ego penetrated beyond phenomenal consciousness into the Absolute.

No Western seeker has fully succeeded in abandoning his Western cultural heritage, not even Lafcadio Hearn. One of the most interesting aspects of Hearn's distant, transoceanic pilgrimage to Buddhism was that he remained a Spencerian evolutionist throughout. He had been an ardent Spencerian in America and he continued to champion the English thinker's views in his books from Japan. In his last word on Buddhism he wrote: "I venture to call myself a student of Herbert Spencer; and it was because of my acquaintance with the Synthetic Philosophy that I came to find in Buddhist philosophy a more than romantic interest" (*Japan,* p. 232). For Hearn there was no incongruity in simultaneously following the doctrines of Buddha and Spencer, however dissimilar the ideas might appear. Both were monistic and evolutionary; one reinforced the other. Much of the argument in the "Higher Buddhism" essay focused on demonstrating the parallels between them. On the other hand, there were some key differences. In Hearn's judgment the most basic was that while Spencer steadily denied that human consciousness would ever succeed in penetrating what the English philosopher termed the "Unknown Reality," Buddhism claimed that through nirvana that reality could be known. Spencer's system remained an "agnosticism," while Buddhism advanced to "gnosticism." If the doctrine of nirvana made it possible to move beyond Spencer, Hearn insisted that the two systems still remained remarkably alike. To him Buddhism was merely a spiritualization of Spencer's Synthetic Philosophy.

VIII. CONCLUSIONS

The following generalizations seem warranted. Most important, Americans first discovered Oriental thought during the course of the nineteenth century. Where Oriental ideas were practically unknown at the century's opening, by its close the world of Eastern thought had been thrown open. The existence of English translations of most of the Oriental classics and of popular explications of the Oriental doctrines brought a general acquaintance with Oriental thought within the reach of the educated reader. Second, the emphasis during the nineteenth century was on the religious thought of the Orient. This was understandable in view of the strong religious preoccupation of Americans during the century. As awareness of Oriental religious thought dawned, Americans were astonished at the size, complexity, and richness of religious life and thought in the Orient. Hinduism and Buddhism were granted the greatest attention, with the interest in Buddhism largely confined to the later decades of the century.

Third, the transcendentalist movement, especially its later followers, played the most decisive role in the introduction of Oriental ideas into American culture. Emerson led the way, but the later, lesser transcendentalists such as James Freeman Clarke and Samuel Johnson were most instrumental in the first popular explanation and discussion of Oriental thought in America. Fourth, while the growth in general American awareness of Oriental thought was appreciable during the century, the visible impact of Oriental ideas was largely limited to individual writers and intellectuals. The thought was too alien for quick public assimilation. Nevertheless, the individuals influenced by it were significant figures in American culture.

Fifth, the impact varied with the individual and served to reinforce rather than replace already-held Western conceptions. Emerson, the idealist, was most influenced by philosophical Hinduism; Thoreau, the practical exponent of transcendentalism, by yoga; Paul Carus, the scientific monist, by "philosophically scientific" Buddhism; and Lafcadio Hearn, the Spencerian evolutionist, by "higher," philosophically mystical Buddhism. Oriental thought was accommodated to both the religious and the positivistic mood. Finally, the nineteenth-century cultural impact of Oriental thought was carried out almost entirely through books and the written word. Knowledge gained was largely second-hand. In the twentieth century communication would become more direct through the increased facilities of travel and commerce; the much expanded contacts between America and the Orient have yielded a growing appreciation and understanding of the cultural and intellectual contributions that East and West may make to one another.

BIBLIOGRAPHY

Van Wyck Brooks, *Fenollosa and his Circle* (New York, 1962), 1–68. Frederic I. Carpenter, *Emerson and Asia* (Cambridge, Mass., 1930). Paul Carus, *Buddhism and Its Christian Critics* (Chicago, 1897). K. R. Chandrasekharan, "Emerson's Brahma: An Indian Interpretation," *New England Quarterly*, 33 (Dec. 1960), 506–12. Edward Tyrrel Channing, "Lalla Rookh," *North American Review*, 6 (Nov. 1817), 1–25. Lawrence W. Chisolm, *Fenollosa: The Far East and American Culture* (New Haven, 1963). Arthur Christy, ed., *The Asian Legacy and American Life* (New York, 1942); idem, *The Orient in American Transcendentalism* (New York, 1932). James F. Clarke, *Ten Great Religions* (Boston, 1871); idem, *Ten Great Religions, Part II* (Boston, 1883). Ralph Waldo Emerson, *Complete Works*, ed. E. W. Emerson, 12 vols. (Boston, 1903–04); idem, *Indian Superstition*, ed. K. W. Cameron (Hanover, N.H., 1954); idem, *Journals*, ed. E. W. Emerson and W. E. Forbes, 10 vols. (Boston, 1909–14); idem, *Letters*, ed. R. W. Rusk, 6 vols. (New York, 1939). Alexander Hill Everett, "Remusat's Chinese Grammar," *North American Review*, 17 (July 1823), 1–13; idem, "Chinese Manners," *North American Review*, 27 (Oct. 1828), 524–62. Edward Everett, "Hindu Drama," *North American Review*, 26 (Jan. 1828), 111–26. John Chipman Gray, "Cochin China," *North American Review*, 18 (Jan. 1824), 140–57. Lafcadio Hearn, *Japan: An Attempt at Interpretation* (New York, 1904). Carl T. Jackson, "The Meeting of East and West: The Case of Paul Carus," *Journal of the History of Ideas*, 29 (Jan.–March 1968), 73–92. Samuel Johnson, *Oriental Religions and their Relation to Universal Religion*, Vol. I: *India* (Boston, 1872); Vol. II: *China* (Boston, 1877); Vol. III: *Persia* (Boston, 1884). Louis H. Jordan, *Comparative Religion* (Edinburgh, 1905). Kurt Leidecker, "Oriental Philosophy in America," *American Philosophy*, ed. Ralph Winn (New York, 1955), pp. 211–20. Earl Miner, *The Japanese Tradition in British and American Literature* (Princeton, 1958). Winfield E. Nagley, "Thoreau on Attachment, Detachment, and Non-Attachment," *Philosophy East and West*, 3 (Jan. 1954), 307–20. Theophilus Parsons, "Manners and Customs of India," *North American Review*, 9 (June 1819), 36–58. Dale Riepe, "Emerson and Indian Philosophy," *Journal of the History of Ideas*, 28 (Jan.–March 1967), 115–22. Sreekrishna Sarma, "A Short Study of the Oriental Influence upon Henry David Thoreau with Special Reference to his *Walden*," *Jahrbuch für Amerikastudien*, 1 (1956), 76–92. William B. Stein, "Thoreau's First Book: A Spoon of Yoga," *Emerson Society Quarterly*, No. 41, Quarter IV (1965), 4–25. Elizabeth Stevenson, *Lafcadio Hearn* (New York, 1961). Henry David Thoreau, *Journal*, ed. Bradford Torrey and F. H. Allen, 14 vols. bound as 2 vols. (New York, 1962); idem, *Writings*, ed. Bradford Torrey and F. B. Sanborn, 20 vols. (Boston, 1906). William Tudor, "Theology of the Hindoos," *North American Review*, 6 (March 1818), 386–93. Brooks Wright, *Interpreter of Buddhism to the West: Sir Edwin Arnold* (New York, 1957). Beongcheon Yu, *An Ape of Gods: The Art and Thought of Lafcadio Hearn* (Detroit, 1964).

CARL T. JACKSON

[See also **Buddhism; China;** Christianity; **Civil Disobedience;** Class; Dualism; Evolutionism; Gnosticism; God; Language; Neo-Platonism; **Peace;** Positivism; Unity of Science.]

ETHICS OF PEACE

AGGRESSIVENESS and hostility have always marked men's behavior, wanting only the labeling; and history could be read as the progressively successful pursuit of the technology and waging of war. In contrast, a long, painful struggle was necessary before the notion of peace could be formulated. This point is readily enough illustrated in the emerging Greek tradition. The concept of peace finds little place among the Homeric Greeks. Hector, for example, bidding his wife farewell, regrets the foolishness and injustice of the Trojan war (from which the listener knows he will never return). Then, gathering his son in his arms, he wishes for him not the vocations of peace but the life of a warrior— gladdening the heart of his mother by bringing home as spoils the bloodied armor of his foes.

A more sophisticated appreciation of peace arises in the classical period of Greek thought. Both the tragedian Euripides and the comedian Aristophanes voice general antiwar sentiment, though it is set in the context of the then-current war between Athens and Sparta. Aristophanes in the *Acharnians* has an Athenian farmer make a private peace and sit gorging himself on imported food while his fellow citizens look on longingly, and in the *Lysistrata* the women are incited to withhold their favors until men make peace. Euripides in his *Trojan Women* offers an early version of the humanitarian's disgust with the cruelties of war.

Plato, though writing to an ideal state, recognizes the desirability of peace. He first describes a society on a marginal level of existence without government or strife. When this is rejected for lack of human amenities from furniture to spice, Plato recasts the republic in Spartan-like terms, so as to control the internal aggression of human appetite in a world of scarcity. Its simplicity makes it unappealing to an external aggressor, and if attacked it can always secure allies by letting them have the spoils. But Plato is too pessimistic to conceive of a world of such republics as his, and even expects human appetite to ensure the corruption of the best state, for the appetites (symbolized by the dragon) are bound to engender a class struggle when the rulers inevitably make mistakes.

Aristotle too seems to regard war as inevitable, but wants basic ethical and educational focus to be on the pursuits and virtues of peace rather than on those of war, and on the arts of leisure rather than those of business. Appreciating the inevitability of social tensions (especially between rich and poor), and accepting the institution of slavery, Aristotle conceives men as essentially social and plastic, in the sense that reason can effectively guide them towards a stable polity. Military training ought to be directed towards defense

alone; its purpose is to prevent enslavement of the citizens by conquerors. The end of a just war is always peace.

The revolutionary program that was implicit in Zeno's doctrine of equality and fraternity dampened as Stoicism matured. Even in the more law-oriented Roman Stoics such as Marcus Aurelius a metaphysical ideal of natural order and harmony led less to the correction of those ills of society which resulted from the imperfect realization of the *logos*, the rational order of nature, than to the development of a personal moral stance with which to confront evil. Even so, the view of a single world community overriding distinctions between Greek and barbarian, slave and master, man and woman remained a powerful ingredient in the history of ideas of peace. It was to some extent, at least insofar as civil peace was guaranteed through a centralized authority, exhibited in the *Pax Romana*, and it was given a Christian statement in Saint Paul.

The Old Testament provides passages which easily match the warlike stance of Homer and in which Jehovah is virtually a Lord of War, jealous of his sovereignty and promising vengeance against the foes of Israel. Yet there emerges, especially in the Prophets, another aspect of God as the Father of all men, a Lord of Peace, enjoining the pursuit of a peace for which the price was sometimes thought to be the sufferings of the Jews themselves. Most stirring and influential of the prophetic utterances comes from Isaiah and is repeated in Micah; it promises brotherhood of man, benevolence of God, and an intimate fellowship with Him.

And he shall judge among the nations, and shall rebuke many people: and they shall beat their swords into plowshares, and their spears into pruninghooks: nation shall not lift up sword against nation, neither shall they learn war any more (Isaiah 2:4).

Pacific themes pervade the Judaic tradition; we need only remember that the daily prayers of the Jews for more than three thousand years have concluded with a petition of peace, while "Jerusalem" came, by folk etymology, to mean "Vision of Peace." This rabbinic tradition was powerfully presented by Hillel who placed love of man on a par with reverence toward God. Hillel intended to include the whole community of man, nonbelievers, the humble, and the poor as well as the believers, the mighty, and the rich. "What is unpleasant to thyself, that do not to thy neighbor; this is the whole of the Law, all else is but exposition."

These attitudes are continued in the early Christian rejection of the *Lex Talionis*, and the replacement of negative commandments such as "Thou shalt not kill" by the positive responsibilities of love. The classic

Christian formulation is of course the Sermon on the Mount with its gentle advocacy of nonviolence, of the love of one's neighbor, of the infinite value of the soul and of humanitarian charity and benevolence. The perplexing issue is why such straightforward and unambiguous teaching came to be ignored, or at least taken as a counsel of perfection impossible of realization in this world. In any case, as the hope of an immediate "Coming" receded, Christians began to accommodate to the social realities of civil government, military service, taxation, etc; and then to develop their own political power. Yet the literal directives of the Sermon were time-resistant and Christian pacifism has not lacked for bold and uncompromising advocates in such early Church Fathers as Clement, Justin, and above all Origen, in sects such as the Quakers, Schwenkfelders, and Doukhobors, and in such modern proponents as Leo Tolstoy, Jacques Maritain, and A. J. Muste. However, even this literal interpretation opens onto two rather different constructions: sometimes the emphasis falls on the responsibility of men to each other and sometimes, rather, on the relation between the individual and God, in which case the duties of love and charity are derivative.

This latter has much in common (not accidentally) with a Stoic search for tranquility and peace of soul. War, anger, hatred, and killing are renounced not so much out of compassion for the suffering they entail, but because they interfere with the individual's capacity to respond to God. "But man is not to be loved for his own sake, but whatever is in man is to be loved for God's sake" (Aquinas, *Summa Theologica*, Part II, Qu. 2, Art. 7). And in the seventeenth century, even George Fox, the founder of the Society of Friends, gave the peace testimony not (as members of the Friends Service Committee sometimes forget) so much because of the pain inflicted on the victims but because violence mars the spiritual condition of the violent doer and thereby his relation with the divine. The Quakers sought to bring about nonviolently the kind of attitude and condition which would remove the occasion of war and inhumanity. Moral antagonism to war and slavery, the advocacy of prison and hospital reform, and the humane treatment of the insane thus all have a common base.

Christian pacifism could also be turned, we noted above, directly toward humanitarian responsibility. In this context, to love one's neighbor entailed obligations of charity and benevolence, in an effort to seek the Kingdom of God on earth. More prosaically this can be regarded as a Christian utilitarianism which had spokesmen among the Cambridge Platonists. Ralph Cudworth, for example, thought that God had constructed the world for the good of man, and that there-fore God's imperative was to contribute to it. "The greatest benevolence of every rational agent towards all constitutes the happiest state of all, and therefore the common good of all is the supreme law" (*Treatise*, Ch. I, Sec. 4).

Yet historical Christianity generally compromised its pacifist commitments. The ideal of the *Pax Romana*—of civil peace secured under a strong central authority—was inherited by the church as it entered organic relations with civil government and control. The issue became not that of outlawing war but of distinguishing just from unjust wars. Augustine translated the Roman view into the new setting. Clearly the literal interpretation of the sermon was inapplicable when all Christendom was facing the barbarian. Defensive and retributive wars and those undertaken by appointment of God are justified when waged by a legitimate sovereign; but the ultimate objective of war must always be peace. Aquinas was somewhat more explicit: offensive wars may not be justly ventured merely, for example, to increase territory; furthermore, the intention must be morally well-formed, that is, that the good sought and the justice to be vindicated must not exceed the injustices committed in the securing of it. Robert Bellarmine restated this last condition with even stronger relevance for the present: war must not cause greater evil in, for example, the destruction of life and property than it was intended to remedy. Major Protestant thinkers such as Martin Luther and John Calvin for the most part followed this lead, although the latter made an influential provision for revolt by peoples under an unjust ruler or under one who commanded unchristian behavior. Apart from this, warfare and police under legitimate authority are considered by Calvin to be essential to retributive justice.

As the theoretical vision of a unified Europe was shattered, and with the emergence of national states and the revival of Roman law (which strengthened the secular at the expense of religious power), it became evident that there was no arbiter to legislate a war's justification. A search was begun for a new kind of authority to fill the vacuum. The choice lay between alternatives: that of a Machiavelli or a Hobbes in which individual sovereigns, owing allegiance only to might, would entail an unending series of wars; or that of a Grotius, which projected Roman Law onto relations between nations. Grotius, doubtless motivated by the horrors of the Thirty Years War, sought the ground rules which might outlaw some of the barbarities. Thus the treatment of prisoners of war or alien property must not go beyond what is needed to break down resistance or to obtain reparations. More optimistically than the Stoics, he believed that there was a superior moral order or "law of nature" beyond force and self-interest which is accessible to reason. Grotius combines the *jus gentium*, the laws and customs common to all peoples, with *jus inter gentes*, the traditional laws governing relations between peoples or nations. Thus, in his view of international law, precedent and reason coalesce as sources for a code to determine when a war is just; but that wars are sometimes legitimate ways of settling disputes is never put in question.

It was left to those writing in the context of an eighteenth-century belief in the perfectibility of man to conceive of the eliminability of war itself and to challenge the morality of any use of force. Early in the century the Abbé Saint-Pierre introduced the novel suggestion that an intelligent understanding of social processes and a true appraisal of the obstacles standing in the way of progress might allow mankind to take a hand in planning its own destiny. The major social obstacle to progress, as the abbé saw it, was war, and he set about planning its elimination. His "Projet de traité pour rendre la paix perpétuelle entre les souverains chrétiens" (1713) proposed an institution much like an international court or society of nations. This alliance was to be a federation of all European states, which, after some adjustments as to boundaries, was to hold to the status quo. The federation was to establish an army from revenue provided by the member states, and it would make civil wars impossible and international wars preventable. Leibniz publicly ridiculed the *Projet* for its impracticability; it reminded him of an inscription "Pax Perpetua" outside a graveyard, for only in death do men cease fighting. But Emmerich de Vattel and Jean Jacques Rousseau took the plan more seriously, for by their time commerce and trade had already made European economic interdependence a fact of life. Rousseau recognized the dictates of reason which warned that international security was a condition for further progress, but feared the stupidity (rather than the immorality) of self-interested national policy. In the end he concluded pessimistically that only force could establish the needed federation—and that at too horrible a cost.

Rousseau and Vattel provided much of the setting for Kant's writings in these matters, but it was Kant's work and prestige which vindicated Saint-Pierre by giving respectability to the notion of international peace. Kant undertook to show that peace was morally and rationally imperative as well as empirically feasible. The individual's duty to seek peace would appear to follow in the critical philosophy from the categorical imperative, whether it is formulated in terms of rational autonomy, the universalization of maxims, or the ultimate value of humanity. Yet Kant reaches far beyond his predecessors by projecting the rules of indi-

vidual morality onto the social domain: nations are moral entities standing in moral relation to one another. States are obligated to develop those institutions which will lead to the abandonment of irrational and wasteful wars as instruments of policy; so much has now become the indispensable condition for progress. Kant's essays on "The Idea of a Universal History from a Cosmopolitan Point of View" (1784), "On the Common Saying" (1793), and "Perpetual Peace" (1795) are not only interesting for the issues at hand but also because they add an empirical reference to his critical ethics, relating the world of science to that of moral behavior, happiness to duty, and integrating his view of the moral agent with a Hobbesian view of human nature.

Hobbes, it will be remembered, regarded human nature when left to itself as egoistic, greedy, and aggressive without limit. This is for Hobbes not a moral reproach, since in his view the laws of human behavior are derived from more general laws of bodies in motion; human bodies being a particular sort of object, and that "artificial body," the state, an extension of human behavior under the pressure of needs and the rational search to satisfy them. Hobbes backs up this essentially deductive position by observations of aggressive individual behavior when unrestrained by fear and of the tendency of social groups to collapse into anarchy whenever a controlling authority is lacking. When he has his physiology well in mind, Hobbes even demotes pleasure-seeking into a secondary place; what is primary is the effort of the organism to preserve itself for reason never alters this objective but merely provides strategies for realizing it.

This ability to sacrifice immediate satisfactions for greater long-term benefits, especially a peaceful order, is what allows men to contract away some liberties to a civil society and thereby avoid what would otherwise be a war of each against all, a life that would not only be ". . . nasty, brutish, and short" but which would lack all the amenities of culture—agriculture, navigation, science, etc. Once the civil society is contracted, the imperative to seek peace is reasonable and in force. Thus "Every man ought to seek peace, for in a condition where every man can injure any man as he pleases there can be no security, and everyone seeks security both by necessity of his nature and by natural right." And, "Every man should renounce his right to defend himself in so far as all agree to renounce their rights to the extent they find it necessary for peace." On the other hand, such imperatives are hypothetical, i.e., binding only when there is an effective authority to insure peace. "Every man, if he fails to find peace, should defend himself as best he can in war" (*Leviathan*, Book I, Ch. 13).

Yet even within an instituted civil society stability is threatened by the omnipresent causes of quarrel: competition, which makes men war for gain; diffidence, which makes men war for safety; and glory, which makes them war for reputation. When the State (as in civil war) loses that coercive power which makes the breaking of promises more costly than the keeping of them, society once again is plunged into war which may be overt struggle or, what is almost as bad, ". . . that intermittent state of active hostility, a ready disposition to fight, or a sustained preparation for conflict" (ibid.). Nations severally have a primary responsibility not only for maintaining internal security but also for the defense against external threats; and since there is no effective super-power, individual nations are in the "state of nature" with respect to one another, that is, in a condition of war of each against all. "Neither if they cease from fighting, is it therefore to be called peace; but rather a breathing time, in which one enemy observing the motion and countenance of the other, values his security not according to pacts, but the forces and counsels of his adversary" (ibid.).

Kant takes the next and obvious step: mechanisms similar to those that lead men to form civil societies are also at work encouraging nations to form federations. Kant supports this thesis with two sorts of considerations. The first, formal and legalistic, has roots in his critical philosophy, and amounts to a projection of the categorical imperative onto the political screen. Here the moral considerations adduced are independent of cultural development and expediency. Whereas Hobbes had thought that morality is instituted with a civil state, Kant held that the essentially contractual relations that make a state possible depend on a prior morality which makes those contracts binding and (morally) validates political relations. Man is free to realize the inner principle of perfection which his own reason sets. Unfortunately, desires and inclinations impede the realization of this self-imposed duty. Civil societies arise to facilitate the realization of that perfection (i.e., to enable the "good will," in Kant's sense, to fulfill the moral imperatives). This is the moral justification of the state. Of all the historical forms of government, the representative-republican best reflects the moral relation in which men stand to one another. In such a government the citizens are equal and they are free because they are committed to laws internalized by their own consent and expressed in legislation of their own making. The state aims not at happiness but at justice; it must support a value system which is justified by reason not merely by anthropology.

The ideal of peace in a modern sense could not even have arisen until the rise of republics. Representative government further implements peace, since men are not likely to consent to wage wars whose cost and horror they must bear. Once a state has become a republic it will bind itself to other states with covenants in a network of moral obligations and rights. After all, nonviolence among the citizens of a single state would avail them little if they remain helpless before the constant threat of international wars. This view is legalistic: member states of the federation, being moral entities, must also be autonomous and equal.

Kant then sketches the rules of a practical science of diplomacy which—given the will—would support the establishment of perpetual peace. For example, when at war nations must seek to minimize the hatred and bitterness which would make final conciliation difficult; when at peace they must avoid the evils of secret diplomacy, avoid maintaining standing armies, and preparing for war. They must cultivate those hospitable attitudes and increase those commercial and cultural activities which transcend national boundaries. In all of these matters, Kant modestly remarks, no one is more helpful than the philosopher, who ought therefore to be free to advise.

Kant advances considerations of a second sort to show that perpetual peace is empirically feasible, and therefore can serve as a practical and regulative ideal. (Kant optimistically shifts *Pax Perpetua* from the Leibnizean epitaph to a sign over a Dutch inn.) Human nature is, at least in part, the unlovely and unsociable attitude which Hobbes portrayed. Man prefers indolence and would live instinctually if he could. His natural inclinations are directed toward his own satisfactions, and his love of possessions sets him in conflict with his neighbor. Ironically, the very effort to outstrip the neighbor drives him into society, which social state he resents all the while. He spreads out and populates the most inhospitable areas and adapts to the most varied conditions. This very spread makes it possible for him to survive and to form larger and larger social groups. Yet man also is affiliative, though somewhat reluctantly, and forges bonds of genuine feeling and sentiment, wishes for peace, prepares to keep his contracts; this mixed sociability introduces a new quality to the happiness he can secure and a chance to plan for it that would have been impossible in a primitive society. The tension, this unsocial-sociability, is a critical part of the dynamics of progressive history and it accounts for the rise of culture and civilization, Kant claims. That men are reasonable is also an empirical fact. Yet reason in this context develops over time and through trial and error; thus it is cumulative, is bound to the particular achievement of a culture—its social forms and its science—and is a characteristic of the species rather than merely of the individual. What is true of science and culture generally holds for morals. History has a moral dimension; it is teleological and evolutionary. Beneath the erratic and uneven movement of history the plan of nature can be discerned and the laws of historical development formulated. The ideal of peace has already emerged. Retrospectively, wars are seen to have served local and parochial ends; they may have stimulated industry and inventiveness and even freedom of inquiry which, since it knows no boundaries, must extend to religion. Wars, or more often force, have had their role in the creating of states, republics, and now, federations. Yet wars and all that they entail prepare the ground for their own transcendence. As wars become more widespread and effective, the fear and fatigue of the people make them progressively reluctant to fight and more prepared to seek other remedies. The ideal of peace as realizable in history arises, and the striving to realize it enters as a new factor in history—a factor which must in time breed its own consequences. Just as religious wars in his day had become anachronistic, Kant foresaw the time when the irrationality of war would also become generally apparent; and peace, which would be no mere truce between powers, no temporary secession of hostilities, but a way of civilized life, would become so rooted that appeal to violence would be inconceivable. The plan of nature with its laws of human and social development does not guarantee peace as inevitable but as sufficiently feasible to make its pursuit reasonable and obligatory.

Kant's influence extended differently through both the legal and the empirical-historical emphases. The legalistic arguments climaxed the continental tradition. English translations of Kant's political writings were popular on both sides of the Atlantic, even in the eighteenth century, and in the nineteenth century, were discussed by Transcendentalists. Many appeared in Frederick H. Hedges' *Prose Writers' of Germany* (1848). Francis Lieber, while teaching Americans the Kantian moral philosophy, worked the premises of *Perpetual Peace* into the code for the conduct of armies which President Lincoln commissioned. This last was only one of the ways that Kant's proposals were shepherded into the international law of the nineteenth and twentieth centuries. Laissez-faire cosmopolitans such as David Hume and Adam Smith had had the same objectives as Kant, if not his metaphysics. They appreciated the interdependence of one nation's prosperity with that of others, and they thought that the peace necessary to wealth could be furthered by those cooperative policies that were in line with the laws of economics.

Jeremy Bentham, with greater faith in legal reform, refashioned these attitudes into concrete proposals for international peace. Bentham's test of an institution by use of the calculus of "the greatest happiness of the greatest number," would have been unacceptable to Kant, but both were equally committed to a federation of nations. Utilitarian concern for public good and happiness extends to the "habitable limits of the globe." Thus international law has as its objective the securing of the common good for all nations. It aims not merely at minimizing evils during times of war, but has a positive task—to maximize benefits across national boundaries—a task which, for Bentham, requires the searching out of the causes of war and a *Plan for an Universal and Perpetual Peace*. Most wars, according to Bentham, are caused by passion or ambition and in either case the remedy lies basically in an appeal to reason, supplemented in the first instance by justice and in the second by self-interest (wars are not compatible with enlightened self-interest). Bentham distinguishes two functions of international institutions: a court without coercive powers beyond those of justice and an international legislature supported by public sanctions, which latter would lead to disarmament, to the publicity of treaties and negotiations, and to the emancipation of colonies (which so often are causes of hostility).

Eighteenth-century America provided a model as well as theorists. For example, James Wilson cast the problem of the Constitutional Convention of 1787 as quite literally one of uniting states not through power but through the multiplicity of interests of the people taken individually. More importantly, the United States provided a heartening example to those concerned about peace; as James Wilson put it, "The United States exhibited to the world the first instance of a nation unattacked by external force, unconvulsed by domestic insurrections, assembling voluntarily, deliberating fully and deciding calmly concerning that system of government under which they and their posterity should live" (speech in Convention, Nov. 24, 1787).

Now it is important to note that the posing of the problem in terms of a relation between nations has important consequences. The area of conflict, the conceptual space in which war and peace operate are thereby defined, and the relevant uses of "war" and "peace" implicitly determined. War and peace become identifiable states separated by a fairly well-marked line. Strictly speaking, the sovereignty of a nation is unbreachable; domestic injustice, civil strife, and the most rampant abuse of nationals by their own governments cannot legally be touched; this also applies to the American and French revolutionists. Equally, commitments to geographically-bounded sovereignty forecloses treatment of the larger-than-national conflicts between races, ideologies, or classes unless they are refashioned in national terms. In fact these commitments also close out the notion of a peace guaranteed by a single sovereign to which some aspects of their position might have led them.

Hegel did move toward such a super-state, building on Kant's dynamics of historical growth but in large measure destroying the pacific conclusions. There is an inevitability to the progressive replacements of powers throughout history. Each nation emerges as a self-contained moral personality without obligations of any sort to other nations. Thus, might certifies right, and war is a legitimate expression of the dominant power of the moment; but war is more than that—it is a force for the good of the state since it discourages internal dissent and corruption, and fosters the spiritual cement of patriotism. Hegel thus lent support to the rising nationalism, justifying at the same time the need for a strong military caste.

Later writers, in expanding their views of social evolution, often go beyond political categories, and view peace as a concomitant of a future more progressive state of the world. Herbert Spencer, for example, distinguished a militaristic state of society which is now giving way to the industrial; in the latter cooperation has selective value in the evolution of man. Security and peace are the necessary conditions for international trade in Spencer's laissez-faire individualism, and he was outraged by the emergence of corporate imperialism. Karl Marx too saw war as a special form, part of an exploitative class society under given conditions of production. Hence war cannot be eliminated and genuine peace secured until a world of socialism based on unleashed productive power has eliminated exploitation. And this socialistic solution of course was not possible till recent times when technology and the organization of production have made possible the elimination of scarcity.

The anarchistic view of history also, as for example in P. A. Kropotkin, emphasized a basic human relation of mutual aid and cooperation as the natural state of man. This is aborted by the emergence of power motivations and institutional power establishments which constitute the source of war. Ultimately the restoration of the basic values of mutual aid will break through the power barrier to establish cooperative organizational forms, federational rather than central in spirit.

The twentieth century has brought with it violence of unprecedented intensity and scope. Earlier wars, although centrally important, were isolable phenomena; now even the quality of peacetime life has been modified by the demands and the anxieties of undeclared wars, cold wars, and military preparations. R. G. Hawtrey early appreciated what is now a commonplace: war is an industry which contributes to the economic prosperity and technological development of a nation. Even apart from standing armies, communications must be organized, railroads and factories maintained, skills taught, and popular attitudes and traditions shaped with a view to future wars. War has become an integral part of the organization of society.

But if total war has been consolidated into the social structure, and is making its bid for supremacy in human life, the twentieth century is not without heirs to the accumulated tradition of the idea of peace. The religious tradition had its strong and radical statement in Tolstoy and Gandhi; theologians such as Maritain and Muste denied the justice of any war, while Freud, Einstein, and Russell deepened the insights of Hobbes and Kant.

Tolstoy sought, in a literal reexamination of the Sermon on the Mount, for the knowledge of how one ought to live. "Resist not evil" means not only that evil is not to be repaid by evil, but that all use of physical force is immoral. From this central imperative other pacifistic injunctions follow as theorems: for example, "Judge not that ye be not judged," means that Christians should take no part even in legal prosecution for it is our laws that make criminals. "Live in peace with all men" and "Love your enemies" also require respect for each man (never regarding him as a "fool") regardless of national loyalties, competing patriotisms, and similarly divisive passions.

Tolstoy's utter rejection of violence does not take root in mere humanism; the wrongness of violence lies in its rupture of the relationship between the individual and God. Men *can* change their attitudes; violence *can* be replaced by love if only the obstacles created by the iniquitous socioeconomic structure of society are done away with. Technological advance depends on morally horrendous factories, prisons, prostitution, and serfdom; our material enjoyments are purchased at too high a moral price. In modern society, the forces of love (the Judeo-Christian tradition) are in continual and equal conflict with those of violence (represented by the power-holders, the armies which support them, the courts which rule in their behalf, etc.).

Tolstoy's position was also grounded in personal experience. In his youth he had seen the banalities and excesses of aristocratic life, juxtaposed with the misery of the serf, and he concluded, in the manner of Rousseau, that the simplicity of the latter was to be preferred. Tolstoy's encounter with military justice in the Crimea was a turning point; he witnessed soldiers dying heroically for a regime that offered them nothing, fighting those against whom there was no complaint. One of them, a young volunteer, had been flogged for a clerical error and had retaliated by striking out at the captain. The uninjured officer forced a court martial which resulted, in spite of Tolstoy's defense, in execution. Tolstoy, even in those youthful moments, was sickened by a social order which permitted the captain's action, the soldier's behavior, as well as the punishment. What was needed was a reconstitution of society to eradicate violence.

Gandhi was influenced by the Sermon on the Mount, especially Tolstoy's interpretation of it, by correspondence with him, and by Thoreau's *Civil Disobedience*. But Gandhi goes far beyond Christian anarchism in his distinctive welding of Western humanism and *ahimsa* ("non-injury") which had been for centuries a part of Buddhism and Jainism. Non-injury is much more than a refusal to kill or do harm; it requires the avoidance even of the wish to harm or embarrass, and the seeking of positive human values which violence, even in intent, destroys. All men including the adversary and the wrongdoer are reasonable and at least latently moral—thus either they can be persuaded by rational argument, or conscience can be aroused by the example of suffering and by nonviolent coercion, which last does not mean demonstrations for the sake of harrassment. One turns the other cheek because this may provoke reflection and call forth from the opponent the soul force.

Non-violence is the law of our species, as violence is the law of the brute. . . . The dignity of man requires obedience to a higher law—to the strength of the spirit (*Autobiography*, p. 62).

Nonviolence was also worked into an effective political tool. Like Tolstoy, Gandhi saw, in industrialization and the concentration of power, sources of the destruction of the moral individual. He wanted a moral reawakening that required a return to the simplicity and asceticism of peasant life. India was to provide the model by which all governments resting on violence and exploitation were to be overwhelmed. It was not that India was so weak she could not win her independence by arms, but that she morally ought not to do so. Internationalism would come, but only after the future member-states had achieved some measure of self-reliance and self-respect. This future federation must be founded not on compromise, but on the forging of genuinely common interests; the peace it serves is a trans-historical and cosmic force.

Bertrand Russell starts with a basically Hobbesian view of human nature as self-interested, aggressive, and above all, fearful; yet he adds the Enlightenment's faith that reason can show a way out of the impending disaster. In the first place self-interest does not necessarily mean total selfishness, and further, although ineradicably aggressive, those passions can be channeled constructively by social institutions. Fear produces the three domains of conflict. The fear of

nature that was justified under primitive conditions is less and less reasonable as science converts mere acceptance of the natural world into control of it. Technology could provide the means to satisfy the material needs of the present population and to render less frightening the spectre of over-population and the despoiling of the planet, thus removing a major cause of wars. Fear of others, that was also inevitable under conditions of scarcity, still atavistically and irrationally determines some of our present attitudes, and is the basis of nationalism, racism, class antagonisms, and religious intolerance. These could be largely erased by the understanding of their origin and the recognition that mankind's basic interests are not only consistent but mutually self-serving. Yet modern social institutions, above all governments, aggravate such fears and institutionalize aggression, when what is needed are new social designs and a new and creative source of political power that will diffuse prosperity and science, control population, and enforce peace.

Rather paradoxically, Russell, like some other advocates of an authoritative international agency, justifies special cases of the display of armed power; for example, he thought the United States, when it was the sole possessor of the bomb, should have forced the rest of the world to disarm under the threat of nuclear punishment. Yet social controls are at best stopgaps; our fear of one another, turned inward as guilt and intra-personal strife, projected outward in war and conflict, remains. A profound reconstruction of personality is required—the replacement of destructive tendencies, such as deep-seated resentment, hostility, and anger (which have their military use), by the expansive, joyous, and generous attitudes appropriate to citizens in a world of peace. Man must discover

. . . how to live in freedom and joy, at peace with himself and therefore with all mankind. This will happen if men will choose joy rather than sorrow. If not, eternal death will bury man in deserved oblivion (Russell [1951], p. 213).

Einstein, Freud, and Dewey are in general agreement with Russell, although they write less comprehensively on the issues. Einstein, in his correspondence with Freud (1932), also thought that governments institutionalize aggressiveness, and are embarked on a cataclysmic course. "The unleashed power of the atom has changed everything save our modes of thinking . . ." If we do not achieve peace, we are faced by nuclear destruction hitherto unimagined. Yet peace cannot, in the modern world, be achieved on a merely national level. An economy built on planning for "security" is inherently pernicious: a society organized for "defense" is one in which war is engendered. Speaking of the United States, Einstein declared: ". . . our own rearmament, through the reaction of other nations to it, will bring about that very situation on which its advocates seek to base their proposals." Einstein calls upon the intellectual community to oppose the advocates of militarism and to find a means of protecting mankind from the curse of war.

Freud responded, adding psychological observations to Einstein's pacifism. Conflicts of interest are inevitably settled by violence, the superior individual being the winner until the weak learn that unified they can outmatch the strength of any individual. Yet the sovereign power of the community thus formed, the enforcement of its rules and regulations, still rests on potential and/or actual violence. Further, the community still has internal conflicts resulting from the unequal strength of its members. Court decisions and common law tend to reflect the interest of the strong, who are ever on the alert to better their situation; while the weak or exploited press steadily, and sometimes turbulently, for justice. At the same time, communities also develop strongly supportive emotional and social bonds.

The divisive and affiliative forces which society exhibits are to be found also in the destructive and death-dealing instincts on the one hand, and the uniting and erotic instincts on the other. In some combination, externalized or internalized, these are ineradicably present in all human behavior. The problem cannot be the extirpating of aggression but as William James had proposed in "The Moral Equivalent of War," the diverting of it to legitimate outlets other than war, and the counterbalancing of it by reinforced impulses toward loved objects and those uniting forces upon which society already rests.

There is yet another factor of importance—that of the evolution of culture with its accompanying psychic modifications. The most striking of these have been the progressive control of instinct by intelligence, and the internalization of aggression. War is the grossest affront to cultural achievement and the psychical attitudes which this achievement has bred; the pacifist's commitment is thus grounded more profoundly than even an intellectual and emotional repudiation of war.

Writers in the latter half of the twentieth century challenged such views as too individualistic, negative, or simplistic. For the most part, modern warfare has only the remotest and most indirect connection with the individual's hostility, either as a cause of war or as an outlet for aggression; thus the fostering of good will, love, sublimation, is an abysmally inadequate remedy. As Dewey recognized, the causes of war are multiple and socio-institutional; a total reconstruction of society and of the consequent interrelation between individual and social determinants is required. Further, a defensive campaign directed merely at the avoidance of war obscures the need for the constructive and creative uses of human resources for which peace is a necessary condition.

Finally, war and peace are complex not only by virtue of the variety of their causes but their multiple connections with the whole fabric of human life. Wars will not be prevented until we have eliminated the overwhelming problems of poverty, population, pollution. Furthermore, war is a possible outgrowth of all the phenomena of conflict that permeate life today. While the forecasts of doom waken us to the newer intensity of our problems, what is needed is an ethics of peace based on the full potential of both the physical and the social sciences.

BIBLIOGRAPHY

The following are the editions used in the text: Jeremy Bentham, *Plan for an Universal and Perpetual Peace*, ed. C. Colombos (London, 1927). John Dewey, "Does Human Nature Change?" *The Rotarian* (1938), reprinted in D. J. Bronstein, Y. H. Krikonan, and P. P. Wiener, *Basic Problems of Philosophy* (New York, 1922). A. Einstein and S. Freud, "Why War?" International Institute of Intellectual Cooperation, League of Nations (Paris, 1933). Eric Erikson, *Gandhi's Truth* (New York, 1969). M. Gandhi, *An Autobiography: The Story of my Experiments with Truth* (Washington, 1948 and reprints). Hugo Grotius, *De jure belli ac pacis*, trans. W. Knight (1625; London, 1922). R. G. Hawtrey, *Economic Aspects of Sovereignty* (London and New York, 1930). William James, "The Moral Equivalent of War," International Concilium, No. 27, (Feb. 1910). G. W. F. Hegel, *Philosophy of Right*, trans. W. Knox (1821; Oxford, 1942). Immanuel Kant, *Perpetual Peace: a Philosophical Sketch*, trans. M. Smith, with an extensive introduction (1795; London, 1903); idem, *The Idea of a Universal History from a Cosmo-political Plan* (1784), trans. T. de Quincy, *London Magazine* (Oct. 1824). For Leibniz, "Observations sur le projet d'une paix perpétuelle de M. l'Abbé de St. Pierre," see *Opera omnia*, ed. L. Dutens, 6 vols. (Geneva, 1768), V, 56; 20, 21; 65–66. A. J. Muste, "War, Politics and Normative Principle," *Ecumenical Review*, 7 (1954). Bertrand Russell, *New Hopes for a Changing World* (London and New York, 1951); idem, *Human Society in Ethics and Politics* (London and New York, 1955); idem, *Why Men Fight* (New York, 1916). Abbé de Saint-Pierre, *Abrégé du projet de paix perpétuelle*, trans. H. Bellot (1713; London, 1927). Leo Tolstoy *The Kingdom of God is Within You* (various editions). Of general interest are: Irving Horowitz, *War and Peace in Contemporary Philosophy* (New York, 1957). Herbert Schneider, "Peace as Scientific Problem and as Personal Experience," *Mensch und Frieden* (Zurich, 1959). See also the Grotius Society Publications, Texts for Students of International Relations.

ELIZABETH FLOWER

[See also Constitutionalism; Enlightenment; Liberalism; **Nationalism; Peace, International;** Perfectibility; Progress; Utilitarianism; **War and Militarism.**]

INTERNATIONAL PEACE

THE WORD "peace" has traditionally been defined as freedom from strife or war. This idealistic or utopian concept has yielded, especially since 1945, to a belief that peace exists in the absence of total war. Thus, despite military engagements usually described as "police action," the world has still been termed peaceful. This attitude of toleration toward armed conflict, while more apparent in recent years, has always existed because warfare has ever been a part of human existence. Since before recorded time, men have engaged in military struggles and have felt impelled at the same time to seek ways to curtail the "scourge of mankind."

The Greek city-states formed amphictyonic councils to stabilize relations between them, and they established a truce to suspend wars during the Olympic games. Later, the Roman government imposed the famous *Pax Romana* or Peace of Rome upon its citizens by suppressing armed conflict throughout the empire. Still later, the Roman Catholic Church, as the dominant secular as well as religious power of the Middle Ages, decreed the famous Truce of God in 1041 which limited warfare to specified times. From then to the present, men have continually revealed a willingness to compromise and accept armed struggle as a part of life even as they fought to reduce or eliminate it.

But peace whether total or partial remained a dream. As the Italian city-states and later nation-states emerged in Europe, as countries thrust outward in pursuit of colonial empires, and as religious differences aroused men to fight, the intensity and scope of conflicts increased rather than diminished. This condition prompted renewed thought on the subject of peace which by the end of the eighteenth century resulted in philosophical and moral stands against war. Persons commonly categorized as pacifists came to believe that nations, like people, should be held accountable for their acts, that mankind should be informed of the evils and injustices of international conflicts, and that everyone should assume an uncompromising stance in opposing the use of arms.

Ideas on Peace and War. Peace workers soon emerged with a number of beliefs. They argued that wars were unnecessary and harmful and that pacifism was thus utilitarian and logical rather than emotional. They adopted a Christian posture, insisted that the taking of life was wrong, and that contrary to popular belief there were no just wars.

They faced a mountainous obstacle in this task, because for centuries men had fought religious battles and been told in the very name of Christianity that they had been right. But peace workers assumed that men possessed noble characteristics, that a common spirit of brotherhood existed, and that human qualities would rise above those of a bestial nature. They relied upon these assumptions in the nineteenth century to refute biological and evolutionary arguments that war was an implicit part of life because human beings possessed aggressive qualities that made them fight.

In arguing against the theory that wars were inevitable, the peace workers relied upon educational programs and propaganda techniques to inform people of the horrors, the evils, and the waste of war in the hope that men and women would turn against it. Beginning in the nineteenth century, peace advocates shifted in their emphasis and tactics and worked to create some type of international machinery or organization to resolve disputes amicably. At the same time, they explored the causes of war in the hope that governments might eliminate inequities and abuses and thus preserve peace. Among their causes they listed economic factors, especially those relating to trade and finance, and they examined nationalism, with its concepts of honor, vital interests, sovereignty, and sensitivity which led to alliances and other treaties involving mutual self-interest. They also recognized that ideological differences, notably those related to racial, religious, and political beliefs, could precipitate clashes. Finally, they exposed militarism and armament-races as causes of war.

The peace movement has thus been built upon two foundations. The traditional pacifist of the nonresistance variety reflected a negative philosophy by assuming an anti-war posture, and by seeking to persuade people to abandon arms as a way of life. The other premiss, of more recent vintage, was positive because it called for solutions to the causes of war and constructive machinery to resolve conflicts. Peace workers have long debated which of these tactics should prevail. The traditionalists have argued that the world will not see peace until a revolution has taken place in the hearts and minds of people. The positive thinkers insist that men cannot await such a millennium and that they must erect machinery which will at least reduce the frequency or intensity of war. Neither group has succeeded in its quest despite centuries of effort.

The Peace Movement. Peace advocates discovered early in the nineteenth century that as individuals they could accomplish little; hence, the history of their efforts since that time has been written largely in terms of organizations. The founding of the New York Peace Society in 1815, the British Peace Society in 1816, and the American Peace Society in 1828 represented landmarks in the movement. Many organizations subsequently appeared. In England, the Workingmen's Peace Association under the leadership of William Randal Cremer emerged in 1871, and the National

Peace Council, formed in 1905, represented a federation of existing groups. French advocates led by Frédéric Passy founded a League of Peace in 1867, and in Germany and Austria Alfred H. Fried and the Baroness Bertha von Suttner organized groups in 1891 and 1892. The latter's book, *Lay Down Your Arms (Die Waffen Nieder*, 1889), became a bible for peace workers everywhere.

The United States kept pace with Alfred Love's Universal Peace Union in 1866, and with a host of new agencies early in the twentieth century—a reorganized New York Peace Society, the Carnegie Endowment for International Peace, the World Peace Foundation, and the Church Peace Union. Pacifists also sought to organize on a worldwide scale with the International Peace Bureau in 1892. The founding of the Inter-parliamentary Union in 1889 further reflected this current. Consisting of representatives of the legislative bodies of individual countries, it reached across national lines directly into the heart of governments. Pacifists also sought broad action through conferences. A series of these had been held between 1848 and 1851, and they were revived in 1889. Thereafter the Universal Peace Congresses met annually in various countries until the First World War, while in the United States National Arbitration and Peace Congresses assembled five times between 1907 and 1915.

This surge of activity, especially in the quarter-century preceding the First World War, reflected a widespread and optimistic belief that armed conflict between civilized nations was declining. Not since the battle of Waterloo in 1815 had there been a major conflagration of comparable scope, and many persons dedicated themselves to the task of eliminating any remnants of war that remained. Likewise, a developing democratic spirit throughout the nineteenth century contributed to the peace movement. Where people rather than rulers determined the policies of nations, it was assumed there would be less likelihood of warfare, and the greatest thrust of the peace workers appeared in the two countries, Great Britain and the United States, where representative governments and firmly established legal systems prevailed. Elsewhere, especially in those states on the European continent where autocratic governments existed, activities did not compare with those in lands which guaranteed freedom of speech.

The tactics of peace advocates in the century between 1814 and 1914 reflected these two molding influences of declining war and democratic principles. Their societies acted as educational agencies to win people to their cause and inform them of work which still needed to be done. They especially sought to persuade the democratically elected parliamentary and congressional bodies in Great Britain and the United States that treaties and laws should be developed to curtail war, and they resorted to the petition as one of their most effective devices. Since the United States Senate played a major role in treaty-making, many peace groups sought to influence its attitudes to insure approval of measures by a favorable two-thirds vote.

During the First World War, activity in most countries centered upon a campaign for a league of nations; thereafter, until 1939, in England and on the Continent societies concentrated upon disarmament and the strengthening of the League. In the United States, some organizations like the League of Nations Association and the American Foundation agitated for League or World Court membership, while others such as the National Council for the Prevention of War, the Committee on the Cause and Cure of War, and the Fellowship of Reconciliation pursued more conventional aims. The latter bodies attracted widespread support as American citizens experienced a reaction against warfare and armaments that contributed to the isolationist stance of their country in the 1930's.

Following the Second World War, peace workers rallied behind the United Nations, but many of them realized that their age-old quest had not ended. Therefore, they created new societies which sought to strengthen the United Nations or to create an even more powerful international agency. Others renewed demands for disarmament as nuclear weapons threatened the annihilation of mankind. The intensity or scope of the movement after 1945, however, did not approach that of the previous seventy-five years until the late 1960's when the war in Vietnam stimulated a renewed interest in the subject of peace.

Peaceful Settlement of Disputes. Once peace workers abandoned their negative posture against war, they argued that nations should act constructively to settle their differences without conflict. Methods, however, had to be devised which governments would accept and utilize, and an array of alternatives appeared—arbitration, conciliation, mediation, inquiry, and good offices. All operated upon the basic principle that a third party or parties should serve as a friendly agent and propose a suitable solution for a particular problem that threatened war.

Arbitration had the most ancient lineage of these methods, and it became exceedingly popular between 1870 and 1914. It called for the third party to suggest a solution which the disputing nations agreed they would accept. The Greek city-states had resolved differences in this way, but the process had virtually disappeared between the sixteenth and nineteenth centuries when intense nationalistic and religious conflicts dominated the European scene. It then became

449

dangerous for an outsider to intervene in any quarrel, for his motives were suspect and he often found himself enmeshed in the controversy.

Attitudes changed, however, so that by the time of the First Hague Peace Conference in 1899 delegates adopted a resolution which acknowledged the honest intention of third parties willing to serve as brokers. The Jay Treaty of 1794 between Great Britain and the United States had started this revolution in attitudes when it reawakened interest in the idea of resolving differences through arbitral processes, and an increasing number of governments subsequently resolved disputes in this way. The most famous instance involved the controversy between Great Britain and the United States over damages claimed by the latter for the depredations of the Confederate cruiser, the *Alabama*, and its settlement in 1872 stimulated further activity. Peace advocates began a quest to persuade statesmen to write into all agreements, even those of trade, a clause that they would resort to arbitration if any problem arose over the accord. This goal soon gave way to a campaign for general obligatory treaties in which governments would agree to arbitrate certain types of disputes. Once this had been achieved, efforts centered on committing nations to broader provisions in which they would submit all differences of whatever nature to arbitration.

This activity resulted in the only achievement of importance at the Hague Peace Conference of 1899. The delegates created a Permanent Court of Arbitration, a panel of judges from which governments could select impartial arbiters to hear and decide a dispute. Between 1828 and 1899, nations had signed approximately forty bipartite treaties of arbitration; from 1899 to 1914, they reached agreement on at least one hundred fifty more.

This superficial evidence of success cloaked a weakness. None of the issues at stake would have led to a major war. Governments usually submitted only inconsequential differences and in most instances refused to sign any instrument which obligated them to refer questions of vital interest, national honor, or independence to third parties. The record of the United States supported that fact, for the Root-Roosevelt arbitral agreements of 1908–09 contained little to commit the nation, and the Senate refused to approve clauses in treaties concluded by the Taft administration in 1911 to broaden the obligations under arbitration procedures.

The weakness of the system became apparent in 1914. Prior to the formal declarations of war, no government suggested that the issues be resolved by arbitration, and none of the major European powers had signed accords with each other which included clauses relating to national honor or vital interests. Their agreements obliged them to submit for settlement only such matters as misunderstandings over the interpretation or application of treaties or questions of a legal nature. Statesmen had been unwilling to commit their countries to effective programs as the peace advocates had suggested.

Many pacifists had perceived the weakness of arbitration and sought to fill in other ways the gap through which nations could still plunge to war. They emerged with another plan—conciliation. Those issues which governments would not submit to arbitration should be referred to another kind of third party whose recommendations would not be binding. This process was greatly strengthened early in the twentieth century by the addition of the "cooling off" principle largely associated with William Jennings Bryan. He discussed the idea at a meeting of the Interparliamentary Union in 1906, suggested it to President Taft, saw it partially incorporated into the arbitration accords of 1911, and wrote it into the conciliation treaties he concluded as Secretary of State in 1914. The latter called for a postponement of hostilities while any commission was at work and a further moratorium, usually of six months, after it had rendered its decision. This process assumed that wars began in moments of passion. If nations would delay and explore their problems calmly and rationally, tempers would cool and there would be no armed struggle. This principle, however, like arbitration, had its limitations. Such agreements did not bind the signers to accept the recommendations of the third party or forbid fighting. Thus conciliation also failed to avert the First World War.

Because both arbitration and conciliation possessed limitations, men devised other ideas to resolve disputes peacefully or to stop wars after they began. These involved mediation, good offices, and inquiry, but the one proposal which seemed most attractive was that associated with an international court of justice. A legal tribunal would operate under commonly accepted practices and perhaps even statutes, and it would thus be distinctive in its procedures and authority. If nations could agree to establish rules of behavior and a genuine judicial court, they would then willingly bring their disputes to the bar of justice.

This idealistic concept possessed flaws, however, the most important of which was the absence of any code of international law. Hugo Grotius, in *De jure belli ac pacis* (1625), had pioneered in exploring the subject and in formulating philosophical principles, especially his assumption that a body of rules or commonly accepted practices did exist which could be determined and on which nations could agree. He argued that these could be codified, and states would then have some basis on which to determine right from wrong. Those in the wrong would rely less upon force to assert their claims because they could be condemned for their actions, and the world would thus see peace through law. Grotius maintained that countries subscribed to certain moral standards of behavior, that many of these could be found in treaty provisions, and that laws could be extracted from conventions and customs and presented in the form of a code. Yet neither men nor governments made headway in ensuing years in compiling a set of acceptable rules.

Not until the nineteenth century did legal scholars progress in this work. First, they divided international law into public and private categories with the latter applying to nongovernmental relations. Trends in business, commerce, and improved communications greatly accelerated this movement in private law, while the arbitration campaigns and the emergence of more democratic governments in western Europe further stimulated interest in public law. Two societies appeared in 1873, the International Law Association and the Institute of International Law. The former concentrated upon the private sector and the latter the public. At the same time, such individuals as J. C. Bluntschli of Switzerland, David Dudley Field of the United States, and John Westlake of England prepared written codes, but no governments accepted these or acknowledged the existence of any rules which restricted their action.

The creation of the Permanent Court of Arbitration at The Hague in 1899, however, encouraged the legalists. Agitation in ensuing years resulted in an effort at the Second Hague Peace Conference of 1907 to establish an International Court of Justice, but this dream faded because the delegates there and later workers could not find a formula to select judges which governments would accept. The ideal persisted, nevertheless, and the creation of the Central American Court of International Justice in 1907 stimulated the legalists to further activity. In the United States the American Society of International Law and the American Society for Judicial Settlement of International Disputes appeared in 1906 and 1910 to promote their goal of a worldwide judicial tribunal. They did not succeed in their quest prior to 1914, but their vision took form in 1921 with the creation of the Permanent Court of International Justice.

This tribunal, authorized under Article 14 of the Covenant of the League of Nations, functioned until April of 1946. It heard sixty-five cases and rendered twenty-seven advisory opinions and thirty-two decisions. The United States never accepted membership but during the Court's life-span fifty-six governments did join. While the Court contributed to the principle

of international law by its existence, operation, and decisions, it faced problems similar to those experienced by arbitral bodies. It never developed a code to be used in the judging of cases, and nations did not entrust major problems to it for settlement. These weaknesses were compounded by its lack of authority to uphold decisions and by those attitudes of sovereignty which kept issues involving vital interests, national honor, and independence outside of the realm of justice.

Such conditions determined that the International Court of Justice under the United Nations would likewise be an ineffective agency for peace. Despite provisions which granted it greater authority than its predecessor, most governments which joined qualified their acceptance. The United States stood in the vanguard of this movement by approving membership in 1946 under the Connally Reservation which allowed that nation to determine what constituted domestic questions. Thus the International Court of Justice heard only minor matters and never considered controversial issues which could result in a major war. Several groups have campaigned since 1946 for a greater acceptance of peace through law, but such efforts, especially those by Grenville Clark and Louis B. Sohn in their book, World Peace Through World Law (Cambridge, Mass., 1958), have been relatively ineffective.

The idea of peace through law has thus suffered adversely. The ambitious hopes of late nineteenth- and early twentieth-century planners did not materialize. A number of reasons can be cited for this condition. First, the Grotian assumption of an international society in basic accord on standards of conduct was proven invalid. The diversity of states, the various levels of development of societies, and the absence of any common worldwide cultural or ideological foundation made it impossible for nations to agree to any code of behavior. Second, war has always been considered a legitimate activity for countries. The Spanish philosopher, Francisco Suárez, late in the sixteenth century argued in one of the earliest discussions on international law that legitimate wars could be waged either to promote justice or to uphold the right of the state on matters vital to its survival. This principle, unfortunately for the cause of peace, became accepted doctrine; thus, nations have considered wars to be legal and justifiable, and they have claimed the right to determine what a "just war" might be.

Third, nations have been unwilling or afraid to rely upon legal machinery to resolve disputes. When they created the Covenant of the League of Nations, they did not establish a system to develop law as most internationalists wished; rather, they relegated justice and courts to the periphery and relied upon political decisions by the major powers to avert wars. The Covenant provided for the Permanent Court of International Justice to function as a separate agency outside the League, not as an essential part of the League's machinery itself.

A further factor behind the failure of law lay in the way it was discredited in the 1930's and 1940's. The first step began in the 1920's with a movement to outlaw war. Led by Salmon Levinson of Chicago, peace workers campaigned successfully to have governments conclude treaties in which they renounced aggressive warfare as an instrument of national policy. The Pact of Paris to which they subscribed contained no provisions for enforcement or for any effective machinery to be employed in time of crisis. Thus when nations resorted to war in the 1930's and the treaties were not upheld, concepts of law suffered. The application of certain standards at the Nuremberg Trials following the Second World War further discredited the idea of international justice. Separate military tribunals heard the cases, not those which had been legally created as courts, and the principles of law applied had still not been embodied in any formal code accepted by nations.

Peace through Diplomacy. The general inability of men to develop successful machinery to resolve disputes and prevent war meant that countries had to rely upon their own resources. Traditionally, they have utilized diplomacy to avoid conflicts, and peace advocates have encouraged statesmen in this task. American pacifists of the nineteenth century often argued that their secretary of state had been misnamed. He should have been called secretary of peace as a counterpart to that of war. They thus revealed a faith in the oldest and most natural method of states to resolve their differences. Diplomats might pursue other aims, but for humanitarian, economic, and practical reasons governments should concentrate upon the pursuit of peace.

Diplomats had long been practitioners of negotiations with both bad and good results. They had devised the balance of power concept as one of their major devices to avert struggles, but rather than deter, it seemed to stimulate a spirit of rivalry among nations which actually encouraged instability. Wars continued as a part of life, and men sought to repudiate the balance of power concept after 1918 when they replaced it with a community of nations organized for peace. Yet by the late 1930's, statesmen returned to their alliances. The Charter of the United Nations recognized this reality of life when in Article 51 it allowed the creation of regional groups after 1945.

Diplomats also resorted to defensive treaties through which they sought to avoid war by threatening any aggressor who might move against any of the signatories. But such arrangements, notably the Locarno Pact, proved to be unreliable; they have been both violated and repudiated. Statesmen have thus followed less formal procedures to avert wars. They have negotiated through exchanges of notes, by informal talks, or by conferences either to prevent or end struggles. The diplomatic pathway to peace, however, while reconciling many differences, has possessed many pitfalls. Too often negotiations have taken place in an atmosphere of mistrust in which governments have sought to attain a preferred position rather than peace. Furthermore, few statesmen have ever placed much faith in treaties as peacekeeping devices. The "scraps of paper" which did not avert the First World War and the agreements in effect in 1938 and 1939, which countries both honored and dishonored, revealed serious shortcomings in traditional diplomacy.

Peace through International Organization. Nations have, therefore, turned more and more toward machinery to keep the peace, and the most significant achievement along these lines can be found in the evolution of an international organization. The modern concept of a world body had to await the rise of the nation-state, and the word "international" did not appear in men's vocabulary until the eighteenth century. The idea of cooperation among countries, however, had emerged in medieval times when it was associated with schemes to strengthen the Roman Catholic Church or to recover the Holy Land from the hands of infidels. Pierre Dubois, about 1255, pioneered in such schemes, and by the sixteenth century several other projects had been written. In the following century, Maximilien de Bethune, duc de Sully (1603), Émeric Crucé (1623), and William Penn (1694) formulated notable proposals.

Most early planners revealed common aims. They thought in terms of some type of assembly or congress, of an arbitration system, and of sanctions to uphold decisions or rules. All but Crucé proposed a union confined to European powers. They also reflected the autocratic spirit of their age and the absolutism of rulers, for they wrote primarily of leagues of princes and often revealed an ulterior motive.

The pattern did not shift appreciably in the proposals of the Abbé de Saint-Pierre in 1712 or Rousseau in 1761. Rousseau, however, reflected ideas of the Enlightenment in suggesting a representative assembly of people rather than of crowned heads or their delegates. He also emphasized voluntary action so that states would enter any association by free will rather than under compulsion. Jeremy Bentham in 1789 and Immanuel Kant in 1795 stressed the idea of confederation, and the latter sought to justify an international organization on moral as well as political grounds. Such thinkers received considerable support for their views from the form of government created in the United States after the American Revolution, for the union there seemed to confirm the belief of those writers who argued that a voluntary society would be possible.

The Congress of Vienna in 1815 represented an important turning point in the evolution of thought. It still reflected autocratic principles, for the major powers operated as virtual dictators in determining policy, but it also encouraged cooperative action on the part of states. Both Tsar Alexander's abortive Holy Alliance and the more practical Concert of Europe gave prominence to the belief that nations could voluntarily work together in deciding important questions. The series of conferences which followed, Aix-la-Chapelle in 1818, Troppau and Laybach in 1820 and 1821, and Verona in 1822 laid the foundation for others throughout the nineteenth century, notably those at London in 1829 and 1830 and at Berlin in 1856, 1878, and 1885.

Men took note of these political gatherings and decided that cooperation on nonpolitical matters would also be beneficial. Over two thousand world conferences prior to 1914 on such diverse subjects as communications, labor, agriculture, business, and social problems reflected a growing spirit of internationalism.

Peace workers in the United States shared in these activities, for leadership in discussing an international organization had largely shifted to the United States by the 1830's. The American Peace Society under the direction of William Ladd became the leading exponent of the ideal of world unity by sponsoring essay contests which elicited considerable response and resulted in Ladd's famous *Essay on a Congress of Nations* (Boston, 1840). He added one distinctive contribution to the already age-old idea of an international organization. There should be two separate operating agencies, both a congress and a court, not one functioning in different ways. Ladd's proposal appealed to many persons, and under the leadership of his disciple, Elihu Burritt, the congress and court theme received widespread endorsement in ensuing decades in Europe and America.

By the 1890's, spokesmen for an international organization appeared in increasing numbers. Andrew Carnegie coined the phrase "League of Peace" to describe their aims, but others preferred to speak of the "Federation of the World." The secretary of the American Peace Society, Benjamin F. Trueblood, advanced the latter ideal in articles, speeches, and a book, and he received considerable support from the Boston minister and editor, Edward Everett Hale. Americans usually thought in terms of a world union,

but on the Continent and in Great Britain advocates reflected their environment by calling for a European federation of states. Journalist W. T. Stead and Prime Minister Lord Salisbury in England, the Baroness von Suttner of Austria, the Baron d'Estournelles de Constant of France, and Jacques Novicow of Russia emerged as the leading exponents of this proposition.

The First Hague Peace Conference greatly advanced the belief that an international organization could be attained. Twenty-six states sent delegates, and although they failed to agree on many proposed items they did create a Permanent Court of Arbitration. This achievement stimulated thought in many lands. In the United States, Trueblood, journalist Raymond Bridgman of Boston, attorney Hayne Davis and editor Hamilton Holt of New York City, United States Representative Richard Bartholdt of Missouri, and Andrew Carnegie spearheaded a propaganda campaign. They obtained a promise from President Theodore Roosevelt in 1904 to seek a second Hague Conference, which Tsar Nicholas subsequently called for 1907. These internationalists sought one basic aim. They wished to see periodic congresses in which governments could discuss common problems and create machinery to avert crises. Arbitral commitments, a court of justice, an agency to formulate and codify international law, and perhaps some form of sanctions might arise from such meetings. Some men explored the subject of an executive and the delicate question of how force should be applied to prevent war, but they aroused few followers.

The Second Hague Peace Conference further encouraged the internationalists. Delegates representing forty-two nations attended and followed the course previously charted. They could not agree upon disarmament proposals, but they did recommend the creation of an international prize court and a court of justice.

Between 1907 and 1914, men made no substantial headway in official circles toward a world organization. The limited scope and application of arbitration was amplified by the failure to achieve a purely judicial tribunal because governments could not agree on a formula to select judges. The propaganda continued with two clear schools of thought. One endorsed the principle of periodic congresses and began a campaign for a third Hague Conference. The other spoke for a permanently functioning body in the form of a league rather than a loose association meeting only on occasion. The latter group also believed in a greater delegation of authority to any agency, but all advocates agreed upon one point. Concepts of justice should lie at the core of its operation.

With the outbreak of the First World War, the idea 453

of some form of union gained widespread currency. In England, many individuals prepared plans and several organizations appeared of which the League of Nations Union, the Fabian Society, and the League of Free Nations Society were the most prominent. These groups reflected prewar thinking as they called for periodic congresses, the creation of machinery to resolve disputes through legal and arbitral processes, and a cautious application of sanctions. British thinkers generally favored force to uphold awards of the authorized bodies and even to defend members from attack, but they preferred that a league in each instance determine whether or not to employ sanctions.

In the United States, groups also appeared, notably the League to Enforce Peace, the World's Court League, and the League of Free Nations Society. Nearly everyone agreed with the formula for regular meetings and machinery to settle differences, but there accord ended. The League to Enforce Peace favored automatic sanctions but called for their application in only one way. Nations should be compelled to submit their disputes to the procedural machinery. Awards should not be upheld and members should not be defended. In the neutral countries of Europe, internationalists created the Central Organization for a Durable Peace, the only body not primarily national in its membership, which suggested a program similar to that of the League to Enforce Peace. Statesmen slowly accepted the idea of a postwar union, and by the war's end it had been embodied in the aims of nearly everyone.

Thus by 1919 men agreed to test this new proposition. Between 1920 and 1946, sixty-five nations joined the League of Nations with thirty-one involved for the entire period. From its headquarters at Geneva and with an average annual budget of six million dollars, the League assumed a number of tasks in its role as a preserver of peace. It attacked the problem of territorial rivalries through a mandate system under which the former colonies of Germany as well as other disputed lands were assigned to various governments as agents of the League. It sought to achieve disarmament, to solve refugee problems, and to cope with major economic and human difficulties. It also served as a peacemaker by settling disputes. Until 1931 it succeeded reasonably well, largely because no vital issue involving a major power came before it. Then the Japanese attack upon Manchuria in 1931 and that of Italy upon Ethiopia in 1935 tested the League and exposed its weaknesses. Its members refused to support the principle of sanctions in Articles 10 and 16 of the Covenant, and from that point until the outbreak of the Second World War in September of 1939 aggressors successfully challenged the League. The idea of collec-

tive security implicit in the Covenant gave way to neutrality and appeasement. Discussions after 1935 to "reform" the League clearly reflected the desire of states to reduce their responsibilities, and the organization became little more than a consultative body.

The idea of an international agency, however, did not die with the collapse of the League of Nations. Again, groups and political leaders emerged to create the United Nations in 1945. In its basic structure, it bore a marked resemblance to the League, but it contained clauses in its Charter which made it distinctive. The United Nations placed much more emphasis on averting wars by improving social, economic, and political conditions that prompt conflict, and it created many agencies to deal with such problems.

On the other hand, the Charter retained the League concept of political rather than judicial action to cope with problems. Chapters VI and XIV of the Charter did provide for the peaceful settlement of disputes along various lines, but other clauses placed the real decision-making in the hands of the Security Council and the General Assembly. The Council received a charge to maintain peace, and the Assembly had the right to discuss any matter relating to the peace and security of the world. The organization displayed its authority most dramatically with a Security Council decision to intervene in Korea in June of 1950, but thereafter when the Council failed to act because of the veto power of members the Assembly assumed the initiative. The Uniting for Peace Resolution in November of 1950 granted the Assembly the authority to reach decisions and even to call for the use of arms when necessary. Thus the Assembly gained significant power as an agency of peace.

This transition elevated the Secretary-General to a position of prominence, and he has served as a personal mediator in disputes or as the instigator of United Nations action. Peacekeeping operations increased with military observers in Kashmir, the Middle East, Greece, and Lebanon and with a police force in the Middle East, Cyprus, and the Congo. Despite such efforts, the United Nations in its first twenty-five years did not always resolve disputes or problems of major importance, especially those involving the great powers. Bypassed in favor of traditional diplomacy, it played the role of an "honest broker" as it sought to stabilize conditions and to persuade the major governments to follow the pathway of common sense. It also influenced discussions involving large countries by increasing the number of participants. Its actions, while notable, have not been impressive, and its ineffectiveness in such "preventive diplomacy" has led to increasing doubts about its efficacy as a peacekeeping agency.

This has prompted suggestions for strengthening the United Nations by granting it greater authority and thus allowing it to escape from its policy of improvisation. Planners have called for increased executive, legislative, and judicial powers to make it more effective. They have noted the discrepancy between international life in 1945 when statesmen drafted the Charter and the later reality of nuclear confrontation, and they have argued that the United Nations should be allowed to cope with the problems of armaments, fissionable materials, and delivery systems. Reformers have exposed other weaknesses: membership concepts which give micro-nations equal weight with great powers; the limitations on agencies seeking to alleviate conditions leading to war; and the financial dependence of the United Nations upon its members, and the insufficient funds available for its extended operations. Governments, however, while aware of these problems, have not been inclined to resolve them.

Peace and Arms. Because the United Nations never received sufficient authority to prevent all wars, governments have had to rely upon their own strength to defend themselves as in the past. And pacifists have always responded with proposals that countries disarm, because that would be the most simple and direct formula for peace. They have long assumed a direct connection between the existence of weapons and fighting and believed that when men prepare for wars they will have them. Pacifists have also associated armaments with militarism. As forces grow, military leaders have assumed a greater role in political affairs and thus advised firmness and aggressive action rather than caution and moderation. The advocates of disarmament have never proven their case, but their arguments have often been heeded. The record of achievement in arms reduction, however, has been disappointing.

The Hague Conferences considered the subject because men at that time worried about the vast expenditures for war preparation in the late nineteenth century, but both in 1899 and 1907 the delegates could not agree upon a program. Their discussions led only to rules which limited or forbade the use of weapons capable of inflicting unusual devastation or cruelty.

The peace treaty in 1919 contained many provisions to limit the forces of the former Central Powers so they could not rearm and again threaten their neighbors. These clauses failed, however, because the German government found ways to circumvent or defy them. The Covenant likewise provided for disarmament through the League of Nations, but commissions and sessions beginning in the 1920's yielded no appreciable results and ended their work in 1934.

The only notable gain of the interwar years came

at the Washington Conference of 1921–22, one of the rare instances in history when governments actually agreed to a program and acted upon it. The formula, in the form of the Five Power Treaty signed by Great Britain, the United States, Japan, France, and Italy, called for naval disarmament according to classes and the total tonnage of ships. Public response appeared in the Republican party platform of 1924 which referred to the agreement as "the greatest peace document ever drawn." Subsequently, at conferences at Geneva in 1927 and at London in 1930 and 1935, the major naval powers partially extended the program of naval disarmament, but the effort collapsed in 1936 after Japan withdrew from the arrangement. Historians have judged the experiment a worthy one, but it did not succeed in keeping the peace.

The Second World War shattered pacifist claims regarding the efficacy of disarmament, and the Charter of the United Nations contained few clauses on the subject compared to the League of Nations Covenant. A few months later, however, with the use of atomic bombs upon Hiroshima and Nagasaki, mankind faced the specter of nuclear annihilation and responded with renewed demands for action. The United Nations at its first regular session created an Atomic Energy Commission which examined the subject of control and inspection of fissionable materials, while at the same time a Commission for Conventional Armaments functioned from 1947 to 1952. After the Soviet Union developed a nuclear weapon in 1949, the United Nations created a new general Disarmament Commission in 1952. Despite many sessions, it failed to discover formulas to limit or regulate the production of nuclear weapons because of an impasse over an inspection system to guarantee that the terms of any agreement would be honored.

For a time, the governments of the United States and the Soviet Union announced moratoriums on the testing of bombs, but they broke these. The United States recognized the scope of the problem when in 1961 it created the Arms Control and Disarmament Agency as an independent office within the government, and the two powers established a Disarmament Committee outside of the United Nations in 1962.

The Soviet Union and the United States also approved a nuclear test-ban treaty in 1963 in which they agreed not to explode devices in the atmosphere, outer space, or under water. It allowed underground testing, however, and contained another escape clause which permitted any signatory to withdraw after three months' notice. Over one hundred countries (excluding France and China) subsequently joined in the accord. In 1964, the General Assembly approved a resolution banning nuclear arms on orbiting space vehicles, and governments then turned to the problem of controlling the spread of fissionable materials and weapons. Then in 1968 the Soviet Union and the United States drafted a nonproliferation pact. Nonnuclear countries which signed promised neither to receive nor develop arms, and in return gained the use of fissionable materials for peaceful purposes. They further secured a pledge from the United States, the Soviet Union, and Great Britain that they would be assisted immediately in the event of a nuclear attack. Many nations signed, but significant ones, including some with atomic and hydrogen weapons, refused to join.

The developments of the 1960's clearly reflected a trend from the idea of disarmament to that of arms control. Statesmen realized that nuclear powers would never destroy their arsenals without an adequate inspection system, and they could not agree on that subject because of mistrust and the concept of sovereignty. Furthermore, as the nuclear "club" grew with the addition of France in 1960 and China in 1964, men realized that they had to allay the fear expressed by President John F. Kennedy "that by 1970 . . . there may be ten nuclear powers instead of four and by 1975 fifteen or twenty." The recent emphasis upon control is thus a new hope applied to an old problem.

The difficulties which governments faced in achieving satisfactory agreements limiting or controlling weapons forced men to attempt another approach—peace through arms. In a refinement of the old balance of power principle, the major nations achieved a military stalemate and injected into their vocabularies such new phrases as massive deterrent, retaliation, overkill, and sufficiency. At the same time, they developed conventional arms and a delivery system for nuclear warheads, spending between one and two hundred billion dollars every year from 1945 to 1969 in the name of peace.

Two basic beliefs lay behind this trend. The first has been expressed as peace through terror, with each power possessing the capacity to annihilate its potential enemy, and with a reprisal system to bring destruction on whatever country strikes first. The second has been described as a philosophy of confrontation in which the world knows neither peace nor war. The delicate balance achieved presupposes sensitive statesmanship, restraint on the part of men and nations, and sufficient rationality to avoid a thermonuclear holocaust.

Since governments may no longer wage major wars, they have had to prepare for lesser conflicts involving conventional weapons, and with these they have sought to stabilize the world so that a greater conflagration does not erupt. They have thus combined many of the ideas of the past. They seek the peaceful settlement of disputes and hope to develop a more advanced legal system; they resort to diplomacy by building and maintaining a collective security system based upon a balance of power principle as reflected in the North Atlantic Treaty Organization, the Warsaw Pact, and the Organization of American States; they strive to make the United Nations a more effective agency both to alleviate the causes of war and to preserve an uncertain peace; they have not abandoned their dream of disarmament or arms control; and they stand confronting each other with the scientific capacity to destroy.

These concepts, however, aside from the recently developed policy of nuclear deterrence, have never prevented war. Other cultural, political, and ideological factors such as nationalism, militarism, and sovereignty have been of greater importance in determining events. Man, therefore, stands at the same threshold he approached centuries ago. Despite improved means of communication, an ominous threat to his survival, an increased awareness of his danger, and the experiences and machinery of the past to aid him, peace still remains a dream. The idea of peace, however, has survived innumerable wars and still motivates men to hope and work for the millennium.

BIBLIOGRAPHY

The peace movement has been traced by A. C. F. Beales, *The History of Peace: A Short Account of the Organised Movements for International Peace* (New York, 1931). American efforts appear in Peter Brock, *Pacifism in the United States: From the Colonial Era to the First World War* (Princeton, 1968), in Merle Curti, *Peace or War: The American Struggle, 1636–1936* (Boston, 1936), and in Lawrence S. Wittner, *Rebels Against War: The American Peace Movement, 1941–60* (New York, 1969). Accounts of developments toward an international organization can be found on Sylvester J. Hemleben, *Plans for World Peace through Six Centuries* (Chicago, 1943); Warren F. Kuehl, *Seeking World Order: The United States and International Organization to 1920* (Nashville, Tenn., 1969); Christian L. Lange, *Histoire de l'internationalisme*, 2 vols. (Kristiana, 1919; New York, 1954); F. S. L. Lyons, *Internationalism in Europe, 1815–1914* (Leyden, 1963); Gerard J. Mangone, *A Short History of International Organization* (New York, 1954); Jacob ter Meulen, *Der Gedanke der internationalen Organisation in seiner Entwicklung*, 2 vols. (The Hague, 1917–29); Edith Wynner and Georgia Lloyd, *Searchlight on Peace Plans* (New York, 1944).

The following specialized studies are also useful: Raymond Aron, *Peace and War: A Theory of International Relations* (New York, 1966); Herbert Butterfield and Martin Wight, eds., *Diplomatic Investigations: Essays in the Theory of International Politics* (London, 1966); Inis L. Claude, Jr., *Swords into Plowshares: The Problems and Progress of International Organization* (New York, 1959); Arthur H. Dean,

Test Ban and Disarmament: The Path of Negotiation (New York, 1966); Clark M. Eichelberger, *UN: The First Twenty Years* (New York, 1965); Stephen D. Kertesz, *The Quest for Peace Through Diplomacy* (New York, 1967); Wilfred F. Knapp, *A History of War and Peace, 1939–1965* (New York, 1967); Arthur Nussbaum, *A Concise History of the Law of Nations* (New York, 1954); M. Stuyt, *Survey of International Arbitrations, 1794–1938* (The Hague, 1939); F. P. Walters, *A History of the League of Nations* (New York, 1952; reprint 1960).

WARREN F. KUEHL

[See also **Balance of Power;** Enlightenment; Ideology; Law, Concept of; Millenarianism; **Nationalism; Peace, Ethics of;** State; **War and Militarism.**]

PERENNIAL PHILOSOPHY

A PERENNIAL philosophy is, as its name implies, one with qualities which assure its survival through time and change, and therefore, by generalization, a permanently significant philosophy. It must therefore be universal and inclusive, internally coherent, fruitful of new insights and applications, and reasoned so conclusively that attacks cannot refute, and written or presented so convincingly that reasonable minds cannot resist it.

It can be seen from this definition that a perennial philosophy has never been formulated in complete detail and with final perfection. But it has been an ideal for many thinkers who have sought to state its basic method and principles. This ideal is itself, therefore, perennial, expressing the persistent hope for finality in the philosophical task.

As such it is opposed to skepticism, to historicism and other relativisms, to all intellectual sectarianism and partisanship, and to all forms of what Berkeley called appropriately "minute philosophizing," or the limiting of aim and method to the analysis of a plurality of small, empirically graspable and unrelated problems. A perennial philosophy must offer a unity which relates the total plurality, in particular the unity of theoretical and practical concerns, of knowledge, wisdom, and piety; it must be theoretically complete and of sufficient detail to guide to successful action. Charles Sanders Peirce, in spite of his indeterminism and fallibilism, expressed his commitment to the ideal of a perennial philosophy for a scientific age in the Preface to his *Principles of Philosophy,* reprinted in *Collected Papers* (1931–35):

To outline a theory so comprehensive that, for a long time to come, the entire work of human reason, in philosophy of every school and kind, in mathematics, in psychology, in physical science, in history, in sociology, and in whatever other department there may be, shall appear as the filling up of its details. The first step toward this is to find simple concepts applicable to every subject (I, vii, Sec. 1).

Traditionally, however, the ideal reaches beyond this intellectual role to offer bases for a more personal value of religious and moral wisdom, thus showing an affinity with Platonism, Stoicism, and the theological appropriations of classical thought in general.

I. HISTORY OF THE TERM PHILOSOPHIA PERENNIS

So far as can be discovered, the term *"philosophia perennis"* is modern, first appearing in the Renaissance. But the ideal of such a philosophy is much older—as old, indeed, as the hope for a definitive resolution of human problems. Though the term *"philosophia perennis"* is widely associated with the philosopher Leibniz, in whose writings it appears and whose thought aims at many characteristics essential to it, he himself found it in Augustinus Steuchius, a theologian of the sixteenth century, librarian of the Vatican, and Regular Canon of the Congregation of the Sacred Savior, who in 1540 published the *De philosophia perenni sive veterum philosophorum cum theologia christiana consensu libri X,* a work which quickly passed through several editions, including that in the *Opera omnia* in 1591. No evidence has been found that Steuch found the term in earlier writers, though cognate terms such as "perennious fountain of God's will" and "perennial wisdom of God" were not uncommon, and the term has been applied retroactively to the Scholastics.

Dedicated to the Farnese Pope, Paul III, initiator of the Counter-Reformation, Steuch's work is an apology for Christian orthodoxy as a return to an originally revealed absolute truth made available to man before his fall, completely forgotten in that lapse, and only gradually regained in fragmentary form in the subsequent history of human thought. Thus from its first use, the term represented an attempt at a perfect thought system, the unity of reason and revelation, but present in the history of thought only as an ideal which may be said to be "regulative" (in Kant's sense) and directive of man's striving for intellectual unity.

The history of the term since Steuch may be said to be fortuitous and infrequent—useful but far from indispensable in the justification of a certain philosophical tradition. It came to Leibniz in the next century only as the title of Steuch's book, and he used it more generally only in the later years of his life as a term for the type of philosophy he himself was striving to formulate. In 1687 Simon Foucher, a Paris friend who had revived the tradition of academic skepticism, called Leibniz' attention to Steuch's book in connection with a discussion of philosophic first principles, saying that Steuch's design seemed to be chiefly to adapt the ancients to Christianity, "which is indeed very beautiful, rather than to order the thoughts of philosophy in their places" (Gerhardt, I, 395). Leibniz had already known of Steuch, however; in the reading notes of his early Mainz years he had several times listed him and his book among "the Christian writers of all times" (Academy ed. VI, i, 532–33; VI, ii, 137, where he quotes Steuch's statement that God is *intelligens intellectum et intellectionem*, "understanding, understood, and still understanding," i.e., as act, as object, and as process). But as in the case of other terms which Leibniz read as a youth and then forgot, only to recall them much later at an opportune time in his own thinking, the term cannot be found again until 26 August, 1714, when, in a letter to Remond de Montmort, he used it in describing what was needed to complete his own system, to which he had referred in earlier correspondence as a hypothesis (Gerhardt, III, 624–25). What was still needed was an eclectic analysis of the truth and falsehood of all philosophies, both ancient and modern. In this process "one would draw the gold from the dross, the diamond from its mine, the light from the shadows; and this would be in effect a kind of perennial philosophy" (*perennis quaedam philosophia*). This is the *locus classicus* for the term in Leibniz, who gives in the same passage a brief sketch of the contributions of the major schools and also makes a reference to the "Orientals, who have beautiful and grand ideas of the Deity."

After Leibniz the term seems to go underground, only to reappear in different philosophical contexts; sometimes in support of the conclusion that a certain tradition—for example, Scholasticism—possesses the quality of unity, adequacy, and time-transcendence which the term implies. Thus it reappeared as the title of a collection of papers on Scholasticism, with some emphasis upon its new development after the Council of Trent, edited by Fritz-Joachim von Rintelen, and presented to Josef Geyser for his sixtieth birthday. Sometimes the term has been used for an eclectic combination of religious and philosophical ideas from East and West, proposed as a way of spiritual revival for modern man, as in Aldous Huxley's *The Perennial Philosophy* (1944). In all cases, the term stands for the notion of a philosophy of philosophies, an enduring set of intellectual and personal insights which is repeated in all variations of thought and conviction and which serves as an ideal of unity for thought and life.

II. HISTORY OF THE IDEA OF A PHILOSOPHIA PERENNIS

As has already been suggested, certain convictions were traditionally regarded as essential to the ideal of a perennial philosophy.

(1) Realism: that is, the view that the aim of philosophy is the knowledge of an independent world, including an order of ideas (universals, forms, laws) as an important aspect of this real order.

(2) Harmony: that human experience in both its cognitive and its practical aspects involves an underlying unity in which all plurality is resolved, this unity itself having an individual nature which makes it the object of religious veneration.

(3) A philosophical method in which analysis is completed in synthesis, but synthesis is itself a means to direct apprehension, through dialectic, intuition, revelation, or mystic vision; that therefore reason and faith are coextensive and mutually supporting.

(4) In particular, an eclectic method which assures this unity of being and truth through a quest for the truths and errors of all historical sects, old and new, seeking to synthesize their truths; thus eclecticism seeks to resolve the conflict between tradition and innovation, "ancients and moderns."

(5) Dualism of the ideally real and the historically real, historical philosophies being imperfect approximations, more or less adequate, to a perfect and complete system of truth. Implicit in this is the eschatological orientation which holds that the end and limit of history must be sought in the complete and eternal. This eschatological position is not utopian, however, for utopias temporalize the eternal and are therefore either philosophical heresies or metaphors.

These characteristic doctrines, of course, point to Platonism as the tradition most adequate for a perennial philosophy, though this Platonism may be that of the negative theology suggested by Plotinus, the Christian theism of Saint Augustine, or an eclectic fusion of Platonism and Aristotelianism. Lovejoy's discussion of the two gods of Platonism (in the last lecture of *The Great Chain of Being*, 1933; published in 1936) is applicable as well to the two philosophies, historical and eternal, implied by this tradition, which finds support also in such doctrines as the degrees of truth and being, the negative or privative theory of error and evil, and the macrocosm-microcosm relation. Though the roots of the ideal of a perennial philosophy may be found in the rise of philosophy itself, the clear conception may be dated from the attempts to use Greek philosophy to explicate the theological traditions of the theistic religions.

1. Ancient and Early Christian Concepts. The eclectic interest shown by Plato in his dialogues, but developed more fully in Aristotle, who built his thought upon an evaluation of the insights and errors of his predecessors, was expanded in the Hellenistic period in opposition to skepticism and in support of the new role of philosophy as handmaiden to religion. But the historical beginnings of the ideal of perenniality in philosophy may with much truth be ascribed to Philo of Alexandria, who found Plato to be Moses speaking Attic. The much looser eclecticism of the so-called Hermetic Corpus, the alleged writings of Hermes Trismegistus, was a collection of Platonic, Pythagorean, and popular wisdom gathered in Egypt, which was later considered an important source. Thus the Eastern tradition of wisdom and mysteries came through the cultural impact of Alexander's conquests to be absorbed into the eclecticism of the West.

It was in the fusion of Greek with the Hebrew-Christian tradition, however, that the redemptive and the theoretical, the historical and the eternal, were more firmly united and justified. The two Platonic traditions—the mysticism of Plotinus with its hierarchy of beings and its negative theology, and the conceptualized and personalized theory of Augustine with its trinity of modalities in God and its history of creation and redemption, were eventually combined in a theology which was at once the highest philosophy and the justification of faith. The perennial philosophy was, for Augustine, the rational Christian faith.

In Augustine, moreover, this religious metaphysics was reinforced with a profound psychology of sin and redemption, and what proved to be the orthodox Christian conception of history as a record of the fall of man, the conflict of good and evil, the successive acts of revelation and redemption, and the culminating judgment and end of time. This pattern of history itself provided the intellectual foundation of the ideal of a perennial philosophy.

2. Scholasticism. Although the late *Retractations* of Augustine involve a surrender of reason to authority, and therefore must have suggested to him that his theology was not absolute and eternal, Christian thought for centuries achieved a stability by discussing the alternative interpretations involved in Augustine's staunch rational fideism, and the Neo-Platonic tradition of mystical vision.

It may therefore be with better reason that the distinction of achieving the principles of a perennial philosophy has been assigned to the great Scholastic *Summas* and commentaries, in which the casuistic work of qualifying, amplifying, and applying this philosophical theology was continued with the aid of Aristotle's logic and metaphysics.

3. The Renaissance and Steuch. The revival of ancient literature and learning in the West led to a criticism of the Scholastic tradition and a widespread development of philosophical sects and controversies. Petrarch humanized Augustine to confront man with his freedom and powers; Nicholas of Cusa developed Christian Platonism in a comprehensive way which acknowledged skepticism but also revived great cosmological and apologetic issues; Stoicism was adapted in various ways to the courtly ideal of the *homo honestatis* through the principles of natural law and the virtue of obedience; Aristotelians, discovering the "true" as opposed to the Scholastic Aristotle, concentrated on his logic and physics, and became forerunners of the new science and its methods. Not until the religious controversies of the sixteenth century did metaphysics have a vigorous revival, largely in Scholastic terms. Meanwhile eclecticism was demanded by the variety of sects, and Platonism undertook the role of harmonizer of positions. In Florence, Ficino, Pico della Mirandola, and others, influenced by Nicholas of Cusa, undertook to reconcile Plato and Aristotle.

By the end of the sixteenth century, the humanistic, creative period of the Renaissance was thus disciplined and intellectualized, so that eclecticism flowered into encyclopedism—an effort, not without eschatological sanction, to exhaust the possibilities of knowledge and to organize it in a logically structured way. Of this encyclopedic movement Francis Bacon was the most popular and influential representative.

For Augustine Steuch, to whom we owe the term *"philosophia perennis,"* metaphysics was still secondary to the Christian history of creation, fall, and redemption; his idea of philosophy identifies it with revelation (*omnium sacrarum literarum philosophia*). This perennial philosophy requires not only wisdom but grace; in a commentary to the first chapters of Genesis Steuch writes, "There never was true philosophy without piety."

Human wisdom, however, has been corrupted in the long history of fallen man, Steuch continues, and the history of God's redemption includes the long quest for this saving wisdom. This historical development itself involves three kinds of philosophy: a common sense one diffused through oral transmission among all peoples; a critical refinement of this "arising in the speculation about the nature and causes of things"; and (a third) the full radiance of truth dispelling darkness everywhere; "this alone is worthy of the name of Wisdom." The rest of Steuch's work is a wide-ranging eclectic examination of the variety of traditions contributing to the chief doctrines of Christian theology, beginning with the Trinity and ending with the end of things and Last Judgment.

4. The Seventeenth Century and Leibniz. At the beginning of the new century, three developments which we have already noted became important in affecting changes in philosophy, and therefore also in the ideal of a perennial philosophy: the revival of metaphysics and the critical examination of first principles of "being as being," which arose from theological controversy; encyclopedism, the impulse, coming from the new spirit of discovery, to exhaust the possibilities of human knowledge and its ordering through a logical method; and the success of a method combining experience and reason (particularly mathematical) in achieving certainty in the new sciences of nature. The total philosophical effect of these projects was to render plausible to the great minds of the century the direct achievement of a complete, unified, and therefore time-transcending, perennial body of knowledge and wisdom. The so-called "rationalists" of the century sought this completion of the philosophical ideal.

The new encyclopedic spirit was widespread, but that part of it which sought to attain its end through a new method is most instructive. The pansophic movement was associated with Amos Comenius but also included, among others, his teacher John Henry Alsted, author of the great *Encyclopaedia* of 1630, and John Bisterfeld, whose many plans for a universal science of characters or symbols and an encyclopedia influenced Leibniz in his early youth. This movement adopted principles of method from Bacon, Ramus, and the revived interest in Raymond Lully's (or Lull) *Ars generalis sive magna* (ca. 1272) and applied them, ineffectually but with a zeal inspired by the conviction of Christ's imminent return.

Futile though their pretentious efforts were, the platforms of these men (for example, Comenius' *Prodromus pansophiae*, written in London in 1641) popularized the ideal of a completed philosophy which should go beyond the traditional fields of logic, metaphysics and physics, ethics and political theory, to embrace all possible knowledge, and which should do this by a unitary and certain method. The sense of urgency with which this method of combining empirical content with logical order was pursued, endured throughout the century.

The historical study of philosophy in a critical sense is closely related to the development of philosophical eclecticism of a soberer and more disciplined kind than that of Steuch. The crowning achievement of eclecticism appeared only later in the Enlightenment in Jacob Brucker's great *Historia critica philosophiae a tempore resuscitatarum in occidente literarum ad nostram temporem* (Leipzig, 1766), a work which Brucker argued would restore to philosophy, through the eclecticism of which Bacon was "parent," the "God of truth which it had until then neglected." But eclecticism had borne earlier fruit in such historical works as the *Origines*

historicae philosophiae et ecclesiasticae (Leipzig, 1665), of Leibniz' teacher Jacob Thomasius, and Gerhard Johann Voss's *De philosophiae et philosophorum sectis libri II* (The Hague, 1658). After describing eighteen philosophical sects with Greek origins, Voss rejects them all, passing over Plato, whose language he finds unfit for philosophizing, but praising Aristotle, who "stands out in sharpness of genius and variety of doctrine above all who preceded him as the light of the sun stands out above that of the moon and lesser stars" (Ch. 21, Sec. 1). Yet he urges acceptance of an eclecticism "which founds no new doctrines but selects its doctrines from others," urging this course as the most productive even though it is also the most difficult. "In the examination of all sects we must first see what is said, why it is said, what can be argued against it, and whether the two sides can be reconciled" (Ch. 21, Sec. 13).

Descartes repudiated the eclectic approach for the supposed certainty of an original logical method, which he nevertheless expected to result in a perennial pattern of thought. Though the other great systematizers of the century rejected Descartes' repudiation of the past as itself sectarian, they shared his confidence in a method which should at last achieve the adequation of thought to things through an insistence upon clear and distinct concepts, and should therefore bring philosophy in its history into identity with eternal truth. Unfortunately their disagreements merely sharpened and broadened the dualism of the actual and the ideal.

Of these thinkers, Leibniz was the most specific in formulating the goal of perenniality, the most thorough in his eclectic examination of historical philosophies, and the clearest in his formulation of adequate method. This method was analytic in its reduction of all experience and all questions to the primary notions and first principles entailed in them. It was then synthetic in its generalizing these principles and their application, through the appropriate definitions, to the various fields of knowledge and practice to be investigated. The unity and harmony of the results were assured by the simplicity and universal applicability of the principles.

Leibniz' development of a plan and program for a perennial philosophy was gradual. Involved from the beginning was a Neo-Platonic world view akin to that of Nicholas of Cusa, of Bruno, and of the Italian Platonists, in which the universal harmony of being and truth is reflected in the greatest possible variety in every created individual being, and man, possessed of the quality of inwardness and created with a nature compounded of the very attributes of God (in finite measure), finds his good in obedience to the order of law established in creation—natural, moral, and civil.

Within this general and incompletely defined theory, Leibniz' early philosophical conceptions were loosely eclectic. In physics he preferred the mechanistic interpretations of the "moderns" to the dynamic forms of the Scholastics, but deliberated on problems of motion, following Suárez and the Cartesians in using motion as a basic argument for the existence of God. In logic (as in jurisprudence) he was strongly influenced by Hobbes, but Leibniz' youthful nominalistic inclinations did not keep him from a conceptualistic theory of combinations, a connotative interpretation of logic, and an Augustinian theology. His own work centered in practical applications: a projected work in Christian apologetics, proofs for the existence of God to refute atheists, essays in education, problems of jurisprudence and of theology as the highest jurisprudence, and interest in the logical foundations of metaphysics and the theory of knowledge. He studied the efforts being made to reconcile Plato and Aristotle, Aristotle and Euclid, Aristotle and the "moderns," substantial forms with mechanism. His inclusive motive may be stated in terms of the phrase borrowed from Galen by Robert Boyle (1626–91, whom Leibniz read in 1671–72): the investigation of truth is the greatest of hymns to the creator.

In the Paris years there emerged the intention to construct a central, unifying philosophical work of inclusive and exhaustive scope, based on an essential unity of metaphysics and logic. Leibniz' synthesizing efforts were stimulated by his intensive study of Plato, Aristotle, and the papers of Pascal and Descartes, and his contacts with thinkers like Boyle, Malebranche, Foucher, and Christian Huygens.

In the early years at Hanover (from 1676 to 1684, perhaps the most creative years of his life), many plans and studies (*Initia* and *Specimina*) were written for such an ultimate decoding and mastery of the whole of truth. Various titles were tried. The papers of the Paris period (1672–76) contain the tentative title *Elementa philosophiae arcanae de summa rerum*. In the years 1679 to 1682, such titles appear as *Aurora seu initia scientiae generalis a divina luce ad humanam felicitatem* (in Gerhardt, VII, 54) and *Initia et specimina scientiae novae generalis pro instauratione et augmentis scientiarum ad publicam felicitatem* (ibid., VII, 64ff., 124ff.), titles obviously influenced by Bacon, Glanvill, or More. While the essays written to fit these titles do not reflect any eschatological convictions, they are impelled by a sense of urgency and show a conviction that, given a universal science of symbols and a combinatorial method (a logic and analysis and synthesis), the end could be achieved within a lifetime. These essays contain the most complete description of the content and procedures of this General Science, including Leibniz' most detailed examination of the traditional sects of philosophy (ibid., 141–56). In this period Leibniz' vision of the practicality of this perennial philosophy seems to have been particularly clear and strong.

The distractions of the years from 1684 to 1695 permitted time only for the perfection of Leibniz' metaphysics and dynamics, with continuing studies in logic and mathematics. The last two decades of his life (1696–1716) were filled with controversies about his opinions which served to clarify them but involved an abandonment of his great projects; his philosophical studies were aimed at winning support for his thought from scholars and leaders of opinion. Although there remain many reflections of his great enterprise in the papers of this period, the distinction between his achievement and the regulative ideal of a perennial philosophy becomes clear. There are impressive brief descriptions of the scope of his philosophical concerns, including compact criticisms of earlier philosophical traditions (for example, in the letters to Gabriel Wagner in 1696, in Gerhardt, VII, 514–27; to Michael Hansch on Platonic Enthusiasm, 1707, in G. W. Leibniz, *Opera omnia*, ed. Louis Dutens, 6 vols. Geneva [1768], II, 222–25; to Korthold, in Dutens, V, 320; to Bouvet, 1697, in Erdmann, p. 146; to Remond in the letters already mentioned; and in the response to the second edition of Bayle's *Dictionnaire*, 1702, in Gerhardt, IV, 554–710). Yet there is no claim of completion or of perenniality. To De Volder and others Leibniz spoke of his philosophy as an hypothesis (though one which had been proved). And in the letter to Remond in which the term "perennial philosophy" occurs, he ventured the remark that given the assistance which he needed, the final system might yet be achieved.

Thus it may be said that although Leibniz' descriptions of the *General Science of the Secrets of the Universe* involve all of the components essential to the perennial philosophy, and his mature philosophy itself gives a coherent account of the first principles and the structure of disciplines involved in such a system, he was unable to complete it, and never claimed to have done so.

5. Perennial Philosophy since Kant. Although the ideal of a perennial philosophy was still effective in the Enlightenment, its role was gradually restricted to the reasonable bringing of order into a narrower, more nominalistic realm of experience and practice. Christian Wolff, it is true, claimed demonstrative certainty for his eclectic union of Scholastic metaphysics with Leibniz' pluralism and Newton's physics, reducing faith to reason and claiming a *philosophia certa et utilis*. But although certain vestiges of the ideal of a transcendent and universal harmony remained in such concepts as the law of nature, the absolutes of science, and moral rights and duties, the acids of subjectivity, nominalism, and skepticism corroded changeless concepts into associated experiences of a passing, atomic kind. Kant's emphasis upon the universal and necessary, and the architectonic which underlies his critiques, still presuppose the ideal of perenniality. But in arguing for the irresolvable antinomies of metaphysics and making mind the key to the first principles of knowledge and right action, Kant confronted philosophy with the dilemma of abandoning the ideal of a perennial philosophy or of forcing it to be sought not in what transcends experience and history but in what is changeless and abiding within them.

What Kant achieved with respect to the first principles of logic and truth, moreover, his idealistic followers, particularly Hegel, achieved for the relation of the perennial to history. Seen critically, Hegel's philosophy may be viewed as a remarkable account of the relation between historical philosophies and the perennial ideal: the absolute is seen in the development of its components in history, and the completion of the historical can be evaluated only in relation to the absolute. But the ambiguities of this relationship led many of Hegel's successors to the conclusion that the ideal of a perennial philosophy is itself a delusion to be rejected (for example, Kierkegaard and Dewey), or that it must be found within the historical and changing rather than in a realm transcending it (for example, Marx, Croce, Jaspers, and followers of Dilthey).

The ideal of a perennial and complete philosophy still haunts the minds of philosophers, probably of a majority even in a positivistic and analytic age. The total effect of the Kantian and Hegelian revolutions of thought have stimulated later philosophers to assume three distinct positions with regard to this ideal.

(1) There is the view of those who have held that the perennial philosophy (in spite of Kant, or through a realistic interpretation of him) is still valid and effective; that its essential structure has been explicated in the thought of many thinkers and constitutes the firm structure, so to speak, about which Western thought and much of Eastern thought has developed. It is an ideal, but one actualized in part, and still in the process of actualization in full.

The Neo-Scholastic movement has in general held this position, as the essays in von Rintelen's work and the dominant theme in Hirschberger's *Geschichte der Philosophie* clearly show.

As an early representative of the same position, Adolf Trendelenberg deserves attention. A critic of Hegel and interpreter of Aristotle, he undertook to recall philosophy from "the humiliating position into which it had been crowded" in his day, and to restore "that philosophy which has been called to unite all peoples and times in a universal human vision and in the necessary task of the sciences, as Plato and Aristotle once did." He condemned the current philosophical tradition in which "a new beginning must be made and a new end reached in each head" (*Logische Untersuchungen*, 2nd ed., 1867, Preface; see also the concluding chapters of the 1st ed., 1840). In a less critical, more loosely eclectic way, the idea of an eternal philosophical order, including a way of redemption, but uniting Western thought with related traditions in the East is offered in Aldous Huxley's *The Perennial Philosophy* (1944).

(2) A second post-Kantian position is that of positivists of a wide variety of types, who follow Hume and Kant in their most empirical and analytic mood, and who reject the entire ideal of a perennial philosophy along with their repudiation of metaphysics. The list of those who have done this, from Comte to Ayer and his contemporaries, is a long one; it includes some of William James's essays on pragmatism, and many existentialists. But it is noteworthy that the internal drive toward metaphysics within these modes of thought (Comte's "unity of the sciences," Spencer's "first principles," the "realms of being" of Santayana, Heidegger's "*Sein des Seienden*," and recent attempts at "descriptive metaphysics") indicate that the hope of perenniality is not entirely dead, even in positivism.

(3) A third point of view about perennial components in philosophy is that which finds the perennial not beyond the history of thought but within it, either as the historical process of thought itself, or as an abstraction of a logical or metaphysical structure from it. In the former group may be considered Dilthey and such followers as Eduard Spranger and Arthur Liebert (for whom philosophy *is* its history), Hegelian temporalists like Benedetto Croce, and existentialists of the Jaspers type, for whom *das Umgreifende* is unattainable, and the perennial philosophy has never been achieved, "and yet such a philosophy always exists in the idea of philosophical thought and in the general picture of the truth of philosophy considered in its history over three millennia which become a single present" (*The Perennial Scope of Philosophy*, p. 25).

On the other hand, Jaspers may also be classed with those recent philosophers who have found perenniality of thought to be an abstraction from its history. "In our temporal transience we know the actuality and simultaneity of essential truth, of the *philosophia perennis* which at all times effaces time" (ibid., p. 169). Perennial meaning is to be found in the dialogue of the few great thinkers, carried on through time. Similarly, Nicolai Hartmann argued more analytically that it is the great problems which constitute the permanent component in philosophy, since they involve the unfolding of apories "without reference to their solvability and without flirting with preconceived results" (*Deutsche Systematische Philosophie* [1931], I, 281), while the depth-psychologist Erich Rothacker finds it in "the critical awareness of the eternal flood of dark and light pictures which arise from the depths of the soul." Among these quests for the permanent (if not the eternal) in the relative and changing, must also be considered the metaphysical methods of process philosophers as diverse as Paul Tillich and Alfred North Whitehead, one reviving Schelling, the other Plato himself, both of whom have sought an eternal through abstraction from the facts of change.

The problem of clarifying a conception of a perennial philosophy thus itself reflects thought about the entire history of philosophy, with respect to the question of the place of this history in the philosophic task itself.

BIBLIOGRAPHY

Jacques Barion, *Philosophia Perennis als Problem und Aufgabe* (Munich, 1936). M. C. D'Arcy, *The Meeting of Love and Knowledge: Perennial Wisdom* (New York, 1957). Paul Haeberlin, *Philosophia Perennis: eine Zusammenfassung* (Berlin, 1952). Johannes Hirschberger, *Geschichte der Philosophie*, 4th ed. (Freiburg, 1960), esp. Vol. 2. Johannes Hoffmeister, *Wörterbuch der philosophischen Begriffe*, 2nd ed. (Hamburg, 1955), article on "philosophia perennis." Aldous Huxley, *The Perennial Philosophy* (New York, 1944). Karl Jaspers, *The Perennial Scope of Philosophy*, trans. Ralph Mannheim (London, 1950). André Lalande, *Vocabulaire technique et critique de la philosophie*, 9th ed. (Paris, 1962), article on "philosophia perennis." Gottfried Wilhelm Leibniz, *Die philosophischen Schriften* . . . , ed. C. I. Gerhardt, 7 vols. (Berlin, 1875–90); idem, *Leibnitii Opera Philosophica quae extant Latina, Gallica, Germanica Omnia* . . . , ed. J. Erdmann (Berlin, 1840); idem, *Sämtliche Schriften und Briefe* . . . , ed. German Academy (Darmstadt and Berlin, 1923–). F. Medicus, "Von der Zeit und vom Ueberzeitlichen in der Philosophie," *Logos*, **12** (1923). Charles Sanders Peirce, *Collected Papers*, ed. C. Hartshorne and Paul Weiss, 6 vols. (Cambridge, Mass., 1931–35). F. H. von Rintelen, ed., *Philosophia perennis: Abhandlungen zu ihren Vergangenheit und Gegenwart* (Regensburg, 1930). Augustinus Steuchius Eugubinus, *De perenni Philosophia* . . . , Libri X (Paris, 1577). Adolf Trendelenberg, *Logische Untersuchungen*, 2nd ed. (Leipzig, 1867).

LEROY E. LOEMKER

[See also Baconianism; God; **Hegelian** . . . ; **Neo-Platonism**; Platonism; Ramism; Skepticism; Stoicism; Utopia.]

PERFECTIBILITY OF MAN

THE CONCEPT of perfectibility is parasitic upon the concept of perfection: to be perfectible is to be capable of being perfected. Perfection itself is a multi-faceted concept. The transcendental metaphysician identifies perfection with the possession of such characteristics as timelessness, immutability, self-sufficiency. To ask whether man is perfectible, from the standpoint of transcendental metaphysics, is to ask whether he can enter into union with the eternal, can rise above change, or can achieve self-sufficiency, at least in his relation with the world around him. From a functional standpoint, in contrast, perfection is identified with the fulfilling of a set task. A perfect man will be one who exercises his function perfectly, it being presumed that men have a function which is set for them whether by the State or by God. Man, that is, is regarded as a superior form of tool. The teleologist thinks of man, rather, as a being whose own inherent nature it is to achieve an ultimate end, e.g., happiness or union with the eternal, the only end in which he can find absolute satisfaction. To be perfect, from a teleological standpoint, is to have achieved such an end, to be fully happy or fully united with the eternal.

The aesthetic definition of perfection looks towards internal structure; the perfect is the orderly, the systematic, the harmonious. Man is perfectible, therefore, in so far as he can conquer every kind of disorder or conflict in his soul. This is linked with the concept of immaculate perfection, for which to be perfect is to be "free from flaw"—a flaw often defined, in theological terms, as "sin." Finally, perfection may be identified with moral perfection, itself diversely defined, whether as perfection in conduct or as perfection in motive. So it is sometimes argued that a man is morally perfect if he always acts in such a way as to produce the greatest happiness for the greatest number, sometimes that he is morally perfect only if he acts from a particular motive, e.g., the love of God. These various types of perfection shade into one another and are often conjoined in a single theory. But to understand the history of perfectibilism they must nonetheless be carefully distinguished.

Perfectibility in Pre-Socratic Thought. For the archaic Greeks, neither man nor god was perfect, metaphysically or morally. On the moral side, Homer and Hesiod were quite willing to ascribe to the gods such acts as stealing, deception, and adultery. As for metaphysical perfection, the gods were certainly both immortal and powerful. But they were not eternal. They were born, if for the most part by somewhat unorthodox methods; they can suffer injury; they are not omnipotent; not even Zeus is entirely self-sufficient. There is not the slightest suggestion that they are immutable, let alone that they possess that infinity of infinite attributes which Christian theologians were to ascribe to the divine. Nor should men try to be perfect, except in relation to a particular skill. To seek self-sufficiency, or perfect happiness, was to display "spiritual pride," *hybris*, and this was certain to attract the unfavorable attention of the gods.

By the sixth century, however, there was a growing dissatisfaction with the Olympian religion. At the same time new ideas were emerging about the infinite, the everlasting, the unchanging, which were profoundly to influence theology, and, through theology, the concept of human perfection. God had first to be perfected, before perfectibility could be ascribed to men. Anaximander's Boundless is not merely immortal, like the gods, but without a beginning. It is infinite and omnipotent. Whether Anaximander himself called the Boundless "divine" is a matter of dispute, but Aristotle, reporting his views, does so, and reflects the way in which Anaximander-type concepts were incorporated into Greek theology (*Physica* 203b 10–15).

In the satirical poetry of Xenophanes, the impact of the new cosmologies upon Olympian religious ideas is made explicit. Anthropomorphism is abandoned; God, as Xenophanes describes him, is in no respect similar to human beings (Kirk and Raven, frag. 173). It is "not fitting" to think of him as committing adultery, for example, not only because it is morally inappropriate to ascribe such qualities to him, but also because it would imply a degree of restlessness which is metaphysically inappropriate to a divine being.

Aristotle wrote of Xenophanes as the teacher of Parmenides and the founder, therefore, of the Eleatic School of Philosophy. That view is now generally rejected. But we can think of Parmenides, all the same, as carrying further Xenophanes' "metaphysical perfecting" of God. Xenophanes' God acts and thinks in ways quite unlike human action and human thought, but he still acts and thinks. Parmenides' "Being," in contrast, does not act: it simply is. Simple, eternal, immutable, devoid of all properties which involve negation or defect, it represents the ideal of metaphysical perfection in its completest form.

Such a "Being" is, on the face of it, completely different from the God of religion, a God to whom men can pray. But the two were nonetheless gradually identified. Or, at least, the properties which Parmenides had ascribed to "Being" were ascribed to the divine. And although the theory of God as "Being" seems to set up an absolute gap between such a "Being" and ordinary human beings, it was at the same time argued that man could, and ought to, perfect himself

by imitating, or uniting himself with, or contemplating, precisely such an Absolute Being. Men were to perfect themselves, that is, by casting off their relationships to the ordinary world, so far as that is humanly possible. Thus it was that Greek thought, and after it, certain forms of Christian theology came closer to the Buddhist conception of perfection, although not, usually, in such a degree as to suggest that the human being ought wholly to extinguish himself in the One.

Developments within religion itself facilitated this transition. The cult of Dionysius and the mystery rites, especially at Eleusis, had already suggested a closer relationship between God and man than the Olympian religion allowed. In the fifth century, Empedocles expounded a religious system of a novel kind, prophetic of what was to come. (How widespread religious ideas of this type were is a matter of dispute; there may have been an "Orphic religion" which they in some degree represent, but the point is hotly disputed.) Man, Empedocles suggests, is a demigod who, at the beginning of human history, committed a dreadful crime for which, ever since, men have had to pay the penalty. His proper home is amongst the gods, but as a result of his crime he is banished to the earth. There he lives in cycle after cycle of reincarnation until, by the exercise of purifying virtues, he finally returns to the earth in one of the higher forms of humanity, as prophet, poet, doctor, or statesman. Then at last he can achieve the state of godlike perfection. So Empedocles is prepared to write of himself that he is "an immortal god, mortal no more."

Pythagoras agreed with Empedocles that men could achieve godlike perfection by way of purifying themselves. But to purify themselves, he thought, men must first learn to philosophize; they can reach perfection only by contemplation, the contemplation of an orderly, harmonious universe. This conception of the perfect life, which identifies it with the life of contemplation, was to dominate Western thought for over two thousand years. It is significant that it also plays so large a part in the religions of the East; its roots lie deep in the human mind.

Plato and Aristotle. As an application of his general metaphysics, one would expect Plato to argue that no human being can ever hope to perfect himself, that nothing except "the Form of humanity" can ever exhibit humanity in its perfection. He avoids this conclusion by drawing a sharp distinction between soul and body (*Phaedo* 79A–D). The soul, he says, is by nature "like the Forms." Normally, this fact is concealed because the soul "is dragged down by the body" into imperfection. To perfect himself man must first subdue the body. Then, by the exercise of reason, he can lift himself to a point at which he can have knowledge of the Forms, and finally, so it is suggested in the *Republic*, of "the Form of the Good." Not everybody can reach this level; only those whose souls are dominated by reason and who have undergone a prolonged education. Perfection, that is, is for an elite; although the ordinary man can achieve "civic goodness," only the fit few can hope to reach the heights of philosophical perfection.

In Plato's later dialogues the theological emphasis is more pronounced. A much-quoted passage in the *Theaetetus* (176C) defines God as "perfect righteousness" and suggests that man can perfect himself only by imitating God. Plato's disciples identified the "God" of the *Theaetetus* with "the Form of the Good" of the *Republic;* and that in turn with the "One" of the *Parmenides* and the "Beauty" of the *Symposium*. So Plato was represented as teaching that man is to perfect himself by subduing the body, and becoming like God by seeing God as he "really is."

It was not too difficult to run together his teachings, thus understood, with Aristotle's, especially as they are propounded in the tenth book of Aristotle's *Nicomachean Ethics*. Aristotle, no doubt, explicitly rejects Plato's theory of forms. For a man to be perfect, on Aristotle's view, is for him to fulfill his natural function, to achieve "the good for man." But at the same time Aristotle's final conclusion is that man is at his best when he imitates God. Since God is entirely devoted to eternal self-contemplation, man perfects himself through the contemplation of God, or, at least, of "heavenly things."

Epicureans and Stoics. Aristotle identifies the contemplative life with happiness in its best and most complete form. Epicurus agrees with Aristotle that perfection lies in the achievement of happiness. But speculative activity, he argues, is necessary to happiness only in so far as it helps men to free themselves from their superstitious fears, their belief in gods who might at any time arbitrarily interfere in their lives, or punish them after death. Once the nonexistence of such gods has been demonstrated, further speculation is useless. Perfection lies not in contemplating the divine, but in the achievement of complete peace of mind by withdrawing from society to live a quiet life with like-minded friends.

It might be objected that men cannot hope to achieve complete happiness, thus understood. As human beings they are subject to the disturbing influence of pain. But the term of pain, Epicurus argues, is relatively brief. It is anxiety, not pain, which destroys men's happiness; they will find pain easy enough to bear if they achieve freedom from anxiety (*Kuriai Doxai*, 21).

The Epicurean ideal is entirely secular; it came into favor again in the seventeenth century, with the rise of secularism. Stoicism, in contrast, is essentially religious. Man is perfectible, for the Stoics, in virtue of the fact that he is rational and so far godlike. In the gods, as Seneca puts the point, reason is already perfected; in man it is capable of being perfected (*Epistulae morales*, 92). "Becoming like God," however, is for Stoicism a very complex concept. God is identified with the Universe. The perfected man, then, submits to the Universe; this is equivalent to obeying God, living according to Nature, being fully rational, becoming godlike. To adopt as one's ruling principle any of these criteria of perfection will be to undertake precisely the same course of action.

The real problem for the Stoics is to explain why man is not, as "a particle of God," automatically perfect. The Stoic solution is that men sometimes fail "to see things as they are." To become perfect, they must become indifferent to those things—everything, that is, but virtue—which do not deserve to be taken seriously. And they cannot do this while they think of such objects of desire, not as they are, but as their imagination gilds them. Men are tempted into avarice, for example, only because they fail to see money as dirty coin. This is a point on which Marcus Aurelius particularly insists (*Meditationes*, 11.16); interestingly enough, it is also to be met with in the Buddhist scriptures (Conze [1959], p. 104).

The perfected Sage will be attached to nothing but virtue, and for that very reason he has complete peace of mind. For if a man sets his heart on any other object of affection, it may at any time be taken away from him, by forces completely outside his control. Virtue alone lies completely under the control of the will. Virtue is indivisible, as Plato had argued; it is impossible for a man to be temperate if he is unjust or cowardly. There can, therefore, be no degrees of perfection; until a man possesses all the virtues, he is simply vicious. Not surprisingly, the Stoics found it hard to nominate examples of perfect men—true Sages—but they usually included Socrates and their founder, Zeno, in that category.

The Neo-Platonists. Philo is sometimes described, for all that he was an Alexandrian Jew, as the first Christian philosopher. He took the momentous step of identifying the Jahweh of the Old Testament, an essentially personal God, with the metaphysical God of the Greek philosophers. In accordance with what he took to be Plato's view, Philo argued that to achieve perfection men must attain to a vision of God, and that to achieve that vision they must shake off all concern with the body. He differed from Plato, however, on two important points: first, as a Jew, he insists on the importance of faith, faith in Revelation, for all that he is forced to interpret Revelation in an allegorical fashion in order to reconcile it with Platonism, and, secondly, he suggests that perfection is dependent on the exercise of divine grace. The Platonic-Stoic assumption is that man perfects himself by his own efforts; if he fails to do so this is out of human weakness. But, for Philo, faith is God's gift—his Revelation, after all, was only bestowed on his Chosen People—even although God grants it, Philo thought, only to those who are worthy of it. Men must first despair of themselves before they can achieve the vision of God (*De somniis*, I, X).

Philo's influence on such fellow-Alexandrians as Clement and Origen was extensive. Plotinus, however, does not seem to have read Philo, and he thinks of himself, indeed, as simply restating Plato's views. Until the eighteenth century, he was taken at his own word: "Platonism" meant, in the centuries to come, what we now call Neo-Platonism, the teachings of Plotinus, as interpreted by his successors, especially his Christian successors.

Men possess, according to Plotinus, not one but two souls: the embodied soul and the "true" soul. Sin and suffering belong only to the embodied soul; the "true" soul is divine. Man perfects himself by "cutting away" whatever holds him to the body, by the exercise first of virtue and then of intense intellectual activity. Spiritual progress consists in climbing a ladder; at the top of the ladder lies "union with the One." Whether at the point of union the individual soul completely disappears into the One—as into Nirvana—remains obscure, as it does in so many subsequent varieties of mysticism and, indeed, even within Buddhism itself.

Augustinians and Pelagians. The New Testament (Matthew 5:48) commands men to imitate God by becoming perfect. Early Christian writings like the *Didache* and such Christian fathers as Ignatius, Irenaeus, and Clement, took it for granted that men are capable of fulfilling this command. But even in the New Testament there are passages (I John 1:8–10) which suggest that men cannot, in this life, be perfect. That view came to represent orthodox Christian teaching, especially, although not exclusively, under the influence of Augustine.

Christian perfection involves loving God with one's whole heart and soul, and since the Fall, Augustine argues, man is incapable of doing so. His will is corrupted by original sin; he cannot succeed in casting off all forms of self-love or wholly freeing himself from the sensual attractions of the world. The Christian can no doubt make some degree of progress towards perfection, but even then not entirely by his own efforts; he is wholly dependent upon the grace of God, who has already determined who shall be members of his perfected elect. Augustine, that is, wholly rejects

Philo's view that grace is given only to those who have already made themselves worthy of it, or the Platonic doctrine that only by a prolonged period of education can men be perfected. No doubt, God could give to his elect such a degree of grace that they could perfect themselves in this life, but he has not chosen to do so: even the elect are to expect perfection only after death.

This interpretation of Christian doctrine did not go unchallenged, most notably by the British monk Pelagius and his followers. The Christian's duty, Pelagius argued, is clear and unambiguous: God has commanded him to be perfect and God would not command him to do anything which lies beyond his powers. As for the suggestion that man is helpless to improve himself morally unless with special grace from God, to take that view is to destroy all moral effort. God helps those who help themselves. Nor are men born corrupted. At birth they are neither virtuous nor vicious; their moral character lies in their own hands, in the free will with which God has endowed them and which he will help them to direct towards the good.

Pelagianism was condemned by the Council of Carthage in 417. Henceforth, it was official Roman Catholic doctrine that men could not perfect themselves without special grace from God. But the precise degree of perfection they could achieve with the help of that grace was still disputed, as was the exact relation between grace and free will. Aquinas tried to settle the question, without departing in any fundamental way from Augustine's teachings. He distinguished between man as he was before the Fall and corrupted man (*Summa theologica* II, i, 109, 3–4). Before the Fall, he argues, man could exercise the ordinary virtues—Plato's "civic goodness"—without divine grace. But even then he needed special grace ("elevating grace") to perform truly moral actions, actions performed entirely out of *caritas*, the love of God. After the Fall, man's position was very different. Even to fulfil the commands of the Law in a purely external way he needed grace—"healing grace." With the aid of grace, man can so far perfect himself that he is free of all those sins, "mortal" sins, which depend wholly on the reason. He cannot, however, avoid all "venial" sins, sins arising out of the flesh. So sinless, immaculate perfection is unattainable by man, even with God's help.

As for absolute perfection, the perfection which consists in the vision of God, that comes, Aquinas argues, only in eternity. Scripture presents Aquinas with some difficulties on this point. He finds himself obliged to admit (*ST*, I, 12, 11) that Moses and Paul had ecstatic experiences which took them out of the body. But with these exceptions, Aquinas denies that the vision of God—mystical perfection—lies within man's reach in this life. What the mystic sees is not God, but some natural object which symbolizes, or stands for, God.

The battle between Augustinians and Pelagians has continued throughout the history of the Christian Church. The Reformers were convinced that Aquinas had allowed too much to man. Man, Calvin argued, is utterly corrupt, from head to toe (*Christianae religionis institutio*, II, 1, 8). It is true that at the purely civic level, he is not entirely devoid of a natural inclination to virtue. But at the spiritual level his corruption is absolute. There is no scriptural ground for any distinction between "mortal" and "venial" sins; all sins are equally mortal.

In the nineteenth century, Pelagianism won its greatest triumphs, culminating in F. R. Tennant's *The Concept of Sin* (1912), as men became more and more conscious of their own power to remake the world. Tennant admits that perfection in the full aesthetic sense of the term—harmonious goodness achieved without effort—does not lie within man's reach. Men cannot be like God, or even like Jesus. But they perfect themselves by the exercise of their free will, insofar as they employ faultlessly the natural talents which they possess, in accordance with the ideals which they recognize.

The counter-reaction to nineteenth-century Pelagianism came after the 1914 war, in the writings of Reinhold Niebuhr and Karl Barth. Man inevitably sins out of pride, Niebuhr argues in *The Nature and Destiny of Man* (1941), because he cannot help trying to overcome anxiety, an anxiety implicit in his ontological situation, by remolding the world to a more secure shape. He is proud of such achievements, pitiful though they are. Karl Barth goes even further. Man, he agrees with Niebuhr, sins out of *hybris*—the sin of sins consists in man's belief that he can lift himself to the level of the divine. But only by recognizing his own complete worthlessness can he find salvation, entirely through God's grace.

Christian Perfectibilists. If orthodox Christianity has usually been antiperfectibilist, at least so far as the present life is concerned, not all Christians have been prepared to abandon perfectibilist hopes. Some of them have been buoyed up by the story told in Matthew (19:21) of the young man who is told that to be perfect he should sell what he owns and give it to the poor. Coupled with similar passages, this has been used to justify, from the time of Ambrose on, the idea of "counsels of perfection" which should govern the lives of the spiritual elite—poverty, chastity, obedience. From an early stage in the history of the Christian Church—adapting Greek precepts and Jewish examples—ardent Christians, intent on perfection, have separated themselves from the temptations of human society, in hermitages or, later, in monasteries. By subduing the flesh, they hoped to achieve a vision of God. It was possible to restrain such asceticism within the bounds of orthodoxy by maintaining that it was only a preparation for a future life, not an attempt to attain to perfection in this life. But Luther was certainly right in suggesting that hermits and monks often sought a perfection which was absolute, as Luther himself had done while still a monk—a perfection not very different from the perfection of the Stoic sage.

Another type of perfectibilism, often closely associated with extremes of asceticism, is mysticism. It was often defended against the charge of heresy by reference to the teachings of such Greek-inspired Church fathers as Clement, and, even more, the writings of Dionysius the Areopagite, sometimes known as "Saint Denys." Dionysius was a fifth-century Neo-Platonic convert to Christianity, wrongly identified by tradition with the Dionysius referred to by Paul (Acts, 17:34) and the French martyr Denys. Thus recommended, Dionysius' writings exerted a tremendous influence, even on Aquinas, and are constantly invoked in reply to charges of heresy levelled against fifteenth- and sixteenth-century Christian mystics. Were it not for his authority, indeed, it is very doubtful whether Christian mystics could ever have claimed orthodoxy for such views as that God can be reached only by passing beyond all knowledge and all rational understanding in order to achieve union with a Being whom it is misleading to describe even as God.

Mystics like Meister Eckhart, even so, found themselves condemned for carrying too far the doctrine that men can become at one with God. However, Eckhart's German disciples, Heinrich Suso and Johannes Tauler, escaped condemnation as did, in Spain, Teresa and John of the Cross—indeed, in varying degrees, they won the warm approval of the Church. Tauler draws a sharp distinction between the ordinary Christian and the "noble ones." The "noble ones" are capable of reaching a degree of "godlike freedom" in which they are entirely free from sin. Similarly, John of the Cross maintained that the soul could be freed by God's grace, preceded by long periods of self-denial and suffering, not only from actual sins but from every kind of imperfection. Both Tauler and John conceded, however, that even the "noble soul" might suffer a relapse into imperfection. As for the vision of God, or union with God, these could not, they admitted, be complete in this life, but they could certainly be attained momentarily and incompletely.

Within Protestantism, the Quakers asserted that men

could be perfected by Christ dwelling within them, in such a way that their actions were Christ's actions. But the most influential form of Protestant perfectibilism is John Wesley's Methodism. Perfection is a theme to which Wesley again and again returns in his writings. In his *Plain Account of Christian Perfection* (1777) he gives a general account of the history of his views on perfection, and grants that he had sometimes expressed himself too strongly. He had carried his perfectibilism to its most extreme point in the preface to a volume of hymns, published in 1741. The perfected Christian is there depicted as a Stoic Sage. He wants for nothing; he does not ask even for relief from pain; he never doubts what to do and is never troubled by temptation. Wesley's more characteristic view, however, is that men can never wholly free themselves from ignorance, or from temptation. But they can reach a point at which they are sanctified throughout, free from all actual sin except such as is based on ignorance. At first Wesley thought that, once achieved, this perfection could never be lost; his own experience in the Methodist movement finally led him to abandon that view.

Perfectibilist Heresies. Running parallel to Christianity throughout its long history—whether it predates Christianity is still disputed—is a heresy which has assumed a great variety of forms, but displays certain persistent features. It condemns the world and the flesh in terms more intransigent than Christian orthodoxy allows; it lays it down that a spiritual elite can reach a condition in which they are entirely incapable of sinning; it asserts that in order to achieve this state they have need of a Revelation which is either additional to, or hidden within, the received Scriptures. One reason why Christianity has, generally speaking, been antiperfectibilist is that it has been forced to set itself against the perfectibilism of such heretical opponents, whether the "Gnostics" or the Manichees, the Albigensians or the Brotherhood of the Holy Spirit.

An ambiguity attaches to the statement: "I can sin no more." It can mean either "I am now so perfect that it is impossible any longer for me to perform those acts which are unlawful" or "I am now so perfect that whatever I do no longer counts as sin." Similarly, "I have conquered the flesh" can mean either "I am no longer in the slightest degree involved in carnal relationships" or "I am now able to engage in carnal relationships without feeling any fleshly desire." The Christian critics of "Gnostic" heresies have always alleged that the heretics interpret these statements, in practice, in the second sense and that their antinomianism is nothing more than an excuse for immorality. In 1650 the English House of Commons found it necessary to pass a bill laying down penalties for those

who argued that the spiritual elite could without sin freely engage in "Whoredom, Adultery, Drunkenness or the like open Wickedness" (Cohen [1957], p. 326). Even the Quaker and Methodist movements knew men and women who interpreted their beliefs in this way (Hannah W. Smith, 1928). The quest for religious perfection has led men in some strange directions.

Perfectibilist Communities. It has led them, too, into some strange communities. Plato argued that only in a perfect State could men become perfect; Epicurus bid his followers desert society to enter communities of like-minded men; the monasteries were communities of men bent on achieving perfection. In the nineteenth century there were innumerable attempts to set up ideal societies, often based on heretical versions of Christianity. So John Humphrey Noyes, the founder of the Oneida community, convinced himself from his devoted reading of scripture that the teachings of the Old Testament had been abrogated since the year A.D. 70. Perfection, now, had to be thought of not as obedience to law but as mystical perfection, destroying all selfishness. The Oneida community was constructed to achieve that end. Men were not allowed to become attached either to property or to persons; they could continue to cohabit, for example, only if they were not seriously in love to a degree which made them possessive. The Stoic ideal, once more, re-emerges: to care for God and for humanity at large, but never to be strongly attached to any particular person or thing. Men should, in other words, seek to achieve a godlike self-sufficiency.

Secular Perfectibilism. Greek metaphysicians and Christian theologians had agreed that if man is to be perfected, this must be as a consequence of his relationship to the metaphysically perfect, his absolute love for, or vision of, or union with, God or with the One. Although, in general, philosophers of the Renaissance accepted these Platonic principles, there was one important exception—Pietro Pomponazzi's *De immortalitate animae* (1516). The intellect proper to man, Pomponazzi argued, is the practical, or moral, intellect, and this is the intellect men should try to perfect. Perfect knowledge and perfect happiness are for God alone, but all men can hope, and should attempt, to achieve moral perfection, here and now, in their present life. In the intensely religious atmosphere of the sixteenth century, so modest a doctrine could not flourish. But in 1601 Pierre Charron's *De la sagesse* set out, in the same spirit, to tell men how to achieve a perfection which was peculiarly moral, not based on metaphysical or religious presuppositions.

Augustine, and Calvin after him, had been prepared to admit that, from a merely external point of view, actions performed out of such theologically deplorable motives as pride and self-love were sometimes indistinguishable from actions performed out of a pure love of God. In his *Essais de morale* (1671–78, III, Second traité, Ch. X), Pierre Nicole put this same point even more forcibly. A society based entirely on self-love might be externally identical, he argued, with a society based entirely on the love of God, however differently they would be judged by God.

In the seventeenth and eighteenth centuries men began to ask whether, if this were so, self-love and pride could be as morally corrupt as Christian moralists had made them out to be. No doubt, there was a bad sort of self-love, a selfish form of pride, but a self-love and a pride on which a humanly ideal society could be constructed were not, on the face of it, to be condemned out of hand. So, whereas Pascal had firmly laid it down (*Pensées* [1670], 617) that "God alone is to be loved, self alone to be hated," Bishop Butler, a half century later, was prepared to maintain that "self-love in its due degree is as just and morally good, as any affection whatever" (*Sermons* [1726], Preface, §34). Thus it was that, in spite of resistance from faithful Augustinians, it gradually came to be assumed that the question whether men are perfectible is identical with the question whether they can reach a condition in which, from whatever motive, they always do the morally right thing.

In classical perfectibilist theories, man is perfected in a sudden breakthrough, a conversion of the soul, even if only after a long period of spiritual preparation. The Stoic Sage, as hostile critics remarked with scorn, might go to bed on Sunday night wholly imperfect and wake up perfect on Monday morning; no less suddenly might a Christian mystic discover God at work in his soul, or the soul of a Platonist be turned towards the Form of the Good. But in the eighteenth century the idea of an absolute, sudden, perfection is gradually replaced by the idea of a gradual, endless perfecting. To assert the perfectibility of man is now to maintain, as Robert Owen put it in his *Book of the New Moral World* (1836, p. iv), that man is capable of "endless progressive improvement, physical, intellectual, and moral, and of happiness, without the possibility of retrogression or of assignable limit." The only question was whether, and how, that "endless progressive improvement" could be brought about.

Perfection by Education. Pelagius thought that man could perfect himself by the exercise of his own free will; Augustine that only God could perfect him. But the Enlightenment assumption is that men can be perfected by other human beings, or by forms of social action. The most obvious candidate for such a role as perfecting agent, from Plato on, had been education. But education, Plato had presumed, could bring only a few men to perfection. What was novel and startling was the suggestion that all men, given the appropriate methods, could be educated to any desired level.

John Locke, in his *Some Thoughts Concerning Education* (1693), entirely rejected the Augustinian concept of original sin. Men, he admits, are born with an individual temperament, and sometimes with a temperament which inclines them to evil. But from the moral point of view, all the same, they are "white paper, or wax, to be moulded and fashioned as one pleases" (§216). Mystics had often suggested that men had first to be purged—reduced to the state of a sheet of white paper—before God could moralize them. Locke maintains that children are born in that condition, and ready therefore to be moralized by education.

As for the manner of moralizing them, it consists in establishing moral habits in the child, by getting him to see that to act badly will bring him shame and to act well will advance his reputation. Men are to be moralized, that is, by developing in them those motives to action which Pascal had regarded with particular horror (*Pensées*, 142)—the desire to avoid public reprobation and to win public esteem.

In his *Observations on Man* (1749), David Hartley supplied a theoretical underpinning for Locke's habit-forming education by developing an associationist psychology and made more explicit its perfectibilist consequences. Hartley set out to show that by appropriate methods of environmental control—"adjusting their associations"—all men, except a very few who suffer from physiological defects, can be elevated to a condition of moral perfection. In essentials, the Hartley type of perfectibilism has been continued into the twentieth century in J. B. Watson's *Behaviorism* (1924) and in B. F. Skinner's Utopia in the guise of a novel, *Walden II* (1948). Men, it is presumed, are completely malleable. Subjected to the appropriate forms of control, therefore, they can be perfected to an unlimited degree.

Perfectibility by Government Action. There is an obvious difficulty in the view that men can be perfected by education. In Christian theology, the only perfecting agent is God, and God is by definition perfect. But the educator is not himself a perfect being; his own education has been imperfect. Furthermore, whereas God is presumed to be omnipotent, the educator has only a limited degree of control over the child's environment. Both Locke's *Some Thoughts Concerning Education* and Rousseau's *Émile* (1762) describe a situation in which a solitary child is educated by a carefully selected private tutor, in an artificially purified environment. But obviously, if these conditions can be fulfilled at all, it will only be in a very few cases. If education is to be generally effective, many environmental perfectibilists have therefore argued, society must first be reformed through-and-through.

So, although in his *De l'esprit* (1758) Helvétius emphasizes the perfecting power of "education," he—like James Mill after him—uses that word very broadly to include any form of deliberate, or even accidental, social influence. In particular, he emphasizes the educative value of legislation. Good laws, he says, will destroy enthusiasm and superstition; it is by laws, too, that men are to be made virtuous—laws which will be designed to ensure that it is in their own interest to pursue the general interest. A problem still remains. Legislators are no more likely than anyone else to prefer the general interest to their own interest. Helvétius put his faith, however, in benevolent despots, of the type of Frederick and Catherine the Great. If only as a result of the laws of chance, he was convinced, such despots are bound to turn up at intervals.

In England, Jeremy Bentham systematized Helvétius' theory of legislation. But Bentham also drew attention to the limits of legislation, especially in his *Essay on the Influence of Time and Place in Matters of Legislation* (*Works* [1843], Vol. I). Legislation cannot, he thought, wholly destroy man's "mischievous passions." By its very nature, too, it employs penalties—a form of pain, and therefore of evil—as its instrument. So it cannot of itself destroy all evils.

As J. S. Mill has pointed out in his *Autobiography* (1873), these reservations served only to confirm Bentham's disciples in their belief that he was a man of exceptional moderation, no fanatic. Bentham's expressed conviction that legislation could lead men into a Promised Land was far more influential than the limitations on legislation to which he also drew attention. For all their disagreement with Bentham on crucial points about the desirable range of legislation, the degree to which it should be used to regulate economic processes, the Fabian socialists can properly be regarded as Bentham's heirs.

Anarchist Perfectibilists. From the standpoint of anarchism, the belief that State action of any kind can ever perfect men is the mistake of mistakes. State action, on the anarchist view, rests by its very nature on force and fraud; State power inevitably corrupts those who use it and wrings from those against whom it is directed nothing more than a servile submissiveness, as remote as can be from true morality. Man, the anarchists agree with Rousseau but in a more radical sense than Rousseau, is born free, but the State puts him in chains; he is born good but degenerates at the hands of society. Only by striking off his chains can man emerge as a fully moral being.

The most philosophical of anarchist writings is William Godwin's *Enquiry Concerning Political Justice*

(1793); the youthful Shelley is Godwin's best known and most devoted disciple. Godwin was a full-blown perfectibilist. Men must, he says, gradually destroy the institutions which corrupt them—government, private property, marriage. This done, men will gradually develop to a point at which they become godlike—not only fearless, truthful, honest, intellectually advanced, but even, Godwin dares to predict, immortal. The old ambition to become godlike recurs, that is, but now in a secularized, naturalistic form. Stoicism, too, found in Godwin a new exponent. One of his best-known novels, generally referred to as *Caleb Williams*, has as its main title *Things as They Are* (1794). It is by "seeing things as they are," seeing through the pomp and ceremony and superstition which surround Church and State, property and marriage, that men, according to Godwin, are to achieve moral perfection.

A peculiarity of Godwin's anarchism—in contrast with such later anarchists as Prince Kropotkin—is his extreme hostility to every form of cooperation. All forms of cooperation, he argues, are in some degree evil (*Political Justice*, Book VIII, Ch. VIII). Even orchestras and theatrical performances are forbidden in Godwin's ideal community, because they involve the musician's submitting himself to the judgment of a conductor, the actor to what other men have written.

The great proponent of perfection by association was Charles Fourier. He was certainly no anarchist, but is scarcely assimilable to any major political tendency, for all that he is often described as a "utopian socialist." In a series of works beginning with his *Théorie des quatres mouvements et des destinées générales* (1808), Fourier suggested a new form of social organization—the phalanx—designed to satisfy man's nature as it actually is, diversely passionate, as distinct from that uniform "true nature" moralists and theologians and metaphysicians try to impose upon him. For once, that is, a perfectibilist does not try to turn human beings either into gods or into mere instruments in the hands of God, the State, or the educator.

The most influential of anarchists, P.-J. Proudhon was, like Godwin, extremely suspicious of every form of "association." A just and free society, he argues, will be entirely based on free contracts, which should apply to every form of human relationships, not only to commerce. Only thus, not by the exercise of State power, and certainly not by setting up Fourier-type associations, can man advance towards that "age of universal fraternity" Proudhon sketches in his *De la justice* (1858). Proudhon, it should be observed, was vehemently opposed to the ideal of a static perfection of the metaphysical type, as was Godwin before him. Constant change, movement from one contract to another, is for Proudhon the very essence of society, in opposition to the Platonic worship of stability, of a form of social organization in which every man has a place and sticks to it.

Godwin rejected revolution; Proudhon thought it possible, at least, that a contractual society might be brought about without revolution, if only the bourgeoisie could be brought to see that it is in their own interests. Michael Bakunin, in contrast, is more like the anarchist of fiction. Society must on his view be utterly and violently destroyed; a more perfect society can arise only out of the ashes of the old. He subscribes, that is, to the myth of the fresh start: if only man was given a fresh start, he would not go wrong as he did before. Or if he does, then he must once more destroy everything and start afresh. For man's nature is good; if he is now corrupt, that is only because his social organizations corrupt him.

Genetic Perfectibilism. Plato, in his *Republic*, advocates State control over marriages, in order to ensure that the right kinds of children are bred; he suggests, indeed, that his ideal State might finally break down just because mistakes are made in breeding. But modern eugenics dates from Francis Galton's *Hereditary Genius* (1869). Galton advocates the formation of a superior race of men by controlled breeding, prohibiting certain matches (negative eugenics) and encouraging others (positive eugenics). In the mid-twentieth century the emphasis has turned, rather, towards modifying the genes themselves. In "Man's Place in the Living Universe" (1956), H. J. Muller has suggested that "by working in functional alliance with our genes, we may attain to modes of thought and living that today would seem inconceivably god-like" (Roslansky [1966], p. 127n.). But other biologists, like P. B. Medawar in *The Future of Man* (1960) have argued that the attempt to limit genetic diversity would destroy man, a conclusion which, so he explicitly draws the moral, sets a limit to any "theoretical fancies we may care to indulge in about the perfectibility of men" (p. 53).

Perfection by Scientific Progress. It is one thing to say that man can, in principle, be perfected by social action; it is quite another thing to say that he will ever in fact be so perfected. The idea of progress is an attempt to bridge this gap; the course of history, it is supposed, is such as to guarantee that man will eventually be perfected. This is either because God is on the side of perfection, and has a plan for man which will not be satisfied until man is perfected, or because there are natural laws inherent in history itself which are bound to issue in man's perfection. The two views may, of course, be combined: God, it may be suggested, is the true agent behind history, but he prefers to work through regularly-operating, empirically-discernible, social laws—not in "mysterious ways" but in ways which are patent once men have learnt to read history aright.

The belief that progress is inevitable got under way in the seventeenth century, developed rapidly in the eighteenth century, and assumed its most characteristic and most influential forms in the nineteenth century. It was at first linked with the conviction that in the seventeenth century there had been a breakthrough in man's intellectual history, a breakthrough which would guarantee man's scientific progress in the future, and, with that progress, his moral and political perfection.

The title Descartes first proposed for his *Discours de la méthode* (1637) was *le projet d'une science universelle qui puisse élever notre nature à son plus haut degré de perfection* ("the plan of a universal science which can raise our nature to its highest degree of perfection"). He was convinced, that is, that his "new method" would lift human nature to the highest possible degree of perfection. Bacon and Leibniz were no less confident that they had discovered a new and immensely fruitful method. Newton's scientific triumphs seemed to demonstrate that this was no idle dream, that man had in fact embarked, with the discovery of the mathematico-empirical method, on a limitless path of scientific discovery.

Progress in science is one thing, progress towards total perfection quite another. In the first place, the Newtonian method was not, on the face of it, directly applicable to the solution of man's moral and political problems. But the Enlightenment had no qualms on that point. The subtitle of David Hume's *Treatise of Human Nature* (1739) describes it as "an attempt to introduce the experimental method of reasoning into moral subjects." Indeed, it was a poor-spirited moral and social theorist, from Hume through to Bentham, who did not set out to be the Newton of the social sciences. Social theorists admitted, no doubt, that the methods which had to be applied to the solution of moral and social problems were not precisely Newtonian. But since the calculus of probability, as developed by Laplace and de Moivre, had proved to be applicable to the decisions of gamblers, it seemed reasonable to conclude that it was also applicable to moral and political decisions, as Leibniz and Hartley and Condorcet all maintained.

Even if mathematico-empirical science could solve all men's problems, however, its solutions still had to be generally communicated, before they could be effective. That is one reason why so many eighteenth-century philosophers interested themselves in the idea of a perfect language. Leibniz had suggested that the invention of such a language would break down the only important barrier to the spread of Christianity throughout the world; Condorcet applied Leibniz' argument to the diffusion of scientific knowledge.

A presumption still remains. Granted that it is possible by mathematical means to determine what it is best for men to do, and that it is possible, also, to express the conclusions thus derived in a language so clear that all men can understand them, they may still prefer to do something else, preferring the satisfaction of their own desires to the perfecting of mankind. Enlightenment perfectibilists, with few exceptions, do not take this possibility seriously. For they subscribe to the Socratic principle—which Godwin works out in detail—that if men go wrong, this is only out of ignorance. Once reason determines what it is best for men to do, the passions cannot but accede, and direct men's actions correspondingly. Progress in knowledge, that is, is automatically progress in virtue, provided only that such knowledge can be made available to all mankind. Ignorance and vested interests are the great enemies. In the end, however, vested interests are bound to be destroyed by science; the darkness of obscurantism will be dispelled by the light of science, however vigorously a reactionary Church and a reactionary State may try to keep men in ignorance.

Perfection by Necessary Laws. Not all Enlightenment philosophers, however, were prepared wholly to rely on the automatic growth of science to guarantee men's final perfection. There was always the risk, after all, that science might be destroyed by a new wave of barbarism. They sought to supplement their confidence in science with arguments derived from other sources, sometimes theological, sometimes historical.

Joseph Priestley, the most convinced of perfectibilists, is a case in point. Himself a distinguished scientist, he saw in the history of science the clearest demonstration that progress, now that the correct method had been discovered, could be continuous to an unlimited degree. He drew attention to such historical changes—for the better, he was sure—as the rise of commerce and the American Revolution, in order to support his claim that human society is steadily advancing towards perfection. But in the long run, it is his confidence in a benevolent, providential God which sustains his perfectibilist hopes. God has promised men that a time will come when they shall beat their swords into ploughshares. His infinite benevolence, too, can be satisfied with nothing less than the secular perfection of all men. Education, political revolution, the growth of science, the spread of commerce, are, in Priestley's eyes, the mechanisms through which God makes his purposes effective.

In the twelfth century Joachim of Floris had already deduced from his reading of Scripture that secular society would eventually be perfected, as part of God's plan for men. Joachim thought he could detect three great stages in human history, the age of the Father, the age of the Son, the age of the Holy Ghost—the last still to come. The first two ages had been ages of servility; the new age would be an age of freedom, in which men would at last be perfected. Each stage of history, he tries to show, contains within itself the seeds of a new age; what, to the superficial glance, looks like decline and destruction is in fact the birth-pangs of a new age.

Joachim's "three-stage" interpretation of history, and particularly his view that history would culminate in an age of freedom, anticipated the Idealist perfectibilism of the late eighteenth century and early nineteenth century. But it was there united with a developmental metaphysics, which Leibniz had sketched in his *De rerum originatione radicali* (1697). Every created thing, he suggests, must eventually realize the potentialities it contains, and will thus perfect itself. Ultimate perfection, that is, is metaphysically guaranteed. Kant's *Idee zu einer allgemeinen Geschichte in weltbürgerlicher Absicht* (1784) took over and developed this metaphysics, drawing the conclusion that, in consequence, man is bound eventually to live in a perfect State in which, alone, his potentialities can be fully realized. Kant's emphasis, it should be observed, is on the perfection of mankind as a whole in a perfect State, not on the perfection of individuals. Man's duty here and now is to sacrifice himself to the construction of such a State—to act as if it is realizable. But progress towards a perfect State does not depend, simply, on human aspirations. Man has, according to Kant, a "radical evil" in his nature which makes it impossible for him to act purely out of a sense of duty. His vices, however, are themselves essential to progress; out of his vices, his pride and ambition and competitiveness, the State emerges. To that extent private vices are (historically speaking) public benefits. In the end, however, to mold into shape the perfect State, there will be need of a perfect legislator; Kant is more confident, for this kind of reason, that it is man's duty to act *as if* the State will finally be perfected than that it will ever in fact be perfected.

Kant was almost certainly provoked into writing his *Allgemeine Geschichte* by the appearance of the first volume of J. G. Herder's *Ideen zur Philosophie der Geschichte der Menschheit* (1784–91), which he reviewed with some asperity. Herder, who had been one of Kant's pupils, replies to his criticisms in the later volume of *Ideen*. Herder has no enthusiasm whatever for the State, nor is he prepared to accept the view that everything must be sacrificed to the perfection of the generations to come. What is to be perfected, according to Herder, is not the State but "humanity," understood as including every potentiality for good of which men are capable. More immediately, however, men should strive for, and can hope to achieve, that kind and degree of perfection characteristic of their times. Every period of human history, according to Herder, has its peculiar potentialities and, in the end, humanity will benefit from their realization. It is ridiculous, for example, to condemn Shakespeare because his tragedies are imperfect when judged by the standards of eighteenth-century classically minded critics; he achieved perfections which the eighteenth century could not achieve, by working within the limits of his times. Thus Herder hoped to solve a problem which had beset Enlightenment perfectibilists. Judging the past by eighteenth-century standards they pronounced it a record of crime and folly. But this way of looking at the past left them, on the face of it, with little reason for believing that such dreadful times would not come again. For Herder, in contrast, every past age, even when it is greatly inferior from certain points of view to its predecessor, still had something new to contribute to the history of humanity as a whole, to its ultimate perfecting. If Roman culture is inferior to Greek culture, it at the same time brought to perfection aspects of humanity which the Greeks could not, in their historic situation, perfect—as did the Middle Ages, in relation to Rome.

Herder's *Ideen*, in seeking to understand the development of human society, placed considerable emphasis on geographical and even on anatomical factors—the separation of societies by mountains, man's upright posture. To such Idealists as Fichte this was an unforgivable concession to materialism. The history of society, as Fichte sketches it, is the history of the Spirit in its progress towards a condition of perfect love, perfect freedom, complete human unity. Material factors are irrelevant; it is the nature of the human spirit which determines what it must become. The old ideal of "union with the One" reasserts itself, but "the One" is now a form of human society, wholly unified, which is at the same time identical with Spirit in its most perfect form.

Hegel took over from Fichte that interpretation of history which sees it as moving through spiritual stages, logically related one to another. But the task of philosophy, on his view, is to understand the past, not to predict the future. It is enough for Hegel that the State has realized its potentialities in Prussia, and the intellect in his own philosophy. That this is not the end of history, he freely admits, but what form Spirit will take next it is impossible to tell. There is no way of determining, for example, what will replace philosophy now that it is perfected. (Some of Hegel's successors were to argue that it would be replaced by the history

of philosophy; others, like Marx, that political economy would take its place.)

Hegel's left-wing successors, with Marx the most influential of them, seek to reject whatever is theological in Hegel's thinking. In an important sense, it is their object to reinstate the humanistic ideals of the Enlightenment, while preserving Hegel's view that history necessarily moves in a particular direction. So they convert Hegelianism into a theory about the development of civilization, under the influence of social, especially economic, forces. They reject, too, the view that human society has perfected itself in the Prussian State, or could perfect itself in *any* State. The human spirit cannot come to perfection, on their view, while it is still restrained by laws imposed on it by the State; it is still not free. Marx remained enough of an Hegelian not to want to draw up a detailed blueprint for the future; it was enough for him that social development must issue in a communist society, a Joachimite kingdom of perfect freedom, in which men would work out of joy, not out of compulsion. Less cautious Marxists, like Trotsky in his *Literatura i revoliutsiia* (1923), did not hesitate, in contrast, to predict the emergence of a form of society in which all men will achieve, as a bare minimum, the intellectual and moral level of an Aristotle, a Goethe, or a Marx.

Evolutionary Perfectibilism. Engels welcomed Darwin's *Origin of Species* (1859) because it helped, he thought, to destroy theology. But the doctrine of natural selection, of itself, does nothing to encourage the view that man can, or will, be perfected. Should his environment alter, man might simply die out. Nevertheless, William Wallace, the co-discoverer of natural selection, indulged in a glowing vision of a perfected future, in which men would come into possession of powers they can as yet only dimly foresee. Herbert Spencer, an evolutionist before Darwin, converted "natural selection" into "the survival of the fittest" and applied it to man's life in society. Man, he argued, has not yet adapted himself to the social condition, which, unlike his pre-social environment, requires him to sacrifice his own interests to the common welfare. Inevitably, as a result of the ordinary processes of evolution, he will in the end do so; evolution must issue, so he thought when he wrote his *First Principles* (1862), in "the establishment of the greatest perfection and the most complete happiness" (Ch. XVI). He was enabled the more readily to come to this conclusion because, unlike Darwin, he continued to believe in the inheritance of acquired characteristics.

In later life, under the influence of the doctrine that "the universe is running down," Spencer was to modify his optimism. The passage quoted above, significantly enough, disappears from later editions of *First Principles*. In, for example, the revised edition of *Social Statics* (1892), he is content to conclude that the evils to which men are subject must gradually be diminished, not that they will ever disappear. More metaphysically minded "emergent" evolutionists like Henri Bergson had no such second thoughts. The universe, Bergson went so far as to argue in his *Les Deux Sources de la morale et de la religion* (1932), is a machine for making gods. Men must help in the task, however, by turning back from the life they now live, which is leading to an evolutionary dead end, towards a simpler life from which they can fan out once more in a new godlike direction. So the old ascetic-mystical ideal reasserts itself within an evolutionary framework.

Although T. H. Huxley vigorously opposed the view that evolution by itself would necessarily perfect man—man, he argued, in his lecture on "Evolution and Ethics" (1893) can progress only by struggling against the amoral tendencies of evolution—the more optimistic interpretation continues to have its supporters. T. H. Huxley's grandson, Julian Huxley, suggests in his *Evolution in Action* (1953) that man has at his disposal a new evolutionary force, education. His future progress is no longer determined by natural selection; with the help of education man can deliberately impose on the Universe the best and most enduring of his moral standards. Indeed, he will finally, Huxley agrees with Wallace before him, develop powers he does not now commonly—unless he be an Eastern mystic—possess. Evolution thus drives man towards becoming what is, by present standards, a superman, a being infinitely more perfect than man as we have so far known him.

Eugen Dühring, under the conjoint influence of Darwin and Marx, had already suggested in his *Der Werth des Lebens* (1865) that it is man's destiny to become a superman. The idea of a superman is more commonly associated with the name of Nietzsche. But while Nietzsche was prepared to say that the Universe "calls for" the Superman, he was not prepared to conclude that, if thus called, he would necessarily come. Indeed, in *Der Wille zur Macht* (1901) Nietzsche explicitly rejects the view that the "Superman" is bound to come into being as a result of the inevitable processes of evolution. If the Superman emerges, it will be because men, through their suffering and striving, have brought him into being. The belief in inevitable progress, Nietzsche suggests, is simply the old doctrine of Providence disguised in scientific clothes.

Hegel presented his philosophy of development, certainly, as if it were "the truth of theology," and the nineteenth century witnessed innumerable attempts to bring religion and science together in a grand evolutionary system. The fundamental mistake of tra-

ditional Christianity, Ernest Renan argues in his *L'Avenir de la science* (written 1848; published 1890) lay in its drawing too absolute a distinction between the sacred and the profane, the natural and the supernatural. As a consequence, Christianity identified perfection with a narrowly conceived ideal of supernatural perfection. For Renan, in contrast, perfection is the realization of all men's powers in an aesthetically unified whole. Man will achieve such perfection, Renan argues, only when he becomes part of a God whom he helps by his own efforts to bring into being. "Union with God," then, consists in becoming part of a divine being whose nature incorporates man's own strivings towards perfection.

At a more popular level, Henry Drummond in *The Ascent of Man* (1894) sought to demonstrate that God—the Christian God, in Drummond's case—worked through evolution to perfect man. In the twentieth century Teilhard de Chardin developed an elaborate Christian-evolutionary metaphysics—summed up in *Le Phénomène humain* (1955)—according to which man is able to perfect himself by cooperating with the natural world in its progress towards a perfect, coherent, love-infused society. But even that is not the final end. Man, according to Teilhard, will eventually be gathered up into the body of Christ; only in direct union with God will he attain his final perfection. Christian-mystical and evolutionary perfectibilism are thus amalgamated by Teilhard in a single system.

Perfectibilism Today. No variety of perfectibilism is yet quite dead, as the popularity of Teilhard's conglomerate sufficiently illustrates. Mysticism flourishes in a variety of forms, traditional and contemporary. There are still those who believe that social forces are at work in history which are bound, ultimately, to bring man to perfection, and still those who put their faith in education, or genetics, or social change, or psychological adjustment, or the fulfilment of prophecies. But that absolute confidence that man is on the way to perfection which permeates Winwood Reade's *The Martyrdom of Man* (1872) or H. G. Wells' *The Outline of History* (1919) is now but rarely paralleled. Men have come to fear, indeed, precisely those social tendencies which the Enlightenment greeted with such enthusiasm.

This is the principal theme of such "dystopias"—the very word is new—as E. I. Zamiatin's *My* (English translation *We*)—written in 1920 in the Soviet Union but first published abroad in 1924, Aldous Huxley's *Brave New World* (1932) and George Orwell's *1984* (1949). They depict a society in which technical perfection has been carried to its highest pitch, mathematics has been universally applied to the conduct of human life, an ideal language has made it impossible any longer for men to talk nonsense—nonsense as defined by the governing powers; happiness lies ready at hand, in the form of drugs; the rulers are an intellectual elite. And the effect is not the flowering, but the death, of freedom and justice. Skinner's *Walden II* will serve to remind us that the malleability of man is not in all quarters contemplated with despair rather than hope, but in *1984* it is the arch-villain who affirms the malleability of man as his fundamental creed.

The explanation of this change of tone is in large part socio-historical, rather than theoretical. The nearer men approach to a technologically perfect society, the less easy it is for them to believe that such a society promises men freedom and justice. The history of the Soviet Union has done much to destroy the naive belief that a despotism can be benevolent, or that once gained, power will ever be willingly surrendered. Even more devastatingly, the rise of Nazism in Germany has demonstrated that a country famous for its poets, its philosophers, its composers, its scientists, can yet degenerate into unprecedented depths of brutality and irresponsibility. Fichte and Winwood Reade looked forward gladly to a time when all men would think and feel alike, for they were convinced that what they would all think would be the truth and what they would all feel would be the noblest of sentiments; unanimity, nowadays, is something we have come to dread. The classical ideals of stability, order, uniformity were precisely the ideals invoked in Nazi Germany.

In general, the pessimistic view of human nature and human potentialities to which Augustine gave expression has in the twentieth century been revived not only by theologians but by Freudian psychologists and by comparative biologists. That man has, at least, a "radical evil" in his nature which society can in part control but can never hope wholly to destroy—and perhaps even, could not destroy without destroying civilization in the process—is now widely maintained. As for confidence in the future, the gloomiest of predictions about the inevitability of nuclear warfare, overpopulation, pollution, are today as commonplace as, forty years ago, was the hopefulness of Wells' *Outline of History*.

On the other hand, however, a curious variety of perfectibilist mysticism, often psychoanalytically tinged, has attracted some forceful adherents. One finds it, for example, in Erich Fromm's *Beyond the Chains of Illusion* (1962) or, very differently, in Norman Brown's *Life against Death* (1959), and in many philosophically oriented novels. Man is to perfect himself, to be once more united with "his own nature" and with nature at large, in perfect freedom.

More modestly, it can still be argued that man is perfectible, if all this means is that there is nothing in his nature to prevent him from becoming, with the help of others, a better person than he now is. That is the faith in which teachers, and parents, work. However often disappointed, it is a faith they cannot afford to abandon. It can survive the destruction of the belief that man is bound someday to live like a god in a perfect world.

BIBLIOGRAPHY

Almost any book on the history of political, social, metaphysical, or religious ideas contains relevant material. This bibliography contains only a small selection of the secondary material, concentrating, for the most part, on recent work which contains further bibliographies. For the theme as a whole see John Passmore, *The Perfectibility of Man* (London, 1970; New York, 1971). On the general concept of perfection see M. Foss, *The Idea of Perfection in the Western World* (Princeton, 1964).

On the Greeks: A. H. Armstrong, ed., *The Cambridge History of Later Greek and Early Mediaeval Philosophy* (Cambridge, 1967); F. M. Cornford, *Plato and Parmenides* (London, 1939; reprint 1950); E. R. Dodds, *The Greeks and the Irrational* (Berkeley, 1951); idem, *Pagan and Christian in an Age of Anxiety* (Cambridge, 1965); W. K. C. Guthrie, *A History of Greek Philosophy*, 3 vols. (Cambridge, 1962–70); G. S. Kirk and J. E. Raven, *The Presocratic Philosophers* (Cambridge, 1957).

On Christianity and perfection, useful general works include: R. N. Flew, *The Idea of Perfection in Christian Theology* (Oxford, 1934; reprint 1968); R. Garrigou-Lagrange, *Perfection chrétienne et contemplation selon saint Thomas d'Aquin et saint Jean de la Croix* (Saint-Maximin, 1923); James Hastings, ed., *Encyclopedia of Religion and Ethics*, Vol. 9 (Edinburgh, 1917): articles on "Original Sin," "Pelagianism," "Perfection"; K. E. Kirk, *The Vision of God*, 2nd ed. (London, 1932; reprint New York, 1966); R. A. Knox, *Enthusiasm* (Oxford, 1950; corr. reprint 1951); B. B. Warfield, *Perfectionism*, 2 vols. (London, 1931–32).

On more specialized topics, see for example: N. Cohn, *The Pursuit of the Millennium* (London, 1957); Hannah Whitall Smith, *Religious Fanaticism*, ed. R. Strachey (London, 1928); N. P. Williams, *The Ideas of the Fall and of Original Sin* (London, 1927); Robert McL. Wilson, *The Gnostic Problem* (London, 1958); H. A. Wolfson, *Philo: Foundations of Religious Philosophy in Judaism, Christianity and Islam*, 2 vols. (Cambridge, Mass., 1947; 1962); R. C. Zaehner, *Mysticism, Sacred and Profane* (Oxford, 1957).

On non-Christian perfectibilism see: E. Conze, ed., *Buddhist Scriptures* (Harmondsworth, 1959); M. Smith, ed., *Readings from the Mystics of Islam* (London, 1950); R. C. Zaehner, ed., *Hindu Scriptures* (London, 1966).

For Enlightenment perfectibilism see: J. B. Bury, *The Idea of Progress* (London, 1924; later reprints); Ernst Cassirer, *Die Philosophie der Aufklärung* (Tübingen, 1932), trans. as *The Philosophy of the Enlightenment* (Princeton, 1951); R. S. Crane, *The Idea of the Humanities*, 2 vols. (Chicago,

475

1967); Peter Gay, *The Enlightenment* (New York, 1966); idem, *The Party of Humanity* (Princeton, 1959; London, 1964); Arthur O. Lovejoy, *The Great Chain of Being* (Cambridge, Mass., 1936); idem, *Reflections on Human Nature* (Baltimore, 1961); J. A. Passmore, "The Malleability of Man in Eighteenth-Century Thought," *Aspects of the Eighteenth Century*, ed. Earl R. Wasserman (Baltimore, 1965); B. R. Pollin, *Education and Enlightenment in the Works of William Godwin* (New York, 1962); Joseph Priestley, *Priestley's Writings on Philosophy, Science and Politics*, ed. J. A. Passmore (New York, 1965).

Post-Enlightenment perfectibilism: Ernst Benz, *Schöpfungsglaube und Endzeiterwartung* (Munich, 1965), trans. as *Evolution and Christian Hope* (New York, 1966); C. P. Blacker, *Eugenics: Galton and After* (London, 1952); A. Bose, *A History of Anarchism* (Calcutta, 1967); D. G. Charlton, *Secular Religions in France, 1815–1870* (London, 1963); Theodore Denno, *The Communist Millennium* (The Hague, 1964); Élie Halévy, *La Formation du radicalisme philosophique*, 3 vols. (Paris, 1901–04), trans. as *The Growth of Philosophic Radicalism*, new ed. corr. (London, 1952); Julian Huxley, *Man in the Modern World* (London, 1947); James Joll, *The Anarchists* (London, 1964); F. E. Manuel, *The Prophets of Paris* (Cambridge, Mass., 1962); idem, *Shapes of Philosophical History* (Stanford, 1965); J. D. Roslansky, ed., *Genetics and the Future of Man*, Nobel Conference Discussion, 1965 (Amsterdam, 1966).

For twentieth-century antiperfectibilist writings, see: T. S. Molnar, *Utopia: The Perennial Heresy* (New York, 1967); Chad Walsh, *From Utopia to Nightmare* (London, 1962).

JOHN PASSMORE

[See also Anarchism; Buddhism; Death and Immortality; Education; **Enlightenment;** Evolutionism; Gnosticism; God; Happiness; Platonism; **Progress;** Sin; Stoicism; **Utopia.**]

PERIODIZATION IN HISTORY

History—the life of mankind in time—is a continuum. Subdivisions of historical time are a product of the human mind; only in this way is the mind capable of appraising the past and of assigning to the present its place within the stream of history. The so-called periodization of history in particular, which has been a recurrent theme for discussion by historians, contains of necessity an arbitrary element and often appears dated: it bears the stamp of the time of its origin. The best historians have warned against our becoming prisoners of a terminology of periodization, of "wrong labels which eventually deceive us about the contents" (Marc Bloch, *Apologie pour l'histoire*, Ch. IV, Part 3), and against our "ending up by giving the signs authority over their contents" (Fernand Braudel, *Annales* [1953], p. 70). For the same reasons Huizinga (*Task,*

Part 5) has come to the conclusion that division of historical time into periods is best served by colorless or emotionally neutral terms.

Three main categories or types of division of historical time are distinguishable, although all three may be applied simultaneously. The first of these types of periodization is merely chronological, that is, the enumeration of centuries and years (B.C., A.D., before and after the Hegira, etc.). The starting point for this kind of periodization—the beginning of an era (Judaic, Christian, Muslim, etc.)—reveals the underlying theology or philosophy of history. The second type of periodization springs from one of the two basic notions of historical thought, evolution. It regards a period as a phase in a larger development, whether of a nation, of a civilization, or of the history of mankind in general. Concepts of growth and decay (or cycles of progress and regress) are inherent in this type.

The third type of periodization bears characteristic features of the other fundamental concept of historical thought, historical individuality. It professes to summarize the essence of an age, and it requires the period to have a meaning in itself. This assumption presupposes an approach to the past resembling the scholastic "realism" of objective values. In using this kind of periodization the historian must be especially alert to the warnings mentioned above. Frequently terms which had been adopted for external reasons have been subsequently filled with contents originally alien to them.

In antiquity neither historical interpretation nor the aggregation of years had led to any periodization. Greek historiography was rational and pragmatic; it concentrated on political analysis and leaned towards a cyclical view of history which in modern times with Machiavelli was again to become a tributary to the stream of historical thinking. Time had been defined for immediate and practical needs, not by counting years over extended periods.

For Rome some scholars have found traces of an official "era" from the founding of the Republic (510 B.C.); yet since the second century B.C. annalists and in Imperial Rome historians such as Livy popularized the chronology *ab urbe condita*, i.e., from the legendary founding of Rome (753 B.C.), the effect was limited. The humanist scholars revived this dating; historians of ancient Rome retained it until the late nineteenth century.

With the Old Testament the theologians of the early Christian Church adopted the cosmological concept of the creation of the world; from the third century they constructed a chronological sequence *ab exordio mundi*. The *aetates* ("world periods") prior to Christ, initially assumed to number six of five hundred years each, were regarded as merely preparatory to the incarnation. This dating from the creation of the world was replaced in the seventeenth and eighteenth centuries by "B.C." (before Christ).

Ab incarnatione Domini, anno Domini (A.D.) for the era since Christ—the dating which was gradually adopted in the early Middle Ages—represents the new Christian world view. The Incarnation is the central event of history, the end of this imperfect world will be the Second Coming, the Day of the Last Judgment. No subdivisions were made; the only date of significance was the Millennium with its eschatological meaning. On the secular, political side this belief was complemented by the doctrine of the four empires which had its base in the prophecy of the book of Daniel, the Roman Empire being regarded as the last. The permanence of Rome and the concept of the *Translatio Imperii* (the transfer of the Empire from the Romans to the Franks by the coronation of Charlemagne, and later of Otto the Great) were integral parts of the medieval world view. World chronicles were based on these Christian and Empire concepts; histories of nonuniversal scope as well as local annals rested likewise on the Christian framework of time.

There was no need for our customary numerical subdivisions. Terms like *Quattrocento* or *Cinquecento* seem not to be traceable back beyond the eighteenth century. *Centuria*, alien to classical and medieval Latin, was coined by the humanists; in the seventeenth and eighteenth centuries it found its way into the vernacular as century and *Jahrhundert*. In a measure it replaced the less precise *saeculum*. *Saeculum*—a sequence of generations or even an infinite sequence of time—was related to ages of the world and to eternity (e.g., *in saecula saeculorum* in the Mass). The very opposite happens in *siècle*, which came to signify a precise arithmetic measuring of time. Voltaire wrote *Le Siècle de Louis XIV;* now we have periodicals such as *XVIIe Siècle*. Division of history into centuries thus proves to be a late product of "modern" scholarship.

The concept of modernity preceded this division into centuries. *Modernus* as a term had not been absent in the Middle Ages: it had been used particularly in contrast to *antiquus*, which referred mostly, if not exclusively, to antiquity, to the pre-Christian as well as to the Fathers of the Church. *Modernus* related most of all to the present, it could be merely descriptive yet could also include a positive as well as negative evaluation. Never did it indicate a division of time.

The first challenge to the Christian concept of the continuity of history under God, in which the period of antiquity was seen only as preliminary to the Christian era, came with the Renaissance. The humanists regarded themselves as initiators of a new epoch. Their concept of *Rinascita*, or rebirth of arts and letters, presupposed and often definitely stated that a decline had occurred in these fields since antiquity. The intermediate time was referred to, in this respect, as a period *medii aevi*, of neglect of letters, even of darkness (Petrarch). For very different reasons Protestant interpreters of the mid-sixteenth century would refer to the period of the medieval Church as an age of darkness. More significantly even, the Italian humanists definitely abandoned the concept of the continuity of the Roman Empire; to them it had been destroyed by the barbarian invasions. This interpretation eventually became interrelated with the revival of the cyclical view of history. In the following centuries the intensive concern with empirical observation and with the analysis of the background of states, law, and society, was bound eventually to undermine the traditional view of history with its eschatological outlook.

For almost two centuries the new insights were gained without shattering the Christian periodization of *aetates* and empires, much as the concepts of Christendom and of Europe coexisted, with the latter prevailing from the middle of the seventeenth century. Until then the old sequence of universal history was still retained in Protestant and Catholic textbooks alike; within this framework, political history in the course of time was allotted more space—the *historia civilis*—and sometimes the literary and artistic development was also periodized.

Only one new concept of periodization of universal history emerged in these times: the distinction between *antiquus* and *modernus*, which in Petrarch had already been related to the ancient and the post-ancient world, was now generally adopted. This entirely secular periodization, presented by the Leyden historian Hornius (*Arca Noae*, 1666), by the turn of the century was popularized in the textbooks of the German Cellarius. The final break came only with the Enlightenment. When in the middle of the eighteenth century Voltaire attempted to fill the gap left after Charlemagne; in Bossuet's *Discours sur l'histoire universelle* of 1681, he abandoned the Christian framework which Bossuet had retained (W. Kaegi, I, 221–48). In the original preface to his work Voltaire speaks expressly of "Modern History, since the decay of the Roman Empire." Modern as well as *neuer* as late as the nineteenth century meant frequently the whole of European history since the end of antiquity; professorships in different countries, such as Guizot's chair of *histoire moderne* (1812) attest to this as much as Ranke's *Epochen der Neueren Geschichte* (i.e., since the late Roman Empire) of 1854. For the period from the end of Rome to the revival of learning the Enlightenment had no common denomination. It was the romantics who applied to these centuries their new idea of historical individuality, and the *medium aevum* became the "Middle Ages" (*Mittelalter, Moyen Age*). In Latin textbooks of history the term *medium aevum* had existed for more than a century; Hornius had made it a subdivision of *historia nova* (*moderna*), and Cellarius had presented his *Historia universalis* as *in antiquam et medii aevi ac novam divisa* (Jena, 1696). But only in the course of the nineteenth century was "medieval" severed generally from "modern history."

Both terms then lost their former meaning: modern was no longer post-ancient history, medieval no longer merely a time of decay of classical languages. In due time professional historians became busy making subdivisions. "Modern" had to be followed by "recent" and "contemporary" (in French historiography *histoire contemporaine* means history since the French Revolution, *histoire moderne* the period prior to it), the Middle Ages were subdivided according to national inclination (French: *haut et bas Moyen Age*, German: *Früh-, Hoch- und Spätmittelalter*).

Whatever the new meaning of the now completely secularized history might be, it could not be derived from these terms any better than from the division into centuries. Thereafter, the two fundamental concepts of mature historicism, evolution and historical individuality, had a bearing on periodization. Since history moves in time its consciousness cannot be separated from the notion of change. When the Christian world view was secularized by the Enlightenment, the idea of progress came to the fore, perhaps to absorb even the older cyclical concept of rise and decline, with new growth emanating from the decline. From then on two main currents of philosophy of history influenced historical periodization: the positivist, which was linear-progressive, and the dialectical, which incorporated conflict. The first, beginning with Saint-Simon, was closely related both to the natural sciences and to the emerging social sciences; it focussed as much on changes in society as on the progress of thought. It found its most influential expression in Comte's "law of the three stages" of historical development—the theological, the metaphysical, the positive or scientific —and in Spencer's interpretation of universal history as leading from integration of society in the militaristic type to differentiation in the industrial type. The dialectical philosophy of history had been conceived by Hegel as the self-realization of the Universal Spirit, but Marx's dialectical materialism provided even more of an answer than positivism to the ever more absorbing questions of the economic and social structure of the nineteenth century.

The impact of these philosophies of history on the notions of periods which professional historians formu-lated is closely related to the dominating concept of civilization. In the Enlightenment the idea of a universal progress towards civilization had replaced the earlier Christian view of history. By the twentieth century, as scholars penetrated deeper into the structure and history of the non-Western world, the concept of civilizations took its place along with civilization. Finally, the ancient idea of necessary phases of political development, an undercurrent of historical-political thinking, was now, under the impact of the social sciences, joined by the notion of necessary stages of social-economic development. The willingness to universalize terms which had emerged from the interpretation of the history of Europe, was the result, and this at the very time when the other constituent element of historicism, the notion of individuality, took deeper root, and when historians strove to endow with content terms such as "Middle Ages," which had previously had only a formal meaning.

As opposed to the identification of the Middle Ages with "Dark Ages," the romantics had exalted the Middle Ages as the age of hierarchy, chivalry, municipal pride. On the other hand, from the latter part of the nineteenth century some scholars regarded the Middle Ages—in analogy to human life—as a general middle phase in the development of civilizations; such terms as the Greek Middle Ages, or the Russian Middle Ages, were coined.

Similarly, the stages of the economic (or so-called materialistic) theory of history which Marx and Engels had culled from their analysis of the European development have been universalized by contemporary Marxian-Leninist historians. Successive changes in control over the means of production are presented as traceable, even if not uniformly, everywhere in the development of mankind: from a primitive communal system via slavery to feudalism and from there to bourgeois capitalism, to be followed by socialism. In this manner the Western model is made into a general pattern of historical evolution. The two key terms in the Marxian-Leninist terminology, "feudalism" and "capitalism," have sometimes been used independently for the periodization of European history. Feudalism, a very specific military and social-political system in the Carolingian Empire and its successors, had become by the eighteenth century a rather indistinct term to denote legal relations between lord and peasant (O. Brunner). As such it entered into the comparative vocabulary. Eventually European historians defined the ninth to the twelfth centuries as characterized by feudalism, sometimes referring to them as "the feudal age." The concept of capitalism began its victorious career with Marx. Sombart's *Der Moderne Kapitalismus* (1902) described capitalism as an economic system which was specifically Western and which, beginning in the late Middle Ages, reached its climax in the late nineteenth century. Other historians have distinguished a period of predominantly commercial capitalism (fifteenth to eighteenth century) and of industrial capitalism which can be equated with the "Machine Age."

Marx's fundamental discovery of the global aspect of industrialization which would destroy or revolutionize all previous social relations has been increasingly accepted by historians as a main component for the further periodization of "modern history." In the present-day view, it is associated with the social-political revolution (which partly preceded, partly paralleled the industrial development), the first expression of which had been the French Revolution: the direction towards legal equality and towards emancipation of social groups from isolation and subservience, leading to political democracy—the central theme of Tocqueville (*De la démocratie en Amérique*, 1835–1840). In the lively opposition which the paper on "The Periodization of World History" by the Soviet historian E. M. Zhukov provoked at the International Historical Congress at Stockholm, 1960, there seemed to be consensus only on one point: that industrialization and technology had initiated a new age which could not be subsumed under "modern history." Whatever terms might be chosen for this last period (*histoire contemporaine, neueste Geschichte*), it seems to have come to an end in our own time, as titles like *The Political Collapse of Europe*, by H. Holborn (1951) or *The Passing of the European Age*, by E. Fischer (1948) suggest, and as G. Barraclough in *An Introduction to Contemporary History* (1964) points out. The entrance of the United States into the First World War and the establishment of the Soviet regime in Russia mark the year 1917 as the turning point. Others regard the irrationalism at the turn of the century as a break with the intellectual traditions of the whole European past and see these years as a pivotal period to usher in a new age.

The evolutionary aspect was less prevalent in other concepts of periodization whose aim was rather to show the distinctive character of a period. Frequently the successors summarized the essence of a previous age from which they had broken away or to which they even stood in conscious contrast. Adam Smith coined "mercantile system" (mercantilism) for the economic policy of the seventeenth and eighteenth centuries. "Absolutism" was an invention of the early nineteenth-century liberals who were critical of the previous governmental system (S. Skalweit in *Historische Zeitschrift* [1957], p. 65). Subsequently these terms were used by historians to characterize an age, overemphasizing by necessity specific features, and thus rendering questionable the usefulness of the terms.

Somewhat less controversial is the term "Enlightenment," "age of reason," for the intellectual characteristics of the eighteenth century. Yet in this case, too, the opposition of the following generation was instrumental in spreading, if not inventing, the term. The French *philosophes* would speak of *les lumières* in reference to their own age; they would even refer to it as *le siècle des lumières*, but the term is not as much in vogue as *Illuminismo, Aufklärung*, Enlightenment. Of these terms only the Italian word, which came into being in the early nineteenth century, appears to have been free from any derogatory connotation. In "Was ist Aufklärung?" (1784), Kant called his own age an age in which, by way of religious tolerance, man could acquire the ability to become enlightened, hence "Zeitalter der Aufklärung." This notion, however, was pushed back by the romantics' negative *Aufklärerei* ("to explain the unexplainable"); only gradually the more positive form of *Aufklärung* took root. A similar process seems to have been at work in English when the German term was adopted and translated as "Enlightenment."

A somewhat parallel transformation can be traced in the term "baroque." Originally of derogatory nature the word was used in the history of art by Wölfflin (*Renaissance und Barock*, 1888) to define the period following the Renaissance. At that time it was still a generic term, Wölfflin originally planned to include also a study of baroque in antiquity. Recently Carl Joachim Friedrich has analyzed most of the seventeenth century in all its manifestations, from statecraft to opera, as *The Age of the Baroque: 1610–1660* (1952).

The most genuine product of historical realism, i.e., of an attempt to penetrate into the essence of an age, is "Renaissance." Nevertheless, hardly any term has become more controversial. The Italian humanists were conscious that they lived in an age where art and letters had been restored. The road from this attitude via the limited concepts of *rinascita dell'arte* (Vasari, 1550) and *renaissance des lettres* (Pierre Bayle, 1695) to the mid-nineteenth-century "Renaissance" as a period has been traced by Wallace K. Ferguson. With Jacob Burckhardt's *Kultur der Renaissance in Italien* (1860), a portrait of Italy from the fourteenth to the sixteenth century was presented which thereafter determined our view of the Renaissance as a period. At the same time Burckhardt made "the discovery of the world and of man" his central piece. He thereby seemed to assign to the Italian Renaissance a place in the development of the European mind, an assignment foreshadowed in eighteenth-century interpretations of history and formulated a few years earlier (1855) in exactly the same way by Michelet for the French Renaissance. The unending discussion about the character of the

479

Renaissance amongst later historians, particularly contemporary scholars, centered around three problems: (1) Did the Italian Renaissance imply a break with the Middle Ages? (2) Is the Renaissance a period in European history; especially, was there a "northern Renaissance" and what was its relation to the Middle Ages? (the latter question became very acute with Huizinga's *Waning of the Middle Ages*, 1919); (3) Was the Renaissance, to use Hans Baron's paraphrase of a formulation of Burckhardt's, the "prototype" of the modern world?

It is apparent that any interpretation of the Renaissance is inextricably connected with each scholar's evaluation of that other term of periodization, the Middle Ages. Indeed, the content and limits of this rather accidental creation of Cellarius have been for a long time the crux of the periodization of European history. Within the so-called modern period most historians are willing to accept two dividing lines: one at the end of the nineteenth or beginning of the twentieth century when global history is the new entity emerging out of European history, the earlier one at the turn from the seventeenth to the eighteenth century (Paul Hazard's *Crise de la Conscience Européenne*, 1935), or else at the time of the French Revolution. But what of the preceding period and its relation to the so-called Middle Ages? If the concept of a medieval period can be made plausible, both its beginning and its end pose a problem.

The transition from antiquity to "European" civilization, involving a shift from the Mediterranean to Western and Central Europe, took on a new aspect after Henri Pirenne, in his *Mahomet et Charlemagne* (1922; 1937), claimed that the breakup of Mediterranean civilization occurred late as a result of the advance of Islam about 700. His thesis, which was based mainly on controversial evidence about the disruption of commerce, was in general not accepted, but it contributed to the growing realization that in the so-called "early Middle Ages" (sometimes referred to specifically as the "Dark Ages"), Byzantium and later on the Islamic World by far outstripped the Occident in strength and attraction, even at the time of the Carolingian Empire. *The Making of Europe* (Christopher Dawson [1932], up to about 1000), and *The Awakening of Europe* (Philippe Wolff [1968], dealing with the time from Charlemagne to Abélard, i.e., from the late eighth to the early twelfth century) are representative titles of recent scholarship. They are indicative of the realization that a long process of gestation preceded the emergence of Europe. On the other hand, it is illustrative that R. W. Southern, who analyzes the formative period of the eleventh and twelfth centuries in the most penetrating way, calls his book *The Making of the Middle Ages* (1953). He equates

the Middle Ages with the social-political order of Europe and its underlying religious and legal thought both of which crystallized in the eleventh and twelfth centuries. *The Renaissance of the Twelfth Century* (C. H. Haskins, 1927) played a decisive part in this crystallization. Institutions and the structure of society in their basic features persisted well into the period of the *ancien régime* (eighteenth century). For this reason some scholars, including the author of this article, have argued that, if we emphasize continuity over a long period of time—the *longue durée* whose problematic character has been stressed by Fernand Braudel (*Annales*, 1958)—we should at least replace the accidental term "Middle Ages" by the concept of the "Old European Order." The end of this period would be identical with the first division within the so-called "modern" period, the turn from the seventeenth to the eighteenth century. Such an interpretation would be based on the assumption that institutions, including educational curricula (including in this case the teaching of Aristotelian philosophy) and the structure of society are the very backbone of a civilization. This interpretation presupposes a "realistic" approach, a concern with historical individuality more than with evolution, with the "what" more than with the "why."

Recently the question of "modernity" has been posed anew with regard to a central problem in the emergence of the "new" society since the eighteenth century: the famous Weber thesis about the relation of Protestantism and capitalism has been under renewed scrutiny, with the result that the Counter-Reformation has been largely held responsible for the halt in the advance of capitalism (H. Luethy, *In Gegenwart der Geschichte*, Cologne, 1967; H. Trevor-Roper, *Religion, The Reformation and Social Change*, London, 1967). Whatever the merits of this thesis may be, it seems that along with the evolutionary question "Why not yet?"—a question which has dominated also the lively discussion about the origins of the Industrial Revolution—an analysis of the persisting attitudes and institutions is a necessity. Such an analysis reveals conceptual and structural features in the seventeenth century which date back to the so-called Middle Ages. If we cannot dispose of the traditional main terms of periodization in European history, "medieval" and "modern," we should remember that originally they were devoid of content and we should keep them, to use Huizinga's formulation, as colorless or neutral as possible.

BIBLIOGRAPHY

A. G. Barraclough, "*Medium Aevum*: Some Reflections on Mediaeval History and on the Term 'The Middle Ages'," in *History in a Changing World* (Oxford, 1956). O. Brunner,

Neue Wege der Verfassungs—und Sozialgeschichte, 2nd enlarged ed. (Göttingen, 1968); review article of the 1st ed. by F. Braudel in *Annales* (1959). A. Dove, "Der Streit um das Mittelalter," *Historische Zeitschrift*, **116** (1916), 209–30. W. Freund, *Modernus und andere Zeitbegriffe des Mittelalters* (Münster, 1957). D. Gerhard, "Periodization in European History," *American Historical Review*, **61** (1956), 900–13; idem, "Regionalismus und ständisches Wesen als ein Grundthema Europäischer Geschichte," *Alte und Neue Welt in Vergleichender Geschichtsbetrachtung* (Göttingen, 1962); idem, "Regionalism," *Studies in Diplomatic History in Memory of D. B. Horn* (London, 1970). O. Halecki, *The Limits and Divisions of European History* (New York, 1950). H. Heimpel, "Ueber die Epochen der mittelalterlichen Geschichte," *Der Mensch in seiner Gegenwart* (Göttingen, 1957). J. Huizinga, "De Taak der Cultuurgeschiedenis," *Verzamelde Werken*, Vol. 7 (Haarlem, 1950); trans. as "The Task of Cultural History," in *Men and Ideas* (New York, 1959). W. Kaegi, *Historische Meditationen*, Vol. I (Zurich, 1942), "Voltaire und der Zerfall des Christlichen Geschichtsbildes." A. Klempt, *Die Säkularisierung der Universalhistorischen Auffassung. Zum Wandel des Geschichtsdenkens im 16. und 17. Jahrhundert* (Göttingen, 1960), with extensive bibliography. W. Rehm, *Der Untergang Roms im abendländischen Denken* (Leipzig, 1930; reprint Darmstadt, 1966). E. Troeltsch, *Der Historismus und seine Probleme* (Tübingen, 1922), esp. Ch. IV, "Ueber den Aufbau der Europaeischen Kulturgeschichte." L. Varga, *Das Schlagwort vom Finsteren Mittelalter* (Vienna, 1932). E. Walder, "Zur Geschichte und Problematik des Epochenbegriffs Neuzeit und zum Problem der Periodisierung der Europäischen Geschichte," *Festgabe Hans von Greyerz* (Bern, 1967). E. M. Zhukov, *The Periodization of World History*, XIe Congrès International des Sciences Historiques (1960), *Rapports*, Vol. I, and *Actes du Congrès* (discussion); cf. E. Werner, in *Annales* (1962), pp. 930–39.

For the relation of antiquity to the Middle Ages, the following collections are helpful. F. Havighurst, ed., *The Pirenne Thesis. Analysis, Criticism, and Revision*, Problems of European Civilization (Boston, 1958). P. E. Hübinger, ed. (Wege der Forschung, Darmstadt): *Kulturbruch oder Kulturkontinuität im Übergang von der Antike zum Mittelalter*, Vol. 201 (1967); *Zur Frage der Periodengrenze zwischen Altertum und Mittelalter*, Vol. 51 (1969); *Zur Bedeutung und Rolle des Islam für den Übergang vom Altertum zum Mittelalter*, Vol. 202 (1969).

Especially for the Renaissance, see the following discussions and collections. D. Cantimori and E. F. Jacob, "La Periodizzazione dell'Età del Rinascimento nella Storia d'Italia e in quella d'Europa," *Comitato Internazionale di Scienze Storiche. X Congresso Internazionale di Scienze Storiche* (Florence, 1955), Relazioni, IV, 306–63, Atti, 536–48. K. H. Dannenfeldt, ed., *The Renaissance. Medieval or Modern?*, Problems of European Civilization (Boston, 1959). T. Helton, ed., *The Renaissance. A Reconsideration of the Theories and Interpretations of the Age* (Madison, 1961). L. Febvre, "Comment Jules Michelet inventa la Renaissance," in *Pour une Histoire à part entière* (Paris, 1962). W. K. Ferguson, *The Renaissance in Historical Thought* (Boston, 1948). D. Hay, *The Italian Renaissance in its Historical Background* (Cambridge, 1961). J. Huizinga, "Het Probleem der Renaissance," *Verzamelde Werken*, Vol. 4 (Haarlem, 1949); trans. as "The Problem of the Renaissance," *Men and Ideas* (New York, 1959). W. Kaegi, *Jacob Burckhardt*, Vol. 3 (Basel, 1956), Ch. VIII. T. E. Mommsen, *Petrarch's Conception of the Dark Ages*, in *Medieval and Renaissance Studies* (New York, 1959). E. Panofsky, *Renaissance and Renascences in Western Art* (Stockholm, 1960).

DIETRICH GERHARD

[See also Classification of the Sciences; Cycles; Evolutionism; Historicism; **Historiography;** Historiography, Influence of Ideas on Ancient Greek; Periodization in Literary History; Positivism; Progress; **Renaissance Literature;** Theodicy.]

PERIODIZATION IN LITERARY HISTORY

PERIODIZATION IN literary history can hardly be discussed apart from periodization in general history. The contrast between the modern age and antiquity was a central issue in literary debates for centuries. *La querelle des anciens et des modernes* at the end of the seventeenth century in France and its echo in England— where it is usually called the "Battle of the Books"— did much to define the idea of progress and demonstrate the emancipation of the moderns from the ancients. But Friedrich Schiller's distinction between naive and sentimental (1795) and the Schlegels' contrast of classical and romantic resume the same debate in different terms. The consciousness of a new age, in what later became to be called the Renaissance, implied as early as Petrarch a conception of the Middle Ages as the dark or monkish ages. It was extended to literature, though the term "Middle Ages" cannot be traced further back than to 1688 when Christophus Cellarius (Keller), in Halle issued *Historia medii aevi*.

In the seventeenth century specific ages of literature established their supremacy and attracted laudatory terms independently of purely political periodizations. For example, John Dryden in his *Original and Progress of Satire* (1693) enumerates the great age of Euripides, Sophocles, Aristophanes, "and the rest among the Greeks" alongside the age of Augustus and that of Lorenzo de'Medici and Pope Leo X (*Essays*, ed. Ker, II, 25). Voltaire in *Le Siècle de Louis XIV* (1751) lists the great French age with the ages of Pope Leo X, Augustus, and Alexander. Characteristically, he ignores the age of Pericles which, later in the eighteenth century, was usually added to the four great ages.

The metaphor of the Golden Age drawn for the scheme of mythical history first found in Hesiod's **481**

Works and Days was during the Renaissance proudly claimed for contemporary Italy. In a letter of Marsilio Ficino (1492) his own age is called golden and Erasmus, in a letter to Pope Leo X (1517) and the dedication of his edition of the Vulgate to the Pope, congratulated him for turning a worse than iron age into a golden one. Similar claims for their own time were not uncommon in the Spain and France of the sixteenth century, but a specific application of this term to the literature of a particular age seems later. Dryden, in the Preface to the *Fables* (1700) says that "with Ovid ended the golden age of the Roman tongue," but this opinion seems to have been common much earlier. Tiraboschi in his *Storia della letteratura italiana* (Modena, 1777), calls the sixteenth century of Italian literature *secolo d'oro* rather casually, and so does Algarotti in a letter of 1752. This must be also an old usage, as Bishop Berkeley refers, in *Alciphron* (1723), to "the golden age (as the Italians call it) of Leo the Tenth." (See Fritz Schalk, "Das goldene Zeitalter als Epoche," in *Exempla romanischer Wortgeschichte,* Frankfurt, 1966.) Bishop Hurd's dialogue "On the Golden Age of Queen Elizabeth" (1759) was an early statement of what to Thomas Warton seemed a commonplace. In his *History of English Poetry* ([1790], III, 490) Warton expressly states "The age of Queen Elizabeth is commonly called the golden age of English poetry." Later, in the context of the romantic revolt, Friedrich Schlegel in *Gespräch über die Poesie* (1800) and *Geschichte der alten und neuen Literatur* (lecture 15, 1815) attacked the concept of the Golden Age and pointed to its relativity. J. C. Gottsched identified the golden age of German literature as the time of Frederick the Great, in poets such as Besser, Neukirch, and Pietsch, completely forgotten even in Schlegel's time. Only in Spain has the term *el siglo de oro* become completely established. It seems to have been used first by Francisco Martínez de la Rosa, a romantic poet, when writing his *Poética* while exiled in Paris. Today it is usually conceived as extending well beyond a century from Garcilaso (who died in 1536) to the death of Calderón (1681).

The concept of the Golden Age suggested the application of a Silver Age to literature. In Ainsworth's *Latin English Dictionary* (1736) we are told that "Tacitus, Pliny the historian, Suetonius, and some other prose writers flourished in the silver age" and this usage must go back to Latin writers of the preceding century. Herder, in 1775 (ed. Suphan, 5, 633), and Friedrich Schlegel (*Kritische Ausgabe,* **11,** 127) refer to this contrast which seems, however, rare before the later nineteenth century. F. A. Wolf in his *Geschichte der römischen Literatur* (1832) does not even allude to it. An echo of this conception is Thomas Love Peacock's

witty little treatise "The Four Ages of Poetry" (1820) of iron, gold, silver, and brass seen as a sequence in antiquity and repeated inexorably by the moderns—which elicited Shelley's *Defense of Poetry* (1822, published 1840). These terms imply a concept of evolution, a scheme of the flowering and decay of literature.

The simplest and one of the oldest methods is the division by calendar centuries, decades, or years in annalistic fashion. "Period" is treated implicitly as merely a linguistic label, as a convenience in the delimitation of a topic or the subdivision of a book. This view, though frequently unintended, underlies many studies even today which religiously respect datelines of centuries or which set exact limitations of years (e.g., 1700–50) unjustified by any reason other than the practical need of some time limits. An extreme nominalism is implied in such practice. "Period" is, in this view, an arbitrary imposition on material which in reality is nothing but a continuous directionless flux. Richard Moritz Meyer (1901) defended his division of nineteenth-century German literary history by decades on theoretical grounds, but such self-consciousness is rare. One must realize, however, that the names of centuries at least in some literatures, particularly in Italian, have assumed an almost symbolic meaning, so that Trecento, Quattrocento, Cinquecento, Seicento, etc., probably under the influence of their meaning in the history of art, continue to be widely used, and also in English the term "Eighteenth Century" seems to have assumed a stylistic meaning about equivalent to neo-classicism.

Many period concepts in literary history presuppose rather a dependence on or parallel to historical, political, and social changes. Literature is implicitly conceived as determined by the historical, political, and social revolutions of a nation and the problem of determining literary periods is handed over to the general historian, whose divisions and periodizations are often adopted without question. Older English literary histories frequently were written in divisions according to the reigns of the English sovereigns. This division could and can hardly be carried out consistently. It would be difficult to defend an account of early nineteenth-century literature which respects the dates of the reigns of George III (d. 1820), George IV (d. 1830), and William IV (d. 1837). The distinctions however, between the literature under Queen Elizabeth (d. 1603), James I (d. 1625), and Charles I (d. 1648) still survive in such terms as "Elizabethan," "Jacobean," and "Caroline" drama.

Among the English monarchs, Queen Elizabeth and Queen Victoria, have come to symbolize the character respectively of their times and their literatures. The exact chronological span of their reigns is, however, usually not respected in practice. The term "Elizabethan" thus often includes dramatists up to the closing of the theaters in 1642, thirty-nine years after the death of the Queen. On the other hand, hardly anybody would refer to a man such as Oscar Wilde as a Victorian though his life falls well within the chronological limits of Queen Victoria's reign.

A special case in literary periodization is presented by the term "Augustan" which was applied early to the period after the Restoration to the death of Queen Anne. It claims comparison with the great age of Rome, flatters the reigning monarch, and congratulates the English poets. It seems first to occur in Bishop Atterbury's preface to Waller's *Poems* (1690); was applied to English literature by Leonard Welsted in 1724 (*Epistles, Odes,* etc. p. 45), and was used as a matter of course in Joseph Spence's sketch of a *History of English Poetry* (written in French about 1732–33, published in 1949): he speaks there of *notre Age Augustaine qui commence avec la Restauration de Charles 2.* Oliver Goldsmith wrote "An Account of the Augustan Age in England" for *The Bee* (24 November 1759) and Anna Seward refers to the age of Pope as "generally called the Augustan age" (in *Gentleman's Magazine* [April 1789], p. 192). The irony of Pope's Epistle to Augustus (i.e., George II, in 1737) must be seen in this context. All these examples precede the date (1819) given for the first occurrence of the term in the *New English Dictionary.*

Similar processes can be observed in other literatures: in French the term: "the age of Louis XIV" (who reigned from 1643 to 1715) is in literary use usually confined to the writings of the heyday of classicism: from Pascal's *Lettres provinciales* (1656–57) to Fénelon's *Télémaque* (1699). In other literatures the attention to monarchs varies with their importance: in Russia the dominance of the Czars assures some significance to distinctions among the ages of Peter, Catherine the Great, the two Alexanders, and the two Nicholases while in Germany only Frederick the Great and possibly the Emperor Wilhelm I have lent their names to literary periods (*das Friedericianische Zeitalter, das Wilhelminische Zeitalter*). Elsewhere (e.g., in Italy) terms of rulers seem almost without significance for literature.

Individual historical events and great social changes associated with them have provided other common period concepts. In England the Restoration of 1660 is also an obvious dividing line in literature; the French revolution of 1789, the fall of Napoleon in 1815, the 1830 and 1848 revolutions, and the establishment of the republic in 1871 are landmarks in French literary history. In Germany the end of the Thirty Years War (1648) and the Seven Years War (1753) are treated as

watersheds in literature. The list could be extended almost indefinitely. It gives rise to debates about the exact relation between these events and the literature of the times.

The dependence of literary periodization on political and social history has, however, never been complete. Periods were and are divided by diverse criteria derived rather from intellectual and art history and from the slogans of the literary movements themselves. In practice, the derivation of these names current today is bewilderingly diverse. A glance at the usual terms of English literary historiography suffices to reveal the lack of consistency in the usual sequence. "Reformation" comes from a movement mainly in ecclesiastical history; "humanism" describes a revolution in classical scholarship; "Renaissance" is a term first used widely in the history of the plastic arts; "Restoration" refers to a single political event; "Augustan" is a self-congratulatory term suggesting an analogy to Rome. "Classicism," "romanticism," "realism," "symbolism," "naturalism" are definitely literary terms. "Modernism," though wider in its implications, has also primarily literary associations.

In other literatures the picture is equally motley. In American literature "the Colonial period" is a well-defined historical term. "Puritanism" and "Transcendentalism" are religious or philosophical notions. "Romanticism," "realism," and "naturalism" are literary slogans. In France the neat literary sequence "Renaissance, classicism, romanticism, realism, symbolism" has prevailed, though *le siècle des lumières* emphasizes rather ideology. In German literary history, "baroque" has won out as a designation for the literature of the seventeenth century, while in the eighteenth century shorter subdivisions are generally accepted. Of these *Sturm und Drang* is a slogan derived from a contemporary play by Friedrich Maximilian Klinger performed in 1777, while *Klassik* is a term dating from the late nineteenth century to match *Romantik* a designation first used derisively for the Heidelberg group in 1808. The term *das junge Deutschland* has stuck though it was imposed by an arbitrary resolution of the German Diet in 1835 on a literary coterie of five authors. "Naturalism" is an established term in German literary history but neither symbolism nor realism have caught on though the term *poetischer Realismus,* invented by Otto Ludwig (1813–65), has made headway as a designation for the literature from about 1848 to 1885. A peculiarity of German literary history is the use of local terms such as *Biedermeier* (derived from a comic figure invented by L. Eichrodt in the 1850's) for the literature between 1815 and 1848 and "expressionism" (first used in 1910) which has begun to spread beyond the confines of the German arts and literature. 483

In Germany the most sustained efforts were made to apply the stylistic terms established or recently devised in art history to literary periods. The art historian Richard Hamann suggested the applicability of impressionism to a period in literature in his *Der Impressionismus in Leben und Kunst* (1907); the Czech art historian Max Dvořák was apparently the first to suggest the term "mannerism" for literature which has been taken up most influentially by Ernst Robert Curtius in his *Europäische Literatur und lateinisches Mittelalter* (Bern, 1948). "Baroque" has completely replaced the old deprecatory terms such as *Schwulst*. "Rococo" as a literary term emerges in the early 1920's even with an application to Pope's *Rape of the Lock*, in Friedrich Brie's *Englische Rokokoepik* (1927). "Gothic" has been used in German literary history largely as a term for the originally "Teutonic" (in defiance of the evidence for the origin of gothic in France) and recently even *Jugendstil* has been applied to literature.

All these terms raise large issues about the parallelism of the arts, of the possibility of a "reciprocal illumination of the arts," as advocated by Oskar Walzel in *Wechselseitige Erhellung der Künste* (1917), and of the existence and nature of a unitary *Zeitgeist*. The difficulties and dangers of the transfer of such categories to literature have been widely recognized: the arts and literature do not always develop step by step, the categories devised in art history lend often only vague and even misleading metaphors in their application to literature. Nevertheless the terms have also spread outside Germany, as the problem of the parallelism of the arts is very real indeed. In English the books by Wylie Sypher, *Four Stages of Renaissance Style* (1955) and *Rococo to Cubism* (1960), and of Roy Daniells, *Milton, Mannerism and Baroque* (1963) testify to the fascination of these transfers.

In Italy the century labels seem to have proved most useful but *Romanticismo* is used alternately with *Il risorgimento*. "Arcadia," derived from the name of an Academy founded in 1690, corresponds roughly to French and English neo-classicism. *Verismo* is the Italian term for naturalism, *Ermetismo* for symbolism. Similar lists could be drawn up for most other literatures.

In defense of this mixture of terms it may be urged that the apparent confusion is caused by history itself. Literary history has to pay heed to the ideas and conceptions, the programs and the slogans, of the writers themselves and must be content with accepting their own divisions. Consciously formulated programs, and self-interpretations cannot, one should grant, be ignored. Still, programs and names are only declarations of intentions which may not conform to performance, and the whole history of criticism provides only a running commentary on the history of literary creation. Contemporary programs and slogans, while offering suggestions and hints to the modern literary historian, cannot prescribe his own divisions, for the modern historian must describe, interpret, and evaluate works of art in his own terms, not always adequately described or even labeled by their contemporaries.

Besides, the terms of so confusingly different origin were usually not established in their own time. In English, according to the *New English Dictionary*, the term "humanism" occurs first in 1832; "Renaissance" in 1840; "Elizabethan" in 1817; "Augustan" in 1819; and "romanticism" in 1844. These dates are not reliable. "Augustan" occurs as early as 1690, "romanticism" in 1831, but they indicate the time lag between the labels and the periods which they designate. "Romanticism" as a term for the English poets of the early nineteenth century which used to be grouped under the "Lake," "Cockney," and "Satanic" schools was established only late in the nineteenth century. One cannot escape the conclusion that the sequence of English literary period names is a motley collection of political, literary, and artistic labels picked up here and there without much rhyme or reason.

Theorists of literary history have therefore argued for the adoption of a consistent scheme derived purely from literary history, from an observation of the decisive changes in literary evolution. A solution of the problem of evolution of literature is presupposed. A period is after all only a subsection of the universal development. Period is thus no metaphysical entity whose essence can be intuited, as conceived by some Platonizing Germans, nor an arbitrary cross-section preferred by nominalists of the British empiricist tradition, but rather a time-section dominated by a set of literary norms (conventions, genres, ideals of versifications, standards of characters, etc.) whose introduction, spread, diversification, integration, decay, and disappearance can be traced. These norms have to be extracted from history itself: we have to discover them in the observable literary process. "Romanticism," for instance, is not a unitary quality which spreads like an infection or a plague, nor is it a mere verbal label, but it is a historical category or, to use the Kantian term, a "regulative" idea (or rather a set of ideas) with the help of which we interpret the historical process. But we have to find this scheme of concepts in the process itself. This concept of the term "period" differs from one frequent use: its expansion to a timeless psychological type which can be taken out of its historical context and transferred anywhere else. Thus speaking of "Greek romanticism," "Latin realism," or "medieval classicism" takes these terms out of their historical context and either assumes some timeless set of types, or suggests a dubious hypothesis of recurrences and regularities in the manner of Oswald Spengler.

Thus a period is not a type or a class but a time section defined by a system of norms embedded in the historical place and irremovable from its historical place. If it were merely a general concept, it could be defined exhaustively. But the many futile attempts to define "romanticism" show that a period is not a concept similar to a class in logic. If it were, all individual works could be subsumed under it. But this is manifestly impossible. An individual work of art is not an instance in a class, but a part which together with all the other works makes up the concept of the whole. No individual work of art will ever realize the concept in its entirety nor can the concept exhaust its meaning. The history of a period will consist in the tracing of changes from one set of norms to another. While a period is thus a section of time to which some sort of unity is ascribed, it is obvious that this unity can be very imperfect. It means merely that during a specific period a certain scheme of norms has been realized most fully, i.e., has been dominant in the eyes of a later observer. If the unity were absolute, periods would lie next to each other like blocks of stone. There would be no continuity of development. Thus the survival of a preceding scheme of norms, and anticipations of a following scheme are inevitable, as a period is historical only if every event is considered a result of the preceding past and if its effects can be traced into the future. The decision about the dominance of specific norms at a specific time will be an act of criticism, as only critical judgment can single out the important works of art and their leading traits.

The critic will have to decide which works present a break with tradition, are genuinely innovating, and which revive older stages of the literary development, present throwbacks, and which simply continue the accepted tradition. Distinctions between epigones, dominant figures, and path-breaking avant-gardists will have to be made.

It will be wise to distinguish the concept of "period" from that of "movement," "current," and "school." "Movement" might be reserved for a self-conscious and self-critical activity which, in its metaphor, has the advantage of suggesting something of the dynamism of history implicit also in "current," a term made popular through Georg Brandes' influential *Main Currents of 19th Century Literature* (originally in Danish, 1872–90), and hence picked up by Vernon L. Parrington for his *Main Currents of American Thought* (1927–30), and many others. "School" might be reserved for a group of writers who derive or owe allegiance to some master. The term comes from art his-

tory and has its obvious dangers. The members of the so-called "school of Donne" did not go to school to Donne in the same way as painters were trained in the workshop of Titian or Rubens. But Alexander Pope's sketch of the history of English poetry, first published in 1769, lists all English poets under headings such as the School of Provence, the School of Petrarch, the School of Dante, followed by the schools of Chaucer, Spenser, and Donne. Thomas Gray's later sketch (in a letter 1770, first printed in 1783) speaks of three Italian schools of English poetry, headed respectively by Chaucer, Surrey, and Donne, and a contemporary School of France which began with Waller and culminated in Pope. The romantic "schools" in Germany and France designate a *coterie,* a *cénacle,* a *Pléïade,* or simply groups of friends and acquaintances with similar aims and ambitions.

Another criterion for the division of literary change has found much favor in the last hundred years. The concept of generations, first elaborated in Cournot's *Considérations sur la marche des idées* (1872), has since been applied to literary history. There are many theoretical discussions, e.g., by Julius Petersen and Eduard Wechssler, and more recently by Henri Peyre. A division by generations appears first in Friedrich Schlegel's *Geschichte der alten und neuen Literatur* (1815) and is carried out for the German nineteenth century in F. Kummer's *Deutsche Literaturgeschichte des 19. Jahrhunderts* (1909), and very skillfully for France in Albert Thibaudet's *Historie de la littérature française de 1789 à nos jours* (1936). But one should realize that generation, taken as a biological entity, offers no solution. If we postulate three generations in a century, e.g., 1800–33, 1834–67, 1868–1900, we must admit that there are equally such series as 1801–34, 1835–68, 1869–1901, etc. Biologically considered, these series are completely equal; and the fact that a group of writers born around 1800 have influenced literary change more profoundly than a group born around 1815 must be ascribed to other than biological causes.

No doubt, at some moments in history literary change has been effected by a group of young people of approximately equal age: the German *Sturm und Drang* or the French romantics around 1830 are obvious examples. Still, the generational unity is achieved by social and historical conditions: only people of a certain age group can have experienced such events as the French Revolution or the First World War at an impressionable age. The fact that Wordsworth was 19 and Coleridge 17 at the outbreak of the French Revolution has obvious bearings on the formation of their political views as has the fact that Byron was 27, Shelley 23, and Keats 20 at the time of the battle of Waterloo, and the victory of the Holy Alliance. In the writing of literary history such groupings by age will always run into difficulties when dealing with authors of longevity and a long productive life such as Goethe or Victor Hugo or with authors who began to publish late like Stendhal or Proust. In Albert Thibaudet's *History* Stendhal and Proust have to appear outside their generational position: Stendhal with the generation born in 1800, though he was born in 1783, and Proust with that of 1895, though he was born in 1871. The only workable concept of a generation is a historical one: the grouping caused by the impact of a great event. The rest is number mysticism.

BIBLIOGRAPHY

Louis Cazamian, "La Notion de retours périodiques dans l'histoire littéraire," *Essais en deux langues* (Paris, 1938), pp. 3–10; idem, "Les Périodes dans l'histoire de la littérature anglaise moderne," ibid., pp. 11–22. Harry Hayden Clark, ed., *Transitions in American Literary History* (Durham, N.C., 1953). Herbert Cysarz, "Das Periodenprinzip in der Literaturwissenschaft," *Philosophie der Literaturwissenschaft*, ed. E. Ermatinger (Berlin, 1930), pp. 92–129. Claudio Guillén, "Second Thoughts on Currents and Periods," *The Disciplines of Criticism*, eds. P. Demetz, T. M. Greene, and Lowry Nelson, Jr. (New Haven, 1968), pp. 477–509. J. Hermand, "Über Nutzen and Nachteil literarischer Epochenbegriffe," *Monatshefte*, **58** (Madison, 1966). Uri Margolin, "The Problem of Periodization in Literary Studies," *Hasifrut*, **2** (Tel-Aviv, 1969); English summary on pp. 269–70. Richard Moritz Meyer, "Prinzipien der wissenschaftlichen Periodenbildung," *Euphorion*, **8** (1901), 1–42. Josephine Miles, "Eras in English Poetry," *PMLA*, **70** (1955), 853–75. J. M. Ritchie, ed., *Periods in German Literature* (London, 1966). Le Second Congrès international d'histoire littéraire, Amsterdam, 1935: les Périodes dans l'histoire littéraire depuis la Renaissance; *Bulletin of the International Committee of the Historical Sciences*, **9** (1937), 255–398. H. P. H. Teesing, *Das Problem der Perioden in der Literaturgeschichte* (Groningen, 1949). René Wellek, "Periods and Movements in Literary History," *English Institute Annual, 1940* (New York, 1941), pp. 73–93. Benno von Wiese, "Zur Kritik des geisteswissenschaftlichen Periodenbegriffes," *Deutsche Vierteljahrsschrift für Literaturwissenschaft und Geistesgeschichte*, **11** (1933), 130–44.

On Generation in Literary History, see: Julius Petersen, "Die literarischen Generationen," *Philosophie der Literaturwissenschaft*, ed. E. Ermatinger (Berlin, 1930), pp. 130–87. Henri Peyre, *Les Générations littéraires* (Paris, 1948). Wilhelm Pinder, *Das Problem der Generation* (Berlin, 1926). Eduard Wechssler, *Die Generation als Jugendreihe* (Leipzig, 1930).

RENÉ WELLEK

[See also Ancients and Moderns; **Classification of the Arts;** Criticism; **Evolution of Literature;** Gothic; **Periodization in History;** Style.]

PHILANTHROPY

Philanthropy. The term "philanthropy," which entered the English language in the seventeenth century as a translation of the Greek φιλανθροπία and the Latin *philanthropia* ("the love of mankind"), has denoted various values and institutions. It has been related to many ethical and religious systems, movements of thought, and social contexts. Associated with charity, civic spirit, humanitarianism, social control, and social work, it has come in the twentieth century to mean, in the main, private and voluntary giving, individually and collectively, for public purposes. Its complex history can best be understood in terms of the related ideas that have characterized its evolution in time and place.

Pre-Greek Foundations. In the nineteenth century, when travelers and early ethnologists reported examples of mutual helpfulness among pre-literate peoples, the widening spectrum of thought about philanthropy was extended backward into prehistoric time. These reports gave support to Peter Kropotkin's contention in *Mutual Aid* (1890–96) that such behavior, whether innate or acquired, had been an indispensable factor in the evolution and survival of the human race and in the development of civilization. Without ignoring this movement in thought, the discussion of the ideas associated with philanthropy in the broadest sense may properly be confined to religious, ethical, and other firsthand written evidences. These, to be sure, can be understood only in relation to changing social, cultural, and institutional (and thus often nonverbal) contexts.

Chinese classical thought exhibited some sophistication and some differences in points of view toward philanthropy. Confucius and Mencius exalted universal benevolence as a personal virtue (Legge, I, 405; II, 485). Hsüntze in his *Essay on Human Nature*, regarded spontaneous sympathy with others as an acquired, rather than as an innate, human quality, but seemed to imply that this trait is within the capacity of all human beings (Dubs, p. 312). On the other hand, the Taoist Chuang-Tzŭ denounced philanthropy as a false outgrowth of human nature that disturbed human well-being (Giles, pp. 165–67). In practice, the maxim "love mankind" seems to have been largely operative in the extended family and in the institution of friendship until the early nineteenth century.

Personal generosity to those in need, especially to strangers, widows, and orphans, was commended or enjoined in the sacred writings and ethical teachings of pre-Greek civilizations. In some instances the practice of charity was advocated as a personal virtue, in others it was enjoined as a religious duty pleasing in the eyes of the gods. In some cases, notably in the Hindu scriptures, giving to the needy, especially to holy men dependent on alms, was an imperative duty, the fulfillment of which also rewarded the donor in a future state of existence. The general tone of admonition suggested that the emphasis was on the effect of giving on the donor, rather than on the recipient, except insofar as poverty was often identified with holiness. The teachings of Gautama, the Buddha (ca. 450 B.C.) not only sanctioned giving as a personal virtue but associated it with self-restraint as an evidence of rectitude. Buddhist institutionalization of philanthropy was evident in the establishment of hospitals, and in the example of King Aśoka in generous giving for the sake of spreading Buddhist truth. References, in more or less general terms, to a concern for the unfortunate appear in the Hammurabic Code (ca. 2000? B.C.), and in the Egyptian *Book of the Dead* in which a good man is identified as one who had given bread to the hungry, water to the thirsty, raiment to the naked, and a boat to one who had none. Egyptian inscriptions indicate that pharaohs regarded acts of benevolence and tomb-building as means of propitiating the gods in the interest of immortality and of insuring their own identity in the minds of succeeding generations.

Greek and Roman Philanthropy. Mercy, regard for others, hospitality and kindness beyond the limits of family, friends, and ethnocentric bounds found some expression in Homer, Hesiod, Herodotus, Thucydides, and the Attic orators, but the word "philanthropy," destined to have so long a history, makes almost its first appearance in Aeschylus' *Prometheus Bound*. Broadly speaking, in Greek thought the word connoted good citizenship and democratic, humanitarian inclinations. Xenophon called Socrates "democratic and philanthropic," that is to say, a friend of mankind. Demosthenes declared that "the laws ordain nothing that is cruel or violent or oligarchic, but on the contrary, all their provisions are made in a democratic and philanthropic spirit" (Macurdy, p. 98). With the Stoics the concept clearly transcended the dominant, ethnocentric emphasis on the rights and privileges of citizenship by emphasizing a kind and compassionate behavior toward all fellow human beings as a necessary corollary of a common humanity. In concrete terms and in an institutional implementation, however, the idea of love of mankind did not take among the Greeks the form of private charitable giving to the needy poor; guiding policy preferred the idea of public responsibility in the form of work relief projects or doles. When a man of wealth gave of his substance for public purposes, the objective was largely civic and cultural, as Alexander's gift of the library in Egypt, and as the endowment of the Academy and Lyceum indicate.

Roman concepts and practices did not greatly differ from Greek precedents although institutions for the sick and needy sometimes enjoyed private as well as public support. The custom of subsidies (*sportula*) by the wealthy and powerful to clients for political and personal reasons was not truly philanthropic in the original sense of the term, love of mankind.

Jewish Philanthropy. The age-old and possibly ubiquitous compassionate impulse to relieve suffering through personal service and the giving of personal substance to the needy, whenever a society developed marked inequality in possessions, found its most notable exemplification among the ancient Hebrews. In marked contrast with the permissiveness of charity in most early religious and ethical systems, and with the relegation to the state of responsibility for the poor in Greco-Roman civilization, Judaism made charity a central and imperative duty for each believer. In the fifth book of Moses (Deuteronomy 14:22) tithing was made a compulsory obligation: "For the poor shall never cease out of the land; therefore I command thee, saying, Thou shalt open thine hand wide unto thy brother, to thy poor, and to thy needy, in thy land." Similarly, it was an obligation to give one's bread to the hungry, to take the outcast into one's home, to clothe the naked (Isaiah 58:7). In making charity to all needy Jews an obligation (however gladly it was executed), Judaism identified charity and justice (*Zedakah*). Amos, Isaiah, and Micah severely attacked the exploitation of the weak by the strong, thus taking an innovating stand in attacking the problem of poverty at its root: a sense of social justice as well as humanitarian feeling is especially evident in the Psalms and in the Wisdom Literature of the Bible. Although the sense of justice was the animating note in the concept of charity, love of one's fellow men as the children of God was a fervent and even passionately expressed value—contrary to the contention of some Christian writers, such as Gehrhard Uhlhorn (*Christian Charity in the Ancient World*, New York [1883], Ch. 2). The idea of righteousness in the interest of ultimate salvation figured only in later Jewish thought. In addition to emphasizing duty, obligation, and ethical love, Judaism very early stressed the organization of charity as a principal institution of the synagogue. Jewish adherence to the religious duty of charity was reinforced by historical experience as an "out-group" in need of social cohesion, a need that was to continue through the Middle Ages and modern times.

The ethical and emotional distinctions in giving were explicated in a voluminous post-biblical, rabbinical literature. The best known medieval writer was Moses

487

Maimonides, who in 1201 codified the Talmudic rules in the Eight Degrees of Charity. The highest sanction was that given to the kind of helpfulness that anticipated charity by preventing poverty: "He who aids the poor to support himself by advancing funds or by helping him to some lucrative occupation" fulfilled a high degree of charity, "than which there is no higher." Charity in which the donor did not know the recipient or the recipient the donor, was more meritorious than types of giving in which the donor could take satisfaction from the appreciation of the recipient. Giving before being asked, was preferable to giving after being asked; and he who gave inadequately but with good grace, was less blameworthy than he who gave with bad grace (Frisch, pp. 62–63). Maimonides as well as other writers were aware of the complexity of motives in giving and, while recognizing utilitarianism and enlightened self-interest, attached supreme importance to religious, ethical, and humanitarian considerations.

The institutionalization of these ideas reflected the problems of the Jews in specific historical contexts. Thus in the Middle Ages particular attention was given to the care of orphans and the ransoming of captives. Jewish philanthropy was adapted to concrete needs by mass-scale efforts and constructive thinking. The far-reaching program of the Baron de Hirsch Fund (1885) in reducing the incidence of persecution of the Jews in Russia by assisted emigration is only one example of the preventive and resourceful quality of modern Jewish philanthropic thought and activity. Another example is the response of worldwide Jewry to the tragedy of coreligionists in Germany and German-controlled areas during the Nazi persecutions. Most striking of all examples is the creative role of philanthropy in the making of the state of Israel with its distinctive civilization.

Semitic influences may in part explain Muslim admonitions to charity in the Koran and, possibly, the establishment of hospitals at Bagdad and other centers. Nevertheless philanthropy in Muslim cultures did not develop an ideology and an institutionalization comparable in any sense to that in Judaic culture.

Christianity. The influence of Judaism on early Christian concepts and practices in philanthropy was positive and direct. Saint Paul developed the Hebrew idea of stewardship, which assumed that the rich man was not the owner but merely the steward of the wealth in his hand, and must therefore use it in accordance with God's commands (I Corinthians 13; II Corinthians 8, 9). Many of the ideas in one of the passages in the New Testament (Matthew 25:35–46) most relevant to Christian philanthropy are closely related to if not identical with Hebrew antecedents. Certain ideas in this passage and in others in the New Testament may, however, be regarded as striking a somewhat new emphasis. One is the idea of reward and punishment in future life for the fulfillment of, or for the failure to fulfil, charitable commands. At the same time Christianity emphasizes the idea that charity enhances life in this world by bringing the giver into closer spiritual relationship with God. If acts of charity, including personal service, were not executed for the most lowly and for those in greatest need, then they were not being executed for God the King.

It might seem that the millennial expectations of the early Christians and the resulting emphasis on the imperative need of readiness for the Coming, would de-emphasize the Jewish tradition of charity as a duty to those in immediate physical distress and need. But such was not the case. The bias of Jesus toward the poor and disinherited, as those most apt to receive the message of God's kingdom, and the feeling that wealth endangers the soul provided an undertone for early Christian precepts and practices in the sphere of charity. The early commitments to those in need, to the equalization of wealth, and to enhancing the sense of fellowship in the community of believers were regarded as expressions of Christian love. At the same time the emphasis on the sanctity and dignity of each individual encouraged the development of the fraternal implications of the doctrine of Christian love. The early appearance of Christian hostels for wayfarers and the incapacitated, and arrangements for mutual aid and group security indicate that the idea of the supreme importance of the care of souls was not entirely disassociated from the care and cure of bodies. This idea was further implemented in A.D. 321 when the emperor Constantine recognized the validity of gifts and bequests for Christian institutions, including charities.

Thus as early as the fourth century the concept of *philanthropia* was well established in Christendom. In the Eastern or Byzantine empire public philanthropy, which owed something to Greek classical tradition, and private charity, largely Christian in inspiration, achieved a notable record in charitable institutions, including monasteries. Yet the Byzantine concept did not include concern for the prevention of poverty; constant almsgiving perpetuated poverty and tended to maintain the status quo in the social structure (Constantelos, p. 284).

In the West the disappearance of the state in the Greek and Roman sense left a vacuum in which no purely secular feudal agency was equipped to provide relief for poverty and disability. Thus the Church found ample scope for institutionalizing the doctrine of love of fellow men by encouraging and sponsoring gifts for charitable hospitals, colleges, and monasteries with well-defined functions for the care of the poor.

The dominance of theology and casuistry as intellectual interests, together with the magnitude of medieval philanthropy, insured the probing of its ethical assumptions and implications. It was undeniable that certain scriptural texts, indicating that generous bestowal of alms is a Christian duty the fulfilment of which would insure heavenly reward, opened the door to self-regard in acts of pious charity. Theologians and canonists held, however, that giving, in order to be pleasing to God, must be an outward manifestation of a genuine feeling of justice and a true act of love. Despite this emphasis, much giving was impulsive, indiscriminate, and perfunctory. Some was motivated by mechanically measured considerations of self-interest: this gift was equal to so much merit, that gift, to so much more or less. It was against all this that Saint Francis of Assisi protested, insisting on the importance, indeed the necessity, of sacrifice, disinterested love, and the dignity and worth of poverty.

According to Church canon, giving was also qualified by consideration of how the donor came by that which he gave. In the thirteenth century, canonists held it meritorious to give property even if it had been improperly acquired, provided that legal title had passed to the donor and that no party was left to claim restitution. Long after the Reformation the ethical criterion of the ways in which wealth flowing into charity had been obtained continued to be a thorny matter. In the twentieth century, Washington Gladden, a Protestant theologian of the Social Gospel, argued, in regard to Rockefeller gifts to Church missions and other charities, that the Church could not properly accept ill-gotten gains or "tainted wealth" no matter how pious the donor nor how worthy the object of donation. This, however, was a minority view.

Finally, contrary to later contentions, medieval canonists considered the effects of charity on recipients. In general, it is true that canonists favored generosity in the execution of the command, "feed the hungry, clothe the naked." But Gratian's *Decretum* (1471), the great summing up of pros and cons on disputed theological points, noted that Saint Ambrose had suggested an order of preference among applicants for charity and that Saint Augustine had opposed donations to able-bodied beggars and vagrants. Thus in theory, if not in practice, medieval charity struck a balance between the interests and spiritual well-being of all concerned—donor, recipient, and community (Tierney, pp. 57–58).

The Transition to Modern Philanthropic Ideas.
While Christianity continued to exert great influence during and after the transition from medieval to modern times, secular conditions altered and finally transformed traditional ideas about charity and philanthropy. What may be regarded as the beginnings of modern philanthropic ideas can be explained in large part by the interlocking of traditional attitudes and values with new social, economic, political, and religious conditions. These included the decline of feudalism, the rise of cities and the middle class, the dislocation of populations resulting from the enclosure movement and other economic changes, and the Reformation itself, related, as it was, to the emergence of national states. The religious foundations, especially after the dissolution of the monasteries in Tudor England, were no longer able to perform their older functions or to meet newer social, economic, and vocational needs. All these changes account in part for the extraordinary development of private philanthropy in Tudor and Stuart England. The merchant and gentry classes poured wealth into charitable and educational institutions, in effect accepting the Tudor policy of shifting to localities and to private donors responsibility for poor relief, and the development of schools and other charitable agencies.

Among the ideas that intermeshed with changing conditions, special importance is to be given to the Protestant rejection, or at least de-emphasis on the doctrine of salvation by good works or individual acts of charity, and the emphasis rather on salvation by faith—the reception of the holy spirit suffusing the entire personality of those worthy of it in God's eyes. This de-emphasized traditional medieval charity. It is true that Calvin, in Reformation Geneva, found biblical warrant for voluntary gifts to the laicized and rationalized welfare agencies previously controlled by the Catholic Church; he also involved himself in the operation of the *Bourse française,* a private fund for helping French refugees. The Calvinistic re-emphasis on the stewardship of riches encouraged giving to needy persons and to Christian charities. Thus Thomas Fuller's *History of the Worthies of England* (1662) provided a special category for donors to public causes. The reliance in England, and to some extent in other Protestant countries, on philanthropy to meet major new social and economic needs was accompanied by the idea of public control over private charitable donations, other current bequests and gifts, and trusts. The Elizabethan Statute of Charitable Uses (1601) summed up much earlier experiment with public supervision. While in England and other Protestant countries the new idea of private responsibility under public supervision for social and economic needs was developing, in Catholic countries the Church in general continued to function in charitable and educational roles with minimal state supervision.

The social as distinct from the personal and religious character of the new philanthropy was exemplified in its nationalistic and class overtones. Fear of the effects of an apparently declining population on the supply of cheap labor inspired greater attention to the establishment of orphanages for foundlings and hospitals (in the modern sense) for the poor. The need of the Royal Navy for personnel was met in part by greater concern for waifs who were salvaged from the dregs of society and given proprietary care and training for national service. To reduce tax costs and to accord with the idea of self-help, philanthropy encompassed a wide spectrum of innovations designed to maintain the class structure. These included various schemes for putting the poor to work rather than permitting them to receive relief for which they rendered no service.

The idea of voluntary organization in charity developed with new social and economic forces associated with overseas commercial expansion, including the slave trade, the industrial revolution, and the need for a cheap but stable and reliable labor force. The prevailing idea that poverty is the result, not of social and economic dislocations, but of a failure of character, the vogue of classical economics with its emphasis on laissez-faire, and the rise of evangelical Christianity with its strong impulse toward social reform, all contributed to the dominance of the idea of voluntary association in philanthropy which, perhaps, was also suggested by the joint stock company. Contributions to voluntary societies that were addressed to specific social problems were now often, made in small sums and anonymously. These, together with larger gifts and bequests, were directed to the relief of distress, to hospitals, orphanages, schools for poor scholars, and agencies for training apprentices. The Society for the Promotion of Christian Knowledge, founded in 1698, which established over two thousand charity schools in the first century of its existence, was typical of the new emphasis on organized, voluntary philanthropy. So was the Society for the Propagation of the Gospel in Foreign Parts. Toward the end of the eighteenth century, with a mounting tide of conservative reaction against the French Revolution, new charity schools, organized by Robert Raikes and Hannah More and supported by voluntary, organized efforts, emphasized moral instruction as a means of reducing crime, and promoted religious teaching as a means of combatting radical innovation and "atheistic" Jacobinism.

Yet social control in associated, voluntary philanthropy was not the only idea underlying the proliferation of eighteenth-century philanthropy. Robert Eden, in *The Harmony of Benevolence: a Sermon on Psalm CXXXVI* (London, 1755), expounded the idea that benevolence is largely instinctive and emotional and that the satisfaction of this instinct is pleasurable. Oliver Goldsmith wrote that "the luxury of doing

good" enhanced self-esteem. And the traditional idea of humanitarian compassion was sometimes expressed with an ironical twist, as in William Blake's poems entitled "Holy Thursday" and "The Human Abstract":

Is this a holy thing to see,
In a rich and fruitful land
Babes reduced to misery,
Fed with cold and usurous hand? ("Holy Thursday").

Pity would be no more,
If we did not make somebody poor,
And mercy no more could be
If all were as happy as we ("The Human Abstract").

Modern philanthropic ideas were given worldwide connotations when the Catholic religious orders undertook to Christianize and civilize indigenous peoples overseas, and to support French, Portuguese, and Spanish colonial empires. The Anglican, Lutheran, Moravian, and Quaker efforts to Christianize Indians and African slaves was the Protestant counterpart. Yet these and other overseas philanthropic interests were not always self-consciously "imperialistic" or even religious. Such considerations, while present in Oglethorpe's venture in founding Georgia, were subordinated to his humanitarian aim of rehabilitating unfortunates who had been imprisoned for debt. Another example of the impact of the new philanthropic spirit on overseas expansion was the comment of Benjamin Franklin, on learning in 1771 of the proposed colonization of New Zealand, that "a voyage is now proposed, to visit a distant people on the other side of the globe; not to cheat them, not to rob them . . . but merely to do them good, and make them, as far as in our power lies, to live as comfortably as ourselves" (*Writings*, ed. A. H. Smyth, V, 342).

The secular and civic tone of Franklin's remarks characterized the newer ideas of philanthropy which he brought to fruit in Philadelphia. In organizing voluntary associations for promoting self-help, such as libraries and discussion groups, in furthering the fortunes of the College of Philadelphia (the University of Pennsylvania) and the Pennsylvania Hospital, Franklin devoted both his means and his services to philanthropy. He also developed practical techniques for fund-raising. These included the listing of prospective donors, personally visiting them and presenting persuasive arguments, following up the visits when results were not forthcoming, and using the new media of communication, especially the public press. In effect he was secularizing and democratizing the Christian concept of the stewardship of wealth, to which his attention had been drawn in his youth in Boston by Cotton Mather's *Essays to do Good* (1710). Franklin's innovating ideas for fund-raising were used throughout the nineteenth century, especially for enlisting support for colleges, and provided the basis for further amplification and refinement by the new professional fundraising organizations of twentieth-century America.

Humanitarian Reform. While the pecuniary element in philanthropy, both in concept and practice, was always an essential and sometimes the central emphasis, the term philanthropy was used in the late eighteenth and early nineteenth centuries in both England and America as a synonym for social and humanitarian reform. This identification was in part explicable by reason of the supporting pillars of social reform: evangelicism, humanitarianism, the idea of progress, and a middle-class awareness of the need for the maintenance of social order. No idea, however, was as important as the conviction that society has no right to advance its own aims and well-being at the expense of the disadvantaged individual. In the sense of social reform, philanthropy expressed itself mainly in the English-speaking countries in the movement for the abolition of the slave trade and, finally, of slavery itself; in the demand for the abolition of capital punishment and the reform of the penal code; in the concern for helpless and exploited children; in the battle for the political, legal, and social rights of women; in the more humane treatment of animals, the mentally ill, and others suffering from inherited or acquired handicaps; and in the elimination of war as a means for solving disputes among nations.

Philanthropy as social reform also expressed itself in charity societies, voluntary agencies for supplementing or even replacing inadequate public provisions for the care of the indigent poor. In both England and America the charity organization movement drew strength from the middle-class conviction that poverty is largely a matter of personal shortcoming and that the bestowal of relief or charity deteriorates the character of the recipient still further. "Human nature is so constituted," wrote a leading figure in the American charity organization movement, "that no man can receive as a gift what he should earn by his own labor without a moral deterioration" (Lowell, pp. 66, 76).

Thus the movement emphasized ways of making the unemployed poor self-supporting. The charity organization movement also sought to eliminate the wasteful duplication of agencies and the prevailing inefficiency in their operation. The idea of efficiency also figured in the emphasis on the careful investigation of the needs of each recipient. But this emphasis was also a function of the feeling that the problems of the poor and needy must be regarded in individual, personal, rather than class terms. To counteract the impersonal, even heartless treatment of those in distress by public agencies, the charity organization movement developed "friendly visiting," in which volunteers not only offered advice to the needy but showed personal interest and understanding. The related social-settlement idea also sought to bring the privileged and underprivileged into mutually rewarding human contacts. When the modern profession of social work developed from the charity organizations and the social settlements, scientific specialization and "expertise" largely supplanted the voluntary character of older practice. The first schools for training professional social workers were called schools of philanthropy.

The New Rationale of Large-Scale Giving. In the later decades of the nineteenth century and in the early years of the twentieth, ideas, in the main new, initiated an almost unprecedented chapter in the intellectual history of philanthropy. While a great deal of giving, both during the lives of donors and in provisions in their wills, continued to be directed toward charitable and religious institutions and causes, an increasing emphasis was put on the use of philanthropy for the prevention of shortcomings in the social order, and for the general improvement of the quality of civilization, especially through the extension of knowledge, the increase of scientific understanding and control through research, and through the enhancement of health and the aesthetic and recreational components of everyday life. This emphasis was expressed in the magnitude of donations by Americans of great wealth for new programs and improvements in existing colleges and universities, and for the establishment of new schools and universities associated with the benefactions of Cornell, Johns Hopkins, Vanderbilt, Vassar, Eastman, Stanford, and Rockefeller. It was also expressed in philanthropic support for art museums, symphony orchestras, parks, and other recreational facilities. Not since the Renaissance and Tudor England had wealth been used on such a scale for the improvement of cultural values.

No less important was the rationale for this philanthropy. In an article in the *North American Review* (1889), Andrew Carnegie, a "self-made" multimillionaire, argued that men of great wealth should, during their lifetime, allocate most of it to purposes other than the relief of individual misfortunes or incompetence, a relief which might be left to the state. Assuming that those who had made great fortunes had demonstrated their competence in the struggle for survival, Carnegie contended that these men had a social obligation to use their acquired wealth to provide opportunities for hardworking, competent, and ambitious youths and adults to advance themselves. This, he felt, could best be done by the use of private wealth for stimulating communities to support public libraries, baths, and recreational and vocational training including that

491

offered, as yet inadequately, for Negro youth. The millionaire, Carnegie concluded, should be ashamed to die rich. This rationale quickly came to be known as "The Gospel of Wealth." While in a sense a further secularization of the Christian doctrine of stewardship, it also emphasized prevention rather than cure, efficiency, and the equalization of opportunity.

Carnegie, together with the Rockefellers and the later Fords, was also a pioneer in the development of the modern foundation. This institution, to be sure, had a long history stretching back into ancient, medieval, and early modern times. But in its American form it differed from its predecessors, not only in the magnitude of its resources and in its use of specialized personnel for the allocation of grants, but in its emphasis less on specific purposes (though these continued to find expression) than on the general prevention of human suffering at home and abroad and on the enrichment of life through the improvement of educational standards, medical and social science research, and city planning, or through the support and dissemination of aesthetic values and opportunities. The promoters of the new foundations were in the main influenced by philanthropic interest and, to some extent, by the value of the foundation for creating a favorable public image of the donor. After 1917 and more particularly 1936, legal provisions in income-tax legislation, exempting gifts from taxation, stimulated much foundation activity, particularly in the case of the so-called family foundations, and in the new development of corporation foundations that directed their largess toward welfare programs, education, and local charities.

The foundation met with a mixed public response. At first, at the high tide of the Progressive movement, fear was expressed that its power and influence might become a bulwark for "conservatism," and inhibit the public assumption of social responsibilities deemed imperative by most liberals. In the early 1950's, during the "McCarthy period," foundations were attacked in some circles as supporters of subversive, "un-American" causes, particularly in the field of social welfare, and in grants given to liberal and radical scholars and other intellectuals. The use and abuse of tax-exemption privileges by many foundations, together with the secretive bookkeeping arrangements in some cases, led to Congressional investigations after mid-century, and to demands for a greater measure of public control.

The development of the welfare state in England, together with the new and large benefactions of the Wellcomes, Nuffields, and others that supplemented venerable trusts, raised again the issue of social efficiency or inefficiency of endowments, and the rela-

tion of these to public responsibility for social welfare and education. On the whole, in England and America, a consensus seemed to hold that by pioneering in needed fields in which government was reluctant to experiment, the foundation at its best had an important and creative role to play in supplementing the state as an agent for social well-being. Although in some noncommunist countries in Europe, Latin America, and Asia philanthropy in the Anglo-American sense showed signs of developing in the mid-twentieth century, in modern times its importance in the history of ideas has largely been confined to Great Britain and the United States, where individual responsibility and the principle of voluntary cooperation for personal and social well-being have been significant values in the culture. Yet, a caveat expressed in the 1930's by Reinhold Niebuhr summed up a criticism almost as old as philanthropy itself: "The effort to make voluntary charity solve the problems of a major social crisis . . . results only in monumental hypocrisies and tempts selfish people to regard themselves as unselfish" (Niebuhr, p. 29).

BIBLIOGRAPHY

The most satisfactory, comprehensive account of pre-Christian philanthropy is Hendrik Bolkestein, *Wohltätigkeit und Armpflege im Vorchristlichen Altertum* (Utrecht, 1939). James Legge's celebrated translations, *The Chinese Classics*, 5 vols. (Oxford, 1893–95), was reissued in Hong Kong in 1960. For Hsüntze's essay, see Homer H. Dubs, *The Works of Hsüntze* (London, 1928). Special studies include Yu-Yue Tsü, *The Spirit of Chinese Philanthropy. A Study in Mutual Aid* (New York, 1912). The literature on Jewish philanthropy is extensive; the best introduction is Ephraim Frisch, *An Historical Survey of Jewish Philanthropy* (New York, 1924). Translations from relevant Greek texts are conveniently accessible in Grace H. Macurdy, *The Quality of Mercy: the Gentler Virtues in Greek Literature* (New Haven, 1940). A sociological approach to the complex and developing ideas in the Christian tradition distinguishes Ernst Troeltsch's *Die Soziallehren der christlichen Kirchen und Gruppen* (Tübingen, 1922), trans. O. Wyon as *The Social Teaching of the Christian Churches*, 2 vols. (London and New York, 1931; reprint New York, 1960). It should, however, be read in connection with Michel Riquet, *Christian Charity in Action*, trans. from the French by P. J. Hepburne-Scott, in a series, *The Twentieth Century Encyclopedia of Catholicism*, Sec. ix (New York, 1961). The first comprehensive study of the subject in the Eastern Church is Demetrios J. Constantelos, *Byzantine Philanthropy and Social Welfare* (New Brunswick, N.J., 1968). A corresponding study for medieval charity in the Roman Church is Brian Tierney, *Medieval Poor Law. A Sketch of Canonical Theory and its Application to England* (Berkeley and Los Angeles, 1959). The earliest modern, and still useful, survey of the whole development of English philanthropy is B. K. Gray, *A His-*

tory of English Philanthropy (London, 1905). It has been corrected at many points and enormously enriched by the indispensable studies of W. K. Jordan, *Philanthropy in England 1480–1660* (London, 1960) and *The Charities of London* (London and New York, 1960), and by David Owen's *English Philanthropy* (Cambridge, Mass., 1964).

The best general introduction to American philanthropy is Robert H. Bremner, *American Philanthropy* (Chicago, 1960). Two basic sources for ideas about early American philanthropy are *The Apologia of Robert Keayne. The Self-Portrait of a Puritan Merchant*, ed. Bernard Bailyn (New York, 1965), and *The Writings of Benjamin Franklin*, ed. Albert Henry Smyth, 12 vols. (New York, 1907). Josephine Shaw Lowell's *Public Relief and Private Charity* (New York, 1884), and Frank D. Watson's *The Charity Organization Movement in the United States* (New York, 1894, and subsequent editions) are standard works. Special aspects of American philanthropy are treated in Roy Lubove, *The Professional Altruist. The Emergence of Social Work as a Career 1880–1930* (Cambridge, Mass., 1965); Merle Curti, *American Philanthropy Abroad* (New Brunswick, N.J., 1963); and Merle Curti and Roderick Nash, *Philanthropy in the Shaping of American Higher Education* (New Brunswick, N.J., 1965). An early critical work on American foundations is Eduard C. Lindeman, *Wealth and Culture* (New York, 1936). More objective is F. Emerson Andrews, *Philanthropic Foundations* (New York, 1956). Andrews' *Corporation Giving* (New York, 1952) is the first and still useful study of a new development in American philanthropy. The comprehensive survey edited and in part written by Warren Weaver, *United States Philanthropic Foundations* (New York, 1967), needs to be supplemented by monographic studies of specific foundations, relatively few having yet been undertaken.

Among the few philosophical analyses of the idea of philanthropy special mention is to be made of T. V. Smith, "George Herbert Mead and the Philosophy of Philanthropy," *Social Service Review*, 6 (March 1932), 37–54, and the study of Pitirim A. Sorokin, *Altruistic Love. A Study of American "Good Neighbors" and Christian Saints* (Boston, 1956).

MERLE CURTI

[See also Buddhism; Christianity in History; Democracy; **Faith, Hope, and Charity;** Millenarianism; Perfectibility; Progress; **Utilitarianism.**]

PIETISM

PIETISM is a movement originating in German Protestantism which sought to restore the genuineness of religious commitment by issuing "a serious call to a devout and holy life." Its influence spread far beyond German Protestantism, in fact far beyond organized religion, affecting men and movements of thought throughout the eighteenth and nineteenth centuries.

The founder of Pietism was Philipp Jakob Spener. His *Pia desideria* of 1675 enunciated six aims that were to become the program of Pietism: biblical study, lay activity, ethical revival, mollification of theological polemics, reform of theological education, renewal of evangelical preaching. Attacking conditions in the Lutheran Church, Spener maintained that an overemphasis upon purity of doctrine had intellectualized faith and had severed the nerve of the moral imperative. He was joined by August Hermann Francke, whose skill as an administrator helped to create institutions of education and of charity where the Pietist stress upon the practical side of Christianity could find expression. From the depth and breadth of the response to their work it is clear that Spener and Francke had uncovered a grave problem in the faith and life of the churches. There was a widespread yearning for authentic Christianity, for the restoration of sincerity and of simplicity, and for a religion based on faith, hope, and charity. The Pietist movement was responsible for the first successful missionary enterprise in Lutheranism. It produced a vast amount of devotional literature and regained the loyalty of many for evangelical faith.

From its German Lutheran origins Pietism reached into the life and thought of many other Christian groups. One of the most active Pietist groups was the Moravians. Johannes Amos Comenius had anticipated many of the themes of Spener's movement and had worked for the reformation of piety in the churches. The exiles of the *Unitas Fratrum* influenced Graf Nikolaus Ludwig von Zinzendorf, who was consecrated a bishop of the *Unitas* and established a renewed Unity of Brethren at Herrnhut. Zinzendorf's "religion of the heart" was an intense devotion to the person of Christ, combined with an emphasis upon Christian life rather than Christian doctrine. In 1738 John Wesley visited Herrnhut and soon thereafter experienced a conversion to a deeper faith. Thus German Pietism helped to launch the Methodist movement in both England and North America. America has, indeed, become the most fertile of fields for Pietism. Many of the immigrant groups had been part of the Pietist element of their mother churches, so that the various Protestant denominations have been represented in the New World by their Pietist interpreters. Even Roman Catholicism in the United States has taken on many Pietist features, such as a suspicion of scholarly theology and a stress upon the conversion of the individual. Such Protestant denominations as the Church of the Brethren and the Nazarenes embody a Pietism separated from its confessional origins, and many of the radical experiments in communal religion (for example, the Rappites and the Amana Community) have grown out of radical Pietism.

Pietism is, therefore, a movement of great importance for the history of modern Christianity. But it is also important for the history of ideas, both in its direct impact upon Christian thought and in its indirect bearing upon such areas as historiography, philosophy, literature, and education.

Both Spener and Francke were theological scholars, the latter having been professor of Scripture at Halle. Most Protestant theologians of the eighteenth and nineteenth centuries were affected in one way or another by Pietism, and even in their rejection of it they continued to bear its marks. Certainly the most impressive contribution of Pietism to theological thought was the theology of Friedrich Daniel Ernst Schleiermacher, who called himself "a Moravian of a higher order." Blending the Pietist doctrine of the primacy of religious experience with a romantic definition of *Gefühl* in contrast to both intellect and action, Schleiermacher defined religion as a "feeling of absolute dependence" and cast his interpretation of the distinctiveness of Christianity in this framework. Religion was neither a special method of knowing nor a way of acting, but a sense of reverence—on this thesis, despite his rejection of his Moravian upbringing as too narrow and the corresponding rejection of him by many Pietists, Schleiermacher and the more orthodox Pietists were in agreement. He was, in turn, "the church father of the nineteenth century" and the one theologian with whom every major Christian thinker after him had somehow to come to terms. Characteristically, more theologians were Pietists in their upbringing than in their mature systems, but Pietism is a factor to be considered in the intellectual development of all of them.

As part of its theological controversy both with dogmatic orthodoxy and with Enlightenment rationalism, Pietism helped to stimulate the rise of modern historiography. Gottfried Arnold, who was a protégé of Spener, applied the Pietist elevation of life over doctrine to the study of church history. In his *Unparteiische Kirchen- und Ketzerhistorie (Impartial History of the Church and Heretics)* of 1699 he showed that dogmatic orthodoxy had not necessarily produced Christian character in its adherents, and that, on the other hand, the heretics had frequently been more sincere and genuine in their devotion than had their persecutors. His work was in many ways an exaggeration of its own central thesis, but Arnold did open up new lines of inquiry into the development of Christian ideas and institutions. The modern attempt to understand ancient heresies in their own terms, rather than as distortions of orthodoxy, owes much to Arnold and thus to Pietism. He also helped to make the history of noninstitutional religion a proper subject for study, thus opening the way for church history to become a history of the Christian people rather than merely of prelates and theologians. Nor was Arnold's importance restricted to ecclesiastical history. Through his work and that of his colleagues, Pietism helped to liberate historical scholarship generally from the dominance of confessional polemics and to make possible the flowering of historical study in the late eighteenth and nineteenth centuries.

The significance of Pietism for the history of philosophical thought is less obvious, but no less important. It must be remembered that many of the leading figures in the history of German Idealism began their intellectual development as students of theology—and this meant a theology strongly tinged with Pietism. Thus it has been suggested that "the whole of Kant's moral philosophy might almost be described under the title of one of his last books as 'religion within the bounds of reason alone.' For him religion is primarily the Christian religion purified" (Paton, p. 196). And this interest in a "religion purified" is one that may well be traced to Kant's early training in Pietism.

The study of Hegel's early theological writings, especially of his work on the life of Jesus, has made it clear that he, too, owed much of his interest in the relation between historical particularity and ideal universality to the Pietist doctrine of the person of Christ. In the words of Richard Kroner, "Hegel's philosophy is in itself a speculative religion—Christianity spelt by dialectic" (Hegel, p. 53). It is ironic that Pietism, with its hostility to the claims of autonomous reason and even to the system-building of traditional theology, should have figured so prominently as a matrix for the systems of German Idealism.

The effect of Pietism on the history of German literature is somewhat more diffuse. Yet, to cite the most ambiguous figure, Johann Wolfgang von Goethe, the effect is undeniable. As Arnold Bergstraesser has suggested, Goethe "concurred with the pietists in their criticism of the established churches. . . . The vision of an evangelical communion of 'those good and wise to the highest degree' was to become the nucleus from which his ideal of a good society developed . . . and the pietist emphasis on the conduct of life rather than upon doctrine was in accord with his inclination toward tolerance" (Bergstraesser, p. 36). This is not to claim that Goethe was a Pietist, nor that Pietism was the sole source of his religious convictions. But much of his outlook on man and society can be read as a kind of secularized Pietism, in which the central emphases of Pietism remain but its specifically christocentric foundation has been replaced by a humanitarian ideal. A similar "afterglow" of Pietism may be seen in other literary figures. There is, for example, some reason to believe that Johann Christoph Friedrich Hölderlin, who was a student of theology at Tübingen, owed some of his religious sensitivity not only to the classicism that was his chief inspiration, but also to the Pietism in relation to which he developed his identity as a poet and a thinker; the later poems of Hölderlin make it clear that he continued to be fascinated by the figure of Christ, as he had learned to know it through his early Christian upbringing and his theological study.

In the field of education, the influence of Pietism was not only great, but deliberate. As noted earlier, one of the six goals set forth in Spener's *Pia desideria* had been the reform of theological education, and Francke had made his most lasting contribution in the schools he established. Like the historians and philosophers referred to in the preceding paragraphs, Johann Heinrich Pestalozzi began as a student of theology, and some students of his pedagogical theories have seen in them the evidence of this early interest. By most standards, Johann Bernhard Basedow must be counted a son of the Enlightenment rather than of Pietism; yet his affinities with Comenius and his concern with education as a means of developing the integrity of the individual suggest that Pietism, albeit in its more radical forms, may have been a factor in his thought. In a more general way, Pietism is evident in the educational development both of Europe and of North America, especially in the nineteenth century. Implicit in much of that development is a stress upon personal commitment that bears a distinct family resemblance to the Pietist preoccupation with individual conversion. And since so much of elementary education in the eighteenth and nineteenth centuries was in fact controlled by churches under the dominance of Pietism, it seems a safe generalization to suggest that Pietistic Protestantism has had a share in nurturing the moral presuppositions of many nations.

These diffuse influences of Pietism are a significant part of its history, but they must not obscure the principal task to which Spener, Francke, Zinzendorf, and other Pietists were pledged: the restoration of seriousness to Christian belief. Therefore the historical achievement of Pietism must still be seen primarily on the basis of its part in the process by which Christianity has been interpreted and reinterpreted since the Enlightenment. It has been blamed, and not without some justification, for the interpretation of religion as purely a private matter at a time when the social consequences of belief have become primary. To the extent that such a movement as "temperance" may be said to stem from Pietistic assumptions about ethics, its preoccupation with individual morality at the expense of the common good has been properly identified

as a source of profound mischief. Nevertheless, the chief residue of Pietism in the history of modern thought is probably to be sought in the deep sense of moral obligation and personal rectitude that has motivated many of the most decisive figures of modern history in their personal lives and in their public careers. The belief that one's life is to be evaluated on the basis not of the abundance of the things which he possesses, but of his service to God and to his fellow man is, to be sure, not an exclusive possession of Pietism; but it is largely through Pietism that this belief has become a part of our culture. Thus, in ways that its founders could not have envisioned and would have repudiated, Pietism has helped to bring about a reformation of human thought and action.

BIBLIOGRAPHY

The most influential work on Pietism is that of Albrecht Ritschl, *Geschichte des Pietismus*, 3 vols. (Bonn, 1880–86), whose violent prejudice against Pietism, and for that matter against any sort of mysticism, makes his account seriously unbalanced. The intellectual development of Pietism is provocatively traced by Emanuel Hirsch, *Geschichte der neuern evangelischen Theologie*, 2nd ed. (Gütersloh, 1960), II, 91–438. The historiography of Pietism is summarized in Johannes Wallmann, "Pietismus und Orthodoxie," Heinz Liebing and Walther Eltester, eds., *Geist und Geschichte der Reformation* (Berlin, 1966), pp. 418–42. Perhaps the most complete bibliography on Pietism is that of M. Schmidt, "Pietismus," *Die Religion in Geschichte und Gegenwart*, 3rd ed. (Tübingen, 1957–62), V, 370–81. The *Pia desideria* of Spener has been edited and translated by Theodore G. Tappert (Philadelphia, 1964), and Kurt Aland's *Spener-Studien* (Berlin, 1943) brings together much of the needed material. F. Ernst Stoeffler, *The Rise of Evangelical Pietism* (Leiden, 1965) is a useful introduction. References have also been made to H. J. Paton, *The Categorical Imperative. A Study in Kant's Moral Philosophy* (Chicago, 1948), and to F. Hegel, *Early Theological Writings*, trans. T. M. Knox, Introduction by R. Kroner (Chicago, 1948), and to Arnold Bergstraesser, *Goethe's Image of Man and Society* (Chicago, 1949). For Hölderlin, see E. Tonnelat, *L'oeuvre poétique et la pensée religieuse de Hölderlin* (Paris, 1950).

JAROSLAV PELIKAN

[See also **Church**; **Reformation**; Romanticism in Post-Kantian Philosophy.]

RHETORIC AND LITERARY THEORY IN PLATONISM

PLATO has been strongly condemned over the centuries for banishing the poets, or most of them at any rate, from his ideal republic and for approaching literature from the moral point of view. Before we join that chorus of critics, however, it will be well to remind ourselves that to discuss the social effects of poetry, and literature in general, is a perfectly legitimate form of criticism provided we do not confuse the moral with the aesthetic. Indeed, where, as in ancient Greece, poetry is a vital educational force—and Homer was still an important part of a Greek boy's education in the fifth and fourth centuries—such an approach is inevitable. It is therefore no surprise to find Greek criticism beginning as moral criticism, with Heraclitus and Xenophanes at the end of the sixth century already blaming Homer for his immoral stories about the gods.

This trend continued through the fifth century and was taken up by the philosophers in the fourth. The belief that the poets were the teachers of men, while first expressed by Aristophanes in our extant text, went back a very long way. Its origin should probably be traced back to the time before writing came into common use, when the epic poems, orally composed and orally transmitted, were indeed the main trustees not only of traditional history but of traditional morality as well.

Moreover, as the founder of the Academy and the spiritual heir of Socrates—who was the apostle of a new kind of education based upon the search for truth, the supremacy of reason in human affairs, and the responsibility of the individual for the state of his own soul—Plato was bound to investigate the claims made on behalf of the poets; that they were the teachers of the art of living, as well as the similar and more recent claims of the Sophists. What knowledge did poets or Sophists have, which they were able to communicate?

When Socrates was told that the oracle of Delphi had declared that no man in Greece was wiser than he, he set out to investigate the knowledge of others, and we are told in the *Apology* that he went to the poets, among others, and found them quite unable to explain their own poetry. Since knowledge to him meant to be able to give a reasonable account of what one knows, he came to the conclusion that the poets wrote their fine poems when inspired, but without knowledge of the things they wrote about. This view is further investigated in the *Ion*. Ion is a rhapsode who claims to recite and to talk about Homer better than anyone else. This should mean, Socrates tells him, that he understands the thought of the poet as well as the words since he must be able to interpret the poem to his audience. Further, he must surely be acquainted with other poets before he is able to judge the quality of Homer's poetry. Ion, however, firmly disclaims any knowledge of other poets. If this is true,

it would seem that he, like the poet himself, relies on inspiration rather than knowledge, and here we find a remarkable simile to describe how inspiration flows from the poet to the rhapsode (or actor), who then communicates it to his audience (*Ion* 533d):

It is no art or craft [*technē*, which requires knowledge] which enables you to talk well on Homer but a divine power which moves you, like the power of a magnet. This not only attracts iron rings but imbues those rings with its own magnetic power to attract other rings, with the result that sometimes a long chain of such rings are suspended from one another, and the power of attraction in all of them is derived from the magnet. So the Muse herself inspires men, and the inspiration is communicated by them to others, until we have a whole chain of men possessed.

We may note here that being possessed by a god was not, to the Greeks, necessarily a good thing, since the gods' purposes were not necessarily good. We need only think of Phaedra's illicit love inspired by Aphrodite, or of Agave killing her own son when possessed by Dionysus. Further, this communication of strong emotion or ecstasy is a purely emotional process without intervention or control by reason or knowledge at any point. It is this which made Plato afraid. We should remember that a wave of powerful emotion sweeping over twenty or thirty thousand spectators in the Greek theater must have been almost tangible in its intensity, and that Plato must often have felt it. *That* is the background of his attacks upon the poets.

In the *Gorgias* Plato turns his attention to the Sophists, the new teachers of the art of prose, and examines what it is they claim to teach. As he is here concerned only with content, much of what he says applies to poetry also, and indeed he identifies poetry and rhetoric as different kinds of public speaking (501d–502d). When told that the art of rhetoric is the art of persuasion Socrates makes an important distinction between two kinds of persuasion: the first is based on knowledge in the persuader and is the art of teaching; the second persuasion aims at making people believe something and requires no knowledge. This last, Socrates maintains, is the art of rhetoric; and since the orator deals with matters of right and wrong the distinction is vital. Gorgias at first accepts this distinction and quite logically suggests that a teacher of rhetoric should not be held responsible if his pupils misuse the skill he teaches any more than a fencing master should be if his pupils use the skill he has taught them to commit murder. However, when he is faced with the consequences of this position, namely that orators need know nothing of good or evil, he changes his mind and says that if a pupil should be so ignorant as not to know good from evil, he will teach him that as well. When the contradiction is pointed out to him he retires from the discussion, which is taken over by his younger disciples.

It is the moral irresponsibility of the rhetoricians which Plato is attacking, for rhetoric does not aim at goodness or truth, only at immediate success. It is not a genuine craft based on knowledge and aiming at the good as gymnastic aims at health, and medicine at restoring it; as lawmaking aims at the good life, (corrective) justice at restoring it. Rhetoric is merely a counterfeit art which aims only at pleasure in an empirical way. For the good of the soul the rhetoricians do not care at all; indeed they have no knowledge of it. Socrates is here obviously thinking of the use of rhetoric in court and the Sophists' claim that they could make the worse appear the better cause. The aim, to Socrates, should be to correct the state of soul of the wrongdoer. Gorgias had claimed that the rhetorician could be more persuasive than the expert. Yes, says Socrates, and so could a pastry cook get more votes than a doctor on a question of diet from an assembly of ignorant children.

In the *Republic* too Plato approaches poetry from the point of view of the educator and gives us in effect the first theoretical discussion of the place of poetry and the other arts in society. Convinced as he is that their influence is great both in the formation of character and upon society generally, he firmly establishes the principle of censorship of literature. For this he has been strongly criticized, and yet every civilized state, except his own Athens, seems to have followed his advice in one form or another.

He attacks, in particular, Homer's tales about gods and heroes—their misbehaviors, their displays of excessive grief, and the like. This criticism was by now traditional, but the educational problem was real since Homer was still the core of Greek education and the Sophists had taught men to argue from the behavior of the gods to justify their own. To Plato, at least from the *Republic* on, gods could not be the source of evil and heroes should behave with dignity and self-control. Hence:

We shall ask Homer and the other poets not to be annoyed if we expunge things of that kind. It is not that these things are not poetical and pleasing for the majority of men to hear; indeed the more poetical they are the less they must be heard by children and by men who must be free and fear slavery more than death (*Republic* 387b).

We note that Plato is well aware that there are other criteria of judgment, with which he is not here concerned. No doubt he would have applied the same moral standard to works of prose but poetry had a much wider appeal, and it is obviously the theater and the epic recitations that he has mainly in mind.

It is in this discussion in the second and third book of the *Republic* that we first come across the Platonic theory of art as "imitation" or *mimesis*. There has been a good deal of confusion about the meaning of this word and for this Plato himself is largely responsible. The word "mimesis" had, in a general sense, been applied both to poetry and the arts long before Plato. We find it in a Homeric hymn about a choral performance where it is usually translated "to mimic." Herodotus and Hippocrates use it of carving and sculpture, and in Xenophon's *Memorabilia* (3.10) Socrates persuades a sculptor, who argues that he can only "imitate" the physical, that he can also "imitate" the emotions since he can represent at least their physical or outward manifestations. In the *Thesmophoria-zusae*, Aristophanes represents the poet Agathon in women's clothes when writing an ode for a female choir, because a dramatist must identify himself with his characters and "what we do not have, *mimesis* will find for us." The dubious jokes of that scene have much more point if Aristophanes is playing on a semi-technical word commonly applied to poetry, as he probably is. Finally, in the *Laws* (668b) Plato himself introduces, as a truism which everybody will accept, the notion that poetry is "imitation" or mimesis. He applies the word in the *Republic* (401b–c) not only to poetry, painting, and sculpture, but to music as well, and even to architecture. In this general sense then it means that poetry and art must represent life, and that the representation must be true, not that the artist can only copy what he has actually witnessed.

It is in this general sense that Plato first uses the word in the *Republic*, where he says that the poet must not "imitate" Zeus weeping (388c) at the death of Sarpedon or Hector, for obviously no one had ever *seen* Zeus weeping, indeed no one had ever seen Zeus. His criticism is that so to represent Zeus is *not true*, for this is not how the gods behave. In this general sense, then, the theory of imitation demands no more than that art must be true to life.

Censorship of content being now firmly established, Plato applies it to literary forms, and in so doing he gives a new meaning to mimesis—that of impersonation. Poets and storytellers, he tells us, proceed either by narration, or by impersonation, or by a mixture of the two. Clearly drama belongs to the second, epic to the third kind. Believing as he does that impersonation makes the emotional impact stronger and that "we become like what we imitate," Plato severely restricts arts which are "imitative" in this sense and

497

forbids all impersonation of evil characters or actions on the stage. When we meet such an "imitative" poet who can impersonate every kind of character

. . . we shall do him reverence as before someone wondrous and sweet. . . . We shall anoint his head with myrrh, crown him with wreaths, and send him away to another city (398a).

Censorship of this kind would of course emasculate both tragedy and epic, and leave little of comedy. It is true that not all poetry is banished, since encomia of good men, hymns to the gods, even dramatization of good actions might remain, but there is little point in exercising our ingenuity as to what would still be acceptable. It is more useful to recognize that, while his solution is totally unsatisfactory to us, Plato is raising for the first time an important social problem— that of the need to censor art and literature, especially drama, a problem to which we have not yet found an entirely satisfactory solution two thousand years later.

That Plato recognized the importance of the problem is clear, for he discusses it again in the tenth and last book of the *Republic*, where he pursues his attack upon the poets with gusto and, one suspects, a good deal of irony. He now attacks poetry on the basis of the psychological and metaphysical theories which he had developed in the intervening books. And again he broadens and changes the meaning of the word "mimesis" or imitation.

The psychological argument offers little difficulty. The human soul has three main parts or functions: the reasonable part which in the good man governs and directs all the rest; the spirited part which rules in the ambitious man (one might call it the feelings, for it is the seat of anger, indignation, and the like); and the lowest or passionate part, the seat of the essential human desires such as hunger, thirst, and sex. This last part rules the soul of the worst type of man whom Plato calls the tyrannical, because this is the rule of Eros in the lowest, most primitive, and most violent sense.

Plato's accusation here is that the poet appeals only to the passionate part, without any rational control, for it is the most violently passionate states of the soul which are the favorite material of tragedy and are most pleasing to the mob. We, the spectators, identify ourselves emotionally with the characters on the stage and the more we are emotionally affected the more we praise the poet. Such identification in the theater will not help us to control our passions and desires in our own lives, as decent people must do, for once more we become like what we "imitate," and mimesis here includes, more clearly than before, the notion of emotional identification, of "suffering with." Essen-

tially, this is the same magnetic power of inspiration described by the simile of the *Ion*.

It is the metaphysical argument of the tenth book, or rather the illustration of it, however, which has caused a good deal of confusion. The whole *Republic* has argued the need for knowledge of the ideal Forms, the only true Realities, on the part of the philosopher, the ruler, and the educator. It is not surprising that Plato denies this knowledge—to him the only true knowledge—to the poets, and this might well have been accepted. Unfortunately, he attempts to clarify his meaning by an oversimplified illustration. There exists, first, the Form of bed created by God (or the gods, the divine, for the word *theos* is used generically); second in truth or reality is the actual bed made by the carpenter with his eye on the Form; and then, third in the degree of truth or reality comes the picture of the bed made by a painter who has no knowledge of the Form nor indeed of the actual bed either, but "imitates" it, as seen from one particular angle only.

If taken literally, this illustration seems to imply that poetry and art can only "imitate" particular things or scenes in a photographic kind of way. However, it is notoriously dangerous to take literally a particular detail in a Platonic myth or a particular Platonic illustration. If we do take this one literally we create a lot of philosophical problems, for nowhere else in Plato do the gods create the Forms; nowhere else would an artisan know the Forms. Yet only too often this particular illustration of the painter and the bed is treated as the only important thing Plato ever said about art or poetry, in spite of the fact that this kind of almost photographic imitation cannot possibly be applied to music or architecture, which Plato categorically asserts also to be "imitations." The only reasonable conclusion is that Plato is only half serious, or at any rate that the illustration must not, in its details, be pressed too far.

Besides, while in his actual discussions of poetry Plato never allows the poet or other artist any knowledge of the Forms—which the poet cannot, therefore "imitate" directly—there are, elsewhere in the *Republic*, hints of a different kind of art, of artists who have such knowledge, as in the *Gorgias* there was a better kind of persuasion. Not only can the artist combine different aspects of existing things to make something which does not exist in the actual world (*Republic* 488a), but when Socrates is challenged as to whether his ideal state could ever exist he says a man who paints a picture of a most beautiful man is surely no less a good painter if he cannot prove that such a man exists (472d). Then again, when defending the philosopher's right to rule (484e), Socrates says that those who do not know the Forms cannot, "as a painter can with their eyes on what is most true," establish laws and customs in the state. Elsewhere again (500e) he compares philosophers to "painters who use the divine model," and the *Republic* itself is "like a pattern laid up in heaven. . . . It matters not whether it exists anywhere, or ever will exist." It seems then that another kind of art, another kind of persuasion could be conceived as is another kind of politics in the *Gorgias*, of which Socrates was the only practitioner. But none of our poets, orators, or politicians practice these higher forms of their own arts.

Yet in spite of these occasional hints, Plato's discussions of both poetry and rhetoric are up to this point essentially negative. He puts all the emphasis upon what the arts do not accomplish, rather than upon what they might achieve. He is afraid of their purely emotional appeal and influence and shows but scant respect for any actual practitioners of these arts. We should not, however, fail to recognize that if Plato insists upon censorship not only of poetry but of music, painting, and even architecture, it is

. . . in order that our guardians shall not be nurtured among images of evil as in an evil pasture, feeding little by little and day by day on evil herbs from many sources and imperceptibly gathering a mass of evil into their very souls. We must seek out artists with an inborn gift to represent what is in its nature beautiful and gracious, so that our youth, living as it were in a healthy place, shall be improved as they see or hear works of beauty on all sides. As a breeze from salubrious climes brings health, so shall our youth from childhood on be led to sympathy and harmony with, and to love of, the beauty of Reason (*Republic* 401b).

In later dialogues, the *Phaedrus* and the *Laws*, Plato's attitude is not so harsh, nor so negative. The *Phaedrus* emphasizes rhetoric, though Plato makes it quite clear that most of what he says applies to poetry as well (258d). We are first given what purports to be a speech by the orator Lysias on the paradoxical subject that a youth should yield to one who does not love him, rather than to one who does—a typical piece of sophistic display rhetoric; then a speech on the same subject by Socrates, who proceeds to criticize both speeches. He interrupts his criticisms, however, with a palinode in praise of Eros, whom he feels he has insulted. (This palinode is the myth on the soul's ascent through love to vision of the eternal Forms.) He then proceeds with his criticism which leads to a search for the true art of rhetoric.

This great myth is in part a vindication of inspiration and of that strong emotion of which Plato has hitherto been so very suspicious. Poetic inspiration is here the third of four kinds of "madness" sent by the gods (the other three being prophecy, mystery rites, and love) and such madness is said to be "a better thing than human sanity" (*Phaedrus* 244d), so that:

whoever comes to the gates of poetry without the Muses' madness, believing that technical skill will make him an adequate poet, is himself ineffectual, and the poetry of this sane man vanishes before that of the man who is mad.

This is the language of myth, and "madness which comes from the gods" means passion properly directed, much the same in fact as what, in the more sober prose of the *Republic* Plato called desire directed by Reason. There is, then, no actual contradiction; but obviously there is a strong change of emphasis, a much clearer recognition of passion as essential to great poetry.

In his first comments on Lysias' speech, Socrates says he admired its manner (*diathesis*) but not its matter, thus establishing a distinction between form and content which soon became a commonplace in rhetorical theory (*Phaedrus* 236a). He then goes on to state some simple but very important critical principles.

The first of these we expect from Plato, namely that the speaker or writer must have knowledge of his subject. Rhetorical theory denied this; all persuasion required was knowledge of the crowd's beliefs. Socrates insists, however, that good advice requires knowledge and adds, with some irony, that even if your intention is to deceive, you will do this more successfully if you yourself know the truth.

The second point is that the writer must define his subject, which Socrates did but Lysias did not.

The third requirement is that every discourse should be like a living organism, with each part in its place and in tune with all the other parts and with the whole. Socrates quotes as bad poetry a four line epitaph:

I am a bronzen maiden, on Midas' grave I lie,
Till stop the flowing waters, as long as trees grow tall,
Forever here remaining, on this lamented tomb,
To those who pass by saying, Midas is buried here.

The order of these lines makes little or no difference. This is bad art.

Fourth, as the various parts of a discourse must each make a significant contribution to the whole, it is essential that the writer should be able to analyze his subject logically, that is, divide it "along the joints" or "according to the Forms."

The fifth requirement is perhaps the most interesting of all, as Plato is here concerned to establish the difference between art and mere technical devices. The elaborate technical vocabulary of the rhetoricians, the claim that they can make things seem important or trivial, speak briefly or at length on any subject, stir up the emotions at will: all this is not the art of rhetoric. It is as if a man claimed to be a musician because he knows the musical notes, or a doctor because he knows the effect of all medicaments without knowing when to apply them:

What if a man came to Sophocles and Euripides and said that he knew how to speak at length on trifling subjects and briefly on important ones, that he could at will make pitiful, frightening or threatening speeches and so on, and that by teaching these things he teaches the making of tragedies.

—I think, Socrates, they would laugh at anyone who considered tragedy to be anything less than the fitting together of those elements so that they harmonize with each other and with the whole work (*Phaedrus* 268c–d).

What is particularly interesting here is that in thus vehemently denying that the rhetoricians have any adequate knowledge of their own art, Plato clearly implies that Sophocles and Euripides (and Pericles as an orator) *were* true artists or craftsmen, for he puts them on a par with Hippocrates as a doctor. This surely is a great advance upon the harsh condemnation of all existing poets in the *Republic*.

Nor does this passage of the *Phaedrus* stand quite alone. In a passage of the *Sophist* which tries to track down the Sophist by a process of dichotomy, Plato has a division for mimesis based on knowledge. Image-making is divided into the making of exact copies and the making of images which only look like the original. The latter class of image makers is then divided into those who use tools to make their images and those who use their own bodies and voices to do so. The word "mimesis" is then applied to this latter class, which surely must include poets, especially dramatists, and rhetoricians as well; for once these are separated from sculptors and painters. A further subdivision separates those imitators *who have knowledge* of their model from those who have not. These last may or may not have the intention to deceive, Sophists and demagogues being among the deliberate deceivers.

Without pressing these somewhat ironic dichotomies too far, it does seem that when Plato here speaks of imitators by voice and gestures with knowledge of their models, he does allow for certain actual practitioners of poetry and rhetoric based on knowledge in much the same way as he ranks Sophocles, Euripides, and Pericles among real artists in the *Phaedrus* passage.

That dialogue goes on to state that the true art of rhetoric will require natural talent, knowledge, and practice. This soon became a favorite formula of the schools, except that knowledge was interpreted by the rhetoricians as knowledge of techniques. This is also what it means to the rhetorician Isocrates, Plato's older contemporary.

Since any art must acquire knowledge of the object of its concern—for without this it is no art or *technē* but a mere empirical routine (270b)—the true rhetorician must acquire a thorough knowledge of human psychology. He must then analyze the different types of arguments, and how they will affect different types of minds. Equipped with this knowledge, and the further knowledge of the proper moment to speak and to remain silent, the true orator will then be able to apply the techniques, which is all that the rhetoricians now teach, in the right way.

That Plato is here trying to be practical is shown by the well-known fact that this is very largely the method followed by Aristotle in his own *Rhetoric*. But Plato, we find at the end of the argument, is not really satisfied with the arguments from probability which will satisfy Aristotle. He wants his true orator to have true knowledge, and to Plato there is only one true knowledge, that of the Forms. So we find our orators (and poets) in danger of becoming philosophers on the way. And then, of course, they will have more important things to do than write poetry or make speeches.

Once more, in the second book of the *Laws*, the work of his old age, Plato returns to the subject of *mousikē* (μουσική), music and poetry. He approaches it as an educator, as he did in the *Republic*, but the discussion is much more positive, and makes a number of points of special interest.

The function of *mousikē* in the formation of character, in training the young to take pleasure in the right things before the age of reason, is still the most important; but to this educational function Plato now adds a second function, the recreational. Even where education has properly trained the emotions in childhood, this proper balance is disturbed and slackened by many things in life, and the gods have granted the festivals of the Muses, Apollo, and Dionysus in order that men might be "put right"—that is, in order that the proper emotional responses may be restored. Clearly this is a new function for poetry and music, and the restoration of emotional balance which this envisages seems to come near to the Aristotelian concept of *Catharsis*.

All this is possible because a sense of rhythm and harmony is a special gift from the gods to mankind, so that men take pleasure in them. Poetry, music, and the dance are then seen as the culmination of the gradual application of rhythm and harmony upon the random cries and uncoordinated movements of the human infant. These arts therefore have their roots deep in human nature (*Laws* 655b).

Plato then allows three criteria by which art may be judged: the first is still the social or moral criterion, and Plato still denies that any representation of evil or vice can legitimately be called beautiful (ibid.).

The second criterion is pleasure, towards which he is much more indulgent, both in this and other contexts, than he was in his earlier works. However, it must be the pleasure of the right people. And it is no use pretending to praise what one does not enjoy—the appeal must be to the whole man (*Laws* 655e). We may doubt Plato's particular application of the pleasure principle—namely that children enjoy puppet shows, older children comedy; youth, educated women, and perhaps the majority prefer tragedy, and old men the epic—as this would seem to make the epic the highest kind of poetry, but we must surely agree to the principle that art is not to be judged by box office receipts. If art is beneficial and a form of education, both poets and judges must educate the audience and not be swayed by it—we must not be a "theatrocracy."

The third criterion is an artistic one, however crudely expressed as "the correctness of the imitation"—how true it is to life. We must not be misled by Plato's use, once again (*Laws* 668d), of sculpture and painting as illustrations, into interpreting this "correctness" too narrowly; it is explicitly said to include at least good and consistent characterization, appropriateness of words and tune to the situation and characters, and is probably meant to include a good deal more. In any case the critic, if he is not to fall into error,

... must know in each case the nature of the work, for if he does not know its essential nature and intention, of what it is truly an image, he can hardly know whether it succeeds or fails in its purpose (*Laws* 668c).

The critic must know the model in order to judge the image. Indeed, one feels that Plato is requiring almost too much from his critic and almost making a philosopher of him too, but the Forms are not mentioned in the *Laws*. He does, however, make one concession to the artist—that he does not need to know whether his work is "good" or "beautiful" in the moralistic sense. But he must then obey the lawgiver, as to whether his work will be performed.

It is obvious, as we have seen, that the *Phaedrus* and the *Laws* display a much milder attitude towards poetry and rhetoric than the earlier dialogues, and equally obvious that these later works make a far more positive contribution to literary theory and criticism. Plato even allows certain artists to be true practitioners of their art. Nevertheless we should not be led by this concession to assume any great change in Plato's basic attitude to poets and rhetoricians, or perhaps even to poetry and rhetoric as such.

Plato has admitted from the very first that poets often say some wonderfully fine things; his criticism was that they speak without knowledge, that they stir up our emotions without knowing whether to do so is good or bad. They are inspired but not responsible. In the *Gorgias* there were two kinds of persuasion, and one of them was based on knowledge, but that was not the persuasion of the rhetorician. He too is irresponsible. The vehement attacks upon the poets in the *Republic* are directed to the same point, the violent emotional effects of poetry without any intervention at any point by reason and true knowledge. Because of the power and influence of such appeals, Plato is afraid of them. Yet we have seen hints even in the *Republic* that there might be another kind of poetry.

Inspiration is certainly spoken of with greater respect in the myth of the *Phaedrus*, at least such inspiration as comes from the Muses, and it has been suggested in this article that Plato here means inspiration directed to the right objects and utterances. This dialogue certainly implies a greater recognition of the value and need for strong emotion; but then already in the *Republic* even the philosophic life is based on passion, the passionate desire for wisdom and truth, the Eros of the *Symposium*. When, in the *Phaedrus*, Plato set out to find the characteristics of the true art of Rhetoric, he concluded that it is based on knowledge and is obviously the first kind of persuasion—that which Gorgias did *not* practice, but which Plato did practice throughout his dialogues and more specifically in the *Laws*, where every law is preceded by a proemium or introduction, the purpose of which is to *persuade* the citizens of the need for it. Here we have persuasion based on knowledge.

Censorship remains to the end in Plato's writings. It is discussed again in the *Laws* and it is not without interest to note that, when asked for an example of the kind of thing the censors will allow, Plato cites as an example the *Laws* itself which is "not unlike poetry of a kind" and "not without some kind of divine inspiration" (811c). This will hardly satisfy lovers of poetry!

The story of Teuth at the end of the *Phaedrus* reminds us forcibly that Plato refused to take even his own writings very seriously. Although in the *Phaedrus* myth the poet rises above the carpenter whose bed he merely "imitates" in the *Republic*, he still remains only the sixth in the scale of lives classified according to the degree to which the souls have shared the vision of true reality (which all human souls have shared to some extent). The poet is ranked below not only the philosopher but also below the law-abiding ruler or general, below the statesman or man of affairs, below the doctor and gymnastic trainer, below the priest or the prophet.

However important art may be in the training of the emotions, especially before the age of reason, the products of art were, to Plato, less important than the characters it formed—less important, that is, than life itself. No one is more aware of the importance of a sense of beauty. Yet in the gradual ascent of the philosopher in the *Symposium* toward the vision of that supreme Beauty which is also Truth and Goodness, the products of art are never mentioned. The same is true in the myth of the *Phaedrus*, where the sense of beauty in nature and life leads to the winged soul's vision of the eternal Forms. Nowhere in his works does Plato envisage an aesthetic divorced from the knowledge of reality, or make a place for poetry and the arts in the curriculum of his philosopher's higher education.

BIBLIOGRAPHY

The reader will find a very complete bibliography in "Plato 1950–1957," by Harold Cherniss in *Lustrum* (Göttingen, 1959, 1960). Plato's theories of aesthetics and art are dealt with in *Lustrum* (1960), 520–54. Cherniss does not restrict himself to the years indicated, but mentions most works of importance from about 1930. The vastness of the literature on our subject can be seen there, and Cherniss' frank comments are a useful guide; they also bring out the startling differences between the interpretations of reputable scholars.

To this we should add: P. Vicaire, *Platon, Critique littéraire* (Paris, 1960), a very full study of the subject. Attention should also be drawn to the chapter on "Plato's Treatment of Art," in N. R. Murphy, *The Interpretation of Plato's Republic* (Oxford and New York, 1951); the chapter on Plato in G. M. A. Grube, *The Greek and Roman Critics* (Toronto, 1965); and I. M. Crombie, *An Examination of Plato's Doctrines*, 2 vols. (London and New York, 1962), I, 143–50, 183–98. A somewhat novel approach will be found in E. A. Havelock, *Preface to Plato* (Cambridge, Mass., 1963), which contends that Greek culture was still very much oral even in the fourth century, and that this affected the nature and meaning of Plato's attack upon the poets.

Translations are by the author of this article, unless otherwise identified.

G. M. A. GRUBE

[See also Catharsis; Criticism; Education; Empathy; Harmony; Language; **Literature; Mimesis;** Myth; **Platonism;** Poetry; Rationality.]

PLATONISM IN PHILOSOPHY AND POETRY

"PLATONISM" does not escape the legacy of all "isms," and one of the many good reasons for distrusting the propriety and alleged value of designating any historical movement by appending *ism* to the name of a man

has been that inevitably historical or simply temporal pressures rapidly distort the aptness of the association. Thus we feel obliged to add classical prefixes such as "neo, ortho, proto, pan"; or temporal adjectives such as "early, late, eighteenth-century, contemporary"; or perhaps content-designators such as "right-wing, left-wing, traditional, or radical," to the *ism*. There may be some very good reasons for avoiding the term "Platonism" entirely. Nevertheless there is some value in tracing the way the label has been used and indeed great value in observing how the thought of this man has influenced the history of Western thought.

Great men not only make great contributions (and sometimes great mistakes), but always engender a great variety of responses. Plutarch identified Plato and philosophy in the most complimentary way, while K. R. Popper has called Plato a totalitarian party-politician who compromised his integrity with every step he took (Popper, p. 169). Whitehead, like Emerson, scorned any supposed revolutionary originality in philosophy since the fourth century B.C., and called all of Western thought a series of footnotes to Plato. And Herbert Spencer, lacking the patience to appreciate Plato as a philosopher and the judgment to rate him above a third-rate novelist in literary skills, considered the reading of Plato a gross waste of time.

A certain arbitrariness is inescapable in deciding upon an appropriate meaning of Platonism. Part of the problem is endemic to all studies of ancient writers: do we really know their doctrines and how they were misunderstood or altered or profaned by their disciples? In the case of Plato the texts generally agreed to be as authentic as can be expected following centuries of recopying, translation, burned libraries, and careless handling, are numerous enough to allay most fears about the writings, but the questions of interpretation continually arise, as in, for instance, Gilbert Ryle's strikingly innovative *Plato's Progress* (Oxford, 1966). Plato, like so many brilliant writers, indeed displays marked changes in beliefs and doctrines throughout the productive years of his life. There is, therefore, as could be expected, a historical line of influence which attaches itself to the earlier writings of Plato which is simply inconsistent with movements which find their genesis in what one must assume to be clearly a later period in Plato's development.

Philosophers tend to treat Platonism as a theory, or as a set of doctrines or beliefs. Whether these doctrines constitute a therapeutic answer to deep human problems or are in some ways the disease itself has been, and will always be, one of the most provocative of academic debates. As one moves away from the philosophical, Platonism becomes more and more a style of life, not a formal theory, but as Walter Pater argued, a tendency to think or feel or speak about certain things in a particular way (Pater, pp. 169ff.). This way is always some sort of transcendentalism or mysticism, and Platonism then becomes some kind of witness to the unseen. The history of Platonism is full of poignant reminders of this tendency.

Yet it would be misleading to polarize this diversity into radical bifurcation. The most transcendental minded Platonists must admit to Plato's deep concern with the sensible world, while on the other hand the sets of doctrines which philosophers arrange and call Platonism, inevitably attribute to Plato absolutes, ultimate entities, and references to the eternal quest. Typical of such quasi-definitions is the effort of William Inge to find the core of Platonism in a belief in absolute and eternal values as the most real things in the universe and the confidence that we can know these, if only we put ourselves to the task with a total dedication of intellect, will, and affection, while holding an open mind toward scientific discovery and a reverent attitude toward the beauty and sublimity of the world as the manifestation of the mind and character of the creator (Inge, pp. 72ff.). Quite apart from the fact that this is undoubtedly technically misleading in its reference to values, as Santayana pointed out in his *Platonism and the Spiritual Life* (pp. 3f.), and in its reference to Plato's open-mindedness to science, which appears to be simply false, this is the kind of account of Platonism which has always been prevalent and not entirely mistaken.

Much of what has been called Platonism did not originate with Plato, and, as is true with any man's thought, much of Plato's thought can be readily traced to those powerful influences to which he himself admitted. Recognizing the spurious reputation of *Epistle II*, we must at least admit that its author, Plato or not, expressed the influence of Socrates with a clear, if exaggerated passion, saying that there never was, nor ever will be any written work of Plato. All that goes by that name is that of Socrates, grown handsome and modernized. Aristotle, whose credentials should make him a knowledgeable commentator on Plato, saw the Heraclitean influence on Plato's ideas, the denial of any stability to the sensible world and the resultant skepticism about scientific knowledge. He noted too, in *Metaphysics A*, the assuming of the Socratic attitude that one should therefore disregard the sensible world and seek the universal in the moral sphere. But most of all, Aristotle sees Plato as a kind of Pythagorean who not only distinguishes between sense objects and universals but postulates the existence of objects of mathematics, both like and unlike each, and takes the Parmenidean One to be a substance, not a predicate. It seems clear that philosophers in the periods following Plato took Platonism to include a doctrine of being in which the Forms, eternal, immutable, simple, perfect, and separate, were the ultimate elements of the universe conceived as a metaphysical system; a doctrine of knowing in which sense data can legitimately function only in the acquisition of fallible opinion, whereas the Forms are the only objects of genuine knowledge; and a doctrine of man in which body and soul are separate and separable elements, and survival after death becomes a pious, although reasonable hope. Plato's consistent concern for the unity of his philosophy, such as his attempt to show how morality is necessarily related to metaphysical knowledge, was shared in varying degrees, but always to some extent, by the Platonists of later periods.

In spite of many philosophers' beliefs in the independence of their discipline and their timeless insights, untouched by the drama of life, philosophical systems are as much the effects of social and political change as they are causes. The changes in the political scene, which had been developing for several generations, had more bearing on the destiny of Plato's philosophical influence in the post-Aristotelian era than one might expect. The ancient ideal declined, not because of any philosophical attack, but at least in part because the city-state disappeared and the new imperialism de-emphasized the Socratic man, demanding new loyalties and a new kind of piety which made "Know thyself" irrelevant. All the influences now were alien to the Greek heritage, and knowing for the sake of knowing became more of a historical curiosity than a viable alternative to the pragmatic commitments of the new schools. Consolation, not speculation, became the goal of the thinker, and even social and ethical thinking was increasingly directed toward the practical problems of living in this hostile world. Nevertheless, death comes hard, if ever, to philosophies, and while it is indeed the case that the teachings of Plato were used during the next five hundred years to support movements and ideals with which he would not have been at all sympathetic, they were surely not ignored, and on occasion showed vigorous signs of life.

Of all the schools like Plato's Academy which flourished in Athens from the death of Aristotle until their ultimate destruction by Justinian in the sixth century A.D., the Cynics, those who chose to escape from an unpleasant world by leaving it alone, represent best the trend toward and the triumph of the practical. Finding their heroic inspiration in Diogenes of Sinope (410–320 B.C.), the Cynics were largely able to circumvent the teaching of Plato, and their solution to living in an evil world was characteristically un-Platonic; to abolish traditional logic, mathematics, music, and social restraints, and to produce *aretē* (ἄρετη) by living like

503

dogs, as their name suggests and their critics insisted. There is meager philosophical substance in the Cynics, and their lean doctrines, hidden or perhaps undogmatically shared, found their way into Stoicism, there to become elements of a more substantial philosophy against which Platonism continually roiled.

One would not be far wrong in simply denying any positive influence of Plato on Epicureanism. Stoicism, however, in spite of its early materialism, and a non-Greek heritage, not only shared a common hero with Plato, but in its later years, several important doctrines. However, admiration for Socrates is not enough to merit the label Platonic, and it must be acknowledged that the theory of Forms never found a home in Stoicism. Yet Chrysippus (280–207 B.C.) held to a very limited theory of survival after death, and it seems clear that some sort of awareness of the Platonic doctrine of the soul came into Stoicism with Panaetius (b. 180 B.C.), and especially through his disciple Posidonius (b. 135 B.C.), whose views of the soul, primitive by Plato's standards, were nevertheless to have an historically important role in the period which led to Neo-Platonism.

After the death of Plato in 387 B.C., the Academy at Athens passed through the hands of Speusippus, Xenocrates, Polemo, and Crates, taking on successively more ethical and less speculative concerns. None of these was any more intent on being radical in his Platonism than was Aristotle, and several considerably less. The Academy under Speusippus and Xenocrates, in spite of its increasing emphasis on morals, shared, in fact, with Aristotle the same interest in the metaphysical problems in Plato, and attempted to overcome the dualism of the intelligible and sensible worlds in ways not always unlike Aristotle's. The radical change in the Academy came after the death of Crates and the influence of his successor Arcesilaus (b. 315 B.C.) in skeptically reconstructing it into what is known as the Middle Academy. The Academy remained basically skeptical for about three hundred years, through various regimes.

The skeptics in the Academy were not all consciously hostile toward Plato. More often than not they felt that they could find in the questioning of Socrates ample justification for their own hesitancy about making cognitive assertions, for Socrates certainly perpetrated some doubts about knowing. Plato's own ironic skepticism has always been a lively topic for philosophers and should not be dismissed without consideration. Why, it is sometimes asked, did Plato write the *Protagoras* if not to show a degree of skepticism as a reasonable, if not indeed inescapable commitment? Hans Wolff, for instance, has raised the questions of both epistemological and moral skepticism in his *Plato:*

Der Kampf ums Sein. Skeptics found a dogmatic source, however, in Pyrrho (365–275 B.C.) who, while agreeing with Plato on the cognitive unreliability of sense perception, went far beyond him in flatly denying that this is rationally corrigible, and, while not absolutely denying the existence of absolute truth, at least denied that any human mind could ever know it. Pyrrho was a relatively unsophisticated skeptic but many of his views, and especially those of his disciple Timon (ca. 320–ca. 230), were so similar to those inside the Academy that by the first century B.C. "Academic" and "Pyrrhonic" skepticism were indistinguishable.

Timon, and probably Pyrrho also, were trained in Megaric dialectic, an outgrowth of early Socratism, and the suspension of judgment so dear to skeptics can without great effort be found in the Platonic Socrates, if one is selective enough. Arcesilaus, in spite of his excellent training in mathematics and the humanities and his sharp critical mind, turned out to be little better than a sophist in his influence on students in the Academy, and was memorialized for his vigorous attacks on the Stoics rather than for any constructive thought. It was Carneades (213–129), moving into leadership in the Academy after it had experienced a long period of intellectual aridity, who paired the critical skills of a philosophical in-fighter with some original work on probability and the relationships between impressions and actions so much ignored by other skeptics. His position is in another respect more compatible with the recognizable Plato. Carneades' pragmatic skepticism differed from that of other skeptics who simply shrugged at life. He allowed events to determine actions so that the wise man would not always withhold judgment nor resist opinions, but would and should permit opinion to be directive of action even in the absence of certain knowledge. Sextus Empiricus, whose skepticism emerged during the second century A.D. and was more tightly reasoned, and of whose thought we know much more, understood these necessities better than the contemporaries of Carneades. Skeptics, he observed, recognize a difference between one's life as a man and as a philosopher. If a skeptic attempted to act only upon his professed philosophy, for example, he could not act at all.

The skeptical thread spun out of the Academy is found, upon further examination, in the fabric of all post-Aristotelian philosophies. Unless the eternal Forms exist, Plato insisted, knowledge is impossible. To believe Plato and to be a skeptic called only for denying the existence of the Forms. Platonism, nevertheless, as an irresistible *idée-force*, is easily recognizable when its formal structures appear in medieval theology, its humanism in the Renaissance, and its metaphysical and epistemological doctrines in later idealism.

The Platonic intrusion into medieval thought, both Christian and non-Christian, was through Plotinus' brand of Platonism, which, in turn, owed something to a recurrent revival of Pythagoreanism. As a religious fraternity, Pythagoreanism had retained adherents long after its decline as a school of philosophy. The cults and the mysteries associated with the school had even rebounded into great popularity by the first century B.C. and, as is often the case, the practice revived interest in the theory. This time, however, elements of Plato as well as of Aristotle and other writers had a share in the influencing of the dogma. The metaphysics of the revived Pythagoreanism contained four principles, three of which were very similar to the later Neo-Platonic ontological trinity; the One, the Logos, and the World-Soul. The fourth, Matter, was radically different from the first three, and the system was quite compatible with Plato's dualism of appearance and reality, and assimilable into the Platonic theory of knowledge. Because the visible space-time world is a copy of intelligible reality, the Platonic strictures on knowing hold. The doctrine of the separable, immortal human soul in Neo-Pythagoreanism is also quite like the hierarchical psychology of Plato, if one ignores Plato's beliefs about reincarnation.

While Plutarch remains the best known writer of the revived Pythagoreanism in the Neo-Platonic school, largely because of the writings of his which have come down to us, perhaps the most interesting of the cluster was Numenius (fl. A.D. 175), whom we know only from secondary sources. He apparently worked out a system very much like that of Plotinus. Numenius used sources prior to Plato to create a structure in which the highest reality appears very much like the Unmoved Mover of Aristotle, too impersonal and distant to be concerned with the world, but delegating creation to a second being (the Demiurge of Plato's *Timaeus*), the middle person in the metaphysical trinity. Moses and Jesus became teachers of importance and the inclusion of Mosaic and Christian concepts sets a different direction for philosophy.

The meeting of the thinking of Moses and Plato found its highest realization in Philo Judaeus (ca. 20 B.C.–A.D. 50), an orthodox believer who had assimilated much of Platonism and also some Neo-Pythagorean beliefs; his contributions were largely in theology, where his method of allegorical interpretation of the scriptures on the one hand and sympathetic handling of Plato on the other, had great influence on the medieval period.

The impact of Plato on early Christian philosophy was surely through Plotinus (205–70), whose metaphysical triad sounds so much like the Christian trinity, of which Plotinus seems to know very little, that the great task of admirers of Saint Augustine turned out to be the defense of Augustine against the charge of being a follower of Plotinus. The concept of emanation, explaining how the parts of the trinity can be related, and the analogy of the light proceeding from the sun, are graphically Platonic and were not ignored by later Christian writers in attempting to conceive how the Son could proceed from the Father. In addition, Plotinus' spiritualism, his antipathy to materialism, the place of illumination in his epistemology, and his mysticism are reminiscent of earlier Platonism.

Augustine is the fountainhead of Platonism in the Christian Middle Ages and surely the Platonism of which he speaks is Neo-Platonism. In the books of the Platonists, he writes in *Confessions*, he read passages paralleling the openings of John's gospel, "In the beginning was the Logos, and the Logos was with God and the Logos was God," but he failed to find the crucial Christian doctrine of incarnation: "The Logos was made flesh and dwelt among us." Platonism provides a truncated theology because it fails to include the Christ-event, although it is quite compatible with the incarnation and can be accommodated to a theological system. Indeed, Augustinians were tireless in looking in Plato for hints that he was a proto-Christian, and finding enough evidence to satisfy, such as turning to the first three words of the *Timaeus* "One, two, three . . ." to find clear indication that Plato knew about the trinity. In fact the writings of many of the early Church Fathers are filled with bizarre references to parts of sentences in Plato as anticipations of Christian doctrine. Yet not all the parallels and symbolisms are continued, and the ethics, politics, and psychology of the early medieval period and even of the Byzantine period reflect without question a familiarity and respect for Platonic texts as they were made available. Medieval mysticism and the monastic movement leaned heavily on Plato's disparagement, if not renunciation, of this world. Nevertheless the un-Platonic elements in primitive Christianity were apparent to Augustine; the populism of Christianity and the aristocracy of Platonism are as different as emotivism and intellectualism, open and closed societies, fire and ice.

There is, of course, a singular justification for the identification of Neo-Platonism and the thinking of Plato during the first part of the Middle Ages. Some of the Platonic writings were safely closeted in Moorish libraries, translated into Latin by Western scholars even before the conquest of Constantinople by the Turks in 1453. Little of Plato except *Timaeus*, *Phaedo*, and *Meno* was extant in Latin during a crucial period of intellectual development in which Greek and Arabic were simply not studied. It is easy, therefore, to see how the influence of the *Timaeus* as an isolated Platonic text could be so powerful in the early scholastic period, both in theology and in the broader cultural areas which were so forcefully molded by the cathedral schools in France, for instance.

During the fifteenth century a number of seemingly unrelated events brought about a dramatic revival of Platonism in Europe. The threatening power of the Turks, after their capture of Constantinople, the increasing commerce between European and Eastern cities, and the dominance of the Medici vision made Florence the center of a revived Platonism which extended its influence throughout Europe. It was Cosimo de' Medici who became so taken with what he could learn of Plato that he chose Marsilio Ficino, the brilliant son of a Medici physician, to be educated and directed to do the primary work of translating the dialogues, as well as being the commentator of the revival of Platonism, and finally to bring into one systematic whole Platonic studies and the Christian faith. To be sure, there was some success on the last point, but the signal achievement of the Medici revival was to influence literature and the arts for centuries.

Ficino's influence upon religious thought was to bring about a non-hierophantic, subtle Platonizing of ethical Christianity rather than a Christianizing of Plato as others had attempted, and sometimes partially achieved. Plato could be used to support numerous detached theological beliefs, and where Plato's conclusions were alien to Ficino's view of the faith, he was not reluctant to suggest that the Greek was capable of error. Still some of the bizarre accoutrements of speculative religion—witchcraft, demonology, astrology—could be tolerated by this kind of Platonism, and, along with more sophisticated formulations, can be seen in its fruits in continental Europe and Great Britain in the succeeding centuries.

The liberal religious tradition of the last several hundred years is rooted in this Platonizing of theology, although it would be mistaken to call all, or even most subsequent religious liberals Platonists. The liberal Christians at Cambridge in the seventeenth century, who as a group have come to be known as the "Cambridge Platonists," represent (in spite of their loose handling of classical sources) this selective Platonizing of ethical Christianity. Like Plato, they saw their times as badly in need of intellectual therapy, with materialism again the dominant illness (Hobbes now being the pathogenic agent). Unlike Plato, they tended toward a dullness of style, and when forceful, tended to be more eloquent in rhetoric than brilliant in philosophy. Like Plato, they leaned to a somewhat mystical theology, holding that wherever one finds beauty, harmony, love, wisdom, one has found God.

Contrary to orthodoxy, they maintained that sin had not extinguished any "natural light," but that the spirit of man, "the candle of the Lord," still shines in all men, leading to the truth which nobler men, like Plato, see with great clarity.

Of the half-dozen or so primary figures who made up the group, Ralph Cudworth (1617–88) was the most philosophical, the most erudite, and the most respected. Along with Benjamin Whichcote, John Smith, Henry More, and other minor members of the school, Cudworth's Platonism was dominantly Neo-Platonic. Nevertheless his attacks on sensations, as an inadequate basis of knowledge, his idealistic interpretation of moral notions, and his ontology were main-line Platonism.

Philosophically Platonism spent itself in the seventeenth century and never really revived as a movement, not because the influence of Plato failed or because the power of his ideas waned. On the contrary, the relevance of Plato to the great systematic philosophies of the nineteenth century is apparent in even the most superficial reading. Nevertheless one cannot call the idealistic edifices of Hegel, Bradley, Royce, or the numerous minor idealisms of the past two hundred years Platonisms, for they bear only in part the Greek hallmark. Their heritage is largely Germanic, and while various interesting parallels exist, it would be simply false to attribute all idealistic metaphysics to Plato. Post-eighteenth-century idealisms have all been hybrids. Furthermore, while the presence of Platonic elements in the philosophies, for instance, of the empirical philosophers, such as Locke's concept of philosophical method, or the plethora of references to Plato in the later writings of Berkeley, has led admirers of Plato to see all serious thought to be merely footnoting, it is clear that finding Plato in a man's thought is not to find Platonism. Platonism is systematically iconic, and not universal, even though Plato might conceivably be everyman.

Florentine Platonism is much more important to letters than to religion or philosophy, however. The quaint legends of the Platonic Academy at Florence, the burning of incense before the bust of Plato, the Symposium-like banquets, the revival of pagan feasts, embellish every account of the Italian Renaissance, and, while of little significance conceptually or with regard to the degree of their truth, they do convey something of the spirit of the times which was to thrust a kind of Platonism into the arts in Europe for centuries to come.

In spite of the scholarliness of some of the followers of Ficino, such as Pico della Mirandola, Renaissance Platonism flourished not so much as an academic endeavor as an alchemistic efficacy, a way of thinking and living which brought the powers of love, inspiration, and creativity to transform the mundane into the sublime. Indeed, the impact of the literary Platonists, such as Dante, had a more powerful effect upon European thought in the eighteenth and nineteenth centuries than any of the philosophical Platonists.

Platonism dominated literary history during the Renaissance and romantic periods because Plato's is perhaps the most poetic of all philosophies. Platonism cannot be simply a collection of correct and well-argued doctrines and still remain true to its heritage. Poetry and philosophy converge in the Dialogues, and most often philosophy finds its rival in sophism or rhetoric, rather than in poetry. To be sure, Meletus, the frustrated tragic poet, angered by Socrates' vicious criticism of the poets, played a major role in his prosecution, but Plato's attack on the poets was a pragmatic move. He knew the political and intellectual dangers of poetry from the inside. Only a poet-philosopher could have written the Dialogues. In them he continually distinguishes between natural knowledge and truth. He insists in the *Phaedrus* that trees and fields cannot teach him anything, but men can, for truth has an inward character foreign to sensation. And men teach not by writing books or by making speeches, but by becoming vitally involved in dialogue, in human relationships. All else is sophistry or soliloquy.

The most vital and intimate of human relationships is love, and the exploration of the Platonic significance of love is one of the dominant themes of literary romanticism. Plato's fanciful identification of *eros* and *pteros* in the *Phaedrus* did not escape the attention of later writers who caught the Platonic vision of the necessity of love in genuine human communication. Words which communicate, Homer taught us, must have wings, and, if communication is a human trait, then the erotic attachment is the crucial human relationship. Friendship, Byron once noted, is love without its wings. Thus literary Platonism leans heavily upon Plato's often mystical concept of love.

Yet, as Plato developed his notion of eros, it became clear that love was not a simple relationship, and the dualistic principle which overarches all of Plato applies here as well. Heavenly love and heavenly beauty stand apart from and above earthly love and earthly beauty, just as the Forms are apart from and above things, although in some curious and relevant way related to them. These two fundamentals of Platonism, the role of eros and the metaphysical dualism of heavenly vs. earthly forms, dominated late Renaissance and post-Renaissance letters.

Commercial and military adventures brought the works of the Italians into France, especially during the reign of Francis I, whose powerful sister, Marguerite of Navarre, it is said, never allowed the works of Castiglione, Ficino, and Dante to be out of her reach. After the death of Francis I, in 1547, Catherine de' Medici became Queen of France, the Pléiade was born, with its sometimes variant Platonic interpretation, e.g., in the poetry of Ronsard and Du Bellay, and the Florentine influence spread more dominantly over France throughout the reigns as kings of Catherine's three sons. Often during these years the Platonic yields to a simple humanistic orientation. The Platonism of Rabelais or Montaigne, from a technical perspective, would have to be quite corrupt. Champier's translations of Ficino's efforts were less in the spirit of Plato than in the spirit of the Middle Ages. And to add to the confusion, the generosity of Ficino toward the bizarre and the occult reaped its consequences in the warren of astrology, cabbalism, and hermeticism which became the home of French Platonism during the Renaissance.

Platonism in English literature before the Renaissance was medieval, indirect, all from secondary sources, and therefore often unrecognizable, as for instance the curious and sometimes absurd references to Plato in Chaucer's *Canterbury Tales*. This very early English Platonism undoubtedly arrived by way of the cathedral schools of France, particularly Chartres. During the Renaissance in England, the Platonism of Linacre, Colet, Grocyn, Ascham, and More was no more than a copy of Italian and French Renaissance Platonism. Spenser too leaned heavily on Ficino and Pico for the Platonic elements of his thought and was perhaps the first major figure in English literature to settle on love and beauty rather than on theology or politics as the major emphases of Platonism. The early indications of Platonism as a philosophical or ethical system in the *Faerie Queene* soon appear of minuscule importance alongside the constant and powerful treatments of the inner vision, the Symposium-like pilgrimage of the soul to true love and beauty which leaves sense far behind.

It is not difficult to learn, often from their own testimonies, which English literary figures had read their Plato and which had not, nor is it difficult, from their writings, to determine which had read it well. Coleridge, for instance, clearly in the camp of those who knew the texts, had incredible difficulty distinguishing Plato from the Neo-Platonists. Philosophically as well as poetically his Platonism was a muddied stream. Another student of Plato, Matthew Arnold, on the other hand, unlike his literary colleagues, rejects the emphasis on love, rarely mentioning the *Symposium* or *Phaedrus*, and can only be significantly Platonic in his religious and ethical views and in his rejection of materialism. Wordsworth was not an avid reader of Plato (if he read him at all), nor of the Neo-Platonists, and the Platonism often ascribed to him is totally unhistorical, indeed, not Platonism at all. True, his references to immortality remind one that Plato was also concerned with that issue, but the romanticism of Wordsworth is alien to the tone and substance of Plato's ideas.

From whichever direction one chooses to consider him, temperament, interest, commitment, doctrine, effort, Shelley is the primary literary Platonist in the English language. From his earliest allusions to the dualism of sense and thought and the doctrine of the soul in *Queen Mab* to the polarity of time and the ideal in *Adonais* and *Hellas*, and *Mont Blanc*, the moral and metaphysical doctrines of *Prometheus Unbound*, and the pervasive aura of eros, Shelley demonstrates his infatuation with Platonism. His translation of the Dialogues, hasty and enthusiastic (his translation of the *Symposium* seems to have been motivated largely by his hope of converting Mary Shelley), are more important to students of Shelley than of Plato, but indicate something of the passion of the poet for the Greek. The imagery and symbolism of the Dialogues is recalled in the poetry in a completely unabashed way and the total effort of the creative life of Shelley is paradigmatic of Plato's poetic inspiration and passion.

So it would seem, in the light of the preceding reflections on Platonism, that the polarity between philosophy and poetry has persisted. But is it really between the philosopher and the poet? Perhaps it is found rather in man as he seeks to learn about his world and to know himself. Plato and his *ism* are not, nor is man, all of one piece. Platonism is metaphysics, but there is also what Lovejoy called "metaphysical pathos," the feeling aspect of or sensibility in philosophy which Plato so clearly saw. The susceptibility to different kinds of metaphysical pathos is determinative of the future of an *ism* and, as Lovejoy argued, the task of discovering these susceptibilities and showing their role in shaping a system or giving an idea currency is part of the task of the historian of ideas.

BIBLIOGRAPHY

John Burnet, *Platonism* (Berkeley, 1928). Frederick William Bussell, *The School of Plato* (London, 1896). Ernst Cassirer, *The Platonic Renaissance in England,* trans. F. C. A. Koelln and James P. Pettegrove (1932; Edinburgh, 1953). William Ralph Inge, *The Platonic Tradition in English Religious Thought* (New York, 1926). Raymond Klibansky, *The Continuity of the Platonic Tradition During the Middle Ages* (London, 1939). Paul Oskar Kristeller, *The Philosophy of Marsilio Ficino* (New York, 1943). Arthur O. Lovejoy, *The Great Chain of Being: A Study in the History of an Idea* (Cambridge, Mass., 1933). Philip Merlan, *From Platonism to NeoPlatonism* (The Hague, 1953). Paul Elmer More, *Platonism* (Princeton, 1917). Joseph Moreau, *Le Sens du Platonisme* (Paris, 1967). John Henry Muirhead, *The Platonic Tradition in Anglo-Saxon Philosophy* (London, 1931). Walter Pater, *Plato and Platonism* (London, 1893). George Santayana, *Platonism and the Spiritual Life* (New York and London, 1927). Paul Shorey, *Platonism, Ancient and Modern* (Berkeley, 1938). Alfred Edward Taylor, *Platonism and Its Influence* (Boston, 1924). Hans Wolff, *Plato: Der Kampf ums Sein* (Berkeley, 1957). Harry A. Wolfson, *Philo: Foundations of Religious Philosophy in Judaism, Christianity, and Islam* (Cambridge, Mass., 1962).

JOHN FISHER

[See also Dualism; Love; **Myth in Antiquity; Neo-Platonism; Platonism;** Pythagorean . . .; Renaissance Humanism; Skepticism; Stoicism.]

PLATONISM IN THE RENAISSANCE

STRICTLY construed, Platonism means the teachings of Plato. While not constituting a formal system of philosophy, Plato's dialogues evince certain recurring themes, characterized by a fundamental dualism of intelligible and sensible objects. Forms or ideas, which are transcendent universals, alone constitute reality as against the shadowy existence of particular material objects; chief among these Forms or ideas is the idea of the Good, supreme both as the goal of knowledge and as the guide to morality. Reason should prevail against sense: the well-ordered soul is a tripartite amalgam of appetite and spirit, represented as two horses, governed by reason, the charioteer. Similarly, the ideal republic is a state in which each class—workers, soldiers, and ruling philosophers—performs its function harmoniously. Knowledge of ideas—the only real knowledge—is pictured mythically as a sort of reminiscence of the transmigrated soul's earlier existence. Plato's spokesman in his dialogues, Socrates, proclaims paradoxically that virtue is knowledge, but that no teachers of virtue are to be found. Love is depicted in the *Phaedrus* as a "divine madness"; in the *Symposium* as a process of ascent from sensual cognition of earthly beauty to the apprehension of the immortal idea of beauty itself.

The nature of Platonism evolved a great deal even during classical antiquity as it was continued by the Academy, the Alexandrian School, by Plotinus, Proclus, and their successors. The alterations and the systematization of Platonism by these thinkers constituted Neo-Platonism. The most complete of these and probably of all philosophical systems is that of the pagan

Plotinus. Its essential concept is that of a hierarchy of being emanating from the godhead. Plotinus' supreme triad consists of (1) the One, morally identified with the Good, transcendent and ultimately unknowable, approachable if at all through negative theology; (2) the ideas or essences, emanating from the ultimate source of all, the One; and (3) the world soul which expresses the divine creative power in the world of natural objects. The material world itself is a shadowy reflection of the celestial world; pure matter itself is next to nonbeing. Corresponding conversely to this downward path of creation is the upward thrust of cognition. Even higher than man's rational, discursive knowledge stands the intuitive knowledge of the intelligences (or minds); the One is above knowledge.

Unfortunately for Renaissance Platonism, both Greek and Italian scholars of the fifteenth century accepted uncritically Plotinus' declaration that in all his writings he was simply a repeater and interpreter of Plato. The adulteration of authentic Platonism by Neo-Platonism colored the history of Platonism throughout the Renaissance. As Plotinus and other Neo-Platonists sought to systematize Plato's dialogues and imbue them with their own ideas, they not only distorted them, but robbed them of their poetic fire. To reduce Plato to dry doctrine is to lose his very essence. Renaissance scholars were not prepared to see in Plato the drama of men's minds; the historical perspective which would have allowed them to do so was achieved much later. They could not believe that some of Plato's imaginative myths were merely suggestive or even playful. Jehudah Abarbanel, known in Italy as Leone Ebreo, writes in his *Dialoghi d'amore* (ca. 1502) of the character of Aristophanes' fable of the halving of primeval man in Plato's *Symposium:* "The fable is beautiful and ornate; and it is not to be doubted that it signifies some fine philosophy."

Platonism continued to influence Western thought not only through the philosophic schools—Aristotle himself was strongly influenced by his teacher Plato—but through Christianity as well. The writings of Saint Paul and the Church Fathers are imbued with the basic Platonic dualism of matter and spirit. Combined with Augustinian asceticism and the sacramental system of salvation, this dualism contributed to the medieval ideal of morality and immortality.

Plato himself saw the spiritual glory of the intelligible in the whole world of life and art that was Athens, but his Orientalized successors turned more and more away from the setting of human life to the higher realm. Even Plato at times was touched by this asceticism, and in the beautiful dialogue of *Phaedo* called the entire aim of man the seeking of death—death to the body and immortal being for the soul (Randall, p. 47).

Saint Augustine asserted that Neo-Platonism possessed all spiritual truths except that of the Incarnation.

Typical Platonist doctrines, such as the eternal presence of the universal forms in the mind of God, the immediate comprehension of these ideas by human reason, and the incorporeal nature and the immortality of the human soul, are persistently asserted in his earlier philosophical as well as in his later theological writings . . . (Kristeller, *Renaissance Thought*, p. 55).

". . . it has been well said that the Middle Ages were full of a spontaneous Platonism, inspired by a mind *naturaliter Platonica*" (Randall, p. 46). Certain structures and recurrent metaphors of Dante's *Divine Comedy* are Neo-Platonic. The angels of the *Paradiso* are analogous in rank and function to the second hypostasis of the Plotinian triad; this canticle is permeated by Neo-Platonic metaphors of light. Some of Dante's notions of hierarchy may have reached him through the anonymous Neo-Platonic *Liber de causis*, which he mentions repeatedly in his *Convivio*, as well as through Christian theologians.

Plato's writings have been preserved in their entirety; yet the only dialogue by Plato available to early medieval readers was the *Timaeus*, in the incomplete version and commentary of Chalcidius. In the twelfth century, the *Meno* and the *Phaedo* were also translated into Latin. But a lively interest in Plato reappeared in Francesco Petrarca (anglicized as Petrarch), who more rightly than any other man may be called the founder of humanism and the inaugurator of the Renaissance. The references to Plato which he found in Cicero and Saint Augustine led him to proclaim, on faith, Plato's superiority to Aristotle and to declare (*De ignorantia*) to four Venetian critics that he possessed a manuscript of "sixteen or more" dialogues by the ancient master. Unfortunately, Western Europe in the fourteenth century could claim few masters of Greek language. Petrarch's dream of a Platonic revival had to await Leonardo Bruni's translation of several of Plato's dialogues in the first half of the fifteenth century and the far more extensive work of Marsilio Ficino a century after Petrarch. The Christianizing tendency of Renaissance Platonists and its emotional raison d'être are foreshadowed in Petrarch: "Of Plato, Augustine does not in the least doubt that he would have become a Christian if he had come to life again in Augustine's time or had foreseen the future while he lived. Augustine relates also that in his time most of the Platonists had become Christians and he himself can be supposed to belong to their number" (ibid.). Augustinian Platonism pervades Petrarch's *Canzoniere*, the most influential lyric poetry of all time. Throughout the Renaissance,

Platonism and Petrarchism were to walk hand-in-hand—Italian Platonic love theorists of the sixteenth century illustrate their works by quoting Petrarch's poetry even more frequently than they quote Plato. Ficino's chief work was his *Theologia Platonica*, whose very title implies an essential agreement between Platonic philosophy and Christian theology (Kristeller, *Ficino*, p. 322).

Pietro Bembo and his followers in the sixteenth century take Petrarch's Laura as their model for the woman whose "celestial" beauty leads the poet or philosopher upward to divine beauty. Yet paradoxically, Petrarch himself saw his sensual love of Laura as conflicting with his love of God. Ultimately he rejected sensual love as unworthy: Laura appears in the final poem of the *Canzoniere* as the fearsome Medusa.

During the Middle Ages Neo-Platonism continued in the Byzantine East in more readily identifiable fashion than in the West. Its impact was felt in Italy in 1438 with the visit of George Gemisthus Pletho to Florence. From him Ficino inherited the tradition that Plato was the continuer of an ancient pagan theology —later shown to be apocryphal—handed down by Hermes Trismegistus, Zoroaster, Orpheus, and Pythagoras.

The Renaissance generally was a less creative age in philosophy than in the arts. Yet Platonism, far from being a sterile repetition of ancient doctrine, played a dynamic role throughout the Renaissance from the time of its introduction by Petrarch as a countervailing force against traditional Aristotelian learning—often repeated almost by rote—to the abandonment of Aristotelian physics at the end of the Renaissance by Platonically influenced innovators such as Telesio, Bruno, and Campanella, to whose animistic, God-reflecting cosmos there corresponded the microcosm of the human spirit. They and their predecessors, Marsilio Ficino and Giovanni Pico della Mirandola, transcend the primarily scholarly and literary objectives of Renaissance humanism. All three, and particularly Bruno, extend Ficino's anthropocentrism into cosmic dimensions, as they unfold a universe to be explored and understood through the unfettered interrogation of nature rather than by a perusal of traditional authors—an ideal consecrated by Bruno's martyrdom. "In other words," writes Giovanni Gentile (*Rinascimento*, p. 293), "the new philosophy and the new science are distinguished from faith not by putting the latter above themselves and attributing to it the privilege of truth unattainable by them, although they too aim at it; but rather by denying it any value in regard to the ends sought by philosophy and science." In this broad sense only, Telesio, Bruno, and Campanella were predecessors of Galileo and Bacon. The Renaissance was preeminently an age of transition.

Plato throughout the Renaissance was seen as a newly-discovered, ancient, pre-Christian sage whose exciting doctrines, wrapped in esoteric myth, challenged the cut-and-dried teachings of a more mundane, less imaginative Aristotle.

North of the Alps an early reviver of Neo-Platonism was Nicholas of Cusa. Following his education at Deventer, Heidelberg, Padua, Rome, and Cologne, he became a leading philosopher and theologian. Combining Neo-Platonic sources with the Christian Fathers and others, he may have exerted some influence on Ficino; he surely influenced Bruno in such doctrines as the coincidence of contraries, the respectively differing infinities of God and the universe, the plurality of worlds, and the motion of the earth. His *De docta ignorantia* Socratically praises wisdom as the awareness of one's own ignorance. However, Italian Platonists generally ignored him in favor of Ficino and Leone Ebreo.

Marsilio Ficino's influence upon Platonism in the Renaissance and later is pervasive and multiple. A translator of Plato and Plotinus as well as several other Neo-Platonists, he was also their interpreter and a Platonic philosopher in his own right.

In his *Platonic Theology* he gave to his contemporaries an authoritative summary of Platonist philosophy, in which the immortality of the soul is emphasized, reasserting to some extent the Thomist position against the Averroists. His Platonic Academy with its courses and discussions provided for some decades an institutional center whose influence was spread all over Europe through his letters and other writings. Assigning to the human soul the central place in the hierarchy of the universe, he gave a metaphysical expression to a notion dear to his humanist predecessors; whereas his doctrine of spiritual love in Plato's sense, for which he coined the term Platonic love, became one of the most popular concepts of later Renaissance literature (Kristeller, *Classics*, p. 59).

Ficino's love doctrine, expounded in his *Commentarium in convivium Platonis de amore* (1469; *Commentary on Plato's "Symposium" about Love*), gave rise to more than a score of Platonic love treatises—a new genre, often more literary than philosophical, which lasted well into the seventeenth century. This commentary in dialogue form is based upon a commemoration of Plato's traditional birthday and date of death, November 7, held under Lorenzo de' Medici's auspices. Ficino's seven orators tend generally to Christianize the *Symposium*. Greek gods and demons are transformed into Christian angels; Socrates' instructress in the meaning of love, Diotima, is said to be inspired by the Holy Spirit. At the basis of Ficino's cosmology is the emanative system of Plotinus. Love is "desire to enjoy beauty"; and nourished by the spiritual senses of sight and hearing alone, it is temperate, ascensive, morally beneficent. "Love is in all things and toward all, creator of all, and master of all." Ficino's threefold classification of love was widely repeated: (1) divine love, the expression of a contemplative life, whose goal is divine knowledge; (2) human love and the active life, which delight in seeing and conversing with the loved person—identified by Pietro Bembo and others as the idealized golden-haired lady of Petrarch; and (3) bestial love and the voluptuous life which deserts the spiritual senses for the "concupiscence of touch." Beauty is "the splendor of divine goodness," present everywhere; personal beauty expresses an interior moral goodness.

While not identical, Ficino's Neo-Platonic love theory is strikingly similar to that of the *dolce stil nuovo* and Dante's *Divine Comedy*. Since Petrarch's poetry was strongly influenced by the *stil nuovo*, it is not always possible to separate Renaissance Platonism from the heritage of medieval Platonizing in poets such as Lorenzo de' Medici, Angelo Poliziano, Girolamo Benivieni, Michelangelo Buonarroti, and a host of others. Both Dante and Ficino believe in a Neo-Platonic hierarchy of being which includes God, intelligences, souls, and bodies. Love, for both, is a process of ascent culminating in union with and knowledge of God. For Petrarch also the central human and divine experience is love; yet he was unable to reconcile the human and divine elements as were Dante, who invested his Beatrice with theological symbolism, and Ficino, who followed Plato to the stars. In both Dante and Ficino human love becomes a *scala coeli* ("ladder to heaven") in which the senses are abandoned for a higher life. However, in Ficino male friendship rather than love of an angel-lady is the basis of the ethereal flight; hence there is no troubadour theme of serving and praising one's lady as in Dante and Petrarch. Ficino ultimately abandons any particular love object; for all of his desire to reconcile Platonism with Christianity, his concept of love is basically Platonic, Dante's Christian and chivalric.

A number of Ficino's tenets, interspersed with motives from Dante and the *stil nuovo*, reappear in the verse and prose of his patron, Lorenzo de' Medici. Lorenzo's genuine attitude toward love, however, lacks the asceticism which generally characterized Christian Neo-Platonism—a fact occasionally masked by the Ficinian terminology employed by Lorenzo in the prose commentary which he wrote to accompany some of his poems. Human love, if not the highest good, nevertheless "occupies the place of good" so long as it is true and enduring. *Gentilezza*, defined by Lorenzo

as the perfect and graceful performance of one's function, is engendered by supernal beauty, identified Platonically with the good and the true. Ultimately, Lorenzo's sensuality reverses the Platonic ladder: "Presupposing that Love motivates all the actions of my Lady that we have named, that is, seeing, singing, talking, laughing, sighing, and ultimately touching; seeing shows less affection than singing, singing less than talking, and so I say of all the others up to touching" (*Comento sopra alcuni de' suoi sonetti*, in *Opere*, Bari [1913], I, 120).

In the *Stanze per la giostra* (1478; *Stanzas for the Tournament*) of Angelo Poliziano, who is like Ficino a protégé of Lorenzo, there is a similar coupling of delicate sensuality with Platonizing conceptions. Love is celebrated in a scheme reminiscent of Petrarch's *Trionfi*, as Love, in the form of fair Simonetta, triumphs over Iulio (Giuliano de' Medici). The exquisite description of the timeless realm of Venus, repeating and eternalizing the idyllic moment of earthly Spring, embodies the Platonic notion that transient, earthly beauty has its origin in a remote celestial world. Iulio in his approach to Simonetta expresses the hope that a divine being may be hidden in her lovely form. The two "Platonic" senses find expression in a preponderance of the verbs of seeing and hearing. The handling of color and light follows Ficino's Neo-Platonic guidelines: most brilliant at their source, both in the worldly scene and in its celestial exemplar.

Poliziano's description in the *Stanze* of the birth of Venus in turn influenced Botticelli's famous painting of that subject. The model for both works is the same Simonetta Cattaneo who inspired verses by Lorenzo and portraits by Pollaiuolo and Ghirlandaio. While Botticelli's *Birth of Venus* has been variously interpreted, its Neo-Platonism appears to be clearly discernible in several features: the luminescence and weightlessness of Venus; the reduction of volume and mass to relatively immaterial line; a pervasive spirituality; and the suggestion, perhaps, of the mantle awaiting Venus that love and beauty are experienced on earth only through a veil.

In 1486 Girolamo Benivieni (1453–1542), a member of the Platonic Academy in Florence which Ficino headed under Medicean sponsorship, wrote a *Canzone d'amore*, an epitome in verse of Ficino's love theory and other elements of Neo-Platonic doctrine. Concise and somewhat obscure, it evoked a learned and exhaustive commentary from Ficino's fellow philosopher and sometime Platonist disciple, Giovanni Pico della Mirandola. A fundamental ambiguity in Renaissance Platonism appears in Benivieni's doubt regarding publication: "There were born in our minds some shadows of doubt as to whether it were proper for a professor

511

of Christ's law, wishing to treat of love, especially heavenly and divine, to treat of it as Platonic and not as Christian" (Benivieni, Introduction to *Canzone d'amore*, in Giovanni Pico della Mirandola, *Opera omnia*, Basel, 1572). Pico sees even the structure of Benivieni's poem as reflecting the Plotinian scheme of universal emanation and return. Love originates in "the divine fount of uncreated good"; when the "divine sun" descends into the angelic mind, the angels, as in Dante's circle, desire and contemplate God. The human soul must die in itself in order to partake of angelic love.

Renaissance Platonists tried to combine the classical ideal of beauty and Platonic morality with the Christian ideal of religious and moral perfection. The difficulty of this fusion is shown by Benivieni's expressed doubts and his eventual composition, under Savonarolan influence, of a *"Canzone* of celestial and divine love according to Christian and Catholic truth." The Platonic intuition of love and life, while far from naturalistic, is not yet Christian. Hence for Ficino, Pico, Benivieni, and later Patrizi, divergences between Platonism and Christianity are recognized as demanding reconciliation.

While Marsilio Ficino is the single most important Renaissance source of Platonism, he was not unrivaled in his influence. The *Dialoghi d'amore* of Leone Ebreo, written almost contemporaneously with Bembo's *Asolani*, are praised by several later writers as an unsurpassed book of love doctrine. Not merely a treatise on love, they are also a detailed restatement of Neo-Platonic philosophy. Though broader than any commentary on Plato's *Symposium*, Leone's book has many themes in common with Ficino's *Commentary*. The upper and lower worlds join in man's soul, a microcosm of the world soul. By knowing beauty man purifies himself, rising in both knowledge and virtue. Bad desires, as for the Platonic Socrates if not for Ficino, derive from erroneous judgment rather than from corrupted will. Man's intellect, like the soul for Pico in his famous *Oration* on the dignity of man, is potentially all things. The ultimate wisdom is to know God—a goal not fully attainable in this life, where intimations of intuitive knowledge are achieved only briefly in a Platonic *raptus* or ecstasy, which Leone calls "copulation with highest God." Like Ficino, he attributes to Plato the Plotinian doctrines of the One, and of emanation. Leone links Plato's cosmology to that of Moses, and Aristophanes' myth in the *Symposium* of the halving of man to the Hebrew story of man's creation in Genesis. Plato's superiority to Aristotle is credited to the influence of Mosaic theology! Leone's formulation of Platonic love theory may have influenced Spinoza's concept of the intellectual love

of God; it is certain that his influence on many minor sixteenth-century authors was profound.

Pietro Bembo and Baldassare Castiglione employ a Christianized Platonism as an antidote for the courtier's excessively mundane preoccupations. Their respective treatises, the *Asolani* (1505) and *Il libro del cortigiano* (1528; *The Book of the Courtier*), are largely void of serious philosophic concerns. They were to have many imitators in the sixteenth century who followed Bembo's lead in making of the Platonic love treatise a vehicle for topical discussions, couched in the fashionable literary style of lively dialogue interspersed with quotations or imitations of Petrarch's love poetry. Castiglione wishes his ideal courtier "to love apart from the custom of the profane crowd": snob appeal helps to explain the popularity of literary expressions of Platonism in the high Renaissance. Both Bembo and Castiglione envelop their Platonism with an air of Christian sanctity. Bembo's penchant for Petrarch, whom he canonized as the model for lyric poetry, encouraged the predominance of literary as against philosophical motives in most subsequent Platonic love treatises. The *Asolani* is gallant, courtly, mundane; yet it manages to repeat a great deal of Ficino's doctrine, in combination with motives from Petrarch, Dante, and Boccaccio.

The goal of Castiglione's book, which also takes the popular dialogue form inherited from Plato and Cicero, is the Platonistic attempt "to form with words a perfect courtier." The exposition of Platonic love in the fourth book by the interlocutor Bembo is a literary restatement without significant philosophical accretions of Ficino's love theory, derived directly from the Florentine *alter Plato* rather than from the historical Bembo. There is no longer, however, any pretense that male friendship or love should provide the starting point for the ascent of Diotima's ladder; the beloved must be a lady. Renaissance Platonists are unanimous in their condemnation of the homosexuality reflected in Plato's *Symposium* and *Phaedrus*. Like Ficino, they either limit male love to the moral and intellectual realms, or, increasingly after Bembo, replace the lover's young male friend with the Laura figure familiar in Renaissance poetry and painting.

Francesco Cattani da Diacceto, Ficino's chief disciple, was active in the Medici Academy, which called itself a revival of the Platonic Academy. His *Tre libri d'amore*, with its insistence upon the superessentiality and unknowability of God and its comprehensive ontological scale ranging from supra-being to non-being, denotes a stronger influence of Plotinus than in Ficino. The human soul from its intermediate position between matter and spirit can achieve happiness through the combined effort of will and intellect to possess God. The universe itself is animated. The angelic nature is completely lucid; man's soul, partly so; the body, altogether dark. Bodily beauty can be either a *scala dei* or the soul's ruination.

The influence of Platonism on Renaissance art is generally acknowledged. As Panofsky writes (p. 180), "With an Italian artist of the sixteenth century the presence of Neo-Platonic influences is easier to account for than would be their absence." Foremost among Platonizing artists was Michelangelo himself, "who adopted Neo-Platonism not in certain aspects but in its entirety"—witness the conception of Julius II's apotheosis not as an orthodox Christian resurrection, "but as an ascension in the sense of the Neo-Platonic philosophy"; and in the Medici Chapel the figures of Dawn, Day, Evening, and Night, demonstrating "the destructive power of time," and the four River-Gods depicting "matter as a source of potential evil."

While flashes of Dante and Francesco Berni appear throughout Michelangelo's poems, it comes as no surprise to find in the majority of them a mixture of Petrarchan and Platonic motives. Among the latter are the soul's desire to return to its parent star, retracing in the upward path of knowledge, as in Plato, Plotinus, and Ficino, the downward thrust of divine creation. The sight of a beautiful human face or form is sufficient, as for Plato, to start the soul on its restless upward journey, which is made possible by the rejection of whatever is vicious or merely material. The origins of Michelangelo's Platonism are as easy to explain in a general way as they are difficult to pinpoint in detail. As a young protégé of Lorenzo he early came under the influence of Ficino and his circle. Add to this his innate spirituality and it is no surprise that his poetry is replete with Platonism—not mere lip service to current literary and artistic fashion, but the expression of his inner nature and beliefs.

The prestige enjoyed by Platonism in the arts if not in philosophy is shown by its curious hold over Torquato Tasso. No reader of his pastoral *Aminta* (1573) or epic *Gerusalemme liberata* (1575; *Jerusalem Delivered*) can fail to appreciate the sensual splendor of the amorous passages. Both in his poetry and in his life he evinces a strain of hedonism uneasily held in check by religious restraints. Yet such was the authority of Platonism in the sixteenth century that when he turned to theoretical writing on love (*Conclusioni amorose*, 1570; *La Molza*, 1583, etc.), he followed the Platonic precepts which his mimetic works contradict. Written over a span of at least fifteen years, his several works on love and related topics combine some Aristotelian motives with a predominant, but gradually

diminishing Platonism. The *Allegory* which he wrote in 1576 in defense of his *Jerusalem* is based upon an analogy between Plato's tripartite soul in the *Phaedrus* and the roles of the leading characters in his epic.

In some ways the tradition of Platonic love treatises culminates in the *Eroici furori* (1585) of Giordano Bruno. The poetic-religious zeal for divine beauty and goodness harks back to Plato himself, surpassing in its intensity and sincerity the commonplaces of earlier Platonizing literati. Philosophical problems, such as the relation of intellect and will, are given greater attention than in the more conventional love treatises; personal allusion and allegory in the work's final dialogue differentiate it from the category of commentary and elaboration upon the classical Platonic writings. Nevertheless, the *Eroici furori* is replete with motives common to most Renaissance Platonists: the Neo-Platonic ontological hierarchy, Diotima's ladder, metaphors of light and fire, man the microcosm, the flesh as a prison, the overwhelming effects of love—to name but a few.

Yet surprisingly Bruno does not call himself a Platonist. He identifies himself with the pristine energy of pre-Socratic natural philosophers, whose opposition and "superiority" to Aristotle he emphasizes. While Platonizing in certain works—the *De umbris idearum* (1582), *De gli eroici furori*, and the *Summa terminorum metaphysicorum* (1595)—Bruno does in other works repudiate certain Platonic doctrines: the separate realm of ideas in the *De immenso et innumerabilibus;* negative theology and Socratic ignorance in the *Cabala del cavallo pegaseo*, in which, however, the real object of attack is the Christian church and priesthood. Matter in the *De la causa, principio e uno* is not subordinated to forms as it is in the *Eroici furori*. We frequently find in Bruno's writings not a development of systematic philosophy but an enthusiastic amalgam of doctrines some of which are in mutual contradiction. A personal echo of Plato's *Phaedo* is discernible in Bruno's execution at the stake: his heroic defiance of Church authority is inevitably reminiscent of Socrates' death. In the *Eroici furori* (I, iii, 369) there is an unconscious presage of his refusal to retract the heresies with which he was charged: "Certainly a worthy and heroic death is better than an unworthy and cowardly triumph."

Unlike Bruno, his rival anti-Aristotelian, Francesco Patrizi of Cherso openly espoused Platonism as true philosophy and was able to occupy a special chair of Platonic philosophy first at Ferrara, and later, through his friendship with Clement VIII, in Rome. It is an irony of history that the pope who later condemned Bruno should have invited Patrizi to Rome as a teacher of Platonism, despite the belief of Bruno's judge, Cardinal Bellarmino, that such teaching was inimical to

Catholic orthodoxy. The condemnation of Patrizi's *Nova de universis philosophia* in the Index of 1595 and the hostility of the Curia to philosophies subversive of Thomistic Aristotelianism apparently did not prevent his continued teaching in Rome. However, during the centuries following the Church's condemnation and their deaths the works of both men became scarce and almost unknown.

Patrizi's *Nova de universis philosophia* is replete with Platonism. In dedicating it to Pope Gregory XIV, Patrizi defends his teaching of Platonic philosophy as a way of promoting the Catholic religion. The Church Fathers, he avers, were Platonists and anti-Aristotelians. He expresses the hope that his teaching of Platonic philosophy at Ferrara will become by papal fiat the pattern for all schools and suggests that should the practice spread to Germany, one result of such teaching would be the return of the Protestants to the Mother Church. Nevertheless, his chief love treatise, *L'amorosa filosofia*, offers a surprisingly un-Platonic analysis of love based on the concept of uncompromising *philautia*, or self-love, deriving ultimately from Aristotle's *Nicomachean Ethics* (IX, 8).

Petrarch and Ficino were quite influential beyond Italy. Symphorien Champier (ca. 1472–1539), physician and scholar, imported Italian humanism and Platonism to Lyons. His *Nef des dames vertueuses* (1503) "contains in its fourth book the first . . . expression in French of Ficinian Neo-Platonism" (Wadsworth, p. 13), including a discussion of Platonic love and the soul's step-by-step ascent to God.

Petrarchism accompanied Platonism into France in the poetry of Maurice Scève, whose *Délie* (1544) "rests on a foundation of Petrarchism to which are added certain Platonic elements" (McFarlane, p. 28). In the poet's elaboration of his spiritual union with Délie and her divine perfection and beneficent influence on the poet and other mortals, the Italian Platonist tradition finds expression. The influence of Sperone Speroni in the latter stanzas is extensive; that of Bembo, Leone Ebreo, and Equicola is also identifiable.

In the sixteenth century in the circle of Marguerite of Navarre, Plato's dialogues were studied and translated into French. Antoine Héroet is strongly influenced by Ficino's version of the *Symposium* in *L'androgyne* (1542) and other works. Louis Le Roy translated and commented upon the *Symposium* and other dialogues. Du Bellay's sonnet, *Si nostre vie est moins qu'une journée*, deals Platonically with ideal goodness and beauty. Petrarchism and Italian Platonism are frequently combined in Du Bellay's and Ronsard's poetry.

John Colet (ca. 1466–1519) brought back to England from his studies in Italy and France an enthusiasm for humanistic learning which he shared with such collaborators as Erasmus and Thomas More. His commentary on the *Hierarchies* of pseudo-Dionysius and his other writings reveal the influence of Ficino and Pico.

Platonic influence is not lacking in Sir Thomas More's combination of humanistic and theological learning, notably in his *Utopia*. Erasmus compared More's household to a Christianized version of Plato's Academy. More's martyrdom, while inspired by that of Christ, repeated Socrates' respect for human law and exaltation of eternal law.

The exposition of love theory in Edmund Spenser's *Four Hymns*, though attributing greater goodness to earthly love than do many of his Italian counterparts, is strongly influenced by Ficino's commentary on the *Symposium*.

The teaching of Plato came to the poet and his contemporaries along a tangle of paths: from the philosopher himself and from his followers Porphyry and Plotinus; from Greek and Latin moralists like Plutarch, Vergil, Cicero, Macrobius and Boethius; from St. Augustine and other fathers of the Christian church; from philosophers and poets of the Italian Renaissance (William Nelson, *The Poetry of Edmund Spenser*, New York [1963], pp. 108–09).

The Renaissance witnessed a continuation of rivalry between Plato and Aristotle, with the latter generally triumphant in the universities and the Church. The Platonistic aesthetics of Patrizi and others made little headway in the face of the sixteenth century's rediscovery and normative application of Aristotle's *Poetics*. Though Torquato Tasso sought to defend the hedonistic liberties of a few passages in his *Gerusalemne liberata* by referring them to Platonic allegory, his Neo-Aristotelian critics eventually forced him to delete the passages in his revision, the *Gerusalemme conquistata*.

There were also instances of anti-Platonism which did not derive from Aristotle or the Church. Ariosto's narrative of the love of Orlando for Angelica in the *Orlando furioso* (1516) carries some vaguely anti-Platonic overtones. Francesco Sansovino's *Ragionamento* (1545) on "the fine art of love" dismissed "the Platonists . . . since their actions are suspect"—an allusion to charges of homosexuality, universally denied by Renaissance Platonists. Machiavelli in affirming the novelty of his political science must surely have had Plato, among others, in mind when he wrote (*The Prince*, XV): "Many have imagined republics and principalities that have never been seen or known actually to exist; because there is such a difference between how men live and how they should live that he who abandons that which is done for that which should be done experiences his own destruction rather than his preservation."

The influence of Platonism, of course, did not die with the Renaissance. The Platonism of Benjamin Whichcote and the Cambridge school derives largely from Renaissance Platonism. Among modern philosophers, as among those of classical antiquity and the Middle Ages, Plato has been so strong an influence that Whitehead (*Process and Reality*, p. 63) could call the history of Western philosophy a series of footnotes to Plato. In the luxuriant flowering of Renaissance culture that centered in Florence—inevitably reminiscent, for all its differences, of ancient Athens—the Platonic rootstock proved amazingly fertile.

BIBLIOGRAPHY

Ernst Cassirer, *The Individual and the Cosmos in Renaissance Philosophy* (Oxford, 1963). Eugenio Garin, *La cultura filosofica del Rinascimento italiano* (Florence, 1961). Giovanni Gentile, *Il pensiero italiano del Rinascimento* (Florence, 1940). E. H. Gombrich, "Botticelli's Mythologies: A Study in the Neo-Platonic Symbolism of his Circle," *Journal of the Warburg and Courtauld Institutes*, **8** (1945), 7–60. Sears Jayne, "Ficino and the Platonism of the English Renaissance," *Comparative Literature*, **4** (1952), 214–38. Paul Oskar Kristeller, *The Philosophy of Marsilio Ficino* (New York, 1943); idem, *The Classics and Renaissance Thought* (Cambridge, Mass., 1955). Paolo Lorenzetti, *La bellezza e l'amore nei trattati del Cinquecento* (Pisa, 1917). Robert V. Merrill with Robert J. Clements, *Platonism in French Renaissance Poetry* (New York, 1957). John Charles Nelson, *Renaissance Theory of Love* (New York, 1958). Erwin Panofsky, *Studies in Iconology* (New York, 1939). John Herman Randall, Jr., *The Making of the Modern Mind* (New York, 1940). Nesca A. Robb, *Neoplatonism of the Italian Renaissance* (London, 1935). John Addington Symonds, *Renaissance in Italy*, 7 vols. (London, 1875–86). Luigi Tonelli, *L'amore nella poesia e nel pensiero del Rinascimento* (Florence, 1933). James B. Wadsworth, ed., *Symphorien Champier, Le livre de vraye amour* ('s-Gravenhage, 1962). Alfred North Whitehead, *Process and Reality* (New York, 1941; various reprints).

The translations of Lorenzo de' Medici and Girolamo Benivieni are by the author of this article.

JOHN CHARLES NELSON

[See also Dualism; Hermeticism; Hierarchy; **Love;** Macrocosm and Microcosm; **Neo-Platonism; Renaissance Humanism.**]

PLATONISM
SINCE THE ENLIGHTENMENT

RENAISSANCE Platonism had received its imprint from the Florentine Academy, notably from the translations, commentaries, and treatises of Ficino. In the seven-teenth century the Florentine tradition was mainly carried on in England by the so-called Cambridge Platonists. After the decline of the Cambridge School of Neo-Platonism, no important philosophical movement or system has arisen which can be unambiguously named Platonism (or Neo-Platonism). It is true that all kinds of mysticism, of pantheism or panentheism, and also of metaphysical idealism have at some time been thus called. But this does not mean more than that certain parts or aspects of a philosophical or quasi-philosophical system betray an impact of Platonic or Neo-Platonic thoughts on its author whether or not the latter was aware of it. On the other hand, since the nineteenth century the designation "Platonists" has often been conferred on scholars who, without a philosophical commitment to the validity of Plato's philosophy, have tried to elucidate "what Plato says." Their case is, however, complex. It is probable that a considerable number of the most thorough and important scholarly works on Plato would not have been completed, unless their authors had been motivated by their belief in the excellence of his philosophy. Yet others were written by scholars who were antagonistic to it, and so it seems sensible to reserve the name for those who as explorers of Plato indicate their assent to what they reasonably believe to be essential in his philosophy.

I

Leibniz ". . . was the first European thinker to emancipate himself inwardly from that conception of Platonism devised by the Florentine Academy, and to see Plato again with his own eyes" (E. Cassirer, *The Platonic Renaissance in England*, p. 154). In order to free Plato from what Ficino had made of him, Leibniz produced a condensed Latin version of the *Phaedo* and the *Theatetus* though he did not publish it. But if Leibniz sought an independent understanding of Plato's thought, he still did not seek it as would a modern critical historian of philosophy. He was attracted to Plato's philosophy because he recognized in it his own ideas and also, perhaps, because Plato helped him to formulate them. He was, however, puzzled by the form in which Plato presented his philosophy. "If someone should bring Plato into a system, he would do a great service to the human race and one would see that I am approaching him a little" (*Letter to Remond*, 2.2 [1715]). One thing which Leibniz admired in Plato was the pluralism of the theory of ideas; Plato, he says in the *Letter to Hansch*, teaches that *objectum sapientiae esse substantias nempe simplices, quae a me Monades appellantur* ("the objects of knowledge are the simplest substances, which I call Monads"). Apparently Leibniz assimilated Plato to his own thinking as much as Ficino

515

had assimilated Plato to his Christian Neo-Platonism. But the greater originality of Leibniz as a thinker made him also a more independent reader. Although he was free from prejudice against the Catholic and indeed the scholastic tradition, he read Plato in a "Protestant" manner.

No important philosopher before F. W. J. Schelling acquired a knowledge of Plato comparable to that of Leibniz or felt a similar affinity to him. Still it was not the discovery of new profundities in Plato by Schelling but the inauguration of a new method of interpretation by his contemporary Friedrich Schleiermacher which gave rise to a new phase of the history of Platonism. In this history, both Leibniz and Schelling are powerful figures outside of the mainstream whose direct influence remained limited.

In the philosophy of the Enlightenment—i.e., the dominating trend of philosophy in the period between Leibniz and Schelling—Schleiermacher was mostly contemptuous of Plato and, when not outright hostile, treated him condescendingly. Condillac, who in the spirit of Locke fought against metaphysical constructs and systems, stated: "His opinions appear to me nothing but delirium," and counted Plato among those who "held up the progress of reason" (*Oeuvres complètes de Condillac*, I, 188f.). Voltaire's comments on Plato vary to some extent, but for the most part he ridicules him as the inventor of "chimeras," an expression that at that time was frequently used to characterize Plato's thoughts. "Platonic love," which by philosophers and poets of the Renaissance was understood in a profoundly mystical sense, was castigated by the enlightened authors of the rococo as the naive enthusiasm of immature adolescents. In Wieland's *Agathon*, a chapter is ironically given the title "Natural History of a Platonic Love." In the same novel, the plot of which is placed in the fourth century B.C., Plato appears as one of the major characters. He is shown at the court of Dionysius II as a naive dreamer who mistakes the flattering reception given him by the tyrant and his courtiers as an indication that they have been seriously converted to his abstruse theories. Plato is compared unfavorably with Aristippus who represents the refined hedonism of the man of the world, and, in a later edition, also with Archytas of Tarentum who preaches a sermon which, surprisingly, contains a great deal of traditionally Neo-Platonic ideas.

Less hostile but still condescending is the treatment of Plato by some of those philosophers who tried to defend the existence of a personal God and the immortality of the soul by common sense rationalism. Moses Mendelssohn, who occasionally pays high tribute to Plato as a writer, says at a certain point in the preface to Mendelssohn's *Phaedo*, an attempt to adapt the Platonic dialogue of the same title to the taste of his century: "In the following I see myself compelled to abandon my guide. His proofs for the immateriality of the soul appear, at least to us, so shallow and chimerical that they hardly deserve a serious refutation. Whether this is due to our better philosophical insight or to our poorer comprehension of the philosophical language of the ancients I am not able to decide" (*Gesammelte Schriften*, ed. G. B. Mendelssohn, Berlin [1843], II, 69).

But the same age which through its representative writers treated Plato so severely also witnessed a new awareness of the phenomenon of history and created new forms of historical analysis which eventually cleared the way for a more understanding approach to Plato also. One of the chief characteristics of the growth of modern historical consciousness was the rising interest in the individual phenomenon as against the exclusive emphasis on unchanging general ideas and on universal laws. Attempts have been made to trace the trend of the new individualism back to a current of Neo-Platonism which survived through the eighteenth century. The aesthetics of Shaftesbury and especially his insistence on intuitive understanding was one of the main sources of this current. Leibniz' Monadology was another one.

The discussions of Platonism by the historians of philosophy of the eighteenth century exemplify the shift from antiquarian polyhistorism and the emphasis on external classification to the search for individual characterization. In the beginning of the century, an historically important distinction was drawn between Plato's doctrine and that of the ancient Neo-Platonists, not in the spirit of Leibniz, but in that of baroque scholarship; that is to say, the distinction served mainly certain theological interests and at the same time was in line with certain antiquarian speculations. Some of the learned readers of Diogenes Laertius were troubled by the fact that he "classifies" a single philosopher as an "eclectic," viz, Potamon of Alexandria (I, 21). As the history of philosophy was conceived in terms of "sects," one looked for other names which might be added to the list of eclectics. The church father Clement appeared to qualify as an Alexandrian who uses the term "eclectic" himself. But it was especially Ammonius Saccas, the teacher of Plotinus and Origen, who was considered likely to have been a member of the school of Potamon. It was common knowledge that Plotinus tried to harmonize Plato with Aristotle. What else was this if not eclecticism? In the Latin translation of Thomas Stanley's *History of Philosophy* (*Historia philosophiae*, Leipzig, 1711), a section on the eclectic sect, which discusses a number of pagan as well as of Christian authors, but which had been absent from the

English original, was added by the translator (G. Olearius).

By this time the problem had gained additional significance. In 1700, a posthumous work of the French protestant preacher N. Souverain (who later became an Anglican minister) appeared under the title *Le platonisme dévoilé*. Souverain was an antitrinitarian who maintained that the dogma of the Trinity was foreign to the teachings of the earliest Christians. He charged that in later antiquity platonizing theologians, who had absorbed the teachings of philosophy before becoming Christians, grafted the senseless doctrine on the pure and simple faith. Souverain carefully distinguishes Plato and the "refined" Platonists for whom the "holy trinity" is a symbolical expression for God's chief predicates—i.e., goodness, wisdom, power—from the "coarse" Platonists who misunderstood the symbolism and interpreted this trinity as one of three persons. Souverain's distinction between Plato's truthful followers and those Platonists who were in truth the corrupters of his doctrine was appropriated by some of his opponents who defended the originality of the trinitarian doctrine of the Church. As they saw it, it was by evil design that those corrupters of Platonism presented themselves as the possessors of the ultimate truth maintaining that their doctrine included and combined whatever is valid in all philosophies and religions. This is especially the view of the famous theologian and church historian, J. L. Mosheim. In his notes to a German version of Ralph Cudworth's *The True Intellectual System of the Universe* (English version 1678), Mosheim shows himself particularly hostile to Ammonius Saccas whom he considers as a renegade and archenemy of the Christian Church whose members he tried to lure away toward his eclecticism.

The classification of the ancient Neo-Platonists as eclectics, their distinguishability from genuine Platonists, and their condemnation as rivals and enemies of the Christian Church are features which were incorporated in the most erudite and the most influential eighteenth-century work on the history of philosophy, Johann Jakob Brucker's *Historia critica philosophiae* (Leipzig, 1742–44). Even before he became interested in the controversy about Souverain's book, Brucker had published a history of the concept of idea, in which he had made a distinction between Plato's genuine theory of ideas and that of the "younger" Platonists, i.e., not only of the Florentines but also of their ancient predecessors (*Historia philosophica doctrinae de ideis* [Augsburg, 1723]; hereafter referred to as *De ideis*). The crucial point is the ontological status of the ideas. Whereas the later ("younger") Platonists mostly interpreted them as notions within the divine mind, the author concludes that the best evidence suggests that

Plato considered them as "products" of the divine mind which had acquired the status of separate substances (*De ideis*, 65–69). Two points ought to be emphasized: first, the "younger" Platonists include both "Middle-Platonists" (such as Plutarch) and "Neo-Platonists" (such as Plotinus); second, even the view which Brucker ascribes to Plato himself is "Neo-Platonic" to the extent that it considers the ideas as products of the divine mind. In the *Historia critica philosophiae*, he even speaks of an "emanation" of the ideas from the divine intellect, while still maintaining their separateness (*Historia critica philosophiae*, I, 699).

In the latter work, "Platonism" is discussed in four different chapters. One of them is devoted to the Academic Sect, i.e., Plato and the members of the Ancient, Middle, and New Academy; another one with the title "The Platonists" discusses those authors who today are sometimes called the "Middle-Platonists"; a third chapter is called "The Eclectic Sect" and deals with Potamon and Ammonius Saccas and most of the ancient Neo-Platonists; a fourth chapter, finally, treats "The Restorers of the Platonic Philosophy," i.e., the Italian Renaissance Platonists.

In Stanley's *History of Philosophy* (4 vols., 1655–62), there is a learned discussion about Plato's life, but the author withholds any personal comment on Plato's thought and instead inserts in his work a translation of the *Introduction* of the so-called Alcinous. Brucker discusses both Plato's life and his thought and his discussion abounds with references to Plato's writings as well as to ancient and modern commentators. But the reader is disappointed by the absence of a synthesis. Although the various themes of Plato's thought are discussed in separate sections and although the author insists on the paramount importance of the theory of ideas, he often does not distinguish the essential from the unessential and does not arrive at a unified picture. His favorite is Socrates, whose genuine teachings, he believes, have been better preserved by Xenophon than by Plato, who has contaminated them with his abstruse speculations. In his preference for Socrates Brucker is a spokesman of his century which, in spite of the increasing number of publications on Plato, can scarcely be called an age of Platonism but may be called an age of Socratism.

Because of its wealth of material, Brucker's *Historia critica* became a standard reference work which was still widely used in the early nineteenth century. Its reputation may be derived from the fact that various articles on ancient philosophy in the famous eighteenth-century *Encyclopédie*, including those on *éclectisme* and *platonisme*, rely heavily on Brucker's work for information. There is of course a marked difference of style; instead of the learned polyhistor, the contributors to the *Encyclopédie* are enlightened men of the world. Diderot, the author of the article on *platonisme*, after mentioning the traditional slander (charges of luxury, sensuality, contentiousness, plagiarism) about Plato's character by such enemies as Antisthenes and Aristippus, adds: "But one line of his work is sufficient to make one forget his faults, if he had any, and the reproaches of his enemies" (XII, 746).

In the second half of the eighteenth century several histories of philosophy were published, mostly in Germany, which more or less successfully tried to substitute a continuous narration and individual characterization for Brucker's formless accumulation of material and for the traditional attribution of philosophical ideas to "sects." At the same time there appeared, in several countries, translations of single and groups of dialogues, synopses of the whole work, e.g., Floyer Sydenham, *Synopsis or General View of the Works of Plato* (London, 1759) and of the individual dialogues, e.g., D. Tiedemann, *Argumenta dialogorum Platonis* (Zweibrücken, 1786), and a great number of articles and monographs on Plato's thought and his art of writing.

An event which exercised a long-lasting influence on Platonism and the Platonic studies was the appearance of Kant's critical philosophy. Several of the histories of philosophy of the later eighteenth century include theoretical discussions on the purpose and meaning of the history of philosophy. Other essays on the same subject were published independently. Although the topic had been debated earlier, the most important of these discussions originated under the impact of the revolution in philosophical thinking brought about by Kant.

Kant himself refers to Plato on various occasions, but it is doubtful whether he was directly acquainted with Plato's writings. Even so it is of great historical importance that in a famous passage of the *Kritik der Reinen Vernunft* (B 370–75) he links his own with Plato's philosophy and defends him, as Rousseau had done previously, against the indictment that Plato's ideas and his "republic" are chimeras. Earlier in the same work Kant had blamed Plato because he "left the world of the senses . . . and ventured out beyond it on the wings of the ideas, in the empty space of pure understanding" (B 9, trans. N. K. Smith). In the later passage he suggests a way how to understand "the sublime philosopher" more profoundly. He admits that in so doing, he may have assumed the right of the interpreter to understand Plato better than Plato had understood himself, and today it seems obvious that Kant, in what we call an unhistorical manner, assimilated Plato to his own thinking. Still, in claiming that a philosopher is to be understood in terms of the truth

toward which he was striving, Kant consciously acknowledged what has been the attitude of many philosophers toward their predecessors since ancient times. Schleiermacher, in the general introduction of his translation of Plato, attacks such a claim as Kant's because it shows too little concern for what Plato actually said; he thus missed the true significance of Kant's words.

By linking his own "theory of ideas" to Plato's, Kant occasioned a long series of attempts to find parallels between Plato's and Kant's philosophy. This was done under such different auspices as Schopenhauer's pessimism and the methodological formalism of the Marburg school. In Kant's lifetime, the most impressive attempt of an assimilation of Plato to Kant was furnished by one of Kant's earliest followers, W. G. Tennemann in his four-volume work, *System der platonischen Philosophie* (Leipzig, 1792–95). In a later work, Tennemann gave an interesting account of his view about the task of a historian of philosophy. In the introductory volume to his *System*, he discusses such topics as Plato's life, the significance and purpose of his philosophy, the dialogue form, the genuineness of the single works, their chronology as an instrument to follow Plato's intellectual development, the tradition about an esoteric Platonic philosophy, etc. All this is done with circumspection but remains entirely separated from his subsequent analysis of Plato's philosophical system. In this analysis, Tennemann dissects Plato's thought without any regard for the way in which it presents itself in the dialogues. Convinced of the absolute validity of the Kantian philosophy, he is mainly interested in showing that Plato was on the path which would have led him to Kant's conclusions but that he deviated from it before reaching the goal. Because Plato assumed that things in themselves can be known, he seems to Tennemann to have confused that which can be conceived in thought with that which can be known as an object.

For a long time, "Platonism" remained affected by Kant, but the turning point in the history of Platonism was not the monograph on Plato by the Kantian Tennemann, but the translation and exegesis of Plato by Schleiermacher, in whom the Kantian philosophy worked only as one among several formative influences.

II

Since antiquity Plato had been praised as a master stylist, the criteria for literary excellence having been derived from ancient rhetoric. When in the second half of the eighteenth century, partly through the influence of Shaftesbury and of Rousseau, new aesthetical criteria gained acceptance, Plato as a writer was also appreciated in a new manner. He could now appear as one of the great geniuses of all time whose charm lies in the unaffected immediacy with which they are able to portray general human situations. Homer and Shakespeare were read in the same spirit. J. J. Winckelmann (1717–68) felt that Plato shared with Xenophon the distinction of each displaying in his writings the same kind of humanity which inspired the great Greek sculptors. There are scattered remarks of Herder which attest to his profound admiration for Plato's creative power. Goethe was occupied with the study of Plato's writings at various periods of his life. At the time when he completed his theory of color (*Farbenlehre*) by the history of its predecessors, he had arrived at the conception of a common foundation of our intellectual culture formed by the writings of Plato, Aristotle, and the Bible. Such an estimate of Plato's significance can hardly be excelled, but it implies that he who expressed it cannot properly be called a Platonist. This conclusion is supported by the observation that Goethe seems never to have been absorbed by the study of Plato as thoroughly as he was at times by that of Spinoza or Plotinus.

The situation was quite different for the early German romanticists. In some of them an exact acquaintance with the Platonic dialogues caused a sustained enthusiasm for the genius who had composed them. Leading these post-Kantian romantic philosophers was Friedrich Schlegel who, as none of his contemporaries, was able to appraise in an original manner the unique character of the great works of literature and of ancient Greek literature in particular. It was Friedrich Schlegel who suggested to Schleiermacher the plan of a translation of the entire work of Plato into German. At first both friends intended to undertake the work in common and it was only Schlegel's incessant delays that eventually led Schleiermacher to carry on the plan alone though without ever completing it.

By a strange coincidence, the first volume of Schleiermacher's German version of Plato appeared in the same year as the first complete English translation of Plato which was, with the exception of some of the shorter dialogues, the work of Thomas Taylor (1804). Comparing the two works is like looking at two different cultural eras. Both translators added to their translations general and special introductions.

Thomas Taylor, frequently called "the Platonist," revived the Neo-Platonic tradition in England in an original manner, adding to it an element of the philhellenism of the late eighteenth century. Platonism for him implied polytheism which he defended against the Christianity of the churches. His authorities were not the Cambridge Platonists but the ancient Neo-Platonists many of whose writings he translated in addition

to those of Plato and Aristotle. Proclus seems to have been his favorite.

Taylor translated Plato in a harsh and undifferentiated style. The translation is accompanied by introductions and notes which for the most part call the reader's attention to the meaning ascribed to Plato's words by the Neo-Platonists. Taylor's writings were mostly ignored by nineteenth-century scholars, but both the English romantic poets and the American transcendentalist philosophers became acquainted with Plato mainly through Taylor's translation and his Neo-Platonic exegesis. Of Schleiermacher's problem Taylor was not aware.

Schleiermacher seeks to determine the distinctive character of Plato's philosophy as it appears in his work, and, second, how it is possible for us to understand it. In answer to the first problem he finds Plato's philosophy to be that of a philosopher-artist. The second problem is solved by Schleiermacher's principle that one must not separate Plato's philosophy from its literary form but must comprehend and appreciate their indissoluble unity. Plato's was neither a systematic nor a fragmentary philosophy but a dialogical one. Schleiermacher is certain that there must have existed some kind of a system in Plato's mind and that it is even possible to reconstruct that system to a certain extent. But the first task, and this is the one which Schleiermacher himself takes up, is to understand the *dialogical* order of his writings. Schleiermacher deliberately omits from his introduction everything which does not directly lead to the study of the texts. Unlike his predecessors, he does not narrate Plato's life or the history of pre-Platonic philosophy. In probing such questions as the relative chronology of the Platonic dialogues, the exclusion of spurious works from the corpus of the genuine dialogues, the existence of an esoteric doctrine, he tries to derive the criteria solely from the analysis of each of the dialogues studied singly and from their various interpretations. No one had analyzed the writings of a philosopher in this manner before.

Schleiermacher was primarily a theologian and perhaps only secondarily a philosopher. On textual problems he was given assistance by the philologist Ludwig Friedrich Heindorf. Yet Schleiermacher's approach toward "understanding" became a milestone in the development of hermeneutics as well as philology. Schleiermacher's one-time student August Boeckh, who himself made important contributions to the interpretation of Plato, defined the aim of philology as the understanding or the recognition of that which had once been known (*die Erkenntnis des Erkannten*). In the same context he stated: "As philologists we ought not to philosophize like Plato but understand Plato's writings and this not only as works of art but also with respect to their content. . . . The philologist must be able to understand a work on the philosophy of nature like Plato's *Timaeus* as much as Aesop's *Fables* or a Greek tragedy" (*Encyklopädie und Methodologie der philologischen Wissenschaft*, Leipzig [1877], p. 13).

The more Schleiermacher's thinking matured, the more he emphasized the necessity of rigorous philological criticism. At the same time he became more and more assured of the preeminence of the Platonic philosophy. In certain periods of Schleiermacher's life Spinoza, Kant, and Schelling had impressed him almost as much as Plato, but in the end he believed that Plato came nearer to the truth than any other philosopher. This emphasis on Plato's excellence, sometimes coupled with a certain opposition to modern philosophy, was shared by several of Schleiermacher's friends and students. With certain important exceptions, it became the typical attitude of scholars who played a leading role in the progress of Platonic research. In spite of the omission of this point from Boeckh's characterization of the ideal interpreter, it seems unlikely that the philological research on Plato in the nineteenth and twentieth centuries would have produced so many outstanding works, if the philological masters had not been inspired by a predilection, whether acknowledged or unconscious, for the Philosopher Artist.

In a sense, the predilection of a nineteenth-century interpreter is, of course, more subjective than the admiration of the Neo-Platonic dogmatist. The danger inherent in the modern attitude was clearly seen by Hegel. He probably had Schleiermacher in mind when he declared: "Thus the Platonic, Aristotelian, etc. philosophy, [indeed] all philosophies have always lived and still live today by their principles; but philosophy has no longer the form and is no longer at the same stage at which the Platonic and Aristotelian philosophy was" (*Werke*, Berlin [1833], XIII, 60). When nowadays philosophy is urged to return to the standpoint of the Platonic philosophy in order to escape "the complications of subsequent ages," this does not bring back the initial situation. It is as if people want to return to a primitive society (cf. XIII, 61f.).

Boeckh's definition of the purpose of philology as the reproduction of knowledge that had once been known does not reveal how such a reproduction is possible. It would be naive to assume that an exact repetition of former acts of thinking could ever take place. All reproduction of previous knowledge is necessarily the production of new knowledge and is, in some manner, related to the thinking of the present age. Hegel's willfulness in applying his insight to the construction of the history of philosophy and of Platonism in particular sometimes obscures what is valid

in it. However an adequate analysis of the relation of Platonism to contemporary thought must not ignore the truth of Hegel's principle.

In the absence of a positive justification of Platonism in the period of methodically refined Platonic research, the polemics of modern anti-Platonists has sometimes exercised a wholesome influence, however crude the polemics may appear. This is especially true for the critique of Plato's political philosophy.

Among several of the authors whose political philosophy influenced the thinking and eventually the practice of the men who made the French Revolution, J. J. Rousseau and Gabriel Bonnet de Mably were great admirers of Plato. To Rousseau, Plato appeared to belong to the same class of lawgivers as the Spartan King Lycurgus, for whom the well-being of the state consisted in the virtue of his citizens. The abbé Mably, who in dialogues between members of the ruling classes praised the excellence of communism, repeatedly referred to Plato as a chief authority on the subject. There can be no doubt that such revolutionary leaders as Robespierre and Saint Just assimilated to their own thinking certain parts of Plato's political thoughts that they found in Rousseau and in Mably.

The same is true for the first communist conspirator, F. N. Babeuf. This fact was clearly realized only when the liberal bourgeoisie, after the revolutions of 1830 and of 1848, saw that its power was even more threatened by revolution and communism than it had formerly been threatened by the aristocracy. At this moment there came into existence a violent anti-Platonic literature which made Plato appear as the true predecessor of the detestable Rousseau. The political passions gave occasion to venomous attacks on Plato's character but also to new scholarly analyses of Plato's political views which caused some erstwhile Platonists to modify their former enthusiasm. The attitude of the French political opponents of Plato after the revolution of 1848 appears now like an anticipation of the charges that Plato was the intellectual ancestor of modern totalitarianism, i.e., of communism or of fascism and national socialism. Although the charges are as far apart as the political objectives of the revolution of 1848 and those of the twentieth-century revolutions, the open hatred of Platonism and the willful handling of the instruments of critical scholarship have in both cases caused some Platonic scholars to reappraise Platonism's possible meaningfulness. In an analogous way, Nietzsche's attack on Plato as the predecessor of Christian transcendentalism eventually served to give new vigor and new depth to the interest in Plato and Platonism, at least in Germany.

Among Schleiermacher's immediate successors, a sudden flourishing of Platonic research obscured the problem of the justification of Platonism in the modern age that was posed by Hegel. In the course of a few decades, there appeared an astonishing number of editions, commentaries, monographs, and comprehensive works which in a short time made most of Schleiermacher's conclusions appear obsolete. His chronology of the dialogues, his rejection of the tradition about an esoteric Platonism, and his neglect of the pre-Socratic philosophy were criticized and often with valid arguments. The most consistent attack on Schleiermacher's position was contained in C. F. Hermann's *Geschichte und System der platonischen Philosophie* (Heidelberg, 1839). To be sure, the author emphatically affirms his indebtedness and that of his contemporaries to Schleiermacher's innovations in the study of Plato. But at the same time Hermann criticized Schleiermacher's reliance on the concept of the Philosopher Artist for the solution of a large number of problems. In particular, Hermann attacked the view that in the composition of the single dialogues Plato followed a preconceived plan for his entire written work. Hermann himself tried to show that about half of the dialogues are documents of the various stages of Plato's intellectual development which culminated in the conception of a philosophical system that is represented in the other half, i.e., in the truly doctrinal works. More than a century of Platonic research since the appearance of Hermann's book has shown that Plato's philosophical development is one of those controversial issues which has never been settled to everyone's satisfaction. Other such issues are the problem of the reputed esoteric philosophy and the genuineness of the Platonic letters. The methodological difficulty of these controversies consists in the almost inextricable mixture of purely linguistic and historical problems with those philosophical problems which Boeckh, without a sufficient analysis, assigned to the domain of philology.

Significant for the development of Platonic research is the position of the author of one of the most learned and most judicious works of the nineteenth century on the Platonic philosophy, Eduard Zeller. Zeller had been a Hegelian, but in his monumental *Die Philosophie der Griechen* which includes his account of Plato's thought, he emphatically criticized Hegel's *a priori* construction of the course of history and unreservedly accepted the standards of the historical school of Schleiermacher and his followers.

The achievements of German philosophy and philology at the beginning of the nineteenth century occasioned new departures in the intellectual history of other countries also, and it is significant that Platonism played an important role in this process. To be sure, the conflict between philosophical constructivism and philological-historical criticism received, outside of Germany, little attention. What impressed foreign readers of German literature and visitors to Germany was rather the existence of a vigorous spiritual movement which seemed to penetrate all spheres of the intellectual life. By a curious coincidence, the beginnings of a direct influence of this movement on the philosophical and philological studies in France and in England are connected with the personalities of two distinguished visitors to Germany, Victor Cousin and Benjamin Jowett, both of whom, in the wake of their journeys, adopted the idea of creating new translations of Plato's works and both of whom were going to play important roles in the development of Platonism and Platonic studies in their countries. Between each of their visits there was a lapse of two decades.

Victor Cousin visited Germany several times in the 1820's and was cordially received by Goethe, Schelling, Hegel, Creuzer, Brandis, and many others. Both Schelling and Hegel were impressed by the young Frenchman who wanted to become acquainted with the new German philosophy. Creuzer advised him to edit some unpublished writings of Proclus. From Brandis he received the suggestion that he should translate the entire written work of Plato into French, taking Schleiermacher's translation as a model. Cousin followed both suggestions. Instead of a general introduction to the French edition of Plato, he planned to write a monograph on Plato's philosophy. This he never did, but he composed individual introductions to most of the dialogues and also a few independent essays on Platonic themes which were the first French studies on Plato that were conceived in the spirit of the new century. Also as a teacher and as an educational organizer, Cousin caused several of his students to undertake further research on Plato and other Greek philosophers. Cousin's own philosophical ideas found expression in a system which he called "eclecticism." In metaphysics, his eclecticism combines ideas about the philosophy of history with a spiritualism which has a Neo-Platonic and more exactly an Augustinian flavor. Although Cousin was hardly the most profound French philosopher of his age, eclecticism became the dominant philosophy at French universities during the years of the reign of Louis-Philippe and of the Second Empire and, what is here of particular interest, to a large extent determined the direction of Platonic studies in France. In agreement with the teachings of this eclecticism, it was almost considered a dogma that Plato's "ideas" were the thoughts of God and had no independent reality.

When Benjamin Jowett visited Germany in 1844 and again in 1845, many of the famous men whom Cousin had met were dead. He still met Schelling, but more important was his contact with several Hegelians, especially J. J. Erdmann. He also visited some of the outstanding philologists of the period such as Karl Lachmann. The parallel to the fate of Cousin is apparent in that one of the consequences of Jowett's journey was an intensified study of Plato which eventually caused him to create a new English translation of Plato in the spirit of Schleiermacher, which appeared in 1871. Jowett's situation, of course, differed from Cousin's in that there already existed the translation by Thomas Taylor. Yet the inspiration of Taylor's Platonism was so different from that of modern Platonic scholarship that, after it had done its mission among the romanticists, its influence in England remained limited to the devotees of ancient mysteries who represent a sometimes profound, sometimes shallow undercurrent beneath the rationalistic mainstream of the Victorian and prewar period.

The introductions to Schleiermacher's translations had already been translated into English in 1836, two years after Schleiermacher's death. Jowett, like Cousin, added his own introductions to his translations. These introductions reveal that Jowett was not only a Platonic scholar but also a devoted Platonist. But Jowett's Platonism is a Hegelian Platonism. This does not mean that he accepted Hegel's interpretation of Plato but that he set out with the conviction that there is a basic harmony in the philosophies of the two thinkers. In contrast to the theistic Neo-Platonism (which in a modified version had survived in Cousin's eclecticism), Jowett and his English disciples understood Platonism as a form of pantheism. This position implies that they denied the existence of a separation (*chorismos*) of the ideas from the perceptual world. Modern English Platonic scholarship was started almost simultaneously by Jowett and by the historian George Grote, who was a utilitarian and who, in his magisterial work on Plato, tried to separate the dialectical critic Plato (whom he admired) from the dogmatic metaphysician (whom he rejected). Modern English Platonism is more conspicuously represented by the Jowett tradition. In its union with Hegelianism it helped to create the intellectual climate which produced the idealistic philosophies of T. H. Green, F. H. Bradley, and B. Bosanquet.

American Platonic scholarship in the modern sense was founded and most successfully represented by Paul Shorey who, as a youth, had studied in Germany. Yet when his Latin dissertation on the theory of ideas appeared in Munich in 1884, a different kind of American Platonism was just about to expire. Among the New England transcendentalists, Thomas Taylor's Neo-Platonic translations had been eagerly studied together with his "Plato." Emerson's Plato essay in

Representative Men is indebted to this tradition, even though it is full of original observations. Bronson Alcott tried to use Platonism, as it was transmitted through Taylor, as the philosophical basis of his educational reform program. After the middle of the century the New England Platonism spread to the Middle West. An Akademe and several Plato Clubs were founded. The culminating achievement of the "Platonism in the West" was the publication of the periodical *The Platonist* (St. Louis, Mo., 1881–87); one of the first issues included a "Life of Thomas Taylor the Platonist" by its editor Thomas T. Johnson. He and his friends considered Platonism as an antidote to the materialism of the age and acted both as allies and rivals of the St. Louis Hegelians. Of the existence of an Hegelian Platonism in England they seem not to have been aware.

Hegelian Platonism had its counterpart in Kantian Platonism. What Tennemann had attempted while Kant was still alive was repeated a century later with considerably more sophistication by the Marburg school. After Hermann Cohen had pointed the way, Natorp's *Platos Ideenlehre* (1903) almost became a classic, as it combined mastery of the philological art with philosophical depth. Still to those who withstood the fascination of the masterful presentation, Natorp's "Plato" was bound to appear as a distortion. This did not prevent a brilliant French scholar (J. Moreau) from making another attempt at proving the basic identity of Platonism and Kantianism, about thirty years after Natorp.

One could multiply the enumeration of claims of reviving Platonism on the basis of its homogeneity with various ancient and modern philosophies, theologies, theories of education, or less conceptualized *Weltanschauungen*. Walter Pater suggested that there is equal justification for defining Platonism as a metaphysical doctrine and as an unsystematic approach to the solution of philosophical problems. More recently, Alfred North Whitehead maintained that "the safest general characterization of the European philosophical tradition is that it consists of a series of footnotes to Plato" (*Process and Reality,* reprint [1955], p. 63). Yet however much he emphasized his own indebtedness to Plato, in his borrowings from Plato's thinking he was quite eclectic and unconcerned about the original context. Like Whitehead, Husserl, Nicolai Hartmann, and Santayana were sometimes classified as Platonists, because they insisted in their teachings on the role of essences or "ideal beings." Hartmann was a Platonic scholar in his own right and always showed a profound admiration for Plato, even though in his ultimate philosophy he wanted to overcome the anthropocentric teleology of the Platonic tradition. In a less radical manner, Santayana excluded moral values from the realm of essences. As he considered the mixing of morals with metaphysics as a main feature of Platonism, his attitude toward Plato was ambivalent.

On the opposite side, Paul Elmer More and the Dean of St. Paul's Cathedral in London, R. W. Inge, gave new expression to the conviction of the basic harmony of Platonism and Christianity. Inge's Platonism has a Neo-Platonic flavor, but in contrast to the disciples of Thomas Taylor, he studied the sources, and especially Plotinus, with the tools of modern philological scholarship. Plotinus rather than Plato also attracted, and to some extent influenced, the thinking of Henri Bergson. At about the same time, Léon Robin renewed the Neo-Platonic interpretation of Plato's thought on the basis of thorough philological investigations. But his conclusions have remained controversial.

Still, in spite of all controversies, Platonic scholars have been able to show that certain forms of alleged Platonism are related to assumptions about the meanings of Plato's words which are demonstratively false. But they have not been able to provide an interpretation of Plato's words which would be generally conceded to offer a safe basis for a new definition of Platonism. Moreover certain scholarly interpretations have been attacked by recent philosophers on the basis that, from the point of view of philosophical analysis, they are meaningless and therefore cannot be imputed to a thinker of Plato's rank. For example, I. M. Crombie tries to save Plato by denying the possibility that he should have questioned the reality of the physical world or assumed the existence of transcendent archtypes.

It might seem to follow that "Platonism" is one of those terms which, due to the refinements of historical criticism and to its abstention from metaphysical commitments, have lost their usefulness as concepts with a clearly defined and generally accepted meaning. Being a Platonist might mean nothing more than that somebody basically accepts as true what he believes or others believe to have been Plato's teaching.

There is, however, something paradoxical in such a position. A common feature in many, though perhaps not in all, uses of the term "Platonism" is that Platonism is opposed to relativism. But then the relativistic view that all doctrinal definitions of Platonism are subjective is un-Platonic itself. It is sometimes assumed that one of the basic philosophical issues of our time is the contrast between a relativistic historicism and the view that there are transhistorical, i.e., permanent ethically relevant ontological structures, and the anti-relativistic and anti-historistic view is sometimes identified with Platonism. No doubt, such an identification of Platonism with an absolutism that is opposite to historical subjectivism lacks that precision which has

been the goal of most Platonic scholars. Indeed, it qualifies as Platonists many philosophers who traditionally have been listed among Plato's opponents. Even so it provides the broadest basis for a doctrinal definition of Platonism which is significant in the present situation.

This is not the place to discuss the metaphysical and methodological reasons why the aspiration for a definite interpretation of a phenomenon like the Platonic philosophy cannot be fulfilled, whatever may have been its importance as a stimulus for Platonic research. Neither is it possible here to argue the case of Platonism as against historicism. It must be sufficient to designate the two central facts which dominate the continuing discussion on the significance of Platonism in our time, i.e., first, the complex and often confusing situation of Platonic research, and, second, the philosophical debate on the existence of permanent ethically relevant ontological structures.

III

A brief note may be added on Platonism in literature. Renaissance Platonism had added a metaphysical dimension to love poetry. In the eighteenth century, Platonic love became an ambiguous phrase, as it was both praised and ridiculed (Wieland). In a different manner Platonism was revived by preromantic and romantic poets and aestheticians. In Germany the writings of the Earl of Shaftesbury, the Platonizing herald of enthusiasm, exercised a profound influence. Among English romantic poets, the Neo-Platonism of Thomas Taylor, sometimes reinforced by Berkeley's Siris, played a similar role. William Blake's poetry is full of Neo-Platonic symbolism much of which seems to have been derived from Taylor's writings. Neo-Platonic ideas still appeared in Blake's poems when, after 1803, he denounced the mathematical spirit of Plato and of all Hellenic thought.

Blake was the first romantic poet who claimed for the poet the role which Plato had assigned to the philosopher. "True poets and philosophers were prophets, who were able to 'describe what they saw in Vision as real and existing men, whom they saw with their imaginative and immortal organs'." (Cf. George M. Harper, The Neoplatonism of William Blake [1961], p. 99; the last part of the sentence is a quotation from Blake's A Descriptive Catalogue.) Coleridge announced "the transcendental deduction of Imagination," and with it the principles of production and genial criticism in the fine arts from a "Dynamic Philosophy" which he believed to be "no other than the system of Pythagoras and Plato revived and purified from impure mixtures" (Biographia Literaria, London and New York [1947], p. 129). The transcendental poetry of Coleridge and of Wordsworth may be called Platonistic in the vague sense of a tendency toward spiritualism accompanied by occasional reminiscences of Platonic dicta and images.

Doubtless the most ardent admirer of Plato among the romantic writers was Shelley. After he had become acquainted with Plato through Taylor's translation, he began to study Greek and to read Plato in the original language, and soon made his own translation of his favorite dialogues. There are several aspects of Shelley's Platonism. Here it must suffice to mention that Plato led him to recognize the misunderstandings of his early "materialism." However even as a Platonist Shelley tried to combine the wisdom of Aristophanes (in the *Symposium*) with that of Diotima. Although he was striving toward "intellectual beauty," he was drawn with equal force toward his human other half that appeared to him as the embodiment of the idea of beauty.

In his poem "Intimations of Immortality from Recollections of Early Childhood" and in the explanatory note which he added to it, Wordsworth had suggested an ingenuous interpretation of the Platonic theory of reminiscence. Compared with Wordsworth's lines the allusions to Platonic thought in the *Méditations Poétiques* (1820) of Lamartine appear conventional. This is equally true for Lamartine's poem *"Immortalité"* which indulges in sentimental rhetoric (*"Laissez-moi mon erreur: j'aime, il faut que j'espère"*), and for the later *"Philosophie"* in which the poet formally abdicates to Plato and transcendental speculation in favor of an Epicurean *Carpe diem*. It is scarcely surprising that the impressionable poet changed his opinion again when, one year after writing *"Philosophie,"* he read the *Phaedo* together with an enthusiastic friend (1822) and subsequently composed *La Mort de Socrate*, a long poem which transposes the *Phaedo* into a romantic showpiece. Having failed as a politician, Lamartine, toward the end of his life, turned into one of Plato's vilifiers, but this scarcely belongs to the history of literature.

The cult of beauty, which in Shelley, Keats, and also Hölderlin was based on the belief in the oneness of divine and human nature and in the correspondence of art and metaphysics, changed its meaning when this belief was weakened. When Schopenhauer explained the Platonic idea as the object of art, he announced the new attitude. In a world in which the faith in an ultimate harmony was vanishing, beauty, mainly understood as the perfection of works of art, became the refuge and consolation of disenchanted romanticists. The new aestheticism was elaborated by the French Parnassians and symbolists, and was subsequently spread by poets and critics to many countries (e.g., Walter Pater).

Although Mallarmé never acknowledged his indebtedness to Plato, critics have often claimed that there is an affinity between his aesthetics and Plato's. There is a famous sentence in his *Divagations* in which the symbolistic creed seems to be condensed and which sounds like the proclamation of a theory of ideas through the mouth of a poet. But this "theory of ideas" is solely aesthetic. (Cf. C. M. Bowra, *The Heritage of Symbolism*, London [1943], p. 5.) The romantic substitution of the poet for the Platonic philosopher seems to have been followed by the symbolistic substitution of the separate and exclusive beauty of objects of the poetic vision, called *idées*, for the unrestricted beauty of the Platonic ideas.

In contrast to his "master" Mallarmé, Paul Valéry paid homage to Plato by composing "Platonic" dialogues in which the names of the speakers are those of Socrates and his friends (*Eupalinos ou l'architecte* and *L'âme et la danse*, 1923). But although he does not oppose the artistic imagination to the analytical activity of the intellect, his Platonism does not transcend aestheticism, as the intellectual process itself is assimilated by him to creativity and is not recognized as the discovery of an eternal order.

At first sight the Platonism of Stefan George, who had also been one of Mallarmé's "disciples," seems to be more comprehensive than Valéry's. Yet it may be asked, whether in the final analysis he did not also substitute creativity (in George's case, the creative will) for the recognition of eternal truth. In Friedrich Gundolf's *George*, which was written while the author enjoyed the poet's confidence, it is stated: "Plato's work is probably the only literary work which George comprehends through a brotherly spirit and not only as myth" (F. Gundolf, *George*, Berlin [1920], p. 52). In his love for a youth whom he called Maximin, George believed to have found the meaning of the Platonic *eros*, which he and his friends defended against the bourgeois notion of "Platonic love." In the same vein George assumed that the true spirit of Platonic *paideia* was akin to his own endeavor to bring about a renaissance of hellenism by the training of an elite imbued with the ideal of *kalokagathia*. As most of George's later poetry is related to his belief in his pedagogic mission, it may be counted as an original form of Platonistic literature.

George's Platonism was directly derived from Plato. He took no interest in Neo-Platonism, even though he was attracted by the "cosmic" symbolism of ancient myth. W. B. Yeats, the Irish bard of English symbolistic poetry felt a similar attraction but was led, mainly through the study of the poetry of Blake, to connect the symbolic wisdom of the myths with the Neo-Platonic tradition. He became an enthusiastic reader of the writings of Thomas Taylor and took a deep interest in the first complete English translation of Plotinus by S. Mackenna. Although it is difficult to disentangle the threads from which Yeats' poems were woven, it seems certain that Neo-Platonic Platonism is one of them. (Cf. Kathleen Raine, *Defending Ancient Springs*, London [1967], pp. 66–87.)

The examples indicate that one can identify various kinds of Platonism in twentieth-century literature, but that there is none which can claim to be representative of the age. There are numerous other works in recent literature which may be called Platonistic for one reason or another, but none has emerged which could be called so in a truly significant manner.

BIBLIOGRAPHY

The first volume of W. B. Tennemann's *System der platonischen Philosophie* (Leipzig, 1792–95) includes a critical bibliography. Heinrich von Stein, *Sieben Bücher zur Geschichte des Platonismus* (Göttingen, 1862–75) pays attention to Platonism as well as to Platonic research. Platonism in literature is stressed by Paul Shorey, *Platonism, ancient and modern*, Sather Lectures, Vol. XIV (Berkeley, 1938).

For surveys of Platonic research, see H. Cherniss, "Plato (1950–1957)," *Lustrum*, **4** (1959), and **5** (1960); A. Diès, *Autour de Platon* (Paris, 1927); Victor Goldschmidt, *Platonisme et la pensée moderne* (Aubier, 1970); E. Hoffmann, "Der gegenwärtige Stand der Platoforschung," appendix to E. Zeller, *Die Philosophie der Griechen*, 5th ed. (Leipzig, 1922), Part II, Vol. 1, 1051–1105; Charles Huit, *La vie et les oeuvres de Platon*, Vol. II (Paris, 1893); H. Leisegang, *Die Platondeutung der Gegenwart* (Karlsruhe, 1929); E. M. Manasse, "Bücher über Platon," I and II, *Philosophische Rundschau*, Sonderheft I (1957) and Sonderheft II (1961); K. Oehler, "Der entmythologisierte Platon," *Zeitschrift für philosophische Forschung*, **19** (1965), 393–420.

Special aspects of Platonism are stressed in Paul R. Anderson, *Platonism in the Midwest* (New York and London, 1963); F. J. Brecht, *Platon und der George-Kreis* (Leipzig, 1929); G. Gentile, *Le origini della filosofia contemporanea in Italia*, 2nd ed., Vol. I, "I Platonici" (Rome, 1925); W. D. Geoghegan, *Platonism in Recent Religious Thought* (New York, 1959); George Mills Harper, *The Neoplatonism of William Blake* (Chapel Hill, 1961); R. W. Inge, *The Platonic Tradition in English Religious Thought* (New York and London, 1926); J. N. Mohanty, *Nicolai Hartmann and Alfred North Whitehead: A Study in Recent Platonism* (Calcutta, 1957); R. M. Mossé-Bastide, *Bergson et Plotin* (Paris, 1956); J. M. G. Muirhead, *The Platonic Tradition in Anglo-Saxon Philosophy* (London and New York, 1931); James Notopoulos, *The Platonism of Shelley* (Durham, N. C., 1949); *Thomas Taylor the Platonist: Selected Writings*, eds. Kathleen Raine and George Mills Harper (Princeton, 1969).

For general background, see E. Cassirer, *The Platonic Renaissance in England*, trans. F. C. N. Koelln and James P. Pettegrove (Austin, 1953); idem, *The Philosophy of the Enlightenment*, trans. F. C. N. Koelln and James P. Pettegrove (Princeton, 1951); W. Dilthey, *Das Leben Schleiermachers* (Berlin, 1870); idem, "Friedrich Daniel Schleiermacher," *Gesammelte Schriften*, 12 vols. (Berlin and Leipzig, 1921), IV, 354–402; H. G. Gadamer, *Wahrheit und Methode*, 2nd ed. (Tübingen, 1965); F. Meinecke, *Die Entstehung des Historismus* (Munich and Berlin, 1936); Ernst Simon, *Ranke und Hegel* (Munich, 1928).

ERNST MORITZ MANASSE

[See also Enlightenment; Hegelian . . .; Ideology of Soviet Communism; Love; **Neo-Platonism; Platonism; Romanticism in Post-Kantian Philosophy;** Totalitarianism.]

POETRY AND POETICS FROM ANTIQUITY TO THE MID-EIGHTEENTH CENTURY

POETRY (*poesis*, "making," since Herodotus) and *Poetics* (*poietikē*, viz., *technē*, since Plato), the words as well as the concepts were created by the Greeks in their endeavor to analyze man and the cosmos rationally. The subsequent evolution of these ideas is determined by their Greek origin, as is evident in the terminology. During the period treated here, the Greek words, or their equivalents, were used in Latin and in the vernaculars; "poetry" being to all purposes identical with verse. Literary prose—oratory, history, philosophy—belonged to the parallel but separate "art" of rhetoric. Prose fiction—novels, short stories—was ignored or explicitly rejected by the theorists.

Poetics like rhetoric is an "art" (*technē*, *ars*), i.e., a part of man's activity by means of which he alters nature or even adds something to it, as is the case here. Until the beginnings of romanticism, the modern concept of art did not exist, though in classical antiquity attempts were made to group poetry together with fine arts. Only in the eighteenth century was the modern system of arts, as well as the concept of "aesthetics," created. Earlier philosophical speculations about "beauty" did not directly concern poetics.

Nor did poetics and rhetoric form a higher unity. The modern concept of "literature" emerges during the eighteenth century. Classical Greek and Latin have no proper word for it. *Grammata* and *litterae* mean, at the utmost, literary education, learning. In some late Latin authors, e.g., Tertullian, *litteratura* can mean writing in general, or upon a certain topic. But the modern sense of *belles lettres* is missing.

I. CLASSICAL ANTIQUITY

1. Sources and Development. In Homer we find the concept of poetry as an activity of its own, and statements about its aim and inspiration. Similar statements occur in later poets, but a rational *technē poietikē* is lacking. The earliest philosophers, on the other hand, seem mainly to have discussed poetry from a logical or ethical point of view.

The true originators of Greek poetics are the Sophists of the fifth century, e.g., Protagoras, Hippias, Prodicus, to whom, on this point, Democritus should be added. Since nearly all of their writings are lost, we cannot exactly estimate their role. But Gorgias' *Praise of Helen*, with its acute analysis of the uncanny power of the *logos*, stresses their importance.

The Sophists' study of poetry—as well as of eloquence—was carried on by later philosophers, of whom only Plato and Aristotle are really known to us. If according to Plato's dialogues no "poetics" is possible, poetry being an entirely sensory phenomenon, then Aristotle's *Poetics* is the one outstanding monument of ancient poetics, though mutilated and not representative of average opinion.

Post-Aristotelian philosophical and critical discussions, though evidently important—e.g., Theophrastus—elude us. The loss of the greatest part of Hellenistic literature, due to Atticist condemnation, is to some extent made good by the fragments of the Epicurean philosopher and poet, Philodemus of Gadara, *On Poems,* and by Horace's *Ad Pisones.* The mutilated *On the Sublime* (first century A.D.), allegedly written by Longinus, is in its way as unique as Aristotle's *Poetics.*

In the fourth century rhetoric was already beginning its conquest of classical culture and education. Owing to their popularity in late antiquity, many rhetorical works have been preserved, such as Aristotle's *Rhetoric,* or the writings of Dionysius of Halicarnassus (first century B.C.), or Cicero's *De oratore, Orator, Brutus,* or Quintilian's *Ars oratoria* (ca. A.D. 95). Rhetoric being close to poetics and forever trying to absorb it, those works often treat problems which directly concern poetry, such as *decorum,* the different kinds of style, metaphors, etc.

In the final phase of classical antiquity, after the great crisis of the third century, poetics is reduced to a subordinate part of rhetoric—e.g., in the *Ars grammatica* of Diomedes—dealing mainly with the division of poetry into different genres and with metrics.

2. The Aim of Poetry. To Homer, poetry is entertainment, though men's reputations are in the poet's keeping. After Hesiod, however, Greek poets claim to be not only creators of beauty and entertainers but also spiritual teachers and leaders: "to make men better in the cities" (Aristophanes, *Frogs,* line 1010). This claim was generally accepted, the more so as the poets, above all Homer, dominated Greek education.

Their domination provoked fierce criticism by a new power, philosophy. After the sixth century, poetry was condemned—e.g., by Xenophanes and Heraclitus—as mendacious, immoral, and inflammatory. These accusations are summed up in Plato's *Republic,* where a new, Platonic argument is added, viz., that poetry, like painting and sculpture, is only an imitation (*mimēsis*) of this sensual world, which, in its turn, is an imitation of real being, the world of ideas. Therefore, traditional poetry should be driven out of the ideal state; the only poetry allowed there, as the *Laws* shows, is tightly controlled state propaganda.

Aristotle in his *Poetics* does not directly polemicize against Plato. But by treating *mimēsis* as something natural and pleasant, and by regarding the excitement caused by tragedy as a sort of purgation (*catharsis*), he silently refutes Plato.

After Aristotle the problem loses its urgency. In the new Hellenistic monarchies the poet is not and does not wish to be a teacher and leader, but stresses the hedonic character of poetry; this hedonism is also maintained by the Epicureans, though not in order to favor poetry. Only in Rome during the few decades of the Augustan age, is the old claim again made. Vergil and Horace regard themselves and are regarded by their contemporaries as spokesmen of Rome. In the *Ad Pisones* we find the formal program of what could be called the "Horatian compromise," but which, in reality, is the old idea: poetry should both benefit and please.

The rise of Christianity meant a sharpening of the old attacks on poetry, although Christians continued to read the poets at school. Against those attacks, the defenders of the old faith and the old civilization appeal to the venerable argument of allegorism, which had been used in the sixth century B.C., and was later systematized and popularized by the Stoics. It is now taken over by the Neo-Platonists to whom as to the Stoics poetry is philosophy in disguise. This applies particularly to Homer and Vergil, who are much allegorized.

This high opinion of poetry is not shared by rhetoric, the real ruler of civilization at the time. Poetry becomes only a part, an indispensable but subordinate part, of rhetorical culture. For poetry only pleases, whereas rhetoric also persuades and moves (Quintilian X.I,28).

3. The Craft of Poetry. After Homer, the Greek poet regarded himself as "inspired" by a divinity, usually the Muses, whom he invoked in his poems. Despite Plato, there is no evidence that any poet ever regarded himself as "possessed" (*manikos*) in the same sense as the Pythia at Delphi. The inspiration never excluded the poet's own activity.

Plato, on the contrary, declared that in the act of creation the poet becomes a passive mouthpiece of a god, unable to understand and explain afterwards what the god had done through him. Serious or not, this paradox—expounded in the *Ion* and the *Phaedrus*—in any case abolishes the poet's authority.

Aristotle shows traces of Plato's teaching, but he is not interested in the question. After Aristotle, in the peripatetic *Problemata* XXX (ca. 250 B.C.), we find an attempt to explain inspiration as characteristic of the "melancholic" temperament, caused by "black bile," one of the four "humours." This theory became very popular later but had scant influence in classical antiquity. Horace pokes fun at it (*Ad Pisones* 301ff.).

An old problem, bound up with that of inspiration, was the relation between the poet's innate capacity or "nature" and his acquired skill or "art." Pindar proclaimed the superiority of nature (IX 01 100ff.), but the Hellenistic poets stressed the importance of art. Here too Horace presents us with a compromise: the poet needs both (*Ad Pisones* 408ff.). Thus also "Longinus."

The Hellenistic age enhanced the status of the artist, who in Greek and Latin terminology is not distinguished from the artisan. At the same time the creative character of poetry and art was stressed against older, mimetic theories. Neither the poet nor the artist imitates external nature but realizes an ideal model in his soul (Cicero, *Orator* II.7–10), if not the Ideas themselves (Plotinus V.8), thanks to his power of visualization (*phantasia*) as "Longinus" (15) says. In this way, poetry or art becomes independent of nature (Philostratus, *Vita Apollonii* VI.19), and the artist as well as the poet is an inspired man (Callistratus, *Imagines* II.1).

4. The Realm of Poetry. For the Greeks and Romans there were distinct varieties (*eidē, genera*) of poetry which constituted a hierarchy. This was so self-evident that Aristotle never bothers to give a definition of *eidos*, mentioned in the first sentence of the *Poetics*. The number and character of the genres were determined by the accidents of literary history, but they tend to be regarded as pre-existent forms whose founders are "finders" (*heuretai*), since all that we call "invention" tended to be regarded as "discovery" by the Greeks, and consciously so by all Platonists.

The genres are not equal. At least since Plato epic and tragedy were regarded as the two highest genres, as analyzed in Aristotle's *Poetics*. Tragedy belongs with comedy and satyric play to drama. The many different kinds of lyrics never acquired a common name. In Hellenistic and Roman times, "lyric poetry" meant poetry, whether monodic or choric, (originally) sung; it did not include elegy or iambics. Later on, some special Roman kinds, e.g., the *atellana,* were added to the list.

Ancient poetics never developed a real system of genres. In Plato (*Republic* III) and in Aristotle poetry is divided according to whether the poet is telling a tale himself (dithyramb), or through others (drama), or both (epic). This primitive classification disregards lyrics but was used until the romantic age. Plato's and Aristotle's attempts to classify poetry with the fine arts (painting and sculpture) as "imitative arts" (*technai mimētikai*) were not successful, however, owing to the original dramatic sense of *mimēsis* and to later reaction against mimetic theories.

The golden rule of all genres is "appropriateness" (*prepon, decorum*), which hovers between ethics and aesthetics. Every genre has its special *decorum*, which is most exacting in the high genres. There was an early tendency to interpret *decorum* as good manners, which especially in Hellenistic and Roman times inspired much criticism of Homer and other old poets. As the *Ad Pisones* shows, *decorum* is the heart of Horatian poetics.

The individual rules of the different genres tend to fix them as they were established by their originators or early masters. Thus the Aristotelian rules of tragedy codify the practice of the great Attic dramatists of the fifth century. The most spectacular proof of this tendency is the use of different dialects in different genres, e.g., the Homeric dialect in epic, or the pseudo-Doric dialect in the choruses of the Attic tragedies.

5. Tradition and Progress. The tendency to immobilize poetry was strengthened by a customary assumption in Greek literature (found also in Sanskrit poetry and the Vedas): the first known of its poets is also the greatest. The prominence of Homer, in spite of philosophical and aesthetical criticism, accepted by public opinion and promoted by education, soon became an obstacle to innovation in epic. But the rise of other genres meant a perpetual new creation, at least until the end of the high classical age.

Looking back upon centuries of Greek poetry, Aristotle in the *Poetics* accepts "progress in literature," but only as the evolution of genres to their predestined goal. He seems, however, to accept the possibility of new genres.

In the early Hellenistic period, the necessity of change and renewal was stressed, e.g., by Callimachus. The old poets were revered as masters but not copied as models. The rise (first century B.C.) and final triumph (second century A.D.) of Atticism signified a return to the "classics." Beginning as a critical and rhetorical movement, Atticism later on conquered the schools and emerged as a radical linguistic reaction, an attempt to restore the pure Attic of the fifth and fourth centuries. Though it was never wholly successful, Atticism dominated Greek literature and education until the end of the Byzantine empire. In poetics its influence hardened the hereditary dislike of innovation. Creative imitation in the spirit of "Longinus" disappeared.

Greek poetics paid no attention to foreign literature. But Roman literature began as imitation of the Greeks and struggled hard to equal them. Hence, as Horace, *Epodes* II.1 and the historian Velleius Paterculus (I.16–17) show, a belief in progress was necessary to Roman writers, at least until their works themselves had become classics, which happened in the Augustan age. Thenceforth, Roman literature, too, became conservative, the schools teaching the imitation of the masters.

II. THE MIDDLE AGES

1. Sources and Development. Both the Greek East and the Latin West inherited poetics as a part of rhetoric or of its preliminary, grammar. In the East, the rhetorical tradition remained uninterrupted until the fall of Constantinople in 1453. Latin literature was neglected but the great Greek poets continued to be read in and outside the schools. The indifference to nonrhetorical poetics appears from the lack of any commentary upon Aristotle's *Poetics* and from the loss of its second book, dealing with comedy.

Owing to the great invasions the cultural level in the West was for many centuries (450–750) much lower. Outside Italy knowledge of Greek and Greek literature nearly disappeared. Much of Roman literature was lost too; but the great classics survived, as did a certain number of rhetorical and grammatical writings. Through them and through such résumés of ancient learning as the *Etymologiae* of Isidor of Seville (ca. 560–633), a scanty knowledge of classical poetics was preserved.

During many centuries poetics virtually meant the art of writing Latin verses in classical meters. It had no place of its own in the system of the Seven Liberal Arts but belonged with grammar or rhetoric to the *Trivium*.

At the end of the eleventh century a great change occurred. With Anselm of Canterbury European philosophy received a new impetus; with the Provençal poets, vernacular poetry began to emulate the classics. In the twelfth century, a closer study of the classics became popular, though the Scholasticism of the thirteenth century pushed them into the background. But at the new universities rhetoric and even poetics were studied as parts of logic, following a tradition which goes back to late antiquity. The Aristotelian *Rhetoric* was translated three times, the last time by William of Moerbeke, who also translated the *Poetics* (1278). However, the latter work was mostly known from Herrmannus Alemannus' bad translation of Averroës' *Commentum medium* (1174) upon Abu Bišr's Arabic

translation. As Averroës knew nothing about Greek poetry, his commentary gives no adequate idea of the *Poetics*.

From the end of the twelfth century on, several Latin *poetriae*—the name is due to a misunderstanding of *poetria*, "poetess"—appeared, e.g., by Geoffroy de Vinsauf (ca. 1210), or by Johannes de Garlandia (before 1250). They were not only manuals of metrics but also treatises of rhetoric applied to poetry, for to their authors as to the classical rhetoricians poetry is versified eloquence.

2. Doctrines. The absence of an autonomous poetics illustrates the precarious position of poetry in medieval thought, in spite of a flowering Latin and vernacular poetry. The theologians and philosophers inherited both the early Christians' hostility to secular poetry and their uneasy acceptance of it as an educational necessity. The Roman poets were read at school, and allegorism Christianized them—not only Vergil but also Ovid. For didacticism was rampant: poetry had its only raison d'être as pleasant teaching.

As to poetical inspiration, the theologians regarded only the Bible as inspired and perhaps devotional poetry, but to a lesser degree. At least according to popular belief pagan poets were inspired by demons. But the reading of the classics in the schools kept the Muses alive, and Christian poets invoked them if only metaphorically.

The classical genres were known by name but not really understood, least of all the dramatic genres, the theater having disappeared. The Platonic tripartition survived, but the real division of genres followed the rhetorical tripartition of the *genera dicendi*—high, middle, low—exemplified by Vergil in the *Aeneid*, the *Georgics*, and the *Bucolics*. This also implied a social stratification—kings, peasants, shepherds—as seen already in late antiquity (Donatus, Servius).

These divisions take no account of vernacular poetry, which develops its own genres, with the *canzone* as the highest. But at this time a vernacular poetics is only just beginning.

The Middle Ages believed in authorities not only in philosophy, law, and theology, but also in literature. The *auctores* read in the schools were a curious mixture of classical authors (Cicero, Vergil, Horace, Ovid), late Latin writers ("Cato," Avienus), and old Christian poets (Iuvencus, Arator, Prudentius). But the reverence for them did not prevent a certain belief in progress. Religion made Christians as such superior to pagans, but it did not exclude the view that the *moderni* (a fifth-century word) could be considered superior to the *veteres* (old Christians included), if only as "pygmies standing upon the shoulders of giants" (Bernard of Chartres, twelfth century).

III. EUROPEAN CLASSICISM

1. Sources and Development. With the Italian writers of the *Trecento*—to whom Dante and the "pre-humanists" of the late *Dugento* must be added—a new epoch begins also in poetics. The literary horizon was immensely enlarged through an intensified study of the classics, first the Roman and then from the end of the *Trecento* on the Greek.

This meant a new and deeper knowledge of ancient rhetoric and poetics. To the *De inventione* of Cicero and the *Rhetorica ad Herennium* which were already well-known, were now added Cicero's great treatises, the *Institutio oratoria* of Quintilian, and later many Greek rhetorical works. In the fifteenth century Aristotle's *Poetics* became known in the original. Giorgio Valla's Latin translation was printed in 1498 and the Greek text in 1508, but only with Alessandro Pazzi's new Latin translation (1536) did neo-Aristotelian poetics really begin.

The break with medieval poetics occurred, however, in Dante's *De vulgari eloquentia* (ca. 1304–05). For all his dependence on medieval rhetoric, Dante voices a new self-esteem for the classics and intimacy with them. After him there were for a long time no Italian attempts at poetics until Bartolomeo della Fonte and Giorgio Valla at the end of the *Quattrocento*. Only Valla's work was printed (1501); it is the first, though confused and desultory, exposition of Aristotelian poetics.

M. G. Vida's *De arte poetica* (1527) is still uninfluenced by Aristotle, and there is little of Aristotle in the first parts of G. G. Trissino's *Poetica* (1529), or in Daniello's *Della poetica* (1536). But with Francesco Robortello's commentary (1548) an overwhelming stream of Italian books about Aristotle's work and about poetics in general emerged, soon to be followed by a less voluminous but still imposing amount of comparable writings in other countries.

The main endeavor of the new theorists and critics was to construct a systematical poetics both for neo-Latin poetry, so much favored by the humanists, and for the different vernacular literatures which tended to rival the classics. In this way Aristotle often, if not always, became a pretext and a point of departure for very un-Aristotelian ideas.

This holds true even of the great Italian commentaries upon the *Poetics*—Maggi (1550), Vettori (1560), Castelvetro (1570), Piccolomini (1575), Beni (1613)—and, naturally, still more of the systematical treatises—Minturno's *De poeta* (1559) and *Arte poetica* (1564), Scaliger's *Poetice* (1561); Patrizzi's *Della poetica* (1586) is openly anti-Aristotelian. To the many poets who expounded their ideas and defended their works—e.g., Giraldi Cinthio, *Discorsi* (1554), Tasso, *Discorsi dell'arte poetica* (1587), Guarini, *Compendio della poesia tragicomica* (1601)—Aristotle is either a convenient ally or an embarrassing obstacle.

Outside Italy Aristotle is revered and studied, mostly in Italian editions, and literary theory is heavily dependent on the Italians. This is true of France—Peletier du Mans (1554), Vauquelin de la Fresnaye (1604)—as well as of England—Ascham (1570), Puttenham (1589)—of Spain—Lopez Pinciano (1596)—and of Germany—Pontanus (1594), Opitz (1624). More interesting and independent are the poets' own utterances, such as Ronsard's *Abrégé de l'art poétique français* (1565) or Sidney's *Apology for Poesy* (1595) or Lope de Vega's *Arte nueva de hacer comedias* (1607).

With the beginning of the seventeenth century, the interest in neo-Aristotelian poetics diminishes, though it is seldom openly rejected. The different nonclassical, "baroque" currents never develop a poetics of their own. In France, which emerges as the new leader of European literature, there are still lively debates about drama—d'Aubignac's *Pratique du théâtre* (1657), Corneille's *Discours sur le poème dramatique* (1660), Molière's and Racine's prefaces to their pieces—and about epic—Le Bossu's *Traité du poème épique* (1675). But Boileau's *L'art poétique* (1674) is an elegant, unpedantic résumé of current opinions. Later discussions show growing dislike of theorizing and a disregard of Aristotle's authority. When Lessing in *Hamburgische Dramaturgie* (1767–68) proclaims Aristotle's infallibility, the reign of neo-Aristotelianism is well on the wane.

2. The Aim of Poetry. One of the signs of a new epoch is the vigor with which in the *Trecento* poets and friends of poetry (Albertino Mussato, Boccaccio, Coluccio Salutati) defend it against theologians and moralists. With increasing self-confidence they declare that poetry, even pagan poetry, is no idle but deep truth hidden under the veil of fables, as Dante said. The poet is once more a teacher and a leader, a theologian and a philosopher: the *poeta doctus*.

In the *Quattrocento*, however, the apologists were confronted with Plato's attacks on poetry, when his works became known and soon translated—in their entirety—by Marsilio Ficino (1484). As in classical antiquity, poetry was defended with allegorism. A more dangerous crisis was caused by the religious fervor of the Reformation and the Counter-Reformation in the sixteenth century.

Fortunately, the rediscovery of Aristotle's *Poetics* gave poetry an authoritative new ally. Horace's *Ad Pisones* was combined with the *Poetics*, and the Horatian compromise was ascribed also to Aristotle: poetry is delightful teaching. This became the prevailing opinion, and Castelvetro's assertion that the only

529

aim of poetry is to amuse "the raw multitude" was the exception which proved the rule. Thus the Aristotelian *catharsis* is interpreted as moral purification, and the theater defended, e.g., by G. E. Lessing, as improving manners.

In other countries, poetry is defended with Italian arguments, Sidney's *Apology* being the most eloquent. But in England and other Calvinist countries, poetry, especially the drama, is fiercely attacked, and the victorious Puritans close the theaters. Milton, however, serenely combines his Puritan faith with a Renaissance belief in the truth and glory of poetry, but a poetry serving God.

In the seventeenth and eighteenth centuries the debate continues, with steadily diminishing fervor. The Horatian compromise remains the official doctrine, to which lip service is paid, e.g., by Boileau. But as theology gradually loses its grip on public opinion, authors and critics—such as Corneille—now dare to state openly that the aim of poetry is to please.

At the end of the seventeenth century, poetry was confronted with a new enemy. The rise of science and the Cartesian philosophy induced many people, especially in France, to condemn poetry as a foolish and useless relic of barbaric ages. This attitude characterized some of the participants in the great quarrel about the Ancients and the Moderns, e.g., Abbé Jean Terrasson. Less extreme and therefore more dangerous was the condescending tolerance of poetry as a social amusement, expressed by Fontenelle. Against this depreciation old Boileau and young Voltaire protested strongly. But early romantic writers accepted the challenge: poetry is, indeed, a creation of barbarism and therefore admirable. The proclamation of this thesis by Giambattista Vico (1730) and Thomas Blackwell (1735) means the end of the concept of the *poeta doctus* and of European classicism.

3. The Craft of Poetry. The rising self-confidence of poets in the late Middle Ages appears also in their renewed insistence on inspiration. The poems of the troubadours and of the *dolce stil nuovo* are inspired by Love and the Lady, as is Dante's *Vita nuova*. In the *Divina commedia* (*Divine Comedy*), Dante's invocations of Apollo and the Muses are no mere metaphors but express his belief in the hidden truth of pagan mythology. His poem is "sacred."

In Petrarch, the idea of poetical ecstasy emerges again, and in the fifteenth century the direct contact with Plato makes the *furor poeticus* a popular idea, developed by Ficino and accepted by many poets and critics, e.g., Scaliger, Ronsard, and Puttenham. This does not imply, as in Plato, any negative or ironical assessment of the poet's own activity, which on the contrary is stressed to the utmost.

The poet is regarded as a second Creator, inferior to God but akin to him. This divinization of Man as Poet—later on applied to the artist—originated in Florentine Platonism and was first stated by Christoforo Landino (1481). It was inspired by Platonic and Hermetic belief in the unique cosmic status of Man, by Christian belief in a Creator, and by Plato's Demiurge. The poet as creator became a metaphor popular with many poets and critics, such as Scaliger, Tasso, and Sidney, though mostly with reservations.

The theologians of the Reformation and the Counter-Reformation could no more than their medieval predecessors accept profane poetry as inspired. Therefore, in their great religious epics both Tasso and Milton invoke a "Heavenly Muse."

But even some critics like Castelvetro rejected inspiration because it made poetics superfluous. Indeed, a few libertines or freethinkers, like Pietro Aretino or Giordano Bruno drew this conclusion. But most authors combined faith in inspiration with obedience to tradition and the rules.

In the seventeenth and eighteenth centuries the idea of poetical inspiration and creativity fades away. It is taken for granted that the poet should be inspired, particularly if he writes an ode and breaks into "Pindaric frenzy." But critics and readers smile or frown at boasts of inspiration and find the usual invocations frigid, as Shaftesbury did. To the new enemies of poetry all talk of inspiration is silly.

Shaftesbury did not belong to them. In spite of his attacks on "Enthousiasm," his *Soliloquy* (1710) exalts the Poet as Creator with a Renaissance fervor. We are on the threshold of romanticism.

For all its glorification of the poet the Renaissance did not call him a "genius." The Latin word was used but in the neutral sense of innate disposition, good or bad. And it was thus used by Boileau and even by Dr. Johnson. In seventeenth-century France, however, *génie* was increasingly used in a positive sense, until the Abbé Du Bos in his *Réflexions critiques sur la poésie et la peinture* (1719) gave it its present absolute meaning. The romantic genius was born.

4. The Realm of Poetry. The old concept of poetry as a hierarchy of genres was generally accepted, but the admission of new genres and their rank in the hierarchy were fiercely disputed.

The study of Roman and Greek literature, poetics and rhetoric, brought forth by humanism, replaced the inherited medieval genres, still embraced by Dante, with the old classical genres. But a real attempt at creating a system of genres was not made before the advent of neo-Aristotelianism. Its point of departure was the combination of the Platonic-Aristotelian tripartition of poetry and the rhetorical tripartition of style with the Aristotelian *mimēsis*, generally understood as "imitation of nature." But this "nature" was not identical with the world of the senses; it also comprised the possible or even the supernatural. On the other hand, it excluded the ugly and the low, especially in the high genres. There was a strong tendency to idealize, generalize, and moralize.

The difficulty in finding a place for lyric poetry—disregarded by Plato and Aristotle—in a mimetic poetics was overcome by Minturno and Beni among others, who regarded lyrics as an imitation of the poet's thoughts and sentiments. Thus the now usual division of poetry into epic, drama, and lyrics was established. It first appears in Daniello. It was combined with the division of styles, so that each of the three main parts of poetry had its high, middle, and low genres. This systematization was never worked out in detail, but it was generally agreed that heroic poetry, tragedy, and the ode constituted the high genres. In spite of Aristotle verse was commonly regarded as essential to poetry, and prose fiction was therefore excluded from poetics by most critics—but not by Minturno and Beni.

As in classical antiquity, *decorum* was the main rule, with its ambiguous ethical-aesthetic-social meaning. In practice this meant a close imitation of established models, especially in the high genres. But the choice of models was disputed and was involved in the battle between the Ancients and the Moderns.

Vergil was the great epic model, but in Italy the existence of a popular vernacular epic poetry—Dante, Boiardo, Ariosto—caused some critics, e.g., Giraldi Cinthio, to prefer epics with national and Christian themes and a different, more loose construction. In tragedy, the theorists had a freer hand, at least in Italy and France. There, the "rules" could be enforced, particularly the "three unities" of action, time, and place, finally established by Castelvetro (1570) but corresponding to the general practice of Greek and Roman tragedy. The unities were imposed in the name of verisimilitude, whereas the epic was freer and admitted the marvellous as well as the episode.

Outside Italy, especially in England and Spain, the dramatists and the public cared little for the rules, even in tragedy. In comedy the liberty was always greater, and the creation of mixed genres like tragicomedy in seventeenth-century France or pastoral drama in Italy—Guarini's *Il pastor fido* (1590)—was condemned by the critics but gladly accepted by the public.

For the neo-Aristotelian system of genres was never completely realized in actual literature. Everywhere, even in Italy and France, it was confronted with already existing genres, which could be fitted into the system only with difficulty or not at all. Only in the early eighteenth century, are the genres generally accepted, but by then the whole system is breaking down. The rise of the novel and the recognition of it as an equal and autonomous genre by such orthodox critics as Lessing and Dr. Johnson is one of the signs of the disintegration of European classicism.

5. *The Ancients and the Moderns.* The Renaissance radically changed the medieval *autores*. The great Roman writers kept their place, but to them many rediscovered authors were added, and in the fifteenth century the works of the Greeks reclaimed their rank as classics. The old literary rivalry between Greece and Rome was renewed, most people showing a strong predilection for the Romans, who were already well-established and more accessible.

The importance of this debate was due to the role which the "imitation of the classics" played. Dante, in the *De vulgari eloquentia*, had demanded imitation of the "regular" (Roman) poets. His own imitation of Vergil in his *Divine Comedy* is the greatest instance of that creative imitation which is the fundamental paradox of European classicism.

But to later generations Dante's imitation seemed too free and unclassical. While in the *Trecento* Italian writers followed medieval tradition in vernacular writings, in the *Quattrocento* neo-Latin poetry and prose closely imitated Roman models. When in the early *Cinquecento* Italian, i.e., Tuscan, was finally accepted as equal to Latin, it adopted its own classics, Petrarch and Boccaccio but not Dante. Their status as linguistic and stylistic models was proclaimed by Pietro Bembo in his *De imitatione* (1512).

Though the word "classic" was seldom applied to vernacular authors before the eighteenth century, the recognition of modern writers as equal to ancient shows that the imitation of the classics implied a hope to equal if not to surpass them. Classicism did not exclude progress.

Thus the comparison between the "Ancients" and the "Moderns" was a standard theme in the literature of this age down to the *Parallèles* (1688-97) of Charles Perrault, which caused the famous *querelle* in France, and to the Battle of the Books in England (1690-98).

The debate quickly transgressed the frontiers of literature and developed into a general discussion of the possibilities of cultural progress. Some debaters, like Bentley and Wotton in England, while accepting the idea of progress, still admired classical literature. But to most people a belief in progress meant a depreciation of this literature, particularly the Greek poets. This view was strengthened by the general contempt of poetry and admiration of science. But the supporters of the Ancients had not lost their faith, as the great success of Pope's *Iliad* (1715) was soon to show. The Greek revival was on the way.

531

BIBLIOGRAPHY

There is no modern comprehensive work on this subject. But see *Momenti e problemi di storia dell'estetica*, Vol. 1, by various scholars (Milan, 1959), with rich bibliographies; Karl Borinski, *Die Antike in Poetik und Kunsttheorie vom Ausgang des klassischen Altertums bis auf Goethe und Wilhelm von Humboldt*, 2 vols., in the series *Das Erbe der Alten*, Vols. 9 and 10 (Leipzig, 1914–24); *Critics and Criticism*, ed. Ronald S. Crane (Chicago, 1952); William K. Wimsatt and Cleanth Brooks, *Literary Criticism* (New York, 1947).

For Greece and Rome, while out-of-date, still the best is Eduard Müller, *Geschichte der Theorie der Kunst bei den Alten*, 2 vols. (Breslau, 1834–37). See also J. W. H. Atkins, *Literary Criticism in Antiquity*, 2 vols. (Cambridge, 1934; reprint New York). Charles S. Baldwin, *Ancient Rhetoric and Poetic* (New York, 1924). J. F. D'Alton, *Roman Literary Theory and Criticism* (London, 1931). Ernesto Grassi, *Die Theorie des Schönen in der Antike* (Cologne, 1962). G. M. A. Grube, *The Greek and Roman Critics* (London, 1965). W. Rhys Roberts, *Greek Rhetoric and Literary Criticism* (New York, 1928). E. E. Sikes, *The Greek View of Poetry* (London, 1931).

For the Middle Ages see especially Edgar De Bruyne, *Études d'esthétique médiévale*, 3 vols. (Bruges, 1946); cf. idem, *Esthétique du moyen âge* (Louvain, 1947); Ernst Robert Curtius, *Europäische Literatur und Lateinisches Mittelalter*, 2nd ed. (Bern, 1953), trans. Willard R. Trask as *European Literature and the Latin Middle Ages* (Princeton, 1953; reprint New York). See also Rosario Assunto, *Die Theorie des Schönen im Mittelalter* (Cologne, 1963). Charles S. Baldwin, *Medieval Rhetoric and Poetic* (New York, 1928). E. Faral, *Les Arts poétiques du XIIe et XIIIe siècles* (Paris, 1924). Franz Quadlbauer, "Die antike Theorie der genera dicendi im lateinischen Mittelalter," *Österreichische Akademie der Wissenschaften. Philosophisch-historische Klasse. Sitzungs-Berichte*, **241**, 2 (1962).

For the Renaissance and later, Joel Spingarn, *A History of Literary Criticism in the Renaissance* (New York, 1899), is out-of-date but still useful; but see Charles S. Baldwin, *Renaissance Literary Theory and Practice* (New York, 1939). See also J. W. H. Atkins, *English Literary Criticism*, Vol. I, *The Renascence* (London and New York, 1947; 1968), and Vol. II, *17th and 18th Centuries* (London and New York, 1951). Karl Borinski, *Die Poetik der Renaissance und die Anfänge der literarischen Kritik in Deutschland* (Berlin, 1886). René Bray, *La formation de la doctrine classique en France* (Paris, 1927). August Buck, *Italienische Dichtungslehren vom Mittelalter bis zum Ausgang der Renaissance*, *Beihefte*, Vol. 94 (1952). Baxter Hathaway, *The Age of Criticism, The Late Renaissance in Italy* (Ithaca, 1962); cf. review by E. N. Tigerstedt, *Lychnos* (1965–66). Bruno Markwardt, *Geschichte der deutschen Poetik*, 2 vols. (Leipzig, 1956–57). Raymond Naves, *Le goût de Voltaire* (Paris, 1938). Warner F. Patterson, *Three Centuries of French Poetic Theory*, 2 vols. (Ann Arbor, 1936). Henri Peyre, *Qu'est-ce que le classicisme?*, revised ed. (Paris, 1965). Bernard A. Weinberg, *A History of Literary Criticism in the Italian Renaissance*, 2 vols. (Chicago, 1961); cf. review by E. N. Tigerstedt, *Lychnos* (1962). Ciro Trabalza, *La critica letteraria, secoli XV–XVI–XVII* (Milan, 1915).

E. N. TIGERSTEDT

[See also Ancients and Moderns; Beauty; **Classification of the Arts;** Comic; Creativity; Literature; Love; **Mimesis;** Platonism; Renaissance; Tragic; *Ut pictura poesis.*]

POSITIVISM IN EUROPE TO 1900

I

THE WORD "positivism" was coined by Auguste Comte in the 1820's. To understand the history of the idea behind the word, however, it is necessary to look at the eighteenth and even at the seventeenth century for at least three reasons. First, because significant component elements of the idea are to be found in those periods; secondly, because Comte himself owed important intellectual debts, both acknowledged and unacknowledged, to earlier figures; and thirdly, because he elaborated his positivist synthesis in response to problems peculiar to his generation.

In a sense which is not merely trivial, positivism as an intellectual attitude characteristic of Auguste Comte is as old as the Platonic tradition in philosophy. In practice, however, it is sufficient to start with the seventeenth century. Without necessarily subscribing to a recent positivist view, expressed by Pierre Ducassé, that the only precedent for Comte's synthesis of the sciences was that of Descartes, we can still say that Descartes as the classic French representative of the *esprit de système* was a part of the air that Comte breathed. More widely than that, the scientific revolution of the seventeenth century in general was an indispensable condition for positivism, although the discoveries and results of the scientific revolution, and even its assumptions and methods, were less important in this connection than the enormously enhanced prestige of the natural sciences and of its practitioners.

It was, however, only in the eighteenth century that, especially in France, this new prestige made itself felt throughout educated society, and this is the first and most general respect in which Comtean positivism, as one expression of the scientism of the nineteenth century, owes a debt to the Enlightenment. Voltaire, whom Comte did not acknowledge, d'Alembert and Condorcet whom he did, and many other *philosophes* made strenuous and successful efforts to familiarize polite salon society with the achievements of French and foreign scientists. Equally important for positivism, they preached and practiced the application of the methods of the natural sciences to social problems in order to create "social physics" (i.e., social science). They were not always clear, and certainly not always agreed, on what exactly "scientific method" consisted of, particularly as to the relative importance of induction and deduction, experiment and mathematics. They tended, especially on social questions, to be less empirical than they professed themselves to be, and in this respect, also, Comte resembled them.

It is both possible and necessary, however, to be more specific concerning Comte's debt to the *philosophes*. From Montesquieu, as he acknowledged, Comte derived the fundamental insight that society was governed by historical and other laws analogous to the laws governing natural phenomena. The great *Encyclopédie* (1751–72) of d'Alembert and Diderot had pioneered the project of a coordination of all knowledge free from theological presuppositions and reinforced the notion of the unity of the natural and social sciences. D'Alembert and Turgot between them had sketched more than rudimentary models of two of Comte's most fundamental assumptions, the Classification of the Sciences and the Law of the Three Stages. The Idea of Progress implicit in the latter and in much Enlightenment thinking generally had been elaborated by Condorcet, of whom Comte called himself the "spiritual son."

Although he eventually became a victim of the French Revolution, Condorcet constituted an important link between the Enlightenment and the intellectual climate of the revolutionary era. In the plans for educational reform that he produced during the first years of the Revolution, Condorcet pressed on the one hand for a greater emphasis on mathematics and the natural sciences in secondary and higher education, and on the other hand for a more intense application of the method of the natural sciences to moral and social problems. Himself a mathematician by profession, Condorcet deliberately cultivated personal as well as intellectual connections both with the tradition of the *philosophes* and with practicing contemporary scientists such as J. L. Lagrange. After Condorcet's death this role was taken up by the group of so-called *Idéologues*, led by Cabanis and Destutt de Tracy, who were particularly concerned with the social and political application of the ideas of Condillac and who disseminated their teachings in an educational system reformed, from 1795, on lines not unlike those suggested by Condorcet, especially in the new École Polytechnique.

These links are important because they sustained the momentum of the Enlightenment and particularly of the idea of "social science" until the day when Auguste Comte himself entered the École Polytechnique. At the same time Comte was at least as much a rebel against the Enlightenment and the Revolution as he was their heir and the beneficiary of one of their institutions. So far as the École Polytechnique was concerned, Comte was not alone in making the inference from an advanced training course for a highly selected group of future engineers to the idea of social engineering by a managerial political élite. So far as the wider issues were concerned, Comte took as his point of departure the premiss that the Enlightenment and the Revolution had undermined the intellectual and the social bases of the *ancien régime* without having put anything viable in their place. (Later, one of his famous aphorisms ran: "You can destroy only what you replace.") He shared, therefore, with men otherwise as far apart as Hegel, Victor Cousin, the "Theocrats" J. M. de Maistre and L. G. A. de Bonald, and Henri de Saint-Simon the conviction that the urgent and paramount task after 1815 was to repair this defect, to reconstruct, to supply new institutions and particularly a new ideology—for social and political anarchy could be remedied only after intellectual anarchy: political authority could be restored only on the basis of general acceptance of a new doctrine.

It would be going too far afield here to investigate Comte's relationship with Hegel, but a discussion of the similarities and differences between Comte and Cousin, Maistre and Bonald, and Saint-Simon should be instructive by leading to a clearer definition of Comte's place in the politics and culture of the French Restoration. Victor Cousin was Comte's senior by a few years and therefore already a teacher at both the École Normale and the Sorbonne when Comte was still a student at the Polytechnique. A brilliant man of letters and master of rhetoric, Cousin was the idol of the liberal youth of the Restoration, and well connected with the liberal political Opposition, especially under Charles X, while Comte wrote in a crabbed style, lectured to tiny audiences, and was despised by such men as F. Guizot both in opposition and in power. Cousin thus was bound to be Comte's chief enemy quite apart from their doctrines, and despite their agreement that what France and Europe needed was a new intellectual and moral consensus to replace orthodox religion. Cousin set out to supply it with a characteristically eclectic philosophy, historically oriented, with an emphasis on introspective psychology and on the autonomy of the mind and man's spiritual nature—a consciously moderate system deliberately designed to serve as support for the political doctrine of the *juste milieu* espoused by the orthodox liberal constitutional monarchists of the Restoration. Cousin had little use for the natural sciences, whose success from Francis Bacon to Condillac, he said, had drawn attention away from human problems. A technocrat and intellectual hermit who read nothing after he began to write his own large works, Comte was the adulator of "science" as he understood it. He thought that a "scientific" psychology must be physiological (here he based himself on the work of such biologists as M. F. X. Bichat and F. J. V. Broussais, and in particular on the phrenology of Franz Gall), scorned eclecticism, and prided himself on the originality and the rigor of his own projected synthesis. Comte could have nothing but contempt for Cousin's "spiritualism" which he regarded as dishonest as well as shallow.

He had far more sympathy for the authoritarian approach to the intellectual, moral, and social legacy of the Enlightenment and the Revolution propounded by Maistre and Bonald. He agreed with them that the fundamental trouble arose from the individualism unleashed by all the loose—and, he would add, metaphysical—talk about "liberty" for two generations or more. This heady wine had done nothing but confuse and excite people and make them unamenable to discipline. Comte agreed with the conception of "counter-revolution" (as distinguished from reaction) advanced by Maistre and particularly by Bonald, who was the more sociologically oriented of the two. Bonald added a new dimension to the social analysis bequeathed by Montesquieu and the Enlightenment— some would say that it was he who discovered the "sociology" that Comte was to place at the pinnacle of his hierarchy of the sciences—by using it in order to shore up the restored Bourbons. Rather than taking seriously the idea of a literal "restoration" (which derived from the Swiss Haller), Bonald argued that since the *ancien régime* had been totally destroyed it was necessary to reconstruct from the ground up. Sociology, not philosophy, could reveal the human condition in all its aspects and thus lead to a discovery of the eternal laws of society which would form the basis of a tradition so firm as to be invulnerable to future enlightenments or attempted revolutions.

While erecting this perfectly rationalistic structure, Bonald shared with Maistre a pessimism about human reason which justified an authoritarianism ultimately backed up by religious sanctions administered by a Church in a Throne-and-Altar alliance with the monarchy, although Bonald was less prepared than Maistre to bother himself with the metaphysics of theism. Comte went farther than either of them in this respect: he subjected religion as well to sociological analysis and integrated it into his political synthesis. Above all, he differed from Maistre and Bonald (as well as from Cousin) in insisting on the natural sciences as a model

and basis for social prescription. Nevertheless, the significance of the emergence of sociology in an atmosphere and with the purpose of "restoration" in some sense should not be underestimated.

Although Comte owed a considerable debt—which he acknowledged—to Maistre and Bonald, particularly in reinforcing his "theocratic" inclinations, there can be little doubt that his real master was Saint-Simon whom, by contrast, he disowned after he left service as his secretary. If it seems strange that the same man could be significantly influenced by such diverse figures as Maistre and Bonald on the one hand and the early socialist Saint-Simon on the other—stranger still if one takes the view that Karl Marx, also, owed his greatest (and likewise unadmitted) debt to Saint-Simon—the answer may be found, not only in Comte's own powerful intellect which enabled him to discern and absorb what he needed and, in contrast to Cousin, to refashion it for his own synthesis, but also in what Maistre, Bonald, Saint-Simon, and Comte himself all shared: the politics of reconciliation, the aim of establishing a consensus and, based on it, an authority above parties and factions, characteristic more recently of the advocates of "presidential" government in the last years of the Weimar Republic and in the Fifth Republic in France. This was a social goal that could be striven for by radicals as well as by counter-revolutionaries. It was, however, precisely Saint-Simon's radicalism that Comte dropped from his intellectual armory.

In almost every other substantive respect, even in the chronology and pattern of his development, Saint-Simon served as Comte's model, however much the latter decried it, and however much Saint-Simon had himself merely been reflecting or summing up a general "pre-positivist" climate. The subordinate role assigned to academic or traditional philosophy; the professed rejection of metaphysics in particular; the Law of the Three Stages and the idea of a hierarchy of the sciences; the worship of natural science and of technology; the commitment to a physiological view of the mind; the subjection of the historical process to laws of human nature; the interweaving and interdependence of scientific and historical method; the increasingly emphatic view of themselves in messianic terms, and the development of a full-blown religion to replace orthodox Christianity, complete with disciples—all these and other teachings were common to the two men. What separated Saint-Simon and Comte above all from the earlier figures on whom they both drew was the French Revolution and their consequently far more urgent insistence that doctrine was merely a means to achieving social ends, an insistence commensurate with the magnitude of the crisis that they conceived the Revolution to have created. But this sense of urgency was combined in Comte with the Cartesian *esprit de système.* Unlike the auto-didact Saint-Simon, who wrote down ideas as they came into his head, Comte had the patience, the self-discipline, and the scholarship to wish to lay down a solid scientific foundation before erecting on it the political and religious synthesis whose prescriptions would rescue a stricken society. For this reason Comte's main teachings are contained in two prolix works of six and four large volumes respectively, although the summary of them in the next section is considerably aided by shorter and sometimes occasional works intended for popular consumption.

II

Appreciation of the sources on which Comte drew for his doctrine should not obscure or detract from his originality. This consisted not in inventing an entirely new system but in assembling many already current ideas in a new arrangement or cluster and adding a few new ideas and emphases. Comte's great strength lay in the uniqueness and internal logic of his system; his great weakness lay in the unaccustomed and uneasy relationship among the ideas making up the system. The strength and the weakness were thus two sides of the same coin minted by Comte's sheer energy and persistence (or obstinacy, according to taste) which derived, in turn, from the strength of his motivation: the urgency of the social problem as he saw it; the need for a complete intellectual system as the means of solving it; and his conception of his own messianic mission. These considerations inspired him throughout a career of almost continuous personal hardship which never diverted him from his ultimate goals. Neither did he change any fundamental aspect of his teachings; alterations of detail, of attitude, and of emphasis appeared, but these never ran counter to his initial premises. They were a result of the chronological coincidence of a profound personal experience with the completion of his intellectual substructure in 1842 and represented, not a sharp *caesura* in his thought but merely a change of gear before he embarked on the politico-religious superstructure. Comte himself, when taxed with inconsistency, indignantly pointed out that he had sketched his basic social design in his earliest writings and reprinted them as an appendix to his second *magnum opus,* the *System of Positive Polity.* Any attempt to separate the often absurd prescriptions of the latter from the scientific analysis of the earlier *Positive Philosophy* was and is doomed to failure. For better or (as almost all unbiased observers agree) for worse, Comte's doctrine from first to last was a unity. Science to him was never an end in itself; a mathematician by profession, he did not really even

understand contemporary science in his infatuation with it for practical social purposes.

An exposition of the doctrine must, however, begin with the "scientific" foundations, and at the center of these, as already indicated, were the interlocking Law of the Three Stages and the Classification of the Sciences. The first of these (in Comte's version) described the inevitable progression of the human mind through three methods of explaining the world: the first, "theological," in terms of the will of anthropomorphic gods; the second, "metaphysical," in terms of philosophical abstractions; and the third, "positive," in terms of scientific truth. Comte substantiated this scheme, and its many subdivisions, with an elaborate though rather arbitrary discussion of the history of universal thought, with emphasis on the development of scientific ideas. The order of subject-matter in which the mind reached the third stage was disclosed by Comte's second fundamental proposition, which arranged the sciences in a hierarchy according to their decreasing generality and increasing interdependence and complexity. With mathematics at the base, this hierarchy set on top of it astronomy, physics, chemistry, and biology, with sociology (a word also invented by Comte, who had little respect or feeling for language) at the pinnacle. Taken together, the two propositions show that sociology is the last discipline to reach the positive or scientific stage; and Comte's specific historical analysis indicated that this development, which would constitute the climax of the evolution of the human mind, was imminent, biology having recently reached the positive stage. Moreover, it would occur in the mind of the man who first recognized the process, Auguste Comte himself.

But—and this was perhaps the most crucial respect in which Comte's vision went beyond Saint-Simon's—it was not only a climax but also a beginning. The conversion of the last and highest of the sciences, sociology, into a positive discipline did not yet overcome the separateness of the six sciences and therefore could not yet yield the synthesis of all the positive sciences which would establish positivism as a total system, as a "conception of the world and of man." Only such a synthesis deserved the name "philosophy." In contrast to Saint-Simon, for whom philosophy became positive when the sciences had shed everything that was not verifiable, Comte's view was that this purification was only an essential preliminary to a recoil or converse movement, so that the sciences become truly positive, and truly unified, only when a philosophy makes them aware of their positiveness. This view involved, in practice, making positive sociology, that is to say the knowledge of mankind (or Humanity, as the positivists preferred) and of the laws of its development, into the point of departure for the construction of a second and this time "subjective" synthesis, an edifice even more imposing than the first, "objective," scientific, and only partial synthesis.

It was subjective because knowledge of mankind included knowledge of its needs. It was a true synthesis or a "philosophy" because it was not merely a coordination of the objective findings of the several sciences but a coordination of them from a "human" and "social" point of view. Conversely, only this subjective synthesis, this coordination of the content of the inferior sciences in the light and from the point of view of positive sociology, the highest of the individual sciences, could avail to solve the pressing problems of the day. But even this, of course, was not enough: the solution had to be not only discovered but also imposed. Since fashioning of the intellectual consensus must precede the reformation of society, the creation of a new spiritual power must precede the establishment of a new political order. This new spiritual power or priesthood was to serve, not some outmoded theology, but Humanity itself; and from there it was only a small further step to the idea of a Religion of Humanity and to Comte's casting of himself in the role of its first High Priest.

This entire construction was contained in the first of Comte's two major works and in the early *opuscules*. It was a work as remarkable for its symmetry as it was formidable in its content. Everything cohered, everything balanced, every loss was compensated by a gain. Progress was the development of order, order was the goal of progress, and positivism alone could reconcile them. The superior sciences, owing to their greater complexity, yielded less reliable knowledge than the inferior, but in return the phenomena with which they dealt were more amenable to human intervention. The word "positive" itself was defined in mutually counterbalancing terms. Whereas on the one hand it meant "precise," "certain," "real," it meant also not only "useful" (reconcilable with rationalism as in the Enlightenment tradition), but in addition, "organic" (i.e., coherent, constructive, systematic) and, finally, "relative," indicating the reverse traverse of the sciences back down from sociology, which made them not merely positive but positivist and established positivism as a total system.

It was after completing this system in the six volumes of the *Positive Philosophy* (1830–42) that Comte, a recluse separated from his wife, fell in love with Clotilde de Vaux, a lady of good family, whom he tried to make his mistress, carried on a platonic relationship with her when she refused, and elevated her to the status of patron saint of the Religion of Humanity when she died young within a year of their meeting. This

"incomparable year" of his life undoubtedly contributed to the more pronounced sentimental and authoritarian characteristics (a most dangerous combination) of his last years and of the four volumes of the *System of Positive Polity* with the minute regulations of religious ritual and of social life which caused John Stuart Mill to compare Comte's tyranny with that of Loyola. But even before this episode Comte had often conveniently forgotten the relatively low predictive value of conclusions in sociology, the most complex of the sciences, and had made not only unproved assumptions but also "useful fictions" and "artificial hypotheses" into the bases of subsequent deductions. When he sometimes declared that in the last analysis positivism was nothing but systematized common sense, this device had both the rhetorical advantage of appealing when necessary from the rigors of scientific reasoning to some axiom of "common sense," and the practical advantage of facilitating his call for the support of workmen and women, who at least did not need to unlearn metaphysical philosophy.

III

Nevertheless, there were those among Comte's disciples who found the details of the *System* so repellent that they set out to depict them as mere embroidery and to rescue both his reputation and his doctrine by repudiating that part of it, the Religion of Humanity including its social and political as well as its ritualistic aspects, at which he had quite overtly been aiming all along. They sought to distinguish Comte's first, valid, "scientific" phase from his second, "subjective" phase, besotted by Clotilde de Vaux and to be discreetly ignored. Comte would certainly have excommunicated these dissidents even if it had not been the case that their leader, Émile Littré, was also championing the rights of Comte's estranged wife. Littré, at one time Comte's chosen successor as High Priest of Humanity, was instead cast into outer darkness, and when Comte died, far short of the life-span of Fontenelle (1657–1757) which he had counted on in order to preach positivism from the pulpit of Notre Dame, no new, more worthy successor had in fact been named.

It would be inappropriate here to become involved with the many intricate internecine squabbles among Comte's disciples. Two principal matters, instead, remain to be discussed: first, the nature of and reasons for discipleship; and secondly, the effectiveness of Comte and of his disciples in spreading his doctrine into the world at large. It should be clear that the word "disciples" is applicable here in no mere figurative sense. Comte himself used it to denote (and demand) not only philosophical agreement, and not only religious dedication, but also personal devotion to himself (so that, for example, he came to assume that he had a right to full financial support). Comte's disciples, totalling perhaps a thousand each in France and England, a scattering elsewhere in Europe and in the United States, and a following of considerable political influence in Latin America, particularly in Brazil (which is outside the scope of this article), were the propagators of a faith which for them filled a need partly intellectual, partly emotional. They were, to begin with, all emancipated, of course, from traditional religion, although they ranged from renegade Anglican priests who had lost their faith to confirmed secularists in search of one.

In France, positivism in addition filled a political as well as a religious vacuum, appealing to those who, like Comte himself, thought that neither the Revolution nor the Restoration nor the bourgeois monarchy provided any constructive political or social framework; although later the disciples fell out among themselves over the attitude to be adopted toward Louis Napoleon and then the Third Republic. In England the positivists were exercised chiefly over two public issues, colonialism and the "condition-of-England" question. The first leader of the English positivists, Richard Congreve, urged the government to give up Gibraltar, and later there were serious cross-Channel disagreements when the French brethren did not take a sufficiently militant attitude against their government's policy in Tunisia. In social matters the English positivists were among the earliest, most active, and most effective supporters of the trade-union movement so long as it was conciliatory and unpolitical but, in accordance with Comte's teaching, shied at the first hint of class struggle and became markedly conservative. In both countries there was a sizable number of working-class disciples, and particular efforts were made by the leadership to recruit more, in view of Comte's emphasis on the unspoiled minds of "proletarians"; but the bulk of the membership and nearly all of the leadership of the movements were middle-class, and mostly academic or professional. In the second rank of the most active positivists, especially in France, were to be found a good many medical men, particularly those interested in psychopathology, for Comte, who railed at ordinary doctors both in his books and in person, had, despite his semi-commitment to the phrenology of Gall and some odd notions on the "cerebral faculties," some very remarkable things to say about the nature and treatment of mental illness and had anticipated something of the assumptions and practices of what we should nowadays call psychosomatic medicine.

When they propagated positivism the disciples did not, however, stick to their specialties but ranged over most if not all of the immense field of knowledge which the master had striven to coordinate, so that much of their literary output is woefully weak. Partly because of their attempt at being as encyclopedic as Comte himself; partly because, with few exceptions, they were not original thinkers even within their specialties; partly because of the fact that the doctrine to whose propagation they were dedicated was a closed system; and partly, no doubt, because they were busy men, the disciples of positivism tended merely to repeat and defend Comte's formulas rather than enrich them. The exceptions were Frederic Harrison (1831–1923), a man of quite obviously independent mind, of immense energy, and of quick temper even in advanced old age, who rejected a few of Comte's most extreme liturgical and social injunctions but built a private chapel in his garden; the mathematician Pierre Laffitte, eventually evolving as High Priest in succession to Comte, administratively inefficient but the only man who thought Comte's system through for himself in its entirety and expressed it with great erudition and lucidity; and Littré, an eminent scholar and man of letters who probably did more than anyone else to make Comte's work and ideas (albeit excluding those of the "second phase") generally known.

Since Comte himself during his lifetime made little impression on the world apart from the circle of personal devotees, with the notable exception of John Stuart Mill who for about five years accepted most of Comte's earlier writings, the task of spreading the gospel was in fact left mostly to the disciples after the master's death. To this task they dedicated themselves most resolutely: journals were launched, free courses of lectures were given, societies, discussion groups, women's auxiliaries and committees were formed, services of positivist worship and of commemoration of Comte were held, books were written, money was raised, Comte's apartment and, later, the house of Clotilde de Vaux were made into shrines. Actually the disciples were undecided whether to concentrate on recruiting more disciples, building up the positivist organization, and preaching to the converted, or on reaching out among the heathen to infiltrate the doctrine; and the two purposes often conflicted with each other, which exacerbated the schisms within the positivist camp which, in turn, reduced the effectiveness of positivist propaganda. In view of this endemic sectarianism, added to the intrinsic abortiveness of Comte's system, the fact that the movement was decidedly not without influence is testimony to the disciples' valiant perseverance.

Even their efforts, of course, would have availed little without a climate of opinion in the late nineteenth century favorable to the absorption of elements, at least, of positivism. Relevant features of this climate of opinion included the more general scientism of which positivism was one expression; the anticlerical heritage of the Enlightenment, especially in France; the decline in the hold over "progressive" opinion in France exercised by the dominant spiritualist philosophy of Victor Cousin, exposed as insufficiently in touch with the natural sciences; the preparatory work performed, in England, by utilitarianism in accustoming people to secular and pragmatic views; and the general sense of social unease brought on by the French and industrial revolutions. Like almost all intellectual systems or clusters of ideas, positivism could usually only reinforce latent tendencies or support existing movements and impart to them new overtones or deviations in direction. The political and social effects already mentioned serve as instances. Similarly, it is doubtful whether positivism gave more nourishment to the general adulation of science than it took from it, but it definitely strengthened a "scientific" outlook, in some sense of the word, in certain specific fields, particularly in ethics and psychology. In France it gave support to anticlericalism and to lay education, and in a number of ways infiltrated the educational system of the Third Republic; in England it increasingly joined forces with the Ethical movement and other humanist and secularist organizations. In France and particularly in Germany small groups of artists and aestheticians adopted Comte's ideas on the social origin and function of art. There is a tenuous link with twentieth-century logical positivism through Ernst Mach as intermediary.

By far the most important intellectual legacy of Comte and his followers, however, is due to his approach to history as a preliminary to a predictive and scientific sociology. This was fundamentally what appealed to Mill. None or almost none of Comte's specific notions about the past have withstood critical scrutiny, but his conception on the one hand of sociology as a unifying and normative discipline, and his insistent emphasis on the other hand on the history of science and of scientific thought, have been enormously fruitful well into the twentieth century. Comte's vision of sociology was blurred by his often absurd prejudices, and his distinctive and genuinely pioneering work in the history of science was marred, like everything he did, by his egocentric point of view and by the necessity of fitting it into his general scheme; but his influence on the foundation of these two academic subjects cannot well be doubted. It is enough to mention here that the first chair in the history of science in France was established specifically for Pierre Laffitte, that George Sarton dedicated *Isis* "*à refaire l'oeuvre de Comte*," among other purposes, and that the first chairs of sociology in France and

England respectively were occupied by Émile Durkheim and L. T. Hobhouse, for both of whom Comte's work was avowedly an inspiration and a point of departure.

Still, when all this has been said perhaps the most important aspect of Comte's influence, both positively and negatively, has not been sufficiently emphasized. This is the religious aspect and the emotional needs to which it appealed, the aspect of Comte himself which he likened to Saint Paul rather than Aristotle. For all that his new religion was in some respects a pastiche of the Roman Catholicism that he had abandoned in his youth—so that T. H. Huxley could ridicule the Religion of Humanity as "Catholicism minus Christianity," and Beatrice Webb could describe a speech of her friend Frederic Harrison as "a valiant effort to make a religion out of nothing; a pitiful attempt by poor humanity to turn its head round and worship its own tail" (Simon [1963], p. 226)—it still evoked a certain response in some quarters, a response which Comte himself explained by his declaration that "mankind is becoming more and more religious," coupled with his emphasis on the etymology of the word "religion" in the sense of "binding together." His Religion of Humanity must take its place among a whole outcropping of "substitute religions" beginning with the new creeds of the French Revolution itself. Comte tried to have it both ways by generating an emotional appeal on behalf of an allegedly scientific religion; but, predictably, he fell instead between stools, since most people who welcomed the "scientific" basis would not accept the ritual or the emotional incantations, while those who came to have their emotional needs satisfied for the most part either did not understand or did not accept the intellectual substructure.

These needs, nevertheless, existed. *Cris de coeur* at the void left when doubt replaced faith are scattered about the letters, essays, and autobiographies of the period. Such a man as Théodore Jouffroy, a disciple of Comte's archenemy Victor Cousin, in a famous essay, part historical, part autobiographical, wrote an obituary of Christian dogma which was at the same time a blackly pessimistic account of the consequences of its demise; and there were plenty of other educated people to whom Christianity was no longer convincing but who still had a need or a hankering for some sort of religion all the same. The disciples of positivism were certainly among them, and many of the other thousands who read positivist literature or who came to positivist meetings without becoming disciples must also be included in this category.

Nevertheless, the difference between the disciples and those who were merely disposed to accept one or more parts of Comte's historical or sociological analysis must not be blurred. Mill, who did more than any other Englishman during Comte's lifetime to spread his reputation and large parts of his teaching and even helped him financially, in the end could not stomach Comte's intellectual arrogance and sacerdotal pretensions. John Morley, the later statesman and biographer of Gladstone, as editor of the *Fortnightly Review* gave generous hospitality to essays by Harrison and other positivists and himself praised Comte's intellectual achievement, but would have nothing to do with the Religion of Humanity. Perhaps the most striking case is that of the novelist George Eliot, who was of a profoundly religious temperament and, having lost her old faith, clung for many years to the Religion of Humanity in the hope of finding in it a satisfactory substitute; but in the end she felt obliged to withdraw: "I cannot submit my intellect or my soul to the guidance of Comte . . ." (Simon [1963], p. 213). The desire for intellectual independence had proved even stronger than the need for spiritual solace. In George Eliot's good friend Frederic Harrison the balance had just tipped the other way.

BIBLIOGRAPHY

The principal texts include J. H. Bridges, *Illustrations of Positivism* (London, 1915); Richard Congreve, *Essays: Political, Social, and Religious,* 3 vols. (London, 1874–1900); Frederic Harrison, *Autobiographic Memoirs,* 2 vols. (London, 1911); Émile Littré, *Auguste Comte et la philosophie positive* (Paris, 1864); and the following works of Auguste Comte: *Appeal to Conservatives* (London, 1889), *The Catechism of Positive Religion* (London, 1858), *Cours de philosophie positive,* 6 vols. (Paris, 1830–42) or the abridged translation *The Positive Philosophy,* 3 vols. (London, 1896), *System of Positive Polity,* 4 vols. (London, 1875–77), the Introduction of which has been published separately as *A General View of Positivism* (London, 1865; various reprints). Consult: Isaiah Berlin, *Historical Inevitability* (London, 1954); D. G. Charlton, *Positivist Thought in France during the Second Empire, 1852–1870* (Oxford, 1959), and *Secular Religions in France, 1815–1870* (Oxford, 1963); Henri Gouhier, *La jeunesse d'Auguste Comte et la formation du positivisme,* 3 vols. (Paris, 1933–41), and *La vie d'Auguste Comte* (Paris, 1931); L. Lévy-Bruhl, *The Philosophy of Auguste Comte* (London, 1903); J. E. McGee, *A Crusade for Humanity* (London, 1931); F. E. Manuel, *The Prophets of Paris* (Cambridge, Mass., 1962); J. S. Mill, *Auguste Comte and Positivism* (London, 1866); W. M. Simon, *European Positivism in the Nineteenth Century* (Ithaca, 1963), and "The 'Two Cultures' in Nineteenth-Century France: Victor Cousin and Auguste Comte," *Journal of the History of Ideas,* **26** (1965), 45–58.

WALTER SIMON

[See also **Classification of the Sciences;** Enlightenment; Historicism; **Positivism in Latin America;** Progress.]

POSITIVISM IN LATIN AMERICA

POSITIVISM is the key to much of the social and political as well as intellectual history of Latin America in the second half of the nineteenth century. It flourished there as nowhere else, not even in France. The Roman Catholic form of society remained, but it was an empty vessel, waiting for something to fill it. Positivism satisfied the needs of Latin American intellectuals who had rejected Spanish and Portuguese culture and were trying to prove their independence by almost slavishly adopting French ideas. Catholicism, they maintained, was a tool of Spanish imperialism, and it had kept Latin America in a state of amoral, chaotic backwardness. The positivism of Auguste Comte promised progress, discipline, and morality, together with freedom from the tyranny of theology. Positivism influenced every country in Latin America, but none as much as Brazil; it was the positivism of Comte rather than that of Herbert Spencer.

In Brazil the positivist "Church and Apostolate" became a reality unique in the world. The founders were Miguel Lemos and Raimundo Teixeira Mendes, but the apostolic succession goes right back to Comte; a Brazilian professor of mathematics, Antônio Machado Dias, studied in Paris under Comte in 1837–38. Other Brazilians were students of Comte, but Machado Dias was a prophet in that he wanted a republic based on positivist ideals to replace the Empire of Pedro II— something which did not happen until 1889. Since Machado Dias lived thirty years in Paris—he took part in the revolution of 1848—he was clearly more deeply imbued with positivist ideas than Brazilians who stayed only briefly in the French capital. However, the first written manifestation of positivism in Brazil was a thesis presented at the University of Bahia in 1844, just two years after the publication of the sixth and last volume of the *Cours de philosophie positive.* The author, Justiniano de Silva Gomes, devoted his thesis to a plan for a course on physiology following the ideas of Comte, under whom he had studied in Paris.

One of the founders of the Brazilian positivist movement was a woman, Nísia Floresta, whom the famous scholar Manoel de Oliveira Lima considered to be "the most notable woman in Brazilian letters." Having won fame as the founder and director of a school in Rio de Janeiro, she and her daughter moved to Paris, where they became close friends of Auguste Comte, who in his "Twelfth Annual Confession" refers to "the noble Brazilian widow" as a "precious pupil." Seven letters, with their replies, remain as a testimony to their friendship. Comte hoped that the two Brazilian women would settle in Paris permanently and found a "positivist salon." In 1857 Nísia made a solemn visit to the tomb of Clotilde de Vaux and wrote a romantic eulogy of her which Comte kept as one of his most treasured documents. Later that same year Comte fell mortally ill. He rejected Nísia's suggestion that he should call specialists and died on September 5. Nísia was one of four women who accompanied his body to Père Lachaise cemetery.

Nísia Floresta published in 1864 a fascinating two-volume work entitled *Trois ans en Italie, suivis d'un voyage en Grèce*, in which she reveals the influence of Comte. In view of the fact that positivism was to provide the philosophical basis for dictatorships in Latin America, it is interesting to note that she repeated Comte's condemnation of Bonaparte at a time when Napoleon III was promoting his cult. In an earlier book, *Itinéraire d'un voyage en Allemagne* (1857), Nísia had denounced the failure of the sword to regenerate humanity; such a regeneration, she said, could be achieved only by the religion of humanity. She died in Rouen in 1885 at the age of 76. In 1953 the Brazilian government brought her remains back to Brazil. They were buried in the northeastern province of Recife, in her native village, which was officially renamed Nísia Floresta.

One of Comte's leading pupils, Louis Auguste Segond, gave up his academic career to become an operatic tenor, and in 1857 his company visited Brazil. Segond wrote letters giving a graphic account of Brazilian society. Although there was no clear color line in Brazil, the proportion of Negro blood was considerably higher than it is today. Positivism in Latin America was essentially a white man's doctrine, and in Brazil it was used as an intellectual weapon by those who overthrew Emperor Pedro II; it is interesting to note that Segond speaks with admiration and affection of the Emperor and laments the ill treatment to which the Negroes, for whom he felt a liking, were subjected.

Segond's report that there was already in 1857 a nucleus of positivists in the naval academy in Rio de Janeiro changes the usual version that Brazilian positivism grew in the military academy. In any case the "spontaneous growth" of the Brazilian positivist movement "some years ago" was praised by Pierre Laffitte, the French positivist, in his seventeenth circular (dated 1865). Laffitte saw in it the confirmation of Comte's belief that the countries of the south, which were still nominally Catholic, would be the most fruitful ground for the positivist movement.

Where exactly the first positivist group in Brazil was formed is not too important. In all the major scientific centers of Rio de Janeiro—the Colégio Pedro II, the military and naval academies, the school of medicine, and the polytechnical school—the positivist approach to science appeared frequently in the decade following

1850, but it was positivism in its stress on mathematics and the exact sciences, technology, and medicine, with no reference to the social and ethical aspects which were to become so important later.

In the same year as Comte's death, 1857, Benjamin Constant Botelho de Magalhães, who was later to be Brazil's greatest positivist leader, joined the movement. His father had named him after the French author who at the time enjoyed great prestige because of his determined republicanism; following the Brazilian custom, he is usually referred to by this given name, Benjamin Constant. He became a professor at the military academy, which, because of him, came to be regarded as the focus of Brazilian positivism. In 1868 he founded a society for the study of positivism. In 1871, when this same Benjamin Constant, who was also director of the Institute for Blind Children, presented a report in which he praised positivism, a conservative deputy demanded that he be dismissed for promoting an atheistic doctrine which had allegedly brought about the horrors of the Paris Commune the previous year. A government spokesman defended Benjamin Constant, saying that one should not confuse positivism and Marxism, "the new philosophy of German materialism." This is apparently the first reference to Marxism in Brazil.

We must mention another woman who had an important role in the origins of Brazilian positivism: Marie de Ribbentrop, the daughter of a Prussian baron who was a German positivist leader. Born in Metz, she traveled widely as a tutor and worked for a while in Venezuela, but she was never in Brazil. However, she was a tutor in a Brazilian family in Brussels, and it was there that she influenced several young Brazilians, especially Luis Pereira Barreto. He became an enthusiastic positivist propagandist, as his correspondence with Pierre Laffitte shows. He attributes his lack of success in winning proselytes to the difficulty of getting Brazilian youths to accept the strict positivist sexual morality. Yet he foresaw little real opposition, since the clergy were "ignorant, shameless, and barely tolerated by the population." Other Brazilians had been married in Paris according to the positivist rites. Pereira Barreto laments that on his father's estate in Brazil he must be married in a Catholic ceremony.

Pereira Barreto finished his medical studies in Rio de Janeiro. His thesis, written according to the positivist concept of science, was dedicated to the memory of Auguste Comte. However, the importance of Pereira Barreto was that he regarded politics as the most difficult of sciences—much more difficult than medicine or engineering—and one which must be developed in the framework of positivism. His two-volume work, *As tres filosofias* (1874, 1876), had a great influence on the students of the period. Pereira Barreto became a regular contributor to the republican newspaper *Província de São Paulo;* through hundreds of articles he was able to spread his positivist interpretation of Brazilian problems. He got into noisy arguments with intellectuals of other persuasions. This led Pereira Barreto to incorporate into his philosophy some of the latest scientific ideas and to abandon certain peculiarities of Comte's doctrine. Thus arose the distinction between "Comtism," which was "personal and ephemeral," and "positivism," which grew with the times. Some "pure" Comtists rejected this thesis, and the result was a series of weird debates on Dr. Edward Jenner and vaccination, which the "pure" Comtists rejected, whereas the progressive positivists merely rejected obligatory vaccination.

Yellow fever was a scourge of Brazil at this time. Pereira Barreto claimed that he had discovered before the Cuban Carlos Finlay that it was transmitted by the anopheles mosquito. Grapes do not grow in tropical Brazil, but, applying Comtian principles, Pereira Barreto succeeded in growing "excellent grapes" in São Paulo. He claimed that Brazilian viticulture was now superior to European, and a famous poet wrote verses praising Pereira Barreto for having given Brazil its wine independence. Something seems to have gone wrong somewhere, since wine is now produced almost exclusively in the temperate south of Brazil, but even in France Pereira Barreto won fame as a wine specialist. Applying positivist principles, he was developing a coffee plant which would grow in colder climates, but he abandoned this experiment when he realized that Europeans might be able to grow their own coffee.

Pereira Barreto's positivism, his dislike of Catholicism, and above all his attacks on the Jesuits involved him in a polemic with conservatives, Catholics, and Monarchists. Miguel Lemos, who claimed to be the head of the positivist apostolate in Brazil, joined the fray and accused him of being a heretical positivist. This dispute coincided with proposals to create a university in Rio de Janeiro. Pereira Barreto took the anti-university position which was common among positivists in Latin America. He argued that the university was a dead institution and that the positivist creed demanded the creation of a new and strictly scientific kind of institution. Brazil must put an end to "the reign of law school graduates." Medicine must be encouraged, but to demand that doctors be approved and registered by the state was an offense to freedom. Pereira Barreto became an exponent of the "positivist morality," to which science is subordinated. Like many Latin American positivists, he regarded the people as ignorant and undisciplined and was therefore contemptuous of universal suffrage.

Whereas most intellectual movements in Brazil were largely confined to Rio de Janeiro and São Paulo, positivist groups sprang up throughout Brazil. In São Luis do Maranhão a weekly, *Ordem e Progresso,* began to appear in 1860. It may have been influenced by the positivist magazine *El Eco Hispano-Americano* published in Paris by José Segundo Flores, a disciple of Comte. It was founded by Francisco Antônio Brandão Júnior, who had lived with Pereira Barreto in Brussels. In 1881 Pereira Barreto published in São Luis a Portuguese edition of the positivist calendar.

In Fortaleza, capital of Ceará, a positivist group formed around the writer Rocha Lima; it was known popularly as "the French Academy." Brazil's great lawyer, Clóvis Bevilaqua, was a member of the group, and he always acknowledged his indebtedness to positivism, although, like John Stuart Mill and Thomas Huxley, he rejected the Comtian belief in the need for positivist religious ceremonies, which were, despite Clóvis Bevilaqua, to flourish in Brazil as nowhere else in the world.

Slavery, which was not abolished in Brazil until 1888, was a burning issue, especially in the Northeast. Pereira Barreto was opposed to immediate and complete abolition. In line with Comte's thesis of social dynamics, he preferred a gradual approach. This was the attitude of most Brazilian positivists, but it was sufficient to anger the landowners. One positivist, Celso Magalhães, was a district attorney; his career was ruined because he prosecuted, unsuccessfully, the wife of a slaveowner who had stabbed a slave baby to death because it was white and because she suspected her husband was the father.

The Northeast around Bahia and Pernambuco is the most colorful part of Brazil. It has the highest percentage of Negroes, a traditional Catholicism, and a variety of cults. The anger of the positivists against universities and the Roman Catholic Church can be understood in the light of the experience of Domingos Guedes Cabral, whose positivist-inspired thesis on *The Functions of the Brain* (1876) could not be presented at the University of Bahia because of the opposition of the Church.

The duel between positivists and Catholics was equally marked in São Paulo, where a Thomist professor of law devoted most of his class time to attacking positivism. He deprived a positivist student of two years of academic credit for having spoken offensively of the Catholic religion. In reply, positivists spread their dogma through the newspapers *A República, O Federalista, A Evolução,* and *A Luta.* Many of the leaders of the Republic belonged to the group who

541

had fought for positivism in São Paulo around 1880. São Paulo remained an important positivist center until 1951, when the Positivist Society there was closed. There was a quaint episode in 1931 when an *interventor* (official appointed by the national government to run the state) issued a long order saying that positivism demanded that beggars be treated with respect and that no one should interfere with their freedom to beg. This episode inspired one of Brazil's best-known plays, *Deus lhe pague* ("God bless you") by Joracy Camargo.

The southernmost state, Rio Grande do Sul, became in a way the most important stronghold of positivism in Brazil. A knowledge of Spanish was more widespread there than in the rest of Brazil, and there were a number of subscribers to the Spanish-language positivist review *El Eco Hispano-Americano*. It was probably because of the proximity of Buenos Aires and Montevideo and because of the virtual absence of slavery that republicanism was much stronger in Rio Grande do Sul than in the rest of Brazil. The two tendencies met and gave rise to the simple equation: positivism equals republicanism. The leader of the positivist elite was Júlio de Castilhos, who preceded Miguel Lemos' apostolate, despite the latter's claim to primacy.

After the republic came in 1889, Júlio de Castilhos prepared the 1891 constitution for the state of Rio Grande do Sul; it survived until the revolution of 1930, when Getúlio Vargas, of positivist background, seized the national government and established his dictatorship, which, while it reflected fascist developments in Europe, was a culmination of the dictatorial trend within the political philosophy of Brazilian positivism. The main feature of the Rio Grande do Sul constitution, derived from positivist principles, was the division of powers and the attempt to achieve a balance between authority and freedom. In fact it was authoritarian, and positivist republicanism in the New World was usually somewhat dictatorial. At the same time it is claimed that the constitution of the state of Rio Grande do Sul was the first in the New World to embody articles defending the rights of workers. For decades Borges de Medeiros was the virtual dictator of the state. One positivist peculiarity of the constitution was that university degrees were not recognized, so that in the name of freedom anyone could practice medicine. This gave rise to a continuous battle between the medical profession of Brazil and Borges de Medeiros. The positivists, who promoted curious forms of social freedom, stressed the authority of the state. Borges claimed that he was following Comte in giving the state unusual power in the fields of finance and taxation. Comte was opposed to laissez-faire and believed in state intervention in economic affairs, and Borges followed this line. In his speeches Borges invoked the name of Comte and positivist morality, and his administration won widespread respect for its rectitude and justice.

Borges had scientific ideas about immigration and held that only assimilable elements should be allowed to enter Rio Grande do Sul. He opposed the immigration of Negroes and was especially hostile to the proposal to allow U.S. Negroes to migrate to Brazil. Positivism in Latin America mixed with Darwinism to produce a "scientific" racial concept of society.

While there were positivist groups in all the states of Brazil, the most important and the most influential one was that in the capital, Rio de Janeiro. The imperial court of Pedro II attracted the social and intellectual elite of the country, and Rio de Janeiro was the principal entry for European culture. The influence of France was preponderant in all matters except politics, a domain in which the Empire cultivated English ideals. However, French positivism was destined to undermine the Empire politically. About 1870 four positivist magazines, *A Idéia, O Debate, A Crença,* and *A Crónica do Império,* began to appear, followed in 1876 by *A Revista do Rio de Janeiro,* an important positivist organ. The positivists made no secret of the fact that the Empire was incompatible with positivist republicanism and told Pedro II so. He, with characteristic broadmindedness, made no attempt to repress the positivist movement. As elsewhere in Brazil, positivism had first developed around 1860 in medical research, especially in the field of cerebral physiology, but it soon affected every phase of thought, including political theory.

The leader of positivist republicanism in Rio de Janeiro was the aforementioned Benjamin Constant Botelho de Magalhães. Positivist republicanism was especially popular among students. Its most vehement enemies were the clergy, but they had been discredited by their long battle with the Freemasons. A major crisis arose in 1874 when the imperial government condemned to four years in jail the bishops of Olinda (Recife) and Belém do Pará because they had attempted without government authorization to put into effect a papal bull ordering Catholics to leave Masonry. Although we have little detailed information about Freemasonry because of its secrecy, there is no doubt that many Brazilian republicans were both positivists and Freemasons.

The Escola Politécnica was a focal point of positivism. At least ten professors, including Benjamin Constant, were positivist leaders. The students they imbued with positivist ideas became teachers in many of the leading schools of Brazil. Whereas earlier positivism had had its most marked impact on medicine, now the instrument of positivism was mathematics, the queen of the sciences.

The positivists were the brains of the republican movement which brought about the fall of the Empire in 1889, and Benjamin Constant was its leading intellectual figure. The peaceful transition from Empire to Republic was facilitated by a mutual respect unique in Latin American history. Despite Benjamin Constant's declared republicanism, the imperial court not only kept him as a royal preceptor, but also offered him a title, which he refused. To Benjamin Constant's dismay, for he openly preached the subordination of the military to civilian authority, the republic was dominated by the Army. The republic came into being because the Army refused to continue capturing fugitive slaves. Slavery thereby broke down, and in 1888, in the absence of Pedro II, the government abolished slavery. The Empire thus lost the support of the landed aristocracy, and it collapsed in 1889. The republican movement had won the decisive support of the Army when Benjamin Constant persuaded Marshal Deodoro da Fonseca to join its ranks. Deodoro da Fonseca accepted the Presidency of the Republic, although he had expected Benjamin Constant to take the post. Benjamin Constant, acclaimed as the founder of the Republic, was named Minister of War in the provisional government, but when the Republic created the Ministry of Education, Postal Service and Telegraphs as one bureau, he moved over to it. He died in 1891, so his role as an active republican leader was cut short.

The oratory and journalism of the first years of the Republic were marked by an abundant use of positivist slogans and catchwords. The division between the "apostolate" of Miguel Lemos and Teixeira Mendes and the orthodox positivism of Pierre Laffitte, which Benjamin Constant followed, continued to divide the republicans. The latter group was more democratic, but even it talked about the need for a "dictatorship," by which it meant a strong executive. There were many young officers in the constituent assembly, all declared positivists, and all in favor of an authoritarian regime. The result was that the assembly adopted a presidential form of government, whereas the Empire had been parliamentarian.

The Church was separated from the State, and religious freedom proclaimed. Traditional militarism was discouraged, and the Army became essentially an organ for civic betterment, thus anticipating the "civic action" roles of Latin American armies in the twentieth century. By a curious quirk of ideology, because of their belief in professional freedom, Brazilian positivists abandoned their teaching positions, thus weakening both Brazilian higher education and the positivist movement. This did not prevent Cândido Mariano Rondon, who had given up his chair in the military school, from carrying on a splendid job opening up the interior of Brazil. The Republic adopted as its flag a representation of the firmament showing the position of the stars, especially of the Southern Cross, at the moment the Republic was proclaimed. Over it appears the positivist motto "Order and Progress." For decades the positivist church in Rio de Janeiro was a gathering place for national leaders. It continued to function long after positivist churches had closed in France and elsewhere. In the latter part of the twentieth century, it leads a precarious existence, non-Catholic religious activity having been diverted to spiritualism and neo-African cults, both of which are booming.

Whereas positivism is the key to much of Brazilian history in the nineteenth century, in Argentina it was intellectually important but had only a vague impact on the course of Argentine history. Because of the ties between England and the River Plate countries, Spencer had more influence in Argentina and Uruguay than in the rest of Latin America, and political leaders like Domingo Faustino Sarmiento proclaimed their indebtedness to him, but the symbiosis between positivism and politics in no way resembles that of Brazil. Carlos Octavio Bunge is credited with having introduced the positivist science of sociology into Argentina, and much of his writing is an unflattering analysis of Argentine, indeed of all Hispanic-American society. Argentine positivists were not dogmatically hostile to the concept of a university, as were many positivists in Brazil and Mexico, and Joaquín V. González was the founder and president of the University of La Plata. José Ingenieros was a psychologist and criminologist. He founded the *Revista de Filosofía*, which served as a mouthpiece for his positivist ideas even after the idealist reaction had set in. Alejandro Korn represented the reaction against positivism, which he criticized for giving man a subordinate place in the universe.

The creation of the University of Chile in 1842 crystalized the intellectual life of the country, and the so-called "Generation of 1842" welcomed positivist ideas along with other manifestations of French culture. José Victorino Lastarria believed that positivism would provide the philosophical basis for the national progress of Chile, although he had a greater faith in political freedom than did many Latin American positivists. Lastarria was not bold enough to reject Christianity, but another positivist, Francisco Bilbao did just that; it got him into trouble at the time, but his radicalism has kept his name alive among twentieth-century liberals. Valentín Letelier, on the contrary, was a more typically Latin American positivist, believing that authoritarianism could be justified if it were a vehicle to bring about progress.

Comtian positivism was brought to Mexico by Gabino Barreda, who spent the years 1847 to 1851 studying medicine in Paris and there met Auguste Comte. Like other Latin Americans who had studied medicine in Paris, on his return he combined the practice of medicine with the propagation of positivist philosophy. In 1867 in Guanajuato, where he had settled, he made a speech which caught the attention of Benito Juárez who named Barreda chairman of a commission to reorganize Mexican education. The education reform law which he drafted was based on positivist ideas. Barreda was a liberal anticlerical, and his positivism was marked by hostility to the Roman Catholic Church as an institution which in the historical process had been superseded. Barreda viewed the defeat of the army of Napoleon III in Mexico as a triumph for liberal positivism, of which Mexico, he thought, was the bulwark. Education would prepare an elite which would bring order and progress to Mexico and put an end to the power of the clergy. However, Barreda changed the motto "love, order and progress" to "liberty, order and progress." A modus vivendi was reached with the Church, which agreed to stay out of politics if the formal cult of the "Religion of Humanity," which led to the founding of positivist churches in Brazil and Chile, were not introduced into Mexico.

It is ironical that positivism, which came to Mexico as a liberal doctrine sponsored by Benito Juárez, should have become an instrument of the dictatorship of Porfirio Díaz, President of Mexico from 1876 to 1911 (except for four years). It should be noted that even under Juárez the positivism of Barreda had defended the concept of private property and was essentially middle-class in its outlook. Indeed, Barreda was a bitter enemy of the wildly liberal ideas of the "Jacobins."

In 1877 Barreda and his disciples founded the Asociación Metodófila "Gabino Barreda." Most of the members of the group were students of medicine. These students were depressed by the condition of Mexico and felt an acute need for a social hierarchy which could impose order and further the progress of the country. After Barreda's death in 1881, this authoritarian tendency became more marked.

Positivism was to provide the dictatorship of Porfirio Díaz with a philosophical garb which gave it respectability. This is not what Mexican positivist writers had intended. Francisco Bulnes was concerned with the threat to Mexican independence presented by an efficient and domineering United States next door. The plight of Mexico and of the other Spanish American countries, according to Bulnes, was due to the Spanish heritage, the Catholic religion, and the aestheticism of writers. Bulnes wanted a Mexico which was positivist in its philosophy, scientific in its intellectual life, and progressive in politics. Bulnes was unusual in that he buttressed his diagnoses of Mexican problems with an array of statistics. He was one of the original *científicos*, i.e., positivist thinkers who believed that only science could bring progress to Mexico and who regarded the Indians as an illiterate mass impeding national progress. In 1892 the Partido de los Científicos was founded, with Justo Sierra as its leading figure. It provided Porfirio Díaz with a political ideology.

It is easy to see how the term *científico* came to be used to describe government leaders who used these ideas to justify the dictatorship of Porfirio Díaz and its harsh attempts to bring material progress to an apathetic nation. This was, however, sufficient to discredit positivism, and when Porfirio Díaz fell, positivism ceased to be virtually the official philosophy of the government and indeed of the nation. The positivists refuted the attacks of men like Antonio Caso, who accused them of guilt by association with the Díaz regime, but their protests were lost in the noise of the Revolution. The ideologues of the Revolution were "the generation of the Ateneo," i.e., the Ateneo de la Juventud, a group of youths separated by a generation gap from the positivists.

Enrique José Varona y Pera is usually regarded as the founder of the Cuban school of positivists. His early writings reveal the influence of Comte, but in his middle years Spencer became the dominant influence and later John Stuart Mill. The best-known figure in Cuban history, José Martí followed Victor Hugo's concept of inspired rather than scientific leadership of humanity. The references to positivist writers in his works are scant, but unwittingly he owed a great deal to the positivist ideas of a regenerated Latin America. The Cuban struggle for freedom, of which Martí was the apostle and which culminated in the war of 1898, caught the imagination of Americans North and South, somewhat as did later the struggle of Fidel Castro against Batista. The interpreter of the Cuban revolutionary movement to the rest of Latin America was the positivist Eugenio María de Hostos y Bonilla, a Puerto Rican who traveled widely throughout Spanish America but who strangely enough never visited Cuba. He became a sociology teacher, one of the first in Latin America, and showed he was ahead of his time by inventing the most unpalatable neologisms.

It is not possible in a brief survey to discuss the rise and fall of positivism in all the republics of Latin

America. The end of the great positivist phase came in the first decade of the twentieth century. The Uruguayan José Enrique Rodó denounced in his famous little book *Ariel* (1900) the whole concept of material progress as exemplified by the United States and proclaimed that man lives by the spirit. Francisco Madero, who led the Mexican Revolution of 1910, was a spiritualist, and the leading writer of the movement, José Vasconcelos, (1882–1959), was philosophically a disciple of Bergson and an idealist. Since the tendency in Latin America has been to follow the latest French intellectual fashion, when Comte's star waned in France it disappeared from the ideological sky of much of Latin America. Only in Brazil was there no sharp reaction against positivism. It was associated with the founding of the Republic and its motto was emblazoned on the Brazilian flag. Some of the grand old men of the Republic, like Marshal Cândido Rondon (1865–1957), were positivists. Unlike Spanish America, with its sharp dichotomies, Brazil is a country where religions and philosophies coexist. While the "Religion of Humanity" was too cerebral and disciplined to survive as a flourishing cult in the tropics, the Brazilian military dictatorship of the 1960's developed out of the "Sorbonne," the intellectuals of the war college in Rio de Janeiro whose historic roots are in positivism. Although they may not regard themselves as practicing positivists, the military leaders of Brazil justify their intervention into politics in terms of the positivist belief in the role of the army as an instrument of "Order and Progress."

BIBLIOGRAPHY

Arturo Ardao, *Espiritualismo y positivismo en el Uruguay* (Mexico City, 1950), Vol. 49 in series "Tierra Firme." Comité Positivista Argentino, *Iniciación positivista* (Buenos Aires, 1938). W. Rex Crawford, *A Century of Latin-American Thought* (Cambridge, Mass., 1961). João Cruz Costa, *Augusto Comte e as origens do positivismo* (São Paulo, 1959); idem, *A History of Ideas in Brazil* (Berkeley, 1964); idem, *O Positivismo na República* (São Paulo, 1956), Vol. 291 in series "Brasiliana." Harold Eugene Davis, *Latin American Social Thought*. The History of Its Development since Independence, with Selected Readings (Washington, D.C., 1963). Luis Beltrán Guerrero, *Introducción al positivismo venezolano* (Caracas, 1956). Ivan Lins, *História do positivismo no Brasil* (São Paulo, 1967), Vol. 322 in series "Brasiliana." Ricaurte Soler, *El Positivismo argentino* (Panama City, 1959). Raimundo Teixeira Mendes, *Benjamin Constant* (Rio de Janeiro, 1937). Leopoldo Zea, *El Positivismo en México* (Mexico City, 1953).

RONALD HILTON

[See also Church, Modernism in; **Positivism in Europe**.]

POSITIVISM IN THE TWENTIETH CENTURY (LOGICAL EMPIRICISM)

THE BASIC ideas of this movement in twentieth-century philosophy of science, had their historical roots in the philosophies of the Enlightenment and more generally in classical British empiricism (particularly in David Hume) as well as in nineteenth-century positivism (notably Auguste Comte, John Stuart Mill, and Richard Avenarius). Equally, if not even more important were the influences that came from outstanding scientist-philosophers of the same century, e.g., G. F. B. Riemann, H. von Helmholtz, Ernst Mach, Heinrich Hertz, Ludwig Boltzmann, Henri Poincaré, David Hilbert—and in the early twentieth century, especially Albert Einstein; the incisive impact of the great mathematical logicians, primarily Gottlob Frege, Bertrand Russell (also through his theory of knowledge), Alfred North Whitehead, together with all the aforementioned influences resulted in the 1920's in the formation of the Vienna Circle of Logical Positivists and The Berlin Society of Scientific Empiricists. The Vienna group was formed in 1924 under the leadership of Moritz Schlick. Its most active members were Hans Hahn (a mathematician, and an admirer of Russell's), Kurt Reidemeister (also a mathematician who called the circle's attention to Ludwig Wittgenstein's *Tractatus Logico-Philosophicus*), Otto Neurath (sociologist-economist and an energetic organizer and propagandist of the Circle), Friedrich Waismann; and, after 1926, especially Rudolf Carnap with his important work in modern logic, the foundations of mathematics, concept-formation in physics, and a logical systematization of the concepts of empirical knowledge in general (cf. his *The Logical Structure of the World*, original German edition, 1928). Schlick had paved the way for much that became the standpoint of logical positivism in his *Allgemeine Erkenntnislehre* ("General Theory of Knowledge"), first edition as early as 1918; second edition 1925. Wittgenstein, though admired by most members of the Vienna Circle, and despite frequent conversations with some circle members (especially Schlick, Waismann, Carnap, Feigl) never joined or even attended the meetings of the Circle. Among the younger members were the mathematicians Kurt Gödel and Karl Menger, and later Gustav Bergmann. Also, despite basic similarities along the lines of philosophical endeavor, there were Edgar Zilsel and Karl R. Popper who, probably because of some divergencies they considered very essential, did not become members—but were close friends with some of them. Victor Kraft was a member from the beginning, but some of his most important published work appeared long after the final disintegration of the Circle. On the whole the group consisted mainly of scientifically or mathematically oriented philosophers, or of philosophically gifted scientists or mathematicians.

The Berlin group was led by Hans Reichenbach whose early training and experience had been, like Carnap's, in modern physics and mathematics. Richard von Mises (a great mathematician, aerodynamicist, and positivist philosopher—very much like his friend Philipp Frank, the Prague theoretical physicist who like von Mises was Viennese by origin and an outstanding disciple of Ernst Mach's) along with Kurt Grelling, Walter Dubislav, and the younger student-members C. G. Hempel and Olaf Helmer were among the principal exponents of the Berlin group.

In highly compressed and somewhat oversimplified form the main ideas (common to the Vienna and the Berlin groups) comprised:

(1) A view—considered then new and revolutionary by its proponents—of the "true" nature and "genuine" task of the philosophical enterprise. In contradistinction to the still largely prevailing speculative (e.g., Hegelian) tendencies in (transcendent) metaphysics, the Viennese and Berliners were convinced that most (if not all) allegedly unsolvable problems of philosophy (the unanswerable "riddles of the universe" regarding which even some nineteenth-century scientists like E. DuBois-Reymond declared a stern *ignoramus et ignorabimus*) rest on conceptual confusions or on closely related misuses of language. It was especially under Wittgenstein's influence that the primary (if not the sole) task of a sound philosophy was considered as a kind of "therapy" of thought. Inspired by this veritable *bouleversement*, H. Feigl impudently defined philosophy as "the disease of which it should be the cure." (This may have been an unwitting plagiarism or paraphrase of the witticism of Vienna's great political satirist, Karl Kraus, who had said that "psychoanalysis is the disease whose therapy it pretends to be"). Reflection upon the very logic of explanation (be it commonsensical or scientific) showed clearly that, for example, the still fashionable existentialist questions: "Why is there anything at all?" or "Why is what there is the way it is?" are unanswerable not because they are too difficult, or surpass the limits of human intelligence altogether, but because all (legitimate) explanation (in contradistinction to tranquilization by means of verbal sedatives) inevitably proceeds from premises which are themselves unexplained, at least in the given context of inquiry. Moreover, explanations of facts (or events) or of the regularities (of facts or events) require premises in the form of (deterministic, or else probabilistic) laws—and these laws depend in their validity

on confirming evidence. And since confirming (or disconfirming) evidence is apt to change—often in rather surprising ways—knowledge-claims (most especially in "higher level" scientific hypotheses or theories) can be held only tentatively ("until further notice"), i.e., they must be kept open for revision. The only "safe" procedure is therefore that of the critical approach or the open mind. Genuine and legitimate explanation of facts, events (and their regularities) is thus *relative* in two ways: (a) only in the light of tentatively assumed premises can we say the facts are "necessarily so" (i.e., are deductively derivable from those premises); (b) the premises themselves stand or fall in the light of observational evidence.

Pseudoproblems in the history of thought (even of scientific thought) have often arisen out of (unwittingly) making some assertions "proof against disproof," i.e., by making completely and essentially untestable assumptions. Many a scientific hypothesis originated as a testable, that is, confirmable or disconfirmable knowledge-claim; but when difficulties arose, often by a shift in meaning, those hypotheses were rendered, in principle, impervious to any conceivable test. Well-known important examples are the doctrines of absolute space and time (Plato, Newton); of substance (Locke); of "necessity" in causality (already incisively and classically criticized by Hume); of the vital force ("entelechies," etc.) assumed by many vitalists as an explanation of the admittedly most puzzling features of organic life; the ether hypothesis in its last desperate stand (Lorentz, Fitzgerald); and so forth. Great scientific innovators (like Lavoisier in the case of the phlogiston theory in chemistry; or Einstein in the case of the ether, and of space and time generally) recognized the spurious nature of such explanations and replaced them by scientifically legitimate ones. According to the Vienna and Berlin positivists and empiricists, the reform of philosophy was to be patterned after the paradigm of those great purifications and clarifications in the sciences.

(2) Perhaps the most distinctive feature of the new empiricism was the pivotal role of its analysis of language and meaning. None of the Europeans were aware (in the middle 1920's) of the important work of Charles S. Peirce, the great American philosopher and logician who had anticipated (in 1878) in an informal way the basic idea of the notorious "verifiability criterion" of meaning. Nor was there—at the time—much awareness of the pragmatism of William James (who was strongly influenced by Peirce's ideas). The Viennese, at least in the manner in which they construed the often obscurely aphoristic *Tractatus Logico-Philosophicus* of Ludwig Wittgenstein, were emphatic in declaring *testability-in-principle* a necessary condi-

tion for the factual meaningfulness of sentences. The sentences in a language (be it the language of common usage, of science, or of metaphysics) were said to make factual sense only if it was logically conceivable that they might be confirmed or disconfirmed (i.e., at least partially and/or indirectly verified or refuted) by empirical evidence. From this point of view (more fully developed in the thirties by the American philosopher Charles Morris, but already contained in the slightly earlier theory of language developed by the great Vienna psychologist Karl Bühler) fundamental distinctions among the various functions of language (or communication quite generally) and the corresponding types of significance were made. Preoccupied with science, the focus of interest was centered upon the informative or representative function of language (and the *cognitive* meanings). This was distinguished from the expression and appeal functions, i.e., mainly the pictorial, the emotional, and the motivative uses of communication. It was granted (even emphasized) that in most cases these various functions of language are fused or combined; and the distinctions made were the result of a logico-philosophical *analysis*. Thus while granting the fusion, the logical positivists warned against *confusion* of one type of significance with another. The sort of metaphysics that was repudiated was said to arise out of mistaking noncognitive (pictorial, emotional, motivative) significance for genuinely cognitive (representative) meaning. Among the genuinely cognitive meanings a further very important distinction was drawn between the purely formal (i.e., logico-mathematical) and the factual (empirical) types of meaning. Full awareness of this distinction led, among other things, to a repudiation of the "conventionalist" doctrine (suggested by H. Poincaré and carried to an untenable exaggeration by Hugo Dingler) according to which the principles of physical geometry and the basic "laws of nature" generally, were considered as "definitions in disguise." The logical empiricist doctrine (later attacked as one of its "dogmas" by the prominent American logician Willard Van Orman Quine) insisted on the indispensable distinction (already contained in Hume's *Treatise*, and explicitly—but rather narrowly drawn in Kant's *Critique of Pure Reason*) between analytic and synthetic propositions. Analytic propositions are true by virtue of presupposed meanings (which can be articulated by explicit definitions or meaning rules), whereas synthetic propositions are nonanalytic, and thus require grounds of validity outside of mere meaning assignments or definitions. The logical positivists—being staunch empiricists—recognized only the data of experience as the grounds of validity for synthetic knowledge-claims. "Pure reason" was considered competent only in the realm of

analytic truth. "Pure intuition" (in Kant's or any other sense) was at best admitted as a *source* of ideas ("hunches") but never as a basis of validity.

In the further development (during the 1930's) of the analyses of language, and mainly in the work of Carnap, it became clear that the language which is the object of discussion (the "object language") must be distinguished from an (especially constructed) *metalanguage* which talks *about* the object-language. Moreover, purely *syntactical* studies regarding the formation and transformation rules (i.e., the purely "structural" aspects of language) soon required (as Alfred Tarski's important work indicated) supplementation by *semantical* analyses (concerned with rules of designation and of truth). The purely syntactical approach was prevalent in the formalist philosophy of mathematics of Hilbert, Bernays, and their disciples. The semantical approach was actually implicit in the work of Frege, Russell, Whitehead, and was made fully explicit by Tarski and Carnap.

The theories of the empirical sciences especially those of physics, were viewed as consisting of erstwhile uninterpreted postulates, containing basic (undefined, or rather only "implicitly" defined) "primitive" concepts; explicit definitions which introduce more complex concepts; and correspondence rules (or, as Reichenbach called them, "coordinative definitions") which provided at least a partial *empirical* interpretation of the "primitive" concepts. The correspondence rules connect the abstract concepts of the postulates with the empirical (experimental, mensurational) concepts of the observation language. Thus the factual-empirical significance "seeps upward" to the originally quite abstract ("formal") concepts of the postulate system.

(3) A characteristic feature, especially of Viennese positivism in epistemology and philosophy of science, was two doctrines or "theses" of reductionism. The first concerned the reducibility of the concepts of the factual sciences to the concepts of a common observation basis. This view may be considered as a *logical* version of the older empiricist (e.g., Humean) doctrine of the relation of ideas to impressions. Influenced by the rather sketchy attempts in this direction by Mach, Avenarius, and the early Russell, Carnap in his early *Der Logische Aufbau der Welt* (now also available in English translation, *The Logical Structure of the World*) presented a systematic rational reconstruction of the major domains of empirical knowledge in terms of concepts introduced by stepwise definitions with a "ground level" of concepts pertaining to the data of direct experience. This was essentially a reconstruction along the lines of an epistemological phenomenalism. A few years later Carnap came to prefer a different

basis for reconstruction (already briefly discussed as one of several possible alternatives in the *Aufbau*): the language that would provide for the "unity of science" in this sense was to be the ("physicalistic") intersubjective observation language. Once this starting point of reconstruction was chosen, the unwelcome associations of the earlier reconstruction with subjective idealism or "methodological solipsism" were obviated. In less technical terms it may be said that this first thesis of physicalism—or of the unity of the language of science simply amounted to asserting common, communicable perceptual experience to be the ultimate testing ground for all sorts of factual knowledge claims. With the help of symbolic logic (essentially Whitehead-Russell's) Carnap elaborated an impressive system of definitions—including some completely worked out examples—that was to show that the concepts of empirical knowledge (especially those of the natural and social sciences, including psychology) were thus reducible to a minimum (in Carnap's system actually a single) basic concept of immediate experience. While the *Aufbau* was regarded by many of its critics a—however brilliant—tour de force, it was patterned after the exemplary sort of reduction presented by Whitehead and Russell in their famous *Principia Mathematica* (3 vols., 1910–13; 1925). There the bold claim was made that all of mathematics (really only set theory, arithmetic, number theory, analysis) could be built up from (or reduced to) a few principles and concepts of modern logic. (Frege had done most of the important spade work in that direction.) If Carnap's analogical attempt for the empirical sciences succeeded, it would represent a formal justification of the phenomenalist epistemology according to which all factual knowledge-claims are re-translatable into statements about actual or possible immediate experience. Carnap, and along with him most of the Viennese positivists (Schlick, then under Carnap's and Wittgenstein's influence, Hahn, Frank, et al.) regarded the issue of realism vs. phenomenalism as a pseudoproblem. Reichenbach, however, insisted on an inductive critical realism according to which the inference to an external world (as well as other persons' mental states) was justifiable on grounds of analogy and probability. This controversy (by staunch positivists regarded as a dispute about the "emperor's clothes") still continues, e.g., in the issue regarding realistic vs. instrumentalistic interpretations of scientific theories. According to the realist viewpoint, "existential hypotheses" (i.e., assumptions concerning the reality of unobserved and even unobservable entities such as atoms, electrons, and the host of other subatomic particles; the unconscious wishes, motives, etc. as formulated in psychoanalytic theories) were to be taken as referring to actually existing

"things" or occurring processes. In sharp opposition, the instrumentalists viewed the concepts of such unobservable entities either as in principle dispensable logical constructions or, in accordance with earlier positivist tendencies, as (at best!) useful auxiliary fictions.

Retrospectively, the first thesis of the unity of science (as championed by Carnap, Neurath, and Hahn, ca. 1928–35) seems relatively obvious (insofar as it is correct), and hardly worth the excitement and opposition it aroused at the time. That thesis asserted neither a unity of method nor a unity of explanatory premises for all of science. As already indicated, it merely insisted on a common empirical basis or testing ground.

(4) The *second* thesis of physicalism or of the unity of science was proposed by Carnap more in the sense of a promising research program than as a truth about science and its relation to the world, let alone as an accomplished achievement along the lines of a unification of the sciences. It did assert the logical possibility and the empirical plausibility of a unitary set of explanatory assumptions from which the empirical laws and (with the help of descriptions of "initial and boundary conditions") even all the individual facts and events of the world could (in principle) be derived. This was, of course, a vast and precarious extrapolation from whatever successes had been scored in the reduction (now in the sense of explanation) of empirical laws to unifying theories; and of theories of lower level to higher level theories. Outstanding examples were the nineteenth-century reduction of optics to electromagnetics; of part of thermodynamics to the kinetic theory of heat (developed in molecular and statistical mechanics); and the strong indications of the reducibility of the laws of chemistry (and the nature of the chemical bond) to atomic theory, implemented especially by the new quantum and wave mechanics (beginning in 1926).

The meaning of this (second) thesis of the unity of science is best understood by considering what it tries to exclude or oppose, viz., the doctrines of Emergent Evolution, and to some extent also the related views of holism. These philosophies of science (or of nature) insist on some absolute irreducibilities, especially that of biology and psychology (and *a fortiori* of the social sciences) to basic physics. Representatives of these ideologies oppose the "reductionism" of physicalism (or of the second unity of science thesis). They maintain that in the course of evolution entirely new levels of reality emerged, whose regularities are autonomous, i.e., insusceptible to explanation on the basis of the theories and laws that seem to suffice for the phenomena of the inorganic world. It is important to note that emergentism need not be combined let alone buttressed with vitalism. The assumption of an extra-physical *vis vitalis* (vital force, entelechy, *élan vital*, etc.), as formulated in most forms (old or new) of vitalism, is usually without any genuine explanatory power. It has served altogether too often as an intellectual tranquilizer or verbal sedative—stifling scientific inquiry rather than encouraging it to proceed in new directions.

Emergentist doctrines, though by no means easy to formulate clearly and positively, need not be transempirical. Just as electromagnetics turned out to be irreducible to classical Newtonian mechanics, so biology, despite the remarkable advances of biophysics and biochemistry (and more recently especially of molecular biology), may ultimately be "emergent" in relation to basic physics. In any case the recognition of the all-important role of organization, structure, configuration stressed at first by the Gestalt psychologists (especially M. Wertheimer and W. Köhler) is entirely compatible with a nonmechanistic physicalism. To be sure, some of the positivists (notably G. Bergmann) opposed any and all holistic tendencies, staunchly maintaining that organic wholes could be analyzed as composed of parts, and their different features could be explained by adducing composition laws (such as those expressible in vector algebra, e.g., in the simplest case: the parallelogram of forces). But while this is entirely appropriate within the theoretical schemes of classical physics (from Newton to Einstein), it fits into neither the conceptual framework of electrodynamic field theory nor (especially) that of quantum physics (with its principle of complementarity and Pauli's exclusion principle—a sort of "Gestalt" law on the atomic level).

Hence, even despite the astonishing and dramatic developments in molecular biology (the double helix model of the gene; the DNA and RNA stories, etc.) the thesis of a unitary explanation for all phenomena of nature is still at best a "promissory note," i.e., a bold conjecture regarding the future development of the sciences. The logical empiricists have always considered that thesis as a general research program that helps in encouraging reduction without being reductionistic in a dogmatic sense.

The difficulties multiply rapidly in regard to psychology and the social sciences. The positivists, along with Bertrand Russell (and some pragmatists like Edgar A. Singer), for a while joined the bandwagon of American behaviorists (J. B. Watson, A. P. Weiss, C. L. Hull, B. F. Skinner, et al.). Actually, Carnap, as early as 1932, formulated in fairly detailed outline a kind of logical behaviorism which only later (and quite independently) was quite elaborately expounded and defended in Gilbert Ryle's *Concept of Mind* (1949), and in a manner designed primarily for psychologists by B. F. Skinner in *Science and Human Behavior* (1953). The basic intention in Skinner's approach was to show that psychology could be presented as a branch of natural science. Ryle's work (no doubt influenced by Wittgenstein—at least as Ryle understood the later work of Wittgenstein) was designed to show that the very "grammar" of our common language requires an intersubjective approach even in regard to such notoriously "private" mental acts as thought, imagery, emotion, etc. Carnap's ideas on the scientific status of psychological knowledge-claims are to be taken as an outcome primarily of the first thesis of the unity of science. Since the testing-basis of psychology if it is to be scientific must be in the data of everyday or experimental observations of behavior (including verbal behavior), the concepts and propositions of the science of mind must be "reducible" (in the sense of the first thesis) to the concepts regarding the overt behavior of organisms (man included, of course). In the spirit of the second thesis Carnap argued that conceivably (in the more or less distant future) the facts and regularities of mind might well become explainable, and thus "reduced" in the other sense, to neurophysiology, and, if the second thesis should prove correct, eventually to basic physics.

Philosophical opposition naturally arose on this last claim. This despite the fact that Carnap always stressed the conjectural character of the second ("unitary") thesis. The traditional mind-body problems thus came to the fore again, having been almost completely suppressed during the reign of (first) phenomenalistic and (later) behavioristic-physicalistic trends of thought. Wittgenstein's arguments against the possibility of a private language together with the prevailing American climate of psychological and philosophical views of "mind" seemed, for quite a few years, to exclude any revival of the well-known controversies of dualism (interactionistic, emergentistic, or parallelistic) with monism (materialistic, mentalistic, neutral, or various forms of double aspect, double-language, twofold knowledge identity theories). Carnap himself reluctantly approved of some formulation of an identity theory. But his preference remained for a view according to which the mentalistic language of immediate experience would be supplanted by a physicalistic language. As a first step here (in approximate agreement with G. Ryle) he tried to show how the many dispositional concepts (designating abilities, capacities, or propensities) could be construed by some sort of conditional definitions (reduction sentences), i.e., by test-situation causally implying test result conditionals. But in an important later essay (1956), Carnap preferred to recognize most scientific concepts as *theoretical* concepts, whose meaning is to be explicated by postulates and correspondence rules. Others (like H.

549

Feigl) attempted to formulate an identity theory patterned after the reductive identifications that are so abundantly present in the natural sciences. Just as we can in physics "identify" the intensity of heat of a substance with the average kinetic energy of the molecular motions, so the mental acts and processes may well be ultimately identified with some neurophysiological processes occurring in the nervous systems (or more specifically in the cerebral cortex) of the mammalian organisms. This "solution"—also formulated in the recent work of J. J. C. Smart and other Australian philosophers of science—is currently very much in the focus of philosophical discussion and dispute.

Some of the more conspicuous difficulties of the new "monism" have to do with the apparently irreducible feature of *intentionality* that seems to characterize *all* or most mental phenomena. The acts of thought, volition, perception, and such emotions as love, hatred, hope, fear, etc., are all directed upon some object or other be it an actually existing or a merely imagined or fancied object. It seems well nigh impossible to find in the neurophysiological (and *a fortiori* physical) processes a structurally similar (isomorphic) counterpart that would suggest an ultimate identity. The only helpful way out was proposed by Wilfrid Sellars who views the intentionality feature as basically linguistic. If this is correct, the act-object relation, though phenomenologically undeniable, is to be analyzed as a case of the semantic relation of designation. If this is correct, then we are here not dealing with the relation of the mental to the physical, but rather with the relation of the logical (semantical) to either the psychological processes, or the physical processes in the brain (or in the electronic computer). Since the logical positivists always agreed with the rejection of psychologism (i.e., the fallacious identification of logical with psychological categories) already forcefully presented by Frege and Husserl, they did not feel that the discussion of intentionality belonged in the domain of the mind-body problem. But in recent discussions, just this is being disputed again.

(5) The most important positive achievements of the logical empiricists are contained in their work in philosophy of the sciences. These cannot be briefly summarized. Hence a few hints and the (appended) notes and references must suffice. Carnap's work in syntax and semantics has already been mentioned. Equally important are his studies and those of Hans Reichenbach, Ernest Nagel, C. G. Hempel, and a host of younger scholars (notably, Adolf Grünbaum, Wesley Salmon, Mario Bunge, Wolfgang Stegmüller, and others) in the logic and methodology of the empirical sciences. Problems of induction and probability, of space and time, of the interpretations of modern physics (especially of the theory of relativity and of quantum mechanics), in the philosophy of biology, (J. H. Woodger, and more recently Morton Beckner and Kenneth Schaffner), and in the logic of modern psychology (C. C. Pratt, S. S. Stevens, H. Feigl, P. E. Meehl, and others)—all these and many other contributions have been growing enormously and have, on the whole, been received with the greatest interest—especially by many scientists in various fields, and by scientifically informed and interested philosophers. Several collaborative groups for research in the philosophy of science have been formed, beginning with the Minnesota ·Center (1953); and later the Departments for Philosophy and History of Science at Indiana and Pittsburgh Universities; the Boston Colloquium; (for a few years also the Delaware Seminar). In most other universities there are outstanding younger scholars pursuing research and engaged in teaching philosophy of science, all of them at least influenced by, or reacting critically to the ideas of the logical empiricists.

The change of designation from "logical positivism" to "logical empiricism" (around 1935) was due to the increasing influence of Reichenbach's and Popper's scientific realism and thus the final abandonment of the (Hume-Mach) phenomenalism or sensationalism. Even the empiricism of the group has been under attack—first by Karl Popper's incisive critique of "inductivism," later by the repudiation of the analytic-synthetic distinction by W. V. O. Quine and Hilary Putnam; and finally the critique of the empiricist views of scientific theories and of scientific explanation by Paul K. Feyerabend and Thomas S. Kuhn. The original line of logical empiricists (with some exceptions) had not sufficiently focussed their attention on the history of science; this made some of their pronouncements open to severe criticisms. The current controversies regarding the level structure of scientific explanation, and the meaning invariance (or variance) of basic scientific concepts reflect some of those recent doubts regarding the adequacy of the logical empiricist approach.

A different school of thought, largely of British origin (represented by S. Toulmin, W. H. Watson, N. R. Hanson, and others), originated under the influence of Ludwig Wittgenstein's later work. Analyses of meaning of this kind are oriented along the lines of making explicit the rules according to which the words or symbols of language (whether of common speech or of the scientific terminologies) are used. This is somewhat akin to the much earlier operationalistic approach that was first explicitly formulated by the Harvard physicist, P. W. Bridgman. In fact at the time Bridgman independently conceived his ideas, the similarities with the contemporaneous Viennese positivism were quite striking. In the author's opinion, both operationalism and logical positivism, along with the earlier pragmatism, were a salutary antidote or preventive in regard to metaphysical speculation, but their lesson has been absorbed and a considerable liberalization has succeeded, especially in the philosophy of science.

BIBLIOGRAPHY

Most of the original "classics" of logical positivism, logical empiricism (and of the related analytic and linguistic philosophy)—both books and articles—are listed in the ample bibliography of A. J. Ayer, ed., *Logical Positivism* (New York, 1959). Among many other important essays, R. Carnap's "Psychology in Physical Language" is contained in this anthology.

Books, mainly in the area of the foundations of the sciences (but also in philosophy of language, epistemology), many by the leading logical empiricists, are listed in the ample, and fairly up-to-date *Bibliography and Index* by Herbert Feigl and Charles Morris, eds., *International Encyclopedia of Unified Science*, Vol. II, No. 10. Of major relevance are the works of R. Carnap, O. Neurath, M. Schlick, P. Frank, H. Reichenbach, E. Nagel, C. G. Hempel, R. von Mises, Charles Morris; and for criticisms, those of Karl R. Popper; and the intellectual autobiography, the twenty-six descriptive and critical essays, and Carnap's replies, in P. A. Schilpp, ed., *The Philosophy of Rudolf Carnap* (LaSalle, Ill., 1963).

For quite recent reactions, see P. Achinstein and S. F. Barker, eds., *The Legacy of Logical Positivism: Studies in the Philosophy of Science* (Baltimore, 1969).

For a brief account of the European movement of logical positivism and its migration and impact in the Unites States, see H. Feigl "The Wiener Kreis in America" in D. Fleming and B. Baylin, eds., *The Intellectual Migration: Europe and America 1930–1960* (Cambridge, Mass., 1969). The early history of Viennese positivism is well told in Victor Kraft's *The Vienna Circle*, trans. A. Pap (New York, 1953); second edition (somewhat expanded and revised) of *The Wiener Kreis* (Vienna and New York, 1968). Another important source is the monograph by J. Joergensen, *The Development of Logical Empiricism*, Vol. II, No. 9 of the *International Encyclopedia of Unified Science* (Chicago, 1951).

HERBERT FEIGL

[See also Newton on Method; **Positivism in Europe;** Pragmatism; **Psychological Schools;** Relativity; **Unity of Science to Kant.**]

PRAGMATISM

I. DIFFICULTIES IN
DEFINING PRAGMATISM

WHEN Arthur O. Lovejoy (in 1908) discriminated thirteen meanings of pragmatism and showed that some of them were in contradiction with one another, he raised the problem of whether there was any coherent core of ideas that could define the doctrine or movement that was so widely discussed by American and European thinkers in various disciplines. Certainly Charles S. Peirce and William James (who credited Peirce in 1897 with inventing the doctrine) had divergent ideas in their "pragmatic" theories of truth. There were also divergences among those writers in the United States and abroad who defended their own particular versions of pragmatism, e.g., John Dewey, George H. Mead, F. C. S. Schiller, G. Vailati, G. Papini, Mario Calderoni, Hans Vaihinger, and others on the fringes of philosophy. The latter group, ranging from scientists like Henri Poincaré and Percy Bridgman to legal, political, and even literary minds such as O. W. Holmes, Jr., Georges Sorel, and Luigi Pirandello respectively, make it especially difficult to include their varieties of pragmatism within the same set of ideas that are common to Peirce, James, and Dewey. At one extremity one can find self-styled pragmatists with a Jamesian tendency to regard their personal experience as a sufficient source and test of truth; the extreme group in the undefined fringe can only charitably be included in Peirce's ideal community of minds whose opinions in the long run are destined to converge on the one unalterable Platonic truth.

From the standpoint of the history of ideas a well tried and useful method of arriving at a common core of component ideas of any group's doctrines is to consider historically the ideas which that group of thinkers was opposing or trying to combat intellectually with regard to some problem viewed in its cultural and historical context. It will become evident that we can discern historically a substantial though complex core of such component ideas that came to the fore in the nineteenth and twentieth centuries in opposition to certain long established traditional modes of belief. Common to this substantial core of pragmatism is an opposition to the absolute separation of thought from action, of pure from applied science, of intuition or revelation from experience or experimental verification, of private interests from public concern—concrete applications of older philosophical problems concerning the relation of universals to particulars. It will also be evident that each alleged historical example of pragmatism shows a wide variety of individual ways of resolving these problems, especially when we include the outer fringe of those calling their very personal effusions "pragmatic."

It is not the intellectual historian's task to decide which of the many variants of pragmatism is the "correct" one. Usage in all its culturally varied ramifications is the primary concern here, and the historical effects of such usages on subsequent intellectual developments in various fields are difficult enough to trace. The usage or core of ideas central to pragmatism that has been most influential historically in many fields is found in contributions to methodology and the theory of value judgments. Against supernaturalism, authoritarianism, and eternally fixed norms of belief and values stand the more flexible method and dynamic values of naturalistic empiricism, temporalism, and pluralistic individualism as the chief component ideas at the center of what is most coherent and enduring in the many varieties of pragmatism. However, we cannot overlook the historical deviations from this central core, especially as they provide evidence of the pluralism, individualism, and relativism defended by our "core" pragmatists. Since some of these ideas are also found in other philosophical schools, we must acknowledge the difficulty of defining the borders of pragmatism.

Hence it is not surprising that there is no one general definition of pragmatism that covers all the historical doctrines that have been given that name. In the comprehensive account of the subject by H. S. Thayer an attempt at a general definition makes pragmatism stand for (1) a procedural rule for explicating meanings of certain philosophical and scientific concepts; (2) "a theory of knowledge, experience, and reality maintaining that (a) thought and knowledge are biologically and socially evolved modes by means of adaptation" and control; (b) reality is transitional and thought is a guide to satisfying interests or realizing purposes; (c) "all knowledge is a behavioral process evaluative of future experience" and thinking is experimentally aimed at organizing, planning, or controlling future experience; and (3) "a broad philosophic attitude toward our conceptualization of experience" (H. S. Thayer [1968], p. 431). However, Thayer's summary outline of a definition of "the aim and formative doctrines of pragmatism," despite its comprehensiveness does not dwell sufficiently on the very varied character and conflicting theories of method, knowledge, and reality maintained by pragmatists of different schools in diverse fields of thought and of diverse cultural and historical backgrounds.

The opening paragraph of G. Papini's work on *Pragmatismo (1905–1911)*, a collection of his articles introducing that doctrine to Italian philosophers, reads: "Pragmatism cannot be defined. Whoever gives a definition of Pragmatism in a few words would be doing the most antipragmatic thing imaginable" (*Il Pragmatismo non si può definire. Chi desse in poche parole una definizione del Pragmatismo farebbe la cosa più antipragmatista chi si possa immaginare*, p. 75). Papini was (in 1906) echoing William James's romantic aversion to fixed definitions, and even mistakenly placed Peirce in the same boat with James, thus overlooking the important difference between James's

nominalism (emphasis on particular perceived consequences of ideas) and Peirce's Scotistic realism (positing the reality of universals in logic and value judgments: truth and justice being two of the most powerful ideas in the world, according to Peirce).

The historical and cultural facets of various pragmatisms do not all fit under any general definition for two reasons. First, the philosophical writings of a leading pragmatist like C. S. Peirce are concerned with and defend theories of truth and reality that are not merely procedural, behavioristic, transitional, or conceptual. Peirce's metaphysical writings contain a speculative, idealistic version of pragmatism which he called "pragmaticism" in order to disassociate his philosophy from the pragmatisms of William James and James's disciple F. C. S. Schiller. Secondly, whole areas of knowledge, other than those mentioned in the general definition above, have been discussed by diverse pragmatists in their interpretations of the nature of history, of law and politics, of language, and of mathematical logic. It is true that some pragmatists have pursued some parts of these subjects, but some have not; some have professed a profound concern for religion and others have not. Hence, instead of trying to find a general definition to cover the conflicting beliefs and widely divergent interests of all pragmatistic philosophies, the historian of ideas will find it more instructive to trace various components of the various doctrines historically held by pragmatists.

Arthur O. Lovejoy was a student of William James at Harvard, and outlined more than sixty years ago the most discriminating criticism of pragmatism in two short articles, "The Thirteen Pragmatisms" (1908, pp. 1–12, 29–39). Lovejoy's analysis of pragmatism into its component ideas yields four groups of internal conflicts and ambiguities: (1) those claims to truth which rest, on the one hand, on the psychological properties of belief as a disposition to act from those, on the other hand, which are based on the changing characters of the *objects* of belief; (2) the identification of knowledge with a form of action based on some form of immediate perception (e.g., James's "radical empiricism") versus knowledge as the result of the mediation of ideas which interpret experience; (3) ethical and aesthetic judgments validated, on the one hand, by subjective emotional criteria, e.g., in the "will to believe" doctrine of William James and the personalism of F. C. S. Schiller; and on the other hand, by objective, verifiable social consequences along utilitarian lines, e.g., in John Dewey's "instrumentalism" and George Herbert Mead's social criteria of meaning; (4) Bergson's and James's appeal to immediate experience versus Peirce's "long run" theory of truth as the opinion that an indefinite community of scientific investigators will ultimately agree upon after continued experimental inquiry.

Lovejoy thus insisted that there are incompatible theories of knowledge, of truth, and of values present in these diverse ideas maintained by different pragmatists. F. C. S. Schiller's dramatic response to Lovejoy's discriminations was to welcome the fact that there are as many pragmatisms as there are pragmatists, but Schiller's response does not eliminate the internal discrepancies among the ideas of pragmatists. Schiller's "humanistic personalism" is diametrically opposed to Peirce's claims for logic, and reduces the definition of pragmatism to the problem of ascertaining whether there are any common ideas shared by all pragmatists in the light of the incompatible components of their philosophies.

One historical investigation of the American founders and evolutionary background of pragmatism (Wiener [1949], Ch. 9), by minimizing the differences and stressing optimistically "the common features," attempted to establish the following general components: (1) a *pluralistic empiricism* or method of investigating piecemeal the physical, biological, psychological, linguistic, and social problems which are not resolvable by a single metaphysical formula or *a priori* system; e.g., Chauncey Wright, William James, John Dewey, C. I. Lewis, John H. Randall, Jr., Sidney Hook, Ernest Nagel, Y. Bar-Hillel, Charles W. Morris; (2) a *temporalistic* view of reality and knowledge as the upshot of an evolving stream of consciousness (W. James) or of *objects* of consciousness (C. S. Peirce), including ideas and claims to truth, processes of observation, measurement, and experimental testing; (3) a *relativistic* or contextualistic conception of reality and values in which traditional eternal ideas of space, time, causation, axiomatic truth, intrinsic and eternal values are all viewed as relative to varying psychological, social, historical, or logical contexts (Chauncey Wright, William James, George Herbert Mead, John Dewey, Stephen C. Pepper, F. P. Ramsey, and C. I. Lewis); (4) a *probabilistic* view of physical and social hypotheses and laws in opposition to both mechanistic or dialectical determinism and historical necessity or inevitability, yielding a fallibilistic theory of knowledge and values opposed to dogmatic certainty and infallibility (W. James, C. S. Peirce, O. W. Holmes, Jr., J. Dewey, Ernest Nagel, Sidney Hook, H. Reichenbach); (5) a secular *democratic* individualism asserting the right of individuals to live in a free society without the sanctions of supernatural theological revelation or totalitarian authority. This pragmatic individualism of the American pragmatists is linked to a political tradition that goes back to John Locke and the European Enlightenment, and is represented historically in the United States by thinkers from all walks of life: John Woolman, Benjamin Franklin, Thomas Paine, Thomas Jefferson, Ralph Waldo Emerson, Henry David Thoreau, Abraham Lincoln, and Walt Whitman.

It is typical of pragmatic ideas that they are not restricted to the ideas of professional philosophers, but often find influential expression among lawyers and judges like Nicholas St. John Green (the "grandfather of pragmatism," according to C. S. Peirce), Oliver Wendell Holmes, Jr., Jerome Frank, Carl Llewellyn; among logicians and scientists like Chauncey Wright, C. S. Peirce, G. Vailati, Pierre Duhem, Henri Poincaré, Edward Le Roy, C. I. Lewis, W. V. O. Quine, Percy Bridgman; among historians like Carl Becker and Charles Beard; among literary figures such as Irwin Edman and Luigi Pirandello; and even the syndicalist Georges Sorel.

We cannot simply equate the "pragmatic" with the "practical" as is so commonly done by popular writers. For technically in philosophy, "practical" may refer to Kant's idea of the categorical imperative in his *Critique of Practical Reason*, which placed the *pragmatische* on a much lower level than the *praktische*. Furthermore, "practical" in ordinary discourse is often synonymous with the "convenient," the "useful," and the "profitable" and thus contributes to enormous misunderstandings of the serious aims of pragmatism. Among the empirical varieties of pragmatism "practical" refers to what is experimental or capable of being tested in action, not quite the same as Marx's use of "praxis" or alleged "identity of theory and practice." The American pragmatists preferred the experimental meaning without the dialectics. At Harvard, in the first decades of the twentieth century, George Santayana criticized William James and John Dewey for failing to subordinate "practical thought" to eternal Platonic values.

Santayana's chapter on "How Thought is Practical" in the first volume of his *Life of Reason* (5 vols., 1905–06) is far from making him a pragmatist. Writing at Harvard as a younger colleague of William James, Santayana did not consider his own peculiar blend of Platonism and naturalism in accord with the pragmatic movement at Harvard; he regarded James as a romantic subjectivist. Santayana, in this first major work, *The Life of Reason*, maintained against the instrumentalist theory of consciousness that "In so far as thought is instrumental it is not worth having, any more than matter, except for its promise; it must terminate in something truly profitable and ultimate which being good in itself, may lend value to all that led up to it. . . . In a word the value of thought is ideal" (I, 218–19). From Santayana's aristocratic standpoint, "thought is in no way instrumental or servile; it is an experience realized, not a force to be used" (ibid., 214). It is no wonder then that neither James nor Dewey could accept Santayana's Platonic naturalism. Santayana was certainly not as democratic as James or Dewey in political theory, but followed the classical tradition of Plato and Aristotle in associating democracy with demagoguery and in favoring a form of intellectual timocracy. Thus the component features of pragmatism discussed above appear in the American variety, deeply hued by its British ancestry, and also in some of the continental European forms of pragmatism to be discussed below. However, each of the component aspects of even the American and British forms of pragmatism has had its antecedents in the more distant cultural and intellectual history of Europe, and may be traced back to some of the ideas of ancient classical and the Enlightenment's versions of both "practical" and speculative thought, yielding among its important fruits a pragmatic transformation of the basis of law in civilization and an empirical theory of value judgments in general. The next section explores some of the "old ways of thinking" for which "pragmatism is only a new name," as James put it.

II. HISTORICAL ROOTS

The very term "pragmatic" with its Greek root *pragma* ("affair, practical matter") was borrowed by the Romans to mean "skilled in business, and especially, experienced in matters of law"; hence, a *pragmaticus* was "one skilled in the law, who furnished orators and advocates with the principles on which they based their speeches" (Cicero, *Orationes* 1, 59; cf. also Quintilian 12, 3, 4; Juvenal 7, 123; Ulpian, *Digest* 48, 17, 9). In late Latin juridical writings a pragmatic sanction (*pragmatica sanctio*) was an imperial decree that permitted an activity in the community's affairs (*Justinian Code* 1, 2, 10).

When James and Peirce generously refer to Socrates as a forerunner of pragmatism, they perhaps had in mind Plato's dramatized Socratic activity of inquiring into the meanings of ideas about friendship, courage, justice, piety, and so forth in dialogues with the young citizens of the Athenian community. However, the logic of Plato was more of a semantic exercise than "pragmatic" in either James's psychological sense or Peirce's experimental methodology. Without going into the philological question raised by W. Lutoslawski's thesis that Aristotle's logic was a continuation of Plato's, it is safe to say that the problems of the syntax and semantics of language were more systematically treated in Aristotle's logical treatises. Plato's inquiry in the *Parmenides* whether "Being is One or Many" and whether "Non-Being is or is not" proceeds semantically to avoid verbal contradictions, but to

imagine that such exercises of language suffice to understand the problems of existence, such as the struggle for existence, would be unfair to Plato's purpose. The semantic analysis is only part of Plato's thinking, but it predominates over any pragmatic intent. For example, viewing the State as "the individual writ large" (*Republic*, Book II) leads metaphorically to an ideal utopia. When Plato seems to be practical in the *Laws*, the pragmatic aspects of his political proposals (e.g., censorship and religious intolerance with possible death penalty) are shocking to modern liberals; the result is that scholars differ in deploring or explaining away the totalitarian aspects of the *Laws*.

Aristotle's use of the "practical syllogism" in ethics and his notion of each subject having its own method belong to the ancient sources of the functional and pluralistic methodology of those pragmatists who link their ideas to an Aristotelianism stripped of medieval supernaturalism (e.g., G. H. Mead; J. H. Randall, Jr.). Aristotle's "practical syllogism" consists in stating in the major premiss the object desired or goal to be achieved, and in the minor premiss the means which experience has shown necessary to attain the desired end, so that one can conclude that a good result may be attained by acting with the means indicated. For example, one who wishes to be a good musician must learn how to play a certain instrument; a practical syllogism would demonstrate that practice in mastering that instrument is necessary in order to achieve the desired goal. The *pluralism* of methods, categories, and goals of human endeavor also characterizes certain "pragmatic" aspects of Aristotle's applied logic. For example, Aristotle states it would be practically foolish for a mathematician to prove theorems in his science by the same methods of argumentation that an orator uses in a political speech, and conversely.

According to G. H. Mead and John Dewey, what is *not* pragmatic in Plato and Aristotle is their belief that nature, especially human nature, was essentially fixed in its eternal features. A Sophist like Protagoras and Sextus Empiricus was closer to the relativistic and empirical view of modern pragmatists, a view that can be found even in "God-intoxicated" Spinoza, namely, that the good is not what eternally determines our nature or desires; it is the variety of natures and desires that determines what is good. "Music is good for the melancholy, bad for the mourner, and neither good nor bad to the deaf" (*Ethics*, Part IV, preface). Again we cannot simply bring under the rubric "pragmatism" the philosophies of Aristotle, Spinoza, or Santayana or of any other thinker who espouses this relativistic view of values, when in fact there are so many nonempirical aspects present in their philosophies, such as Aristotle's "unmoved mover," Spinoza's "intellectual love of God," or Santayana's eternal "realms of being."

Medieval and modern forms of casuistry are considered by some writers as "pragmatic" insofar as general rules are adapted to practical situations; but we should not therefore regard the Tartuffes as pragmatists. Critics of pragmatism often wish to condemn the doctrine as sheer opportunism, or as "guilt by association" with such self-styled "pragmatic" theories as Georges Sorel's doctrine of violence.

In his "Lessons from the History of Science," Peirce viewed science as an outgrowth of the thinking of ancient and medieval philosophers; Peirce was more appreciative of medieval logic in the history of the sciences than nearly all his contemporaries. (Pierre Duhem, of course, is an outstanding exception among partly pragmatic philosophical historians of medieval science.) Peirce adopted Duns Scotus' theory of true universals as inherent in particulars, and called it "Scotistic realism." Peirce had translated Petrus Peregrinus' difficult manuscript on the magnetic properties of the lodestone. In these medieval thinkers Peirce saw some continuity with the modern scientific method of treating hypotheses (based on analogical comparisons of present with past observations), drawing inferences (preferably mathematically) from these conjectured hypotheses, and testing the deduced consequences by experiment. However, he rejected the scholastics' recourse to the authority of the Church Fathers and to their version of Aristotle, and favored the "self-corrective method" of experimental inductive science. His logic of relations went far beyond the classical logic, Peirce developing logic as a continuation and generalization of the subject-predicate logic of statements, after De Morgan and Boole.

Among the Renaissance precursors of the pragmatic union of experimental action and theoretical contemplation we may surely place the experimentalism in art and science represented by the works of such masters as Leonardo da Vinci and Galileo. Rudolfo Mondolfo, in his essay on the idea of manual and intellectual work, following a Hippocratic text which declared that man knows best what he makes (an idea developed in the *Scienza nuova* [1725] by G. B. Vico), has suggested a plausible Renaissance source of this interrelationship in Galileo's development of an intuition expressed in Ficino's *Theologia platonica*: "What is human art? A kind of nature that treats matter from the outside." This external treatment of nature takes the place of the scholastic idea of nature as "being within matter itself; but human art can produce any reality produced by nature, so long as man can struggle successfully with matter and with the necessary instruments. . . . Leonardo had already expressed his view

of mechanics as the noblest and most useful of the sciences as well as the paradise of mathematical sciences because it yields the harvested fruit of these sciences in practical application" (R. Mondolfo [1950], p. 22, notes 9 and 10).

Of course, the Renaissance sources pertinent to the roots of pragmatism go back to the revival of classical ideas of natural processes and ways of living with them such as were explored by the pre-Socratics, Plato, Aristotle, Archimedes, the Epicureans, and the Stoics, and include those medieval thinkers who (like Roger Bacon and the Padovan Averroists) saw the advantages of combining experimental activity with theoretical speculation. Philosophy in the seventeenth and eighteenth centuries developed rival schools, later labelled "empiricism" and "rationalism" depending on the emphasis given to sense-experience or "pure" reasoning, but that these two aspects of knowledge are inseparable in scientific knowledge was the great achievement of Immanuel Kant before the pragmatists developed their philosophical versions of the interplay of thought and experience in all scientific and value judgments.

A sharp separation of theory and practice, however, is reflected in Kant's distinction between ethical and "pragmatic" rules. Kant's ethical rule is a "categorical imperative" based on the individual's inner "pure practical" reason, free will, and universal consciousness of one's a priori duty to respect all persons as ends in themselves; Kant's pragmatic (*pragmatische*) rule is practical in the very different sense of having to do only with rules of prudence which belong to the technical imperatives or means required to achieve desired ends: "For what is prudence but the skill to use free men and even natural dispositions and inclinations for one's own purposes?" (Kant, *Critique of Judgment*, Introduction). This Kantian distinction so sharply separates subjective from objective considerations, ends from means, and pure reason from social experience that post-Kantian thinkers, including the romantic Schelling, as well as Schopenhauer and Hegel and some of the American pragmatists (especially C. S. Peirce and John Dewey) were led to seeking a closer and more organic relationship between morality and mankind's other intellectual and cultural concerns.

Knowing that Chauncey Wright and C. S. Peirce daily discussed Kant's philosophy for two years at Harvard in the third quarter of the nineteenth century, the historian of pragmatism is not surprised to find that Kant's limitation of our knowledge of nature to what is observable became a cardinal empiricistic principle of some of the Harvard pragmatists, along with controversies about the role of a priori categories in interpreting the sensory manifold. There was also critical discussion of Kant's absolute separation of means and ends in ethics. Peirce, for example, could accept the *a priori* elements in Kant's theory of knowledge but not his categorical imperative in ethics; for Peirce, as for James and Dewey, all value judgments are hypothetical, of the form: if men desire to attain certain ends in any harmonious way, they will probably achieve these ends by acting in accord with certain specifiable empirical conditions. Only by conducting themselves according to such hypothetical rules, will men discover after "trial and error" (often painful) experience, whether they really find the attained ends desirable.

Hegel made an impressive attempt to establish the unity of means and ends, of the subjective and objective aspects of experience and thought, of the individual and the state, and of universal reason and particular events in his monistic metaphysics and philosophy of history. In this respect Hegelianism is part of the intellectual background of early forms of pragmatism and of Marxism.

"Pragmatic history," is a subspecies of "reflective history" in Hegel's classification of three kinds of history: (1) "original history" written by those historians observing events in their own lifetime; (2) "reflective history," not limited to the time of the historian "whose spirit transcends the present"; and (3) "philosophical history," which allegedly shows that "Reason is the Sovereign of the World." *Pragmatic history* consists of didactic reflections on the past for the purpose of drawing lessons from it that can be applied to moral and political problems of the present. Examples of pragmatic history appear in patriotic histories and the biographies of heroes and spiritual leaders that are supposed to teach rulers, statesmen, and moralists how to be guided by the experience of the past. However, Hegel clearly shows his contempt for this pragmatic kind of history when he states emphatically:

But what experience and history teach is this—that peoples and governments never have learned anything from history, or acted on principles deduced from it (*Philosophy of History*, Introduction, trans. W. Sibree).

This sentence is often quoted by antihistorical writers; they fail, however, to note that Hegel obviously draws this meta-historical statement from his rather extensive study of history. They fail also to note that Hegel concludes his remarks on pragmatic history by observing that the more objective reflective historian will insist on the distinctiveness of his own age as well as of the age whose history he depicts. Pragmatic historians still insist that our knowledge of the past is or should be determined by the interest and problems of the present, thus ignoring Hegel.

Peirce, in his later years, and Dewey, in his early

career, show the influence of the Hegelian ideas of organic unity and historical continuity in the cultural life of mankind. However, their pragmatic attitudes toward experience and history diverge radically from Hegel's absolutism and dialectical method: Peirce was sharply critical of Hegel's logic and deficiency in mathematics, although he shared with Josiah Royce sympathy for Hegel's spiritual monism:

My whole method [of using triadic categories] will be found to be in profound contrast with that of Hegel; I reject his philosophy *in toto*, nevertheless, I have a certain sympathy with it, and fancy that if its author had only noticed a very few circumstances he would himself have been led to revolutionize his system. . . . He has usually overlooked external Secondness, altogether. In other words, he has committed the trifling oversight of forgetting that this is a real world with real actions and reactions. Rather a serious oversight that. Then Hegel had the misfortune to be unusually deficient in mathematics (*Collected Papers*, 1.368, "A Guess at the Riddle," ca. 1890).

While Peirce criticized Hegel's logic and neglect of physics and mathematics, Dewey abandoned Hegel's *a priori* dialectical method because it was not experimental and had too fixed a conception of human nature, society, and history. In the United States from the 1860's to the 1880's we can trace the growth of the impact of Hegelianism. John Dewey's *Psychology* (1885) reflected the impact of the St. Louis School of W. T. Harris and Denton J. Snyder. Hegelian ideas mark the first writings of the positivist J. B. Stallo, and the Spencerian Hegelian, Francis Ellingwood Abbot. Also, among the origins of the American pragmatists was an antimetaphysical "back to Kant" movement in a reaction to Hegel, stimulated by the rapid growth of the physical sciences and Darwin's evolutionary theory (Wiener [1949], pp. 2f.).

Kant's separation of phenomena from the metaphysical unknowable "thing-in-itself" (*Ding an sich*) led to the positivistic element in empiricistic pragmatism. It appears in Chauncey Wright's antimetaphysical attack on both the Hegelian absolutists and the Spencerian "social Darwinists" (as they were later called; Wright, after reading Haeckel, labelled their ideas "German Darwinism"). There is also a positivistic strain in the early work of William James, as he admits in the Preface to his first book, *Principles of Psychology* (1890).

III. PRAGMATISM AS OPERATIONAL LOGIC

Early twentieth-century developments in logic and philosophy of science led away from Comte's positivism and Mill's psychologism to the Viennese school of logical positivists with whom many pragmatists share an operational and antimetaphysical viewpoint. Later, on removal to England and the United States, as well as in Poland and other countries in Europe, logical positivists preferred the name "logical empiricists." Rudolf Carnap offered a definition of "pragmatics" following "syntactics" and "semantics" in order to show the relationship of formal logic to empirical and psychological aspects of meaning, as well as to distinguish all three. "Syntactics" is the formal study of the logical rules of formation and transformation of statements. In any formal language, e.g., of logic or mathematics, the "rules of formation" determine what statements are "well formed" combinations of the elements of the language used. The syntactical "rules of transformation" determine the equivalences, inferences, and forms of proof which are logically acceptable within a system whose elements and elementary or basic statements conform to the principles of formation. "Semantics" (in logic) is concerned with the relationship of well formed statements or of ordinary language to what they designate. The interpretation or application of a set of axioms in pure mathematics, for example, would be a semantic question. Finally we come to "pragmatics" which deals with the behavioral or experimental conditions for verifying the inferences or testing the truth claims of hypotheses, laws, and theories. "Pragmatics" will ask for specification of the *operations* that need to be performed and the empirical conditions that should be met by all experimenters if their findings are to be acceptable to others. This "operational" requirement is what is meant by the criterion of "intersubjectivity" or public verifiability.

Pragmatism then, in this twentieth-century version, is another name for the operational theory of scientific method, and is closely linked to logical empiricism. This operational variety of pragmatism is the historical outcome of the many attempts of philosophers, mathematicians, and experimental scientists to avoid sterile speculation, subjective intuitions, and unverifiable hypotheses (of the sort Newton rejected when he said *hypotheses non fingo*, although he accepted absolute space and time as the ultimate framework of the physical universe). Bar-Hillel has criticized the separation of syntax and semantics from the pragmatic elements of language; he and Roman Jakobson refer to Peirce's theory of signs (*Linguaggi nella società e nella tecnica*, Milan [1970], pp. 3–16, 269–84), and find useful Peirce's classification of signs as icons, indices, and symbols.

Among the mathematical philosophers, especially in France, Italy, England, and Germany for the last hundred years, the study of formal axiomatic systems and their relation to experience led to a rejection of Descartes' view of intuitively self-evident truth based on his criterion of clear and distinct ideas. This crite-

rion of intuitive self-evidence had been employed to justify the indubitable metaphysical truth of Euclid's axioms epitomized in Galileo's view that the book of nature was written in the language of Euclid's geometry. The advent of non-Euclidean geometries in the first part of the nineteenth century put an end to the exclusive ontological claims of Euclid's axioms, and reopened fundamental questions in the philosophy of science about the grounds for determining the meaning and truth of axiomatic sets. The proofs of the consistency and isomorphism of non-Euclidean and Euclidean systems made it clear that self-evidence was not an adequate test of meaning or truth, since the non-Euclidean axioms were not obvious or self-evident, e.g., that through a point outside a line no lines or (in an alternative system) an infinite number of lines can be drawn parallel to a given line. The meaning of such abstract axioms can only be ascertained by working out the deducible theorems or logical consequences of the axioms, and their interpretation or application. This orientation of the mind to developing the consequences of logically primitive statements instead of attempting to grasp their meaning in an immediate mental act of intuition provides the basis for the views of those German, French, and Italian mathematical philosophers (e.g., Leibniz, Dedekind, Frege, Hilbert, Cantor; Poincaré, Herbrand, Couturat; Peano, Vacca, Vailati) who explored the logical foundations of axiomatic systems of the theory of numbers. By establishing alternative sets of axioms and tests of internal consistency, mutual independence, and completeness of axiom-sets, these scientists showed little or no concern for any "indubitable" self-evidence of their axioms. Felix Klein and Henri Poincaré also made it clear that in pure mathematics no axioms are privileged; the upshot of these developments is to support a sort of democratic equality among axioms with respect to claims of truth (Vailati, *Scritti*). Thus, in pure mathematics, historically the "queen of the sciences," meaning was reducible to the "pencil and paper operations," as Percy Bridgman called them in his operational theory of meaning, for the purely-mathematical and logical aspects of scientific research. The experimental aspects that yield more concrete empirically applicable meanings for hypotheses about "matters of fact" depend on specifying what must be done experimentally to test the logical consequences of the hypotheses in question.

C. S. Peirce was the best equipped of the American founders of pragmatism to develop the operational logic of mathematical and physical science, and to extend it to the analysis of philosophical concepts and problems of meaning. As a first-rate mathematician, astronomer, physicist, and chemist, he kept in touch with the new views of Dedekind, Cantor, Mach, Ostwald, and others who were digging deep into the foundations of mathematics and physical science. Peirce translated the chapter on weights and measures of Mach's important history of the science of mechanics (1883; trans. 1893), and even claimed prior discovery of the principle of the "economy of thought" before Mach.

IV. CHARLES S. PEIRCE'S "PRAGMATICISM"

Alexander Bain, whom Peirce regarded as the Scottish ancestor of pragmatism, had in his psychological writings defined an idea or belief as a disposition to act in a certain way under certain conditions. Applying this definition to the problem of meaning, Peirce formulated his famous prescription for fixing the meaning of a concept: "Consider what effects that might conceivably have practical bearings you conceive the object of your conception to have. Then your conception of those effects is the WHOLE of your conception of the object." This rule for attaining a higher grade of clarity than Cartesian intuition or Leibnizian calculus of reasoning is the *locus classicus* of Peirce's form of pragmatism. He stated it first in the early 1870's before the informal "Metaphysical Club" in Cambridge, Massachusetts, where a group consisting of the mathematical empiricist Chauncey Wright, the psychologist William James, three lawyers (Oliver Wendell Holmes, Jr., Nicholas St. John Green, Joseph B. Warner), the historian John Fiske, and the "scientific theist" Francis E. Abbott met from time to time to discuss the philosophical questions of the day. Among those questions the Darwinian controversy loomed large and led to disputes about science and religion, positivism and metaphysics, scientific method and the introspective investigation of the mind, ethics and legal institutions, the roles of the individual and the environment in history. The writings of Hume, Bentham, Bain, Mill, Kant, Comte, Hegel, Spencer, and Darwin furnished these Harvard Square thinkers with the fuel for illuminating problems and issues in their various fields of interest. After much crossfire and heated discussion, they found themselves more concerned with problems of method than with agreeing on a single system. The experimental method for matters of fact and logical analysis for relations of ideas were accepted as the best instruments of investigation for the natural and social sciences.

Peirce began philosophizing by discussing problems of method. His two now classic papers "The Fixation of Belief" and "How to Make Our Ideas Clear," (*Popular Science Monthly*, 1877–78) were the first two of a series of "Illustrations of the Logic of Science." He

claimed, about twenty years later, that these two articles were the first formulations of his variety of pragmatism (although that term does not appear in either paper). Peirce challenged traditional "seminary" types of bookish learning and contrasted them with the "laboratory" type of thinking which he advocated (in 1905) as "pragmaticism," his own brand of pragmatism. Peirce said (about thirty years after his Metaphysical Club papers) of his variety of pragmatism:

It will serve to show that almost every proposition of ontological metaphysics is either meaningless gibberish—one word being defined by other words, and they by still others, without any real conception ever being reached—or else is downright absurd; so that all such rubbish being swept away, what will remain of philosophy will be a series of problems capable of investigation by the observational methods of the true sciences—the truth about which can be reached without those interminable misunderstandings and disputes which have made the highest of the positive sciences a mere amusement for idle intellects, a sort of chess—idle pleasure its purpose, and reading out of a book its method ("What Pragmatism Is," *Monist* 15 [1905], 171).

Peirce went on to deny that he was "merely jeering at metaphysics, like other prope-positivists" because "the pragmaticist extracts from it [metaphysics] a precious essence, which will serve to give life and light to cosmology and physics. At the same time, the moral applications of the doctrine are positive and potent and there are many other uses of it not easily classed" (ibid.).

Peirce's "Classification of the Sciences" was composed for his Lowell Institute Lectures in 1903. The adult education movement in the United States had taken to talks on the growth of sciences with their Baconian "promise of providing the relief of man's estate" as seriously as the older generation had taken their Bible lessons. These lectures reveal the progressive or futuristic outlook of Peirce's philosophy of science. There were for Peirce three classes of science in a descending order of importance: (a) Sciences of Discovery, (b) Sciences of Review, (c) Practical Sciences. It is well known that classifications of sciences vary with each new period in the history of science, but such classifications are a clue to the cultural role and value of various sciences and the philosophy of each period. To Peirce, the "Sciences of Discovery" were first and foremost because Peirce conceived of science primarily as a method of inquiry, as the most promising way of exploring the nature of Kant's "starry heavens above and the moral world within." The method of science was not a Baconian new instrument, because science for Peirce had always been an organon of the mind, although Peirce would agree with Bacon's idea that we moderns are the true ancients since we in our evolution have accumulated the knowledge and fruits of the experience of our predecessors.

In his experimentalism, Peirce placed great importance on the neglected role of Hypothesis as a mode of reasoning. He called the discovery of hypotheses "Abduction" to supplement what logic books previously had been mainly concerned with, viz., "Deduction" and "Induction." The reason for this novel importance which Peirce attached to the role of hypothesis is based on the logical ground that all generalizations from particular facts of observation have to be continuous extensions of what is typical or representative in these facts as gathered from previous experience. For example, although the life span of man has increased, the historical fact of man's mortality is the basis of the major premiss of the argument that proves that even Socrates was a mortal. No historical record of all human lives is complete, so that our general judgment that all men are mortal is a well grounded hypothesis on the rather large sample of what our limited historical records and observation have shown. To the extent that the randomly sampled cases are alike, some ground for their similarity may be "abducted" as a probable hypothesis. "Abduction" and "retroduction" were Peirce's synonyms for the form of reasoning leading to conjectural hypotheses. All historical statements about individual events are hypotheses drawn ("abducted" or "retroducted," in Peirce's terminology) from documents, monuments, remains which serve as our only links to the past if interpreted carefully. Every medical diagnosis consists of a hypothesis about the observed "symptoms" of a disease. Deciphering a secret code or strange language starts with hypotheses interpreting certain recurrent signs with the aid of frequency tables. Predictions or prognoses are hypotheses which when verified become scientific generalizations.

Peirce defined laws of nature as predictive generalizations with varying degrees of probability according to experimental tests. Peirce's contribution to the logic of hypothesis was regarded by him as the keystone of his variety of pragmatism; his "pragmaticism," armored with symbolic logic, attacked the more psychological and nominalistic views of William James and F. C. S. Schiller. Facts or the truth about reported events are always subject to and inseparable from the interpretations or hypotheses assumed by the interpreter in his reports, which are signs. To Peirce, James's "radical empiricism" as a form of direct immersion in facts lacked logical awareness of the role of hypotheses or interpretation of signs in such allegedly immediate forms of perception. The theory of signs is central to Peirce's pragmaticist logic. Peirce's pragmaticism is a theory of meaning based on the logical analysis of the conceivable consequences of adopting an hypothesis in so far as its signs and their implications affect the conduct of the inquirer in relation to what is designated by the signs. For example, if a student is puzzled over the meaning of an abstract set of axioms, and asks a mathematician to explain or justify his adoption of such a queer set of "postulates," the pragmatist's answer generally will take several forms. From the standpoint of technique, the axioms enable one to prove with the aid of acceptable rules of inference a body of theorems or consequences deducible from the axioms, thus reducing a large number of theorems to what is contained in a small number of axioms. This reduction is a practical aid to the memory. Another explanation or justification would consist in seeking out and showing by concrete interpretations (in which the axioms are all true) that the axioms are consistent; hence, the whole system of axioms and theorems must be consistent (this assumes a metalogical rule that only consistent results can be deduced from consistent axioms). Again, we may be told pragmatically that this axiomatic set permits certain "interpretations" or applications to empirical domains. Euclid's geometry is still useful to surveyors and engineers, whereas non-Euclidean geometry is applicable in modern applications of relativity theory to atomic physics and cosmology. Proof of the consistency of non-Euclidean geometry establishes the consistency of Euclid. Peirce's formulation of his pragmaticism repeatedly applied to formal sciences the above mentioned test of meaning: *Consider what conceivable consequences the object of your conception has in its bearing on human conduct. Then the sum total of all these conceivable consequences constitute the total meaning of your conception.*

The notion of *conceivability* rather than of actual perception plays a central role in Peirce's analysis of meaning in which he tried to generalize criteria of meaning to cover both formal systems and empirical statements (in physical sciences and everyday expressions). For example, "diamonds are hard" is explicated by considering what conceivable experimental consequences the hypothesis of the constant hardness of diamonds has on the bearing of that hypothesis in human conduct. To an experimenter the conduct involved would consist chiefly in testing the hypothesis by trying to penetrate or scratch a diamond with other materials or with another diamond. There is a Moh's scale of hardness, based on the results of such laboratory testing of different substances, from which it becomes predictable which substance can penetrate or scratch others. The need to specify the *operations* required to test such properties led scientific thinkers from Charles Babbage (1792–1871) to Percy Bridgman to defend a generalized operational methodology. It is therefore historically justifiable to claim that the hard core of the American, British, French, German, and Italian varieties of pragmatism was largely a generalization of the reflections of mathematical logicians and philosophical experimenters in the nineteenth and twentieth centuries.

G. Vailati in 1906 was the first European to recognize Peirce's importance as greater than James's in the formulation of pragmatism. In his article in the journal *Leonardo* (1906): "Pragmatismo e Logica Matematica," Vailati saw three intimate relations between pragmatism and symbolic or mathematical logic; symptomatic of this close connection, he said, "is the fact that the very inaugurator of the term and conception of pragmatism, Charles S. Peirce, is also at the same time the initiator and promoter of an original direction of logico-mathematical studies" (Vailati [1957], p. 197). He indicated three points of contact between modern operational logic and pragmatism: (1) "Their common tendency is to regard the validity and even meaning of any assertion as something intimately related to the use that one could or wished to make of it through the deduction or construction of definite consequences or sets of consequences" (p. 198); postulates and axioms would then no longer be privileged in any autocratic or aristocratic fashion but be "simple employees in great 'associations' that constitute the various branches of mathematics" (p. 199). (2) "The common concern of Pragmatism and modern logic is to avoid vague and imprecise generalities by reducing or analyzing every assertion into its simplest terms: those referring directly to facts or to relations among facts." The laws of science can thus be seen as expressions of hypothetical relations, contingent on such facts as "boundary conditions." The classical opposition of "facts" and "laws" begins to disappear. (3) "A third point of contact between pragmatists and mathematical logicians is their interest in historical inquiry into the development of scientific theory and in the importance that many of them attribute to such inquiry as a means of recognizing the equivalence or identity of theories which have appeared in diverse forms at various times or in different fields, though expressing substantially the same facts and serving the same purposes" (p. 200).

A further common feature is the interest in economy of expressions in order to enhance their instrumental value. Vailati's friend, a mathematical logician, G. Vacca, reported (ibid., p. 206) that when concepts or terms introduced in a theory grow arithmetically, the number of corresponding propositions to be verified grows much more rapidly in a geometrical progression according to an exponential law, stated by W. K. Clifford, and cited by G. Peano (*Calcolo geometrico*, 1888).

What distinguishes Peirce's "pragmaticism" is his elaboration of metaphysical categories going far beyond his proclaimed adherence to the logic of the "laboratory mind" of the experimenter, and even beyond his attempt to revive the medieval doctrine of objective universals (Scotistic realism). His unpublished "Hume on the Laws of Nature" was rejected by the scientific director of the Smithsonian Institution, Samuel P. Langley, as too abstruse. Instead of defending the "laws of Nature" as absolute, Peirce insisted on the absolute reality of one of his favorite metaphysical triads: (1) Immediately felt Qualities, (2) Brute Existence, and (3) Ordered Reasonableness, so that the laws of nature discovered by scientists were approximations, probable guesses (hypotheses) whose logical consequences had been tested by controlled experiments. Peirce, at various times in his metaphysical thought-experiments, stated his categories in various triads: Feeling, Habit, Purpose; Sensation, Resistance, Order; Spontaneity, Contingency, Law; and in evolutionary terms, Sporting Mutation, Habit, and Adaptation. The generalization of these triadic categories was simply Firstness, Secondness, and Thirdness. Peirce offered applications of these very broad categories in many fields, e.g., in logic: terms, propositions, inferences; in his theory of signs: icons, indices, symbols; in his metaphysical doctrines: tychism, synechism, agapism—Greek-derived words for Chance, Continuity, and Love.

Critics of Peirce have no difficulty showing the confusing ambiguities of his categories. "Chance" shifts meaning as Peirce applies it to spontaneity, feeling, contingency, approximation, random distribution of energy, unpredictability, individuation, uniqueness, inexplicability; "Continuity" is ambiguously applied to the laws of natural phenomena, to human habits, to all evolution including the history of scientific discoveries, and to the history of civilization. "Evolutionary Love" is a very speculative use of the Platonic idea of the attraction of all things for order emerging in millenarian fashion out of a primordial chaos of sporting feelings. No wonder then that Peirce's "Guess at the Riddle of the Universe" was not taken seriously by the more hardheaded utilitarian followers of John Stuart Mill, Herbert Spencer, and the "Social Darwinists" of his day.

It remains nevertheless true that Peirce made pioneer contributions to the logic of relations, to the foundations of mathematics, to the theory of probability and induction, and to the theory of signs—contributions which have paved the way for rapid progress in mathematical logic and the logic of the sciences. Only in 1967, for example, was it discovered (by the mathematical logician A. R. Turquette) that

Peirce had, in his unpublished papers, worked out a truth-table for a three valued logic, together with a proof of its completeness (*Transactions of the Charles S. Peirce Society*, III, 66–73). Whitehead and Russell have acknowledged their debt to Peirce's calculus of relations; Frank P. Ramsey paid tribute to Peirce's theory of probable inference as truth-frequency and instrumentalist view of theories in science as "leading principles." Whether or not Peirce would have made his discoveries (e.g., in his physical and psychological experiments, in his symbolic logic, etc.) without his restless metaphysical speculations is a difficult historical and psychological question, even though one can easily prove that *logically* there is no necessary connection between his truth-frequency analysis of probability and his tychistic cosmology.

Josiah Royce, in his *The Problem of Christianity* (2 vols., 1913, Preface), paid tribute to Peirce: "I owe much more to our great and unduly neglected American logician, Mr. Charles Peirce, than I do to the common tradition of recent idealism, and certainly very much more than I have ever owed, at any point of my own philosophical development to the doctrines which . . . can be justly attributed to Hegel" (ibid., p. xi). In fact, Royce by defining an idea as a "plan of action" developed a theory of knowledge and reality with the outcome "a sort of absolute pragmatism, which has never been pleasing either to rationalists or to empiricists, either to pragmatists or to the ruling type of absolutists" (ibid., II, 122f.). Royce's theory of knowledge was, like Peirce's, based on a social theory of inquiry, meaning, and truth. Both he and Peirce were very critical of the subjective individualism of William James. Royce's "absolute pragmatism" required an ideal community of minds as a logically necessary condition for knowledge and reality.

V. WILLIAM JAMES'S PRAGMATISM AND "WILL TO BELIEVE"

It was William James who, in 1897, credited Charles S. Peirce, his friend and admirer, with having originated pragmatism. James made this announcement in a public lecture (at the Philosophical Union of the University of California in Berkeley) entitled "Philosophical Conceptions and Practical Results." In subsequent correspondence between Peirce and James, both acknowledged their debt to Chauncey Wright. Wright's stimulating analytical mind and empiricist methodology had been inspired by John Stuart Mill's critical examination of the Scottish intuitionism of Sir William Hamilton, and by Charles Darwin's theory of natural selection. Wright was a mathematician for the *Nautical Almanac,* and had applied his knowledge to a theory about the optimal arrangement of leaves around the stems of plants (phyllotaxis) to obtain maximum exposure to air and sunlight. The paper interested Charles Darwin, who thanked Chauncey Wright for this evidence of evolutionary adaptation.

Wright also argued for a neutral view of science with regard to moral and religious values, and for John Stuart Mill's utilitarian, relativistic theory of objective morality. William James, under the influence of his Swedenborgian father's religious philosophy, argued against Wright's skepticism. The "right" and later "duty" and "will to believe," which James defended, was the counterpoise to Wright's positivistic and "nihilistic" agnosticism. However, James admitted Wright's influence on his own scientific approach in the preface to the *Principles of Psychology* (1890), the forerunner of nearly all of James's ideas as developed in his later formulations of his doctrines of the will to believe, of "radical empiricism," and of pluralism—the three major components of his variety of pragmatism and of his general philosophy.

James's article "The Function of Cognition," written for a psychological journal in 1885, shows the influence of Peirce's realism as well as elements of the operational theory of knowledge developed later by John Dewey and Percy Bridgman. James's realism and "radical empiricism" went beyond Berkeley's idealistic view that external objects are merely passive groups of sensations or ideas. That nothing exists "without the mind" was for James a totally inadequate expression of the creative dynamism and transformative powers of the mind. The same critique was levelled at the classical rationalists (Descartes, Spinoza, Leibniz) who maintained that the order and connections of things were simply reflected by the order and connection of ideas. The mind, for James, Peirce, Dewey, and Mead—and their followers—is active in knowledge, operating on and transforming its experience in order to grasp the changing relations of things and events, utilizing ideas tested experimentally as tools needed to understand and to adapt the mind to nature. We know the earth's physical properties only when we can take some of its materials into our laboratories, break down compounds into elements, discover and create new ones by experimental activities that control some of the conditions governing nature's secret powers. So long as philosophers refer knowledge to antecedent untouched sensations and eternal ideas, which do nothing and give the mind nothing to do, they will discover nothing new and continue to produce static, unproductive models of mythical ontologies. *Homo faber* can best understand what he can create, but in order to understand nature man must learn to create and control the processes at work in nature. While Peirce, astronomer, mathematical physicist, and chemist, was concerned with cosmic evolution, James, physiological psychologist and humanist, was drawn to the trials and tribulations of the individual mind, perplexed by the complexity of environing forces and seeking the freedom to create a life worth living.

After much pondering over metaphysical and theological arguments—especially influenced by R. H. Lotze, Charles Renouvier, and Jules Lequier—James offered his "will to believe" as a solution to the age-old problem of the freedom of the will. Wright's early influence on James's thought here had been twofold. First, Wright followed Kant's and Mill's antimetaphysical views that absolute freedom of a disembodied will was beyond logical or empirical proof, but held that a practical justification for the belief in free will was to be sought in the moral benefits of holding the self responsible for the knowable empirical consequences of one's deliberate actions. James agreed with Wright's empirical approach, and explored the psychological and physiological experimental facts that might throw light on the force of instincts, habits, and association of ideas resulting from previous sensations, and on the Will, in various chapters of the *Principles of Psychology* but emerged with a negative result. The last chapter ("Necessary Truths and the Effects of Experience") concluded that the scientific study of the human mind yielded no decisive idea about the precise relation of bodily behavior to states and acts of consciousness, and thus left James with the "dilemma of determinism."

In his paper bearing this title, James distinguished "soft" from "hard" determinism. The "hard" determinist (James preferred to deal with persons rather than with doctrines) was one who denied absolutely that any act was "free" from complete determination by strict causation, so that freedom of the will was simply an illusion due to ignorance of the causes behind one's actions and decisions. The "soft" determinist was less of a pessimist by admitting the impossibility of knowing *all* the determining causes of one's actions, and by affirming a positive knowledge only of the probable empirical consequences of choosing between equally determined alternatives. Soft determinism appealed to James as more in harmony with the common-sense belief in the freedom to make some practical, moral, and religious decisions. The will to believe might then help release untapped energies.

Furthermore, there are occasions when one is confronted empirically by what James called "genuine, live, momentous, and forced options" with vital consequences foreseeable with some degree of probability as one chooses on the basis of previous experience and present feeling among two or more apparent alternatives. And there are many human situations when all the scientifically foreseeable consequences are so equally balanced between two alternatives that there is no decisive preponderance of evidence in favor of one over the other. Wright would have argued that *scientific* evidence is neutral with regard to moral decisions about ultimate valuations, and—as the mathematician W. K. Clifford later advocated—would suspend judgment if there were no further evidence to favor one alternative as more useful, socially or individually, than another. At this point William James departed from Wright's negative neutrality and Clifford's paralyzing suspension of judgment, because for James action is demanded in genuine, live, momentous, and forced options, and because it is absurd to expect human beings to suspend their natural inclinations indefinitely.

The criticisms made by both Chauncey Wright and C. S. Peirce did affect James's doctrine of "the will to believe" to the extent that James was led to laying down a condition for the application of his doctrine, namely, that no belief was to be accepted as true if it went contrary to available evidence. In other words, the appeal to the emotional willingness to believe was, in James's critical judgment, applicable and relevant only when all the available evidence for and against a possible decision or action was equally balanced or indecisive. James's position is saved from the charge of "mere" subjectivism by his adherence to this condition, although at times it seems as though he ignored it, especially when he insists that the very desire to act in the direction of one's natural inclinations is part of the objective situation. Such insistence on the objective status of emotional factors is not surprising for a philosopher who had devoted so many years to the scientific study of psychology. The famous "James-Lange theory of the emotions" is a forerunner of the objective approach of behaviorists. We tremble not because we are afraid, but we are afraid because we tremble. James was not an extreme behaviorist; he would not dismiss or reduce to physical symptoms the immediate experience of conscious states or the effects of subconscious forces. He was willing to adopt the dual language of physiological and introspective methods of psychologizing. With G. Stanley Hall, he early recognized the importance of Freud's ideas.

Later criticisms of the James-Lange theory of emotions by W. B. Cannon and other psychologists show that James oversimplified the physiological conditions by referring only to visceral and muscular states. While James would have welcomed further knowledge and physiological research on glandular, neurological, and psychoanalytical conditions of emotional responses, he would still have left open the question whether conscious voluntary effort (such as the "will to believe" entails) is not also a possible cause for producing emotions that can be beneficial to the human organism. Like Freud, who accepted analysis of a patient's history, while awaiting physiological details, William James accepted introspective reports as equally important as behavioral data. His sympathy for Freud's approach was similar to the way in which he opened his mind to philosophical arguments for free will by the neo-Kantians Renouvier and Lotze, and even by the more mystical views of Lequier and Henri Bergson.

Although James died (1910) before the appearance of Bergson's *Two Sources of Morals and Religion* (Paris, 1932; London, 1935), he would have approved Bergson's defense of the "open" as against the mechanistically "closed" world as well as his sympathetic account of the Christian mystics. Bergson's "creative evolution" and dynamic spiritualism were not alien to James's own pluralistic and open-ended world view and interest in the varieties of religious experience. For James could argue passionately for pluralistic, democratic individualism and at the same time feel deeply the self's need for spiritual unity. The many kinds of "self" (material, social, moral, and spiritual) which he analyzed in his *Principles of Psychology* were not simply Hume's "bundles of habits" and atomistic sensations; they were the varied organic forms and directions of the stream of consciousness of an organism striving not only to survive but to create meaning and value in its finite existence. James's pragmatism was as unfinished as his open universe. He died knowing that he had not solved the eternal enigmas of the relationship of the Many to the One, of the Material to the Spiritual. In his own romantic way he had found spiritual excitement in the quest for truths which are practically unattainable with either certainty or final satisfaction, but worth pursuing if only for the glimpses of their transcendent, elusive values.

VI. EUROPEAN VERSIONS OF PRAGMATISM

James's democratic temper and tender-minded sensitivity to human suffering and political injustice were clearly evidenced in his attack on the curse of bigness in the rapid growth of America's giant monopolistic industries, on the military expansion in the Philippines and Latin America, and the growing agnosticism and cynicism. It is, therefore, surprising to note that some European thinkers referred to James's emphasis on feeling and action in their own violently antidemocratic programs of political action. For example, Mussolini, in his socialistic days, said that he admired James's philosophy though there is no evidence that he had ever read or understood it. Giovanni Papini, an enthusiastic supporter of a "magical pragmatism," had been hailed earlier by James as a leader of the

pragmatic writers of articles in *Leonardo*, the philosophical journal founded by Papini in 1903.

Although Papini had said that it was impossible to give a unique and precise definition of pragmatism, he offered to indicate ". . . the dominant feature which forms the internal unity of all the various elements that go together under the mantle of its name" (. . . *il carattere dominante che forma l'unità interna di tutti i vari elementi che vanno riuniti sotto il mantello del suo nome*) namely, "*the plasticity or flexibility of theories and beliefs*, that is, the recognition of their purely *instrumental value*; . . . their value being only *relative* to an end or group of ends which are susceptible to being changed, varied, and transformed when needed" (Papini's emphases, *Pragmatismo*, p. 91).

The elements united thus by Papini turn out to be more Jamesian than Peircean, more romantic and "magical" than classical and realistic. He enumerates six such component ideas: (1) *nominalism*, (2) *utilitarianism*, (3) *positivism* (antimetaphysical scientific method), (4) *kantianism* (emphasis on the "practical reason" of the free will), (5) *voluntarism* of a Schopenhauerian sort (ontological priority of the will over science), (6) *fideism* or Pascalian apologetics aimed at restoring religious faiths. Papini adds that different emphases and combinations of these elements go to make up the "variety of pragmatism" (ibid., p. 92), but he lumps Peirce and James together as emphasizing in the theory of meaning the *particular* consequences of ideas in future *practical* experiences, thus ignoring the criticism of nominalism by Peirce (ibid., p. 93).

Papini's "magical" pragmatism owes the adjective to his own emphasis on the personal power of ideas to transform what we experience by a romantic activity of the "imitative" imagination. He leans heavily on James's notion that "*faith in a fact can help create the fact*" (quoted with emphases by Papini, ibid., p. 145). He agrees also with James's statement in "The Sentiment of Rationality" (*Will to Believe*, pp. 63–110), that truths cannot become true till our faith has made them so" (ibid., p. 96). The confusion between meaning and truth remains a common feature of James's and Papini's versions of pragmatism. Papini found James' *Will to Believe* "among the most exciting and fruitful theories of contemporary thought" (Papini, p. 153), but regretted that in James "there is no trace of the belief in *magical* powers, that is to say, in the possibility that certain men have the power to change by their will external things and natural phenomena; for James restricted this power to internal psychological reality" (Papini's emphasis, ibid., p. 151).

An interesting brief chapter of Papini's book is entitled "Il Pragmatismo e i parti politici" ("Pragmatism and Political Parties," written in 1905), in which the eight Italian political parties of his day (Catholic, Conservative, Liberal, Radical, Republican, Socialist, Democratic, and Anarchist) are taken to task for using common locutions but acting differently. They all talk of aiming at Italy's *unity, freedom, prosperity* but pragmatically these terms must have as many different meanings as the various means or actions that are specifically proposed and pursued by each party's leaders. On this point, Dewey, Mead, and Hook would surely agree with Papini in applying the instrumentalist interpretation of social and political programs as no better than possible hypotheses. But the American pragmatists would also reject Papini's resort to an antimodernistic and mystical Catholicism, a far cry from his initial subjective pragmatism.

Although Luigi Pirandello (1867–1936) was not a professional philosopher, his many plays, translated in many languages and successfully performed in many countries in the 1920's and 1930's, almost always contain a Protagorean relativism with respect to truth and values. The conversations of Pirandello's characters reflect the version of the subjective relativism in the pragmatism made current in Italy by Papini's personalism and Mario Calderoni's "corridor theory" of truth. Pirandello himself disavowed any philosophical content in his plays:

> In Italy people seem to be intent on following the misleading line (*la falsariga*) of some critic who believed he discovered a philosophical content in my things that isn't there (*un contenuto filosofico che non c'è*), I guarantee its non-existence (quoted in L. Pirandello, ed. C. Simioni, p. xxvii; trans. P. P. Wiener).

Yet there was a stormy, philosophical controversy over so-called Pirandellism; Pirandello's relativism was criticized by followers of Benedetto Croce, Italy's dominating metaphysician of the absolutistic Hegelian type against which the *Leonardo* group led by Papini, had led a rebellion in the first decade of the century. Croce had himself accepted Adriano Tilgher's (one of Croce's epigoni's) dialectical analysis of "the central problem" of Pirandello's art, viz., the antithesis of Life and Form (A. Tilgher, *Teoria della critica d'arte*, 1913). A. Gramsci, on the other hand, suggested that Pirandello was merely displaying his satirical sense of humor, by creating "philosophical" and nasty doubts about truth and goodness in order to flaunt subjectivism and philosophical solipsism (ibid., p. xxviii).

The most extreme form of this abuse of James's notion of the usefulness of ideas as adaptive means of action is the theory of the syndicalist Georges Sorel in his *Réflexions sur la violence* (Paris, 1908); in what he took to be a pragmatic justification of using the weapon of a general strike to bring about the revolu-

tionary overthrow of the existing capitalistic system, Sorel argued as follows: "The myth must be judged as a means of acting on the present; any attempt to discuss how far it can be taken literally as future history is devoid of sense. . . . The question whether the general strike is a partial reality, or only a product of popular imagination, is of little importance." Thanks to revolutionary leaders, "we know that the general strike is indeed what I have said: the *myth* in which Socialism is wholly comprised, i.e., a body of images capable of evoking instinctively all the sentiments which correspond to the different manifestations of the war undertaken by Socialism against modern society. Strikes have engendered in the proletariat the noblest, deepest, and most moving sentiments that they possess . . ." (pp. 360–61).

Sorel's pragmatic conclusion to his peculiar "scientific ethics" and revolutionary myth of the general strike, reveals the missionary zeal of the syndicalist's hopes: "It is to violence that Socialism owes those high ethical values by means of which it brings *salvation* to the modern world" (ibid., p. 365). This variety of revolutionary pragmatism—surely on the extreme fringe of the solid core of pragmatism—makes a dangerous appeal to men's instincts and to irrational disregard of the consequences of the means employed. Sorel's appeal to violence, so common to extreme militants of both fascistic and communistic camps, is certainly confuted by our core pragmatists who are concerned as reformers about the human effects or social consequences of resort to violence which so often breeds greater violence. Sorel owes some of his ideas, especially the appeal to instinctive drives, to Bergson's *élan vital* and emphasis on action, although Bergson never advocated violence, and preferred the mystical road to salvation.

Further illustration of the rich variety to which pragmatism lends itself, within the French group of pragmatic thinkers as well as among other nationalities, is provided by the dispute between Abel Rey and Pierre Duhem on the philosophical foundations of physical theory. Professor Rey defended an antimetaphysical, positivistic principle of verifiability against Duhem's attempt to weld experimental physics to a neo-Thomistic theory of knowledge and reality. Duhem was perfectly willing and even anxious to have physical science aim at convenient theories that "save the appearances," provided however, that the structure of physical theories reflected the overarching ultimate nature of the supernatural invisible reality of God. Abel Rey, of course, dismissed such theological overtones as irrelevant to the aims and structure of physical theory.

A French fascist, Drieu La Rochelle, in 1927, took

pride in his epistemological "pragmatism" which to him meant that "knowledge is the product only of experience," that is, of *personal* experience, as Robert Soucy explains in his article on "Romanticism and Realism in the Fascism of Drieu La Rochelle," in the *Journal of the History of Ideas* (**31** [Jan. 1970], 78 and notes 30, 31). Truth had to be "lived," thus La Rochelle espoused "a kind of fascist existentialism" without knowing anything of existentialist philosophy (ibid.).

Bergson's form of pragmatism only tenuously merits that label (which he did not adopt for his philosophy); his metaphysical and spiritualistic theory of action bears all the marks of the *fin-de-siècle anti-scientisme* which appears in his criticism of the analytical, conceptual, abstract, and static modes of scientific understanding. The flux of immediate experience (*les données immédiates de la conscience*, the subject of his dissertation) could not be grasped by the abstract intellect but required an immersion in the real moving duration (*durée*) of the vital impulse (*élan vital*) which surges through the dynamic universe. William James was greatly impressed and awed by the imaginative sweep and psychological insights of Bergson's ardent defense of concrete intuitive data of consciousness so similar to James's "stream of consciousness." Bergson's *Creative Evolution* (1907) was Lamarckian, however, and was not compatible with James's defense of August Weismann's refutation of the Lamarckian theory of the inheritance of acquired characters. Despite their many differences, the kinship of Bergson's and James's pragmatic philosophies is based on their common concern to transcend static, impersonal conceptual analysis and to make of man's active, dynamic, emotional nature the source of a creative moral and spiritual order. This aim was a far cry from Sorel's appeal to the myth of a violent class war on the Marxist ground of historical materialism, but the dynamism is there, and the existentialists claim Bergson as one of their own.

Sorel, in his work on the *Utility of Pragmatism* (*De l'utilité du pragmatisme*, 1917), during World War I and nine years after his *Réflexions sur la violence*, hoped "to convince readers of this book that the pragmatic manner of considering the pursuit of truth is bound to become one of the essential elements of modern thought" (Sorel [1908], p. 4). He noted that Peirce in his 1878 essay, "How to Make Our Ideas Clear," had said that Catholics and Protestants ought not be concerned about the idea of transubstantiation so long as they agree on the effects on moral conduct of the real Presence. He noted also that Édouard Le Roy (1870–1954), the Bergsonian physicist, interpreted Catholic dogmas in Peircean fashion when Le Roy maintained that these "dogmas would impose strict rules of conduct on the faithful, but would leave a great

deal of freedom for the intellectual representation of things" (ibid., pp. 5–6, with reference to Le Roy's *Dogme et critique*, pp. 19–23, 32). To Peirce, of course, "conduct" referred to "conduct of the mind," whereas James broadened the scope of the term to include, and indeed to emphasize, moral and religious behavior.

Sorel defended James's idea of the "will to believe" against the critics who misinterpreted it to mean "the will to make-believe" or to indulge in wishful thinking. Sorel also took to task those critics who had picked on James's phrase "cash value of an idea" as a reflection of Yankee commercialism. Against this gross and yet common European misinterpretation of James's lively rhetorical way of discussing epistemological theories of truth, Sorel as a political thinker and Marxist, looked with favor upon James's condemnation of undemocratic State authority and of an infallible Church that imposed its dogmas upon its members.

Sorel's brand of pragmatism was critical of Bergson's spiritualism, although Bergson shared with him an admiration for William James's break away from traditional, eternalistic metaphysics. What further distinguishes Sorel's from Bergson's pragmatic ideas is Sorel's unwavering confidence in the certainty of scientific knowledge and of historical materialism. He could find no value in Bergson's vitalism, antiscientific intuition, and religious mysticism. He did, however, praise Bergson's theory of intelligence as "the faculty of manufacturing artificial objects, especially tools for making tools, and for varying their manufacture indefinitely" (quoted by Sorel from Bergson's *L'évolution créatrice*, p. 151).

Sorel's revolutionary, syndicalist brand of pragmatism appealed strongly to Mussolini and the fascists. Of course, the very different varieties of pragmatism of James, Peirce, Mead, and Dewey can hardly be held responsible for either the Marxist or fascist interpretations of James. The very opposite defence of liberal democracy is at the cultural base of the American, British, Italian (pre-Mussolini), German (H. Vaihinger), and French varieties of pragmatism.

Communistic ideologists have criticized pragmatism as a bourgeois capitalistic doctrine of American imperialism despite James's attacks on big business and American policies in the Philippines, Cuba, and Venezuela. At the same time communist philosophers urge the union of theory and practice in very narrowly practical terms. "Praxis" occurs often in their theory of truth; it is the title of a philosophical periodical in Yugoslavia, edited by more liberal Marxists than in the USSR or Red China. So long as philosophy is chiefly an ideological tool among communist theoreticians, it is subject to modification by the leaders of the party or state. Thus Soviet philosophy becomes instrumental in the worst opportunistic sense, the polar opposite of Dewey's instrumentalism and Peirce's pragmaticism or of any of the other liberal varieties of pragmatism, so crudely regarded by its critics as advocating crass opportunism with respect to truth and human values.

For the social and political forms of pragmatism, more moderate or liberal than Sorel's or other Marxist versions of praxis, we must turn to the legal writings of philosophers like Vaihinger, and the American pragmatic realists.

In the years 1876 to 1878, while Oliver Wendell Holmes, Jr. was preparing the chapters of his work *The Common Law*, the Kantian commentator Hans Vaihinger was writing a pragmatic masterpiece, *Die Philosophie des Als Ob*. It was not published until 1911, and not translated into English until 1924. The legal philosopher, Lon L. Fuller, has devoted the last third of his work on *Legal Fictions* to explaining the contribution to legal thinking made by Vaihinger's "as if" philosophy. Though conceived independently, Vaihinger's pragmatic philosophy is similar to James's and Holmes's views in showing how the mind tends to project or reify its own conceptual constructions, which are primarily evolutionary means of adaptation to a changing world. Whatever and whenever such adaptive ideas serve to help us confront reality, they are regarded *as if* they were real properties. Perhaps Vaihinger may be considered "more pragmatic than the American school because . . . he has obtained his generalizations about human thinking, not by deduction from some premise concerning the nature of thought in general, but from an examination of the ways and byways of thought in particular sciences" (Fuller [1967], p. 96). These sciences range from the mathematical to the legal. "Imaginary numbers" (roots of negative numbers) can be treated as if they were quantitative properties of electromagnetic fields. The fictive "personality" of a corporation is regarded by the courts as if it were a person subject to specific laws of liability, bankruptcy, and so forth. In short, "Vaihinger taught German legal science how to use its own intellectual tools" (ibid.).

VII. PRAGMATISM IN THE LAW

Three of the members of the Metaphysical Club at Harvard in the 1870's, where Peirce claimed "pragmatism saw the light of day," were concerned, as students, practitioners, or teachers of law, with the cultural evolution and philosophical foundations of the law. They were Nicholas St. John Green (the "grandfather of pragmatism" who followed A. Bain's idea of belief as a disposition to act), Oliver Wendell Holmes, Jr. (busily editing the twelfth edition of Kent's *Commentaries on the American Law*, 4 vols.), and Joseph B. Warner (future lecturer in the Harvard Law School, 1886–87, and who in 1896 before the American Bar Association gave an address on "The Responsibilities of the Lawyer"). A fourth law student, John Fiske, who occasionally came to the Metaphysical Club, turned from law to history. He was a disciple of Comte and Spencer and wrote a four-volume survey, *Outlines of Cosmic Philosophy* (1874), developing an evolutionary philosophy of civilization along Spencerian lines.

The law schools were steeped in classical syllogistic methods of applying the law to individual cases as previously decided and in the Hobbesian-Austinian view that the law was "the command of the sovereign." The Lockean view of the social contract was mingled with the Puritan idea of the Covenant with God. Sir Henry Maine's *Ancient Law* (1861) and *History of Early Institutions* (1875) were reviewed by Chauncey Wright in the *Nation* (July 1, 1875) after he had previously remarked: "In the Law School there is a vigor of thought and a stimulus to study which can't be found elsewhere" (Wiener, p. 272). Maine's work emphasized the evolution of the law as paralleling the evolution of society from slavery and feudalism to modern free enterprise: "from status to contract." A similar emphasis on historical development as an essential key to understanding the cultural role and evolution of the law was the prominent feature of Holmes's great work *The Common Law* (1881):

> The felt necessities of the time, the prevalent moral and political theories, intuitions of public policy, avowed or unconscious; even the prejudices which judges share with their fellow-men have had a good deal more to do than the syllogism in determining the rules by which men should be governed. The law embodies the story of a nation's development through many centuries, and it cannot be dealt with as if it contained only the axioms and corollaries of a book of mathematics. In order to know what it is, we must know what it has been, and what it tends to become. We must alternately consult history and existing theories of legislation. But the most difficult labor will be to understand the combination of the two into new products at every stage. The substance of the law at any given time pretty nearly corresponds, so far as it goes, with what is then understood to be convenient; but its form and machinery and the degree to which it is able to work out desired results, depend very much upon its past (Holmes, p. 1).

Holmes illustrated his evolutionary and pragmatic approach by tracing the change from the primitive basis of revenge in the punishment of criminals to the more pragmatic justification of deterring future crimes. In civil cases, Holmes explained, the evolution of the laws of liability is shaped mainly by "considerations of what is expedient for the community concerned" (ibid., pp. 15, 35).

A progressive combination, and at times radical application, of British empiricism and utilitarian ethics was deployed by the American legal pragmatists against the metaphysical idealism of the German romantic variety that had come to the United States in the Hegelian school (mentioned above) of W. T. Harris in St. Louis, where the *Journal of Speculative Philosophy* was launched in 1868. The upshot of pragmatic jurisprudence was the dissociation of the law from its scholastic accretions of eternal theological standards and imputations of original sin and hell-fire for the nonconformist and iconoclast. The criminal law with its medieval system of punishment and torture "for the good of one's soul" was subjected to unsparing criticism by Nicholas St. John Green (1830–70) in his *Essays and Notes on the Law of Tort and Crime* (published in 1933). He insisted on an historical approach in his projected annual publication of criminal law reports and cases in both the United States and the British Empire. Before Green's death he had completed the editing and annotation of the first two volumes (1874–75) of this bold venture in historical jurisprudence. Peirce showed the influence of Green's analytical use of legal history when he pointed out, as Green had in the *American Law Review* (4 [Jan., 1870], 201), that key terms like "proximate cause" could not simply be transferred from Aristotelian physics to the laws of liability. "The idea of making the payment of considerable damages dependent on a term of Aristotelian logic or metaphysics is most shocking to any student of these subjects, and well illustrates the value of Pragmatism" (C. S. Peirce, "Proximate Cause and Effect," *Baldwin's Dictionary of Philosophy*). "Proximate cause" in civil law has to do with the negligence of a party with respect to the legal rights of others and nothing to do with spatio-temporal contiguity or a mechanical chain of causes. Rights and liabilities are determined by the civil law in the case of property damages which can even be inflicted at a distance, e.g., by hiring others to commit arson.

Green's influence on the shaping of legal pragmatism is not as well known as that of Oliver Wendell Holmes, Jr. (Wiener, pp. 164ff.). Common to their legal philosophies were: (1) a behavioristic method of determining intention by regarding an act "as a voluntary muscular contraction and nothing else" (Holmes, *American Law Review*, 14, 9) or consisting "as such of inward feelings and outward motions, the motions forming the evidence of the feelings" (Green, *Essays and Notes*, p. 192); (2) the irrelevance of the internal phenomena of conscience (Holmes, *Common Law*, pp. 62, 110; Green, *Essays and Notes*, p. 67); (3) the primacy of public policy over individual idiosyncrasies. Holmes applied a tough-minded principle of interpreting the law by the external standard of the consequences for public policy as set by the legislature, regardless of the private feelings or moral ideals that might be affected. The rule of eminent domain might seem harsh to a property owner not compensated with as much as he thinks "just," but the public interest must prevail, if the community or state budget is too limited to award more compensation. The right of free speech must be limited in time of war, or denied to a mischievous person crying "Fire" in a crowded theater. But the same right must be rigorously protected against self-appointed censors of public morality, because (as John Stuart Mill had shown in his *Essay on Liberty*) in the long run the harm to the public will be greater if ideas are suppressed than if some allegedly harmful or "immoral" ones are tolerated. The test of how good or bad a new law is becomes a matter of predicting the social consequences or public effects of enacting and enforcing the proposed law. Since every judicial decision as to how the acts of the legislature should be interpreted or applied may modify the meaning of the law, Holmes argued that judges make the law as much as the legislature. The constitution of 1789 is not the same as that of 1865 or of 1965, not simply because amendments have been added, but because both the original articles and amendments have been interpreted differently by judges at various times in new cases having aspects unforeseen by the original makers of the law. Holmes's predictive theory of the law was offered as advice to lawyers in doubt about the meaning or applicability of a law. Holmes's counsel amounted to the rule that the law in any particular case would mean what one could predict the judges would decide in that case. Such predictions would vary with the temperament, education, prejudices, or mood of the judges. Obviously, however, this predictive theory will not help a judge who is pondering over what he should decide, for it is tautologous to state that the law will be or mean what he will decide. Holmes's realistic dictum that the law is what the courts will predictably decide also runs afoul of legislation that aims at curbing the latitude of judicial freedom. Hence, the pragmatist is faced with the practical questions of social and political values, and criteria for judging them, in a rapidly changing society.

VIII. PRAGMATIC THEORIES OF VALUE

One common feature of all the varieties of pragmatism is the idea or "the premise that valuation is a form of empirical knowledge" (C. I. Lewis, Preface, p. vii). However, the diversified range of empirical theories of knowledge, due largely to the blurred and indefinite boundaries of "experience," leaves the idea rather vague and the premiss hardly unequivocal. For example, James's *Varieties of Religious Experience* does not exclude revelations of the supernatural, and Peirce includes purely logical and mathematical reasoning as forms of "diagramatic experimentation." In ethical theory, pragmatists will be either "emotivists" (following Wright, James, F. C. S. Schiller), or "cognitivists" (following Dewey, Mead, or C. I. Lewis). Outside this variety of pragmatic theories of value—and we must specify the type or theories of value that are excluded from the "pragmatic" if this term is to have any identifiable meaning—we can point to *a priori* or transcendental ideas of the *summum bonum* which can only be known by pure reason, by political or theological authority, or by a transcendental inner conscience or Ego untouched by common experience, and in any case, claiming moral jurisdiction not subject to any appeal to public verification.

William James, F. C. S. Schiller, and Luigi Pirandello (the latter not as a systematic philosopher, of course, but as illustrated in his play, *Six Characters in Search of an Author*) based their pragmatic humanism on the relativism of knowledge and values. On the other hand, C. I. Lewis aimed to avoid "the errors of Protagorean relativism or the moral skepticism which would destroy the normative by reducing it to merely emotive significance" (ibid., p. viii). Pragmatic ethics, for C. I. Lewis, is concerned with the nature of justice, and we have seen that legal pragmatists like Holmes always insisted on applying the "external standard" of social expediency in determining what the law considers "just."

Whether there is a "higher law" above what the law courts decide is "right" depends on whether we can appeal to a more general idea of the good or *summum bonum* that subsumes or overrides the legal idea. While it is not difficult to understand the social nature of justice in the sense of what is considered legally right or correct, it requires much more argument to accept a pragmatic criterion of public verification for the more general theory of values. But that is the kind of criterion that Peirce, Dewey, G. H. Mead, and C. I. Lewis have defended against the emotivists and the apriorists.

The verifiability theory of knowledge is shared by the core pragmatists (Peirce, James, Dewey, C. I. Lewis, and their followers) and logical empiricists (M. Schlick, R. Carnap, A. J. Ayer, and their followers) but the two schools of thought differ basically on whether value judgments are verifiable. The pragmatists affirm the idea that value judgments are verifiable to the extent that such judgments are implicit hypotheses about what is valued as desirable or enjoyable. Hypotheses, as possible truths about what objects or activities will satisfy desires or yield the enjoyments

anticipated, have logical consequences that will either be falsified or verified by future experiences of such objects or activities. This view of value judgments as verifiable hypotheses is known as the "cognitivist" view. It is opposed to the "emotivist" view of those logical empiricists and others who regard value judgments as expressions of personal taste, feeling, or preference without any reference to knowledge claims. John Dewey and C. I. Lewis and their pragmatistic followers have criticized the "emotivist" view by showing how ideas, reflection, and knowledge of the consequences of actions modify emotional responses and behavior. For example, knowing that some mushrooms are poisonous will lead even a hungry person to desist from eating them until he learns to distinguish them from a nonpoisonous variety. In aesthetics, the art critic and connoisseur of music, by informed comments on the art object or musical score, the artist's or composer's, conductor's, or performer's techniques, can call attention to aspects of the works contemplated which would be overlooked or ignored by the uninformed spectator or listener, and thus enhance his enjoyment. "By their fruits, ye shall know them" was Peirce's epitome of the pragmatic logic of ethical judgments. Dewey's pragmatic analysis of aesthetic judgment in his *Art as Experience* (1934) applied a similar maxim to criticisms of works of art. William James in his *Varieties of Religious Experience* (Gifford Lectures, 1902) applied the same pragmatic justification of religious beliefs of all creeds whenever he saw evidence of their effects on transforming the lives of believers.

The general theory of values comprehends not only the legal and ethical ideas of "right" and "good" but also the logical grounds of aesthetic judgment, thus pursuing in greater detail the analysis of the ancient ideals of the true, the good, and the beautiful. Peirce had gone so far in his addiction to the romantic idealism of Friedrich Schiller and Schelling as to argue that logical theory rested ultimately on ethics because logic aims to determine what sort of reasoning we ought to adopt in conducting our inquiries into truth, and ethics is the science of what we *ought* to do. Moreover, what we ought to do ultimately depends on what goals we desire to achieve, and what is desirable in the end is a question of aesthetic judgment. Peirce, however, cannot offer any criterion of what would constitute a reasonable basis for aesthetic judgment, although he defends reasonableness as the ultimate end of all existence. If logic determines what is "reasonable," we are back to where we started in Peirce's hierarchical triad of logic, ethics, and aesthetics.

There is a more fruitful development of the pragmatic logic of valuation in Dewey, C. I. Lewis, and their followers by assuming that our value judgments are essentially *hypotheses* or tentative claims to knowing what is good or bad, either for an individual or for a society.

By assuming that value judgments are hypotheses, we make them subject to verification by individual or public experience. There seems to be for Dewey and for Mead no absolute demarcation between "private" and "public" experience, but all verification is or should be "intersubjective," i.e., common to and communicable by all persons capable of testing an idea of what is proposed as "good" by their past, present, and anticipated future experiences and feelings of satisfaction or dissatisfaction. By regarding all value judgments as tentative, while being tested or verified, we make it possible to modify the claims on our approbation or disapprobation implicit in the value judgment. The modification after verification may range from complete rejection to some compromise or adjustment, but always with the reservation that further experience may make it necessary to reappraise the situation.

Dewey continually emphasizes the need for facing the peculiar complexities of each specific situation, the problematic and indeterminate nature of each initial stage of valuation, and the tentative character of any solution or resolution resulting from publicly testing our value judgments. Dewey had the temerity to attempt to apply his pragmatic instrumentalism to the complex psychological and social problems of education (in the experimental schools of Chicago in 1902, with George Herbert Mead), to the analysis of the turbulent scene of political revolutions in Russia, China, and Mexico, and in trying to form a third party in the United States during the depression in the 1930's, in combatting fascism and communism in the 1940's, and finally in grappling with the momentous issues of war and peace. Like James, Dewey argued for channeling the aggressive impulses of men towards combatting the common enemies of mankind: ignorance, poverty, disease, and injustice. A liberal democracy for Dewey is a social order that can be achieved in a common faith by uniting thought and action against political, economic, and social injustice.

Peirce's tychism and fallibilism, James's soft determinism, O. W. Holmes's "bet-abilitarianism," and Dewey's instrumentalism are sharply opposed to the economic determinism associated with Marxian dialectical necessity and historical materialism. Only a simplistic fallacy would link the social liberalism of these pragmatists to the totalitarianism of Marxian determinists. The fallacy consists in linking these very different views by finding a common feature in the fact that the pragmatists and Marxian determinists were both opposed to "formalism." To state that individualists like Justice O. W. Holmes, Thorstein Veblen, Charles Beard, James Harvey Robinson, and John

Dewey were "all products of the historical and cultural emphases of the nineteenth century" (Morton G. White, quoted by Thayer, p. 444) is to minimize their role as shapers of nineteenth- and twentieth-century thought in the United States.

In the field of aesthetics, Peirce regarded Friedrich Schiller's *Letters on the Aesthetic Education of Mankind* (1794–95) as one of the first philosophical influences on his own intellectual development, and regarded the play element, to which Schiller attributed so much educational value, as a major factor in art and even in religious contemplation. (See Peirce's essay on "A Neglected Argument for the Existence of God" [*Hibbert Journal*, **7** (1908), 90–112] in which "musement" over the order and beauty in nature leads by a play of ideas to the idea of a divine being.)

The more detailed problems of artistic and literary criticism are treated pragmatically by Dewey in *Art as Experience* (1934), and by Stephen C. Pepper in *Aesthetic Quality: A Contextualistic Theory of Beauty* (1937). The common basis again of pragmatic criticism in aesthetics is that aesthetic judgments should not be based on fixed *a priori* ideas of classical or avant-garde models but on experimenting with every possible means or media for communicating the subtle nuances of feeling and meanings that elude the ordinary means of expression.

Knowledge and feeling, meaning and action, are organically fused in aesthetic experience and artistic creation, which finally exemplify in the most immediately enjoyable sense the pragmatic notion that knowledge can and should be instrumental to the enhancement of human values. In both the appreciation and creation of art, Dewey's pragmatism appeals to the possibilities of greater public participation than the elitist conception of art displayed in art galleries with a "holier-than-thou" aloofness. Against such an esoteric sanctuary for the arts, but without denying the artist's need for complete freedom to experiment, Dewey's pragmatic view aims to extend the field of artistic experimentation to every human from early childhood to adult life at home, in the schools, in the community and world. Knowledge of the history and problems of artistic creation can help improve our understanding of artistic values, and such understanding can also help refine our taste and make us more sensitive to the values that creative intelligence can elicit from the untapped potential capabilities of human nature. The realization of all values for Dewey is inseparable from his faith in the unlimited possibilities of a liberal civilization based on social and economic justice as well as on political democracy. Both intelligence and action—neither subordinated to the other—become creative instruments for the realization of these values in Dewey's experimentalist version of pragmatism. **569**

BIBLIOGRAPHY

A very full historical account of pragmatism with a comprehensive bibliography is H. S. Thayer's *Meaning and Action: A Critical History of Pragmatism* (Indianapolis and New York, 1968). A. J. Ayer, *The Origins of Pragmatism* (San Francisco, 1968) is less historical and mostly critical of James and Peirce. Alexander Bain, *The Emotions and the Will* (Edinburgh, 1859). P. W. Bridgman, *The Logic of Modern Physics* (New York, 1927). Mario Calderoni, *I postulati della scienza positiva ed il diritto penale* (Florence, 1901); idem, *Scritti*, ed. O. Campa, 2 vols. (Florence, 1924). P. Duhem, *La théorie physique—son objet et sa structure*, 2nd ed. (Paris, 1914), trans. P. P. Wiener as *The Aim and Structure of Physical Theory* (Princeton, 1954). John Dewey, "The Development of American Pragmatism," *Studies in the History of Ideas*, 3 vols. (New York, 1925), II, 353–77, repr. in *Philosophy and Civilization* (New York, 1931); idem, "The Pragmatism of Peirce," Supplementary Essay to *Chance, Love and Logic, Philosophical Essays by the Late Charles S. Peirce*, edited with Introduction by Morris R. Cohen (New York, 1923). *The Philosophy of John Dewey*, ed. P. A. Schilpp (Evanston, 1939). Southern Illinois University Press has been publishing a definitive edition of Dewey's works. Lon L. Fuller, *Legal Fictions* (Stanford, 1967). Nicholas St. John Green, *Essays and Notes on the Law of Tort and Crime* (Menasha, Wisc., 1933). G. Gullace, "The Pragmatist Movement in Italy," *Journal of the History of Ideas*, 23 (1962), 91–105. O. W. Holmes, Jr., *The Common Law* (Boston, 1881). Sidney Hook, *The Metaphysics of Pragmatism* (Chicago, 1927). Roman Jakobson, "Language in Relation to Other Communication Systems," *Linguaggi nella società e nella tecnica* (Milan, 1970), pp. 3–16; see also Y. Bar-Hillel, "Communication and Argumentation in Pragmatic Languages," ibid., pp. 269–84. William James, *The Principles of Psychology*, 2 vols. (New York, 1890); idem, *The Will to Believe and Other Essays in Popular Philosophy* (New York, 1897); idem, *The Varieties of Religious Experience* (New York and London, 1902); idem, *Pragmatism, A New Name for Some Old Ways of Thinking* (New York, 1907). C. I. Lewis, *An Analysis of Knowledge and Valuation* (La Salle, Ill., 1946). Karl N. Llewellyn, *Jurisprudence: Realism in Theory and Practice* (Chicago, 1962). Arthur O. Lovejoy, *The Thirteen Pragmatisms* (Baltimore, 1965; reprint of his articles in the *Journal of Philosophy* of 1908). George H. Mead, *Mind, Self, and Society: From the Standpoint of a Social Behaviorist*, ed. with introduction by Charles W. Morris (Chicago, 1934), bibliography in pp. 390–92; see also Maurice Natanson, *The Social Dynamics of George H. Mead* (Washington, D.C., 1956); Charles Morris, *The Pragmatic Movement in American Philosophy* (New York, 1970); John W. Petras, ed., *George Herbert Mead: Essays on His Social Philosophy* (New York, 1968). R. Mondolfo, "Trabajo manual y trabajo intelectual desde la antigüedad hasta el renacimiento," *Revista de la Historia de las Ideas*, 1 (1950), 5–26. Ernest Nagel, *Principles of the Theory of Probability* (Chicago, 1939); idem, *Logic Without Metaphysics* (Glencoe, Ill., 1956); idem, *The Structure of Science* (New York, 1961). G. Papini, *Pragmatismo 1903–1911* (Milan, 1913; 3rd ed.,

Florence, 1927); idem, *Crepùscolo dei Filosofi* (Florence, 1925). Charles S. Peirce, *Collected Papers*, Vols. 1–6, ed. C. Hartshorne and P. Weiss; Vols. 7–8, ed. A. W. Burks (Cambridge, Mass., 1931–58). *Transactions of the Peirce Society* is a quarterly edited and published by University of Massachusetts Press and contains a supplementary list of Peirce's unpublished papers as well as articles on his philosophy. Max H. Fisch is preparing a biography of Peirce, a book to supplement Paul Weiss's valuable article in the *Dictionary of American Biography*. L. Pirandello, *La vita che ti diedi, Ciascuno a suo modo*, ed. C. Simioni, with the chronology of Pirandello's life and times, an introduction and bibliography (Verona, 1970). Frank P. Ramsey, *The Foundations of Mathematics* (London, 1931). Francis E. Reilly, *Charles Peirce's Theory of Scientific Method* (New York, 1970). George Santayana, *The Life of Reason*, 5 vols. (New York, 1905–06). A. Santucci, *Il pragmatismo italiano* (Bologna, 1963). F. C. S. Schiller, "William James and the Making of Pragmatism," *Personalist*, 8 (1927), 81–93. H. W. Schneider, *A History of American Philosophy* (New York, 1946). Georges Sorel, *Réflexions sur la violence* (Paris, 1908), trans. T. E. Hulme, *Reflections on Violence* (New York, 1920); idem, *Les illusions du progrès* (1908), trans. J. and C. Stanley as *The Illusions of Progress* (Berkeley, 1969); idem, *De l'utilité du Pragmatisme* (Paris, 1917; 2nd ed. 1928). Hans Vaihinger, *Die Philosophie des Als Ob* (Berlin, 1911), trans. C. K. Ogden as *The Philosophy of As If* (New York, 1924). Giovanni Vailati, *Il metodo della filosofia*, ed. F. Rossi-Landi (Bari, 1957), with bibliography, pp. 29–36; see also F. Rossi-Landi, article on Vailati in *Encyclopedia of Philosophy*, ed. Paul Edwards, 8 vols. (New York, 1967), Vol. 8. G. Vailati, *Scritti*, ed. M. Calderoni, U. Ricci, and G. Vacca (Florence, 1911). Philip P. Wiener, *Evolution and the Founders of Pragmatism*, with Introduction by John Dewey (Cambridge, Mass., 1949; repr. Gloucester, Mass., 1969). Ludwig Wittgenstein, *Philosophical Investigations*, 3rd ed. trans. G. E. M. Anscombe (Oxford, 1953; New York, 1968). Chauncey Wright, *Philosophical Discussions*, ed. Charles E. Norton (New York, 1877); idem, *Letters of Chauncey Wright, with an Account of His Life*, ed. James B. Thayer (New York, 1878).

PHILIP P. WIENER

[See also Evolutionism; Law, Concept of; Positivism; Relativism in Ethics; **Utilitarianism.**]

PRE-PLATONIC CONCEPTIONS OF HUMAN NATURE

1. The term "pre-Platonic" has been chosen here in preference to pre-Socratic, on the grounds that the only natural terminal point for a survey of early Greek thought is provided by the events of the end of the fifth century B.C.; the death of Socrates in 399, almost coincides with the collapse of the Athenian Empire

(404 B.C.) and with the passing of the great Athenian tragic dramatists, Euripides and Sophocles (ca. 406 B.C.). Any earlier dividing line, separating Democritus and the Sophists from the mainstream of early Greek speculation, would obscure the continuity of the development. The first tangible sign of the new period is not the lifetime of Socrates but the appearance after his death of Socratic literature, and above all of the dialogues of Plato.

In the strict sense, a conception of human nature presupposes a conception of nature, or *physis*. The term occurs once in Homer, for the distinctive physical aspect or form of a plant with powerful magical properties (*Odyssey* 10. 303: "And Hermes showed me its *physis*," namely, that of the *moly* plant). In accordance with this early usage, the phrase "the *physis* of man" would mean his visible stature or appearance (so in Pindar, *Nemean* 6.5; cf. *Isthmian* 4.53 Bowra). On the other hand, the concept of nature as the true, inner structure or character of a thing, not immediately visible, is a product of Ionian natural philosophy. Thus Heraclitus, who promises to "distinguish each thing according to its *physis* and point out how it [really] is" (frag. 1), also remarks that "*physis* loves to hide" (frag. 123). Theories of human nature in this sense, as an object for scientific knowledge or philosophic insight, appear for the first time in Heraclitus and his fellow philosophers. And it is such theories which are generally reflected in the use of the Greek phrases from which we have received "human nature" and "the nature of man" as loan-translations (φύσις ἀνθρωπεία, φύσις ἀνθρωπίνη, φύσις ἀνθρώπου). This terminology does not become common in Greek literature before the late fifth century, for example in Thucydides and the Hippocratic Corpus, where the influence of philosophic speculation is obvious.

As an explicit concept with a fixed terminology, the idea of human nature is thus a product of the scientific and philosophical development which begins in Miletus in the sixth century B.C. For the purposes of the present survey, however, we may understand "conceptions of human nature" more broadly, to include not only these philosophical theories but also the less explicitly formulated views of the nature and condition of man which we find in early poetry and in a nontechnical author like Herodotus. In this broader perspective, the various pre-Platonic conceptions of man can be located between two extreme positions: on the one hand, an archaic view of mankind as wholly subject to the arbitrary power and decision of the gods, as expressed in the *Iliad;* and, on the other hand, a late fifth-century view which ignores the gods completely and holds, as Protagoras puts it, that "Man is the measure of all things." After a brief description of the archaic conception, we shall consider the various ways in which it was altered, both inside and outside the philosophical tradition.

2. The archaic Greek view of man is dominated by a polar opposition between mortals and immortals, between men who walk upon the earth and the gods who dwell in the sky. The gods are not only superior to men; they are in the last analysis their masters. Fate (*moira*) is not a power which stands above the gods: in Homer, at least, it is simply the instrument by which divine control is exercised. A man's fate is literally the "share" which the gods have alloted him, his portion of good and evil, his share of life and death. (The notion of a Fate or Necessity more powerful than Zeus, which is once hinted at in Hesiod and explicitly developed by Aeschylus in *Prometheus Bound*, is unknown in Homer.) At *Iliad* 16.443, Hera says quite clearly that Zeus, if he insisted, could change the *moira* of Sarpedon by postponing his appointed day of death; so also for the death of Hector at *Iliad* 22.181. The arbitrary nature of divine decision is emphasized in the words of Achilles to Priam in *Iliad* 24.525ff.: "Two vessels stand at the threshold of Zeus, one full of evil gifts and the other of good ones." When Zeus mixes these and bestows them on a man, his life is a blend of prosperity and misfortune. But when Zeus gives from the vessel of sorrows, the man's life is sheer disaster. In this view, the only consolation for mortality is undying fame (such as Achilles obtains, and Priam too in his own way); but this in turn is largely the gift of the gods. Although some room is left for human decision, the efficacy of man's action depends in the last resort upon divine favor or support. In typical cases human virtues and vices, achievements and failures, are themselves interpreted in terms of divine intervention. Thus it is a god who puts fury and valor in a warrior's breast; it is Athena who lures Hector to his death at Achilles' hands; and Athena again who guarantees Odysseus' triumph over the suitors in the *Odyssey*. On the negative side, Agamemnon blames Zeus and Fate and the Fury for his folly in insulting Achilles; and the poet himself represents Helen's submission to Paris as a direct result of the personal intervention of Aphrodite (*Iliad* 3.380ff.).

This archaic view of man as totally and permanently exposed to divine forces beyond his control can be abundantly illustrated from Greek literature down to the fifth century B.C. It is this helplessness of man in the face of superhuman power which is expressed in the various references in archaic poetry to the "ephemerous" condition of man, changing day by day as the gods determine; it is this again which is formulated in Pindar's aphorism: "What is he? What is he not? Man is the dream of a shadow" (*Pythian* 8.95;

see Fränkel, 1960). This sense of the immeasurable gulf between god and man is codified in the wisdom of the seven sages: "Know thyself," namely, that you are a mortal and not a god. New motifs are added in different authors, but the old view can still be discerned in Sophocles' *Oedipus Rex* and in Herodotus' whole conception of human history as a pattern of cyclical reversion between good and evil fortune. When Herodotus uses the term "human nature," he generally has in mind these limitations on human power and fortune in contrast with the unrestricted strength and blessedness of divine beings (III 65.3, VIII 38, 83.1).

This polar opposition between gods and men takes an epistemological form in early philosophic literature. In one of the first explicit generalizations about human nature as such (as distinct from statements about the human condition or situation), Heraclitus says: "Human character (*ēthos*) has no insights, but the divine does" (frag. 78). According to Xenophanes, man can only have guesswork or conjecture (*dokos*) on most matters, where the gods have knowledge of the truth (frag. 34 with A24; cf. Alcmaeon frag. 1). Parmenides' doctrine of true knowledge and reality is presented as the revelation of a goddess, and contrasted with the delusive beliefs (*doxai*) of mortals.

3. The preceding summary of an archaic view of man which emphasizes human helplessness and the arbitrary character of the divine assignment of good and evil fortune is a simplification designed to bring out certain fundamental traits in early Greek thought. Some qualifications are clearly required. For instance, the cult of heroes such as Heracles, Theseus, or Oedipus was an integral part of Greek religious practice (although not recognized as such in Homer). This implies a status and power for certain men *after their death* which tends to blunt the sharp contrast between mortals and immortals as sketched above. Furthermore, the princes and warriors of the Homeric poems are not *slaves* of the gods, as men are said to be in Mesopotamian thought: Athena gives advice to Achilles with courteous respect, like one nobleman speaking to another (*Iliad* 1.207–14). In some aspects of the Homeric hero, and above all in the portrayal of Achilles himself, the notion of the individual as an autonomous moral agent responsible for the consequences of his action is almost as fully developed as in Attic tragedy. Yet it is precisely because mortals live out their lives in the shadow of death and disaster that their action can have the quality of nobility, dignity, and courage; for the gods who know no death, nothing is *serious*.

A more important qualification or alteration of the archaic view is the moralizing tendency in the conception of the gods, or at least in the relations between god and man, with a corresponding emphasis on Justice (*dikē*) as a fundamental principle in human life, a principle which guarantees prosperity or disaster as the retribution for human merit or crime. There are occasional traces of such a view in the *Iliad*, and perhaps in all mythopoetic literature in every land. But it becomes more systematic and conspicuous in the *Odyssey*, where the suitors play the role of villains who are justly punished for their hubris, their reckless transgression of normal restraints, while Odysseus and his son are presented as the wronged parties whose revenge is assured by divine intervention in the person of Athena. This moralizing tendency is underscored by Zeus' remarks in the opening scene of the poem (*Odyssey* 1.32ff.): "Mortals are always blaming the gods; they say their troubles come from us. But they themselves suffer beyond what is allotted to them, because of their own folly." It is above all in Hesiod that we find the principle of Justice personified as a goddess, the daughter of Zeus; and this principle plays a central role in Hesiod's conception of human life and labor. The prospect of the righteous suffering while the wrongdoer goes unpunished seems to Hesiod incompatible with the government of human affairs by Zeus: the dispensation of Zeus to fishes, beasts, and birds is that they eat one another, for there is no Justice among them, but to men he has given *dikē* (*Works and Days* 276ff.). This view of a moral order in human life is developed in Solon's poems with a new application to social and political circumstances. For Solon it is above all the oppression of the poor and weak by the rich and mighty which is characterized as hubris and as an assault upon the holy foundations of Justice (frag. 3.7–14).

On the other hand, in lyric poetry we find a deeper insight into the emotional nature of men. Human passion may still be seen as the action of divine power (sexual passion as the work of Aphrodite, drunkenness as that of Dionysus, and so forth), but the perception of this action is now internalized to such an extent that we may perhaps speak of the "discovery" of emotional experience as such, as an intrinsic property of the human subject rather than an intervention of forces from outside (Snell, Ch. III).

In some poetry which is otherwise not influenced by philosophy, and notably in Pindar, we find a new view of the human soul or *psychē* as immortal, and therefore divine. This view is closely associated with the name of Pythagoras, and hence it might be regarded as part of the philosophic development. Unlike other philosophic doctrines, however, this view became popular or at least widely known at an early date. In some form it seems to have been connected with the promise of blessedness for the initiates in the state

Mysteries of Eleusis; and a similar view of the soul as divine was propagated in certain private cults generally described as "Orphic." The specifically Pythagorean notion of a transmigration of souls is mentioned by Xenophanes and appears to have exerted some influence on Heraclitus and Parmenides. Its most systematic statement in the pre-Platonic period is to be found in the *Katharmoi* of Empedocles. This notion of a deathless *psyche* implies a completely new conception of human nature in its relation to the divine. But the mystic view of the soul, although familiar to authors such as Herodotus and Euripides, does not become a major factor in Greek intellectual history until it is taken up into the myths of Plato.

4. The view of man in Attic tragedy can largely be seen as a working-out of the orthodox archaic conception (above all in Sophocles), under the impact of the more demanding view of divine justice as formulated by Hesiod and Solon. This notion of divine justice is predominant in Aeschylus; it operates in a more problematic or negative way in Euripides, who often seems to be insisting that the destiny of men does *not* conform to any morally acceptable pattern of divine governance. In Sophocles we have "the last great exponent of the archaic world-view" (Dodds, p. 49). All three playwrights are concerned with the inwardness of human experience, insofar as it can be represented on the stage. But Sophocles focuses our attention on the personal strength which is required for a hero to assume and master a role assigned to him by fate or temperament; Aeschylus is above all concerned with the crucial moment of a choice between alternative courses of action (Pelasgus in the *Suppliants;* Agamemnon in his decision to immolate Iphigeneia, symbolically re-enacted by his decision to walk upon the purple carpet spread by his wife). More than the other two, Euripides is concerned with the irrational, destructive power of human passion as such. An occasional trace of philosophic influence may be discerned in Aeschylus and Sophocles; but only in Euripides do we find the decisive impact of new conceptions of human nature worked out or popularized in what we may call the Greek Age of Enlightenment, in the last third of the fifth century B.C. It is the philosophic background of these new views which we must now consider.

5. From the beginning, the philosophic interpretation of nature turns its back on the traditional conception of human life and destiny based upon the fundamental contrast between mortal and immortal, between the helpless human subject and his Olympian masters. The break with this traditional or Homeric view is, as far as we know, only tacit in the Milesian attempt to explain the natural world (including thunder, lightning, earthquake, and other events previously interpreted as the work of the gods) according to physical principles operating in an orderly, intelligible way. The break with the religious tradition becomes explicit in Xenophanes' attack on Homer's and Hesiod's picture of the gods. We cannot follow here the new conceptions of divinity, but we must note that something analogous to the archaic opposition between mortals and immortals is often preserved within the philosophical systems, with a new cosmic power (the Boundless *apeiron* of Anaximander, cosmic Fire of Heraclitus, *Nous* of Anaxagoras) occupying the position of the old Olympian gods. But on the side of mortality the conception of man is an integral part of the conception of nature as a whole, as a system within which things come to be and perish according to principles that are the same for the heavenly bodies, for the whole cosmos, and for the microcosmos which is man. The human condition is still seen as one of exposure to forces which are largely beyond man's control, but these are now the rationally defined forces which constitute the natural order: the hot and the cold, the winds, the waters, and the sun. And within this rational view man is seen, without reference to the gods, as a special kind of animal.

It is in the late fifth century B.C. with Democritus, Thucydides, and the Sophists, that the typically new conceptions of human nature are formulated. These conceptions are conditioned by four notions, three of which derive from the tradition of Ionian natural philosophy going back to Miletus.

In the first place, the physical origin and structure of man is thought of as determined by general forces which operate in the formation of all physical bodies, including the cosmos as a whole. We have a glimpse of this in the doxography for Anaximander, which reports that human beings were first formed in the wet element (perhaps the sea), enclosed in membranes which protected them until they were fully grown and could take up life on land (A30; cf. A11.6 and A10). Thus the emergence of men is part of the general cosmic separating-out of the dry from the moist, the same trend which produces dry land in the first place. In the theory of Empedocles, the tissues or organs of the human body are produced by the combination, in simple proportions, of the same four elements which produce all other bodies in the world. We have an echo of some of these early theories in later accounts of the origin of life, such as that given by Diodorus of Sicily.

In these early theories it is often difficult to distinguish phylogeny, or the origin of the species as such, from ontogeny, or the origin of any given individual. In line with a general tendency to understand structure in terms of genetic development, the world-order is 573 explained by way of a cosmogony and the human organism is explained by an account of its embryonic development. There are traces of such explanations for Parmenides, Empedocles, and others; and we possess more detailed accounts in the Hippocratic Corpus. The etymological sense of *physis* ("nature") is "growth" or "development." On the other hand, the word also designates the mature structure or constitution of an organism (or any other body), e.g., its composition, which results from elements being blended and balanced in various ways. In the medical treatises, health is generally regarded as a symmetrical blend or equilibrium of opposing powers, while disease is explained by the excess or predominance of some one power or constituent. The earliest known instance of such a view of health is assigned to Alcmaeon of Croton, who is probably to be dated in the early fifth century. A full account is given in the treatise *On the Nature of Man*, ascribed to Polybus the son-in-law of Hippocrates. According to this author (writing about 400 B.C., i.e., at the end of our period), the structure of the human body in health and disease is determined by the interaction of four fluids, which bear a certain analogy to the four elements of Empedocles. "The body of man contains blood and phlegm and yellow bile and black bile, and these are the nature (*physis*) of his body; and it is because of these that he suffers or enjoys health. He is most healthy when these are mingled in due proportion to one another in power and quantity; he suffers when there is too little or too much of one of these, or when one is separated in the body and not blended with the rest" (Ch. 4). This author does not discuss questions of intelligence or consciousness; in other treatises such as *On the Sacred Disease*, these phenomena are explained by the presence of air in the brain and veins. The theory of a connection between air and intelligence (a theory mocked in Aristophanes' *Clouds*) can be traced back to the Ionian tradition of natural philosophy, where we find it expressed by Diogenes of Apollonia (frag. 4: "men and other animals live by breathing the air, and this is their *psychē* and their thought or intelligence"; cf. frag. 5). The earliest known statement is that of Anaximenes, whose view is quoted by a later writer as follows: "As our soul which is air controls us, so breath and air surround and control the whole world-order" (frag. 2). Other authors identify intelligence or thought (*nous*) with the entire constitution of the body, as organized in the mixture of elements. Thus Parmenides identifies mortal thinking with "the *physis* of men's limbs," consisting of a combination of Night and Light as the two elementary physical principles (frag. 16). Empedocles echoes this doctrine and situates human thinking (*noēma*) above all in the blood around the heart, as

the place where the four elements are most perfectly blended (frag. 105): as the *physis* or physical constitution varies for different men, so does their character or *ēthos* (frag. 110.5).

6. So far we have considered only physical and biological theories of human nature. But even more important for the new view of man are certain sociological theories which also develop in connection with philosophic speculation as to the origin of things. The physical doctrines just described seek to explain the origin of the species; but how did men come to live as they do today (i.e., in the fifth century B.C.), in cities governed by laws and binding customs (*nomoi*)? More generally, how did human *culture* arise? Again, we find systematic discussion of these questions only in much later authors, in Lucretius *On the Nature of Things*, Book V, and in the introduction to the Universal History of Diodorus of Sicily. But there is good reason to believe that the early versions of these theories were formulated in the fifth century. We have hints of speculation concerning the origin of human culture and society in a few early fragments, for example, Xenophanes frag. 18: "The gods certainly did not show all things to men from the beginning, but by seeking they find what is better in the course of time." We know that Protagoras wrote on "The situation [of man?] in the beginning," but we do not know how his account ran. (Many scholars have used the mythological account of the origin of human civilization given by Protagoras in Plato's dialogue of that name to reconstruct the doctrine of Protagoras' lost work on "the state of nature." But since Plato's version involves the direct intervention of the gods, it cannot be an *exact* account of Protagoras' own view. And we have really no way of knowing how far Plato has adapted Protagoras' doctrine to his own purposes in the dialogue.)

Aeschylus' *Prometheus Bound* contains a long and important speech (vv. 458–84) in which the god enumerates the arts which he bestowed upon man. This passage probably reflects some philosophical account of human culture which is older than Protagoras; it may well be the theory of Anaxagoras. But whereas the poet ascribes the development of civilization to Prometheus, Anaxagoras seems to have attributed it to the special *physis* of the human hand, which makes man alone a tool-using or tool-making creature, and hence the most intelligent and "cultivated" of animals. (Anaxagoras, frag. 21B; the context in Aristotle, *De partibus animalium* 687 A7–23 makes clear that it was the acquisition of arts or *technai* that Anaxagoras had in mind.) It is the same admiration for the achievements of human culture—measured not against the gods but by reference to other animals—that we find echoed in the famous ode of Sophocles: "Many are the marvels (of the earth), but none more marvelous than man" (*Antigone* 332ff.).

The fifth-century philosophical theories concerning the origin of culture are mostly lost, though we have a brief doxographical account of one such theory for Archelaus, a pupil of Anaxagoras (Diels-Kranz, 60.A1.16, 4.6). The most important surviving text from the fifth century is a fragment of the *Sisyphus* of Critias, which is concerned not with technological but with moral and political culture. Written by the future leader of the Thirty Tyrants, these verses describe, first, a time in which "the life of men was disorderly, bestial, and subject to [the rule of] strength, when there was no prize for good men nor any punishment for evil." Then men established laws (*nomoi*) and punishment "so that justice might rule and hold crime (*hybris*) as her slave." But these laws prevented only open wrongdoing. To prevent wrongdoing in secret, some clever man invented the fear of the gods as a deterrent. He declared that the gods are omniscient and that they dwell in the most impressive region, the sky, whence come the terrors of lightning and thunder and the blessings of rain and sunshine. Thus he quenched lawlessness with "the sweetest of teachings, and concealed the truth with a false tale" (Critias, frag. 25).

The verses of Critias present us with a definite theory as to the man-made origin of human law (*nomoi*) as well as of the belief in the gods. This may count as the second basic notion derived, indirectly, from Ionian natural philosophy. A third comes from Miletus by way of the world travellers and ethnologists Hecataeus and Herodotus. The interest in strange lands leads to an interest in strange customs, and to a realization that men differ even more in their notions of the right and wrong ways to honor the dead, for example, than they do in their physical characteristics. Hence comes an awareness of the great force of custom or convention, on the one hand ("*nomos* is king of all men," says Herodotus, III, 38.4, echoing Pindar), with an increased sense of the relative uniformity of man's *physis*, or physical nature. "We are kinsmen and fellow-citizens by nature," says the Sophist Prodicus of Ceos in Plato's *Protagoras* (337 C–D); it is only "*nomos*, which is a tyrant among men," that has made the participants in the dialogue strangers to one another, since they come from different cities. The point is made even more generally by Antiphon: "by nature we are all alike, both Greek and barbarian" (frag. 44, Diels-Kranz).

The final ingredient in the new conception of man in the late fifth century seems to be derived from common sense and shrewd observation rather than from any explicit philosophic theory. This is a view of human beings as basically motivated by self-regarding and essentially anti-social appetites, of which the most conspicuous are sexual passion and the intrinsically unlimited desire for wealth and power.

7. In summing up now the new view of man in the Greek Enlightenment (or in the so-called Age of the Sophists), for simplicity two phases will be distinguished: a more conservative view formulated by Protagoras (ca. 450–30 B.C.), and a more radical view to be found after 430 B.C. in Antiphon, in Aristophanes' *Clouds*, and (in various forms) in Thucydides' *History*. It is the second view which is expressed by the basic opposition between *nomos* and *physis*, such as we find for example in the great speech of Callicles in Plato's *Gorgias*.

An evolutionary or naturalist view of *nomoi* as man-made need not be subversive of traditional institutions in its intended moral and political application. (We may compare this first view with the conservative doctrines of the social contract in Hobbes and Hume.) For Protagoras, the doctrine that man is the measure of all things seems to have meant that what a given society regards as right and good really is right and good (for the members of that society). There is no other criterion of evaluation or obligation; the institutionalized judgment of men expressed in their *nomoi* is the only criterion, and it is valid as such. (This is at least the interpretation of Protagoras' view given by Plato in *Theatetus* 167C.)

From similar factual premises as to the human origin of moral standards, other fifth-century thinkers drew a much more radical conclusion. This is baldly stated by Antiphon the Sophist as a direct opposition between a man's natural interests and the conventional restraints which society would impose upon him. The formula for this opposition is *physis* versus *nomos*, Nature against Convention (or Nature against Law and Custom). The idea of a fundamental divergence between human *nomos* and the nature of things can be traced back as far as Parmenides, who describes the erroneous views of mortals in terms of their "customary beliefs" (*nomizein*, frag. 6.8) and the words or names which they have mistakenly imposed on the objects of opinion (8.38, 8.53, 9.1, 10.3; compare *nomizein* and *nomos* for a misleading form of speech about physical processes in Anaxagoras, frag. 17 and Empedocles, frag. 9.5). Thus the *nomos-physis* antithesis first emerges as an epistemological formula for the contrast of Appearance and Reality. The most striking and important expression of this view is in the famous statement of Democritus (frag. 9): "By custom (*nomos*) there is sweet, by custom there is bitter, by custom hot, by custom cold, by custom color; in truth there are atoms and void."

It is this antithesis which is restated as a moral theory in Antiphon's discussion of Justice: "Most of the things 575 which are just by law (*nomos*) are hostile to nature (*physis*). . . . Those acts which the laws prohibit are no more agreeable or more akin to nature than those which they command. . . . The advantages which are established by laws are chains upon nature, but those which are established by nature are free." Since there is no divine sanction for human prescriptions, the lucid man will ignore them and do as he pleases, taking measures simply to avoid punishment. We find this view in comic parody in Aristophanes: since it is a man who first made the *nomos* against striking one's father by persuading other men, says Pheidippides, why can't I make a new law in turn? (*Clouds* 1421ff.). It is with reference to such thowing-off of conventional chains that the speaker called "Unjust Argument" urges his disciples to deprive themselves of no pleasure, including adultery, but to yield to "the necessities of nature": "Follow me, enjoy nature, frolic, laugh, deem nothing shameful" (ibid. 1071–78). It is essentially the same view which we find more seriously stated by Callicles in the *Gorgias* and by Glaucon in Book II of the *Republic*. In the Platonic statements this view is connected with the assumption of an original compact, such as we find hinted at in the fifth-century passage of Critias quoted above: vexed at being taken advantage of by a few strong and unscrupulous characters, the mass of men agreed to outlaw certain forms of conduct and to impose penalties upon them. But the strong and clever man is not bound by these restrictions, which are designed only to hold him down and to prevent him from getting what he is strong enough to take.

It would be inaccurate to say that this view (which is that of the historical Antiphon and probably of the historical Critias, as well as that of the Platonic Callicles and of some characters in Aristophanes' comedy) is also the view of Thucydides. But the picture of human nature and conduct in Thucydides' *History* is determined by the presence of such a view in the background. We can see this most clearly in the words of the Melian Dialogue: "Justice is a consideration among men only when the forces are equal; but the strong do what they can and the weak suffer what they must." (For, as Hobbes was later to point out, there is no pretense of a social compact between nations.) More generally, "Of gods we believe, and of men we know, that by a necessity of their nature they rule as far as their power permits" (Thucydides, V. 89, 105.2). In the growth of the Athenian empire Thucydides sees the action of the permanent motivating forces in human nature: fear, honor or ambition, and the accumulation of economic profit leading to political power (I. 75–76; cf. 1–19). In the disaster of Melos as in the later disaster of Athens he sees the result of

such forces aided and abetted by human folly with the concomitant action of chance or the unexpected turn of events. It is because of the constancy of human nature—or more exactly of the human condition (*to anthrōpinon*), the interaction of man's natural desires and fears, his plans and folly, with his changing circumstances—that the future must resemble the past, so that an accurate and perceptive history can be a permanently useful possession for the one who seeks to understand (but is not always able to alter) the course of events (I. 22). In the last analysis, Thucydides' view of human nature as revealed in human history may be closer in spirit to the archaic conception of mortal helplessness than one could suppose, but rendered more tragic by the total absence here of any positive contrast of the kind provided by the traditional notion of the gods. The historian's view of man as defined by his action is ultimately that of a creature "incapable of comprehending his position within the limitations of a present moment" in which he is obliged to act (Stahl, p. 171).

8. Like Thucydides, Democritus and Socrates are men of the Greek Enlightenment, and their views of human nature are conditioned by the collapse of the traditional sense of supernatural control over human action and destiny. Like Thucydides, both men grew up in the generation which had heard or read Protagoras' statements, that man is the measure of all things and "concerning the gods, I am not able to know whether they exist or do not exist" (frag. 4). For both men the response takes the form of a reassertion of traditional Greek values such as justice and temperance or moderation (*sōphrosynē*), but on a purely naturalistic basis, in other words, on the basis of a view of human nature which claims that moral action towards other men and towards the political community as a whole is in a man's *own* best interest. Democritus argued his case on the grounds of an enlightened hedonism: "If one oversteps due measure, the things which are most pleasant will become most unpleasant." "Moderation (*sōphrosynē*) increases enjoyment, and makes pleasure even greater" (frags. 233 and 211). Bodily needs are limited and easily satisfied; what causes distress and hardship is excessive desire due to a misdirected aim of the mind (frag. 223; cf. 159). For Democritus as for Socrates, "happiness and unhappiness belong to the *psychē*" (frag. 170), and wisdom heals the soul of passion as medicine cures the body of disease (frag. 31). Since the happiness of the individual depends upon the common good and the well-being of the city, the life of rational pleasure or "cheerfulness" for the individual coincides with the life of just and lawful action with a mind at ease (frags. 174, 252, 287). Since the soul or mind is itself explained in terms of atoms in motion, it is probable that Democritus founded his theory of happiness and moral action on a thoroughgoing materialism, but the details of his doctrine on this point are not clear.

In the absence of reliable independent evidence, it is impossible to separate an account of Socrates from an interpretation of the Platonic dialogues. (The former view that Xenophon was a reliable source for our knowledge of the "historical" Socrates is now largely abandoned; in many cases Xenophon is not even independent of Plato.) It is in the *Apology* and *Crito,* if anywhere, that we catch a glimpse of the real Socrates. A few characteristic features of his view of human nature may be noted here. If we set aside the corporealist account of the soul offered by the atomists and the emphasis upon pleasure, a certain general similarity to Democritus' moral position is very striking. All good things for the individual and the community depend upon excellence (*aretē*) of the soul (*Apology* 29D–30B). The fundamental reason for refusing to do an unjust act is that it would corrupt that part of us "which is harmed by injustice and benefited by what is just"; and the life of one whose soul is corrupt is not worth living (*Crito* 47E). Thus the moral life is self-regarding, and ultimately secure: "no evil can happen to a good man, whether in life or in death" (*Apology* 41D). Hence no one does wrong willingly, but in ignorance of the good—of the morally good, which is the good life itself. In this view moral virtue is simply knowledge of what is good for a man, and the life of philosophy is the life of inquiry. If the *Apology* is to be trusted, Socrates embedded this intellectual and individualistic ethic within the old contrast of mortal and immortal, insisting paradoxically that his only wisdom lay in the recognition of his ignorance: no man is wise, but only the god (23A). Socrates set the seal upon this extraordinary teaching by his own life and death. It was left for Plato (in the myths of the afterlife, the doctrine of intelligible Forms, and the moral psychology of the *Republic*) to provide a fuller philosophical justification for the view of man enshrined in the Socratic paradoxes.

BIBLIOGRAPHY

For the pre-philosophical conceptions of human nature, see Hermann Fränkel, *Dichtung und Philosophie des frühen Griechentums,* 2nd ed. (Munich, 1962), and idem, *Wege und Formen frühgriechischen Denkens,* 2nd ed. (Munich, 1960), esp. pp. 23–35; Bruno Snell, *Die Entdeckung des Geistes,* 3rd ed. (Hamburg, 1955); trans. T. G. Rosenmeyer as *The Discovery of the Mind* (Cambridge, Mass., 1953), esp. Chs. I, III, VII, and VIII; E. R. Dodds, *The Greeks and the Irrational* (Berkeley, 1951), esp. Chs. I–II; an excellent summary with fuller references in J. Mansfeld, *Die Offenbarung*

des Parmenides und die menschliche Welt (Assen, 1964), Ch. I, pp. 1–41.

Fragments of the early philosophical writings are quoted from Diels and Kranz, *Fragmente der Vorsokratiker,* 7th ed., 2 vols. (Berlin, 1954). For secondary literature see the references in W. K. C. Guthrie, *A History of Greek Philosophy,* Vol. I. (Cambridge and New York, 1962), and Vol. II (Cambridge and New York, 1965). For the Sophists, see Guthrie, Vol. III (1969) and Werner Jaeger, *Paideia,* trans. Gilbert Highet (New York, 1939), I, 286–331. See also: Felix Heinimann, *Nomos und Physis* (Basel, 1945); W. K. C. Guthrie, *In the Beginning* (Ithaca, N.Y., 1957); Thomas Cole, *Democritus and the Sources of Greek Anthropology* (Cleveland, 1967), with full bibliography. For Thucydides see Hans-Peter Stahl, *Thukydides. Die Stellung des Menschen im geschichtlichen Prozess* (Munich, 1966).

CHARLES H. KAHN

[See also **Cultural Development in Antiquity;** Historiography, Influence of Ideas on Ancient Greek; Macrocosm and Microcosm; **Platonism.**]

PRIMITIVISM

Primitivism is a name for a cluster of ideas arising from meditations on the course of human history and the value of human institutions and accomplishments. It is found in two forms, chronological and cultural, each of which may exist as "soft" or "hard" primitivism.

I. FORMS OF PRIMITIVISM

Chronological primitivism maintains that the earliest stage of human history was the best, that the earliest period of national, religious, artistic, or in fact any strand of history was better than the periods that have followed, that childhood is better than maturity. In short, it argues that to discover the best stage of any historical series one must return to its origin. Primitive man, for instance, was better than civilized man, primitive Christianity was better than later developments of Christianity, the arts of savages and children are better than those of educated men and adults.

Cultural primitivism maintains that whatever additions have been made to what is called the "natural" condition of mankind have been deleterious. Unfortunately the meanings of the natural are so multiple that cultural primitivists vary widely in what they consider to be the state of nature. They are often chronological primitivists as well, but this is not inevitable. One may believe that a complete absence of civilized institutions is a blessing and yet think that primitive man was as much beset by them as modern man. Or one may think that man as he first appeared on earth was gifted with all that man requires to live well and yet not to believe that such requirements are sufficient for modern man. Logically one may be both a chronological and a cultural primitivist, a chronological but not a cultural primitivist, a cultural but not a chronological primitivist, or neither one nor the other.

Hard primitivism is the doctrine that man is happiest when he is not burdened with arts and sciences, lives with the fewest possible needs, is satisfied with the simplest of lives. A cave suffices for a house, acorns for food, the skins of wild beasts for clothing, a heap of dried leaves for a bed. The hard primitivist is likely to hold up the animals as exemplars; for they ask, he will say, for no more than Mother Nature has given them at birth. When the hard primitivist is also a chronological primitivist, he will maintain that at the earliest period of human history man lived as the animals do, without luxuries. But he is not forced to be a chronological primitivist; he may simply believe that men are overburdened with unnecessary desires and that they should "return to Nature" or to the "simple life."

Soft primitivism maintains that the best life is the life without toil, the sort of life that was sometimes depicted as characteristic of the islands of the South Seas where the climate is gentle, the earth spontaneously productive, the animals friendly, the sea full of fish easily caught. Soft primitivism often accompanies chronological primitivism, as it did in the legend of the Golden Age or in one version of life before the Fall.

II. CHRONOLOGICAL PRIMITIVISM

1. Chronological Primitivism in Classical Antiquity.

Chronological primitivism in occidental culture is found in two forms, that of classical antiquity and that of Christianity. In classical antiquity this doctrine was first expressed in the legend of the Ages. Our earliest version of this legend is that given by Hesiod in his *Works and Days*. In this version, which is probably a fusion of two different myths, there are five ages, beginning with the Golden Age—or the "Golden Race" as Hesiod himself puts it—proceeding through the Silver, the Bronze, the Age of Heroes, and our own, the Iron Age. The insertion of the Age of Heroes breaks the series of progressive degeneration, for the Heroes are demigods who, instead of dying, are translated to the Islands of the Blessed. But the other ages indicate a steady worsening of mankind. In the Golden Age Kronos is king, life is free from work and is merry, the earth produces its fruits spontaneously, and there is neither war nor violence. Thus the lot of mankind is easy and morals are good.

The men of the Silver Age are not descendants of their historical predecessors, but a fresh creation. Why the Golden Age disappeared is not told us by Hesiod but the Silver Race has a very protracted infancy, though it does not fit them for a vigorous maturity. On the contrary, they are mentally retarded, violent, irreligious, and are destroyed by Zeus because of their impiety. Nothing is said of the economic condition of these men; the emphasis is on their physiological and moral deterioration. People of this race are wiped out because of their wickedness.

The Bronze Race is also a new creation. Hesiod's text is not clear about how its members compare in qualities with the Silver Race, but in themselves they are strong and terrible. Their strength, which would seem to be an improvement on the debility of the Silver Race, is not praised by Hesiod, and indeed his dislike of them comes out when he says that they ended in mass suicide and not through any action of Zeus. The Heroes are obviously superior to both the Bronze and the Silver Races. They are the men who fought in the Trojan War and figured in the great mythical cycles. In spite of their superiority to their predecessors, they too fell victim to war. Their life in the Islands of the Blessed, however, is free from sorrow and, like the Golden Race, they enjoy fruits plentifully produced from the earth. Whether Earth produces these fruits spontaneously or not is not clearly stated, but it is likely that the Islands of the Blessed reproduced the land of the Golden Race.

Our own race, that of Iron, is the worst. It is a period of greater and greater degeneration and our race will disappear when it is "born with greying temples." It is characterized by intrafamily quarreling, unfilial behavior, violence, war, disregard for moral qualities, high regard for insolence. "Right will be might and modesty will no longer exist," is Hesiod's prophecy. The two goddesses Shame (*aidos*) and Indignation (*nemesis*) will leave the earth in disgust and evil will prevail. At that point we shall disappear. Thus the cause of the race's destruction is its own wickedness coupled with physical degeneration.

The elements of this myth are greatly mixed. The use of the four metals to name the ages would seem to be an indication that one factor in the story is the theme of steady deterioration, perhaps inherent in human nature. But the fact that the gods destroyed the first two races and created new ones to take their places breaks the series; and the first race, that of gold, did nothing to merit destruction. The first age, moreover, is that governed by Kronos and the later are all governed by Zeus, so that one of the elements of the myth may be the dethronement of Kronos by his son and the theme of two ages only, as it appears in some

of the later writers. But the castration and dethronement of Kronos by his son does not seem to fit in with
the other theme of progressive deterioration. Nor does
it seem fitting that a god as bloodthirsty as Zeus is in
castrating his father should have been powerful at so
blessed a time. But Hesiod is not remarkable for consistency. The interpolation of the Age of Heroes is
another discordant note. It is actually better than the
Silver Age, if not the Golden, and a special creation
of Zeus. But since the poet was not an admirer of
warlike men, it is strange to find these extraordinarily
brave warriors praised and given terrestrial immortality with some of the pleasures of the Golden Age.
Subsequent writers omit this period of history, presumably to smooth out the inconsistencies. Again, there
is no reason why this period should have been followed
by the worst of ages. Hesiod seems simply to have
transferred his dislike for his contemporaries to his
myth of historical development.

Hesiod's story must have lingered on in the minds
of seventh-, sixth-, and fifth-century writers, for we find
echoes of it in the *Alcmaeonid* as well as in Theognis.
But, as far as is detectable now, these writers emphasize
the moral deterioration of mankind rather than the
physiological. So Aratus, a third-century didactic poet,
in his *Phaenomena* (lines 96–136), removes most of the
inconsistencies of Hesiod by reducing the number of
ages to three and telling a story of increasing wickedness. He also inserts a blood relationship between the
races. Each is a descendant of the preceding one and
none are fresh creations. Why the generations should
have deteriorated morally is not explained, but that
they did is stated dogmatically. There are, however,
hints of innovations which Aratus probably thought
were causes of "injustice." There was, for instance, no
international trade in the Golden Age: ships "did not
carry men's livelihood from afar." Men lived a simple
agricultural life. The goddess Justice dwelt among men.
But when the Silver Race appeared, she mingled seldom and no longer with great eagerness, "longing for
the manners of the ancient people." She did her best
to keep men in her path, but they were wayward and
soon there appeared the Bronze Race which, for
Aratus, is the worst. Its people were the first to forge
swords and to eat meat, and Justice was so disgusted
that she went off to heaven where she appears in the
skies as the constellation Virgo. The factors of vegetarianism and pacifism had come into the myth earlier
in the works of Empedocles, the Sicilian philosopher
(fl. ca. 444 B.C.), who does not write a story of four
ages but of two, that of Love and that of Strife, each
of whom in turn governs history. In the reign of Love
(*Cypris*) all warfare ceases and there is no sacrifice of
animals, for men think slaughter and the eating of flesh

an abomination. But this is a cyclical account of history
and the reign of Love occurs indefinitely, cycle after
cycle. It is worth pointing out in passing that the steady
emphasis by all writers on the vegetarianism of primitive man is characteristic of ancient primitivists and
reappears as late as Pope's *Essay on Man* (III, 147–60).

The poem of Aratus, which as a whole was about
astronomy and not about history, had considerable
popularity in ancient times. Achilles Tatius is said to
have written an introduction to it as well as a commentary, and another commentary was written by
Hipparchus. There were three known Latin translations: one by Cicero in his *De natura deorum* (II, 41),
one ascribed to Germanicus Caesar, and one to Festus
Avienus. Such works were really astrological. There
were also parodies of the Golden Age, "when Kronos
was king," in the Greek comic poets, the burden of
which was the legendary soft primitivism of the period.
Life was described as in the legend of the Land of
Cockaigne, in which rivers of porridge flowed through
the land and roast hams and fish, pigs' ribs already
roasted stood ready to be eaten. Clearly there were
Greeks who were as skeptical of such legends as they
were of the whole Greek mythology.

In Latin literature as it has come down to us, the
ages were usually reduced to two, that of Saturn and
that of Jupiter. In Tibullus, for instance (*Elegies* II, iii,
35–46, 63–74) the Golden Age, as in Empedocles, was
the Age of Love, whereas the Iron Age was that of
pillage. Pillage is the source of war, navies, large estates, and luxury. But in the Age of Gold, love was
free; "there was no guardian, no gate to shut out
grieving lovers." This was presumably enough to his
way of thinking to recommend a return to it. Now
in the Iron Age there are strife, slaughter, foreign trade,
and private property: the fields are hemmed in to feed
countless flocks. But there is a faint hint of hard primitivism when Tibullus wishes that the vineyards which
keep girls in the country might disappear and "the
acorn and water would be our food *prisco more* ['in
the ancient manner']." Our primitive ancestors made
love openly in shady nooks; there was none of the
artificiality of modern times.

The more obvious continuator of the Hesiodic-
Aratean tradition in Latin literature was Ovid, who
in his *Metamorphoses* (I, 76–215) outlines the story. In
Ovid, however, our own race is descended from none
of those named by Hesiod; it is the progeny of the
stones thrown behind their backs by Deucalion and
Pyrrha. Ovid's Golden Age is free of almost all the
institutions which characterize his own time. Men were
faithful and righteous by nature and thus had no need
for laws. There were no punishments for evil deeds
since there were no evil deeds. Again, shipping had

not been invented and towns were without walls. There was no need of armies to guard them. And Earth, as in Hesiod, "untouched by the hoe and unwounded by the ploughshare," gave food freely to her children. Striking a note of hard primitivism, Ovid points out that the first men were satisfied with wild fruits and berries along with acorns. "Spring was eternal and the placid Zephyrs with warm breezes lightly touched the flowers, born without seeds . . . rivers of milk and rivers of nectar flowed, and yellow honey dripped from the green oaks." Here then we have what might be called "juristic primitivism," pacifism, the absence of foreign trade and travel, technological primitivism, and vegetarianism together with echoes of soft primitivism, primeval innocence in the Land of Cockaigne.

But, according to Ovid, this was not to endure. Jupiter took over the throne from his father Saturn and the Silver Race appeared. The year was divided into four seasons, men began to live in houses, agriculture was instituted, and "bullocks groaned under the weight of the yoke." Then came the Bronze Race, more savage than its predecessor and more belligerent, "yet not utterly wicked." Like Aratus Ovid omits the Age of Heroes. The utterly wicked are men of the Iron Age. Shame, truth, and faith all fled. Deceit, trickery, and treachery took their place. Shipping was invented and also property. Agriculture wounded Mother Earth and, worse than that, mining was started; mining which by bringing up gold, "more noxious than iron," paved the way for war. Men lived by plunder and no one was safe from either stranger or kinsman. Men lost their sense of duty (*pietas*) and the Virgin Astraea, Justice, left the earth. There followed the War of the Giants and finally a Deluge wiped the evil race from off the face of the earth. Nor does Ovid, like some other poets, suggest that the Golden Age may return in some future near or remote.

It was no doubt Ovid who kept the Hesiodic legend alive in medieval Europe, for the Greek poets were largely lost. It was Ovid who transmitted the notion that in primitive times land was owned in common. The emphasis moreover is upon two ages, not four or five: the Age of Saturn and that of Jupiter.

In fact the Age of Saturn became synonymous with the ancient past. And there are intimations that Jupiter gave us a better age than his father had been able to provide. But that side of the story belongs to a history of the idea of progress. Now Saturn was originally a Latin god and it is difficult, if possible, to reconcile some of his traits with those of Kronos, though the two were fused. Like Kronos he ruled the world before Jupiter or Zeus did and his reign was noted for its blessings: leisure, peace, abundant food, absence of private property, evil passions, and sometimes of slaves.

But nevertheless he was a bloodthirsty god who swallowed his children and castrated his father. By turning him into a culture-hero and eliminating the supernatural elements in the myths, it was possible to think of him as a primitive king who had taught his subjects how to live in communities, gave them laws, no longer a curse, and brought them out of primeval barbarism. But this version, which is not purely primitivistic, we owe to Vergil (*Aeneid* VIII, 314–27). Before Vergil's Age of Saturn there existed a race of men born of tree trunks and hard oak, who were utterly uncivilized, had no agriculture or wealth, and lived by hunting and gathering food. This race is not praised by Vergil nor does he show any sympathy for cultural primitivism in this place. His contemporary, Tibullus, however, thinks of the Saturnians as the most primitive of peoples and he describes their life in glowing terms and generally as soft. In line with the tradition we have already mentioned, he describes them as knowing nothing of shipping, foreign trade, agriculture, private property. "The oaks themselves gave honey and ewes offered their udders full of milk to untroubled men" (*Elegies* I, iii, 35–52). These men were pacific and friendly. But now, under Jupiter, their descendants have become belligerent, murderous, laying out "a thousand roads to sudden death."

There is a second version of primitive life in Ovid where he tells of Pythagoras (*Metamorphoses* XV, 75–142). Here the philosopher is represented as exhorting men to give up their animal diet and to live on fruits and berries, milk, and wild honey. This was what the Golden Race had done. They treated the animals, moreover, as fellow farmers (*vestros colonos*). These accounts of primitive times could be duplicated by passages in other works of Ovid (*Amores* III, viii, 35–56) and even of Lucian (*Saturnian Letters* I, 20). But quotation from such passages one by one would be otiose.

It is more important to turn to Juvenal (*Satire* XIII, 28–59), where a fierce attack on contemporary society is made in favor of early times. Our own age, he says, is so base that there is no metal base enough to name it. One is called a simpleton when one demands that oaths be held sacred; our crimes are nameless. But under Saturn men lived without arts and luxuries and there was no need of instruments of torture to make men tell the truth. A heap of acorns was sufficient for food. Juvenal does not hesitate to represent primeval life as close to that of the animals. In his sixth *Satire* (1–24) he points out that an icy cavern was home enough for a man, a mass of leaves for a bed. The wife "bore breasts to feed great children and was often more savage than her acorn-belching mate." These men had no private property and they knew nothing of adultery.

Thus the hard primitivism of Juvenal is mitigated by certain features of the more idyllic versions of history. And he carries on as well the Hesiodic story that after the Golden Age Shame and Justice fled from earth to live in heaven.

Ironically Saturn, who had conferred upon mankind so many benefits, became a ludicrous figure later on. The Greeks used the name of Kronos in compounds and derivatives to mean dim-sighted, senile foolishness, nonsense, antiquated ideas. The planet Saturn became a malignant body. The fact that Kronos (and presumably Saturn) was the oldest of the gods identified him with very ancient times, and it was easy to equate antiquity with senility. Possibly it was the identification of Saturn with Moloch, who also swallowed little children, that gave the planet its bad name. Yet when the planet became the symbol of philosophy and mathematics, to say nothing of melancholy, a more favorable view could be taken of the god. But to consider the transformation of the ancient gods into planets and stars would take us beyond our range.

2. *The Return of the Golden Age.* One form of chronological primitivism locates the best period of history at the beginning of each cycle. We have already seen this suggested in Empedocles. The Stoics in particular maintained that history on a grand scale manifested an eternal recurrence. They usually held that they derived their theory of cycles from Heraclitus, who may be interpreted as believing that each cycle ended with a cosmic conflagration (the *ekpyrosis*), after which all things would begin once more and continue to repeat the history of the previous cycles. This version dates back at least to the fourth century B.C., though it is by no means certain that Heraclitus, a sixth-to fifth-century figure, held any such theory. As for Empedocles, we have already mentioned his Age of Love. Whether this is to be thought of as the beginning or end of a cycle is disputable, for the image of eternal recurrence by its very nature excludes beginnings. Yet there need be no uncertainty that in the mind of Empedocles the Age of Love would return with all its blessings, and these blessings were those of the traditional Golden Age. So the Sybilline Oracles foretold a return to a period of happiness when "all-bearing earth will give her best fruit without end to mortals, bread, wine, and wild olive." All the old refrains are heard again, the disappearance of war and violence as well as a return to peace and plenty. But since these *Oracles* are as a whole apocalyptic prophecies and show no firm evidence that they were based on a doctrine of cycles—though the language used in some of them is affiliated with that of Stoicism—they may be out of place here. But one document that must be included is Vergil's famous *Fourth Eclogue.* The pur-

pose of this poem and its use by Christian apologists, beginning with Constantine, are too much a matter of debate to be dealt with here. We mention simply as a case of predicting the return of the Golden Age when in Shelley's words, in the concluding chorus of *Hellas,* "the world's great age begins anew." Vergil predicts that the Golden Age is at hand in the consulship of Pollio and that a child will be born on whom Earth "untilled" will bestow her blessings. All the evils both of human nature and of the Iron Age will disappear and the regime of soft primitivism will once more be instituted. But the *Fourth Eclogue* and its many imitations belong to the story of Millenarianism rather than to that of primitivism and we leave it here with this simple mention.

3. *Chronological Primitivism in Christianity.* The condition of Adam before the Fall in the Garden of Eden is the Judeo-Christian equivalent of life in the Golden Age. In the first chapter of Genesis Adam, created in the image and likeness of God, is given dominion over the earth and all its creatures; in the second chapter he is ordered to "dress and keep" the Garden. The amount of work involved was presumably thought of as light and pleasant, prelapsarian life as easy and delightful. There are, however, very few details given in Scripture of just what Adam and Eve did before they met the Serpent; but later writers filled in the gaps, as Milton was to do, by imagining what was most pleasant and by asserting that it existed at the earliest period of human history. On the whole they excluded from primitive life all forms of hard primitivism. Man's condition before the Fall was, when dwelt upon in any detail, like life in the Golden Age, accounts of which the Christian writers could get from Ovid, if they had no text of Hesiod. There was a complete absence of whatever an author believed to be an evil, whether a defect of human nature or of the natural landscape.

The early Fathers paid little attention to the original condition of man. With one exception—the *Epistle to Diognetus,* which is later than the second century—the name and mention of Adam and the Tree of Knowledge do not appear in any of the patristic writings. But when we come to a late second-century writer, Theophilus, we find in his letter to Autolycus an account of the life of the first human couple which is in part well in the tradition of soft primitivism. Adam, we are told, was created innocent and happy, had no suffering, and knew no toil; earth, as in the Golden Age, gave him spontaneously of her fruits and the beasts were friendly. But at the same time man's original condition was not intended by God to be permanent. It was meant to be the first stage in man's continuous moral improvement, an idea which was to recur in Lessing in the eighteenth century. Whether this applied to the whole human race or to Adam alone is not clear, but there is a hint that Theophilus believed that history was to exhibit an educational process in religion at least. It should be noted that in this account Adam stands for man in the state of childhood. That is why God forbade him to eat of the fruit of the Tree of Knowledge; he was not yet ready to digest it. In the words of Theophilus, "When a child is born, it is not able to eat bread, but is first fed on milk, and then with its advance in years it proceeds to solid food. So it was with Adam." In our own time the innocence of childhood has been repeatedly held up as a model for adults (see below), and we find here, in this description of Adam, an anticipation of a kind of anti-intellectualism which was not intended by its author.

In Tertullian an additional bit of information is given us. Man up to the time of the Deluge was a vegetarian, for God disapproved of eating flesh. But after the Deluge God extended the permissible diet of men on the ground that morality demands freedom of choice: though it was better to be a vegetarian than a carnivore, it was best to be free to choose one's diet. Adam and Eve before the Fall were emotionally and even physically children; they had neither attained the age of reason nor even puberty. Yet Tertullian elsewhere asserts that the human soul was created in a purely rational condition and that our irrational faculties were added after we had yielded to the temptation of the Serpent. It was impossible to reconcile the idea of our primordial juvenility with rationality and our rationality with our yielding to the gullet, as he puts it, to our appetite for sensual pleasure. But Tertullian was not too respectful of logical consistency, and he gives us a picture of primitive man as sexually immature, rational, and mentally a child; and furthermore, the image of God.

Similar confusions can be found in the Pseudo-Clementine *Homilies* and *Recognitions,* which are now generally believed to date from the third century. Basically they all assert that Adam was created in the most perfect of conditions, so perfect in fact that Saint Peter is made to say in the *Homilies* that since Adam was created in the image of God, he must have possessed foreknowledge and could not have sinned through ignorance. But Eve on the other hand was the very principle of evil, and it was through her that death and war and false prophecy came into the world. This seems to be the beginning in extant Christian literature of the attribution to woman of whatever things were thought evil. All primitivists agree that in the beginning everything was good and, in view of Adam's likeness to a divine model, he could not have brought evil into existence. Elsewhere in the *Clementina* the life of our primordial parents and those of several generations of their descendants duplicate life in the Golden Age. But upon becoming accustomed to the free gifts of Nature, men forgot their divine benefactor and proceeded to introduce the seeds of evil into the world, as if they were advantageous to men. But the *Clementina* do not develop this theme and pass on to another version of our earliest historical stage. Based upon the descent of the Sons of God to earth, where they were married to the Daughters of Man, the story says that they descended with the best of motives, to show men the error of their ways. But the angels too lost their power to regain their perfection, though they did retain their supernatural knowledge of magic. They, moreover, acquired the sexual appetites of man and united, as in the Bible, with women.

All sorts of arts were invented to please their mistresses, and the technological state of nature was lost. The children of these unions, the giants, became bestial, began to eat animal food—were even cannibalistic—and the earth, defiled by blood, bred disease along with carnivorous and destructive beasts. The persistent dread of sexuality which appears in so many of the early Fathers, as contrasted with the Pagans, finds in sexuality the cause of all human troubles. There is nothing in Genesis, as Saint Augustine was to say, that forbade procreation. Quite the contrary. But the evil lay in man's sexual desires, not so much in their satisfaction or consequences. In any event the first stage in human history began in perfection and ended in failure. Men, with the exception of Noah and his sons, were wiped out by the Deluge and a new start was made.

It is worth pointing out, in view of later developments of the same theme, that in the *Recognitions* (VIII, 48) there is a passage that suggests that some races of men still exist in relative purity and in the enjoyment of primeval felicity. They may be the literary ancestors of imaginary peoples who turn up in later writings.

The notion of Adam's childlike nature is also to be found in Clement of Alexandria (third century). It was indeed his childlike quality which allowed him to succumb to the wiles of the Serpent. For the Serpent is a symbol of pleasure. The true Christian in becoming like a child, returns to Adam's condition. This opinion opened the way for many other primitivistic ideas, anti-intellectualism, the *docta ignorantia,* and the general depreciation of learning (see below).

In Novatian (third century), a schismatic, the diet of primitive man is not merely confined to vegetable foods but to the fruits of trees. Thus, being made upright in stature, he will not have to stoop to the ground for sustenance. The cultivation of grain and the eating of flesh came after the Fall. For then labor was man's lot and he needed stronger food. Hence a carnivorous diet and toil are associated, and nothing is made of the verse in the second chapter of Genesis which specifically says that Adam was put into the Garden to tend it. The emphasis is upon Genesis 3:19: "In the sweat of thy face shalt thou eat bread." The dream of toilless happiness was the dream of a return to primeval innocence and it was to take centuries before men could introduce the notion of the dignity of labor into common belief. Work was punishment.

A new conception was introduced into the accounts of man's original condition by Gregory of Nyssa (late fourth century). Gregory draws a picture of human perfection in which there were no hints of defect. Adam knew neither old age nor sickness nor passion; he had no sexual intercourse, conception, parturition, impurity, evacuation, gradual growth, disease, nor death. He was perfectly beautiful, physically and morally, without envy or other evil emotions. The contempt which the early Fathers had for everything that is specifically human comes out strongly in this writer; and since almost all human traits, as distinguished from the angelic or divine, have their origin in the emotions, Adam is depicted as a Stoic Sage, rational, free, and apathetic. Yet envy entered the scene with the Serpent, and Adam, in spite of his perfect rationality and his ability to see truth face to face, yielded to that emotion and hence brought all imaginable evils into the world. He became mortal rather than immortal and subject to all the ills of the flesh. Yet Gregory still thought that we could return to the age of innocence, and his primitivism turns into a program rather than remaining simply a historical description. We should renounce marriage, then agriculture, then the life of sensation, "the wisdom of the flesh," and follow God's commandments alone. We see here a similarity to the life advocated by the Greek Cynics, but cynicism was not motivated by a desire to expiate an inherited primordial sin. Both Cynic and saint, however, agreed in their contempt for civilized life and in the belief in the possibility of rejecting it while remaining alive. This will be treated below under *Cultural Primitivism*.

Gregory's brother, Saint Basil, also thought of Adam before the Fall as a Stoic Sage. Basil's ideal was the apathetic life, the life without emotion. He also thought it could be regained by renunciation. The fundamental problem to such a writer is how a perfectly rational being could have yielded to temptation. Oblivious of this Basil goes so far as to assert, as Tertullian had, that Adam fell through literal gluttony, "the lust of the belly." Why a Stoic who was enjoying the fruits of all the trees but one should have wanted the pleasure of an extra sensation is never explained, though maybe that would be to ask too much. On the contrary, Basil simply accepts the fact and urges us to return to something approximating original happiness by fasting and other forms of penance. We must especially avoid the eating of flesh, for in a work of the Basilian school even the beasts were not originally carnivorous. We must, moreover, learn to do without superfluities and to restrict ourselves to necessities, thus becoming, like the Cynic in his wine jar, free from wants and needing but little. Adam was free from all wants, needed no clothes nor house, and enjoyed perfect health. But with the Fall even the climate deteriorated.

In Lactantius these themes are repeated, as they were to be repeated throughout the later history of Christian thought. Life in the Garden was free from toil; man was immortal; no evil existed. But Lactantius also refers to secular history and bases some of his ideas upon pagan legends. In the Age of Saturn there was, he says, a general acceptance of monotheism and charity. But the Fall is analogous to the assumption of power by Jupiter, a man full of hybris and pride. Jupiter wished to be deified and worshipped; hence polytheism began. Whereupon images were made and worshipped and a general decline of morality was initiated. Man lost his original feeling of fraternity, his sense that we are all children of one parent, and cupidity was born, the source of all the evils that were to follow. But mankind could not have been truly virtuous without having at least some knowledge of other possibilities. In short, there is no virtue in obligatory innocence. Hence the knowledge of the body was useful, but unfortunately man made poor use of it.

In Saint Ambrose we have once more the old stories of man's felicity based not only on Genesis but also on the classical poets. The tone is that of soft primitivism. Ambrose is in fact such an ultraprimitivist that he believes man to have been happiest before the creation of Eve, in spite of Genesis 2:18: "It is not good that man should be alone." If he had been left in solitude, he would not have fallen. But this must have been a passing remark, for Ambrose could not deny that the multiplication of the human race was part of the divine plan. The trouble lay in Adam's immaturity; he was not yet ready for a thorough knowledge of the truths for which he had a craving. God's purpose was to educate the human race step by step. In this way the new revelation of Christianity surpasses the Old Law. If Adam had not been so precipitate, he would not have sinned. Virtue is the overcoming of temptation, and if the Devil entered Paradise at all, it must have been with God's consent. In fact the Fall was a cryptic blessing, for it permitted the incarnation and redemption; it was a *felix culpa*

583

("happy fault"). That neither would have been needed without the Fall is true; but does one praise crime for permitting expiation?

With Ambrose's pupil, Saint Augustine, one may terminate the patristic period. Augustine is one of those great figures into whom streams of thought from many sources flow, and out of whose works scores of authors derive their fundamental notions. He was learned in the pagan authors, the philosophers as well as the poets; and it would require a lifetime of labor to sort out all the sources for his many ideas. As far as human history is concerned, Augustine thought of all events under two aspects, the temporal and the spiritual or allegorical. The Garden of Eden was indeed a spatio-temporal locality in which our first parents were born and sinned, but it is also a figure of speech symbolizing the pleasures of the spiritual life. "For [Eden]," he says in *De Genesi contra Manicheos* (Book II, Ch. 9), "may mean either delights or pleasures or feasts, if it is translated from Hebrew into Latin." The trees that were growing in the Garden signify every spiritual joy, for they tower over the earth, that is, over matter. And the Tree of Life planted in the center of the Garden means "that wisdom, by which the soul ought to know that it is placed in the center of things . . . so that although it have all corporeal nature subjected to it, yet may know that above it is God's nature, and it should neither bend to the right, arrogating itself to what is not, nor to the left, negligently disdaining what is." Similarly the Tree of Knowledge is a symbol, a symbol of "the centrality of the soul and its ordered integrity." But eating of its fruit is forgetting God upon whom we depend for all things and we swell up with pride in our own endowment. Having committed this sin (of pride), we then know evil, into which we have fallen, and the good which we have abandoned. If we now ask just what Adam was like before the Fall, we are told, in Augustine's treatise on free will (Ch. 24), that he was midway between wisdom and stupidity, capable of either, like a child, but actually enjoying neither. Yet he did not live an entirely spiritual life. Our parents had bodies, as the animals do, but they kept them well disciplined. Before the Fall they lived in a state of innocence, in perfect sinlessness. When they decided to have children, "those parts were moved by that act of will which moves the other members, and without the ensnaring stimulus of hot desire, in tranquillity of soul and no loss of corporeal integrity did the husband pour forth his seed into the womb of his wife" (*City of God*, Book XIV, Ch. 26). And just as there was no pleasure in procreation, there was no pain in childbirth. All bodily acts were under the control of the will and man was not forced by emotion to do anything whatsoever.

Yet such a picture of apathetic happiness did not include idleness, as might be expected. Adam did a certain amount of agricultural work, but since the climate of Eden was as perfect as the nature of its inhabitants, the work was pleasant. Adam in tending the Garden was simply cooperating with his Creator. Pain, like all other evils, was a consequence of the Fall. Not only are all sins, crimes, and misdemeanors attributable to this one act, but also all catastrophes over which Adam could have no control: accidents of travel, poisons, harmful insects, famines, nightmares. The only escape from this terrestrial hell is through God's grace. Some of these evils cannot be avoided by a man; they are rooted in the nature of the physical universe. Yet they were brought into existence by one man's sin. The Pagans had usually attributed evil to one man's acts and confined it to his life. But in Augustine evil had cosmic relevance, though caused by one man, and was passed on to his descendants. To explain the inheritance of evil, if not its cosmic importance, Augustine devised the theory that all mankind was included in Adam as particulars are included in a universal, even as triangles—equilateral, scalene, and isosceles—are included in the concept of triangularity. But how a flesh and blood human being could be thought of as a universal concept living in space and time, created and dying at given moments, was never clarified by this Father.

Chronological primitivism continued in the Christian tradition, as might be expected, throughout the Middle Ages. Like all beliefs based on a sacred text, Christianity could be subjected to detailed exposition and clarification, but not to fundamental criticism. Inner contradictions were to be illuminated but never rejected and when one came upon apparent inconsistencies one could accept them with resignation as evidence of mysteries. Hence the medieval apologists spent their time elaborating details of life before the Fall and its evil consequences. None could assert that human beings were better off since that unfortunate event. And since God could not have created anything evil, all must have been perfect before the Serpent entered the stage. But even his entrance was not in itself an evil, for it gave Adam and Eve the chance to resist temptation and remain virtuous.

To read medieval literature on this topic is to be entertained with a variety of fantastic dreams, dreams of a soft primitivistic life which were not exceeded by those of any of the Pagans. Yet the delights of such a life might seem to some readers in direct opposition to what we have come to think of as essential to Christianity, the utmost control of our sensual desires. There is no need to string out expositions of such dreams, for they are in the nature of the case largely similar. What is more important is to see how they kept alive the *contemptus mundi* ("contempt for worldly things") and to an extent that made most of the outstanding figures of that period, whether they knew it or not, enemies of what the Church was teaching as basic doctrines.

III. CULTURAL PRIMITIVISM

Cultural primitivism came to the fore in the Greek Cynics who apparently had no interest in appraising contemporary life. In spite of the fundamental differences in the Greek and Latin ethical schools, they all agreed that the end of life was personal self-sufficiency (*autarky*), freedom from all claims made by the external world upon the soul of the individual. The Platonist found this in the life of reason, freedom from the demands of the senses; the Aristotelian found it in the Golden Mean, freedom from extremes; the Epicurean found it in freedom from pain and indeed from all but the simplest pleasures; the Stoic found it in apathy, freedom from any emotional attachments. The emphasis on freedom from something or other is the essential point; and one might reasonably conclude that the ancient philosophers had become weary of society, of family, of friends.

1. Cynicism. The most extreme form of *autarky* was sought and found by Diogenes of Sinope, whose teacher, if tradition is correct, was Antisthenes (ca. 444–365 B.C.), a member of the Socratic circle. Though we have no writings of Diogenes and only scattered fragments of dubious authenticity from his master, it is fairly well established that their principal axiom was that life according to nature was the best of life. "Nature," however, is one of the most ambiguous words in either Greek, Latin, or English. It may refer to that which distinguishes one class of things from all others, or to the geological landscape. It may name that which is congenital as contrasted with the unnatural and the supernatural as well. It is both descriptive and normative. For the very reason of its invincible ambiguity it has taken on a strong emotional color, and arguments about the value of human behavior are based on whether it is natural or unnatural, natural or merely customary, instinctive or deliberate. One is always hard put to it to know precisely what a man means when he calls an act "unnatural" or "natural."

To the early Cynic one of the basic meanings of the natural was that which distinguishes it from the customary, that is, *physis* vs. *nomos*. (Later *nomos* in the sense of "law" came to be divided into the Law of Nature and the Law of the State.) And if we read the tradition correctly, we should have to conclude that for Diogenes the natural was that which he could not discard and still live. Thus we could discard clothing

and throw a rag about us to keep off the cold; we could discard a house and creep into a wine jar; we could discard all family ties, wives and children, and procreate like the animals; we could even discard cooked meat and eat food raw. Those things that could be discarded without committing suicide are all the contributions of civilization, and it might be assumed that mankind as it came from the hands of the Creator was without them. As far as Diogenes was concerned, he had only to look at the beasts to see what was natural and what unnatural; and, looking at them, he threw away his clothes and his cup, wrapped a length of cloth round his body, and lapped up water like a dog. To carry out this program to its logical consequences was to renounce all social life whatsoever, to give up schooling, the arts and sciences, all crafts except the simplest (for the birds built nests and the spiders spun webs), and to roam about in solitude.

The revolt of the Cynic was above all a revolt against the intellect. The use of reason might seem to be natural to man in that most of the ancients believed rationality to be man's *differentia*, the one thing that distinguished him from the animals. But it was perhaps easier to follow one's instincts and appetites than to reason to what ends one wished to attain. So the Cynic deprecated any attempt to supersede instinct by learning. If one did not follow one's instincts and appetites, one could substitute something else which would do just as well: intuition, direct communication with revelation, momentary desires. And there are grounds for believing that this is precisely what Diogenes did. Hence stories began to circulate about the Cynics that seemed obscene to their contemporaries: doing "the works of Demeter and Aphrodite" in public. If the charge was founded, the Cynic *was* obscene. And if his program eventuated in such practices, it followed that the arts and sciences were an evil and should be discarded. When he assumed that primeval man was more natural than civilized man, he turned to chronological primitivism and attributed to our primordial ancestors only those forms of behavior which were not based on learning, or, as he would have said, on art. The natural desires are then defined as those which can be gratified by all men regardless of their state of civilization: the universal, the biologically irrepressible, the primary. Hence shame and modesty must be repressed, as Aratus had said the Iron Race had repressed them, for they obstruct the satisfaction of our fundamental drives. Cynicism was the most extreme form of cultural primitivism.

Platonists, Aristotelians, and Stoics, having accepted reason as essential to humanity, could not indulge in this kind of moral philosophy. Reason is above all a critical faculty, whether it is employed in logic, science, or ethics. In Aristotle it chastens our instinctive appetites by holding them to the mean; in Plato it teaches us to reject the temporary for eternal goods; in the Stoics it clarifies our duties and corrects passionate and willful behavior. The Epicurean with his emphasis on pleasure and his dislike of "culture" nevertheless saw, by using his reason, that most pleasures are the prelude to pain and that the avoidance of pain is the sanest form of hedonism. Antirationalism was an inherent part of cultural primitivism as it appeared in pagan thought.

Occasionally Socrates was held up as an exemplar by the Cynics. He was represented as being contented with simple pleasures, being neither an ascetic nor a voluptuary. He could withstand cold and hunger and yet did not disdain the comforts of life. He was about as self-sufficient as a man could be and yet he enjoyed the company of friends and philosophic discussion. He was rational and yet listened to the controlling voice of his *daimon* ("guiding spirit"). The true Cynic, however, could not follow Socrates, for he could not admit that any desire which was "natural" should be controlled. He could not disapprove of incest, as Dio Chrysostom puts it in his *Discourses* (X, 29–30), for "cocks do not see anything wrong in such unions, nor do dogs or asses, nor yet the Persians." Diogenes even approved of cannibalism, since some nations indulge in it.

Perhaps the best account of the Cynic life is that given by Lucian in his *Cynicus*, though it dates from a much later period (second century A.D.). Here the Cynic is pictured as unshorn, shirtless, barefoot, roaming from place to place, sleeping alone on the hard ground, dirty and in rags. He is proud of his economy, for he needs no money. He has everything he requires. He is chided for rejecting the good things that Nature has given him—the wool of sheep, wine, oil, and honey —but replies that like a temperate man he uses those goods that he needs and does not gorge himself with delicacies that are superfluous. Lucian launches into a criticism of luxury that was to be repeated over and over again in the course of history. "Embroidered clothes are no warmer than others, houses with gilded roofs keep out the rain no better; a drink out of a silver cup—or a gold one for that matter—is no more refreshing, and sleep is no sweeter on an ivory bed—the reverse in fact is true." The enjoyment of these supposed delights simply involves one in endless trouble, whereas the simplicity of the Cynic's life is free from worry and anxiety.

The fusion of the simple life with life in the Golden Age was made by the essayist, Maximus of Tyre (second century A.D.), in his question, "Whether the Cynic life is to be preferred." Maximus was a paradoxist and it is doubtful that his conclusions were to be taken seriously. But whether this is so or not, some people did take them seriously. When man was created, by Prometheus, he was "in mind approaching very near to the gods, in body slender, erect and symmetrical, mild of aspect, apt for handicraft, firm of step." He had at his disposal an environment with abundant food such as Earth "is accustomed to bear when undisturbed by husbandsmen. . . ." Strife was unknown, peace reigned, health was in every body, all was perfection itself. But then in another age men began to divide up the earth, built walls and fortifications, made soft clothes for their bodies, hung gold about their necks and on their fingers, built houses, and invented locks and keys. They molested the earth with mining, built ships for war and foreign trade, caught birds out of the air, slaughtered the animals, and filled their bellies with blood, and, seeking wealth and pleasure, they fell into poverty and misery. Maximus gives us here a picture of man's unhappiness which might apply to any century, whether pagan or Christian.

The remedy for this condition is obviously the simple life. Compare the men who live naked, without a house, without arts, who have all the earth for their city and their household, with the men who have all the clothes, the kind of house, the arts and contrivances of civilization. Who is the happier? Obviously the former. For he is free, whereas the latter is as a man in a dark prison, weighted down with irons. He will relieve his misery by singing, guzzling food, and sexual indulgence. Yet he is always afraid of the consequences and is never really free. His antithesis is the Cynic, the man of the Golden Age, who "is living in the clear light of day, whose hands and feet are free, who can turn his neck in any direction, can lift his eyes to the rising sun, look at the stars. . . ." In short, he is Diogenes. There follows a eulogy of the early Cynic describing him as the one free man.

If then Cynicism is the natural program of life, it must be the program followed by all who are not corrupted by civilization. Hence it is the universal philosophy, much as the "religion of nature" was believed to be the universal religion in the eighteenth century. Its universality sufficed to recommend it and in a time when cosmopolitanism was being preached, not only by the Stoics but by the Christians as well, the search for a universal philosophy was of paramount interest. It was not surprising that the monks should have been identified later on with the followers of Diogenes and that they should have adopted as their uniform the Cynic cloak, the *tribon*, a cloth wrapped loosely about the body.

2. Epicureanism. But before entering into the

Christian version of cultural primitivism, we must say a few words about Epicureanism, Stoicism, and the simple life. Though this doctrine sometimes has been interpreted as urging involvement in all sorts of pleasures and the very name of its founder has become a synonym for the ultrahedonist, the original sources of the doctrine, as far as we have them, tone down the note of pleasure seeking. Epicurus himself urged men to simplify their desires and to search for the attainment of only those which are necessary for the free life. He did not refuse to partake of the pleasures that were offered to him so long as he had to make no effort to get them. But as a free agent, seeking *autarky*, he would be content with very simple pleasures. "Bread and water," he says in his *Third Letter* (Diogenes Laërtius, Book X, 130–31), "yield the very acme of pleasure to a man who is really hungry and thirsty." And the same frugality of corporal delights was to be paralled in the delights of the spirit. But there was certainly no anti-intellectualism and the Epicurean seldom went to the extremes of the Cynic in shocking his neighbors.

The Epicurean who is best known is Lucretius (first century B.C.). And though he is in some ways an anti-primitivist, assenting to man's technological progress through the discovery of fire, yet he had a streak of hard primitivism in him which comes out when he is relating the life of primitive man. Lucretius clearly admires the physical strength of the first man "created out of hard earth," who was able to stand the cold or heat and was not assailed by illness. He lived like an animal, roving about, and had neither agriculture nor cooking, but fed on acorns and berries, which were then more plentiful than they are now. He drank water from the streams, had no fire, no system of laws, no settled customs. "Whatever booty or chance gave to each," he says (Book V, 958ff.), "that each bore off at his own pleasure, taught to be strong and live for himself alone. And in the woods Venus united the bodies of lovers; for each woman was won either by mutual desire, or by the violence of a man and his vehement lust or at a price of acorns." These men chased the wild beasts with stones and heavy clubs, lying on the naked ground when fatigued and sleeping until dawn awoke them. But their Spartan regimen was no preventive of lamentation; for they often met death through encounters with wild beasts which caught and mangled them, and they died "in wild convulsions." But at the same time they were not bothered with foreign trade and navigation, which apparently most primitivistic authors disdained, and rather than seek food in foreign lands they let themselves die of famine. "In those days men often took poison in ignorance; now, better instructed, they give it to others."

In such a passage as this Lucretius admires the vigor of our primordial ancestors and their ability to do without some of the superfluities of life which his contemporaries thought of as necessities. But he is no chronological primitivist. For he goes on to relate the story of man's progress from savagery to civilization, beginning with the discovery of fire. This part of the story properly belongs to the history of the idea of progress and we shall leave Lucretius here. But we should point out that he regrets man's lapse from primitive simplicity. Our greatest misfortune seems to have been the discovery of gold, "for the majority follow the party of the richer" (V, 1113–15). The idea of wealth stirs men to seek position and power and they forget that it is better to live as a subject and in peace than as the governors of others. Men, moreover, having discovered metals, had the means to make weapons, and war began; Lucretius dilates upon our departure from primitive pacifism. Yet he also praises learning and the arts.

But best of all was the philosophy of Epicurus, which freed men from their supernatural terrors, "set bounds to both desire and fear," and showed us the chief good which we all seek. It is clear that Lucretius is ambivalent about primitive conditions, admiring physical strength and the ability to do without luxury, but also regretting the absence of the arts that enlighten men. He definitely rejects chronological primitivism, for the first stage of history was far from the best. He wavers also about the value of cultural primitivism, for the best period was the second stage of history when men lived a simple pastoral and agricultural life. Men then for the most part lived at peace with one another and only later did ever more horrible wars begin. His attitude is very similar to that of Rousseau in the *Second Discourse*. Both men are on the whole cultural but not chronological primitivists.

Though Lucretius' contemporary Cicero favored antiprimitivism to primitivism, there were certain primitivistic strains which appear in his writings. He too uses "nature" as a catchword, without any definite meaning, goes back to antiquity for authoritative knowledge, looks for the natural in the child. But he also believes in the value of racial experience, holds up the light of nature as a guide which has been diverted from the true path by prejudices, and often has recourse to the *consensus gentium* ("general agreement") as a criterion of truth. The Law of Nature has been corrupted by man, who has invented statutes which are as poisons to the body politic (*De legibus* II, v, 13). None of this is systematic and it would be misleading to try to organize such ideas into a system.

3. Stoicism. The early Stoics—Zeno, Cleanthes, and Chrysippus—are said to have agreed with the Cynics about some of their tenets. For instance, Zeno and Chrysippus are said to have believed in the community of wives and the permissibility of incest. Zeno even is reported to have approved of cannibalism "in certain circumstances," and to have argued that money is needed neither for travel nor for exchange and that the reputation and the esteem of others are not goods. These resemble Cynic doctrines and all seem to issue from the initial axiom, "follow nature."

Along with such ideas went a positive adoration of the cosmic scene, as expressed in the *Hymn to Zeus* of Cleanthes. This religious attitude towards the cosmic order led to a contempt for man, to whom all evils were attributed. Yet since man had been created by Nature and therefore was created good, evil must be due to a Fall. But how explain the fall of a perfect man? This problem was solved by the Stoic invention of cycles, according to which doctrine things went from good to bad indefinitely, with a cosmic conflagration putting an end to the world's Great Year. Since the rise of evil is inherent in natural law, it was one of many reasons for remaining in a state of apathy and taking things as they come. But unfortunately for the consistency of the system, the Stoic was more apathetic about evil than he was about good. And among the goods of life was the use of reason. The Stoic was not indifferent to philosophy nor to the pleasant aspects of civilization. His apathy was internal. He accepted or rejected goods as they occurred. Stoicism in fact was a doctrine with many shades of meaning, some members of the school being closer to Cynicism than others, and some, like Seneca, now being more, now less "cynical."

Seneca emphasizes the physical superiority of primitive man and the advantages of the absence of the arts and of private property. But at the same time, the primitives were obviously not Stoics and their resemblances to Stoics in their way of life were instinctive rather than rational. Seneca was a strong believer in the value of knowledge: it is better to know why a certain course is right and then to pursue it than it is to pursue it without knowing why. The innocence of the savage, like that of the child, is good but not so good as the conscious virtue of the Sage. Most of this can be found in Seneca's ninetieth *Moral Epistle*, addressed to Lucilius, which begins with the opinion that though life is a gift of the gods, the good life is a gift of philosophy. The first men followed nature, had the strongest man as their chief; but his strength lay in his mind as well as in his body. Therefore in the Golden Age the wisest man was the leader. Seneca's description of such a leader would correspond to what was later said about benevolent despots: they were all-powerful but used their power for the benefit of the tribe. Yet, as in so many political philosophies, one had to admit that degeneration could set in and the benevolent despot become a tyrant; the rule of law had to take the place of the rule of a king.

So far Seneca says that he is following Posidonius. But since Posidonius says that philosophy gave men all the arts, of which Seneca has a low opinion, he is abandoned as a guide at this point. Seneca cannot believe that architecture and the use of iron, from both of which only evil has resulted, could have come from philosophy. Here his cultural primitivism shows itself strongly. On the contrary, Seneca believes that it was man's cunning (*sagacitas*) that invented these things. The wise or philosophic man can do without houses and rare foods. He is content with little, for most of the things we prize are encumbrances. Seneca launches into a typical diatribe against luxury in the vein of the early Cynics, a diatribe which is the more amusing in that its author was enjoying all the luxuries of the imperial court while writing this. "Luxury has abandoned nature; day by day she grows greater, age after age she has been gathering strength and making intellect the minister of vice."

Almost everything which civilized men value is subjected to the philosopher's scorn. The only way to reconcile the acceptance of all these evils rationally is to see that they follow from the cosmic law, the steady degeneration of mankind. It was probably from Seneca that Rousseau found his source for his *First Discourse*, if one was needed. For Rousseau too took as his theme the depreciation of all the arts and sciences (see also Seneca's eighty-eighth *Moral Epistle*). Though there are less woeful passages in Seneca, in the end his teaching leads to despair. In each cycle the earth is destined to senescence and decay, and all that a man may accomplish will be in vain if he hopes that his accomplishments will be lasting. As he puts it in *Natural Questions* (III, xxx, 7–8), once the cycle is ended, men will be created anew, "born under happier auspices, knowing naught of evil." But their innocence will endure only so long as they are new. Wickedness creeps in quickly.

4. *Christianity and Cynicism.* The cultural primitivism of the Christians appears in the influence of Cynicism upon the ideas which they held concerning the best life. Unlike the Pagans, however, they had a sacred text which told them at least the rudiments of a moral philosophy. Their problem was mainly a rationalization of the doctrine and the drawing of inferences from its basic principles. For just as the Pagan believed in a fundamental distinction between nature and custom, so the Christian believed a conflict to exist between the laws of God and those of man. There was a further contrast found in Christianity, one arising from the Platonistic inference that the creation was inferior to the Creator. Nature, in every sense except that which equated it with God, was part of creation and, though inferior to God, yet it showed traces of its Maker's hand. But there were other traces of the Greek use of the term "nature" in Christianity. Saint Paul, for instance, when he tells the Corinthians that women should cover their heads, bases his lesson not on Scripture but on the unnaturalness of a woman's hair being her covering. The "teachings of Nature" also turn up in the Epistle to the Romans, where the Gentiles are described as doing by nature the things that are commanded by the Law.

This became customary in the patristic period. When one comes to a man like Tertullian, who was born a pagan, it is not surprising to find him resorting to an appeal to nature when he can find no scriptual support for his teachings. He uses the argument when he is preaching against the wearing of wreaths as decorations for the head; such usage is unnatural. But he equates the Law of Nature with the Law of God, the Creator of nature. In general one can say that Tertullian turns to nature about as often as he turns to Scripture. So Lactantius, attacking philosophy, uses a type of epistemological primitivism, arguing that philosophy is too recently founded a practice to be followed. True wisdom, he maintains, must be innate, and what is acquired must thus be rejected in favor of the innate. In fact, if philosophy were true wisdom, then before its appearance on earth men would have lived *sine ratione*. But this is absurd, for by definition man is a rational animal. The Carpocratians, an heretical sect, appealed to nature in support of equalitarianism. This heresy, which seems to have recurred in the thirteenth century, and appears in the *Roman de la Rose*, supported the marital status of nature, for the community of goods demands the community of wives. The Marcionites, on the other hand, saw Nature as an evil deity and did not contrast nature and custom, but Nature and God. Hence that which was natural and good to the Carpocratians was on that very account evil to the Marcionites.

Out of this confusion Saint Ambrose draws a conclusion which had definite effects. He puts this cultural primitivism to special use in arguing that the Law of Nature decreed that all things should be owned in common; but wives were not among the things owned. We have already seen that it was common among the Pagans to oppose private property; indeed many of them maintained that its initiation in early times was the source of most of our ills. Now there was no basis in the Old Testament for the belief that private property is unnatural or that God had ordained the earth to be owned by all in common. But certain texts of the New Testament, such as Matthew 19 and its parallels, condemned riches, though even these texts did nothing more than advocate an extreme form of charity. But by seeing Adam, as Saint Augustine also was to do, as the entire human race and God's gifts to Adam as of the earth and the fruits thereof as a gift to all mankind, Ambrose was able to preach primitive communism as a Christian doctrine. Mankind thus becomes a corporate person bound together by the Law of Nature. It is for that reason that charity has the position that Saint Paul gave it. But, says Ambrose, there is no distinction between the Law of Nature and the Law of God. Both appear in the operation of instinct, though sometimes we fail to follow instinct. If we had continued to follow it as the first men did, we should have had no need for statute. He is so convinced of this that he is almost unique in early writers in finding in children a model for the kind of behavior of which he approves. The child, who is innocent, follows the Law of Nature (*lex naturae*); he is a living example of what Adam was like before the Fall. He is, in Cicero's language, a mirror of nature (*speculum naturae*). And like Adam he is neither avaricious, guileful, cruel, ambitious, or insolent. He is the opposite of such things because he follows nature, not because he has received any instruction. Saint Ambrose has his own interpretation of the word "knowledge." Knowledge for him is cunning (*astutia*). The commandment not to eat of the Tree of Knowledge was the commandment not to be cunning, thus avoiding all the vices attendant upon its use. The good Christian then is a man in the state of nature, childlike and unreasoning. Thus the same type of argument which in Cynicism produced the ragged and wanton Diogenes, produced the saint in Christianity.

The cultural primitivism of the Cynic also comes out in the Christian doctrine of the simple life. The Cynic had rejected almost everything which civilization had given mankind. But this contempt for the worldly things of life was also shared by some of the Christians. Justin Martyr, for instance, continued to wear the philosopher's cloak, the *tribon*, after his conversion, and it was easy for a third- or fourth-century man to confuse the monks with the Cynics; both wore soiled garments and carried wallet and staff. Even Saint Basil confuses Cynics and saints from time to time, as when he compares the ethical ideals of the Pagans and the Christians. The teachings are highly similar but their motivation is quite different.

Moreover some of the early Fathers did not hesitate to use pagan as well as biblical sources in support of their ideas. One of the best examples is Constantine's using Vergil as a prophet, in the *Fourth Eclogue*, of the birth of Christ. Another is the legend that Saint

589

Paul and Seneca had been friends, a legend that produced their correspondence. In fact the use of pagan sources grew to such a point that Saint Jerome protested vigorously against it. But that did not prevent him from listing Seneca among the saints. The similarity between the two sets of doctrine was so great that some writers explained it away as plagiarism on the part of the pagans. So Philo Judaeus (first century A.D.) had spoken of Plato as "Moses speaking Greek."

It must be granted that the Christian who followed the way of poverty and chastity, who was free internally while a slave externally, was indeed hard to distinguish from a Cynic or a Stoic. And when monasticism was instituted, the resemblance was all the greater. The hermit for that matter was not unlike Diogenes in his wine jar; the monk in his monastery reminded one, as the Essenes had, of the Golden Race, sharing all things in common, having few if any wants, and living a life of freedom from external goods. But the resemblance was superficial. For the Christian lived not in dependence on himself alone, but in full dependence on God. The pagan ascetic was not an ascetic because he was doing penance, but because he wanted to be free from all social ties. In reality the Cynic or Stoic reduced his wants as a gesture of self-assertion, the Christian as self-denial. One of the clearest examples of the Christian motivation, and practice as well, is in the *Pseudo-Clementina* (*Homilies* XII, vi), where Peter says, "I eat only bread and olives and rarely vegetables—and my wrap and cloak (*tribon*) are this very thing which is thrown about me. Nor have I any other nor need I others. For in these I have more than enough, for my mind, looking upon all the eternal goods over yonder, sees none of the things here below." With the exception of the last sentence, this might have been said by any Cynic, by Epictetus, or even by Epicurus.

This difference in motivation sharply distinguishes Christian cultural primitivism from pagan. The pagan would be free not only of wants for material things, but, as we have said above, from the claims of family and friends. The Christian would be free of the former but hardly of the latter, since brotherly love or *caritas* was one of the virtues which Saint Paul had most earnestly commended. In Saint Basil's *Longer Rules* it is made clear that a communal life was to be instituted for the monks, but within the community living was on a par with what one had learned from pagan cultural primitivists. Dress should be as simple as possible and a single cloth ought to suffice for protection against the weather; the rule of poverty should be strictly enforced and it was pointed out that there is virtue in living a hard life. Basil actually refers to Hesiod as a teacher of this rule and offers the Cynic hero, Her-

cules, as an exemplar. But he was schooled in the classics and did not hesitate to use even the language of the Cynics when it suited his purposes. Nor does he refrain from the Cynic argument that desiring only the bare necessities is in accordance with nature. But he, as a saint, exceeds their limitations, for the Cynic permitted the gratification of bodily needs, including the sexual, whereas he suppresses all pleasures and is suspicious even of good health.

The hard primitivism of the monks, regardless of its motivation, so closely resembled that of the Cynics that it was easy to confuse the two. But after the Dark Ages the Cynic was forgotten and the ascetic monks stood in his place as models of the virtuous life. In the twelfth century we find a man like Alain of Lille writing a *Summa of the Art of Preaching* in which (Ch. 25) he refers to nature without any mention of those biblical passages which one might expect him to quote. He urges self-sufficiency (*autarky*) and indicates that it can be attained by checking concupiscence, rejecting pleasures, being moderate in eating and drinking, and limiting one's wants to those that Nature demands, that is, to sustaining life. The basis of this passage is Seneca, not the Bible, and earlier in the same work (Ch. 5) he almost reproduces a speech of the Cynic Antisthenes in saying, "If you live in accordance with Nature, you will never be poor." But Alain had read his Latin authors and held them in greater respect than was customary in the earlier period of Christianity. So Peter Cantor (twelfth century), whose *Verbum abbreviatum* is a sort of anthology, sets forth not only passages such as Luke 6:20 and Matthew 8:20, but alongside these, long quotations from Seneca's epistles. This is a way of bringing pagan and biblical authority into harmony.

More typically Christian was Guigo the Carthusian (early twelfth century). Addressing his fellow monks and extolling poverty, he recalls the hermits and their life of hard work and abstinence. He was impressed by the communism of the primitive church and the sacrifice of possessions. Yet, as might be expected, the hard primitivism of his appeal is based on the need for self-humiliation rather than on the Law of Nature.

Another aspect of the cultural primitivism of the Middle Ages was a strain of anti-intellectualism which, though never dominant, was nevertheless strong. It could not be denied that Adam fell because he wished to know something which he had been forbidden to learn. In Tertullian the sacrifice of rationality is no more than any saint should be willing to make. Pope John XIII took another stance: living in the tenth century, he pointed out that the vicars of Peter and his disciples had no need for pagan authorities, that God had not chosen orators and philosophers to preach his word, but illiterate and unpolished men. But these words, which were only the faint echo of a philosophy, were repeated by none other than Saint Anselm in his *De contemptu mundi*. And Saint Bernard in the twelfth century put intellectual curiosity in the same class as the sin of Eve. Self-knowledge, he insisted, was alone worth seeking—paradoxically enough a pagan goal—but knowledge about external things is vain. As for that knowledge which is necessary for the Christian life, self-knowledge and the knowledge of God, these may be had without technological or scientific training. In his *The Steps of Humility and Pride* (II, 10) we find him praising ignorance of both the mechanical and the liberal arts on the ground that the Apostles were ignorant of both. A pure conscience and unsullied faith are enough to win salvation.

Similar views are expressed by Helinandus, the Venerable Guibertus, Hildebert, and even Pope Innocent III. The Pope almost preached ignorance on the plea that we are made sick by too much learning. "Let scholars," he says in his *De contemptu mundi* (I, xiii), "scrutinize, let them investigate the heights of heaven, the stretches of the earth, the depths of the sea, and let them dispute over each particular and explore whole subjects, let them spend their time in learning and teaching. For what shall they discover from this occupation but labor and pain and affliction of the spirit?" And he refers back to Ecclesiastes. This is followed by a diatribe against all the arts and sciences, a diatribe which was to be made again in the sixteenth century by Agrippa von Nettesheim. It was in itself a repetition of the thoughts of the Greek Cynics.

IV. THE NOBLE SAVAGE

One of the problems that confronted the primitivist was the discovery, if possible, of the natural man—the man who followed nature rather than custom or opinion, and who was a living exemplar of the primitivistic life. The Greeks found such persons among the savages, both real and imaginary. The Scythians, the "blameless Ethiopians," the inhabitants of the Fortunate Islands, and the Hyperboreans were fair samples of what they found or invented. Life in the Fortunate Islands, as in the Land beyond the North Wind, was characterized as softly primitive: the climate was pleasant, earth gave its fruits spontaneously, the goats, as Horace put it (*Epode* XVI, lines 40ff.), came to be milked unbidden. In short, all the delights of the Golden Age seen through the magnifying glass of the poetic imagination are attributed to these lands. And as for the Hyperboreans, they live until they have found their pleasant life sufficient—not boring, according to Mela in his *Chorographia* (III, 35–37). They then wreathe their heads with garlands and fling themselves into the sea. The Scythians, like most Noble Savages, lived a hard

primitivistic life. They were nomads, ate meat, and drank mare's milk, and, though they grew fat and indolent, they had no need for luxuries. In Herodotus (IV, xix, 46–47) they emerge as a somewhat praiseworthy people for they have produced at least one sage, Anacharsis.

But in later writers they are described as very pious, never injuring anyone, nomadic, and communistic. So Pseudo-Scymnus, in his *Orbis descriptio* (A.D. 850–59), describes them. Similar remarks are made by Strabo, the geographer; and the tradition of the hardy and wise Scythian passes on into Latin in Cicero, Horace, and Vergil. Ovid, however, who knew whereof he was speaking, despises the savages of the Pontus, region of the Scythians, and can find nothing good to say of them. It is interesting that when the colonists came to America, their views of the Noble Savage were similarly modified by direct acquaintance. They may have been touched by the glowing accounts of the native American which had been made by the first explorers, but they were quickly disillusioned.

The most famous passage in Latin literature on a savage people is in the *Germania* of Tacitus. But the Germans had already been described by Julius Caesar in his *Gallic Wars* (VI, 21–23) as men who admire chastity, live mainly on milk, cheese, and meat, have no private property, and are noticeably brave in war. The tradition that idealizes them begins in Seneca's *De providentia* (IV, 14–15). Though Seneca admits the harshness of the German climate, he admires the people for walking in the path of nature. Tacitus gives us more details. The Germans are a cattle raising people; they have no pride in adornment; are particularly brave; have no cities; are chaste and in general monogamous, knowing little of adultery; are very hospitable; are communistic; and have no elaborate funerals. They are thus contrasted with the Romans. But at the same time, they have certain weaknesses: belligerency, gluttony, drunkenness. In short he is describing this people as he believes them to be and is not imagining a culture to fit a preconceived theory.

The Christian writers were not so fond of Noble Savages as the pagans were. After all they had tried to convert them and had suffered directly at their hands. Many of the twelve Apostles had been sent beyond the frontiers of the Mediterranean Basin and had not been welcomed by the inhabitants. Above all the barbarians had not received the Revelation and, though they could hardly be blamed for that, they could not be thought of as on a par with Jews and Christians. But sometimes one finds an early Christian author who will see some good in them. Saint Jerome for one used the barbarians as a standard of comparison with Christians, excusing to some extent their injustice, their avarice, and their general wickedness, since they knew no better, whereas the Christians did know better and hence were less excusable for their sins. Salvianus (fifth century) goes a bit farther in his *De gubernatione Dei* (III, i, 2) citing the Goths as models of sexual decency. The Romans, he says, are unchaste, the Goths are pure, and that is precisely why God permitted them to conquer the Romans.

The Greek Fathers also occasionally refer to the barbarians in terms of praise. Clement of Alexandria, for instance, admits their moral weaknesses, drunkenness, idolatry, belligerency, but at the same time says that they are superior to the Christians in invention. He even brings up the case of that preeminent Noble Savage, Anacharsis, as a model for Christians to observe with shame. But his point usually is that if the savage can achieve excellence, the Christian ought to do as well. This, as a matter of fact, was the general tendency of Christian writers until the twelfth century when the reading of classical texts was revived. Then one finds, for instance, Hugh of Saint Victor writing of the Scythians in his *Excerptiones priores* (V, ii) in the same vein as his Greek forebears had done, emphasizing Scythian virtues, their Spartan endurance, their abstemious diet of milk and honey, and their great corporeal strength. By this time the Scythians had become a legendary people.

The idea that somewhere there was a people living in accordance with nature never died out. Though the Christian writer could not find a real Noble Savage, he could find a few imaginary ones. The Camerini, for instance, have never been identified with any real tribe, but in the *Liber junioris philosophi* (ca. fifth century A.D.) we are told that they receive their food as a gift from heaven, live in a juristic state of nature, know no evil, do no work, and die happy at the age of one hundred and twenty years. At the same time, along with this mild form of cultural primitivism, the author reports that their country abounds in precious stones, something no pagan author had ever imagined. The emeralds, pearls, and sapphires remind one of Saint John's heaven.

The Camerini did not survive, as far as is known, in medieval literature; the Brahmins who, though real, were treated with as much fantasy as the Camerini, became known in Western Europe as early as the fourth century B.C. through the histories of Alexander's wars. In the *Gesta Alexandri* of Pseudo-Callisthenes, a work influenced by Christianity, the Brahmins take the place of the Scythians. They are withdrawn from the world like monks, live in nakedness, have neither domestic animals, agriculture, iron, buildings, fire, bread, wine, clothing, "nor anything pertaining to the productive arts or to pleasure." Their diet is vegetables,

fruits, and water. They sleep on beds of leaves. The passage describing them ends with a dialogue between the Brahmins and Alexander, in which the former talk like Greek Cynics who have learned some manners. Their aim, they say, is to live in accordance with nature, which means to have no wealth, to withstand the cold and the heat, to conquer oneself rather than others. They have no love of money, of pleasure, of fornication, murder, or wrangling. In short the main difference between the regimen of the Brahmins and that of Diogenes is that it is communal rather than solitary. The story of this encounter was repeated and with repetition grew until by the twelfth century the Brahmins were proto-Christians.

Yet it is fair to say that medieval writers were not enthusiastic about savages. The main function of these writers in the history of cultural primitivism was to keep alive the idea that it was possible to live in a hard primitivistic fashion and at the same time be virtuous, in fact exemplary in behavior. And it goes without saying that such men would also be happy. The more remote the savage, the more likely was it that he would be virtuous. The Icelanders win the palm, for they live on the young of their flock exclusively, are clothed in skins, inhabit caves, and, as Adam of Bremen (eleventh century) put it in his *Description of the Islands of the North*, they lead "a life holy in its simplicity." They ask for no more than nature yields and are especially happy in their poverty. They own all in common and practice charity to all. But, says Adam, they are now all Christians.

The desire to find somewhere or to believe that somewhere there exists a really virtuous and happy people may have been the stimulus in the Middle Ages to invent islands in the Atlantic where a life in accordance with nature would be lived. The Fortunate Islands, the Earthly Paradise, the Islands of the Blessed, Saint Brendan's Island, Perdita, the country of Prester John (though not an island in this case)—these were some but not all of these happy lands, far, far away. When it was a question of the Earthly Paradise, clearly the apocalyptic visions of early Christianity played their role in describing these lands. But the belief in such lands persisted up to the time of Columbus and indeed beyond that time. In fact Columbus' account of his third voyage almost if not quite identifies the West Indies with the Earthly Paradise. The people, he says, are graceful, shrewd, intelligent, and courageous. But they are also timid, and this was a trait that made them little to be feared. They are the best people in the world, "so unsuspicious and so generous with what they have, that no one who had not seen it would believe it." With Columbus we are at the beginning of the Renaissance and modern views of primitivism.

V. MODERN PRIMITIVISM

By the end of the fifteenth century the explorers had changed men's minds about the inhabitants of the globe, having found men who had never heard of the Gospel and who nevertheless seemed to be living in relative decency. The invention of printing moreover had given more men access to the accounts of these people and when combined with all the inventions and discoveries of the sixteenth century, permitted people to doubt a good portion of what they had always accepted on authority. But the proliferation of books, which were now preserved instead of being lost, makes it impossible to enter into details about the history of a point of view which was widely adopted and as widely combated. Hence what follows attempts to be no more than a sketch of the various kinds of modern primitivism.

Saint Augustine had laid it down as an outline of history that there would be seven ages of the world, of which the first, from Adam to Noah was the best. This age corresponded to infancy; and Augustine drew a parallel between the life of a human being, from babyhood to senescence, and the life of the race. This parallel has been used in historical accounts of civilization up to our own times by a writer like Spengler and in a modified form by Arnold Toynbee. To Augustine all would end in a cosmic Sabbath corresponding to the seventh day of Creation on which God rested. His outline was repeated without significant variation throughout the Middle Ages, and in modern times vestiges of it appear in speculations on the senescence of the world, of which the outstanding example is Thomas Burnet's *Theory of the Earth,* of which the first edition appeared in 1681. By emphasizing the decay of all the physical forces, proved by the diminution in size of the animals, including man, the book gave additional reason for looking backwards with longing to the first age when all was fresh and vigorous.

But by the end of the fourteenth century the submerged social classes had revolted in England, France, and a bit later in Germany. The famous cry of Wat Tyler,

> When Adam delved and Eve span,
> Who was then the gentleman?

recalled to his listeners that social class was not in the order established by God, and was a stimulus to return to the original plan according to which the Creator ordained the life of his people. One found much the same thing in the Proto-Protestant and Protestant movements in the fifteenth and sixteenth centuries, when only primitive Christianity and the words of the Bible as "uncorrupted" by commentators were considered authoritative. Of these movements in their most

primitivistic form one might select the Adamites. From then on the idea that the best condition of anything was its primordial condition was often taken for granted; and we find that there is a tradition not only of seeking the earliest form of religion as the best, but also the earliest form of the state, of the arts, even of the individual.

Columbus' accounts of his voyages were given currency in the works of Peter Martyr (Pietro Martire d'Anghiera, 1459–1526), whose *Decades* were frequently translated and reedited. Peter Martyr gave detailed accounts of the conduct of both the Spaniards and the Indians; and though those of the Indians were not always to their credit, nevertheless he kept alive the tradition that the natives resembled the men of the Golden Age. The islanders of Hispaniola, for instance, would be well nigh perfect if only they were Christians. They go about naked, like the Adamites, know nothing of weights and measures, "nor of the source of all misfortunes, money . . . living in the golden age, without laws, without lying judges, without books, satisfied with their life, and in nowise solicitous for the future." They are like men who were living before the social compact and yet with no need for government. The description is one which could well be written by a cultural primitivist but for one particular: the Hispaniolians are ambitious and fight among themselves. The Cubans are similarly described. They hold the land in common and know no difference between *meum* and *tuum.* Peter Martyr compares them also to the men of the Golden Age, and they apparently differ from their neighbors in Hispaniola only in that they are naturally equitable and never injure one another. If one believed this writer, and many did, one saw that ideas that might have been thought of as simply literary conventions or legend were in fact true. The Indians were primitive in the concrete sense of preserving the manners of the first age of man. They were real people living in a state of nature.

But the idea of the Golden Age was also kept alive in belles lettres. Italian literature of the fifteenth century is full of allusions to that happy period, and the following custom, started by Vergil in his *Fourth Eclogue,* was often used to celebrate the advent of any new ruler. All the well worn clichés about the earth producing without toil, the community of goods, the happiness of mankind, the beauty of men and women, their goodness, were brought out of storage and put into liquid verse. Sannazaro's *Arcadia* (1504) was a case in point with its fairylike land, peopled by exquisite shepherds and shepherdesses, all of whom speak in exquisite tropes. This classical theme, derived from Theocritus and Vergil, was reinforced by the reading of travelers' tales. Gilbert Chinard in his *L'Exotisme américain dans la littérature française au XVIe siècle* has shown how such reports extended the imagination of poets, even when they were using the idiom and mythology of the ancients.

It would be impossible to list all the contributors to the progress of modern primitivism for they survive in too great quantity. We shall therefore confine ourselves to mentioning a few of the most influential and let them stand for the rest. Of these Michel de Montaigne must head the list, for his *Essais* (1580) not only went through several editions and were widely translated, but one of them, *On the Cannibals* (Book I, 31), was hotly disputed by his seventeenth-century critics and was thus called to the attention of men who might not otherwise have read it.

There was, however, little in this essay that had not been anticipated by reputable classical writers, though they would not have been writing about American Indians. Montaigne's main thesis is simply that civilization does not improve morals. He points out that all that is barbarous among American natives is their strangeness, for we always think that the strange is barbarous. These people are wild (*sauvages*) in the same way that berries and flowers are wild: they are the product of "our great and powerful mother, Nature." They are living as men lived in the Golden Age, without trade, letters, mathematics, courts of justice, political ranks, servitude, riches or poverty, contracts, legacies, leisure occupations, individual kinship, clothing, agriculture, metallurgy, wine, or grain. They have no words for lying, treason, dissimulation, avarice, envy, belittlement, pardon, or misunderstanding. And, quoting Vergil (*Georgics* I, 20), he says, "These ways of life were first taught by Nature." Their country enjoys a mild climate, so that it is rare to see illness or any defects of bodily structure. They live on the coast and have plenty to eat. Their food is cooked without artificial embellishments. Their houses and clothes are simple, and they rise with the sun and eat their single meal immediately. They pass their time in dancing, while their youth are at the chase.

After relating their regard for women, the discourses of their old men, and their wars against a transmontane people, Montaigne comes to their cannibalism. He excuses this on the ground that they eat only their enemies, and they eat them not for sustenance but for vengeance. (This would seem to show that they could do things for which they had no names.) But this was no worse than what the Portuguese were doing, which was to bury their captives waist-deep and then shoot at them with arrows. There is no sense in our being horrified at their behavior if we can accept our own. "I think," Montaigne says, "it is more barbarous to eat a man alive than to eat him dead, to tear to pieces by torture and pain a body still capable of feeling, of roasting it bit by bit, of letting it be bitten and torn by dogs and swine"—here he cites what he had seen during the wars of religion—"than to roast and eat him after his decease." In any event cannibalism is better than our ordinary defects: treason, disloyalty, tyranny, and cruelty.

Montaigne here is not embellishing the life of his primitives; on the contrary he accepts all their blemishes but maintains that in comparison with our own, they are either no worse than we, or not bad at all. The primitive thus serves as a basis of contrast, and this service is founded on the premiss that morality is not to be judged by an absolute standard but by the context in which deeds are done. The argument may not be solid if acts are considered in isolation. But Montaigne was one of the first to think of the total regimen of peoples and he uses his law of nature as a standard for that. To take this attitude is to challenge one of the traditional premisses of the Church, that the foundation for morality lies in the *Decalogue* and the words of Christ. It might also be argued that these words are at the same time the Law of Nature and the Law of God. But in that case the goodness of savage life would be an accident of history and in no sense a paradigm for civilized people. Montaigne, it should also be noted, contributed to that side of primitivism which looked to the animals for models of good behavior, and to children.

The feeling spread that if goodness could be found in men who were supposed to be living in a state of nature, then one had but to revert to the Greek ideal. The problem was to find exemplifications of that which was natural. As a result of this search new concepts of primitivism arose. The savage began to lose his prestige as soon as more reports came in from, for instance, the North American settlers. No one who had been through the Deerfield Massacre could feel friendly towards the Indians. They became simply a bloodthirsty lot. Their behavior showed that they had not received the word of God and knew nothing of the theological virtues. Someone had to take their place. And when the islands in the Atlantic became exhausted as a source for primitivism, men turned to the Pacific. When there were no more imaginary lands to be inhabited by imaginary saints, instead of abandoning the notion, writers turned elsewhere.

First to be endowed with the characters of the Noble Savage, probably because of the influence of Rousseau, was the Peasant, living a simple, pastoral life as was lived in the pastoral period of history. The Peasant lived close to nature in the sense of the nonartificial. He was primitive only in degree, for after all he plowed his fields, sowed them, reaped the harvest, bought and sold; but he was innocent of most of the arts and sciences and, until advanced methods of agriculture were introduced, he could be endowed with simplicity, innate wisdom, guilelessness, and, by the time Wordsworth came along, with poetic insight. He seemed to be living in intimate communion with forces over which men had no control, the wind and the rain. It was the urban dweller who represented Custom as opposed to Nature.

Sometimes a ballad would play on the Peasant's shrewdness, his ingenuity, even his ability to outwit the city man. Men of education, like Montaigne or Agrippa von Nettesheim (1486–1535), along with some of the Protestant mystics, insisted that learning was a cover for a higher kind of knowledge which needed no schooling to emerge. This was a reversion to that form of anti-intellectualism which had appeared now and then in the Middle Ages, when writers pointed out that Christ had not chosen scholars for his disciples but fishermen. Only four of the Apostles, as far as is known, were actually fishermen, but since the occupation of only one of the others, that of Matthew (a tax collector, *publican*) was known, no one could be contradicted who held to this opinion.

At the same time there was a current of thought that was definitely antipeasant. It appears, to take but one instance, in the vogue for emblems, whose supporters insisted that the deepest truths were too important to be revealed to all and sundry, that Christ had spoken in parables not to teach the unlearned, but to conceal his real meaning from them. The sixteenth century had as one of its marked traits the antagonism between learning and folly, and Erasmus was not alone in praising the latter. Agrippa's *Eulogy of the Ass* was in line with the tradition of the Wise Fool; and the party of the Wise Fool could appeal to Saint Paul, "the Fool in God," or for that matter to Tertullian if they knew about him. Montaigne was bitterly attacked in the seventeenth century for his anti-intellectualism.

But in a time when one side of Protestantism was emphasizing any man's ability to interpret the Bible, the other side could only take refuge in insisting that the truths of Scripture were too complicated, too recondite, for the understanding of anyone but a scholar. Yet just as the American Indian could be peaceful, gentle, kind, able to do without law and judges, so the farmer knew instinctively the essentials of religion, and the inessentials could be reserved for those who wanted to study them. It would be absurd to see in this no more than an epistemological quarrel. The fourteenth and fifteenth centuries were, as we have said, periods of armed revolt, revolt not only against the State but also against the Church. And once the Peasant had the audacity to declare that he had the same rights as the landed proprietors, the magnates, and was willing to fight for them, the truth would be proved pragmatically. As in the case of the Noble Savage, closer acquaintance with the Peasant led to doubts. The Peasant, like the urban ruffian was soon to be just as evil as the noble, the burgess, or the small employer.

The lower classes had to wait until the nineteenth and twentieth centuries to become fully rehabilitated. And by that time they were on the wane, slowly rising in the social hierarchy. But there was another candidate for the position of primitivistic paradigm waiting in the wings, ready to enter the stage when the cue came. That was the Child. The Child might have come into his own with Christianity, for the verses of Matthew 18:3, beginning, "Except ye be converted, and become as little children, ye shall not enter into the kingdom of heaven," might have been expected to be an incentive to put childhood on a pedestal. But that did not take place and, though it may seem strange from the modern perspective, even the cult of the infant Jesus was relatively late (sixteenth century). It was Montaigne again who first began calling attention to the rights of the child to be a child and not an immature man. And in Rousseau's *Émile* this right was accentuated and developed into a theory of pedagogy. Rousseau did not urge men to turn into children—that was to come in the middle of the twentieth century. But he did insist on the evil of treating children as if they were only potential adults. And since there was a strong streak of anti-intellectualism in him, it was easy to infer that he meant education to be nothing more than allowing a child to do as he would.

It is true that Rousseau believed in a source of truth that was nonempirical and which he called the heart. One could always argue that, if men were simply rational, then the present person without schooling was defective. But this would never do, for society needed men of all grades of intelligence, and there must be at least a minimum of knowledge accessible to us all. We have quoted Cicero on the Child as a *speculum naturae*. This meant that one did not have to go to the Scythians to gather information about universal beliefs in order to discover what Nature had to say to us. One had but to look at the Child.

This form of cultural primitivism contained within itself an element of chronological primitivism. The Child stood for Adam before the Fall. He was innocent and pure and the fact that his innocence depended on his impotence was irrelevant. He was like an angel. In the words of John Earle in his *Microcosmographie* (1628), he is "the best copy of *Adam* before he tasted of Eve or the apple. . . . He is nature's fresh picture newly drawn in oil which time, and much handling, dims and defaces." The process of growing up is degeneration. The history of individual men reproduces the history of the race. And if we wish to understand what has happened to mankind since the Fall, we have only to watch the Child as he matures. He gradually loses his primeval innocence and innate wisdom; in Wordsworth's words, the "shades of the prison-house begin to close" about him. During the nineteenth and twentieth centuries the Child loomed larger as an exemplar; and children's rights took on greater importance, not only in the eyes of educators but also in those of moralists. The twentieth century, said Ellen Key, was to be the "century of the child." The Child, she maintained, instinctively knows both what is right and what is true. The totem of this school of thought might well be Hans Christian Andersen's child who saw that the Emperor was naked.

From the Savage to the Peasant to the Child would seem a fairly steep descent, but there was one more step to be taken, the step into animality. Diogenes the Cynic had already taken the beasts as his model. And it had been said that man had learned his arts from the spider and the bird; that the beasts never went to extremes of eating and drinking and sexuality; never made war upon their own kind; and, according to some writers, were not only as rational as men but more so. During the Middle Ages when men believed that the animals had been created for the use of mankind, this sort of infraprimitivism was recessive. But during the Renaissance it was revived. How seriously admiration for animals was preached is questionable. But the problem of their intelligence, as of the existence of their souls, was very seriously debated. For if they had souls, those souls might be immortal; and if they were intelligent, what became of man's differentia?

To treat the beasts with kindness is modern and it would be senseless if the creatures had no feelings, as the Cartesians maintained. But since the development of theories of evolution, men have tended to integrate themselves into the whole biological order and to feel their kinship with the other animals. This tendency would by no means allow us to infer that animals had rights which were equal or superior to our own. But it would lead men to protect them from cruelty, to study their ethology, to admire their ingenuity. One thing above all was true of them: they could not be called unnatural. They had developed no culture which might lead them away from that which was "in accordance with Nature," and even more than the Child, the animal was a mirror of Nature's designs.

One other strain of cultural primitivism should be mentioned, though it was short-lived. That is the strain of epistemological feminism. At the end of the eighteenth century, especially among the romanticists, it was believed that women had a kind of insight into the truth which was lacking in man; it was called "intuition." Intuition usually was directed towards character reading, the arts, and the concealed motives of human behavior. The story of the rehabilitation of Eve does not belong here. But it is not out of place to recall that most of the evils which beset mankind had been attributed to her weakness when faced with the Serpent. Christ as the Second Adam had redeemed mankind from the sin of the first Adam; the Blessed Virgin as the Second Eve had been the immaculate vessel of the Redeemer. But somehow or other woman had to wait for some centuries to pass before the German romanticists saw in the sex those dark enigmatic forces which are unperceived by the more active and rational male. This very attractive point of view was not of long duration. With the economic and political emancipation of women, they were given something approaching equality and hence lost what mystery they had previously possessed.

Chronological primitivism today has lost most of its force. Few take the story of either the Golden Age or prelapsarian Adam literally. Life in the Islands of the Blessed has become simply a literary decoration, at most a wistful dream, and there are no Noble Savages left to admire. But the theory of social evolution as framed by nineteenth-century writers like Herbert Spencer led some people to believe that preliterate tribes were really primitive, as children or eggs prior to adults or freely living individuals. According to this view there ought to be no significant differences among such tribes. Yet one could hardly lump together the Polynesians and the Bantus, the Eskimos and the Patagonians without noting important differences in manner of life, social organization, kinship rules, sanctions, in short, ideals. The use of the word "primitive" to characterize all such people was scientifically unfortunate, for there was no evidence that any civilized group had ever literally evolved from any condition identical with that of the so-called primitives. But psychologically the misfortune was not so great, for it satisfied those who had primitivistic leanings. It induced men to look upon the arts of the Africans and the American Indians, the South Sea Islanders and the Eskimos, with greater sympathy and, though the reasoning about such matters was usually weak, the results of the reasoning were to broaden our sympathies and understanding. The South Sea Islands were usually described in terms of soft primitivism, but soon the detection of yaws and elephantiasis balanced the notice taken of beautiful women and the abundance of fruit and flowers.

The extension of our field of aesthetic appreciation,

moreover, was helped by the opening of caves in France and Spain, by the discovery of the rock paintings of North Africa and southern Mexico. Where some saw in these works of art the persistent need for self-expression, others saw in them a degree of "naturalness" which was lacking in what came out of the academies. Consequently there was an aesthetic movement back to what was believed to be primitive; and the drawings of children, as well as the masks and images of the Africans or Maoris, became the inspiration of artists like Paul Klee, Miró, and Picasso. Some of these men have denied this influence, but an artist is seldom aware of all of the forces which have been most powerful in forming his style.

There has also been a reversion to a form of anti-intellectualism with primitivistic overtones in the work of both Freud and Jung. Freud was a bitter critic of civilization and found in it the unconscious vestiges of primitive mentality. Yet he never urged us to act either as uncivilized human beings or as children. Jung on the other hand with his theory of archetypes tended towards a definite aesthetic primitivism. The archetypes were supposed to be a limited number of universal symbols possessed by the collective unconscious. The collective unconscious by its very nature is the common property of all human beings, regardless of their culture. Hence to uncover these symbols is to see directly into the minds of all one's fellowmen. But it was also to discover within one's psyche an identity with the primitives. Thus we had a form of cultural primitivism which led its proponents to interpret all myths, all forms of scientific theory, all artistic expressions of aspirations and fears, all ethical commandments, in a manner independent of linguistic barriers. Since the archetypes tend to be covered with layers of cultural accretions, they are most clearly found in the child or the childlike adult, who are not inhibited by convention from seeing and speaking primitive truth.

There was also a strain of cultural primitivism in the two outstanding forms of fascism, that of Italy and that of Germany. Mussolini was heavily influenced by anarchism and the theory of violence. The emphasis upon leadership, that which was later to be called by the Nazis the *Führerprinzip*, was a throwback to the model of the horde governed by the will of a strong man. Mussolini emphasized the need for strength and power. Bitterly opposed to any form of humanitarianism, a kind of neo-Darwinism was his ideal. Man was a superior form of ape and must remember this.

In Nazism the animal origin of mankind was even more strongly emphasized. The motto *"Blood and Soil"* was supposed to indicate the continuing link between the blond beast of today and the blond beast of primitive times. Men like Ludendorff and Rosenberg even urged a return to the religion of the Nordics, the worship of Odin and Thor, as a fit religion for the German people. The Nazis would readily have claimed that civilization had detracted men from their original condition, for it was no longer the civilization of the Germans; it was an international style of culture. But his primitivistic vocabulary did not prevent the Nazi from using all the modern methods of destruction when he made war.

Finally, it might be conceded that some forms of extreme "progressive education" are based on primitivistic postulates. If the child is to be permitted to satisfy all his desires, however contrary to the general peace, he will obviously act in a totally undisciplined manner. Discipline is something imposed from outside; it rarely, if ever, originates from within. Hence it cannot be called "natural." But progressive education was also based on the hope, which had been expressed by Rousseau, that the child would soon grow out of its anarchic state, just as society was believed to have done. In fact, some theories of pedagogy were derived from transferring the Law of Recapitulation out of embryology into sociology. It was then maintained that the growth of the individual recapitulated the history of the race. Hence the child must be allowed to repeat all the stages through which mankind had grown to maturity.

Since some historians, Spengler for instance, had utilized the basic metaphor of the life cycle as a picture of a nation's progress, there seemed to be some evidence that would justify this educational process. But though the American child might begin his schooling with studying the American Indian, building tepees, dancing corn dances, making Indian costumes, none seem to have been made to live in a cave, eat his fellows' flesh, or hunt with stone-tipped arrows. At the time of writing a similar movement has set in among certain sociologists to erect the animals again as exemplars of civilized behavior. Thus the "territorial imperative" is used to interpret what civilized nations are doing on the international scene. But it is not always clear whether this is an interpretive description or a program.

There always remain residues of earlier cultural periods in every period and these tendencies may not be of long duration. Primitivism now seems to exist mainly in the arts, perhaps because it is no longer reasonable to deny the benefits of scientific discovery and technological inventions. It appears as if modern man were committed to civilization with all its weaknesses and lack of picturesqueness.

BIBLIOGRAPHY

A. O. Lovejoy and G. Boas, *Primitivism . . . in Antiquity* (Baltimore, 1935), gives in Greek, Latin, and English all the passages pertinent to the subject. G. Boas, *Essays on Primitivism and Related Ideas in the Middle Ages* (Baltimore, 1948), cites English translations of similar texts for the medieval period. For the eighteenth century, see Lois Whitney, *Primitivism and the Idea of Progress in English Popular Literature of the Eighteenth Century* (Baltimore, 1934). Other books covering aspects of the subject: Gilbert Chinard, *L'Exotisme américain dans la littérature française au XVIᵉ siècle* (Paris, 1911); and idem, *L'Amérique et le rêve exotique dans la littérature française au XVIIᵉ et au XVIIIᵉ siècles* (Paris, 1933); G. Boas, *The Happy Beast* (Baltimore, 1933); and idem, *The Cult of Childhood* (London, 1966). For the rise of the pastoral and its relations to primitivism, see Walter W. Greg, *Pastoral Poetry and Pastoral Drama* (London, 1906); for primitivism in art, see Robert J. Goldwater, *Primitivism in Modern Painting* (New York, 1938).

GEORGE BOAS

[See also Allegory; Astrology; Christianity; Cosmic Fall; Cycles; Cynicism; Education; Epicureanism; Happiness and Pleasure; Impiety; Law, Natural; Millenarianism; Myth; **Nature;** Progress; Rationality; Sin and Salvation; Skepticism; **Stoicism;** Women.]

PRIMITIVISM IN THE EIGHTEENTH CENTURY

THE NOTION of primitivism gained new significance in the eighteenth century because of the popularity of certain allied notions with which it was compatible. One of these was the doctrine of the so-called natural goodness of man, expounded in the first decade of the century by Shaftesbury and later by Rousseau. Obviously if man is inherently good, he must certainly be so in the primitive state before he is exposed to corrupting influences of any sort. Exponents of man's natural virtue such as Lord Shaftesbury and Richard Steele blamed defective education for acquired vices, and others such as Rousseau found science and civilization at fault.

Primitivism also merged with deism in a type of rationalism which implied, that the truths of "reason" or "nature," since they are universal, must be at least as well known to uncivilized men as to those in society and that since the unsophisticated man is protected from the corrupting forces of society, his insight into God and nature will be all the more direct and certain. In 1700 a Swedish missionary delivered a sermon to a tribe of Indians in Pennsylvania. A native spokesman in reply exposed Christian doctrine to such searching questions that the episode was reported in a history of the Swedish church in America printed in Uppsala in 1731. An enterprising American deist translated literally the reasoning of the Indian orator, who among other points had asserted that since he and his ancestors had always believed that a good life would be pleasing to God, this opinion must have come to them directly from heaven; and that although it may be possible that the Christians have superior knowledge, it is at the same time certain that their morals are depraved. When this colloquy appeared as a deistical essay in several American newspapers, it inspired Benjamin Franklin's *Remarks Concerning the Savages of North America* (1784), in which an Indian replies to a doctrinal sermon on original sin, "What you have told us . . . is all very good. It is indeed bad to eat apples. It is better to make them all into cyder."

A further major impetus to primitivism consisted in the accounts of travels, real or imaginary, to uncivilized regions of the world. By far the most influential were those concerning North America and the Pacific Islands, especially the sentimental romances of Chateaubriand, and the sociological speculations induced by the discoveries of Captain Cook.

The first major philosopher to rely extensively on evidence concerning primitive tribes, John Locke, actually used it to refute suppositions of natural goodness and wisdom. In order to destroy the doctrine of innate ideas in his *Essay Concerning Human Understanding*, Book I, Ch. III, Sec. 9 (1690) he cited a variety of monstrous beliefs and religious customs existing among savage tribes in Africa. At the same time Locke anticipated modern anthropology in recognizing that the crude superstitions of backward peoples represent definite stages in the evolution of thought. "Doctrines that have been derived from no better original than the superstition of a nurse, or the authority of an old woman, may, by length of time and consent of neighbours, grow up to the dignity of principles in religion or morality" (ibid., Book I, Ch. XI, Sec. 22). Shaftesbury, however, attacked Locke's credulity, without attributing the least glamor or superiority to primitive society as later thinkers would do. He charged that books of travel were to people of his day what books of chivalry had been to their ancestors. Their leisure hours were filled with "*Barbarian* customs, *savage* manners, *Indian* wars, and wonders of the *terra incognita.*" According to Shaftesbury, "they have far more pleasure in hearing the monstrous accounts of monstrous men, and manners; than the . . . lives of the wisest and most polish'd people." Rather than the accounts of diversity in religious observances which Locke had used to attack innate ideas, Shaftesbury advised philosophers "to search for that simplicity of manners, and innocence of behaviour, which has been often known among mere savages; ere they were corrupted by our commerce" (*Advice to an Author*, Part III, Sec. III). Shaftesbury was not praising the savage, but arguing that his example could be used to support uniformitarianism just as well as diversitarianism. He thus prepared the way for later authors who cited the savage to prove natural goodness and the universality of belief in God.

One of the most remarkable of the author-travelers who drew upon personal experience to promote primitivism was the Jesuit Father Joseph François Lafitau, who had lived in North America and who wrote his *Manners of the American Natives Compared with the Manners of Earliest Times* (*Moeurs des sauvages amériquains, comparées aux moeurs des premiers temps*, 1724) in order to protest against travelers who spoke of barbaric people as though they had no notion of religion. Lafitau affirmed that both the barbarians of the times of ancient Greece and Rome and the savages of his time had the concept of God. He denied the possibility that these nations, widely separated in their customs and manners of thinking, would concur in the same opinion if God had not "engraved the sentiment in the heart of all men at the same time that it is depicted without by the beauty of his works." This, he affirmed is what Lactantius calls "the evidence of peoples and nations" (*De falsa religione*, Book I, Ch. 2). After citing the aphorism of Cicero and Seneca that the universal belief in the truth of something is an assured and infallible evidence that it is indeed true, Lafitau quoted an earlier deistical work, Guedeville's *Dialogues or Conversation of a Native and the Baron de la Hontan* (*Dialogues ou Entretiens d'un sauvage et du baron de la Hontan*, 1704) to prove the existence of religion among the Hurons.

Giambattista Vico also believed in the existence of "universal and eternal principles," including the belief in God "on which all nations were founded and still preserve themselves." He lashed out, therefore, in his *Principles of the New Science* (*Principi di scienza nuova*, 1725, 1744) at "the modern travelers who narrate that peoples of Brazil, South Africa, and other nations of the New World . . . live in society without any knowledge of God." Vico argued simply that "these are travelers' tales, to promote the sale of their books by the narration of portents."

One of the major literary works of the century, Swift's *Gulliver's Travels* (1726), provides a convincing example of the pervasiveness of primitivistic conceptions even though Swift himself was highly mundane and sophisticated. His ridiculing of the passion for precious metals—represented by the odious Yahoos digging for days to extract them from the earth and then hiding them by heaps in their kennels—had been preceded in Gueudeville's *Dialogues* by a passage in which a Huron Indian condemns the prizing of precious metals and characterizes money as "the demon of demons." Swift's concept that only vicious nations have words to express the vices of humanity, that the vocabulary of the Houyhnhnms is totally inadequate to portray "the desire of power and riches, of the terrible effects of lust, intemperance, malice and envy," had been applied by Montaigne to the Brazilians: "The very words that signify lying, treachery, falsehood, avarice, envy, detraction and pardon were unheard of among them" ("Of Cannibals"). Swift's most fundamental concept that the natural reason which the Houyhnhnms possess penetrates directly to the truth, that it strikes with immediate conviction, "as it must needs do where it is not mingled, obscured, or discoloured by passion and interest," had been previously suggested by Lafitau in *Moeurs des sauvages amériquains:* "They think precisely about their concerns, and better than the masses among us: they go immediately to their ends by direct routes."

Rousseau, who was generally considered during the century as being almost fanatical in his dedication to the natural man, actually depicted man in the primitive state as little better than a brute or animal in his first two major works. His primary doctrines, nevertheless, supported primitivistic suppositions. In his *Discourse on the Sciences and Arts* (*Discours sur les sciences et les arts*, 1749), in which he gave a negative answer to the query whether the development of the sciences and arts has helped to purify morals, Rousseau paradoxically argued that the achievements of man's intellect have brought about a corresponding decline in man's happiness. This decline he attributed to the failure of man's passions to adjust to his intellectual progress. Man's inherent flaw consists in his perpetual need to elevate himself above his peers. In his *Discourse on Inequality* (*Discours sur l'inégalité*, 1755), which traces social imbalance to the establishment of the concept of property, Rousseau touched on an argument frequently used to vindicate primitivism in economic theory—that luxury is an evil of mundane society productive of most of its vices. Otherwise he portrayed man in a struggle for self-preservation so fierce that, had he remained in the savage state, the human race would have been in danger of extermination. In common with Lord Monboddo, he wondered whether the orangutang should be considered a savage man. The only difference between man and brute animals, he declared, was man's faculty of perfecting himself, a concept obviously antiprimitivistic.

Rousseau vigorously denied, however, that human perfection consisted in science or belles-lettres. In the preface to a comedy, *Narcissus or the Lover of Himself* (*Narcisse ou l'amant de lui-même,* 1752), he emphasized the doctrines of his first discourse: that the taste for the refinements of society leads to idleness and vainglory and that science corrupts the mental processes.

Although it is true that Rousseau did not exalt the mythical state of nature, he nevertheless almost constantly portrayed the advantages of life removed from society. The famous opening sentence of his *Émile or Concerning Education* (*Émile ou de l'éducation,* 1762) epitomized his confidence in nature as the strongest force in education: "Everything is good in leaving the hands of the creator of things; everything degenerates in the hands of man."

The classical concept of the Golden Age continued to flourish, particularly in England. James Thomson, in *The Castle of Indolence* (1748), described the idyllic state of the biblical patriarchal age.

> Toil was not then. Of nothing took they heed,
> But with wild beasts the silvan war to wage,
> And o'er vast plains their herds and flocks to feed:
> Blest sons of nature they! true golden age indeed!
> (Canto I, Stanza 37)

Pope in *An Essay on Man* (1733–34) stressed the benevolence of life in a mythical prehistorical period.

> Nor think, in Nature's State they blindly trod:
> The state of Nature was the reign of God: . . .
> (III, 149–50)

Thomson in "Spring" (1730) gave essentially the same portrayal of the prime of days before injurious acts or surly deeds were known among the "happy sons of Heaven." Reason and benevolence were law, and manners were pure, white, and unblemished (lines 272–308).

Joseph Warton in *The Enthusiast: or, The Lover of Nature,* (1744) paraphrased Lucretius' *De rerum natura* V to produce the same effect.

> Happy the first of Men, ere yet confin'd
> To smoaky Cities; who in sheltering Groves,
> Warm Caves, and deep-sunk Vallies liv'd and lov'd,
> By Cares unwounded (lines 78–81).

Closely related to the Golden Age is another classical concept that even in one's own day a richer way of life may be found in rural retirement than in urban centers, a concept which may be called domestic primitivism. In English its best expression is the poem *The Choice* (1700) by John Pomfret. The Georgic tradition in English verse similarly celebrates agricultural life for its wholesomeness, simplicity, and virtue. Examples are John Philips' *Cyder* (1708) and John Dyer's *The Fleece* (1757).

The transition from the Golden Age of fable to a state of nature in modern times is well illustrated in the poem *The Alps* (*Die Alpen,* 1729) by Albrecht von Haller in praise of his native Swiss mountains. He described first of all the "happy golden age, gift of the first good," when wheat grew of its own accord, honey and milk ran in the streams, and lambs lay down with the wolves. But most to be prized in this idyllic existence which might be called soft primitivism was the absence of superfluous luxury and lust for wealth. In the modern world as well, according to Haller, the state of nature (represented by life in the country or the mountains) is to be preferred to urban conditions because of its simplicity and even its hardship. Life in the Alps provides bodily health and inculcates virtues of independence, self-reliance, courage, and fortitude, the same virtues extolled by the Stoics.

> Die Arbeit füllt den Tag und Ruh besetzt die Nacht.
> ("Work filled the day, and rest possessed the night.")

A humble Swiss peasant later attained considerable celebrity for rising to the "sublime heights of philosophy" entirely by devoting his genius to agricultural pursuits. This unlearned but shrewd farmer named Jacob Kleinjogg had turned a debt-ridden property into a profitable enterprise. His achievements were heralded by Hans Caspar Hirzel in *Die Wirthschaft eines philosophischen Bauers* (1761) which was later translated into English as *The Rural Socrates* (1770). Herzel argued that "in the country, humanity presents itself to our view, in a state of innocent simplicity, resembling in some degree, the state of nature." The older Mirabeau together with the physiocrats regarded Kleinjogg as a modern hero, and Benjamin Franklin's disciple Benjamin Vaughan edited an American edition of *The Rural Socrates* in 1800. No doubt a considerable amount of the homage accorded to "the ploughboy poet," Robert Burns, as well as to such pedestrian versifiers as Stephen Duck can be traced to this vogue for living close to nature in the domestic environment.

An English novel of revolutionary tendencies in education *Sandford and Merton* (1783–89), by Thomas Day, contrasts a young farm boy, Sandford, a British counterpart of Jacob Kleinjogg, with a wealthy scion of an aristocratic family, Merton. The tutor of the two boys, the Reverend Mr. Barlow, a disciple of Rousseau's *Émile,* instructs them according to a pattern of close contact with nature, and inculcates lessons through practical experience. Day complements the domestic primitivism of the English farm with innumerable moral tales celebrating the virtues of faraway Negroes, Laplanders, and Indians.

A more famous panegyric of the virtues of English country life is Oliver Goldsmith's *The Deserted Village*

(1770) which celebrates "Sweet Auburn, loveliest village of the plain." Thomas Gray in similar vein drew attention in his *Elegy Written in a Country Churchyard* (1750) to the virtues and unrealized talents of the rural dweller, "Far from the madding crowd's ignoble strife."

Other English poets recognized that the rugged life of the soil which may be called hard primitivism is not always idyllic, but they found it nevertheless admirable and salutary because of the Spartan character it developed. William Collins in his *Ode on the Popular Superstitions of Scotland*, written about 1749, described the "bleak rocks" and "rugged cliffs" of the Hebrides which contribute to the "sparing temp'rance" of the inhabitants.

> Thus blest in primal innocence they live,
> Suffic'd and happy with that frugal fare
> Which tasteful toil and hourly danger give,
> Hard is their shallow soil, and bleak and bare.

These lines are based on Martin Martin's *Voyage to St. Kilda* (1698), an influential treatment of domestic primitivism.

Even Warton in *The Enthusiast* tempered his rhapsodic portrayal of nature by recognizing that the fierce north wind often smites the shivering limbs of shepherds and that wild animals may fright them from their caves to rove "houseless and cold in dark, tempestuous Nights." But these rigorous conditions were, nevertheless, to be prized because they develop corresponding virtues.

The primitivism based on the appeal of a simple life in far away places may be termed exotic, the chief characteristic of which is praise of "the noble savage," a phrase which seems to have been introduced into the English language by Dryden in *The Conquest of Granada*, Part I (1669).

> I am as free as Nature first made man,
> Ere the base laws of servitude began,
> When wild in woods the noble savage ran.

This is, of course, a description of the assumed political state of nature rather than a portrayal of actual faraway lands. The latter Dryden had earlier supplied in a reference to the discoveries of Columbus in *To My Honour'd Friend Dr. Charleton* (1663).

> The fevrish aire fann'd by a cooling breez,
> The fruitful Vales set round with Shady Trees;
> And guiltless *Men*, who danc'd away their Time,
> Fresh as their *Groves* and *Happy* as their *Clime*.

The Spanish conquest of Mexico and Peru does not seem to have inspired any depiction of the noble savage in Spanish literature, with a single exception, a treatise on the *Virtues of the Indian* (*Virtudes del Indio*), by Juan de Palafox first printed secretly around 1650 in the town of Puebla, Mexico. It was republished in Spain in 1661 and translated into French in 1666. The work, written for the purpose of extolling the qualities and virtues of the Indians of New Spain, stressed their contentment with poverty, their frugality, modesty, piety, and innocence. The Indian nevertheless did not play a major role in Spanish or Spanish-American literature until he was introduced in the nineteenth century under the influence of Chateaubriand. In France and England, however, translations of Spanish chronicles of the *conquistadores* led directly to several eighteenth-century dramatic and fictional representations of noble Aztecs and Incas. Most important was Marmontel's philosophical novel, *The Incas, or The Destruction of Peru* (*Les Incas, ou la destruction de l'empire du Pérou*, 1779), which affirmed the moral superiority of the state of nature.

The first influential work of prose fiction devoted to exotic primitivism was an English work, *Oroonoko; or, The Royal Slave* (1688) by Aphra Behn, which concerns the stoic sufferings of a princely African Negro brought by trickery to Surinam in Dutch Guiana. The author not only extols the handsome looks, intelligence, and courage of Oroonoko, but also lauds the Indians of Surinam.

> These people represented . . . an absolute Idea of the first State of Innocence, before man knew how to sin: and 'tis most evident and plain, that simple Nature is the most harmless, inoffensive, and virtuous Mistress. 'Tis she alone, if she were permitted, that better instructs the World, than all the Inventions of Man: Religion would here but destroy that Tranquillity they possess by Ignorance; and Laws would but teach 'em to know offenses, of which they have no notion.

Undoubtedly the most famous literary savage of all times is Friday of Daniel Defoe's, *Life and . . . Adventures of Robinson Crusoe* (1719), a work which Rousseau considered the best textbook of the natural sciences in print and the only book which he allowed Émile to read during the period of developing reason, from 12 to 16 years. Crusoe, who in the novel is described as living alone for twenty-five years on an island near the mouth of the Oroonoko River, had no high opinion of the natives of the area, who were cannibals, but he acquired a strong affection for Friday whom he had saved from death at the hands of two other natives.

Crusoe himself may not have appeared to Defoe as a happy child of nature, but he was considered in this light by the Yverdon *Encyclopédie*. "After four years, this European felt himself eased of the great burden of social life, when he had the good fortune of losing the habit of reflection and thought which used to take him back to the past or torment him with the future" (article "Sauvages").

Most of the noble savages who appear as characters in literature are masculine, but a notable exception appears in Richard Steele's story of "Inkle and Yarico" which appeared in the *Spectator* (No. 11, 1710/1711). Based on Richard Ligon's *True and Exact History of the Island of Barbados* (1657), the story concerns the sacrificial love of a beautiful native princess, Yarico, for an avaricious English trader, Inkle. Fleeing a party of hostile Indians on the American mainland, Inkle is befriended by the nude and innocent Yarico. For several months she shelters him in the woods and finally leads him to the coast, where he embarks on an English vessel along with the protectress, promising faithfully to take her with him to England. At Barbados, however, Inkle sells her into slavery despite her tearful revelation that she is carrying his child. For the benevolent Steele, the story illustrated the pernicious effects of the love of gain overcoming natural impulses. The sentimental overtones of the story were developed in over forty-five imitations or variants in poetry and drama in English, German and French produced before 1830 (Lawrence M. Price, *Inkle and Yarico Album*, 1937).

An entirely new element was added to exotic primitivism when the French explorer Louis Antoine de Bougainville touched at Tahiti in 1768, followed shortly thereafter by an English scientific expedition, including in its personnel, Joseph Banks, Daniel Carl Solander, and Captain James Cook. Tahiti offered to the delighted Europeans a beneficent climate with food in abundance, a race of natives extremely handsome even by European standards, an apparent community of property, and sex habits which approached free love. In addition, the Tahitians followed a religion rich in fertility rites. All this contrasted sharply with the various Indian tribes of America, who for the most part lived in difficult climates, were hostile and cruel toward foreign tribes, and aroused very little sex interest in each other or in their European visitors. Bougainville gave *Tahiti* the French name "Nouvelle Cythère" because of the sexual appetites of its inhabitants as well as "the beauty of its climate, its soil, its situation and its produce" (Chinard, *Supplément . . .* , p. 29).

When Diderot reviewed Bougainville's report on his expedition, *Voyage Around the World* (*Voyage autour du monde*, 1771), he affirmed that this was the only account of a voyage which had given him the taste for any country other than his own. Aware of the dangers of corrupting the island paradise of Tahiti, he implored Bougainville to leave the innocent and fortunate natives in peace and happiness, free to follow their way of life based on "the instinct of nature." For Diderot, this meant that they had no conception of "the baleful distinction between yours and mine" and that their wives and daughters were shared in common without the furors of love and jealousy which existed in European society. Changing any of this, according to Diderot, would be equivalent to forging the chains of their future slavery. (Chinard, *Supplément . . .* , p. 207).

The voyage of the English scientists was described first of all in a work in French, *Supplement to the Voyage of Bougainville, or Journal of a Voyage Made Around the World by Messrs. Banks and Solander* (*Supplément au voyage de M. de Bougainville, ou Journal d'un voyage autour du monde fait par MM. Banks et Solander,* 1772) by de Fréville. The author described the South Sea islands as "a happy land," with "the best built and most handsome inhabitants one could ever see. The women especially seemed to have been embellished with all the graces." More important, de Fréville also found among these islanders "humanity, rectitude, and the frankness of the Golden Age." In 1773 John Hawkesworth compiled and adapted the observations of Cook, Banks, and Solander in a single narrative, *New Voyage Round the World*. In describing the happiness of the natives of Tahiti, he formulated the essential dilemma of the theory of progress. "If we admit that they are upon the whole happier than we, we must admit that the child is happier than the man, and that we are losers by the perfection of our nature, the increase of our knowledge, and the enlargement of our views."

Bougainville brought back to France with him a native of Tahiti, Aotourou, whom a minor social critic, Nicolas Bricaire de La Dixmerie, used as an instrument for satirizing French culture and the ideas of Rousseau in *The Native of Tahiti to the French People; with a message to the philosopher, friend of the natives* (*Le Sauvage de Taiti aux Français; avec un envoi au philosophe ami des sauvages,* 1770). Another Tahitian, Poutaveri, was described poetically by Jacques Delille in *The Gardens* (*Les Jardins*, 1782), as visiting the royal gardens and breaking out in tears at seeing a tree which reminded him of his own land.

> *Les champs de Taiti si chère à son enfance,*
> *Où l'amour sans pudeur n'est pas sans innocence.*
> ("The fields of Tahiti so dear to his childhood,
> Where love without bashfulness is not without
> innocence.")

The English similarly brought back to London a handsome and agreeable young man, Omai, who was lionized and portrayed in several poems, dramatic performances, and paintings.

Diderot took advantage of the vogue of Tahiti to publish a *Supplement to the Voyage of Bougainville* (*Supplément au voyage de Bougainville*, 1796) in which he unequivocally denounced the evils of private property and the restraints of the Christian religion. He attributed to Tahiti the concept which a century earlier Aphra Behn had applied to the Indians of South America, that "Religion would here but destroy that Tranquillity they possess by Ignorance; and laws would but teach 'em to know offenses of which they have no notion." Diderot's *Supplément*, bearing the subtitle, *On the Inconvenience of Attaching Ethical Concepts to Certain Physical Actions to which They are not Appropriate*, enlarges the erotic and exotic elements suggested by Bougainville. The notions of jealousy, fidelity, chastity, and modesty associated with sexual gratification represent, according to Diderot, moral concepts improperly attached to a physical act. In protesting against the taint of vice being associated in civilized societies with the sexual act, Diderot wrote caustically: "Bury yourself, if you wish, in the dark forest with the perverse companion of your pleasures, but allow the good and simple Tahitians to reproduce without shame in the sight of heaven in broad daylight" (Chinard, *Supplément* . . . , p. 125). Like Rousseau, Diderot attributed all violent sex passions to the restraints placed on indiscriminate lovemaking in society. For both authors, the limitation of one man to one woman was a type of unhealthy restraint. The moral principle of Diderot's subtitle, however, certainly does not apply to any work of Rousseau. Indeed, it represents an opinion which Shaftesbury in his *Characteristics* (1711) had particularly condemned travel writers for affirming: "That all actions are naturally indifferent; that they have no note or character of good, or ill, in themselves; but are distinguish'd by mere fashion, law or arbitrary decree." In the dialogue itself, Diderot comes to no conclusion concerning whether a distinction exists between vice and virtue—or whether some vices may also appear in a state of nature as well as in artificial society. Taking just the opposite position to Saint Paul's in the dichotomy between the natural man and the spiritual man, Diderot described the inner conflict raging within each man in society between his natural impulses and his moral prejudices. "There existed a natural man; inside this man an artificial man has been introduced, and there takes place in the cavern a civil war which lasts throughout life." By extolling the sexual freedom existing in Tahiti, Diderot gave his answer to a question which Hawkesworth had raised in his *New Voyage* . . . : "Whether the shame attending certain actions, which are allowed on all sides to be in themselves innocent, is implanted in Nature, or superinduced by custom?" Diderot pro-

vided a further answer to this question by inserting in the midst of his dialogue on Tahitian sexual rites a translation of Benjamin Franklin's hoax, *The Speech of Polly Baker* (1747). Franklin's mythical Polly had supposedly been tried in New England on charges of bearing five bastard children. In defending herself before the court, she pleaded that she had merely been performing her religious duty—"the Duty of the first and great Command of Nature, and of Nature's God, *Encrease and Multiply*." The story combines two of Franklin's favorite themes, rational religion and philoprogenitiveness, the latter of which is a theme of Diderot's *Supplément* as well.

Before the discovery of Tahiti, Lafitau had merged the concepts of chronological and cultural primitivism by drawing a parallel between the Greeks and Hebrews of the ancient world and the American Indians of the modern. A traveler to Africa, Michel Adanson in his *Natural History of Senegal* (*Histoire naturelle du Sénégal*, 1758) saw the blacks in the same light. Their "ease and indolence" together with "the simplicity of their dress and manners" brought to his mind the concept of "the first man," and he "seemed to see the world at its birth." After Cook's voyages, Lord Monboddo similarly observed in his *Origin and Progress of Language* (1774) that the "golden age may be said yet to exist . . . in the South Sea, where the inhabitants live, without toil or labour, upon the bounty of nature in those fine climates."

At the turn of the century, Chateaubriand's sentimental romances *Atala* (1800) and *René* (1802) concerning incredibly noble Indians of North America left an indelible impression on his readers and kept the stream of primitivism alive in literature until it was later again replenished by James Fenimore Cooper's *Leatherstocking Tales*. The portrayal in *René* of "happy savages," seated tranquilly under their oaks, letting their days pass without counting them, is idealized and sentimental. According to Chateaubriand, the rational activity of the happy Indians is limited to satisfying their needs, and they "arrive at the result of wisdom, like a child, between play and sleep." Their excess of happiness occasionally induces a transitory melancholy, from which they are diverted by looking toward the sky for God. Despite this idyllic portrayal, Chateaubriand admitted in his later account of his travels in the United States (*Voyage en Amérique*, 1827) that the American Indian had passed the savage state long before the eighteenth century and that European civilization had, therefore, not been brought to bear upon "the pure state of nature," but upon a native American civilization then beginning. For Chateaubriand as well as for Rousseau and most eighteenth-century authors, no matter how rhapsodically they pursued the themes of primitivism, exotic or domestic, the pure state of nature was largely myth.

Antiprimitivism. Because of the popularity of the Noble Savage, it was only natural that the Ugly or Ignoble Savage should also be introduced in literature. Polyphemus in classical antiquity followed by Shakespeare's Caliban are the prototypes. In the eighteenth century, the Ugly Savage was represented by the Negro as portrayed in many travel books. Apologists of the slave trade used a brutish stereotype to argue that the blacks were better off as slaves in the New World than in the cruel environment of their native Africa (J. R. Constantine, "The Ignoble Savage, an Eighteenth Century Stereotype," *Phylon*, **27**, 171–79). William Bosman, in his *New and Accurate Description of the Coast of Guinea* (1705), charged for example that the "Negroes are all without exception, crafty, villainous, and fraudulent, and very seldom to be trusted." A former governor of Jamaica, Philip Thicknesse, based racism upon biology in his *Memoirs and Anecdotes* (1778). He admitted that Negroes are "a species of the human race," but of "an inferior and very different order." Their bile, he observed, is black; that of the white man, yellow, "proof of their being of a very distinct race of the human kind."

Theories of climate which attribute physical and intellectual backwardness to the Negro also represent important aspects of antiprimitivism. Other strains contrary to primitivism exist in portrayals of the rigors of climate and dangers from wild animals in distant lands. Captain Cook himself declared that the natives of Tierra del Fuego at the tip of South America were "perhaps as miserable a set of people as are this day upon Earth."

Goldsmith in *The Deserted Village* (1770), portrayed the "dreary scene" and "various terrors" of the "horrid shore" of Georgia. "Matted woods are filled with silent birds and silent bats; and poisonous fields" crawl with snakes and scorpions.

> . . . crouching tigers wait their hapless prey,
> And savage men, more murderous still than they.

In *Animated Nature* (1774) Goldsmith viewed the naked savage as "a poor contemptible being, standing on the beach of the ocean, and trembling at its tumults!" He is incapable of converting its terrors into benefits or aesthetic pleasure. "He considers it an angry deity, and pays it the homage of submission." According to Goldsmith, the savage remains without dignity in this degraded condition until he begins to use his mental powers. Another English poet, William Falconer, gives a similarly denigrating portrait of the primitive state in *The Shipwreck* (1788). Here poetry is the civilizing influence which elevates the savage from his degraded condition.

> When in a barbarous age, with blood defiled,
> The human savage roamed the gloomy wild;
> When sullen ignorance her flag displayed,
> And rapine and revenge her voice obeyed;
> Sent from the shores of light the Muses came
> The dark and solitary race to tame.

The Hottentots, inhabitants of the southern tip of Africa, were widely considered as the most disgusting of all primitive peoples. Sir William Petty regarded them as the most beastlike of all men encountered by travelers, and Sir John Ovington described them as "the very reverse of Human Kind," wondering whether they should be classed as midway "between a Rational Animal and a Beast" (A. O. Lovejoy, *Great Chain of Being*, p. 363). A satirical essay in *The Connoisseur* (No. 21, 1754) portrayed the infatuation of a Hottentot prince with a virgin of his species. "He was struck with the glossy hue of her complexion, which shone like the jetty down on the black hogs of Hessaqua; he was ravished with the prest gristle of her nose; and his eyes dwelt with admiration on the flaccid beauties of her breasts, which descended to her navel." Lessing in *Laokoön* (1766) cited this and a related passage as an example of the disgusting mixed with the sentimental to produce laughter. Quite possibly it was intended as a burlesque of the story of Inkle and Yarico.

James Boswell scattered throughout his *Life of Samuel Johnson* (1791) numerous remarks of the great lexicographer, directed against "cant in defense of savages." Johnson apparently overlooked the fact that early in his career he had portrayed a wise Indian chief in the manner of the deists, except that he allowed his philosophical Indian to repeat Christian doctrine (*Idler*, No. 81). Johnson nevertheless insisted that Indians have no physical superiority over civilized man, attributing their reputed health and development to a high incidence of infant mortality. "As to care of mental uneasiness, they are not above it, but below it, like bears." Rhapsodies over the state of nature, Johnson dismissed as gross absurdity. "It is sad stuff; it is brutish. If a bull could speak, he might as well exclaim,—Here am I with this cow and grass; what being could enjoy greater felicity?" In response to the often-repeated argument that savages scorn the complications and cares of civilized life, Johnson roundly declared that their opinion comes from ignorance alone. If savages were told about the labor, time, and risk involved in building a house, Johnson averred, "they would laugh heartily at our folly in building; but it does not follow that men are better without houses."

The strongest voice raised anywhere against primitivism was the ultra-sophisticated and highly cultivated Voltaire. In his poetic defense of luxury, *Le Mondain* (1736), developing the theories of Mandeville's *Fable* of the Bees (1727), Voltaire cleverly mocked both cultural and chronological primitivism. It is true, according to Voltaire, that in the earliest times our ancestors lived in ignorance, not recognizing private property. Indeed they could not, for they were naked and had no property of any kind. He who has nothing has no sharing to worry about. Later in the article "Homme" of his *Philosophical Dictionary* (*Dictionnaire philosophique*, 1765), Voltaire seriously and vehemently repudiated the notion of man's nobility in the pure state of nature. Such a man he argued would be far below the Iroquois of America. "The inhabitants of Kamchatka and the Hottentots of our days, clearly superior to the completely savage man, are animals who live six months of the year in caves, where they eat with their bare hands the vermin by whom they are eaten in turn." Like Rousseau, Voltaire recognized that the "pure state of nature" does not exist, and he was fervently persuaded that if it did, it would be wretched.

BIBLIOGRAPHY

An extensive bibliography appears in Paul Hazard, *La Pensée européenne au XVIIIᵉ siècle* (Paris, 1946). A pioneer study, still not superseded, is Gilbert Chinard's *L'Amérique et le rêve exotique* (Paris, 1913). A discussion from a sociological perspective is René Gonnard's *La Légende du bon sauvage* (Paris, 1946). Studies primarily devoted to English literature are H. N. Fairchild, *The Noble Savage* (New York, 1928) and M. M. Fitzgerald, *First Follow Nature* (New York, 1947). A superb study of the "Gothic" background is *Northern Antiquities in French Learning and Literature* by Thor J. Beck, 2 vols. (New York, 1934–35). E. A. Runge covers the German phase in *Primitivism and Related Ideas in Sturm and Drang Literature* (Baltimore, 1946). Two of the most valuable sources are editions of Diderot's *Supplément au voyage de Bougainville* edited by Gilbert Chinard (Paris, 1935) and by Herbert Dieckmann (Geneva, 1955).

A. OWEN ALDRIDGE

[See also Deism; **Nature; Primitivism;** Progress; **Romanticism in Literature;** Social Contract.]

PROBABILITY: OBJECTIVE THEORY

I. THE BEGINNING

1. Games and gambling are as old as human history. It seems that gambling, a specialty of the human species, was spread among virtually all human groups. The Rig Veda, one of the oldest known poems, mentions gambling; the Germans of Tacitus' times gambled heavily, so did the Romans, and so on. All through history man seems to have been attracted by uncertainty. We can still observe today that as soon as an "infallible system" of betting is found, the game will be abandoned or changed to beat the system.

While playing around with chance happenings is very old, attempts towards any systematic investigation were slow in coming. Though this may be how most disciplines develop, there appears to have been a particular resistance to the systematic investigation of chance phenomena, which by their very nature seem opposed to regularity, whereas regularity was generally considered a necessary condition for the scientific understanding of any subject.

The Greek conception of science was modelled after the ideal of Euclidean geometry which is supposedly derived from a few immediately grasped axioms. It seems that this rationalistic conception limited philosophers and mathematicians well beyond the Middle Ages. Friedrich Schiller, in a poem of 1795 says of the "sage": *Sucht das vertraute Gesetz in des Zufalls grausenden Wundern/Sucht den ruhenden Pol in der Erscheinungen Flucht* ("Seeks the familiar law in the dreaded wonders of chance/Looks for the unmoving pole in the flux of appearances").

2. However, the hardened gambler, not influenced by philosophical scruples, could not fail to notice some sort of long-run regularity in the midst of apparent irregularity. The use of loaded dice confirms this.

The first "theoretical" work on games of chance is by Girolamo Cardano (Cardanus), the gambling scholar: *De ludo aleae* (written probably around 1560 but not published until 1663). Todhunter describes it as a kind of "gambler's manual." Cardano speaks of chance in terms of the frequency of an event. His mathematics was influenced by Luca Pacioli.

A contribution by the great Galileo was likewise stimulated directly by gambling. A friend—probably the duke of Ferrara—consulted Galileo on the following problem. The sums 9 and 10 can be each produced by three dice, through six different combinations, namely:

$$9 = 1 + 2 + 6 = 1 + 3 + 5 = 1 + 4 + 4 = 2 + 2 + 5$$
$$= 2 + 3 + 4 = 3 + 3 + 3,$$
$$10 = 1 + 3 + 6 = 1 + 4 + 5 = 2 + 2 + 6 = 2 + 3 + 5$$
$$= 2 + 4 + 4 = 3 + 3 + 4,$$

and yet the sum 10 appears more often than the sum 9. Galileo pointed out that in the above enumeration, for the sum 9, the first, second, and fifth combination can each appear in 6 ways, the third and fourth in 3 ways, and the last in 1 way; hence, there are altogether 25 ways out of 216 compared to 27 for the sum 10. It is interesting that the "friend" was able to detect empirically a difference of $\frac{1}{108}$ in the frequencies.

3. Of the same type is the well-known question

posed to Pascal by a Chevalier de Méré, an inveterate gambler. It was usual among gamblers to bet even money that among 4 throws of a true die the "6" would appear at least once. De Méré concluded that the same even chance should prevail for the appearance of the "double 6" in 24 throws (since 6 times 6 is 36 and 4 times 6 is 24). *Un problème relatif aux jeux de hasard, proposé à un austère Janséniste par un homme du monde a été l'origine du calcul des probabilités* ("A problem in games of chance, proposed to an austere Jansenist by a man of the world was the origin of the calculus of probability"), writes S. D. Poisson in his *Recherches sur la probabilité des jugements* . . . (Paris, 1837). The Chevalier's experiences with the second type of bet compared unfavorably with those in the first case. Putting the problem to Blaise Pascal he accused arithmetic of unreliability. Pascal writes on this subject to his friend Pierre de Fermat (29 July 1654): *Voilà quel était son grand scandale que lui faisait dire hautement que les propositions [proportions (?)] n'étaient pas constantes et que l'arithmétique se démentait* ("This was for him a great scandal which made him say haughtily that the propositions [proportions (?)] are not constant and that arithmetic is self-contradictory").

Clearly, this problem is of the same type as that of Galileo's friend. Again, the remarkable feature is the gambler's accurate observation of the frequencies. Pascal's computation might have run as follows. There are $6^4 = 1296$ different combinations of six signs a, b, c, d, e, f in groups of four. Of these, $5^4 = 625$ contain no "a" (no "6") and, therefore, $1296 - 625 = 671$ contain at least one "a," and $671/1296 = 0.518 = p_1$ is the probability for the first bet. A similar computation gives for the second bet $p_2 = 0.491$, indeed smaller than p_1.

Both Fermat and Pascal, just as had previously Galileo, found it natural to base their reasoning on observed frequencies. They were interested in the answers to actual problems and created the simplest "theory" which was logically sound and explained the observations.

4. Particularly instructive is another problem extensively discussed in the famous correspondence between the two eminent mathematicians, the *problème des parties* ("problem of points"), which relates to the question of the just division of the stake between players if they decide to quit at a moment when neither has definitely won. Take a simple case. Two players, A and B, quit at a moment when A needs two points and B three points to win. Then, reasons Pascal, the game will certainly be decided in the course of four more "trials." He writes down explicitly the combinations which lead to the winning of A, namely *aaaa*,

aaab, *aabb*. Here, *aaab* stands for four different arrangements, namely *aaab*, *aaba*, . . . and similarly *aabb* stands for six different arrangements. Hence, $1 + 4 + 6 = 11$ arrangements out of 16 lead to the winning of A and 5 to that of B. The stake should, therefore, be divided in the ratio $11:5$. (It is worthwhile mentioning that mathematicians like Roberval and d'Alembert doubted Pascal's solution.)

The same results were obtained in a slightly different way by Fermat. The two greatest mathematicians of their time, Pascal and Fermat, exchanged their discoveries in undisturbed harmony. In the long letter quoted above, Pascal wrote to Fermat: *Je ne doute plus maintenant que je suis dans la vérité après le rencontre admirable où je me trouve avec vous. . . . Je vois bien que la vérité est la même à Toulouse et à Paris* ("I do not doubt any longer that I have the truth after finding ourselves in such admirable agreement. . . . I see that truth is the same in Toulouse and in Paris"). In connection with such questions Pascal and Fermat studied combinations and permutations (Pascal's *Traité du triangle arithmétique*, 1664) and applied them to various problems.

5. We venture a few remarks regarding the ideas on probability of the great philosophers of the seventeenth century. "Probability is likeness to be true," says Locke. "The grounds of it are in short, these two following. First, the conformity of anything with our knowledge, observation, and experience. Secondly, the testimony of others" (*Essay concerning Human Understanding*, Book IV). This is the empirical viewpoint, a viewpoint suggested by the observation of gambling results as well as of deaths, births, and other social happenings. "But," continues Keynes "in the meantime the subject had fallen in the hands of the mathematicians and an entirely new method of approach was in course of development. It had become obvious that many of the judgments of probability, which we, in fact, make do not depend upon past experience in a way which satisfied the canon laid down by the logicians of Port Royal and by Locke" (*"La logique ou l'art de penser . . . ,"* by A. Arnauld, Peter Nicole, and others, 1662, called the "Port Royal Logic"). As we have seen, in order to explain observations, the mathematicians created a theory *based on the counting of combinations*. The decisive assumption was that the observed frequency of an event (e.g., of the "9" in Galileo's problem) be proportional to the corresponding relative number of combinations (there, 25/216).

6. We close our description of the first steps in probability calculus with one more really great name, though his fame was not due to his contributions to our subject: Christian Huygens. Huygens heard through friends, about the problem of points but he had difficulty in obtaining reliable information about the problem and the methods of the two French mathematicians. Eventually, Carcavi sent him the data as well as Fermat's solution. Fermat even posed to Huygens further problems which Huygens worked out and later included as exercises in a work of his own. In this work, *De ratiociniis in aleae ludi* ("On reasoning in games of chance") of 1657, he organized all he knew about the new subject. At the end of the work he included some questions without indicating the method of solution. "It seems useful to me to leave something for my readers to think about (if I have any readers) and this will serve them both as exercises and as a way of passing the time." Jakob (James) Bernoulli gave the solutions and included them in his *Ars conjectandi*. The work of Huygens remained for half a century *the* introduction to the "Calculus of Probability."

7. A related type of investigation concerned mortality and annuities. John Graunt started using the registers of deaths kept in London since 1592, and particularly during the years of the great plague. He used his material to make forecasts on population trends (*Natural and Political Observations . . . upon the Bills of Mortality*, 1661). He may well be considered as one of the first statisticians.

John de Witt, grand pensioner of Holland, wrote on similar questions in 1671 but the precise content of his work is not known. Leibniz was supposed to have owned a copy and he was repeatedly asked by Jakob Bernoulli—but without success—to let him see it.

The year 1693 is the date of a remarkable work by the astronomer Edward Halley which deals with life statistics. Halley noticed also the regularity of the "boys' rate" (percentage of male births) and other constancies. He constructed a mortality table, based on "Bills of Mortality" for the city of Breslau, and a table of the values of an annuity for every fifth year of age up to the seventieth.

The application of "chance" in such different domains as games of chance (which received dignity through the names of Pascal, Fermat, and Huygens) and mortality impressed the scientific world. Leibniz himself appreciated the importance of the new science (as seen in his correspondence with Jakob Bernoulli). However, he did not contribute to it and he objected to some of his correspondent's ideas.

II. JAKOB BERNOULLI AND THE LAW OF LARGE NUMBERS

1. The theory of probability consists, on the one hand, of the consideration and formulation of problems, including techniques for solving them, and on the other

hand, of general theorems. It is the latter kind which is of primary interest to the historian of thought. The intriguing aspect of some of these theorems is that starting with probabilistic assumptions we arrive at statements of practical certainty. Jakob Bernoulli was the first to derive such a theorem and it will be worthwhile to sketch the main lines of argument, using, however, modern terminology in the interest of expediency.

2. We consider a binary alternative (coin tossing; "ace" or "non-ace" with a die; etc.) to this day called a Bernoulli trial. If q is the "probability of success," $p = 1 - q$ that of "failure," then the probability of a successes followed by b failures in $a + b$ trials performed with the same die is $q^a p^b$. This result follows from multiplication laws of independent probabilities already found and applied by Pascal and Fermat. The use of laws of addition and multiplication of probabilities is a step beyond the mere counting of combinations. It is based on the realization that a calculus exists which parallels and reflects the observed relations between frequencies.

The above probability $q^a p^b$ holds for any pattern of a successes and b failures: fssfffsf. . . . Lumping together all of these, writing x for a and $a + b = n$, we see that *the probability $p_n(x)$ of x successes and $n - x$ failures regardless of pattern* is

$$p_n(x) = \binom{n}{x} q^x p^{n-x}, \qquad x = 0, 1, 2, \ldots, n, \quad \text{(II.1)}$$

where $\binom{n}{x}$ is the number of combinations of n things in groups of x, and the sum of all $p_n(x)$ is 1.

Often we are more interested in the relative number $z = x/n$, the *frequency* of successes. Then

$$p_n(x) = p'_n(z) = \binom{n}{nz} q^{nz} p^{n(1-z)}. \quad \text{(II.1')}$$

This $p'_n(z)$—that is, the function that gives to every abscissa z the ordinate $p'_n(z)$—has a maximum at a point z_m, called the *mode* and z_m is equal to or very close to q. In the vicinity of z_m the $p'_n(z)$, as function of n, becomes steeper as n increases.

3. It was Bernoulli's first great idea to consider increasing values of n and a narrow neighborhood of q or, in other words, to investigate the behavior of $p'_n(z)$ in the neighborhood of $z = q$ as n increases; this he did at a time when the interest in the "very large" and the "very small" was just awakening. Secondly, he realized that we are not really interested in the value of $p'_n(z)$ for any particular value z but rather in the total probability belonging to all z's in an interval. This interval was to contain q which, as we remember, is our original success probability and at the same time

607

the mode of $p'_n(z)$ (for large n) and likewise its so-called "mean value."

Now, with ε a very small number, we call P_n the probability that z lies between $q - \varepsilon$ and $q + \varepsilon$, or, what is the same, that $x = nz$ lie between $nq - n\varepsilon$ and $nq + n\varepsilon$. For this P_n one obtains easily the estimate

$$P_n \geq 1 - \frac{pq}{n\varepsilon^2}. \qquad \text{(II.2)}$$

And from this follows immediately the fundamental property of P_n:

$$\lim_{n \to \infty} P_n = 1. \qquad \text{(II.3)}$$

This result can be expressed in words:

Let q be a given success probability in a single trial: n trials are performed with the same q and under conditions of independence. Then, no matter how small an ε is chosen, as the number n of repetitions increases indefinitely, the probability P_n that the frequency of success lie between q − ε and q + ε, approaches 1. (See *Ars conjectandi*, Basel [1713], Part IV, pp. 236–37.)

The above theorem expresses a property of "condensation," namely that with increasing n an increasing proportion of the total probability (which equals 1) is concentrated in a fixed neighborhood of the original q. The term "probability" as used by Bernoulli in his computations is always a *ratio* of the number of cases favorable to an occurrence to the number of all possible cases. About this great theorem, called today the "Bernoulli Theorem," Bernoulli said: ". . . I had considered it closely for a period of twenty years, and it is a problem the novelty of which, as well as its high utility together with its difficulty adds importance and weight to all other parts of my doctrine" (ibid.). The three other parts of the work are likewise very valuable (but perhaps less from a conceptual point of view). The second presents the doctrine of combinations. (In this part Bernoulli also introduces the polynomials which carry his name.)

4. It will be no surprise to the historian of thought that the admiration we pay to Bernoulli, the mathematician, is not based on his handling of the conceptual situation. In addition to the above-explained use of a quotient for a mathematical probability his views are of the most varied kind, and, obviously, he is not conscious of any possible contradiction: "Probability calculus is a general logic of the uncertain. . . . Probability is a degree of certainty and differs from certainty as the part from the whole. . . . Of two things the one which owns the greater part of certainty will be the more probable. . . . We denote as *ars conjectandi* the art of measuring (*metiendi*) the probability of things as precisely as possible. . . . We estimate the proba-

bilities according to the number and the weight (*vis probandi*) of the reasons for the occurrence of a thing." As to this certitude of which probability is a part he explains that "the certitude of any thing can be considered *objectively* and in this sense it relates to the actual (present, past, or future) existence of the thing . . . or *subjectively* with respect to ourselves and in this sense it depends on the amount of our knowledge regarding the thing," and so on. This vagueness is in contrast to the modern viewpoint in which, however, conceptual precision is bought, sometimes too easily, by completely rejecting uncongenial interpretations.

5. There appears in Bernoulli's work another conceptual issue which deals with the dichotomy between the so-called *direct* and *inverse* problem. The first one is the type considered above: we know the probability q and make "predictions" about future observations. In the *inverse* problem we tend to establish from an observed series of results the parameters of the underlying process, e.g., to establish the imperfection of a die. (The procedures directed at the inverse problem are today usually handled in mathematical statistics rather than in probability theory proper.) Bernoulli himself states that his theorem fails to give results in very important cases: in the study of games of skill, in the various problems of life-statistics, in problems connected with the weather—problems where results "depend on unknown causes which are interconnected in unknown ways."

It is a measure of Bernoulli's insight that he not only recognized the importance of the inverse problem but definitely planned (ibid., p. 226) to establish for this problem a theorem similar to the one we formulated above. This he did not achieve. It is possible that he hoped to give a proof of the inverse theorem and that death intercepted him (Bernoulli's *Ars conjectandi* was unfinished at the time of his death and was published only in 1713); or that he was discouraged by critical remarks of Leibniz regarding inference. It may also be that he did not distinguish with sufficient clarity between the two types of problems. For most of his contemporaries such a distinction did not exist at all; actually, even an appropriate terminology was lacking. We owe the first solid progress concerning the inverse problem to Thomas Bayes. (See Section IV.)

The Bernoulli theorem forms today the very simplest case of the Laws of Large Numbers (see e.g., R. von Mises [1964], Ch. IV). The names Poisson, Tchebychev, Markov, Khintchine, and von Mises should be mentioned in this connection. These theorems are also called "weak" laws of large numbers in contrast to the more recently established "strong" laws of large numbers (due to Borel, Cantelli, Hausdorff, Khintchine,

Kolmogorov) and their generalizations. The "strong" laws are mainly of mathematical interest.

III. ABRAHAM DE MOIVRE AND THE CENTRAL LIMIT THEOREM

1. Shortly after the death of Jakob Bernoulli but before the publication (1713) of his posthumous work books of two important mathematicians, P. R. Montmort (1673–1719) and A. de Moivre (1677–1754), appeared. These were Montmort's *Essai d'analyse sur les jeux de hasard* (1708 and 1713) and de Moivre's *De mensura sortis . . .* (1711) and the *Doctrine of Chances* (1718 and 1738). We limit ourselves to a few words on the important work of de Moivre.

De Moivre, the first of the great analytic probabilists, was, as a mathematician, superior to both Jakob Bernoulli and Montmort. In addition he had the advantage of being able to use the ideas of Bernoulli and the algebraic powers of Montmort, which he himself then developed to an even higher degree. A charming quotation, taken from the *Doctrine of Chances,* might be particularly appreciated by the secretary. "For those of my readers versed in ordinary arithmetic it would not be difficult to make themselves masters, not only of the practical rules in this book but also of more useful discoveries, if they would take the small pains of being acquainted with the bare notation of algebra, which might be done in the hundredth part of the time that is spent in learning to read shorthand."

2. In probability proper de Moivre did basic work on the "duration of a game," on "the gambler's ruin," and on other subjects still studied today. Of particular importance is his extension of Bernoulli's theorem which is really much more than an extension. In Section II, 3 we called P_n the sum of the $2r + 1$ middle terms of $p_n(x)$ where $r = n\varepsilon$ and $p_n(x)$ is given in Eq.(II.1). In Eq.(II.2) we gave a very simple estimate of P_n. (Bernoulli himself had given a sharper one but it took him ten printed pages of computation, and to obtain the desired result the estimate Eq.(II.2) suffices.)

De Moivre, who had a deep admiration for Bernoulli and his theorem, conceived the very fruitful idea *of evaluating P_n directly for large values of n,* instead of estimating it by an inequality. For this purpose one needs an *approximation formula for the factorials of large numbers.* De Moivre derived such a formula, which coincides essentially with the famous *Stirling formula.* He then determined P_n "by the artifice of mechanical quadrature." He computed particular values of his asymptotic formula for P_n correct to five decimals. We shall return to these results in the section on Laplace. Under the name of the *de Moivre-Laplace formula,* the result, most important by itself, became

the starting point of intensive investigations and far-reaching generalizations which led to what is called today the central limit theorem of probability calculus (Section VIII). I. Todhunter, whose work *A History of the Mathematical Theory of Probability . . .* (1865) ends, however, with Laplace, says regarding de Moivre: "It will not be doubted that the theory of probability owes more to him than to any other mathematician with the sole exception of Laplace." Our discussion of the work of this great mathematician is comparatively brief since his contributions were more on the mathematical than on the conceptual side. We mention, however, one more instance whose conceptual importance is obvious: de Moivre seems to have been the first to denote a probability by one single letter (like p or q, etc.) rather than as a quotient of two integers.

IV. THOMAS BAYES AND INVERSE PROBABILITY

1. Bayes (1707–61) wrote two basic memoirs, both published posthumously, in 1763 and 1765, in Vols. 13 and 14 of the *Philosophical Transactions of the Royal Society of London.* The title of the first one is: "An Essay Towards Solving a Problem in the Doctrine of Chances" (1763). A facsimile of both papers (and of some other relevant material) was issued in 1940 in Washington, edited by W. E. Deming and E. C. Molina. The following is from Molina's comments: "In order to visualize the year 1763 in which the essay was published let us recall some history. . . . Euler, then 56 years of age, was sojourning in Berlin under the patronage of Frederick the Great, to be followed shortly by Lagrange, then 27; the Marquis de Condorcet, philosopher and mathematician who later applied Bayes's theorem to problems of testimony, was but 20 years old. . . . Laplace, a mere boy of 14, had still 11 years in which to prepare for his *Mémoires* of 1774, embodying his first ideas on the "probability of causes," and had but one year short of half a century to bring out the first edition of the *Théorie analytique des probabilités* (1812) wherein Bayes's theorem blossomed forth in its most general form." (See, however, the end of this section.)

2. We explain first the concept of *conditional probability* introduced by Bayes. Suppose that of a certain group of people $90\% = P(A)$ own an automobile and $9\% = P(A,B)$ own an automobile and a bicycle. We call $P(B|A)$ the conditional probability of owning a bicycle for people who are known to own also a car. If $P(A) \neq 0$, then

$$P(B|A) = \frac{P(A,B)}{P(A)} \qquad \text{(IV.1)}$$

609

is *by definition the conditional probability of B given A.* (This will be explained further in Section VII,9.) In our example

$$P(B|A) = \frac{9/100}{90/100} = \frac{1}{10};$$

hence, $P(B|A) = 10\%$. We may write (IV.1) as

$$P(A,B) = P(A) \cdot P(B|A). \qquad (IV.2)$$

The *compound probability* of owning both a car and a bicycle equals the probability of owning a car times the conditional probability of owning a bicycle, given that the person owns a car. Of course, the set AB is a subset of the set A.

3. We try now to formulate some kind of inverse to a Bernoulli problem. (The remainder of this section may not be easy for a reader not schooled in mathematical thinking. A few rather subtle distinctions will be needed; however, the following sections will again be easier.) Some game is played n times and n_1 "successes" (e.g., n_1 "aces" in n tossings of a die) are observed. We consider now as known the numbers n and n_1 (more generally, the statistical result) and would like to *make some inference* regarding the unknown success-chance of "ace." It is quite clear that if we know nothing but n and n_1 and if these numbers are small, e.g., $n = 10$, $n_1 = 7$, we cannot make any inference. Denote by $w_n(x,n_1)$ the compound probability that the die has ace-probability x and gave n_1 successes out of n. Then the conditional probability of x, given n_1, which we call $q_n(x|n_1)$ equals by (IV.1):

$$q_n(x|n_1) = \frac{w_n(x,n_1)}{\int_0^1 w_n(x,n_1)\, dx}. \qquad (IV.3)$$

Here, x is taken as a continuous variable, i.e., it can take any value between 0 and 1. The $\int_0^1 w_n(x,n_1)\, dx$ is our $P(A)$. It is to be replaced by $\Sigma_x w_n(x,n_1)$ if x is a discrete variable which can, e.g., take on only one of the 13 values 0, $\frac{1}{12}$, $\frac{2}{12}$, . . . , $\frac{11}{12}$, 1.

Let us analyze $w_n(x,n_1)$. With the notation of Sec. II.1 we obtain $p_n(n_1|x) = \binom{n}{n_1} x^{n_1} (1-x)^{n-n_1}$, the conditional probability of n_1, given that the success chance (e.g., the chance of ace) has the value x. Therefore,

$$w_n(x,n_1) = v(x)p_n(n_1|x). \qquad (IV.4)$$

Here $v(x)$ is the *prior* probability or prior chance, the chance—prior to the present statistical investigation—that the ace-probability has the value x. Substituting (IV.4) into (IV.3) we have

$$q_n(x|n_1) = \frac{v(x)p_n(n_1|x)}{\int_0^1 v(x)p_n(n_1|x)\, dx}, \qquad (IV.5)$$

where, dependent on the problem, the integral in the denominator may be replaced by a sum. This is Bayes's "inversion formula." If we know $v(x)$ and $p_n(n_1|x)$ we can compute $q_n(x|n_1)$. Clearly, we have to have some knowledge of $v(x)$ in order to evaluate Eq.(IV.5). We note also that the problem must be such that x is a *random variable*, i.e., *that the assumption of many possible x's which are distributed in a probability distribution* makes sense (compare end of Section IV, 6, below).

4. In some problems it *may be justified to assume that v(x) be constant,* i.e., *that v has the same value for all x.* (This was so for the geometric problem which Bayes himself considered.) Boole spoke of this assumption as of a case of "equal distribution of ignorance." This is not an accurate denotation since often this assumption is made not out of ignorance but because it seems adequate. R. A. Fisher argued with much passion against "Bayes's principle." However, Bayes did not have any such principle. He did not start with a general formula Eq.(IV.5) and then apply a "principle" by which $v(x)$ could be neglected. He correctly solved a particular problem. The general formula, Eq.(IV.5), is due to Laplace.

How about the $v(x)$ in our original example? Here, for a body which behaves and looks halfway like a die, the assumption of constant $v(x)$ makes no sense. If, e.g., we bought our dice at Woolworth's we might take $v(x)$ as a curve which differs from 0 only in the neighborhood of $x = \frac{1}{6}$. If we suppose a loaded die another $v(x)$ may be appropriate. The trouble is, of course, that sometimes we have no way of knowing anything about $v(x)$. Before continuing our discussion we review the facts found so far, regarding Bayes: (a) he was the first to introduce and use conditional probability; (b) he was the first to formulate correctly and solve a problem of inverse probability; (c) he did not consider the general problem Eq.(IV.5).

5. Regarding $v(x)$ we may summarize as follows: (a) if we *can* make an adequate assumption for $v(x)$ we can compute $q_n(x|n_1)$; (b) if we ignore $v(x)$ and have no way to assume it and n is a small or moderate number we cannot make an inference; (c) Laplace has proved (Section V, 6) that *even if we do not know v(x) we can make a valid inference if n is large* (and certain mathematical assumptions for $v(x)$ are known to hold). This is not as surprising as it may seem. Clearly, if we toss a coin 10 times and heads turns up 7 times and we know nothing else about the coin, an inference

on the head-chance q of this coin is unwarranted. If however, 7,000 heads out of 10,000 turn up then, even if this is all we know the inference that $q > \frac{1}{2}$ and not very far from 0.7 is very probable. The proof of (c) is really quite a simple one (see von Mises [1964], pp. 339ff.) but we cannot give it here. We merely state here the most important property of the right-hand side of Eq.(IV.5)—writing now $q_n(x)$ instead of $q_n(x \mid n_1)$. Independently of $v(x)$, $q_n(x)$ *shows the property of condensation*, as n increases more and more, a condensation about the observed success frequency $n_1/n = r$. Indeed the following theorem holds:

If the observation of an n times repeated alternative has shown a frequency r of success, then, if n is sufficiently large, the probability for the unknown success-chance to lie between r − ε and r + ε is arbitrarily close to unity.

This is called *Bayes's theorem*, clearly a kind of converse of Bernoulli's theorem the observed r playing here the role of the theoretical q.

6. We consider a closely related problem which aroused much excitement. Suppose we are in a situation *where we have the right to assume that* $v(x) =$ constant *holds*, and we know the numbers n and n_1. By some additional considerations we can then compute the ace-probability P itself *as inferred from these data* (not only the probability $q_n(x)$ that P has a certain value x), and we find that P equals $(n_1 + 1)/(n + 2)$, and correspondingly $1 - P = (n - n_1 + 1)/(n + 2)$. This formula for P is called *Laplace's rule of succession*, and it gives well-known senseless results if applied in an unjustified way. Keynes in his treatise (p. 82) says: "No other formula in the alchemy of logic has exerted more astonishing powers. It has established the existence of God from the basis of total ignorance and it has measured precisely the probability that the sun will rise tomorrow." This magical formula must be qualified. First of all, if n is small or moderate we may use the formula *only if we have good reason to assume a constant prior probability.* And then it is correct. A general "Principle of Indifference" is not a "good reason." Such a "principle" states that in the absence of any information one value of a variable is as probable as another. However, no inference can be based on ignorance. Second, if n and n_1 are both large, then indeed *the influence of the a priori knowledge vanishes* and we need no principle of indifference to justify the formula. One can, however, still manage to get senseless results if the formula is applied to events that are not random events, for which therefore, the reasoning and the computations which lead to it are not valid. This remark concerns, e.g., the joke—coming from Laplace it can only be considered as a joke—about

using the formula to compute the "probability" that the sun will rise tomorrow. The rising of the sun does not depend on chance, and our trust in its rising tomorrow is founded on astronomy and not on statistical results.

7. We finish with two important remarks. (a) The idea of inference or inverse probability, the subject of this section, is not limited to the type of problems considered here. In our discussion, $p_n(n_1 \mid x)$ was $\binom{n}{n_1}$ $x^{n_1}(1 - x)^{n - n_1}$, but formulas like Eq.(IV.5) *can be used for drawing inferences on the value of an unknown parameter from* $v(x)$ *and some* p_n *for the most varied* p_n. This is done in *the general theory of inference* which, according to Richard von Mises and many others finds a sound basis in the methods explained here (Mises [1964], Ch. X.). The ideas have also entered "subjective" probability under the label "Bayesean" (Lindley, 1965). Regarding the unknown $v(x)$ we say: (i) if n is large the influence of $v(x)$ vanishes in most problems; (ii) if n is small, and $v(x)$ unknown it may still be possible to make some well-founded assumption regarding $v(x)$ using "past experience" (von Mises [1964], pp. 498ff.). If no assumption is possible then no inference can be made. (The problem considered here was concerned with the posterior chance that the unknown "ace-probability" has a certain value x or falls in a certain interval. There are, however, other problems where such an approach is not called for and where—similarly as in subsection 6—we mainly want a good *estimate* of the unknown magnitude on the basis of the available data. To reach this aim many different methods exist. R. A. Fisher advanced the "maximum likelihood" method which has valuable properties. In our example, the "maximum likelihood estimate" equals n_1/n, i.e., the observed frequency.)

(b) Like the Bernoulli-de Moivre-Laplace theorem the Bayes-Laplace theorem has found various extensions and generalizations. Von Mises also envisaged wide generalizations of both types of Laws of Large Numbers based on his theory of Statistical Functions (von Mises [1964], Ch. XII).

V. PIERRE SIMON, MARQUIS DE LAPLACE: HIS DEFINITION OF PROBABILITY, LIMIT THEOREMS, AND THEORY OF ERRORS

1. It has been said that Laplace was not so much an originator as a man who completed, generalized, and consummated ideas conceived by others. Be this as it may, what he left is an enormous treasure. In his *Théorie analytique des probabilités* (1812) he used the powerful tools of the new rapidly developing analysis to build a comprehensive system of probability theory. (The elements of probability calculus—addition, multiplication, division—were by that time firmly established.) Not all of his mathematical results are of equal interest to the historian of thought.

2. We begin with the discussion of his well-known *definition* of probability as the number of cases favorable to an event divided by the number of all equally likely cases. (Actually this conception had been used before Laplace but not as a basic definition.) The "equally likely cases" are *les cas également possibles, c'est à dire tels que nous soyons également indécis sur leur éxistence* (*Essai philosophique*, p. 4). Thus, for Laplace, "equally likely" means "equal amount of indecision," just as in the notorious "principle of indifference" (Section IV, 6). In this definition, the feeling for the empirical side of probability, appearing at times in the work of Jakob Bernoulli, strongly in that of Hume and the logicians of Port Royal, seems to have vanished. The main respect in which the definition is insufficient is the following. The counting of equally likely cases works for simple games of chance (dice, coins). It also applies to important problems of biology and—surprisingly—of physics. But for a general definition it is much too narrow as seen by the simple examples of a biased die, of insurance probabilities, and so on. Laplace himself and his followers did not hesitate to apply the rules derived by means of his aprioristic definition to problems like the above and to many others where the definition failed. Also in cases where equally likely cases can be defined, different authors have often obtained different answers to the same problem (this result was then called a paradox). The reason is that the authors choose different sets of cases as equally likely (Section VI, 8).

Laplace's definition, though not unambiguous and not sufficiently general, fitted extensive classes of problems and drew authority from Laplace's great name, and thus dominated probability theory for at least a hundred years; it still underlies much of today's thinking about probability.

3. Laplace's *philosophy* of chance, as exposed in his *Essai philosophique* is that each phenomenon in the physical world as well as in social developments is governed by forces of two kinds; permanent and accidental. In an isolated phenomenon the effect of the accidental forces may appear predominant. But, in the long run, the accidental forces average out and the permanent ones prevail. This is for Laplace a consequence of Bernoulli's Law of Large Numbers. However, while Bernoulli saw very clearly the limitations of his theorem, Laplace applies it to everything between heaven and earth, including the "favorable chances tied with the eternal principles of reason,

justice and humanity" or "the natural boundaries of a state which act as permanent causes," and so on.

4. We have previously mentioned Laplace's contributions to both Bernoulli's and Bayes's problems. It was de Moivre's (1713) fruitful idea to evaluate P_n (Section III, 2) directly for large n. There is no need to discuss here the precise share of each of the two mathematicians in the *de Moivre-Laplace formula*. Todhunter calls this result "one of the most important in the whole range of our subject." Hence, for the sake of those of our readers with some mathematical schooling we put down the formula. *If a trial where $p(0) = p$, $p(1) = q$, $p + q = 1$, is repeated n times where n is a large number, then the probability P_n that the number x of successes be between*

$$nq - \delta \sqrt{npq} \qquad \text{and} \qquad nq + \delta \sqrt{npq} \quad \text{(V.1)}$$

or, what is the same, that the frequency $z = x/n$ of success be between

$$q - \delta \sqrt{pq/n} \qquad \text{and} \qquad q + \delta \sqrt{pq/n} \quad \text{(V.1}')$$

equals asymptotically

$$2 \frac{1}{\sqrt{2\pi}} \int_0^\delta e^{-t/2} \, dt + \frac{e^{-\delta^2/2}}{\sqrt{2\pi npq}}. \qquad \text{(V.2)}$$

Here, the first term, for which we also write $2\Phi(\delta)$, is twice the famous *Gauss integral*

$$\Phi(\delta) = \frac{1}{\sqrt{2\pi}} \int_0^\delta e^{-t^2/2} \, dt,$$

or, if δ is considered variable, the celebrated *normal distribution function*. For fairly large n the second term of Eq.(V.2) can be neglected and the first term comes even for moderate values of δ very close to unity (e.g., for $\delta = 3.5$ it equals 1 up to five decimals). *The limits in Eq.(V.1') can be rendered as narrow as we please by taking n sufficiently large and P_n will always be larger than $2\Phi(\delta)$.*

This is the first of the famous *limit theorems of probability calculus*. Eq.(V.2) exhibits the phenomenon of *condensation* (Sections II and IV) about the midpoint, here the mean value, which means that *a probability arbitrarily close to 1 is contained in an arbitrarily narrow neighborhood of the mean value*. The present result goes far beyond Bernoulli's theorem in sharpness and precision, but conceptually it expresses the same properties.

5. Thus, the distribution of the number x of successes obtained by repetition of a great number of binary alternatives is asymptotically a normal curve. As previously indicated more general theorems of this type hold. If, as always, we denote success by 1, failure by 0, then $x = x_1 + x_2 + \cdots + x_n$, where each x_i is either 0 or 1. It is then suggestive to study also cases where the distributions of the $x_1, x_2, \ldots, x_n$ are not as simple as in the above problem (Section VIII, 2).

6. We pass to Laplace's limit theorem for Bayes's problem. Set (Section IV, 3) $q_n(x|n_1) = q_n(x)$ and $\int_{x_1}^{x_2} q_n(x)\, dx = Q_n(x_2) - Q_n(x_1)$; let n tend towards infinity while $n_1/n = r$ is kept fixed. The difference $Q_n(x_2) - Q_n(x_1)$ is the probability that the object of our inference (for example, the unknown "ace"-probability) be between x_1 and x_2. Laplace's limit result looks similar to Eq.(V.1′) and Eq.(V.2). *The probability that the inferred value lies in the interval*

$$(r - t \sqrt{r(1 - r)/n},\, r + t \sqrt{r(1 - r)/n}$$

tends to $2\Phi(t)$ *as* $n \to \infty$. Bayes's theorem (Section IV, 5) follows as a particular case. The most remarkable feature of this Laplace result is that *it holds independently of the prior probability*. This is proved without any sort of "principle of indifference." This mathematical result corresponds, of course, to the fact that any prior knowledge regarding the properties of the die becomes irrelevant if we are in possession of a large number of results of ad hoc observations.

7. To appreciate what now follows we go back for a moment to our introductory pages in Section I. We said that the Greek ideal of science was opposed to the construction of hypotheses on the basis of empirical data. "The long history of science and philosophy is in large measure the progressive emancipation of men's minds from the theory of self-evident truth and from the postulate of complete certainty as the mark of scientific insight" (Nagel, p. 3).

The end of the eighteenth and the beginning of the nineteenth century saw the beginnings and development of a "theory of errors" developed by the greatest minds of the time. A long way from the ideal of absolute certitude, scientists are now ready to use observations, even inaccurate ones. Most observations which depend on measurements (in the widest sense) *are* liable to accidental errors. "Exact" measurements exist only as long as one is satisfied with comparatively crude results.

8. Using the most precise methods available one still obtains small variations in the results, for example, in the repeated measurements of the distance of two fixed points on the surface of the earth. We assume that this distance *has* some definite "true" value. Let us call it a and it follows that the results $x_1, x_2, \ldots$ of several measurements of the same magnitude must be incorrect (with the possible exception of one). We call $z_1 = x_1 - a$, $z_2 = x_2 - a$, $\ldots$ the *errors* of measurement. These errors are considered as *random deviations* which oscillate around 0. Therefore, there ought to exist a *law of error*, that is a probability $w(z)$ of a certain error z.

It is a fascinating mathematical result that, by means of the so-called "theory of elementary errors" we obtain at once the form of $w(z)$. This theory, due to Gauss, assumes that each observation is subject to a large number of sources of error. Their sum results in the observed error z. *It follows then at once from the generalization of the de Moivre-Laplace result* (Section V, 5, Section VIII, 3) *that the probability of any resulting error* z *follows a normal or Gaussian law* $w(z) = (h/\sqrt{\pi})e^{-h^2 z^2}$. This h, the so-called *measure of precision*, is not determined by this theory. The larger h is, the more concentrated is this curve around $z = 0$.

9. The problem remains to determine *the most probable value of x*. The famous *method of least squares* was advanced as a manipulative procedure by Legendre (1806) and by Gauss (1809). Various attempts have been made to justify this method by means of the theory of probability, and here the priority regarding the basic ideas belongs to Laplace. His method was adopted later (1821–23) by Gauss. The last steps towards today's foundation of the least squares method are again due to Gauss.

10. Any evaluation of Laplace's contribution to the history of probabilistic thought must mention his deep interest in the applications. He realized the applicability of probability theory in the most diverse fields of man's thinking and acting. (Modern physics and modern biology, replete with probabilistic ideas, did not exist in Laplace's time.) In his *Mécanique céleste* Laplace advanced probabilistic theories to explain astronomical facts. Like Gauss he applied the theory of errors to astronomical and geodetic operations. He made various applications of his limit theorems. Of course, he studied the usual problems of human statistics, insurances, deaths, marriages. He considered questions concerned with legal matters (which later formed the main subjects of Poisson's great work). As soon as Laplace discovered a new method, a new theorem, he investigated its applicability. This close connection between theory and meaningful observational problems—which, in turn, originated new theoretical questions—is an unusually attractive feature of this great mind.

VI. A TIME OF TRANSITION

1. The influence of the work of Laplace may be considered under three aspects: (a) his analytical achievements which deepened and generalized the results of his predecessors and opened up new avenues; (b) his definition of probability which seemed to provide a firm basis for the whole subject; (c) in line with the rationalistic spirit of the eighteenth century, a wide field of applications seemed to have been brought within the domain of reason. Speaking of probability,

Condorcet wrote: *Notre raison cesserait d'être esclave de nos impressions* ("Our reason would cease to be the slave of our impressions").

2. Of the contributions of the great S. D. Poisson laid down in his *Recherches sur la probabilité des jugements* . . . (1837), we mention first a generalization of James Bernoulli's theorem (Section II). Considered again is a sequence of binary alternatives—in terms of repeatedly throwing a die for "ace" or "not-ace"—Poisson abandoned the condition that all throws must be carried out with the same or identical dice; he allowed *a different die* to be used for each throw. If $q^{(n)}$ denotes *the arithmetical mean* of the first n ace-probabilities $q_1, q_2, \ldots, q_n$ then a theorem like Bernoulli's holds where now $q^{(n)}$ takes the place of the previously fixed q. Poisson denotes this result as the Law of Large Numbers. A severe critic like J. M. Keynes called it "a highly ingenious theorem which extends widely the applicability of Bernoulli's result." To Keynes's regret the condition of independence still remains. It was removed by Markov (Section VIII, 7).

3. Ever since the time of Bernoulli one could observe the duality between the empirical aspect of probability (i.e., frequencies) and a mathematical theory, an algebra, that reflected the relations among the frequencies. Poisson made an important step by stating this correspondence explicitly. In the Introduction to his work he says: "In many different fields we observe empirical phenomena which appear to obey a certain general law. . . . This law states that the ratios of numbers derived from the observation of very many similar events remain practically constant provided that the events are governed partly by constant factors and partly by variable factors whose variations are irregular and do not cause a systematic change in a definite direction. Characteristic values of these proportions correspond to the various kinds of events. The empirical ratios approach these characteristic values more and more closely the greater the number of observations." Poisson called this law again the Law of Large Numbers. We shall, however, show in detail in Section VII that this "Law" and the Bernoulli-Poisson theorem, explained above, are really two different statements. The sentences quoted above from Poisson's Introduction together with a great number of examples make it clear that here Poisson has in mind a generalization of empirical results. The "ratios" to which he refers are the frequencies of certain events in a long series of observations. And the "characteristic values of the proportions" are the chances of the events. We shall see that this is essentially the "postulate" which von Mises was to introduce as the empirical basis of frequency theory (Sections VII, 2–4).

4. Poisson distinguished between "subjective" and "objective" probability, calling the latter "chance," the former "probability" (a distinction going back to Aristotle). "An event has by its very nature a *chance*, small or large, known or unknown, and it has a *probability* with respect to our knowledge regarding the event." We see that we are relinquishing Laplace's definition in more than one direction.

5. Ideas expressed in M. A. A. Cournot's beautifully written book, *Exposition de la théorie des chances et des probabilités* (Paris, 1843) are, in several respects similar to those of Poisson. For Cournot probability theory deals with certain frequency quotients which would take on completely determined fixed values if we could repeat the observations towards infinity. Like Poisson he discerned a subjective and objective aspect of probability. "Chance is objective and independent of the mind which conceives it, and independent of our restricted knowledge." Subjective probability may be estimated according to "the imperfect state of our knowledge."

6. Almost from the beginning, certainly from the time of the Bernoullis, it was hoped that probability would serve as a basis for dealing with problems connected with the *"Sciences Morales."* Laplace studied judicial procedures, the credibility of witnesses, the probability of judgments. And we know that Poisson was particularly concerned with these questions. Cournot made legalistic applications *aux documents statistiques publiés en France par l'Administration de la Justice*. A very important role in these domains of thought is to be attributed to the Belgian astronomer L. A. J. Quételet who visited Paris in 1823 and was introduced to the mathematicians of *la grande école française*, to Laplace, and, in particular, to Poisson. Between 1823 and 1873 Quételet studied statistical problems. His *Physique sociale* of 1869 contains the construction of the "average man" (*homme moyen*). Keynes judged that Quételet "has a fair claim to be regarded as the parent of modern statistical methods."

7. It is beyond the scope of this article to delve into statistics. Nevertheless, since Laplace, Poisson, Cournot, and Quételet have been mentioned with respect to such applications, we have to add the great name of W. Lexis whose *Theorie der Massenerscheinungen in der menschlichen Gesellschaft* ("Theory of Mass Phenomena in Society") appeared in 1877. He was perhaps the first one to attempt an investigation whether, and to what extent, general series of observations can be compared with the results of games of chance and to propose criteria regarding these questions. In other words, he inaugurated "theoretical statistics." His work is of great value with respect to methods and results.

8. We return to probability proper. The great prestige of Laplace gave support to his concept of equally likely events and actually to the "principle of insufficient reason" (or briefly "indifference principle") on which this concept rests (Section IV, 6). The principle enters the classical theory in two ways: (a) in Laplace's definition (Section V, 2) and (b) in the so-called Bayes principle (Section IV, 4). However, distrust of the indifference principle kept mounting. It is so easy to disprove it. We add one particularly striking counter-example where the results are expressed by continuous variables.

A glass contains a mixture of wine and water and we know that the ratio $x =$ water/wine lies between 1 and 2 (at least as much water as wine and at most twice as much water). The Indifference Principle tells us to assume that to equal parts of the interval $(1, 2)$ correspond equal probabilities. Hence, the probability of x to lie between 1 and 1.5 is the same as that to lie between 1.5 and 2. Now let us consider the same problem in a different way, namely, by using the ratio $y =$ wine/water. On the data, y lies between $\frac{1}{2}$ and 1, hence by the Indifference Principle, there corresponds to the interval $(\frac{2}{2}, \frac{3}{4})$ the same probability as to $(\frac{3}{4}, 1)$. But if $y = \frac{3}{4}$, then $x = \frac{4}{3} = 1.333 \ldots$ while before, the midpoint was at $x = 1.5$. The two results clearly contradict each other.

With the admiration of the impressive structure Laplace had erected—supposedly on the basis of his definition—the question arose how the mathematicians managed to derive from abstractions results relevant to experience. Today we know that the valid objections against Laplace's equally likely cases do not invalidate the foundations of probability which are not based on equally likely cases; we also understand better the relation between foundations and applications.

9. One way to a satisfactory foundation was to abandon the obviously unsatisfactory Laplacean definition and to build a theory based on the empirical aspect of probability, i.e., on frequencies. Careful observations led again and again to the assumption that the "chances" were approached more and more by the empirical ratios of the frequencies. This conception—which was definitely favored by Cournot—was followed by more or less outspoken statements of R. L. Ellis, and with the work of J. Venn an explicit frequency conception of probability emerged. This theory had a strong influence on C. S. Peirce. In respect to probability Peirce was "more a philosopher than a mathematician." The theory of probability is "the science of logic quantitatively treated." In contrast to today's conceptions (Section VII, 5) the first task of probability is for him to compute (or approximate) a probability by the frequencies in a long sequence of observations; this is "inductive inference." The prob-

lem considered almost exclusively in this article, the "direct" problem, is his "probable inference." He strongly refutes Laplace's definition, and subjective probability is to be excluded likewise. He has then—understandably—great difficulty to justify or to deduce a meaning for the probability of a single event (see Section IV of Peirce's "Doctrine of Chances"). The concept of probability as a frequency in Poisson, Cournot, Ellis, Venn, and Peirce (see also Section VII, 6) appears clearly in von Mises' so-called "first postulate" (Section VII, 4). These ideas will be discussed in the context of the next section.

VII. FREQUENCY THEORY OF PROBABILITY. RICHARD VON MISES

1. As stated at the end of Section VI, the tendency developed of using frequency objective as the basis of probability theory. L. Ellis, J. Venn, C. S. Peirce, K. Pearson, et al. embarked on such an empirical definition of probability (Section VI, 9 and 3). In this direction, but beyond them in conceptual clarity and completeness, went Richard von Mises who published in 1919 an article "Grundlagen der Wahrscheinlichkeitsrechnung" (*Mathematische Zeitschrift*, **5** [1919], 52–99). Probability theory is considered as a scientific theory in mathematical form like mechanics or thermodynamics. Its subjects are *mass phenomena* or *repeatable events,* as they appear in games of chance, in insurance problems, in heredity theory, and in the ever growing domain of applications in physics.

2. We remember the conception of Poisson given in Section VI, 3. Poisson maintains that in many different fields of experience a certain *stabilization of relative frequencies* can be observed as the number of observations—of the same kind—increases more and more. He considered this "Law of Large Numbers," as he called it, the basis of probability theory. Following von Mises, we reserve "Law of Large Numbers" for the Bernoulli-Poisson theorem (Sections II, and VI, 2), while the above empirical law might be denoted as Poisson's law.

3. The essential feature of the probability concept built on Poisson's Law is the following. For certain types of events the outcome of a single observation is (either in principle or practically) not available, or not of interest. It may, however, be possible to consider the single case as embedded in an ensemble of similar cases and to obtain for this mass phenomenon meaningful global statements. This coincides so far with Venn's notion. The classical examples are, of course, the games of chance. If we toss a die once we cannot predict what the result will be. But if we toss it 10,000 times, we observe the emergence of an increasing constancy of the six frequencies.

A similar situation appears in social problems (observed under carefully specified conditions) such as deaths, births, marriages, suicides, etc.; in the "random motion" of the molecules of a gas; or in the inheritance of Mendelian characters.

In each of these examples we are concerned with events whose outcome may differ in one or more respects: color of a certain species of flowers; shape of the seed; number on the upper face of a die; death or survival between age 40 and 41 within a precisely defined group of men; components of the velocity of a gas molecule under precise conditions, and so on. For the mass phenomenon, the large group of flowers, the tosses with the die, the molecules, we use provisionally the term *collective* (see complete definition in subsection 7, below), and we call *labels*, or simply results, the mutually exclusive and exhaustive properties under observation. In Mendel's experiment of the color of the flower of peas, the labels are the three colors red, white, pink. If a die is tossed until the 6 appears for the first time with the number of this toss as result, the labels are the positive integers. If the components of a velocity vector are observed the collective is three-dimensional.

4. Von Mises assumed like Poisson that to the various kinds of repetitive events characteristic values correspond which characterize them in respect to the frequency of each label. Take the die experiment: putting a die into a dice box; shaking the cup; tossing the die. The labels are, for example, the six numbers 1, 2, . . . , 6 and it is assumed that there is a characteristic value corresponding to the frequency of the event "6." This value is a *physical constant* of the event (it need, of course, not be $\frac{1}{6}$) and it is measured approximately by the frequency of "6" in a long sequence of such tosses and is approached more and more the longer the sequence of observations. We call it *the probability of "6"* (Poisson says "chance") *within the considered collective.* If the die is tossed 1,000 times within an hour we may notice that the frequency of "6" will no longer change in the first decimal, and if the experiment is continued for ten hours, three decimals, say, will remain constant and the fourth will change only slightly. To get rid of the clumsiness of this statement von Mises used the concept of *limit.* If in n tosses the "6" has turned up n_6 times we consider

$$\lim_{n \to \infty} \frac{n_6}{n} = p_6 \qquad \text{(VII.1)}$$

as the probability of "6" in this collective. Similarly, a probability exists for the other labels. The definition (VII.1), which essentially coincides with Poisson's, Ellis'

and Venn's assumptions, is often denoted as *von Mises' first postulate.* It is of the same type as one which defines "velocity" as $\lim_{\Delta t \to 0} \Delta s / \Delta t$, where $\Delta s / \Delta t$ is the ratio of the displacement of a particle to the time used for it.

5. Objections of the type that one cannot make infinitely many tosses are beside the point. We consider frequency as an approximate measure of the physical constant probability, just as we measure temperature by the extension of the mercury, or density by $\Delta m / \Delta v$ as Δv the volume of the body decreases more and more (containing always the point at which the density is measured). It is true that we cannot make infinitely many tosses. But neither do we have procedures to construct and measure an infinitely small volume and actually we cannot measure any physical magnitude with absolute accuracy. Likewise, an infinitely long, infinitely thin straight line does not "exist" in our real world; its home is the boundless emptiness of Euclidean space. Nevertheless, theories based on such abstract concepts are fundamental in the study of spatial relations.

We mention a related viewpoint: as in rational theories of other areas of knowledge it is not the task of probability theory to ascertain by a frequency experiment the probability of every conceivable event to which the concept applies, just as the direct measurement of lengths and angles is not the task of geometry. Given probabilities serve as the *initial data* from which we derive new probabilities by means of the rules of the calculus of probability. Note also that we do not imply that in scientific theories probabilities are necessarily *introduced* by Eq.(VII.1). The famous probabilities $\frac{1}{4}$, $\frac{1}{2}$, $\frac{1}{4}$ of the simplest case of Mendel's theory *follow from his theory of heredity* and are then verified (approximately) by frequency experiments. In a similar way, other *theories*, notably in physics, *provide theoretical probability distributions* which are then verified either directly, or indirectly through their consequences.

6. We have mentioned before that von Mises' conception of a long sequence of observations of the same kind, and even definition Eq.(VII.1), are not absolutely new. Similar ideas had been proposed by Ellis, Venn, and Peirce. Theories of Fechner and of Bruns are related to the above ideas and so is G. Helm's *Probability Theory as the Theory of the Concept of Collectives* (1902). These works did not lead to a complete theory of probability since they failed to incorporate some property of a "collective" which would characterize randomness. To have attempted this is the original and characteristic feature of von Mises' theory.

7. If in the throwing of a coin we denote "heads" by 1 and "tails" by 0 the sequence of 0's and 1's generated by the repeated throwing of the coin will be a "random sequence." It will exhibit an *irregular* appearance like 0, 0, 1, 1, 1, 0, 0, 0, 1, 0, 0, 1, 1, . . . and not look like a regular sequence as 0, 1, 0, 1, 0, 1, ... Attempting to characterize a random sequence von Mises was led to the concept of a *place selection*. *From an infinite sequence* ω: x_1, x_2, . . . *of labels an infinite subsequence* ω': x'_1, x'_2, . . . *is selected by means of a rule which determines univocally for every* x_ν *of* ω *whether or not it appears in* ω'. *The rule may depend on the subscript* ν *of* x_ν *and on the values* x_1, x_2, . . . , $x_{\nu-1}$ *of terms which precede* x_ν *but it must not depend on* x_ν *itself or on subsequent terms.* We call a sequence ω *insensitive* to a specific place selection s if the frequency limits of the labels which by Eq.(VII.1) exist in ω, exist again in ω' and are the same as in ω. The simplest place selections are the *arithmetical* ones where the decision whether or not x_ν is selected depends only on ν. "Select x_ν if ν is even." "Select x_ν if ν is not prime," etc. Another important type of selection is to use some of the x's preceding x_ν. "Select x_ν if each preceding term equals 0." "Select x_ν if ν is even and three immediately preceding terms are each equal to 1." It is clear that such place selections are "gambling systems" and with this terminology von Mises' *second postulate* states that *for a random sequence no gambling system exists.* Sequences satisfying both postulates are called *collectives* or simply *random sequences.*

8. Von Mises' original formulation (1919, p. 57; see above, Section VII, 1) seems to imply that he had in mind insensitivity to all place selections. It can, however, easily be seen that an unqualified use of the term "all" or of an equivalent term, leads to contradiction, a set-theoretical difficulty not noticed by von Mises. Formulating the second postulate more precisely as insensitivity to *countably many* place selections the mathematician A. Wald has shown in 1937 that *the postulate of randomness in this form together with the postulate of the existence of frequency limits are consistent.* (If "countably many" is specified in an adequate sense of mathematical logic we may even say: if one can explicitly indicate *one single* place selection which alters the frequency limit of 0, say, then ω is not a random sequence.) Wald proved actually much more, namely, that collectives are, so to speak, the rule. A particular result: *almost all* (in a mathematical sense) *infinite sequences of 0's and 1's have the frequency limit* $\frac{1}{2}$ *and exhibit the type of irregularity described by the second postulate* (*von Mises* [1964], Appendix One; *or von Mises* [1957], p. 92).

9. The concept of sequences which satisfy the two postulates is only the starting point of the theory. In

his 1931 textbook von Mises has shown that from this starting point by means of precisely defined *operations* a comprehensive system of probability theory can be built. First, the definition yields a reasonable *addition theorem.* Consider the probability P that *within one and the same collective* a result belonging to either of two disjoint sets A or B is to occur. The corresponding frequency is in an immediately understandable notation $(n_A + n_B)/n = n_A/n + n_B/n$ and by Eq.(VII.1) $P = \lim_{n \to \infty} n_A/n + \lim_{n \to \infty} n_B/n = P(A) + P(B)$. Previous theories that did not use some concept like frequency "within one and the same collective" could not be counted on to provide a correct addition theorem. Indeed the probability of arbitrary "mutually exclusive" events can have any sum, even greater than 1. We also understand better now the definition of "conditional probability" introduced in Eq.(IV.1). The proportion of people who owning an automobile also own a bicycle clearly equals n_{AB}/n_A and if n is the size of the population under consideration then $n_{AB}/n_A = n_{AB}/n : n_A/n$, and if we take the limits as $n \to \infty$, Eq.(IV.1) follows. By means of these and other "operations" new random sequences are derived from given ones.

It is obvious that random sequences are generated as the results of repeated independent trials. However, the theory of the collective is by no means limited to problems of independence. In von Mises (1964, pp. 184–223), under the heading "some problems of nonindependent events," an outline of a theory of "arbitrarily linked" (= compatible but dependent) events is given, followed by applications to Mendelian heredity where the important concept of a "linkage" distribution of genes is introduced, and by an introduction to the theory of "Markov chains," where the successive games depend on n conditional probability-distributions, so-called transition probabilities. All these problems can be considered within the framework of von Mises' theory. The key to the understanding of this apparent contradiction is, in my opinion, the working with more-dimensional collectives; $p(x, y, z)$ may well be the probability in a three-dimensional collective without its being necessarily equal to $p_1(x)p_2(y)p_3(z)$. If we denote a triple x, y, z by $\vec{x}$ then the sequence ω in the randomness definition of subsection 7, above, is a sequence $\vec{x}_1$, $\vec{x}_2$, . . . *of such triples* and the x'_1, $\vec{x}'_2$, . . . occurring in a place selection are selected by a rule *for the triples*, while the three components of the triples can be arbitrarily linked with each other.

Owing to the initially built-in relations between basic concepts and observations the theoretical structure conserves its relation to the real world.

We also note that it is very easy to show that in cases where Laplace's equally likely cases exist (games of chance, but also certain problems of biology and of physics), the von Mises definition reduces to that of Laplace.

10. We finish by discussing Bernoulli's theorem (Section II) in terms of Laplace's and of von Mises' definition. Set, for simplicity, $p(0) = p(1) = \frac{1}{2}$. We have from Eq.(II.1) that $p_n(x) = \binom{n}{x} (\frac{1}{2})^n$ and the theorem states that *with increasing n the proportion of those sequences of length n for which the frequency of 0's, n_0/n, deviates from $\frac{1}{2}$ by less than ε, approaches unity.* This formulation corresponds to Laplace's definition. Let us consider it more closely. Take $\varepsilon = 0.1$; then the just-described interval is $(0.4, 0.6)$ and we denote, as in Section II, by P_n the probability that the frequency of 0's out of n results (0's and 1's) be between 0.4 and 0.6. Now compute, for example, P_n for $n = 10$. We find easily $P_{10} = {}^{676}/_{1024} = 0.656$. That means in Laplace's sense that of the $2^{10} = 1,024$ possible combinations of two items in groups of ten, 676 have the above property (namely, that for them n_0/n is between 0.4 and 0.6). Likewise we obtain $P_{1000} = 1.000$ and with the classical definition this means that most of the 2^{1000} combinations of two items in groups of 1,000 have the above property. But since the days of Bernoulli the result for P_{1000} has been interpreted in a different way, saying: *"If n is large, the event under consideration* (here $0.4 \leq n_0/n \leq 0.6$) *will occur almost always.* This *is an unjustified transition from the combinatorial result*—which Laplace's theory gives—*to one about occurrence.* The statement about occurrence can be justified only by defining "a coin of probability p for heads" *in a way which establishes from the beginning a connection between p and the frequency of the occurrence of heads; and one must then adhere to this connection whenever the term probability occurs.* In von Mises' theory the fact that $P_n \to 1$ means, of course: *if groups of n trials are observed very often then the frequency of those groups which show an n_0/n very close to p tends towards unity.* This is the generally accepted meaning of the law of large numbers and it results only in a frequency theory.

We recognize now also the difference between Poisson's law and the Law of Large Numbers. The latter states much more, namely that the *"stabilization" which according to Poisson's law appears ultimately, happens in every group of n trials if n is large.* The reason for this difference is as follows: in von Mises' theory the law of large numbers follows from Poisson's law *plus randomness,* and in the classical theory it follows from Laplace's definition *plus the multi-*

plication law. In both instances it states more than Poisson's law.

To summarize: (a) if we use Laplace's definition, Bernoulli's theorem becomes a statement on binomial coefficients and says nothing about reality; (b) if we start out with a frequency definition of probability (equivalent to Poisson's law) and assume in addition either an adequate multiplication law or randomness, then Bernoulli's theorem *follows mathematically* and it has precisely the desired meaning; (c) Bernoulli's theorem goes beyond Poisson's law; (d) often Bernoulli's theorem has been used as a "bridge" between Laplace's definition and frequency statements. This is not possible, because, as stated in (b) above, we need a frequency definition in order to derive Bernoulli's theorem with the correct meaning.

11. It would lead us much too far if we went beyond a mere mentioning of the influential and important modern statisticians R. A. Fisher, J. Neyman, E. Pearson, and others. Their interest is not so much in formulations (both, frequency definition and classical viewpoint is used) as in problems of statistical inference (see the important work of H. Cramér; and von Mises [1964], Ch. X).

R. Carnap has advanced the concept of a *logical* probability which means "degree of confirmation" and which is similar to Keynes's "degree of rational belief." He assigns such probabilities also to nonrepeatable events, and in his opinion it is this logical probability which most probabilists have in mind. However, Carnap accepts also the "statistical" or frequency definition and he speaks of it as "probability$_2$" while the logical one is "probability$_1$." Considerations of space limit us to only mentioning his theory as well as Reichenbach's idea (similar to Carnap's) of using a probability calculus to rationalize induction. We agree with von Mises in the belief that induction, the transition from observations to theories of a general nature, cannot be mathematized. Such a transition is not a logical conclusion but a creative invention regarding the way to describe groups of observed facts, an invention which, one hopes, will stand up in the face of future observations and new ideas. It may, however, be altered at any time if there are good reasons of an empirical or conceptual nature.

VIII. PROBABILITY AS A BRANCH OF PURE MATHEMATICS

1. The beginning of the twentieth century saw a splendid development of the mathematics of probability. A few examples follow which are interesting from a conceptual point of view.

At the end of Section III and in Section V, 4 we

discussed the de Moivre-Laplace formula, the first instance of the so-called Central Limit Theorem. In Eq.(II.1) we denoted by $p_n(x)$ the probability to obtain in n identical Bernoulli trials x 1's and $n - x$ 0's, or equivalently, *to obtain in these n trials the sum x.* Denote by $Q_n(x)$ the probability to obtain in the n trials a sum less than or equal to x; then the de Moivre result is that *the distribution $Q_n(x)$ tends asymptotically towards a normal distribution.*

2. Generalizations of this result might at first go in two directions. (a) The single game need not be a simple alternative, and (b) the n games need not be identical. (We do not mention here other generalizations.) Mathematically: denote by $V_\nu(x_\nu)$ the probability to obtain in the νth game a result less than or equal to x_ν, $\nu = 1, 2, \ldots, n$ (this definition holds for a "discrete" and a "continuous" distribution—regarding these concepts remember Section IV, 3). One asks for the probability $Q_n(x)$ that $x_1 + x_2 + \cdots + x_n$ be less than or equal to x; in particular as $n \to \infty$. The first general and rigorous theorem of this kind was due to A. Liapounov in his "Nouvelle forme du théorème sur la limite de probabilité" (*Mémoires de l'Académie des Sciences, St. Petersbourg,* **12** [1901]), who allowed n different distributions $V_\nu(x)$ which satisfy a mild and easily verifiable restriction. If this "Liapounov condition" holds, $Q_n(x)$ *is asymptotically normal* just as in the original de Moivre-Laplace case. In 1922 J. W. Lindeberg gave necessary and sufficient conditions for convergence of $Q_n(x)$ towards a normal distribution.

3. Obviously, this general proposition gives a firm base to the theory of elementary errors (Section V, 8) and thus to an important aspect of error-theory. Gauss applied error theory mainly to geodetic and astronomical measurements. The theory applies, however, to instances which have nothing to do with "errors of observations" but rather with fluctuations, with variations among results, as, for example, in the measurement of the heights of a large number of individuals. (Many examples may be found in C. V. Charlier, *Mathematische Statistik . . . ,* Lund, 1920.) Apart from its various probabilistic applications the Central Limit Theorem is obviously a remarkable theorem of analysis.

4. We turn to considerations which lie in a very different direction. We remember that in the derivation of Bernoulli's theorem we used the fundamental concept of probabilistic (or "stochastic") *independence.* Independence plays a central role in probability theory. It corresponds to the daily experience that we may, for example, assume that trials performed in distant parts of the world do not influence each other. In the example of independent Bernoulli trials it means mathematically that the probability of obtaining in n

such trials x heads and $n - x$ tails in a given order equals $q^x p^{n-x}$.

In 1909, É. Borel, the French mathematician, gave a purely mathematical illustration of independence. Consider an ordinary decimal fraction, e.g., 0.246. There exist 1,000 such numbers with three digits, as 0.000, 0.001, . . . , 0.999. The Laplacean probability of the particular number 0.246 equals therefore $\frac{1}{1000}$, or (Π denoting "probability"): $\Pi(d_1 = 2, \ d_2 = 4, \ d_3 = 6) = \frac{1}{1000}$, where d_i means ith decimal digit. Now obviously: $\Pi(d_1 = 2) = \frac{1}{10}$, $\Pi(d_2 = 4) = \frac{1}{10}$, etc. Hence, $\Pi(d_1 = 2, \ d_2 = 4, \ d_3 = 6) = \Pi(d_1 = 2) \cdot \Pi(d_2 = 4) \cdot \Pi(d_3 = 6)$ and we may then say with Borel that *"the decimal digits are mutually independent."* The meaning of $t = 0.246$ is $t = x_1(t)/10 + x_2(t)/100 + \cdots$, where $x_1(t) = 2$, $x_2(t) = 4$, $x_3(t) = 6$. Now we define analogously the *binary expansion* of a decimal fraction t between 0 and 1, namely $t = \varepsilon_1(t)/2 + \varepsilon_2(t)/4 + \varepsilon_3(t)/8 + \cdots$ where the $\varepsilon_i(t)$ are 0 or 1. For example, $\frac{1}{3} = 0.0101010 \ldots$. *The binary digits are mutually independent;* this is proved just as before for the decimal digits.

Now a sequence $0.\varepsilon_1\varepsilon_2\varepsilon_3 \ldots$ is, on the one hand, the binary expansion of a number t (between 0 and 1) and, on the other hand, a model of the usual game of tossing heads or tails, if, as always, 0 means tails, and 1 means heads. Hence this game becomes now *a mathematical object* to which a calculus can be applied without getting involved with coins, events, dice and trials. The existence of such a model was apt to calm the uneasiness felt by mathematicians and, at the same time, to stimulate the interest in probability.

5. In 1919 von Mises' "Grundlagen" (Section VII, 1) appeared, followed by his books of 1928 and 1931. His critical evaluation of Laplace's foundations (Section V, 2) his distinction between mathematical results and statements about reality, his introduction of some basic mathematical concepts (label space, distribution function, principle of randomness, to mention only a few) brought about a new interest in the foundations and, at the same time, pointed a way to an improved understanding of the applications whose number and importance kept increasing.

6. A few comments on the most important modern applications of probability which, in turn, strengthened the mathematics of probability, may seem in order. We have seen in our consideration of the theory of errors that, in the world of macro-mechanics, physical measurements have only a limited accuracy. It was the aim reached by Laplace and by Gauss to link error theory to probability theory. A more essential connection between probability and a physical theory emerged when statistical mechanics (Clausius, Maxwell, Boltzmann, and Gibbs) embarked on a probabilistic interpretation of thermodynamical magnitudes; in particular, entropy was given in probabilistic terms, and for the first time a major law of nature was formulated as a statistical proposition. Striking success of statistical arguments in the explanation of physical phenomena appeared in the statistical interpretation of Brownian motion (Einstein, Smoluchovski). However, the great time of probability in physics is linked to quantum theory (started by Max Planck, 1900). There, discontinuity is essential (in contrast to continuity—determinism—differential equations, the domain of classical physics). In the new microphysics, differential equations connect probability magnitudes. Probability permeates the whole world of microphysics.

Another important field of application of probability is genetics. The beginning of our century saw the reawakening of Mendel's almost forgotten probability theory of genetics which keeps growing in breadth as well as in depth.

7. We return to probability as a piece of mathematics proper. Early, in Russia, P. L. Chebychev (1821–94) carried on brilliantly the work of Laplace. His student, A. A. Markov investigated various aspects of nonindependent events. In particular, the "Markov chains," which play a great role in mathematics as well as in physics, are still vigorously studied today. The great time of mathematical probability continued in Russia and re-emerged in France, and other countries. Paul Lévy initiated the theory of so-called "stable" distributions. De Finetti introduced the concept of "infinitely divisible" distributions, a theory forcefully developed by P. Lévy, A. N. Kolmogorov, A. Khintchine, and others. These are but a few examples. Probability became very attractive to mathematicians, who felt more and more at home in a subject whose structure seemed to fit into real analysis, in particular, measure theory (subsection 8, below).

It became also apparent that methods which probability had developed lead to results in purely mathematical fields. In M. Kac's book *Statistical Independence in Probability, Analysis and Number Theory* (New York, 1959) chapter headings like "Primes play a game of chance" or "The Normal Law in number theory" exhibit connections by their very titles. "Probability theory," comments M. Kac (in an article in *The Mathematical Sciences. A Collection of Essays*, Cambridge [1969], p. 232), "occupies a unique position among mathematical disciplines because it has not yet grown sufficiently old to have severed its natural ties with problems outside of mathematics proper, while at the same time it has achieved such maturity of techniques and concepts it begins to influence other branches of mathematics." (This is certainly true for probability, but it is less certain that it applies *only* to probability.)

8. The impressive mathematical accomplishments of probability, along with its growing importance in scientific thought, led to the realization that a purely mathematical foundation of sufficient generality, and, if possible, in axiomatic form, was desirable. Various attempts in this direction culminated in A. N. Kolmogorov's *Grundbegriffe der Wahrscheinlichkeitsrechnung* (Berlin, 1933). Kolmogorov's aim was to conceive the basic concepts of probability as ordinary notions of modern mathematics. The basic analogy is between "probability" of an "event" and "measure" of a "set," where set and measure are taken as general and abstract concepts.

Measure is a generalization of the simple concepts of "length," "area," etc. It applies to point sets which may be much more general than an interval or the inside of a square. The generalization from "length" to "Jordan content" to "Lebesgue measure" is such that to more and more complicated sets of points a measure is assigned. In a parallel way the "Cauchy integral" has been generalized to the "Riemann integral" and to the "Lebesgue integral."

9. In what precedes, our label space S has been a finite or countable set of points in an interval. For Kolmogorov, the label space is a general set S of "elements" and T, a "field" consisting of subsets of S, is the field of "elementary events" which contains also S and the empty set $\emptyset$. To each set A of S is associated a nonnegative (n.n.) number $P(A)$ between 0 and 1, called the *measure* or the *probability* of A and $P(S) = 1$, $P(\emptyset) = 0$. Suppose now first that T contains only finitely many sets. If a subset A of T is the sum of n mutually exclusive sets A_i of T, i.e., $A = A_1 + A_2 + \cdots + A_n$ then it is assumed that $P(A) = P(A_1) + P(A_2) + \cdots + P(A_n)$ and P is then called an *additive set function* over T. The above axioms define a *finite probability field*. An example: S is any finite collection of points, e.g., 1, 2, 3, . . . , 99, 100. To each of these integers corresponds a nonnegative number p_i between 0 and 1 such that the sum of all these p_i equals 1. T consists of *all* subsets of this S and to a set A of T consisting of the numbers i_1, i_2, . . . , i_r the $P(A)$ is the sum of the r probabilities of these points. This apparently thin framework is already rather general since S, T, and P underlie only the few mentioned formal restrictions.

10. Kolmogorov passes to *infinite probability fields*, where T may contain infinitely many sets. If now a subset A of T is a sum of countably many disjoint sets A_i of T, i.e., $A = A_1 + A_2 + \cdots$, then it is assumed that $P(A) = P(A_1) + P(A_2) + \cdots$ and P is called a *completely additive* or σ-*additive* set function. A so-

called σ-*field* is defined in mathematics by the property that *all countable sums of sets* A_i *of the field belong likewise to it.* It seems desirable to Kolmogorov to demand that the σ-additive set functions of probability calculus be defined on σ-fields. The simplest example of such an infinite probability field is obtained by taking for S a countable collection of sets, for example, the positive integers, and assigning to each a n.n. number p_i, such that $\Sigma p_i = 1$. For T one takes *all* subsets of S and for a set A of T as its probability $P(A)$ the sum of the p_i of the points which form A. Another most important example is obtained by choosing a n.n. function $f(x)$, called *probability density*, defined in an interval (a, b) [or even in $(-\infty, +\infty)$] such that $\int_a^b f(x)\,dx = 1$. T is an appropriate collection of sets A in (a, b), for example, the so-called Borel sets, and $P(A) = \int_A f(x)\,dx$. The integrals in these definitions and computations are Lebesgue integrals.

Such probability fields may now be defined also in the plane and in three-dimensional, or *n*-dimensional space.

The next generalization concerns *infinitely-dimensional* spaces where one needs a countable number of coordinates for the definition of each elementary event.

The above indications give an idea of the variety and generality of Kolmogorov's probability fields. His axiomatization answered the need for a foundation adapted to the mathematical aspect of probability. The loftiness of the structure provides ample room to fill it with various contents.

11. These foundations are not in competition with those of von Mises. Kolmogorov *axiomatizes the mathematical principles of probability calculus,* von Mises *characterizes probability as an idealized frequency in a random sequence.* Ideally, they should complement each other. However, the integration of the two aspects is far from trivial (Section IX).

One must also remain conscious of the fact that from formal definitions and assumptions which the above axioms offer, only formal conclusions follow, and this holds no matter how we choose the S, T, and P of subsections 9 and 10. In measure theories of probability the relation to frequency and to randomness is often introduced as a more or less vague afterthought which neglects specific difficulties. On the other hand, a definition like Mises' cannot replace the fixing of the axiomatic framework and the measure-theoretical stringency. We shall return to these points of view and problems in our last section.

IX. SOME RECENT DEVELOPMENTS

1. In Section VII, 4–8 we introduced and explained the concept of probability as an *idealized frequency.* In Section VIII, 8–10 we indicated an *axiomatic set-*

theoretical framework of probability theory. We have seen in this article that these two aspects—frequency and abstract-mathematical theory—were present from the seventeenth century on. However, this duality was not considered disturbing. We have only to think of Laplace: his aprioristic probability definition, his mathematics of probability and his work on applications (for both of which his definition was often not a sufficient basis) coexisted peacefully for more than a hundred years although in some respects not consistent with one another. It is only in this century that the Laplacean framework was found wanting. The erosion started from both ends: the scientists using probability and statistics found Laplace's concept insufficient, and the development of mathematics greatly outstripped Laplacean rigor. Clarity about probability as a branch of mathematics, on the one hand, and of its relation to physical phenomena, on the other hand, was reached only in the twentieth century. These two aspects are rightly associated with the names of Kolmogorov and von Mises.

2. It would be a mistake to think that either von Mises or Kolmogorov negated or were not conscious of the problems arising from this duality. It might be more adequate to say that each man considered the questions connected with the other aspect as somehow of second order and not in need of strong intellectual effort on his part. We illustrate this point by examples.

We remember that von Mises' collective is defined by two postulates: (α) existence of frequency limits, (β) insensitivity to place selections. His work introduces a wealth of clarifying concepts, also of a purely mathematical nature, which are used today by most probabilists. In places, however, mathematical precision was lacking; we mention two instances.

As the first one we recall the difficulty reported and discussed in Section VII, 8. The second concerns a gap that has hardly been referred to by the critics of von Mises' system, namely that his collective, in its original form, applied only to the *discrete* label space, a space consisting of a finite or countable number of points. A *continuous* label space contains as subsets a wide variety of *sets of points.* In most, if not in all of his publications, von Mises does not bother about the adaption of his theory to general point sets, but considers this an obvious matter once the concept of collective has been explained. (He spoke, for example, of "all practically arising sets.") We shall return to this matter in subsections 4 and 5 below.

Kolmogorov's set-theoretical foundations were accepted gladly by the majority of probabilists as the definitive solution of the problem of foundations of probability. With respect to the interpretation of his abstract probability concept Kolmogorov points explicitly and repeatedly to von Mises' frequency theory. However, within the framework of Kolmogorov's theory this interpretation meets serious difficulties.

Kolmogorov's theory is built on Lebesgue's measure theory. Now it can be shown that *a frequency interpretation of probability* (whose desirability Kolmogorov emphasizes) *is mathematically incompatible with the use of Lebesgue's theory*. One cannot have it both ways: Lebesgue-Kolmogorov generality *is not consistent with a frequency interpretation*.

3. Von Mises' label space was too unsophisticated. Kolmogorov's mathematics is too general to admit always a frequency interpretation (and no other interpretation is known) of his probability. Analysis of these shortcomings should lead to a more unified theory. The following is a report on some attempts in this direction.

As stated in Section VII, 8, Wald has proved—under certain conditions—the consistency of the concept of collective. Being both a student of von Mises and of the set theoretician K. Menger, Wald in the course of this work could not fail to discern those fields of sets to which a probability with frequency meaning can be assigned. Before Wald, E. Tornier, the mathematician, presented an axiomatic structure, different from both von Mises' and Kolmogorov's, and compatible with frequency interpretation. H. Geiringer, much influenced by Tornier and Wald, took a fairly elementary starting point where concepts like "decidable" and "verifiable" play a role. (The following paper by Geiringer is easily accessible and contains all the quotations, on pp. 6 and 15, of Wald's and Tornier's works, which are all in German: H. Geiringer, "Probability Theory of Verifiable Events," *Archive for Rational Mechanics and Analysis*, **34** [1969], 3–69.)

4. (a) Our eternal die (true or biased) is tossed and we ask for the probability that in $n = 100$ tosses "ace" will turn up at least 20 times. The event A under consideration is "at least 20 aces in 100 tosses." (The problem is of the type of that of Monsieur de Méré, discussed in Section I, 3.) The single "trial" consists of at least 20 and at most 100 tosses. If in such a trial "ace" turns up at least 20 times we say that the "event" (or the set) A has emerged; otherwise non-$A = A'$ resulted. Clearly, after *each* trial we know with certainty whether the result is A or A'. Hence, repeating the trial n times we obtain n_A/n, the frequency of A, which we take as an approximation to $P(A)$. Problems like (a) are strictly *decidable*.

(b) Next remember the elementary concept of a rational number: it is the quotient of two integers; and we know that the decimal form of a rational (between 0 and 1, say) is either finite like 0.7, or periodic like 0.333 . . . = $\frac{1}{3}$, or 0.142857142857 . . . = $\frac{1}{7}$. Call R

the set of rationals between 0 and 1 and R' that of irrationals in this interval. We want a frequency approximation to $P(R)$, the "probability of R."

Imagine an urn containing, in equal proportions, lots with the ten digits 0, 1, 2, . . . , 9. We draw numbers out of the urn, note each number before replacing it and originate in this way a longer and longer decimal number. The single "trial" consists of as many draws as needed to decide whether this decimal is rational or not (belongs to R or to R'). It is, however, *impossible* to reach this decision by a finite number of draws—and we cannot make infinitely many. If after $n = 10,000$ draws a "period" has not emerged it may still emerge later; if some period seems to have emerged the next draw could destroy it. *Not one single trial leads to a decision*. The problem is *undecidable*.

5. In Lebesgue's theory, R has a measure (equal to 0). But, assigning this measure $|R|$ to R as its probability means renouncing any frequency interpretation of this "probability." A probability should be "verifiable," i.e., an approximation by means of a frequency should be in principle possible. But any attempt to verify $|R|$ fails. The conclusion (Tornier, Geiringer) is that to the set R (and to R') *no probability can be assigned* in a frequency theory. This is not a quibble about words but a genuine and important distinction. If somebody wants to call $|R|$ a probability then we need a new designation like "genuine probability" for sets like those in (a).

It is easy to characterize mathematically sets like R which have measure but not a verifiable probability. However, such a description would not be of much help to the nonmathematician.

(c) *There is a third class of sets which are more general than* (a) *but admit verifiable probabilities*. It is this class of sets which, in von Mises' theory, should have been added to class (a). Again we have to forego a mathematical characterization.

6. Von Mises dealt exclusively with sets of the strictly decidable type (a). This, however, does not imply that a von Mises-probability can be ascribed to no continuous manifold. Consider, e.g., an interval or the area of a circle. An area *as a whole is verifiable*. Imagine a man shooting at a target. By assigning numbers to concentric parts of the target, beginning with "1" for the bull's eye including its circular boundary, and ending with the space outside the last ring, we can characterize each shot by a number and, we have a problem similar to that of tossing dice.

Similarly, on a straight line a label space may consist, for example, of the interval between 0 and 10. We can then speak of the *probability* of the interval (2.5, 3.7) or any other interval in (0, 10). These are problems of type (a), although the data are given in a different way (Section VIII, 10). We ought to understand that the total interval (0, 1) say, *has* a probability, but certain *point sets* in (0, 1), like R or R', are of type (b) and have no probability, although they have Lebesgue measure. The distinction which we sketched here very superficially (subsections 4 and 5, above), shows in what direction von Mises' theory should be extended beyond its original field and up to certain limits. But these same bounds should also restrain the generality of measure theories of probability insofar as these are to admit frequency interpretation.

7. Reviewing the development we can no longer feel that the measure-theoretical axiomatics of probability has solved all riddles. It has fulfilled its purpose to establish probability calculus as a regular branch of mathematics but it does not help our understanding of randomness, of degree of certainty, of the Monte Carlo method, etc.

It thus feels remarkable but understandable that in 1963 Kolmogorov himself again took up the concept of randomness. He salutes the frequency concept of probability "the unavoidable nature of which has been established by von Mises." He then states that for many years he was of the opinion that infinite random sequences (as used by von Mises) are "not close enough to reality" while "finite random sequences cannot admit mathematization." He has, however, now found a formalization of finite random sequences and presents it in this paper. The results are interesting, but, of necessity rather meager.

Further investigations on random sequences by R. I. Solomonov, P. Martin Löf, Kolmogorov, G. J. Chaitin, D. L. Loveland, and, particularly, C. P. Schnorr are in progress. These investigations (which are also of interest to other branches of mathematics) use the concepts and tools of mathematical logic. The new random sequences point of necessity back to von Mises' original ideas and some of them study successfully the links between the various concepts.

8. In this section we have sketched two aspects of recent development. The first one concerned attempts to work out the mathematical consequences of the postulate (or assumption) that a frequency interpretation of probability is possible. This postulate, basic in von Mises' theory, had been considered by Kolmogorov as rather obvious and not in need of particular study. Our second and last subject gave a few indications regarding the analysis of randomness in terms of mathematical logic. The problems and results considered here in our last section seem to point towards a new synthesis of the basic problems of probability theory.

BIBLIOGRAPHY

Jakob (James) Bernoulli, *Ars conjectandi* (Basel, 1713; Brussels, 1968). R. Carnap, *Logical Foundations of Probability* (Chicago, 1950). H. Cramér, *Mathematical Methods of Statistics* (Princeton, 1946). F. N. Davis, *Games, Gods, and Gambling* (New York, 1962). R. L. Ellis, *On the Foundations of the Theory of Probability* (Cambridge, 1843). J. M. Keynes, *A Treatise on Probability* (London, 1921). A. N. Kolmogorov, *Grundbegriffe der Wahrscheinlichkeitsrechnung* (Berlin, 1933). D. V. Lindley, *Introduction to Probability and Statistics from a Bayesian Viewpoint* (Cambridge, 1965). R. von Mises, *Wahrscheinlichkeit, Statistik und Wahrheit* (Vienna, 1928); trans. as *Probability, Statistics and Truth*, 3rd ed. (New York, 1959); idem, *Wahrscheinlichkeitsrechnung und ihre Anwendung in der Statistik und theoretischen Physik* (Vienna, 1931); trans. as *Mathematical Theory of Probability and Statistics*, ed. and supplemented by Hilda Geiringer (New York, 1964). E. Nagel, "Principles of the Theory of Probability," *International Encyclopedia of Unified Science* (Chicago, 1939), I, 6. C. S. Peirce, "The Doctrine of Chances," *Popular Science Monthly*, **12** (1878), 604–15; idem, "A Theory of Probable Inference," reprinted in *Collected Papers* (Boston, 1883), II, 433–77. H. Reichenbach, *The Theory of Probability* (Istanbul, 1934; 2nd ed. Los Angeles, 1949). I. Todhunter, *A History of the Mathematical Theory of Probability, From the Time of Pascal to that of Laplace* (Cambridge, 1865; reprint New York, 1931). J. Venn, *The Logic of Chance* (London, 1866). E. T. Whittaker and G. Robinson, *The Calculus of Observations* (London, 1932).

HILDA GEIRINGER

[See also Certainty; **Chance**; Determinism; **Game Theory**; Infinity.]

PROGRESS IN CLASSICAL ANTIQUITY

"THE ANCIENTS had no conception of progress: they did not so much as reject the idea; they did not even entertain the idea." So wrote Walter Bagehot (*Physics and Politics*, p. 41) in the year 1872, and his assertion has often been echoed since. Yet it was possible for the late Ludwig Edelstein, in his posthumous book *The Idea of Progress in Classical Antiquity* (1967), to declare that "The ancients formulated most of the thoughts and sentiments that later generations down to the nineteenth century were accustomed to associate with the blessed or cursed word—'progress'" (p. xxxiii); and this is a view to which many contemporary scholars would subscribe. The explanation of this seeming conflict of opinion lies partly in the Greek vocabulary and the Greek habit of thought, partly in the ambiguity of the concept itself. It must be conceded to Bagehot that classical Greek had no word for progress: the nearest equivalent is προκοπή, literally "pushing forward"; but this term appears to be a Hellenistic coinage (though the corresponding verb is older). It must also be conceded that if the idea of progress be strictly defined, as suggested in 1935 by A. O. Lovejoy and George Boas (p. 6), as "a general and necessary *law* of progress" governing man's past, present, and also future development, it would be difficult to produce an ancient text which directly disproved Bagehot's generalization. While speculation about man's past is an important element in Greek thought of all periods, speculation about his future is surprisingly rare. As B. A. van Groningen has pointed out in an interesting essay, the typical Greek was a backward-looking animal: the future was to him the domain of total uncertainty (τύχη), to which man's only guide was delusive expectation (ἐλπίς). He was therefore much inclined to follow the advice of the poet Simonides: "Being but man, never try to say what to-morrow brings." The chief exceptions, as we shall see, are to be found among the scientists, and their predictions are usually confined to the field in which they claim to have expert knowledge. For the others, we can as a rule do no more than infer their expectations about the future from their attitude to the past and the present.

A further difficulty lies in the inherent ambiguity of the concept of progress. Progress implies a goal, or at any rate a direction; and a goal or direction implies a value judgment. By what scale of values, then, is progress to be measured? Is happiness to be the yardstick, or power over nature, or gross national product? Is moral advance the true criterion, or is it the advancement of learning? On this question the ancients were no more unanimous than men are today, and different criteria suggested conflicting conclusions. Then as now, the field in which past progress was most obvious was that of technology; but the view that technological advance has been accompanied by moral failure or moral regress was, as we shall see, at least as widely held in antiquity as it is at present. Some went further and posited a direct causal relation between the two: for them technological advance had actually induced moral decay, and was thus not a blessing but a curse—a line of thought which issued logically in an extreme form of primitivism.

The idea of progress—even in the restricted sense of technological progress—is not one which comes early or easily to men. In primitive societies, custom-bound as they are, and lacking historical records, progress does not readily develop a generalized mean-

ing. Such societies may ascribe particular inventions or discoveries to individual culture-heroes or culture-gods, as popular Greek thought did from the Archaic Age onwards; but they do not think of them as forming a continuous ladder of ascent, and still less do they conceive such a ladder as extending into the present and the future. It is therefore not surprising that the idea of progress should be missing from the oldest Greek literature. And it must be remembered that when it did emerge it found the field already occupied by two great anti-progressive myths which threatened to strangle it at birth, the myth of the Lost Paradise—called by the Greeks "the life under Kronos," by the Romans the *Saturnia regna* or Golden Age—and the myth of Eternal Recurrence. These are dealt with elsewhere in this dictionary, but they must be mentioned here because of the distorting influence they exerted, whether by way of competition or of conflation, upon the development of the idea of progress.

Both of them would seem to have been already known to Hesiod (ca. 700 B.C.), who was the first Greek to generalize about man's past, present, and future. His much-discussed tale of the Five Races (*Works and Days* 109–201) is a story of progressive though not uninterrupted degeneration, starting from the Lost Paradise "under Kronos" and extending into the present and the future. Its backbone is the myth of the four metals—gold, silver, bronze, and iron—symbolizing four stages of material and moral decline, which he appears to have derived from an oriental source (see Gatz, pp. 7–27). He has combined this with an historical tradition of the heroic world described in early Greek epic, which interrupts the pattern of continuous decline. In the oriental version the story usually ended with the completion of a *magnus annus* and an abrupt return to the Lost Paradise. And it seems likely that this was so also in Hesiod's source; for he wishes that he had either died before the present Age of Iron or *been born later* (174–75; cf. 180–81, where he foresees its end). The cyclic interpretation of human history was not, however, what interested Hesiod; his concern was to emphasize the degeneracy of his own time. And later poets followed his example: they have much to say about the Lost Paradise but almost nothing, until Vergil, about Paradise regained. The cyclic view is most often found in the service of pessimism.

Xenophanes. How far the rest of archaic Greece accepted Hesiod's gloomy prognosis we have no sure means of knowing. All we can say is that the first explicit statement to the contrary appears at the end of the Archaic Age in two well-known lines of the Ionian poet-philosopher Xenophanes: "Not from the beginning did the gods reveal everything to mankind, but in course of time by research men discover improvements" (frag. 18, Diels-Kranz). This is a genuine affirmation of progress: the writer conceives it as a gradual process which extends into the present and presumptively into the future, and one which is dependent on man's own efforts, not on the arbitrary gift of any "culture-god." We do not know whether the couplet was a casual *obiter dictum* or formed part of a fuller historical statement. It may well have been prompted by Xenophanes' observation of recent cultural advances (we are told that he mentioned somewhere the invention of coinage by the Lydians, and that he admired the astronomical discoveries of Thales). It is also relevant to recall that he was a much-travelled man who took an interest in the red-haired gods of the Thracians and the snub-nosed gods of the Ethiopians. Such comparison of different cultures suggested to him, we know, the idea that religious beliefs are relative to the believer; it may also have suggested the idea of man's slow and uneven upward movement from barbarism to civilization.

Aeschylus. The pride in human achievement which we can feel in the few words of Xenophanes found more vivid expression a generation later in the great speech which Aeschylus put into the mouth of Prometheus (*Prometheus Vinctus* 442–506). It is true that Prometheus credits the achievement not to man but to himself: that was implicit in the dramatic situation. But the contrast between man as he once was and man as he now is has never been more proudly or more eloquently expressed. Man is no exile from a Lost Paradise. On the contrary, he has come up from a state in which he was not yet capable of coherent thought but drifted aimlessly through life "like a figure in a dream," unable to interpret the message of eyes and ears, his only shelter a cave. And consider him now! Not only has he set the animals to work for him, conquered the sea, discovered the secret mineral wealth of the earth, but he has learned to record his own achievements and has mastered difficult sciences —astronomy, arithmetic, medicine, divination.

This passage has surprised some critics, and has even been adduced as an argument against the authenticity of the play. Wilhelm Schmid, who held that the play was composed by an anonymous atheist some twenty years after Aeschylus' death, saw in the speech on progress "our earliest evidence for the existence of the sophistic movement and its radicalism about the middle of the fifth century" (pp. 95f.). This view rests on a misconception. Considered as a piece of anthropology, the speech is archaic in the extreme. There is no attempt to mark the stages of evolution, no recognition of the decisive influence of the food-producing techniques (cattle-herding and agriculture), no reference to the origins of community life. Technology takes a

very minor place: even the potter's wheel, which Attic tradition associated especially with Prometheus, is left out as too unimportant or too banal. What the poet has chosen to stress is man's intellectual progress: the spur of economic necessity, which figures prominently in later Greek accounts as ἀνάγκη or συμφέρον, receives no emphasis from Aeschylus: instead, his hero undertakes to relate "how I made men rational and capable of reflection, who till then were childish." And the science on which he dwells at greatest length is that of divination, lovingly described in all its various branches. This is in keeping with Aeschylus' attitude elsewhere, but would be very surprising in a pupil of Protagoras.

There has been much speculation about the "authority" to whom Aeschylus owed his anthropological notions. But perhaps no authority need be assumed. The list of sciences was easy to make, and there is nothing in the description of man's original unhappy state which suggests special knowledge. If we ask how the poet came to substitute the idea of progress for the Hesiodic regress, part at least of the answer must surely lie in the triumphant *experience* of political, social, and cultural progress which fell to the lot of Aeschylus and his generation. The influence of this experience is equally apparent in the *Eumenides* (458 B.C.), where Athena's gift of law is the counterpart, and the completion, of Prometheus' gift of reason. In that play Aeschylus appears not only to look back upon his country's past but to look forward with confidence to its present and its future. For contrast, he had available to him the reports of barbarian peoples brought home by Greek travellers like Aristeas and Hecataeus, and several passages in his work show him making free use of them.

One difficult question remains: Did Aeschylus actually believe that the arts of civilization were taught to man by a divine being called Prometheus, or is his Prometheus just a symbol of human reason? The question may be thought illegitimate: so long as mythmaking is a living mode of thought, to confront it with this sort of brutal "either-or" is to force upon it a choice which destroys its being. But later antiquity was in no doubt about the answer. For all Greek writers after Aeschylus, Prometheus is purely a symbol of man's restless intelligence, to be admired or condemned according to the author's outlook.

The earliest statement of this opinion appears in a line from the comic poet Plato (frag. 136 Kock) which in so many words equates Prometheus with "the human mind." But it is suggestive that the line should have occurred in a play called *The Sophists*. In view of this and of the myth in Plato's *Protagoras* (see below) it is a natural guess that Protagoras was the man who first made the symbolism explicit. But it can be argued that in Aeschylus it is already implicit. So far as we know, it was he who first made such an interpretation possible, by crediting Prometheus not merely with the gift of fire but with all the arts of civilization, including some which are assigned to other culture-heroes by other writers and even by Aeschylus himself in other plays (cf. Kleingünther, pp. 78ff.). By thus transfiguring the serio-comic trickster whom Hesiod had portrayed (*Theogony* 510–616; *Works and Days* 42–89) he created one of the great symbolic figures of European literature. The symbolism, however, was not for him, as it was for Protagoras, something which could be stripped away without loss of significance. The belief that man's achievements are not purely his own but are the outcome and the expression of a divine purpose was to Aeschylus—at least in the present writer's view—a basic religious postulate.

The Teleological View. After Aeschylus the literary tradition branches in two opposed directions. The religious interpretation of progress as a manifestation of divine providence (πρόνοια) appears in a speech that Euripides in his *Suppliants* (195–218; ca. 424–420 B.C.) put into the mouth of Theseus, the type of Athenian conservative orthodoxy. To refute the view of those who hold that there is more evil than good in human life, Theseus lists the most obvious human assets and achievements and asks if we should not be grateful to the god who so ordered man's life, raising it from incoherence and bestiality. He then proceeds to reprove those persons who in their conceit of human intelligence "imagine themselves wiser than the gods," i.e., think they know better what is good for them. This pretty certainly reflects some contemporary controversy, not the personal views of the poet. The opinions criticized may be those of the Sophist Prodicus; the standpoint of the speaker is that of orthodox piety. He singles out divination as man's crowning achievement, and he admits past progress only to enforce the old lesson that man should accept his station and be content. This line of thought developed into the argument from design which Xenophon attributed to Socrates, and issued ultimately in the Stoic and Christian conception of history as providentially guided.

The Humanistic View. The first full statement of the opposing assumption, that man's achievements are his own, is to be found, surprisingly enough, in Sophocles. In a celebrated ode (*Antigone* 332–75), he set forth man's conquest of earth and sea, of beasts, birds, and fishes, of speech and thought and the arts of communal life, representing these things not as a providential endowment but as the result of man's own efforts. This had led some scholars to speak of Sophocles' "humanistic philosophy" and to conclude

that he is "tinged with the rationalism of his age." But to draw that conclusion is to ignore the implications both of the lyric as a whole and of the play as a whole. The poet's praise of man's "cleverness" (δεινότης, a morally ambiguous word) leads up to the warning that cleverness can bring destruction as easily as it can success; and the warning is reinforced in the next ode (586–625), where the picture of man's achievement is balanced by the companion picture of his utter helplessness when our human purposes come into conflict with the inscrutable purposes of God. Sophocles was no humanist, and the *Antigone* is no Protagorean tract for the times. We can, however, legitimately infer that by the date of the play (441 B.C.) the humanistic interpretation of progress was already current at Athens.

A much more radical assertion of this view appears in a well-known fragment of the poet-politician Critias where the speaker explains, after the manner of an eighteenth-century *philosophe*, how "some wise man" invented the gods as a prop to public morality. Among later dramatists, Chaeremon (frag. 21, Nauck) echoes in almost the same words the sentiment of Xenophanes, and Moschion (frag. 6), describing man's progress from cannibalism to civilization, treats Prometheus as the mythological equivalent of "necessity" or "experience"—by then the accepted catchwords.

Fifth-Century Anthropology. It is evident that behind these poetic utterances there lies a substantial amount of serious anthropological speculation which had excited public interest. And we know who the leading figures in this movement were: the philosophers Anaxagoras and Democritus, both of whom emphasized the role of human intelligence in man's emergence from the animal level; Anaxagoras' Athenian pupil Archelaus, who described the origin of "leadership and laws and skills and city states and the rest" (Diels-Kranz 60 A 4); and the Sophist Protagoras, reputedly the author of a work "On Man's Original Condition" (Diogenes Laërtius ix. 55). Unfortunately the writings of all these men are lost, and what they had to say on this subject is represented only by the scantiest of fragments. There are, however, two prose texts from which scholars have thought to recover the fifth-century doctrine of progress, though neither of them belongs to that century.

The Platonic "Protagoras." The first of these is the myth which Plato in his *Protagoras* (320C ff.) put into the mouth of the great Sophist. The difficulty of using this as evidence lies not so much in its mythical form (which does not pretend to be more than allegory) as in the impossibility of deciding with any precision how much is Protagoras and how much Plato. Some scholars have treated the passage as an exact report of Protagoras' views, or even as a verbatim excerpt from his alleged work "On Man's Original Condition." This is unjustified: Plato was no scissors-and-paste composer; the style (despite assertions to the contrary) is not notably different from that employed in other Platonic myths, and certain of the ideas seem much more Platonic than Protagorean. (See further Havelock's critical bibliography, pp. 407–09.) The utmost that can safely be inferred is that Protagoras did somewhere express opinions on the origins of society; that in doing so he emphasized the poverty of man's physical endowment (of which design-mongers like Xenophon made much) and insisted that early man owed his survival ultimately to his capacity for communal life; and that this in turn depended in his view on the development of the social virtues, αἰδώς and δίκη—respect for the feelings and the rights of others. Since Protagoras also believed that virtue can be taught, this may well have led him to take a rosy view of man's prospects; Plato makes him claim (327C, D) that the very worst citizen of modern Athens is already a better man than any savage. In the same spirit Democritus seems to have held that man's natural endowment was malleable and could be "re-shaped" by education (frag. 33). In the great days of the fifth century such optimism was natural; by the time Plato wrote, faith in the common heritage of αἰδώς and δίκη had been shattered by the Peloponnesian War and its aftermath, and the reproachful phantom of the "Noble Savage" was waiting in the wings.

Anonymus Diodori. The other relevant text presents even greater problems, which cannot be adequately discussed here. It consists of a cosmogony, a zoogony, and an anthropology which Diodorus inserted into the preface (I. 7–8) to his *Universal History* (ca. 60–30 B.C.), on the authority, as he tells us, of "the most generally recognized natural scientists" (φυσιολόγοι). It is distinguished from most other productions of its period both by its consistently rationalist approach (no supernatural agencies are invoked at any point) and by its consistent use of terms and ideas characteristic of fifth-century speculation. K. Reinhardt in 1912 argued ingeniously that its ultimate source was Democritus; this view was long accepted, and the passage still appears as fragment 5 among the fragments of Democritus in Kranz's collection. But doubts have since accumulated (most fully summarized by Spoerri, pp. 1–33). The cosmogony is nonatomist; the account of the origin of animal life has closer parallels in other pre-Socratic texts than it has in Democritus; some features of the anthropology may be Democritean, but the author's reference to the crucial significance of the human hand (8. 9), which has made man the only tool-using animal, seems to go back to Anaxagoras (Aristotle, *De partibus animalium* 687a 7; cf. also Xenophon, *Memorabilia* 1.4.11). A

possible view is that Diodorus or some Hellenistic predecessor, being no philosopher, consulted one of the current "doxographic" manuals and out of what he found there put together a not very up-to-date précis in general terms of the opinions most often attributed to rationalist thinkers. If this is so, any hope of reconstructing in detail a "Democritean" anthropology (as attempted most recently by Thomas Cole) seems doomed to failure.

The Idea of Progress in the Professions. Whatever may be the truth about the source used by Diodorus, it is in any case fairly clear that at least in the latter half of the fifth century the fact of man's gradual rise from an animal (θηριώδης) level was very widely accepted. The cyclic view of history was not dead (it had been given a new interpretation by Empedocles) and the dream of the good old days "under Kronos" survived in the imagination of poets (e.g., Cratinus, frag. 165 Kock; Sophocles, frag. 278). But the weight of "scientific" opinion was against them, and so was the continuing experience of progress, particularly in the skilled professions (τέχναι). Plato represents Socrates as agreeing with the Sophist Hippias that there have been advances in all the τέχναι such that "the old practitioners cut a poor figure in comparison with to-day's" (*Hippias major* 281D). Thucydides makes his Corinthian envoy warn the conservative Spartans that "In politics, as in any τέχνη the latest inventions always have the advantage" (1.71.3). The professionals themselves were apparently full of confidence, not only about the present but about the future.

The author of the essay *On Ancient Medicine* (Littré I. 570ff.), which is usually assigned to the last third of the fifth century, asserts that "many splendid medical discoveries have been made over the years, and the rest will be discovered if a competent man, familiar with past findings, takes them as a basis for his enquiries" (c. 2). The progress of medicine is for him neither accidental (c. 12) nor god-given (c. 14) but has resulted from systematic research. In the same spirit the essay *On the Art of Medicine* (Littré VI. 2ff.), which probably dates from the same period, declares that "To make new discoveries of a useful kind, or to perfect what is only half worked out, is the ambition and the task of intelligence." A similar but wider confidence is expressed in the proposal of the architect Hippodamus that a special award of merit should be given to those "who discovered something of advantage to the State" (Aristotle, *Politics* 1268a 6). The passion for research had been awakened: Democritus was not unique in feeling that he had rather solve a single problem than become King of Persia (frag. 118, Diels-Kranz).

Limitations on Progress. But however buoyant the expectations of the anthropologists and the specialists, thoughtful minds in the fifth century were aware of the limitations imposed on progress by the human condition. Each of the two great historians expressed this awareness in his own way. Each of them, it is true, took pride in the past achievements of his people: for Herodotus, the Greeks had long since outgrown the "silly nonsense" associated with barbarism (1.60.3); and Thucydides saw the past history of Greece as pursuing a gradual upward course. But Herodotus writes "as one who knows the instability of human prosperity" (1.5.4), and this conviction haunts his imagination as it did that of his friend Sophocles. He explains it in the old religious manner: man is at the mercy of a Power which forbids him to rise above his station. Thucydides, on the other hand, finds the limitation in the psychological structure of man himself. Certain kinds of disaster, he tells us, "occur and will always occur while human nature remains the same" (3.82.2); and he adventures the more general statement that "In all human probability events of much the same kind [as those he is about to describe] will happen again in the future" (1.22.4). It is a mistake to conclude from these passages that Thucydides "finally adopted a cyclical view of history very much like Plato's" (John H. Finley, Jr., *Thucydides*, p. 83; cf. A. Momigliano, pp. 11f.). His expectation of recurrence is based not on cosmic cycles but on the permanence of the irrational and unteachable elements in human nature. He also recognizes the importance in history of sheer chance: "It is possible for the fortunes of events to develop just as unpredictably ($\dot{\alpha}\mu\alpha\theta\tilde{\omega}\varsigma$) as the designs of men" (1.140.1).

Progress and Primitivism in the Fourth Century. When we pass from the fifth century to the fourth we enter a recognizably different atmosphere. There is no falling off in creative energy: the fourth century produced the greatest philosophers and the greatest orators of antiquity; it invented new art forms, prose dialogue, and domestic comedy; it witnessed great advances in mathematics and astronomy. Yet it is hard to deny (as Edelstein does) that something at least of the old confidence had been lost. The feeling of insecurity expressed itself in a variety of ways. Men looked over their shoulders to a supposedly more stable past, to the "ancestral constitution" or beyond that to a state of primal innocence no longer to be found save among remote peoples. Plato, as we shall see, celebrated the virtues of Stone Age man; Xenophon those of the early Persians; the historian Ephorus discovered such virtues among the Scythians, while Ctesias attributed them to the Indians.

Alternatively, the dream could be projected as a blueprint for the future, one of those "rational Utopias" of which Plato's *Republic* is only the most famous example. Utopias of this kind are less a sign of confidence in the future than of dissatisfaction with the present; their authors seldom have much to say about the practical steps by which Utopia is to be achieved. Others took a more radical line. Starting from the ideal of "self-sufficiency" ($\dot{\alpha}\upsilon\tau\dot{\alpha}\rho\kappa\epsilon\iota\alpha$) which Socrates had commended, the Cynics preached rejection of all social conventions and a return to the simple life in its crudest form. They were the "beatniks" or "hippies" of antiquity: they had opted out not only from the rat race but from civilization itself. Like their modern counterparts they were an unrepresentative minority, but like them they were symptomatic of a social malaise, something which was to become widespread in the Hellenistic Age. Primitivism was not "on the wane" (Edelstein [1967], p. 69); it was on the way to a revival.

The Theory of Recurrent Catastrophes. The myth of the Eternal Return was also on its way to revival, assisted by Babylonian astrology. The doctrine of the Great Year had been imported from the East by the Pythagoreans together with its sister doctrine of identically recurrent world periods separated by recurrent catastrophes. Both Plato (*Timaeus* 39D) and Aristotle (*Meteorologica* 352a 28) know about the Great Year and attach some importance to it, but they reject the idea of total world destruction and identical recurrence (which excludes all free will). In its place both of them postulate *partial* natural catastrophes which have destroyed and will destroy successive civilizations without destroying mankind.

This theory appears first in the dialogues of Plato's old age (*Timaeus, Critias, Laws*); whether it was his own invention is uncertain (see Cole, p. 100 n. 5). The myths of Deucalion and Phaethon may have suggested it, but its value for Plato and Aristotle lay in enabling them to retain their metaphysical belief in the endless duration of the human race while recognizing that civilization, at any rate in Greece, was of comparatively recent origin (cf. Plato, *Laws* 677C, D). The theory allowed for temporary and limited progress between catastrophes: the fifth-century picture of humanity's upward struggle need not be completely jettisoned. But it led Aristotle to the discouraging conclusion that "In all likelihood every skill and every philosophy has been discovered many times over and again perished" (*Metaphysica* 1074b 10).

The Theory of Forms. A more fundamental limitation on the idea of progress was imposed by the theory of Forms, both in the Platonic and in the Aristotelian version. For Plato, all progress consists in approximation to a preexisting model; the model has been and will be there to all eternity, in the unchanging world of transcendent Forms. There is thus, strictly speaking, no open future and no such thing as invention; what we call invention is but "recollection" of a reality which is already there: nothing entirely new can ever come into being. For Aristotle, again, progress can never be more than the actualization of a Form which was already present potentially before the progress began. He traces, for example, the development of tragedy from rude beginnings to its contemporary state; but once it has "attained its natural Form" development ceases, apparently forever (*Poetics* 1449a 14). Similarly in Nature his doctrine of immutable Forms excluded any possibility of biological progress: in the absence of any concept of evolution his *scala naturae* is a static sequence, not a ladder of ascent.

Plato and the Noble Savage. Despite this, Plato has recently been claimed as a believer in the idea of progress (Edelstein [1967], pp. 102–18). This is hard to accept. The passage in the *Politicus* (299B ff.) where he defends the autonomy of the professional skills against meddlesome dictation by democratic politicians is not really relevant, and is in any case cancelled out by the very severe restrictions which he himself suggests imposing on these skills in the *Laws*. More significant are his speculations about the emergence of civilization, playfully sketched in his theoretical picture of "the genuine and healthy city" in *Republic* II (368E–372E) and more seriously described, on rather different lines, in *Laws* III. Plato was no literal believer in the Lost Paradise, though he repeatedly toyed with the idea on a mythical level (*Cratylus* 398A, *Politicus* 271C–272D, *Laws* 713A–714A, and the Atlantis myth in the *Critias*). Up to a point he accepted the view of the fifth-century anthropologists that the emergence of civilization had been slow and difficult. But just as Engels projected his utopian vision of the future on to the remote past in the form of an imaginary "primitive communism," so Plato projected on to the earliest human society certain features of his Ideal State: the same simplicity of living which he would impose on his Guardians; the same absence of wealth and poverty which is his recipe for avoiding internal conflict; the same freedom from the corrupting influence of foreign trade. The experience of these early men was incomplete, since they were innocent alike of the vices and the virtues of city life (*Laws* 678A, B), but they were simpler, more courageous, more self-controlled, and in all ways more righteous than men are to-day (679E, cf. *Philebus* 16C). With these words the aged Plato ushers in the Noble Savage. Subsequent history appears to him in this passage as a story of technical progress combined with moral regress—a pattern which we shall find constantly reasserted later. Elsewhere in the *Laws* he sees human history as largely chance-directed,

for "practically all human affairs are matters of chance," even though this "chance" may serve the mysterious ends of Providence (709A–C). Thus it is that one society grows better over the years while another deteriorates (676C): there is no consistent direction of change. (See further Lovejoy and Boas, Ch. V; Havelock, pp. 40–51.)

Aristotle and his Pupils. Deeply interested in the history of culture, they made large collections of material bearing on it. These are unfortunately lost, and outside the field of social organization dealt with in the *Politics* Aristotle's view of human development has to be inferred from one or two passing allusions. His account of the growth of society from the individual household through the clan to the city-state (*Politics* I.2) follows the lines of fifth-century anthropology and is free from the equivocations of Plato's version. His interpretation of it is teleological: only in the city-state does man become what Nature intended him to be, a "civic" animal, and only there can he live the good life. There is no suggestion of a Lost Paradise: on the contrary, early man was "in all probability similar to ordinary or even foolish people today," and this is confirmed by the foolishness of such remnants of ancient custom as still survive (*Politics* 1268b 38–1269a 8). In this latter passage Aristotle also mentions the great advances which have been achieved in sciences like medicine "and in general in all professional skills and abilities." As we have seen, however, a limit is set to any advance by the attainment of "the appropriate Form." The city-state was for Aristotle such a Form; he never envisaged any wider type of social organization, though a wider society was in fact in process of emergence in his own day. And if we can believe Cicero (*Tusculanae Quaestiones* 3.69) philosophy had in his opinion made such progress in recent years that it would within a short time be "completely worked out (*plane absolutam*)," i.e., would have reached its appropriate Form (see, however, the doubts of I. Düring, *Aristotle's Protrepticus* [1961], pp. 229–31). Progress on this showing is real enough, but it is the fulfillment of a predetermined and limited possibility—one which has been fulfilled many times before and will be fulfilled many times again. Aristotle's pupils Theophrastus and Dicaearchus shared his interest in cultural history but idealized early man in a way which would surely have surprised their master. Theophrastus, writing on vegetarianism, traced the origin of corruption to the discovery of fire, which led to animal and human sacrifice and ultimately to war. Dicaearchus, rationalizing Hesiod, asserted that "the ancients" were the best endowed by nature and lived the best life, "so that they were considered a Golden Race compared with the men of to-day" (frag. 49,

Wehrli). In this shift of emphasis they reveal themselves as true children of the Hellenistic Age. A similar combination of open-minded enquiry and backward-looking sentiment appears later in Agatharchides.

The Philosophies of Resignation. The great social changes which accompanied the advent of the Hellenistic Age reinforced the new attitudes towards both the past and the future whose emergence is already foreshadowed in the fourth century. The loosening of the traditional political and religious bonds which had attached the citizen to his small city-state, and the development of vast monarchies bureaucratically administered, left the individual with an increased sense of isolation and helplessness and forced his thoughts inwards upon himself and his personal salvation. At the same time the new conditions of urban life, with the widening gap between rich and poor and the development of artificial wants stimulated by commercial greed, induced a nostalgia for a simpler and less "civilized" existence which found literary expression in the Idylls (third century B.C.) of Theocritus, while its counterpart on the mythical level appears in Aratus' description of the Golden Age and in the utopian accounts of distant or imaginary lands presented by writers like Onesicritus, Megasthenes, and Iambulus. Its application to real life was enforced by Cynic, Stoic, and Epicurean preachers, who saw themselves as psychiatrists confronted with the task of healing a sick culture. Since all else was subordinated to the aim of inducing freedom from anxiety (ἀταραξία), they had little interest in promoting scientific advance save insofar as it might contribute to this aim. Zeno is said to have considered "the ordinary education" (τὴν ἐγκύκλιον παιδείαν) useless (Diogenes Laërtius 7.32), and Epicurus expressed a frank contempt for science as such (*Epistola* 1.79, 2.85; frags. 163, 227). The Stoics, moreover, were systematic determinists, and most of them accepted the theory of identically recurrent world periods, which excluded all genuine human initiative. It is therefore not surprising that the idea of progress played little part in early Stoic teaching. For Epicurean views on the subject our only substantial source is Lucretius (see below).

The Expectation of Scientific Progress. This, however, is only half the story. Despite the philosophers' contempt, the period between the death of Alexander and the Roman conquest of Greece was the greatest age of scientific discovery that Western man was to know until the Renaissance; and the scientists speak with another voice than the philosophers. The greatest among them were not only proudly conscious of past and present progress; they expected it to continue. Thus Archimedes wrote that by using his method "I apprehend that some either of my contemporaries or

of my successors will be able to discover other theorems in addition, which have not yet occurred to me" (*Method;* Heiberg, *Archimedis opera,* II, 430). And the great astronomer Hipparchus (second century) compiled a list of all the fixed stars known to him in order that future astronomers might be able to compare his observations with their own and thus determine what changes if any had occurred in the population of the heavens (Pliny, *Natural History* II. 95; cf. Edelstein [1967], pp. 140–55). Nor was this confidence entirely confined to scientific specialists. Polybius notes contemporary advances in technology and expects further improvements (10.43–47). He also expects his own historical work to be of practical value to future generations (3.31), e.g., by providing posterity with the material for a final judgment on Roman rule (3.4). And while holding (at least sometimes) a cyclic view of history he nevertheless describes the origins of civilization in terms which make no concession to primitivism. Starting like Plato from the theory of recurrent partial catastrophes, he offers an account of the genealogy of morals which is much more tough-minded than Plato's: man is distinguished from the other animals only by his intelligence, which causes him to develop elementary ideas of right and wrong in the interests of self-preservation (6.5–7).

Posidonius and the Philosopher Kings. The revived interest in human beginnings which shows itself in this passage of Polybius appears in the first century B.C. in the work of the Stoic Posidonius and the Epicurean Lucretius, both of whom have been acclaimed by some scholars as champions of the idea of progress. Posidonius is the greatest polymath of antiquity, at once philosopher, historian, geographer, and natural scientist. He may also be called the first true *field* anthropologist. His interest in cultural origins seems to have arisen out of his personal studies among the semi-civilized Celts of Gaul and the barbarous tribes of Lusitania, in whose way of life he saw a clue to the original condition of mankind (Reinhardt [1921], pp. 397–99). The rather odd picture of human development which resulted is known to us from Seneca's *Ninetieth Letter,* where these views are quoted and criticized. Posidonius knew too much about the ways of contemporary "primitives" to treat man's earliest days as a Golden Age. But at some stage of the development (it is not clear just where) he postulated the emergence of wise philosophers (*sapientes*) who invented the useful arts and ruled the people for their good, not out of a lust for power but, like Plato's philosopher kings, out of a sense of duty; this was the true Golden Age (90.5), when men were, in a phrase which echoes Plato, "fresh from the hands of the gods" (*a dis recentes,* 90.44; cf. Plato, *Philebus* 16C, and

Sextus Empiricus, *Adversus physicos* 1.28). Later, however, tyrannies arose, and thus the need for laws to hold them in check; these too were the work of wise men like the Seven Sages of Greece, but for Posidonius, as for Plato, the rule of law is only a second-best (90.6). His further account seems to have been largely taken up (to Seneca's disgust) with a detailed description of the growth of the various practical skills, such as house-building (where his ideas found an echo in Vitruvius), weaving, milling, etc. This interest in technology, nourished by his ethnographic observations, is a welcome change from the usual Greek contempt for manual occupations. But it hardly justifies us in crediting either Posidonius or his predecessor Panaetius with a belief in "the idea of endless progress" (Edelstein [1967], p. 169). No doubt, like the Alexandrine scientists, Posidonius expected a continuing increase in professional skills, but morally his own age seems to have represented for him a decline from the ideal standards of his primitive *sapientes*. Whether these were originally suggested to him by Plato's philosopher kings, or by the "learned men" to whom Democritus (frag. 30, Diels-Kranz) had ascribed the origin of religion, or by his own encounters with Gaulish druids, they show that for all his scientific empiricism he never completely liberated himself either from the myth of the Lost Paradise or from the moralizing tendencies of his school.

Progress and Regress in Lucretius. The tension between the idea of technological progress and the idea of moral regress appears in an even more acute form in the fifth book of Lucretius, the fullest account of prehistory which has come down to us from antiquity. How much of it goes back to Epicurus or beyond him to Democritus, how much is Lucretius' own contribution, is not easy to determine with any certainty. As a good materialist Lucretius refuses to see the hand of providence at any point in the story: the human race is the product of accident, and its achievements are its own, brought about in response to the spur of necessity by "men who excelled in understanding and were strong in mind" (5.1107). Progress in all the skills of civilization has been steady and gradual (*pedetemptim*, 5.1453); some are still advancing (5.332–37), but in general they are said to have attained their perfection (*summum . . . cacumen*, 5.1457). All this is very much in the spirit of Democritus. But civilization has brought with it the seeds of corruption. Where necessity was once the mother of invention, invention has now become the mother of necessity: every fresh invention creates a new need (5.1412–15), whereas the only true riches is "to live frugally with a contented mind" (5.1118f.). Worse still, modern society offers new opportunities to senseless ambition (5.1120ff.), includ-

ing what Lucretius had experienced in his own lifetime, the opportunity of large-scale war (5.999f., 1434f.). Thus he plays off morals against technology, Epicurus against Democritus and against Hellenistic scientists.

On one point the two conflicting currents in his thought appear to land him in flat self-contradiction. In one place (5.330f.) we are told that the world is still in its first youth, with the implication that it still has great possibilities before it; yet elsewhere we learn that Nature is now worn out, like a woman past the age of childbearing, so that for all his modern tools the farmer can scarcely wring a livelihood from the soil which once yielded crops spontaneously and in abundance (2.1150–74; 5.826f.). The idea that the generative powers of the earth have diminished was a traditional one (Diodorus 1.7.6, it can no longer generate large animals as it must once have done), but it is here given an alarmist turn which is seemingly new. Despite certain critics, Lucretius was no whole-hearted apostle of progress (it would have been a little surprising if he had been, considering the times he lived in). See further Robin, and Edelstein (1967), pp. 160–65.

Growth of Anti-Progressive Sentiment. The age of civil war and corruption which destroyed the Roman Republic had a lasting effect on men's valuation of the past and present and on their expectation of the future; it reinforced existing anti-progressive tendencies and stimulated new ones. The immediate reaction was conveyed by Horace when he compressed into eleven lapidary words the advancing moral decline of four generations, of which the last and worst was still to come (*Odes* III.6.46ff.). This is "crisis poetry" (Edelstein [1962], p. 54; cf. Eduard Fraenkel, *Horace* [1957], pp. 286–88): we should not read into it a general philosophy of history. But the mood of depression strengthened existing doubts about the values of Greek civilization. We see this in the popularity of the supposed *Letters of Anacharsis* (one of which is quoted by Cicero, *Tusculanae quaestiones* 5.90); in Strabo's view (after Posidonius?) that the Greek way of life has corrupted even the neighboring barbarians (7.3.7); in the opinion of Pompeius Trogus that Nature has done more for the Scythians than philosophy has for the Greeks (Justin, *Epitome* 2.2); in the judgment of Dio Chrysostom that Prometheus was rightly punished for introducing man to the arts of civilization (6.25).

Others, influenced by the prevailing belief in astrology, saw in the disturbing events of their time the symptoms of a *Weltwende*, a fresh turn of the Great Year. This could be interpreted in an optimistic sense: Vergil believed or half believed the Sibylline prophecy which announced the immediate return of the Golden Age (*Eclogues* iv. 4ff.; cf. *Aeneid* 6. 791ff.). To the

Greco-Roman world this was, so far as we know, a novel idea: cyclic theories implied an eventual recurrence of the Golden Age, but no pre-Vergilian text suggests that it is imminent. And the vision soon faded to a formula; it became a standard form of flattery to describe the rule of the existing Emperor as a Golden Age (Seneca applied the term to Nero's reign, *Apocolocyntosis* 4.1). At the opposite extreme, Juvenal can find no metal base enough to symbolize man's present condition (13.28–30), and Lucian thinks that "the Race of Lead" would be too flattering a description (*Saturnalia* 20). This is rhetorical hyperbole. More seriously meant is the apocalyptic passage in Seneca's *Natural Questions* (III.27–30) where the displaced and disappointed ex-minister, using oriental sources, contemplates with something unpleasantly like glee the prospect of "the single day which shall destroy the human race" (III.29.9).

That such a day must come was traditional Stoic doctrine, and probably troubled believers no more seriously than the eventual cooling of the earth disturbed the optimism of nineteenth-century thinkers (Guthrie, p. 78). What is new, as in the case of Vergil, is Seneca's conviction that the day is not far off (III.30.5); this and his gloating description of it in terms which suggest modern visions of atomic destruction: "Cities that an age has built an hour destroys" (III.27.2). To this expectation of evil two other sentiments made their contribution. One was the belief which we have already met in Lucretius that the earth itself is growing old and losing its vigor; it reappears in Seneca (*Epistolae* 90.40,44) and in many later writers. The other was the more specific feeling that the might of Rome—which good patriots from Vergil onwards declared to be eternal—had in fact like all things mortal its fixed life span and was already declining into impotent old age. This too goes back in principle to Seneca (see Lactantius, *Divinarum institutionum libri vii.* 7.15.14ff.), though his language is prudently obscure, and perhaps beyond him to the age of civil war (cf. Häussler, and Gatz, pp. 108–13). Already Cicero in a similar vein had likened the Roman State to an old and faded picture which through neglect had lost its color and even its outline (*De republica* 5.2).

Testimony of the Roman Scientists. Where sentiments of this sort prevail little interest in the idea of progress can logically be expected. Even the mystical faith in the eternity of Rome to which many clung for support in good times and bad, from Vergil (*Aeneid* 1.279, etc.) down to the fifth-century poet Rutilius Namatianus (*De reditu suo* 1.133ff.), did not carry with it any necessary belief in progress; it was essentially a faith in the perpetuation of a static present. Such testimony to progress as we find in the Roman Imperial Age comes, as in the Hellenistic period, chiefly from the scientists and technologists. Vitruvius (first century B.C.) in his book on architecture and Manilius in his poem on astronomy describe the gradual rise of their respective sciences from crude beginnings in terms which exclude any hint of a past Golden Age. Manilius shares Lucretius' pride in scientific achievement without his moral despondency. "Man's capacity for learning," he tells us (*Astronomica* 1.95ff.), "has by effort vanquished every difficulty, and did not count its task finished until reason had scaled the heavens and grasped the deep nature of things and seen in its causes all that exists." As for the future, the elder Pliny—again in an astronomical context (*Natural History* II.62)—remarks that no one should lose hope that the ages will continually make progress.

But the most confident pronouncements come, surprisingly, from that same Seneca who predicted the early demise of the present world. Elsewhere in the *Natural Questions* (VII.25) he declares that science is still in its infancy: "The day will come when time and longer study will bring to light truths at present hidden . . . when our descendants will be astonished at our ignorance of what to them is obvious." The same expectation of indefinite progress appears in other passages of *Natural Questions* (VI.5.3; VII.30.5) and in *Letter* 64.7, where we are assured that "No one born a thousand ages hence will lack the opportunity to add to the store of knowledge." But Seneca's enthusiasm is limited to pure science, whose aim is simply "the knowledge of Nature" (*Natural Questions* VI.4.2); applied science he thinks positively harmful (*Epistolae* 90.7ff.); the liberal arts he judges in the old Stoic manner as worthless save insofar as they conduce to moral improvement (ibid., 88). And in his own day he sees only decadence: far from advancing, science and philosophy are actually on the retreat (*Natural Questions* VII.32). The question of his sources and of his consistency is too complex for discussion here (see the references in Edelstein [1967], Ch. IV, notes 80, 81).

Eclipse of the Idea of Progress. All the writers quoted in the preceding paragraph belong to the Early Empire. The two centuries which followed were the final period of consolidation and unification in all the sciences: thus medicine was unified and systematized by Galen, geography and astronomy by Ptolemy, Roman law by Papinian and Ulpian, and lastly philosophy by Plotinus. But in all these fields consolidation, necessary and valuable though it was, gradually turned to petrifaction (Edelstein [1962], p. 56). Men stood with their backs to the future; all wisdom was in the past, that is to say in books, and their only task was one of interpretation. Even Plotinus, the most original mind of the period, saw himself as a schoolman rather than a creative thinker: his doctrines, he says, "are no novelties, no inventions of to-day"; he can prove their antiquity by Plato's own testimony (5.1.8). Where men can build their systems only out of used pieces the notion of progress can have little meaning—the future is devalued in advance. And in the hands of the philosophers the devaluation was gradually extended to cover almost every aspect of man's activity except the contemplative, of which mundane action is merely the outward shadow (Plotinus 3.8.4); thus history is reduced to a puppet-play (Marcus Aurelius 7.3; Plotinus 3.2.15–18), so that future and past alike are emptied of significance. "In a sense," says Marcus Aurelius, "the man who has lived for forty years, if he has any intelligence at all, has seen all that has been and all that will be, since all is of one kind" (11.1). This is the epitaph on the ancient idea of progress.

Conclusions. The reader has been warned of the difficulty of generalization in this field. But a few simple conclusions may be thought to emerge from the evidence we have presented.

1. It is untrue that the idea of progress was wholly foreign to antiquity. The earliest trace of it appears at the close of the Greek Archaic Age (Xenophanes), and there is reason to think that it became widespread in the course of the fifth century, though our evidence for this is incomplete and largely indirect. At all periods the most explicit statements of it refer to scientific progress and come from working scientists (*Ancient Medicine*, Archimedes, Hipparchus) or from writers on scientific subjects (Lucretius, Pliny, Seneca).

2. After the fifth century B.C. the influence of all the major philosophical schools was in varying degrees hostile to, or restrictive of, the idea of progress. In particular, all save the Epicureans held cyclic views of one type or another; and a belief in moral regress was common to Cynics, Stoics, Epicureans, many Platonists, and some Aristotelians.

3. The tension between acceptance of scientific or technological advance and acceptance of moral regress is perceptible in many ancient writers (most acutely in Plato, Posidonius, Lucretius, Seneca).

4. There is a broad correlation between the expectation of progress and the actual experience of progress. Where culture is advancing on a wide front, as in the fifth century, faith in progress is widely diffused; where progress is mainly evident in specialized sciences, as in the Hellenistic Age, faith in it is largely confined to scientific specialists; where progress comes to a virtual halt, as in the last centuries of the Empire, the expectation of further progress vanishes.

BIBLIOGRAPHY

Primary sources. The most important texts, in the original and in translation, are collected in the fundamental book of A. O. Lovejoy and G. Boas, *Primitivism and Related Ideas in Antiquity* (Baltimore, 1935). Fragments, etc., are quoted from the following standard collections: H. Diels, *Die Fragmente der Vorsokratiker,* 7th ed., ed. by W. Kranz, referred to as Diels-Kranz (Berlin, 1954); T. Kock, *Comicorum Atticorum Fragmenta* (Leipzig, 1880); É. Littré, *Oeuvres complètes d' Hippocrate* (Paris, 1839); A. Nauck, *Tragicorum Graecorum Fragmenta,* 2nd ed., (Leipzig, 1888); A. C. Pearson, *The Fragments of Sophocles* (Cambridge, 1917); F. Wehrli, *Dikaiarchos* (Basel, 1944).

Secondary literature. J. Baillie, *The Belief in Progress* (Oxford, 1950). J. B. Bury, *The Idea of Progress* (London, 1920). T. Cole, *Democritus and the Sources of Greek Anthropology* (A.P.A. Monograph 25, 1967). L. Edelstein, "The Greco-Roman Concept of Scientific Progress," *Ithaca* (1962); *The Idea of Progress in Classical Antiquity* (Baltimore, 1967). B. Gatz, *Weltalter, Goldene Zeit und sinnverwandte Vorstellungen* (Hildesheim, 1967). B. A. van Groningen, *In the Grip of the Past* (Leiden, 1953). G. Grossmann, *Promethie und Orestie* (Heidelberg, 1970), 111–27. W. K. C. Guthrie, *In the Beginning* (London, 1957). R. Häussler, "Vom Ursprung und Wandel des Lebensaltervergleichs," *Hermes,* **92** (1964), 313–41. E. A. Havelock, *The Liberal Temper in Greek Politics* (London, 1957). A. Kleingünther, Πρῶτος Εὑρετής (Leipzig, 1933). F. Lämmli, *Homo Faber* (Basel, 1968). A. Momigliano, "Time in Ancient Historiography," *History and Theory,* Beiheft 6 (1966). K. Reinhardt, "Hekataios von Abdera und Demokrit," *Hermes,* **47** (1912), 492–513; repr. *Vermächtnis der Antike* (Göttingen, 1960), pp. 114–32; *Poseidonios* (Munich, 1921). L. Robin, "Sur la conception épicuréenne du progrès," *Revue de Métaphysique et de Morale,* **23** (1916), 697ff.; reprinted in *La pensée hellénique* (Paris, 1942), pp. 525–52. Jacqueline de Romilly, "Thucydide et l'idée de progrès," *Annali Pisa,* **35** (1966). Wilhelm Schmid, *Untersuchungen zum Gefesselten Prometheus* (Stuttgart, 1929). E. E. Sikes, *The Anthropology of the Greeks* (London, 1914). W. Spoerri, *Späthellenistische Berichte über Welt, Kultur und Götter* (Basel, 1959). E. N. Tigerstedt, "The Problem of Progress in Literature in Classical Antiquity," in P. Demetz, T. Greene, and L. Nelson, Jr., *The Disciplines of Criticism . . .* (New Haven, 1968). W. von Uxkull-Gyllenband, *Griechische Kultur-Entstehungslehren* (Berlin, 1924). R. Vischer, *Das Einfache Leben* (Göttingen, 1965). Translations are by the author of the article.

E. R. DODDS

[See also Astrology; Chance; Christianity; **Cycles**; Epicureanism; Humanism; Myth; Nature; Necessity; Platonism; Pre-Platonic Conceptions; Primitivism; **Progress in the Modern Era; Pythagorean . . .** ; Rationality; Utopia.]

PROGRESS IN THE MODERN ERA

THE BELIEF in progress, the idea that human history forms a movement, more or less continuous, towards a desirable future, began to take shape late in the seventeenth century. Despite persistent criticism it gained steadily in strength. The culminating point was reached towards the end of the nineteenth century. Thereafter a reaction set in and in the interval between the World Wars I and II there was a widespread impression that it was about to be relegated to the realm of exploded myths. Like all powerful ideas the idea of progress drew from a number of different streams of thought—the belief that there was a necessary connection between advances in knowledge and social betterment emanating from the Enlightenment, the philosophical theories of development in their Hegelian or Marxist form, the extension of the theory of organic evolution to the sphere of mind and society.

These movements of thought, combined with the buoyant hopefulness inspired by the plainly visible advances in science and the even more obvious consequences in material civilization gave the belief in progress a commanding position, and for many it provided a basis for a working faith of great vitality. This faith has been deeply eroded by contemporary skepticism, arising mainly from the growing recognition that advances in technical knowledge are not sufficient to ensure moral and social progress and the fear that the use of science for destructive purposes might outpace and arrest the growth of its powers for good.

Historians seem to be agreed that the references made occasionally by ancient writers to advances in knowledge of nature and the probability of future additions to it hardly amount to an anticipation of a theory of progress. This view goes back to Auguste Comte's discussion of the origins of the idea in the *Cours de philosophie positive* (Vol. IV). The Greeks, he thought, were not in possession of sufficient historical or observational data and they were dominated by the idea that "humanity was doomed to an arbitrary succession of identical phases, without ever experiencing a new transformation directed towards an end determined by the whole constitution of human nature" (Comte [1875], p. 45). No coherent theory of such a transformation could arise before its direction had been indicated by the experience of the French Revolution and before the emergence of the positive sciences in the seventeenth century.

The argument that the climate of ancient thought was not congenial to ideas of progress was developed by J. B. Bury and has gained wide acceptance. Bury argued that the Greek thinkers had only very limited historical experience to serve as a basis for such ideas and that the presuppositions of their thought, their suspiciousness of change, their theories of Moira, of degeneration and cycles suggested a view of the world incompatible with notions of progressive development (Bury [1920], p. 19). On the evidence accumulated since the publication of Bury's book there is much to be said for the carefully balanced judgment reached

by Robert Flint towards the end of the nineteenth century. His position may be briefly summarized thus: the view that the Greeks and the Romans conceived of the course of history only as a downward movement is not borne out by the facts; they conceived of it in many different ways—as a process of deterioration, as a progress, and as a cycle, though none of these conceptions were worked out fully or consistently or supported by a survey of historical data (Flint [1893], pp. 89–96). However this may be, the influence of Greek thought on the idea of progress is to be sought not in what they had to say about the course of history, but in their belief in the value and potency of rational inquiry (Edelstein, 1967).

On the connection between Hebrew and Christian ideas about the destiny of man and ideas of progress historians differ widely. Comte attributed to Christianity the "first dawning sense of human progression." By proclaiming the superiority of the law of Jesus to that of Moses it gave form to the idea of a more perfect form replacing a less perfect, which had been necessary as a preparation (Comte [1875], p. 54). He thought this idea belonged essentially to Catholicism. Protestantism distorted it by recurring irrationally to the period of the primitive Church and by offering for guidance "the most barbarous part of the Scriptures—that which relates to primitive antiquity." On the whole, however, he blamed Christianity for barring its own way to progress by claiming to be the final stage in man's progress and for "the mischief and vague obscurantism which belong to all applications of the theological method." In essentials, therefore, he thought the idea of progress was modern and could not receive effective expression before the rise and expansion of the positive sciences.

Comte's brief comments were taken up and developed by J. Delvaille (1910). He was deeply influenced by Ernest Renan's *History of the People of Israel* (1887–91) and by Charles Renouvier's philosophical and historical studies, and had a deeper understanding than Comte of Hebrew beliefs. His account has the merit of distinguishing clearly between the prophetic and the later apocalyptic visions of the future. He showed that the prophetic teaching contained no reference to the fall of man or original sin hindering the growth of well-being and justice on this earth. He traced in some detail the visions offered by the prophets of an age of social justice and universal peace, when nature as well as man would be renewed and when Israel would become the divine instrument of bringing the nations to repentance and to the knowledge of the true God.

Delvaille followed Renouvier in showing how in the last two centuries before Christ prophecy gave way to apocalyptic eschatology—a movement which from the point of view of its effect on theories of progress Delvaille considered a "degradation" (Delvaille, p. 29). In dealing with Christianity Delvaille, following Pierre Leroux (*Doctrine de la perfectibilité et du progrès continu, Oeuvres;* 1850) held that in the early period there were in the Christian teaching the germs of a theory of progress; thus the parables of the Kingdom contained passages declaring that the manifestations of God in Christ were to be a seed which was to grow and progress, to produce results beyond hope and imagination and to act in humanity like leaven in meal till the whole mass was transformed. Later, however, the notion of the kingdom was taken to refer to or even to be identified with the Church, and increasing stress was laid on the helplessness and sinfulness of man and on the contrast between life on this earth and the state of heavenly blessedness. Beliefs of this sort could hardly provide an effective basis for theories of progress in their modern form.

On the whole, Delvaille's verdict on the contribution of early Christianity to the belief in progress is somewhat vague and inconclusive. The difficulty may be illustrated by his discussion of Saint Augustine. He draws attention to Augustine's references to the advances made by man in the knowledge of nature, in the arts and skills, in the means of communication, in methods of healing, in agriculture and navigation (*De civitate Dei* XXII. 24). Yet it is clear from Delvaille's own account that to Augustine "progress" of this sort was of little significance. There was only one progress: that towards salvation. What happens in the course of history is made intelligible only by the hope of a final triumph of the city of God over the city of men. But the city of God is an ideal which could not become real in this world.

Later developments of the doctrine of the kingdom of God cannot be examined here. They oscillate between intramundane and supramundane conceptions of the future, but throughout there persists the belief that the final consummation is "beyond history" and that on this earth there can be no assurance of continuing betterment. In recent theological writings the claim is often put forward that modern beliefs in progress are secularized versions of Hebrew and Christian eschatology. But precisely what is meant is not quite clear. It seems to involve a confusion of different universes of discourse or "genres," as Renouvier pointed out. We must avoid the error of reading our own ideas of historical interpretations into the views of history perhaps implicit in the Old and New Testaments. Neither the prophets of Israel nor the apocalyptic writers believed in progress as a continuous and cumulative process of inner transformation. It was God and not the power of man that shaped the course of history. Nothing is said of any slow moral development

or the cumulative use of natural resources to serve human needs. The whole setting is one of miraculous and sudden divine intervention and there is not even a hint of any conception of the struggle of mankind towards rational self-determination (Renouvier [1896], pp. 553f.).

It remains to be added that both Christian and Jewish theologians only became interested in the idea of progress after it had become a dominant element in modern thought. The Catholic Church has on occasion explicitly repudiated it. It was, for example, included among the errors censured in the famous *Syllabus* published by the Vatican in 1864 (Bury [1920], p. 323). In early Protestantism the idea appears only in the old apocalyptic form of a supernatural millenarianism, and mainly among proscribed sects, such as the Anabaptists (Dawson [1929], p. 182). Since the eighteenth century Protestant theologians have sought to come to terms with doctrines of progress, but always with a certain misgiving. The belief in original sin and the helplessness of man cannot be easily reconciled with the belief in perfectibility and the power of man to make himself, nor the notion of gradual development with the sudden or unique intervention of God in the course of history. Dean Inge writing in 1920 was of the opinion that the doctrine of progress had "distorted Christianity almost beyond recognition" and dismissed it as a "superstition which is nearly worn out." Yet he leaves open the possibility that there may be "an immanent teleology which is shaping the life of the human race towards some completed development which has not yet been reached."

Recent writers, for example Reinhold Niebuhr, retain the idea of development and admit that there has been genuine advance in history, both in thought and practice. At the same time he and others stress the finitude and limitations inherent in the nature of man and dismiss as intolerable hubris the claim that man can ever become master of his fate. They agree that there is good evidence for the view that in the course of history we can trace growing efforts to extend the area of freedom and harmony. But this extension, it is argued, may at the same time increase the power and destructiveness of self-love. It follows that "no solution can be found for the meaning of history within history itself." "The antinomies of good and evil increase rather than diminish in the long course of history." Apart from the belief in the *agape* of Christ the contemplation of history cannot but drive man to despair (Niebuhr [1949], p. 264).

Jewish thinkers appear to have become interested in the nineteenth century in the idea of progress. It is easy to see that in their efforts to reinterpret the principles of prophetic Messianism they did not face the difficulties that troubled Christian theologians.

Thus Jewish teaching on the whole rejects the notion of inevitable and ineradicable sin. The prevailing view in the Old Testament and in the Talmud is that man by his own inward power can conquer sin and that while sin is general, it is not uncontrollable. Next, the temperate ethical optimism of Jewish teaching and its "this-worldly" interpretation of the messianic future harmonize well with modern ideas of progress. This future was always conceived as a phase of history on this earth, purified and ennobled but still human. The kingdom of God was to be a universal reign of peace and justice overriding all political divisions.

The reinterpretation of messianic beliefs in the light of the idea of progress can best be followed in the writings associated with the rise of Reform and Liberal Judaism. Three points deserve special attention. First, emphasis is laid on the universalistic elements in the prophetic teaching. Secondly, the belief in a personal Messiah, a descendant of David who will lead the Jews back to their ancient land, is abandoned in favor of what may be fairly claimed to be the earlier view, that mankind as a whole is advancing to a better and purer knowledge of God and his laws and to a fuller application of the ideals of righteousness and love. Thirdly, the notion of the gradual moralization of mankind, to some extent anticipated in the Rabbinic insistence on the need for repentance as a condition of the coming of the Messiah, replaces the notion of the sudden and miraculous beginning of the messianic age (Montefiore, 1923; Wiener, 1928; Wilhelm, 1967).

On the whole question of the relations between religion and ideas of progress Renouvier's comments retain their importance. He showed that beliefs about the destiny of man were an essential element in all religions. But the end to be attained is not to be reached by their own efforts or without divine intervention. In this sense the belief is a matter for theologians and cannot be regarded as a recognizable historical law. On the other hand, those who build their hope for the temporal destiny of man on a vague optimism insensitive to the existence of evil run the risk of turning progress itself into a God and indulging in a religiosity repugnant alike to deeper faith and to science and history (Renouvier [1896], pp. 553f.).

On the relation of the belief in progress to the belief in Providence, Bury's verdict holds good; that the former could not take a firm hold over men's minds while the latter was indisputably in the ascendant. Bury allowed that the two beliefs might, and, in a future age would be, combined (Bury, 1920). It is interesting to note that Lord Acton in his later writings virtually identified them. "Progress was Providence: unless there was progress there could be no God in history" (Butterfield [1955], p. 130). Nevertheless, the fundamental

assumptions were incongruous. According to the one, man makes himself, according to the other "it is He that hath made us and not we ourselves." The idea that man has the ability and the duty to shape his own future could hardly obtain wide credence until attention was shifted from the kingdom to come to the kingdom of this world, and until the notion of law was extended from the sphere of nature to the sphere of man. The belief in progress was essentially linked with the growth of science and its applications, with the spread of the rationalist and humanitarian outlook, and with the struggle for political and religious liberty.

The vagueness of the idea of progress was noted early by its critics. Thus Étienne Vacherot wrote in 1864: "To speak of progress without defining it is to utter a word which covers as many errors as truths and which can therefore be denied or affirmed or discussed interminably" (*Essais de philosophie critique*). Similar complaints are still made. For example, the theologian John Baillie wrote: "It is truer of the votaries of progress than of the adherents of any of the great religions that they believe without knowing either quite what they believe or why they believe in it" (Baillie [1950], p. 88). It would seem that the hold ideas of progress had on the popular mind was due not so much to the theories propounded by philosophers as to the impression made by the vast social and material achievements in Europe and America—the increase in wealth and population, the transformation of daily life in the new urban centers, the spread of European culture, the growth of democratic institutions, universal education, the changes connected with the rise of humanitarian ideals, such as the abolition of slavery and the reform of the criminal law, the emancipation of women. The movement seemed all-powerful and irreversible. Even if disliked and feared, it was accepted as inevitable. It is not uncommon for a disturbing new invention to be met with the remark: "it is progress and can't be helped."

In dealing with the historical development of the idea of progress no attempt can be made here at a detailed chronological analysis of the works of its chief exponents. Instead there will be a discussion of some of the definitions that have been given of the idea at different times, the aim being to disentangle the ingredients that have gone into its making and their latent presuppositions. This will be followed by an inquiry into the answers that have been given to the problems thus raised and an estimate of their importance in the general development of theories of progress.

A well-known definition is that given by Bury: the idea of progress means that civilization has moved, is moving and will continue to move in a desirable direction (Bury, 1920). This implies that progress is taken to be continuous and general, a view repudiated by many important supporters of the doctrine. A more serious difficulty is that raised by the criterion by which what is desirable is to be judged, which Bury takes to be "increasing happiness." But this would not have been considered decisive by either Comte, Kant, or even Spencer. In Comte's view it was not possible to compare the happiness of men at different stages. Happiness depended on a certain harmony or equilibrium between men's faculties and the possibilities offered by their environment. The harmony is experienced by individuals in different ways and as experiences are not comparable (Comte [1875], p. 48). For Kant the end of development was moral perfection achieved through freedom. This might bring happiness with it but what was important was not merely that we should be happy but that we should make ourselves worthy of being happy (Kant [1930], p. 252). For Spencer the end of development was the greatest happiness, but the criteria of progress were growing individuation and increasing mutual dependence (Spencer [1902], pp. 249–55; [1901], I, 8f.).

Other problems are raised by the definition offered by A. O. Lovejoy: in contemporary usage the law of progress denotes "a tendency inherent in nature or man to pass through a regular sequence of stages of development in past, present, or future, the later stages being—with perhaps occasional retardations or minor regressions—superior to the earlier" (Lovejoy and Boas [1935], I, 6). Here the idea is generalized to include nature as well as man, and it is not clear how the superiority of the more developed to the other stages is to be judged. More serious is the inclusion of the notion of a regular sequence of stages. There is no evidence that this notion has always or generally been considered essential. A. R. J. Turgot, one of the earliest and most brilliant exponents, maintained that progress was unequal among nations, that different levels coexisted and that it is only by considering mankind as a whole that the general lines of growth could be traced (Turgot, 1808; 1895). In a similar vein Herbert Spencer explained that there was no uniform ascent from lower to higher and that it was only by taking into consideration the entire assemblage of societies that the law of evolution could be confirmed (Spencer [1897], pp. 599f.). The anthropologist E. Reclus, in an article on Ethnography contributed to the ninth edition of the *Encyclopaedia Britannica* (1879), wrote: "The course of progress runs not incessantly onwards in a straight line at a uniform speed. It proceeds in irregular motions and sometimes by curves, by broken or even by spiral lines." In 1870 Edgar Quinet in his work *La création* argued that progress was not effected along a single line, was not continuous and did not proceed

in the same direction or at the same rate. There were times of relapse, aberration, and decadence, and not every species or generation was an improvement on that which preceded it (cited in Flint [1893], p. 558).

A striking account of progress emphasizing its moral content and its dependence on free choice is given by Proudhon. Progress is neither universal nor inevitable; decadence and regression are as real. Progress is not to be measured by increase in wealth or population, or advance in the arts and the sciences. While all these advance man may be deteriorating. True progress must come from man's own energy. Man makes and unmakes himself, in proportion as what he does tends to freedom and justice or equality. Progress is "the self-justification of humanity under the impulsion of the ideal." It is "the march of freedom" spurred on by revolutions whose success, however, is never assured. It is essentially a moral phenomenon and morality in Proudhon's view is independent of religion which, he thought, perverted reason and conscience and was the source of weakness and disorder (Proudhon, 1861).

Renouvier in his long sustained studies of the history of the idea of progress also in his own way stressed the effects of moral freedom on the destiny of peoples and he denied the universality and necessity of progress. He showed that historians had relied on very inadequate data and had made no serious investigation of moral beliefs, religions, and political organizations on a scale sufficient to justify any generalized theories of progress. Nevertheless, he thought that as far as Europe was concerned progress was both a palpable fact and a worthy ideal. By its aid Europe had become conscious of itself as the heir of the moral conquests and achievements of the various peoples of the world and as capable of promoting even further advance (*perfectionnement*).

Two other attempts at definition may be mentioned, taken from more recent discussions. The historian E. H. Carr defines progress as "the development of human potentialities in so far as it moves towards the right goals." These, it seems, can only be defined "as we advance towards them and the validity of which can be verified only in the process of attaining them." That is best which in fact "works best"; the test, in short, is "success." If we ask how this is to be applied in shaping policy, the answer is that the politician has to consider not only what is morally or theoretically desirable, but also what is possible with the forces available. It is not clear, however, whether the test of what is morally desirable is also taken to be "success" or "what works best" and whether no policy can be adjudged progressive until it has been shown that it works best (Carr [1961], Ch. V). Carr makes light of the distinction between fact and values, and, on his own showing, inquiry into what is morally desirable would lapse into inquiry concerning what is historically or sociologically possible.

A balanced and comprehensive view of progress was that expounded by J. M. Robertson. Progress, he showed, does not mean "that human affairs must constantly improve in virtue of some cosmic law, but that a certain advance in range of knowledge, of reflection, of skill, of civic amenity, or general comfort is attainable and desirable, that such advances have clearly taken place in former periods; and that the due study of these periods and of present conditions may lead to a further and indefinitely prolonged advance." The general test is the rise in the quantity and quality of pleasurable and intelligent life (Robertson, 1913). This has the merit of distinguishing between progress as fact and ideal and of avoiding the implication that progress is general or inevitable or directed towards a fixed or predetermined end.

We must now consider some of the movements of thought which in various ways gave content to the general ideas of progress.

Universal History and the Unity of Mankind. The idea of the unity of mankind emerges, and the possibility of a "universal history" distinct from the combined history of different peoples. The idea is developed with varying degrees of emphasis during the eighteenth century in the works of Vico, Voltaire, Turgot, Herder, and Kant. Vico conceived of history as the study of "the modifications of the human mind." He tried to trace the patterns followed by the peoples of the world in their rise, progress, maturity, decline, and fall. The typical course of change is a progress from anarchy to order, from savage and "heroic" ages to the ages of civilization. The different ages have each their own mentality. In the age of savagery feeling rather than thought is predominant; in the higher barbarism of the heroic age the mental state is imaginative knowledge, "poetical wisdom"; in the age of civilization conceptual knowledge plays an ever greater part. Each of these stages has its own typical institutions, law, language, and literature, shaping the character of men. The progress, however, is without end or fulfillment. The course is cyclical: civilized societies decline into an anarchical state of nature, pass to the higher barbarism and thence again to civilization. Vico does not venture any prediction regarding the civilization of his own time, but it is probable that he thought that it would follow the general pattern. It seems therefore that Croce was right in saying that Vico had "missed the idea of progress," though allowance must be made for the fact that in Vico's view the cyclical movement is not a mere rotation of fixed phases but a spiral ascent (Croce [1913], p. 133. See

also R. G. Collingwood, *The Idea of History* [1946], pp. 67–68).

Voltaire's *Essai sur les moeurs et l'esprit des nations* ("Essay on the Manners and Mind of Nations") was published in 1756, but written in great part in 1740, ten years before the delivery of Turgot's "Discours" at the Sorbonne. In this Voltaire set out to "trace the history of the human mind" by comparing the achievements of European peoples with those of China, India, Persia, and Arabia. In developing his ideas he had in mind Bossuet's *Discours sur l'histoire universelle* (1681). Voltaire attacked this work on the ground that so far from being "universal," it distorted world history by dealing with the rise and fall of empires mainly from the point of view of their relations to the people of Israel and the Christian Church, and by neglecting the achievements of great civilizations beyond the bounds of Christendom, such as China and India. Even more emphatic was Voltaire's repudiation of Bossuet's doctrine of Providence. He could see in history no evidence of a comprehensive plan, a pervasive order, attributable to a Divine Will. He not only rejected final causes but he frequently wrote as if there were no law at all in human affairs, as if they were the domain of *Sa Majesté le Hasard.*

Yet Voltaire did believe in progress, clearly visible in the growth of the sciences, arts, morals and laws, commerce and industry. The great obstacles to progress were wars and religions. If they were abolished and the prejudices which engender them removed, the world would rapidly improve.

Voltaire was not a systematic thinker and he offered no clear-cut theory of the forces at work in history. The accounts he gave of human nature were uncertain and conflicting, cynical and generous in turn; they provided no sure basis for a theory of progress. Repeatedly he dwelt on the folly and credulousness of the masses and the selfishness and unscrupulousness of the ruling few. On the other hand, he disliked intensely the gloomy view of human nature given by the "sublime misanthrope," Blaise Pascal, dismissed as completely unfounded the doctrine of original sin, and took justice and pity to be fundamental in the life of man. Voltaire's conclusions about the future were necessarily tentative. Progress was liable to be interrupted by periods of regression, and great crises in history had often been decided by accidents. In the end, however, Voltaire held on to his trust in the power of reason to guide progress, "in spite of all the passions which make war on it, in spite of all the tyrants who would drown it in blood, in spite of the imposters who would annihilate it by superstition" (*Oeuvres complètes,* Paris [1877–85], XVI, 35).

Perhaps the most cogent and clearest exposition of

the idea of a universal history is that provided by Turgot in his two discourses of 1750. He conceived of universal history as concerned with the rise and fall of nations and empires, their mutual relations in wars and commerce, the development of the sciences and arts, of religions, morals and manners, "Humanity being ever the same amidst all these confusions and ever marching to its perfection." He raised questions of continuing importance today, such as the part played by war in civilization at different stages, the factors making for growth in some spheres and for retardation in others, the interaction of the various sciences and the mechanical arts and the possible reasons for the differences in their rates of growth. He showed progress to be unequal and its story to be full of bloodshed and struggles dominated by tumultuous and dangerous passions. Yet despite these ravages, in their day unavoidable (in Turgot's opinion) and perhaps even necessary as goads to progress, "manners become more gentle, the human mind becomes more enlightened, isolated nations draw nearer to each other, commerce and politics connect all parts of the world and the whole mass of the human race, alternating between calm and agitation, good and bad conditions, marches always, though slowly, towards greater perfection" (Turgot, 1895).

The belief in the unity of mankind did not in Turgot's view necessarily imply that men did not differ in capacity. There were differences, due partly to innate equipment and partly to education. But Turgot was more cautious than many later investigators: "The causes of inequality will always be unknown." Furthermore, though abilities differ their distribution was probably much the same in all races, places and times. High ability might remain undeveloped owing to the hazards of education and environment.

Differences in innate endowment are stressed by J. G. Herder. Each race has its own permanent inborn characteristics, each develops in its own way, within the limits prescribed by its innate constitution and physical environment. He followed G. E. Lessing in maintaining that life is an education for humanity and he urged that evils are self-corrective and that reason and justice tend to become more powerful. Herder's conception of universal history is, as we should now say, "pluralistic." Each people has its own ideals and its own conception of happiness. He rejected the hypothesis of a final and unique state of perfection and maintained that it could not be right to expect existing generations to suffer in order to ensure the happiness of a remote posterity. It is not clear whether *Humanität* or *Menschlichkeit* is the same for all men, or whether each people or stage of civilization has its own conception of *Menschlichkeit* as it has its own forms

of happiness. Europe, it seems, was in a privileged position, being alone capable of indefinite progress. Other peoples, for example, the Negro and the Chinese, have remained static, having realized all that they had it in them to become. On this as in some other issues Herder adopted a fatalistic attitude inconsistent with the emphasis he placed elsewhere on spontaneity and freedom (Herder, 1803).

By contrast with Herder's view, Immanuel Kant's conception of universal history is linked essentially with that of the unity of mankind. Kant's approach is frankly ethical and teleological. The end of history is the rationalization and moralization of man. The full realization of this, he thought, was only possible in a "universal civil society" founded on justice. "It is only in a society in which there is the greatest freedom and therefore antagonism between all the members, and at the same time the most exact determination of the limits of this freedom in each, so that it is consistent with equal freedom in all the rest, that the highest end of nature in man, i.e., the full development of all his natural capacities can be attained" (*Ideen* . . . [1784]; *Idea of a Universal History from a Cosmopolitan Viewpoint*). The impetus to development Kant found in the restlessness arising from the conflict in man between his social and antisocial tendencies, in what he calls the unsocial sociableness of man, his desire for gain and power, his greed and competitiveness. These antagonisms drive men to seek a master and to form societies, which in turn are driven by greed and ambition to form wider units. States may eventually, if they can avoid mutual destruction, abandon their "barbaric freedom" and seek equilibrium in some form of international authority.

The unification of mankind is for Kant an ethical postulate. Whether there is any evidence that mankind is in fact moving in this direction is quite a different question. He is well aware that we cannot with any certainty infer future trends from what has been observed in the relatively short period of history known to man, and he put forward suggestions for a universal history on a scale which he himself was unable to undertake. His own view is far from optimistic. He suggested that mankind may be like the sick man who died by getting better and better (*vor lauter Besserung*). Yet he did find ground for hope in the growing recognition (illustrated by the impression made by the French Revolution) of the importance of freedom and enlightenment for the internal efficiency of states and therefore for their external relations also. So out of the very vices of men, their competitiveness and power-seeking, conditions may yet emerge for the fulfillment of the highest end, the rationalization and moralization of man. Yet in the *Lectures on Ethics* (1913, p. 252), "the hope of it is still distant; it will be many centuries before it can be realized."

Auguste Comte's attitude to history is somewhat ambiguous. He complained that it had more of a literary and descriptive than of a scientific character, that it had not been able to establish "a rational filiation in the series of social events," so as to admit of any systematic prevision of their future succession. He even says that "every actual attempt to constitute directly the highly complex history of human societies" is to be regarded as "chimerical" (Comte [1875], p. 387). Yet, of course, the "Historical or Comparative Method" which Comte himself adopted had to make use of generalizations from history, though these were to be verified by deduction from the laws of human nature.

Law in History. Bury has drawn attention to the importance of the notion of the invariability of the laws of nature for the idea of progress. Unless this hypothesis is accepted, there can be no certainty that either scientific or social progress will continue indefinitely. Bury showed that Montesquieu was among the first to extend the Cartesian notion of natural law to social facts. In this Bury followed Comte, who somewhat condescendingly praised Montesquieu for "treating political phenomena as subject to invariable laws, like all other phenomena." He added that Montesquieu had made no effective use of this idea except in those portions of his work in which he had considered the influence of climate (Comte [1875], p. 208). This ignores important aspects of Montesquieu's work, *The Spirit of the Laws* (1748), especially his views of the structure of societies and of the laws of social change. Each society, Montesquieu had held, had a specific structure and its own constitutive principle. Social phenomena had to be viewed as interdependent and could only be interpreted by examining their relation to the constitutive principle. This applied also to social change. Changes in any part of the structure set up strains which affect the rest and disturb the balance of the society as a whole, as for example, when the Roman republic was corrupted by its physical expansion. It seems that ultimately the strains are psychological in character. The more power men have, the more greedy they become for still more power. Beyond a certain point, opposing forces are set in motion and these in turn change the structure. "There is in every nation a general spirit, upon which power itself is founded. When it shocks this spirit, power disturbs its own foundations and thus necessarily checks itself" (Montesquieu, 1949).

According to Bury, "Montesquieu was not among the apostles of the idea of progress" though he contributed to its growth by his theory that political like physical phenomena are subject to general laws. The laws that Montesquieu enunciated are not laws of progress. In one or two places he formulated a cyclical theory: barbarism, conquest, consolidation, conquest, consolidation, beginning corruption, dissolution. But as Franz Neumann has pointed out, he never used the cyclical theory in any relevant manner (Montesquieu, 1949).

In the introduction to his essay on the idea of a universal history Kant argued that whatever metaphysical views may be held about the freedom of the will, it was clear that human actions are as subject to invariable laws as any other phenomena. The statistics of births, deaths, marriages, so much influenced by the will of individuals, nevertheless show the same sort of regularity as that of occurrences in the world of nature (a point later taken up by Adolphe Quételet, J. S. Mill, and Henry Thomas Buckle in the nineteenth century). Hence, Kant thought that historical events which individually seem incoherent and lawless, may, when considered in relation to the whole species, be seen to follow a regular course (*einen regelmässigen Gang*), a slow but steady realization of human potentialities. What the laws of historical development are, he did not profess to know. He suggested that perhaps some future genius might do for social phenomena what Kepler and Newton did for the heavenly bodies. For his part he found a clue to history in the notion of a hidden plan whereby nature (or Providence) utilizes the conflicting passions of man to bring about his moralization and rationalization, a goal whose full realization is only possible in a "universal civil society founded on political justice" (Kant [1913], IV, 156).

The attempt to formulate laws of development which Kant deemed hazardous in view of the vastness of the period and the limitations of our historical knowledge was boldly undertaken by French thinkers in the next generation. The outstanding names are those of Fourier, Saint-Simon, and Comte.

Charles Fourier's law of passional attraction which he believed to be a rigorous deduction from Newton's law need not be discussed here. The laws formulated by Saint-Simon and Comte, on the other hand, are generally regarded as still of value, at least as offering suggestions for further inquiry. Both expressed their indebtedness to Condorcet, while censuring him for his exaggerations and inconsistencies. They certainly have in common certain leading ideas, such as that man must be studied as a species and not only as an individual, that human development is subject to law and that it has been and will continue to be, on the whole, progressive. The main difference is that Saint-Simon and Comte both lay greater stress on continuity in development. For example, they held that the Middle Ages, which Condorcet and his followers had regarded as periods of chaos and confusion, had in fact constituted a valuable and necessary stage in human progress.

Saint-Simon's teaching, so far as relevant, may be briefly summarized: (1) Society is not an aggregate of individuals, but a whole *sui generis;* (2) to study societies scientifically it is necessary to inquire how the parts of which they are composed contribute to the life of the whole at a given time and above all, to ascertain how the stages through which they pass are linked in their historical development; (3) though, except for an illuminating analysis of the history of some European societies, Saint-Simon did not undertake any comparative study of other societies on the scale that would be needed to establish general laws of development, he was convinced that the dominating fact in the life of societies is the fact of progress; (4) the law of progress has been stated in different forms by Saint-Simon, prior to his death in 1825, and by his school (*Mémoire sur la science de l'homme,* 1859).

There is, first, the law of the two states. According to this human thought passes out of a conjectural and theological state into a positive and properly scientific state. Religion passes through a succession of phases —fetishism, polytheism, deism. The sciences can be arranged in a series based on the order in which they pass from theological conjecture to positive knowledge. Physiology was on the eve of becoming positive and when this process has been completed it will be possible for philosophy, conceived as a synthesis of all the special sciences, to become positive and to provide an adequate basis for the rational organization of society. How all this is related to Comte's classification of the sciences and his law of the three states is another question.

A second form of the law of progress, partly stated by Saint-Simon but more fully elucidated in his *Exposition . . .* (1830) by S.-A. Bazard, is that in history there is an ever-recurring alternation between organic and critical periods. In the organic periods there is a common body of beliefs strong enough to resist the dispersive tendencies that threaten to divide society and to create a mood of stability and unity. In the critical periods, on the other hand, there is no creed commanding the assent of all, there is widespread discontent, egoistic tendencies gain in strength and anarchy results. Thus pre-Socratic Greece was organic, post-Socratic Greece, critical. In Rome the organic period ended with Augustus. With the constitution of the Christian Church in the sixth century began a new organic period of feudalism: in the sixteenth century the Reformers inaugurated another critical period. This has now (i.e., the beginning of the nineteenth century) reached its highest point and what society needs next is not a continuance of destructive criticism but a fresh

effort to reconstruct social institutions and a new system of beliefs to serve as a moral basis for these changes.

There is yet a third aspect of the law of progress emphasized by Bazard in his *Exposition . . .* (1830). This is the continual extension of the area of association from small groups of families, to cities, nations, confederations, a supernational church. This trend towards unity must eventually result in a still vaster association comprehending the whole race. It is part of Bazard's argument that the enlargement of the area of association makes for improved social relations within the smaller groups; "conflicting elements within each association are weakened to the degree that several associations unite into one." His view of the future was highly optimistic. The part played by force was steadily diminishing; governmental and military types of organization will be replaced by an industrial and administrative regime; while in the past human relations were based on the exploitation of man by man, in the future the concerted efforts of a united mankind will be directed to increasing the power of man over nature (Halévy, 1848; Durkheim, 1928).

Comte's theory of progress is far more comprehensive and elaborate than Saint-Simon's and, though no one would now concede his claim that his laws of social evolution were more "fully verified than any essential law of natural philosophy" (Comte [1875], II, 387), there can be no doubt of the enormous influence his work had in promulgating the idea that the history of civilization was subject to general laws and that a science of society was possible. In essentials Comte's theory of progress was summed up by himself in the law that human thought passes through three stages, the theological, the metaphysical and the positive, and in the more general statement that the development of man, individual and collective, consists in the growing ascendancy of our human attributes over our animal or purely organic ones and that this is achieved by the increasing command of the intellect over the passions and of the sympathetic over the self-regarding tendencies.

Comte's law of the three stages has been subjected to a good deal of criticism. In Bury's view it is "discredited." A more balanced estimate will be found in the valuable analysis made by J. S. Mill (*Auguste Comte and Positivism* [1866], pp. 9f.), by A. Fouillée in *Le mouvement positiviste* (1896), and by L. T. Hobhouse (*Democracy and Reaction,* 1904). A few comments will be offered on points of current interest. The first concerns the relations between monotheism and science. There is a widely held view that the basic assumptions of science, the orderliness or regularity of nature, were made acceptable by the belief in the unity and rationality of God (Whitehead, 1926). As far as the earlier stages are concerned Comte favored the reverse relation. It was the nascent positive spirit, encouraged by the emergence of geometry and astronomy that familiarized the educated mind with the conception of invariable laws and thereby facilitated the transition from the belief in a plurality of arbitrary and unpredictable gods to the belief in one God, the source of unity and order, though still capable of reversing the course of nature by miraculous interpositions (Comte [1875], II, 208). In regard to later ages, however, Comte maintained that though monotheism owed its first stirrings to the scientific spirit "it was itself indispensable to its further progress, both in regard to its improvement and propagation" (idem, II, 339). At this point his argument falters. He overrated the contribution of Catholicism to the growth of science, and ignored the fact that the Arab contributions were based on the recovered thought of polytheistic Greeks.

Next, a brief comment on the principle of consensus governing both social statics and dynamics. In the former, the state of any part of a social whole is intimately connected with the contemporaneous state of all the others. Dynamically, the principle implies that a change in any one sphere of social life, e.g., religion, science, philosophy, the fine arts, the industrial arts, commerce and government, is likely to be connected with a parallel change in all the others. For these principles, as for the law of the Three Stages, Comte made large claims.

His method, however, provided no procedure for distinguishing between different kinds and degrees of interdependence, with the result that many of the connections which he thought safely established, had no sound basis. This applies to the association or correlation he sought to establish between the theological stage and militarism, between metaphysical modes of thought and "defensive" warfare and between the growth of positive science and the phase of industrialism and the cessation of war. He did not foresee the clashes that would result from the intensification of nationalism, the industrialization of the non-Western communities or the complicated interactions between militarism and technological advances in the arts of war. Herbert Spencer, who also believed in the ultimate supersession of war by peaceful industry, nonetheless predicted a recrudescence of militarism. Comte and his followers were confident that at any rate in Western Europe the period of war was rapidly coming to an end.

In the event, it was Western Europe that became the center of the most terrible wars in history. If advances in industry do not necessarily make for peace, neither do advances in positive science. The sciences nowadays tend to be morally neutral or indifferent, and to be used as readily for evil as for good. It is plain from these and other examples that Comte had devised no reliable method for testing alleged correlations, or for passing from correlations to deeper underlying connections.

Finally, something must be said of the way in which the theory that the main agent of progress is intellectual advance was received by his contemporaries and immediate successors. In France a similar view was put forward by T. S. Jouffroy. The passions of individuals tended, he thought, to neutralize each other by their opposition, thus enabling general ideas on which all are agreed to rule with comparatively little resistance. The effects of individual passions are transient and secondary in the life of communities. "Nothing great, nothing permanent can ever be produced among a people, whatever be its government, except by the force and with the support of the convictions of that people" (*Mélanges philosophiques*, 3rd ed. [1860], p. 50). On the other hand, Émile Littré, Comte's most noted disciple, maintained that developments in industry, morality and art were separate from and antecedent to intellectual development. In England J. S. Mill stoutly defended Comte's view against the attacks made on it by Herbert Spencer. Mill's main point is that Comte did not deny, as Spencer implies, that intellectual changes were to some extent conditioned by changes in other elements in society. What he was concerned to show was that these were themselves consequences of prior intellectual changes.

As to Spencer's argument that feelings rather than ideas govern the world, Mill replied that while the feelings supply the motive power they are ineffective if not shaped and directed by some form of intellectual conviction. In view of the stress laid nowadays on "ideologies," in the sense of beliefs shaped by hidden "interests," some of Mill's remarks deserve special attention. He pointed out that the disturbing or distorting influence of the passions and interests was confined to morals, politics, and religion, while it is intellectual movement in other regions than these which is the root of great changes in human affairs. "It was not human emotions which discovered the motion of the earth, or detected the evidence of its antiquity, which exploded Scholasticism and inaugurated the exploration of nature, which invented printing, paper or the mariner's compass. Yet the Reformation, the English and French Revolutions and still greater moral and social changes yet to come, are direct consequences of these and similar discoveries" (Mill [1866], pp. 101–04). The issues thus raised are still actively discussed, as, for example, in the studies devoted to the relations between Calvinism and capitalism or between the Enlightenment and the Reformation (Trevor-Roper, 1967).

Determinism and Indeterminism. Opinions differ widely on how far progress is necessary or contingent, and even those who on the whole favored a deterministic interpretation were by no means committed to the view that the future of man is taken entirely out of his hands. In France, Renouvier, Cournot, Proudhon, Bouillier (see below), and many others definitely rejected fatalistic theories of progress. In England Walter Bagehot insisted that progress depended on a rare combination of energy and balance of mind, hard to attain and harder to keep. The notion of automatic or necessary progress is wholly foreign to Hobhouse's theory of social development. On the other hand, Comte and Spencer both stressed the certainty or "necessity" of progress. Nevertheless even they did not believe that progress was "inevitable" in the sense that it would take its own course no matter what we do. It was part of Comte's teaching that the greater the complexity of any order, the more it admits modification. Since social phenomena are the most complex of all, they are the most liable to perturbation, but they are also most open to rational control.

Within limits set by the conditions of social development growing knowledge of the positive laws of social life would enable us to exercise effective control, just as advances in the physical sciences give us greater power over the forces of nature. Spencer's argument goes deeper. The thoughts and actions of individuals are among the factors that arise in the course of evolution and they therefore play a part in producing changes. The analogy of individual development is instructive. An organism will gradually unfold its potentialities in a manner characteristic of its type in an approximately uniform manner. Nonetheless the process can be facilitated by maintaining favorable conditions or deranged by neglect. In the same way social development may be aided or hindered, retarded or accelerated, "without, however, being in any essential way diverted from its general course" (Spencer [1892], p. 401). It is interesting to note that Engels, from an entirely different approach, reaches a somewhat similar conclusion. What happens in history is the result of conflicts between many individual wills; each of these has been shaped by past conditions and all interact in such a manner that what emerges is something that no one has willed. Yet each individual contributes something and his actions must therefore be regarded as part-causes of the result (Engels, n.d.).

Human Nature and Perfectibility. The belief in perfectibility was linked by the Encyclopedists such as Helvétius and d'Holbach with a theory of human nature derived mainly from Locke and Condillac but influenced also by Leibniz (Hubert, 1923). According to this theory the dogma that human nature is unchangeable must be rejected. Man is by nature neither good nor bad. Circumstances and institutions, especially education, determine in which direction he is to develop. Change the institutions and this will change human nature. Helvétius further thought, though in this he was not followed by other Encyclopedists, that men do not differ in innate endowment.

All differences of intelligence and character are due to education or other environmental influences. These may act very subtly: "no two men ever receive precisely the same education" (*De L'esprit* [1758], iii. I). Princes, Holbach tells us, are like gardeners who can by varying systems of cultivation alter the character of men as they would alter the form of trees. In England this doctrine was adopted and developed by Godwin. But unlike the French philosophers he did not think that the transformation of human character could be attained by compulsory state education. State schools would only strengthen the power of kings and would be used to perpetuate prejudices and prevent the growth of independent thought (Godwin, 1796; Brailsford, 1913).

It will be seen that the belief in perfectibility rests on two presuppositions, namely that human nature is plastic and can be molded by changes in the environment, and that the progress of knowledge necessarily brings with it improvement in conduct. The first of these presuppositions harmonized very well with the empiricist doctrine of mental contents adopted by the Encyclopedists. The basis of the second, on the other hand, is vague and obscure. There are according to them no innate ideas, intellectual or moral. Morality is based on the capacity to experience pleasure and pain and to reflect on this experience. But they undertook no exact investigation of the way in which, under the influence of ideas and their associations, the feelings come to be modified. They also made no attempt to deal with the problem raised by philosophers in the post-Socratic period and repeatedly since then by religious teachers, of accounting for the fact that men can know what is good and choose the bad. To ascribe moral evil to the corrupting influence of bad institutions and to ignorance only pushes the problem a stage further back, since it does not account for the evil in institutions or for the failure to make use of whatever wisdom is available.

The problems thus raised were not resolved by Condorcet, though he was more aware than the Encyclopedists of the need of accounting for the persistence of prejudices and bad institutions. His views on perfectibility, however, were based not so much on a psychological analysis of human nature as on his belief in the possibility of discovering universally valid truths in the area of morals, politics, and economics as certain as those reached in the physical sciences and of using the knowledge thus gained in dispelling prejudices and guiding action. "Just as the mathematical and physical sciences contribute to improve the arts that are employed for our most simple wants, is it not equally," he asks, "the necessary order of nature that the progress of the moral and political sciences should exercise a similar influence upon the motives that direct our sentiments and our actions?" (Condorcet, *Esquisse . . . ,* Dixième Époque, 1795). Knowledge, if widely diffused, would make for greater freedom and equality. *La discussion générale et publique conduit à la vérité et ces mots vérité, liberté, égalité sont synonymes* (cited by W. Alff from an article in the *Chronique de Paris,* November 1791; Condorcet [1963], p. 380).

Comte's views of the relations between the intellectual and affective elements in human nature are less optimistic. The intellect has no energy of its own. It is moved to action by the instincts and among these the egoistic or self-regarding are more powerful than the social or other regarding. Nevertheless, in the course of development the intellect and the social impulses tend to support each other. The division of labor brings home to men their need of and dependence upon one another. Stimulated by increasing social contact and by the larger problems set before it, the intellect gains in strength. Reciprocally the altruistic tendencies are invigorated by the greater command which the intellect gives man over his passions and the deeper insight which it makes possible into the needs of others. A historical survey, Comte argued, shows that altruistic tendencies have in fact grown in strength and that this justifies the conclusion that they have the capacity for "indefinite extension." Furthermore, altruism is not only a dominant trend in social development, it is also a supreme ethical principle. "Living for others" Comte takes to be the ultimate aim and standard of conduct, rather than the mere increase of happiness, though he holds that the more altruistic any man's sentiments and habits can be made, the greater will be the happiness enjoyed by himself as well as by others.

Moral Progress. By the end of the seventeenth century the applicability of the idea of progress to the growth of scientific knowledge and its applications was generally accepted. Whether "perfectibility" could be extended to other spheres of social life was not so clear. Thus Fontenelle, who is generally regarded as having been among the first to formulate a definite theory of the progress of knowledge, denied that there was a parallel advance in the aesthetic arts. He was even

more definite in rejecting the notion of moral progress. Men's passions he thought would always remain the same, the proportion of "reasonable" men would always be small; civilization was little more than a veneer. Among the Encyclopedists, Diderot restricted the idea of development to the individual. Existing societies had rules and institutions so contrary to reason that he could only suppose them to have arisen out of superstition and lust of power. Societies did indeed grow larger and more complex. But while this growth generated new duties and widened the scope of moral obligations, it also increased the strength of inordinate desires. "In the state of nature there were few choices to be made, few desires to combat . . . the growth of new arts, of new needs and desires have deadened the spirit of hospitality and generosity and replaced it by a spirit of cupidity, venality and avarice" (Diderot, 1751). On the other hand Turgot and more fully, Condorcet, maintained that intellectual progress was the cause and instrument of a parallel development in the arts of life, morality, and happiness. In Comte's view religion, philosophy, science, the fine arts, the industrial arts, economic and political institutions were taken as in close mutual dependence and the progress of society from one state to another was not an aggregate of partial changes, but the product of a single impulse acting through all the partial agencies.

In the nineteenth century the moral elements in progress were emphasized by many French philosophers, notably by Renouvier and by the historian of Cartesian philosophy, F. Bouillier (1876). E. Reclus, in the article on Ethnography in the *Encyclopaedia Britannica* in 1879, sums up current opinion in the statement that "whilst material and intellectual development is not in dispute, this is not the case regarding moral progress." He quotes a remark of Mrs. J. S. Mill: "the world is very young, and has only just begun to cast off injustice" and another by Dr. Henry Maudsley: "morality, the last acquired faculty of man, is the first which he is liable to lose."

Much of the discussion of the part played by morals in social development was occasioned by Buckle's *History of Civilization in England,* published in 1857–61. In this he set out to show that progress in Europe "was entirely due to its intellectual activity. . . . In what may be called the innate and original morals of mankind there is, in so far as we are aware, no progress" (Buckle [1904], p. 128). The debate has been studied in great detail by J. M. Robertson (1895). In estimating the outcome of these highly complicated arguments a number of important distinctions have to be made.

First, we must distinguish between morality in the sense of conscientiousness, that is, steadiness in acting in accordance with one's sense of duty, and morality in the sense of the body of rules and obligations binding on the individual and the ideals set before him as models to emulate. It is clear that conscientiousness does not lend itself to comparative study: we have no direct access to the inner side of morality. Second, even as far as outward conduct is concerned, we cannot estimate with any accuracy the extent to which in our own times practice corresponds to precept. For earlier times the evidence would completely fail us. Third, we have no reason for believing that there has been any improvement in genetic makeup. Men are not born with a better moral equipment than in earlier times. Fourth, if there is such a thing as moral progress it must consist in: (1) fuller knowledge of the nature of purposive acts, of responsibility, of the ends of action and of the order of social relations most likely to be conducive to their fulfillment; (2) the progressive use of the knowledge thus attained in the criticism and reconstruction of social, political, and economic institutions; (3) the building up of cognitive, emotional, and affective systems needed to sustain the sense of moral obligations, to extend the range of imaginative sympathy and to provide the energy and drive required for the pursuit of ideals.

As to (1), those who deny the reality of moral progress must be ready to write off the whole history of reflection on human nature and its possibilities as of no significance. The dictum that "morality admits of no discoveries" can hardly be justified. Hobhouse has pointed to at least four discoveries of capital importance. The first is the establishment of the impartial rule, the foundation of common sense morality. The second is the establishment of universalism, the foundation of religious idealism. The third is the social personality (if we may use a modern phrase to express the real center of the Greek doctrine) which governs the first stage of philosophic ethics. The fourth is the idea of freedom as the basis of personal development and social cooperation which emerges in the modern reconstruction of ethico-religious idealism (Hobhouse [1927], p. 186). As to (2) and (3), the vast data available were examined by Hobhouse and Westermarck in the beginning of this century. Since then no survey on a comparable scale has been attempted and no adequate study exists of the impact of moral ideas on changes in the law, social and economic institutions, or on religious beliefs and practices.

There are two sets of problems now urgently in need of clarification. One concerns the ethical aspects of technological advance and in particular the social responsibilities of scientists. The other relates to the moral elements in the "ideologies" now dividing the communist and Western world alike. Their leaders speak in moral terms, but it is not at all clear whether they have different conceptions of the ultimate ends of life, or of the order of their importance, or of the types of institutions needed to attain them. In general, the problem of the causes of the variations in moral insight and the part played by ignorance or distortion of the relevant facts and the confusion of factual assertions with moral assertions proper requires much fuller investigation if further light is to be thrown on the reality or possibility of moral progress (Hobhouse, 1951; Westermarck, 1906; Macbeath, 1952; Ginsberg, 1956).

Marxism and Progress. Marxist writers tend to regard the idea of progress as the reflection, in the social consciousness of the time, of the forces at work in the ascendant phase of capitalist production. Likewise they attribute what they take to be its decline or demise to the pessimism induced by the failures of capitalism to solve the problems which it had itself generated. Accordingly they claim further that it is socialist thought alone which has kept alive what was rational in the idea, and which is now proving its validity in practice by the triumphant achievements of revolutionary socialism. The doctrine of progress now held by communist writers is set out in some detail in the official Soviet textbook *Fundamentals of Marxism-Leninism* (Kuusinen [1961], pp. 238ff.).

The main points as understood are formulated in this way: (1) progress consists in the growth of man's power over nature and of his ability to reduce or eliminate man's power over man (cf. the Saint-Simonians). (2) This growth depends upon and is correlated with the development of the forces of production. A society is progressive if it opens up fresh possibilities for the development of the productive forces and ensures a faster rate of growth, and if these changes in the forces of production are followed by social changes tending to reduce the various forms of personal dependence and oppression of the working classes. (3) The main difficulty in reducing man's power over man lies in the private ownership of the means of production. Only under socialism passing into communism is liberation possible. (4) It is taken as established that the development of the productive forces and the resulting changes in social relations has been of necessity progressive, since at each stage the level of the productive forces has grown and every advance has opened up possibilities of further development. From this it is deduced that "the forward movement of society is a historical necessity . . . that neither individuals nor classes can halt this movement or change its direction." Despite this "necessity" communists do not abandon the belief of the early rationalists that man can make himself. They look forward confidently to an age "when the true realm of freedom will blossom out of the realm of necessity in the fully developed communist society of the future." (5) The ultimate goal may be defined in the words of the concluding sentence of the second section of the *Communist Manifesto:* "an association in which the free development of each member is the condition for the free development of all."

On the evidence it is clear that the Marxists have not succeeded in revealing "the economic law of motion of modern society." Capitalist states have revealed powers of reconstruction and adaptation not foreseen by Marx. Furthermore, experience of communist societies has shown that the problem of power is not resolved by transferring the ownership in the means of production to the state. For this results in a concentration of political power and economic power, and renders the individual more helpless than in capitalist systems in which power and responsibility are more widely diffused. Finally, in Western societies property for power is of less importance than it was when political power was directly linked with property, and freedom of association was limited or nonexistent. Nowadays the direct power of employers over workers is kept in check by trade unions, and workers have learned to use the political machine to remodel the economic system (Korsch, 1938; Meissner, 1963).

Evolution and Progress. Of the three main ideas which enter into the theory of evolution, namely variation, heredity, and selection, it is the last that has had the most profound repercussions in its application to human affairs. Darwin himself made no extravagant claims for natural selection in his account of the evolution of man. He maintained that while in the formative period man had acquired his intellectual and moral faculties under the influence of natural selection, their further development owes much more to training, education, and tradition. In dealing with the "civilized" nations Darwin attached only subordinate importance to natural selection, since "such nations do not supplant and exterminate one another as do savage tribes." He added that it is very difficult to say "why one civilized nation rises, becomes more powerful and spreads more widely than another, nor why the same nations progress more quickly at one time than another" (Darwin [1909], p. 216).

Darwin's followers made no such reservations. Thus Karl Pearson confidently asserted that "selection is the sole effective process known to science by which a race can continuously progress." Similar statements were frequently made by writers belonging to the movement misnamed "Social Darwinism." This movement took various forms: (1) It purported to provide a biological basis for theories of race and class as the main agencies in the rise and fall of civilizations, and, readily passing from what is or is coming to be to what ought to be,

it pretended to find in biology an ethical justification for existing inequalities and for condemning all efforts at mitigating struggle within and between groups as "interference" with natural laws. (2) In its milder forms the ideas underlying Social Darwinism gave rise to the various forms of the Eugenic movement, the main aim of which is to replace natural by rational selection. (3) Politically its teaching was highly ambiguous. It was used by some to justify laissez-faire individualism on the ground that competitive struggle is the key to progress. For others it provided a scientific basis for socialism on the ground that societies being organisms, it was necessary to subject all their parts to central control.

It is now clear, after many years of controversy, that Social Darwinism suffered from an uncritical use of the notion of natural selection. In the main social change is not effected by the selective elimination of genetic variants and their replacement by others, but by changes in organization and tradition having little to do with the transformation of biological types. Changes in the structure of the family, in the forms of government, or the class system can be brought about without changes in the inherited structure, under the influence of selection.

Recently some biologists have claimed that the concept of progress can be fruitfully used in biology and even that from evolutionary theory an ethic can be derived. Various criteria have been proposed. Evolution is said to be progressive when it produces types that are more dominant or varied and abundant; have greater control over the environment and greater independence of its chances and changes; or develop powers of awareness which enable them to respond with greater plasticity and discrimination to their environment. Such criteria are obviously useful in describing certain lines of evolution. Whether they can provide the basis for an ethic is quite another question.

It is clear that progress in the sense defined is not a universal law of evolution, since the history of life provides examples not only of progress but also of retrogression, degeneration, and decay. In social change as in biological change, many trends can be traced. Among these we have to choose, but the ground of the choice cannot be deduced from the trends. An independent value judgment has to be made. Thus we cannot say on the grounds of general evolutionary theory that human society is moving inevitably to collectivism, as Joseph Needham claims (*Integrative Levels*, 1937), or that the progress of man requires the maintenance of class distinctions, as William Bateson suggested (*Biological Fact and the Structure of Society*, 1912), or that totalitarianism or authoritarianism is wrong, as G. G. Simpson maintained in *The Meaning of Evolution* (1950). Assertions of this kind assume that the laws of social change are already known and they imply ethical judgments which may or may not be valid, but which cannot be shown to follow from general evolutionary theory.

A survey of the history of the ideas of evolution and progress from Spencer onwards shows the importance of keeping them distinct. Progress means the realization of an ethical order; evolution is ethically neutral. Increasing complexity or growing differentiation are not necessarily progressive. A caste system may be a product of social evolution and may become highly complex and differentiated, but whether it is good or not cannot be decided by tracing its history. There is an evolution of imperialism, of socialism, of nationalism, of militarism and of many other trends, but the fact that they have evolved is no evidence of their value. The verdict of T. H. Huxley holds that from the facts of evolution, including the evolution of morals, no ethics of evolution can be derived (Hobhouse, 1928; Richard Hofstadter, 1945; Sorley, 1885; Julian Huxley, 1947).

Doubt and Disillusion. From the end of the nineteenth century onwards doubt about the reality of progress began to be heard more and more frequently. The writings of L. T. Hobhouse—a staunch believer in a humanitarian ethics—are of great interest in this context. In 1904 he drew attention to the widespread reaction against humanitarianism which was affecting every department of life and thought. He traced the rise of jingoistic imperialism and brought out its impact on domestic policy. In the world of thought he pointed to the various movements which, on the one hand, tended to erode the claims of individual personality and, on the other, to glorify self-assertion and to hold up to derision everything that savored of altruism and social justice (Hobhouse, 1904). During the first world war he contributed a series of articles to the *Manchester Guardian* (later reprinted in *The World in Conflict*, 1915) in which he examined in some detail the changes in outlook which were to be observed everywhere in his own life time, the growing impatience with reason, the glorification of "action," vital impulse, or instinct, the greater readiness to resort to violence as an instrument of politics both within states and between them. He was not, however, without hope that the outcome of World War I would be a restoration of the fundamental rules of justice, and faith in the principles of humanitarianism. In this he was to be disappointed. Reviewing the international situation in 1924 he thought that the forces making for a peaceful world policy and those making for growing tyranny, confusion, and the renewal of ever more destructive wars were evenly balanced. In 1927 his doubts persisted. There was the danger not only of the cessation of progress but of the break-up of our distinctive civilization. "Humanity would have to go back upon its traces, as it has done before" (Hobhouse [1927], p. 232).

Hobhouse died before the Nazis had done their worst. There can be no doubt that it was the horror and savagery of the Nazi period, all the more terrible for its cold-blooded and systematic ruthlessness, that shook or shattered the hopes that many still entertained for future progress. What importance is to be attached to this period in estimating the long-range trends of Western civilization is a problem on which opinions differ. There are those who, like Peter Geyl, hold that Mussolini and Hitler came to power only with the aid of exceptional political and economic circumstances which confused the masses and that their regimes were overthrown without having any lasting impact on the mentality of their peoples (Geyl, *Encounters in History* [reprint 1961], p. 293). Others are more skeptical and would agree with Arnold Toynbee, who argues that what happened in this period points to a radical inadequacy or weakness which will not be remedied by a revival of the ideals of the eighteenth century (Toynbee [1961], XII, 532).

Next we must note yet another wave of skepticism and disillusion. In the thirties there were many in Western countries who looked forward hopefully to the achievements of the Russian Revolution. They believed that Marxism-Leninism provided not only a theory of progress but a technique for promoting it in the event "their God failed them." They realized that the means employed defeated the ends of the Revolution, and that there were grave dangers of new and self-perpetuating forms of tyranny as difficult to control as those they had displaced. In this context too the state of later opinion is far from clear. It is interesting to note that in 1927, with the experience of the emergent dictatorships before him, Hobhouse expressed the opinion that these would prove unstable, and that some measure of political freedom could be deemed the norm for the advanced nations. He might have strengthened his case by stressing the fact that the dictatorships had only arisen in countries in which democracy had no deep roots. The Soviet dictatorship appeared to him as a normal stage in the development from autocracy to democratic institutions (Hobhouse [1927], p. 223). Tending in the same direction was Toynbee's opinion (in 1961) that "Communism as well as Liberalism was a product and expression of the modern Western civilization and the difference between the Liberal and the Communist way of Western life might be expected to diminish progressively with each additional decade of 'coexistence'" (Toynbee [1961], XII, 546). This view, however, is widely disputed: there are many who think that the two ways of life differ radically and are not reconcilable.

Finally, those who believe that the growth of knowledge is the chief or sole determinant of social progress have to face the charge that advances in science and technology can be and have been used for evil as for good, and indeed that they may bring mankind to the point of self-destruction. As against theories of "inevitable" progress, or of step by step correspondence between intellectual and moral progress, arguments of this sort have their importance. But as a basis for estimating the role of intellectual development in the history of civilization they are far from impressive. They fail to take into account the enormous contributions to human well-being due to the growth of knowledge and its applications, and they underestimate the strength of the movements for peace and for the control of nuclear power. More generally, they make no allowance for the resilience and resourcefulness of our age, shown by the success with which the peoples of the world have recovered from two devastating wars, by the development of policies of social welfare, and by the liberalizing forces at work in the communist world.

Conclusion. Looking back on the elements of progressivist thought which have been most influential, we may consider first the idea of the unity of mankind. This had a double significance, methodological and ethical. Methodologically it implied a belief in the possibility of a universal history as distinct from the history of particular peoples. In fact the data used by the early progressivists were, as judged by modern standards, grossly inadequate. The Encyclopedists gave some attention to the ethnographic material then available and, for the civilizations, they relied mainly on what they could learn from the Greek historians about ancient Egypt. Comte confined his synthesis to the "elite" nations of Europe and ignored China, India, and even the Muhammadan peoples. Nowadays there is an abundance of data, archeological, historical, and contemporary and, though we do not hear much about "universal" history, comparative sociology, which rests on the same presuppositions, is actively pursued. It is true that much emphasis has recently been placed on the distinctiveness of civilizations; but this does not necessarily preclude the notion of the development of mankind as a whole (Toynbee [1934], III, 390).

On the ethical side, the unity of mankind was conceived as an ideal of equal justice for all men, independent of class or race distinctions. Unity as an ideal was often combined with the belief that in fact human nature was in essentials the same in all men, and that the differences between them were not such as to justify relegating any of them to perpetual inferiority, or to disqualify them from playing a useful part in the progress of mankind. Of the vitality of this idea there can surely be no doubt. It is true that group morality persists; it survives in race discrimination, in war and the precarious rules supposed to govern its conduct, in chauvinistic nationalism. Still, universalism has grown; the scope of common principles and the impartiality shown in their application have expanded despite setbacks and reversals.

Next in importance is the belief in perfectibility, in the power of reason not only to utilize the forces of nature in the service of human needs, but also to bring about improvements in human relations and in the conduct of men. It is this belief which has aroused the sharpest criticism. Thus it has been argued that the increase in man's power over nature can be and has been used for evil and for good, and that there is no ground for confidence that they are more likely to be used in the future for the latter than for the former. Arguments of this sort, as noted above, vastly underestimate the great contributions of the natural sciences to human well-being, and their resourcefulness in dealing with problems of their own making. Furthermore, they ignore the fact that what the early progressivists relied on was not only progress in the natural sciences but also in the moral and political sciences and the influence that these might have on the motives directing action (Condorcet, 1795).

The real difficulties lie deeper. It is not at all clear whether the early thinkers believed that the social sciences could of themselves provide an ethic or whether independent moral judgments were involved. Thus Condorcet's principle of equality is stated as at once an ideal and a historical trend. Is the one derived from the other? Comte passes readily from the indicative to the imperative mood. His view that in the course of development altruistic tendencies gradually predominate over the selfish is stated not only as a fact but as a guide to action. In these and in many other cases the relation between progress as an ethical ideal and as statement of fact remains ambiguous.

A further, and even more serious weakness is to be traced to the failure of the early theories to inquire more fully into the relations between knowledge and feeling, between reason and passion. They were much too ready to take it for granted that "enlightenment" would bring virtue and happiness with it, and they made no serious effort to deal with the sources of irrational behavior. In this context Comte is an exception. In his view the preponderating power in human conduct belongs not to the intellect but to the instincts and emotions. The intellect has no energy of its own. It is moreover inherently anarchic and egoistic. It can be of service to humanity only under the influence of the altruistic emotions. Comte is thus not open to the charge of overstating the power of reason. The difficulty is rather that his analysis provides no assurance that the intellect has sufficient strength to ensure the triumph of benevolent over egoistic impulses.

In the last resort the validity of the belief in progress turns upon the question whether we can form an intelligible conception of a good common to humanity and have the ability to shape the conditions needed to secure this end. Bury, in introducing his historical analysis, insisted that the question is not one of ideals but of fact, "which man's wishes or labours cannot affect any more than his wishes or labours can prolong life beyond the grave." This fatalistic attitude is the precise contrary of the view taken by progressivists who see no cause of progress except in the human will. The facts are relevant insofar as they can throw light on the possibilities open to mankind. But Kant's verdict still holds good, that the short periods of history so far studied are not sufficient to establish laws of social development. It is further now generally held that we cannot pass directly from facts to values. The question therefore remains: By what standards is progress to be estimated? Those who reject the idea of progress do so because they believe that all such standards are "subjective" or "relative," and must always remain so. Rationalists, on the other hand, believe that principles of appraisal are available, and that our knowledge of them is itself progressive. In other words they believe that our knowledge of the nature of ideals and of the principles of justice and the conditions of their fulfillment has grown and will continue to grow. On this view the belief in progress consists primarily in the belief that man makes himself, that he has the power and the duty to control and direct future development. The history of the idea shows that in this sense it is relatively new and that it stands in need of development before it can direct development. Obviously, there can be no assurance of ultimate success, but there can be no real test of progress through conscious effort until the effort is made on a world scale. The ideas inherent in the belief in progress, the ideas of freedom, self-determination, and the rational use of natural forces to meet human needs have spread all over the world. This has meant a release of energies; but as usual, has also brought with it collisions, violence, and the justification of violence.

The immediate task is to rid the world of the now palpable irrationality of war. Once freed from the fear of war, the problem of world unity will assume a different character. Cultural diversity will be seen to constitute no danger. Peoples will feel free to develop each in its own way and to cooperate in the problems of common concern—the conquest of disease and poverty and the removal of the barriers that divide men. It may then become possible to work out more fully the practical implications of the conception of a self-directing humanity, to deepen our knowledge of the causes making for conflict, or onesidedness and discrepancies in development, and to use the knowledge thus gained in guiding future developments.

BIBLIOGRAPHY

J. Baillie, *The Belief in Progress* (London, 1950). Saint-Amand Bazard, *Exposition de la doctrine saint-simonienne* (Paris, 1830). F. Bouillier, *Morale et progrès*, 2nd ed. (Paris, 1876). H. N. Brailsford, *Shelley, Godwin and their Circle* (London, 1913). H. T. Buckle, *Introduction to the History of Civilization in England*, ed. J. M. Robertson (London, 1904). J. B. Bury, *The Idea of Progress* (London, 1920). H. Butterfield, *Man on his Past* (Cambridge, 1955). E. H. Carr, *What is History?* (London, 1961). Auguste Comte, *Cours de philosophie positive*, 6 vols. (Paris, 1836–42); idem, *The Positive Philosophy*, trans. Harriet Martineau, 2 vols. (London, 1875). M. J. A. N. de Condorcet, *Esquisse d'un tableau historique des progrès de l'esprit humain* (Paris, 1795); idem, German edition, ed. W. Alff (Frankfurt, 1963). B. Croce, *The Philosophy of Giambattista Vico*, trans. R. G. Collingwood (New York, 1913). Charles Darwin, *Descent of Man* (1871; London, 1909). Charles Dawson, *Progress and Religion* (London, 1929). J. Delvaille, *Essai sur l'histoire de l'idée de progrès* (Paris, 1910). D. Diderot, "Société," in *Encyclopédie* (Paris, 1751). É. Durkheim, *Le socialisme* (Paris, 1928). Ludwig Edelstein, *The Idea of Progress in Classical Antiquity* (Baltimore, 1967). F. Engels, "Letter to Bloch," in Marx and Engels, *Selected Correspondence* (Moscow, n.d.). R. Flint, *Philosophy of History* (Edinburgh and London, 1893). A. Fouillée, *Le mouvement positiviste* (Paris, 1896). M. Ginsberg, *On the Diversity of Morals* (London, 1956). W. Godwin, *Political Justice* (London, 1796). Léon Halévy, *Histoire du socialisme européen* (Paris, 1848). J. G. von Herder, *Ideen zur Philosophie der Geschichte der Menschheit*, 4 vols. (Riga, 1784–91), trans. T. O. Churchill as *Outlines of a Philosophy of the History of Man*, 2nd ed., 2 vols. (London, 1803). L. T. Hobhouse, *Democracy and Reaction* (London, 1904); idem, *Development and Purpose* (1913), revised ed. (London, 1927); idem, *Social Evolution and Political Theory* (London, 1911); idem, *Sociology and Philosophy: A Centenary Collection of Essays and Articles* (London, 1966), Ch. 3; idem, *Morals in Evolution* (1906), 7th ed. (London, 1951). R. Hofstadter, *Social Darwinism in American Thought* (Philadelphia, 1955). R. Hubert, *Les sciences sociales dans l'Encyclopédie* (Paris, 1923). T. H. Huxley and Julian Huxley, *Evolution and Ethics, 1893–1943* (London, 1947). Immanuel Kant, *Ideen zu einer allgemeinen Geschichte in weltbürgerlicher Absicht* (1784), in *Kants Werke*, ed. Ernst Cassirer, Vol. 4 (Berlin, 1913); idem, *Ob das menschliche Geschlecht in bestándigem Fortschreiten zum Bessern sei*, in *Kants Werke*, ed. Ernst Cassirer, Vol. 7 (Berlin, 1916); idem, *Lectures on Ethics* [from students' notes], trans. L. Infield (London, 1930). K. Korsch, *Karl Marx*

(London, 1938). O. Kuusinen, ed., *Fundamentals of Marxism-Leninism* (London, 1961). H. Liebeschutz, *Das Judentum in deutschen Geschichtsbild* (Tübingen, 1967), pp. 9ff. A. O. Lovejoy and G. Boas, *Primitivism and Related Ideas in Antiquity* (Baltimore, 1935), I, 6. A. Macbeath, *Experiments in Living* (London, 1952). B. Meissner, *Die Idee des Fortschritts*, ed. E. Burck (Munich, 1963). J. S. Mill, *Auguste Comte and Positivism*, 2nd ed. (London, 1966). C. G. Montefiore, *Outlines of Liberal Judaism* (London, 1923). Baron de Montesquieu, *Oeuvres*, ed. E. Laboulaye, 7 vols. (Paris, 1875–79); idem, *The Spirit of the Laws*, trans. T. Nugent, Introduction by Franz Neumann (New York, 1949), p. xxxvi. R. Niebuhr, *Faith and History* (New York, 1949). P. J. Proudhon, *De la justice dans la révolution et dans l'église*, 3 vols. (Paris, 1858; ed. M. Rivière, 1927). Charles Renouvier, *Introduction à la philosophie analytique de l'histoire* (Paris, 1896). J. M. Robertson, *Buckle and his Critics* (London, 1895); idem, *The Evolution of States* (New York and London, 1913). Henri de Saint-Simon, *Mémoire sur la science de l'homme*, in *Oeuvres choisis* (Paris, 1859), Vol. II. H. Spencer, *The Study of Sociology* (1873; London, 1892); idem, *Principles of Sociology*, 3 vols. (London, 1876–96); idem, *Essays Scientific and Speculative* (London, 1901); idem, *Social Statics* (1851; London, 1902). W. R. Sorley, *Ethics of Naturalism* (London, 1885). A. Toynbee, *A Study of History*, 12 vols. (London, 1934–61). H. R. Trevor-Roper, *Crisis of the Seventeenth Century: Religion, the Reformation and Social Change* (London, 1967). A. R. J. Turgot, *Oeuvres* (1808); *Life and Writings of Turgot*, ed. W. Walker Stephens, 2 vols. (London, 1895). G. Vico, *La Scienza nuova prima*, trans. T. G. Bergin and M. H. Fisch as *The New Science of Giambattista Vico* (Ithaca, 1948). F.-M. A. de Voltaire, *Essai sur les moeurs et l'esprit des nations* (1756), in *Oeuvres* (Paris, 1792). E. Westermarck, *Origin and Development of Moral Ideas* (London, 1906). A. N. Whitehead, *Science and the Modern World* (New York, 1925; Cambridge, 1926), Ch. I. M. Wiener, "Der Messiasgedanke und seine Umbiegung," Festgabe für C. G. Montefiore (Berlin, 1928). K. Wilhelm, "The Idea of Humanity in Judaism," *Studies in Rationalism, Judaism and Universalism*, ed. R. Loewe (London, 1967).

MORRIS GINSBERG

[See also Causation, Final Causes; Cycles; Education; **Evolutionism;** Justice; Law, Natural; Nationalism; **Perfectibility;** Primitivism; Prophecy; Socialism.]

PROPERTY

I. INTRODUCTORY OBSERVATIONS

IN ITS WIDEST sense, property denotes the exclusive relationship of a person or a group of persons to an object or a complex of objects of material value. Therefore the history of property accompanies the history of mankind, from the dawn of civilization. From time immemorial man has searched for and consumed food. He has worn clothes and ornaments. A slightly more advanced stage of civilization means the exclusive occupation of some piece of land or some dwelling, however modest, for shelter. In this primitive sense some form of exclusive personal property is essential to human life. But the social, economic, and legal history of property, as one of the major aspects of the evolution of civilization, begins with the appropriation and use of land for purposes of exploitation. In this sense the history of property may be dated from the time when man, thousands of years ago, began to abandon his exclusive reliance on hunting and the gathering of wild fruit for the raising and use of domestic animals. The nomadic phase of economic organization—which in certain parts of the world endures to the present day—makes it necessary to apportion certain pastures for a while, for exclusive use by the tribe or any other group, and thus brings with it the first problems of equity in the use of the resources for the benefit of the group. This is carried much further when man begins to settle and to cultivate the soil. The permanent association of a man, a family, or a group with a piece of soil for purposes of economic exploitation intensifies the problems of distribution. It is probable that, in this phase, the notion of private ownership, meaning the exclusive control over a piece of land, becomes articulate and raises the age-old problem of private versus collective property. The question of ownership of agricultural land also begins to introduce into the concept or idea of property the two distinctive aspects of exclusive control over a certain thing or complex of assets of material value which have gained increasing significance with the evolution and the manifold ramifications of property in more modern times: on the one hand, the privileges and benefits flowing from the exclusive *use* of property for its owner; and, on the other hand, the *power* which control of property, beyond personal needs, puts into the hands of one person or group over others. The age of feudalism—when, in an elaborate hierarchy, the feudal owner, in proportion to his rank and place on the ladder, acquired not only superior wealth through his enjoyment of the produce of the land but also had, by virtue of his tenure, power over the ones below him, especially the peasants—clearly illustrates these two aspects of property. Both these privileges of property raised in an acute form the social problems of property: inequality in the satisfaction of the needs of life, and a growing gap between the governors and the governed through the power that the former exercise over the latter.

The social and economic problems flowing from

increasing inequalities in the enjoyment of the things that life offers, as well as in the degree of power that property conveys, are enormously magnified in the industrial age. It is now that the exclusive control over things and assets, collectively described as property, not only widens the gap between the rich and the poor, but also multiplies the power over an industrial complex that property gives to the property owner. The inevitable reaction to this phase—starkly illustrated by the early phases of the Industrial Revolution—is the social revolution which expresses itself in a multiplicity of forms: social reform legislation, redistribution of property, and most of all, socialization of the means of production.

This brief preliminary survey indicates that while property in a general sense is as old as the history of mankind, its meaning and function have varied, and steadily become more complex, with the evolution of society. In order to understand this evolution even in its broadest outline, the following pages will attempt to survey some of the principal developments from three perspectives: first, the evolution of the social and economic function of property; second, the ideology of property; third, the various legal concepts of property. Some brief concluding observations will sketch the probable evolution of property in our changing contemporary society.

II. STAGES IN THE SOCIAL AND ECONOMIC FUNCTION OF PROPERTY

Although we know little about the status and function of property in most of the earlier, and especially the non-Western civilizations, it is likely that even without any customary or statutory legal sanction, the more purely personal objects especially clothes, jewels, and other prized personal things have always been recognized as "belonging" to that particular person. It is equally likely that in the primitive economies of scarcity, in which man has lived as a hunter and a nomad, there must have been some form of collective ownership and use of beasts hunted for food or of cattle put to pasture by a nomadic tribe. Exclusive or privileged claims on the hunted beasts or the produce of domesticated animals are probably the concomitant of a developing hierarchy, in which the chieftain or king receives a share of the wealth produced by the group, as a symbol of his privileged status.

But apart from such privileges of rank or leadership, it is significant to note to what extent various agricultural economies of societies different in vocation, nationality, race, and political structure have had collective ownership of the assets needed for their sustenance. It is both difficult and fruitless to attempt to analyze how far the sharing of these essential things

can be described as community of ownership or community of use. The differentiation of the degrees of legal control—such as the distinction between ownership and possession—is essentially an aspect of more advanced civilizations and in most respects dates from the history of Rome. The early Roman *gens* combined its members under a common name, in a common cult, and above all served as a collective organization for the cultivation and maintenance of the land, e.g., by irrigation. The absence of private property in land in the Germanic tribes—as described by Caesar and later by Tacitus, has often been contrasted, as an early example of socialism, with the individualistic development of private property in Roman society.

Whatever the reason—whether it be the fact that the Germans changed at a relatively late stage from a nomadic forest and pasture economy to the static cultivation of soil by agriculture, or certain social and racial characteristics of the Germanic tribal traditions— it appears that the German *Genossenschaft* stood for collective ownership and distribution of cattle and other goods. Again, the Russian *Mir*—which has often been described as a precursor of the contemporary collective farm system of the Soviet Union—is an ancient Russian rural institution. It was composed of the heads of families who, in a village or a group of villages, directed the cultivation of the land, controlling the size of the different fields as well as the method of cultivation and agricultural maintenance. Its functions extended to pastures and forests.

In yet another environment characterized by the overwhelming need for cultivating and sharing available food resources in a given community, the Chinese village has for many centuries constituted a basic unit of common cultivation control. It should be added that such collective institutions could and did survive the growing development of a class structure, when princes and feudal lords acquired the overall dominion over large lands, while the peasants, forced to work not only for their own minimum needs but for the demands of their overlords, preserved communal institutions.

Generally, and in awareness of the inevitable oversimplification that characterizes a brief general survey, it may be said that some form of community of property predominates in primitive agricultural economies, at least on the level of those who have to work and live on the land by agriculture or cattle raising in order to survive. Private property, even in the preindustrial age, is essentially the hallmark of a more structured society, in which almost inevitably those who accumulate land not only become the rich members of the society, but also its political and social leaders.

It is the history of Rome—a society that developed from a self-supporting agricultural tribal economy to

651

a complex multinational commercial empire—that contributed decisively to the evolution of Property as a theoretical concept. The Roman legal concepts dominate the legal systems of a large part of mankind to the present day. It is Roman law that developed the concept of the *Dominium ex iure Quiritium*, a concept denoting absolute control over a piece of land and the sky above it. Much of this was created by the conversion of the *Ager Publicus* ("public land"), conquered in war, from possession to the right of exclusive control. Until the agrarian reforms initiated by the Gracchi, this was predominantly a privilege of the patricians, but gradually the plebeians acquired rights in some of these properties. In contrast to the Quiritian property —which was subject to very formal procedures of transfer—the gradual expansion and commercialization of the Roman Empire created another form of property, the so-called bonitarian property, easier to transfer and appropriate to the age of trade and commerce which requires mobility of goods.

The history of the social and political conflicts of Rome is to a large extent the history of the conflicts between patricians and plebeians for the control of land and other forms of property. In the process, the Romans developed a clear contrast between public and private property, the former denoting the domain of state ownership and the latter of private ownership. As will be shown in the subsequent section, the Romans also developed a dichotomy between ownership as a complete right of control over things movable and immovable and all other forms of economic interests. It is equally clear that this theoretical distinction has no particular relationship to the social, political, and economic struggle, which marks the history of Rome as of any other civilization. It is more significant that as a society develops from a predominantly rural and agricultural one to a commercial one, the forms and modalities of ownership multiply, and with it the increasing distribution of property among a growing section of the population. Things that can be bought and traded such as handicraft, commercial merchandise, ships, and many other articles, change hands more easily and ubiquitously than land.

Nevertheless, it is the control over land that remains by far the predominant form of property until the advent of the commercial and industrial age, which marked the transition from the Middle Ages to modern Western history. The age of feudalism is characterized by the degrees of dominion over land in its political and legal as well as its economic and social aspects. The hierarchy that, at the height of the Middle Ages, leads from the emperor through the regional princes to the lesser lords down to the peasant who cultivates the land, is marked by the degree of legal control over

the land. The emperor has—an increasingly theoretical—control over the entire realm which is both *political* control (sovereignty) and *economic* control in the sense that he exacts dues and tribute from those who hold the land under him. The political, social, and economic hierarchy descends to the level where the peasant, who produces the fruits of the earth by his labor, has not only the most limited measure of right over the land that he cultivates but also the lowest standard of living and the lowest social status.

In escaping from the bondage of feudal land tenure to the cities, the peasant not only acquires more freedom of movement but also the ability to produce and own more freely by virtue of craftsmanship, commerce, or other forms of work. This corresponds to the gradual displacement of an economy based predominantly on the self-sufficiency of the rural household—producing its own food, weaving its clothes and making the things used by the household—by a commercial economy, in which land increasingly loses its exclusive or predominant position. But it is an equally important hallmark of the growing commercial economy that property no longer means only land and other physical objects but also a complex of assets (*Vermögen*). The big merchant of the sixteenth century not only owns houses, land, and ships but he also has claims on the money that he lends to emperors and princes, and on his deposits in the banks which are developing rapidly in the age of commerce. He also increases his control, by means of wage contracts, over the growing number of persons who work for him in his various commercial and maritime enterprises.

But it is the Industrial Revolution that decisively increases not only the diversity of the modalities of property but also, and above all, the function of property as a means of controlling the lives of others who do not own property beyond their immediate personal needs and are dependent for their living on those who do. The concentration of workers in factories not only increases the wealth aspects of property, by enabling the very few who own the complex of assets—land, buildings, machines—that make up the means of production to draw the new proletariat away from the relative self-sufficiency of land and rural life but also immensely increases the power enjoyed by the owner of the means of production over those whom he employs. In the Marxist theory of property, this becomes the *Mehrwert*, the surplus value, which the owner of the means of production appropriates to himself above the minimum needed to keep the workers alive and capable of working. At later stages of the Industrial Revolution this growing gap is somewhat mitigated by public law, i.e., by public restrictions on the freedom to use property, resulting in a growing body of social legislation and restrictions on the use of property which gradually lead to the modern welfare state.

For the evolution of the concept and function of property, a more significant development is the gradual separation in a more advanced stage of the enjoyment and power aspects of property. The catalyst of this divorce is the modern corporation in which ownership becomes depersonalized and diversified in the multitude of shareholders who jointly have the title to the property represented by the corporation and become increasingly the recipients of dividends and interest while the power of command enjoyed by the early capitalists passes to modern management, a self-perpetuating oligarchy. The managers of the contemporary corporation do not need the formal title to the property represented by the shares in order to direct the enterprise.

Various attempts have been made—covering the entire spectrum of modern political and economic theory—to overcome this divorce between power and property. One approach—in essence the contemporary liberal philosophy—is to spread property as widely as possible, by limitations on the size of landholdings, and measures against monopoly or other concentrations of industrial property. An indirect way to reach a similar goal is progressive taxation designed to reduce the inequalities of property by redistribution through the state. Another more limited attempt is to increase the role of labor in the management of the modern corporation, by giving the workers a share in its direction—an experiment carried out in the postwar German legislation which gives the workers' representatives a fixed share in the management of certain industries (coal and steel).

By far the most radical attempt to counter the power conferred by property in the industrial society is socialization. It goes to the root of the property problem by expropriating the private owners of property and vesting the title as well as the power of management in the state. While in the original Marxist doctrine the expropriation of the owners of industrial property was intended to lead to the abolition of the entire coercive apparatus of the state, seen as a symbol of capitalist expropriation, in modern socialist or communist systems the change over property has essentially been the vesting of the ownership of industry and business in the state, either direct or through the instrumentality of state corporations.

Generally, then, the effect of the commercial, and later the industrial, revolution has been to divorce property increasingly from the function that, by and large, it had in the earlier agricultural economy. Then work and the means of subsistence were centered around property and land, the home and the tools of farming, craft, and primitive manufacture, although even in that phase the accumulation of large properties in the hands of princes, nobility, and other large owners created the social inequalities that made property an instrument of inequality and the ability of a few to dominate the many. In contemporary industrial society the enormously increased potential of property as a vehicle of both wealth and power is countered by a growing use of public power to mitigate the inequalities, through a limited redistribution of the benefits of property or, more radically, by the socialization of private property and the means of production. In contemporary Soviet society, some of the original functions of property are restored insofar as private property is permitted in private houses, a limited agricultural acreage for personal consumption, and the tools of personal craft, while the major means of production are owned by the state.

III. THE IDEOLOGY OF PROPERTY

The acknowledgment of the importance of property as perhaps the most significant single determinant of the conditions of life, liberty, and the pursuit of happiness is an idea shared by the many conflicting ideologies of property. But, depending on their philosophies of life and the human condition, they have developed starkly contrasting theories. At one end of the spectrum, the right to own private property is regarded as one of the most basic "natural rights," essential to the existence and dignity of man. At the other end, private property is condemned as an evil, as the most important single instrument of oppression of the many by the few, and it is the common use of goods by all members of the community, the counterpart to the abolition of private property, that is regarded as a natural condition of man.

The most important ideological justification of property is that property is seen as a sum product of the labor of man, who mixes his sweat with the soil and is entitled to reap the rewards of his work. Ironically, this philosophy has been most articulately expressed by the social philosophers of the commercial and industrial age at a time when the conditions of society increasingly divorced the opportunities for accumulation of property from the products of a man's toil. Not only John Locke and the philosophers of the American Revolution, but also the German philosopher Hegel and the doctrine of the modern Catholic church extol the right of private property on this ground. In all these ideologies, the social and economic facts, i.e., the increasing divorce of labor and property, is ignored. They are essentially idyllic pictures of a society that no longer exists. But perhaps the most powerful and practically influential justification of private property is a religious philosophy, which not only accepts the inequalities of property, but regards them as based on the will of God. Calvinism is a branch of Protestantism which—in contrast to the Lutheran branch—sees the accumulation of wealth as a sign of the grace of God, and poverty as a condition equally imposed and deserved by the will of God. The practical result of such an ideology is of course the rejection of any moral or social duty to equalize the conditions for acquisition of property. By contrast the earlier Catholic philosophy of Saint Thomas Aquinas and his immediate successors regards private property not as a natural right but as a social condition. The nineteenth-century doctrine of the Catholic church, however, postulates the right of private property as a natural right, tempered only by the Christian duty of charity.

On the other side, philosophies demanding the complete equalization or abolition of private property have been formulated throughout history, from the early stages of Greek civilization through Thomas More's *Utopia* (1516) and the Christian Socialists of the nineteenth and twentieth centuries. Marxist socialism is, of course, the most radical of the anti-property theories. However, it postulates the abolition of private property not as an ideology but as a dialectical necessity resulting from the increasing concentration of industrial property, which reduces itself *ad absurdum* through increasing monopolization. However, insofar as Marxism demands action by the proletariat "to expropriate the expropriators," it must in effect be ranged among the philosophies of collectivism. The difference between the Utopia of Thomas More and the dialectical socialism of Marx is not so much due to the tension between ideology and necessity as to the difference in the social substratum. The problem of the function and redistribution of property is very different in the rural and essentially self-sufficient society of the sixteenth, as compared with the increasingly industrialized and urbanized society of the mid-nineteenth century. The socialist Utopia of Thomas More can envisage the abolition of all private property and money. Each family, consisting of forty persons, is to obtain all its needs on the public market. But in the complex industrial society, the abolition of the inequalities and injustices of private property can only be envisaged not in the form of the *abolition* of property, but in its *transfer* from private to public hands.

The ideology of private property, as the "natural" and untouchable expression of personal freedom, reaches its peak in the latter part of the nineteenth century, i.e., at the time when the social conditions of modern industrialized Western society had already radically altered the assumptions on which the ideology

of private property had built: the identification of man with land and things within his reach, which he had essentially acquired, or was capable of shaping, through the sweat of his brow. Under the fifth and fourteenth Amendments of the United States Constitution, "No person shall be . . . deprived of life, liberty, or property, without due process of law; . . ." In numerous cases, the Supreme Court of the United States interpreted these essentially procedural provisions as constituting an absolute prohibition against interference with complete freedom of contract—seen as an aspect of property. This meant, for example, the invalidation of elementary social welfare statutes, such as a maximum ten-hour working day or provisions regulating children's and women's labor. Not only did this interpretation—which, on the whole, prevailed until the days of the New Deal—mean a complete identification of the right of private property with the extreme principles of a laissez-faire economic philosophy; it also extended, as a matter of course, the individual rights formulated by eighteenth-century philosophies for the human individual, to the modern corporation. The ideology of the log-cabin pioneer was applied to corporate entities controlling hundreds of millions of dollars and employing tens of thousands of persons. The contemporary American jurist and sociologist Thurman Arnold has termed this ideology "the folklore of capitalism."

About the same time, the first of the modern Encyclicals of the Catholic Church issued by Pope Leo X in 1891 elevated the right of property to an absolute natural right—departing in this from Saint Thomas Aquinas. Significantly, both the modern jurisprudence of the Supreme Court—roughly from 1936 onwards—and the most recent Encyclicals issued by Pope John XXIII and Pope Paul VI substantially depart from this ideology. The former has long accepted the constitutionality of social and economic legislation, while tending to emphasize more strongly the untouchability of personal noneconomic freedoms. The latter acknowledge the legitimacy of social and economic legislation for the sake of public welfare and the necessity of appropriate restrictions on the scope and use of private property. This leads to many economic and social systems, ranging from predominantly free enterprise to predominantly state-directed systems, short only of the complete abolition of private property.

While capitalist systems have increasingly modified the formerly near-absolute ideological and practical protection of private property, by a complex system of social welfare legislation, of progressive taxation, of the transfer of basic industries and utilities to public ownership (e.g., in Britain, France, Italy, India), socialist systems have considerably widened the scope of private property for personal use. In the U.S.S.R., all industrial production beyond small artisans' shops is state-owned and operated by state corporations, while farming is run either by collective or by state farms. However, individual ownership of houses and a few acres, as well as their cultivation and some livestock, and the ownership of personal implements are permitted and play a not inconsiderable part in the economy.

As has been pointed out earlier, a significant aspect of the contemporary industrial society is a divorce between titular ownership and the control of enterprises. Hence the question of the legal title to property is no longer as significant as it was. Publicly and privately owned enterprises coexist and often compete with each other while the state controls both through a variety of devices. This, in the view of many contemporary economists and social philosophers, makes the question of the formal transfer of property from private into public hands a matter of relatively minor importance. The power once conveyed by the ownership of the means of production is not only no longer necessarily linked with formal ownership but it is also curtailed by the controlling powers, planning devices, and other directive measures of the state. The privileges conferred by the unlimited use of private property—leading to a great gap between a rich minority and a destitute majority—are countered by a variety of measures, all aimed at a partial redistribution of property. Progressive taxation siphons off some of the benefits of property and uses them for public purposes or services, such as a national health service, while anti-trust laws, labor legislation, and other public controls restrain, though by no means eliminate, the power of the modern corporation.

IV. LEGAL CONCEPTS OF PROPERTY

Although the social and economic functions of property are determined by the character of the society in which it operates rather than by legal concepts, the latter have significantly influenced different developments in the forms and modalities of property. The principal difference is between the large number of civil law systems, which are derived from the Roman law, and the common law systems, which have developed pragmatically and historically, essentially from the English political and social environments. Romanistic systems define property as the ownership of things, movable and immovable, while excluding from "property" in a legal sense any other kind of economic right, i.e., such intangible rights as patents, copyrights, trademarks, claims against other persons, as the creditor has against the debtor, the mortgagee against the mortgagor, the employer against the employee, the landlord against the tenant (and vice versa).

The Roman law concept is embodied in the definitions of property in the Continental civil codes, such as Article 544 of the French Civil Code which defines ownership (*propriété*) as "the right to enjoy and dispose of the things in the most absolute manner. . . ."

Such a definition, though repeated with relatively modest variations in the more modern German, Swiss, and other contemporary codifications, is inadequate in two ways: in the first place, it artificially divides tangible objects—movable or immovable—from the increasingly important and manifold types of economic assets which are of a different character. In the second place it ignores the extent to which the most important functions of property can be divorced from the legal title. As the Austrian jurist and sociologist Karl Renner pointed out in a book published in 1905, *The Institutions of Private Law and Their Social Function*, in industrial society the actual functions of property are increasingly exercised by those who have acquired the economic substance but not the legal title: mortgagees, bankers, and other money lenders, shareholders, and others. As mentioned earlier, an even more recent development tends to divorce the control functions of property from legal ownership altogether, a development which is sometimes characterized as the "managerial society."

The Anglo-American concept of property has always been more pragmatic and elastic. Property is a bundle of powers, and it may include the claim for the repayment of a loan, the title to a mortgage on another man's land, or a share in a company, as much as the ownership over a piece of land or a chattel. Moreover, the continuous development of the common law from the medieval land tenure system has led to the recognition of various *degrees* of ownership in land. In theory the full right of property is vested in the Crown—i.e., the State—while the others hold "estates" in land measured in terms of duration. There are freeholds or leaseholds of 999 or 99 years duration and a variety of other forms. In substance, this does not greatly affect the extent and function of ownership. Finally, English law has developed the concept of the Trust, which is a splitting up of ownership between a "legal" and an "equitable" owner, a concept unacceptable to the civil law systems. The trustee has the powers of the legal owner, especially the right to administer and sell the assets, while the beneficiary is entitled to the fruits of the property. The concept of Trust—which pervades all spheres of life in the Anglo-American legal world, such as the administration of estates or club properties—has no parallel in the world of civil law.

On the other hand, the Continental law, and in particular French law, distinguishes between public property (*domaine public*) and private property (*domaine privé*). This distinction—which is not accepted in all the Continental systems and has no parallel in the common law—corresponds to the time honored and sharp divisions between public and private law, which has only much more recently been introduced into the common law systems. An entire system of administrative jurisprudence has been built around the distinction between legal relations between public authority and the citizen on the one hand and those between private subjects of law on the other hand. Generally, in the formulation of a modern authority on the French administrative law, a public domain means "the totality of assets of public entities and institutions which are either put directly in public use or affected by a public service. . . ." This comprises public utilities of all kinds from public waters to railways, roads, public markets, public libraries, and other services or entities dedicated to public use.

Contemporary developments in the comparative jurisprudence of the civil law and the common law countries show that the conceptual distinctions in the definitions of property have become increasingly less significant as compared with the socially and economically much more important question of the relation of public power to private property. In common law as in civil law systems many public utilities such as railways, electric power, coal and steel, or shipping have been transferred from private to public ownership generally through the instrumentality of government controlled semi-autonomous public corporations. In common law as in civil law systems, the governments have extensive powers of expropriation of private property in the public interest (eminent domain). The extent as well as the form of the exercise of these powers are determined by political and economic considerations, not by the legal form. Even the once extremely sharp distinction between the civil law and the common law concepts of property—as it has been briefly described earlier—is no longer absolute. Thus, modern French law has developed the concept of *propriété commerciale*. Under modern French legislation both businessmen and farmers who rent their premises and land enjoy certain rights, as against the titular owner, the essence of which is the claim of the occupier against the owner for renewal of the lease. To that extent the owner is deprived of his legal power to dispose of his property, in favor of the lessee's right to the continuity of his enterprise. This is a recognition of the fact—more dramatically illustrated in the development of the modern giant corporation—that the conduct of the enterprise, with or without legal title, represents the substance of property rights, while the titular ownership may be reduced to the receipt of certain rents, dividends, or interest payments.

V. THE FUTURE OF PROPERTY

In many countries, depending on the state of their historical and cultural traditions, the necessities of contemporary society have led to public policy restraints which have imposed many restrictions upon the unfettered use of property rights. The traditional privileges of property, i.e., the more or less unlimited use and enjoyment of the objects of ownership, incorporeal and corporeal, have been severely curbed. The curbs extend over a wide range, from restrictions on the free determination of wages, of statutory minimum standards for food, drugs, machines, factory conditions, and many more, through the power of expropriation by public authority for public purposes, to wholesale socialization and transfer of private property into public hands. This does not however mean the end of the concept or of the significance of property. The protection of property rights is today spread over the community as a whole where it has, in the past, essentially benefited the very limited class of owners of land and commercial property. The effect of the older law was to give excessive protection—often at the expense of the essential necessities and liberties of the rest of the community—to the owners of large estates and industrial enterprises. The balance is to a large extent being restored in contemporary society. This corresponds to a wider conception of property, influenced by new social and economic philosophies. For the vast majority of people the most essential economic interest is the right to use one's labor and skills and the assurance by the law that the minimum needs of human existence will be protected. It is to that end that modern states today have minimum wage statutes, a legal machinery protecting collective bargaining agreements, public credit institutions that facilitate the ownership of homes, and statutory protection against oppressive conditions in installment (hire purchase) transactions. In the field of family law, almost all legal systems give statutory minimum rights to dependent wives and children, and thereby limit the freedom of the owner of the matrimonial home or other property assets to dispose of them freely. Thus a deserted wife is now widely protected, in common law as in civil law systems, in her occupancy of a house that may be legally owned by her husband. The big landowner and the industrial entrepreneur are unquestionably today far more restricted in the free use of their property than in earlier times, even where the property is not transferred into the hands of the state or another public entity. But for the average person, who disposes of limited physical assets and depends for his own and his family's livelihood mainly on the ability to work, on fair conditions of trade, and on the enjoyment of minimum standards of living, property in the wider, nontechnical sense, i.e., the right and the ability to enjoy the minimum conditions of human existence, is today probably far more effectively implemented than in earlier times. In that sense the intermeshing of private rights and public law has led to a much more complex concept and regulation of property, with the object of giving legal protection and facilities for the widest possible utilization of a power to create economic values to the largest number of people.

BIBLIOGRAPHY

Wolfgang Friedmann, *Law in a Changing Society* (London, 1959; 2nd ed. 1972), Chs. 3, 4, 8, 9 survey concepts, functions, and changes of property law in the context of the evolution of contemporary industrial society. Vinding Kruse, *The Right of Property*, 2 vols. (Oxford, 1939; 1953), deals with both the broader and the technical aspects of the right of property, its origins and limits, its functions in production and circulation, and the various forms of transfer. Much of it is based on the pioneer Danish Real Property Act of 1926. F. H. Lawson, *Introduction to the Law of Property* (Oxford, 1958), gives a concise survey of the various legal aspects of property predominantly against an English background. Franco Negro, *Das Eigentum* (Munich and Berlin, 1963), gives a more recent but much more compressed survey of the legal and social function of property in history, and for the future. C. R. Noyes, *The Institution of Property* (London, 1936), gives an historical and analytical survey of property, both in its economic and legal aspects, with particular emphasis on the Roman and English systems of property and the substance and structure of modern property. Karl Renner, *The Institutions of Private Law and Their Social Functions* (1905; London, 1949), is a sociological analysis of changes in the function of property, from a Marxist point of view. The fifty-page introduction by O. Kahn-Freund to the English edition puts this classical study into a comparative and contemporary perspective. Richard Schlatter, *Private Property, The History of an Idea* (New York, 1951), is a special study. *Transactions of the Third World Congress of Sociology*, edited by the International Sociological Association (Amsterdam, 1956), has a major part devoted to changes in property relationships, with contributions from American, Dutch, German, and Soviet authors.

WOLFGANG G. FRIEDMANN

[See also **Class**; Economic History; **Equality**; Ideology; Individualism; Law, Ancient Roman, Natural; Marxism; **Socialism**; State; Utopia.]

PROPHECY IN HEBREW SCRIPTURE

ONLY THREE modes of prophecy (in the sense of Greek *prophēteia,* "speaking for a god and interpreting his will") are recognized in Hebrew Scripture. All other traffic with the occult is stigmatized as unlawful, devious behavior that has nothing to do with God. It is a consequence of biblical monotheism, that there is only one source of divine communication with man, which cannot be evoked except on its own terms and as it wills. Traffic with the occult realm (e.g., necromancy) is ascribed to Israelites as well as to pagans, but it is severely deprecated as ungodly. Ideally "there is no augury (*naḥaš*) in Jacob, no divining (*qesem*) in Israel," but only God's direct communication of his messages to men (Numbers 23:23). The three modes are monotheistic adaptations of common Near Eastern usages; one of them—prophecy proper in the Hebrew sense (see the discussion of *nabi,* below, §1)—underwent an elaboration peculiar to Israel (§2).

This article focuses on the sanctioned modes of prophecy; unlawful modes of inquiry into the occult —in the biblical view not prophecy in any sense— are referred to only for contrast and illustration.

1. The Sanctioned Modes of Communication with God. The regular modes of obtaining oracles from God (as opposed to *ad hoc* signs—Genesis 24:12ff.; Judges 6:36ff.; I Samuel 14:8ff.; II Samuel 5:24) were three: dreams, the *Urim,* and prophets (*nebiʾim;* I Samuel 28:6). Through these God responded (*ʿana*) to those who inquired of (*šaʾal*) or resorted to (*daraš*) him.

God might speak through a dream or vision to a man directly (Genesis 20:6; 28:12; 31:24; I Kings 3:5, apparently an incubation dream), or to a medium—a dreamer-prophet (Numbers 12:6; Deuteronomy 13:2ff.; Jeremiah 23:27ff.). Though God is regularly said to have appeared in these visions, only rarely is an apparition described (e.g., Genesis 28:12; cf. Job 4:13ff.; later an angelic interlocutor appears: Daniel 7; 10), the divine speech being the essential feature of the narrative. Often the verbal message alone is called a "vision" (I Samuel 3:15; II Samuel 7:17; Isaiah 1:1; 21:2).

A dream or vision might also be symbolic, a visual allegory—such as those of Pharaoh (Genesis 41) or Nebuchadnezzar (Daniel 2) through which God revealed the future (cf. also Joseph's dreams, Genesis 37, those of Pharaoh's servants, Genesis 40, the Midianite's, Judges 7:13ff., and Daniel's, Chs. 7, 8). It is characteristic of the biblical view that when the enigmatic dreams occur to pagans, who resort (unsuccessfully) to wizards to interpret them, they are finally solved by God-inspired Israelites. The lesson is that both the dream and its interpretation belong to God, and that not occult arts, but trust in God reveals its meaning (Genesis 40:8; 41:16, 39; Daniel 2:17ff.; 27ff.). When prophets have symbolic visions, they are always interpreted by God or an angel (e.g., Amos 7:1ff.; 8:1ff.; Zechariah 1:8ff.; 2:1ff.; 4:2ff., etc.).

The *Urim* and *Thummim* (etymology and meaning uncertain) were probably sacred lots; they were carried in the breastplate of the chief priest, which was attached, in turn to the *ephod*, a vest-like garment (Exodus 28:30). The priest consulted God through them on state affairs (Numbers 27:21). The same instrument seems to be called *ephod* in narratives of the time of the Judges and early kings (Judges 18:14ff.; I Samuel 2:28; 23:6, 9; 30:7). No king after David is said to have consulted the *Urim;* prophetic oracles only are recorded—evidence of a tendency to prefer rational to mechanical oracles. The reference to *ephod* in Hosea 3:4 suggests that it had not altogether disappeared later, though Ezra 2:63 shows that by the age of the Restoration the *Urim* were no longer extant.

How the *Urim* were used is unknown. What emerges from the narratives is an instrument designed to indicate which of two statements framed as simple alternatives was to be followed: "If this guilt lie in me or in my son Jonathan, O YHWH God of Israel, let it be *Urim;* if it lie in your people Israel, let it be *Thummim*" (I Samuel 14:41, restored by the Greek text); or "'. . . Will Saul come as I have heard?' YHWH answered, 'He will' . . . 'Will the citizens of Keilah surrender me and my men to Saul?'" . . . YHWH answered, 'They will'" (23:9ff.). A priest was needed for the manipulation of the oracle, but there was no technique or art of interpretation comparable to pagan divinatory lore that had to be mastered. When used by the priest, God spoke plainly through the *Urim-ephod*, without the mediation of man's art or science.

The third mode of obtaining oracles was through a prophet (*nabi,* perhaps "proclaimer"; cf. Akkadian *nabu,* "to call," Arabic *naba'a,* "to announce"). Clues to the essential meaning of *nabi* are the description of his role in Deuteronomy 18:18 ("I will put my words in his mouth and he will speak to them all that I command him"), and the interchange of *nabi* and "mouth" in Exodus 4:16; 7:1 (cf. Jeremiah 15:19): the *nabi* is God's mouth, his spokesman to men. Further aspects of his role are indicated by synonyms: *ro'e,* "seer" (archaic, according to I Samuel 9:9; cf. Isaiah 30:10; II Chronicles 16:7) and *hoze,* "seer" (II Samuel 24:11; Amos 7:12f.); *'iš (ha)'elohim,* "man of God" (I Samuel 9:6ff.); *'iš haru^ah,* "man of (God's) spirit" (Hosea 9:7).

Multiplicity of terms and diversity of roles may indicate a merging of originally distinct functionaries in the biblical prophet. "Seer" evokes a clairvoyant, a visionary gifted with the power of seeing the occult (Balaam has been compared, Numbers 24:15ff.). Traces of such a power are found in the *nabi:* Elisha is credited

by pagans (II Kings 6:12) and claims for himself (5:26) the ability to know what is far off. More characteristically biblical, however, is the view that the prophet's occult knowledge is God-given (cf. I Kings 14:5ff.). Unless informed by God, the prophet may be ignorant and in error (I Samuel 16:7; II Kings 4:27). The popular view of the prophet's inspired omniscience is stated doctrinally in Amos 3:7: "The Lord YHWH does nothing without disclosing his intention to his servants the prophets."

"Man of the spirit" evokes a different type: the "touched" man, whose conduct seems "mad" (Hosea 9:7; Jeremiah 29:26) as a result of the divine spirit that rested (II Kings 2:15) or sprang (*salah,* cf. Greek at I Samuel 10:6, 10) upon him. In early times spiritual possession betokened election to eminence. Some of Moses' spirit was laid upon the seventy elders who were to help him govern the people, and they "prophesied" for one time only (Numbers 11:16ff., 24ff.). Saul was marked for kingship by "turning into another man" in an ecstasy caught from a band of minstrel *n^ebi'im* (I Samuel 10:5f., 10ff.). Such ecstasy is usually a group phenomenon, sometimes an overflow of the spirit of a "man of God" who, though present, is not himself swept up in it (Numbers 11:24ff.; I Samuel 19:20ff.). Its contagiousness is graphically portrayed in I Samuel 19:20–24. The aim and social effect of this sort of spiritual activity is obscure. No speech of ecstatics has been recorded. Similar phenomena have been found in Israel's ancient environment (cf., e.g., Pritchard, *Ancient Near Eastern Texts,* 26c).

The later attested prophetic companies (*b^ene hann^ebi'im*) of the northern kingdom may have developed from such ecstatic bands. These companies lived together in various towns (II Kings 2), sometimes with an eminent master (6:1–7), who cared for them (4:38ff.), and for whom they ran errands (Ch. 9). Service to a "man of God" might be rewarded by a gift of his spirit (II Kings 2:9, 15); direct inspiration of members of a prophetic company occurred (I Kings 20:35). In contrast to the ecstatic bands, the inspiration of members of a prophetic company is not depicted as contagious or technically inducible. Elijah cannot bequeath his spirit to Elisha, but merely gives him a sign by which to tell whether God will bestow it (II Kings 2:10). The disposition of the spirit is clearly up to God (for a singular example of inducing the spirit through music, cf. II Kings 3:15).

The commonest synonym of *nabi* is "man of God" (in II Kings 4:9, "holy man of God"); Samuel, Elijah, and Elisha are frequently given this epithet. It suggests all the features of the *nabi*—his special intimacy with God as confidant and servant, his possession of uncanny gifts. The two terms are coextensive; neither seems to have been specialized for one particular aspect of prophecy.

The prophet was consulted by both the individual and the community. He was sought out for healing (II Kings 2:19ff.; 4; 5; 6:1–7), for advice about the future (I Kings 14:1ff.; II Kings 1:6; 8:8ff.), about lost items (I Samuel 9:6ff.). For such individual service he received pay (I Samuel 9:7f.; II Kings 5:5, 15; 8:9); the abuse that this invited is excoriated in Micah 3:5, 11. Important state matters were not undertaken before consultation with him. Replacing the priestly oracle in post-Davidic times, the prophet gave oracles before battle (I Kings 22:5ff.; II Kings 3:11); in crises he was asked what the future held (II Kings 22:12ff.; Jeremiah 38:14).

As an intimate of God, the prophet was often called upon to act as intercessor on behalf of the people; this role is indeed so essential to the prophet that to refrain from performing it is counted a sin (I Samuel 12:23). The unique reference to Abraham as a *nabi* occurs in connection with intercession (Genesis 20:7; cf. 18:23ff.). The prophet Moses and Samuel were archetypal intercessors (Jeremiah 15:1, with reference, e.g., to Exodus 32:11ff., 31ff.; Numbers 14:13ff.; 21:7; Deuteronomy 9:18ff.; I Samuel 7:8f.; 12:19ff. Cf. also II Kings 19:4; Jeremiah 14:11; 27:18; 37:3; Ezekiel 13:3ff.; 22:30.).

Temple and palace had their prophets. The prophet Gad had served as David's advisor in his outlaw days (I Samuel 22:5); when David became king, Gad served as "the king's seer" (II Samuel 24:11). The prophet Nathan too appears as the king's confidant and advisor (II Samuel 7:3; I Kings 1). Northern kings had hundreds of prophets (I Kings 22:6ff.; II Kings 3:13), presumably as pensioners (cf. I Kings 18:19). That the temples too had prophetic functionaries is suggested by the fixed word pair "priest—prophet" (e.g., Hosea 4:5; Jeremiah 4:9; 8:10), and especially by passages locating both in the temple (Jeremiah 23:11; 26:7; Lamentations 2:20). In late times, we hear of a priestly officer of the Jerusalem temple whose duty it was to check "madmen and prophesyers" (Jeremiah 29:26). The sons of a "man of God" had a room in that temple (Jeremiah 35:4). A clue to the role of temple prophets is suggested by the post-exilic usage of the verb "prophesy" (*nibba*) with reference to the work of the singers' guilds in the Jerusalem temple (I Chronicles 25:1–5). In view of the relation of prophecy to song (II Kings 3:15; Ezekiel 33:32; cf. I Samuel 10:5f.), such usage may well have originated in poetic oracles that were delivered in the course of the temple worship. II Chronicles 20:14ff. describes a temple scene in which, after the king's public prayer for help against a foe, a temple singer is inspired on the spot to deliver an oracle of victory. The abrupt change from plea or lament to confident assurance in some psalms (e.g., 20:7) has been taken to imply the intervening of an encouraging oracle by a temple prophet.

In the late Judahite monarchy, the prophets were listed in the ruling hierarchy after "kings, officers, priests" and before the citizenry (Jeremiah 8:1; 13:13; 32:32). Evidently institutionalized, these prophets shared in the making of—or they at least supported—national policy; they are almost invariably condemned by the classical prophets (see below).

This completes the discussion of the modes of obtaining oracles of YHWH. Of these, Deuteronomy 18:9–22 focuses on the *nabi* as the quintessential mode of the religion of YHWH, in contrast to diverse pagan mediums of inquiry into the occult:

Let no one be found among you who consigns his son or daughter to the fire, or who is an augur, a soothsayer, a diviner, a sorcerer, one who casts spells, or one who consults ghosts or familiar spirits, or one who inquires of the dead. For anyone who does such things is abhorrent to YHWH. . . . You must be wholehearted with YHWH your God. Those nations that you are about to dispossess do indeed resort to soothsayers and augurs; to you, however, YHWH your God has not assigned the like. YHWH your God will raise up for you a prophet from among your own people, like myself [Moses]; him you shall heed. . . .

The practice by Israelites of these outlawed forms of occult inquiry is dutifully recorded in Scripture (e.g., I Samuel 28:3ff.; II Kings 16:3; 17:17; 21:6; Isaiah 8:19); it is nowhere supposed, however, that YHWH is responding through these means. Biblical thinkers did not, then, discount occult inquiry as futile—on the contrary, they believed in its efficacy (e.g., I Samuel 28:3ff.)—but condemned it as ungodly. Occult practices are heathen self-sufficiency in contrast to recommended wholehearted reliance upon the will of YHWH. Such perfect reliance is ideally expressed through recourse to the *nabi*, the spokesman of YHWH. For in the *nabi* all is dependence upon God; man merely listens.

2. The Prophet as the Messenger of God. The Israelite modes of obtaining oracles from YHWH are paralleled in ancient Near Eastern paganism, though nowhere else is there such a rejection of techniques and occult arts. One may compare, for example, the Hittite triad: omens, dreams, prophets, in which the first involved highly developed techniques (Pritchard, 394f.). A distinctively biblical phenomenon is the dominant role of the prophet as the messenger or agent of God to promote a religious ideology—the ideology of Israel's election by and covenant relation with YHWH.

Instances of lay and cult persons carrying messages from gods (usually to the king) occur among the west

Semites of Mari, a city in North Syria, in the eighteenth century B.C. (Pritchard, 623ff., 629ff.). In Israel, Moses was regarded as founder and pinnacle of a prophetic succession of apostles of God extending from the thirteenth to the fifth centuries B.C. (Numbers 12:6ff.; Deuteronomy 18:15ff.; 34:10ff.; curiously, Moses is alluded to as a *nabi* only in Hosea 12:14, while elsewhere he is called "man of God" [Deuteronomy 33:1; Psalms 90:1], or YHWH's "servant" [Numbers 12:8; Deuteronomy 34:5]; the Egyptian oracle priest too was called "servant of god"). He was sent by God on a mission to Pharaoh and Israel (Exodus 3:10ff.), and ever after it was characteristic of Israel's prophets that they appeared as the messengers of God—the verb "send" figuring in their calls (cf. I Samuel 12:8, 11; 15:1; 16:1; II Samuel 12:1; 24:13; I Kings 14:6; Isaiah 6:8; Jeremiah 1:7; Ezekiel 2:3f.). Prophetic utterances regularly begin with the message formula "Thus said YHWH" (cf. Genesis 32:5; 45:9).

The mission of these prophets fills their lives, and they are ready to give their lives for it. This prophecy . . . involved a new conception of the revelation of the word of God, and it ousted the earlier forms of manticism. The distinctive feature of apostolic prophecy is that it champions a religious and moral doctrine. These prophets are stirred by a religious-moral passion . . . ; the continuing evolution of the religion of Israel . . . found expression in their utterances. . . . Nowhere else was the *mantis* the bearer of a religious-moral ideology. Nowhere else did apostles of a god appear in an ages-long, unbroken succession (Kaufmann, p. 215, fn. 1).

The prophet's apostolic role colored all his traditional functions. His oracles, his miracles, and his wonders brought glory to YHWH whose agent he was. Thus the wonders of the archetypical Moses attest to his divine mission and display the might of his sender ("that the Egyptians may know that I am YHWH" [Exodus 7:5; cf. 8:18; 9:14], superior to the mere magic of the Egyptians [8:14f.]). Moses' speeches to Pharaoh are messages from God—"Thus said YHWH" (5:1; 7:17, etc.). The wonders Moses performs for Israel are signs of YHWH's care for them; they aim to create trust in and loyalty to God (Exodus 14:31; cf. Numbers 14:11, 22). Moses mediates YHWH's covenant with Israel, teaches them its stipulations, and chastises them when they fall away from it. Through him God liberated and protected Israel (Hosea 12:14).

In the images of other prophets, mantic and apostolic features mingle—there can be no question of pure types in the historical reality. Samuel was accredited as a prophet of YHWH on the basis of his inerrancy—presumably with respect to the ordinary mantic services he performed for pay (I Samuel 3:19f.; 9:6f.). But when Saul arrived to consult him about some lost asses, Samuel, having been put on notice by a prior revelation, acted as YHWH's agent to anoint Saul as king to rescue Israel from the Philistines (9). Ahiah the Shilonite was God's messenger to announce to Jeroboam his election to kingship of the northern tribes (I Kings 11:29). But he is also a mantic to whom a distressed mother repairs with a gift for word about her sick child (14:1ff.). Elijah is God's agent for scourging Ahab, but he also champions the therapeutic role of prophecy against Ahaziah's appeal in his sickness to Baalzebub (II Kings 1:2ff.). Elisha is consulted for pay about the fate of ailing Benhadad, but while responding he suddenly utters a dire message from YHWH concerning Hazael's coming oppression of Israel (II Kings 8:7ff.). The popular tales about the mantic and wonder-working deeds of the prophets have been preserved in the Bible precisely because in them God's power is manifest: it is important for Naaman, for example, to know that "there is a prophet in Israel" so that he might be led to confess that "there is no God throughout the whole earth except in Israel" (II Kings 5:8, 15).

As Israel's sovereign and patron by virtue of the covenant, YHWH governed his people by means of the prophets. Israel's political and cultic institutions were shaped by prophecy—i.e., ideally, by God: its law, its forms of worship, and clerical hierarchy, its civil administration were given to it by Moses. Its monarchy was established by Samuel. The Davidic dynasty was certified as YHWH's elect by Nathan. Northern dynasties were made and unmade with the inspiration of prophets. Throughout, faithfulness to the covenant was the object of prophetic activity.

One aspect of the covenant was the promise of God's protection; that entailed an identification of Israel's well-being and security with the will and authority of YHWH. Early prophets called for war to save Israel from enemies or avenge wrongs done to it: Moses stirred up the people against Midian (Numbers 31), Deborah stirred up Barak against the Canaanites (Judges 4), Samuel called on Saul to wipe out Amalek (I Samuel 15)—all as the bidding of YHWH. During the century of struggle with the Arameans, victory of the northern kingdom was a condition for the survival of Israel and YHWH's covenant. Hence victories might be prophesied for the sake of establishing YHWH's authority ("That you may know that I am YHWH" [I Kings 20:13, 28]). Elisha predicted that Joram and Jehoshaphat would defeat Moab (II Kings 3:18) and that Joash would triumph over the Arameans (13:14ff.). Jonah prophesied the recovery of Israel's lost territories by Jeroboam (14:25ff.), and Isaiah eloquently asserted YHWH's authority over arrogant Sennacherib (19:21ff.).

Apart from the covenant ideology, such prophecy does not seem essentially different from other victory oracles delivered by prophets outside Israel (e.g., Assyrian, in Pritchard, 449f.; West Semitic [Mari], ibid. 629f.). More distinctively Israelite is the religio-moral censure of the people and their leaders by prophets arraigning them in God's name for breach of covenant. The earlier motif of such arraignments is disloyalty to YHWH and apostasy. Thus Moses castigates and purges the people for making the golden calf (Exodus 32); anonymous prophets rebuke the people for apostasy in the time of the Judges (Judges 2:1ff.; 6:8ff.; cf. 10:11ff.); Samuel rebukes them for apostasy and for rejecting God's kingship (I Samuel 7:3ff.; 12). During the monarchy, kings become the focus of censure in the narratives of the Book of Kings (I Kings 11:31ff.; 14:7ff.; 18:18; II Kings 9:6ff., etc.); only a few general condemnations represent the prophets as reproaching the people at large for apostasy (II Kings 17:13; 21:10ff.).

The narratives also show the prophets censuring the kings for gross moral offenses, and condemning them to punishment for them: the classic instances are Nathan's rebuke of David for his adultery with Bathsheba (II Samuel 12:1ff.), and Elijah's rebuke of Ahab for the murder of Naboth and the confiscation of his land (I Kings 21:17ff.).

In their opposition role, prophets risked and sometimes met death. The first martyrs were the zealous prophetic opponents of Jezebel's imported Phoenician Baal cult in Samaria (I Kings 18:13; 19:10; II Kings 9:7). Prophetic radicalism reached a peak here in violent encounter, careless of consequences, with royal power. Its voice is that of Elijah, who, for the sake of God's authority, was ready to subject Israel to ruthless decimation and subjugation to its enemies (I Kings 19:15ff.).

During the century-long struggle with the Arameans the threatening breach between state policy ("the national interest") and the radical covenant ideology championed by some prophets became a reality. To be sure, some prophets spoke for the national interest (e.g., Jonah, in II Kings 14:25ff.), and in the breast of Elisha conflicting tendencies were evidently at work. But the continuing politico-military crisis, and the deepening rift between impoverished masses and an oligarchy who ruled them exploitatively gave rise, in the mid-eighth century, to a burst of new prophetic idealism, in which the issues of the current crises generated a new level of sensibility. This is the level of classical or literary prophecy, whose productions fill the books of the "Latter Prophets" from Isaiah to Malachi.

3. New Ideas of Literary Prophecy. The literary prophets drew out several heretofore latent implications of the earlier religion.

(a) Whereas the covenant laws ascribed to Moses did not discriminate between socio-moral and religio-cultic obligations, literary prophecy characteristically stressed the former over the latter. Amos, the first of the new breed, denounced the moral corruption of his audience, contrasting it with their zeal in fulfilling the cultic requirements of religion.

I hate, I spurn your feasts (says YHWH),
And I take no pleasure in your festal gatherings.
Even though you bring me your burnt offerings
And your meal offerings, I will not accept them . . .
Take away from me the noise of your songs;
To the melody of your lyres I will not listen.
But let justice roll down like waters,
And righteousness like a mighty stream (Amos 5:21–24).

Isaiah's arraignment of Judah is similar:

Of what use is the multitude of your sacrifices to me,
    says YHWH;
I am sated with burnt-offerings of rams and the fat of
    fed beasts . . .
Bring no more worthless offerings,
Foul smoke it is to me.
New moon and sabbath, the holding of assemblies—
I cannot endure evil with festival . . .
So when you spread out your hands, I will hide my eyes
    from you;
Though you make many prayers, I will not listen;
Your hands are full of blood.
Wash yourselves clean!
Put away the evil of your doings from before my eyes!
Cease to do evil, learn to do good;
Seek justice, right the oppressed,
Uphold the right of the fatherless,
Defend the cause of the widow! (Isaiah 1:11–17).

The subordination of the issue of cult-loyalty to YHWH (doubtless reflecting the general orthodoxy of the national religion) reached a culmination in a soliloquy of Micah, in which the demand of YHWH is concentrated on morality alone:

Wherewith shall I come before YHWH,
Shall I bow myself before God most high?
Shall I come before him with burnt-offerings,
With calves a year old?
Will YHWH be pleased with thousands of rams,
With myriad streams of oil?
Shall I offer my first-born for my transgression,
The fruit of my body for the sin of my soul?
You have been told, O man, what is good,
And what YHWH desires of you:
But to do justice, and love fidelity,
And to walk humbly with your God (Micah 6:6–8).

661

(b) Having fallen short of this standard, the community deserved punishment, and the literary prophets boldly applied the dire threats found in the tradition for the sin of apostasy to the morally corrupt people of their day. Deriding the reliance of the people upon the efficacy of the cult to ward off wrath, the literary prophets predicted the fall and exile of Israel for its social-moral offenses (Amos 3:9—6:14; Isaiah 1; 3–5). Micah shocked his (to him emptily) pious audience by predicting the destruction of Jerusalem on their account:

Hear this, now, you heads of the house of Jacob,
And rulers of the house of Israel,
Who abhor justice, and distort what is right;
Who build Zion with blood,
And Jerusalem with guilt—
Her chiefs pronounce judgment for a bribe,
Her priests give oracles for hire,
Her prophets divine for cash.
Yet they lean upon YHWH, saying
"Is not YHWH in our midst?
No misfortune can befall us."
So then, because of you Zion shall be plowed like a field,
Jerusalem shall become ruins,
And the temple mount a forested height (Micah 3:9–12).

A century later, the precedent of Micah saved Jeremiah from death for having prophesied the same in the court of the Jerusalem temple (Jeremiah 26).

(c) Along with false reliance on the cult, the literary prophets denounced trust in human devices, in military power, in political alliances.

Israel forgot his maker and built palaces
And Judah multiplied fortified cities;
But I will send a fire upon his cities,
And it shall devour his palaces (Hosea 8:14).

The prophetic policy for the nation beset by powerful enemies was uncompromisingly radical: eschew trust in power and cast your burden on God!

In placid rest you shall be saved;
In quiet confidence shall be your strength (Isaiah 30:15).
If you have not firm faith you shall not stand firm!
(ibid., 7:9).

Moses' exhortation on the shores of the sea, "Stand still and see the salvation of YHWH" (Exodus 14:13) became the guideline of the national policy of the prophets. In the radical dichotomy of trust in God or trust in man, idolatry came to be lumped with silver and gold, towers and ships, horses and chariots—all the man-made recourses in which the heathen (in and out of Israel) trusted. Thus the failure of man-made power and security would at the same time be the end of idolatry (Isaiah 2).

(d) The quietism of the literary prophets was based on a faith in the imminent intervention of God in events, which would put to nought all earthly powers and show the futility of the idols. There would be a great purge of sinners in Israel; later, under the rule of a new David, a remade Israel, with hearts informed by knowledge of God, would live in idyllic peace (Isaiah 11; Jeremiah 31; Ezekiel 36). But God's plan extended beyond Israel, to the redemption from violence and ignorance of all mankind. Isaiah articulated the vision of the reunification of men under God in its classic form: when the heathen might of Assyria would be broken on the mountains of Israel, the worldwide impact would shatter faith in idols forever. Then all men would turn to YHWH in Zion, saying

"Come! let us go up to the mountain of YHWH
To the house of the God of Jacob;
That he may instruct us in his ways,
And that we may walk in his paths;
For out of Zion goes forth instruction
And the word of YHWH out of Jerusalem."
Then will he judge between the nations,
And arbitrate for many peoples;
And they will beat their swords into plowshares,
And their spears into pruning-hooks:
Nation will not lift up sword against nation,
Nor will they experience war any more (Isaiah 2:3f.).

The conversion of the nations to the worship of YHWH (cf. also Isaiah 19:23ff.) was expressed by Zephaniah (3:9), recurs in Jeremiah (3:17) and Habakkuk (2:14), and is a major theme of the Second Isaiah (e.g., 45:23). It is the natural complement to the early religion's notion of a primeval unity of men that was shattered by the hybris of the builders of the tower of Babel.

4. Conflict and Tension. The continuing and deepening crisis that set in during the Aramean wars and ended in the exiles of Israel and Judah bred an endemic conflict between prophets who said yea and those who said nay to the national policy. The issue of false prophecy arose.

The black-and-white terms of the Deuteronomic law on the subject were hardly adequate for meeting the far more complicated reality. "If a prophet speaks in YHWH's name and the oracle does not come true, that oracle was not spoken by YHWH; the prophet has uttered it presumptuously" (Deuteronomy 18:22). What if one could not wait for the issue, but must know at once if the prophet was true? Or if the oracle was not predictive but prescriptive? On the latter subject, Deuteronomy 13:1ff. lays it down that a prophetic call to apostasy, even if supported by a miracle, must be discredited; the miracle is but a test of the people's faithfulness to YHWH.

Accounts of actual prophetic conflicts show how perplexing the reality was. A complicating factor was the notion that God might deceive an audience purposely in order to punish it by means of a false prophecy. Micaihu ben Imlah, standing alone as a prophet of doom against 400 court prophets predicting victory for the kings of Israel and Judah, explained the prophecy of the 400 as a divine lure to lead the king of Israel to battle and death (cf. Ezekiel 14:9). Micaihu was put under arrest pending the outcome of the battle (I Kings 22). Jeremiah gave an ironic blessing to Hananiah ben Azzur who confuted Jeremiah's predictions of doom. He admonished him that only the issue of events could validate his prediction of restoration. Onlookers can not have known which of the two prophets was to be believed, but Hananiah's death within the year, as subsequently predicted by Jeremiah, must have settled the issue (Jeremiah 28). Jeremiah once sought to exonerate the Judahites by pleading that God himself had (through false prophets) seduced them into complacence (4:10). Quite mysterious is the point of the story in I Kings 13 telling how a northern prophet misled a southern man of God into violating his charge, then prophesied truly that he would be punished therefor.

However perplexed onlookers might have been in the face of prophetic conflicts, the prophets themselves are not likely to have been doubtful of the reality of their mission. Amos compares the compulsion to prophesy to the terror inspired by a lion's roaring (3:8). Jeremiah compares God's word to fire, to a "hammer that shatters rock" (23:29); it is like "a burning fire, shut up in my bones" that cannot be contained (20:9; cf. 6:11). To such men, counter-oracles must be false, hence virtually all references to other $n^eb\hat{i}^{\,}im$ in prophetic writings are derogatory (e.g., Isaiah 9:14; 29:10f.; Ezekiel 13; Zechariah 13:2ff.). Other prophets are deceitful, venal charlatans who pander to their audience (Ezekiel 13:10); if fed, they say "peace," if not, "war" (Micah 3:5, 11); their visions are mere figments (Jeremiah 14:13f.), often plagiarized (23:25ff.); they are a mendacious, adulterous lot (23:32; 29:23). Favored epithets for them and their utterances are "diviner" (qasam) and "divination" (miqsam; Micah 3:6f., 11; Ezekiel 13:7). Now, while it is true that the prophets of weal had a basis for their optimism—God's election of Israel—it is also true that their prophecy, by telling the people what they wished to hear, encouraged self-delusion and complacency in both prophet and audience. To the extent that dissent requires courage and strength of conviction, the moral quality of the dissenting prophets may be assumed to have been on the whole higher than their opponents.

The political disasters of Israel validated the dissenting prophecy of doom. The worthlessness of the mass of pre-exilic prophets was then acknowledged in terms drawn directly from the diatribes of the literary prophets:

Your prophets prophesied to you
Delusion and folly;
They did not expose your iniquity
So as to restore your fortunes,
But prophesied to you oracles
of delusion and blandishment (Lamentations 2:14).

Popular reception of the prophets was ambivalent. The power of the oracle (cf. Isaiah 55:10f.) was so feared, on the one hand, that an unfavorable one was to be avoided (I Kings 22:8; Amos 2:12; 7:16; Micah 2:6, 11; Jeremiah 29:26; II Chronicles 25:15–16). Once uttered, however, awe of the prophet was usually enough to protect him from serious harm, though insult and mockery might follow (Isaiah 28:9; II Chronicles 36:16). In times of great stress, demoralizing oracles might lead to imprisonment (Jeremiah 29:26f.; 32:1ff.; 37) or even death (26; 38; cf. 2:30).

On the other hand, their eccentric behavior (I Kings 20:35) and dress (II Kings 1:7f.; Zechariah 13:4) made the prophets objects of (anxious) derision: "The prophet is a fool, the man of spirit, mad" (Hosea 9:7; cf. II Kings 9:11).

5. The Extinction of Prophecy. Since prophecy and oracle were regarded as prime expressions of God's favor, their absence was a sure sign of divine wrath (I Samuel 14:37f.; 28:6). The end of oracles was one of the calamities threatened by the prophets for Israel's sin (Micah 3:6f.; Amos 8:11f.; Jeremiah 18:18; Ezekiel 7:26) and materialized in the period of the fall of Judah (Lamentations 2:9). It was far from final, however, and one senses that the presence of prophets among the exiles was taken by them as a harbinger of speedy restoration (Jeremiah 29:8f., 15, 21f.). Similarly the Second Isaiah combines the advent of the spirit with the announcement of an imminent liberation (61:1), and Joel 3:1f. depicts an eschatological outpouring of the spirit of prophecy upon all men.

Since the reality of the restoration in Persian times fell far short of the anticipated glory (cf. Ezra 3:12; Zechariah 4:10), a feeling of continued disfavor of God seems to have persisted among the people. That, more than anything else, dried up the well-spring of prophecy in its traditional form. Concentration on fulfilling the covenant stipulations became the leading concern of the restored community (cf. Malachi 3:22), in the hope that full reconciliation with God and a final, glorious redemption of Israel, would ensue therefrom. The renewal of prophecy was deferred to the eschaton (cf. I Maccabees 4:46; 14:41); the belief in its imminent renewal appeared among certain Jews at about the time of the rise of Christianity (John 1:21, 25; 6:14; 7:40; Matthew 16:14; 21:11).

663

BIBLIOGRAPHY

Renderings of biblical passages, when not by the author of this article, have been adapted from *The Torah: A New Translation* (Philadelphia, 1962), *The Old Testament: An American Translation*, ed. J. M. Powis Smith (Chicago, 1927), and the Jewish Publication Society, *The Five Megilloth* (Philadelphia, 1969).

M. Buber, *The Prophetic Faith* (New York, 1949; and reprint). *La divination en Mésopotamie ancienne, et dans les régions voisines*, XIVe Rencontre Assyriologique Internationale (Paris, 1966). Abraham J. Heschel, *The Prophets* (New York, 1962). Yehezk Kaufmann, *The Religion of Israel* (Chicago, 1960), pp. 157–66, 212–16, 273–86, 343–446. J. Lindblom, *Prophecy in Ancient Israel* (Philadelphia, 1962). H. Wheeler Robinson, *Inspiration and Revelation in the Old Testament* (Oxford, 1946; reprint 1962). R. B. Y. Scott, *The Relevance of the Prophets*, rev. ed. (New York and London, 1967). G. von Rad, *Old Testament Theology*, trans. D. M. G. Stalker (Edinburgh and London, 1965), II, 3–300. W. Zimmerli, *The Law and the Prophets*, trans. Ronald E. Clements (Oxford, 1965).

MOSHE GREENBERG

[See also God; Music as Divine Art; Myth in Biblical Times; **Prophecy**; Religion, Ritual in; **Sin and Salvation**.]

PROPHECY IN THE MIDDLE AGES

MEDIEVAL prophecy belonged to Christian eschatology. The belief in death, judgment, heaven, and hell engendered different notions of how their sequence would occur. These included the idea of a final age of peace and concord before the end of the world and the Last Judgment. As an apocalyptic expectation of a violent and sudden end to the present order, it had its source in the Prophetic Books of the Old Testament—above all the Book of Daniel—and the Book of Revelation of Saint John of the Apocalypse. Together they transmitted to Christian thinking the Jewish legacy of a messiah who would deliver his people from tribulation after untold suffering. God having punished those who had deserted him would reign over those who had remained true to him from a New Jerusalem for a thousand years (though this number was not invariable) until the final destruction of the world.

Such visions were the invariable accompaniment of persecution, both in Jewish and early Christian times and during the Middle Ages. They offered redress for present sufferings. As projections of desires which could not be realized in the here and now they derived their power from being invested with divine agency. The prophecies of the Old and New Testaments were in the form of inspired dreams and divine revelations; moreover they were on a cosmic scale, involving the whole world in a struggle between the righteous and unjust, the oppressed and the oppressors. It would culminate in the ending of the present dispensation. This theme unites Jewish and Christian prophecy from the Book of Daniel, written ca. 165 B.C., to the sixteenth century; it stressed the conviction in a coming denouement to be followed by a new and better dispensation on earth.

The Book of Daniel was among the earliest and the most formative elements in this tradition. In its imagery and pattern it formed the prototype of much of subsequent prophecy, above all the struggle between the forces of evil and goodness. The former, representing the four world empires, were symbolized by four beasts, albeit mythical. The fourth and most terrible anticipates the later figure of Antichrist: it "was different from all the beasts that were before it; and it had ten horns . . . and, behold, there came up among them another horn, a little one before which three of the first horns were plucked up by the roots; and behold, in this horn were eyes like the eyes of a man, and a mouth speaking great things" (Daniel 7:8). This horn represented a future king who will "exalt himself and magnify himself above every god and shall speak astonishing things against the God of gods" (Daniel 11:36); he would make war against the saints and prevail over them until "judgment was given for the saints of the Most High, and the time came when the saints received the kingdom" (Daniel 7:22). This would be by "one like the son of man," coming with the clouds of heaven, who would overthrow this false king. These different symbols prefigured Antichrist and Christ and the form their conflict would take; it would be one both of open tyranny and deceit in which Antichrist would claim to be God. Already there is the notion of some world kingdom of God, under the son of man, "that all peoples, nations and languages should serve him" (Daniel 7:14).

It was with the Book of Revelation, composed ca. A.D. 93, during the Christian persecutions of the emperor Domitian (51–96), that Daniel's figures became firmly established as the dramatis personae of Christian apocalyptic. The Book of Revelation went beyond any of the other canonical writings among which indeed it was accepted only through misconception. Its importance for subsequent Christian and medieval belief cannot be exaggerated. Diffused through commentaries and mingling with other legends it penetrated the outlook of the Middle Ages and inspired much of its prophecy. Through its imagery of the opening of the scroll sealed with seven seals it unfolded the sequence which "must soon take place." With the undoing of each seal a new phase was revealed, which would culminate in a thousand years of Christ's reign on earth before a final struggle with Satan, followed by the Last Judgment. "This first glory was reserved for those who had been beheaded for their testimony to Jesus and for the word of God, and who had not worshipped the beast or its image and had not received its mark on their foreheads or their hands. The rest of the dead did not come to life until the thousand years were ended. This is the first resurrection. Blessed and holy is he who shares in the first resurrection! Over such the second has no power, but they shall be priests of God and Christ and they shall reign with him a thousand years" (Revelation 20:5–6). And the new Jerusalem in which they would live would come down from heaven; it would only be attained after Satan had been bound and thrown into a pit for a thousand years. Before this he would reign over the world, inflicting terrible sufferings and causing men to worship him and to blaspheme against God. The fourth beast of the Book of Daniel now becomes the great red dragon with seven heads and ten horns and firmly identified with Satan thrown down to earth with his minions (Revelation 12:9). The dragon persecuted the faithful in the form of two beasts: "a beast rising out of the sea with ten horns and seven heads . . . to it the dragon gave his power and throne and great authority" (Revelation 13:1–2); and "another beast which rose out of the earth; it had two horns like a lamb and spoke like a dragon. It exercises the authority of the first beast in its presence, and makes the earth and its inhabitants worship the first beast" (Revelation 13:11–12). These two beasts stood for the Roman empire, which made "war on the saints," and the priests who served it; together with the Dragon they henceforth constituted the figure of Antichrist. Where Christ remained always clearly conceived as God and man—depicted as a divine warrior and as the lamb "with seven horns and seven eyes which are the seven spirits sent into all the earth" (Revelation 5:6)—Antichrist was demonic and bestial. Thus the second beast attempts to beguile the faithful by appearing like the lamb yet speaking "like a dragon." Like the serpent in Paradise it works by deceit, at the same time wreaking destruction. Just as, in orthodox belief, man's redemption came through having first sinned, so in Christian apocalyptic, deliverance would be after the dragon had conquered. "If anyone is to be taken captive to captivity he goes; if anyone slays with the sword, with the sword must he be slain. Here is call for the endurance and faith of the saints" (Revelation 14:10). Antichrist was thus a presence on the same cosmic scale as Christ; he

represented a universal power for evil, which could take diverse human manifestations.

This was the form as transmitted by the Book of Revelation in which the Middle Ages received the Jewish-Christian apocalyptic legacy. It was one which was more mythological than theological. In being concerned with the future it relied upon imagination rather than reason; its rich and often extravagant imagery acted as an intoxicant, often upon those not themselves apocalyptic. But it flourished mainly amongst the visionaries and the persecuted. There was also a tributary stream from the so-called Sibylline writings. These, too, derived originally from Judaism, but in this case from its Hellenic branch. Composed initially in Greek hexameters they purported to be pronouncements from Greek oracles designed to convert the Greeks to Jewish belief. They sought to do so by trying to show that the present emperor was the last; since both the Greeks and the Romans by then worshipped the emperor as divine they hoped to make them accept the (Jewish) messiah who would succeed their ruler.

The oldest Sibyl known to the Middle Ages was the Tiburtina, written in the mid-fourth century A.D. Together with seventh-century pseudo-Methodius— purporting to be by the fourth-century bishop and martyr of that name—it introduced a similar apocalyptic note. There would be a time of impending sorrows, from which after dreadful struggles a world emperor would emerge, bringing peace and joy to all the nations until the final struggle between Christ and Antichrist. As later developed in the thirteenth and fourteenth centuries the legend was used to depict both future emperors and popes; they, however, could be the instrument of either Christ or Antichrist.

The development of these ideas into a distinctive outlook during the Middle Ages only becomes significant in the twelfth century. At one level it could be said that some kind of apocalyptic belief was common to the greater part of medieval society. Conviction in the existence of the devil was integral to the Christian recognition of the pervasiveness of sin; the struggle between Christ and Antichrist expressed the dualism between the flesh and the spirit. God's retribution was as real as his love; and in times of stress or tension the sense of impending doom came easily to the surface, among the learned and the sophisticated as well as the illiterate and poor. Adherence to God or rejection of him marked the difference between the saved and the damned, which Saint Augustine (354–430) in the *City of God* identified with the difference between the heavenly and earthly cities. What distinguished the apocalyptic outlook as such was not only a belief in imminent and violent change but a perspective upon the future; what was occurring now, and would occur in the future, belonged to the same sequence within which alone events could be measured.

In that sense prophecy was historical, however idealized, as well as eschatological; for it drew upon what had already happened in order to point to what was about to come. Not surprisingly, therefore, the idea of prophecy as more than periodic outbursts of fear and distress which punctuated periods of disturbance—such as the People's Crusade at the end of the eleventh century or peasant risings from that time onwards—was grounded in an interpretation of history. While throughout the earlier Middle Ages there had been writings on Antichrist, such as by Adso in the tenth century, medieval prophecy only became significant with the renewed study of history in the twelfth century.

The Middle Ages are commonly believed to have lacked historical awareness. In the modern understanding of history as a discipline that is true, but as a recognition of temporal sequence and change it is not. Like the Judaic-Christian tradition on which it drew, medieval prophecy saw in the impending dissolution of the present order the climax of the world's history. It differed in giving that history a new pattern which it owed to Saint Augustine more than to anyone else. In the *City of God* he had taken the seven days of Genesis as the paradigm of the seven ages of the world.

The first age, as the first day, extends from Adam to the deluge; the second from the deluge to Abraham, equalling the first not in length of time but in the number of generations, there being ten in each. From Abraham to the advent of Christ there are, as the evangelist Matthew calculates, three periods, in each of which are fourteen generations—one period from Abraham to David, a second from David to the captivity, a third from the captivity to the birth of Christ in the flesh. There are thus five ages in all. The sixth is now passing, and cannot be measured by any number of generations. . . . After this period God shall rest as on the seventh day, when he shall give us (who shall be the seventh day) rest in himself . . . the seventh shall be our sabbath which shall be brought to a close, not by an evening, but by the Lord's day, as an eighth and eternal day, consecrated by the resurrection of Christ, and prefiguring the eternal repose not only of the spirit but also of the body (*City of God*, Book XXXII, Ch. 30).

This periodizing of Christian history from the Bible formed the basis of the world histories of the twelfth century. They were particularly in vogue among German writers, like Anselm of Havelberg, Geroch of Reichersberg, Otto of Freising, and Rupert of Deutz. Germany, as the seat of the medieval empire since the tenth century, had been the focus of the struggles between its kings and the papacy; each side in its claim for precedence over the other sought for antecedents and historical precedents which stimulated the study of history. But this was also part of a European-wide revival of learning, speculation, and the study of law; and Calabria not Germany was the scene of a new apocalyptic conception of history which was to be the most influential for over two centuries.

Its author, Joachim of Floris, was a Cistercian monk, who, after becoming abbot of the Calabrian monastery of Curazzo, founded his own monastic order in 1196. Joachim arrived at his interpretation through biblical exegesis. Drawing upon the separation of history into seven epochs, he combined it with another and larger trinitarian division into the three ages of the Father, the Son, and the Holy Spirit, which Rupert of Deutz had also adopted (*De Trinitate*). This enabled Joachim to go beyond the present. Saint Augustine in the *City of God* had treated the *Book of Revelation* as allegory: the millennium had begun with Christ and was maintained in the sacramental life of the Church which would endure until the end of time. Joachim also treated the Apocalypse allegorically; but he translated it differently because of his tripartite framework. In his three main works, *The Concord of the Old and the New Testaments*, the *Exposition of the Apocalypse* and *The Psaltery of the Ten Chords*, Joachim, by means of elaborate parallels and calculations, established the relation between the three great ages. That of the Father corresponded to the period of the Old Testament; the age of the Son roughly covered that of the New Testament, running from King Ozias (Matthew 1:9) until around the middle of the thirteenth century—beyond Joachim's own lifetime; it would be followed by the third and final age of the Holy Spirit, which would last for 1000 years until the world's destruction and the Last Judgment. Each age was symbolized by a particular group of men: the patriarchs or married men in the first age; the clerics in the second age; the third age would be the age of spiritual monks of whom the Benedictines were the precursors. Each age also had or would have three great men; but whereas those for the first two ages were actual figures drawn from the Old and the New Testaments—Abraham, Isaac, and Jacob, and Zachariah, John the Baptist, and Christ—the three for the coming third age were symbolical: the man clothed in linen, taken from Daniel, and two angels of the Apocalypse, from the Book of Revelation.

The distinction between the first two ages and the third is central to Joachim's outlook. From the relation between the first two he was able to deduce the patterns which could be transposed to the future third age. This applied especially to the way in which the transition from the first to the second age had occurred.

The third age was taken as the consummation of what had gone before. It was this which changed the traditional perspective. For Joachim it meant superseding the existing forms and replacing them by a higher state. In a series of antitheses he sought to characterize the differences between the three ages. The first had been under the law, the second was under grace, but the third would have still greater grace. The first age had been of knowledge, the second was of partial wisdom, the third would be of full understanding; servile servitude and filial servitude would give way to liberty. In these and other examples Joachim drew upon metaphor, which makes his precise meaning elusive. It seems clear, however, that he envisaged the new order still to come as one of spiritual renewal in which, to use his own recurrent phrase, the spirit would triumph over the letter. Joachim did not specify what this would entail; but he was emphatic that the change would be in man's understanding of the Bible and the sacraments rather than in a new faith or a new church.

Paradoxically it was here that Joachim's thinking was to be most betrayed by those who called themselves his disciples. His symbolic terms such as a new "spiritual church" and new "spiritual men," his frequent contrast between the outward "figures" of the sacraments and their inner meaning came to stand independently and to be opposed to their existing visible forms. By the end of the thirteenth century, among some of the Franciscan Spirituals and their followers in Provence and Italy, the spiritual church had come to stand for their opposition to the carnal church at Rome under the pope, which they condemned as the Whore of Babylon and the congregation of Antichrist. The spiritual church was the bearer of a new gospel and possessed a new spiritual insight.

Not only was the terminology from Joachim; so also was the significance of the confrontation between the spiritual and carnal churches. This related directly to Joachim's subdivision of the first two ages, of the Father and Son, into seven phases or epochs. From the concordance of the Old and New Testaments he deduced the order of succession from one phase to the next. First, he saw something like a dialectical interplay between them; within an existing phase the new was already germinating and would finally supersede that from which it arose. Thus the spiritual men who were to typify the third age of the Holy Spirit had their harbingers in Saint Benedict's (d. ca. 547) monastic order, which had been founded in the fourth phase of the second great age. Since Joachim computed that the age of the Son would end in about the year 1260, the bearers of the new age had coexisted with the old for 600 years. They were the agents by which the dualism between the flesh and the spirit, characterizing the age of the Son, would be overcome when the Spirit triumphed in the third great age. In the second place, this transformation would be through struggle between the old and the new.

From the first two ages Joachim distinguished between periods of quiescence and disturbance. As each main age drew to a close the latent antagonism between the forces of the old order and the new came to a head; only after their collision could the new age finally emerge. Joachim placed the conflict in the sixth and penultimate phase of the expiring age. As Christ and his disciples had been persecuted, and he had been crucified before his message had finally prevailed, so Christ's successors, the new spiritual monks, would have to suffer the attacks of Antichrist before they, too, emerged to inaugurate a new golden age on earth, in the seventh and last phase of the second age. Accordingly, the pattern which Joachim presented was of an underlying continuity through discontinuity, of a series of consummations, or periods of sabbatical calm as he called them, preceded by periods of violent struggle, until some time after the middle of the thirteenth century a new and final era of sabbatical peace would reign.

Now it was in the transition from the second to the third age that Joachim's teaching was so relevant for the thirteenth century and beyond; for by his own computation the present age of the Son should end around 1260 with the completion of the forty-second generation from the birth of Christ (counting each generation as thirty years). The beginning of the thirteenth century thus also marked the opening of the sixth phase of the second age culminating in the struggle between the old and the new. For the generations immediately succeeding Joachim's they appeared to be living in the center of the upheaval. Hence the immediacy of his message to those who, like the Franciscan Spirituals and others, were suffering either persecution or the effects of the devastating papal-imperial war in Italy; their miseries found a vindication in Joachim's predictions and his stress upon the tribulations which would precede the advent of the third age. He had foretold that the years from 1200 to 1260 would be worse than the preceding centuries of the second age put together. They would be filled with the evil doings of Antichrist. The sixth phase would contain great persecutions culminating in the seventh with the appearance of the first Antichrist. (The second would appear at the end of the world and the Last Judgment.) The same sixth epoch, however, would also see the first heralding of a new spiritual understanding of the Old and New Testaments, which would be consummated in the final defeat of Antichrist. This would be followed by a second incarnation of Christ and the period of sabbatical calm which would inaugurate the third great age of peace on earth and the rule of the Spirit.

Joachim, then, offered an interpretation of the present which at once explained its tribulations and gave hope in suffering them. Like all apocalyptic visions it provided a cosmic setting to the struggles of the various reforming and apostolic groups; they were enacting the final struggle between the forces of Christ and Antichrist, Jerusalem and Babylon. Nor was the impact of Joachim's teaching initially confined to sects or opposition groups. It is to be found among thinkers like Robert Grosseteste, Adam Marsh, William of St. Amour, Saint Bonaventure, and John Pecham (or Peckham), among others. Many members of the new orders of friars identified themselves with Joachim's prophecy of the new spiritual monks. One thirteenth-century pope at least, John XXI, was sympathetic to Joachite ideas.

By the middle of the thirteenth century, however, as the time allotted for the close of the second age approached, Joachism became increasingly a focus of dissent. The extent to which it had become subversive was first revealed in the so-called affair of the Eternal Gospel at Paris in 1254. A young Franciscan, Gerard of Borgo San Donnino, published an *Introduction to the Eternal Gospel* (*Introductorius in evangelium eternum*, 1254) in which he substituted Joachim's three main writings for the authority of the Bible; they had become the everlasting gospel in the year 1200 when "the spirit of life had departed from the two gospels." The change marked the beginning of the sixth epoch of the age of the Son. Joachim's images in turn became translated into contemporary Franciscan Spiritual terms: Saint Francis (1182–1226) and those true to him were the new order of spiritual monks and the renewers of Christ's teachings. The Roman church was the carnal church characterized in the language of the Apocalypse as the Whore of Babylon, drunk with the blood of martyrs; its persecutions of those who upheld Saint Francis' ideal of absolute poverty represented the struggle between the forces of Christ and Antichrist. The year 1260 would bring the denouement of the present second age with the appearance of Antichrist. After unspeakable ravages and destruction Christendom would be reunited and a new era would open.

Gerard's *Introduction* was a direct challenge to the Church. It was condemned and he was imprisoned. Although disavowed by other adherents of Joachim among his order Gerard represented an extreme tendency which grew with the persecution of the Franciscan Spirituals during the later thirteenth century. They turned Joachim's teaching into a doctrine of dissent which sought the supersession of the Church rather than its renewal. Inevitably this threatened it as an institution. Although Joachim's teachings were never officially banned, Gerard of Borgo revealed them in another light. The first outbreak of the Flagellant movement in 1260, the year of Joachist prophecy, the emergence of the heretical semi-Joachist sect of the False Apostles, condemned in 1274, and above all the conflict within the Franciscan order, all helped to discredit Joachism and identify it with subversion by the end of the thirteenth century.

What Gerard did in 1254, transposing Joachim's doctrines into an apologia for poverty, was done repeatedly over the next century. Among the Franciscan Spirituals, Saint Francis was in the imagery of the Apocalypse, the angel of the sixth seal "who had the seal of the living God upon him" (Revelation 10:4). With him the sixth age had begun. He was the renewer of Christ's life and teaching, the center of which was poverty. The test of loyalty to Christ thus became loyalty to the Franciscan rule of absolute poverty; and persecution of its adherents was the mark of Antichrist. Poverty accordingly took on a cosmic significance. It represented the struggle between the forces of Christ and Antichrist. To suffer for it was to be of Christ; it was the badge of those who would triumph not in some distant and timeless void, but in the imminent change from the second to the third eras. For Spirituals like Peter John Olivi, his follower, Ubertino of Casale, and Angelo of Clareno such a conviction did not lead to indiscriminate identification of the church hierarchy with Antichrist. But for their less sophisticated followers the distinction became blurred; popes like Boniface VIII and John XXII became either Antichrist or his forerunners—Boniface for rescinding in 1295 his predecessor Celestine V's recognition of the Spirituals as a separate order; John for declaring heretical in 1323 the Franciscan doctrine of Christ's absolute poverty.

It was at this point that the apocalyptic tradition of Joachim mingled with the Sibylline tradition, mentioned earlier. This produced the two other figures of a Last World Emperor and a line of Angelic Popes. The role of the first was now usually reversed from that in the original Sibylline books. Generally called Frederick III—as last in the line of the Hohenstaufen emperors of whom Frederick II (1194–1250) in the first half of the thirteenth century was the archetype—he was often identified with the sixth or seventh head of the dragon. The revival of the notion of a Last World Emperor came from the revival of the Sibylline genre of writings. It began in Italy where the destructive effects of Frederick II's wars against the North Italian cities and the papacy fed Joachist prophecy. From the early decades of the thirteenth century there was a growing stream of pseudo-Joachist writings, which also incorporated the older Sibylline tradition. Notable among them were the so-called *Oracle of the Angel Cyril* and the *Erithrean Sibyl*, both of which saw in Frederick II and his descendants the precursors of Antichrist, whose coming would be presaged by the future Frederick III. These works were taken up by leading Franciscan Spirituals like Angelo of Clareno. But they also found popular expression, above all in the *Liber de Flore* written in the early fourteenth century. It contains the other aspect of pseudo-Joachist prophecy: a line of angelic or redeeming popes who would reform the Church and return it to its true apostolic state. For this it drew upon a Byzantine legend, from the ninth and tenth centuries, known as the Leo Oracles; these consisted in a series of prophecies over the future of the Byzantine empire, falsely ascribed to the emperor Leo the Wise. They, too, were incorporated into Joachist prophecy during the thirteenth century. Among the earliest works in which they were found in the West were the *Prophecies of Merlin* (ca. 1275)—a glorification of Venice—again of Italian provenance. They entered the Joachist canon in the form of compilations—ascribed either to Joachim or an apocryphal bishop Anselm—of popes both historical and yet to come; these popes were depicted by portraits, usually of animals drawn from the Apocalypse, accompanied by captions, in the case of future popes as prophecies. They thereby served at once to condemn past popes for having served Antichrist and to exalt in future popes the evangelical virtues which would triumph after the Antichrist's defeat. These future popes were thus the agents of the new era, fulfilling the positive role which had been given to a Last World Emperor in the original Sibylline Books. Such collections continued to circulate in new up-to-date versions down to the seventeenth century. Not the least significant of these later developments is that Joachim's works were among some of the first to be printed at Venice in the early part of the sixteenth century.

By the fourteenth century, then, Joachist prophecy had become the umbrella for a syncretism of apocalyptic belief. If little of it was authentically Joachim's it owed to him the almost universal expectation of the coming end to the present age, and its displacement by a new golden age, which would endure for the rest of time. Although in this form it was the preserve of the dissidents, the sense of impending upheaval was very strong in the later Middle Ages. It was stimulated by natural disasters such as the Black Death from 1348 to 1350, the endemic social and political disturbances of the period, and then by the nearly forty years of the Great Schism (1378–1417), which led many thinkers and ecclesiastics to see in the two rival popes of Rome and Avignon the advent of Antichrist. The defeat of the Franciscan Spirituals by about 1325 ended the open association of Joachism with an organized sect; but it continued among its dissident remnants—the Fraticelli—as well as prominent individuals such as John of Rupescissa, imprisoned in the papal court at Avignon (ca. 1350) for his prophetic writings.

Prophecy, however, extended far beyond Franciscan circles; it is to be found among diverse groups and individuals: the Flagellants in the fourteenth and fifteenth centuries, the heretical semimystical sect of the Men of Intelligence in the first decade of the fifteenth century, many of the Czech Reformers, as well as mystics like Catherine of Siena. It reached its climax in the early years of the Hussite Revolt in 1419 and 1420 in the Taborite movement which was organized upon the assumption of the imminent end of the world. Such proclamations continued to be made during the fifteenth century, especially in Germany, where in the sixteenth century they culminated with Thomas Münzer (or Müntzer), (ca. 1489–1525), a German Anabaptist and popular leader.

Prophecy in the Middle Ages, then, as at other times, was a state of belief. If it derived its inspiration from the prophetic writings of the Bible it lent itself to other influences which were consonant with the experiences of the epoch. Foremost among these was Joachism, which by the fourteenth century embraced almost the whole range of prophetic belief. In providing an historical framework it served to explain the sufferings and aspirations of any group or individual, even when many went beyond it. Together they transmitted the apocalyptic legacy to the succeeding age.

BIBLIOGRAPHY

Saint Augustine, *Basic Writings of St. Augustine*, ed. W. J. Oates (Edinburgh and New York, 1948), II, 663. O. Holder-Egger, "Italienische Prophetien des 13 Jahrhunderts," *Neues Archiv*, **15** (1890), 143–78; **30** (1904), 324–86; **33** (1907), 95–187. E. Jordan, "Joachim de Flore" in *Dictionnaire de Théologie Catholique*, Vol. 8, Part II, Cols. 1425–58. F. Kampers, *Die Deutsche Kaiseridee in Prophetie und Sage* (Münster im Westfal, 1896). G. Leff, *Heresy in the Later Middle Ages*, 2 vols. (Manchester, 1967), with bibliography. M. E. Reeves, "Joachimist Influences on the Idea of a Last World Emperor," *Traditio*, **17** (1961), 323–70. M. E. Reeves, "The *Liber Figurarum* of Joachim of Fiore," *Mediaeval and Renaissance Studies*, **2** (1951), 57–81; idem, *Influence of Prophecy in the Later Middle Ages* (Oxford and New York, 1969).

GORDON LEFF

[See also Allegory; **Christianity in History;** Dualism; God; Historicism; Metaphor; Myth; **Prophecy in Hebrew Scripture;** Sin and Salvation.]

669

PROTEST MOVEMENTS

THE RELATIONSHIP between ideas and protest in history has always been complex. Before modern times most protest ideologies were religious and few were specifically intended for social protest; this suggests already the common distinction between the grievances that caused popular unrest and the ideologies that might be invoked by it. In modern times, the rise of explicit protest ideologies compounds the interpretive problem in many ways, for it becomes deceptively easy to assume that actual protest was caused by what ideologists said it was caused by, and intended what they said it intended. The leading question, then, is always the causal relationship between ideas and protest. This should lead to tests of the extent to which ideas had filtered down to popular levels and of the links between protesting intellectuals and other groups.

Relatedly, the more elaborate forms of protest required organization. Protest ideas and intellectual leaders could help shape such organization, but the requirements of effective organization could force ideological compromises, even radical distortions, as well. The evolution of protest movements, quite obviously, has more often been an accommodation of ideas to the demands of constituents and of organization than an application of any undiluted ideology. Skepticism is a prerequisite for a study of ideas and protest: protesters might seize on ideas despite intentions diametrically opposed to these ideas; clearly enunciated protest ideas might have no impact on actual protest; ideas initially important in protest, to which lip service might even later be paid, might decline in actual impact surprisingly rapidly. On the other hand, a wide variety of ideas has undeniably played a role in many forms of protest.

Until the late eighteenth century, religion was almost always the link between formal ideas and popular social and political protest. European aristocrats and, frequently, town burghers had a sense of local rights and status that could be used to justify protest, or even rebellion, against the growing powers of central rulers, but until the rise of liberalism political theory offered scant support for their efforts. For the sporadic protests of the common people, which became an important part of European history from at least the fourteenth century onward, specifically political ideas had even less relevance. Religion was the only formal system of ideas that had any hold on the common people, and a protest ideology before 1789 meant either the theories of a sectarian Christian leader or the common man's interpretation of Christianity's social message.

Christianity could serve as a vehicle for social protest for a variety of reasons. Like any effective protest ideology, it could combine bitter denunciation of the present order and belief that a better way, even a utopia, could be found for the future; and it could overlay these with deep emotion and a passionate confidence that could sustain leaders and inspire followers as well. The egalitarian message of gospel Christianity recurred in many types of protests, from the peasant jacqueries of the late Middle Ages, through the Levellers and Diggers of the English Civil War, to the late nineteenth-century peasant uprisings in southern Europe. The common people now and again claimed in violent uprisings that Christ had condemned the rich and preached the sharing of goods. The Church itself was a frequent object of attack for its opulence and the worldliness of its clergy. The major heresies from the Albigensian movement to the Reformation, with their appeals to a purer Christianity and their attacks on the corruption of the present order, were to a significant extent embodiments of social protest by the common people. More rarely, under impassioned leadership, limited popular protest could invoke not only the Christian social gospel, not only anticlericalism, but also the desire to set up a separate community of the pure, free from the religious as well as the social inadequacies of the outside world. This was the impulse behind the Anabaptists in the sixteenth century and, to an extent, the most revolutionary groups in the English Civil War.

Christianity as a protest ideology differed in many ways from the protest ideologies of the last two centuries. The Christian churches, including all the major Protestant sects, were set against protest. The Christian message to the common people, with its focus on heavenly rewards, lulled discontent more often than it inflamed it. This ambiguity with regard to protest has some parallels in modern ideologies; socialism, for example, quickly developed an institutional outlook that discouraged violent protest. We may have witnessed, in the student rebellions of the 1960's, one of the first of many rebellions in the name of socialist purity, apart from or even against organized socialism. But it is too soon to say if the parallel will expand; the modern ideologies, even when institutionalized, have been far more tolerant of protest and of social change than was institutional Christianity. Christianity as an ideology of protest, though well suited to this role in many ways, was a deviation from the religious mainstream and a recurrent rather than persistent force. Christian protest also looked backward rather than forward. It stressed that the present had fallen away from past standards and strove for a better future that would restore these standards at least in earthly society. Lower-class protest that used Christian ideas was also apolitical, in the usual sense of this term. It might seek major change in the most relevant local political relationships, those between lord and serf; but it did not specifically discuss alterations in political structure, and its participants typically venerated the central ruler. Only with Protestantism did Christianity become clearly relevant to violent protest over constitutional issues, particularly in seventeenth-century England. Even then, the rebels most impelled by Christian concerns (and many in the lower classes), were more intent on religious purity and social justice than on changes in the position of Parliament and the courts. Christian protest typically tried to ignore the state rather than to alter it.

From the Enlightenment on, the principal ideologies of protest were non-Christian and often explicitly anti-Christian. Liberalism, radicalism, and socialism differed in crucial respects but, as protest ideologies, had important points in common. They were vigorously political, seeing changes in the organization and control of the state as the basis for achieving social justice; only a few Enlightenment-derived ideologies, such as syndicalism, dissented from this view. They were avowedly progressive and spent little time measuring the present by the past. Often, as in Marxist socialism, the existing order was admitted to be in many ways an improvement over the past. Their main point was that an unprecedentedly good society could be built in the future, and of course on this earth. The new ideologies also countenanced protest directly, even urged it in many circumstances; they were, at least in the early stages of their existence, truly protest ideologies and did not have to be reinterpreted or taken out of the mainstream to be used as such.

Furthermore, the new ideologies depended heavily on formal intellectuals not only for their articulation but also for their adaptation to actual protest efforts. This was part of the broader transition from Christian to secular culture and helps explain the extraordinary proliferation of protest ideas. Intellectuals, no longer priests, lost their traditional channel of communication within the larger society. Books written for sale to the public and leadership of political movements—both ways of using ideas to stir protest—became the new channels for intellectuals. In many ways they were less satisfactory channels than religion had been, for they long continued to be weaker organizationally than the churches and narrower than religion in emotional commitment, and hence less effective in reaching either the mass of the people or the wielders of power. Intellectuals therefore moved to spread political awareness and build massive organizations out of protest movements. Their concern about their status and their relationship with society frequently became in itself a motive for protest. This meant that protesting intellectuals were not moved by their ideas alone and that leaders of quite different, even opposing, protest movements might be concerned about similar problems

in their role as intellectuals. It meant also that intellectuals were often more aggrieved than other groups and might misinterpret broader protest movements.

Because of the changes in the content of protest ideologies and in the position of their advocates, the function of ideas in protest changed and increased as well. The sheer expansion of protest ideas and ideologists, clearly related to a rising tide of actual unrest, was as important as the new stress on secular progress. The first new functional connection between ideas and protest was at the level of leadership. From the ranks of intellectuals or their immediate adherents, the self-proclaimed advocate of protest emerged for the first time. At an extreme, the professional revolutionary came from this environment, armed in some cases with devotion to disorder and little else. Filippo Michele Buonarroti and, even more, Louis-Auguste Blanqui preached revolution for revolution's sake, with only the vaguest suggestion of the social and political justice that would ensue. Theirs was a minimal ideology which won few followers. It proved impossible to foment revolution so directly, and only in the Paris Commune did the pure revolutionaries play much role even in a movement not of their making. But the revolutionaries' organizational notions, particularly their stress upon a strict hierarchy descending from central control to small local unit, and something of their spirit influenced more elaborate protest ideologies and more successful leaders.

There were also signs that ideas were becoming increasingly involved in popular protest, a natural result of the radical intellectuals' efforts to be relevant and of the unrest caused by population growth and industrialization. Every modern revolution involved one or more ideologies, of course. There was in fact something of an ideological buildup before each revolution. This consisted of an increased outpouring of dissenting ideas and a growing diversity in the ideas themselves, resulting from a new or newly-important left wing. The proliferation of political tracts which were increasingly specific in content, and the birth of socialist theory helped prepare the French Revolution of 1789. Histories of this revolution, stressing its liberal or radical or socialist legacy, combined with rising agitation in the press and pamphlets to set the stage for the revolutions of 1830 and 1848. Ideas helped spur leaders like Louis Adolphe Thiers and A. M. L. de Lamartine. They provided goals, or at least slogans, for supporters of a revolution and for actual rioters, though by 1848 at least the multiplicity of ideologies helped divide the revolutionary ranks and set one group against another.

Dissemination of ideas before a revolution also helped create organizations capable of taking charge of the revolutionary effort once it began. Groups like the

Masons, and even simple reading societies that formed initially to discuss ideas and circulate tracts, often in secret, developed revolutionary cadres in western and southern Europe in the late eighteenth and early nineteenth centuries, and in the Balkans later on. Efforts by a regime to stifle the effervescence of ideas could, finally, trigger the revolution itself. New censorship laws set off the French revolution of 1830, while the Austrian government's restrictions on intellectual life created the student revolutionaries of 1848.

Ideologies played an increasing role in protests that fell short of revolution. There had always been, and continued to be, lower-class agitation without any connection with formal doctrine. Bread riots, banditry, theater riots, and the like were directed at specific targets and needed no larger goals; or at most they expressed a traditional belief in natural justice and a hatred of the rich, related perhaps to the radical Christian social ethic but long since separated from any reasoned theories. In the nineteenth century, however, traditional rioting declined, partly because elements of the lower classes gained a new contentment, but also because better-organized outlets developed. For workingmen, strikes became the chief form of protest. They were often conducted, with or without a formal organization, for purely bread-and-butter goals; organizations like the practical New Model Unions in Britain might have no ideological motivation, but strikes did teach workers that they needed organization and could make doctrines of class warfare seem appropriate. Socialist and syndicalist leaders had growing contacts with ordinary workers, and persuaded many of them of the importance of ideas. From about 1900 strikes for ideological goals became more common; even before, the leading labor organizations had been ideologically inspired. Rioting, though at lower levels than before the industrial revolution, precisely because it was seldom appropriate for expressing large goals, also came under the influence of ideas. Not only socialists but also nationalists and anti-Semites were able to call forth riots by the later nineteenth century. Finally, protest voting added a new dimension to lower-class agitation and was surely open to ideological direction.

The growing connections between protest ideas and protest movements developed partly because of the growing experience of the lower classes and their exposure to new conditions in the cities and in industry. Rising literacy and new freedoms of the press and of association obviously aided the process. But the vigorous efforts of the propagandists themselves played a vital role. Hence eastern and southern Europe, though far behind the West in industry, literacy, and civil rights, by the end of the nineteenth century matched or surpassed the West in the extent and ideological

fervor of protest. Under the impact of agrarian socialism or of nationalism many east European peasants gained real political awareness before their French or German counterparts did. More generally, the various ideas of protest moved the lower classes on the southern and eastern fringes of Europe to a revolutionary excitement. The same groups in the West in a comparable early stage of industrialization never achieved such intensity because the link between ideas and protest had not been completed. Here is a clear indication both of the importance of ideas in altering protest patterns and of the problems in spreading protest ideas.

Beneath the broad patterns of modern protest movements, the role as well as the specific content of the leading ideologies varied greatly. The multiplicity of protest ideas was itself an important new development, and its products require a brief description in terms of the history of protest. There was a fairly clear chronological progression from one group of ideologies to the next, in the nineteenth and early twentieth centuries, though most of the significant ideologies had been sketched by 1850, in the extraordinary exploration of the social systems suggested by the Enlightenment and the French Revolution. There was no necessary connection between the birth of an ideology and a real protest movement. Utopian socialism, for example, has little importance in the history of European protest, though it looms large in the evolution of social thought. The Owenites in Britain briefly attracted a following; Parisian artisans were aware of some slogans from Louis Blanc's writings, but probably of little more. Many utopian socialists spent more time appealing to industrialists than to workers, but even those who went to the factories found few supporters. Socially-radical, lower-class protest had long existed, but it became open to ideologies only in the late nineteenth century, when it produced the second stage of modern protest history.

Liberalism and radicalism were the first significant ideologies of protest, partly because both could appeal to rising middle-class elements, capable of sensing and expressing grievances, and yet not close the door to lower-class participation. Liberals wanted specific reforms in law and the economy; furthermore, their demands for parliaments and extensions of the suffrage implied an overturning of the ruling class that could be genuinely revolutionary. On the other hand, liberalism as a protest ideology had a number of crucial weaknesses. Liberals disliked disorder and violence, preferring evolutionary reform, partly because of their ideas and partly because most of them were comfortable property-owners. Hence liberals started very few violent protests; more often they were in the position of countenancing a protest already under way and were trying to pick up the pieces to their own benefit and that of public order. Hence, liberal revolutions almost always failed, for liberals lacked the toughness of spirit and authoritarian stamp to carry them through.

Two other ideologies supplemented liberalism in the first half of the nineteenth century, however, and gave it more muscle. Radicalism—a vague designation for a number of movements—preached more vigorous methods, such as massive demonstrations. It drew into its own organizations some elements of the most discontented lower classes, particularly the artisans. And in preaching democracy, with a hint often of social reform, radicals sought far more sweeping change than did liberals. From the Jacobins through the democrats of 1848 (including the Chartists) radicals played a vital role in political rioting and revolutions; if they lacked a single or elaborate ideology, they were clearly moved by ideas.

Political nationalism also spurred agitation, particularly in areas under foreign rule. Nationalism did not significantly touch the lower classes before the later nineteenth century; but it could unite the upper classes, including aristocrats, and move them to direct violence as liberalism never could. This was the vital ingredient of all those "revolutions" that were primarily patriotic wars, from Belgium and Poland in 1830 to Italy and Hungary in 1848.

The first set of radical ideologies had practically burned itself out by 1848. Nationalism was to inspire new protest at the end of the century, but this was a distinct movement under a different nationalist ideology. Only the nationalist wars of the 1860's, which captured or transformed some of the motives and violence of social protest, served as a partial transition. For liberals and many radicals, direct protest had proved ineffective and sufficient gains had been won to permit work through the existing order. Only a few groups in the radical tradition, particularly in France and Italy, were dissatisfied with the new parliamentary system and turned to socialism to express their discontent in voting, changing the nature of socialism somewhat in the process.

There were three clusters of protest ideologies from the later nineteenth century onward: socialism-communism, radical nationalism-fascism, and anarchism-syndicalism—a trio considerably more diverse than that of the earlier period. All, however, tried to reach the masses directly. All carried a social message which, with the partial exception of fascism, outweighed political demands. All preached violence at least at some point, and all paid considerable attention to the methods and organization of protest. All reflected, then, the shift from the middle to the working classes as the most numerous and persistent constituents

of a protest movement (though the fascists countered by playing on new middle-class grievances) and the related preeminence of social issues. All recognized the difficulties of revolution against an industrial state; hence the concern for tactics which ranged from assassination through small-scale gang violence to general strikes and protest voting. And, in fact, none of the new protest ideologies produced a true revolution in an industrial country, though they may be said to have produced revolutionary change by other means.

Socialism most resembled the liberal-radical ideologies of previous decades, though it battled them in theory. It was progressive, rational, and political. As a result, like liberalism, it rather rapidly turned away from protest to evolutionary reform. This process dissatisfied the guardians of the revolutionary socialist ideas and led to many divisions, including the communist spin-off in the 1920's; but communism itself underwent a similar process within twenty years, if not in accepting piecemeal reforms alone, at least in renouncing revolution in favor of political action. Broadly speaking, three factors turned socialism and ultimately communism from persistent protest even when a theoretical commitment to agitation was maintained. The constituency of the movement, primarily the working classes, was interested in sweeping rebellion only in the now rare years of economic misery; ordinarily it expected limited but rapid gains from the socialists. A minority wanted more, and socialist theorists talked about the importance of the minority as the vanguard of the proletariat; but they could not resist recruiting a broader following, and everywhere, this forced them to greater moderation, by requiring pragmatic compromises in order to win votes, and by opening the possibility of real if limited power and achievement through parliamentary position. The socialists' commitment to politics also dulled the edge of protest. Finally, learning both from Marx and from the necessities of resisting an initially hostile society, socialists and later communists stressed strong organizations. Initially designed as a basis for protest, the organizations rapidly asserted their own imperatives, requiring administrators rather than idealists, routine and accommodation rather than revolutionary zeal; their very existence gave leaders and members a stake in the existing order. Only where repression inhibited the development of extensive organization did socialism remain a revolutionary force in Europe. Elsewhere the ideological impetus in socialism declined, as it had earlier in liberalism, in part because of the orientation of the original ideas themselves.

Anarchism and syndicalism, hostile to any kind of extensive organization from the state down, avoided the perils of bureaucracy, but at the price of effective action. Theirs were the most radical protest doctrines developed in the modern era, for they rejected the whole direction of industrial society, and often urged individual and collective violence virtually for its own sake. They appealed particularly to artisans and peasants in areas where industrialization was just beginning to take hold; Andalusian anarchism was in fact the first non-Christian ideological current involved in rural protest. Neither anarchism nor syndicalism had a long life outside Spain, for they could not marshal enough force to accompany their goals. The glorification of violence lived on in fascism, however, which also picked up many of the vague currents of late nineteenth-century nationalist protest. Ideas of racial purity, national strength, authoritarian leadership, and social harmony, directed against both capitalism and the labor movement, had already spurred unrest before World War I. Until the 1890's, sporadic rioting was the most tangible result of these ideas but thereafter tentative approaches were made toward the protest methods of the fascists themselves: organized but selective violence by special shock troops combined with protest voting. Anti-Semites in Germany and Austria developed the latter while the *Action française* stressed the former. It remained for the fascists and Nazis to combine the methods. Fascism must be ranked as one of the most effective of all protest ideologies, for it attracted many groups that prided themselves on their respectability and had hitherto shunned any form of protest. It did this with a deliberately vague set of ideas that combined a radical attack on modern society from ethics to economics, a high level of emotion, and unprecedented attention to tactics and to organization.

Growing diversity of protest ideas and the groups to which they appealed, increasing radicalism, and explicit focus on the act of protest itself, until the ultimate absurdity of fascism in which ideas scarcely veiled the quest for power—these elements could provide a dramatic ending to an essay on ideas and protest, but it would be an inaccurate one. A number of problems must still be raised, not the least of which is the question of what has happened since the salad days of the second generation of modern protest ideologies just described. This relates to more basic questions about the historic role and novelty of modern protest ideologies.

A description of modern protest ideologies, following comments on Christianity in protest, inevitably suggests sharp differences between modern and pre-modern situations. Recent students of protest have noted a break, sometime during the nineteenth century, between modern and pre-modern (or industrial and pre-industrial) protest that is clearly linked to the ideological change. Protest turns to demands for new rights instead of claims for past ones, a reflection of the idea of progress; forms of protest change, as from riots to strikes, due among other things to the new attention to protest tactics and organizations. Appealing as a division into modern and pre-modern may be, however, it must be challenged at this point, above all, because it takes the content of modern protest ideologies too literally. The actual relationship of ideologies to protest changed, but less rapidly, completely, or obviously than the ideologies themselves.

There was a lag between the new ideas and popular attitudes. Christianity continued to express protest directly. Conversions to a more rigorous religion reflected intense social grievance at least through the nineteenth century; one need only cite the spread of Methodism among the British lower classes or the adhesion of several million Russian peasants to the Old Believers. In these cases religion expressed discontent but deflected or delayed active protest. But in the mid-nineteenth century, the Lazzarretti in Italy revived the gospels' social message for direct protest, while peasant rioters in southern Italy and southern Spain clearly thought in terms of Christian justice, although this moved them to attack the Church among other things. The lower-class religions were ultimately a major source of British socialism. Beyond these direct connections, many ostensibly secular protest movements maintained or developed a significant religious tone. Early in the nineteenth century many liberal or radical groups and many labor organizations claimed religious inspiration and conducted elaborate, church-like rituals. In southern Italy the leaders of the Carbonari were convinced liberals or democrats, but many ordinary members were drawn primarily by the secret rites; and the whole organization claimed derivation from Jesus Christ.

The transition from "religious" to "modern" protest was not sudden, but it is true that appeals to religious inspiration and mystical rituals faded as the new protest ideologies gained greater hold. More important for interpretive purposes are the similar characteristics of Christian and modern ideologies in protest. The similarities exist for two reasons. First, the attitudes of the constituents of modern protest movements were not completely transformed. Many protesters, like the avid German artisan-socialists of the 1890's who really hoped for a return to an older economy, did not take their ideologies at face value; they sought, in their protest movements, traditional as well as novel satisfactions. The conversion of workers from Christianity to socialism or communism was a genuine change, but it was also a transference of durable sentiments: hope for a glorious if remote future, desire for authoritative doctrine and guidance, and so on. Hence the most rigorous socialism or communism often spread in traditionally religious areas.

In many cases traditionalism among ordinary participants and within the forms if not the ideas of a protest movement long reinforced each other. Beyond this, ideas, whatever their content, must perform several broadly common functions whenever they are successfully involved in a protest movement. Whether Christian or secular, they must vigorously condemn the existing order; more people will be drawn to them on this basis than on any other. They must at least suggest dramatic tactics for overthrowing the existing system; and of course Marxism like Christianity adds a suggestion of inevitability as well, merely by replacing the hand of God with the hand of history. The protest ideology must offer some promise of a more perfect future society. To be successful, it must appeal to a variety of social groups and personality types. It needs to attract people willing to engage in violence, at least when particularly aroused. It must inspire a leadership willing to make sacrifices for the cause. Leaders of the modern protest ideologies displayed not only a fervor similar to that of dissident Christians, but frequently a comparable moral strictness, a desire for purity in their own lives and in society at large. Protest ideologies reflect and promote such moral sense; successful modern revolutions, like major religious revolts, have as a result invariably gone through a period of moral rigor. But protest ideologies must be sufficiently inclusive, indeed sufficiently vague, to enlist supporters whose interests are practical and immediate. The need to balance an ultimate vision with practical reforms has increased with the secularization of popular attitudes, for nothing has replaced religion as a widespread inducement to hold out for a more perfect future.

The characteristics of protest ideology have not completely changed; it is possible to offer a very broad definition of its role regardless of time or place. The needs and possibly the personality types of protest leaders retain important common elements. So do the varied demands of ordinary followers upon a protest ideology. Socialism has often been termed a modern religion, though we must repeat that, like Christianity, institutional socialism is not necessarily a protest ideology. The religious analogy holds for other protest ideas as well.

The most successful of modern protest ideologies helped reduce direct, and particularly violent, protest; this was one of their most basic, if unexpected, contributions to the character of industrial as opposed to pre-industrial society. Their advocates helped wean the common people from the traditional, largely spontaneous forms of agitation, replacing them with strikes

and political action that depend upon formal leadership. As the leadership became bureaucratic and turned from the ideological impulse, the followers could only follow; apart from sporadic wildcat action they too had learned that strength lay in organization. At the same time, of course, strikes and political action won important gains. Finally, socialism and particularly communism created something of a separate world, in which the most discontented could find comfort even when the total society still seemed hostile.

The combination of doctrine, ritual, diversified group activities, and material benefits within the socialist or communist organization limited the sense of isolation on which popular protest traditionally depended. The analogy with the Christianity of the common people is again obvious. The ideas that remake the popular mentality may begin as a protest but they cannot stop there; they must provide their own satisfactions, for a protest stance is too difficult to maintain over long periods of time.

Indeed, the currents of protest developed in the later nineteenth century and amplified in the early twentieth have not found successors. Syndicalism failed, fascism was defeated by war, socialism and communism express protest but in a limited and controlled form. We may in the later twentieth century be witnessing a new wave of protest, the ideological and other dimensions of which are still unclear; but it is not certain that the most durable of the older ideologies, now institutionalized, can yet be shaken.

It may be, then, that the period of direct protest stemming in part from the ideas derived from the Enlightenment will turn out, in a broad historical perspective, to have been surprisingly short. Certainly, one of the most decisive and novel results of the modern protest ideologies—one which contemporary student unrest falls far short of overturning—has been to encourage adaptation to modern, industrial society, not necessarily to its precise form at any given time, but to its broad principles. Liberals, radicals, and socialists believed in a progress that was consistent with the advance of industrial life. They helped teach the benefits of material improvements. They urged acceptance of technical change. The labor movements particularly stressed the importance of discipline, temperance, even family morality. They increased their own effectiveness as a result, by improving the stability of their constituents, but at the same time they helped train an efficient modern work force and reduced the multitude of individual resistances to industrial society, ranging from idling on the job to theft and sabotage, that suggested far more fundamental hostility to modernity than the dictates of reason could countenance. New expectations were aroused—again one of the truly novel if painfully slow products of modern protest movements—particularly the desire for new levels of material well-being that was foreign to the collective traditions of the common people, but these expectations have been manageable within the framework of industrial society.

From the early nineteenth century (and particularly in romanticism and its successor movements), a multitude of theories and theorists started with an opposition to rationalism and went on to oppose the whole tenor of industrial life. They logically opposed liberalism and socialism as well. In the ideas of a Nietzsche there was protest far more basic than anything that developed as a protest movement. Resistance to machines and commercialism and the corruption of parliamentary politics—that is, a popularized version of an anti-industrial philosophy—had potential popular appeal. In Luddism and similar movements there had been spontaneous protest along these lines in early industry. Yet with one exception no anti-industrial protest movement developed in an industrialized nation; and that exception, Nazism in Germany, when in power promoted further industrialization and may have opened the way for a more thorough acceptance of its consequences among the German people.

Aside from this, the anti-industrial philosophies failed to make that connection with a popular constituency that produces a real protest movement. They came too late for western Europe, where adaptation to industrial society had considerably advanced. They failed to make full connection with the Christian impulse and so lost a huge potential following. In the intensity of their alienation their advocates failed to organize, for they rightly sensed that this would necessitate some compromise; and they often scorned the common people anyway, which a successful protest ideology, dependent on numbers and violence that only the common people can produce, cannot afford to do. Yet this current of intellectual protest has continued in many forms in the twentieth century, winning largely intellectual converts. In the 1890's and again in the 1960's it won masses of students, and this could lead to outright rioting. Yet at least until the 1960's this current of rejection of modernity separated its advocates from the rest of society, including potential rebels on other grounds. This is yet another reason that the association of ideas and protest, so vigorous in the nineteenth century, has declined in the twentieth. One is tempted to add that successful protest ideas and their advocates must swim with a broader tide of social change.

This leads, in conclusion, to a renewed emphasis on the fragility of the link between formal ideas and protest. The difficulty in judging the relationship lies in the separate strands of causality involved. The development of protest ideas, although not independent of economic factors, rests primarily on the interpretation of previous movements of ideas by intellectuals, and on their concern with their own special status in society. Popular protest depends in its goals as well as in its timing on economic conditions above all. In its most elaborate expressions it rebels against the organization and even the guiding motives of the economy, rather than against material hardship, but it remains dependent on economic trends.

This means that most active protests, not only those concerned with bread-and-butter issues, have done without formal ideas. Some have generated their own, as Luddism did, building on conceptions based on tradition and natural justice. It means, at the other extreme, that many protest ideologies have never developed into protest movements. The failure of the Populists in Russia provides a prime example of ideas that failed to take hold despite widespread unrest. It means, finally, that many protest movements do not intend what the formal ideas involved seem to intend.

Syndicalism in France developed as an ideology for quite good intellectual and political reasons, but most of its working-class constituents, who were really rather moderate, never followed its precepts, for they wanted only its guidance in practical strike tactics; in other words, the followers needed leaders, and the most readily available leaders were syndicalist for good cause, but the cause did not extend to the followers. The movement ultimately had to turn from its ideology, but not until after almost two decades of confusion in which it is common, but almost completely inaccurate, to call French workers syndicalist. German liberalism briefly, in 1848, caught the attention of an older middle class that actually wanted above all to resist liberal trends. These, of course, are extreme examples. But other ideologies, more in tune with the goals of their constituents, like anarchism in Spain or socialism in Germany, still had to be modified to adapt more completely. Hence a successful protest ideology leads to quite diverse protest movements in different regions, among different social groups, even among different personality types. Socialism among stubborn but practical miners, to use one example, was never the same as socialism among more visionary textile workers.

Ideologies, then, can never fully define or describe a protest movement. The association became particularly complex during the last two centuries, when ideas were modernized more rapidly than popular attitudes and intellectuals were moved, whether consciously or not, by growing uncertainty about their social role. Historians, ostensibly intellectuals and often committed to the ideology they study, have too often looked at the intellectual origins of a movement and its most formal pronouncements and left their accounts at that. They tend to neglect the variety of interests that the ideology served, and its emotional impact upon its followers. They can grossly exaggerate the importance of ideas, like the historians who correctly note the presence of syndicalist ideas in Britain after 1910 and the rise of labor agitation, and therefore assume without further examination that syndicalism had a widespread audience. Or they can take ideological fervor too literally. Again, the approach must be skeptical, not through denial of the vital role of ideas in many forms of protest, but through recognition of the complexity involved. The future of the study of ideas and protest lies in the admittedly difficult examination of the actual contacts between ideas and those who use them.

BIBLIOGRAPHY

There are few explicit studies of the relationship between ideas and protest. The spread of ideas before three major revolutions has been treated in the following: Christopher Hill, *Intellectual Origins of the English Revolution* (Oxford and New York, 1965); Daniel Mornet, *Les origines intellectuelles de la révolution française* (Paris, 1933); Avrahm Yarmolinsky, *Road to Revolution: A Century of Russian Radicalism* (New York, 1959). Correctives to the temptation to overstress the role of ideas in the first two revolutions are: Michael Walzer, *The Revolution of the Saints; A Study in the Origins of Radical Politics* (Cambridge, Mass., 1965; London, 1966) and Georges Lefebvre, *The French Revolution*, 2 vols. (New York, 1962–64). Two treatments of the German Revolution of 1848 suggest the difficulties of interpreting the role of ideas: Jacques Droz, *Les révolutions allemandes de 1848* (Paris, 1957) stresses ideological factors in a careful assessment, while Theodore Hamerow, *Restoration, Revolution, Reaction; Economics and Politics in Germany, 1815–1871* (Princeton, 1958) notes that the formal ideas involved had little to do with the motives of most participants in the revolution. Ernst Troeltsch, *Social*

Teaching of the Christian Churches, 2 vols. (London, 1950) includes a comprehensive treatment of the relationship between Christianity and protest, both before and after Protestantism. For medieval protest and its heritage see also Sylvia Thrupp, ed., *Millennial Dreams in Action; Essays in Comparative Study* (The Hague, 1962). Two studies which provide vital insights into pre-industrial protest are: George Rudé, *The Crowd in History, 1730–1848* (New York, 1964), and Eric Hobsbawm, *Primitive Rebels; Studies in Archaic Forms of Social Movement in the Nineteenth and Twentieth Centuries* (New York, 1957). Three books on protest leaders, of quite different sorts, contribute to an understanding of the role of ideas in modern protest: Elizabeth L. Eisenstein, *The First Professional Revolutionist: Filippo Michele Buonarroti . . .* (Cambridge, Mass., 1959); Eric Hobsbawm, *Labouring Men; Studies in the History of Labour* (New York, 1965); James Joll, *The Anarchists* (New York, 1964). On the labor movement significant books are: Asa Briggs, *Chartist Portraits* (London, 1959); Guenther Roth, *Social Democrats in Imperial Germany; A Study in Working Class Isolation and National Integration* (Totowa, N.J., 1963); Gerhard Ritter, *Die Arbeiterbewegung in wilhelminischen Reich* (Berlin, 1959). Harvey Mitchell and Peter N. Stearns, *Workers and Protest* (Itasca, Ill., 1971) deals with the relationship between ideas and the European labor movement, and provides a convenient bibliography. Barrington Moore, *Social Origins of Dictatorship and Democracy; Lord and Peasant in the Making of the Modern World* (Boston, 1966) is perhaps the most useful single book on the conditions and nature of modern protest, though more concerned with the impact than the process of unrest; there is an extensive bibliography. New and rather tentative efforts to generalize about protest attribute little importance to formal ideas, as opposed to economic conditions and aspirations: see Ronald G. Ridker, "Discontent and Economic Growth," *Economic Development and Cultural Change*, **15** (1962–63), 1–15; Ted Gurr, *The Conditions of Civil Violence; First Tests of a Causal Model*, Center of International Studies Research Monograph No. 28 (Princeton, 1967).

PETER N. STEARNS

[See also **Anarchism;** Church as an Institution; Democracy; Heresy; Ideology; Nationalism; Progress; Reformation; **Revolution;** Skepticism; **Socialism;** Utopia.]